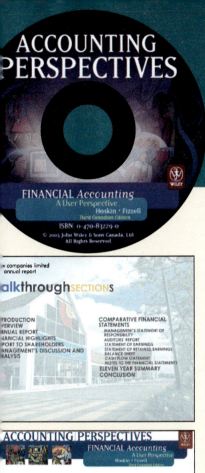

Accounting Perspectives CD

Accounting Perspectives is an exciting CD packaged exclusively

with Hoskin, Fizzell, *Financial Accounting: A User Perspective*,

*Third Canadian Editi*on and is included free with this text!

In the Accounting Perspectives CD, you will find a variety of simulations, exercises, reference guides, and tutorials. Content is divided into six main sections: Annual Report Walkthrough, Accounting Cycle Tutorial, Study Tools, Analyst Tools, Professional Tools, and Ethics in Accounting. You can access the contents by entering one section at a time, or navigate via the Study by Chapter option.

ANNUAL REPORT WALKTHROUGH

The Loblaw Annual Report Walkthrough helps you master the intricacies of annual reports. Voice-overs and animations take you step-by-step through the entire 2001 Annual Report.

ACCOUNTING CYCLE TUTORIAL

This interactive tutorial will reinforce your understanding of the accounting cycle. Voice-overs explain in further detail the material that appears on screen. Interactive questions are also available throughout.

STUDY TOOLS

The Study Tools section of the CD includes a variety of interactive materials to help you expand your knowledge of accounting, practise and prepare for tests, and maximize the benefits of the text. Tools include Demonstration Problems, Multiple Choice Quizzes, Rapid Review Sheets, PowerPoint ® Presentations, Checklists of Key Figures, a Glossary, and a link to the text website.

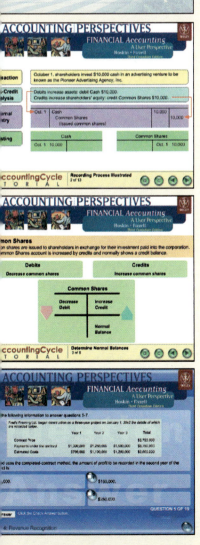

ANALYST TOOLS

You can develop your analytical skills through practice with the Analyst Tools. In this section, you will be asked to analyze real accounting data in a variety of situations. Tools include Working with Annual Reports, a Case Primer, and Technology Tools for Time Value Problems.

PROFESSIONAL TOOLS

This section provides you with additional resources and reference material related to the accounting and business fields. Tools include Careers in Accounting, Professional Profiles, a Writing Handbook, and Surviving the Group Project.

ETHICS IN ACCOUNTING

This portion of the CD provides expanded discussion of ethics and ethical issues as they relate to accounting and the financial reporting environment. It includes an Ethical Analysis Framework and Ethics Cases with suggested solutions.

FINANCIAL
Accounting

A User Perspective

Third Canadian Edition

Robert E. Hoskin

University of Connecticut

Maureen R. Fizzell

Simon Fraser University

JOHN WILEY & SONS CANADA, LTD

This textbook was created entirely by electronic means using the Macintosh platform — QuarkXpress, Illustrator, and Photoshop. Film was produced using disk-to-film technology.

National Library of Canada Cataloguing in Publication

Hoskin, Robert E., 1949-
    Financial accounting : a user perspective / Robert E. Hoskin, Maureen R. Fizzell. -- 3rd Canadian ed.

Includes bibliographical reference and index.
ISBN 0-470-83227-4

    1. Accounting. I. Fizzell, Maureen. II. Title.

HF5635.H68 2002   657'.044   C2002-904847-8

Production Credits
Publisher: John Horne
Publishing Services Director: Karen Bryan
Developmental Editor: Leanne Rancourt
Marketing Manager: Carolyn Wells
New Media Editor: Elsa Passera
Publishing Services Supervisor: Ian J. Koo
Publishing Services Coodinator: Michelle Marchetti
Editorial Manager: Karen Staudinger
Editorial Assistant/Permissions Coordinator: Gail Brown
Cover Illustration: Anson Liaw
Cover and Interior Design: Interrobang Graphic Design Inc.
Printing and Binding: Tri-Graphic Printing Limited

Printed and Bound in Canada
10 9 8 7 6 5 4 3

For my family

About Maureen Fizzell

Maureen R. Fizzell

Maureen R. Fizzell, B.Ed., B.Comm., M.Sc., CMA has been teaching at the university level for 18 years, nine years at the University of Saskatchewan and nine years at Simon Fraser University, where she is now Associate Dean of the Faculty of Business Administration. Over her university teaching career she has taught financial accounting from the introductory to the advanced level. Maureen is an active CMA member serving on the B.C. Board of Directors and the Management Accounting Institute Board from 1997 to 1999. She is currently a member of the CMA Canada National Board of Examiners. As well, she has been a member of the Saskatchewan Provincial Council, critiqued exams and acted as liaison between university students and the Society. During her 18 years, she has received numerous teaching awards. Some of them are: Most Effective Professor in the Classroom Award at the University of Saskatchewan in 1990; Canada Trust Distinguished Teaching Award in 1996; and membership in the Teaching Honour Roll in 1997 at Simon Fraser University.

Preface

Background

Financial Accounting: A User Perspective sets out to teach students about accounting information and how it affects decision-making by complementing the fundamental procedural aspects of accounting with discussions about who uses accounting information and what decisions they make from it. This unique balance has been widely appreciated and has, therefore, been maintained in the third edition. Furthermore, in response to feedback from instructors from across the country, the content has been enhanced even more with new features, new technology, and an all-new four-colour design that make the text even more relevant to today's student.

New to this Edition

Prior to the preparation of the third edition, research was conducted by contacting users of the text. The two points that came up almost unanimously were that an increase in the user focus of the material presented in each chapter was needed to better prepare students to successfully complete the problems and an increase in the number of cases at the end of each chapter was desired to allow students to further hone their analytical skills.

We therefore:

- Added a **new User Relevance** section at the start of each chapter from Chapter 2 onward that describes why the content of the chapter is important to users of accounting information as they make business decisions. It prepares the students to view the material from a user perspective as they read. Also, throughout the chapter there are now frequent references to what users will see on financial statements and how that information is relevant to decision-making.

- More than tripled the number of **Cases** presented at the end of each chapter. There are now over 50 cases in all. Even more cases can be found on the companion website. A web icon found in the text directs students to the site.

We also introduced other new features to enhance the text, most notably the **Accounting Perspectives CD**, which includes:

- An **Annual Report Walkthrough** that takes students through the entire report of Loblaw Companies Ltd. and a Working with Annual Reports section that includes a database of over 20 company reports and Excel templates to work with the data from those reports.

- An **Accounting Cycle Tutorial** to reinforce the basics of accounting, especially for those who plan to continue studying in the area.

- **Ethics in Accounting** provides expanded discussion of ethics and ethical issues as they relate to accounting and the financial reporting environment. It includes an Ethical Analysis Framework and Ethics Cases with suggested solutions.

- A **Case Primer** to help students successfully work through the cases found in the text and on the CD.

- A selection of **Study Tools** including PowerPoint Presentations, Rapid Review Sheets, Checklists of Key Figures, a Glossary, and Demonstration Problems that provide models for students as to how the end-of-chapter material in the text should be presented.

- A variety of **Professional Tools** that will help students develop the skills needed in the workplace. These include a Writing Handbook and material on group work.

- An in-depth explanation of the **Time Value of Money,** complete with problem material to test students skills in this area. A Technology Tools for Time Value of Money module is also featured.

 This icon directs students to the CD. It appears throughout the text when there are tools available on the CD that enrich the text coverage. For instance, the icon appears in the margin next to the discussion of Sears Canada's annual report. It directs them to the Annual Report Walkthrough so they can review another report to reinforce what they have learned.

And all chapters have been updated to reflect the latest standards and practices. Most notably, Chapters 5 (Cash Flow Statement), 8 (amortization requirements for intangibles), 9 (liability method for future income taxes), and 11 (stock options) and Appendix B have been updated to reflect the latest *CICA Handbook* changes.

Text Organization

In order to focus on the understanding and use of financial statements and to emphasize the importance of topics such as decision-making, cash flows, and ratio analysis, this text is organized in a unique manner.

Chapter 1 lays the conceptual groundwork for the mechanics of the accounting system, and guides students through the annual reports of Sears Canada Inc. and Sun-Rype Products Limited. Students learn basic accounting terminology and are introduced to the three major financial statements: income statement, balance sheet, and cash flow statement. This chapter also presents background material on the standard setting process and the conceptual framework underlying accounting. The section on who the users of financial statements are has been revised so that students have a better understanding of who the people are, what kind of decisions they make, and how the financial statements can provide that information.

Chapters 2 and 3 build on the basics from Chapter 1, portraying the traditional presentation of the accounting system using the basic accounting equation and a full description of the double entry accounting system and the accounting cycle. The early introduction of the cash flow statement enables students to appreciate the differences between the income statement and cash flow statement that are crucial to understanding accrual basis financial statements.

Chapter 4 caps the discussion of the income statement with revenue recognition criteria and methods. This topic is often not emphasized in introductory texts. However, the authors recognize that the revenue recognition policies established by a company can have a major impact on its operating results. It is, therefore, important for students to have some understanding of these policies early in the course.

Chapter 5 reflects the importance of the cash flow statement in at least two ways: it is unique in covering the interpretation as well as the construction of the statement, and secondly, the coverage occurs earlier than in other introductory texts. Because this topic is a difficult one for many students, the chapter explains the linkage of the cash flow statement to the operating policies of the company (accounts receivable, inventory, and accounts payable policies) helping students to interpret the information in the operating section of the cash flow statement. By the end of Chapter 5 students will have a basic understanding of the three major financial statements. Because of the complexity of the cash flow statement, some instructors prefer to teach the topic later in the course. The chapter has been designed so that it can be taught after chapter 11 instead of after chapter 4.

Chapters 6 through 11 discuss the major asset, liability, and equity accounts that students will see in published financial statements. In each of these chapters, students are alerted to the important aspects of these items so that they can better interpret financial accounting information. The chapter material and the questions at the end provide numerous examples of disclosures from the financial statements of real companies.

Financial statement analysis issues are discussed in all chapters and are summarized and extended in Chapter 12 after students have learned about the major asset, liability, and equity accounts. Financial ratios associated with the topics under discussion are introduced in each chapter. From their first exposure to accounting, students are given tools that they can use to analyze financial statements. By the time they reach Chapter 12 where all the ratios are summarized and extended, they have worked with all the ratios. Chapter 12 gives them an opportunity to pull the analysis together and work with the total corporate entity. In some cases, this takes the coverage slightly beyond what is usual in introductory texts.

Because real corporations are complex, and generally prepare consolidated financial statements, an appendix that covers long-term investments in other corporations and the consolidation process is included. Recognizing that consolidation procedures are complicated and beyond the scope of an introductory textbook, this discussion is kept very simple. In keeping with the user orientation, the financial statement impacts of the consolidation policies are considered.

Features of This Book

The text's user orientation aims to prepare students for their future in business no matter what their area of concentration and has been successfully followed at universities across Canada. In addition to the content and organization, a variety of pedagogical features support the approach.

The Use of Financial Statements

Virtually all introductory accounting students, both graduate and undergraduate, will become users of accounting information, while only a few will become preparers. The user perspective that continues in this text focuses on the understanding and use of corporate financial statements as a primary source for accounting information. Over the years, instructors across the country have found this approach to be an effective way of preparing students to work with accounting information. As well, it provides a solid foundation for students who continue on in accounting.

Integral to this approach is the extensive use of real financial statement data. Throughout the text you will find excerpts from the annual reports of actual corporations, reprinted exactly as they originally appeared. The annual report of Sears Canada Inc. is presented in its entirety, along with a variety of excerpts from over 55 Canadian and international corporations. The icon in the margin identifies material from the annual reports of these companies. In addition, the annual report of Sun-Rype Products Limited and a database of over 50 other Canadian companies are available on the *Accounting Perspectives CD*. Each chapter provides a unique set of problems in the "Reading and Interpreting Published Financial Statements" section, which requires students to analyze and interpret corporate financial statement disclosures.

An International Perspective: Reports from Other Countries

International issues are integrated into the text in several ways. Where appropriate, international differences are discussed in the main body of the text. Additional international material is set off from the main body in boxed-in areas that often feature "NAFTA Facts." Actual foreign financial statements are included in some of the boxed-in areas and are included in some of the problems at the end of the chapters.

Ethics in Accounting

Ethical issues are raised in most chapters by special boxed-in sections. These exhibits are designed to raise the reader's consciousness on ethical issues, and to provide a source of in-class discussion topics. The focus of these boxes is what students need to think about in order to act responsibly. This feature is complemented by additional material on the *Accounting Perspectives CD*.

Critical Thinking & Communication

While many of the problems in the "Reading and Interpreting Published Financial Statements" sections are challenging problems, special critical thinking problems and a large selection of new cases have been included at the end of most chapters. These problems require students to critically analyze issues. They can be used as the basis for term papers, class discussion, or debates, providing opportunities for students to polish written and oral communication skills.

In-Text Student Aids

Each chapter includes the following sections: text, summary problems, synonyms & abbreviations, glossary, and problems:

Summary Problems The summary problem at the end of each chapter is designed to illustrate the main points in the chapter. Many of these problems elaborate on topics discussed in the chapter and provide an example for students to aid them when tackling the end-of-chapter problems. Additional demonstration problems are included on the *Accounting Perspectives CD*.

Synonyms & Abbreviations This section contains terms used in the chapter and their common synonyms as well as any common abbreviations that are used in the chapter.

Glossary There is a glossary at the end of each chapter that defines the key terms introduced in the chapter. Key terms are boldfaced in red the first time they are used in a chapter. A searchable glossary is also available on the *Accounting Perspectives CD*.

Problems The problem section of each chapter is divided into seven parts: Assessing Your Recall, Applying Your Knowledge, User Perspective Problems, Reading and Interpreting Published Financial Statements, Beyond the Book, Cases, and Critical Thinking Questions. As mentioned earlier, the number of cases in this edition has more than tripled.

- The *Assessing Your Recall* section is designed to assess the understanding of basic terms and concepts introduced in the chapter.

- The *Applying Your Knowledge* section asks students to apply the concepts and procedures discussed in the chapter in a hypothetical situation. These problems are most like those found in a traditional text and will often reinforce the technical side of accounting.

- The *User Perspective Problems* let students assume the role of a particular user and consider and discuss chapter topics from that perspective.

- The *Reading and Interpreting Published Financial Statements* section is unique to this book and contains problems that make use of corporate financial statement disclosures. The problems typically involve some type of analysis and interpretation of financial statement data.

- The *Beyond the Book* section provides an opportunity for the instructor to have students do individual or group research. The Beyond the Book section in Chapter 1 gives several library and internet sources of corporate financial statements that students can use throughout the course. Students are asked to find financial information about a company of their choice and to answer questions about topics introduced in each chapter.

- The *Cases* are hypothetical scenarios in which students are asked to identify problems, evaluate situations, and make recommendations. The required part of the cases often asks for a written report.

- The *Critical Thinking Questions* often take students beyond the structured data in the chapter by asking them to consider controversial areas associated with one or more of the chapter's topics.

Acknowledgements

I would like to thank Robert Hoskin who developed the original concept for this book and who put so much thought and energy into its construction.

I would like to acknowledge the many reviewers who provided very valuable comments on the second edition and on the revised chapters of the third edition as they were written. As a result of their comments, several changes were made to the organization of material in the book and within chapters. As well, their comments helped me simplify some areas and provide clearer descriptions in others.

Respondents to our pre-writing research survey were:

Marilyn Adams, McMaster University
Mariann Glynn, Ryerson University
Charlotte Heywood, Wilfrid Laurier University
George Kanaan, Concordia University
Fred Phillips, University of Saskatchewan
Peter Secord, St Mary's University
Mohammed Shehata, McMaster University
Karen Touche Lightstone, St Mary's University

Reviewers were:

Hilary Becker, Carleton University
Bryan J. Bessner, DeVry Institute of Technology
Christopher Burnley, Malaspina University College
Judy Cumby, Memorial University
Charles Draimin, Concordia University
Murray Hilton, University of Manitoba
Stuart H. Jones, University of Calgary
Fred Phillips, University of Saskatchewan
Aziz Rajwani, Lanagara Community College
David K. Scallen, Wilfrid Laurier University
Shu-Lun Wong, Memorial University

I am very grateful to everyone at John Wiley and Sons Canada, Limited. John Horne and Karen Staudinger got me going on the third edition and found me two great developmental editors: Hal Harder and Leanne Rancourt, who worked tirelessly to keep me to a schedule and to find the help I needed to complete the third edition. I also want to thank the many people who worked behind the scenes producing material that makes this book unique: Francoise Giovannangeli, who researched and wrote the vignettes that open each chapter about real Canadian companies; Aleli Balagtas, who found and summarized many of the numerous news articles that bring the real world into the book; Alan Johnstone, the copyeditor who made the important grammatical decisions; Zofia Laubitz, who proofread all of the pages; Enola Stoyle, who checked all of the solutions; and Edwin Durbin, who produced the index. I want to thank Carolyn Wells who is working to develop creative ways of marketing this edition of the text. No thank you of Wiley people is complete without a thank you to all of the university/college representatives who talk to instructors about the merits of the book.

There are several people who worked on supplemental material for the text that also deserve a special thank you: Tashia Batstone who wrote the additional cases and prepared the test bank; Anne Macdonald who prepared the solutions manual; Hilary Becker who prepared the instructor's manual; Suzanne Coombs who prepared the PowerPoint material; and George Fisher who prepared sample multiple choice questions.

I want to extend a special thank you to Don Cherry who created and revised many of the chapter problems, giving me time to concentrate on the text material. Thank you, Don.

I also need to thank Michelle Czornobay and Jennifer Van Elslande who worked with me getting permissions from companies for inclusion of their financial statement information in the book.

Concluding Remarks

I hope that both students and instructors will find the material contained in this book useful as they attempt to understand the extremely complicated world of corporate financial reporting. I have tried to be careful in the editing of the book and the associated solutions manual and instructors' manual so that there are a minimum number of errors. The remaining errors are, of course, mine and I look forward to hearing from you concerning any that you find so that I can improve upon the product.

Maureen Fizzell
Simon Fraser University, December, 2002

Brief Table of Contents

TABLE OF CONTENTS

It's Like Your Scorecard

Raj Randhawa admits accounting wasn't his favourite class at the University of Saskatchewan, where he received his Bachelor of Commerce degree. But as general manager and co-owner of Horizon Computer Solutions, a computer hardware, software, and services provider in Saskatoon, he uses it every hour of his business life.

Beginning in 1995 with three employees, by 2001 Horizon had 32 employees and $10 million in sales annually. This rapid growth has been made possible by sound finance decisions, all of which rely on accounting information. For example, Horizon recently began focusing more on service—programming, network support, and so on—than on hardware sales. "Profit margins in hardware are about 10% or 11% in this business," explains Mr. Randhawa, "whereas in services they can be much higher. In addition, by selling customers a whole package—the computer and the service—we provide better value and gain loyalty." While the recent downturn in PC sales has been felt by many other Canadian computer resellers, this carefully planned shift in focus helped Horizon's overall sales grow by 12% in 2001.

By contrast, Mr. Randhawa regrets not thinking through all of the relevant financial accounting issues when, in 1997, Horizon renovated its first store. "We paid for the renovation with our line of credit," he says. "Bad idea." It would have been cheaper and simpler, he now realizes, to obtain a loan for the purpose. "It seemed like it was going to be a small job at first," he explains, "but it got bigger and bigger."

He learned his lesson. When Horizon moved into a larger downtown location in

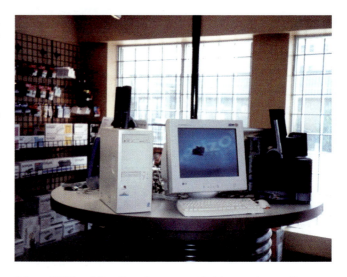

May 2001, Mr. Randhawa and his partner, Duane Carruthers, covered a large part of the $400,000 required for renovations and improvements with a bank loan, using the company's equity for the rest. "Again, we ran into cost overruns with things our engineers hadn't forecast," he says. "But by renegotiating with the landlord for a few extra rent-free months and injecting some more money into the company, we were able to offset some of the extra costs and keep our ratios in line."

"Nothing in school could have prepared me for the real world of business," he sighs. But a good grasp of accounting helps him make a lot of decisions. "Say you want to invest in a lot of new training for your staff. It's expensive—is it worth it? If it will increase your revenue and result in cost savings, then yes," he says. Regularly analyzing Horizon's accounting data has also enabled Mr. Randhawa to establish profit centres, allowing him to track growth areas or pinpoint problems. For example, service—which has grown 25% in the past year—is now a separate department for accounting purposes.

"Accounting is like your scorecard," Mr. Randhawa muses. "It lets you know what's going on at any moment. It shouldn't be at the forefront of your business; you must concentrate on what you do or make, like a player concentrates on the game. But it is in the background all the time so that you can check to see how you are doing and it provides you with input to your next strategy. Everything has to work together to make a business successful."

OVERVIEW OF CORPORATE
FINANCIAL REPORTING

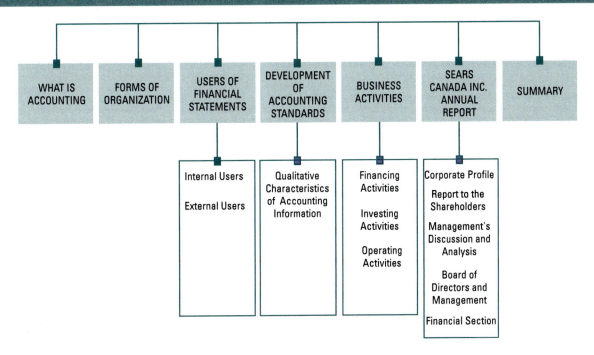

Learning Objectives:

After studying this chapter, you should be able to:

1. *Define accounting and understand its relationship to economic decision-making.*
2. *Understand what an annual report is and what it contains.*
3. *Describe the major forms of organization in which accounting is used.*
4. *Identify several users of financial statements and begin to understand how they use accounting information.*
5. *Know what Generally Accepted Accounting Principles (GAAP) are.*
6. *Identify the qualitative characteristics of accounting information.*
7. *Describe the three fundamental business activities.*
8. *Identify the major financial statements and describe their major components.*
9. *Begin to understand the role of ethics in financial accounting.*

The opening story tells how accounting and business success work hand in hand. Whether you are performing day-to-day operations, borrowing money for expansion, planning a new avenue of operations, deciding to purchase or lease, etc., you need to have information which will enable you to make the most advantageous decisions. One of the most important sources of that information is the accounting system.

Learning Objective

❶

Define accounting and understand its relationship to economic decision-making.

WHAT IS ACCOUNTING?

Accounting is an information system in which the underlying economic conditions of organizations and, indeed, individuals, are recorded, summarized, reported, and understood. Accounting can be as simple as balancing your individual cheque book or as complex as recording and reporting on the economic condition of a multinational corporation such as Microsoft or a government such as the Federal Government of Canada. All of these entities need to know economic information in order to continue to operate efficiently and effectively. Accounting is the system that provides the information. It provides the very framework around which people and organizations make decisions. It is therefore important that you, as future users, have at least a basic understanding of what accounting is (and is not), what it is trying to accomplish, and how it goes about doing so.

Learning Objective

❷

Understand what an annual report is and what it contains.

The focus of this book is going to be on the accounting information produced by profit-oriented organizations, although we will occasionally make reference to not-for-profit organizations or governments. We will concentrate mainly on the **financial statements**, which are the reports from the management of companies to their owners summarizing how the company performed during a particular period. The financial statements are the final set of documents produced at the end of an accounting period. They are included in a larger **annual report** that is the main method management uses to report the results of the company's activities during the year. The annual report is sent to all owners, but many other parties that have an interest in the company—for example, lenders, analysts, and credit-rating agencies—use it as well. Many companies have created websites and include their most recent financial statements as part of the information users can access.

The primary goal of this book is to help you become an intelligent user of accounting information by enhancing your ability to read and understand corporate financial statements. You may become a manager, accountant, banker, or financial analyst, and even if you don't, you probably will become an investor in the shares or bonds of a company at some point in your career. Whatever your business role, you will make decisions about companies, such as whether or not to invest in their shares, lend them money, or sell them goods or services on credit. In making these decisions, it will be important for you to understand the information that is presented in corporate financial statements. You must know not only what each piece of information tells you about the company, but also what it doesn't tell you. You should also recognize that some important information is not contained in the financial statements, yet is useful in certain decision-making contexts.

We have written this book for a broad readership, understanding that many of you will play multiple roles as owners (shareholders), creditors, and managers of companies. We have assumed that you know little or nothing about accounting.

We have not assumed that you are training to be an accountant, although that may be your objective. Therefore, this book does not emphasize accounting procedures. Instead, the underlying concepts of accounting and the analysis of financial statements are emphasized. However, a complete understanding of the end result of the accounting process is probably not possible without an overall view of how the accounting system works. For this reason, the first few chapters present the mechanics of the accounting system. Subsequent chapters are devoted to accounting issues and concepts, and to analyzing financial statements.

Throughout the book, information from real companies is used to illustrate the topic at hand. In addition to numerous examples of financial statement information from a variety of companies, the complete annual report of **Sears Canada Inc.** for 2001 is included in Appendix A at the end of book. A second complete annual report, that of **Sun-Rype Products Ltd**. for 2001, has been included on the *Accounting Perspectives CD*, which is the disk that is included inside the front cover of the text. The inclusion of two complete annual reports, one for a retailer (Sears Canada) and one for a manufacturing company (Sun-Rype Products), will provide you with more reference material. Many references will be made to the Sears Canada (SC) report and the Sun-Rype Products (SRP) report throughout the text. Page numbers from these annual reports will be preceded by "SC-" or "SRP-"; that is, page 10 from an annual report will be referred to as "SC-10" or "SRP-10." At the end of each chapter, additional problems, labelled "Beyond the Book," require that you find a company of your own choosing or one suggested by your instructor. At most universities, annual reports of other companies may be accessed through electronic means. Reports are also currently available on the Internet through the SEDAR filings. Your instructor may provide you with information about how to access this information on your campus, or you can contact your university librarian.

**Sun-Rype
Products Ltd.
Annual Report**

Because different companies use slightly different terminology to refer to items in their financial statements, it is sometimes confusing to read their statements. To assist you in interpreting these financial statements, lists of abbreviations and synonyms are provided at the end of most chapters. A glossary that briefly defines or explains the terms used is also provided at the end of each chapter.

AN INTERNATIONAL PERSPECTIVE

Reports from Other Countries

Because we live in a global environment, another goal of the book is to expose you to financial statement requirements in countries other than Canada. Integrated into the discussion of most chapters are examples of how accounting standards in other countries might differ from those in Canada. These sections are set off from the main text, as is this paragraph, so that you can easily identify discussions of international standards rather than Canadian ones. Some of these international boxes are used to highlight accounting principles used in the United States and Mexico, which we have labelled "NAFTA FACTS."

**Learning Objective**

3

Describe the major forms of organization in which accounting is used.

FORMS OF ORGANIZATION

Financial information is used in many different types of organization: profit-seeking entities like corporations; governing organizations like federal, provincial, and municipal governments; service entities like hospitals and academic institutions; and not-for-profit entities like charities and clubs. Although all of these entities have different objectives, they all need information that tells their users whether they are still viable, whether they are meeting their goals, and whether they have a future. Financial statements attempt to capture financial information about an **entity** and present it to users so that they can make informed decisions. Because these entities have different objectives, the underlying accounting approaches associated with them may be different. To try to capture the variations adequately would make this book too complicated. We are, therefore, concentrating on the profit-seeking entities, although we will occasionally add information about the other types of entity.

Many different types or forms of organization conduct business in Canada. Although the accounting issues discussed in this book apply to some degree to all these forms of organization, attention is directed primarily toward the accounting issues facing *corporations*. Almost every large business in Canada is a corporation. Other forms of business include *sole proprietorships, partnerships, limited partnerships, joint ventures,* and *Crown Corporations*. These forms of organization are discussed in more detail in Chapter 11.

In all business organizations, the owners make some type of initial investment in the business entity in the form of cash or property. In sole proprietorships and partnerships, this ownership interest is referred to as the *owner's* or *partners' capital*. In a corporation, owners make similar investments in the company but their ownership interest is referred to as **shareholders' equity** and is represented by a document known as a *share*. A share is simply a document that represents a small part of ownership in the corporation. The owners therefore are referred to as **shareholders**. One advantage of the corporate form of business is that the shares can be easily transferred to another investor, allowing one investor to sell and another to buy ownership in a given company. It is not as easy to transfer ownership in a sole proprietorship or a partnership. Corporations whose shares are held by a small number of individuals are sometimes referred to as **privately held corporations**. The shares in these corporations do not trade on the public stock exchanges, which makes the transfer of ownership more difficult. Corporations whose shares are held by a larger number of individuals or entities and trade on a public stock exchange (such as the Toronto Stock Exchange) are referred to as **publicly traded corporations**. Some portion of their ownership often changes hands on a daily basis.

Except for some small corporations, shareholders typically do not become involved in the day-to-day operation of the business. Because of the large number of shareholders and their lack of involvement in day-to-day activities, the shareholders typically elect a **Board of Directors** to represent them. The Board of Directors then hires (and fires) individuals known as senior management to manage the day-to-day operations. These senior managers, along with the managers they hire, are collectively referred to as **management**. To keep shareholders informed of the performance of their investment in the company, management reports periodically to the shareholders. This periodic information is sent to share-holders on a quarterly basis (every three months) in a quarterly report. The fourth-quarter report is combined with the prior three quarters to produce financial statements that cover the entire fiscal year. These annual financial statements are included in the company's annual report. It is these annual statements that we will be studying.

USERS OF FINANCIAL STATEMENTS

Learning Objective

4

Identify several users of financial statements and begin to understand how they use accounting information.

Accounting is primarily concerned with the communication of financial informa-tion to users. Accountants must first identify what information should be commu-nicated to users, then must ensure that the company's accounting system will accurately collect and record this information so that the desired communication is possible. Because businesses are involved in many thousands of transactions each year, accountants must summarize this information in a format understandable, and therefore useful, to users. Accountants are very concerned that the information they provide is both reliable and relevant to users.

Although annual reports and corporate financial statements are prepared by managers primarily for shareholders, other users of financial data who are both external and internal to the company also analyze them. The various users do not have the same goals with respect to the information that they need. As mentioned previously, in the future you will probably be a user of financial information. What kind of user is still unclear. It is important, therefore, at this stage that you under-stand who the typical users of financial information are and what they want to know. At the end of each chapter there are a series of questions entitled "User Perspective Problems" that describe situations for you to consider from different user perspec-tives. Exhibit 1-1 lists some of these users.

Users of Financial Statement Information

Internal users:

    Management

    Board of Directors

External users:

    Shareholders

    Potential investors

    Creditors (for example, bankers and suppliers)

    Regulators (for example, a stock exchange)

    Taxing authorities

    Other corporations, including competitors

    Security analysts

    Credit-rating agencies

    Labour unions

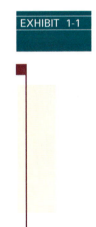

EXHIBIT 1-1

Internal Users

Management and the Board of Directors

Management and the Board of Directors, as primary internal users, make use of accounting data to make many decisions such as pricing products, expanding operations, deciding whether to buy or lease equipment, and controlling costs. Because of their position inside the company, managers have access to many sources of financial information beyond what is included in the financial statements that external users see. Their uses of these additional accounting data are important, but are generally covered in courses and books devoted to **managerial accounting** or **cost accounting** and will not be discussed in this text. Our primary focus will, therefore, be on the value of accounting data to external users. **Financial accounting** courses are oriented primarily to the study of the accounting data provided to these outside users through the use of financial statements. In most academic programs, both a financial and a managerial accounting course are required to expose students to both types of accounting information.

External Users

The information disclosed in financial statements is sensitive to external users' needs because management, who prepares the statements, wants to communicate information to shareholders, creditors, and others about the financial status of the company. Management can, therefore, disclose almost any information it considers important for an understanding of the company, subject to some limitations set by various regulatory bodies.

Shareholders and Potential Investors

Shareholders and potential investors need information that will enable them to assess how well management has been running the company. They want to make decisions about buying more shares or selling some or all of the shares they already own. They will be analyzing the current share prices (as reflected on the stock exchange) and comparing them to the original price that was paid for the shares. Are they worth more now or less? They will also be comparing the share price to the underlying value of the company as reflected in the financial statements and in other sources of information they have about the company. They also want to decide if the people currently sitting on the Board of Directors are adequately overseeing the management team they have selected. Is the company heading in the right direction? Is it making decisions that result in value to the shareholders? Information in the financial statements will contribute to those decisions. Other sources of information for these users include press releases, websites, business newspapers and magazines, and experts like stockbrokers and financial advisors. Because shareholders are concerned with the company as a whole, they probably have the broadest need for information of all of the external users.

Creditors

Creditors usually come from three major groups. The first group includes those who sell goods or services to the company and are willing to wait a short period of time for payment. Examples of these users are suppliers, employees, and government (with respect to payroll deductions). These users focus on the short-term cash level in the company because they want to be paid. The second group consists of financial institutions, such as banks, that have loaned money to the company. The loans can either be short-term or extend over several years. Like the people in the first group, they are also interested in the cash level of the company, but they often need to assess the cash flow further into the future, so their need for information is broader. They want not only the principal of the debt repaid, but also an interest charge paid. The third group is made up of investors who have purchased long-term debt instruments such as corporate bonds from the company. Similar to banks, these users have both a long-term and a short-term interest in the cash level. These creditor groups use the financial statements as a source of information that enables them to assess the future cash flows of the company. They will make their lending or investing decisions and establish interest levels based on their assessment of the risk of non-collection.

Regulators

The regulators who are interested in the financial statements are numerous. For example, the government establishes regulations for how a business becomes incorporated and for its conduct after incorporation. It is, therefore, interested in ensuring that the company follows those regulations. The stock exchange on which the shares are traded establishes regulations about the timing and format of information that must be conveyed to it and to investors. If companies do not comply with those regulations they could be de-listed (their stocks can no longer trade on the stock exchange), which greatly affects their ability to raise capital. Environmental groups, as well, monitor the activities of companies to ensure that environmental standards are being met.

Taxing Authorities

The federal taxing authority in Canada, the Federal Parliament, has established the Canada Customs and Revenue Agency (CCRA) as its collection agency. Parliament establishes the rules for how taxable income should be measured. The tax rules use accounting financial statements extensively in the assessment of the amount of tax to be paid by businesses, but there are several areas in which they vary. Later in this text we will describe some of those variations and explain their impact on the financial statements.

Other Users

Additional users of financial statement information include other companies, security analysts, credit-rating agencies, and labour unions. Other companies may want information about the performance of a company if they enter into cooperative agreements or contracts with that company. If it is a direct competitor, the company may want information that will enable it to assess the strength and future plans of the competitor. Security analysts and credit-rating agencies use the information in financial statements to provide information about the strengths and weaknesses of companies to people who want to invest. Labour unions need to understand the financial health of the company in order to negotiate labour issues with management.

All of these users, with their various needs, use the same set of financial statements. It is therefore important that the financial statements provide information to the widest possible group of users. As you would guess, however, there are many pieces of information particular users may want but cannot find in the financial statements. They must therefore develop alternate sources of information.

Learning Objective

5

Know what Generally Accepted Accounting Principles (GAAP) are.

DEVELOPMENT OF ACCOUNTING STANDARDS

When management begins the task of measuring, collecting, recording, and reporting financial information for users, it needs some guidelines to follow so that users can read and understand the financial statements. If there were no guidelines, each company would develop its own information reporting system and it would be very difficult for users to evaluate the statements and to compare them with other companies as they attempt to make knowledgeable decisions. Each country has developed guidelines for this purpose.

In Canada, the **Accounting Standards Board (AcSB)** of the Canadian Institute of Chartered Accountants (CICA) sets accounting recommendations and guidelines, which are published in the *CICA Handbook*. These accounting recommendations and guidelines have the force of law as they are recognized in both federal and provincial statutes that regulate business corporations. In the United States, the **Financial Accounting Standards Board (FASB)** sets accounting standards for American corporations.

The set of accounting recommendations and guidelines that corporations use is referred to as Generally Accepted Accounting Principles, or **GAAP** (usually pronounced as "gap"). Many different methods of deriving these principles have been used over time. Deductive methods have been used that start with some generally accepted definitions (of assets, liabilities, and income, for instance) and concepts, and then logically derive accounting methods and other accounting principles from them. These methods are similar to the process mathematicians use in the development of mathematical theory. The problem with this approach has been the difficulty in achieving a consensus on the underlying definitions and concepts. Inductive approaches have also been used. These approaches generally take into consideration the methods in current practice and attempt to develop (induce) general principles from these methods. Current standard-setting under the CICA combines both an inductive and a deductive approach. On the deductive side, the CICA has developed a set of underlying objectives and concepts called financial statement concepts, or the **conceptual framework**. This framework has then been used deductively to justify new accounting standards and to revise old ones. On the inductive side, the conceptual framework and the new accounting standards have all been established by a political process of reaching consensus among the various users of financial information.

AN INTERNATIONAL PERSPECTIVE

Reports from Other Countries

The development of accounting standards has, in general, been a country-specific process. Each country has developed its own standards, which reflect its political, social, and economic environment. However, with the development of world markets for both products and financial capital, there has been an increasing need for better understanding among countries with regard to financial reporting. Over the years, numerous organizations have attempted to set international accounting standards. There are currently several groups involved in the process of trying to formulate international accounting standards. Predominant among them is the **International Accounting Standards Board (IASB)**. The IASB is an independent, private-sector body that is funded by donations from accounting organizations around the world and from the **International Federation of Accountants (IFAC)**. By the end of 2001, the IASB had issued 41 **International Accounting Standards (IASs)**. The IASB has developed relationships with the primary standard-setting bodies in numerous countries, including the CICA in Canada, in order to promote the development of international accounting standards. The IASB encourages countries to change their accounting standards so that they more closely resemble the international standards. Through its deliberations about new standards and the revisions of old standards, the AcSB has attempted to realign Canadian standards more closely with the IASB and with the FASB in the United States.

As a future user of accounting information, it is important that you understand the concepts that underlie financial accounting. The conceptual framework in which these concepts lie is used to develop accounting guidelines from which financial statements are prepared so that external users can find information on which they can base decisions about the entity. The financial statements should describe what the entity owns, to whom it has obligations, and what is left over after the obligations are satisfied. They should also show how cash flowed in and out of the entity. The final purpose of financial statements should be to describe the results of the operations of the entity.

Learning Objective
6

*Identify the qualitative
characteristics of accounting
information.*

Qualitative Characteristics of Accounting Information

Accounting data should possess four essential characteristics. Exhibit 1-2 provides a hierarchy of these characteristics.

Characteristics of Accounting Information

Understandability
Relevance
    Predictive value and feedback value
    Timeliness
Reliability
    Representational faithfulness
    Verifiability
    Neutrality
    Conservatism
Comparability

Understandability, the first qualitative characteristic, simply means that the information must be understandable to the user. For example, if you see an item called "Current portion of long-term debt" listed on a financial statement, you should understand that this means that over the next year, the amount listed for this item will be paid in cash to the group that loaned the money to the company. If preparers of the financial statements were not interested in understandability, they would show the amount of long-term debt in total without backing out the amount that has to be paid back in the next year. Then, users would not be able to assess the probable cash outflow from the company in the coming year. The underlying assumptions behind this qualitative characteristic are that the users are reasonably well informed about accounting terminology and procedures and that they have a reasonable understanding of the business environment. It is unlikely that you have such a background, which means that initially you will find the financial statements difficult to understand.

Relevance refers to whether the information is capable of making a difference in a decision. If you were told that you had an exam next week, that would be relevant to you. However, if you were told that it was snowing at the North Pole, you would probably not find that relevant. It is not always easy for management to know what information will be relevant to users. In some cases, there are accounting guidelines that direct management to disclose certain information. For example, the market value of a short-term investment is likely a relevant piece of information to a user. If the investment is short-term, it means that the company intends to sell it in the near future. Knowing what its market value is at a point in time enables the user to estimate the potential cash inflow from its sale. Management is required to disclose this information.

Relevant information may have three kinds of value: predictive value, feedback value, and timeliness. **Predictive value** means that the information is useful in predicting future results and, therefore, should be helpful to users who make decisions that depend on accurate predictions of future events. Predictive value is based on an underlying assumption that the past is a good predictor of the future. The example in the previous paragraph has potential predictive value in that the market value of the investment may be a good predictor of future cash inflows. **Feedback value** is information that allows users to assess the outcomes of previous decisions, providing them with feedback on decisions made in the past. This can be helpful as users learn from their past successes and failures. Following the investment example, if the user saw financial statements following the sale of the investment, the user could determine whether the investment sold for the market value previously disclosed. If it did, the user would be confident that relying on the market value was a reasonable decision. If the investment sold for less or more, the user might decide that the market value was one piece of information, but that other sources of information are needed to make a better prediction of future cash inflows. Finally, **timeliness** is important because old information quickly loses its relevance to users. If the information is not timely, it may lose its ability to make a difference in a decision. For example, if you were interested in investing in a company, one of the things you would want to see would be its financial statements. Companies produce financial statements for the public every three months (quarterly) and annually. If you request information from a company, this is what you will receive. If it is June and the most recent financial statements you can get are dated March 31, is this timely information? With the rapid changes in the business environment that are evident around us, timeliness will become even more important in decision-making. It may be that, in the future, companies will publish monthly financial statements in order to satisfy the demand of users for timely information.

accounting in the news

On February 6, 2001, Cisco Systems Inc. surprised the business world when it announced its second quarter results, complete with financial statements, for the quarter ending January 31, 2001. Most companies take about three weeks to produce the previous quarter's results. Providing information within one week enabled users to make decisions based on actual results rather than speculation. How was Cisco able to report so fast? Its accounting system utilizes the Internet and it enables near-real-time financial reporting. It continued this fast reporting by announcing on May 8, 2001, its third quarter results and on August 7, 2001, its fourth quarter and annual results for the period ended July 28, 2001.

Source: "Speed Matters. Cisco Systems pocketed $86 million last year thanks partly to virtual-close financial reporting," by Desirée de Myer, *Smart Business*, May 2001; also news releases by Cisco Systems on February 6, 2001, May 8, 2001, and August 7, 2001.

accounting in the news

O n November 20, 2001, a financial analyst on ROB TV was asked why Nortel Networks shares had risen so dramatically in the last month and whether it was a good time to buy the shares. The shares were trading around $9.50 on October 27, 2001, and by November 20, 2001, they had risen to around $13.00, an increase of over 35%. The analyst said that he did not know what information was leading investors to pursue the shares so much that the demand was driving up the price. The most recent financial statements were included in the third quarterly report dated September 30, 2001, which was released October 18. In that report, Nortel reported a net loss from continuing operations of US $3.5 billion. Since October 18, Nortel had several news releases about various activities of the company but there had been no further financial statement information. Did the investors in late October and early November use the third quarterly report as a basis for buying or selling their shares? It is extremely unlikely. That information was no longer timely.

Reliability of information rests on four fundamental characteristics: representational faithfulness, verifiability, neutrality, and conservatism.

Representational faithfulness means that the information faithfully represents the attribute, characteristic, or economic event that it purports to represent. For example, suppose the accounting system produces a dollar total for sales that is supposed to represent all sales made during a single year. This amount should include all sales made in that year and exclude all sales made in any other year. If it does, the information has representational faithfulness.

Verifiability means that independent measurers using the same measurement methods should agree on the appropriate value. Determining the cost of an item based on evidence such as invoices and cancelled cheques possesses a high degree of verifiability. Determining the market value of a piece of real estate possesses a much lower degree of verifiability because it is based solely on opinions.

Neutrality means that the information is not calculated or presented in a way that would bias users towards making certain desired decisions and not making other, undesired decisions. For example, an inflated estimate of the value of inventory on hand is biased and not neutral. On the other hand, recording inventory at what you paid for it is neutral.

Conservatism means that, if estimates must be made in financial statements, they should err on the side of understating rather than overstating net assets and net income. For example, if a company bought a piece of land for $50,000, it would be on its records at $50,000. If there was a downturn in the economy and the market value of the land dropped to $40,000, the company would be required to reduce the land on the records to $40,000 and recognize a loss in the value of the land. This write-down is necessary even though the company has no intention of selling the land in the near future. The write-down illustrates conservatism. If, instead of declining to $40,000, the market value of the land increased to $100,000, no change would be made in the company's records unless the company actually sold the land for $100,000. This also represents conservatism. Note that conservatism may conflict with neutrality. If conflict occurs, conservatism overrides neutrality.

Comparability generally refers to the ability of information produced by different companies, particularly within a given industry, to be compared. A high degree of comparability allows for better comparisons across companies and potentially better decisions. Within Canadian GAAP, however, there are no guidelines that require all companies in an industry to use the same accounting methods. Because different methods will produce different financial statement amounts, it is important for users to understand what methods are available to companies and how the various methods will impact on the accounting numbers. Comparability is enhanced with the consistent application of accounting methods by a given company over time. Much of the predictive value of accounting information depends on the long-term trends of the data. If different methods are used to produce that information over time, the predictive value of the information is diminished.

Finally, there are two overriding constraints that impact the information provided by management: the cost/benefit constraint, and the materiality criterion. The **cost/benefit constraint** states simply that the value of benefits received from information should exceed the cost of producing it. The value of benefits received from information, however, is very difficult to measure. This can lead to problems because the company bears the cost of producing the information, yet the benefits are perceived mainly by outside users. For example, a company could consider publishing financial statements every week instead of every three months. To publish the financial statements every week would be very costly in terms of hours required to produce the financial statements and ensure their accuracy. It is likely that it would take at least a week to produce the statements and then the company would have to start again on the week just ended. The company could measure how much it would cost to engage in this activity. It would then have to estimate the amount of benefit users would get from seeing weekly financial statements. If there was perceived to be very little benefit from weekly financial statements, the company would not provide them because the cost would exceed the benefit.

Materiality is a pervasive concept that affects many aspects of the production of information. It is generally thought of as the minimum size of a transaction that can significantly affect decisions. For example, when a company purchases a building, the amount spent is usually substantial. Because the building will be used for several years, it is appropriate to spread that cost over several years, which affects the company's profitability. The effect on profitability over a period of years may affect an investor's decision to buy shares. On the other hand, if the company purchases a pencil sharpener, the cost is so small that it will not affect an investor's decision. Materiality is used by the company's **external auditors** in their annual audit of the financial statements. Auditors are an independent third party that the shareholders hire to review the financial statements presented by management. They provide a professional opinion as to whether the financial statements fairly present the results of the company's operations. In their tests of the financial statements, auditors will ignore discrepancies below a certain dollar level because the explanation of the discrepancy would not significantly change their opinion about the financial statements. More is said about the work of the auditor later in the chapter. Both materiality and the cost/benefit constraint are kept in mind as the CICA adopts and implements new accounting guidelines and as accountants apply those guidelines.

These qualitative characteristics and constraints help form the underlying basis on which accounting recommendations and guidelines are established. As we discuss these in the book, referring back to these characteristics and constraints should help you understand and remember the recommendations and guidelines being used.

Learning Objective

Describe the three fundamental business activities.

BUSINESS ACTIVITIES

To understand the information in financial statements, it is useful to think about the fundamental types of activities that all businesses engage in and report on. The basic activities of businesses are **financing**, **investing**, and **operating**.

Financing Activities

Financing refers to the activity of obtaining **funds** (cash) that can be used to buy major assets such as the buildings and equipment used by virtually every business. This activity is necessary, of course, to start the business, but it is also a continuing activity as the business grows and expands its operations. Funds are obtained from two primary sources outside the company: **creditors** and **investors**. Creditors expect to be repaid on a timely basis and very often charge the business in the form of interest for the use of their money, goods, or services. The amount to be repaid is generally a fixed amount. Examples of creditors are banks that offer both short-term and long-term loans, and suppliers who are willing to provide goods and services today with the expectation of being paid for those products later. Investors, on the other hand, invest in the company in the hope that their investment will generate a profit. They earn profits either by receiving **dividends** (withdrawals of funds from the company) or by selling their shares to another investor. Of course, investors may experience either a gain (receive more than the initial amount paid for the shares) or a loss (receive less than the initial amount paid for the shares) when the sale occurs.

A primary internal source of new funds to the company is the profit generated by the business that is not paid out to shareholders in the form of dividends. These profits are called **retained earnings**. If the company is not profitable, or if all profits are distributed to shareholders in the form of dividends, the only way the company can expand is to either get more funds from investors (existing shareholders or new investors), or borrow more from creditors. How much to borrow from creditors and how much to obtain from investors are important decisions that the management of the company must make. Those decisions can determine whether a company grows, goes bankrupt, or is bought by some other company. Examples of financing activities follow.

TYPICAL FINANCING ACTIVITIES

Borrowing money
Repaying loans
Issuing shares
Repurchasing shares
Paying dividends on shares

Investing Activities

Once the company obtains funds, it must invest those funds to accomplish its purposes. Most companies make both long-term and short-term investments. Most short-term investments are considered operating activities, such as the purchase of raw materials and inventories. Some short-term investments, such as the investment in the shares of other companies (called marketable securities) and most long-term investments are considered investing activities. Long-term investment in property, plant, and equipment to produce goods and services for sale is one such investing activity. Long-term investments in the shares of other companies would also be considered an investing activity. Examples of investing activities follow.

TYPICAL INVESTING ACTIVITIES

Purchase of property, plant, and equipment
Sale of property, plant, and equipment
Investments in the shares of other companies
Sale of investments in the shares of other companies

Operating Activities

Operating activities are those associated with developing, producing, marketing, and selling the products and/or services of the company. While financing and investing activities are necessary to conduct operations, they tend to occur on a more sporadic basis than the activities thought of as operating activities. The day-to-day continuing activities are generally classified as operations. Examples of operating activities follow.

TYPICAL OPERATING ACTIVITIES

Sales to customers
Collections of amounts owed by customers
Purchase of inventory
Payment of amounts owed to suppliers
Payment of expenses like wages, rent, and interest
Payment of taxes owed to the government

Financial statements provide information about the operating, financing, and investing activities of a company. By the end of this book, you should be able to interpret financial statements as they relate to these activities. To start you on the journey to becoming a successful user of financial statement information, we have included for you, in Appendix A at the back of the book, the annual report of a Canadian corporation, **Sears Canada Inc.** A survey of the various types of information contained in the Sears Canada Annual Report follows.

SEARS CANADA INC. ANNUAL REPORT

Annual Report Walkthrough

The 2001 annual report for **Sears Canada** constitutes Appendix A at the back of the book. As mentioned earlier, references to its page numbers are prefixed by "SC-". The Sears Canada annual report will probably appear very complex, particularly if you have never before been exposed to accounting. The fact is, however, that Sears Canada is a fairly simple company. We selected it because it is a good example of annual reporting, it illustrates almost all the reporting issues discussed in this book, and it offers a challenge to you, the reader, to understand a modern company. The "pain" in trying to understand Sears Canada will be rewarded by the "gain" in your understanding of real, complex business organizations.

A survey of the various types of information contained in the Sears Canada Annual Report follows.

Corporate Profile

The annual report starts with a short section describing the business activities of the company during the year. Sears Canada sells merchandise to consumers through department and specialty stores. Its headquarters are in Toronto, Ontario.

When you evaluate a company for the first time, it is extremely important to know what kind of businesses it is in so that you can assess the risk level of the company. You may be deciding whether to invest in the company or whether to lend it money. The decision will be heavily influenced by the risk being taken. An investment in an oil exploration company, for instance, would have a much greater risk than an investment in a grocery store chain. When you read the financial statements, you must weigh the financial results against the level of risk of the investment. On page SC-1, Sears Canada shows a map of Canada with all of its various selling outlets. This section gives you information about the range of its retail products (from automobile parts, to travel, to clothing) and where it is currently selling them. This information should help you in your risk assessment.

Report to the Shareholders

The report to the shareholders appears on pages SC-4 and SC-5. The report is written by the chairman and chief executive officer, Mark A. Cohen. The chairman has the opportunity to give a global view of where the company has been, what it accomplished last year, and where it is going in the future. You can see that he has highlighted his report with information about the conversion of Eaton's stores to Sears, its focus on inventory management and reduced expenditures, and the strength of its people.

Management's Discussion and Analysis

Many companies use this report (page SC-6 to SC-29) to make more extensive detailed comments on the company and its operating results. This report provides an opportunity for senior management to discuss the company's performance with shareholders. Often the information is presented from the perspective of the various divisions of the company. Sears Canada has general comments about various segments of the business from pages SC-6 to SC-14. From pages SC-15 to SC-29, the discussion and analysis focuses on the financial aspects of the various business segments. On page SC-16 it includes an 11-year summary that highlights for the user the changes that have occurred in Sears Canada over an extended period of time. Such a summary allows a user to identify possible trends that may continue into the future. Some companies include this summary in the notes to the financial statements.

This section of the annual report is one of the few places in the annual report where you will find prospective (i.e., forward-looking) information. As you will discover shortly, most of the information presented in the annual report is retrospective (i.e., based on past events). If your interest is in the future of the company, management's discussion and analysis is a good place to get management's opinion about the future directions and prospects of the company. The report should be read sceptically, however, since much of what is said reflects top management's opinion. In such a report, there is an inherent bias toward presenting results to the shareholders in the best possible light.

Board of Directors and Management

Somewhere in every annual report there is a list of the Board of Directors of the company. Sometimes the report also includes their pictures. The directors often hold positions in other companies as well. These directors are elected by shareholders to serve as their representatives, and as such they provide advice and counsel to the management of the company. They also have broad powers to vote on issues relevant to shareholders (e.g., the declaration of dividends), and to hire and fire management. A listing of the senior management of the company is also often included in the report; for Sears Canada, the list of the Board of Directors and senior management can be found on page SC-51.

Financial Section

The remainder of the annual report contains all the financial information about the performance and status of the company (SC-30 through SC-49). In general, this section contains the following major components:

COMPONENTS OF THE FINANCIAL SECTION:

Statement of Management Responsibility
Auditor's report
Financial statements:
    Income Statement
    Balance Sheet
    Statement of Retained Earnings
    Cash Flow Statement
    Notes to the financial statements
Statement on Corporate Governance

Each of these components is discussed at some length in the sections that follow. Virtually all the disclosure contained in this section of the annual report is in compliance with either the recommendations in the *CICA Handbook* or the Ontario Securities Commission (OSC), although management would surely disclose most of this information voluntarily to shareholders in the absence of requirements by the CICA or the OSC.

There are three major statements that appear in all sets of financial statements. They are the **income statement**, the **balance sheet**, and the **cash flow statement**. In addition to these, a company will often include a *statement of retained earnings*. In this chapter, only the income statement, balance sheet, and cash flow statement will be discussed.

Learning Objective

Identify the major financial statements and describe their major components.

INCOME STATEMENT   The income statement (SC-32) is also known as the statement of earnings. This statement describes the results of the operating activities of the current period. The results of those activities add up to the **net income** amount, or bottom line. In companies, net income is defined as **revenues** (money or resources flowing into the company as a result of sale transactions) less **expenses** (money or resources flowing out of the company related to sale transactions). This is different from the concept of income used in preparing individual income tax returns. Income to individuals, for tax purposes, is generally the gross amount of money earned by the individual (salary) with very few deductions allowed. Individuals cannot, for example, deduct the cost of groceries or clothing. In a business, the rules are such that almost all expenditures qualify as expenses in the determination of earnings. There may be a delay in recognizing some expenditures as expenses. Because items such as machinery contribute to the generation of revenues over several years, we will normally recognize as an expense a portion of the original cost of the machine each period over its life. This expense is called **amortization**. Eventually, the entire expenditure will have been expensed in the determination of net income.

Refer to the Consolidated Statement of Earnings for Sears Canada (SC-32). Note that this statement is followed by a retained earnings statement. Companies will sometimes produce a combined statement instead of two separate ones. The statement covers a period of time as indicated at the top of the statement where it reads, "For the 52 week periods ended December 29, 2001 and December 30, 2000." The revenues and expenses are the amounts recognized during each of the years ended December 29, 2001 and December 30, 2000. The activities reported in this statement are primarily the operating activities of the corporation. The statement is a report of the operating performance of the corporation during the year and measures the inflow of revenues and the outflow of expenses from the shareholders' point of view. For this reason, it is sometimes called a **flow statement**. Another way of putting it is that the earnings statement captures the net change in the shareholders' wealth, as measured in the accounting records, across a designated time period. In this case, that time period is one year.

As you will note in the statement, there is one revenue category called Total Revenues which represents the inflow of resources from the sale of inventory in its various stores. Depending on the operating activities of a company, you might also find revenue from performing services or earning interest. The level of detail provided in a company's statement depends on the usefulness of the disclosure. Since Sears Canada is involved only in the retail department store business, the statement can be quite simple.

Another related reason for the breakdown into different types of revenues is that shareholders (and other users of financial statements) want to forecast the future performance of the company. The amounts that are reported in the financial statements are largely historical in nature. For example, the values reported for the assets of the company are generally based on what the company historically paid for them, not on what they are currently worth on the market. These historical numbers may be useful to forecast the future. Because of the differences in the nature of various aspects of a company, the growth rates of the different types of revenues and expenses may differ greatly. If the reader of the financial statements is not provided with any detail about the breakdown in revenues and expenses, it will be very difficult to forecast them accurately.

Costs and expenses are also listed under various categories, including cost of sales or cost of goods sold or cost of merchandise sold (the expenditures for goods sold during the period) and operating expenses. These cost and expense categories are also provided to explain to the shareholders, in more detail, the performance of the company. Sears Canada's income statement has a couple of interesting expenses that likely require further explanation. The Depreciation and Amortization Expense represents the allocation of the original cost of a long-lived asset like a building. Sears Canada owns buildings and equipment that it uses to sell its inventory to generate revenue. The cost of using the buildings and equipment, the depreciation or amortization, is included every year as an expense. The Unusual Items represents a Gain on the Sale of a distribution facility less the cost of closing 14 auto centres. Sears Canada sold an investment in a distribution centre for an amount that was above the recorded amount on the books. The value of this item had risen above its carrying value on the records of Sears Canada. The last expenses, Income Taxes (Current and Future), which represent the provision for income taxes, are listed as separate expenses because they depend on both the revenues and expenses reported. Taxes are calculated on the amount by which revenues exceed expenses.

At the bottom of the income statement is an **earnings per share** disclosure. Basic earnings per share is the net income of the company divided by the average number of common shares that are outstanding during the year. Shareholders find this calculation useful since it puts the performance of their investment in the company into proper perspective. In other words, a shareholder who holds, say, 1,000 shares of Sears Canada can determine his or her share of the earnings during the period. In 2001, Sears Canada earned $0.88 per share. Therefore, that investor's share of the earnings for 2001 would be $880. Sears Canada also has a fully diluted earnings per share amount which indicates that the company has either debt, shares, or share options that can be converted into common shares (Note 10, page SC-41, states that there are common share options outstanding). If they were exercised, the earnings per share would stay the same at $0.88 per share. In other words, when the additional shares are issued there will be no effect on the earnings per share.

For a second example of an income statement, review Exhibit 1-3, the Consolidated Statements of Earnings and Retained Earnings of **Sun-Rype Products Ltd.** for 2001. This is an example of a combined statement of earnings and retained earnings. Note that, like Sears Canada's, it is an uncomplicated income statement. Sun-Rype also has fully diluted earnings per share, which means that it holds some potentially dilutive financial instruments. Use the Sun-Rype Statement of Earnings to review the components of the income statement.

EXHIBIT 1-3

Sun-Rype Products Ltd.

CONSOLIDATED STATEMENTS OF EARNINGS AND RETAINED EARNINGS

For the years ended December 31 (in thousands of dollars except per share amounts)

	2001	2000
Net sales	$ 101,092	$ 94,670
Cost of sales	61,030	58,695
Gross profit	40,062	35,975
Selling, general & administrative expenses	29,178	25,358
Amortization	2,926	3,526
Interest expense, net (note 10)	4	375
Other (note 11)	(308)	(831)
Earnings before income taxes	8,262	7,547
Income taxes (note 13)	3,048	2,695
Net earnings	5,214	4,852
Retained earnings, beginning of year	5,427	575
Retained earnings, end of year	$ 10,641	$ 5,427
Earnings per share (note 16)		
Basic	$ 0.49	$ 0.49
Fully diluted	0.49	0.48

Sears Canada is a simple company with all of its operations concentrated in retail sales, credit card finances, and investments in shopping malls. Sears Canada is the parent and it runs and controls its financial operations out of a subsidiary company. Both of these companies are separate business entities, but when Sears Canada prepares its annual financial statements, it prepares **consolidated financial statements**. These consolidated financial statements are the combination of all the elements of the subsidiary's financial statements with the elements of the parent's financial statements. More detail concerning consolidated financial statements is contained in Appendix B at the end of the book. When businesses expand, they will often establish other companies, or buy shares in other companies. This enables them to expand operations and diversify the risk.

When the subsidiary company is in a business that is fairly similar to the parent company's business, consolidated financial statements provide much more useful information. However, when the business of a subsidiary is very different from that of the parent company, the combined set of financial statements may not be easy to interpret because of the complexity of the combined companies. In Canada, parent companies must prepare consolidated financial statements unless there is some impediment that prevents the earnings of the subsidiary from flowing to the parent.

Reviewing the income statement for Sears Canada, you can see that the earnings (net income) for 2001 were $94.1 million. You will notice that the net income has decreased from the $225.8 million of the previous year. Companies provide the previous year's results along with the current year's so that users can better evaluate the current year. They will often round amounts to the nearest $100, $1,000, or in the case of very large companies, $1,000,000. The units in which the numbers are expressed must be stated somewhere on the statement. Usually, they can be found in parentheses at the top of the statement. This brings up an issue that was discussed earlier in the development of accounting standards section: materiality. If an auditor were to find a $2,000 mistake when trying to verify how fairly the statements presented the earnings of a company, how much difference would it make assuming the company rounded its amounts to the nearest $1,000? The answer is, it would not make much difference in the overall analysis of the financial status of the company. On the other hand, a $2,000 mistake in the tax reporting of an individual's earnings would certainly get the attention of the Canada Customs and Revenue Agency. How material an item is often depends, in part, on the size of the entity being considered.

Below is a list of some of the more common items you can expect to see on an income statement.

COMMON INCOME STATEMENT ITEMS:

Sales Revenues	The total amount of sales for the period.
Other Income	Various types of revenues or income to the company other than sales.
Cost of Goods Sold	The cost of the units of inventory that were sold during the period.
Selling, General, and Administrative Expenses	The total amount of other expenses of the company during the period that do not fit into any other category (e.g. salaries, rent).
Amortization Expense	The allocation of part of the cost of long-lived items like equipment.
Interest Expense	The amount of interest incurred on the company's debt during the period.
Income Tax Expense (Provision for Taxes)	The taxes levied on the company's profits during the period.

BALANCE SHEET   The balance sheet (SC-31) is also known as the statement of financial position, which is what Sears Canada calls it. Financial position suggests that this statement represents the financial status of the company at a particular point in time. In fact, at the top of the statement, the words "December 29, 2001 and December 30, 2000" appear. The amounts in the statement are those that exist on December 29, 2001 and December 30, 2000, respectively. These dates may also be thought of as the beginning and end points of the current accounting period. In the transition from one accounting period to the next, the ending balances of one accounting period become the beginning balances of the next accounting period. This statement has been described by various authors as a snapshot of the financial position of the company at a particular point in time.

So what makes up the financial position of the company? Individuals, if asked about their own financial position, would probably start by listing what they own—such as a car, a computer, or a house—and then listing what they owe to other people, such as bank loans and credit card balances. What is owned less what is owed would be a measure of their net worth (wealth or equity) at a particular point in time. A company lists exactly the same types of things in its balance sheet. In Sears Canada's statement, there are two major categories: the first is a category for **assets**, and the second is a category for **liabilities** and **shareholders' equity**.

Assets   When asked for a simple definition of an asset, many people reply that it is something of value that the company either owns or has the right to use. In fact, the accounting definition of an asset is very similar. In this book, assets will be those things that meet the following criteria: (1) the company owns or has the right to use them; (2) they have probable future value which can be measured; and (3) the event that gave the company the ownership of or right to them has already happened. The word "future" has been added to value since the company would not want to list things that had value in the past, but do not have value in the future. "Probable" has been added because businesses exist in an uncertain world and the value of an asset is subject to change. One of the risks of ownership of an asset, in fact, is that its value may change over time.

CHARACTERISTICS OF AN ASSET:

1. Something that has probable future value that can be measured.
2. The company owns or has the right to use the probable future value.
3. The event that gave the company the ownership or right has already occurred.

The assets that Sears Canada lists in its balance sheet include cash and short-term investments, accounts receivable, inventories, prepaid expenses and other assets, current portion of future income tax assets, investments and other assets, capital assets, deferred charges, and future income tax assets. A full discussion of how each of these meets the criteria of ownership and probable future value is left to later chapters. As an example, however, ownership of inventory by the company is evidenced either by possession or by legal documentation. It has future value because the company can later sell the inventory and receive cash in the amount of the selling price. The presence of the inventory or the documents indicates that the event that gave ownership to the company has already happened. The cash, in turn, has value because the company can use it to obtain other goods and services. The total assets of Sears Canada as at December 29, 2001, were $3,880 million. Following is a list of assets normally found in a balance sheet.

COMMON BALANCE SHEET ASSETS

Cash	The amount of currency that the company has, including amounts in chequing and savings accounts.
Short-Term (Temporary) Investments	Short-term investments in securities of other companies, such as treasury bills, shares, and bonds.
Accounts Receivable	Amounts owed to the company that result from credit sales to customers.
Inventory	Goods held for resale to customers.
Prepaid Expenses	Expenses related to items that have been paid for but have not yet been used. An example is prepaid insurance.
Capital Assets	Investments in land, buildings, and intangibles that the company uses over the long term. Intangibles are investments in assets such as patents, trademarks, and goodwill.

Sears Canada prepares a **classified balance sheet**. A classified balance sheet is one in which the assets and liabilities are classified as **current** and **noncurrent**. For assets, current means that the asset will be turned into cash or consumed (used up) in the next year or operating cycle. The **operating cycle** of a company refers to the time period between the initial investment of cash in products or services and the return of cash from the sale of the product or service. Assets such as cash, accounts receivable, and inventories are classified as current, and assets such as capital assets are classified as noncurrent.

Assets and liabilities are listed on the balance sheet in *liquidity order*. **Liquidity** refers to how quickly the company can turn the asset into cash. Noncurrent assets are the least liquid because they will be used over a long period of time and will not be quickly turned into cash. Accounts receivable, on the other hand, are amounts owed to the company by its customers who bought goods or services on credit. The company hopes that these will be collected quickly (many companies have collection policies that give customers 30 days to pay). Therefore, accounts receivable are fairly liquid. In the case of Sears Canada, its accounts receivable are from credit card sales. Interest is charged on any amounts that are not fully paid for within a month. Inventories are less liquid than receivables since they must be sold first, which normally results in an account receivable. Cash is then received when the account receivable is collected.

An **unclassified balance sheet** is, then, a balance sheet in which current assets or liabilities are not distinguished from noncurrent assets or liabilities. Even in an unclassified balance sheet, however, assets and liabilities are still listed primarily in the order of their liquidity. For instance, the cash, receivables (current receivables), inventories, and capital assets will have the same order as in the Sears Canada report even if they are not specifically identified as current or noncurrent.

Using the information you have just been given about assets, examine the balance sheet of Sun-Rype Products Ltd. in Exhibit 1-4. You will notice that it has fewer assets listed than Sears Canada has. Is it a classified balance sheet? The current assets are identified but the noncurrent ones are not, although they are in a separate section. They do follow the current ones and the liquidity order has been maintained.

EXHIBIT 1-4

Sun-Rype Products Ltd.

CONSOLIDATED BALANCE SHEETS

As at December 31 (in thousands of dollars)

	2001	2000
ASSETS		
Current assets		
Cash	$ 950	$ –
Accounts receivable (note 2)	10,882	8,727
Income taxes receivable	290	79
Inventories (note 3)	13,126	10,144
Prepaid expenses	566	425
Future income tax benefit (note 13)	391	347
	26,205	19,722
Property, plant and equipment (note 4)	15,359	14,857
Deferred expenses (note 5)	1,970	687
	$ 43,534	$ 35,266
LIABILITIES AND SHAREHOLDERS' EQUITY		
Current liabilities		
Bank indebtedness (note 6)	$ –	$ 800
Promissory note (note 7)	725	725
Accounts payable and accrued liabilities	12,567	9,055
Current portion of long-term obligations (note 8)	72	100
	13,364	10,680
Long-term obligations (note 8)	217	247
Future income taxes (note 13)	661	541
	14,242	11,468
Shareholders' equity		
Share capital and contributed surplus (note 9)	18,651	18,371
Retained earnings	10,641	5,427
	29,292	23,798
	$ 43,534	$ 35,266

Commitments (note 15)

APPROVED BY THE BOARD OF DIRECTORS

D. Selman, Director   J. Alfonso, Director

Liabilities A simple definition of liabilities might be "amounts that the company owes to others." The accounting definition of liabilities encompasses this concept and, consistent with the earlier definition of assets, will be used to refer to items that require a probable future sacrifice of resources. In most cases, the resource is cash, but recognize that a company could satisfy a liability with services or goods. For example, a warranty liability could be satisfied with a new part or with the services of a repair person.

Sears Canada, in its classified balance sheet, lists among its liabilities accounts payable, accrued liabilities, income and other taxes payable, principal payments on long-term obligations due within one year, current portion of deferred debt, long-term obligations, deferred credit, and future income tax liabilities. Note that Sears Canada labels the current liabilities as such, and then lists the long-term liabilities in a separate section in its balance sheet. Current liabilities are those that will require the use of current assets or will be replaced by another current liability in the next year or operating cycle. The following list includes some of the more common liabilities found in financial statements.

COMMON BALANCE SHEET LIABILITIES

Bank Indebtedness	Amounts owed to the bank on short-term credit.
Accounts Payable	Amounts owed to suppliers from the purchase of goods on credit.
Notes Payable	Amounts owed to a creditor (bank or supplier) that are represented by a formal agreement called a note (sometimes called a promissory note). Notes payable often have an interest component whereas accounts payable usually do not.
Dividends Payable	Amounts owed to shareholders for dividends that are declared by the Board of Directors.
Accrued Liabilities	Amounts owed to others based on expenses that have been incurred by the company but are not yet due, such as interest expense and warranty expense.
Taxes Payable	Amounts owed to taxing authorities.
Long-Term Debt	Amounts owed to creditors over periods longer than one year.
Future Income Tax Liabilities	Amounts representing probable future taxes the company will have to pay to the Canada Customs and Revenue Agency (sometimes called deferred taxes).

Refer back to Sun-Rype's balance sheet in Exhibit 1-4 and review the liability items listed there. Notice that Sun-Rype has bank indebtedness and a promissory note. A promissory note is like a note payable. The company will be required to repay the principal amount of the note along with an interest component.

Shareholders' Equity   The last major category in the balance sheet is the section called **equity**. It is frequently referred to as shareholders' equity. In Sears Canada's section on shareholders' equity, note the listings for capital stock and retained earnings. This section captures the value of the shareholders' interest in the company as measured by the accounting recommendations and guidelines. Note that the total assets equal the total liabilities plus the equity. Both are listed as $3,880 million by Sears Canada on December 29, 2001. This relationship is described by the **basic accounting equation**:

BASIC ACCOUNTING EQUATION

Assets = Liabilities + Shareholders' Equity

This equation gives meaning to the description of this statement as the *balance sheet*. If the equation is rearranged, it can be seen that shareholders' equity is equal to assets minus liabilities:

BASIC ACCOUNTING EQUATION (REARRANGED)

Shareholders' Equity = Assets − Liabilities
(Net Assets)

To state this relationship another way, shareholders' equity is the difference between what the investors own and what the company owes to others, as measured in the **accounting records**. Because of this relationship, shareholders' equity is sometimes referred to as the *net assets* of the company (net refers to the net value of the assets less the liabilities) or the *net book value* of the company. It is the equivalent of an individual's personal net wealth. The shareholders' wealth as measured by the accounting statements is a residual concept. The shareholders can claim the assets that are left over after paying all of the liabilities. You should note that the market value of the shares of a company is another measure of the shareholders' wealth in the company. By **market value**, we mean the price at which the shares trade in the stock market. This value could be very different from the book value of shareholders' equity because accounting records are not necessarily based on market values.

We can look at the proportion of liabilities and shareholders' equity on the balance sheet to better understand the financing strategy used by the company. For Sears Canada, total liabilities are $2,260.1 million and total shareholders' equity is $1,619.9 million. The proportion of liabilities is 58.3% ($2,206.1/$3,880), which is greater than 50%. This means that Sears Canada uses more debt than shareholders' equity to finance activities in the company.

Shareholders' equity is generally made up of two accounts: **share capital** and **retained earnings**. The first, share capital (Sears Canada uses the term *capital stock*), is used to record the amount that the investors originally paid (invested) for the shares that the company issued. The retained earnings account is used to keep track of the earnings of the company less any amounts that are paid from the company to the shareholders in the form of **dividends**. Dividends will be paid to shareholders only when approved by a vote of the Board of Directors. The change in the retained earnings of a company during a given period can be explained by the net income less the dividends declared as follows:

CHANGE IN RETAINED EARNINGS

Change in Retained Earnings = Net Income − Dividends

Other accounts can appear in this section. During the early part of this book, these other accounts will be ignored in order to concentrate on common share capital and retained earnings. The other accounts will be discussed in later sections of the book. Following is a list of some of the more common account titles that appear in the shareholders' equity section.

COMMON BALANCE SHEET SHAREHOLDERS' EQUITY ACCOUNTS

Share Capital	Represents the shares that have been issued by the company and is usually stated at an amount equal to what was originally paid by investors for the shares. This can be referred to as capital stock. Shares can be of different types, with different rights and privileges attached to each.
Retained Earnings	The earnings of the company (as measured on the Income Statement) that have been kept (retained) and not paid out in the form of dividends.

Refer back to the balance sheet of Sun-Rype Products in Exhibit 1-4. Note that Sun-Rype uses the term "Share capital and contributed surplus" to refer to the share portion of shareholders' equity. Contributed surplus is one of those other accounts in share capital that will be explained later in the book. Other terms that you might see are Common shares or Preferred shares, which refer to the type of shares that the company has issued.

CASH FLOW STATEMENT The cash flow statement, sometimes called the statement of cash flows or the statement of changes in financial position (SC-33), is a flow statement that is, in some ways, similar to the income statement. It measures inflows and outflows of cash during a specific period of time. Note how the words at the top of the statement indicate that the statement is for "the 52 week periods ended December 29, 2001 and December 30, 2000," which is the same terminology used on the income statement. The difference is that instead of measuring the increase and decrease in shareholders' wealth, this statement measures the increase and decrease in cash and highly liquid assets and liabilities called cash equivalents. Remember that a liquid item is one that can be converted very quickly to cash. Since cash is very important to the operations of the company, this statement is vital to any user's evaluation of it.

The cash flow statement has three sections that report the sources and uses of cash and cash equivalents for the three business activities described earlier: operating, financing, and investing.

SUBSECTIONS OF THE CASH FLOW STATEMENT

Cash from operating activities
Cash from financing activities
Cash from investing activities

In order to evaluate the liquidity position of a company, users need to evaluate where cash is coming from and where it is being spent. Sears Canada generated a positive cash flow of $241.7 million from its operating activities in 2001.

Operating activities include all inflows and outflows of cash related to the sale of goods and services of the company. The starting point in this section is net income (net earnings), which is a summary of the income from operating activities from the income statement. There are adjustments to this number because the recognition of revenues and expenses (as will be seen in future chapters) does not necessarily coincide with the receipt and payment of cash. For instance, sales could be either cash sales or sales on account (i.e., the customer can pay at a later date, resulting in an account receivable rather than cash). Expenses may also be paid later if the company is given credit by its suppliers (this would result in an account payable). Because the operating activities are the backbone of the company, a positive cash flow from operations is essential to its health. Sears Canada's liquidity position has declined somewhat from the previous year, when its cash flow from operations was $310.4 million.

The positive cash flow of $65.9 million from financing activities indicates that Sears Canada used outside sources for more cash during the year; the long-term obligations were greater than the repayments and it raised $2.8 million by issuing more shares. **Financing activities**, as you will recall, are those transactions that either generate new funds from investors or return funds to investors. Investors can be either shareholders or lenders, and the typical activities in this category are the issuance and repurchase of shares and the issuance and repayment of debt. Note as well that Sears Canada paid $25.6 million in dividends to its shareholders in 2001.

Investing activities generally involve the purchase and sale of long-term assets such as property, plant, and equipment, and investments in other companies. These typical activities can be seen from the disclosure by Sears Canada. The negative cash flow of $113.8 million from investing activities indicates that Sears Canada made a substantial investment in new capital assets during the year. In the future the company will use the new capital assets for operating activities. It also spent $23.5 million to purchase Eaton's. In 2001, Sears Canada generated enough cash flow from operations to cover its investment activities (a good sign), and although it went to outside sources to raise additional cash, it did not need to do so to cover its investing activities. If the current year is an indicator of future results, the future operating activities will generate a positive cash flow and the company's investment in new capital assets will have been a worthwhile investment. These amounts in 2001 indicate that Sears Canada is doing quite well with respect to cash flow.

Examine the cash flow statement for Sun-Rype Products Ltd. in Exhibit 1-5. You can see that in 2001, it generated enough cash from operating activities ($5,969 thousand) to pay for all of its investing activities ($4,411 thousand). This new investment was financed almost entirely from internally generated funds. Sun-Rype did issue new shares ($280 thousand) but it also paid off a portion of the capital lease ($88 thousand). These activities leave an inflow of cash from financing of $192 thousand. Sun-Rype and Sears Canada are both successful, but are operating under different financing policies.

Sun-Rype Products Ltd.

CONSOLIDATED STATEMENTS OF CASH FLOWS

For the years ended December 31 (in thousands of dollars)

EXHIBIT 1-5

	2001	2000
Cash provided by (used in):		
Operating activities		
Net earnings	$ 5,214	$ 4,852
Non-cash items:		
Amortization of tangible assets	2,289	2,487
Amortization of goodwill and product launch costs	637	1,039
Gain on sale of trademark (note 11)	–	(835)
(Gain) loss on capital dispositions (note 11)	(308)	4
Future income taxes (note 13)	76	(64)
Shares issued for services (note 9)	–	73
Other	20	(2)
	7,928	7,554
Changes in non-cash working capital items (note 14)	(1,959)	(3,021)
	5,969	4,533
Financing activities		
Proceeds from issue of long-term debt	–	3,100
Repayment of long-term debt	–	(3,583)
Capital lease payment	(88)	(82)
Shares purchased and cancelled	–	(1,169)
Proceeds from issue of shares	280	1,750
	192	16
Investing activities		
Deferred expenses	(1,939)	(884)
Proceeds on capital dispositions (note 11)	441	113
Capital expenditures	(2,913)	(3,806)
Net proceeds on sale of trademark (note 11)	–	835
	(4,411)	(3,742)
Increase in cash position	1,750	807
Bank indebtedness, beginning of year	(800)	(1,607)
Cash (bank indebtedness), end of year	$ 950	$ (800)
Supplemental information on cash flows		
Interest paid	$ 74	$ 241
Income taxes paid	3,460	4,627

See accompanying notes to these financial statements

The preparation and interpretation of the cash flow statement is discussed in greater detail in Chapter 5. Until you study the statement in more detail, confine your study of this statement to understanding what the three sections of the statement are measuring.

SUMMARY OF FINANCIAL STATEMENTS

Income Statement
- Measures the operating performance of a company over a period of time.

Balance Sheet
- Measures the resources controlled by a company (assets) and the claims on those resources (liability and equity holders) at a given point in time.

Cash Flow Statement
- Measures the change in cash flow through operating, financing, and investing activities over a period of time.

NOTES TO THE FINANCIAL STATEMENTS   You may have noticed that various items in the financial statements direct the reader to specific notes. In such notes to the financial statements (SC-34 to SC-48), management has a chance to provide more detail about the referenced items. For example, on Sears Canada's income statement, the income taxes item includes a reference to Note 4. Note 4 goes into greater detail about taxes owed, future income taxes, and tax rates. Financial statements are thus kept simple and uncluttered by including additional explanations in notes rather than on the financial statements themselves.

A full discussion of notes will be left to succeeding chapters, but some attention should be paid to the note that discusses the Summary of Accounting Policies. It is usually the first or second note. It is the first note in Sears Canada's financial statements. Within GAAP there are choices and judgements to be made by management. This note describes the choices that were made. The auditors, of course, review these choices for conformity with GAAP. As you progress through the book, you will learn that the choices made by management have important implications for the interpretation of the statements. As an example, note how, on page SC-34, Sears Canada changed its method of valuing inventories from the retail inventory method to the average cost method. The average cost method will produce a different balance in the inventory account on the balance sheet from that produced by a similar company using an alternative method, such as the first-in, first-out, or FIFO, method. Comparing the two companies using these two different methods would be difficult. To aid users in comparing various companies, management must disclose their major accounting policies in this note. You will learn more about inventory valuation methods in Chapter 7.

SEGMENTED INFORMATION   Information about various segments of the company is provided as a part of the notes to the financial statements. This is a requirement for any company that has more than one significant segment. A segment represents a business activity. Sears Canada has three operating segments: merchandising, credit financing, and the real estate joint venture. If it made sales outside of Canada, it would also report the percentage of those sales. This information is important to users because it helps to explain the kinds of risks an investor takes when buying Sears Canada shares. Segments can differ significantly with regard to risk and are affected in different ways by economic factors such as commodity prices, inflation, exchange rates, and interest rates. It is important to know the relative amounts invested in these segments if an overall assessment of the risk of this company is to be made. Because companies produce consolidated financial statements which provide aggregate information, it would be difficult to assess segment risks without this additional information.

ethics in accounting

Ethics in Accounting

> ■ The management of a company, through the direction given to it by the Board of Directors, has both a moral and a legal obligation to safeguard the investment shareholders have entrusted to it. To ensure that management fulfills this stewardship function with regard to the resources of the company, shareholders typically provide some incentives for and controls over management. You have probably heard about stock option plans and bonuses given to top management. These additional compensation arrangements are often tied to the financial performance of the company and provide incentives for management to make decisions that are in the best interests of the shareholders. The shareholders also hire auditors to review the financial statements to ensure that they adequately reflect the transactions of the company and that GAAP has been followed. There are also legal responsibilities placed on the behaviour of management.

STATEMENT OF MANAGEMENT RESPONSIBILITY This section, which is often included with the financial statements, contains a statement by management that it is responsible for the contents of the annual report. In addition, it discusses the steps management has taken to ensure the safekeeping of the company's assets and to assure the shareholders that management is operating in an ethical and responsible way. Sears Canada (page SC-30) and Sun-Rype both include this statement in the annual report. Review Exhibit 1-6, Sun-Rype's statement, to see what a typical statement conatins.

MANAGEMENT'S RESPONSIBILITY

EXHIBIT 1-6

The management of Sun-Rype Products Ltd. is responsible for the preparation and integrity of the consolidated financial statements of the Company. The financial statements have been prepared in accordance with Canadian generally accepted accounting principles using management's best estimates and judgements where necessary. The financial information contained elsewhere in this annual report is consistent with that in the balance sheet, earnings and cash flow statements.

Sun-Rype Products Ltd. maintains a system of internal accounting controls designed to provide reasonable assurance that assets are safeguarded against loss or unauthorized use and that financial records are adequate and can be relied upon to produce financial statements in accordance with Canadian generally accepted accounting principles. The concept of reasonable assurance is based on the recognition that the cost of maintaining our system of internal accounting controls should not exceed benefits expected to be derived from the system. The system is supported by written policies and guidelines, and is continuously reviewed.

Deloitte & Touche LLP, independent auditors, are retained to audit Sun-Rype Products Ltd.'s financial statements. Their audit is conducted in accordance with Canadian generally accepted auditing standards and provides an independent assessment that helps assure fair representation of the Company's financial position, results of operations and cash flows. Their opinion on the financial statements is published below.

The Board of Directors, through its Audit Committee, comprised of non-management directors, exercises a monitoring role in the Company's financial affairs and statements. The Committee meets with management regularly and the independent auditors as required. These meetings include discussions of internal accounting control and the quality of management and financial reporting. The Finance & Administration department of the Company and the independent auditors have full and free access to the Audit Committee.

Management recognizes its responsibility to conduct Company business in accordance with high ethical standards. Our policy statements and ongoing communications and review programs are designed to ensure this responsibility is fully carried out.

Lawrence Bates
President & Chief Executive Officer

Robert McGowan
Vice President Finance & Administration, Chief Financial Officer

INDEPENDENT AUDITOR'S REPORT   The financial statements are prepared by the management of the company. Independent auditors are hired by shareholders to provide an opinion about the fairness of the presentation and the conformity to accounting guidelines. **Auditors** are professionally trained accountants who add credibility to the financial statements by expressing their professional opinion as to whether the financial statements fairly present the results of the company.

Companies such as Sears Canada are not audited by one person alone, but by a firm of auditors. Auditors apply a set of procedures to test the financial statements to determine if they comply with generally accepted accounting principles and to assess the fairness of the presentation. Audit reports are often expressed in a standard format of three paragraphs. The first paragraph states which financial statements have been audited, that the financial statements are the responsibility of management, and that the auditors' responsibility is to express an opinion about the financial statements. The second paragraph explains how they conducted the audit using generally accepted auditing standards. The third paragraph is the auditors' opinion about the financial statements. The audit report of Sears Canada (SC-30) follows this format. We have included the auditors' report from Sun-Rype Products Ltd. in Exhibit 1-7 so that you can see the similarities between the two. A standard format like this is called an **unqualified opinion**. It means that the financial statements present fairly, in all material respects, the financial position, results of operations, and cash flows of the entity in conformity with Generally Accepted Accounting Principles.

EXHIBIT 1-7

AUDITORS' REPORT

To the Shareholders of Sun-Rype Products Ltd.

We have audited the consolidated balance sheets of Sun-Rype Products Ltd. as at December 31, 2001 and 2000 and the consolidated statements of earnings and retained earnings and cash flows for the years then ended. These financial statements are the responsibility of the Company's management. Our responsibility is to express an opinion on these financial statements based on our audits.

We conducted our audits in accordance with Canadian generally accepted auditing standards. Those standards require that we plan and perform an audit to obtain reasonable assurance whether the financial statements are free of material misstatement. An audit includes examining, on a test basis, evidence supporting the amounts and disclosures in the financial statements. An audit also includes assessing the accounting principles used and significant estimates made by management, as well as evaluating the overall financial statement presentation.

In our opinion, these consolidated financial statements present fairly, in all material respects, the financial position of the Company as at December 31, 2001 and 2000 and the results of its operations and cash flows for the years then ended in accordance with Canadian generally accepted accounting principles.

Chartered Accountants
Vancouver, British Columbia
February 1, 2002

In Canada the **unqualified** or **"clean" opinion** is the most commonly seen opinion. Companies prefer to have a clean opinion attached to their financial statements. If the auditors are considering an opinion other than an unqualified one, management is informed about the reason(s) for the opinion prior to the issuance of the financial statements. Management then has an opportunity to change the financial statements to resolve the problem(s) the auditors have detected. If the issue is controversial, there may be some negotiation between management and the auditors as to how best to resolve the problem. If no resolution is reached and management decides to issue the statements as originally prepared, a **qualified** or **adverse opinion** will be included with the statements. This rarely happens in practice because the problems are often resolved prior to statement issuance. As the enclosed article indicates, sometimes the auditors withdraw from an audit if they do not think they can find enough information to verify the amounts on the financial statements.

accounting in the news

AUDITORS RESIGN BEFORE CERTIFYING STATEMENTS

In relatively rare cases, a company is not able to provide audited financial statements. In January 2001, Ernst & Young LLP resigned as auditors to CINAR Corporation after the company indicated that "its management will not be able, until at least the completion of fiscal 2001, to make the necessary representations regarding the accuracy of the Company's financial statements." The financial statements for the years ended November 30, 1999 and 2000, had not been audited. Throughout 2001, the company produced unaudited financial statements for its shareholders. In November 2001, it announced that new auditors had been hired. CINAR Corporation is a Montreal company. Its shares are not traded on a stock exchange, which means that it is subject to the corporate legislation under which it is incorporated, but it is not subject to the regulations of a stock exchange.

Source: News Releases from CINAR Corporation by L. Sansregret, VP Investor Relations and Public Affairs, January 26, 2001, and November 26, 2001.

In any set of financial statements, the auditors' report should be read because it can alert the reader to major problems the company may be experiencing. In other words, it can provide a "red flag." Readers must then investigate further to make their own assessments of the extent of the problems the company is facing. Also, recognize that there may be significant problems that the auditors did not identify with their tests or that are beyond the responsibility of the auditors.

Most large companies are audited by large accounting firms because of the size and expertise needed on the audit team. Until the late 1980s, the eight largest accounting firms were known as the Big Eight. The Big Eight audited virtually all the large companies in Canada and, as international firms themselves, many companies in other parts of the world. In the late 1980s, two mergers among the Big Eight resulted in what became known as the Big Six. In 1997, merger talks began between two of the Big Six, Price Waterhouse and Coopers & Lybrand. In 1998, that merger was finalized to form PricewaterhouseCoopers, the largest public accounting firm in Canada. This created the Big Five. In 2001, however, Enron, which was audited by Arthur Andersen, went bankrupt. In the subsequent investigation, it was determined that the auditors had shredded Enron documents; Andersen was thus charged with obstruction of justice and found guilty. Many Andersen partnership groups around the world have since left Andersen and joined one of the remaining Big Four, which are, in alphabetical order, Deloitte & Touche, Ernst & Young, KPMG, and PricewaterhouseCoopers. There are also several large and medium-sized national accounting firms that perform audits in Canada.

In Canada, there are three professional accounting organizations that establish the professional standards followed by accountants. The members of the Canadian Institute of Chartered Accountants are called Chartered Accountants (CAs). The organization of the Certified Management Accountants (CMAs) is CMA Canada. The Certified General Accountants' Association of Canada establishes the standards for the Certified General Accountants (CGAs). These professional accountants perform audits, supervise and perform accounting functions inside organizations, and provide decision-making functions inside and outside organizations. Canada is one of the few countries in the world that has more than one professional accounting body. In the past, there have been attempts to combine the three bodies into one, but so far these attempts have been unsuccessful.

What do professional accountants do? Accountants, whether they are in public practice (work in an accounting firm) or in industry, government, or education, provide their clients and employers with information and advice so that they can make effective, informed decisions. They are often strategic advisors who are part of a company's management team. Much of the day-to-day recording of transactions and events is not performed by accountants, although some of them may have some supervisory role over those who do perform this function. Today, most financial information is collected in computer systems that enable the rapid summarization of the data into financial statements and other reports. Computer systems enable managers to access financial statements as often as they want. With up-to-the-minute data, financial statements can be updated in real time.

Ethics in Accounting

ethics in accounting

■ Auditors are hired by the shareholders to review the financial statements presented to the shareholders by the management of the company. The auditors, as they conduct their review, must maintain their independence from the management. In order to ensure their independence and encourage ethical behaviour, the professional accounting organizations have developed codes of professional conduct. The codes state the responsibilities of auditors to the public, clients, and colleagues. For example, accountants normally cannot audit companies in which they own shares. In addition, the codes describe the scope and nature of the services provided by auditors. Each professional accounting organization has also developed a peer review process to monitor its members in the performance of audit work.

SUMMARY

In this chapter, we discussed what accounting is and what financial statements are. We looked at the activities in which companies engage. We discussed the various users of financial accounting information and provided an overview of the types of information that they would need. A brief introduction to the development of accounting standards which underlie accounting recommendations and guidelines was included so that you can begin to understand the basic concepts that govern how we collect and report financial information. The majority of the chapter was used to provide a detailed explanation of the various components of an annual report using Sears Canada Inc. as an example. In the annual report, you discovered the information components of three major financial statements: the income statement, balance sheet, and cash flow statement. Subsequent chapters will build on this framework. In Chapters 2 through 5, the mechanics of preparing these statements and more information about their decision-making capabilities are discussed. Details of each individual asset, liability, and shareholders' equity account are discussed in Chapters 6 through 11. Chapter 12 considers financial statement analysis to provide some tools to interpret and link the major financial statements. To provide some understanding of complex business organizations and the major accounting issues related to mergers, acquisitions, and consolidated financial statements, Appendix B goes into these issues.

SUMMARY PROBLEM

The major financial statements of **Petro-Canada** from its 2001 annual report are included in Exhibit 1-8.

Additional Demonstration Problems

PETRO-CANADA (2001)

EXHIBIT 1-8
PART A

CONSOLIDATED STATEMENT OF EARNINGS

(stated in millions of Canadian dollars)

For the years ended December 31,	2001	2000	1999
REVENUE			
Operating	$ 8 582	$ 9 372	$ 6 095
Investment and other income (Note 5)	108	149	52
	8 690	9 521	6 147
EXPENSES			
Crude oil and product purchases	4 687	5 537	3 436
Operating, marketing and general (Note 6)	1 670	1 619	1 512
Exploration	245	171	78
Depreciation, depletion and amortization	568	584	558
Interest	135	144	141
	7 305	8 055	5 725
EARNINGS BEFORE INCOME TAXES	1 385	1 466	422
PROVISION FOR INCOME TAXES (Note 7)			
Current	528	363	147
Future	(47)	210	42
	481	573	189
NET EARNINGS	$ 904	$ 893	$ 233
EARNINGS PER SHARE (dollars) (Notes 3 and 8)			
Basic	$ 3.41	$ 3.28	$ 0.86
Diluted	$ 3.38	$ 3.25	$ 0.85

EXHIBIT 1-8

PART B

PETRO-CANADA (2001)

CONSOLIDATED STATEMENT OF RETAINED EARNINGS

(stated in millions of Canadian dollars)

For the years ended December 31,	2001	2000	1999
RETAINED EARNINGS AT BEGINNING OF YEAR, as previously reported	$ 897	$ 288	$ 147
Adjustment for the cumulative effect of change in accounting policy on prior periods (Note 3)	—	(175)	—
RETAINED EARNINGS AT BEGINNING OF YEAR, as restated	897	113	147
Net earnings	904	893	233
Dividends on common shares	(106)	(109)	(92)
RETAINED EARNINGS AT END OF YEAR	$ 1 695	$ 897	$ 288

CONSOLIDATED STATEMENT OF CASH FLOWS

(stated in millions of Canadian dollars)

For the years ended December 31,	2001	2000	1999
OPERATING ACTIVITIES			
Net earnings	$ 904	$ 893	$ 233
Items not affecting cash flow (Note 9)	539	806	653
Exploration expenses (Note 13)	245	171	78
Cash flow	1 688	1 870	964
Decrease (increase) in operating working capital related to operating activities and other (Note 10)	55	87	(148)
Cash flow from operating activities	1 743	1 957	816
INVESTING ACTIVITIES			
Expenditures on property, plant and equipment and exploration (Note 13)	(1 681)	(1 203)	(1 021)
Proceeds from sales of assets (Note 5)	127	722	81
Increase in deferred charges and other assets, net	(10)	(8)	(5)
Decrease (increase) in operating working capital related to investing activities (Note 10)	96	(44)	(13)
	(1 468)	(533)	(958)
FINANCING ACTIVITIES			
Reduction of long-term debt	(475)	(4)	(3)
Purchase of common shares (Note 17)	(362)	(134)	—
Dividends on common shares	(106)	(109)	(92)
Proceeds from issue of common shares	34	33	6
(Increase) decrease in operating working capital related to financing activities (Note 10)	—	(1)	6
	(909)	(215)	(83)
(DECREASE) INCREASE IN CASH AND SHORT-TERM INVESTMENTS	(634)	1 209	(225)
CASH AND SHORT-TERM INVESTMENTS AT BEGINNING OF YEAR	1 415	206	431
CASH AND SHORT-TERM INVESTMENTS AT END OF YEAR	$ 781	$ 1 415	$ 206

PETRO-CANADA (2001)

CONSOLIDATED BALANCE SHEET

(stated in millions of Canadian dollars)

As at December 31,	2001	2000
ASSETS		
CURRENT ASSETS		
Cash and short-term investments (Note 11)	$ 781	$ 1 415
Accounts receivable	758	1 289
Inventories (Note 12)	455	455
Prepaid expenses	15	20
	2 009	3 179
PROPERTY, PLANT AND EQUIPMENT, NET (Note 13)	7 460	6 660
DEFERRED CHARGES AND OTHER ASSETS (Note 14)	352	291
	$ 9 821	$ 10 130
LIABILITIES AND SHAREHOLDERS' EQUITY		
CURRENT LIABILITIES		
Accounts payable and accrued liabilities	$ 1 158	$ 1 561
Income taxes payable	234	194
Current portion of long-term debt	5	454
	1 397	2 209
LONG-TERM DEBT (Note 15)	1 396	1 320
DEFERRED CREDITS AND OTHER LIABILITIES (Note 16)	481	477
FUTURE INCOME TAXES (Notes 3 and 7)	1 486	1 533
COMMITMENTS AND CONTINGENT LIABILITIES (Note 22)		
SHAREHOLDERS' EQUITY (Notes 3 and 17)	5 061	4 591
	$ 9 821	$ 10 130

Approved on behalf of the Board

Ronald A. Brenneman
Director

Claude Fontaine
Director

1. Find the following amounts in the statements:
   a. Total revenues in 2001
   b. Total operating costs (from Crude oil and product purchases through to Depreciation, depletion, and amortization) in 2001
   c. Interest expense in 2001
   d. Income tax expense in 2001
   e. Net income (earnings) in 2001
   f. Inventories at the end of 2001
   g. Accounts payable and accrued liabilities at the beginning of 2001
   h. Shareholders' equity at the end of 2001
   i. Future income taxes at the beginning of 2001
   j. Cash provided from operating activities in 2001

k. Cash payments, net of disposals (sales), to acquire capital assets in 2001
l. Dividends paid in 2001
m. Cash proceeds from issuing new shares in 2001
n. Cash provided from investing activities in 2001

2. Does Petro-Canada finance its business primarily with debt or with shareholders' equity? Support your answer with appropriate data.

3. List the two largest sources of cash and the two largest uses of cash in 2001. (Consider operations to be a single source or use of cash.)

4. Does Petro-Canada use a classified balance sheet? Explain.

SUGGESTED SOLUTION TO SUMMARY PROBLEM

All answers are in millions of dollars unless otherwise stated.

1. The following answers are found on the financial statements included in Exhibit 1-8:
    a. Total revenues in 2001 = $8,690

    b. Operating costs in 2001 = $7,170 ($4,687 + $1,670 + $245 + $568)

    c. Interest expense in 2001 = $135

    d. Income tax expense in 2001 = $481

    e. Net income (earnings) in 2001 = $904

    f. Inventories at the end of 2001 = $455

    g. Accounts payable and accrued liabilities at the beginning of 2001 = $1,561 (The end of 2000 is the same as the beginning of 2001.)

    h. Retained earnings at the end of 2001 = $5,061

    i. Future income taxes at the beginning of 2001 = $1,533

    j. Cash provided from operating activities in 2001 = $1,743

    k. Cash payments, net of disposals (sales), to acquire capital assets in 2001 = ($1,554) (Expenditures on property, plant and equipment and exploration less Proceeds from sales of assets under the investing activities). Putting the amount in parentheses indicates that it is a negative number.

    l. Dividends paid in 2001 = ($106) (Listed under the financing activities on the Statement of Cash Flows)

    m. Cash proceeds from the issuing of new shares in 2001 = $34

    n. Cash provided from investing activities in 2001 = ($1,468)

2. Petro-Canada uses slightly more shareholders' equity to finance its business than debt. You can see this when you compare the total liabilities to the total shareholders' equity (balance sheet) as shown below:

    Total liabilities (12/31/01) $4,760

    Total shareholders' equity (12/31/01) $5,061

    Total liabilities and shareholders' equity $9,821

    Total liabilities are, therefore, 48.5% ($4,760/$9,821) of the total sources of financing for Petro-Canada.

3. The two largest sources of cash are proceeds from the operating activities, $1,743, and proceeds from the sale of assets, $127. The two largest uses are expenditures on property, plant, and equipment and exploration, ($1,681) and the purchase of common and variable voting shares, ($362).

4. Petro-Canada does use a classified balance sheet. It has labelled a section for current assets and current liabilities but not for the noncurrent assets and liabilities. It has included the noncurrent assets and liabilities in bold type after the total of the current assets and liabilities. It has not, however, given you a total for the non-current assets or liabilities.

ABBREVIATIONS USED

AcSB	Accounting Standards Board	GAAP	Generally Accepted Accounting Principles
CA	Chartered Accountant		
CCRA	Canada Customs and Revenue Agency	IAS	International Accounting Standards
CGA	Certified General Accountant	IASB	International Accounting Standards Board
CICA	Canadian Institute of Chartered Accountants	IFAC	International Federation of Accountants
CMA	Certified Management Accountant	OSC	Ontario Securities Commission
FASB	Financial Accounting Standards Board		

SYNONYMS

Accounts Receivable/Current Receivables/Credit Accounts Receivable

Balance sheet equation/Accounting equation

Capital Assets/Property, Plant, and Equipment/Plant Assets/Fixed Assets

Cash Flow Statement/Statement of Changes in Financial Position/Statement of Cash Flows/Consolidated Statement of Cash Flows

Common Shares/Share Capital/Capital Stock

Earnings Statement/Statement of Earnings/Income Statement/Net Income Statement/Consolidated Statement of Earnings/Profit and Loss Statement

Equity/Owners' Equity/Shareholders' Equity

Financial reporting books/Books/Accounting records/Accounting information system

Liabilities/Debt/Obligations

Managerial accounting/Cost accounting

Net Income/Profit/Net Earnings

Retained Earnings/Earnings Retained in the Business/Earnings Reinvested in the Business

GLOSSARY

Accounting Standards Board (AcSB)   The CICA committee in Canada that sets accounting standards.

Adverse opinion   Synonym for qualified opinion.

Assets   Elements of the balance sheet that have probable future value that can be measured, are owned or controlled by the company, and are the result of a past transaction.

Auditor   A professionally trained accountant who examines the accounting records and financial statements of the company to determine whether they fairly present the financial position and operating results of the company in accordance with GAAP.

Balance sheet   A financial statement showing the asset, liability, and shareholders' equity account balances of the company at a specific point in time.

Basic accounting equation   The equation that describes the relationship between assets, liabilities, and shareholders' equity. It is as follows:

Assets = Liabilities + Shareholders' Equity

Board of Directors   The governing body of a company elected by the shareholders to represent their ownership interest.

Books   The accounting records of the company. Usually this term refers to the records reported to shareholders rather than to any other body, such as the tax authority.

Capital stock   Synonym for Share Capital.

Cash flow statement   A financial statement that shows the cash flows of the company during the accounting period, categorized into operating, investing, and financing activities.

Classified balance sheet   A balance sheet in which the assets and liabilities are listed in liquidity order and are categorized into current and noncurrent sections.

Clean opinion   Synonym for unqualified opinion.

Common shares   The shares issued by a company to its owners. Shares represent the ownership interest in a company.

Comparability   A quality of accounting information that improves the ability of financial statement readers to compare different sets of financial statements.

Conceptual framework   The framework set out in section 1000 of the *CICA Handbook* to guide the AcSB as it sets new accounting standards.

Conservatism   A quality of accounting information stating that when estimates are made in financial statements,

they should err on the side of understating rather than overstating net assets and net income.

Consolidated financial statements   Financial statements that represent the combined financial results of a parent company and its subsidiaries.

Cost accounting   A branch of accounting that studies how cost information is used internally within the company.

Cost/benefit constraint   A constraint that states that the cost of implementing a new accounting standard should be less than the benefits that will be derived.

Creditors   Individuals or entities that are owed something by the company.

Current asset/liability   For assets, current means that the asset will be turned into cash or consumed in the next year or operating cycle of the company. For liabilities, current means that the liability will require the use of cash or the rendering of a service or will be replaced by another current liability within the next year or operating cycle of the company.

Dividends   Payments made to shareholders that represent a return on their investment in the company. Dividends are paid only after they are declared by the Board of Directors.

Earnings   Synonym for net income.

Earnings per share   A ratio calculated by dividing the earnings for the period by the average number of shares outstanding during the period.

Entity   The business reported by the financial statements, usually a company.

Equity   A term sometimes used to describe the sum of liabilities and shareholders' equity; sometimes also used to refer simply to the shareholders' equity section, which can lead to some confusion in the use of this term.

Expenses   The resources used in the production of revenues by the company, representing decreases in the shareholders' wealth.

Feedback value   A quality of accounting information that gives it relevance to decision makers. The information provides feedback on previous decisions.

Financial accounting   The study of the accounting concepts and principles used to prepare financial statements for external users.

Financial Accounting Standards Board (FASB)   The regulatory body that currently sets accounting standards in the United States.

Financial reporting books The accounting records that are summarized and reported to shareholders and other users via the financial statements.

Financing activities Activities of the company in which funds are raised to support the other activities of the company. The two major ways to raise funds are to issue new shares or borrow money.

Flow statement A statement that describes certain types of inflows and outflows of the company. The cash flow statement and the income statement are both examples of this type of statement.

GAAP Generally Accepted Accounting Principles.

Income statement A financial statement that measures the results of the operating activities of a company over a period of time.

Investing activities The activities of the company involved with long-term investments, primarily investments in property, plant, and equipment, and in the shares of other companies.

Investors Individuals or entities that acquire shares of a company as an investment.

Liability An element of the balance sheet characterized by a probable future sacrifice of resources of the company.

Liquidity The length of time required to turn assets into cash.

Management The individuals responsible for running or managing the company.

Managerial accounting The study of the preparation and uses of accounting information by the management of the company.

Materiality A concept used to indicate items that will affect decision-making. In auditing, it means those items that are large enough to have a significant effect on the evaluation of the presentation of the financial results of a company.

Net income The profits generated by a company during a specified time period. Net income is determined by subtracting expenses from the revenues of the company.

Neutrality A quality of accounting information indicating that the methods or principles applied should not depend on the self-interest of the company being measured but be neutral with regard to the potential outcomes for the company.

Noncurrent asset/liability Assets or liabilities that do not fit the definition of current assets and liabilities.

Operating activities The activities of the company that involve the sale of goods and services to customers.

Operating cycle The time period between the initial investment of cash in products or services and the return of cash from the sale of the product or service.

Owners Synonym for shareholders.

Predictive value A quality of accounting information that makes the information relevant to decision makers. Its relevance stems from its ability to predict the future.

Privately held corporation A company whose shares are held by a few individuals and do not trade in an active stock market.

Publicly traded corporation A company whose shares are traded in a public stock market.

Qualified opinion An audit opinion that finds some exception to the fair presentation of the financial results.

Relevance A quality of accounting information indicating that the information should have an impact on the decisions of the user.

Reliability A quality of accounting information indicating that the information should be reliable in order to be of use to decision makers.

Representational faithfulness A quality of accounting information indicating that the information should accurately represent the attribute or characteristic that it purports to represent.

Retained earnings Earnings that are retained within the company and not paid out to shareholders in the form of dividends.

Revenues Inflows of resources to the company that result from the sale of goods and/or services.

Share capital The investment in a company by the shareholders.

Shareholders The individuals or entities that own shares in a company.

Shareholders' equity The section of the balance sheet that represents the shareholders' wealth; equivalent to the assets less the liabilities.

Statement of cash flows Synonym for cash flow statement.

Statement of changes in financial position Synonym for cash flow statement.

Statement of Earnings Synonym for income statement.

Statement of financial position Synonym for balance sheet.

Taxing authority An agency that assesses and collects taxes from the company.

Timeliness A quality of accounting information indicating that information must be timely in order to be relevant to decision makers.

Unclassified balance sheet A balance sheet that does not classify assets and liabilities into current and noncurrent categories.

Understandability   A qualitative characteristic that states that accounting information should be understandable to users.

Unqualified opinion   An audit opinion that states that the financial statements present fairly the financial position and operating results of the company in conformity with GAAP.

Verifiability   The capability of accounting information to be verified by an independent measurer.

Working capital   The difference between the current assets and the current liabilities.

Assignment Material

Multiple Choice Quizzes

Assessing Your Recall

1-1   Explain the difference between a public corporation and a private corporation.

1-2   Identify at least three major users of corporate financial statements, and briefly state how they might use the information from the statements.

1-3   List three types of information that users should be able to learn from financial statements.

1-4   Discuss the meaning of Generally Accepted Accounting Principles, and describe the organizations that establish these principles.

1-5   List and briefly describe the major qualitative characteristics that accounting information should possess, according to the CICA conceptual framework.

1-6   Describe and illustrate the three major types of activities in which all companies engage.

1-7   Describe and illustrate the three major categories of items that appear in a typical balance sheet.

1-8   Describe the purpose of the three main financial statements that are contained in all annual reports.

1-9   Explain the purpose behind the notes to the financial statements.

1-10   What is the purpose of an auditor's opinion, and what types of opinion can they render?

Applying Your Knowledge

1-11   (What is accounting?)
In the opening story to this chapter, Raj Randhawa compared accounting to a scorecard.

Required:

a. Write a paragraph explaining why this comparison is appropriate.

b. Describe two major business decisions made by Mr. Randhawa for which he used accounting information.

1-12   (Identification of financing, investing, and operating transactions)
For a company like **Sears Canada**, provide two examples of transactions that you would classify as financing, investing, and operating.

1-13 (Identification of financing, investing, and operating transactions)
For a company like **Bombardier Inc.**, provide two examples of transactions that you would classify as financing, investing, and operating.

1-14 (Application of qualitative characteristics)
The AMAX Company purchased land several years ago for $100,000 as a potential site for a new building. No building has yet been constructed. A comparable lot near the site was recently sold for $120,000.

Required:

a. At what value should AMAX carry the land on its balance sheet? Support your answer with consideration for the relevance and reliability of the information that would result.

b. If AMAX wanted to borrow money from a bank, what information about the land would the bank want to know? Explain your answer.

1-15 (Application of qualitative characteristics)
Matrix Technologies designs and installs computer software for businesses. Recently, it learned that one of its major customers, representing 20% of annual sales, is in financial difficulty and is unlikely to be ordering for some time. Matrix is about to issue its quarterly report to shareholders.

Required:
Do you think the information about the customer should be disclosed in the quarterly report? Support you answer by referring to the qualitative characteristics described in this chapter.

1-16 (Comparison of the income statement and the cash flow statement)
Compare and contrast the statement of income and the statement of cash flows with regard to their purpose. Outline how they are similar.

1-17 (Identifying items on financial statements)
Use the following abbreviations to respond to this question.

CA   Current Assets
NCA   Noncurrent Assets
CL   Current Liabilities
NCL   Noncurrent Liabilities
SC   Share Capital
RE   Retained Earnings
IS   Income statement item
SCF   Statement of cash flows item

Required:
Classify the following items according to where the item would appear in the financial statements:

a. Accounts receivable

b. Taxes payable

c. Interest expense

d. Inventory

e. Dividends paid to shareholders

f. Sales to customers

g. Manufacturing equipment

h. New issuance of common shares

i. Cash

j. Bonds payable (debt due in 10 years)

1-18   (Identifying items on financial statements)
Use the following abbreviations to respond to this question.

CA   Current Assets
NCA   Noncurrent Assets
CL   Current Liabilities
NCL   Noncurrent Liabilities
SC   Share Capital
RE   Retained Earnings
IS   Income statement item
SCF   Statement of cash flows item

Required:
Classify the following items according to where the item would appear in the financial statements:

a. Wages payable

b. Administrative expenses

c. Purchase of equipment

d. Amounts owed to suppliers

e. Short-term bank loan (debt due in six months)

f. Cost of inventory sold to customers

g. Building

h. Net income for the year

i. Prepaid expenses

j. Amounts owed by customers to the corporation

1-19   (Identifying items on financial statements)
Use the following abbreviations to respond to this question.

CA   Current Assets
NCA   Noncurrent Assets
CL   Current Liabilities
NCL   Noncurrent Liabilities
SC   Share Capital
RE   Retained Earnings
IS   Income statement item
SCF   Statement of cash flows item

Required:
Classify the following items according to where the item would appear in the financial statements:

a. Intangible assets

b. Interest revenue

c. Sale of land

d. Bank loan due in three years

e. Earnings over the years which have not been paid to shareholders as dividends

f. Revenue from sales inventory

g. Rent payable

h. Total increase or decrease in the cash balance for the year.

i. Office supplies

j. An investment in the shares of another corporation (the intent of the investment is not to sell it in the near future)

1-20 (Classifying items on the cash flow statement)
Use the following abbreviations to respond to this question.

OA   Operating Activities item
FA   Financing Activities item
IA   Investing Activities item

Required:
Classify each of the following transactions according to whether they are operating, financing, or investing activities:

a. Cash collected from customers

b. Repayment of debt

c. Payment of dividends

d. Purchase of a truck for use in deliveries

e. Change in the accounts receivable balance

f. Purchase of shares of another company

g. Sale of a building

h. Issuance of shares

1-21 (Classifying items on the cash flow statement)
Use the following abbreviations to respond to this question.

OA   Operating Activities item
FA   Financing Activities item
IA   Investing Activities item

Required:
Classify each of the following transactions according to whether they are operating, financing, or investing activities:

a. Repurchase of a corporation's own shares

b. Net income

c. Sale of machinery no longer needed in the business

d. Acquisition of a long-term bank loan

e. Amortization of a building

f. Repayment of a bond payable

g. Purchase of land

h. Payment of dividends

1-22   (Identifying items on the balance sheet and income statement)
Indicate whether each of the following items will be reported in the balance sheet (BS), income statement (IS), neither the balance sheet nor the income statement (N), or both the balance sheet and the income statement (B).

   a. Cash

   b. Accounts receivable

   c. Prepaid expenses

   d. Interest income

   e. Sales of goods and services

   f. Dividends distributed to shareholders

   g. Rent expense

   h. Sales anticipated next period

   i. Payment made to reduce the principal amount of a bank loan

   j. Common shares

1-23   (Identifying items on the balance sheet and income statement)
Indicate whether each of the following items will be reported in the balance sheet (BS), income statement (IS), neither the balance sheet nor the income statement (N), or both the balance sheet and the income statement (B).

   a. Loans payable

   b. Interest expense

   c. Retained earnings

   d. Current portion of long-term debt

   e. Purchasing property, plant, and equipment

   f. Revenue earned from selling inventory

   g. Office supplies expense

   h. Long-term investments

   i. Securing a new short-term bank loan

   j. Future income tax

1-24   (Determine missing balance sheet amounts)
Calculate the missing balance sheet amounts in each of the following independent situations:

	A	B	C	D
Current Assets	?	$ 450,000	$ 130,000	$ 90,000
Noncurrent Assets	450,000	?	500,000	?
Total Assets	?	1,000,000	?	310,000
Current Liabilities	100,000	300,000	100,000	60,000
Noncurrent Liabilities	?	250,000	?	70,000
Shareholders' Equity	225,000	?	240,000	?
Total Liabilities and Shareholders' Equity	550,000	?	?	?

1-25 (Determine missing balance sheet amounts)

Calculate the missing balance sheet amounts in each of the following independent situations:

	A	B	C	D
Current Assets	$ 600,000	?	$120,000	$420,000
Noncurrent Assets	?	650,000	?	750,000
Total Assets	1,500,000	?	470,000	?
Current Liabilities	400,000	300,000	80,000	200,000
Noncurrent Liabilities	350,000	?	190,000	?
Shareholders' Equity	?	400,000	?	600,000
Total Liabilities and Shareholders' Equity	?	950,000	?	?

1-26 (Determine missing retained earnings amounts)

The change in retained earnings from the beginning of the year to the end of the year is caused by net income minus dividends. Calculate the missing amounts in the reconciliation of retained earnings in each of the following independent situations.

	A	B	C	D
Retained Earnings Dec. 31, Year 1	$120,000	$300,000	?	$230,000
Net Income	30,000	?	700,000	100,000
Dividends Declared and Paid	6,000	35,000	250,000	?
Retained Earnings Dec. 31, Year 2	?	460,000	1,200,000	320,000

1-27 (Prepare a simple income statement)

Jackson Wong operates a florist shop called Bouquet Scents Ltd. During the month of July, the following things occurred: he spent $160 on the telephone system and $370 on electricity and water; the rent on the premises was $1,500; he took in $24,730 from selling flowers and plants; the cost of the flowers from a local grower was $10,733; he paid $329 for gas and repairs to the delivery vehicle; he paid his employees $7,000 in wages.

Required:

a. Prepare an income statement to determine how much Jackson Wong earned in July.

b Are there any other costs that you think Jackson Wong might have incurred in July that were not listed?

1-28 (Prepare a simple income statement)

Janice Fontelle runs an outdoor adventure company called Call of the Wild, Ltd. Her busiest months are June through September, although she does operate some limited excursions later in the fall. For the month of August, she recorded the following items: she paid $24,980 for employee wages; she spent $7,320 on advertising; people paid her $84,200 for excursions in August; the supplies used in August cost $12,674; the telephone and electricity in the office came to $740; it cost $1,500 for gas and repairs on the vehicles.

Required:

a. Prepare an income statement for Janice Fontelle to determine how much she earned in August.

b. Are there any other costs that you think Janice Fontelle might have incurred in August that were not listed?

1-29 (Prepare a simple balance sheet)

Problem 1-27 introduced Jackson Wong and his florist shop. At the end of July, the following items were in his records:

Inventory	$1,100
Wages owed to employees	950
Bank loan owed to the bank	8,000
Cash held in the chequing account	8,361
Cost of the refrigerators used to store the flowers	18,695
Prepaid rent for August	1,500
Common shares	18,000
Retained earnings	2,706

Required:

a. Identify each of the items in his records as an asset, liability, or shareholders' equity item.

b. Prepare a balance sheet for the end of July.

c. Jackson Wong does not have accounts receivable in his records. Suggest an explanation for why it is unlikely that he will have an account called "accounts receivable." Under what business circumstances would it be necessary for him to have such an account?

1-30 (Prepare a simple balance sheet)

Problem 1-28 introduced Janice Fontelle and her outdoor adventure company. At the end of August, the following items were in her records:

Bank loan owed to the bank	$14,000
Supplies on hand to be used in September	5,220
Cash in bank accounts	17,450
Common shares	12,000
Tents, rafts, etc.	18,600
Retained earnings	33,200
Vehicles	34,400
Amounts paid for trips to be taken in September	16,470

Required:

a. Identify each of the items in her records as an asset, liability, or shareholders' equity item.

b. Prepare a balance sheet for the end of August.

c. Does Janice Fontelle have any inventory? Explain.

d. Janice Fontelle does not have accounts receivable in her records. Explain why it is unlikely that she will have an account called "accounts receivable." Under what business circumstances would it be necessary for her to have such an account?

1-31 (Identification of assets and liabilities)

For each of the following companies, list at least two types of assets and one type of liability that you would expect to find on its balance sheet (try to include at least one item for each company that is unique to its business):

a. **Suncor Energy Inc.** This company is involved in oil recovery in the Alberta tar sands.

b. **Ballard Power Systems Inc.** This company is involved in the development and commercialization of fuel cells and related power generation systems.

c. **Danier Leather Inc.** This company designs and sells leather clothing.

d. **Quebecor Inc.** This company has several business interests: printing, newspapers, leisure and entertainment, web integration/technology, broadcasting, and Internet/portals.

e. **Bombardier Inc.** This company manufactures transportation equipment and other industrial products.

f. **Royal Bank** This is a major commercial bank.

g. **Westjet Airlines Ltd.** This is an airline company.

1-32 (Identification of income statement items)
For each of the companies listed in Problem 1-31, list at least two line items that you would expect to find on its income statement (try to include at least one item for each company that is unique to its business).

1-33 (Identification of statement of cash flow items)
For each of the companies listed in Problem 1-31, list at least two line items that you would expect to find on its statement of cash flows (try to include at least one item for each company that is unique to its business).

User Perspective Problems

1-34 (Use of accounting information)
You are a junior accountant in a transportation company. Your company transports people (buses travelling between cities in eastern Canada) and goods (trucks used for the transportation of merchandise across Canada). The company has to replace its buses and trucks on a regular basis. The controller (the person in charge of the overall accounting system) needs information about whether it would be more advantageous for the company to lease the vehicles rather than buy them. She has asked you to do some research on the issue.

> *Required:*
> A lease is a long- or short-term contract with a dealer that sells and leases vehicles. The company doing the leasing (the lessee) usually pays a monthly fee that includes an interest charge. At the end of the lease term, the company can either return the vehicle to the dealer or pay an additional amount to the dealer to buy the vehicle. What kind of information about leasing and the financial situation of the company do you think the controller would need before a decision could be made about leasing the vehicles?

1-35 (Use of accounting information)
Using the information provided in problem 1-34, assume the controller wants you to do the background work for a buy decision instead of a leasing one. What kind of information about the purchase and the financial situation of the company do you think the controller would need before a decision could be made about buying the vehicles?

1-36 (Use of accounting information)
You are the accounting manager for a Canadian company that has just been acquired by a German company. Helmut Schmidt, the CEO of the German company, has just paid you a visit and is puzzled as to why Canadian companies use different information when reporting to the Canada Customs and Revenue Agency and their shareholders. In Germany, the same set of information is sent to both parties.

Required:
Draft a memo explaining to Mr. Schmidt why the two users accept different information. In answering this question, consider the reporting objectives of the two users.

1-37   (Information for decision making)
Suppose that the CICA proposed that inventory be accounted for at its current market price (i.e., what you could sell it for) rather than its historical cost. Provide an argument that supports or opposes this change on the basis of relevance and reliability.

1-38   (Information for decision making)
Suppose that you started your own company that assembles and sells laptop computers. You do not manufacture any of the parts yourself. The computers are sold through orders received over the Internet and through mail orders.

Required:
Make a list of the information that you think would be relevant to running this type of business. When you are through, discuss how you would reliably measure the information that you would want to keep track of.

1-39   (Information for decision making)
Suppose that you own and operate your own private company. You need to raise money to expand your operation and you approach a bank for a loan. The bank loan officer has asked for financial statements prepared according to GAAP.

Required:

a. Why would the loan officer make such a request?

b. Assuming that your statements were prepared according to GAAP, how could you convince the loan officer that this was so?

c. What items on your financial statements would be of the most interest to the loan officer?

1-40   (Value of auditors)
In order for a company's shares to be listed (i.e., traded) on a Canadian stock exchange, the company's annual financial statements must be audited by an independent auditor. Why?

1-41   (Raising new capital)
Suppose that your best friend wants to start a new business providing website construction services to customers. Your friend has some savings to start the business but not enough to buy all of the equipment that she thinks she needs. She has asked you for some advice about how to raise additional funds.

Required:
Give her at least two alternatives and provide the pros and cons for each alternative.

1-42   (Value of future-oriented information)
From time to time there have been calls from the user community for management to disclose its own forecasts of future expectations such as net income.

Required:
As an external user of the financial statements, discuss the relevance and reliability of this type of information.

1-43   (Distribution of a dividend to shareholders)
The Board of Directors of a public company is having its monthly meeting. One of the items on the agenda is the possible distribution of a cash dividend to shareholders. If the board decides to issue a cash dividend, its decision obligates the company to issue cash to shareholders based on the number of shares each shareholder owns.

Required:
Before making its decision, what kinds of information about the company should the board consider? Think of the items on the financial statements that you saw in this chapter.

Reading and Interpreting Published Financial Statements

Base your answers to problems 44–49 on the financial statements for **Sears Canada Inc.** in Appendix A at the end of the book.

1-44   (Find dividends declared)
Determine the amount of dividends that Sears Canada declared in 2001. On which financial statement(s) did you find this information?

1-45   (Verify basic accounting equation)
Verify that total assets equal total liabilities and shareholders' equity for Sears Canada in 2001.

1-46   (Find financial statement balances)
Find the following amounts in the statements of Sears Canada:

   a. Revenues from the sale of merchandise in 2001

   b. Cost of merchandise sold and operating, administrative, and selling expenses in 2001

   c. Interest expense in 2001

   d. Income tax expense in 2001 (include both current and future in your answer)

   e. Net earnings in 2000

   f. Inventories at the end of 2000

   g. Accounts payable at the beginning of 2001

   h. Retained earnings at the end of 2001

   i. Long-term obligations at the beginning of 2001 (include "principal payments on long-term obligations due within one year" in your total amount for long-term obligations)

   j. Cash flows generated from operations in 2001

   k. Cash payments to acquire capital assets in 2001

   l. Cash proceeds from the issuance of new long-term obligations in 2001

   m. Cash flows generated from (used for) investment activities in 2001

   n. Cash payments to reduce long-term obligations in 2001

1-47   (Identify sources and uses of cash)
List the two largest sources of cash and the two largest uses of cash in 2001. (Consider operations to be a single source or use of cash.)

1-48   (Net income versus cash from operations)
Suggest some reasons why net earnings were $94.1 million in 2001 yet cash flows generated from operations were $241.7 million.

1-49   (Comparison of change in sales with change in net income)
During 2001, total revenues were approximately $370 million higher than they were in 2000. However, net earnings in 2001 were approximately $132 million lower than in 2000. By examining the statement of earnings, suggest some explanations as to where the additional revenue went.

Base your answers to problems 50–57 on the 2001 financial statements for **Canadian Tire Corporation Limited** in Exhibit 1-9.

EXHIBIT 1-9
PART A

CANADIAN TIRE CORPORATION LIMITED (2001)   →   **Consolidated Statements of Earnings and Retained Earnings**

(Dollars in thousands except per share amounts) For the years ended		December 29, 2001		December 30, 2000
Gross operating revenue	$	**5,374,759**	$	5,207,574
Operating expenses				
Cost of merchandise sold and all other operating expenses except for the undernoted items		**4,854,801**		4,729,112
Interest				
Long-term debt		**81,389**		74,851
Short-term debt		**6,647**		19,836
Depreciation and amortization		**136,301**		127,021
Employee profit sharing plans (Note 8)		**18,645**		16,067
Total operating expenses		**5,097,783**		4,966,887
Earnings before income taxes		**276,976**		240,687
Income taxes (Note 9)				
Current		**102,445**		97,370
Future		**(2,733)**		(4,705)
Total income taxes		**99,712**		92,665
Net earnings before minority interest		**177,264**		148,022
Minority interest (Note 15)		**611**		—
Net earnings	$	**176,653**	$	148,022
Net earnings per share	$	**2.25**	$	1.89
Diluted earnings per share (Note 7)	$	**2.23**	$	1.89
Weighted average number of Common and Class A Non-Voting Shares outstanding		**78,652,610**		78,349,097
Retained earnings, beginning of year	$	**860,129**	$	763,651
Net earnings		**176,653**		148,022
Dividends		**(31,482)**		(31,328)
Repurchase of Class A Non-Voting Shares (Note 7)		**(32,250)**		(20,216)
Retained earnings, end of year	$	**973,050**	$	860,129

CANADIAN TIRE CORPORATION LIMITED (2001)

Consolidated Statements of Cash Flows

EXHIBIT 1-9

PART B

(Dollars in thousands) For the years ended		December 29, 2001		December 30, 2000
Cash generated from (used for):				
Operating activities				
Net earnings	$	**176,653**	$	148,022
Items not affecting cash				
Depreciation and amortization of property and equipment		**125,592**		119,726
Net provision for credit charge receivables		**82,469**		73,665
Amortization of other assets		**10,709**		7,295
Post retirement benefits (Note 6)		**1,701**		1,432
Gain on sale of credit charge receivables (Note 2)		**(15,437)**		—
Gain on disposals of property and equipment		**(9,184)**		354
Gain on sale of subsidiary (Note 14)		**(8,128)**		—
Future tax liability		**(2,733)**		1,820
Cash generated from operations		**361,642**		352,314
Changes in other working capital components (Note 10)		**(174,699)**		150,024
Cash generated from operating activities		**186,943**		502,338
Investing activities				
Additions to property and equipment		**(358,229)**		(382,172)
Investment in credit charge receivables (Note 2)		**(317,597)**		(253,043)
Long-term receivables and other assets		**(22,256)**		(24,800)
Proceeds on sale of subsidiary (Note 14)		**135,590**		—
Proceeds on disposition of property and equipment		**93,659**		29,085
Cash used for investing activities		**(468,833)**		(630,930)
Financing activities				
Proceeds on sale of limited partnership interest (Note 15)		**300,000**		—
Issuance of long-term debt		**225,000**		65,000
Sale of Associate Dealer receivables (Note 10)		**188,594**		—
Securitization of credit charge receivables		**53,115**		115,217
Commercial paper		**—**		(234,025)
Dividends		**(31,482)**		(31,328)
Class A Non-Voting Share transactions (Note 7)		**(5,262)**		5,999
Repayment of long-term debt		**(315)**		(200,292)
Cash generated from (used for) financing activities		**729,650**		(279,429)
Cash generated (used) in the year		**447,760**		(408,021)
Cash and cash equivalents, beginning of year		**130,999**		539,020
Cash and cash equivalents, end of year (Note 10)	$	**578,759**	$	130,999

EXHIBIT 1-9
PART C

CANADIAN TIRE CORPORATION LIMITED (2001)

Consolidated Balance Sheets

(Dollars in thousands) As at		December 29, 2001		December 30, 2000
ASSETS				
Current assets				
Cash and cash equivalents (Note 10)	$	578,759	$	130,999
Accounts receivable (Note 10)		433,825		515,130
Credit charge receivables (Note 2)		525,317		453,412
Merchandise inventories		440,935		412,381
Prepaid expenses and deposits		14,297		15,777
Total current assets		1,993,133		1,527,699
Long-term receivables and other assets (Note 3)		134,414		122,867
Property and equipment (Note 4)		2,243,609		2,097,095
Total assets	$	4,371,156	$	3,747,661
LIABILITIES				
Current liabilities				
Accounts payable and other	$	1,009,598	$	1,038,471
Income taxes payable		70,425		85,965
Current portion of long-term debt (Note 5)		30,027		315
Total current liabilities		1,110,050		1,124,751
Long-term debt (Note 5)		1,310,000		1,115,027
Long-term liability for post retirement benefits (Note 6)		28,280		26,579
Future tax liability (Note 9)		19,132		21,865
Total liabilities		2,467,462		2,288,222
Minority interest (Note 15)		300,000		—
SHAREHOLDERS' EQUITY				
Share capital (Note 7)		622,104		595,116
Accumulated foreign currency translation adjustment		8,540		4,194
Retained earnings		973,050		860,129
Total shareholders' equity		1,603,694		1,459,439
Total liabilities and shareholders' equity	$	4,371,156	$	3,747,661

Gilbert S. Bennett   Director

Maureen J. Sabia   Director

1-50 (Find dividends declared)
Determine the amount of dividends that Canadian Tire declared in 2001. On which financial statement(s) did you find this information?

1-51 (Verify basic accounting equation)
Verify that total assets equal total liabilities and shareholders' equity for Canadian Tire in 2001.

1-52 (Calculation of current assets – current liabilities)
Canadian Tire prepared a classified balance sheet, although it did not provide a subtotal for either noncurrent assets or noncurrent liabilities. Calculate the difference between the current assets and current liabilities at the end of 2001. This amount is referred to as **working capital**. State explicitly what assets and liabilities you have included as current for the purpose of your calculation.

1-53 (Find financial statement balances)
Find the following amounts in the statements of Canadian Tire:

a. Gross operating revenues in 2001

b. Cost of merchandise sold and all other operating expenses in 2001

c. Interest expense (long-term and short-term) in 2001

d. Income tax expense (current and future) in 2001

e. Net earnings (income) in 2001

f. Merchandise inventories at the end of 2001

g. Accounts payable and other at the beginning of 2001

h. Retained earnings at the end of 2001

i. Long-term debt at the beginning of 2001 (ignore the current portion of long-term debt)

j. Cash produced from operating activities in 2001

k. Cash payments to acquire capital assets (property and equipment) in 2001

l. Cash proceeds from the issuance of long-term debt in 2001

m. Cash produced or used for investing activities in 2001

1-54 (Determine financing strategy)
Did Canadian Tire finance the company mainly from creditors (total liabilities) or from shareholders (shareholders' equity) in 2001? Support your answer with appropriate data.

1-55 (Identify sources and uses of cash)
List the two largest sources of cash and the two largest uses of cash in 2001. (Consider cash generated from operating activities to be a single source or use of cash.)

1-56 (Net income versus cash from operations)
Suggest some reasons why net earnings were $176,653 thousand in 2001 yet cash generated from operating activities was $186,943 thousand.

1-57 (Firm valuation)
The prices of Canadian Tire's common shares in the fourth quarter of 2001 ranged from $30.50 to $42.00 per share. There were 3,423,366 common shares outstanding at the end of 2001. Calculate the average total market value of the common shares of Canadian Tire in the fourth quarter of 2001. Compare this with the value of shareholders' equity

at the end of 2001 as represented in the balance sheet. If these numbers are different, offer an explanation for this discrepancy.

Base your answers to Problems 58–64 on the 2001 financial statements of **Mosaid Technologies Incorporated**, which are in Exhibit 1-10. Mosaid Technologies, an Ontario corporation, designs memory chips and supplies engineering test systems around the world.

EXHIBIT 1-10

PART A

MOSAID TECHNOLOGIES INCORPORATED
(incorporated under the Ontario Business Corporations Act)

CONSOLIDATED BALANCE SHEETS
(in thousands)

As at	April 27, 2001	April 28, 2000
CURRENT ASSETS		
Cash and cash equivalents	$ 5,769	$ 6,046
Short-term marketable securities	13,470	25,101
Accounts receivable	23,112	9,486
Income taxes receivable	–	1,721
Revenues recognized in excess of amounts billed	78	1,860
Inventories (NOTE 2)	6,144	4,690
Prepaid expenses	2,075	1,163
	50,648	50,067
CAPITAL ASSETS (NOTE 3)	22,996	18,107
LONG-TERM INVESTMENTS (NOTE 4)	6,897	1,482
FUTURE INCOME TAXES RECOVERABLE (NOTE 9)	8,462	4,627
	$ 89,003	$ 74,283
CURRENT LIABILITIES		
Accounts payable and accrued liabilities	$ 13,897	$ 10,836
Mortgage payable (NOTE 5)	163	150
Deferred revenue	1,030	1,618
	15,090	12,604
MORTGAGE PAYABLE (NOTE 5)	5,390	5,553
	20,480	18,157
SHAREHOLDERS' EQUITY		
Share capital (NOTE 6)	43,971	38,576
Retained earnings	24,552	17,550
	68,523	56,126
	$ 89,003	$ 74,283

See accompanying Notes to the Consolidated Financial Statements.

Thomas I. Csathy
Director

Robert F. Harland
Director

MOSAID TECHNOLOGIES INCORPORATED

EXHIBIT 1-10

PART B

CONSOLIDATED STATEMENTS OF EARNINGS AND RETAINED EARNINGS

(in thousands, except per share amounts)

Year ended	April 27, 2001	April 28, 2000
REVENUES		
Operations	$ 81,640	$ 47,044
Interest	1,286	1,065
	82,926	48,109
EXPENSES		
Labour and materials	13,367	8,181
Research and development (NOTE 7)	31,428	18,450
Selling and marketing	18,250	11,839
General and administration	8,338	7,015
Bad debt	139	–
Unusual item (NOTE 8)	694	(206)
	72,216	45,279
Earnings from operations	10,710	2,830
Income tax expense (NOTE 9)	3,708	926
NET EARNINGS	7,002	1,904
RETAINED EARNINGS, beginning of year	17,550	15,646
RETAINED EARNINGS, end of year	$ 24,552	$ 17,550
EARNINGS PER SHARE (NOTE 10)		
Basic	$ 0.79	$ 0.26
Fully diluted	$ 0.76	$ 0.26
WEIGHTED AVERAGE NUMBER OF SHARES		
Basic	8,889,863	7,374,469
Fully diluted	10,445,596	8,880,413

See accompanying Notes to the Consolidated Financial Statements.

EXHIBIT 1-10

PART C

MOSAID TECHNOLOGIES INCORPORATED

CONSOLIDATED STATEMENTS OF CASH FLOWS
(in thousands)

Year ended	April 27, 2001	April 28, 2000
OPERATING		
Net earnings	$ 7,002	$ 1,904
Items not affecting cash		
Amortization	7,146	5,361
Loss on disposal of capital assets	22	23
Future income taxes recoverable	(3,835)	(2,179)
	10,335	5,109
Change in non-cash working capital items (NOTE 11)	(10,016)	1,875
	319	6,984
INVESTING		
Acquisition of capital assets – net	(12,057)	(7,966)
Acquisition of short-term marketable securities	(19,674)	(26,651)
Proceeds on maturity/disposal of short-term marketable securities	31,305	14,677
Long-term investments	(5,415)	(1,566)
	(5,841)	(21,506)
FINANCING		
Repayment of mortgage	(150)	(139)
Repurchase of shares	–	(271)
Issue of common shares and warrants	5,395	17,402
	5,245	16,992
NET CASH (OUTFLOW) INFLOW	(277)	2,470
CASH AND CASH EQUIVALENTS, beginning of year	6,046	3,576
CASH AND CASH EQUIVALENTS, end of year	$ 5,769	$ 6,046

See accompanying Notes to the Consolidated Financial Statements.

1-58   (Fiscal year end)
When is the business year end for Mosaid Technologies?

1-59   (Find financial statement balances)
Find the following amounts in the statements of Mosaid Technologies:

    a.   Revenues from operations in 2001

    b.   Research and development in 2001

    c.   Interest revenue in 2001

    d.   Income tax expense in 2001

    e.   Net income in 2001 (net earnings)

    f.   Inventories at the end of 2001

    g.   Accounts payable and accrued liabilities at the beginning of 2001

    h.   Retained earnings at the end of 2001

   i. Mortgage payable at the end of 2001 (current and long-term)

   j. Cash produced from operating activities in 2001

   k. Cash payments to acquire capital assets in 2001

   l. Cash used to repay the mortgage in 2001

  m. Cash proceeds from new share issuances in 2001

   n. Cash produced or used for investing activities in 2001

1-60 (Determine financing strategy)
Did Mosaid Technologies Inc. finance its business primarily from creditors (total liabilities) or from shareholders (shareholders' equity) in 2001? Support your answer with appropriate data.

1-61 (Identify sources and uses of cash)
List the two largest sources of cash and the two largest uses of cash in 2001. (Consider operations to be a single source or use of cash.)

1-62 (Net income versus cash from operations)
Suggest some reasons why net earnings were $7,002 thousand in 2001 yet cash flow from operations was $319 thousand.

1-63 (Dollar changes in assets and liabilities)
List the three assets and the three liabilities that experienced the largest dollar changes from the end of 2000 to the end of 2001.

1-64 (Determine financing strategy)
Total assets of Mosaid Technologies Inc. at April 28, 2000, and April 27, 2001, were $74,283 thousand and $89,003 thousand, respectively. Total shareholders' equity at these same two dates was $56,126 thousand and $68,523 thousand, respectively. Calculate the ratio of debt to total assets for each of the years 2000 and 2001. How has Mosaid Technologies Inc. been financing its business?

Base your answers to problems 65–70 on the 2001 financial statements of **METRO INC.**, which are included in Exhibit 1-11. METRO INC., a Quebec company, is involved in the food industry.

1-65 (Fiscal year end)
When is METRO INC.'s fiscal year end?

1-66 (Find financial statement balances)
Find the following amounts in the statements of METRO INC.:

   a. Sales in 2001

   b. Cost of sales and operating expenses in 2001

   c. Interest expense in 2000 (both short-term and long-term)

   d. Income tax expense in 2001

   e. Net earnings in 2001

   f. Inventory at the beginning of 2001

   g. Prepaid expenses in 2001

   h. Retained earnings at the end of 2001

   i. Long-term borrowings at the beginning of 2001 (both current and long-term portions)

   j. Cash flows from operating activities in 2001

k. Cash payments to acquire capital assets in 2001

l. Dividends paid in 2001

m. Cash produced or used for financing activities in 2001

EXHIBIT 1-11

PART A

METRO INC. (2001)

CONSOLIDATED BALANCE SHEETS

As at September 29, 2001
(Millions of dollars)

	2001	2000	1999
ASSETS			
CURRENT			
Accounts receivable	$ 236.1	$ 186.3	$ 177.7
Income taxes recoverable	10.3	–	–
Inventories	242.0	221.8	195.7
Prepaid expenses	3.0	4.3	1.2
Future income taxes *(note 5)*	13.1	9.4	–
	504.5	421.8	374.6
Investments and other assets *(note 6)*	28.3	23.1	26.9
Future income taxes *(note 5)*	–	7.8	–
Capital assets *(note 7)*	481.9	430.9	413.9
Goodwill	171.3	176.1	180.8
	$ 1,186.0	$ 1,059.7	$ 996.2
LIABILITIES AND SHAREHOLDERS' EQUITY			
CURRENT			
Bank loans *(note 8)*	$ 31.7	$ 1.7	$ 12.6
Accounts payable	455.4	427.6	387.8
Income taxes payable	–	12.0	19.7
Current portion of long-term debt *(note 8)*	5.0	6.3	4.9
	492.1	447.6	425.0
Long-term debt *(note 8)*	55.3	88.6	144.2
Future income taxes *(note 5)*	80.6	61.8	–
Deferred income taxes	–	–	34.7
	628.0	598.0	603.9
SHAREHOLDERS' EQUITY			
Capital stock *(note 9)*	162.3	160.1	159.3
Retained earnings	395.7	301.6	233.0
	558.0	461.7	392.3
	$ 1,186.0	$ 1,059.7	$ 996.2

See accompanying notes

On behalf of the Board:

PIERRE H. LESSARD
Director

GILLES LAMOUREUX
Director

METRO INC. (2001)

EXHIBIT 1-11

PART B

CONSOLIDATED STATEMENTS OF EARNINGS

Year ended September 29, 2001
(Millions, except for earnings per share)

	2001 *52 weeks*	2000 *53 weeks*	1999 *52 weeks*
SALES	$ 4,868.9	$ 4,657.5	$ 3,995.5
Cost of sales and operating expenses	4,618.3	4,438.0	3,808.2
Depreciation and amortization *(note 3)*	61.4	52.5	44.3
	4,679.7	4,490.5	3,852.5
OPERATING INCOME	189.2	167.0	143.0
Financing costs			
Short-term	0.6	0.7	0.2
Long-term	4.6	8.5	5.7
	5.2	9.2	5.9
EARNINGS BEFORE INCOME TAXES AND UNUSUAL ITEMS	184.0	157.8	137.1
Unusual items *(note 4)*	–	–	15.0
EARNINGS BEFORE INCOME TAXES	184.0	157.8	122.1
Income taxes *(note 5)*	61.2	60.5	45.7
NET EARNINGS	$ 122.8	$ 97.3	$ 76.4
EARNINGS PER SHARE *(note 4)*			
Basic	$ 2.45	$ 1.94	$ 1.51
Fully diluted	$ 2.36	$ 1.86	$ 1.45
WEIGHTED AVERAGE NUMBER OF SHARES OUTSTANDING	50.1	50.2	50.5

See accompanying notes

CONSOLIDATED STATEMENTS OF RETAINED EARNINGS

Year ended September 29, 2001
(Millions of dollars)

	2001 *52 weeks*	2000 *53 weeks*	1999 *52 weeks*
BALANCE AT BEGINNING OF YEAR	$ 301.6	$ 233.0	$ 183.6
Adjustment due to adoption of new accounting standards: income taxes and employee future benefits	–	(7.1)	–
RESTATED BALANCE AT BEGINNING OF YEAR	301.6	225.9	183.6
Net earnings	122.8	97.3	76.4
Dividends	(17.3)	(14.6)	(12.6)
Share redemption premium	(5.4)	(3.2)	(9.7)
Stock options settled in cash, net of income taxes	(6.0)	(3.8)	(4.7)
BALANCE AT END OF YEAR	$ 395.7	$ 301.6	$ 233.0

See accompanying notes

METRO INC. (2001)

EXHIBIT 1-11

PART C

CONSOLIDATED STATEMENTS OF CASH FLOWS

Year ended September 29, 2001
(Millions of dollars)

	2001 52 weeks	2000 53 weeks	1999 52 weeks
CASH FLOWS FROM OPERATING ACTIVITIES			
Net earnings	$ **122.8**	$ 97.3	$ 76.4
Items not requiring cash flows			
Equity earnings in a company subject to significant influence	**(3.5)**	(2.5)	(2.0)
Depreciation and amortization	**61.4**	52.5	44.3
Losses (gains) on disposal and writeoffs of capital assets	**5.1**	4.9	(0.9)
Future taxes/deferred income taxes	**22.9**	10.3	4.8
Excess of amounts paid for employee future benefits over expenses recognized	**(1.5)**	(0.6)	(1.4)
	207.2	161.9	121.2
Net change in non-cash working capital related to operations	**(61.0)**	(6.0)	72.7
	146.2	155.9	193.9
CASH FLOWS FROM INVESTING ACTIVITIES			
Business acquisition *(note 2)*	**–**	–	(157.0)
Net change in investments	**(2.4)**	(0.4)	1.5
Net purchase of capital assets *(note 7)*	**(106.7)**	(63.2)	(81.5)
	(109.1)	(63.6)	(237.0)
CASH FLOWS FROM FINANCING ACTIVITIES			
Increase (decrease) in bank loans	**30.0**	(10.9)	(20.5)
Issue of capital stock	**3.1**	1.5	2.2
Redemption of subordinate shares	**(6.3)**	(3.9)	(11.6)
Stock options settled in cash	**(6.0)**	(3.8)	(4.7)
(Decrease) increase in long-term debt	**(40.6)**	(60.6)	90.3
Dividends paid	**(17.3)**	(14.6)	(12.6)
	(37.1)	(92.3)	43.1
NET CHANGE IN CASH AND CASH EQUIVALENTS AND BALANCES AT BEGINNING AND END OF YEAR	$ **–**	$ –	$ –
OTHER INFORMATION			
Interest paid	$ **4.5**	$ 9.6	$ 5.4
Income taxes paid	$ **57.2**	$ 55.4	$ 7.3

See accompanying notes

1-67 (Determine financing strategy)
Did METRO INC. finance its business primarily from creditors (total liabilities) or from shareholders (shareholders' equity) in 2001? Support your answer with appropriate data.

1-68 (Identify sources and uses of cash)
List the two largest sources of cash and the three largest uses of cash in 2001. (Consider operating activities to be a single source or use of cash.)

1-69 (Determine causes of change in retained earnings)
Explain the change in retained earnings from the end of 2000 to the end of 2001.

1-70 (Net earnings versus cash balance changes)
Net earnings have increased in 2001 compared to 2000, yet the cash balance has not increased over the same period. Instead, the bank loans have increased. METRO INC. has no cash but rather short-term bank loans with the bank. From the major categories presented on the statement of cash flows, can you suggest reasons why METRO INC. has experienced this increase in debt?

Base your answers to problems 71–74 on the 2000 financial statements of **DaimlerChrysler AG** presented in Exhibit 1-12. DaimlerChrysler is a German company that produces its financial statements using U.S. GAAP. In 2000, DaimlerChrysler presented two monetary amounts on each of its financial statements, U.S. dollars and Euros.

1-71 (Fiscal year end)
When is DaimlerChrysler's fiscal year end?

1-72 (Find financial statement balances)
Find the following amounts in the consolidated statements of DaimlerChrysler (express your answers in Euros):

   a. Net revenues in 2000

   b. Cost of sales in 2000

   c. Financial income in 2000

   d. Total income taxes in 2000

   e. Net income in 2000

   f. Inventories at the end of 2000

   g. Accounts payable (trade liabilities) at the end of 2000

   h. Retained earnings at the end of 2000

   i. Capital stock at the beginning of 2000

   j. Property, plant, and equipment in 2000

   k. Cash and cash equivalents in 2000

   l. Earnings per share on net income in 2000

1-73 (Determine financing strategy)
Did DaimlerChrysler finance its business primarily from creditors (total liabilities) or from shareholders (shareholders' equity) in 2000? Support your answer with appropriate data.

1-74 (Format of balance sheet)
The balance sheet of DaimlerChrysler is organized differently from the Canadian balance sheets that you have seen in this chapter. Describe the areas where there are major differences. (Notice that Deferred Taxes are listed under both the assets and the liabilities and shareholders' equity sections of the balance sheet. The former represents taxes recoverable in the future from the government.)

EXHIBIT 1-12

PART A

DAIMLERCHRYSLER AG (2000)

Consolidated Balance Sheets

(in millions)	Note	Consolidated At December 31, 2001 (Note 1) $	Consolidated At December 31, 2001 €	Consolidated At December 31, 2000 €	Industrial Business* At December 31, 2001 €	Industrial Business* At December 31, 2000 €	Financial Services* At December 31, 2001 €	Financial Services* At December 31, 2000 €
Assets								
Intangible assets	12	2,548	2,863	3,113	2,662	2,907	201	206
Property, plant and equipment, net	12	36,641	41,165	40,145	41,016	40,043	149	102
Investments and long-term financial assets	18	11,015	12,375	12,107	11,349	10,967	1,026	1,140
Equipment on operating leases, net	13	32,046	36,002	33,714	3,004	3,047	32,998	30,667
Fixed assets		82,250	92,405	89,079	58,031	56,964	34,374	32,115
Inventories	14	14,913	16,754	16,283	15,338	15,333	1,416	950
Trade receivables	15	5,723	6,430	7,995	6,134	7,617	296	378
Receivables from financial services	16	44,071	49,512	48,673	26	30	49,486	48,643
Other receivables	17	14,409	16,188	14,396	7,512	6,414	8,676	7,982
Securities	18	2,739	3,077	5,378	2,636	4,195	441	1,183
Cash and cash equivalents	19	10,172	11,428	7,127	8,057	6,445	3,371	682
Non-fixed assets		92,027	103,389	99,852	39,703	40,034	63,686	59,818
Deferred taxes	9	2,679	3,010	2,436	2,930	2,350	80	86
Prepaid expenses	20	7,660	8,606	7,907	8,480	7,782	126	125
Total assets (thereof short-therm 2001: €68,676; 2000: €71,300)		184,616	207,410	199,274	109,144	107,130	98,266	92,144
Liabilities and stockholders' equity								
Capital stock		2,322	2,609	2,609				
Additional paid-in capital		6,485	7,286	7,286				
Retained earnings		23,536	26,441	29,461				
Accumulated other comprehensive income		2,374	2,668	3,053				
Treasury stock		–	–	–				
Stockholders' equity	21	34,717	39,004	42,409	29,009	35,825	9,995	6,584
Minority interests		371	417	519	403	506	14	13
Accrued liabilities	23	37,001	41,570	36,441	40,534	35,772	1,036	669
Financial liabilities	24	80,917	90,908	84,783	15,701	9,508	75,207	75,275
Trade liabilities	25	12,601	14,157	15,257	13,773	14,875	384	382
Other liabilities	26	9,135	10,262	9,621	7,431	7,068	2,831	2,553
Liabilities		102,653	115,327	109,661	36,905	31,451	78,422	78,210
Deferred taxes	9	4,318	4,851	5,480	(2,212)	(639)	7,063	6,119
Deferred income	27	5,556	6,241	4,764	4,505	4,215	1,736	549
Total liabilities (thereof short-term 2001: €80,874; 2000: €81,516)		149,899	168,406	156,865	80,135	71,305	88,271	85,560
Total liabilities and stockholders' equity		184,616	207,410	199,274	109,144	107,130	98,266	92,144

*) Additional information about the Industrial Business and Financial Services is not required under U.S. GAAP and is unaudited.

The accompanying notes are an integral part of these Consolidated Financial Statements.

| Consolidated Statements of Income (Loss) | | DAIMLERCHRYSLER AG (2000) | | | | EXHIBIT 1-12
PART B |

			Consolidated Year ended December 31,			
	Note	2001 (Note 1) $	2001 €	2000 €	1999 €
(in millions, except per share amounts)					
Revenues	32	136,072	152,873	162,384	149,985
Cost of sales	5	(114,283)	(128,394)	(134,370)	(119,688)
Gross margin		21,789	24,479	28,014	30,297
Selling, administrative and other expenses	5	(16,317)	(18,331)	(18,303)	(16,063)
Research and development		(5,281)	(5,933)	(6,337)	(5,737)
Other income	6	1,079	1,212	946	827
Turnaround plan expenses – Chrysler Group	7	(2,727)	(3,064)	–	–
Income (loss) before financial income		(1,457)	(1,637)	4,320	9,324
Financial income (expense), net (therein gain on issuance of associated company stock of €747 in 2001)	8	137	154	156	333
Income (loss) before income taxes		(1,320)	(1,483)	4,476	9,657
Effects of changes in German tax law		–	–	(263)	(812)
Income taxes		692	777	(1,736)	(3,721)
Total income taxes	9	692	777	(1,999)	(4,533)
Minority interests		39	44	(12)	(18)
Income (loss) before extraordinary items and cumulative effects of changes in accounting principles		(589)	(662)	2,465	5,106
Extraordinary items:	11				
Gains on disposals of businesses, net of taxes (therein gain on issuance of subsidiary and associated company stock of €2,418 in 2000)		–	–	5,516	659
Losses on early extinguishment of debt, net of taxes		–	–	–	(19)
Cumulative effects of changes in accounting principles: transition adjustments resulting from adoption of SFAS 133 and EITF 99-20, net of taxes	10	–	–	(87)	–
Net income (loss)		(589)	(662)	7,894	5,746
Earnings (loss) per share	33				
Basic earnings (loss) per share					
Income (loss) before extraordinary items and cumulative effects of changes in accounting principles		(0.59)	(0.66)	2.46	5.09
Extraordinary items		–	–	5.50	0.64
Cumulative effects of changes in accounting principles		–	–	(0.09)	–
Net income (loss)		(0.59)	(0.66)	7.87	5.73
Diluted earnings (loss) per share					
Income (loss) before extraordinary items and cumulative effects of changes in accounting principles		(0.59)	(0.66)	2.45	5.06
Extraordinary items		–	–	5.44	0.63
Cumulative effects of changes in accounting principles		–	–	(0.09)	–
Net income (loss)		(0.59)	(0.66)	7.80	5.69

Beyond the Book

The Beyond the Book problems are designed to give you the opportunity to find and utilize company information found outside the book.

1-75   (Using the library and other sources to find company information)
Familiarize yourself with the resources that are available at your university to acquire information about corporations. Most universities have some type of electronic database that contains financial statement information. The following is a short list of resources that may be available:

LEXIS/NEXIS Database—This is an incredibly large database that contains all sorts of news and financial information about companies. It contains information about Canadian, U.S., and international companies. The financial information is in full text form.

Carlson On-line Service—A directory site with Canadian investment information. Research any company traded on a Canadian exchange for links to other sites that have reliable and up-to-date information on that company.

Compact/Disclosure Canada—Contains descriptive and financial data for over 8,500 public, private, and Canadian government–owned (Crown) corporations. Provides more than 60 financial items including assets, liabilities, sales, profits, number of employees, and selected ratios.

CD-Disclosure—This database contains full-text financial footnote information for thousands of companies, but does not contain full text of the major financial statements.

EDGAR Filings—The EDGAR filings are electronic forms of the SEC filings which are included in the Lexis/Nexis database but are also accessible through the Internet at www.sec.gov/edgar.shtml.

ABI Inform (UMI, Inc.)—This database contains full-text information from numerous business periodicals.

You can also surf the web for sites that list information about companies. The **SEDAR** website (www.sedar.com) contains most securities-related information required by the Canadian securities regulatory authorities and is probably your best source for financial statements of Canadian companies on the Internet. The **Wall Street Research Net** (www.wsrn.com) lists over 17,000 companies on the NYSE, NASDAQ, AMEX, OTC Bulletin Board, TSE, CDNX, ME, and Alberta Stock Exchanges.

1-76   (Find information about a new company)
For a company of your choosing, answer the following questions:

a. What are the products (or product lines) and/or services which your company sells? Please be as specific as possible.

b. Who are the customers of your company?

c. In what markets, domestic and global, does your company sell its products and/or services?

d. Who are the major competitors of your company?

e. What are the major inputs your company needs to produce its product? What are the suppliers of these inputs?

f. Are any of the items listed in the questions above changing substantially? Use a two-year time span as a window to address this question.

To answer these questions, it will be useful to collect a series of articles concerning your company over the most recent two-year period. Try to find at least five reasonably sized articles. Use these as references to write a two- to three-page background paper about your company. If your company has a website (most companies do), it will probably have its news releases accessible there.

1-77   (Find information about a new company)

For a Canadian company of your choosing, find its most recent annual report and answer the following questions:

a. What are the major sections included in your annual report?

b. What are the three most important points made in the letter to the shareholders?

c. What are the titles of the major financial statements included in the report?

d. What are the total assets, total liabilities, and total shareholders' equity of the company? What percentage of the company's total assets is financed through liabilities?

e. Is the balance sheet classified or nonclassified? If classified, what are the major categories used?

f. What were the net sales in the most recent year? Is this up or down from the previous year (answer in both dollar and percentage amounts)?

g. What is the net income and earnings per share in the most recent year? Is this up or down from the previous year (answer in both dollar and percentage amounts)?

h. What is the net cash provided (used) by operating, financing, and investing activities for the most recent year?

i. What is the last day of your company's fiscal year?

j. Who are the independent auditors and what type of opinion did they give the company?

Cases

Additional Cases

1–78   Weible Inc.

Weible Inc. is a small manufacturing company located in northern Canada. The company prepares its financial statements on an annual basis. Weible is currently owned privately by the members of the Weible family. They have very little debt and the main purpose in preparing the financial statements has been to assist in the preparation of annual tax returns. Consequently, the financial statements have never been audited.

You are an accountant employed by a local accounting firm and Weible Inc. has been your client for several years. Karen Weible, president of the company, has recently approached you to advise you of a large investment Weible Inc. is planning to undertake. To complete this project, the company will have to make significant investments in property and equipment. Additionally, over 100 employees will have to be hired. To raise capital for this project, she would like to sell shares to outside investors and is also looking for financing from a local bank.

Karen has approached you because she is interested in knowing how the planned changes will impact the preparation of Weible Inc.'s financial statements. Specifically, she wants information about who may be using the company's financial statements and whether the cost of having the financial statements prepared will change dramatically.

Required
Prepare a memo to Karen Weible addressing her concerns.

1-79   Rust Consulting
Heather Rust is the owner-operator of a small consulting business. She has recently taken a brief accounting seminar and was introduced to the idea of the qualitative characteristics of accounting information. She is having some difficulty understanding the concept of materiality. Her question to you is: "How can certain accounting rules apply in some situations and not in others—doesn't this lead to inconsistent financial reporting?"

Required
Using the concepts discussed in the text, draft a brief reply to Heather's question.

Critical Thinking Question

1-80   (The Role of the Auditor General of Canada)
Peter Diekmeyer (*Management*, November 2001) comments on the appointment of Sheila Fraser, CA, as the first woman Auditor General of Canada.

1. Briefly describe the responsibilities of the Auditor General of Canada. To whom and on what does she report?

2. Explain why it is critically important to have an Auditor General.

3. In the article it states that "government accounting is different than private sector accounting." Using the example given in the article, describe one aspect of how they are different.

A Recipe for Success—
Starting Up a Business

Ever since meeting in high school 16 years ago, Chris Emery and Larry Finnson knew they wanted to go into business together. Sure enough, one day Mr. Emery's grandmother came up with an irresistible recipe for a vanilla fudge treat and Krave's Candy Co. was born. In 1996, with $20,000 scraped together from family and friends, the two Winnipeg entrepreneurs set up some old kettle cookers in a tiny industrial space and started churning out 80-lb. batches of the sweets, which they called Clodhoppers.

In its first year of operation, Krave's recorded sales of $59,000. Mr. Emery and Mr. Finnson sold their product mostly through local retailers and craft fairs. Today, Chris & Larry's Clodhoppers are found in stores across Canada—including Wal-Mart, Zellers, Safeway, The Bay, and Shoppers Drug Mart—and sales for 2002 are expected to be well over $4 million.

While their company has enjoyed remarkable success—it now employs a staff of 15 in a spacious 20,000-square-foot facility—Mr. Emery and Mr. Finnson, neither of whom had any prior business experience, have learned a lot along the way. "At the beginning, we just thought we'd fire up a manufacturing plant and start making millions of pounds of candy and be rich within two years," said Mr. Finnson. "It didn't work out that way. It's been step by step for everything from manufacturing to money."

As Mr. Emery recalled, during the company's start-up period, the pair ran into expenses they hadn't anticipated. "First, we needed a computer, then there was the development of the packaging and artwork, plus we had to hire people to help us make the candy," he said. "Before we knew it, the money was pretty much spent." Meanwhile, as their sales continued to climb, the two had to come up with more cash to finance their expansion, including much-needed upgrades to their production equipment—the large mixers, cooling tunnels, and other devices used in the manufacturing process.

Currently, Mr. Emery and Mr. Finnson keep their financing balanced among an array of sources, including a venture capitalist, a traditional bank, and the Business Development Bank of Canada, from which the company secured a $100,000 loan back in 1999. In 2001, following a major deal to supply Wal-Mart's 2,700 stores in the United States, Krave's needed a new $300,000 form-and-fill machine to weigh and package the candy. "We couldn't take that out of our working capital," explained Mr. Finnson. "So what we did was raise some more equity."

Fortunately, the company's accounting records, which are kept using Accpac's Simply Accounting, help them not only with decisions like these, but also with things like pricing and inventory management. To establish sales forecasts, they use Palo Alto's Business Plan Pro. "We simply put data from our balance sheets into the business plan software and manipulate it for cash flow," explained Mr. Finnson. "We're always working two years ahead, so we adjust our projections all the time. The most important thing is to know your numbers—and know how your business works from A to Z."

TRANSACTION ANALYSIS AND ACCOUNTING ENTRIES

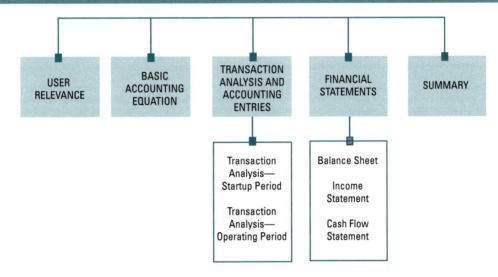

Learning Objectives:

After studying this chapter, you should be able to:

1. *Understand the basic accounting equation.*
2. *Analyze simple transactions and describe their effect on the basic accounting equation.*
3. *Describe the difference between accrual-basis accounting and cash-basis accounting.*
4. *Describe how inventory is accounted for when it is purchased and when it is sold.*
5. *Identify operating activities and describe their impact on retained earnings.*
6. *Describe the revenue recognition and matching criteria.*
7. *Prepare a balance sheet, income statement, and cash flow statement after a series of transactions.*
8. *Calculate three profitability ratios.*
9. *Begin to analyze the information on a cash flow statement.*

Chris Emery and Larry Finnson started small and grew their business through hard work and effective marketing. They started with a product that they thought customers would want, and they were right. They are in their seventh year and seem well on the way to being a successful business. What did they do that made them a success when many new businesses do not survive the first five years? First, they had a product that people liked. Second, they worked hard. They had to make sure that the quality of the product remained consistent as they moved to larger batches. They had to get the product to consumers. They chose to go to craft fairs and to convince local retailers to carry their product. As the name Clodhopper became known, they were able to convince multi-outlet retailers like The Bay to carry their product. This was the start of their real growth. However, along with growth comes a need for additional funding. It is funding problems that often cause young companies their greatest problems. Krave's was no exception. Within a short time, they had exhausted their original investment of $20,000; however, by that time, they were able to convince a bank that they were an acceptable credit risk. Today, they are using multiple sources of funds. Investors are convinced that they have a good product, that the company is well managed, and that there is growth potential. Behind all of its success and through all of its decisions, Krave's had to rely on its accounting information. Sometimes as young companies grow, especially if the growth is rapid, the owners lose track of the numbers. Mr. Emery and Mr. Finnson did not do that. They knew that they had to keep track of all aspects of their business and that the accounting numbers were the tool that would enable them to do that.

The way Mr. Emery and Mr. Finnson started their business is typical of the way many small businesses start. Their original source of funding is from personal savings, family, and friends. Financial institutions are often reluctant to take a chance on a new company until they see some indicators of success. Note the following story. It is about high-tech start-ups, but it applies to most new small businesses.

accounting in the news

LOVE MONEY, ANGEL INVESTING, AND VENTURE CAPITAL

Money is a persistent worry for fledgling companies that need to prove themselves before securing financing from traditional sources such as banks.

Initial funding often comes from family and friends; hence, its name: "love money."

Then there are angel investors, a group who have gained a reputation for mentoring high-tech start-ups into viable businesses. Many angel investors are high-tech millionaires who offer valuable business experience with their dollars. In one study, more than half of the companies that received angel financing later received venture capital dollars; in contrast, only 10 percent of companies that received no angel funding received venture capital funds.

Venture capital financing provides start-ups with large amounts of capital. In Ottawa, a hub of start-up activity, local companies attracted almost $922 million in venture capital in 2001—more than 12 times the amount received in 1998.

However, the year 2001 proved to be slower for Ottawa start-ups looking for financing. Some people attribute a slowdown in angel investing to lower returns on angels' equities portfolios. And while venture capital financing topped $900 million, it did not come near the record $1.3 billion that poured into Ottawa-area companies in 2000.

Sources: "Ottawa pull weakens for startup cash," by Jill Vardy, *National Post, Financial Post*, Jan. 26, 2002; "Angel investors keep flying low," by Brian Salisbury, *Ottawa Business Journal*, Nov. 26, 2001.

USER RELEVANCE

In order for users like Mr. Emery and Mr. Finnson to understand the information that is provided on financial statements, they must have some knowledge of the accounting system—what items are identified, measured, and recorded, how those items are recorded, and how financial statements are generated from the recorded data. Without that knowledge, they will have difficulty understanding the importance (relevance) of the numbers and may not be able to make the best decisions.

The accounting system measures, records, and aggregates the effects on the company of numerous economic events. To interpret the information in financial statements, you must be able to understand the process by which accounting information is obtained, and the guidelines by which it is classified and aggregated for financial statements. Only then can you use accounting information sensibly to make decisions. Chapter 1 provided an overview of the types of information that are presented in financial statements. This chapter and the next are devoted to explaining how accountants collect, classify, and aggregate that information. It is a chapter that is necessarily technical in nature.

Learning Objective

Understand the basic accounting equation.

BASIC ACCOUNTING EQUATION

There are several possible approaches to understanding the accounting systems that companies use. The approach taken in this chapter is to focus on the balance sheet, which will demonstrate how a typical set of **transactions** would be reflected in the financial records and also how the three major financial statements would be prepared using the transaction information. We will use the basic accounting equation discussed in Chapter 1.

The basis of all accounting systems is the basic accounting equation. This equation was stated in Chapter 1 as:

BASIC ACCOUNTING EQUATION
Assets = Liabilities + Shareholders' Equity

When transactions are recorded in the accounting system, the equality of this equation must always be maintained. The balance sheet provides readers with information about this equality at the beginning and at the end of the current accounting period by showing amounts from the previous year in the outside column, and amounts from the current year in the inside column. A statement with the amounts for two years is called a comparative statement (see Sears Canada's balance sheet in Appendix A at the end of the book). The users of financial information typically want to know more than just the balance sheet amounts. They usually want to know something more about how the company's financial position changed from the beginning to the end of the year. An income statement and a cash flow statement are both useful for this purpose. The balance sheet equation will be used to record a set of typical transactions for a hypothetical company, and an income statement and a cash flow statement will be constructed from this information.

In Chapter 1, we showed you that retained earnings (one of the components of shareholders' equity) increased when the company earned net income (revenues minus expenses), and decreased when the company declared a dividend (a payment of earnings back to the investors). To help you understand the linkages between the financial statements and how the various items are affected by transactions, we are adding the following notations beside the amounts: R–revenue, E–expense, and D–dividend. Similarly, to help you understand the cash flows, we will designate them as follows: O–operating, F–financing, and I–investing.

TRANSACTION ANALYSIS AND ACCOUNTING ENTRIES

Learning Objective

Analyze simple transactions and describe their effect on the basic accounting equation.

The basic accounting equation can now be used to illustrate the functioning of the accounting system and the preparation of financial statements. We will use the typical transactions of a retail sales company to demonstrate the analysis and recording of transactions in the accounting system.

Assume that the Demo Retail Company Ltd. is formed as a company in

December of 20x0[1] with the issuance of common shares for $7,500.[2] Before the end of December, Demo uses $4,500 of the cash received from that issuance to buy equipment. It also buys $2,500 of inventory on account. ("On account" means that Demo has been extended credit by its suppliers and will be required to pay for the inventory at some later date. Typical terms for this type of credit include payment within 30 days.)

Transaction Analysis—Startup Period

On December 31, 20x0, just prior to commencing operations, Demo would like to prepare financial statements. Because Demo has not yet begun its normal operation of selling goods to customers, it has not yet earned any income. Therefore, it has no need for an income statement. It could, however, prepare a cash flow statement and a balance sheet. The cash flow statement for December would simply show the cash inflow from the issuance of shares ($7,500), a financing activity, and the outflow to buy equipment ($4,500), an investing activity. To prepare the balance sheet, we would use the basic accounting equation developed earlier.

Balance sheet preparation begins with an analysis of the transactions. In December 20x0, there were three transactions to record. They are as follows:[3]

A. Issuance of common shares for $7,500.

B. Purchase of equipment for $4,500.

C. Purchase of inventory for $2,500, on account.

Each of these transactions is analyzed in the following subsections and recorded in the balance sheet equation that appears in Exhibit 2-1. Note that the beginning balances in all the accounts are zero because this is a new company.

DEMO RETAIL COMPANY LTD.

EXHIBIT 2-1

BASIC ACCOUNTING EQUATION

(Amounts in Dollars)

	Cash	+	Inventory	+	Assets Equipment	=	Liabilities Accounts Payable	+	Shareholders' Equity Common Shares	+	Retained Earnings
Balances	0	+	0	+	0	=	0	+	0	+	0
Transaction #											
A	+7,500 F					=			+7,500		
B	−4,500 I				+4,500	=					
C			+2,500			=	+2,500				
Ending											
Balances	+3,000	+	2,500	+	4,500	=	+2,500	+	7,500	+	0
Totals					10,000	=	10,000				

---

[1] The problems and examples in the text that do not use data from real companies are given artificial dates so as not to confuse them with real companies. Therefore, a designation of "20x0" represents year zero, "20x1" represents year one, and so on.

[2] The amounts used in this and most other made-up examples are stated in small round numbers for ease of presentation. If you want to think of them in more realistic terms, you might multiply all numbers by one thousand or one million.

[3] We will designate these transactions with letters to distinguish them from the numbered transactions in January, which are discussed later in this chapter.

Transaction A

Demo issued common shares for $7,500.

ANALYSIS   The shareholders of the company have contributed $7,500 to the company in exchange for ownership rights. The cash received by the company increases its cash asset, and the ownership interest is represented by an increase in common shares. Look again at Exhibit 2-1. The entry can be summarized as follows:

EFFECTS OF TRANSACTION A

Assets (Cash) increase by $7,500
Shareholders' Equity (Common Shares) increases by $7,500

See Exhibit 2-1 for the recording of this transaction. The transaction can be summarized as follows:

EFFECTS OF TRANSACTION A ON THE BALANCE SHEET (EXHIBIT 2-1)

Assets =	Liabilities	+	Shareholders' Equity
Cash + Inventory + Equipment =	Accounts Payable +		Common Shares + Retained Earnings
+7,500 F =			+7,500

Note that the entries maintain the balance in the basic accounting equation. Also note that the cash transaction has been designated with an "F," indicating that this is a financing-type cash flow.

Transaction B

Demo purchased equipment for $4,500.

ANALYSIS   Because the purchase of equipment requires an outflow of cash, cash decreases. The equipment purchased is generally regarded as a long-term asset because it will be used by the company over several future periods. The asset will be used up or consumed over those future periods, and the annual amount that is consumed or used will be shown as an amortization expense. The expensing of part of this amount is shown later in the transactions for January. By the end of December, however, none of the asset has been used up or consumed and the full amount should be reported as an asset. The entry can be summarized as follows:

EFFECTS OF TRANSACTION B

Assets (Cash) decrease by $4,500
Assets (Equipment) increase by $4,500

See Exhibit 2-1 for the recording of this transaction. The transaction can be summarized as follows:

**EFFECTS OF TRANSACTION B ON THE BALANCE SHEET
(EXHIBIT 2-1)**

	Assets	=	Liabilities	+	Shareholders' Equity	
Cash +	Inventory + Equipment	=	Accounts Payable	+	Common Shares +	Retained Earnings
−4,500 I	+4,500					

Note that the cash outflow has been designated with an "I," indicating that it is an investing cash flow.

GAAP   The treatment of this transaction under GAAP is based on an assumption of **accrual-basis** accounting. Under accrual accounting, costs (such as the cost of the equipment) are only represented as decreases in the shareholders' wealth (expenses) when the item is consumed or the company relinquishes its ownership of the item (such as in a sale transaction). In this transaction, therefore, the view under GAAP is that one asset (cash) has been exchanged for another asset (equipment) and there has been no change in the shareholders' wealth. **Accrual-basis** accounting is different from **cash-basis** accounting, in which costs are represented as decreases in shareholders' wealth (expenses) when the cash is paid. In the cash-basis system, therefore, this transaction would result in an expense that would be reported on the income statement. However, cash-basis accounting is not GAAP. GAAP requires accrual-basis accounting. It is discussed in more detail in the context of transaction 1, which appears later in this chapter.

Learning Objective
3

Describe the difference between accrual-basis accounting and cash-basis accounting.

Transaction C

Demo purchased $2,500 of inventory on account.

ANALYSIS   The substance of this transaction is that Demo has received an asset (inventory) from its supplier and in exchange has given the supplier a promise to pay for the inventory at a later date. The promise to pay represents an obligation of the company and is therefore recorded as a liability. This liability is usually referred to as an **account payable**. The inventory is usually recorded at the amount the company will have to pay to acquire it (its cost). The entry can be summarized as follows:

EFFECTS OF TRANSACTION C

Assets (Inventory) increase by $2,500
Liabilities (Accounts Payable) increase by $2,500

See Exhibit 2-1 for the recording of this transaction. The transaction can be summarized as follows:

EFFECTS OF TRANSACTION C ON THE BALANCE SHEET (EXHIBIT 2-1)		
Assets =	Liabilities +	Shareholders' Equity
Cash + Inventory + Equipment =	Accounts Payable +	Common Shares + Retained Earnings
+2,500	= +2,500	

GAAP   As with Transaction B, this transaction involves the purchase of an asset, but this time no cash changes hands immediately. The inventory will be held until it is sold and GAAP requires that the inventory be recorded at its cost and held as an asset until it is sold. The cost is, therefore, recorded as an asset until the company relinquishes title to it. There is no immediate income statement impact from this transaction. It will affect the income statement only in the period in which the inventory is sold. Note that the transaction also has no impact on the cash flow statement in December, since no cash changed hands. Cash flow will be affected when the company pays the supplier.

At the bottom of Exhibit 2-1, you can see the net result of transactions A, B, and C. These figures represent the balance sheet at the end of December 20x0. The balance sheet could be formally represented as shown below. Note that the total assets of Demo equal the sum of the liabilities and shareholders' equity, as they should, to satisfy the basic accounting equation.

DEMO RETAIL COMPANY LTD. Balance Sheet As at December 31, 20x0			
Assets		**Liabilities**	
Cash	$ 3,000	Accounts payable	$ 2,500
Inventory	2,500		
Equipment	4,500	**Shareholders' equity**	
		Common shares	7,500
Total assets	$10,000	Total liabilities and shareholders' equity	$10,000

Note that, because the retained earnings has a zero balance, it was not included in the balance sheet.

Now that you have seen how a few simple transactions are analyzed and reported on the financial statements, we are going to continue with the example. Assume that during January the following events occurred that affect Demo's account balances:

1. Demo sold units of inventory to customers, on account,[4] for $2,500.[5] The units sold were from the inventory purchased in December.

2. The cost of the units removed from inventory for sales in January totalled $1,800.

3. Purchases of new inventory to replace the units sold in January totalled $2,100. All of these purchases were made on account.

4. During the month, Demo received $2,200 from customers as payments on their accounts.

5. Demo made payments of $2,700 on its accounts payable.

6. Demo paid $360 in cash on January 1 for an insurance policy to cover its inventory from January 1, 20x1, through June 30, 20x1.

7. Demo's accountant determined that the equipment should be amortized by $150 for January.

8. On the first day of January, Demo purchased land for $15,000 as a site for a future retail outlet. In order to pay for the land, Demo raised money by borrowing $10,000 from the bank and issuing new shares for $5,000.

9. The interest rate charged on the loan from the bank in transaction 8 is 6%.

10. Dividends in the amount of $250 were declared and paid in January.

Transaction Analysis—Operating Period

For each of the events or transactions that affect the company, the accountant must analyze the economic substance of the transaction. The accountant must decide what accounts are affected and by how much. We call this **transaction analysis**. We have already done this for transactions A, B, and C which occurred in December. It is at this stage of the accounting process that the accountant's training and knowledge are most needed. Not only must the economic substance of the transaction be analyzed, but the accountant must know which accounting guidelines apply to the transaction.

For each of the preceding transactions, the substance will be analyzed and an appropriate entry proposed. GAAP for the transaction will then be discussed. The transaction will be entered into the "accounting system" (the basic accounting equation). The recording of the transactions appears in Exhibit 2-2, but you may want to try to construct your own exhibit as you work through the transactions.

---

[4] The term "on account" in a sales transaction means that the company is granting the customer credit. The customer will then pay for the goods at some later date based on the agreement with the seller about the terms.

[5] The dollar amounts here are aggregate totals of all units that were sold during the month. Information about individual units would likely be recorded daily and would be of use to the sales or marketing manager, but we are interested in the aggregate effect of sales in this example.

DEMO RETAIL COMPANY LTD.

BASIC ACCOUNTING EQUATION
(Amounts in Dollars)

	Cash +	Accounts Receivable +	Inventory +	Prepaid Insurance +	Land +	Equipment =	Accounts Payable +	Interest Payable +	Bank Loan +	Common Shares +	Retained Earnings
Balances	3,000 +	0 +	2,500 +	0 +	0 +	4,500 =	2,500 +	0 +	0 +	7,500 +	0
Transaction #											
1		+2,500				=					+2,500 R
2		−1,800				=					−1,800 E
3		+2,100				= +2,100					
4	+2,200 0	−2,200				=					
5	−2,700 0					= −2,700					
6a	−360 0			+360		=					
6b				−60		=					−60 E
7						−150 =					−150 E
8a	+5,000 F					=				+5,000	
8b	+10,000 F					=			+10,000		
8c	−15,000 I				+15,000	=					
9						=		+50			−50 E
10	−250 F					=					−250 D
Ending Balances	1,890 +	300 +	2,800 +	300 +	15,000 +	4,350 =	1,900 +	50 +	10,000 +	12,500 +	+190
Totals						24,640 = 24,640					

Column group headers: **Assets** = **Liabilities** + **Shareholders' Equity**

EXHIBIT 2-2

Learning Objective 4

Describe how inventory is accounted for when it is purchased and when it is sold.

Transaction 1

Demo sold units of inventory to customers, on account, for $2,500. The units sold were from the inventory purchased in December.

ANALYSIS   The substance of a sale transaction is that the company has exchanged an asset that it possesses for an asset that the customer possesses. The asset given up by the company may be an item of inventory if the company is a retailer or a manufacturer, or it may be some type of expertise or service if the company is a service provider. In this case, Demo is a retailer and the asset given up is inventory. The asset received in exchange from the customer is generally cash, but other possibilities exist. For example, when a new car is purchased, the buyer's old car is often traded in as part of the deal. Also, the customer may exchange a promise to pay later. This is typically called a **sale on account**, and it results in the company receiving a promise to pay, that is, an **account receivable**, in exchange for the inventory. The name "account receivable" means an account that will be received in the future. It is "receivable" on the day the inventory is sold. This transaction is a sale on account.

Because this is an exchange, there are two parts of the transaction to consider: the inflow of the asset received in the exchange and the outflow of the asset given up. The inflow increases the wealth of the shareholders and increases assets (accounts receivable). The outflow decreases assets (inventory) owned by the company and decreases the wealth of the shareholders (retained earnings). If the inflow is worth more than the outflow in the exchange, the company has generated a **profit** from the sale transaction. If the inflow is less than the outflow, a **loss** results. The increases and decreases in shareholders' wealth in this transaction are typically called the **sales revenue** (inflow) and **cost of goods sold** (outflow), respectively. Because the analysis shown in Exhibit 2-2 focuses only on the balance sheet, the effects of both the sales revenue and the cost of goods sold will be shown as affecting the retained earnings portion of the shareholders' equity. Remember that net income (revenue minus expenses) increases retained earnings. It should, therefore, be logical that revenues will increase retained earnings and expenses will decrease retained earnings. This approach of letting revenues and expenses increase or decrease retained earnings is a temporary shortcut we are going to use to introduce you to transactions.

The question remaining in the analysis is how to value the inflow and the outflow. Based on the information in Transaction 1, the total selling price of the goods sold was $2,500. Therefore, sales revenue (retained earnings) and accounts receivable both increase by $2,500. There is no information given in Transaction 1 regarding the cost of goods sold. This is covered in Transaction 2. It may seem odd to analyze and record these two simultaneous events separately. Nonetheless, it is necessary because the transactions occur at two different value levels, retail and cost. For example, in a department store, when a clerk rings up a sale, a record is made of the sales revenue amount and the increase in cash (or accounts receivable in the case of a sale on account). The salesperson does not know the cost of the item sold at the time of sale. The cost is determined at the end of the period as described under Transaction 2. To summarize:

Learning Objective

5

Identify operating activities and describe their impact on retained earnings.

> ### EFFECTS OF TRANSACTION 1
>
> Assets (Accounts Receivable) increase by $2,500
> Shareholders' Equity (Retained Earnings) increases by $2,500

GAAP The timing of the recognition of revenues and expenses is an important decision that management must make in preparing financial statements. There is an underlying conflict between reporting income information in a timely manner and being assured that the transaction is a bona fide sale. To take two extreme positions, it might be argued at one extreme that a company should recognize a sale when a customer signs a contract for the future delivery of the product. At the other extreme, it might be argued that the company should wait until cash is collected before recognizing the transaction as a sale. In the first case, the company is counting on delivering the product and ultimately collecting the cash from the sale. These are both uncertain events and, if they do not materialize, shareholders may be misled by the income statement into thinking the company is doing better than it really is. In the second case, by delaying recognition of the sale until cash is collected (assuming that it isn't collected when the goods change hands), it is clear that by that time the transaction is a bona fide sale, but it may not be providing shareholders with a very good measure of the company's business activity (on the income statement) during the period prior to collection of the cash. Sales that had been made but were in the process of collection would not appear on the income statement.

The two extremes just discussed have evolved over time into two bases on which accountants generally prepare financial statements: the *accrual basis* and the *cash basis*. The accrual basis attempts to measure performance (i.e., revenues and expenses) in the period in which the performance takes place rather than when the cash is collected. When the accrual basis is used, **revenue recognition criteria** are considered to determine if performance has been achieved. These criteria are discussed in detail in Chapter 4. In brief, the criteria state that revenue can be recognized as earned when (1) the company has performed the majority of the things it has to do associated with the sale (i.e., completed the work, transferred the inventory to the buyer, etc.), (2) the amount that has been earned is known, and (3) there is reasonable assurance that the amount will be collected. You can see from these criteria that when a customer signs a contract, as described in the previous paragraph, revenue would not be recognized because the first criterion, that of completion of the work, was not achieved. The company must still deliver the product, which is a major part of the earning process. Once the product is delivered, however, revenue could be recognized even if cash was not received at that point, provided the other two criteria were met. The criteria are set to provide shareholders with assurance that the amounts stated as revenues and expenses are reasonable and that there is a high probability that the revenues and expenses recorded will ultimately result in similar cash flows. The accrual basis is used by most businesses and will be used throughout this book.

When the cash basis is used, events are recorded only when their cash effects occur. For example, sales revenue is recorded only when cash is received from the customer, and the cost of goods sold is recorded only when the cash is paid out for inventory. You can see that on this basis you could be recording expenses for inventory earlier than you recorded the revenue for selling it. Or, if the company purchased its inventory on account (to be paid for later), you could be recording the cash from the sale before you record the expense for the inventory. In either case, if the financial statements were prepared between the cash collected for the sale and the payment of cash for the inventory, you would have revenue in one period and its associated expense in another. The mistiming of recording activities such as this would make it difficult for managers to make decisions about pricing and inventory acquisition. Because of the potentially misleading information produced by the cash basis, it is not used very often. It is, however, still used by some farmers, lawyers, and professional service companies to account for their businesses. In the past, most not-for-profit organizations used the cash basis, but today most of them have switched to the accrual basis.

In a business such as Demo, the revenue recognition criteria are generally met when the product is exchanged with the customer. Therefore, in the preceding analysis, the result of Transaction 1 is to recognize revenues (increase retained earnings). Demo should not wait until the cash is collected (see Transaction 4). On a cash basis, of course, Demo would not recognize revenue as a result of Transaction 1.

Another aspect of accrual-basis accounting is the **matching concept**. This concept requires that all costs associated with generating sales revenue should be matched with the revenue earned on the income statement. That is, the cost of goods sold related to this revenue should be recognized in the same period as the sales revenue. See the analysis of Transaction 2 for the recording of the cost of goods sold.

Refer to Exhibit 2-2 and the following summary for the proper recording of Transaction 1 in the basic accounting equation. Note that the equation is balanced after the entry is made. The effects on the basic accounting equation can be summarized as follows:

EFFECTS OF TRANSACTION 1 ON THE BALANCE SHEET (EXHIBIT 2-2)

	Assets					=	Liabilities			+	Shareholders' Equity	
	Accounts		Prepaid				Accounts	Interest	Bank	Common	Retained	
Cash +	Receivable +	Inventory +	Insurance +	Land +	Equipment =		Payable +	Payable +	Loan +	Shares +	Earnings	
	+2,500					=					+2,500 R	

Note that this transaction has no effect on cash. The cash effects of the sale of goods will be felt by the company only in the period in which the receivable is collected. This will lead to a difference between the cash received from operations and the net income for the period. Note also that the entry to the retained earnings account has been designated with an "R," indicating that this is a revenue that will be reported on the income statement for the accounting period.

Transaction 2

The cost of units removed from inventory for sales in January totalled $1,800.

ANALYSIS   As explained in the analysis of Transaction 1, there are two parts to the sale transaction. Transaction 1 included information about the revenue side of the transaction. Here in Transaction 2, the costs that are to be matched with the revenue are given. The effect of the outflow of the inventory is to decrease the inventory asset and to decrease the shareholders' wealth by the cost value of the inventory because the company no longer holds title to it. The decrease in shareholders' wealth (that is, retained earnings) by the cost of goods sold is one of the many expenses that the company shows on its income statement. To summarize:

EFFECTS OF TRANSACTION 2

Assets (Inventory) decrease by $1,800
Shareholders' Equity (Retained Earnings) decreases by $1,800

GAAP   As explained earlier in the analysis of Transaction 1, when the revenues from the sale are recognized, the matching concept requires that the costs associated with that revenue be recognized as well. For a retailer such as Demo, the cost of the inventory is simply the wholesale price that Demo paid to acquire the inventory. Under accrual-basis accounting, the cost of the inventory is held in the inventory account until it is sold. Typically, the cost of goods sold is determined at the end of the period by physically counting the number of units still available in inventory and then attaching unit costs to those units. Knowing the cost of the inventory that is still unsold at the end of the period (ending inventory) and the cost of the inventory with which the period began (beginning inventory), as well as the purchases during the period, the accountant can calculate the cost of those units that were sold, as follows:

COST OF GOODS SOLD CALCULATION

	Beginning Inventory
+	Purchases
=	Cost of Goods Available for Sale
−	Ending Inventory
=	Cost of Goods Sold

The determination of the cost of the units of inventory sold is discussed in greater depth in Chapter 7.

Refer to Exhibit 2-2 for the recording of this transaction. The entry is summarized as follows:

EFFECTS OF TRANSACTION 2 ON THE BALANCE SHEET (EXHIBIT 2-2)

		Assets				= Liabilities		+ Shareholders' Equity		
	Accounts		Prepaid			Accounts	Interest	Bank	Common	Retained
Cash +	Receivable +	Inventory +	Insurance +	Land +	Equipment =	Payable +	Payable +	Loan +	Shares +	Earnings
		−1,800				=				−1,800E

Note that this transaction has no effect on cash. The cash flow effects of inventory occur at the time payment for the inventory is made. This leads to a difference between the cash from operations and the net income for the period. Note further that the entry to the retained earnings account has been designated with an "E," indicating that this is an expense that will be reported in the income statement for this accounting period.

Transaction 3

Purchases of new inventory to replace the units sold in January totalled $2,100. All these purchases were made on account.

ANALYSIS   The purchase of inventory has the effect of increasing the inventory asset. Because the inventory is bought on account, Demo has given the seller a promise to pay at some time in the future. Demo should record an increase in accounts payable to indicate its liability to the seller. The name "account payable" means an account that will be paid in the future. It is "payable" on the day the inventory is purchased. Note that on the seller's books, this transaction results in a corresponding account receivable. To summarize:

EFFECTS OF TRANSACTION 3

Assets (Inventory) increase by $2,100
Liabilities (Accounts Payable) increase by $2,100

GAAP   With the accrual basis of accounting, inventory is considered an asset until the revenue recognition criteria are met. The valuation principle for inventory under GAAP is that it be recorded at its acquisition cost (i.e., the price paid to obtain it). When inventory is purchased on account, it is valued at the amount of the liability incurred in the transaction, that is, the value of the account payable. Accounts payable are liabilities that are generally settled in a short amount of time (30 to 60 days) and are valued at the gross amount owed. There is generally no recognition[6] of interest on accounts payable even though they are "loans" from the seller. Occasionally, inventory is purchased on longer-term credit, which results in a formal loan document called a **note payable**. In the case of a note payable, interest is usually explicitly recognized. The interest would be recorded as an expense and as either an outflow of cash, if it is paid, or as a new liability on its own, if the interest is going to be paid in the future. The accounting for interest is explained further in Transaction 9.

See Exhibit 2-2 for the recording of this transaction in the accounting system. The entry is summarized as follows:

EFFECTS OF TRANSACTION 3 ON THE BALANCE SHEET (EXHIBIT 2-2)

	Assets					=	Liabilities		+	Shareholders' Equity	
Cash +	Accounts Receivable +	Inventory +	Prepaid Insurance +	Land +	Equipment =		Accounts Payable +	Interest Payable +	Bank Loan +	Common Shares +	Retained Earnings
		+2,100					=+2,100				

Note that this transaction had no effect on cash. The cash effects of purchasing inventory will be shown when the account payable is paid. Also note that it had no effect on shareholders' wealth (retained earnings). Income will be affected only when the inventory is sold.

Transaction 4

During the month, Demo received $2,200 from customers as payments on their accounts.

ANALYSIS   The receipt of cash from customers means that cash increases. Because the customer no longer owes this amount to the company, the value of the customer's account receivable decreases by the amount of the payment. The entry can be summarized as follows:

EFFECTS OF TRANSACTION 4

Assets (Cash) increase by $2,200

Assets (Accounts Receivable) decrease by $2,200

GAAP   Accounts receivable are generally short-term loans from the seller to the buyer and do not typically result in the recognition of interest. The amount of the receivable is stated at the selling price to the buyer. If this were a **note receivable**

---

[6] The term "recognition" means an item in the accounting system.

that explicitly included interest, the cash received would be more than the selling price, and the excess amount above the selling price would represent interest revenue. See Exhibit 2-2 for the recording of this transaction. The transaction can be summarized as follows:

EFFECTS OF TRANSACTION 4 ON THE BALANCE SHEET (EXHIBIT 2-2)											
Assets						=	**Liabilities**			**+ Shareholders' Equity**	
	Accounts		Prepaid				Accounts	Interest	Bank	Common	Retained
Cash +	Receivable +	Inventory +	Insurance +	Land +	Equipment =		Payable +	Payable +	Loan +	Shares +	Earnings
+2,200 O	−2,200					=					

Note that this transaction does affect cash but not shareholders' wealth (retained earnings). The income effect related to accounts receivable was recorded earlier when the original sale occurred. Note further that the cash entry has been designated with an "O," indicating that this is an operating cash flow.

Transaction 5

Demo made payments of $2,700 on its accounts payable.

ANALYSIS   Cash payments result in a decrease in cash. In this case, because the payment is on an account payable, there is a corresponding decrease in the accounts payable account. To summarize:

EFFECTS OF TRANSACTION 5
Assets (Cash) decrease by $2,700
Liabilities (Accounts Payable) decrease by $2,700

GAAP   Note that no part of the payment is interest. When longer-term loans are involved, the payment would have to be divided between the amount that represents interest and the amount that represents repayment of the original amount of the loan. See Exhibit 2-2 for the recording of the transaction. The transaction can be summarized as follows:

EFFECTS OF TRANSACTION 5 ON THE BALANCE SHEET (EXHIBIT 2-2)											
Assets						=	**Liabilities**			**+ Shareholders' Equity**	
	Accounts		Prepaid				Accounts	Interest	Bank	Common	Retained
Cash +	Receivable +	Inventory +	Insurance +	Land +	Equipment =		Payable +	Payable +	Loan +	Shares +	Earnings
−2,700 O						=	−2,700				

Note that cash is affected by this transaction but shareholders' equity (retained earnings) is not. The income effects of inventory are shown in the period in which the inventory is sold. The period of sale could be either prior to or after the payment of cash. The cash flow will be reported in the operating section of the cash flow statement.

Transaction 6

Demo paid $360 in cash on January 1 for an insurance policy to cover its inventory from January 1, 20x1, to June 30, 20x1.

ANALYSIS This transaction is an example of a **prepaid expense**. The cost of the insurance coverage is paid in advance of the coverage period. At the date of the payment (January 1, in this case) the cost of the policy should be shown as an asset since it has not been used up yet. Another way to think about this as an asset is to consider what would happen if you cancelled the policy immediately after it was paid. Except for any cancellation and/or processing fees, you should be entitled to get your money back because the insurance company has not provided any coverage yet. Only as time passes is the coverage "consumed." In this example, the amount of the coverage that is consumed in January is one month's worth, or $60, assuming that we simply spread the coverage out evenly over the six-month period. Therefore, by the end of January, $60 of the insurance should be treated as an expense to represent the month that has been consumed and the rest ($300) should be treated as an asset representing the coverage to which the company is still entitled as of the end of January.

PREPAID EXPENSES

EXHIBIT 2-3

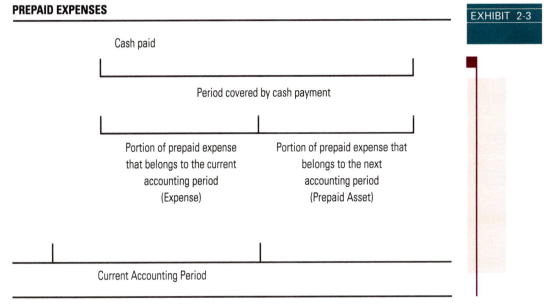

Cash paid

Period covered by cash payment

| Portion of prepaid expense that belongs to the current accounting period (Expense) | Portion of prepaid expense that belongs to the next accounting period (Prepaid Asset) |

Current Accounting Period

Exhibit 2-3 displays a timeline that highlights the effects of a prepaid expense and the timing issue involved. Note that the proportions illustrated in the exhibit are not representative of the situation for Demo. Part of the cash payment results in an expense being recognized in the current period with the remaining portion still seen as an asset for the following period.

There are several ways that a company might record this transaction. One way would be to record the initial cash outflow of $360 on January 1 as a decrease in cash and an increase in a prepaid asset account (Transaction 6a). Then, on January 31, the company would have to record a decrease in the prepaid asset account and a decrease in retained earnings for the $60 that is now an expense (Transaction 6b).

The net result would be to record a decrease in cash of $360, a decrease in retained earnings of $60, and an increase in a prepaid insurance account of $300. This set of effects is shown below:

EFFECTS OF TRANSACTION 6A
Assets (Prepaid Insurance) increase by $360
Assets (Cash) decrease by $360

EFFECTS OF TRANSACTION 6B
Shareholders' Equity (Retained Earnings) decreases by $60
Assets (Prepaid Insurance) decrease by $60

An alternative to this treatment would be to record the transaction as a net result of the analysis above in one entry. A third possible treatment would be to initially show all of the cash outflow as an expense and then at the end of the month adjust the expense from $360 to $60 and at the same time record an increase in a prepaid asset account of $300. All three of these treatments would result in the same net effect on the accounts. For our purposes, we will use the first approach in recording the transaction, but recognize that different companies might follow different methods.

GAAP   The handling of the prepaid expense as part expense and part asset is dictated by the accrual basis of accounting and the concept of attempting to match expenses with revenues in the proper accounting period. See Exhibit 2-2 for the recording of this transaction. The transaction can be summarized as follows:

EFFECTS OF TRANSACTION 6 ON THE BALANCE SHEET (EXHIBIT 2-2)

	Assets					=	Liabilities			+ Shareholders' Equity	
Cash +	Accounts Receivable +	Inventory +	Prepaid Insurance +	Land +	Equipment =		Accounts Payable +	Interest Payable +	Bank Loan +	Common Shares +	Retained Earnings
Transaction 6a											
−360 O			+360			=					
Transaction 6b											
			−60			=					−60 E

Note that these transactions decrease cash flow by $360, which represents an operating cash flow, and decrease income by $60 in January.

Transaction 7

Demo's accountant determined that the equipment should be amortized by $150 for January.

ANALYSIS   Whenever an expenditure is made by a company to acquire an asset, there are three general questions to ask regarding the nature of the transaction:

1. Has an asset been created?
2. If so, what is the value of the asset?
3. How does the asset get used up over time, and when does it cease to exist?

To address the first question, the criteria for an asset must be evaluated. Does the item have probable future value, and does the company own it or have the rights to use it? If the answer to both of these questions is yes, an asset exists and should be recorded. When Demo originally purchased its equipment, the answers to both recognition criteria questions were yes. Demo owned the equipment (because it held title to the equipment), and the equipment had future value (because it was to be used to sell products and thus generate revenues). The equipment, therefore, qualified as an asset.

The answer to the second question is that, under GAAP, the equipment is valued at its acquisition cost (sometimes called *historical cost*). In the example, assume that the $4,500 value of the equipment at December 31, 20x0, represents its historical cost.

The third question is a little more difficult to answer. For an asset such as inventory, the answer is relatively simple: the asset ceases to exist when it is sold and the company gives up title to the asset. The inventory stays on the books until it is sold, and then the cost appears as an expense (cost of goods sold) on the income statement. For equipment, the answer is more complicated. The equipment is used up as time passes and the equipment is used to generate revenues from the sale of the company's products. Equipment has an estimated useful life. For example, it may last for only five years, at which time it is sold, discarded, or traded in for a new piece of equipment.

Because the asset is used up over time, some of the cost of the asset should be shown as an expense in each period in which it is used. Another reason to show some of the cost as an expense is that the expense of using the equipment should be matched (the matching concept) with the revenues generated from the use of the equipment. How much should be shown as an expense in any period is a function of how much of the asset gets used up during that period of time. The amount shown as an expense in any period is called the **amortization** of the asset. There are numerous ways to calculate how much amortization should be taken in a given period. These methods are discussed in detail in Chapter 8. The most common method used is **straight-line amortization**, which assumes that an asset is used evenly throughout its life and that the same amount of amortization should be taken in every time period. The formula for calculating straight-line amortization is:

$$\text{Straight-Line Amortization} = \frac{\text{Original Cost} - \text{Estimated Residual Value}}{\text{Estimated Useful Life}}$$

Two estimates are required to perform the calculation. The **useful life** of the asset must be estimated. This could be expressed in years or months, depending on the length of the accounting period. In the Demo example, this would be months. The second estimate is **residual value**. This is an estimate of what the asset will be worth at the end of its useful life. The quantity in the numerator of the calculation is sometimes called the **amortization value** of the asset because it is the amount that should be amortized over the asset's useful life (or depreciable cost).

In the case of Demo Retail Company Ltd., if it is assumed that the equipment had an original cost of $4,500, an estimated useful life of two years (24 months), and a residual value at the end of two years of $900, the monthly amortization would then be calculated as:

$$\text{Straight-Line Amortization} = \frac{\$4,500 - \$900}{24 \text{ months}}$$
$$= \$150/\text{month}$$

At the end of each month, Demo should reduce the value of the equipment by $150 and show a $150 expense on the income statement (amortization expense). To summarize:

EFFECTS OF TRANSACTION 7

Assets (Equipment) decrease by $150

Shareholders' Equity (Retained Earnings) decreases by $150

GAAP Several amortization methods are commonly used by companies and are discussed in Chapter 8. The choice of methods is influenced by the pattern of use of the asset and the most appropriate method to capture that pattern of use. See Exhibit 2-2 for the recording of this transaction. The transaction can be summarized as follows:

EFFECTS OF TRANSACTION 7 ON THE BALANCE SHEET (EXHIBIT 2-2)

		Assets				=	Liabilities			+ Shareholders' Equity	
Cash +	Accounts Receivable +	Inventory +	Prepaid Insurance +	Land +	Equipment	= Payable +	Accounts Interest Payable +	Bank Loan +	Common Shares +	Retained Earnings
					−150	=				−150 E

Note that the reduction in the equipment account is taken directly out of this account. In practice, the reduction in a capital asset due to amortization is kept in a separate account called *accumulated amortization*. Over time, this account collects all of the reductions in the asset account. It is shown with the capital asset account and is called a *contra asset account* because the accumulated amortization has a balance that is the opposite of the capital asset balance. When the accumulated amortization account is added to the capital asset account, the net amount is reduced. By creating this special account, we can keep the original cost of the capital asset intact. Users find that the original cost of a capital asset is a piece of information that helps them in their decision-making. For now, however, to keep things simple, the number of accounts is being kept to a minimum and we are going to reduce the asset directly. In Chapter 3, we will start to use an accumulated amortization account. Note that this transaction has no effect on cash. The cash outflow due to equipment is shown in the period in which cash is used to purchase the asset. There might also be a cash inflow in the future when the equipment is sold.

Transaction 8

On the first day of January, Demo purchased land for $15,000 as a site for a future retail outlet. In order to pay for the land, Demo raised money by borrowing $10,000 from the bank and issuing new shares for $5,000.

ANALYSIS   It is instructive to view Transaction 8 as a combination of three transactions: the issuance of shares, the borrowing of money, and the purchase of land. These three are discussed as if each occurred separately.

Issuance of Shares   One way for a company to raise money is to issue new shares. New shareholders will provide cash to the company in exchange for share certificates that signify ownership in the company. In this case, the shares are worth $5,000. The shares could be directly exchanged for the land (if the previous landowner was willing to accept them in the exchange), or they could be issued to a new group of investors to obtain cash and then the cash paid to the landowner. We will assume the latter. In either case, the appropriate way to value the shares is at their **fair market value** at the date of the transaction. The effect of the transaction is that cash increases by $5,000 and shareholders' equity increases by $5,000. The new shareholders have made a contribution to the company.

In Canada, shares are generally recorded at the amount that the shareholders paid for them. To summarize (this part of the transaction is referred to as Transaction 8a):

EFFECTS OF TRANSACTION 8A

Assets (Cash) increase by $5,000
Shareholders' Equity (Common Shares) increases by $5,000

Borrowing Money   A second method for raising money is to borrow it. In this case, Demo has borrowed $10,000 from the bank. The effect of this transaction is that cash increases and a new obligation is created to show the amount owed to the bank. The amount of the loan is called the *principal of the loan*. The principal does not include interest. Interest will be added to the amount owed to the bank as time passes. For example, if the interest rate on this loan is 8% per year (interest rates are generally stated on an annual basis), the interest added in the first year of the loan will be 8% of the principal of $10,000, or $800. The terminology is that *interest accrues on the loan at 8%*. The accrued interest at the end of the first year will be $800. At the point of acquiring the loan, the accountant records only the principal because no time has passed since the loan was taken out. To summarize (Transaction 8b):

EFFECTS OF TRANSACTION 8B

Assets (Cash) increase by $10,000
Liabilities (Bank Loan) increase by $10,000

Purchase of Land   The purchase of land for cash means that cash decreases by the amount of the purchase price and land increases by the same amount. GAAP requires that land be recorded at its acquisition cost. Land is an asset because it has probable future value and the company holds title to it. The probable future value can be viewed as either its future sales price or its future use (in this case, its use as a site for a retail outlet). Land is not amortized because it is not consumed the way other capital assets, like equipment, are. Buildings and equipment will wear out from use but land usually stays in a useable condition. To summarize (Transaction 8c):

EFFECTS OF TRANSACTION 8C

Assets (Cash) decrease by $15,000

Assets (Land) increase by $15,000

GAAP   Cash transactions are usually easy to value under GAAP because there is an objective measure of the value given up. In exchange transactions, where cash is not involved, the "cost" is not as easily determined. If, for example, in this transaction the loan had been made by the original owner of the land and the shares had been issued to the original owner of the land and no cash had changed hands, it might be difficult to assign values to the shares and the loan. These types of transactions are called **nonmonetary exchanges**. Under GAAP, the general rule is that these transactions should be valued at the fair market value of the consideration given up in the transaction. In this example, that would be the fair market value of the shares and the loan. In our example, it is assumed that the share issuance and bank borrowing are separate from the purchase of the land. The transaction is, therefore, a monetary exchange, even though there is no net effect on cash. See Exhibit 2-2 for the recording of the net effects of this transaction in the basic accounting equation. Remember that the transaction has been split up into three separate transactions labelled 8a, 8b, and 8c. The transaction can be summarized as follows:

EFFECTS OF TRANSACTION 8 ON THE BALANCE SHEET (EXHIBIT 2-2)

	Assets					=	Liabilities			+ Shareholders' Equity	
Cash +	Accounts Receivable +	Inventory +	Prepaid Insurance +	Land +	Equipment =		Accounts Payable +	Interest Payable +	Bank Loan +	Common Shares +	Retained Earnings
Transaction 8a											
+5,000 F						=				+5,000	
Transaction 8b											
+10,000 F						=			+10,000		
Transaction 8c											
−15,000 I				+15,000		=					

Note that these transactions do not affect income (retained earnings) but do affect cash, although in this case, the effects on cash are offsetting. As we will point out in Chapter 5, this particular transaction would qualify as a noncash transaction and as such would not be reported directly in the cash flow statement. It would, however, be given more complete disclosure in the notes to the financial statements. For the purposes of this chapter, however, we will treat the components of this transaction as separate and report them all in the cash flow statement.

Transaction 9

The interest rate charged on the loan from the bank in Transaction 8 is 6% and is paid quarterly (at the end of every three months).

ANALYSIS   Interest is the amount charged by lenders for the use of their money. From the point of view of the borrower, interest is an expense and therefore results in a decrease in the shareholders' wealth during the period in which it is incurred. By the end of January, the $10,000 loan has been outstanding for one month and, therefore, one month's interest expense should be recognized. Since the interest has not been paid yet (and will not be paid until the end of March), Demo will have to recognize a liability for its obligation to pay the interest at the end of the quarter. This is an example of an *accrued expense*. As illustrated in Exhibit 2-4, accrued expenses are expenses that are recognized on the income statement in the period in which they are incurred, which is prior to the period in which they are paid in cash. Note that the proportions illustrated in the exhibit are not representative of the situation for Demo.

ACCRUED EXPENSES   EXHIBIT 2-4

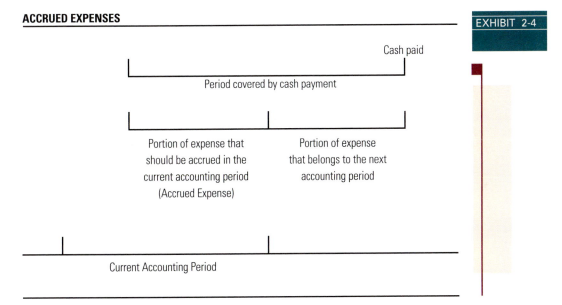

To calculate the amount of interest expense, you multiply the amount of the loan (known as the *principal*) by the interest rate and then by the fraction of the year that has passed (since the interest rate is always expressed as a yearly rate). In Demo's case, the amount of interest incurred in January is $50 [$10,000 $\times$ 6% $\times$ 1/12]. Shareholders' equity (retained earnings) should therefore decrease by $50 to recognize the interest expense, and liabilities (interest payable) should increase by $50 to recognize the obligation to pay the interest. To summarize:

EFFECTS OF TRANSACTION 9

Shareholders' Equity (Retained Earnings) decreases by $50
Liabilities (Interest Payable) increase by $50

GAAP   Accrual-basis accounting requires that expenses be recognized in the period in which they are incurred rather than the period in which they are paid. Accrued expenses, therefore, typically result in a liability that appears on the balance sheet at the end of the period representing the amount of expenses that have been accrued by that date, which will be paid in the subsequent period. See Exhibit 2-2 for the recording of this transaction. The transactions can be summarized as follows:

ASSETS						=	LIABILITIES			+	SHAREHOLDERS' EQUITY	
	Accounts		Prepaid				Accounts	Interest	Bank		Common	Retained
Cash +	Receivable +	Inventory +	Insurance +	Land +	Equipment =		Payable +	Payable +	Loan +		Shares +	Earnings
						=		+50				−50 E

EFFECTS OF TRANSACTION 9 ON THE BALANCE SHEET (EXHIBIT 2-2)

Note that this transaction affects income (retained earnings) but it does not affect cash. Because the interest is paid quarterly, the effect on cash will occur at the end of the quarter.

Transaction 10

Dividends in the amount of $250 were declared and paid in January.

ANALYSIS   Dividends are payments to the shareholders of the company as authorized by the company's board of directors. They are a return to the shareholders of part of the accumulated earnings of the company. They are not expenses of doing business because they are not incurred for the purpose of generating revenues. The effect of Transaction 10 is to reduce the shareholders' equity (retained earnings) and either to increase liabilities (dividends payable), if they have not been paid, or to decrease assets (cash), if they have been paid.

> **EFFECT OF TRANSACTION 10**
>
> Assets (Cash) decrease by $250
> Shareholders' Equity (Retained Earnings) decreases by $250

GAAP   Dividends are declared by a vote of the board of directors of a company. At the date of declaration, they become a legal liability of the company. As just illustrated, the accounting records should show a decrease in retained earnings (usually through an account called the **dividends declared** account) and an increase in the dividends payable account. The dividends declared account affects retained earnings. The change in this account explains part of the change in the retained earnings account from the beginning of the period to the end of the period. It is very important, however, to note that dividends are not an expense and do not appear on the income statement. They will appear on a cash flow statement when they are paid, and many companies prepare a statement of retained earnings, which shows the dividends declared during the period.

There is generally a delay between the date the dividends are declared and the date they are paid, and therefore the cash effects are not recognized until the payment date. In the case of Demo, dividends are declared and paid in the same accounting period, so that the dividends payable account is ignored. See Exhibit 2-2 for the recording of the effects of this transaction in the balance sheet equation. The transaction can be summarized as follows:

EFFECTS OF TRANSACTION 10 ON THE BALANCE SHEET (EXHIBIT 2-2)

		Assets				=	Liabilities			+ Shareholders' Equity	
Cash +	Accounts Receivable +	Inventory +	Prepaid Insurance +	Land +	Equipment =		Accounts Payable +	Interest Payable +	Bank Loan +	Common Shares +	Retained Earnings
−250 F						=					− 250 D

Note that dividends are not part of income but do appear on the cash flow statement because they affect cash.

FINANCIAL STATEMENTS

Balance Sheet

This completes the analysis of the ten transactions of the Demo Retail Company Ltd. The balance sheet for Demo could now be constructed as follows:

Learning Objective 7

Prepare a balance sheet, income statement, and cash flow statement after a series of transactions.

DEMO RETAIL COMPANY LTD.
Balance Sheet

	January 31, 20x1	December 31, 20x0
Current Assets		
Cash	$ 1,890	$ 3,000
Accounts receivable	300	0
Inventory	2,800	2,500
Prepaid insurance	300	0
Total current assets	5,290	5,500
Land	15,000	0
Equipment	4,350	4,500
Total assets	$24,640	$10,000
Current Liabilities		
Accounts payable	$ 1,900	$ 2,500
Interest payable	50	0
Total current liabilities	1,950	2,500
Bank loan	10,000	0
Total liabilities	11,950	2,500
Shareholders' Equity		
Common shares	12,500	7,500
Retained earnings	190	0
Total shareholders' equity	12,690	7,500
Total liabilities and shareholders' equity	$24,640	$10,000

Note that the Demo balance sheet is a classified balance sheet in which current assets and liabilities are distinguished from noncurrent. Because the accounting period involved is one month, the balances for both the beginning of the month[7] and the end of the month are shown.

Income Statement

The income statement can be constructed from the information on the transactions recorded in the retained earnings account in Exhibit 2-2 (refer back to chapter 1 for a description of the income statement). Note that the dividend amount does not belong on the income statement because it is not an expense used to derive net income. Rather, it is a payment of earnings to the shareholders. The income statement would be constructed as follows:

DEMO RETAIL COMPANY LTD. Income Statement For the month ended January 31, 20x1	
Sales revenues	$2,500
Less: Cost of goods sold	(1,800)
Gross profit	700
Amortization expense	(150)
Insurance expense	(60)
Interest expense	(50)
Net income	$440

Demo operated profitably during the month of January, earning a net income of $440.

By itself, a net income of $440 tells users very little about a company other than that it has a positive income flow. To understand the profitability of a company more fully, users will often use ratio analysis, a technique you will see used frequently throughout this text. A ratio divides one financial statement amount by another financial statement amount. This allows users to understand how some amounts are related to other amounts. As you have seen from the financial statements illustrated so far, there are many numbers from which meaningful relationships can be derived. Ratios allow users to compare companies that are of different sizes, or to compare the same company over time. Ratio analysis can be used to assess profitability, the effectiveness of management, and the ability of the company to meet debt obligations. As we introduce new topics to you, we will be showing you ratios that can help users understand and evaluate a set of financial statements. A complete discussion of these ratios can be found in Chapter 12.

We are going to start by using the Demo example to examine profitability ratios. Profitability ratios are usually constructed by comparing some measure of the profit (net income) of the company to the amount invested or by comparing it to the revenues of the company. We will calculate three such measures.

---

[7] Note that the beginning balances in January are the same as the ending balances from December.

Profitability Ratios

The **profit margin ratio** is calculated by dividing the profit generated by the company by the revenues that produced that profit. For Demo, this ratio is 17.6% (net income/revenues = $440/$2,500). This indicates that Demo earned, as profit, 17.6% of the revenue amount. Stated another way, of the $2,500 in initial revenues generated by the company, Demo retained 17.6% and increased the company's wealth by this amount.

The **return on assets** invested is another measure of profitability. It is calculated by dividing the profit of the company by the average total assets invested in the company. Total assets is a balance sheet amount that is determined at a point in time. Thus, to get a measure of the balance over the year, we use the average. The average assets can be calculated using the information in the balance sheet. For Demo, the average is $17,320 [($10,000 + $24,640)/2]. In January of 20x1, the return on assets was 2.5% (net income/average total assets = $440/$17,320). Remember that a company invests in assets so that it can use them to generate profits. Demo's return of 2.5% means that for each $100.00 invested in assets, Demo earned $2.50 of profit.

The third measure of performance is the **return on equity**. This measure compares the return (profit) with the amount invested by the shareholders (average total shareholders' equity). The measure is 4.4% (net income/average shareholders' equity = $440/$10,095) for Demo. The $10,095 is the average of the sum of the shareholders' equity accounts (common shares and retained earnings). The average is calculated as [($7,500 + $12,690)/2]. This measure means that the shareholders have earned a 4.4% return on their investment in one month.

These ratios must be interpreted either within the context of the past performance of the company or in comparison with other companies in the same industry. More will be said about these ratios and their interpretation in Chapter 12.

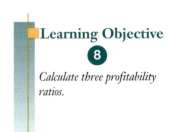

Learning Objective
8

Calculate three profitability ratios.

Cash Flow Statement

A cash flow statement can now be constructed from the information in the cash column in Exhibit 2-2. The cash flow statement explains the changes in cash flow by detailing the changes in operating, financing, and investing activities (refer back to Chapter 1). Remember that we marked all of the cash transactions in the exhibit with an O, I, or F to make the preparation of this statement easier. The operating section of Demo's cash flow statement appears somewhat different from that of Sun-Rype Products, shown in Chapter 1. The reason is that GAAP allows for this section to be prepared using a direct or an indirect method. The direct method has been used here, whereas Sun-Rype used the indirect method. The explanation for this difference is presented in Chapter 5.

DEMO RETAIL COMPANY, LTD.
Cash Flow Statement
For the Month Ended January 31, 20x1

Cash from operating activities:		
Cash receipts from customers	$2,200	
Cash disbursement to suppliers	(2,700)	
Cash disbursement for insurance	(360)	
Cash flow from operating activities		$ (860)
Cash from investing activities:		
Purchase of land		(15,000)
Cash from financing activities:		
Proceeds from issuance of common shares	5,000	
Proceeds from bank loan	10,000	
Dividends paid	(250)	
Cash flow from financing activities		14,750
Decrease in cash		$(1,110)

Learning Objective

9

Begin to analyze the information on a cash flow statement.

The important part of the cash flow analysis is interpreting what the cash flow statement shows about the health of the company. Subsequent chapters discuss many of the detailed analyses that can be done with the data in the cash flow statement. For now, there are two basic questions that can serve as a start for the analysis of this statement. The first is: is the cash from operations sufficient to sustain, in the long run, the other activities of the company? A company can be healthy in the long run only when it produces a reasonable amount of cash from operations. Cash can be obtained from financing activities (issuance of new debt or shares) and from investment activities (the sale of investments or capital assets), but these sources cannot sustain the company forever because there are limits to the company's access to them.

The second question relates to the first: of the sources and uses of cash, which are continuing items from period to period, and which are simply sporadic or non-continuing? A large source or use of cash in one period may not have long-run implications if it does not continue in the future. To address this question, the historical trend in the cash flow statement data must be considered. The cash flow statement for **Sleeman Breweries** is shown in Exhibit 2-5. Note that cash from operations generated a positive amount in each of the two years presented and that the amount increased over those two years.

To assess whether the cash from operations is adequate to meet Sleeman Breweries' needs, look at the major uses of cash. In 2001, the three largest uses of cash were as follows:

Principal repayments of long-term debt	$19,039
Additions to property, plant, and equipment	12,677
Business acquisitions	2,179
	$33,895

EXHIBIT 2-5

SLEEMAN BREWERIES LTD.
Consolidated Statements of Cash Flows
(in thousands of dollars)

	Fiscal Year Ended	
	December 29, 2001	December 30, 2000
NET INFLOW (OUTFLOW) OF CASH RELATED TO THE FOLLOWING ACTIVITIES:		
OPERATING		
Net earnings	$ **9,765**	$ 8,969
Items not affecting cash		
Depreciation and amortization	**7,087**	6,371
Future income taxes	**1,100**	3,100
Gain on disposal of equipment	**-**	(586)
	17,952	17,854
Changes in non-cash operating working capital items (Note 14)	**1,032**	(5,432)
	18,984	12,422
INVESTING		
Business acquisitions (Note 3)	**(2,179)**	(1,054)
Additions to property, plant and equipment	**(12,677)**	(11,433)
Additions to intangible assets	**(1,402)**	(846)
Additions to long term investments (Note 6)	**-**	(4,780)
Proceeds from disposal of equipment	**22**	807
	(16,236)	(17,306)
FINANCING		
Net proceeds from bank operating loans	**6,179**	1,438
Stock options exercised	**769**	-
Common shares repurchased (Note 11)	**-**	(5,168)
Long-term debt - proceeds	**9,343**	15,280
Long-term debt - principal repayments	**(19,039)**	(6,666)
	(2,748)	4,884
NET CASH FLOW AND CASH BALANCE, END OF YEAR	**-**	-
Supplemental disclosures of cash flows:		
Interest paid	$ **6,620**	$6,663
Income taxes paid, net of cash refunds of $898 (2000 -$225)	$ **1,016**	$858

The total of these uses was more than the cash produced from operations of $18,984 thousand. To make up for the shortfall from operations, Sleeman Breweries used proceeds from the disposal of equipment of $22 thousand, borrowed $15,522 thousand (part from bank operating loans and part from long-term debt), and received cash from the exercise of stock options, $769 thousand, for a total of $16,313 thousand. In trying to forecast whether future operations will be sufficient to cover these major uses, the company must assess whether these uses are likely to continue at the same level. If they continue at the same level, Sleeman Breweries will have to make up for the shortfall from operations with other sources of cash. This would not be good because it would require further borrowings or issuances of shares.

All three of the uses—the business acquisition, the acquisition of property, plant, and equipment, and the repayment of long-term debt—seem to be greatly increased in the current year. Replacing capital assets is typical of most companies, especially for a company in the manufacturing industry, since there is a continuing need to replace them if the company wants to continue its current activities or to grow. Sleeman Breweries also seems to borrow and repay long-term debt. Judging by the information for 2001 and 2000, Sleeman Breweries has not used the issuance of shares very extensively as a way of generating cash. If the net cash provided by (used in) financing activities is considered, it is obvious that, over the last two years, Sleeman Breweries has been borrowing and repaying its debt.[8]

Returning to the analysis of Demo Retail Company, even though the company was profitable based on the income statement ($440), the analysis of cash flow indicates a negative cash flow from operations of $860 and an overall decrease in cash of $1,100. Considering the starting balance in cash of $3,000, it is clear that Demo could operate for a few more months at this rate and still have some cash remaining. It cannot, however, continue to operate indefinitely with a negative cash flow (i.e., net cash outflow). The company would run out of cash in a little over three months. This should raise questions about why Demo has this cash drain, even though it appears to be profitable. When we look at the three types of activities, the biggest concern is the negative cash flow from operations. Analyzing why Demo is having difficulty generating cash from operations is beyond the scope of this chapter, but Demo's problem represents an important issue that will be addressed in various sections of this book, most thoroughly in Chapter 5. In fact, problems related to cash flows are key reasons why new businesses fail in their first year. For now, it is important to understand that, while the income statement provides important information about the changes in the shareholders' wealth, it does not reveal everything that is important to know about the company. The cash flow statement can provide additional useful information about the company's operations that is not adequately captured by the income statement. With only one month's worth of data for Demo, it is impossible to comment on the continuing nature of the items on Demo's cash flow statement.

---

8 One caveat should be stated here: a complete analysis of Sleeman Breweries' cash position is not possible without a review of all of the financial statements and related footnotes.

SUMMARY

This chapter has introduced the accounting system using the basic accounting equation. A basic set of transactions were examined in detail and the effect of the transactions on the basic accounting equation was demonstrated. A retail company served as the example in this explanation, but the same procedures would be used in any for-profit organization. From the transactions, the three basic financial statements were developed. The additional explanations that accompanied the financial statements build on the information provided in Chapter 1. In the next chapter, we will use the same example to expand on the operation of the accounting system in a more formal way.

SUMMARY PROBLEM

Additional Demonstration Problems

The balance sheet of Sample Retail Company Ltd. as of January 1, 20x1, is shown in Exhibit 2-6.

EXHIBIT 2-6

SAMPLE RETAIL COMPANY LTD.
Balance Sheet
January 1, 20x1

Cash	$ 4,500
Accounts receivable	500
Inventory	7,500
Prepaid rent	1,200
Total current assets	13,700
Equipment	9,200
Total assets	$22,900
Accounts payable	$ 5,400
Accrued salaries payable	400
Income tax payable	360
Total current liabilities	6,160
Bank loan	800
Total liabilities	6,960
Common shares	3,600
Retained earnings	12,340
Total shareholders' equity	15,940
Total liabilities and shareholders' equity	$22,900

The following transactions occurred during 20x1:

1. Goods with an aggregate selling price of $80,000 were sold, all on account.

2. A review of accounts receivable showed that $750 remained uncollected as at December 31, 20x1.

3. Salaries totalling $20,500 were earned by employees. Cash payments for salaries totalled $20,375.

4. Purchases of inventory, all on account, totalled $39,700. (Assume that this is the only item that affects accounts payable.)

5. Payments on accounts payable totalled $37,300.

6. A count of inventory at December 31, 20x1, revealed that $9,700 remained unsold in ending inventory.

7. Rent for each month is prepaid on the last day of the preceding month. Monthly payments during 20x1 were $1,300/month.

8. Interest on the bank loan accrues at 9% and is payable at the end of each month. On December 31, 20x1, $200 of the principal of the loan was repaid.

9. Amortization expense on the equipment totalled $2,000.

10. New equipment was purchased for $4,500.

11. The tax rate is 40% for 20x1. Taxes are calculated at the end of each quarter and are paid one month later. Assume that the taxes on income in 20x1 were evenly spread across the four quarters of the year.

12. Dividends of $210 were declared and paid.

Required:
Analyze the effect of the transactions above using the basic accounting equation. Prepare an income statement, balance sheet, and cash flow statement.

SUGGESTED SOLUTION TO SUMMARY PROBLEM

The basic accounting equation analysis is shown in Exhibit 2-7. The entries are numbered to correspond with the transaction numbers in the problem. Financial statements are shown in Exhibits 2-8, 2-9, and 2-10. One note regarding the cash flow statement: under GAAP, companies report interest and tax payments as operating items even though you could think of interest as a part of financing activities and tax payments as being spread over all types of activities. When the amounts paid for interest and income taxes are not listed separately in the operating section or in the notes, companies need to disclose these items and they usually do so at the bottom of the cash flow statement. In our example, all interest and tax amounts are shown in the operating section of Exhibit 2-10, so no further disclosure is necessary.

The following detail is provided for selected transactions:

Transaction 2. The ending balance of $750 is provided in the problem. The cash receipts from customers are then determined using this and other information about the beginning balance of accounts receivable and the sales on account given in Transaction 1.

Transaction 3. Salaries earned during the period should be shown as expenses. Salaries paid during the period reflect the payment of salaries from the previous period (i.e., the beginning balance in the accrued salaries payable account) as well as the payment of salaries during the current period. The ending balance in the salaries payable account reflects the salaries that were earned during the current period but not paid at year end.

Transaction 6. The physical count of unsold inventory provides the ending balance in the inventory account. The cost of goods sold is then determined by considering the beginning balance, the purchases of inventory, and the ending balance. Refer back to the explanation given for Transaction 2 for Demo Retail if you want to review the calculation of cost of goods sold.

Transaction 7. The beginning balance ($1,200) in prepaid rent is the payment made on December 31 of the prior year that covers rent expense in January of 20x1. This, along with 11 months of payments (11 × $1,300/month = $14,300) during 20x1, constitutes the rent expense for the year of $15,500 ($1,200 + $14,300). The final payment in 20x1 of $1,300 applies to the first month in 20x2 and is, therefore, the ending balance in the prepaid rent account.

Transaction 8. Because the interest expense is paid at the end of each month, there is no accrued liability to be shown at the end of the period. The cash payments for interest, in this case, are the same as the expense. The expense is calculated by multiplying the principal ($800) times the interest rate (9%) times one year. Remember that interest rates are expressed as an annual rate.

Transaction 11. To determine the tax expense for the period, income before taxes must first be determined. The income before taxes is $4,428. The tax expense is then calculated by taking 40% of this number, resulting in $1,771 for the year (40% × $4,428 = $1,771). The beginning balance in the taxes payable account is the tax calculated for the last quarter of the previous year that is paid in January of 20x1. The quarterly payments in 20x1 are $443 ($1,771/4), assuming the income is evenly distributed across the quarters. The payment for the beginning balance in the tax payable account and three of the quarterly payments constitute the payments for taxes in 20x1 of $1,689 [$360 + (3 × $443)]. The last quarter's amount of $442 ($1 less than the other three quarterly payments due to rounding) is still payable at December 31, 20x1, and is, therefore, the ending balance in the taxes payable account. It will be paid in January of 20x2.

SAMPLE RETAIL COMPANY LTD.

EXHIBIT 2-7

BASIC ACCOUNTING EQUATION

(Amounts in Dollars)

	Cash	+ A/R	+ Inv	+ Prepaid Rent	+ Equip	=	A/P	+ Accrued Salaries	+ Tax Payable	+ Loan	+ CS	+ RE
				Assets		=	Liabilities				+Shareholders' Equity	
Beginning Balance	4,500	+500	+7,500	+1,200	+9,200	=	5,400	+400	+360	+800	+3,600	+12,340
Trans #						=						
1		+80,000				=						+80,000 R
2	+79,750 O	−79,750				=						
3a						=		+20,500				−20,500 E
3b	−20,375 O					=		−20,375				
4			+39,700			=	+39,700					
5	−37,300 O					=	−37,300					
6			−37,500			=						−37,500 E
7a	−15,600 O			+15,600		=						
7b				−15,500		=						−15,500 E
8a	−72 O					=						−72 E
8b	−200 F					=				−200		
9					−2,000	=						−2,000 E
10	−4,500 I				+4,500	=						
11a						=			+1,771			−1,771 E
11b	−1,689 O					=			−1,689			
12	−210 D					=						−210 D
Ending Balance	4,304	+750	+9,700	+1,300	+11,700	=	7,800	+525	+442	+600	+3,600	+14,787
Totals					27,754	=	27,754					

EXHIBIT 2-8

SAMPLE RETAIL COMPANY LTD.
Income Statement
For the year ended December 31, 20x1

Revenues		$80,000
Expenses:		
Cost of goods sold	$37,500	
Salary expense	20,500	
Rent expense	15,500	
Amortization expense	2,000	
Interest expense	72	
Total expenses		75,572
Income before taxes		4,428
Tax expense		1,771
Net income		$ 2,657

EXHIBIT 2-9

SAMPLE RETAIL COMPANY LTD.
Balance Sheet
As at December 31

	20x1	20x0
Assets		
Current assets		
Cash	$ 4,304	$ 4,500
Accounts receivable	750	500
Inventory	9,700	7,500
Prepaid rent	1,300	1,200
Total current assets	16,054	13,700
Equipment	11,700	9,200
Total assets	$27,754	$22,900
Liabilities		
Current liabilities		
Accounts payable	$ 7,800	$ 5,400
Accrued salaries	525	400
Taxes payable	442	360
Total current liabilities	8,767	6,160
Bank loan	600	800
Total liabilities	9,367	6,960
Shareholders' equity		
Common shares	3,600	3,600
Retained earnings	14,787	12,340
Total shareholders' equity	18,387	15,940
Total liabilities and shareholders' equity	$27,754	$22,900

EXHIBIT 2-10

SAMPLE RETAIL COMPANY LTD.
Cash Flow Statement
For the year ended December 31, 20x1

Cash from operating activities:		
Cash receipts from customers	$79,750	
Cash disbursements to suppliers	(37,300)	
Cash disbursements for salaries	(20,375)	
Cash disbursements for rent	(15,600)	
Cash disbursements for interest	(72)	
Cash disbursements for taxes	(1,689)	
Cash flow from operating activities		$4,714
Cash from investing activities:		
Purchase of new equipment		(4,500)
Cash from financing activities:		
Repayment of bank loan	(200)	
Dividends paid	(210)	
Cash flow from financing activities		(410)
Decrease in cash		($ 196)

ABBREVIATIONS USED

A/P	Accounts payable
A/R	Accounts receivable
CS	Common shares
Equip.	Equipment
GAAP	Generally Accepted Accounting Principles
Inv.	Inventory
RE	Retained earnings
SE	Shareholders' equity

SYNONYMS

Amortization/Depreciation
Profit/Net Income/Return/Earnings

GLOSSARY

Accounts payable   The liabilities that result when the company buys inventory or supplies on credit. They represent a future obligation.

Accounts receivable   The assets that result when a customer buys goods or services on credit. They represent the right to receive cash from the customer.

Accrual basis   The accounting basis used by almost all companies, which recognizes revenues and expenses in the period in which they are earned or incurred and not necessarily in the period in which the cash inflow or outflow occurs.

Amortization   The expense taken each period based on the use of a noncurrent asset, such as plant or equipment. Amortization is a process that uses a systematic and rational method, such as the straight-line method, to allocate the cost of a noncurrent asset to each of the years of its useful life. Amortization is sometimes referred to as depreciation.

Amortization value   The portion of the cost of a noncurrent asset, such as plant or equipment, that is to be amortized over its useful life. The amortization value is equal to the original cost of the asset less its estimated residual value.

Cash basis   The accounting basis used by some entities , in which revenues and expenses are recognized when the cash inflow or outflow occurs.

Cost of goods sold   The expense that is recorded for the inventory sold during the period.

Depreciable cost   A synonym for amortization value.

Depreciable value   A synonym for amortization value.

Depreciation   A synonym for amortization.

Dividends declared   A distribution of assets (usually cash) to the shareholders of a company. The Board of Directors of the company votes to formally declare the distribution, at which point it becomes a legal obligation of the company. The distribution of cash occurs at a date specified at the time of declaration.

Fair market value   The value of an asset or liability based on the price that could be obtained from, or paid to, an independent third party in an arms-length transaction.

Matching concept   A concept in accounting that requires all expenses related to the production of revenues to be recorded during the same time period as the revenues. The expenses are said to be matched with the revenues.

Net income   The difference between the revenues and the expenses recognized during the period.

Nonmonetary exchange   An exchange of goods or services in which the assets or liabilities exchanged are not cash.

Note payable   A formal document representing the amount owed by a company. There is usually interest on this type of debt.

Profit   A synonym for net income.

Profit margin ratio   A ratio that compares the profit (net income) during an accounting period with the related revenues.

Residual value   The estimated value of an asset at the end of its useful life. The estimate is made when the asset is purchased.

Return on assets   A ratio that compares the net income for the period with the investment in assets.

Return on equity   A ratio that compares the net income for the period with the investment shareholders make in the company.

Revenue recognition criteria   Criteria established within GAAP that stipulate when revenues should be recognized in the financial statements.

Sale on account   A sale in which the seller receives a promise to pay at a later date from the buyer.

Sales revenue   The amount of sales recognized during the accounting period based on the revenue recognition criteria.

Straight-line amortization   An amortization method that calculates the amount of amortization expense for each period by dividing the amortization value by the estimated number of years of useful life.

Transaction   An exchange of resources with an outside entity or an internal event that affects the balance in individual asset, liability, or shareholders' equity accounts.

Transaction analysis   The process by which the accountant decides what accounts are affected, and by how much, by an economic transaction or event.

Useful life   The estimate of the expected life over which an asset will be used.

ASSIGNMENT MATERIAL

Assessing Your Recall

Multiple Choice Quizzes

2-1   Describe how the basic accounting equation is used when transactions are recorded in the accounting system.

2-2   Discuss why dividends do not appear on the income statement but do appear on the cash flow statement.

2-3   What advantages and disadvantages are there in using the cash basis of accounting rather than the accrual basis?

2-4   Identify the three major sections in the cash flow statement and briefly describe the nature of the transactions that appear in each section.

2-5   Respond to each of the following statements with a true or false answer:

a. Revenues increase shareholders' equity.

b. Cash receipts from customers increase accounts receivable.

c. Dividends declared decrease cash immediately.

d. The cash basis recognizes expenses when they are incurred.

e. There is no such thing as a prepaid rent account on the cash basis.

f. Dividends are an expense of doing business and should appear on the income statement.

g. On the accrual basis, interest should be recognized only when it is paid.

h. Interest paid on bank loans is reported in the operating section of the cash flow statement.

2-6   Briefly describe how a company typically calculates the cost of goods sold.

2-7   What are revenue recognition criteria and how does the matching concept relate to these criteria?

2-8   Explain how a prepaid expense (like rent) gets handled under accrual-basis accounting.

2-9   Explain how an accrued expense (like interest) gets handled under accrual-basis accounting.

2-10   Suppose that a company had an accounting policy that recognizes warranty expense only when warranty service was provided. Discuss whether this meets the matching concept under accrual-basis accounting and suggest other ways that this transaction might be handled.

2-11   Explain what amortization is and how it is calculated using the straight-line method.

Applying Your Knowledge

2-12 (Aspects of a successful business)
Using the information in the opening vignette about **Krave's Candy Company**, describe the aspects of the business that are indicators of growth and success. Identify any areas of the operation where you think Mr. Emery and Mr. Finnson will have to be vigilant so that they continue to be a successful enterprise.

2-13 (Cash basis versus accrual basis)
Given the following transactions, what income would be reported on the cash basis and on the accrual basis:

- Credit sales to customers totalled $36,000. ⌐
- Cash sales totalled $105,000.   a + c
- Cash collections on account from customers totalled $34,000. ᵔ
- Cost of goods sold during the period was $79,000. a ⌐
- Payments made to suppliers of inventory totalled $75,500. C
- Wages of $23,000 were paid during the year; wages of $900 remained unpaid at year end; there were no wages unpaid at the beginning of the year.
- Half-way through the year, insurance premiums on a two-year policy were paid in the amount of $900. C

2-14 (Cash basis versus accrual basis)
Given the following transactions, what income would be reported on the cash basis and on the accrual basis: ⌐

- Inventory costing $65,000 was purchased on account.
- Inventory costing $61,000 was sold for $106,300. Eighty percent of the sales were for cash.
- Cash collected from customers who bought inventory on account totalled $19,000.
- Rent of $1,000 was paid on the last day of each month. The rent was to cover the following month. The rent for the first month of the year was paid on the last day of the previous year.
- Office supplies costing $6,800 were purchased for cash. At the end of the year, $400 of the office supplies were still unused.
- Wages of $18,000 were paid during the year; wages of $200 remained unpaid at year end; wages of $300 were unpaid at the end of the previous year.

2-15 (Nature of retained earnings)
Explain why you agree or disagree with the following statement: "Retained earnings are like money in the bank; you can always use them to pay your bills if you get into trouble."

2-16 (Income statement and cash flow statement)
Compare and contrast the income statement and the cash flow statement with regard to their purpose. Outline how they are similar, and briefly describe their relationship to the balance sheet.

2-17 (Transaction analysis)
For each of the transactions below, indicate which accounts are affected and whether they increase or decrease:

    a. Issue common shares for cash

    b. Buy equipment from a supplier on credit (short-term)

    c. Buy inventory from a supplier partly with cash and partly on account

    d. Sell a unit of inventory to a customer on account

e. Receive a payment from a customer on his or her account

f. Borrow money from the bank

g. Declare a dividend (to be paid later)

h. Pay a dividend (that was previously declared)

i. Recognize wages earned by employees (to be paid at the end of the next pay period)

j. Buy office supplies using cash

2-18 (Transaction analysis and the basic accounting equation)
For each of the following transactions, give the effect on the basic accounting equation:

a. Issuance of shares for cash

b. Payment of a liability

c. Purchase of land for cash

d. Purchase of equipment on credit

e. Payment of cash to shareholders reflecting a distribution of income

f. Receipt of a loan from the bank

g. Payment of interest on a bank loan

h. Purchase of inventory on credit

i. Payment of insurance to cover one year

j. Payment to a delivery company for the delivery of goods to a customer

2-19 (Transaction analysis)
For each of the following transactions, indicate how income and cash flow are affected (increase, decrease, no effect) and by how much:

a. Issue common shares for $60,000.

b. Sell, on account, a unit of inventory for $450 that cost $205. The unit was already in inventory prior to its sale.

c. Purchase equipment for $1,200 cash.

d. Amortize plant and equipment by $500.

e. Purchase a unit of inventory, on account, for $300.

f. Make a payment on accounts payable for $950.

g. Receive a payment from a customer for $100 for inventory previously purchased on account.

h. Declare (but do not pay yet) a dividend for $2,000.

i. Pay a dividend for $2,000 that was declared.

2-20 (Transaction analysis and the basic accounting equation)
Show how each of the following transactions affects the basic accounting equation:

a. Buy land for $50,000 in cash.

b. Declare a dividend of $9,000.

c. Issue common shares for $150,000.

d. Buy inventory costing $35,000 on account.

e. Sell inventory costing $32,500 to customers, on account, for $52,000.

f. Borrow $15,000 from the bank.

g. Receive a payment from a customer for $300 representing a down payment on a unit of inventory that must be ordered.

h. Amortize equipment by $1,200.

i. Make a payment of $210 to the electric company for power used during the current period.

2-21 (Transaction analysis and the basic accounting equation)
Show how each of the following transactions affects the basic accounting equation:

a. Bought supplies for $15,000 on account. The inventory is to be used in the repair of vehicles. The company repairs and services vehicles.

b. Completed the repair and service of several vehicles and received $25,000 in cash. In the repair of the vehicles, $8,000 of the supplies inventory was used.

c. The owners invested a further $25,000 in the business. Shares were issued to them in exchange.

d. Some of the inventory that was used in the repair of the vehicles carried 90-day to two-year warranties. The company estimates that $500 in warranty costs will be necessary in the future. *Hint*: This is a possible future cost to the company. If the sale is recognized in the current period, all associated expenses should be matched to that revenue in the same period.

e. Paid $14,000 to suppliers of the inventory.

f. Received the utility bills (electricity, water, telephone), which totalled $650. Paid all but one bill for $75, which will be paid next month.

g. Borrowed $50,000 from the bank. It is intended that the money be used to purchase a new hoist.

h. Bought a new hoist for $48,000. Used the cash that had been borrowed from the bank.

i. Paid the wages of the employees, $7,000.

2-22 (Transaction analysis and the basic accounting equation)
For each of the following transactions, indicate how each immediately affects the basic accounting equation and what other effects there will be in the future as a result of the transaction:

a. Purchase equipment for cash.

b. Borrow money from the bank.

c. Purchase inventory on account.

d. Pay rent in advance for a warehouse.

e. Pay for an insurance policy on an office building.

f. Sell inventory to customers for cash.

g. Sign warranty agreements with customers that cover products that were sold to them. See 21d) for more information about this type of transaction.

h. Buy a patent for a new production process.

2-23 (Transaction analysis and the basic accounting equation)
Indicate the effects of the following transactions on the basic accounting equation developed in the chapter. The fiscal year end of the company is December 31.

a. Borrowed $12,500 from the bank on Jan. 1, 20x1.

b. Paid interest on the bank loan described in a) on Dec. 31, 20x1. The interest rate is 8%.

c. Bought equipment on Jan. 1, 20x1, for $8,000 cash. The equipment has an estimated useful life of six years and an estimated residual value at the end of five years of $800.

d. Recorded the amortization for the equipment as at Dec. 31, 20x1, assuming the company uses the straight-line method.

e. Sales for the period totalled $35,500, of which $7,500 were on account. The cost of the products sold from inventory was $21,600.

f. Collections on account from customers totalled $6,800.

g. Purchases of inventory on account during 20x1 totalled $24,700.

h. Payments to suppliers totalled $22,900 during 20x1.

i. Employees earned wages of $2,400 during 20x1 (recorded as Wages Payable).

j. All employee wages were paid by year end except the wages for the last week in December, which totalled $50.

k. Dividends were declared and paid in the amount of $400.

2-24 (Transaction analysis and the basic accounting equation)
Indicate the effects of the following transactions on the basic accounting equation developed in the chapter. The fiscal year end of the company is December 31.

a. Issued common shares for $25,000.

b. Paid an insurance premium of $600 on July 1 that provides coverage for the 12-month period starting July 1.

c. Recognized the amount of insurance expense that had been used from July 1 through December 31, assuming the facts in transaction b).

d. Sales recorded for the period totalled $60,000, of which $25,000 were cash sales.

e. Cash collections on customer accounts totalled $37,000 (including some from the previous year).

f. Signed a contract to purchase a piece of equipment that cost $1,200, and put a down payment of $100 on the purchase.

g. Dividends of $1,300 were declared.

h. Dividends of $1,150 were paid.

i. Amortization of $3,300 was taken on the plant and equipment.

j. Purchased $31,350 of inventory on account.

k. Inventory costing $35,795 was sold (including some from the previous year).

2-25　(Transaction analysis and the basic accounting equation)
Sunshine Company Ltd. reported assets of $150,000, liabilities of $85,000, and shareholders' equity of $65,000 on January 1, 2004. During the year, Sunshine Company:

 a. Purchased land for $40,000 cash.

 b. Purchased equipment on November 1 costing $20,000 by signing a three-month note payable.

 c. Paid liabilities of $27,000.

 d. Issued new common shares for $50,000 cash.

 e. Borrowed $10,000 from a local bank on September 1 on a six-month note payable.

Required:
Calculate the totals reported in each of the three major categories of the basic accounting equation following the transactions.

2-26　(Basic accounting equation evaluation)
Ballentine Company Ltd. has assets of $100,000, liabilities of $40,000, and shareholders' equity of $60,000. Using the basic accounting equation, answer each of the following independent questions:

 a. At what amount will shareholders' equity be stated if Ballentine pays off $6,000 of liabilities with cash?

 b. At what amount will assets be stated if total liabilities increase by $2,600 and shareholders' equity remains constant?

 c. At what amount will assets be stated if total liabilities decrease by $3,000 and shareholders' equity increases by $2,000?

 d. What would be the impact on the accounting equation for Ballentine if the shareholders received $4,000 in cash as a dividend?

 e. At what amount will liabilities be stated if total assets increase by $3,000 and shareholders' equity remains constant?

2-27　(Preparation of an income statement)
Sara's Bakery had the following account balances at the end of December 20x1:

Wage expense	$22,000
Sales	95,000
Cash	26,000
Cost of goods sold	52,000
Accounts payable	6,000
Rent expense	9,600
Common shares	60,000

Required:

 a. Prepare an income statement for the year ended December 31, 20x1. Follow the format given in the chapter.

 b. You did not need to use all of the items listed. For every item that you did not use, explain why you did not use it.

2-28 (Preparation of an income statement)

The Wizard's Corner, a company that sells adventure games, figures, cards, and clothing, had the following account balances at the end of June 20x1:

Wage expense	$ 35,000
Sales	160,000
Accounts receivable	14,000
Rent expense	12,000
Cost of goods sold	100,000
Common shares	30,000
Advertising expense	6,000
Dividends declared	3,000

Required:

a. Prepare an income statement for the year ended June 30, 20x1. Follow the format given in the chapter.

b. You did not need to use all of the items listed. For every item that you did not use, explain why you did not use it.

2-29 (Preparation of an income statement)

The Garment Tree Ltd. sells sports clothing. At the end of December 20x1, it had the following account balances:

Miscellaneous expense	$ 5,000
Wages expense	32,000
Wages payable	500
Cost of goods sold	52,000
Sales	120,000
Rent expense	9,600
Inventory	18,000
Advertising expense	5,000

Required:

a. Prepare an income statement for the year ended December 31, 20x1. Follow the format given in the chapter.

b. You did not need to use all of the items listed. For every item that you did not use, explain why you did not use it.

2-30 (Preparation of a balance sheet)

The Tree Top Restaurant Ltd., a restaurant chain that has several restaurants in cities across Canada, had the following account balances at December 31, 20x1:

Accounts payable	$ 80,000
Prepaid insurance	20,000
Common shares	90,000
Cash	63,000
Land	120,000
Inventory	44,000
Retained earnings	65,000
Wages payable	12,000

Required:
Prepare a classified balance sheet for Tree Top Restaurant Ltd. for December 31, 20x1. Follow the examples in the chapter.

2-31   (Preparation of a balance sheet)
At the end of its *first year* of operations, Minute Print Company had the following account balances at December 31, 20x1:

Equipment	$230,000
Sales	488,000
Bank loan	30,000
Wage expense	62,000
Supplies on hand	18,000
Cash	44,000
Supplies used	204,000
Retained earnings	?
Prepaid rent	2,000
Other expense	9,000
Amortization expense	30,000
Dividends declared	3,000
Accounts payable	8,000
Common shares	100,000
Rent expense	24,000

Required:

a. Identify the income statement accounts and calculate net income.

b. Subtract the dividends declared from the net income you calculated in part a) to find the amount of retained earnings at December 31, 20x1.

c. Prepare a classified balance sheet for December 31, 20x1, following the format given in the chapter. Use the amount calculated in part b) for retained earnings.

2-32   (Preparation of a balance sheet)
Little Tots Ltd. sells children's clothing. At the end of December 20x1, it had the following account balances:

Cash	$ 3,000
Wages payable	500
Display counters	4,000
Wage expense	15,000
Cost of goods sold	32,000
Sales	55,000
Rent expense	3,600
Bank loan	1,800
Advertising expense	800
Telephone expense	100
Electricity expense	200
Dividends declared	1,200
Common shares	9,000
Accounts payable	2,000
Inventory	8,000
Other expenses	400
Retained earnings	?

Required:

a. Prepare a calculation to determine the amount of retained earnings.

b. Use what you need to prepare a classified balance sheet following the format given in the chapter.

2-33 (Transaction analysis and financial statement preparation)
The T. George Company started business on Jan. 1, 2004. Listed below are the transactions that occurred during 2004.

Required:

a. Use the basic accounting equation to analyze the transactions for 2004.

b. Prepare a balance sheet, an income statement, and a cash flow statement for 2004.

Transactions:

1. On Jan. 1, 2004, the company issued 10,000 common shares for $175,000.

2. On Jan. 1, 2004, the company borrowed $125,000 from the bank.

3. On Jan. 2, 2004, the company purchased (for cash) land and a building costing $200,000. The building was recently appraised at $140,000. *Hint:* because the building will be amortized in the future and the land will not, you must record the land and building in separate accounts.

4. Inventory costing $100,000 was purchased on account.

5. An investment was made in Calhoun Company Ltd. shares in the amount of $75,000.

6. Sales to customers totalled $190,000 in 2004. Of these, $30,000 were cash sales.

7. Collections on accounts receivable totalled $135,000.

8. Payments to suppliers totalled $92,000 in 2004.

9. Salaries paid to employees totalled $44,000. There were no unpaid salaries at year end.

10. A physical count of unsold inventories at year end revealed inventory costed at $10,000 was still on hand.

11. The building was estimated to have a useful life of 20 years and a residual value of $20,000. The company uses straight-line amortization.

12. The interest on the bank loan is recognized each month and is paid on the first day of the succeeding month; that is, January's interest is recognized in January and paid on February 1. The interest rate is 9%.

13. The investment in Calhoun Company paid dividends of $5,000 in 2004. All of it had been received by year end. The receipt of dividends from an investment is treated as investment income, a revenue.

14. Dividends of $15,000 were declared on Dec. 15, 2004, and were scheduled to be paid on Jan. 10, 2005.

2-34 (Transaction analysis and financial statement presentation)
The Hughes Tool Company started business on October 1, 2003. Its fiscal year runs through to September 30 of the following year. Following are the transactions that occurred during fiscal 2004 (the year starting Oct. 1, 2003, and ending Sept. 30, 2004).

Required:

a. Use the basic accounting equation to analyze the transactions for 2004.

b. Prepare an income statement, a balance sheet, and a cash flow statement for fiscal 2004.

c. Comment on the results of the first year's operations.

Transactions:

1. On Oct. 1, 2003, J. Hughes contributed $120,000 to start the business. Hughes is the only owner. She received 10,000 shares.

2. On Oct. 2, 2003, Hughes Tools borrowed $300,000 from a venture capitalist (a lender who specializes in start-up companies). The interest rate on the loan is 12%.

3. On Oct. 3, 2003, Hughes Tools rented a building. The rental agreement was a two-year contract that called for quarterly rental payments (every three months) of $20,000, payable in advance on Dec. 31, March 31, June 30 and Sept. 30. The first payment was made on Oct. 3, 2003, and covers the period from Oct. 3 to Dec. 31.

4. On Oct. 3, 2003, Hughes Tools purchased equipment costing $240,000 cash.

5. On Oct. 3, 2003, Hughes purchased initial inventory with a cash payment of $100,000.

6. Sales during the year totalled $800,000, of which $720,000 were credit sales.

7. Collections from customers on account totalled $640,000.

8. Additional purchases of inventory during the year totalled $550,000, all on account.

9. Payments to suppliers totalled $495,000.

10. Inventory on hand at year end amounted to $115,000.

11. The company declared and paid a dividend of $40,000 to J. Hughes.

12. Interest on the loan from the venture capitalist was paid at year end, Sept. 30, 2004, as well as $20,000 of the principal.

13. Other selling and administrative expenses totalled $90,000 for the year. Of these, $10,000 were unpaid as at year end.

14. The equipment purchased on Oct. 3 had an estimated useful life of seven years and a residual value of $30,000. Amortization for the year was recorded.

15. The income tax rate is 30%. Assume that Hughes made payments during the year equal to three-quarters of the ultimate tax bill, and the rest is accrued at year end. Also, assume that the way net income is calculated for tax purposes does not differ from the method used for reporting purposes.

2-35   (Transaction analysis and financial statement preparation)
The A.J. Smith Company started business on Jan. 1, 20x1. Following are the transactions that occurred during 20x1.

Required:
a. Use the basic accounting equation to analyze the transactions for 20x1.

b. Prepare a balance sheet, an income statement, and a cash flow statement for fiscal 20x1.

Transactions:
1. On Jan. 1, 20x1, the company issued 25,000 common shares at $15 per share.

2. On Jan. 1, 20x1, the company purchased land and buildings from another company in exchange for $50,000 in cash and 25,000 common shares. The land's value is approximately one-fifth of the total value of the transaction. *Hint:* you need to determine a value for the common shares using the information you were given in transaction 1 and you must record the land and building in separate accounts.

3. Equipment worth $100,000 was purchased on July 1, 20x1, in exchange for $50,000 in cash and a one-year, 10% note, principal amount $50,000. The note pays semi-annual interest, and interest was unpaid on Dec. 31, 20x1.

4. The equipment is amortized using the straight-line method, with an estimated useful life of 10 years and an estimated residual value of $0. Because the equipment was purchased on July 1, only a half year of amortization is recognized in the first year.

5. The buildings purchased in transaction 2 are amortized using the straight-line method, with an estimated useful life of 30 years and an estimated residual value of $40,000.

6. During the year, inventory costing $200,000 was purchased, all on account.

7. Sales during the year were $215,000, of which credit sales were $175,000.

8. Inventory costing $160,000 was sold during the year.

9. Payments to suppliers totalled $175,000.

10. At the end of the year, accounts receivable had a positive balance of $10,000.

11. On March 31, 20x1, the company rented out a portion of its building to Fantek Company. Fantek is required to make quarterly payments of $5,000. The payments are due on March 31, June 30, Sept. 30, and Dec. 31 of each year, with the first payment on March 31, 20x1. All scheduled payments were made during 20x1.

12. Selling and distribution expenses amounted to $30,000, all paid in cash.

13. The company pays taxes at a rate of 30%. During the year, $3,000 was paid to the Canada Customs and Revenue Agency.

14. Dividends of $4,000 were declared during the year, and $1,000 remained unpaid at year end.

2-36 (Preparation of cash flow statement)
Following are descriptions of line items that should appear on a cash flow statement for Gordon Company. Organize these items in a formal cash flow statement and comment on the health of the company to the extent that you can.

Cash flow line items:
Cash receipts from customers $5,000
Purchase of equipment $12,000
Proceeds from the issuance of shares $20,000
Investment in WestJet Airline shares $3,000
Cash disbursements to suppliers $3,400
Cash payments to employees (salaries) $1,900
Proceeds from the sale of equipment $6,000
Dividends paid $2,500
Repayment of bank loan $8,000

2-37   (Transaction analysis)
Many transactions take place between two independent entities. How you record a particular transaction depends on whose perspective you take.

Required:
For each of the following transactions, comment on how it would affect the basic accounting equation from each of the perspectives given:

a. Purchase of inventory from a supplier (buyer's and seller's perspectives)

b. Loan from the bank (borrower's and bank's perspectives)

c. Deposit by customer on the purchase of a unit of inventory to be delivered at a later time (company's and customer's perspectives)

d. Company A invests in shares of Company B and obtains the shares directly from Company B (Company A's and Company B's perspectives)

e. Company A invests in shares of Company B and obtains the shares by buying them on the Toronto Stock Exchange, that is, they had previously been issued by Company B and now trade in the stock market (Company A's and Company B's perspectives)

f. Prepayment of insurance premiums (company's and insurance company's perspectives)

User Perspective Problems

2-38   (Areas of risk in a new company)
Assume that you are a commercial loan officer at a bank. The two owners of **Krave's Candy Company** (see the opening story) come to the bank for a loan shortly before the last of their initial $20,000 is gone. Draft a list of items that you would want to know about the operations of the company before you decide on whether to loan them any money.

2-39   (Accrual versus cash basis with respect to manipulation of earnings)
Under the accrual basis of accounting, revenues are recognized when the revenue recognition criteria are met and expenses are then matched with the revenues under the matching concept. Discuss the opportunities that management has to manipulate income reported to shareholders under the accrual basis as compared to the cash basis.

2-40   (Revenue recognition)
Suppose that your company sells appliances to customers under instalment contracts which require them to pay for the appliance over as much as two years using monthly payments. Two potential methods of revenue recognition would be to either recognize the full purchase price at the time of the sale or to defer recognition of the revenue until

you receive the cash from the payments. Discuss the incentives that management might have to choose one method of revenue recognition over the other from both a tax perspective and the perspective of reporting income to shareholders.

2-41 (Cash basis of accounting)
Under the cash basis of accounting, the purchase of a new piece of equipment for cash would be treated as an expense during the accounting period in which it was purchased.

a. From the perspective of the shareholder of a company, how would this treatment affect your assessment of the income of the company and the value of the remaining assets on the balance sheet?

b. From the perspective of a buyer of the company (someone who wanted to purchase all of the outstanding shares of the company), how would this treatment affect your assessment of the value of the company as a potential acquisition?

2-42 (Warranty expense and tax implications)
Under accrual-basis accounting, warranty expenses are typically estimated at the time of the sale and accrued. If you were allowed to determine tax law, would you allow companies to deduct warranty expenses at the time of the sale or would you make the company wait until it actually provided the warranty service? Why?

2-43 (Calculation of the value of a company)
One of the shareholders of The Really Sinful Cookie Shop is considering selling his ownership and wishes to determine his equity in the cookie shop using good accounting principles. The shareholders know the following transactions have occurred since they started operations at the beginning of the year:

1. $35,000 was borrowed from the bank to help get the business started and $10,000 was repaid by year end. In addition, the shareholders contributed $15,000 to get the business started.

2. Ingredients costing $40,000 were purchased during the year, and 80% were used in goods baked during the year. All but $6,000 of the ingredients were paid for by the end of the year.

3. Cookie ovens were rented during the year for $13,000. At year end, an option to purchase the ovens was exercised and $37,000 was paid to acquire ownership.

4. Wages of $20,000 were earned by employees during the year; all were paid except income taxes of $3,000 which had been withheld from their paycheques and will be forwarded to the Canada Customs and Revenue Agency early next year.

5. After collecting $86,000 for goods sold (which was the full sales amount), the cash balance at the end of the year was $25,000, and net income of $21,000 was reported.

Required:

a. List each of the assets and liabilities of the bakery at the end of the year.

b. Calculate the amount of the shareholders' equity at year end.

c. Prepare a simple balance sheet for the bakery at year end.

d. For what amount should the shareholder be able to sell his 25% interest?

Reading and Interpreting Published Financial Statements

2-44 (Determination of items from a Canadian company's financial statements)
Base your answers to the following questions on the 2001 financial statements of **Enerflex Systems Ltd.** that you will find in Exhibit 2-11.

EXHIBIT 2-11

PART A

CONSOLIDATED BALANCE SHEETS

ENERFLEX SYSTEMS LTD. (2001)

		December 31	
(Thousands)		**2001**	2000
Assets			
Current assets			
Accounts receivable		$ **67,987**	$ 58,842
Inventory	(Note 3)	**59,343**	51,136
Future income taxes	(Note 9)	**2,521**	1,812
Total current assets		**129,851**	111,790
Rental equipment	(Note 4)	**39,042**	31,740
Property, plant and equipment	(Note 5)	**45,149**	47,273
Future income taxes	(Note 9)	**1,138**	639
Intangible assets		**2,815**	—
Goodwill, net of accumulated amortization		**4,151**	1,299
		$ **222,146**	$ 192,741
Liabilities and Shareholders' Equity			
Current liabilities			
Bank loans	(Note 6)	$ **23,886**	$ 24,638
Accounts payable and accrued liabilities		**43,880**	29,075
Current portion of long-term debt	(Note 6)	**—**	200
Total current liabilities		**67,766**	53,913
Long-term debt	(Note 6)	**30,000**	30,000
Future income taxes	(Note 9)	**5,879**	4,717
		103,645	88,630
Commitments and contingencies	(Note 8)		
Shareholders' equity			
Share capital	(Note 7)	**35,412**	35,617
Retained earnings		**83,089**	68,494
		118,501	104,111
		$ **222,146**	$ 192,741

See accompanying notes to the Consolidated Financial Statements.

CONSOLIDATED STATEMENTS OF INCOME

		Years Ended December 31	
(Thousands, except share amounts)		**2001**	2000
Revenue		$ **375,040**	$ 286,283
Cost of goods sold		**301,816**	232,369
Gross margin		**73,224**	53,914
Selling, general and administrative expenses		**35,151**	33,227
Gain on sale of assets		**(1,088)**	(599)
Income before interest and taxes		**39,161**	21,286
Interest, net		**2,680**	3,583
Income before income taxes		**36,481**	17,703
Income taxes	(Note 9)	**14,027**	6,391
Net income		$ **22,454**	$ 11,312
Net income per common share — basic		$ **1.51**	$ 0.76
— diluted		$ **1.49**	$ 0.75
Weighted average number of common shares		**14,916,964**	14,968,887

CONSOLIDATED STATEMENTS OF RETAINED EARNINGS   ENERFLEX SYSTEMS LTD. (2001)

EXHIBIT 2-11

PART B

(Thousands)		Years Ended December 31	
		2001	2000
Retained earnings, beginning of year		$ **68,494**	$ 67,763
Net income		**22,454**	11,312
Common shares purchased for cancellation	(Note 7)	**(1,807)**	(3,125)
Stock options purchased	(Note 7)	**(87)**	(1,467)
Dividends		**(5,965)**	(5,989)
Retained earnings, end of year		$ **83,089**	$ 68,494

CONSOLIDATED STATEMENTS OF CASH FLOWS

(Thousands)		Years Ended December 31	
		2001	2000
Operating Activities			
Net income		$ **22,454**	$ 11,312
Depreciation and amortization		**8,636**	7,570
Future income taxes		**(46)**	200
Gain on sale of assets		**(1,088)**	(599)
		29,956	18,483
Changes in non-cash working capital		**(889)**	(2,324)
		29,067	16,159
Investing Activities			
Acquisition of Landré Ruhaak bv	(Note 2)	**(9,154)**	—
Purchase of:			
Rental equipment		**(16,293)**	(12,443)
Property, plant and equipment		**(3,150)**	(4,503)
Proceeds on disposal of:			
Rental equipment		**6,310**	4,558
Property, plant and equipment		**678**	185
		(21,609)	(12,203)
Changes in non-cash working capital		**126**	(922)
		(21,483)	(13,125)
Financing Activities			
(Decrease) increase in bank loan		**(752)**	9,398
Repayment of long-term debt		**(200)**	(2,000)
Common shares purchased for cancellation		**(2,012)**	(3,369)
Stock options purchased		**(141)**	(2,482)
Stock options exercised		**—**	657
Dividends		**(5,965)**	(5,989)
		(9,070)	(3,785)
Changes in non-cash working capital		**1,486**	751
		(7,584)	(3,034)
Increase in cash		**—**	—
Cash, beginning of year		**—**	—
Cash, end of year		$ **—**	$ —
Supplemental disclosure of cash flow information			
Interest paid		$ **3,918**	$ 3,584
Interest received		$ **807**	$ —
Income taxes paid		$ **6,620**	$ 6,134
Income taxes received		$ **337**	$ —

a. Determine the amount of cash dividends *declared* during fiscal 2001. Where did you find this information?

b. Determine the amount of dividends *paid* during fiscal 2001. Where did you find this information?

c. Assuming that all revenue was on account, determine the amount of cash collected from customers in 2001.

d. Assuming that the only transactions that flow through the accounts payable and accrued liabilities are purchases of inventory, and assuming that all additions to the inventory account were purchases of inventory, determine the cash payments made to suppliers in 2001.

e. Under current liabilities on the balance sheet there is an item called "Current portion of long-term debt." What do you think this represents? What information is it telling users?

f. What was the cash generated from operating activities in 2001? Did it increase or decrease from the previous year?

2-45   (Determination of items from a Canadian company's financial statements)
Base your answers to the following questions on the 2001 financial statements of **Sears Canada** in Appendix A at the end of the book.

a. Determine the amount of dividends declared during fiscal 2001.

b. Assuming that all revenues were on account, determine the amount of cash collected from customers in 2001.

c. Assuming that the only transactions that flow through the accounts payable are purchases of inventory, and assuming that all additions to the inventories account were purchases of inventory, determine the cash payments made to suppliers in 2001.

d. Calculate the following ratios for 2001 and 2000. Use total assets and shareholders' equity for each year in the ratios rather than average total assets and average shareholders' equity.

   1. profit margin ratio

   2. return on assets

   3. return on equity

e. What happened to the profitability in 2001? Search through the annual report and see if you can find an explanation for these results.

**Sun-Rype
Products Ltd.
Annual Report**

2-46   (Determination of items from a Canadian company's financial statements)
Base your answers to the following questions on the 2001 financial statements of **Sun-Rype Ltd.** on the *Accounting Perspectives CD*.

a. Determine the amount of dividends declared during fiscal 2001.

b. Assuming that all sales were on account, determine the amount of cash collected from customers in 2001.

c. Assuming that the only transactions that flow through the accounts payable and accrued liabilities are purchases of inventory, and assuming that all additions to the inventory account were purchases of inventory, determine the cash payments made to suppliers in 2001.

d. Calculate the following ratios for 2001:

1. profit margin ratio

2. return on assets

3. return on equity

2-47 (Determination of items from a Canadian company's financial statements)
Base your answers to the following questions on the 2001 financial statements of **Big
Rock Brewery Ltd.** that you will find in Exhibit 2-12.

a. Determine the amount of dividends declared during fiscal 2001.

b. Assuming that all sales were on account, determine the amount of cash collected
from customers in 2001. Should you use Sales less Government taxes and commissions in your answer or should you use just the Sales amount?

c. Assuming that the only transactions that flow through the accounts payable and
accrued liabilities are purchases of inventory, and assuming that all additions to
the inventory account were purchases of inventory, determine the cash payments
made to suppliers in 2001.

Consolidated Balance Sheets

BIG ROCK BREWERY (2001)

EXHIBIT 2-12
PART A

As at March 31

	2001 $	2000 $
	(Denominated in Canadian Dollars)	
ASSETS [notes 5 & 6]		
Current		
Cash and cash equivalents	1,602,202	106,492
Accounts receivable	1,593,984	1,872,064
Inventories [note 3]	2,701,982	2,676,790
Prepaid expenses and other	400,985	237,656
Investments	156,035	19,060
	6,455,188	4,912,062
Capital assets [note 4]	24,844,994	24,954,398
Deferred charges and other	45,619	51,779
	31,345,801	29,918,239
LIABILITIES AND SHAREHOLDERS' EQUITY		
Current		
Bank indebtedness [note 5]	1,362,907	2,244,903
Accounts payable and accrued liabilities	1,393,068	1,264,073
Income tax payable	151,869	—
Current portion of long-term debt [note 6]	1,567,862	1,496,189
	4,475,706	5,005,165
Long-term debt [note 6]	3,469,976	4,378,224
Future income taxes [note 8]	4,362,400	3,905,400
Total liabilities	12,308,082	13,288,789
Commitments [note 9]		
Shareholders' equity		
Share capital [note 7]	11,553,637	10,077,900
Retained earnings	7,484,082	6,551,550
	19,037,719	16,629,450
	31,345,801	29,918,239

EXHIBIT 2-12

PART B

Consolidated Statements of Operations & Retained Earning   BIG ROCK BREWERY (2001)

Years ended March 31

	2001 $	2000 $
	(Denominated in Canadian Dollars)	
Revenue		
Sales	32,238,035	31,707,142
Government taxes and commissions	(9,038,357)	(8,990,216)
	23,199,678	22,716,926
Cost of sales	9,240,503	9,154,929
Gross profit	13,959,175	13,561,997
Expenses		
Selling, general and administrative	10,176,689	9,415,955
Interest on long-term debt	451,921	481,400
Interest on short-term debt	91,998	36,360
Amortization	1,230,994	1,167,163
	11,951,602	11,100,878
Income before income taxes	2,007,573	2,461,119
Current income tax expense	198,000	42,000
Future income tax expense [note 8]	457,000	958,000
Net income for year	1,352,573	1,461,119
Retained earnings, beginning of year	6,551,550	5,975,448
Redemption of common shares [note 7]	(420,041)	(885,017)
Retained earnings, end of year	7,484,082	6,551,550
Net income per share [note 2]		
Basic and fully diluted	0.29	0.31

Consolidated Statements of Cash Flows

Years ended March 31

	2001 $	2000 $
	(Denominated in Canadian Dollars)	
OPERATING ACTIVITIES		
Net income for year	1,352,573	1,461,119
Items not affecting cash		
Amortization	1,230,994	1,167,163
Future income taxes	457,000	958,000
	3,040,567	3,586,282
Net change in non-cash working capital [note 12]	370,423	(1,150,883)
Cash provided by operating activities	3,410,990	2,435,399
FINANCING ACTIVITIES		
Increase (decrease) in bank indebtedness	(881,996)	1,619,994
Repayment of long term debt	(836,575)	(1,601,587)
Share repurchase [note 7]	(744,304)	(1,358,205)
Shares issued by private placement [note 7]	1,800,000	—
Shares issued on exercise of options [note 7]	—	78,879
Cash used in financing activities	(662,875)	(1,260,919)
INVESTING ACTIVITIES		
Aquisition of investments	(136,975)	—
Additions to capital assets	(1,121,590)	(1,143,222)
Deferred charges and other assets	6,160	—
Cash used in investing activities	(1,252,405)	(1,143,222)
Net increase in cash	1,495,710	31,258
Cash and cash equivalents, beginning of year	106,492	75,234
Cash and cash equivalents, end of year	1,602,202	106,492

d. Calculate the following ratios for 2001:

1. profit margin ratio (use Sales less Government taxes and commissions)

2. return on assets

3. return on equity

e. What happened to the profitability in 2001? How did that profitability translate into cash flow from operations?

2-48 (Determination of items from a Canadian company's financial statements)
Exhibit 2-13 includes two 2001 financial statements from **Canada Bread Company Ltd.**

Required:

a. Refer to the consolidated statements of cash flows and compare the net income in each of the last two years to the cash flow from operations in the last two years.

b. In general, why are there differences between cash flows from operations and net income? Refer specifically to the differences due to sales transactions and amortization.

c. Comment on Canada Bread Company's ability to pay for its cash needs over the last two years using its cash from operations. Do you think that the company is in a favourable cash flow position? Support your answer.

CANADA BREAD COMPANY LTD. (2001)
Consolidated Financial Statements

EXHIBIT 2-13

PART A

Consolidated Statements of Earnings

(in thousands of Canadian dollars, except per share amounts) Years ended	December 31, 2001
Sales	$ 678,348
Earnings from operations	$ 36,397
Other income (note 10)	1,312
Earnings before interest and income taxes	37,709
Interest expense (note 11)	1,324
Earnings before income taxes	36,385
Income taxes (note 12)	15,261
Earnings before minority interest	21,124
Minority interest	271
Net earnings	$ 20,853
Earnings per share (note 8)	$ 0.97

EXHIBIT 2-13
PART B

CANADA BREAD COMPANY LTD. (2001)

Consolidated Financial Statements

Consolidated Statements of Cash Flows

(in thousands of Canadian dollars) Years ended	December 31, 2001	December 31, 2000
Cash Provided By (used in):		
Operating Activities		
Net earnings	$ 20,853	$ 17,240
Items not affecting cash:		
Depreciation	20,027	17,385
Amortization	3,135	3,265
Minority interest	271	—
Future income taxes	(138)	(310)
Undistributed earnings of an associated company	8,986	(843)
Loss on sale of property and equipment	102	—
Other	(1,731)	—
Changes in non-cash operating working capital	43,105	(11,069)
	94,610	25,668
Financing Activities		
Dividends paid	(5,140)	(5,140)
Increase (decrease) in long-term debt, net	29,711	(14,601)
	24,571	(19,741)
Investing Activities		
Additions to property and equipment	(11,729)	(7,771)
Proceeds from sale of property and equipment	313	—
Acquisition of Multi-Marques Inc. (note 15)	(105,150)	—
	(116,566)	(7,771)
Decrease (increase) in bank indebtedness	2,615	(1,844)
Bank indebtedness, beginning of year	(3,280)	(1,436)
Bank indebtedness, end of year	$ (665)	$ (3,280)

2-49   (Determination of items from a Canadian company's financial statements) Base your answers to the following questions on the financial statements of **WestJet Airlines Ltd.** that you will find in the Exhibit 2-14.

WESTJET AIRLINES LTD. CONSOLIDATED BALANCE SHEETS

EXHIBIT 2-14

PART A

December 31, 2001 and 2000
(Stated in Thousands of Dollars)

	2001	2000
Assets		
Current assets:		
Cash and cash equivalents	$ 58,942	$ 79,025
Accounts receivable	12,211	6,447
Income taxes recoverable	779	-
Prepaid expenses and deposits	11,643	6,099
Inventory	2,155	604
	85,730	92,175
Capital assets (note 2)	300,685	239,320
Other long-term assets (note 3)	7,488	5,677
	$ 393,903	$ 337,172
Liabilities and Shareholders' Equity		
Current liabilities:		
Accounts payable and accrued liabilities	$ 42,019	$ 43,616
Income taxes payable	-	10,471
Advance ticket sales	28,609	18,764
Non-refundable passenger credits	12,599	6,996
Current portion of long-term debt (note 4)	8,470	9,336
Current portion of obligations under capital lease (note 5)	3,398	1,597
	95,095	90,780
Long-term debt (note 4)	41,305	40,953
Obligations under capital lease (note 5)	14,400	8,519
Future income tax (note 7)	20,933	15,828
	171,733	156,080
Shareholders' equity:		
Share capital (note 6)	129,268	125,390
Retained earnings	92,902	55,702
	222,170	181,092
Commitments (notes 5 and 8)		
Subsequent events (note 10)		
	$ 393,903	$ 337,172

See accompanying notes to consolidated financial statements.

On behalf of the Board:

Clive Beddoe   _(signature)_   Director

Wilmot Matthews   _(signature)_   Director

EXHIBIT 2-14
PART B

CONSOLIDATED STATEMENTS OF EARNINGS AND RETAINED EARNINGS

Years ended December 31, 2001 and 2000
(Stated in Thousands of Dollars, Except Per Share Data)

	2001	2000
Revenues:		
Passenger revenues	$ 452,910	$ 315,931
Charter and other	25,483	16,588
	478,393	332,519
Expenses:		
Passenger services	95,613	64,090
Aircraft fuel	84,629	55,875
Maintenance	72,317	49,512
Amortization	34,332	17,959
Sales and marketing	30,862	21,763
Flight operations	20,916	13,923
General and administration	20,893	12,147
Reservations	17,777	12,497
Aircraft leasing	15,284	6,770
Inflight	16,104	10,972
Employee profit share (note 8(b))	10,311	13,549
	419,038	279,057
Earnings from operations	59,355	53,462
Non-operating income (expense):		
Interest income	2,837	2,463
Interest expense	(5,086)	(2,937)
Gain (loss) on disposal of capital assets	187	(282)
Gain on foreign exchange	986	-
	(1,076)	(756)
Earnings before income taxes	58,279	52,706
Income taxes (note 7):		
Current	15,974	18,102
Future	5,105	4,350
	21,079	22,452
Net earnings	37,200	30,254
Retained earnings, beginning of year	55,702	25,448
Retained earnings, end of year	$ 92,902	$ 55,702
Earnings per share:		
Basic	$ 0.81	$ 0.72
Diluted	$ 0.79	$ 0.69

a. Determine the value of new shares issued during 2001.

b. Determine the amount of dividends paid during fiscal 2001.

c. Assuming that all operating revenues were on account, determine the amount of cash collected from customers during 2001.

CONSOLIDATED STATEMENTS OF CASH FLOWS

EXHIBIT 2-14

PART C

Years ended December 31, 2001 and 2000
(Stated in Thousands of Dollars)

	2001	2000
Cash provided by (used in):		
Operations:		
Net earnings	$ 37,200	$ 30,254
Items not involving cash:		
Amortization	34,332	17,959
Gain on disposal of capital assets	(187)	(633)
Unrealized loss on foreign exchange	50	-
Future income tax	5,105	4,350
	76,500	51,930
(Increase) decrease in non-cash working capital	(9,139)	35,483
	67,361	87,413
Financing:		
Increase in long-term debt	8,947	22,417
Repayment of long-term debt	(9,461)	(8,019)
Issuance of common shares	3,878	57,689
Share issuance costs	-	(2,369)
Increase in other long-term assets	(2,230)	(3,818)
Decrease in obligations under capital lease	(2,483)	(137)
	(1,349)	65,763
Investments:		
Aircraft additions	(60,518)	(97,269)
Aircraft disposals	-	12,239
Other capital asset additions	(26,271)	(40,043)
Other capital asset disposals	694	182
	(86,095)	(124,891)
Increase (decrease) in cash	(20,083)	28,285
Cash, beginning of year	79,025	50,740
Cash, end of year	$ 58,942	$ 79,025

d. A company such as WestJet has an extensive investment in noncurrent property and equipment (capital assets). From 2000 to 2001, the Capital assets on the balance sheet changed from $239,320 thousand to $300,685thousand, an increase of $61,365thousand. Using the three statements, find as many items as you can that will help explain this change. There is not enough information in the financial statements to totally explain the change, so do not be concerned if you cannot explain everything.

e. Calculate the following ratios for 2001:

1. profit margin ratio (use total revenues)

2. return on assets

3. return on equity

2-50 (Determination of items from an international company's financial statements) Base your answers to the following questions on the 2001 financial statements of **McDonald's Corporation**, a global company headquartered in the United States, that you will find in Exhibit 2-15.

a. Refer to the cash flow statement and compare the net income in each of the last three years to the cash flow from operations in the last three years.

b. Using the cash flow statement, list the items that McDonald's used to convert the accrual-based net income to cash from operations.

c. From the financial statements, discuss how important inventory is in relationship to other assets on the company's balance sheet. Knowing what McDonald's does, explain why the inventory amount is reasonable.

d. Calculate the following ratios for 2001 (use total revenues):

1. return on assets

2. return on equity

EXHIBIT 2-15

PART A

MCDONALD'S CORPORATION (2001)

Consolidated statement of income

IN MILLIONS, EXCEPT PER SHARE DATA	Years ended December 31, **2001**	2000	1999
Revenues			
Sales by Company-operated restaurants	**$11,040.7**	$10,467.0	$ 9,512.5
Revenues from franchised and affiliated restaurants	**3,829.3**	3,776.0	3,746.8
Total revenues	**14,870.0**	14,243.0	13,259.3
Operating costs and expenses			
Food and packaging	**3,802.1**	3,557.1	3,204.6
Payroll and employee benefits	**2,901.2**	2,690.2	2,418.3
Occupancy and other operating expenses	**2,750.4**	2,502.8	2,206.7
Total Company-operated restaurant expenses	**9,453.7**	8,750.1	7,829.6
Franchised restaurants–occupancy expenses	**800.2**	772.3	737.7
Selling, general & administrative expenses	**1,661.7**	1,587.3	1,477.6
Special charge–global change initiatives	**200.0**		
Other operating (income) expense, net	**57.4**	(196.4)	(105.2)
Total operating costs and expenses	**12,173.0**	10,913.3	9,939.7
Operating income	**2,697.0**	3,329.7	3,319.6
Interest expense–net of capitalized interest of $15.2, $16.3 and $14.3	**452.4**	429.9	396.3
McDonald's Japan IPO gain	**(137.1)**		
Nonoperating expense, net	**52.0**	17.5	39.2
Income before provision for income taxes	**2,329.7**	2,882.3	2,884.1
Provision for income taxes	**693.1**	905.0	936.2
Net income	**$ 1,636.6**	$ 1,977.3	$ 1,947.9
Net income per common share	**$ 1.27**	$ 1.49	$ 1.44
Net income per common share–diluted	**$ 1.25**	$ 1.46	$ 1.39
Dividends per common share	**$ .23**	$ .22	$ .20
Weighted-average shares	**1,289.7**	1,323.2	1,355.3
Weighted-average shares–diluted	**1,309.3**	1,356.5	1,404.2

MCDONALD'S CORPORATION (2001)

Consolidated balance sheet

EXHIBIT 2-15

PART B

IN MILLIONS, EXCEPT PER SHARE DATA	December 31, **2001**	2000
Assets		
Current assets		
Cash and equivalents	$ **418.1**	$ 421.7
Accounts and notes receivable	**881.9**	796.5
Inventories, at cost, not in excess of market	**105.5**	99.3
Prepaid expenses and other current assets	**413.8**	344.9
Total current assets	**1,819.3**	1,662.4
Other assets		
Investments in and advances to affiliates	**990.2**	824.2
Goodwill, net	**1,419.8**	1,278.2
Miscellaneous	**1,015.7**	871.1
Total other assets	**3,425.7**	2,973.5
Property and equipment		
Property and equipment, at cost	**24,106.0**	23,569.0
Accumulated depreciation and amortization	**(6,816.5)**	(6,521.4)
Net property and equipment	**17,289.5**	17,047.6
Total assets	**$22,534.5**	$21,683.5
Liabilities and shareholders' equity		
Current liabilities		
Notes payable	$ **184.9**	$ 275.5
Accounts payable	**689.5**	684.9
Income taxes	**20.4**	92.2
Other taxes	**180.4**	195.5
Accrued interest	**170.6**	149.9
Other accrued liabilities	**824.9**	608.4
Current maturities of long-term debt	**177.6**	354.5
Total current liabilities	**2,248.3**	2,360.9
Long-term debt	**8,555.5**	7,843.9
Other long-term liabilities and minority interests	**629.3**	489.5
Deferred income taxes	**1,112.2**	1,084.9
Common equity put options and forward contracts	**500.8**	699.9
Shareholders' equity		
Preferred stock, no par value; authorized–165.0 million shares; issued–none		
Common stock, $.01 par value; authorized–3.5 billion shares;		
issued–1,660.6 million shares	**16.6**	16.6
Additional paid-in capital	**1,591.2**	1,441.8
Unearned ESOP compensation	**(106.7)**	(115.0)
Retained earnings	**18,608.3**	17,259.4
Accumulated other comprehensive income	**(1,708.8)**	(1,287.3)
Common stock in treasury, at cost; 379.9 and 355.7 million shares	**(8,912.2)**	(8,111.1)
Total shareholders' equity	**9,488.4**	9,204.4
Total liabilities and shareholders' equity	**$22,534.5**	$21,683.5

EXHIBIT 2-15

PART C

MCDONALD'S CORPORATION (2001)
Consolidated statement of cash flows

IN MILLIONS	Years ended December 31, **2001**	2000	1999
Operating activities			
Net income	**$ 1,636.6**	$ 1,977.3	$ 1,947.9
Adjustments to reconcile to cash provided by operations			
Depreciation and amortization	**1,086.3**	1,010.7	956.3
Deferred income taxes	**(87.6)**	60.5	52.9
Changes in operating working capital items			
Accounts receivable	**(104.7)**	(67.2)	(81.9)
Inventories, prepaid expenses and other current assets	**(62.9)**	(29.6)	(47.7)
Accounts payable	**10.2**	89.7	(23.9)
Taxes and other liabilities	**160.0**	(45.8)	270.4
Other	**50.4**	(244.1)	(65.1)
Cash provided by operations	**2,688.3**	2,751.5	3,008.9
Investing activities			
Property and equipment expenditures	**(1,906.2)**	(1,945.1)	(1,867.8)
Purchases of restaurant businesses	**(331.6)**	(425.5)	(340.7)
Sales of restaurant businesses and property	**375.9**	302.8	262.4
Other	**(206.3)**	(144.8)	(315.7)
Cash used for investing activities	**(2,068.2)**	(2,212.6)	(2,261.8)
Financing activities			
Net short-term borrowings (repayments)	**(248.0)**	59.1	116.7
Long-term financing issuances	**1,694.7**	2,381.3	902.5
Long-term financing repayments	**(919.4)**	(761.9)	(682.8)
Treasury stock purchases	**(1,068.1)**	(2,023.4)	(891.5)
Common stock dividends	**(287.7)**	(280.7)	(264.7)
Other	**204.8**	88.9	193.0
Cash used for financing activities	**(623.7)**	(536.7)	(626.8)
Cash and equivalents increase (decrease)	**(3.6)**	2.2	120.3
Cash and equivalents at beginning of year	**421.7**	419.5	299.2
Cash and equivalents at end of year	**$ 418.1**	$ 421.7	$ 419.5
Supplemental cash flow disclosures			
Interest paid	**$ 446.9**	$ 469.7	$ 411.5
Income taxes paid	**773.8**	854.2	642.2

Used with permission of McDonald's Corporation.

Beyond the Book

2-51   (Find items from a Canadian company's financial statements)
Find the annual report of a Canadian company in the retailing business. Answer the following questions:

    a. From the financial statements, discuss how important inventory is in relation to other assets on the company's balance sheet.

    b. How does the company finance its business?

    c. Read through the management's discussion of operations and determine if there is any information there that is not included in the financial statements. If you were a shareholder, would you want to know the extra information? Why?

    d. How many directors does the company have? What positions do they hold? Are any of them directors of other companies?

e. Who are the independent auditors? Was the company given an unqualified opinion by the auditors?

2-52 (Research about a Canadian company)

For the company you selected to answer Problem 51, find at least three articles in the financial press that discuss the nature of the markets for this company and the forecast of what the future may be for this sector of the economy. If the company has a website, you may find recent articles about the company posted there. Write a one-page summary of your findings.

Cases

Additional Cases

2-53 Saskco Chicken Products

Saskco Chicken Products is a new company established by four entrepreneurs from Moose Jaw. They intend to purchase live chickens, process them, and sell them as frozen pieces and whole chickens. They initially anticipate hiring three workers to process the chickens. The four owners will work in the business and have the following titles: President (oversees the whole operation including finance and accounting), VP Marketing, VP Operations (in charge of the processing operations), and VP Procurement (in charge of purchasing chickens from farmers). The President of Saskco Chicken Products has hired you for three months to help the company set up its accounting system. In anticipation of establishing a computerized accounting package, develop a list of account titles that you think this company will need to start operations. For each account title, write a brief one-line explanation of its inclusion in the list of accounts.

2-54 Daisy Dry Cleaning

Daisy Dry Cleaning is in the process of preparing its annual financial statements. The owner of the business is not an accountant, but likes to prepare the financial statements himself. Most of the transactions of the business are straightforward and can be easily recorded; however, the owner is having trouble determining how to account for two events that occurred in 2004:

1. On January 1, Daisy Dry Cleaning paid $3,600 for a three-year insurance policy. The owner has expensed the entire amount in the current year.

2. On October 31, the company paid a dividend of $10,000. The owner has recorded this payment as dividend expense.

   Required

   It is now December 31, 2004, and the owner is getting ready to prepare Daisy's financial statements. Advise him as to how the above transactions should be recorded.

2-55 Grill and Associates

Grill and Associates has prepared the following financial ratios based on the company's 2004 and 2003 financial statements. Briefly explain each ratio and comment on the company's performance.

	2004	2003	INDUSTRY AVERAGE
Profit Margin Ratio	18%	16%	18%–20%
Return on Assets	9%	7%	8%–10%
Return on Equity	12%	10%	10%–12%

Critical Thinking Question

2-56 (Comparison of financing strategies)
Using the cash flow statements for **Sierra Wireless Inc.** (Exhibit 2-16) and **BCE Inc.** (Exhibit 2-17), compare the methods used by the two companies to finance their activities. What are the future implications of the method(s) of financing used? By referring to the statements, explain why the companies need outside financing.

EXHIBIT 2-16

SIERRA WIRELESS, INC.

Consolidated Statements of Cash Flows

(Expressed in thousands of United States dollars)
(Prepared in accordance with United States GAAP)

Years ended December 31,	1999	2000	2001
Cash flows from operating activities:			
Net earnings (loss)	$ 3,212	$ (3,118)	$ (24,269)
Adjustments to reconcile net earnings (loss) to net cash provided by operating activities			
Loss on disposal	30	—	—
Amortization	892	3,068	6,661
Expense in-process research and development costs	—	1,000	—
Deferred income taxes	(1,100)	448	(15)
Accrued warrants	—	—	671
Changes in operating assets and liabilities			
Accounts receivable	(1,727)	(17,646)	12,084
Inventories	(537)	(5,644)	(13,031)
Prepaid expenses	(187)	(943)	59
Accounts payable	1,697	7,237	(6,945)
Accrued liabilities	226	7,069	3,420
Deferred revenue and credits	(6)	559	300
Net cash provided by (used in) operating activities	2,500	(7,970)	(21,065)
Cash flows from investing activities:			
Business acquisitions	(506)	(7,250)	—
Purchase of fixed assets	(1,261)	(6,692)	(10,523)
Increase in intangible assets	(624)	(3,118)	(3,328)
Increase in other assets	—	(340)	(143)
Purchase of short-term investments	(38,991)	(212,438)	(69,411)
Proceeds on maturity of short-term investments	42,615	140,294	109,676
Net cash provided by (used in) investing activities	1,233	(89,544)	26,271
Cash flows from financing activities:			
Issue of common shares	29,370	66,557	499
Increase in long-term liabilities	—	—	255
Repayment of long-term liabilities	(389)	(744)	(766)
Net cash provided by (used in) financing activities	28,981	65,813	(12)
Effect of foreign currency exchange rates on cash and cash equivalents	(37)	—	—
Net increase (decrease) in cash and cash equivalents	32,677	(31,701)	5,194
Cash and cash equivalents, beginning of year	5,915	38,592	6,891
Cash and cash equivalents, end of year	$ 38,592	$ 6,891	$ 12,085

CONSOLIDATED FINANCIAL STATEMENTS – BCE INC.

EXHIBIT 2-17

CONSOLIDATED STATEMENTS OF CASH FLOWS

For the year ended December 31 ($ millions)	2001	2000
Cash flows from operating activities		
Earnings from continuing operations	2,419	312
Adjustments to reconcile earnings from continuing operations to cash flows from operating activities:		
Amortization expense	4,691	3,631
Restructuring and other charges	963	–
Gains and losses on reduction of ownership in subsidiaries and joint ventures and on disposal of investments	(3,964)	77
Future income taxes	498	(139)
Other items	(508)	(93)
Changes in non-cash working capital components	546	(1,473)
	4,645	2,315
Cash flows from investing activities		
Capital expenditures	(7,396)	(4,118)
Investments	(1,165)	(4,674)
Divestitures	4,961	717
Other items	246	(209)
	(3,354)	(8,284)
Cash flows from financing activities		
Increase (decrease) in notes payable and bank advances	(2,098)	3,481
Issue of long-term debt	2,607	2,593
Repayment of long-term debt	(1,582)	(1,636)
Issue of common shares	71	36
Purchase of common shares for cancellation	(191)	(384)
Dividends paid on common and preferred shares	(1,033)	(928)
Issue of common shares, preferred shares, convertible debentures and equity-settled notes by subsidiaries to non-controlling interest	1,460	568
Redemption of preferred shares by subsidiaries	(471)	(295)
Dividends paid by subsidiaries to non-controlling interest	(385)	(260)
Other items	62	87
	(1,560)	3,262
Effect of exchange rate changes on cash and cash equivalents	7	(69)
Cash used in continuing operations	(262)	(2,776)
Cash provided by discontinued operations	571	641
Net increase (decrease) in cash and cash equivalents	309	(2,135)
Cash and cash equivalents at beginning of year	260	2,395
Cash and cash equivalents at end of year	569	260
Supplemental disclosure		
Interest paid on long-term debt	1,381	1,309
Income taxes paid	1,348	1,329
Cash restricted to collaterize short-term bank loans	233	–

From Quill Pens to Computers

In the 1840s, when the maple-sugar operation on this picturesque spot in Lanark County, Ontario (some 60 km west of Ottawa) first went into business, accounting records were kept with quill pens dipped in ink, debits on the left and credits on the right of the pages of a handmade book. Today, bookkeeper Jean LeClaire enters all the accounts for Fulton's Pancake House and Sugar Bush using the Accpac Simply Accounting program on a Pentium computer.

But, really, not much has changed. Four generations later, the sugar bush is still in the same family—its accounting records still follow essentially the same principles, although they are now kept electronically. In fact, many of the accounts in the general ledger would look very familiar to the farm's first owners: income from sale of syrup and food, expenses for containers, equipment repairs, payroll, advertising, and so on. And the business still makes most of its over $300,000 of revenue each year from direct sales. "It's unusual today for a producer to sell straight to the buyer, with no middle person," points out owner Shirley Duego.

Of course, those early books probably didn't include huge evaporators, which cut down the boiling time of sap into syrup using a reverse osmosis process, among the capital assets. Nor did they have to include a system for tracking GST! But they had to be flexible enough to account for the vagaries of Canadian weather—a nineteenth-century page might well have included, just as Ms. LeClaire's electronic records for 1998 did, a special account for "ice storm expenses."

Essentially, even the simplest and most old-fashioned of accounting systems had the same aim as the most up-to-date electronic one does today: to provide its users with the information they need to make sound decisions. For Ms. Duego and her co-owner, husband George, these decisions have included diversifying their operations to include a restaurant, craft sales, international group tours, and even an outdoor low-ropes challenge course.

By carefully tracking each of these activities, the Duegos have been able to adapt their efforts as needed. "When the high-tech sector in Ottawa suffered a downturn, that affected our challenge course. But it wasn't a problem because our farm tours were doing well. Then September 11 hit, and many international groups cancelled," says Ms. Duego. "So now we're shifting our marketing strategy to focus on North America."

To accommodate their growing business, Ms. Duego and her husband moved their office into a larger space in one of two portable classrooms acquired in 1999. They also purchased three new computers, a new phone system and a broadcast fax machine, and recently launched a website. Together, the farm's attractions bring some 40,000 visitors to Fulton's each year. With luck—and careful accounting—they will bring in many thousands of visitors for another four generations.

DOUBLE ENTRY
ACCOUNTING SYSTEMS

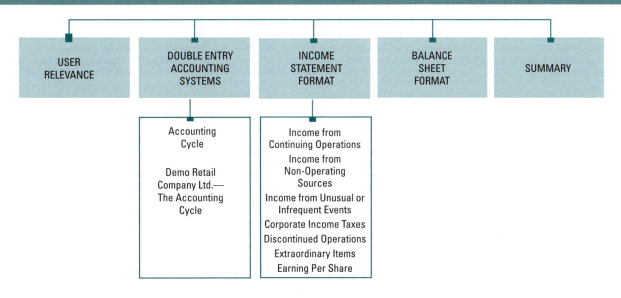

USER RELEVANCE	DOUBLE ENTRY ACCOUNTING SYSTEMS	INCOME STATEMENT FORMAT	BALANCE SHEET FORMAT	SUMMARY

DOUBLE ENTRY ACCOUNTING SYSTEMS

Accounting Cycle

Demo Retail Company Ltd.— The Accounting Cycle

INCOME STATEMENT FORMAT

Income from Continuing Operations

Income from Non-Operating Sources

Income from Unusual or Infrequent Events

Corporate Income Taxes

Discontinued Operations

Extraordinary Items

Earning Per Share

■ *Learning Objectives:*

After studying this chapter, you should be able to:

1. *Understand the relationship of debits and credits in the recording of transactions.*
2. *Understand the difference between permanent and temporary accounts.*
3. *Identify the steps in the accounting cycle.*
4. *Analyze transactions and record them in journal format.*
5. *Post transactions to T-accounts and prepare a trial balance.*
6. *Understand the necessity of adjusting entries and determine how they should be recorded.*
7. *Describe why closing entries are necessary.*
8. *Understand the difference between a single-step income statement and a multistep one.*
9. *Calculate a profit margin ratio.*
10. *Describe the criteria for unusual items, discontinued operations, and extraordinary items.*
11. *Understand the criteria for listing items on a balance sheet.*

As you read in the opening story, the accounting records kept by Ms. Duego and her family have evolved from keeping accounts in a handmade book to keeping accounts using a computer accounting system. The double entry system that we are going to show you in this chapter can be traced back to the late fifteenth century. Although the mode of keeping the records, pen and paper to computers, has changed, the system has not.

Now that you understand the basic accounting equation and can work through the analysis of some transactions, we are going to take you one step deeper into the practical side of accounting. We are going to show you how to get the amounts into the records in a way that will enable you to pull out information that you need and summarize it into statements. The computer accounting system being used by Ms. Duego enables her to pull out information on a daily basis because of the automated functions embedded in the program.

When you were working through the problems in Chapter 2, you were establishing spreadsheet frameworks of the basic accounting equation. You could see that once you expanded beyond about 10 accounts and about 20 transactions, the spreadsheet framework would become unmanageable. Companies have hundreds of accounts and thousands of transactions. Recording, summarizing, and reporting information about their economic activities requires something more elabourate than a spreadsheet.

USER RELEVANCE

Why is it important for users to have a more in-depth understanding of how accounting data is collected, stored, and reported? A business owner, like Ms. Duego, should have an understanding of how the various business activities will be reflected in financial statements, especially if the owner intends to use the financial results to make decisions. A financial analyst, who advises others on buying or selling shares, should have an in-depth knowledge of how the accounting system works. An analyst needs to understand what the numbers on financial statements mean, how they are measured, and how relevant they are in understanding the overall profitability of a company. Creditors, like loan officers, need an in-depth understanding so that they can assess whether future cash flows will be adequate to meet the lending obligations already in place and any future ones being contemplated by the company. They need to understand what types of transactions affect which financial statement amounts. Decisions should not be made on single amounts or ratios. Rather, decision makers should review the total results because changes in one area of a financial statement will often have implications for other areas which could impact the conclusions drawn.

DOUBLE ENTRY ACCOUNTING SYSTEMS

The recording of transactions in the basic accounting equation is sufficient if the entity has only a few transactions to record. We call this type of system a **synoptic journal**. It is used by clubs that only need to maintain information about dues collected and activities undertaken. However, the plus and minus system used in the spreadsheets becomes confusing and somewhat cumbersome when large numbers of accounts and transactions are considered. To overcome this confusion, accountants have developed an alternative system to record transactions. This alternative system is known as a **double entry** or **dual entry accounting system**. We will demonstrate the system by using a device known as a **T-account**. To translate from the equation system to the T-account system, imagine replacing the equality sign in the basic accounting equation with a big "T," as follows:

Replace the basic accounting equation:

$$\text{Assets} = \text{Liabilities} + \text{Shareholders' Equity}$$

With a T-account:

| Assets | Liabilities + Shareholders' Equity |

Note that assets appear on the left side of the T-account and liabilities and shareholders' equity appear on the right side. The equality expressed in the basic accounting equation must still be maintained in the T-account system. Translated, this means that the totals from the left side of the T-accounts must equal the totals from the right side of the T-accounts. The left side of the account is known as the **debit** side, and the right side as the **credit** side. The words *debit* and *credit* have no meaning in accounting other than "left" and "right." Do not try to attach any other meaning to these terms as it will likely lead you astray in your thinking about the accounts of the company. The abbreviations for debit and credit are Dr. and Cr., respectively. The balance in the accounting system can now be expressed in terms of debits and credits rather than in terms of the left and right side of the basic accounting equation. The balance sheet equality requires that debits equal credits.

The T-account concept also carries over into the accounting for specific asset, liability, and shareholders' equity accounts. Each asset, liability, and shareholders' equity item has its own T-account; these accounts, added together, result in the big T-account. See Exhibit 3-1.

Learning Objective

1

Understand the relationship of debits and credits in the recording of transactions.

EXHIBIT 3-1

■ INDIVIDUAL T-ACCOUNTS

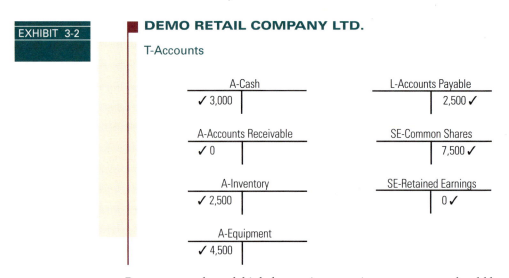

In Exhibit 3-1, note that there are letters preceding the account names. These letters will be used throughout this book to designate the type of account. At this point, there are only three designations to worry about: A represents an asset account, L a liability account, and SE a shareholders' equity account. We will periodically add other designations as we proceed through the book. These letters will be a helpful reminder of the nature of the account with which you are dealing.

Because assets are listed on the debit side of the large T-account by convention, they normally have balances on the debit side of the individual T-accounts. Likewise, liabilities and shareholders' equity accounts have credit balances. In Exhibit 3-2, the beginning balances for Demo Retail Company Ltd. are entered into a set of T-accounts. Beside each balance, you will see a check mark (✓), which is used to show a balance in the account rather than a new entry. Also, note that the sum of the debit balances ($10,000) equals the sum of the credit balances ($10,000), which means that the system is balanced.

EXHIBIT 3-2

■ DEMO RETAIL COMPANY LTD.

T-Accounts

A-Cash		L-Accounts Payable	
✓ 3,000			2,500 ✓

A-Accounts Receivable		SE-Common Shares	
✓ 0			7,500 ✓

A-Inventory		SE-Retained Earnings	
✓ 2,500			0 ✓

A-Equipment	
✓ 4,500	

Because assets have debit balances, increases in asset accounts should be entered on the debit side of the account. Decreases in assets should be entered on the credit side. For liabilities and shareholders' equity, the reverse is true. Increases are entered on the credit side of the account, and decreases are entered on the debit side. Exhibit 3-3 lists the appropriate entries for asset, liability, and shareholders' equity accounts.

ENTRIES TO T-ACCOUNTS

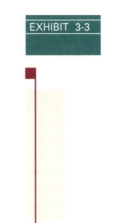

EXHIBIT 3-3

Assets	
✓ Beginning balance Increases	Decreases
✓ Ending balance	

Liabilities	
Decreases	Beginning balance ✓ Increases
	Ending balance ✓

Shareholders' Equity	
Decreases	Beginning balance ✓ Increases
	Ending balance ✓

One way to think about the accounts and debits and credits is to imagine that the accounting system is a large warehouse that is balanced on a central point (like the equal sign between the two parts of the basic accounting equation). Inside the warehouse, the company has boxes stacked on either side which maintain the balance. The boxes themselves are weightless, which means that you do not need to have the same number of boxes on each side. The weight is added when something is put in a box. Each box represents an account. When the company needs to keep track of information about a specific financial item, it creates a new box and labels it so that everyone knows what is in that box. For example, there would be a box labelled Cash on one side of the warehouse and another box labelled Common Shares on the other side. As financial activities are recorded, things are added to or removed from the appropriate box. Therefore, if you add something to an asset box on one side of the warehouse, you would need to take something out of a different asset box that is on the same side or you would need to go to the other side of the warehouse and add something to one of the boxes there (a liability or a shareholders' equity box). Debiting and crediting accounts is like putting things into boxes and taking things out. If the box is on the left side of the warehouse, it is an asset box. Each time you add something to the box, you debit it; each time you take something out of the box, you credit it. If the box is on the right side of the warehouse (liabilities and shareholders' equity boxes), the opposite is true. Each time you put something into one of these boxes, you credit it; each time you take something out, you debit it. If you are careful to ensure that the debits are balanced with credits, your warehouse will not tilt to one side. Periodically you can check all the boxes, record what is in each one, and prepare a balance sheet.

The accounts shown in Exhibits 3-2 and 3-3 are all balance sheet accounts. They have balances that carry over from one period to the next. These accounts are sometimes called **permanent accounts**. One of the permanent accounts is the retained earnings account. You learned in Chapter 1 that the change in the retained earnings account during a given period is the net of the revenues and expenses for the period and the decrease due to dividends declared. In order to keep track of the individual revenue and expense amounts, as well as the dividends declared during the period, the

Learning Objective

2

Understand the difference between permanent and temporary accounts.

retained earnings account can be subdivided into several separate accounts. These separate accounts are called **temporary accounts** because they are used temporarily, during the accounting period, to keep track of revenues, expenses, and dividends. The balances in these accounts ultimately have to affect the retained earnings account. Exhibit 3-4 shows the subdivision of the retained earnings account into the temporary revenue, expense, and dividends declared accounts.

EXHIBIT 3-4

■ Retained Earnings: Income Statement Accounts

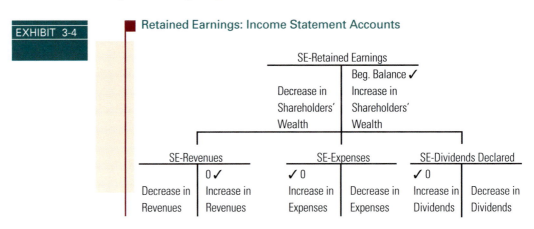

Several things should be noted concerning the revenue, expense, and dividends declared accounts. First, notice that the beginning balance in each of these accounts is zero. Because these accounts are used to keep track of revenues, expenses, and dividends declared during the period, their beginning balances must be zero so that the last period's data are not combined with those of the current period. At the end of the period, the balance in each of the temporary accounts will be used to help prepare the income statement, but then must be transferred into the permanent retained earnings account to produce the final ending balance in the retained earnings account. In this way, the retained earnings account keeps track of the cumulative amounts of revenues and expenses less dividends, and the temporary accounts keep track of only the current year amounts. In other words, using our warehouse example, the contents of the revenue, expense, and dividends declared boxes are all dumped into the retained earnings box. A revenue box with a credit balance will add to the retained earnings box, which also has a credit balance. An expense or dividends declared box with a debit balance will reduce the contents of the retained earnings box.

Note further that while revenues, expenses, and dividends declared are all shareholders' equity accounts, increases and decreases correspond to different entries. For revenues, credits represent increases, and debits represent decreases. For expenses and dividends declared, the opposite is true: debits represent increases, and credits represent decreases. The logic of this is directly connected to the eventual effect on shareholders' wealth: revenues increase it and are thus shown as credits, while expenses decrease it and so are shown as debits. Therefore, by the end of a given accounting period (prior to transferring the balances to the retained earnings account), revenues have credit balances, expenses have debit balances, and dividends declared (if any) has a debit balance. The debit balances in the expense and dividends declared accounts are probably best understood if we remember that they both represent decreases in the shareholders' equity. Because shareholders' equity is represented by a credit balance, the decreases therein must be represented by debit balances. Further, because these are temporary accounts and their balances will be transferred to retained earnings, the debit balances will not persist in the permanent accounts. They will be offset by the credit balance revenue accounts. It is possible to have a debit balance in the retained earnings account if expenses have exceeded revenues (i.e., the company has suffered losses). If you look at the balance sheet of **Ballard Power Systems Inc.** in Exhibit 3-5, you will see that its retained earnings amount in 2001 and 2000 was a deficit (a debit balance). Most companies do not have a deficit position in their retained earnings. However, it is not unusual for a company like Ballard to have a deficit. The company is in the process of developing new fuel cell technology; it will be several years before it has perfected the technology to the stage where it can commercialize it and begin to generate revenue.

CONSOLIDATED BALANCE SHEETS

BALLARD POWER SYSTEMS INC. (2001)

EXHIBIT 3-5

December 31 *(Expressed in thousands of U.S. dollars)*		**2001**		2000
			Change in currency – note 2	
ASSETS				
Current assets:				
Cash and cash equivalents	$	**140,774**	$	181,294
Short-term investments		**280,475**		301,987
Accounts receivable *(notes 4 and 15)*		**17,312**		14,476
Inventories *(note 5)*		**28,046**		11,078
Prepaid expenses		**873**		419
		467,480		509,254
Property, plant and equipment *(note 6)*		**109,006**		54,480
Intangible assets *(note 7)*		**170,453**		26,849
Goodwill *(note 3)*		**184,930**		—
Investments *(note 8)*		**26,241**		73,697
Other long-term assets		**1,209**		1,067
	$	**959,319**	$	665,347
LIABILITIES AND SHAREHOLDERS' EQUITY				
Current liabilities:				
Accounts payable and accrued liabilities *(notes 9 and 15)*	$	**59,307**	$	18,336
Deferred revenue		**1,944**		492
Accrued warranty liabilities		**16,622**		16,387
		77,873		35,215
Long-term liabilities *(note 10)*		**7,723**		3,881
Minority interest		**36,517**		10,294
		122,113		49,390
SHAREHOLDERS' EQUITY:				
Share capital *(note 12)*		**1,051,811**		734,165
Accumulated deficit		**(214,369)**		(118,208)
Cumulative translation adjustment		**(236)**		—
		837,206		615,957
	$	**959,319**	$	665,347

Commitments and contingencies *(notes 12 and 13)*

See accompanying notes to consolidated financial statements.

Approved on behalf of the Board

Director

Director

**Accounting
Cycle Tutorial**

Learning Objective

3

*Identify the steps in the
accounting cycle.*

Accounting Cycle

We are now ready to look at the whole system in which transactions are measured, recorded, and communicated. This system is called the **accounting cycle.** Envision for a moment a company that has just been formed and whose managers need to install an accounting system. What is the first thing they need to decide? One of the first decisions they must make is what information they need to run the business. What information is important for them to make decisions? What information do outside users need to know about the company? What does GAAP require? Accounting systems are information systems, so managers should decide at the start what information they want and need to operate the business. Although companies may be in the same industry, each company will develop its own unique information system. As we proceed through a discussion of the accounting cycle, we are going to demonstrate each stage using the transactions of Demo Retail Company Ltd. from Chapter 2

Chart of Accounts

The types of accounting information to be recorded in the accounting system are generally summarized in a **chart of accounts**. Exhibit 3-6 lists the chart of accounts for Demo Retail Company Ltd. The chart of accounts should be viewed as dynamic and not something that can never be changed. As the business changes, there may be a need for a different type of account. For example, suppose that the company originally was unwilling to provide credit to its customers. There would be no need for an accounts receivable account because the company was strictly a cash business. Later, if the company decided to allow customers to buy on credit, it would need to add an accounts receivable account to the chart of accounts. A key point to note is that the design of the chart of accounts can facilitate additional information or be a handicap, depending upon how carefully it is conceived.

EXHIBIT 3-6

■ DEMO RETAIL COMPANY LTD.

Chart of Accounts
Permanent Accounts
    Assets
        Cash
        Accounts Receivable (A/R)
        Inventory (Inv.)
        Prepaid Insurance
        Land
        Equipment
    Liabilities
        Accounts Payable (A/P)
        Interest Payable
        Bank Loan
    Shareholders' Equity
        Common Shares
        Retained Earnings (RE)

Temporary Accounts
    Income Statement Accounts
        Sales Revenues
        Cost of Goods Sold
        Insurance Expense
        Interest Expense
        Amortization Expense
    Dividends Declared

EXHIBIT 3-6 CONT.

In an actual system, each account in the chart of accounts would be identified by a number that would facilitate the ordering of the accounts and the recording of transactions within a computer system. In this book, accounts will be designated by their names and not by account numbers. An account can be given any name that makes sense and is descriptive of its purpose. Commonly used terms for each type of account will be discussed throughout the book. Several of these names, such as accounts receivable, inventory, accounts payable, and retained earnings, have already been mentioned. Going back to our warehouse example, putting a name on an account is like putting a label on one of the boxes. In order to find a box (or an account) so that you can put something into it or take something out, you need to know what is written on the label.

The chart of accounts is the starting point for the company's accounting cycle. The complete cycle is illustrated in Exhibit 3-7. Each of the steps in the cycle is discussed in the following subsections.

ACCOUNTING CYCLE

EXHIBIT 3-7

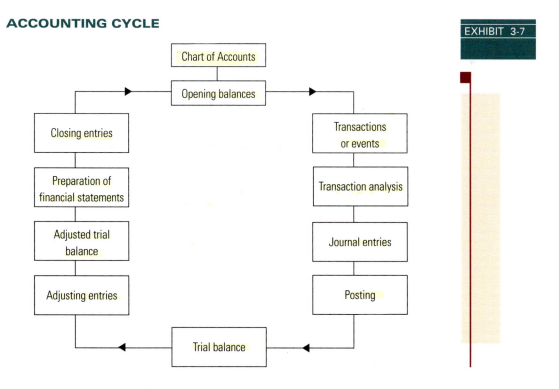

OPENING BALANCES   After the chart of accounts has been established and the company commences business, the accountant needs to record in the accounting system the results of the various transactions that affect the company. The system could be as simple as a notebook with sheets of paper representing the accounts and entries made by hand, or it could be as sophisticated as an on-line computer system in which entries are made via computer terminals. For the purpose of this book, a manual system will be used, but the same entries apply to any accounting system, no matter how simple or how sophisticated.

In the first year of operation of a company, the first step in the cycle would be to initialize the accounts by entering zero balances in all of them. In subsequent accounting periods, the beginning balances will be the balances carried forward from the end of the last accounting cycle. Demo's opening balances at the beginning of 20x1 are shown in Exhibit 3-8.

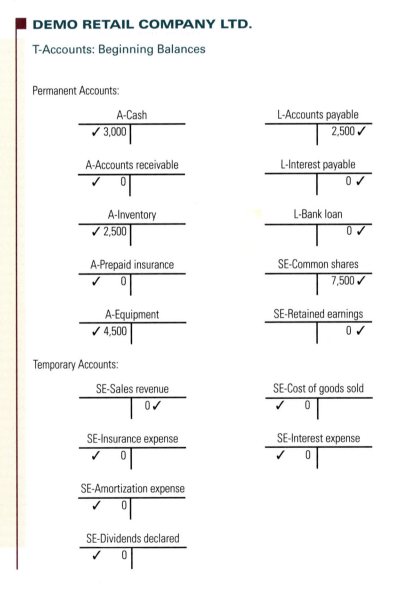

DEMO RETAIL COMPANY LTD.

T-Accounts: Beginning Balances

Permanent Accounts:

A-Cash		L-Accounts payable	
✓ 3,000			2,500 ✓

A-Accounts receivable		L-Interest payable	
✓ 0			0 ✓

A-Inventory		L-Bank loan	
✓ 2,500			0 ✓

A-Prepaid insurance		SE-Common shares	
✓ 0			7,500 ✓

A-Equipment		SE-Retained earnings	
✓ 4,500			0 ✓

Temporary Accounts:

SE-Sales revenue		SE-Cost of goods sold	
	0 ✓	✓ 0	

SE-Insurance expense		SE-Interest expense	
✓ 0		✓ 0	

SE-Amortization expense	
✓ 0	

SE-Dividends declared	
✓ 0	

Note that the temporary accounts for revenues, expenses, and dividends declared have been segregated from the permanent accounts and have zero balances.

TRANSACTIONS OR EVENTS   The next step in the cycle is to recognize that some event or transaction has occurred that affects the assets, liabilities, and/or shareholders' equity of the company. The transaction or event is usually evidenced by some sort of signal such as a source document—a piece of documentation received or created by the company. Examples of source documents would be invoices, cheques, cash register tapes, bank deposit slips, or purchase order forms. For publicly traded companies, the first transaction signalled would be the receipt of cash from the shareholders and the issuance of common shares. This first transaction provides the first inflow of cash, which can then be used to buy the assets that are necessary to operate the business.

TRANSACTION ANALYSIS   After a signal has been received that a transaction or event has occurred, the accountant must analyze the transaction or event to decide what accounts have been affected and by how much. This phase of the process is called **transaction analysis**. We engaged in this activity in Chapter 2 when we analyzed the effect of various transactions on the basic accounting equation. For routine transactions, such as the purchase and sale of goods, the transaction needs to be analyzed only once. After that, each subsequent sale or purchase transaction is the same and can be entered into the accounting system without further analysis. Unique and unusual transactions require further transaction analysis, and generally require the services of a professional accountant who understands the use of appropriate (GAAP) accounting methods. For routine transactions, an accountant is probably not needed, and an accounting clerk could record the transactions in the accounting system.

Learning Objective

4

Analyze transactions and record them in journal format.

JOURNAL ENTRIES   After the accountant has decided how to account for the transaction, an entry must be made in the system. The initial entry is usually made in what is known as the **journal**. The journal is a chronological listing of all the events that are recorded in the accounting system. The entry made to the journal is called a **journal entry**. The journal could be as simple as a piece of paper on which is recorded a chronological list of the transactions that have occurred. The transactions are dated and assigned a transaction number. The journal entry then consists of the date, the transaction number, the accounts affected (and their account numbers), and a listing of the appropriate debits and credits. Exhibit 3-9 demonstrates what a journal entry might look like for the first two transactions for Demo Retail Company Ltd. in January. For simplicity, assume that all transactions in January took place on January 31. By convention, in a journal entry, the debit entries are listed first and credit entries second. Credit entries are also indented from the debit entries. Note that each complete journal entry maintains the balance in the system, that is, debits equal credits. A proper journal entry must always maintain this balance. Accounting software generally contains internal subroutines that check for balanced journal entries and alert the user to any problems before he or she can proceed. An explanation is included with each transaction so that the circumstances of the transaction are available for future reference.

■ DEMO RETAIL COMPANY LTD.

Journal Entries

Transaction	Date 20x1	Account name	Debit	Credit
1	Jan. 31	A-Accounts receivable	2,500	
		SE-Sales revenue		2,500
		Sold inventory on account		
2	Jan. 31	SE-Cost of goods sold	1,800	
		A-Inventory		1,800
		Recorded cost of inventory sold		

Note that in Transaction 1 there is a debit to Accounts receivable. Accounts receivable is an asset account and a debit to it will increase it. Sales revenue is a shareholders' equity account. Because shareholders' equity accounts normally have a credit balance, a credit to this account will increase it. The increase in these two accounts is appropriate because Demo has a new asset (customers owe it $2,500) and shareholders' wealth has increased by the sale price of the goods sold. Consider the second transaction and see if you can follow the same kind of logic to explain why a debit to Cost of goods sold and a credit to Inventory are appropriate.

Learning Objective

5

Post transactions to T-accounts and prepare a trial balance.

POSTING TO THE LEDGER   Once the journal entries are recorded, the information needed to run the business would be recorded in the accounting system (in the journal) but it would not be very accessible. If, for example, the manager wanted to know the balance in the cash account, the accountant would have to take the beginning balance in cash and add or subtract all the journal entries that affected cash. If a company has recorded hundreds of journal entries, this could take a long time. To make the individual account information more accessible in a logical and deliberate way, the accountant then proceeds to the next step in the accounting cycle. In this step, the journal entries are **posted to the ledger**.

The **ledger** is a system (in a simple case, a set of notebook pages) in which each account is listed separately on an individual page. In our warehouse analogy, each account would have its own box. In a computerized system, each account would be represented by a separate computer file accessible by the account number. **Posting** is the process of transferring the information from the journal entry to the ledger accounts. Each page of the ledger represents a specific T-account. The ledger account would include the name (and number) of the account, its beginning balance, and then a listing of all the postings that affected the account during the period. Each listing would include the transaction number reference, the date, and the appropriate debit or credit. The transaction number reference would allow a user to go backward in the system to determine the source of an amount in an individual account. Note that, if the journal entries are posted properly, the balance in the ledger system is preserved (debits will equal credits). Exhibit 3-10 shows four ledger T-accounts and the posting of the first two January transactions for Demo Retail Company Ltd.

DEMO RETAIL COMPANY LTD.

EXHIBIT 3-10

Posting to the Ledger

Ledger

A-Accounts receivable		SE-Sales revenue	
Balance 0			Balance 0
Jan. 31 1 2,500			2,500 1 Jan. 31

A-Inventory		SE-Cost of goods sold	
Balance 2,500		Balance 0	
	1,800 2 Jan. 31	Jan. 31 2 1,800	

The posting to the ledger can take place on a monthly basis, a weekly basis, a daily basis, or any frequency desired. The timing of the postings is determined to some extent by the management's (or the shareholders') need for up-to-date information. If managers need to know the balance in a particular account, say inventory, on a daily basis, then the postings should be done at least daily. If management needs to know the amount of inventory on an hourly basis, then the posting has to be done more frequently. Many computer systems account for transactions in what is called "real time," which means that accounts are updated instantaneously. Once the data entry person has completed the journal entry, the system automatically posts the information to the designated accounts. Other computer systems collect journal entries in "batches" and post them all at one time. In general, managers like to have information sooner rather than later and, as the cost of computer technology continues to decrease, there has been a proliferation of "real-time" systems in the corporate world. Remember the news story in Chapter 1 about how fast Cisco Systems gets its financial statements out at the end of the quarter. It uses a "real-time" system to record its transactions.

At this point, it is important to note that a system consisting only of journal entries would make it difficult to determine the balance in any one account. A system of only ledger accounts, without the original journal entries, would make it difficult to understand the sources of amounts in individual accounts. We need both journal entries and ledger accounts in order to collect information in a way that makes it readily accessible and as complete as possible.

TRIAL BALANCE   While most errors should be detected at the journal entry and posting phases of the accounting cycle, some errors may persist. As stated earlier, in most computerized systems, the system will not post a journal entry unless the debits equal the credits. This type of system catches many errors at the input stage. In a manual system, errors may not be detected at the journal entry stage. If the debits equal the credits at the journal entry stage, it is possible for the amounts to be posted incorrectly to the accounts. One device for detecting errors is to produce a **trial balance**. The trial balance is a listing of all debit and credit balance accounts in the general ledger at a specific point in time. To use our warehouse example, we would look into each box and make a list of what we find. A check can then be done to ensure that the total of the debit balances equals the total of the credit balances. If these are not equal, a mistake has been made at some point during the process and must be corrected. The trial balance assists in detecting balance errors, but it does not, in general, allow detection of errors in which the wrong account was debited or credited. Errors such as these can be detected by examining the accounts and their balances for reasonableness. However, if one minor entry was made to a wrong account, it may not be detected in this phase. The trial balance process will also be unable to detect the omission of a required journal entry, as the totals on the trial balance will nonetheless be equal to each other.

In a computerized system, a trial balance can be generated by the system at any time. Exhibit 3-11 illustrates the appearance of a trial balance using the data from the Demo Retail Company Ltd. example.

EXHIBIT 3-11

DEMO RETAIL COMPANY
Trial Balance

Account	Debit	Credit
Cash	$ 1,890	
Accounts receivable	300	
Inventory	2,800	
Prepaid insurance	300	
Land	15,000	
Equipment	4,350	
Accounts payable		$ 1,900
Interest payable		50
Bank loan		10,000
Common shares		12,500
Retained earnings		0
Dividends declared	250	
Sales revenues		2,500
Cost of goods sold	1,800	
Amortization expense	150	
Insurance expense	60	
Interest expense	50	
Totals	$26,950	$26,950

Note that this trial balance was prepared before the revenue, expense, and dividends declared accounts were put into retained earnings. Retained earnings still has a zero balance. More importantly, the revenue, expense, and dividends declared accounts still have amounts in them. Note, as well, the order in which the accounts are listed on the trial balance. They are in the order in which they will appear on the balance sheet and income statement. Accounts will be kept in the ledger in this order so that it is easier to prepare financial statements. If account numbers are assigned to the accounts, as they will be in a computerized system, a set of account numbers will be assigned to a section of the financial statement, say the current assets section of the balance sheet, and all of the accounts given those numbers will be current assets. When the computer system prepares a balance sheet, it will list the current assets in the current asset section of the balance sheet in numerical order according to the account number they were assigned. For example, many companies using four-digit account numbers will assign numbers between 1000 and 1999 to current assets only.

ADJUSTING ENTRIES   If an error is detected in the trial balance phase, it must be corrected. A journal entry to correct an error is one type of **adjusting entry** that is made at the end of the accounting period. A second type of adjusting entry is made for transactions or events that were not recognized and recorded during the period. Examples of this type of event are the amortization of the capital assets, the recognition of interest that is owed on loans, and the recognition that wages are owed to some employees. Accountants in most businesses have a set of this second type of adjusting entry that they typically make at the end of every period. Care must be taken to ensure that all events and transactions have been accounted for. The adjusting entry phase of the accounting cycle is used to ensure that the appropriate revenues and expenses have been recorded and reported for the period. Adjusting entries are journalized and posted in the same way as other accounting entries. In our Demo example, the transactions that would be adjusting entries are the use of insurance in January, the amortization of the equipment, and the recording of the interest owed on the bank loan.

Under GAAP, companies take care to measure their revenues so that all the revenues earned in a period are recorded and reported in that period. Also, the expenses incurred to generate those revenues are recorded and reported (matched). The final adjustments to the revenues and expenses are achieved through the adjusting entries. Although profit-oriented companies adhere to these requirements, governments have been slower to move to accrual accounting as the following report illustrates:

Learning Objective
6

Understand the necessity of adjusting entries and determine how they should be recorded.

accounting in the news

ACCRUAL-BASED ACCOUNTING

In its February 1995 budget, the Federal Government announced its intention to adopt full accrual-based accounting. The Auditor General had been raising concerns with respect to the accounting for capital assets, environmental liabilities, and government investments. The change to accrual-based accounting has taken several years. The phase-in process began in April 1999 and was completed on April 1, 2001. The financial statements for 2001–2002 will use full accrual accounting. Check your financial newspapers for 2002 for statements from the Auditor General about how successful this transition has been. Do you think that taxpayers will have a better understanding of the financial position of the Federal Government now?

Sources: "Backgrounder: Implementation of Full Accrual Accounting in the Federal Government's Financial Statements," The Department of Finance Canada, 2001. "FIS INFO: Full Accrual Accounting," Government of Canada, September 2001.

Ehics in Accounting

ethics in accounting

■ Many adjusting entries require estimates and judgements by management. These estimates and judgements provide an opportunity to manipulate both balance sheet values and income. Suppose that you, as a staff accountant, are asked to postpone the write-off of some old plant and equipment that is currently idle. It is clear to you that the equipment will never be used again. The write-off would need to be recognized as a loss (like an expense on the income statement—it reduces net income) and would, therefore, have a significant negative impact on the income statement. Management has asked you to postpone the write-off because the company has applied for a large loan from the bank and the loss from the write-off could significantly affect the company's reported performance. What should you do? As you consider your response to this ethical question, it is sometimes helpful to think about who will be affected by your decision (including yourself) and how they will be helped or hurt by your decision. Particularly, think of who the users/potential users of the financial statements are. This should help you structure your understanding of the situation and justify your decision in the context of these effects.

ADJUSTED TRIAL BALANCE   After all the adjusting entries have been recorded and posted, an **adjusted trial balance** is prepared. This is done to ensure that debits still equal credits and that any imbalance is corrected before financial statements are prepared.

FINANCIAL STATEMENT PREPARATION   After the adjusted trial balance has been prepared and any corrections have been made, the financial statements for the period can be prepared. Note that, at this point, the temporary accounts still have balances in them and the retained earnings account has the same balance as it did at the beginning of the period. No entries have been made directly to the retained earnings account. The income statement can, therefore, be prepared from the information in the temporary accounts. Note also that the dividends declared account is not a part of the income statement. Dividends are not an expense of doing business; they are a return to shareholders of part of their accumulated wealth in the company.

   The balance sheet can be prepared from the balances in the permanent accounts with the one exception of retained earnings, which does not, at this point, include the effects of revenues, expenses, and dividends. The preparation of the cash flow statement could be done in a simple case from the information in the ledger account for cash. The preparation of the cash flow statement in a more complex case is discussed in greater detail in Chapter 5. Refer back to Chapter 2 to see the income statement and balance sheet for Demo Retail Company Ltd.

CLOSING ENTRIES   After the income statement is prepared, the balances in the temporary accounts must be transferred to the retained earnings account (a permanent account). This will reset the balance in each temporary account to zero to start the next accounting cycle. The entries that accomplish this are called **closing entries**. Closing entries will be distinguished from other entries in the examples in this book by lettering them (using A, B, C, etc.) rather than numbering them. Sometimes companies use a single temporary account to accumulate all the income statement accounts. This account is usually called an **income summary account**. The balances from all the individual revenue and expense accounts are closed to this summary account. The balance in the income summary account is then closed to retained earnings. This will be demonstrated for the Demo Retail Company Ltd. in the next few pages. Again, because the dividends declared account is not an income statement account, it would be closed directly to retained earnings and would not affect the income summary account. In a computerized system, the accounting program would perform the closing process automatically when instructed to do so. You would want to make sure that you have finished all of the adjusting entries and asked the system to prepare the financial statements before you instructed the program to close the books for the year because most computer systems will not let you go back.

Learning Objective

7

Describe why closing entries are necessary.

ACCOUNTING CYCLE FREQUENCY   One final issue with regard to the accounting cycle is: how often should the cycle be completed? That is, how often should financial statements be prepared? Another way to put it is: how long should an accounting period be? The answer is that financial statements should be prepared as often as necessary to provide timely information to management and shareholders. Since this preparation is not without cost, especially in a manual system, a balance must be struck between the benefits of having up-to-date information and the cost of preparing the statements. In some businesses, the need for up-to-date information is great, in which case daily reports may be necessary. In other businesses, a monthly statement is probably sufficient. Regardless of what time period is selected, the procedures described above are appropriate.

For companies whose shares are traded on a public stock exchange, there is a requirement that the companies file financial statements quarterly, as well as on an annual basis. The frequency with which financial statements are prepared is sometimes expressed in terms of how often a company **closes its books**. If it closes its books monthly, the accounting cycle for the company is one month long, and the temporary accounts are reset on a monthly basis. Adjusting entries, such as those for amortization, interest, and wages, are then made once a month. In a computerized system, the accounts are not reset monthly. Instead, the system produces an income statement just for the month. The system can isolate all of the transactions that were recorded for the month and then prepare an income statement recording only the appropriate transactions. The ease and frequency with which financial statements can be prepared in a computerized system helps reduce the preparation costs significantly.

Demo Retail Company Ltd.—The Accounting Cycle

Return now to Demo Retail Company Ltd. We are going to demonstrate the various stages of the accounting cycle by using the same transactions for January that we used in Chapter 2. The beginning balances in the accounts (the balances that carried over from the end of December 20x0) were already displayed in Exhibit 3-8.

We now want to show you the rest of the transactions for Demo. The transactions from January 20x1 are listed here again for your convenience. They are described in detail in Chapter 2.

1. Demo sold units of inventory to customers, on account, for $2,500. The units had been in inventory. (Already journalized in Exhibit 3-9.)

2. The cost of the units removed from inventory for the sales in January totalled $1,800. (Already journalized in Exhibit 3-9.)

3. Purchases of new inventory to replace the units sold in January totalled $2,100. All of these purchases were made on account.

4. During the month, Demo received $2,200 from customers as payments on their accounts.

5. Demo made payments of $2,700 on its accounts payable.

6. Demo paid $360 in cash on January 1 for an insurance policy to cover its inventory from January 1, 20x1, through June 30, 20x1.

7. On the first day of January, Demo purchased land for $15,000 as a site for a future retail outlet. In order to pay for the land, Demo raised money by borrowing $10,000 from the bank and issuing new shares for $5,000.

8. Dividends in the amount of $250 were declared and paid in January.

9. Demo's accountant determined that the equipment should be amortized by $150 for January.

10. The interest rate charged on the loan from the bank in transaction 7 is 6%.

11. One month of insurance was used up in January.

Note that the transactions have been organized differently from the way they were described in Chapter 2. Instead of recording the purchase of the insurance and the insurance expense for January as part of the same transaction, we have listed the insurance expense as a separate transaction—Transaction 11. We have also moved the amortization of the equipment and the interest transaction to Transactions 9 and 10. These three entries are the **adjusting entries** and will be recorded and posted separately in the adjusting entry phase of the accounting cycle.

Exhibit 3-12 shows the first eight transactions for Demo in January in journal entry form.

DEMO RETAIL COMPANY LTD.

Journal Entries for Transactions in January 20x1

EXHIBIT 3-12

1.	A-Accounts receivable	2,500	
	SE-Sales revenue		2,500
	Sold inventory on account		
2.	SE-Cost of goods sold	1,800	
	A-Inventory		1,800
	Recorded cost of inventory sold		
3.	A-Inventory	2,100	
	L-Accounts payable		2,100
	Bought inventory on account		
4.	A-Cash	2,200	
	A-Accounts receivable		2,200
	Collected on accounts receivable		
5.	L-Accounts payable	2,700	
	A-Cash		2,700
	Paid amounts owed on accounts payable		
6.	A-Prepaid insurance	360	
	A-Cash		360
	Purchased a six-month insurance policy		
7a.	A-Cash	5,000	
	SE-Common shares		5,000
	Issued common shares		
7b.	A-Cash	10,000	
	L-Bank loan		10,000
	Borrowed from the bank		
7c.	A-Land	15,000	
	A-Cash		15,000
	Purchased land		
8.	SE-Dividends declared	250	
	A-Cash		250
	Declared and paid dividends		

In Exhibit 3-13, all these journal entries have been posted to the ledger T-accounts. Notice how the transactions have been numbered so that it is easy to determine which entries are associated with one another. The title of Exhibit 3-13 indicates that the accounts are in the trial balance phase, which means that the adjusting entries have not been recorded and posted and the temporary accounts have not been closed to retained earnings. The term given to calculating the balance in an account is **footing the account**.

DEMO RETAIL COMPANY LTD.

T-Accounts After Posting

A-Cash					L-Accounts payable			
✓	3,000						2,500	✓
(4)	2,200	2,700	(5)	(5)	2,700		2,100	(3)
(7a)	5,000	360	(6a)					
(7b)	10,000	15,000	(7c)				1,900	✓
		250	(8)					
✓	1,890							

A-Accounts receivable					L-Interest payable		
✓	0					0	✓
(1)	2,500	2,200	(4)				
✓	300						

A-Inventory					L-Bank loan		
✓	2,500					0	✓
(3)	2,100	1,800	(2)			10,000	(7b)
✓	2,800					10,000	✓

A-Prepaid insurance				SE-Common shares		
✓	0				7,500	✓
(6)	360				5,000	(7a)
✓	360				12,500	✓

A-Land				SE-Retained earnings		
✓	0				0	✓
(7c)	15,000					
✓	15,000					

A-Equipment	
✓	4,500
✓	4,500

Temporary Accounts:

EXHIBIT 3-13 CONT.

SE-Sales revenue		
	0	✓
	2,500	(1)
	2,500	✓

✓	SE-Cost of goods sold	
	0	
(2)	1,800	
✓	1,800	

SE-Insurance expense	
✓ 0	

SE-Interest expense	
✓ 0	

SE-Amortization expense	
✓ 0	

SE-Dividends declared	
✓	0
(8)	250
✓	250

After the month's transactions have been posted, a trial balance is prepared to ensure that debits equal credits. Exhibit 3-14 shows the trial balance before the adjusting entries:

DEMO RETAIL COMPANY LTD.

EXHIBIT 3-14

Trial Balance

Account	Debit	Credit
Cash	$ 1,890	
Accounts receivable	300	
Inventory	2,800	
Prepaid insurance	360	
Land	15,000	
Equipment	4,500	
Accounts payable		$ 1,900
Bank loan		10,000
Common shares		12,500
Dividends declared	250	
Sales revenues		2,500
Cost of goods sold	1,800	
Totals	$26,900	$26,900

Note that the accounts which have zero balances have not been listed on the trial balance.

The accountant would then move to the next stage of the accounting cycle and record the adjusting entries. For Demo, those entries are for the amortization of the equipment, the recording of interest for January, and the recording of the use of insurance for one month. Exhibit 3-15 shows the adjusting entries for January.

EXHIBIT 3-15

■ **DEMO RETAIL COMPANY LTD.**

Adjusting Entries

9.	SE-Amortization expense	150	
	XA-Accumulated amortization		150
	Recorded the amortization of the equipment for January		
10.	SE-Interest expense	50	
	L-Interest payable		50
	Recorded the interest owed on the bank loan for January		
11.	SE-Insurance expense	60	
	A-Prepaid insurance		60
	Recorded the use of insurance for January		

Note that in Transaction 9, a new account, Accumulated amortization, has been introduced. Its account type, XA, is also different. In the detailed explanation of this transaction in Chapter 2, we told you that rather than reduce a capital asset directly as it is used up, we instead collect the used part in an account called **accumulated amortization**. This is a **contra asset account**, which is why we have labelled it XA. A contra asset account normally has a balance opposite to an asset account. Therefore, it normally has a *credit* balance. Over the life of the equipment, this account will grow by the amortization each year. A contra asset account is shown on the balance sheet contra to the asset account to which it is associated. On the balance sheet you would see:

Equipment	$4,500	
Less: accumulated amortization	150	$4,350

From now on, we will always use an accumulated amortization account when we are amortizing capital assets.

Exhibit 3-16 shows the accounts after the adjusting entries have been posted. Note that the posted adjusting entries are in bold type.

EXHIBIT 3-16

■ **DEMO RETAIL COMPANY LTD.**

T-Accounts After Posting of Adjusting Entries

	A-Cash				L-Accounts payable		
✓	3,000					2,500	✓
(4)	2,200	2,700	(5)	(5)	2,700	2,100	(3)
(7a)	5,000	360	(6a)				
(7b)	10,000	15,000	(7c)			1,900	✓
		250	(8)				
✓	1,890						

EXHIBIT 3-16
CONT.

A-Accounts receivable			
✓	0		
(1)	2,500	2,200	(4)
✓	300		

A-Inventory			
✓	2,500		
(3)	2,100	1,800	(2)
✓	2,800		

A-Prepaid insurance			
✓	0		
(6)	360	**60**	**(11)**
✓	300		

A-Land			
✓	0		
(7c)	15,000		
✓	15,000		

A-Equipment			
✓	4,500		
✓	4,500		

XA-Accumulated amortization			
		0	✓
		150	**(9)**
		150	✓

L-Interest payable			
		0	✓
		50	**(10)**
		50	✓

L-Bank loan			
		0	✓
		10,000	(7b)
		10,000	✓

SE-Common shares			
		7,500	✓
		5,000	(7a)
		12,500	✓

SE-Retained earnings			
		0	✓

Temporary Accounts:

SE-Sales revenue			
		0	✓
		2,500	(1)
		2,500	✓

SE-Insurance expense			
✓	0		
(11)	**60**		
✓	60		

SE-Cost of goods sold			
✓	0		
(2)	1,800		
✓	1,800		

SE-Interest expense			
✓	0		
(10)	**50**		
✓	50		

SE-Amortization expense		
✓	0	
(9)	**150**	
✓	150	

SE-Dividends declared		
✓	0	
(8)	250	
✓	250	

EXHIBIT 3-16 CONT.

Exhibit 3-17 shows the Adjusted Trial Balance after the adjusting entries have been posted.

EXHIBIT 3-17

DEMO RETAIL COMPANY LTD.

Adjusted Trial Balance

Account	Debit	Credit
Cash	$ 1,890	
Accounts receivable	300	
Inventory	2,800	
Prepaid insurance	300	
Land	15,000	
Equipment	4,500	
Accumulated amortization		$ 150
Accounts payable		1,900
Interest payable		50
Bank loan		10,000
Common shares		12,500
Dividends declared	250	
Sales revenues		2,500
Cost of goods sold	1,800	
Amortization expense	150	
Insurance expense	60	
Interest expense	50	
Totals	$27,100	$27,100

Note that the balance of accumulated amortization, the contra asset account, is listed in the credit column.

At this stage in the accounting cycle, the financial statements would be prepared. The income statement, balance sheet, and cash flow statement for Demo Retail Company Ltd. for this accounting period were shown in Chapter 2. Because of the introduction of the new account, accumulated amortization, the balance sheet would be slightly different. See the explanation on page 160 about how the change affects the statement. The income statement and balance sheet can be prepared directly from the balances in Exhibits 3-17. The cash flow statement can be prepared using the transactions identified in the cash account in Exhibit 3-16. Exhibit 3-18 shows one additional statement that many companies prepare, a statement of retained earnings. Note that dividends are shown on this statement.

DEMO RETAIL COMPANY LTD.

EXHIBIT 3-18

Statement of Retained Earnings
For the month ended January 31, 20x1

Retained earnings, January 1, 20x1	$ 0
Add: Net income	440
	440
Deduct: Dividends declared	250
Retained earnings, January 31, 20x1	$190

The format and order of presentation of the line items on the income statement and balance sheet are addressed in more detail in the remainder of this chapter. The format of the cash flow statement is discussed in more detail in Chapter 5.

The temporary accounts now need to be closed. In Exhibit 3-19, the closing entries to transfer the balances from the temporary accounts to the permanent account, retained earnings, are shown, as are the temporary accounts and the retained earnings account from Exhibit 3-16. Note that these entries have been lettered to distinguish them from the regular entries for the period. An income summary account has also been used to collect all the revenue and expense balances before closing the net amount ($440) to the retained earnings account. The dividends declared account has been closed directly to retained earnings.

DEMO RETAIL COMPANY LTD.

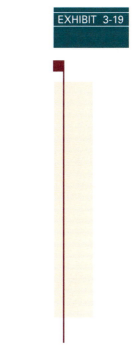

EXHIBIT 3-19

Closing Journal Entries at January 31, 20x1
Journal Entries and Posting of Entries to the Accounts

Journal Entries:

A.	SE-Sales revenue	2,500	
	SE-Income summary		2,500
B.	SE-Income summary	1,800	
	SE-Cost of goods sold		1,800
C.	SE-Income summary	60	
	SE-Insurance expense		60
D.	SE-Income summary	150	
	SE-Amortization expense		150
E.	SE-Income summary	50	
	SE-Interest expense		50

EXHIBIT 3-19
CONT.

| F. | SE-Income summary | 440 | |
| | SE-Retained earnings | | 440 |

| G. | SE-Retained earnings | 250 | |
| | SE-Dividends declared | | 250 |

Temporary Accounts:

SE-Sales revenue

		0	✓
		2,500	(1)
		2,500	
(A)	2,500		
		0	✓

SE-Cost of goods sold

✓	0		
(2)	1,800		
	1,800		
		1,800	(B)
✓	0		

SE-Insurance expense

✓	0		
(11)	60		
	60		
		60	(C)
✓	0		

SE-Interest expense

✓	0		
(10)	50		
	50		
		50	(E)
✓	0		

SE-Amortization expense

✓	0		
(9)	150		
	150		
		150	(D)
✓	0		

SE-Income summary

		0	✓
		2,500	(A)
(B)	1,800		
(C)	60		
(D)	150		
(E)	50		
		440	
(F)	440		
		0	✓

SE-Dividends declared

✓	0		
(8)	250		
		250	(G)
✓	0		

SE-Retained earnings

		0	✓
(G)	250	440	(F)
		190	✓

Note that in Exhibit 3-19, each of the revenue and expense accounts has been closed individually. Remember that you must name the account in the journal entry so that you can post the amount to the right account and reduce the account balance to zero. We used four separate journal entries to close all of the expense accounts. We could have used one.

B.	SE-Income summary	2,060	
	SE-Cost of goods sold		1,800
	SE-Insurance expense		60
	SE-Amortization expense		150
	SE-Interest expense		50

This typical journal entry, referred to as a compound entry, demonstrates that journal entries can have more than two accounts identified. Even though there are four credits to four different accounts, debits still equal credits.

Note as well that when we closed the revenue account, we debited the account. Revenues normally have credit balances, so to empty the account, we must debit it for the total amount in the account. The expense accounts normally have debit balances, which means that in order to close them, we must credit them for their account balances. Once these amounts are posted, each revenue and expense account is back to a zero balance and is ready for the next accounting period.

At this stage, the company would normally prepare a post-closing trial balance. This trial balance would only include the permanent accounts because all of the temporary accounts now have zero balances. This is the final check on the system to ensure that debits equal credits before transactions for the next period are entered into the system.

Now that you have a better idea about the source of the numbers on the financial statements, we are going to have a more detailed look at the income statement and balance sheet. Up to this point, we have kept the preparation of the two statements as simple as possible. Now that you know more about how the numbers are collected, you are ready to expand your knowledge of the statements.

INCOME STATEMENT FORMAT

One of the most fundamental objectives of financial reporting is to ensure that financial statements provide information that is useful to the user. To be useful, information should help current and potential investors, creditors, and other users assess the amount, timing, and certainty of prospective net cash flows to the enterprise.

As you learned in Chapter 1, the purpose of the income statement is to provide information about the performance of the company. The basic format of the income statement summarizes all revenues and expenses to show the net income. The information provided is primarily historical. The revenues are the historical amounts received or receivable from the sale of goods and services, and the expenses are based on the amounts actually paid or payable in the future for the goods and services used to produce the revenues. Some of the expenses may represent very old costs, such as the amortization of very old assets such as buildings.

For the income statement to provide information about future cash flows of the company, the connection between the amounts presented in the income statement and those future cash flows must be understood. Accrual-basis accounting requires that revenues and expenses be recorded at amounts that are ultimately expected to be received or paid in cash. For example, to estimate the actual amount of cash that will be collected from sales, the company estimates the amount of sales that will not be collected (bad debts) and deducts that amount from sales. On the expense side, estimates are made for some expenses where amounts are not yet paid, such as interest or tax expenses. In both cases, the figures reflect management's estimates about future cash flows. In this sense, the income statement provides information to the reader about management's assessment of the ultimate cash flows from the business of the period. This means that the income statement, on an accrual basis, provides more information about future cash flows than an income statement prepared on a cash basis, which only reflects cash flows that have already occurred.

A second aspect of providing information about future cash flows is the forecasting ability of the income statement. If the trends in revenues and expenses over several time periods are examined, the revenues and expenses that will occur in the future may be predicted, assuming of course that earning trends in the past continue into the future. An understanding of the relationship of revenues and expenses to future cash flows will allow a reasonable prediction of the amount of cash flows that will result in future periods.

The ability to predict future revenues and expenses depends on the type of item considered, the industry, and the company's history. The sales revenue and cost-of-goods-sold figures are reasonably predictable if the business is in a fairly stable product line. New businesses and new products make this type of forecasting more difficult. Other types of items are not as predictable. Sales of plant and equipment, for example, tend to be more sporadic than the normal sales of goods or services. Some items may occur only once and will, therefore, not be repeated. The closing of a plant or the sale of a business unit is an event that has income statement implications in the current period but will likely not be repeated.

To enable readers of the income statement to make the best estimates of future results, the continuing items should be separated from the noncontinuing items. For this reason, the format of the income statement is designed to highlight these differences.

The result of all this is that the normal income statement format is designed to provide information about continuing and noncontinuing operations. Exhibit 3-20 provides an overview of the major sections of a typical income statement. Each of these is discussed in the following subsections.

INCOME STATEMENT FORMAT

EXHIBIT 3-20

Sample Company Ltd.
Income Statement
For the year ended December 31, 20xx

Income from continuing operations:	
Operating revenues (i.e., sales or service revenue)	$XXX
Operating expenses (i.e., cost of goods sold, selling expenses,	
and administrative expenses)	(XXX)
Income from continuing operations	XXX
Income from non-operating sources:	
Financing revenue (i.e., interest revenue)	XXX
Financing expenses (i.e., interest expense)	(XXX)
Gain (loss) on sale of capital assets or investments	XXX
Other	XXX
Income from non-operating sources	XXX
Income before unusual or infrequent sources	XXX
Income from unusual or infrequent sources	XXX
Income before income tax	XXX
Provision for income tax	(XXX)
Income before discontinued operations and extraordinary items	XXX
Income from discontinued operations (net of tax)	XXX
Income from extraordinary items (net of tax)	XXX
Net income	$XXX

Income from Continuing Operations

This section provides information about the revenues and expenses resulting from the sales of goods and services to customers. The operations reported are those that represent the normal operating activities of the company and that are expected to continue in the future. A separate section later in the income statement contains the results of those operations that management has decided to discontinue.

Income statements can be either **single-step** or **multistep**. In Exhibit 3-21, the income statement of **Purcell Energy Ltd.** provides an example of a single-step income statement. In this type of statement, all the revenues are listed together and all the expenses (except income tax expense) are listed together. Thus, Purcell Energy shows revenues from oil and gas sales of $30,253,587 plus interest and other revenue of $152,311, for total revenues of $30,405,898 for the year ended December 31, 2001. The four different expenses total $19,613, producing income before income tax expense and non-controlling interest of $10,792,653. After income taxes of $3,378,975, Purcell Energy shows a net income for the year of $7,413,678.

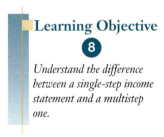

Learning Objective
8

Understand the difference between a single-step income statement and a multistep one.

PURCELL ENERGY LTD. (2001)
CONSOLIDATED STATEMENTS OF OPERATIONS AND RETAINED EARNINGS
For the years ended December 31

	2001	2000
Revenue		
Revenues (Note 13)	$ 30,253,587	$ 24,723,963
Interest and other income	152,311	26,424
	30,405,898	24,750,387
Expenses		
Production	6,392,797	4,145,886
Depletion, amortization and site restoration	10,220,000	4,755,000
General and administrative, net	2,024,126	1,478,157
Interest on long term debt	976,322	977,293
	19,613,245	11,356,336
Income before corporate taxes	10,792,653	13,394,051
Corporate taxes (Note 8)		
Capital taxes	292,442	259,394
Future income taxes	3,086,533	4,908,819
	3,378,975	5,168,213
Net income for the year	7,413,678	8,225,838
Retained earnings (deficit), beginning of year		
As previously reported	1,993,305	(2,483,729)
Adjustment for change in accounting policy (Note 11)	–	470,888
As restated	1,993,305	(2,012,841)
Purchase price of common shares repurchased in excess of book value (Note 7)	(4,943,508)	(4,219,692)
Retained earnings, end of year	$ 4,463,475	$ 1,993,305
Earnings per common share – basic	$ 0.294	$ 0.335
– diluted	$ 0.282	$ 0.320

On the other hand, in Exhibit 3-22, the statement of earnings of **CHC Helicopter Corporation** illustrates a multistep income statement. In this type of statement, the results of different types of operations are segregated. In the top sections of the statement, the results of the main business of the company are reported, resulting in the net line item called "Earnings before undernoted items" of $116,549 thousand. Below that, other continuing operations are reported, such as "Depreciation and amortization" and "Gain (loss) on disposal of capital assets." Other items that could be included after operating income would be income from equity investments and/or unusual items.

Consolidated Statements of Earnings

CHC HELICOPTER CORPORATION (2001)

EXHIBIT 3-22

Year Ended April 30 (in thousands of Canadian dollars, except per share amounts)

	2001	2000
Revenue (Note 2)	$593,849	$534,049
Operating expenses	477,300	440,237
Earnings before undernoted items	116,549	93,812
Depreciation and amortization	(19,980)	(21,577)
Gain (loss) on disposal of capital assets	998	(93)
Earnings from operations	97,567	72,142
Financing charges (Note 9)	(55,483)	(45,250)
Equity in (loss) earnings of associated companies	(416)	1,998
Earnings from operations before undernoted items and income taxes	41,668	28,890
Gain on sale of operations and investments (Note 5)	5,761	5,259
Debt settlement and restructuring costs (Note 11)	(21,904)	(7,447)
Earnings before income taxes recovery (provision) and non-controlling interest	25,525	26,702
Income taxes recovery (provision) (Note 17)	6,395	(5,919)
Non-controlling interest (Note 7)	–	(757)
Net earnings	$ 31,920	$ 20,026
Net earnings per share (Note 18)	$2.03	$1.30

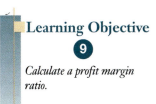

Learning Objective
9

Calculate a profit margin ratio.

Another distinguishing feature of multistep income statements is that the statement often starts with sales less cost of sales to arrive at a **gross profit** or **gross margin** amount. If a company's major source of revenue is selling goods, it must make enough profit or margin to cover all of the other costs of the business. By examining the gross margin, users can assess the profitability of the company. You can calculate a gross margin percentage, which is the gross margin divided by the sales. You can use this percentage to evaluate a company over time (has this percentage been increasing, decreasing, or remaining stable?) and to compare it to other companies in the same industry. If a company creates a multistep income statement and shows users the gross margin, it makes the statement easier to assess. CHC Helicopter does not disclose cost of goods sold. Instead, it deducts operating expenses, which include many different expenses, including cost of goods sold.

Usually, when a company discloses the sales minus cost of goods sold section, it will then include the other operating expenses that it incurred to generate the revenue.

Additional information regarding the performance and profitability of various operating units and operations in different geographical areas can usually be found in the notes to the financial statements under a section called "Segmented Information" if the company has different lines of business that are easily separated, or operations in several geographical areas. Additional information may be necessary if the company is very diverse or if it has global operations.

Income from Non-Operating Sources

In this section of the income statement, the results of transactions that do not involve the normal sale of goods and services are reported. The typical types of items found here are interest income and expense, the gain or loss on the sale of capital assets such as property, plant, and equipment, restructuring expenses, and other, mainly one-time events or transactions. Examples can be seen in the Consolidated Statements of Earnings for CHC Helicopter presented in Exhibit 3-22. The two items in the section following Earnings from operations are being treated as non-operating items. They include financing charges of $55,483 thousand and equity in (loss) earnings of associated companies of $416 thousand. The GAAP guidelines do not strictly specify what should be included in each section of a multistep income statement.

Income from Unusual or Infrequent Events

Learning Objective

10

Describe the criteria for unusual items, discontinued operations, and extraordinary items.

Sometimes unusual or infrequent events occur that the company would like to segregate from the rest of the results so the reader of the income statement can understand the nature of the event and make an assessment of its continuing or noncontinuing status. These types of items are reported either with the other non-operating events or in a section by themselves.

An example of unusual and infrequent items can be found in CHC Helicopter's Consolidated Statements of Earnings. It lists two items: gain on sale of operations and investments of $5,761 thousand and debt settlement and restructuring costs of $21,904 thousand.

Corporate Income Taxes

At the end of the income statement sections that have been discussed so far, there has been a line item for the corporate income **tax expense** calculated on the net of all the items listed above. An example can be seen in the income statement of **Purcell Energy Ltd.** shown in Exhibit 3-21, with income taxes of $3,378,975. Sometimes the term *provision for income taxes* is used instead of income tax expense. Taxes are calculated on the basis of aggregate income and are not listed separately for each operating and non-operating item. The tax expense listed on a company's income statement may not be the actual taxes that are owed to the Canada Customs and Revenue Agency. The rules used to calculate the taxes owed to the government are included in the *Canadian Income Tax Act*. Many of these rules parallel the accounting guidelines but there are some that are not the same. The income tax disclosure of Purcell Energy Ltd. in Exhibit 3-21, shows income tax as "capital" and "future." This means that the total income tax expense calculated on the accounting income is $3,378,975; $292,442 of this will be paid to the government this year (based on the rules in the *Canadian Income Tax Act*) and $3,086,533 will likely result in additional taxes in future years (the amount is positive; if it had been negative, it would have meant that there would have been a tax reduction in the future) as some of the revenues and expenses that were recognized under accounting become taxable in the future. More will be said about these dual calculations in future chapters.

Two additional items may appear after the calculation of tax expenses: **discontinued operations** and **extraordinary items** (although extraordinary items are very rarely found). These items appear below the income tax items (they are sometimes called "below the line" items) because of their unusual or unique nature. Because they appear after the calculation of taxes, the tax effect of these transactions must be reported along with the item itself. The company must pay taxes on these items just as it does on the operating and non-operating items, so they are reported on what is known as a **net of tax basis**. This means that the tax effects of the item have been netted against the before-tax numbers to produce a net, after-tax number. If, for example, discontinued operations result in a loss of $1,000 before taxes and save $400 in taxes (due to the deductibility of the loss), the net of tax amount would be a $600 loss ($1,000 – $400). The tax effects of these "below the line" items are not included in the line item called tax expense.

Discontinued Operations

Discontinued operations are significant segments of the company that management has decided to discontinue. There are criteria for deciding what constitutes a discontinued operation. Once management has decided to discontinue a line of business, there are two types of results that must be reported in the income statement. During the time it takes to dispose of the business segment, which may be considerable, the segment may continue to operate. The income from operating these discontinued operations must be reported separately from other income. In prior years, income from these segments was included with regular operations. It is therefore important to show users the income effect of discontinuing this segment. In addition, if the segment is being sold, either in whole or in part, there will be a gain or loss on the disposal of the segment. This gain or loss must also be reported separately from the results of the operations up to the time of disposal. The disclosure of both types of results is illustrated in Exhibit 3-23 for **Brascan Corporation**. In 2000, the company discontinued a segment of its operations. Note that the details of the income and gain from discontinued operations of $260 million in 2000 included the applicable taxes. Although the amount of the taxes is not disclosed on the income statement, it is given in Note 18. The disposal in 2000 resulted in a gain of $250 million and income of $10 million which was after a provision for taxes and other items of $152 million. Brascan has a whole series of amounts from 1999 to 2001 labelled as "pro forma." In 2001, it purchased additional shares in a company in which it already owned some shares. The additional shares brought its interest in the company to over 50%, which means that Brascan has to include the new company in its consolidated financial statements starting December 31, 2001. To give users some indication as to the impact of consolidating the new company, Brascan retroactively restated its 1999 through 2001 financial statements to include its results.

EXHIBIT 3-23

BRASCAN CORPORATION (2001)
CONSOLIDATED STATEMENT OF *INCOME*

| YEARS ENDED DECEMBER 31 | | Pro forma (Note 2) | | | | |
CDN$ MILLIONS, EXCEPT PER SHARE AMOUNTS	Note	2001	2000	1999	2001	2000
Total revenues		$4,676	$4,205	$3,575	$1,229	$1,216
Net operating income	15					
Commercial property operations		1,087	960	868	130	186
Financial operations		303	275	263	303	275
Power generating operations		142	123	91	142	123
Residential property operations		140	118	94	8	3
Other		90	92	75	25	25
		1,762	1,568	1,391	608	612
Expenses						
Interest expense		724	667	625	266	280
Minority share of income before non-cash items	17	454	416	362	116	132
Other operating costs		79	84	100	11	18
Income before non-cash items		505	401	304	215	182
Depreciation and amortization		157	139	111	39	38
Taxes and other provisions	16	122	137	93	(7)	15
Minority share of non-cash items	17	(123)	(115)	(80)	–	–
Equity accounted loss (income)		38	(148)	(106)	(128)	(259)
Income from continuing operations		311	388	286	311	388
Income and gains on sale of discontinued operations	18	–	260	137	–	260
Net income		$ 311	$ 648	$ 423	$ 311	$ 648
Per common share – diluted						
Income from continuing operations	13	$ 1.52	$ 1.96	$ 1.38	$ 1.52	$ 1.96
Net income		$ 1.52	$ 3.41	$ 2.15	$ 1.52	$ 3.41
Per common share – basic						
Income from continuing operations	13	$ 1.54	$ 1.96	$ 1.38	$ 1.54	$ 1.96
Net income		$ 1.54	$ 3.47	$ 2.17	$ 1.54	$ 3.47

Extraordinary Items

Although extraordinary items are rarely found in income statements, they are interesting. To be classified as extraordinary, items must be unusual, infrequent, and not resulting from management decisions. A recent example was a company that lost money when the provincial government expropriated some of its property in order to expand a road. The amount paid to the company was less than the carrying value of the land in the company's accounting system. Extraordinary items sometimes arise as a result of natural causes such as earthquakes or floods. Because management may have an incentive to place all of its "bad news" events in this category, the above criteria were developed to restrict what should be included as extraordinary. For example, we noted that losses due to floods might be considered extraordinary. If you had business operations in Saskatoon, Saskatchewan, and the South Saskatchewan River overflowed its banks, any losses you incurred would likely be extraordinary because the South Saskatchewan River rarely floods in Saskatoon and management could not have prevented or caused the flood. If, however, your business operations were in the Red River Valley south of Winnipeg, Manitoba, damage from a flood might not be considered extraordinary. It is beyond management's control, but the Red River often floods, causing extensive damage.

Extraordinary items are shown separately because they are beyond the control of the company and are not expected to recur in the future. It is important to segregate them because they may have a material effect on net income, and users need to know that the income is not likely to be affected by this item again in the near future. They should, therefore, put more weight on the income before the extraordinary item than they put on the net income after the extraordinary item.

AN INTERNATIONAL PERSPECTIVE

Reports from Other Countries

In the United States, there are only two criteria necessary for an item to be classified as extraordinary. It must be both unusual and infrequent. One would assume that losses directly associated with the events of September 11, 2001, would meet the criteria set out under GAAP. However, in a surprise move on October 2, 2001, the Emerging Issues Task Force (EITF) directed the accounting community not to treat them as extraordinary. Their reasoning was that although the events were both unusual and infrequent, if companies treated them as extraordinary, then the full impact of the losses, which could have many facets, would be shown as only one number on the financial statements. The EITF thought that users would need more information than could be gained from a one-line item. They also thought that in many instances it would be very difficult to separate direct effects of September 11 from indirect effects in a consistent way. They therefore directed the accounting community not to treat such losses as extraordinary.

Source: "US EITF decides against extraordinary treatment for terrorist attack costs," by FASB, www.fasb.org, October 1, 2001.

Earnings Per Share

In addition to net income, **earnings per share** is shown either in the income statement or in a note to the financial statements. Earnings per share relates the net income to the common shares outstanding. In many cases, this is a simple calculation that consists of dividing the net income of the company by the average number of common shares outstanding during the year. A weighted average is used if the number of common shares outstanding changed during the year. Note the disclosure of earnings per share in Exhibits 3-21 and 3-22 for Purcell Energy Ltd. and CHC Helicopter. For Purcell Energy, the basic earnings per share is $0.294 in 2001. For CHC Helicopter, the basic earnings per share figure is $2.03. Another earnings per share figure is also disclosed by Purcell Energy, fully diluted earnings per share. The fully diluted earnings per share is usually lower than the basic earnings per share. For Purcell Energy Ltd., the fully diluted amount is $0.282. The inclusion of a fully diluted earnings per share figure is a signal to users that the company has some financial instruments (i.e., convertible debt or shares) or some obligations like stock options given to its employees that could result in more common shares being issued. Remember that earnings per share is calculated by dividing the income by the number of shares outstanding. If more shares are issued, it is possible that the return to current shareholders could decline. The fully diluted earnings per share tells current shareholders the maximum amount that the return would decline if all of the new shares were issued. These issues are discussed in more detail in Chapter 12.

An example of additional earnings per share figures can be found in Exhibit 3-23. Brascan Corporation discontinued some operations in 2000. It disclosed an earnings per share from continuing operations and one for net income. The disclosure of the two earnings per share figures enabled users to better assess the impact of the decision to discontinue the operations. When companies have either discontinued operations or extraordinary items, they must show users the earnings per share before and after such items.

An International Perspective

Reports from Other Countries

NAFTA Facts:
The criteria used in other countries to identify extraordinary items are different from those used in Canada. As noted in the previous International Perspectives box on the United States, transactions or events that are both unusual and infrequent are classified as extraordinary. Note that they do not have the third condition of no management influence. Mexico's criteria for classifying an item as extraordinary are the same as in the United States. The transactions must be both unusual and infrequent. When evaluating an income statement from any of these three countries you would need to know by which criteria an extraordinary item was classified.

BALANCE SHEET FORMAT

The format of the balance sheet is less varied than that of the income statement. There are separate sections for assets, liabilities, and shareholders' equity. The most commonly used format presents assets on the left side of the page, and liabilities and shareholders' equity on the right-hand side. Alternatively, assets may be at the top of the page, and liabilities and shareholders' equity at the bottom.

Learning Objective
11

Understand the criteria for listing items on a balance sheet.

Within both current asset and current liability sections, the individual items are generally listed in the order of their **liquidity**. In the case of assets, liquidity refers to the ability to convert the asset into cash. For liabilities, liquidity refers to how quickly the liability will require the use of cash. Current assets and liabilities are generally listed from most liquid to least liquid.

Within the noncurrent asset section, the assets are listed in order of permanency. The asset that will last the longest is listed first. Within the capital asset group, the assets will be listed as land, buildings, and then equipment, because of the time over which they will be useful to the company.

In the noncurrent liability section, accountants do not follow a fixed guideline. The noncurrent liabilities are listed in the order the company thinks is most informative. If you look at **Sears Canada's** balance sheet (SC-31) in Appendix A at the end of the book, you will see that Long-term obligations are listed before Deferred credit and Future income tax liabilities.

Some companies choose not to follow the balance sheet format described above. For example, **Rogers Communications Inc.** in its 2000 balance sheet does not start with current assets, but instead with fixed assets, goodwill and other intangibles, and investments. Accounts receivable is somewhere in the middle. This format is more commonly seen in Europe. The liabilities also start with noncurrent items and then move to current ones. In Europe, the liability and shareholders' equity sections would be reversed. This part of the balance sheet often starts with shareholders' equity and then moves to liabilities.

What we have talked about here are conventions in format. Rogers Communications Inc. shows you that not all companies in Canada follow the conventions. Which format do you think is more understandable? Which format would you find easier to use? Why?

The balance sheet of **DaimlerChrysler**, a German/U.S. transportation products manufacturer (in Chapter 1, Exhibit 1-12), illustrates a European balance sheet. Note that assets start with Intangible assets and end with Cash and cash equivalents. This is exactly opposite to what you would normally see in Canada. Also, two assets, Deferred taxes and Prepaid expenses, are separated from the other assets and shown at the end. The liabilities and shareholders' equity starts with the Capital stock and ends with current liabilities such as trade and other liabilities. Again, this is almost exactly opposite to what you would see in Canada. Two items, deferred taxes and deferred income, are segregated at the end of the liabilities. Do you see how this format has some similarities to that used by Rogers Communications Inc.?

SUMMARY

This chapter adds to your understanding of the procedures underlying how financial information is collected, recorded, and summarized. You now understand about journal entries, debits and credits, ledger accounts, posting, trial balances, adjusting entries, and closing entries. This structure, whether in a manual system or a computerized one, is the same. In a computerized system, the computer takes over more of the mechanical tasks like posting, closing, and preparing trial balances and financial statements. People are still required to formulate and input the actual journal entries.

After the in-depth discussion of the accounting cycle, we built on your previous understanding of the income statement and balance sheet. We showed you some of the complexities of the income statement such as operating income, non-operating income, unusual items, income taxes, discontinued operations, and extraordinary items. As we move through the text, you will have some of these items explained more fully. For now, an awareness of what these items are is sufficient. With the balance sheet, we elaborated on its format, talking about the conventional way of preparing the statement and then showing you some other formats used in Canada and in Europe. By now you should be starting to be more familiar with accounting language and procedures. Remember as you work through the problems at the end of this chapter that the more effort you put in here, the easier the course will become later.

SUMMARY PROBLEMS

Additional Demonstration Problems

1. Use the data from Sample Retail Company Ltd. from the summary problem in Chapter 2.

   Required:
   Record the effects of the transactions in journal entries, number the entries made, post them to T-accounts, and close the temporary income accounts first to an income summary account and then to retained earnings.

2. The balance sheet of Template Company Ltd. as at December 31, 20x1, is given in Exhibit 3-24.

   Required:

   a. Prepare T-accounts for Template Company Ltd., and enter the opening balances from the December 31, 20x1, balance sheet. Using the transactions for 20x2 outlined below, prepare journal entries for the transactions for 20x2. Open new accounts as you need them. Post the journal entries to the T-accounts. Identify the transactions that represent adjusting entries.

   b. Prepare classified balance sheets (beginning and ending of the year) and a single-step income statement for Template Company Ltd. for 20x2.

   c. Prepare journal entries for the closing entries and post them to the T-accounts. Use an income summary account.

TEMPLATE COMPANY LTD.
Balance Sheet
December 31, 20x1

EXHIBIT 3-24

Assets

Current Assets

Cash		$ 55,000
Accounts receivable		39,500
Inventory		43,000
Prepaid rent		15,000
Total current assets		152,500

Capital Assets

Plant and equipment	$350,000	
Less: Accumulated amortization	100,000	
	250,000	
Office furniture	76,000	
Less: Accumulated amortization	16,000	
	60,000	310,000
Total assets		$462,500

Liabilities

Current Liabilities

Accounts payable	$ 33,000
Wages payable	9,000
Taxes payable	16,000
Total current liabilities	58,000

Noncurrent Liabilities

Notes payable	8,000
Long-term debt	75,000
Total noncurrent liabilities	83,000
Total liabilities	141,000

Shareholders' Equity

Common shares	$185,000	
Retained earnings	136,500	
Total shareholders' equity		321,500
Total liabilities and shareholders' equity		$462,500

Transactions for 20x2:

1. Sales for the year totalled $760,000, all of which were on account.

2. A review of accounts receivable at the end of the year showed a balance of $35,000.

3. Amortization of $19,600 was incurred, 80% of which was due to the building and equipment, and the remainder to office furniture.

4. Purchases of new equipment totalled $40,700, all paid in cash.

5. Rent is paid for leased equipment. Payments are made quarterly, in advance, on March 31, June 30, September 30, and December 31. Two payments of $15,000 each were made through the end of June. Rent increased to $16,500 per quarter, starting with the September 30 payment.

6. Employees earned wages of $150,000 during the year. As at December 31, 20x2, $11,000 was owed to employees.

7. Purchases of inventory, all on account, amounted to $431,000 (assume that this is the only item that affects accounts payable).

8. The company owed inventory suppliers $36,000 as at December 31, 20x2.

9. A count of ending inventories revealed $57,000 in ending inventory.

10. The note payable carries a 9% interest rate, and interest is due annually on December 31. On June 30, 20x2, the company paid off $6,000 of the principal, plus accrued interest. The rest of the principal is not due until June 30, 20x3.

11. Long-term debt at December 31, 20x1, carried an interest rate of 10%, with interest payments due semi-annually on June 30 and December 31. On January 1, 20x2, the company paid off $25,000 of the principal of this long-term debt. On September 30, 20x2, the company issued $27,000 of additional long-term debt at an interest rate of 12% with interest payment terms identical to the existing borrowings.

12. Other selling and administrative expenses of $45,000 were paid in cash.

13. The company's net income is taxed at 30% and, as at December 31, 20x2, $7,442 was owed to the Canada Customs and Revenue Agency.

14. The company declared $5,000 in dividends each quarter during 20x2; dividends were payable on April 14, 20x2, July 15, 20x2, October 15, 20x2, and January 15, 20x3.

SUGGESTED SOLUTION TO SUMMARY PROBLEMS

1. Exhibit 3-25 shows the solution to the Sample Retail Company Ltd. problem.

EXHIBIT 3-25

SAMPLE RETAIL COMPANY LTD.

Journal Entries

1.	A-Accounts receivable	80,000	
	SE-Revenue		80,000
	Sold inventory on account		
2.	A-Cash	79,750	
	A-Accounts receivable		79,750
	Collected accounts receivable		
3a.	SE-Salary expense	20,500	
	L-Accrued salaries payable		20,500
	Salaries owed to employees		
3b.	L-Accrued salaries payable	20,375	
	A-Cash		20,375
	Paid salaries		
4.	A-Inventory	39,700	
	L-Accounts payable		39,700
	Purchased inventory on account		

EXHIBIT 3-25
CONT.

5.	L-Accounts payable	37,300	
	A-Cash		37,300
	Paid accounts payable		
6.	SE-Cost of goods sold	37,500	
	A-Inventory		37,500
	Recorded inventory sold		
7a.	A-Prepaid rent	15,600	
	A-Cash		15,600
	Paid monthly rent		
7b.	SE-Rent expense	15,500	
	A-Prepaid rent		15,500
	Recorded monthly rent used		
8a.	SE-Interest expense	72	
	A-Cash		72
	Paid interest owed on loan		
8b.	L-Bank loan	200	
	A-Cash		200
	Paid part of principal on loan		
9.	SE-Amortization expense	2,000	
	XA-Accumulated amortization		2,000
	Amortization of equipment		
10.	A-Equipment	4,500	
	A-Cash		4,500
	Bought new equipment		
11a.	SE-Tax expense	1,771	
	L-Tax payable		1,771
	Income tax owed		
11b.	L-Tax payable	1,689	
	A-Cash		1,689
	Paid income tax		
12.	SE-Dividends declared	210	
	A-Cash		210
	Declared and paid dividends		

EXHIBIT 3-25
CONT.

■ **T-Accounts**

A-Cash			
✓	**4,500**		
2	79,750	20,375	3
		37,300	5
		15,600	7a
		72	8a
		200	8b
		4,500	10
		1,689	11b
		210	12
✓	4,304		

A-Accounts Receivable			
✓	**500**		
1	80,000	79,750	2
✓	750		

A-Inventory			
✓	**7,500**		
4	39,700	37,500	6
✓	9,700		

A-Prepaid Rent			
✓	**1,200**		
7a	15,600	15,500	7b
✓	1,300		

A-Equipment			
✓	**9,200**		
10	4,500		
✓	13,700		

XA-Accumulated Amort. – Equip.			
		0	✓
		2,000	9
		2,000	✓

SE-Revenue			
		0	✓
		80,000	1
A	80,000		
		0	✓

L-Accounts Payable			
		5,400	✓
5	37,300	39,700	4
		7,800	✓

L-Accrued Salaries			
		400	✓
3b	20,375	20,500	3a
		525	✓

L-Tax Payable			
		360	✓
11b	1,689	1,771	11a
		442	✓

L-Bank Loan			
		800	✓
8b	200		
		600	✓

SE-Common Shares			
		3,600	✓
		3,600	✓

SE-Retained Earnings			
		12,340	✓
D	210	2,657	C
		14,787	✓

SE-Dividends Declared			
✓	**0**		
12	210	210	D
✓	0		

SE-Cost of Goods Sold			
✓	**0**		
6	37,500		
		37,500	B
✓	0		

SE-Salaries Expense			
✓	**0**		
3a	20,500		
		20,500	B
✓	0		

SE-Amortization Expense			
✓	**0**		
9	2,000		
		2,000	B
✓	0		

SE-Rent Expense			
✓	**0**		
7b	15,500		
		15,500	B
✓	0		

SE-Interest Expense			
✓	**0**		
8a	72		
		72	B
✓	0		

SE-Income Tax Expense			
✓	**0**		
11a	1,771		
		1,771	B
✓	0		

SE-Income Summary			
		0	✓
B	77,343	80,000	A
		2,657	
C	2,657		
		0	✓

EXHIBIT 3-25 CONT.

Closing Entries (already posted)

A.	SE-Revenue	80,000	
	SE-Income summary		80,000
B.	SE-Income summary	77,343	
	SE-Cost of goods sold		37,500
	SE-Salary expense		20,500
	SE-Rent expense		15,500
	SE-Amortization expense		2,000
	SE-Interest expense		72
	SE-Tax expense		1,771
C.	SE-Income summary	2,657	
	SE-Retained earnings		2,657
D.	SE-Retained earnings	210	
	SE-Dividends declared		210

2. a. The journal entries are shown in Exhibit 3-26. The T-accounts for Template Company Ltd. are shown in Exhibit 3-27. The December 31, 20x1, balances are shown in bold. The posted transactions from 20x2 are numbered. Additional explanations for various transactions are given below:

Transaction 2. The information given is the ending balance in the account. Cash collections are calculated based on the beginning and ending balances in the account and the debit for sales on account as follows:

Beginning balance	$ 39,500
Sales	760,000
Total	799,500
Less: Ending balance	35,000
Payments received	$764,500

Transaction 3. The amortization for the period is split between the plant and equipment and the office furniture account. Both of these could use the same amortization expense account, but accumulated amortization must be recorded in the appropriate contra asset account.

Transaction 5. The beginning balance in the prepaid rent account on December 31, 20x1, of $15,000 represents the payment made on December 31, 20x1, that covers rent for the first quarter of 20x2. The first two payments in 20x2 of $30,000 (2 × $15,000) cover quarters two and three. The third payment of $16,500 on September 30, 20x2, covers the fourth quarter. Therefore, the rent expense during 20x2 (entry 5b) should be the sum of these amounts, or $61,500 [(3 × $15,000) + $16,500]. The last payment of $16,500 on December 31, 20x2, applies to the first quarter of 20x3 and should be the ending balance in the prepaid rent account (entry 5b). The total cash payments during the period total $63,000 [(2 × $15,000) + (2 × $16,500)].

Transaction 6. The amount of wages earned by employees ($150,000) and the ending balance in the wages payable account ($11,000) given in the problem allow the calculation of the amount paid for wages during 20x2 as follows:

Beginning balance	$ 9,000
Wages earned	150,000
Total	159,000
Less: Ending balance	11,000
Wage payments	$148,000

Transaction 9. The beginning and ending balances in inventory and amount of inventory purchased are used to determine cost of goods sold as follows:

Beginning inventory	$ 43,000
Purchases	431,000
Total	474,000
Less: Ending inventory	57,000
Cost of goods sold	$417,000

Transaction 10. The interest is paid for six months on the initial balance of $8,000. For the last six months of the year, the interest is calculated on the new balance in the account, $2,000. It can be calculated according to the following schedule:

$8,000 × 9% × 6/12 =	$360
$2,000 × 9% × 6/12 =	90
Interest expense	$450

Transaction 11. The interest incurred during the year on the initial long-term debt is calculated on the new balance of $50,000 after the principal was reduced by $25,000 on January 1, 20x2. The interest on the new debt that was taken out on September 30, 20x2, is calculated only on the last three months of the year. The interest is calculated as follows:

$50,000 × 10% × 12/12 =	$5,000
$27,000 × 12% × 3/12 =	810
Interest expense	$5,810

Transaction 13. Taxes are calculated on the income before taxes, which is $60,640 in 20x2 (see the income statement in Exhibit 3-28). The tax expense is $18,192 (30% x $60,640). The ending balance in the taxes payable account is then used to calculate how much Template paid in taxes in 20x2 as follows:

Beginning balance	$16,000
Tax expense	18,192
Total	34,192
Less: Ending balance	7,442
Tax payments	$26,750

Transaction 14. Because the last dividend declared in 20x2 is still payable as at December 31, 20x2, a new account, dividends payable, must be created. The first three dividends are paid in cash.

TEMPLATE COMPANY LTD.

Journal Entries for 20x2

EXHIBIT 3-26

		Debit	Credit
1.	A-Accounts receivable	760,000	
	SE-Sales revenue		760,000
	Sold inventory on account		
2.	A-Cash	764,500	
	A-Accounts receivable		764,500
	Recorded receipt of accounts receivable		
3.	SE-Amortization expense	19,600	
	XA-Accumulated amortization—plant and equipment		15,680
	XA-Accumulated amortization—office equipment		3,920
	Amortization of capital assets		
4.	A-Plant and equipment	40,700	
	A-Cash		40,700
	Purchased new equipment		
5a.	A-Prepaid rent	63,000	
	A-Cash		63,000
	Paid rent in quarterly instalments		
5b.	SE-Rent expense	61,500	
	A-Prepaid rent		61,500
	Recorded rent for the year		
6.	SE-Wage expense	150,000	
	L-Wages payable	9,000	
	A-Cash		148,000
	L-Wages payable		11,000
	Recorded wages owed to employees		

**EXHIBIT 3-26
CONT.**

7.	A-Inventory	431,000	
	L-Accounts payable		431,000
	Bought inventory on account		
8.	L-Accounts payable	428,000	
	A-Cash		428,000
	Paid suppliers		
9.	SE-Cost of goods sold	417,000	
	A-Inventory		417,000
	Recorded cost of inventory sold		
10a.	L-Notes payable	6,000	
	SE-Interest expense	360	
	A-Cash		6,360
	Paid on principal of notes payable plus accrued interest		
10b.	SE-Interest expense	90	
	A-Cash		90
	Recorded interest paid on notes payable		
11a.	L-Long-term debt	25,000	
	A-Cash		25,000
	Paid on principal of long-term debt		
11b.	A-Cash	27,000	
	L-Long-term debt		27,000
	Borrowed additional funds		
11c.	SE-Interest expense	5,810	
	A-Cash		5,810
	Recorded interest paid on the long-term debt		
12.	SE-Selling and administrative expenses	45,000	
	A-Cash		45,000
	Paid selling and administrative expenses during the year		
13a.	SE-Income tax expense	18,192	
	L-Taxes payable		18,192
	Income taxes owed for the year		
13b.	L-Taxes payable	26,750	
	A-Cash		26,750
	Paid income taxes		
14a.	SE-Dividends declared	20,000	
	L-Dividends payable		20,000
	Dividends declared during the year		
14b.	L-Dividends payable	15,000	
	A-Cash		15,000
	Paid dividends		

Transactions 3, 5b, the part of 6 that records the amount of wages unpaid at the end of the year, and 13a would be adjusting entries.

TEMPLATE COMPANY LTD.

EXHIBIT 3-27

T-Accounts with Posted Balances

A-Cash

✓	55,000		
2	764,500	40,700	4
11b	27,000	63,000	5a
		148,000	6
		428,000	8
		6,360	10a
		90	10b
		25,000	11a
		5,810	11c
		45,000	12
		26,750	13b
		15,000	14b
✓	42,790		

L-Accounts Payable

		33,000	✓
8	428,000	431,000	7
		36,000	✓

L-Wages Payable

		9,000	✓
6	9,000	11,000	6
		11,000	✓

A-Accounts Receivable

✓	39,500		
1	760,000	764,500	2
✓	35,000		

L-Taxes Payable

		16,000	✓
13b	26,750	18,192	13a
		7,442	✓

A-Inventory

✓	43,000		
7	431,000	417,000	9
✓	57,000		

L-Dividends Payable

		0	✓
14b	15,000	20,000	14a
		5,000	✓

A-Prepaid Rent

✓	15,000		
5a	63,000	61,500	5b
✓	16,500		

L-Notes Payable

		8,000	✓
10a	6,000		
		2,000	✓

A-Plant and Equipment

✓	350,000		
4	40,700		
✓	390,700		

L-Long-term Debt

		75,000	✓
11a	25,000	27,000	11b
		77,000	✓

XA-Accumulated Amort. – P & E

		100,000	✓
		15,680	3
		115,680	✓

SE-Common Shares

		185,000	✓
		185,000	✓

EXHIBIT 3-27

A-Office Furniture

✓	**76,000**	
✓	76,000	

SE-Retained Earnings

		136,500	✓
D	20,000	42,448	C
		158,948	✓

XA-Accumulated Amort. – Off. Furn.

		16,000	✓
		3,920	3
		19,920	✓

SE-Dividends Declared

✓	**0**		
14a	20,000		
		20,000	D
✓	0		

SE-Sales Revenue

		0	✓
		760,000	1
A	760,000		
		0	✓

SE-Cost of Goods Sold

✓	**0**		
9	417,000		
		417,000	B
✓	0		

SE-Wage Expense

✓	**0**		
6	150,000		
		150,000	B
✓	0		

SE-Amortization Expense

✓	**0**		
3	19,600		
		19,600	B
✓	0		

SE-Rent Expense

✓	**0**		
5b	61,500		
		61,500	B
✓	0		

SE-Interest Expense

✓	**0**		
10a	360		
10b	90		
11c	5,810	6,260	B
✓	0		

SE-Selling & Admin. Expense

✓	**0**		
12	45,000		
		45,000	B
✓	0		

SE-Income Tax Expense

✓	**0**		
13a	18,192		
		18,192	B
✓	0		

SE-Income Summary

		0	✓
B	717,552	760,000	A
		42,448	
C	42,448		
		0	✓

2. b. The financial statements for Template Company Ltd. are included in Exhibit 3-28.

TEMPLATE COMPANY LTD.

EXHIBIT 3-28

Financial Statements

Template Company Ltd.
Income Statement
For the year ended December 31, 20x1

Sales revenue		$760,000
Less operating expenses:		
Cost of goods sold	$417,000	
Wage expense	150,000	
Amortization expense	19,600	
Rent expense	61,500	
Interest expense	6,260	
Selling and administrative expense	45,000	
Total operating expenses		699,360
Income before income tax		60,640
Income tax expense		18,192
Net income		$ 42,448

Template Company Ltd.
Balance Sheet
December 31, 20x2 and 20x1

		20x2		20x1
Assets				
Current Assets				
Cash		$ 42,790		$ 55,000
Accounts receivable		35,000		39,500
Inventory		57,000		43,000
Prepaid rent		16,500		15,000
Total current assets		151,290		152,500
Capital Assets				
Plant and equipment	$390,700		$350,000	
Less: Accumulated amortization	115,680		100,000	
	275,020		250,000	
Office furniture	76,000		76,000	
Less: Accumulated amortization	19,920		16,000	
	56,080	331,100	60,000	310,000
Total Assets		$482,390		$462,500

EXHIBIT 3-28
CONT.

Liabilities

Current Liabilities

Accounts payable	$ 36,000	$ 33,000
Wages payable	11,000	9,000
Taxes payable	7,442	16,000
Dividends payable	5,000	—
Notes payable	2,000	—
Total current liabilities	61,442	58,000

Noncurrent Liabilities

Notes payable	—	8,000
Long-term debt	77,000	75,000
Total noncurrent liabilities	77,000	83,000
Total Liabilities	138,442	141,000

Shareholders' Equity

Common shares	$185,000		$185,000	
Retained earnings	158,948		136,500	
Total Shareholders' Equity		343,948		321,500

Total Liabilities and Shareholders'

Equity	$482,390	$462,500

Note that notes payable is classified as a current liability in 20x2 but it was a noncurrent liability in 20x1. The reason for the different treatment is that the last $2,000 of notes payable is due in 20x3, which means that it is now current. The current portion of any long-term debt is classified as current.

2. c. The closing entries are included in Exhibit 3-29. These transactions are labelled with letters instead of numbers. They have been posted to the T-accounts in Exhibit 3-27. Note that after posting all of the revenue and expense accounts and the dividends declared account have zero balances. They are now ready for transactions in 20x3.

EXHIBIT 3-29

TEMPLATE COMPANY LTD.

Closing Entries

A	SE-Sales revenue	760,000	
	SE-Income summary		760,000
B	SE-Income summary	717,552	
	SE-Cost of goods sold		417,000
	SE-Amortization expense		19,600
	SE-Wage expense		150,000
	SE-Rent expense		61,500
	SE-Interest expense		6,260
	SE-Selling and administrative		45,000
	SE-Income tax		18,192
C	SE-Income summary	42,448	
	SE-Retained earnings		42,448
D	SE-Retained earnings	20,000	
	SE-Dividends declared		20,000

ABBREVIATIONS USED

A	Asset	L	Liability
A/P	Accounts payable	PP&E	Property, plant, and equipment
A/R	Accounts receivable	S&A	Selling and administrative
GAAP	Generally Accepted Accounting Principles	SE	Shareholders' equity
		XA	Contra asset account

SYNONYMS

Tax expense/Provision for taxes/Tax provision

GLOSSARY

Accounting cycle   The sequence of steps that occurs in the recording of transactions and events in the accounting system.

Accrued expense   An expense that has been incurred and recognized in the financial statements but has not yet been paid for.

Accumulated amortization   The total amortization that has been taken on an asset to a particular point in time.

Adjusted trial balance   A listing of the account balances after adjusting entries are made but before the closing entries are made.

Adjusting entry   An entry made at the end of the period to record an event or transaction that has not been recorded during the current accounting period. Events or transactions that are not signalled in any other way are recorded through adjusting entries.

Chart of accounts   A listing of the names of the accounts used in the accounting system.

Close the books   The process by which the company makes closing entries to complete one accounting period and sets the balances in the accounts to start the next period. The temporary accounts are closed into the retained earnings account.

Closing entries   Entries made at the end of the accounting period to transfer the balances from the temporary income statement and dividend accounts to the retained earnings account.

Contra asset account   An account used to record reductions in a related asset account. An example is accumulated amortization.

Credit   An entry made to the right side of an account or a reference to the right side of an account.

Debit   An entry made to the left side of an account or a reference to the left side of an account.

Discontinued operations   Operations of the company that are being phased out and will, therefore, not continue in the future.

Double entry accounting system   An accounting system that maintains the equality of the balance sheet equation. Each entry requires that equal amounts of debits and credits be made.

Dual entry accounting system   Synonym for the double entry accounting system.

Earnings per share   A calculation in which the earnings of the company are divided by the average number of common shares outstanding during the period.

Extraordinary items   A gain or loss appearing on the income statement that meets three criteria: (1) it is unusual, (2) it is infrequent, and (3) it is not caused primarily by a decision made by someone inside the company.

Footing the account   Calculating the balance in a T-account.

Future income tax asset/liability   A tax entry made to the books of a company for tax effect on the difference between the accounting balance of assets/liabilities at a given point in time and the tax balance of the same assets/liabilities at the same time. These differences arise when the company uses one accounting method for accounting reporting purposes and a different method for tax reporting purposes.

Gross margin   Sales minus cost of goods sold.

Gross profit   Synonym for gross margin.

Income summary account   An account used to summarize all the temporary income statement accounts prior to their being closed to retained earnings.

Journal   A place where transactions and events are originally recorded in the accounting system.

Journal entry   An entry made to the journal to record a transaction or event.

Ledger   A place where transactions and events are summarized in account balances. Entries are recorded in the ledger by a process known as posting.

Liquidity   A quality of an asset that describes how quickly it can be converted into cash.

Multistep income statement   An income statement in which revenues and expenses from different types of operations of the company are shown in separate sections of the statement.

Permanent accounts   Accounts whose balance carries over from one period to the next. All balance sheet accounts are considered permanent accounts.

Posting   A synonym for posting to the ledger.

Posting to the ledger   The process of transferring the information recorded in a journal entry to the ledger system.

Provision for taxes   A synonym for tax expense.

Single-step income statement   An income statement in which all revenues are listed in one section and all expenses except income taxes in a second section.

Synoptic journal   A journal in which transactions are recorded in a spreadsheet format. Each account is assigned its own column and amounts are added or subtracted inside the columns.

T-account   A device used to represent a ledger account.

Tax expense   The expense for income taxes calculated on the accounting income (revenues minus expenses).

Temporary accounts   Accounts used to keep track of information temporarily during an accounting period. Balances in these accounts are eventually transferred to a permanent account at the end of the period using a closing entry.

Transaction analysis   The process by which the accountant decides what accounts are affected, and by how much, by an economic transaction or event.

Trial balance   A listing of the accounting balances.

ASSIGNMENT MATERIAL

Multiple
Choice
Quizzes

Assessing Your Recall

3-1   Why is it important for users of financial information to have an understanding of how transactions are recorded, summarized, and reported?

3-2   In the adjusted trial balance phase of the accounting cycle, the retained earnings account has its beginning of period balance, whereas the rest of the permanent accounts have their proper end of period balance. Explain why this is the case.

3-3   Respond to each of the following statements with a true or false answer:

   a. Credits increase asset accounts.

   b. Revenues are credit entries to shareholders' equity.

   c. Cash receipts from customers are debited to accounts receivable.

   d. Dividends declared decrease cash at the date of declaration.

   e. The cash basis recognizes expenses when they are incurred.

   f. There is no such thing as a prepaid rent account on the cash basis.

   g. Dividends are an expense of doing business and should appear on the income statement.

3-4   Indicate whether each of the following accounts normally has a debit or a credit balance:

   a. Accounts Receivable

   b. Accounts Payable

   c. Sales Revenue

   d. Dividends Declared

   e. Dividends Payable

   f. Amortization Expense

   g. Common Shares

   h. Prepaid Rent

   i. Retained Earnings

3-5 Indicate whether each of the following accounts normally has a debit or credit balance:

   a. Wage Expense

   b. Cash

   c. Cost of Goods Sold

   d. Interest Revenue

   e. Equipment

   f. Long-Term Debt

   g. Common Shares

   h. Future Income Tax Asset

   i. Inventory

3-6 Draw the accounting cycle, and briefly describe each step.

3-7 "Expense accounts have debit balances, and debit entries increase these accounts." Reconcile this statement with the normal effects of entries on shareholders' equity accounts and the resulting balances.

3-8 Discuss why one company might close its books monthly and another might close them weekly.

3-9 Identify and briefly describe the major sections of the income statement.

3-10 What is the standard format of the balance sheet?

3-11 Explain the meaning of the terms "current" and "noncurrent" as they apply to the balance sheet.

3-12 Explain the meaning of the term "liquidity."

3-13 What two types of disclosures are made in the income statement with regard to discontinued operations?

3-14 What is an extraordinary item and why is it disclosed separately on the income statement?

Applying Your Knowledge

3-15 (Debit and credit balance identification)
For each of the following accounts, indicate whether the account would normally have a debit or a credit balance:

a. Cash

b. Accounts Payable

c. Common Shares

d. Sales Revenue

e. Inventory

f. Cost of Goods Sold

g. Wage Expense

3-16 (Debit and credit balance identification)
For each of the following accounts, indicate whether the account would normally have a debit or a credit balance:

a. Accounts Receivable

b. Retained Earnings

c. Accumulated Amortization

d. Interest Revenue

e. Prepaid Insurance

f. Amortization Expense

g. Bank Loan

3-17 (Construction of journal entries)
For each of the following transactions, construct a journal entry:

a. Inventory costing $3,100 is purchased on account.

b. Inventory costing $1,800 is sold on account for $2,700.

c. Accounts receivable of $2,000 are collected.

d. The company borrows $12,000 from the bank.

e. The company issues common shares for $20,000.

f. New equipment costing $7,500 is purchased with cash.

3-18 (Construction of journal entries)
For each of the following transactions, construct a journal entry:

a. Wages totalling $6,300 were paid to employees.

b. Office supplies costing $1,400 were purchased on account.

c. The company made a payment of $2,000 on its bank loan, $150 of which was an interest payment.

d. The company sold inventory for $13,300. Cash was collected immediately for the sale. The inventory cost the company $7,900. (Two journal entries are required.)

e. Land costing $23,000 was purchased. The company paid $3,000 in cash and the remainder was financed with a mortgage.

f. The company paid $2,500 for the monthly rent on its leased premises.

3-19   (Journalize, post, and prepare a trial balance)
Sweet Dreams Chocolatiers Ltd. began operations on January 1, 20x1. During 20x1 the following transactions occurred:

1. Issued common shares for cash, $200,000.

2. Purchased inventory on credit, $460,000.

3. Sold inventory on credit for $650,000. The original cost of the inventory that was sold was $380,000.

4. Collected $580,000 from customers.

5. Paid $440,000 to the suppliers for inventory previously purchased on account.

6. Paid the rent for the year of $24,000.

7. Paid other expenses, $24,000.

8. Paid wages to employees, $46,000.

9. Bought a delivery vehicle for cash, $36,000.

10. Declared and paid dividends of $8,000.

Required:

a. Prepare journal entries to record each of the above transactions.

b. Create T-accounts and post the journal entries to the T-accounts.

c. Prepare a December 31, 20x1 trial balance.

3-20   (Journalize, post, and prepare a trial balance)
Sparkling Clean Dry Cleaners Inc. began operations on January 1, 20x1. During 20x1 the following transactions occurred:

1. Issued common shares for cash, $150,000.

2. Purchased equipment to use in the operations. The company paid $76,000 for the equipment.

3. Purchased supplies on credit for $7,500.

4. Collected $125,300 from customers for dry cleaning.

5. Used $6,000 of the supplies for the cleaning process.

6. Paid $23,500 for utilities including telephone, electricity, and water.

7. Paid $48,500 for wages to employees.

8. Amortized the equipment by $950 for the year.

9. Borrowed $10,000 from the bank at 8% interest.

10. Paid interest charges of $400 on the bank loan (the loan was taken out on July 1, 20x1).

Required:

a. Prepare journal entries to record each of the above transactions.

b. Create T-accounts and post the journal entries to the T-accounts.

c. Prepare a December 31, 20x1 trial balance.

3-21   (Journalize, post, and prepare a trial balance)

The Riders Shop Ltd. repairs motorcycles. It has two major sources of revenue, one from the sale of repair parts (parts are sold for twice their cost) and the other from the performance of repair service. The company began operations in March 20x1 with the following chart of accounts:

Cash

Accounts receivable

Parts inventory

Shop supplies on hand

Prepaid insurance

Equipment

Accumulated amortization, equipment

Accounts payable

Advances from customers

Common shares

Retained earnings

Sale of parts

Service revenue

Cost of parts sold

Wage expense

Rent expense

Other expenses

During March the following transactions occurred:

March   1   Issued common shares for $100,000.

2   Paid the March rent, $2,100.

5   Purchased spare parts from a supplier on credit for $24,000.

7   Purchased shop supplies for cash, $11,100.

9   Billed a customer $310 for parts and $220 for labour in repairing a motorcycle.

11   Purchased additional motorcycle parts from a supplier, paying $750 cash.

12   Paid the supplier for the spare parts purchased on March 5.

15   Charged a customer $190 for parts and $310 for labour for repairing a motorcycle. The customer paid in cash.

15   Paid the wages for the first two weeks which totalled $900.

16   Signed an agreement with Cruising Wheels Ltd., a local used motorcycle dealer, to perform maintenance repairs on all used motorcycles to make them available for sale. The dealer agreed to pay $750 per quarter for the work. All parts used will be extra. The contract started on March 16. The dealer paid the first quarter's $750.

20   Purchased a one-year fire insurance policy for cash for $540. The policy comes into effect on April 1.

22   Repaired several motorcycles, charging $846 for parts and $1,400 for labour. The customers paid in cash.

25   Billed Cruising Wheels Ltd. $510 for parts used in repairing some motorcycles.

28   The customer whose work was completed on March 9 paid the amount owed.

31   Paid wages for the last half of March, $925.

Required:

a. Prepare the journal entries to record the above transactions and any adjustments which may be needed as at March 31.

b. Draw a T-account for each account. Organize them in the order in which they will appear on the financial statements. Post the journal entries to the T-accounts.

c. Prepare an adjusted trial balance for March 31.

d. From the trial balance, prepare an income statement and balance sheet for the month of March.

3-22 (Journalize, post, and prepare a trial balance and closing entries)
Refer back to Problem 33 in Chapter 2, T. George Company. (1) Prepare journal entries for each of the transactions listed in the problem. (2) Prepare the necessary T-accounts and post the transactions to them. (3) Prepare a trial balance. (4) Prepare the closing entries and post them to the T-accounts.

3-23 (Journalize, post, and prepare a trial balance and closing entries)
Refer back to Problem 34 in Chapter 2, Hughes Tool Company. (1) Prepare journal entries for each of the transactions listed in the problem. (2) Prepare the necessary T-accounts and post the transactions to them. (3) Prepare a trial balance. (4) Prepare the closing entries and post them to the T-accounts.

3-24 (Journalize, post, and prepare a trial balance and closing entries)
Refer back to Problem 35 in Chapter 2, A. J. Smith Company. (1) Prepare journal entries for each of the transactions listed in the problem. (2) Prepare the necessary T-accounts and post the transactions and adjustments to them. (3) Prepare an adjusted trial balance. (4) Prepare the closing entries and post them to the T-accounts.

3-25 (Income statement determination)
Jake Redding owns and operates a tire and auto repair shop named Jake's Jack'em and Fix'em Shop. During the month the following activities occurred:

1. The shop charged $8,300 for repair work completed. All but one of his customers had paid and collected their vehicles. The one customer who had not paid owed Jake $250. Jake still has the car parked in the shop's parking lot and he intends to keep it until the customer pays the bill. The $250 is included in the $8,300.

2. The total cost of parts used in repair work during the month was $2,700. Jake usually pays for the parts with cash. For items like fan belts and oil, which he orders in bulk, he buys from a supplier with 30 days credit. At the end of the month, he still owes $450 to his supplier.

3. Jake earned $40 in interest on the company's bank account.

4. Jake paid $600 monthly rent on the repair shop. He pays on the first day of each month.

5. Jake paid the previous month's utility bills of $250 on the 10th of the month. At the end of this month, he has this month's utility bills totalling $198, which he intends to pay on the 10th of next month.

6. Jake paid his friend David $350 for helping him in the repair shop.

7. Other expenses related to operating the repair shop for the month totalled $990. All of these have been paid.

Required:
Using the concepts discussed so far in the text, determine the amounts that would properly be reported in the income statement for Jake's shop. If an item is excluded, explain why.

3-26   (Income statement determination)
Janice Wylkie owns a cycle and ski store named Jan's Outdoor Blast. Besides equipment, she sells clothing and other accessories. During the month of June, the following activities occurred:

1. The business took in $32,600 from the sale of bicycles, clothing, and accessories. Half of this business was for cash and the other half was paid for with credit cards. By month end, the money had been collected from the credit card company less a 3% charge.

2. The merchandise that was sold originally cost $19,430.

3. Jan purchased new merchandise on credit for $21,800.

4. By month end, Jan had paid $18,000 to the suppliers of the new merchandise.

5. The telephone, electricity, and water for the month came to $480. At the end of the month, one bill for $120 had not yet been paid.

6. At the end of May, Jan had a 9% loan for $5,000 outstanding with the bank. On the last day of June, Jan paid the interest that was owed on the loan and also paid $200 on the principal of the loan.

Required:
Using the concepts discussed so far in the text, determine the amounts that would properly be reported in the income statement for Jan's shop. If an item is excluded, explain why.

3-27   (Determination of expenses using matching)
For each of the following independent cases, indicate how much of the cost should be recognized as expense in the months of September and October, applying the matching concept:

1. Employees work Monday through Friday and are paid on Monday for the previous week's work. The total payroll is $8,000 per week. September 30 falls on a Wednesday.

2. A new lease for the business premises goes into effect on October 1 and increases the rent from $900 to $1,000. Rent for the next month is always prepaid on the last day of the current month.

3. The company borrowed $7,000 on September 1. The loan is to be repaid on the last day of October along with $90 interest.

4. The company purchased several large barrels of lubricant for $2,100 on September 1. The lubricant is to be used in the company's operations and is expected to last until the middle of October.

3-28 (Journalize, post, prepare an income statement and balance sheet, and prepare closing entries)

On December 31, 20x1, Clean and White Linen Supplies Ltd. had the following account balances:

Cash	$210,000
Accounts receivable	85,000
Uniforms for sale	20,000
Supplies on hand	12,000
Investment	100,000
Equipment	340,000
Accumulated amortization	80,000
Accounts payable	40,000
Wages payable	9,000
Long-term bank loan, 8%	150,000
Common shares	300,000
Retained earnings	188,000

During 20x2 the following transactions occurred:

1. Two years before Dec. 31, 20x1, the company bought its equipment for cash, $340,000. The equipment was expected to last for eight years and have a residual value of $20,000.

2. On January 1, 20x2, the company paid $3,300 for a three-year fire insurance policy.

3. Purchased additional uniforms on credit for $120,000.

4. Sold uniforms for $160,000 on account. The inventory that was sold originally cost $95,000.

5. Performed cleaning for customers for a total of $520,000. One-quarter of the customers paid in cash and the remainder received their cleaning on account.

6. Received $580,000 from customers in settlement of amounts owed to the company.

7. Paid $130,000 to the suppliers to settle some of the accounts payable.

8. Paid $15,000 for advertising.

9. Paid $24,000 for utilities for the year.

10. Paid $102,000 for wages over the year. In December, the company still owed $8,500 to the employees for the last 10 days of work in December.

11. Received a $4,000 dividend from the investment.

12. Paid the interest on the bank loan for the year and paid $30,000 on the principal at the end of 20x2.

13. Amortized the equipment for the year.

14. Paid dividends of $20,000.

Required:

a. Prepare the journal entries to record the above transactions. Be sure to include the adjusting entries for the amortization of the equipment, the expiration of the insurance, and the amount of wages owed.

b. Create T-accounts. Enter the beginning balances from 20x1 and post the 20x2 transactions.

c. Prepare a trial balance.

d. Prepare an income statement and a balance sheet for 20x2.

e. Prepare the closing entries and post them to the T-accounts.

3-29 (Journalize, post, prepare an income statement and balance sheet, and prepare closing entries)
On the Go Pizza had the following account balances at December 31, 20x1:

Cash	$150,000
Accounts receivable	5,000
Supplies inventory	15,000
Prepaid rent	36,000
Equipment	60,000
Delivery vehicles	80,000
Wages payable	4,000
Common shares	200,000
Retained earnings	142,000

During 20x2, the following transactions occurred:

1. Sales of pizzas for cash, $480,000. Sales of pizzas on account, $50,000.

2. Purchase of ingredients for the pizzas and other supplies (supplies inventory), $220,000. All of these items were paid for.

3. During 20x2, supplies inventory valued at $215,000 was used.

4. During 20x2, the company paid $75,000 in wages.

5. During 20x2, $52,000 was used for other expenses.

6. Collected $52,000 on the accounts receivable.

7. At the end of 20x2, a dividend of $10,000 was declared and paid.

Adjusting entries:

8. Wages owed to employees at the end of the year were $2,000.

9. By the end of 20x2, half of the prepaid rent had been used.

10. The equipment had a useful life of eight years with no residual value at the end of the eight years. Record the amortization.

11. The delivery vehicles had a useful life of five years with a residual value of $5,000 at the end of the five years. Record the amortization.

Required:

a. Prepare journal entries for transactions 1 through 7. Create new accounts if necessary.

b. Create T-accounts. Enter the beginning balances from 20x1 and post the 20x2 transactions.

c. Prepare a trial balance.

d. Prepare journal entries for adjusting entries 8 through 11. Post these journal entries and prepare an adjusted trial balance.

e. Prepare an income statement and a balance sheet for 20x2.

f. Prepare the closing entries and post them to the T-accounts.

3-30 (Journal entries, trial balances, and closing entries)
Evergreen Retail Company had the following transactions. Assume that the fiscal year end of the company is December 31.

1. Borrowed $6,500 from the bank on January 1, 20x1.

2. Bought equipment on January 1, 20x1, for $12,000.

3. Purchases of inventory on account during 20x1 totalled $24,600.

4. Sales for the period totalled $34,500, of which $19,300 were on account. The cost of the products sold was $19,900.

5. Collections from customers on account totalled $17,700.

6. Payments to suppliers for the inventory totalled $18,800.

7. Employees were paid $6,300 during the year.

8. Dividends were declared and paid in the amount of $2,500.

9. Paid the interest on the bank loan on December 31, 20x1. The interest rate was 9%.

Adjusting entries (you may need to use information recorded in the first nine transactions):

10. The equipment purchased on January 1 has an estimated useful life of five years and an estimated residual value at the end of five years of $1,000. Record the amortization for the equipment as at December 31, assuming the company uses the straight-line method.

11. Wages in the amount of $400 were owed to employees at the end of the year. They will be paid early in 20x2.

Required:

a. Prepare journal entries for transactions 1 through 9.

b. Create T-accounts and post the 20x1 transactions.

c. Prepare a trial balance.

d. Prepare journal entries for adjusting entries 10 and 11. Post these journal entries and prepare an adjusted trial balance.

e. Prepare the closing entries and post them to the T-accounts.

3-31   (Journal entries, trial balances, and closing entries)
Genesis Sportswear Ltd. designs and manufactures sports clothing that it sells to various retail stores. It had the following transactions during its first period of operations. The fiscal year end of the company is December 31.

1. Issued common shares for $40,000.

2. Paid an insurance premium of $1,200 on July 1 that provides coverage for the 12-month period starting July 1.

3. Purchased $18,500 of material on account.

4. Paid $26,900 in wages to employees who designed and manufactured the clothing.

5. Sales recorded for the period totalled $85,000, all on credit.

6. Cash collections on customer accounts totalled $76,000.

7. Inventory costing $41,800 was sold (the total cost of making the clothing is the cost of the material used plus the cost of the wages of those who made the clothing).

8. Payments to suppliers for material purchased totalled $17,100.

9. Purchased some new sewing machines that cost $11,000. Paid cash.

10. Dividends of $1,300 were declared but not yet paid.

Adjusting entries (you may need to use information recorded in the first 10 transactions):

11. Recognize the amount of insurance expense that was used from July 1 through December 31.

12. Amortization of $4,500 was taken on the equipment (this includes amortization on the old sewing machines and the new ones).

Required:

a. Prepare journal entries to record transactions 1 through 10.

b. Create T-accounts and post the transactions.

c. Prepare a trial balance.

d. Prepare journal entries for adjusting entries 11 and 12. Post these journal entries and prepare an adjusted trial balance.

e. Prepare the closing entries and post them to the T-accounts.

3-32   (Adjusting entries)
The trial balance for Snowcrest Ltd. for December 31, 20x1, is presented below:

	Debit	Credit
Cash	$ 11,000	
Inventory	24,000	
Advances to salespersons	1,000	
Prepaid rent	5,000	
Office supplies	2,000	

Equipment	20,000	
Accumulated amortization, equipment		$ 4,000
Deposits from customers		1,500
Common shares		40,000
Retained earnings		7,500
Sales		220,000
Cost of goods sold	130,000	
Salespersons' commissions	35,000	
Office salaries	25,000	
Miscellaneous expense	15,000	
Dividends declared	5,000	
Totals	$273,000	$273,000

Adjusting entries:

1. The sales include deposits from customers of $2,000. As at December 31, the total deposits from customers should be $2,500.

2. Half of the advances to salespersons have been earned by December 31.

3. Office salaries owed at year end but not paid are $600.

4. Half of the prepaid rent was used in 20x1.

5. A count of the office supplies revealed that $500 was still on hand at year end.

6. Amortization on the equipment for 20x1 was $1,000.

7. Income tax for the year should be calculated using a tax rate of 25%. (*Hint*: you will have to determine income before income tax so that you have a basis on which to calculate the 25%. Remember that you have to calculate this amount after you finish the other adjusting entries.)

Required:
Prepare the adjusting entries.

3-33 (Adjusting entries)
The trial balance for Cozy Fireplaces Inc. for December 31, 20x1, is presented below:

	Debit	Credit
Cash	$ 109,000	
Accounts receivable	25,000	
Inventory	95,000	
Office supplies	7,500	
Prepaid rent	3,000	
Land	80,000	
Building	140,000	
Accumulated amortization, building		$ 20,000

Accounts payable		18,400
Deposits from customers		12,400
Bank loan, 8%, long-term		40,000
Common shares		150,000
Retained earnings		6,700
Sales		850,000
Cost of goods sold	480,000	
Salaries and wages	95,000	
Rent expense	43,000	
Miscellaneous expense	15,000	
Dividends declared	5,000	
Totals	$1,097,500	$1,097,500

Adjusting entries:

1. The sales include deposits from customers of $4,500. As at December 31, the total deposits from customers should be $15,500.

2. The bank loan was taken out on March 1, 20x1. The first instalment of interest is due on March 1, 20x2.

3. Salaries and wages owed at year end but not paid are $2,200.

4. Rent is paid in advance on the last day of the month. The $3,000 in prepaid rent represents the monthly rent for January 1, 20x1. At the end of January, 20x1, $3,000 was paid for the February rent and was debited directly to rent expense. All payments during the year were treated the same way. The rent for July to December increased to $4,000. (*Hint*: Rent expense of $43,000 includes five months at $3,000 and seven months at $4,000.)

5. A count of the office supplies revealed that $500 was still on hand at year end.

6. The building is being amortized over 24 years with a residual value of $20,000.

7. Income tax for the year should be calculated using a tax rate of 30%. (*Hint*: you will have to determine income before income tax so that you have a basis on which to calculate the 30%. Remember that you have to calculate this amount after you finish the other adjusting entries.)

Required:
Prepare the adjusting entries.

3-34 (Prepare income statement and balance sheet)
You have been retained by the Downunder Company to straighten out the company's accounting records. It seems that the company's trusted accountant for the past 25 years, Icabod Cranium, has just run off to the Bahamas. Unfortunately, in his rush, he seems to have misplaced the company's books. Now the bank is asking for the latest financial statements so it can determine whether or not to renew the company's loan. Luckily, you manage to find a listing of accounts and balances Cranium left on the back of a travel brochure:

Cash on hand (in third desk drawer)	$ 120	BS
Accounts receivable from customers	24,200	BS

Sales to customers *I/S*	71,500 ✓
Loan balance owed to Last National Bank *B/S*	15,000
Wages owed to employees (not yet paid) *B/S*	1,215
Cash in bank account *B/S*	725
Wage expense — *I/S*	3,500 ✓
Interest income *I/S*	515 ✓
Equipment *B/S*	51,500
Cost of inventory sold *I/S*	40,000 ✓
Inventory still on shelves *B/S*	8,900

Required:

a. Prepare an income statement for the end of the current year, 20x4.

b. Prepare a balance sheet as at December 31, 20x4.

3-35 (Effect of transactions on balance sheet accounts)
Ann and Greg Fenway run a small art gallery and custom framing business. Using the basic balance sheet accounts of assets, liabilities, and shareholders' equity, explain how each of these would be affected by the following transactions and activities:

a. The Fenways purchased five pictures for cash.

b. Framing materials are purchased on credit.

c. A loan from the bank is repaid (ignore interest).

d. A picture is sold for cash at an 80% profit.

e. A plaster statue falls from a shelf and is broken and discarded.

f. A receivable is collected on a major framing project completed last month for a local law office.

g. Payment is made for the framing materials previously purchased.

3-36 (Effect of transactions on balance sheet accounts)
Gagnon's Autobody Ltd. repairs and paints automobiles after vehicular accidents. Using the basic balance sheet accounts of assets, liabilities, and shareholders' equity, explain how each of these would be affected by the following transactions and activities:

a. Gagnon's Autobody purchases new spray painting equipment. The supplier has given the company 60 days to pay.

b. The company paid for one year's worth of liability insurance.

c. The company pays its employees for work done during a two-week period.

d. A car is repaired and repainted. The customer pays the $200 deductible required by her insurance and the remainder of the bill is sent to her insurance company.

e. Supplies such as paint, putty, etc., are acquired on credit.

f. Cash is collected from the customer's insurance company.

g. The company pays for the new spray painting equipment at the end of the 60 days.

3-37   (Prepare income statement)

Prepare an income statement, in proper form, from the following information concerning the results of Biggs & Company Ltd. (a company located in a part of Nova Scotia where earthquakes are not common but windstorms are) for the year ended December 31, 2004. The income tax rate is 40%.

Cost of goods sold	$ 125,000
Dividends declared	3,500
Dividend revenue	500
Gain on expropriation of land	6,000
Gain on sale of land	1,200
Interest expense	5,000
Loss due to earthquake damage	4,500
Loss from windstorm damage	2,300
Loss on discontinued operations	32,000
Operating expenses	45,000
Sales revenue	195,000

3-38   (Prepare balance sheet)

Prepare a classified balance sheet for Novasco Manufacturing Corporation as at December 31, 2004, based upon the following trial data at that date. Ignore income taxes.

	Debits	Credits
Accounts receivable	$ 107,000	
Administration and general expenses	55,000	
Cash	80,000	
Cost of goods sold	450,000	
Dividends declared	35,000	
Finished goods inventory	160,000	
Interest expense	25,000	
Loss on sale of equipment	1,900	
Prepaid insurance	3,000	
Property, plant, and equipment	280,000	
Raw materials inventory	55,000	
Selling expenses	95,500	
Temporary investments	85,000	
Work-in-process inventory	95,000	
Accounts payable		$ 75,000
Accrued salaries payable		28,000
Accumulated amortization		65,000
Common shares		150,000
Dividends payable		7,000
Interest revenue		10,000
Long-term debt		300,000
Retained earnings		117,400
Sales revenues		650,000
Short-term borrowings		125,000
	$1,527,400	$1,527,400

User Perspective Problems

3-39   (The year-end closing process)
The accounting system closing process takes some time at the end of the accounting period in order to check for errors, make adjusting entries, and prepare the financial statements. In recent years, there has been a real push to speed up this process for most companies. Discuss the incentives that companies might have to make this a faster process.

3-40   (Correction of errors and omissions revealed during the audit)
During the auditing process at year end, the auditing firm may find errors and omissions in the recording of transactions and will then ask management to make an adjusting entry to correct these errors. In light of the purpose of the audit opinion (see discussion in Chapter 1), discuss plausible arguments that management might give to convince the auditor to waive making these suggested adjustments.

3-41   (Understanding financial statement information)
Recently, a financial advisor was asked if his firm had recommended the purchase of **Enron** shares to its clients. (In 2001, Enron declared bankruptcy (to the surprise of many investors) and questions were raised about the accounting followed by the company and the credibility of the audit firm that performed the audit.) The financial advisor said that his firm had not advised any clients to buy Enron because the company was just too complex and, therefore, it was too difficult to read and understand the financial statements. He would not advise any clients to buy shares in a company in which it was not possible to analyze the financial information. Your knowledge of financial statements is still very limited. Even fairly simple financial statements are probably still overwhelming. Based on your limited knowledge, comment on the policy established by this financial advisor's firm. What are the advantages of following such a policy? Are there any disadvantages that you can think of?

3-42   (Revision of income statement amounts)
Leadfoot Al decided to retire from stock car racing and invest all his winnings in a fish farm. He had majored in genetics in college and experimented with many different species of fish before coming up with a catfish that had the texture and taste of ocean trout. Moreover, contacts from his previous profession made it possible for him to acquire feed for his unique form of fish at very low prices. After operating for two years, Al decided to explore expansion possibilities. He talked with his banker about getting a loan and presented an income statement for the past year, based strictly on cash flows, as follows:

Cash collected from sale of Al's Gourmet Fish		$520,000
Less: Feed purchases	$470,000	
Purchase of new fish tank	40,000	
Wages paid	70,000	580,000
Operating loss		(60,000)
Plus: Sale of land		120,000
Net income		$ 60,000

From discussions with Al, the banker learned the following:

- $120,000 of the cash collected from the sale of fish in the current period was from shipments delivered prior to the start of the year. All the sales this year were paid for prior to year end.

- The feed can be stored indefinitely, and about 40% of this year's purchases remains on hand at year end.

- Two fish tanks were purchased the previous year at a total cost of $80,000. These tanks, along with the one purchased at the beginning of this year, were used all year. Each tank is expected to last five years.

- The land sold for $120,000 had been purchased two years earlier for $55,000.

Required:

Provide Al and his banker with responses to the following:

a. Why is the matching concept important in this case?

b. What amount of revenue from the sale of merchandise should be included this period?

c. What amount of expense for fish food should be reported this period? How should the remainder of the food purchased be reported?

d. Should some amount for the fish tanks be included in calculating income for the current period? How much?

e. The land was sold for more than its original purchase price. This difference is called a gain and is usually included on the income statement. What is the amount of the gain on the sale of the land that should be included in income this period?

f. Should Al stay in the fish business or go back to auto racing? What factors other than the income calculations would be relevant to evaluating the potential future for Al's fish farm?

3-43   (Multistep income statement)
Northland Enterprises sells snowmobiles and recreational equipment and has reported the following revenues and expenses in 20x2:

Equipment sales	$6,500,000
Cost of parts and equipment sold	4,200,000
Wages and salaries	1,000,000
Sales of replacement parts	900,000
Revenue from labour charges for repair work	700,000
Income tax expense	730,000
Shipping and delivery costs	690,000
Property taxes	100,000
Interest expense on mortgage payable	90,000
Interest income on investments	70,000

Required:

a. Prepare a 20x2 multistep income statement for Northland Enterprises.

b. In 20x1, Northland reported net income of $1,050,000 and earned an 18% return on total revenue (net income divided by revenue). The goal for 20x2 was to earn income in excess of $1,150,000 and earn a 20% return on total revenue. What amounts were reported? Did Northland attain its goals in 20x2?

c. In setting its goals for net income and return on sales for future periods, what types of factors should Northland take into consideration?

Reading and Interpreting Published Financial Statements

3-44   (Income statement and balance sheet items)
Finning International Inc. "sells, rents, finances, and provides customer support services for Caterpillar and complementary equipment on three continents around the world." Refer to its 2001 income statement and balance sheet in Exhibit 3-30 and answer the following questions:

FINNING INTERNATIONAL INC. (2001)

EXHIBIT 3-30

PART A

For the years ended December 31 ($ in thousands, *except per share amounts*)

Consolidated Statements
of Income and Retained Earnings

	2001	2000
Revenue		
New mobile equipment	$ 896,466	$ 796,503
New power & energy systems	238,287	193,906
Used equipment	355,733	342,734
Equipment rental	691,202	166,770
Operating leases	95,715	98,451
Customer support services	956,313	842,244
Finance and other	13,327	19,424
Total revenue	3,247,043	2,460,032
Cost of sales	2,342,308	1,835,644
Gross profit	904,735	624,388
Selling, general and administrative expenses	634,939	461,059
Other expenses/(income) (Note 12)	18,226	(3,789)
Income before interest, income taxes, non-controlling		
interests and amortization of goodwill	251,570	167,118
Finance cost and interest on other indebtedness		
(Notes 8 and 9)	85,550	58,552
Income before provision for income taxes,		
non-controlling interests and amortization of goodwill	166,020	108,566
Provision for income taxes (Note 14)	29,021	33,320
Non-controlling interests (Note 6)	23,113	-
Amortization of goodwill (Note 7)	9,969	1,855
Net income available to shareholders	103,917	73,391
Retained earnings, beginning of year	521,569	502,028
Dividends on common shares	(15,155)	(15,452)
Premium on common share repurchase (Note 10)	(19,742)	(38,398)
Retained earnings, end of year	$ 590,589	$ 521,569
Earnings per share (Note 16)		
Basic	$ 1.37	$ 0.95
Diluted	$ 1.34	$ 0.94
Basic before amortization of goodwill	$ 1.50	$ 0.97
Diluted before amortization of goodwill	$ 1.47	$ 0.96
Weighted average number of shares outstanding	75,854,866	77,436,109

a. Has Finning International used a single-step or a multistep income statement? What aspects of the statement influenced your answer?

b. Explain why Finning International has two earnings per share amounts for each year.

c. Finning International has $1,494,935,000 in capital assets at the end of 2001. However, there is no separate disclosures on the income statement of amortization or depreciation expense of capital assets other than goodwill. In the cash flow statement, there are two line items in the operating section indicating that depreciation (of the buildings and equipment) and amortization of goodwill amounted to $308,533,000 and $9,969,000, respectively, in 2001. Explain why you do not see these expenses on the income statement.

EXHIBIT 3-30
PART B

FINNING INTERNATIONAL INC. (2001)

Consolidated Balance Sheets

As at December 31 ($ in thousands)

Assets	2001	2000
Current assets		
Accounts receivable and other	$ 513,599	$ 375,208
Inventories		
On-hand equipment	418,672	395,420
Parts and supplies	237,557	203,579
Current portion of instalment notes receivable	67,350	66,476
Total current assets	1,237,178	1,040,683
Finance assets		
Instalment notes receivable	70,468	72,569
Equipment leased to customers (Note 2)	233,375	253,949
Total finance assets	303,843	326,518
Rental equipment (Note 3)	776,832	311,019
Land, buildings and equipment (Note 4)	312,359	189,961
Investment (Note 5)	-	218,050
Future income taxes (Note 14)	2,825	7,465
Goodwill (Note 7)	405,744	63,945
	$ 3,038,781	$ 2,157,641

Liabilities		
Current liabilities		
Short-term debt (Note 8)	$ 372,360	$ 398,208
Accounts payable and accruals	758,009	495,239
Income tax payable	11,364	4,883
Current portion of long-term debt (Note 8)	132,986	67,224
Total current liabilities	1,274,719	965,554
Long-term debt (Note 8)	540,756	477,217
Future income taxes (Note 14)	22,443	16,414
Total liabilities	1,837,918	1,459,185

Non-controlling interests (Note 6)		
	425,000	-

Shareholders' equity		
Share capital (Note 10)	212,122	200,629
Retained earnings	590,588	521,569
Cumulative currency translation adjustments (Note 11)	(26,847)	(23,742)
Total shareholders' equity	775,863	698,456
	$ 3,038,781	$ 2,157,641

d. At the end of 2001, what percent of Finning International's total assets is invested in inventory? What kind of inventory does Finning International have?

3-45 (Income statement items)

Use **Sears Canada's** financial statements in Appendix A at the end of the book to answer the following questions:

a. Explain whether Sears prepares a single-step or multistep income statement.

b. Sears Canada lists its earnings per share as "Earnings per share" and "Fully diluted earnings per share." What do you think this means?

c. Identify the two largest assets in the balance sheet. Why is it reasonable that these two assets would be the largest?

3-46 (Income statement and balance sheet items)

Refer to the 2001 financial statements of **Brampton Brick Limited**, Exhibit 3-31, and answer the following questions:

BRAMPTON BRICK LIMITED (2001)

EXHIBIT 3-31
PART A

CONSOLIDATED STATEMENTS OF INCOME AND RETAINED EARNINGS

For the years ended December 31, 2001 and 2000 (in thousands of dollars, except per share amounts)	2001	2000
Net sales	$ 59,815	$ 47,828
Cost of sales, selling, general and administrative expenses	36,463	26,818
Depreciation and amortization	5,600	4,746
	42,063	31,564
Operating income before the undernoted items	17,752	16,264
Other income (expense)		
Interest on long-term debt	(1,085)	(306)
Other interest (expense) income – net	(40)	41
Equity income from Richvale York Block Inc. (note 3)	1,261	1,169
Other (expense) income	(141)	212
	(5)	1,116
Income before income taxes	17,747	17,380
Provision for income taxes (note 9)		
Current	3,476	4,992
Future	1,403	1,115
	4,879	6,107
Net income for the year	12,868	11,273
Retained earnings – Beginning of year	29,946	19,694
Premiums paid on repurchase of capital stock (note 7)	(600)	(1,021)
Retained earnings – End of year	$ 42,214	$ 29,946
Net income per Class A and B share (note 8)		
Basic	$ 1.20	$ 1.03
Fully diluted	$ 1.18	$ 1.03

BRAMPTON BRICK LIMITED (2001)

EXHIBIT 3-31

PART B

CONSOLIDATED BALANCE SHEETS

For the years ended December 31, 2001 and 2000 (in thousands of dollars)	2001	2000
Assets		
Current assets		
Cash and cash equivalents	$ 2,968	$ 802
Accounts receivable	7,014	7,199
Inventories	4,384	3,597
Other current assets	486	441
	14,852	12,039
Property, plant and equipment, at cost (note 2)	114,941	105,227
Less: Accumulated depreciation	(38,308)	(33,441)
	76,633	71,786
Other assets		
Investment in Richvale York Block Inc. (note 3)	7,477	7,361
Property held for sale	1,600	1,600
Investment in Futureway Communications Inc. (note 4)	2,000	2,000
Deferred start-up costs – net of accumulated amortization of $252 (2000 – $219)	–	33
	11,077	10,994
	$ 102,562	$ 94,819
Liabilities		
Current liabilities		
Bank operating advances (note 5)	$ 300	$ –
Accounts payable and accrued liabilities	7,732	11,604
Income taxes payable	923	1,465
Long-term debt, current portion (notes 5 and 6)	1,572	1,455
	10,527	14,524
Long-term debt, less current portion (notes 5 and 6)	10,362	12,019
Minority interest	150	119
Future income taxes (note 9)	6,684	5,281
	27,723	31,943
Shareholders' Equity		
Capital stock (note 7)	32,625	32,930
Retained earnings	42,214	29,946
	74,839	62,876
	$ 102,562	$ 94,819

a. Has Brampton Brick used a single-step or a multistep income statement? What aspects of the statement influenced your answer?

b. You will notice that Brampton Brick lists cost of sales, and selling, general, and administrative expenses together. Is it possible to determine a meaningful gross profit? Explain your answer.

c. Does Brampton Brick prepare a classified balance sheet? What aspects of the statement influenced your answer?

d. Identify the items on the balance sheet that appear to be noncurrent liabilities. What influenced your answer?

3-47 (Income statement items)
Use the 2001 statement of operations of **Intrawest Corporation** in Exhibit 3-32 to answer the following questions:

INTRAWEST CORPORATION (2001)

EXHIBIT 3-32

CONSOLIDATED STATEMENTS OF OPERATIONS

For the years ended June 30, 2001 and 2000
(in thousands of United States dollars, except per share amounts)

	2001	2000
Revenue:		
Ski and resort operations	$ 492,202	$ 447,350
Real estate sales	415,336	341,455
Rental properties	8,935	6,905
Interest and other income	3,547	12,449
Income from equity accounted investment	2,790	2,333
	922,810	810,492
Expenses:		
Ski and resort operations	383,864	353,662
Real estate costs	338,856	281,845
Rental properties	4,426	3,641
Interest (note 16)	44,490	35,217
Depreciation and amortization	57,934	51,399
Corporate general and administrative	9,793	7,985
	839,363	733,749
Income before undernoted	83,447	76,743
Provision for income taxes (note 13)	10,014	15,394
Income before non-controlling interest and discontinued operations	73,433	61,349
Non-controlling interest	9,904	9,258
Income from continuing operations	63,529	52,091
Results of discontinued operations (note 4)	(2,942)	(99)
Net income	$ 60,587	$ 51,992
Income per common share:		
Income from continuing operations	$ 1.45	$ 1.20
Net income	1.45	1.20
Weighted average number of common shares outstanding (in thousands)	43,665	43,362

a. Has Intrawest Corporation used a single-step or a multistep income statement? What aspects of the statement influenced your answer?

b. You will notice that Intrawest's first three revenues have three corresponding expenses listed by the same name. For each of these revenues, calculate the gross profit [(revenue − expense) / revenue] for 2001 and 2000. Has the gross profit increased, decreased, or stayed the same over the two years?

c. In 2000 and 2001, Intrawest had a loss from discontinued operations. Briefly explain what kind of activity results in an amount for discontinued operations. Why is this item reported at the very end of the income statement? It does not say that the discontinued operations amount is net of tax. Is it? Explain your reasoning.

d. In 2000 and 2001, Intrawest reports two earnings per share amounts. Explain why each of those earnings per share is important to users.

3-48 (Income statement items)

Use the statements of operations and retained earnings of **Big Rock Brewery Ltd.** in Exhibit 3-33 to answer the following questions:

EXHIBIT 3-33

BIG ROCK BREWERY LTD. (2001)

Consolidated Statements of Operations & Retained Earning

Years ended March 31

	2001 $	2000 $
	(Denominated in Canadian Dollars)	
Revenue		
Sales	32,238,035	31,707,142
Government taxes and commissions	(9,038,357)	(8,990,216)
	23,199,678	22,716,926
Cost of sales	9,240,503	9,154,929
Gross profit	13,959,175	13,561,997
Expenses		
Selling, general and administrative	10,176,689	9,415,955
Interest on long-term debt	451,921	481,400
Interest on short-term debt	91,998	36,360
Amortization	1,230,994	1,167,163
	11,951,602	11,100,878
Income before income taxes	2,007,573	2,461,119
Current income tax expense	198,000	42,000
Future income tax expense [note 8]	457,000	958,000
Net income for year	1,352,573	1,461,119
Retained earnings, beginning of year	6,551,550	5,975,448
Redemption of common shares [note 7]	(420,041)	(885,017)
Retained earnings, end of year	7,484,082	6,551,550
Net income per share [note 2]		
Basic and fully diluted	0.29	0.31

See accompanying notes

a. Has Big Rock Brewery used a single-step or a multistep income statement? What aspects of the statement influenced your answer?

b. Calculate the gross profit percentage (gross profit divided by sales less government taxes and commissions) for 2000 and 2001. Has the gross profit percentage increased or decreased?

c. Big Rock Brewery lists its earnings per share as "Basic and fully diluted." What do you think this means?

Beyond The Book

3-49   (Financial statement disclosures)
Find the annual report of a Canadian company that is listed on a Canadian stock exchange. Answer the following questions:

a. From the financial statements, discuss how important inventory is in relation to other assets on the company's balance sheet. Also address how important capital assets are to the company.

b. How does the company primarily finance its business (debt or equity)?

c. Does the company prepare a single-step or multistep income statement? How do you know?

d. Does the company have any unusual items, discontinued operations, or extraordinary items? If so, search through the information provided with the financial statements and explain why these items were classified in the manner they were.

e. Has the company prepared a classified balance sheet? Using the items in the balance sheet, explain what liquidity is and how it is used in the balance sheet.

f. How many directors does the company have? How old are they and what percentage of the board is female?

3-50   (Finding additional information about companies)
For the company you selected in problem 49, find at least three articles in the financial newspapers that discuss the nature of the markets for this company and the forecast of what the future may be for this sector of the economy. Write a short, one-page summary of your findings.

Cases

Additional Cases

3-51   Exploits Corporation

Exploits Corporation, a manufacturing facility located in Grand Falls, Newfoundland, had the following two events occur in 2001:

1. The company incurred damages of $200,000 resulting from a nearby river flooding. Since the river has not flooded in the past 50 years, Exploits carried no flood insurance and was therefore required to pay all the repair costs itself.

2. Two years ago the company purchased land in a local neighbourhood for $50,000. The property value has fallen dramatically due to general economic decline in the area and management has therefore decided to write down the value of the land to $25,000.

The management of Exploits Corporation is currently preparing its financial statements and would like to report both these events as extraordinary items. Discuss whether or not the company can record each of these events as extraordinary.

3-52   Peeble's Hardware

In January 2004, Mark Peeble, the owner of Peeble's Hardware, decided to expand the business by buying out a local lumberyard. To finance the purchase, Mark will have to obtain financing from a local bank. As support for the loan application, the bank has asked Mark to provide financial statements for the year ended December 31, 2003. Mark is very busy managing the store and has not made time to review the financial operations of the store over the last year.

When the bookkeeper provides Mark with the hastily prepared financial statements, Mark is pleasantly surprised to learn that the hardware store has had a significant increase in net income over the past year. He comments, "with financial results like these, we should have no trouble obtaining the bank loan."

In January 2004, the following transactions occurred:

1. Salaries of $20,000 were paid on January 2. A review of the time cards shows that the salaries relate to work performed in the last two weeks of December 2003.

2. On January 1, 2004, Mark repaid a $100,000 loan. The loan, a one-year, 10% term loan, was repaid in full including interest. No interest expense was recorded in 2003.

3. Peeble's received a bill for utilities on January 5, 2004, for $700. The bill was for the period ending December 31, 2003. The bill was recorded as an account payable in January 2004.

Mark is concerned that some of these transactions may affect the ability of Peeble's to obtain the necessary bank financing and has instructed the bookkeeper not to make any adjustments to the 2003 statements for these amounts.

Required

1. Calculate the overall effect of these transactions on Peeble's reported net income for 2003.

2. How should Mark proceed, given this information?

3. Does the bank have any responsibility to ensure that it is being provided with accurate financial information?

Charting a Course— When to Recognize Revenue

"An adventurous and realistic look at the world and how people travel through it," is what *Outpost* magazine strives to offer readers through real-life narratives of journeys off the beaten track. Since its launch in March 1996, the Toronto-based publication has grown from a quarterly to six issues per year and seen its circulation climb steadily to more than 28,000. But with all the variables involved in running a magazine, what does it take to keep the business running smoothly? With little prior experience in publishing, partners Chris Frey, Kisha Ferguson, and Matt Robinson quickly learned it pays to have a good grasp of accounting—including a revenue recognition policy that makes sense.

"Like most magazines, advertising is our principal source of revenue," explains Mr. Frey. "We always bill on a per-issue basis, even with long-term contracts. If we were to take payment too far in advance, that would create a liability if anything ever happened and we had to stop printing." Because the company only triggers a new set of invoices every eight weeks, it depends on those revenues to tide it over that two-month period. Still, because *Outpost's* advertisers can take anywhere up to 45 days or more to pay, the magazine has very little control over when the money actually comes in. Meanwhile, its principal suppliers—the printer, landlord, and contributors—all have to be paid.

With subscriptions, it makes more sense to count the amount for the entire subscription as revenue right away. "Although it's not on our revenue sheets, we have to make sure that somewhere on the books we indicate the liability—in other words, how much of the subscription remains unfulfilled," says

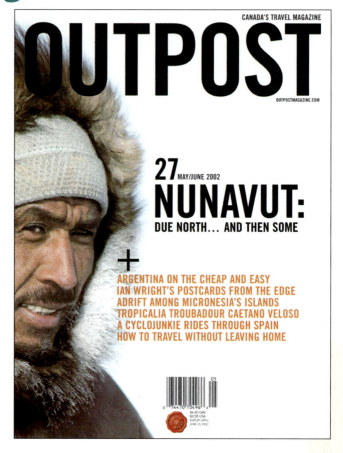

Mr. Frey. "Since subscriptions can begin and end with any issue, keeping track of things for each individual subscriber can be complicated for a small company like ours." As for newsstand sales, the company typically receives payment from distributors six months after an issue has gone out, based on the number of copies left over.

In 2001, *Outpost*, whose partnership has now grown to include an outside minority equity partner, also recorded revenue from its website, consumer shows, radio spots, and a pilot episode it produced for a television series. Whenever there's a bit of extra cash on hand, Mr. Frey and his partners try to invest in circulation promotions, although readership revenues are not that significant. "It's really quite simple," he says, "our number one focus is on continuing to grow the magazine while keeping our payables up-to-date."

REVENUE RECOGNITION

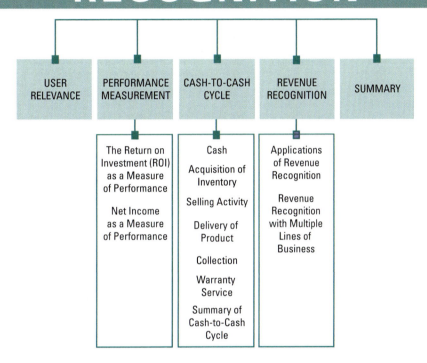

Learning Objectives:

After studying this chapter, you should be able to:

1. *Understand how return on investment can give you one measure of performance.*
2. *Calculate the return on investment under some basic scenarios.*
3. *Describe the cash-to-cash cycle of a retail company.*
4. *Explain the relationship between performance and revenue recognition.*
5. *Describe the criteria for revenue recognition.*
6. *Describe various applications of the revenue recognition criteria.*
7. *Calculate amounts to be recognized under the completed contract method and the percentage of completion method.*
8. *Explain the impact various revenue recognition methods have on earnings recognition.*

■ The opening story describes a new company that has three distinct forms of revenue: first, advertising revenue. *Outpost* has signed contracts from advertisers for the displaying of ads in future issues of its magazine. When should it recognize this revenue? It has chosen to send an invoice to the advertiser and recognize the revenue as each issue is published. This delays both the recognition of revenue and the receipt of cash from the advertiser. The second form of revenue is from individual subscribers. These people pay in advance. Subscriptions are of varying length and start at different times during the year. *Outpost* recognizes this revenue when it receives the subscription request and the money. However, it also recognizes that not all of this revenue should be included in an accounting period if the company must provide additional issues to the subscriber in the following period. The third form of revenue is from sales of magazines to distributors who supply retailers who sell individual copies. In this case, the company does not even know how much revenue it has earned until about six months after it sends the magazines to the distributor. It receives revenue from the number of issues sold and gets the unsold issues back from the distributor. *Outpost* has little choice here as to when to recognize the revenue. It must wait until it knows how much has been earned. In this chapter, we are going to provide you with some guidelines that companies can use when making decisions about when to recognize revenue.

In Chapters 1 through 3, the basic financial statements of a company were discussed. Two of those statements, the income statement and the cash flow statement, measure the performance of the company across some time horizon. In this chapter, some of the problems inherent in the measurement of performance are considered, and the accounting concepts and guidelines for the recognition of income are discussed. Chapter 5 discusses the cash flow statement and the measurement of performance using cash flows in more detail.

USER RELEVANCE

Why is knowledge about the **recognition** of revenue important to users? First, the revenue amount often represents the largest single amount on the financial statements. Total revenues need to be large enough to cover all of the other expenses. When users see that total revenues are greater than total expenses (the company has a positive net income), they take this as a signal that the company is viable, that it has the ability to take advantage of opportunities, and that it is growing. Companies can and do sometimes experience losses. This is a signal that all is not well with the company. When losses occur, it is important for users to evaluate both the size and cause of the loss. They need to observe the company over time to see how serious the problems are.

Users would also want to evaluate the quality of the earnings. All earnings must, at some time, translate into cash. Cash is essential to the ultimate survival of a company. We determine the quality of earnings by comparing the cash flow from operations (cash flow statement) with the net income. If these two amounts are moving together (both up or both down) and if the cash flow is greater than the net income, we consider the earnings to be of high quality. If the two amounts do not move together and if the cash flow is less than the net income, we consider the earnings to be of low quality.

The second reason users need to be aware of the revenue recognition policies of the company is that, as we have illustrated in our opening story, revenues earned by companies are not all the same. Sometimes cash is received at the time the revenue is recognized, sometimes it precedes it or comes after it. A company can have different revenue recognition policies associated with different types of revenue. Users need to be aware of the revenue recognition policies being used by the company so that they can make a judgement about the validity of the revenue amount being reported. Over the last several years, there have been occasional newspaper articles commenting on the revenue recognition policies used by many high-tech companies. Look at the following article:

accounting in the news

AUDITORS RESIGN BEFORE CERTIFYING STATEMENTS

The pressure to deliver a healthy financial picture to the investing world makes it hard for public companies to resist giving their revenue figures a boost.

High-tech companies received low marks for their revenue recognition and reporting methods in a 2001 review by the Ontario Securities Commission (OSC). The OSC, which issued its initial report after reviewing the annual reports of 75 companies, said its findings might even trigger some restated financial statements.

In its initial report, the OSC said it found instances of revenue recognition before products were sold; instances of products shipped and counted as revenue without accounting for returns; and some cases in which software contracts came with obligations such as maintenance or training, boosting revenue without including related expenses.

One of the major problems was the simple lack of information in the notes accompanying companies' financial statements that explain how a company accounts for its revenue—as required by the *Canadian Institute of Chartered Accountants Handbook*.

An OSC official said each public company the OSC oversees would be reviewed at least once every four years. The OSC also wanted feedback from the accounting profession so it can issue a final report giving companies guidance on revenue reporting.

Source: "The OSC gets tough on revenue reporting: Annual reports reviewed: 'There's a whole universe of issues to look at'," by Garry Marr, *National Post, Financial Post*, Mar. 19, 2001, p. C3.

As you will see later in this chapter, there are guidelines under GAAP for revenue recognition. Those guidelines can be applied in various ways. Even within the same industry, companies may choose to recognize the same type of revenue in a different manner. As a user, it is therefore very important to understand the implications on the financial statements of various revenue recognition policies and also to read the disclosures about revenue recognition that accompany the financial statements so that you can evaluate a company's performance.

PERFORMANCE MEASUREMENT

Learning Objective

1

Understand how return on investment can give you one measure of performance.

Let's have a closer look at how we can measure performance. After making an investment, investors generally want to know how well their investment is performing. To put this in a simple context, suppose an investment is made in a savings account at a bank. The money is put in the bank so that it can earn something and it is safe. Periodically, statements are received from the bank that detail any new deposits or withdrawals and any interest earned on the savings. The interest earned can then be compared with the balance in the account to give an indication of the performance of the investment. The comparison of the interest earned to the balance in the account is called a ratio. Ratios can help us assess performance.

The Return on Investment (ROI) Ratio as a Measure of Performance

A common measure of performance used in business is a ratio called the **return on investment (ROI)**, which is generally calculated as follows (in Chapter 12 we will discuss several other ratios that also calculate returns):

$$\text{ROI} = \frac{\text{Return}}{\text{Average investment}}$$

Learning Objective

2

Calculate the return on investment under some basic scenarios.

In the case of the bank account, the numerator is the interest earned during the period, and the denominator is the average amount invested over the time period. By averaging the denominator, additional deposits or withdrawals made during the period are taken into account. A simple average of the beginning balance and the ending balance in the investment is often used; however, more sophisticated averaging methods may be more appropriate. Suppose the average investment in a bank account was $1,000, and the return was $50. The ROI from the investment would be:

$$\text{ROI} = \frac{\$50}{\$1,000} = 5\%$$

Based on this return, two questions might be asked: (1) is this a good return on investment? and (2) how confident is the investor that this really is the return?

To answer Question 1, the return on this investment should be compared with the returns that could have been earned on other, alternative investments, or with the returns that other, similar investors are earning. If the next best alternative would have returned only 4%, the bank account was a good investment. If, however, other similar investors are earning 6.5% for investments of similar risk, it would seem that the best investment was not made.

To answer Question 2, the investors must assure themselves that their $1,000 investment plus their $50 return is really worth $1,050 today. Ultimately, the only way to be sure that the investment is worth $1,050 is to sell the investment; that is, to withdraw the $1,050 from the bank. If the investors do not sell the investment, there is still some chance that the bank will not have the money to repay them; the bank might, for example, file for bankruptcy. In the late 1980s and early 1990s, this was not an inconceivable event, as several small Canadian banks went out of business. In banks insured by the Canada Deposit Insurance Company (CDIC), small accounts (those up to $60,000) are insured so that, even in the event of a bank collapse, the investor would still be repaid by the CDIC. A bank account of this type is about as safe an investment as can be made. An uninsured account would not give the same comfort level with regard to the failure of the banking institution.

Now suppose that instead of investing in a savings account, an investment is made in a house. Assume that the house is bought for investment purposes for $200,000. The buyer is hoping the value of the property will rise. Assume also that there are no further cash outlays or inflows during the year from this investment. To assess the return on the investment, the value of the investment at the end of the period must be determined. This value could be estimated by getting an appraisal of the house by a real estate agent, or by comparing the house with other comparable houses in the area that have recently sold. The selling prices of those houses could serve as a basis for estimating the value of the investment. In either case, the value will be an estimate. Confidence in these estimates will surely be lower than the confidence in the return earned from the investment in the savings account at the bank. In fact, the only certain way to determine the return on the house would be to sell it. If the investor does not want to sell the property, however, the only alternative would be to use an estimate of the selling price to measure performance. If the investor estimates the selling price to be $225,000, the ROI will be:

$$\text{ROI} = \frac{\$225{,}000 - \$200{,}000}{\$200{,}000} = 12.5\%$$

Measuring the performance of a business is much like estimating the return on the investment in a house. The business makes investments in capital assets (property, plant, and equipment), inventory, accounts receivable, and other assets, and periodically measures the performance of these investments. However, it does not want to sell its investment in these assets at the end of every accounting period simply to determine the proper ROI. It must, therefore, estimate any changes in the value of its assets and liabilities that may have occurred during the accounting period, and report these as net income. We then use that net income amount to calculate a couple of ROIs that you will see later in the book. The first is a return on assets (ROA). This ratio measures the amount of income earned per $1 of assets. It attempts to provide the user with information about how effectively the assets are being used to generate income. A second ratio is the return on equity (ROE). This ratio measures the amount of income earned per $1 invested in shares in the company. It provides users with information about the amount of return being earned by shareholders. They can compare this ROE with investments of other types and risks to determine if investing in this company is still a good idea.

Some of the changes in value (returns) are easy to measure, such as the interest earned on a savings account. Other changes, such as the change in the value of property, plant, and equipment, are not as easily measured, as the example concerning the investment in a house demonstrates. Because accounting data should be reliable as well as relevant (in Chapter 1 we discussed these terms), accountants have established concepts and guidelines for recognizing the changes in value of assets and liabilities to ensure that the measure of performance most commonly used (net income) provides a reliable measure of the effects of the transactions that took place during the period.

Net Income as a Measure of Performance

The income statement attempts to measure the return to the shareholders on their investment in the company; that is, it measures changes in shareholders' wealth in the company. The accounting value of this shareholders' wealth is measured by the value of shareholders' equity accounts. Remember that these accounts include common shares and retained earnings.

Shareholders' equity accounts are typically affected by three general types of transactions: shareholder investment activities, the declaration of dividends, and transactions that result in profits or losses. Shareholders may invest more money in the company by buying, for example, new shares when they are issued. This does not directly affect their return on the investment, but does affect the amount of investment they have in the company. Second, shareholders may declare themselves a dividend (via a vote by the board of directors), which reduces their wealth in the company by reducing the total assets of the company. This also does not directly affect the return on investment, but again affects the amount of the investment. Finally, those transactions that result in profits or losses will affect shareholders' wealth through their effects on retained earnings. It is this last set of transactions and their impact on value that are measured by the income statement.

Because the company does not want to sell its investments each period to determine its performance, some concepts and guidelines have been developed to show how estimates of changes in value can be determined. These guidelines and concepts are sometimes called revenue recognition principles. To understand them, it is useful to understand the corresponding relationship between the cash-to-cash cycle of the company and the estimation of changes in value. The cash-to-cash cycle of a typical retail company is used as an illustration.

CASH-TO-CASH CYCLE

Learning Objective
3

Describe the cash-to-cash cycle of a retail company.

As we have seen, corporate managers engage in three general types of activities: financing, investing, and operating. Let us focus for a moment on operating activities.

Operating activities include all of the normal, day-to-day activities of every business, which almost always involve cash. Operating activities include the normal buying and selling of goods and/or services for the purpose of earning profits, for which the business was created. The typical operation of a business involves an outflow of cash that is followed by an inflow of cash, a process commonly called the **cash-to-cash cycle**. In Exhibit 4-1, the cash-to-cash cycle of a typical retail company is shown. Each phase in the cash-to-cash cycle is discussed in the following subsections.

CASH-TO-CASH CYCLE OF A RETAIL COMPANY

EXHIBIT 4-1

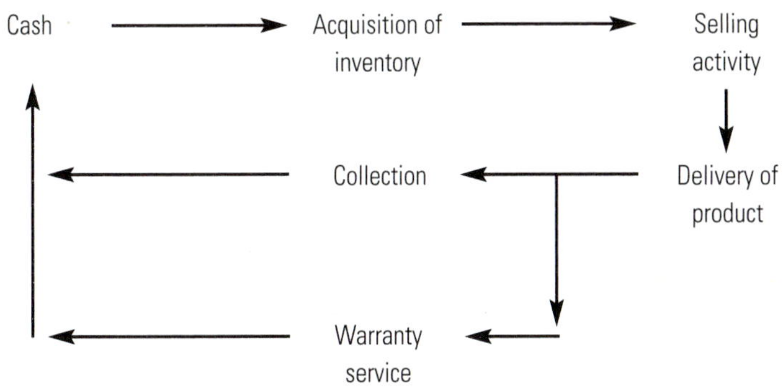

Cash ⟶ Acquisition of inventory ⟶ Selling activity ⟶ Delivery of product ⟶ Warranty service ⟶ Collection ⟶ Cash

Cash

We have already discussed how the initial amount of cash in a company comes from the initial investment by shareholders and from any loans that the company may have taken out to provide the initial financing. In Chapter 12, the difference between the return on the investment made by the shareholders and the investment made by the lenders is considered; at this point, however, no distinction will be made between them. To simplify matters, you might think of the company as being totally financed by shareholders; that is, there are no loans.

Acquisition of Inventory

Before the company acquires the inventory needed to sell to customers or to provide its services, it must first undertake the investing activities of acquiring property, plant, and equipment. Next, labour is hired and the first shipments of inventory are purchased (or contracts are signed to acquire them). Note that in a retail company, the costs involved in this initial phase may be larger than those of a service-oriented company. If you visualize even a small retail store, the amount of inventory that must be purchased to initially fill the shelves can be substantial.

Selling Activity

The selling phase includes all those activities designed to promote and sell the product. These may include pricing the product, advertising the product, hiring and managing a sales force, establishing retail sales outlets, contracting with agencies, signing supply agreements, and attending trade shows, among other activities. The end results of this phase are sales contracts between the buyer and seller. These may be verbal agreements or formal written documents. For most retail outlets selling to customers, the agreement occurs when the goods are paid for in the sales outlet (the store). Some retail outlets, however, sell to other businesses or to large enterprises such as hospitals or schools. For these sales, it is more likely that a formal contract is drawn up specifying prices, times of delivery, and methods of payment.

Delivery of Product

Once a sales contract has been agreed upon, the product must be delivered to the customer. Depending on the type of product, this may be instantaneous (as in a grocery store), or it may take months (as with a car dealership). Some sales contracts require periodic deliveries of inventory (as with fresh produce to a hospital).

Collection

Upon delivery of the product, collection of the sales price in cash may be immediate, as in a grocery store, or it could take place at some later date, resulting in an amount owing at the time of delivery, which is called an **account receivable**. Payment at a later date is the same as the seller making a loan to the buyer and accepting the risk that the buyer will not pay (this is called credit risk). The loan to the buyer may carry explicit interest charges, but usually no interest is charged if payment is made within a specified short period of time (typically 30 to 60 days). If the buyer does not pay within the specified period of time, the seller may try to obtain the product back (repossession) or may try other methods to collect on the account, such as turning it over to a collection agency.

Other events could also occur that would affect the collection of cash. The goods may be returned for various reasons, resulting in no cash collection. The goods may be damaged in shipment, and the buyer may ask for a price adjustment (generally called a **price allowance**). There may also be an incentive built in to encourage prompt payment of cash, such as a **cash discount**, which means that less than the full amount will be accepted as full payment. For example, a seller may offer a 2% price discount if the account is paid within 10 days instead of the usual 30 days. These terms are sometimes stated as "2/10 net 30," which means that a 2% discount is offered if payment is made within 10 days; otherwise, the total amount is due at the end of 30 days.

Warranty Service

Some goods carry a written or implied guarantee of quality. Automobiles, for example, are warranted for a certain number of years or for a certain number of kilometres. During this period, the seller is responsible, to some extent, for replacement or repair of the product. Because the provision of warranty work often involves additional outlays of cash for employees' time and for the purchase of repair parts, warranty service affects the ultimate amount of cash that is available at the end of the cycle.

Summary of the Cash-to-Cash Cycle

The net amount left in cash after this cycle is completed is then available to purchase more goods and services in the next cycle. If the cash inflows are less than the cash outflows, the amount of cash available is reduced, and the company may be unable to begin a new cycle without getting additional cash from outside the company in the form of equity or debt. To the extent that cash inflows exceed cash outflows, the company can expand its volume of activity, add another type of productive activity, or return some of the extra cash to shareholders in the form of dividends.

Note that the order of the phases in the cash-to-cash cycle may be different from one company to the next. For example, a transportation contractor such as Bombardier may do most of its selling activity early in the cycle to obtain contracts to deliver products at a future date, with much of the acquisition of raw materials and production taking place after the contract is signed. Also, in some companies, the separate phases may take place simultaneously. In Safeway, for example, the delivery of goods to the customer and the collection of cash take place at the same time.

REVENUE RECOGNITION

Managers do not want to wait until the end of the cash-to-cash cycle to assess the performance of their company, because they must make day-to-day decisions that will ultimately affect the final cash outcome. If they wait until the end, they may not be able to make appropriate adjustments. For example, if the first few items sold result in significant uncollected accounts or require significant warranty service, they might want to rethink their policies on granting credit and providing warranties. If the cost of warranty service is too high, they might also want to purchase a better quality of inventory so that the products last longer. Furthermore, the cash-to-cash cycle is a continual process that is constantly beginning and ending for different transactions. There is no specific point in time at which all of the cash-to-cash transactions reach an end.

Learning Objective
4

Describe the relationship between performance and revenue recognition.

To measure operating performance as accurately as possible, accountants divide normal operating activities into two groups, called revenues and expenses. **Revenues** are the inflows of cash or other assets from the normal operating activities of the business, which usually involve the sale of goods or provision of services. **Expenses** are the costs incurred to earn revenues. The difference between revenues and expenses, called **net income**, is one of the key measurements of performance. The expression "in the red" is related to net income. In the past, if a company had a negative net income (expenses > revenues), the net loss figure was actually written in red ink. The expression came to mean that a company had experienced a loss. Similarly, but less commonly used, the expression "in the black" meant that you had a positive net income.

The need for timely information to make decisions argues for recognizing revenue as early as possible in the cash-to-cash cycle. The earlier in the cycle revenue is recognized, however, the greater the number of estimates needed to measure the net performance. For example, if the company chooses to recognize revenue at the time of delivery of the product to customers (a common practice for many businesses), it will have to make estimates regarding the collectibility of the receivables, the possibility of returns, and the costs of warranty service. To measure the return (profitability) on the sale of a product accurately, these items should be considered; otherwise, the company may be overestimating the return on the sales of its products. To produce the most accurate measurement of net operating performance, all costs incurred to earn revenues are matched to the revenues they helped earn. In accrual accounting, this is called the **matching principle** (refer to Chapter 2). The matching principle requires that all costs incurred or to be incurred (in the past, present, or future) to produce the revenue must be recognized in the same period as the revenue is recognized.

The question of when to recognize revenue is quite straightforward for some industries (i.e., clothing retailers). Revenue is recognized when the customer buys the goods in the store. Normally customers pay cash or use a debit or credit card, which means that the collection of cash for the sale is not an issue. There are no warranty costs to consider. Returns are often handled by giving the customer another article of clothing, if one is available, or the value of the returned clothing as a credit to buy a different article. Clothing stores also usually put a time frame on returns (typically customers have two weeks to return merchandise), which means the issue of returns is a known quantity very quickly. For other industries, the decision is not as clearly defined. For a manufacturing company like Bombardier, contracts are signed, merchandise such as a train car is manufactured, the merchandise is delivered, money is collected from the customer (usually some time after delivery), and warranty services are provided on the merchandise sold. When should such a company recognize revenue—when the contract is signed, when the goods are delivered, when the cash is collected, or when the warranty period expires such that all obligations with respect to the sale have been satisfied?

The earlier in the cash-to-cash cycle the company chooses to recognize revenues, the less reliable is the company's estimate of the effects of future events. In return, however, the company receives more timely information. To reduce the uncertainty inherent in estimating future events, the company would need to recognize revenues later in the cash-to-cash cycle when those estimates are more reliable, but the information would be less useful for making management decisions. The decision about when to recognize revenue is a very important one for managers. Knowing about the revenue recognition policy is also important for users so that they can assess the reliability of the information.

There is obviously a conflict between the desire to measure performance on a timely basis (early in the cycle), and the ability to measure performance reliably (late in the cycle). **Revenue recognition criteria** have been developed within GAAP to resolve this conflict, and to produce a measure of performance that is intended to balance the need for timely information with the need for reliable information. The issue is further complicated when the company is involved in two or more lines of business in which the cash-to-cash cycles may differ. A revenue recognition policy must be developed for each line and they may not be the same.

AN INTERNATIONAL PERSPECTIVE

Reports from Other Countries

In countries other than Canada, income recognition may be based on different attributes. For instance, in Mexico, Argentina, Brazil, and the Netherlands, income is determined on a current-cost basis; that is, net income reflects adjustments of the inventory and property, plant, and equipment to their current replacement costs. The following excerpt from the annual report of **Grupo Bimbo, S.A.** (a Mexican company that produces, distributes, and markets breads, cakes, cookies, candy, chocolates, snacks, and processed foods) illustrates the income recognition principles:

> The companies restate all of their financial statements in terms of the purchasing power of the Mexican peso as of the end of the latest period, thereby comprehensively recognizing the effects of inflation.
>
> Costs and expenses associated with nonmonetary items [items that change value as the economic environment changes] are restated as follows:
> - Cost of sales is restated . . . based on the replacement costs [of the inventory] at the time of sale.
> - Depreciation is calculated on the restated value of the corresponding property, plant, and equipment.
> - Expenses associated with nonmonetary items are restated through year end, as a function of the restatement of the nonmonetary assets that are being consumed or sold.

Source: Grupo Bimbo, S.A. 2000 financial statements.

There are three specific factors considered before a revenue can be recognized. The first factor is whether the revenue has been **earned**. A revenue is considered to have been earned when the company has substantially completed what it must do to be entitled to the benefits of the revenue. This is sometimes referred to as "the earnings process being substantially complete." In general, this would mean that the company has completed most of what it agreed to do and there are very few costs yet to be incurred in the cash-to-cash cycle, or that the remaining costs are subject to reasonable estimation, or both. Another way to consider this factor is to determine if all of the risks and rewards of the goods or service have been transferred to the buyer. If they have, there can be very little left for the seller to do.

The second factor to consider is whether it is possible to measure how much has been earned. This is often a straightforward matter. When goods or services are sold for cash or an agreed selling price, the **measurement** issue is easy to determine. Sometimes, however, goods or services are sold in exchange for other products, services, or assets (other than accounts receivable). Now the measurement problem is more difficult. The accountant must examine the value of the goods or services sold and compare them with the value of the products, services, or assets received. In deciding which of these values to use, the accountant will look for the most reliable amount, the amount which can be most objectively determined.

The third factor is that there must be reasonable assurance that the amounts earned can be collected from the buyer. If cash is tendered at the time of sale, this third factor is automatically satisfied. If, however, the goods or services are sold on credit, the seller must be reasonably assured that the amount that is owed will be collected. Companies will rarely sell goods or services on credit without a credit check on the buyer. This is to provide assurance of the probable future collection of the accounts receivable. Even with this assurance, it is possible that some customers will not pay the amounts owed. Because of this possibility, companies that recognize credit sales as revenue must, in the same period, recognize an expense that measures the probable uncollectibility of the accounts receivable. This is to keep the revenues from being overstated. We call this expense "bad debt expense." More will be said about this expense in Chapter 6.

Learning Objective

5

Describe the criteria for revenue recognition.

REVENUE RECOGNITION CRITERIA

1. The revenue has been earned. (The company has completed substantially everything it has to do with respect to the sale.)
2. The amount earned can be measured.
3. There is reasonable assurance of collectibility of the amount earned.

In conclusion, if revenues have been earned, the amounts earned can be measured, and there is reasonable assurance that they will be collected, they should be recognized in the financial statements. These conditions are usually met at the time of delivery of the product to the customer, so this is the point at which many companies recognize their revenues. The following sections discuss various applications of revenue recognition, including at the point of sale to the customer as well as at other points on the cash-to-cash cycle.

Learning Objective

6

Describe various applications of the revenue recognition criteria.

Applications of Revenue Recognition

The revenue recognition criteria can be met at different points on the cash-to-cash cycle. Therefore, the point at which different companies recognize revenues varies, as you observed in the opening story about *Outpost* magazine. Several different applications that you will see in practice are discussed in the following subsections.

Revenue Recognition at the Time of Sale

The most common point at which revenues are recognized is the time of sale and/or shipment of goods to the customer. Once the goods have been taken by or shipped to the customer, the company has completed everything that it has to do with respect to the transaction. The title to the goods has been transferred and the revenue has been earned. The first criterion has been met. At the time of sale, the amount that is earned is known. Often the customer will pay cash, which is easy to measure. If the company sells the goods on credit, the amount owed is still fairly easy to determine, which means the second criterion is met. Lastly, the company will have to be reasonably assured of collection of the account receivable before revenue can be recognized. Most companies will not sell on credit if they have doubts about the future collectibility of the amount.

Outpost magazine recognizes two of its revenues at the time of sale. For *Outpost*, the time of sale occurs when an issue of the magazine is completed and sent to subscribers and distributors. At this point, it has completed the earning process on that issue. It recognizes the revenue from individual subscribers and the revenue from advertisers on a per-issue basis. Prior to the issuance of a magazine, it knows how much it has earned because subscribers have paid in advance and advertisers have signed a contract that outlines how much will be paid for advertisements in each issue. The only unknown at the point of sale is whether the advertisers will pay when they receive the bill from the magazine. The company would need to estimate the likelihood of uncollectibility of its advertising revenue.

In annual reports, most companies state their revenue recognition policy as part of the first footnote, which includes a summary of the company's significant accounting policies. For example, in its 2001 financial statements, **Corel Corporation** states its revenue recognition policy in Note 1 to the financial statements:

COREL CORPORATION (2001)
SOFTWARE REVENUE RECOGNITION

The Company recognizes revenue from packaged software and licence fees when the software is delivered, there is persuasive evidence that an arrangement exists, the fee is fixed and determinable, and collection is probable. Sales to distributors are subject to agreements allowing various rights of return and price protection. The Company establishes provisions for estimated future returns, exchanges, and price protection. Where telephone support is included for a limited time (post contract support or "PCS," generally for 90 days) together with the licence fee, the entire licence fee is recognized upon delivery of the product and the insignificant costs to provide the support are accrued. Where support is provided together with an annual licensing fee, the entire fee is deferred and recognized ratably over the term of the licence agreement since the Company does not have vendor specific objective evidence of fair-market value of this PCS. Revenue from professional services and other services are recognized as the services are delivered.

This is a very detailed statement from Corel. Because it creates and distributes software, there is often additional support, short-term or long-term, that occurs after the sale. Remember the matching concept. For short-term support, it recognizes all of the fee revenue on delivery of the product. The subsequent cost of the support is considered to be insignificant so it is accrued as it occurs. For annual contracts, the licence fee is deferred and recognized over the year in equal instalments. Like *Outpost*, Corel has different types of revenue and must establish different revenue recognition policies to recognize them.

If a company's revenue is very homogeneous, it will only need a simple statement about revenue recognition. **Sleeman Breweries Ltd.**, in Note 2 to its 2001 financial statements, has the following statement: "Revenue is recognized upon delivery of product to the customer." Sleeman Breweries manufactures and sells beer. It has a single source of revenue which does not require lengthy disclosure.

Sometimes when you read a description of a company's revenue recognition policy, you will see reference to the term "F.O.B." "F.O.B." means "free on board" and is a legal term used to describe the point at which title to the goods passes. It is used by companies like Sleeman Breweries that deliver goods to customers. If the goods are shipped *F.O.B. shipping point*, the title passes after the goods leave the seller's loading dock (the shipping point). If they were shipped *F.O.B. destination*, the goods would remain the property of the seller until they reached their destination, the buyer's receiving dock. The way the goods are shipped will affect the point at which revenue can be recognized. The point at which title to the goods passes is a clear indication that the seller has earned the revenue. Prior to that point, the seller is still responsible for the goods.

To illustrate revenue recognition at the time of sale, assume that Hawke Company sells 1,000 units of its product during the year 20x1 at $30 per unit. Assume further that the costs of these units totalled $22,000 and that, at the time of sale, Hawke estimated they would cost the company an additional $500 in warranty expenses in the future. The income statement for Hawke for 20x1 would appear as in Exhibit 4-2.

EXHIBIT 4-2

■ **REVENUE RECOGNITION AT TIME OF SALE**

HAWKE COMPANY
Income Statement
For the period ended December 31, 20x1

Revenues	$30,000
Cost of goods sold	22,000
Gross profit	8,000
Warranty expense	500
Net income	$ 7,500

Note that although Hawke Company may not have incurred any actual warranty expenses yet, it recognizes an expense equal to its estimate of what the future warranty costs might be. Recognizing the warranty expense is appropriate because the future warranty costs are directly related to the revenue. Therefore, if the company wants to recognize the revenue before it knows the actual warranty cost, it must estimate what those costs might be so that the revenue is not overstated. At the same time as it recognizes the warranty expense, it recognizes a liability for these future costs. When actual costs are incurred, the liability is reduced and no further expense is recognized.

In some cases, a company might receive a deposit on an order for a product to be delivered in the future. Because it is unlikely that the revenue recognition criteria would be met by this transaction (until the product is delivered, the company has *not* earned the revenue), the revenue from this order would not be recorded until the goods are delivered (title passes). The deposit is therefore recorded as revenue received in advance or unearned revenue (a liability account that represents an obligation either to deliver the goods or to return the deposit). For example, if Hawke Company received a $500 deposit on an order, it would make the following entry:

A-Cash	500	
L-Unearned revenue		500

When the goods are delivered, the liability to provide the product is satisfied (the company has completed what it had to do with respect to completing the sale), and the deposit can then be recognized as a revenue with the following entry:

L-Unearned revenue	500	
SE-Sales revenue		500

Businesses that require deposits or advance payments on products or services may disclose this in their footnote on revenue recognition. Typical disclosures for this type of situation are shown here for **WestJet Airlines Ltd.** (2001). Note that liabilities are created for the obligation to provide the service or product in the future.

WESTJET AIRLINES LTD. (2001)

1. Significant Accounting Policies
c) Revenue recognition:
Passenger revenue is recognized when air transportation is provided. The value of unused tickets is included in the balance sheet as advance ticket sales under current liabilities.

Users should be aware of one other aspect of revenue recognition: sales returns. In many retail stores, customers are allowed to return merchandise. Usually a time period is specified—10 days, one month, etc. When goods are returned, the company either returns the amount paid or provides the customers with a credit that allows them to buy new merchandise. Technically, the company should take into consideration the cost of possible returns when it recognizes revenue, otherwise the revenue may be overstated. In reality, the time period in which returns are allowed is usually short, which means that the revenue is not materially misstated if the returns are recorded when they happen. For companies that sell to other companies, business-to-business sales, the amount of returns can be substantial. For example, in the book-selling business, publishers often accept back from booksellers the books that have not been sold. This can result in a substantial amount of returns depending on how well a book has sold. If such companies want to recognize revenue when they ship books to a bookseller, they must estimate the probable extent of the returns and recognize that amount when the revenue is recognized. The issue of returns has been particularly problematic for companies that sell through the Internet. Note the following example:

accounting in the news

E-TAIL RETURNS

Returns have always been a common source of frustration among traditional retailers. Today, as consumers discover the conveniences of cyber-shopping, on-line retailers are coping with the challenges of cyber-returns.

In certain sectors of the e-tail industry, such as the apparel and shoe business, the problem is compounded by consumers who overcome the lack of a changing room by buying the same pair of pants in different sizes, for example, and keeping the ones that fit the best. The rest go back to the retailer.

One retail consultant says apparel return rates can be as high as 30 percent of on-line sales, and shoe return rates even higher. The return rate for the same items purchased in stores might be 10 percent or less.

Hbc.com, the on-line sales site for Hudson's Bay Co., which owns The Bay and Zeller's, carries very few items of apparel or shoes, a deliberate effort to avoid the problem. The site's overall return rate is about 10 to 15 percent of sales, similar to those of a catalogue business.

But for items that do not need to be tried on or do not offer colour choices, return rates are closer to 5 percent, according to industry observers—not so different from rates at traditional bricks-and-mortar stores.

Source: "Merchants learn to cope with new world of cyber-returns," by Marina Strauss, *The Globe and Mail*, Feb. 8, 2002, p. B11.

Revenue Recognition at the Time of Contract Signing

Even though the point of sale, or more correctly, the point at which title to the product is transferred to the buyer from the seller, is the most common method used to recognize revenues, several situations exist that require exceptions to this application of revenue recognition. Over the years, certain types of transactions have caused concern among investors and accountants because of the revenue recognition practices employed. Two of those were in the areas of franchising and retail land sales. Both of these industries initially recognized revenues at the date of contract signing. In the case of franchisors, this contract was the initial franchise agreement. In the case of retail land sale companies, it was the land sale agreement.

The problem was that, in both cases, a considerable amount of uncertainty existed with regard to future costs on the seller's part subsequent to contract signing, and to the collectibility of the receivables from buyers. Questions were raised as to whether any of the revenue recognition criteria were being met.

The uncertainty stemmed from industry practices. Franchisors (such as McDonald's) typically agree to provide a significant amount of service, such as assistance in locating and designing the franchise facility and in training the staff, subsequent to the signing of a franchise agreement and prior to the opening of the business. Therefore, at the time of contract signing, is the earning process complete? In addition, the initial franchise fee is typically paid in instalments, which raises questions about the reasonableness of future collectibility.

Retail land sale companies often sell land before it is developed and therefore have yet to incur the development costs. This means that the seller has not completed all of the things that must be done; the earning process is not substantially complete. There is also the problem of matching the future development costs to the revenues. Remember that if you want to recognize revenue before all of the costs associated with the sale are incurred (note the warranty example), you must be able to estimate those future costs so that they can be recognized at the same time as the revenue (matching). Sales contracts typically require low down payments and sometimes below-market interest rates to entice buyers to sign contracts. These conditions make it relatively easy for a buyer to back out of the transaction before all the cash is collected, thereby negating the sale.

Given the fact that the earning process was rarely complete, coupled with the uncertainties with regard to future costs and the collectibility of the receivables, revenue for franchisors and retail land sale companies is now recognized at the time of contract signing only if certain minimum criteria are met. These criteria require, first, that there be only minimal costs yet to be incurred (this means that the seller has completed substantially all of the things that have to be done to conclude the sale), and, second, that the receivables created in the transaction have a reasonable chance of being collected. These industries have special accounting guidelines because of the special nature of the activities surrounding revenue recognition. The following excerpts from the financial statements of **Comac Food Group Inc.** and **Intrawest Corporation** typify the revenue recognition policies of franchisors and land sale companies.

COMAC FOOD GROUP INC. (2001)

Franchise revenue

Income from the sale of franchised stores is recognized when the franchise commences store operations. Revenue received for franchised store locations not open at year end is recorded as deferred revenue.

Franchise royalties are based on retail store sales of the franchises and recorded as earned.

INTRAWEST CORPORATION (2001)

Revenue recognition

(ii) Revenue from the sale of properties is recorded when title to the completed unit is conveyed to the purchaser and the purchaser becomes entitled to occupancy.

(iv) Revenue from revenue-producing properties is recognized upon the earlier of attaining break-even cash flow after debt servicing or the expiration of a reasonable period of time following substantial completion. Prior to this time, the properties are categorized as properties under development, and incidental operations related to such properties are applied to development costs

Revenue Recognition at the Time of Production

Revenue recognition at the time of production is common in two different kinds of industries: mining and long-term construction. If the market value and the sale of the product are both fairly certain at the time of production, as in certain mining operations, then the inventories produced can be valued at their net realizable value (selling price) and the resulting revenues can be recognized immediately. The reason for this practice is that the critical event in the revenue earning process for the mine is not the sale of the ore, but the *production* of the ore. Because the market for the ore is well-established with fairly stable prices, the sale is assured as soon as the ore is produced. By recording the revenues as soon as possible, these companies have more timely information for making decisions.

An example of this revenue recognition method is **Bema Gold Corporation**, which operates gold and silver mines.

BEMA GOLD CORPORATION (2000)

Revenue Recognition

Revenue is recorded at the estimated net realizable value when the gold is shipped and title has passed. Adjustments to these amounts are made after final prices, weights, and assays are established. The Company may fix the price it will receive for part or all of its production by entering into forward or option contracts.

Note that for Bema Gold Corporation, the earning process is complete when the gold is shipped. At this point the final amount of the sale is fairly certain but it can still change as a result of final prices, weights, and assays. Although the exact amount earned may not be known, Bema Gold is able to make a reasonable estimate of the amount and adjusts future revenues for any differences that occur. If it uses forward or option contracts, the amount earned is known for certain. A forward or option contract is a contract that stipulates the amount that will be paid for the gold in the future.

The second type of industry that recognizes revenue at the time of production is one where the production period is long, such as in the long-term construction industry. The disclosure below for **Bombardier Inc.** illustrates this type of revenue recognition:

BOMBARDIER INC. (2001)

Revenue recognition

Revenues from long-term contracts are recognized using the percentage of completion method of accounting in accordance with Statement of Position 81-1 "Accounting for Performance of Construction-Type and Certain Production-Type Contracts." For the Transportation segment, the degree of completion is generally determined by comparing the costs incurred to the total costs anticipated for the entire contract, excluding costs that are not representative of the measure of performance whereas for new business aircraft, it is determined in relation to green aircraft deliveries.

Estimated revenues from long-term contracts include future revenues from claims when it is reasonably assured that such claims, resulting from work performed for customers in addition to the work contemplated in the original contracts, will result in additional revenues in an amount that can be reliably estimated.

Revenues from commercial aircraft and other products and services are recognized upon delivery of products or when the services are rendered.

In the long-term construction industry, two methods of recognizing revenue are generally accepted: the **completed contract method**, and the **percentage of completion method**. The completed contract method defers the recognition of revenue until the contract is completed and is generally used for projects that are completed in a reasonably short period of time. Longer-term projects are generally accounted for using the percentage of completion method (you will have noticed that Bombardier uses this method), which recognizes a portion of the revenues and expenses of a project during the construction period based on the percentage of completion. The basis for determining the percent complete is usually the costs incurred relative to the estimated total costs.

As an example, suppose that Solid Construction Company agrees to construct a building for $100,000 thousand that will take three years to build, and the company expects to incur costs of $25,000 thousand, $35,000 thousand, and $10,000 thousand in Years 1, 2, and 3, respectively. The total expected costs are $70,000 thousand and, therefore, the profit on the project is expected to be $30,000 thousand. If all goes according to plan, Solid Construction would recognize the revenues and expenses (and related profits) shown in Exhibit 4-3 during the three years with the percentage of completion method.

Learning Objective

7

Calculate amounts to be recognized under the completed contract method and the percentage of completion method.

| EXHIBIT 4-3 |

REVENUE RECOGNITION WITH THE PERCENTAGE OF COMPLETION METHOD

(Amounts in thousands)

Year	Degree of Completion	Revenue Recognized	Expenses Recognized	Profit
1	$25,000/$70,000 = 36%	36% x 100,000 = $ 36,000	$25,000	$11,000
2	$35,000/$70,000 = 50%	50% x 100,000 = $ 50,000	35,000	15,000
3	$10,000/$70,000 = 14%	14% x 100,000 = $ 14,000	10,000	4,000
	100%	$100,000	$70,000	$30,000

The formulae to arrive at these amounts are as follows:

$$\frac{\text{Expenses for this period}}{\text{Total cost of project}} = \text{Percentage completed}$$

Percentage completed $\times$ Total revenue = Revenue to be recognized this period

How well does the percentage of completion method apply the revenue recognition criteria? The first criterion is that the amount has been earned (or the work the company agreed to do has been performed). Instead of waiting until all of the contract work has been completed (which can take several years), this method allows the company to measure how much work has been completed so far and then recognize as revenue the same percentage of the total contract price. The expenses for the period and the percentage of revenue earned are recognized each period, which provides information to users sooner. The second criterion is that you can measure how much you have earned. We do that using the formulae given above. The third criterion is that there is a reasonable probability of collection. For many long-term construction contracts, the buyer is billed periodically through the construction process. The periodic billing and collection provide the seller with the ability to estimate collectibility. Because the revenue recognition criteria have been satisfied, the percentage of completion method is preferable to waiting until the contract work is complete.

If Solid Construction had used the completed contract method, all the revenues and expenses would have been deferred and recognized at the time of completion. That is, the entire $100,000 thousand in revenue, $70,000 thousand in expenses, and $30,000 thousand in profit would have been recognized in Year 3. Knowing how the percentage of completion method works and that it satisfies the revenue recognition criteria, under what circumstances would it be appropriate to use the completed contract method? Some contracts take less than a year to complete. For such contracts, it might be just as informative for users to wait until the entire contract is finished. If the contract took longer than a year, the company would choose to use the completed contract method if one or more of the revenue recognition criteria were not met. It may not be possible to measure how much of the project is completed, which would make it difficult to measure the revenue earned. There could also be a question about the future collectibility on the contract, although it is doubtful if a company would continue to work on a project if it was concerned about the future payment for its work.

With either the percentage of completion method or the completed contract method, if an overall loss is projected on the project, GAAP requires that the loss be recognized as soon as it can be estimated. For example, if it turned out that, at the end of Year 2, the total estimated costs to complete the Solid Construction contract were $105,000 thousand ($60,000 thousand in year 2, and $20,000 thousand in year 3, plus the $25,000 thousand already incurred in year 1, instead of the original $70,000 thousand), an overall loss of $5,000 thousand would be indicated for the contract. At the end of Year 2, Solid Construction would have to recognize a loss of $16,000 thousand. This loss would offset the $11,000 thousand profit reported in Year 1 and would result in a net loss at this point of $5,000 thousand on the contract. If the actual costs equalled the new estimated costs in Year 3, no additional profit or loss would be recorded in Year 3, as the overall loss on the contract would already have been recognized.

The recognition of the estimated loss in the preceding example is partially a result of the conservative nature of accounting. Conservatism requires that losses generally be recognized as soon as they can be estimated, but profits are seldom recognized until they are realized.

Revenue Recognition at the Time of Collection

Except for cash sales, it is seldom the case that the revenue recognition criteria will not be met prior to the collection of cash. Therefore, for reporting purposes, the collectibility of cash rarely delays the recognition of revenue. *Outpost* magazine has one of those rare circumstances. When it sends magazines to a distributor for sale on newsstands, it does not know how much it has earned until it receives the money from the distributor some six months later. It has no choice but to delay the recognition of revenue.

There are other circumstances under which the collection of receivables is so uncertain that GAAP would require that revenue recognition be postponed until cash is actually collected. In these rare situations, the **instalment method** can be used. This method delays the recognition of revenue until the actual cash is received.

In an instalment type of sale, the buyer agrees to pay for the goods or service over time, sometimes over many months or years. The seller sets the payments that the buyer makes so that all costs incurred can be recovered, a profit is made on the sale, and suitable interest is charged for the loan the seller is making to the buyer. Therefore, the payments received by the seller can be viewed as covering three things: cost recovery, interest, and profits.

The instalment method can be illustrated with a simple example. Assume that the Sunshine Land Company sells a home site for $100,000 that has a cost of $70,000. Further, assume that the buyer has agreed to make three instalment payments over the next three years of $40,000, $40,000, and $40,000, for a total of $120,000. The excess of the payments over the selling price, $20,000, represents interest. Assume that Sunshine decides to recognize interest evenly over the three years, or $6,667 per year. This is not generally done, but it will simplify matters for the purposes of this example. Exhibit 4-4 shows the amount of income that will be recognized with the instalment method.

EXHIBIT 4-4

REVENUE RECOGNITION WITH THE INSTALMENT METHOD

Profit %   = ($100,000 − $70,000)/$100,000 = 30%

Gross profit = Payments applied to principal × profit %

              = (Cash received − interest) × profit %

Year	Gross Profits	Interest
1	($40,000 − $6,667) × 30% = $10,000	$ 6,667
2	($40,000 − $6,667) × 30% = $10,000	6,667
3	($40,000 − $6,666) × 30% = $10,000	6,666
Total	$30,000	$20,000

In Year 1, an Account Receivable of $100,000 would be recognized along with a Deferred Gross Profit of $30,000. The Deferred Gross Profit would be included with the liabilities and represent profit that will be recognized in the future. When the first payment of $40,000 is received, the following journal entry would result:

A-Cash	40,000	
L-Deferred gross profit	10,000	
A-Accounts receivable		33,333
SE-Revenue		10,000
SE-Interest revenue		6,667

In subsequent years, as payments are received, the accounts receivable and the deferred gross profit will be reduced and revenue will be recognized.

Although we have shown you some of the accounting behind the instalment method, we do not expect that you will be required to learn the details behind the method, for two reasons. First, it is quite complicated and more appropriately handled in an intermediate accounting course. For an introductory course, it is only important that you understand a little about the method so that you will understand how revenue is recognized in a company that is using the instalment method. Second, this method is not used very often in Canada. If you think about companies where the instalment method might be used such as Sears Canada, which allows customers to use their credit cards and pay over time, you would probably be surprised to learn that Sears does not use this method. Remember that this method is only used if there is a question about the potential collectibility of the amount owed. Sears has been using credit card sales for a long time and has developed reliable estimation methods that it uses to estimate uncollectibility. If it can estimate potential uncollectibility, it can recognize both the revenue and potential uncollectibility at the point of sale. Therefore, the instalment method becomes unnecessary.

Revenue Recognition with Multiple Lines of Business

In businesses that have multiple lines of business or that sell products in either standard or customized models, the revenue recognition criteria may be met at different points for different products. The disclosures for **CHC Helicopter Company** illustrate this point.

CHC HELICOPTER COMPANY (2001)

Revenue Recognition

Revenues from helicopter operations are recognized based on the terms of customer contracts, which generally provide for revenue on the basis of hours flown at contract rates or fixed monthly charges or a combination of both.

Revenue from engine and component repair and overhaul operations is recognized on the percentage of completion basis, measured on the basis of the sales value of the actual costs incurred and work performed. The repair and overhaul operation invoices customers in advance for "power-by-the-hour" ("PBH") contracts. This revenue is recognized only as the work is performed.

ethics in accounting

Ethics in Accounting

■ Pressures to show profit or growth in revenues, or both, can create ethical dilemmas for managers and accountants. Some of these pressures are self-imposed, particularly if the manager's compensation is tied to reported profits or revenues. Other pressures may be externally imposed by someone more senior in the organization or by the shareholders. Suppose, for example, that you are the accountant of a division of a company and that the manager of the division has asked you to make an adjusting entry for the period to recognize a large order. Revenue in your company is usually recorded when the goods are shipped, not when the order is placed. The manager has indicated that this order will bump the division over its sales target for the year and that the bonuses of several managers in the division will be significantly affected. She has also said that the company is about to issue more common shares and that her boss would like to show improved results from last year to get the most favourable price for the shares that will be issued. What should you do? Identify the individuals who will be helped and hurt by your decision in order to help you determine what to do.

The choice of a revenue recognition policy is one of the critical policy decisions made by a company. Current and future profitability measures will be affected by when revenue is recognized. Companies must choose a revenue recognition policy that is appropriate for their revenue streams and must tell users what that policy is so that they can make informed decisions.

An International Perspective

Reports from Other Countries

In the United States, the revenue recognition policy established by the FASB requires that revenue should be recognized when it is realized or realizable and when it is earned. Other standards have additional requirements that must be met. In light of conflicting requirements, the FASB has decided to revisit the revenue recognition criteria in 2002.

Source: "Proposal for a New Agenda Project: Issues Related to the Recognition of Revenues and Liabilities," from Financial Accounting Standards Board, January 28, 2002.

SUMMARY

In this chapter, we first discussed some measures of performance, or ROIs. This discussion led to an explanation of the cash-to-cash cycle and its importance in understanding a company's performance. Tying in with the cash-to-cash cycle are the concepts underlying the recognition of revenue. We looked at revenue at the time of sale, at contract signing, at the time of production, and at the time of collection. These concepts were explored to improve your understanding of net income as a measure of performance for a business. Companies use different revenue recognition criteria according to the type of revenue they are generating. When assessing the performance of a company, it is important to understand the type of revenue it is generating and the revenue recognition policy it has established. If you know these two things, you will be better able to understand its cash-to-cash cycle.

While net income is a useful measure of performance, it is not the only measure in which users of financial statements should be interested. In the next chapter, the cash flow statement is considered. We had a brief look at this statement in Chapter 1. Now we will explore it in more detail. The construction of the statement itself, as well as the interpretation of the information contained therein, will be discussed. The implications regarding the health of the company above and beyond matters shown on the income statement will also be discussed.

Additional Demonstration Problems

SUMMARY PROBLEMS

1. Jonathan, Anthony, and Kendra operate a bicycle shop, The Silver Spoke. They sell assembled bicycles and bicycle accessories. They have a shop in the back where Kendra repairs bicycles. Occasionally they are given a contract to assemble 20 to 50 bicycles for one of the major retailers like The Bay. Customers use either cash or

credit cards when buying bicycles or bicycle accessories. For minor repairs, the customer pays at the completion of the repairs. For major repairs, The Silver Spoke asks for a down payment equal to 25% of the estimated cost of the repair. The remaining 75% is paid when the work is complete. When the company assembles bicycles for another retailer, it bills the other retailer at the completion of the work. The company normally receives payment within 30 days of the bill submission.

Required:

Using the revenue recognition criteria, recommend when The Silver Spoke should recognize revenue for each of its various revenue generating activities.

2. Suppose that Guenther Construction Ltd. is in the construction business and enters into a contract with a customer to construct a building. The contract price is $10 million, and the estimated cost of the building is $6 million. The construction is estimated to take three years to complete.

Required:

Prepare a schedule of the revenues and expenses that would be recognized in income in each of the three years with each of the following methods:

a. Recognition of income at contract signing

b. Percentage of completion method, assuming the following schedule of estimated costs:

Year	Amount
1	$3,000,000
2	$1,800,000
3	$1,200,000

c. Completed contract method

SUGGESTED SOLUTIONS TO SUMMARY PROBLEMS

1. Sales of bicycles and bicycle accessories: the company should recognize revenue at the time of the sale. At this time, the customer leaves with the merchandise (title transfers); therefore, the company has completed what it has to do, the amount that has been earned is measurable, and it has been collected either in cash or through a credit card.

Minor repairs: the company should recognize revenue when the work is completed. Similar to the situation with the sale of bicycles, the company has completed the work, the amount owed has been measured, and the customer has already paid.

Major repairs: the company should recognize revenue when the work is completed. When the customer makes the 25% down payment, the work has not yet been completed. As well, the total amount owed is still unknown. Therefore, two of the criteria have not been met. The company should record the down payment as unearned revenue. When the repairs are done, the company will have completed the work (therefore earned the revenue), the total amount owed is known, and the customer pays for the work with cash or a credit card. At this time, all three of the criteria have been met.

Assembly contract: the company should recognize revenue when the assembly work is complete. At the time of the contract signing, although the company knows how much it will receive and is confident that it will receive that amount, it has not assembled any bicycles. Because a substantial amount of work is yet to be done, the company has not earned the revenue. When the work is complete, the amount it has earned is known and it is reasonable to assume that it will collect the amount owed. At this time, the revenue recognition criteria have been met and revenue should be recognized.

2. a. Recognizing revenue at the time of contract signing would probably not be allowed under GAAP because of the extended construction period of the contract. If it were allowed, all the profit, $4 million, would be recognized in the first year and none in later years.

b. Percentage of completion method (answers in thousands)

Year	Degree of Completion		Revenue Recognized		Expenses Recognized	Profit
1	$3,000/$6,000 =	50%	50% × $10,000 =	$ 5,000	$3,000	$2,000
2	$1,800/$6,000 =	30%	30% × $10,000 =	$ 3,000	1,800	1,200
3	$1,200/$6,000 =	20%	20% × $10,000 =	$ 2,000	1,200	800
		100%		$10,000	$6,000	$4,000

c. Completed contract method (answers in thousands)

Year	Revenue	Expense	Profit
1	0	0	0
2	0	0	0
3	$10,000	$6,000	$4,000
	$10,000	$6,000	$4,000

ABBREVIATIONS USED

FASB	Financial Accounting Standards Board	ROA	Return on assets
		ROE	Return on equity
GAAP	Generally accepted accounting principles	ROI	Return on investment

GLOSSARY

Account receivable   An amount owing as a result of the sale of a product or service.

Cash discount   A reduction in the amount that has to be paid on an account payable or receivable if payment is made within a specified time limit.

Cash-to-cash cycle   The operating cycle of the company that describes the operating activities of the company from the initial outlays of cash to buy a product or to provide a service, to the replacement of cash through collections from customers.

Completed contract method   A method of revenue recognition used in the construction industry in which the revenues from a contract are recognized only when the contract is completed.

Cost   The value of whatever is given up to acquire an item.

Earned   A term used to indicate that the company has completed its earnings process sufficiently to allow the recognition of the revenues from the sale.

Expenses   The costs incurred to earn revenues.

Instalment method A method of revenue recognition based on cash collections in which each payment received is viewed as part profit and part recovery of costs. A fraction of each payment received is recorded as profit.

Matching principle A concept that requires all expenses related to the production of revenues to be recorded during the same time period as the revenues. The expenses are said to be matched with the revenues.

Measurement The process of determining an appropriate amount or value for some attribute of the item being measured.

Net income The difference between revenues and expenses.

Operating activities Those activities involving the cash effects of the normal operations of a business, such as the buying and selling of goods and services.

Percentage of completion method A method of revenue recognition used in the construction industry in which a percentage of the profits that are expected to be realized from a given project is recognized in a given period, based on the percentage of completion of the project. The percent complete is typically measured as the fraction of costs incurred to date relative to the total estimated costs to complete the project.

Price allowance An adjustment made to the selling price of a good or service to satisfy a customer, typically for some defect in the good or service provided.

Recognition Recognizing an item for inclusion in a financial statement, including both the description and the amount.

Return on investment (ROI) A measure of the performance of the an investment, calculated as the ratio of the return from the investment to the average amount invested.

Revenues The inflows of cash or other assets from the normal operating activities of the business, which mainly involve the sale of goods or provision of services.

Revenue recognition criteria Criteria developed in GAAP that specify the conditions under which revenue should be recognized.

ASSIGNMENT MATERIAL

Assessing Your Recall

Multiple Choice Quizzes

4-1 Explain how ROI measures performance.

4-2 Diagram a typical cash-to-cash cycle of a retail company and briefly explain the various components of the cycle.

4-3 List the three major revenue recognition criteria that exist under GAAP.

4-4 Explain the meaning of revenue being "earned."

4-5 Explain the difference between the percentage of completion method and the completed contract method.

4-6 Describe how the instalment method is implemented and explain why it is rarely used in practice.

4-7 Explain the meaning of the matching principle.

4-8 Describe the accounting treatment for a deposit made by a customer for the future delivery of inventory. Using the revenue recognition criteria, explain the rationale for this treatment.

Applying Your Knowledge

4-9　(Revenue recognition criteria)

In the opening story to this chapter, the owner of *Outpost* magazine explained how the company recognized revenue. Using the revenue recognition criteria described in this chapter, explain the appropriateness of the revenue policy the company has adopted for revenue from advertisers and revenue from subscribers.

4-10　(Calculate the ROI)

Calculate the ROI for the following investments:

a. William Gustovson bought a GIC (Guaranteed Investment Certificate) on June 1 for $2,000. The certificate reached maturity on December 1 (it was a six-month certificate). On December 1, he cashed in the certificate and received his original $2,000 back plus $45 in interest.

b. Rodney Lee bought 10 shares of City Financial Services Ltd. for $7.00 a share. At the end of the year, he received a dividend of $0.30 per share. At that time, the shares were trading for $7.20 per share.

c. Joylene Keller bought a 20% interest in a medical partnership for $80,000. During the year, the partnership earned net income of $240,000.

d. The Sunshine Brick Company had $450,000 in net assets (shareholders' equity) at the beginning of the year, and $490,000 at the end. During the year it earned net income of $50,000.

e. Karen Agnew received $50.00 from an aunt for her birthday. She opened a savings account at the bank. A year later she had $51.25 in her account.

4-11　(Calculate the ROI)

Calculate the ROI for the following investments:

a. The Bainbridge family bought a home in Calgary for $180,000. Two years later, a real estate agent told them that they could probably sell their home for $210,000.

b. The Melrose Motor Company bought an investment in a supply company for $110,000. During the year it received dividends equal to $4,000.

c. Jack Valaas bought 5,000 shares in his sister's retail company for $20,000. The company earned net income of $72,000 which resulted in an earnings per share of $3.75.

d. Margot Chan bought 10 shares in Air Canada for $6.60 per share. One year later she had not received a dividend but the shares were selling at $8.10 per share.

e. The Down Rite Dirty Disposal Company had $1,340,000 in assets at the beginning of the year, and $1,150,000 at the end. During the year it earned net income of $120,000.

4-12　(Revenue recognition and the income statement)

Sheila Mayers and Bailey Klassan started a website development company. They purchased two new computers for $1,800 each and determined that they would probably last three years and then would have a residual value of $150 each. During the year they developed 48 websites and received a total of $60,600 from customers for website development. At the end of the year, they had six websites in various stages of completion. They had received $500 each in advance for these sites and this amount was included in the $60,600 they had received during the year. During the year they spent $15,750 for various things like printing, disks, computer programs, and office supplies. They also spent $8,300 for Internet connections, telephone and fax services, and other utilities.

Required:
Prepare as much of the income statement for Mayers and Klassan as you can, showing the proper amount of sales and any other amounts that should be included. Show all calculations. Do you have a cost of goods sold? Why or why not?

4-13 (Revenue recognition and the income statement)
The Tinder Box Furnace Company installs furnaces and air conditioners in homes and businesses. Each of the furnaces carries a five-year warranty and the air conditioners have a four-year warranty. During 2004, the company had sales of $1,230,000. Customers paid half of the sales price when they made arrangements for the installation of a furnace or air conditioner and paid the other half after it was installed. At the end of the year, $65,000 of the sales amount represented amounts paid for furnaces or air conditioners that were not yet installed and the second half of the payment had not been received yet. The cost associated with the sales was $580,000 for the actual furnaces and air conditioners that had been installed that year. An additional cost of $245,000 was incurred for the labour costs associated with the installation. The accountant estimated that total future warranty costs associated with the installed items would likely be $65,000 over the next five years.

Required:
Prepare as much of the income statement for Tinder Box Furnace Company for 2004 as you can, showing the proper amount of sales, cost of goods sold, gross profit, and any other amounts that can be included. Show all calculations.

4-14 (Revenue recognition on long-term contract)
Smith Brothers Construction Company signs a contract to construct a bridge in three years for $40 million. The expected costs for each year are (in millions):

Year 1:	$ 9.5
Year 2:	$ 7.5
Year 3:	$ 7.0
Total	$24.0

The bridge is completed in Year 3.

Required:
Calculate for each year the total revenue, expense, and profit using each of the following methods:

a. The percentage of completion method

b. The completed contract method

4-15 (Revenue recognition on instalment sale)
Jean's Buy and Sell Store bought used merchandise from people in need of cash and then resold it. Often the merchandise was sold for cash but sometimes larger ticket items were sold on instalment. Although Jean did her best to determine whether a customer was going to be able to make the payments, she knew that most of her customers had low-paying jobs and were sometimes laid off. For these reasons, Jean decided to use the instalment method to account for the revenue from this type of sale. On Tuesday, Jean sold a television set to a customer for $450. She had bought the television set from another customer for $225. The buyer agreed to pay $90 a month for the next five months. (We will ignore any interest costs in the problem.)

Required:

Calculate the account receivable, unearned profit, and earned profit at the end of each of the five months assuming that the profit is earned evenly over the five months.

4-16 (Revenue recognition on instalment sale)

Imperial Company purchases a factory from Superior Manufacturing Company for $1.5 million. The cost of the factory in Superior's records is $975,000. The terms of the agreement are that yearly payments of $705,000, $505,000, $455,000, and $255,000 will be made over the next four years. Each of these payments includes an interest payment of $105,000 per year.

Required:

a. Under what conditions would it be reasonable for Superior to recognize all of the profit on the sale in the first year?

b. Under what conditions would it be important to delay recognition until the actual cash payments are received?

c. Calculate the accounts receivable, interest revenue, and profit at the end of each of the four years assuming all of the profit is recognized in the first year.

4-17 (Revenue recognition on long-term contract)

Cruise Shipping Inc. agreed to rebuild the *Santa Marice*, an old cargo ship owned by the Oceanic Shipping Company. Both parties signed the contract on November 28, 2003, for $120 million, which is to be paid as follows:

$10 million at the signing of the contract

$20 million on December 30, 2004

$40 million on June 1, 2005

$50 million at completion, on August 15, 2006

The following costs were incurred by Cruise Shipping Inc. (in millions):

2003:	$21.2
2004:	36.4
2005:	26.0
2006:	12.4
Total	$96.0

Required:

a. Calculate the revenue, expense, and profit (ignoring interest) that Cruise Shipping Inc. should report for each of the four years using each of the following methods:

   1. Percentage of completion method

   2. Completed contract method

b. Which method do you think should be employed by Cruise Shipping Inc. to show the company's performance under the contract? Why?

4-18 (Revenue recognition on long-term contract)

Computronics Company received a contract on March 3, 2004, to set up a central information system for a college. The contract price was $1 million, which was to be paid as follows:

$200,000 at the signing of the contract

$ 60,000 on July 1, 2004

$ 50,000 on December 31, 2004

$ 50,000 on March 25, 2005

$100,000 on August 25, 2005

$150,000 on December 31, 2005

$390,000 on June 30, 2006

The system was completed on June 30, 2006

Estimated and actual costs were:

$140,000	for the four months ending June 30, 2004
210,000	for the six months ending December 31, 2004
240,500	for the six months ending June 30, 2005
90,000	for the six months ending December 31, 2005
69,500	for the six months ending June 30, 2006
Total $750,000	

Required:

a. Calculate the revenue, expense, and profit that Computronics should report for each of the six-month periods ending June 30 and December 31 using each of the following methods:

1. Percentage of completion method

2. Completed contract method

b. Which method should Computronics Company use? Why?

4-19 (Revenue recognition on long-term contract)
Solid Builders Ltd., a construction company, recognizes revenue from its long-term contracts using the percentage of completion method. On June 30, 2003, the company signed a contract to construct a new city library for $1,500,000. The company estimated that it would take three years to complete the contract and estimated the cost to the company at $800,000. The expected costs in each of the three years are as follows:

Year	Cost
2003	$220,750
2004	400,500
2005	178,750
Total	$800,000

Solid Builders closes its books every December 31. The project was finished on June 30, 2005, as per the schedule.

Required:

a. With respect to this contract, calculate the revenue, expense, and profit/loss as at December 31 for each of the three years.

b. Is it appropriate for Solid Builders to use the percentage of completion method? Explain.

4-20   (Revenue recognition on long-term contract)

On June 21, 2003, Tristar Electric Company signed a contract with Denton Power Incorporated to construct a small hydroelectric generating plant. The contract price was $10 million, and it was estimated that the project would cost Tristar $7,850,000 to complete over a three-year period. On June 21, 2003, Denton paid Tristar $1 million as a default deposit. In the event that Denton backed out of the contract, Tristar could keep this deposit. Otherwise, the default deposit would apply as the final payment on the contract (assume, for accounting purposes, that this is treated as a deposit until completion of the contract). The other contractual payments are as follows:

Date	Amount
October 15, 2003	$3,150,000
April 15, 2004	1,350,000
December 15, 2004	1,800,000
March 15, 2005	1,755,000
August 10, 2005	945,000
Total	$9,000,000

Estimated construction costs were as follows:

Year	Amount
2003	$3,532,500
2004	2,747,500
2005	1,570,000
Total	$7,850,000

The contract was completed on November 30, 2005. Tristar closes its books on December 31 each year.

Required:

Calculate the revenue, expense, and profit to be recognized in each year using each of the following methods:

a. The percentage of completion method

b. The completed contract method

4-21   (Revenue recognition decision)

Jocelyn Black started a catering service in February 2003. She started by catering small functions in homes and businesses. By June she was providing food for weddings and graduation functions for up to 500 people. She hired three other people who helped cook and serve at the larger functions. For small functions of under 20 people, she took the order, prepared the food, and delivered it. She was paid when the food was delivered. For functions of over 20 people, she took the order and requested a 20% deposit from the customer. The remaining 80% was required at the end of the function. For each function, Jocelyn kept a record of who placed the order, the quantity and type of food ordered, the cost of the materials used to prepare the food, the time spent by the hired people to cook and serve the food, the deposit received, and the final cheque. So far, she has not had trouble with customers failing to pay or of cheques not being good, but she knows that, as she expands the business, such things could happen.

Required:

It is the beginning of December and Jocelyn Black would like to have some financial statements prepared by December 31. She has asked you to help set up her records and to provide her with some accounting advice. As one small part of that, advise her about how she should account for the revenue she earns from the small and the large jobs. At what stage should she recognize revenue? Support your answer using the revenue recognition criteria.

4-22 (Revenue recognition decision)

Sonya's Christmas Tree Company began operations on April 1, 2000. She bought a parcel of land on which she intended to grow Christmas trees. The normal growth time for a Christmas tree is six years, so she divided her land into six plots. In 2000 she planted the first plot with trees and watered, cultivated, and fertilized her trees all summer. In 2001 she planted her second plot with trees and watered, cultivated, and fertilized both planted plots. She continued with her plantings and cultivation every year through 2005, when she planted the last plot. On November 1, 2005, she harvested the first plot of trees that she had planted in 2000. In 2006 she replanted the first plot.

Required:

a. Describe Sonya's cash-to-cash cycle.

b. What revenue recognition options are open to her? Which one would you recommend and why?

c. Using your recommended revenue recognition policy, how would Sonya account for all of her costs for growing the trees?

4-23 (Revenue recognition decision)

After graduating with a degree in computer systems and design, Terry Park set up a business to design and produce computer games for use in arcades. Terry hired two other designers because of the anticipated volume of business. One designer, Kim, is paid an hourly wage. The second, Sandy, is paid 50% of the revenue received by Terry on the games designed or redesigned by Sandy. Terry rents an office where they all work and provides all the necessary equipment, supplies, and other items. Terry is not paid a wage but keeps all of the profits earned.

Terry quickly realized there were two kinds of business: speculative design and custom design. For the speculative designs, Terry or one of the designers would think of a new game and design, program, and test it. Terry would then try to sell it to a distribution company, for either a fixed price or a percentage (which ranges from 10% to 25%) of the total revenues earned by the games. To date, Terry has sold three of the four games produced. Terry is currently negotiating the sale of the fourth game.

For the custom design business, Terry would receive an order from a distribution company for either the design of a new game or the redesign of an existing game (which occurs frequently because games have a useful life of only six months as players quickly get bored with them). Terry negotiates either a fixed fee payable upon completion, or an hourly rate based on the estimated length of time it should take to redesign the game. Terry sets the hourly rate based on the perceived difficulty of the project, but the rate is always at least triple the amount paid to Kim. For the hourly-rate contracts, Terry submits monthly invoices showing the number of hours worked on the project.

Required:

a. Describe Terry's cash-to-cash cycle.

b. What revenue recognition options are open to Terry? Which one(s) would you recommend and why?

c. Using your recommended revenue recognition policy, how would you account for all of the costs incurred by Terry?

d. What recommendations would you make to Terry about the running of this business?

User Perspective Problems

4-24   (Revenue recognition and earnings)
Financial analysts frequently refer to the "quality" of a company's earnings. By quality, they mean that the earnings are showing growth and that they are good predictors of future earnings. Discuss how the quality of two companies' earnings might differ depending on the revenue recognition method that the two companies use.

4-25   (Changing revenue policy to affect earnings)
Suppose that a company is currently private (its shares do not trade on a public stock market) but it is thinking of going public (issuing shares in a public stock market). Discuss the incentives that the company might have to misstate its income statement via its revenue recognition policies. If a company decided to change its revenue recognition policy so that its earnings would be enhanced, would the investors realize what it was doing? Where would a new investor look for information about the changes?

4-26   (Revenue policy and management performance measurement)
Suppose that you are the sales manager of a company with an incentive plan that provides a bonus based on meeting a certain sales target. Explain how meeting your sales target is affected by the revenue recognition principles of the company.

4-27   (Revenue policy and sales targets)
Suppose that you are the vice-president in charge of marketing and sales in a large company. You want to boost sales, so you have developed an incentive plan that will provide a bonus to the salespeople based on the revenue they generate. At what point would you recommend that the company count a sale—when the salesperson generates a purchase order, when the company ships the goods, or when the company receives payment for the goods? Explain your answer.

4-28   (Revenue policy for accounting and tax purposes)
Explain the incentives that a company is affected by in choosing its revenue recognition method for both financial reporting and tax purposes.

4-29   (Revenue policy and return policies)
In the toy industry, it is common to allow customers (retail stores) to return unsold toys within a specified period of time. Suppose that a toy manufacturer's year end is December 31 and that the majority of its products are shipped to customers during the last quarter of the year in anticipation of the Christmas holiday. Is it appropriate for the company to recognize revenue upon shipment of the product? Support your answer, making reference to revenue recognition criteria.

4-30   (Revenue policy and modes of shipping goods)
Suppose that an exporter in Vancouver sells goods to a customer in Australia. The goods are shipped by cargo vessel. For goods that are in transit at year end, what recognition should the Vancouver exporter make in its financial statements? Support your answer based on revenue recognition criteria.

4-31   (Revenue recognition for apartment rentals)
Suppose that you are the owner of several apartment buildings. When new tenants rent apartments they are required to sign a one-year lease. A one-year lease is a contract whereby the tenants agree to rent the apartment for at least one year. There are penalties if the tenant decides to leave before the end of a year. Monthly rental payments are required to be paid in advance on the first day of each month. The tenants are also required to pay half a month's rent up front as a damage deposit. When the tenants leave, the apartment is inspected for damage and the damage deposit is either returned or used to repair the damage. Using revenue recognition criteria, explain when you would recognize the revenue from the monthly rent payments and the damage deposit. How does the one-year lease affect your decision?

4-32 (Advertising revenue recognition)
Suppose the sports channel on television sells $10 million in advertising slots to be aired during the games that it broadcasts during the World Cup. Suppose also that these slots are contracted out during the month of October with a down payment of $2 million. The ads will be aired in June and July of the following year. If the fiscal year end of the sports channel is December 31, how should it recognize this revenue in its financial statements?

4-33 (Revenue recognition for gift certificates)
Suppose that **The GAP** (a clothing retailer) sells gift certificates for merchandise. During the Christmas holiday period, suppose that it issues $500,000 in gift certificates. If the company's fiscal year end is December 31, how should it recognize the issuance of these gift certificates in its financial statements at year end? Explain your answer in relationship to the revenue recognition criteria.

4-34 (Revenue recognition on software sales)
Suppose that the Solution Software Company produces inventory tracking software that it sells to retail companies like Canadian Tire. The software keeps track of what inventory is on hand and where it is located. It automatically adjusts the information when items are sold and alerts the company when new inventory needs to be ordered. The software package sells for $100,000 and the company agrees to customize it to the buyer's operations, which can take several months. If the fiscal year end is September 30 and the company sells 10 units of the product in August, how should it recognize these sales in the financial statements at year end? Use the revenue recognition criteria to support your answer.

4-35 (Revenue and expenses associated with obsolete inventory)
Suppose that you are the auditor of Nichol's Department Store and during your audit of the company's inventory you observe a significant amount of inventory that appears to be extremely old. How would you recommend that the company deal with this inventory, and how will it affect the revenues and expenses recognized during the period? Explain the incentives that the management of the company might have for keeping the inventory in its warehouse.

Reading and Interpreting Published Financial Statements

4-36 (Revenue recognition for multiple products)
Brampton Brick Limited's main area of operation is in the manufacture of clay and concrete bricks that it sells for residential and industrial construction. It has expanded its operations into truck transportation services and the disposal of biomedical and pharmaceutical wastes.

> *Required:*
> Using the revenue recognition criteria, describe how you think Brampton Brick should recognize revenue for its brick sales, its trucking operations, and its medical waste disposal. You might find it useful to know more about the company by going to its website at www.bramptonbrick.com.

4-37 (Catalogue production, revenue recognition, and matching)
Eddie Bauer, Inc. sells clothing and other items from retail stores through catalogue mailings and over the Internet. The cost of catalogue production and mailing is fairly substantial for a company such as Eddie Bauer. Discuss how the costs associated with catalogue production and mailing should be treated for accounting purposes. Frame your answer in terms of the revenue recognition criteria and the matching principle discussed in the chapter.

4-38   (Application of revenue recognition criteria)

Refer to the statement of financial position (balance sheet) of **Air Canada** in Exhibit 4-5. In the notes to the financial statements, Air Canada states its Air Transportation Revenue policy as:

> Airline passenger and cargo sales are recognized as operating revenues when the transportation is provided. The value of unused transportation is included in current liabilities.

Required:

a. Referring to the balance sheet in Exhibit 4-5, what is the value of the unused transportation in 2001 and 2000?

b. Referring to the revenue recognition criteria, explain why Air Canada's revenue recognition policy is appropriate.

c. Air Canada has a frequent flyer program where customers earn travel miles that can be exchanged at a later date for trips. Suggest how you think Air Canada should account for these free trips.

4-39   (Application of revenue recognition criteria)

According to Note 2 to its 2001 financial statements, the revenue policy used by **IPSCO**, a steel manufacturer, is as follows:

Revenue Recognition

> Sales and related costs are recognized upon transfer of ownership which coincides with acceptance of or shipment of products to customers.

Required:

a. Describe IPSCO's revenue recognition policy and explain how it satisfies the revenue recognition criteria.

b. Explain why you think it has specified "acceptance of or shipment of products."

4-40   (Application of revenue recognition criteria)

The revenue recognition policy of **IEI Energy Inc.**, a mining company, from Note 1 to its 2001 financial statements is as follows:

> Estimated mineral revenue, based upon prevailing metal prices, is recorded in the financial statements when the concentrates are loaded on trucks or rail cars for shipment to a smelter. The estimated revenue is subject to adjustment upon final settlement, which is usually four to five months after the date of shipment.
>
> These adjustments reflect changes in metal prices, changes in currency rates, and changes in quantities arising from final weight and assay calculations. When recording this estimated revenue, the Company makes a provision for these potential adjustments.

Required:

a. Explain why this revenue recognition conforms to GAAP. Include consideration of the treatment of estimated revenues and settlement adjustments (adjustments caused by changes in metal prices, changes in currency rates, and changes in quantities arising from final weight and assay calculations).

b. What alternative revenue recognition policies and recording could IEI Energy use that would also conform with GAAP?

AIR CANADA (2001)

Consolidated Statement of Financial Position
(in millions)

EXHIBIT 4-5

December 31		2001		2000
Assets				
Current				
Cash and cash equivalents (note 1d)	$	1,067	$	437
Accounts receivable		764		909
Spare parts, materials and supplies		344		403
Prepaid expenses		60		33
Future income taxes (note 14)		–		447
		2,235		2,229
Property and equipment (note 3)		2,830		4,174
Future income taxes (note 14)		404		239
Deferred charges (note 4)		1,773		1,319
Goodwill (note 1a)		510		527
Other assets (note 5)		1,149		1,244
	$	8,901	$	9,732
Liabilities				
Current				
Bank indebtedness and short term loans	$	–	$	264
Accounts payable and accrued liabilities		1,857		2,269
Advance ticket sales		481		498
Current portion of long-term debt and capital lease obligations (note 7)		531		529
		2,869		3,560
Long-term and subordinated perpetual debt and capital lease obligations (note 7)		4,215		3,611
Future income taxes (note 14)		60		86
Other long-term liabilities (note 10)		1,279		1,175
Deferred credits (note 11)		1,416		984
		9,839		9,416
Shareholders' Equity				
Share capital (note 12)		977		977
Contributed surplus		15		15
Deficit		(1,930)		(676)
		(938)		316
	$	8,901	$	9,732

See accompanying notes.

Approved by the Board:

Robert A. Milton
President and Chief Executive Officer

John F. Fraser, OC
Chairman of the Board

4-41　(Application of revenue recognition criteria)

The revenue recognition policies used by **Canadian Pacific Railway Limited**, a transportation provider, according to Note 2 to its 2001 financial statements, is as follows:

> Railway freight revenues are recognized based on the percentage of completed service method. Other revenue is recognized as service is performed or contractual obligations are met.

Required:

Explain how you think the percentage of completed service method would work for a railway transportation provider. Why do you think Canadian Pacific Railway chose this method for its freight revenues rather than waiting until all of the service was provided? You might find it useful to know more about the company by going to its website at www.cpr.ca/english.

4-42　(Revenue recognition decision-making)

There are companies today that are set up to provide additional funds to retired individuals. They offer reverse mortgages. A reverse mortgage is a loan against the person's home that requires no repayment for as long as the person lives there. The person still owns the home and must pay for property taxes, insurance, and upkeep. However, when the person stops living in the home, the loan comes due. The person receives the loan either as an immediate cash advance, as a creditline account, as monthly cash payments, or as a combination of the other options. The amount that must be paid back cannot be higher than the equity in the home, which means that the company cannot seek additional funds from the owner or the owner's heirs. The company runs the risk of the person staying in the home a long time and/or of the equity in the home not growing as quickly as anticipated.

Required:

a. If you were a manager in a company offering the reverse mortgages, how would you decide how much money you should loan to a homeowner?

b. Having decided on the amount, how would you recognize revenue over the life of this agreement?

c. Given your revenue recognition method outlined in b), how would you treat the payments made to the homeowner and the various expenses incurred in administering the agreement?

d. Are there any ethical dilemmas that the managers of such a company might face in contracting reverse mortgages?

Beyond the Book

4-43　(Revenue recognition policies used)

Using an electronic database, select a company in the oil and gas industry. Using the information on its financial statements and in the notes to the financial statements, answer the following questions:

a. Describe the types of revenue generated by the company.

b. Describe the policies used by the company for revenue recognition for its various revenues. Using the revenue recognition criteria, explain how the policies selected are suitable for the revenues generated.

4-44   (Change in revenue recognition criteria)

Using an electronic database, search for a company that has changed its revenue recognition methods during the last three years. Using that company, answer the following questions:

a. Describe the method that was used before the change as well as the new method.

b. Does the company give a reason for the change? If so, describe the reason; if not, speculate on why the change occurred.

c. How significant an effect did the change have on the company's financial statements? As in investor, how would you view this change?

d. Did the auditor agree with the change? Do you agree? Why or why not?

Cases

Additional Cases

4-45   Quebec Supercheese Company (QSC)

Quebec Supercheese Company (QSC) produces many varieties of cheese that are sold in every province in Canada, mainly through large grocery stores and specialty cheese shops. The cheese is produced at its factory in Montreal and shipped across Canada using commercial refrigerated trucks that pick up the cheese at the factory loading dock. All cheese is shipped F.O.B. shipping point, meaning that the purchasers pay for the trucking and assume responsibility for the cheese as soon as the trucks pick it up at the factory. In accordance with generally accepted accounting principles, QSC recognizes the sale as soon as the trucks load the cheese, as the purchasers have title and responsibility for the cheese at this point.

QSC is not happy with these arrangements because it has received many complaints from purchasers about spoilage. Even though the purchasers and their truckers have full responsibility for this spoilage, many disputes have occurred because the truckers insist the cheese is spoiled when they pick it up. QSC is considering setting up its own fleet of trucks to deliver its cheese across Canada. It estimates the additional freight costs can be regained through the higher prices it would charge for including shipping in the price (F.O.B. destination).

If the company makes the deliveries, the title to the cheese will not transfer until the cheese is delivered. QSC's president was not happy when she learned that sales would be recognized and recorded only upon delivery to the customer, since she knew that an average of five days' sales are in transit at all times because of the distances involved. One day's sales total approximately $100,000 on average. The effect of this change would be an apparent drop in sales of $500,000 and a $50,000 decrease in net income in the year of the change.

Required:

a. Advise the president about revenue recognition guidelines.

b. Do you see a solution to the problem of changing the shipping method while avoiding the resulting effect on the income statement?

4-46   Windsor Contracting Ltd.

Windsor Contracting Ltd. currently uses the completed contract method to record revenue. In the past the company has focused on performing small renovation and home improvement jobs that typically lasted from two weeks to three months. The company has a very good reputation for quality work and fair pricing. Due in large part to its strong reputation, the company has begun to expand its operations to encompass larger contracts, some of which may take up to two years to complete. Dan Fielding, the company's president, is thrilled with the success of the company but is a little concerned about accepting these larger contracts. He contacts you, John Philpot, a local accountant, to obtain some advice concerning the accounting for these larger long-term contracts.

"John, I'm concerned about accepting these long-term contracts. If I cannot recognize any of the revenue associated with these jobs until they are completed, my income statement is going to look very poor for the years in which the contracts are in progress but not completed. I will need financing to undertake these large jobs and the bank needs a yearly income statement to support my line of credit. What do you suggest?"

Required:
Write a memo to Dan Fielding as John Philpot addressing his concerns. Your memo should focus on a discussion of the percentage of completion method of accounting for revenue recognition and how this method would meet the needs of Windsor Contracting. The memo should also include a discussion of any estimates that Windsor will have to make to apply this method of revenue recognition.

4-47
John Young and Sandra Grill are both CEOs of very successful businesses. John Young runs a plant that manufactures lawnmowers and sells them wholesale to a variety of hardware stores in Western Canada. Sandra Grill, on the other hand, is a speculator and her company mines gold in various provinces across Canada. Both companies are very successful and recognize significant amounts of revenue annually.

At a recent charity golf tournament, the two ended up on the same team and began discussing their companies' performance in the last quarter.

Grill: "Our company had exceptional performance over the past quarter due to a large strike in central Newfoundland. We have been able to mine several thousand ounces of gold and now have significant reserves. It has really helped our bottom line being able to record so much revenue in this quarter."

Young: "Did I hear you right? You are able to record revenue when the gold is produced? My accountant told me that our company couldn't record revenue until we have actually sold our inventory. I am going have a long talk with my accountant this week and demand that we get to record sales at the time of production as well!"

Required:
Discuss why there is a difference between the ways in which these two companies recognize revenue. Is John Young's accountant correct in requiring that inventory be sold before recognizing revenue? If so, then why can the mining company record revenue as soon as the gold is produced?

4-48   Furniture Land Inc.
Furniture Land Inc. is a producer and retailer of custom-designed and -built high-end furniture. The company only produces to special order and requires a one-third down payment before any work begins. The customer is then required to pay one-third at the time of delivery and the balance is to be paid within thirty days following delivery.

It is now February 1, 2004, and Furniture Land has just accepted $3,000 as a down payment from H. Gooding, a wealthy stockbroker. As per the contract, Furniture Land is to deliver the custom furniture to Gooding's personal residence by June 15, 2004. Gooding is an excellent customer and has always abided by the contract terms in the past. If Furniture Land cannot make the delivery by June 15, the contract terms state that Gooding has the option of cancelling the sale and receiving a full reimbursement of any down payment.

Required:

As Furniture Land's accountant, your job is to decide when revenue should be recorded and to prepare all journal entries related to the sale in a manner that supports the revenue recognition policy selected.

Critical Thinking Questions

4-49   (Inclusion of items in revenue)

The statement of operations and the revenue recognition note from **Big Rock Brewery Ltd.** for the year ended March 31, 2001, are shown in Exhibit 4-6.

Required:

a. Explain what the "Government taxes and commissions" are.

b. Argue why they should (or should not) be included in the revenues of Big Rock Brewery.

BIG ROCK BREWERY LTD. (2001)

EXHIBIT 4-6

Consolidated Statements of Operations & Retained Earning

Years ended March 31

	2001 $	2000 $
	(Denominated in Canadian Dollars)	
Revenue		
Sales	32,238,035	31,707,142
Government taxes and commissions	(9,038,357)	(8,990,216)
	23,199,678	22,716,926
Cost of sales	9,240,503	9,154,929
Gross profit	13,959,175	13,561,997
Expenses		
Selling, general and administrative	10,176,689	9,415,955
Interest on long-term debt	451,921	481,400
Interest on short-term debt	91,998	36,360
Amortization	1,230,994	1,167,163
	11,951,602	11,100,878
Income before income taxes	2,007,573	2,461,119
Current income tax expense	198,000	42,000
Future income tax expense [note 8]	457,000	958,000
Net income for year	1,352,573	1,461,119
Retained earnings, beginning of year	6,551,550	5,975,448
Redemption of common shares [note 7]	(420,041)	(885,017)
Retained earnings, end of year	7,484,082	6,551,550
Net income per share [note 2]		
Basic and fully diluted	0.29	0.31

See accompanying notes

Revenue Recognition

Revenue is recognized upon shipment of product at the gross sales price charged to the purchaser. Invoices for sales to Canadian customers are submitted to the respective provincial Liquor Control Boards who pay the Company after deducting Liquor Control Board commissions. Excise taxes, which are assessed on production, and Liquor Control Board Commissions, which are assessed on sales, are recorded as reductions to gross sales prices.

4-50   (Revenue recognition decision-making)

An article by Mahendra Gujarathi ("Bridging the GAP in GAAP: A Case Study of Accounting for Frequent Flyer Plans," *Accounting Horizons*, September 1991) examines accounting for frequent flyer plans offered by airlines.

Required:

a. Briefly summarize the three alternative methods proposed to account for frequent flyer plans. Describe how, and examine why, the revenue recognition alternatives are linked to liability recognition.

b. Do you agree with the recommendations made by the author?

4-51   (Revenue recognition decision-making)

Alliance Atlantis Communications Company is a fully integrated supplier of entertainment products to the television and motion picture production industries. It produces, among other products, series for television that it sells to television networks. Some of these series involve the incurring of costs to develop an idea and produce a pilot show, followed by attempts to market the show to television stations. If the series is sold, weekly shows are produced for later airing by participating stations.

Required:

Discuss the revenue generation process of this kind of television series, emphasizing the critical points in the revenue recognition process and pointing out the similarities and differences between the revenue process for Alliance Atlantis and for a company manufacturing television sets.

Expect the Unexpected

Just because an organization isn't out to make a profit doesn't mean it can ignore its accounting. In fact, in today's tough financial climate, a charity or any other not-for-profit organization needs to watch its money more carefully than ever.

Just ask Dorothy Hooper, controller for the Manitoba Theatre Centre (MTC), the oldest English-language regional theatre in Canada. Since 1957, this widely acclaimed establishment has presented top-quality shows to Winnipeg audiences as well as touring productions and co-productions with other theatre companies—though outside Winnipeg the MTC is perhaps best known for its 1995 production of *Hamlet*, which headlined movie star Keanu Reeves.

Not surprisingly, that season sold out completely. But most years, income from ticket sales at the MTC is very hard to predict. "You can never accurately determine how the public will respond to the shows we've selected," explains Ms. Hooper. "Of course the artistic director always tries to make choices that are both artistically interesting and appealing to the public. And he's very, very good. But you just can't tell what people are going to want to see."

This uncertainty makes cash flow a real accounting challenge for a theatre. The costs for the season are pretty much fixed once the plays have been chosen, and most of the expenses of mounting a show must be paid up front: sets must be built, costumes created, designers paid, and marketing materials prepared long before the curtain rises on the first performance, when box office revenues, which account for about 50% of MTC's income, are still a great unknown. Income from subscribers, which used to come in at the beginning of the season, is now often paid in instalments throughout the year. Grant money usually comes in instalments also.

So how does the theatre deal with major expenses such as building repairs? "In 1999, we launched a very successful $5-million capital campaign, raising money from government, corporations, and individuals," explains Ms. Hooper. "Since donors will make their pledge payments over a number of years, it's a question of timing: we only spend the money as we collect it." By 2001, the funds had enabled MTC to renovate the main lobby, build a loading dock, and make much-needed improvements to the Warehouse, its second facility. "We even replaced the old seats there—everybody loved that!"

Amazingly, the MTC has very rarely had to borrow to make ends meet. "We plan very carefully," says Ms. Hooper. "Everyone gets involved." And if there's a cash crunch? "We count on everyone to get us through it. We make an announcement to all the senior staff and they defer any expenses they can. One department will put off its purchase of a computer so another one that needs the cash can get it sooner. We all pitch in; people will bring in their own pens if that's what it takes."

CASH FLOW STATEMENT

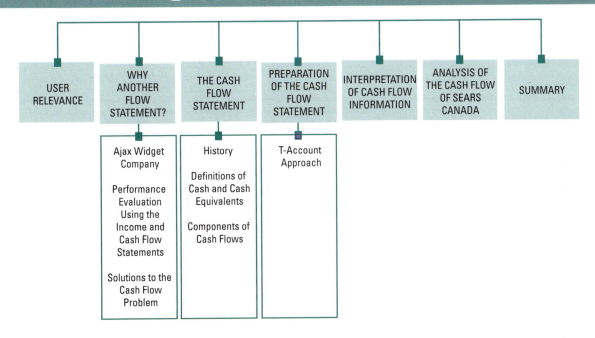

Learning Objectives:

After studying this chapter, you should be able to:

1. *Understand the importance of cash to the financial health of a company.*
2. *Describe the relationship between the cash flow statement and the income statement in assessing management performance.*
3. *Describe the cash-to-cash cycle for a retail company through a discussion of the lead/lag relationship.*
4. *Identify some solutions to cash flow problems.*
5. *Identify the three major activities disclosed in the cash flow statement and describe the components of each activity.*
6. *Prepare a cash flow statement from a company's balance sheets and income statement.*
7. *Provide a basic analysis of a company's financial health using a cash flow statement.*

Every organization, whether a profit-oriented business or a not-for-profit theatre company like the one described in the opening story, needs to manage its cash flow. The health of the organization depends on its ability to predict when cash is coming in and when it needs to be spent. For a not-for-profit organization like the Manitoba Theatre Centre, cash prediction and management is a fine balancing act. Most not-for-profit organizations have a fixed access to funds from either granting agencies or donations. If they experience a cash shortage, they can't just sell more items or provide more services. When not-for-profit organizations provide services, they may or may not get paid for them. They can't issue shares and often cannot borrow money. This greatly limits their choices and makes management of cash essential to their survival.

Profit-oriented companies have similar concerns with respect to cash. They need to know how cash is flowing in and out. If a profit-oriented company has difficulty paying its debts on time, it soon loses its credit rating, and suppliers and lenders will be reluctant to continue to sell goods on credit or loan money to it. These actions will affect its ability to grow and could contribute to an eventual slide into bankruptcy.

In Chapter 4, the basic concepts underlying the recognition of revenue were discussed from the point of view of the shareholders of the company. Although this is an important perspective, other measures of performance that affect the overall health of the company are not adequately captured by the income statement. Because the income statement is based on accrual accounting, the flows represented on the income statement do not necessarily correspond to the cash flows of the company. Because the company cannot operate without cash, it is important to understand its cash-generating performance during the period. Knowing the importance of cash flow, outside users need some way to assess the future cash position of an organization. For example, creditors use cash flow information to assess the company's ability to pay periodic interest and the principal of debt as it comes due. This chapter discusses the second major measure of performance, the cash flows that are summarized in the statement called the cash flow statement. The cash flow statement is quite simple in intent, but a bit more difficult to prepare and understand properly. Because of this difficulty, you may find that your instructor has chosen to leave this chapter until later in the course.

USER RELEVANCE

Some users consider the cash flow statement to be the most important statement in determining the future prospects of a company. Remember the three basic activities of a business that were described in Chapter 1:

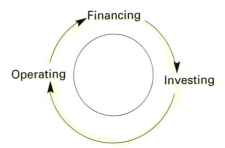

Users will examine these activities on the cash flow statement to assess the financial health of a company. They will examine the statement to see whether the operations of the company are generating a positive **cash flow**. Operations represent the life blood of the company. These are the activities for which the company was first established and it will grow or decline based on those activities. A positive cash flow indicates that more cash is flowing into the company than is flowing out as a result of operations. That cash may be used for other activities such as purchase of new assets, payment of debt, or payment of dividends to shareholders. A negative cash flow indicates that external sources of cash may have to be found such as new debt or the issuance of additional shares.

Other users still consider the income statement as the most important statement, but they will examine the income statement in conjunction with the cash flow statement in an attempt to understand and analyze a company.

As a future user of financial information, it is important for you to know what to look for on the cash flow statement and to understand what the amounts in the various categories in the statement mean. For this reason, we are going to show you how the statement is developed and also talk about how you should analyze it.

WHY ANOTHER FLOW STATEMENT?

The income statement was the first flow statement we examined. The need for another flow statement is probably best conveyed by the use of an example, the Ajax Widget Company (a fictitious company). The assumptions for the example are listed in the boxes below.

Learning Objective

Understand the importance of cash to the financial health of a company.

Ajax Widget Company

PRODUCT LINE

The Ajax Widget Company sells widgets. A widget* is a hypothetical product for this example.

*Widget is also the trade name for a paint scraper produced by the Gillette Company.

SUPPLIER CREDIT

Widgets cost Ajax $4 apiece. Since Ajax's suppliers do not allow it credit, all inventory must be paid in cash when it is ordered.

SALES/CUSTOMER CREDIT

The widgets currently sell for $5 apiece. Ajax allows its customers up to 30 days to pay for the widgets they buy. For the purpose of this example, it is assumed that all customers pay Ajax on the 30th day after a sale.

 Ajax is a relatively new company and has been experiencing fairly rapid growth in sales. Exhibit 5-1 shows this growth during the first three months of 20x1. Ajax expects that sales will continue to grow at the rate of 600 units per month for at least the next year.

INVENTORY POLICY

Ajax's supply of widgets is such that it cannot get them from the supplier instantaneously. Therefore, it must maintain a certain level of inventory so that units are available when a customer comes to buy one. Ajax's policy is to maintain inventory at the end of the period equal to 50% of the current month's sales. The relationship can be seen in the data in Exhibit 5-1, which lists the sales in units for each month and the ending inventory.

EXHIBIT 5-1

■ AJAX WIDGET COMPANY

Sales/Inventory Data
(Data in units)

	January	February	March
Beginning inventory	250	500	800
New inventory purchases	1,250	1,900	2,500
Goods available for sale	1,500	2,400	3,300
Sales	1,000	1,600	2,200
Ending inventory	500	800	1,100

Learning Objective

Describe the relationship between the cash flow statement and the income statement in assessing management performance

Performance Evaluation Using the Income and Cash Flow Statements

As we have discussed earlier in the text, Ajax's performance can be measured by constructing an income statement. Assuming that the revenues are recognized at the time of sale and that no expenses are incurred other than inventory costs, Exhibit 5-2 shows the income statement for each of the first three months of 20x1.

AJAX WIDGET COMPANY

Income Statement

	January	February	March
Revenues	$5,000	$8,000	$11,000
Cost of goods sold	(4,000)	(6,400)	(8,800)
Net income	$1,000	$1,600	$ 2,200

As can be seen from Exhibit 5-2, net income is growing at a predictable rate—the shareholders and managers should certainly be happy with this growth. Assuming that sales continue to increase at a rate of 600 units per month, this growth in income should continue. In the long run, the investment in Ajax should be profitable.

Exhibit 5-3 provides some information about Ajax's balance sheet The trends in cash, accounts receivable, and inventory shown in Exhibit 5-3 reflect rapid business growth. Accounts receivable reflects an increased level of sales, as does inventory, because ending inventory is a function of sales. The disturbing trend in Exhibit 5-3 is, of course, the decline in the amount of cash on hand for Ajax. To understand the decline in cash, Ajax's cash-to-cash cycle must be considered. Exhibit 5-4 shows the cycle for Ajax.

AJAX WIDGET COMPANY

EXHIBIT 5-3

Partial Balance Sheet

	Dec. 31	Jan. 31	Feb. 28	Mar. 31
Cash	$8,000	$5,500	$2,900	$ 900
Accounts receivable	2,500	5,000	8,000	11,000
Inventory	1,000	2,000	3,200	4,400

AJAX WIDGET COMPANY

EXHIBIT 5-4

Cash-to-Cash Cycle

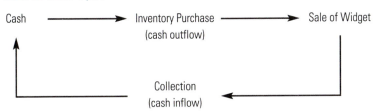

The cash-to-cash cycle illustrates the **lead/lag relationship** between the cash paid out to buy inventory and the cash coming in from collections of accounts receivable. The lag between inventory purchase and sale varies depending on which units are involved. Some units are bought and sold in the same month. Other units are bought in one month, remain in ending inventory, and are sold in the following month. This creates a one-month lag between the outflow of cash for inventory purchases and the sale of those widgets that are carried over in ending inventory.

Learning Objective

3

Describe the cash-to-cash cycle for a retail company through a discussion of the lead/lag relationship.

Therefore, considering both units purchased and units sold in the same period, as well as those that end up in ending inventory, the average lag between purchase and sale is somewhat less than a month. Once a widget is sold, the lag between sale and collection is one month because the collection policy is to allow customers 30 days to pay. Consequently, the total lag between cash outflow and cash inflow is somewhere between one and two months.

Because the income statement measures performance over a particular period of time in the cash-to-cash cycle, it ignores all the timing differences between revenues and expenses recognized and the related cash flows. Therefore, the income statement is not very useful in tracking the cash flows of the company. The income statement will continue to be positive as long as sales are increasing for Ajax. The growth in sales, however, forces Ajax to buy more and more units each month. It is possible that the inventory costs paid in cash in a given month could exceed the cash collections from the previous month's sales. It is evident from the decline in the cash balance in Exhibit 5-3 that this has happened during the first three months of 20x1. Thus, even though net income is increasing each month, the cash position of the company is declining. Because Ajax cannot operate without enough cash, it would make sense to prepare a separate statement in addition to the income statement to measure the company's performance on a cash basis. Hence the need for a cash flow statement.

The cash flow statement cannot replace the income statement; each provides useful information. The income statement summarizes the profitability of the company's operations, while the cash flow statement summarizes the cash flows. To analyze the operations of any company properly, you must consider both profits and cash flows. In the long run, the total profits and net cash flows will be very similar, but they may be quite different for any single year or even over a period of several years.

To understand the usefulness of the information provided by the cash flow statement, think of managing cash as one of the basic duties of the company's management, which must ensure that sufficient cash is maintained on hand both to generate profits now and to invest in assets that will produce profits in the future. Simply producing profits now is not sufficient to ensure the company's long-term survival. Without enough cash to make investments in revenue-producing assets, the long-term viability of the company may be in doubt.

EXHIBIT 5-5

AJAX WIDGET COMPANY

Cash Flow Statement

	January	February	March
Receipts (collections)	$2,500	$5,000	$ 8,000
Payments (inventory costs)	(5,000)	(7,600)	(10,000)
Net cash flow	($2,500)	($2,600)	($ 2,000)

Exhibit 5-5 shows Ajax's cash flow statement for the first three months in 20x1. As can be seen from Exhibit 5-5, the cash flow of the Ajax Widget Company has been negative for the first three months of 20x1. The receipts in the cash flow statement are the collections from the previous month's sales, and the payments are the inventory purchase costs for the month. The inventory costs can be calculated by taking the units purchased in Exhibit 5-1 and multiplying them by the unit cost of $4.

The cash flow statement paints a very different picture of the performance of Ajax during the first quarter of 20x1 than does the income statement. Cash flow is obviously a problem for Ajax. Because Ajax has only $900 left in its cash account, the question it faces is whether cash will run out in April and, if so, how will it be able to buy more inventory so that it can continue doing business? In order to decide whether the problem will persist, Ajax should prepare a forecast for the next several months. In practice, companies prepare these forecasts for 12-, 24-, and even 36-month periods. This provides them with the information needed to manage their cash flows.

Assuming continued growth in sales of 600 units a month and no change in the collection, inventory, and payment policies of the Ajax Widget Company, Exhibit 5-6 illustrates the forecast for the months of April to June.

AJAX WIDGET COMPANY

EXHIBIT 5-6

Net Income, Cash Flow, and Cash Balance Forecast

	April	May	June
Revenues	$ 14,000	$ 17,000	$ 20,000
Cost of goods sold	(11,200)	(13,600)	(16,000)
Net income	$ 2,800	$ 3,400	$ 4,000
Receipts (collections)	$ 11,000	$ 14,000	$ 17,000
Payments (inventory costs)	(12,400)	(14,800)	(17,200)
Net cash flow	$ (1,400)	$ (800)	$ (200)
End of month cash balance	$ (500)	$ (1,300)	$ (1,500)

As can be seen from Exhibit 5-6, income continues to grow by $600 each month, reflecting the growth in sales of 600 units times the net profit margin of $1 per unit. The cash flow statement indicates that net cash flow will be negative for the next three months, but the trend is that net cash flow is improving and it looks as though it will be positive by July. The ending cash balance is projected to be negative for the next three months and will take longer to return to a positive cash balance. This is a problem because Ajax cannot operate with a negative cash balance. Operating with a negative cash balance is feasible only if the bank permits a company to overdraw its bank accounts; that is, if it allows more cash to be withdrawn than was deposited. A negative cash balance is really a loan from the bank. Companies will often make arrangements with the bank for circumstances like this. The loan arrangement is called a **line of credit**. The bank will set a maximum limit on how much can be borrowed in this way and will also establish the repayment schedule if the line of credit is used.

The problem is perhaps best portrayed by Exhibit 5-7, which graphs the situation with regard to net income, cash flow, and cash balance for the entire year 20x1. Note the cash balance line, which drops below zero in April and returns to a positive balance in September. In reality, the company cannot have a negative cash balance without making special arrangements with its bank, and something must be done to prevent the problem from continuing for too long. Nevertheless, the graph clearly shows the magnitude and duration of Ajax's cash flow problem.

EXHIBIT 5-7

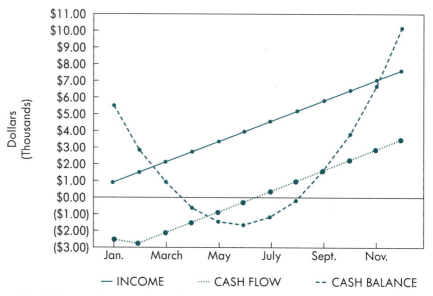

— INCOME   ⋯⋯ CASH FLOW   -- CASH BALANCE

Cash flow problems such as the one just described may appear to be extreme and, indeed, we developed it so that you could easily see that Ajax had a cash flow problem. The following report about **Nortel Networks Corp.**, a telecommunications company, illustrates how cash flow problems can affect a real company.

accounting in the news

LONG-TERM DEBT USED TO OVERCOME CASH FLOW PROBLEM

In August 2001, Nortel Networks Corp. issued $1 billion (U.S.) in convertible bonds. As a result of a drop in sales caused by a decline in consumer spending, Nortel was experiencing a shortage of cash. It had already reduced its workforce by about one third (30,000 jobs) and needed the cash to continue its operations until consumer spending improved. The bonds were issued at an interest rate of 4.75% and are convertible into Nortel shares at the option of the bondholder. This type of bond is very popular with investors because it provides an interest payment (a fixed return to the investor) and enables the investor to convert the bonds to shares if the market value of the shares increases. If the bondholders do convert their bonds, there will be an increase in the total number of shares outstanding, which will dilute the value of the shares held by the current shareholders.

Source: "Nortel moves to raise cash," by Simon Tuck, *globeandmail.com*, August 8, 2001, 8:05 pm edt.

Update: In June of 2002, Nortel Networks was again in need of cash. More employees had been laid off, but continued slow sales meant it needed additional cash to carry it until sales improved. This time it issued shares, raising over $1 billion.

Nortel Networks is attempting to manage its cash flow problem through borrowing, curtailing expansion, and reducing costs. Would these solutions work for Ajax? There are many ways in which Ajax can address its cash flow problem. Before you read on, you might want to take a few moments to think about how you would solve Ajax's cash flow problem.

Solutions to the Cash Flow Problem

Learning Objective
4

Identify some solutions to cash flow problems.

The cash flow difficulties that Ajax is experiencing are typical of many new companies. These problems have three fundamental causes: high growth rates in sales, significant lead/lag relationships in cash inflows and outflows, and under capitalization. The use of the term **capitalization** in this situation refers to how much cash the company has to start with. Start-up companies generally experience rapid growth of sales. This increase in sales requires them to buy or produce more and more inventory as well as to expand their storage or operating capacity. Buying more inventory and expanding capacity both require cash.

Compounding the growth problem is the presence of significant lead/lag relationships between the company's cash inflows and outflows. If there were no lead/lag relationship, then, as long as the product could be sold for more than it cost to produce or buy, there would be no cash flow problem. Most companies, however, do have some significant lead/lag relationships in their cash flows, which are magnified in periods of high growth.

Finally, start-up companies tend to be undercapitalized, that is, they do not have a large pool of cash to start with. When the large cash needs appear, imposed by rapid growth and the lead/lag relationships, the company has no cash reserves to get it through prolonged periods of cash outflows. Start-up companies (as well as other companies in rapid growth phases) will experience cash flow problems at some point. In Ajax's case, the problems create a crisis during the month of April. Solutions to the three causes of Ajax's cash flow problems are discussed in the following subsections.

Growth One way to solve Ajax's problem is to slow down the rate of growth of sales. Exhibit 5-8 shows graphically what happens when the rate of growth in sales is 500 units per month rather than 600. All other facts and assumptions are considered to be unchanged. You can see from the graph that this solves the cash flow problem because the cash balance line does not dip below zero in any month. Cash flows are still negative in some early months, but the balance in cash is sufficient to absorb these cash outflows. Limiting growth may not be the proper response in this case because it may be detrimental to the company in the long run. Limiting growth is likely to divert customers to competitors, and those customers may develop loyalties to those competitors and reduce the company's long-run potential in terms of developing a strong customer base.

EXHIBIT 5-8

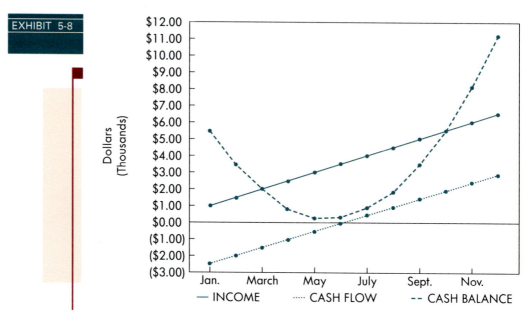

Capitalization   A second way to solve the cash problem is to address the undercapitalization problem; that is, to start with more cash. This larger amount of cash may be obtained in numerous ways. Two typical ways are to issue additional shares (equity) in the company and to borrow the cash (debt). If Ajax issues new shares, the cash flow projections will have to be adjusted to incorporate the additional cash inflow from the issuance and any subsequent outflows for dividends. If money is borrowed, the cash flow projections will have to be adjusted for the initial inflow from the borrowing as well as for the subsequent payments of principal and interest that will occur in the future. Exhibit 5-9 shows what will happen if an additional $2,000 is obtained at the beginning of January from the issuance of shares. For simplicity, it is assumed that there are no dividends. Note, again, that this solves the cash flow problem.

EXHIBIT 5-9

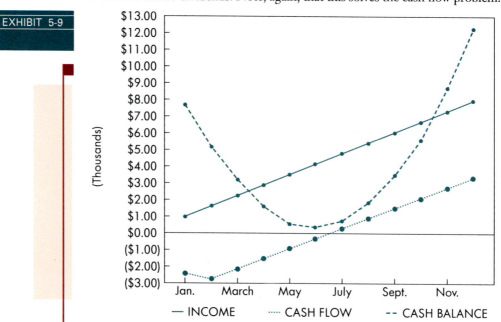

This solution of increased capitalization is not without its own problems. The first is that if shares are issued, the current shareholders of Ajax will be giving up control of some portion of their investment in the company, and they may not want to do that. It may also be difficult to find additional investors willing to take the risk of buying shares in the company. Second, if Ajax decides to attempt to borrow the additional capital, it may not be able to convince a lender that it is worthy of a loan. Lenders are typically very sceptical of new ventures.

Lead/Lag Relationships   The third way to solve Ajax's cash flow problem is to change the lead/lag relationships between the cash inflows and outflows. There are numerous ways to do this. One is to change Ajax's accounts receivable, accounts payable, or inventory policies. Collecting on accounts receivable sooner or selling for cash or via credit card, paying accounts payable later, or reducing the amount of inventory on hand would all reduce the difference between the cash outflow and inflow in a given month. Exhibit 5-10, for example, shows what will happen if the accounts receivable policy is changed to require customers to pay within three weeks rather than one month.

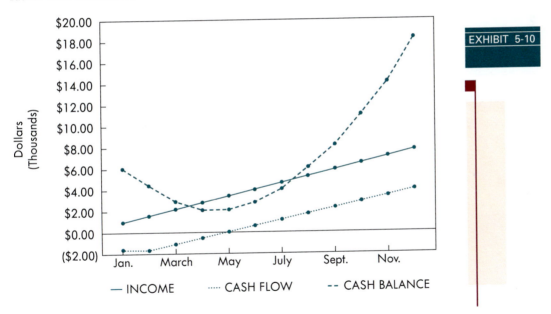

EXHIBIT 5-10

This change would be sufficient to solve the cash flow problem, assuming everything else remains the same. Of course, everything else may not stay the same. If Ajax institutes this change, it is likely that some customers will no longer do business with it if they can get better payment terms from a competitor. Thus the rate of growth in sales may be affected. Ajax, therefore, may need to make changes in some other assumptions before it can realistically conclude that this will solve its problem. In this case, however, you know from Exhibit 5-8 that slowing the rate of growth will actually help solve the cash flow problem.

In our example, Ajax must pay cash for the inventory that it buys from its supplier. A supplier may be reluctant initially to sell inventory to a new company on credit. The company has no track record on which the supplier can gauge its creditworthiness. Once Ajax has proved to the supplier that it can pay cash for increasing amounts of inventory, the supplier may be willing to grant 30-day credit terms. Establishing this creditworthiness takes time, however, and does not solve Ajax's initial cash flow problem.

Besides changing Ajax's receivables, payables, and inventory policies, there are other ways to affect the lead/lag relationship. Changing either the price or cost of a widget would affect the amounts in the lead/lag relationship and could therefore solve the problem. Remember, however, that changes in these items may also affect other assumptions, such as sales growth.

Decisions about cash management are not always about handling a cash shortage. More often they are about how to spend the cash that has been generated. Note the following example:

accounting in the news

WESTJET AIRLINES

Posting record profits for the year your industry lost US $10 billion is one measure of success. Another is knowing your business operations well enough to gauge how best to grow.

This was the task facing Clive Beddoe, head of WestJet Airlines, soon after the Calgary-based discount air carrier reported 2001 earnings of $37.2 million, 23% more than the year before.

While other air executives sweated through cost-cutting measures, Beddoe was weighing the risks of spreading WestJet's wings, as cities dangled attractive financial incentives for the air carrier's service.

WestJet has followed a steady expansion pattern of allotting a third of its growth to new destinations, a third to more frequent flights, and a third to new connections among existing destinations. Yet the company has consistently grown beyond its capacity since it first took to the air in 1996.

For the moment, plans included an expansion into eastern Canada, most notably into Toronto, Air Canada's hub. WestJet's fleet, which numbered 27 Boeing aircraft, was to more than triple by 2008. For Beddoe, the trick was incorporating each new city into the network while maintaining aircraft and staff efficiencies.

But the big challenge Beddoe saw was not to give in to the temptation to grow beyond the company's ability to sustain the growth.

Source: "WestJet wary of growing too fast," by Peter Fitzpatrick, *National Post, Financial Post*, Feb. 7, 2002, p. FP4.

To summarize, it is clear that a cash flow statement provides additional information that is not captured by the income statement and balance sheet alone. For a shareholder, manager, or other user of the financial statements, it is important to understand the relationship between the company's income, its cash-to-cash cycle, and its cash flow statement. Also, understanding how receivables, payables, and inventory policies affect the company's cash flows is extremely important in evaluating its performance. We discuss in greater detail how users interpret cash flow information later in the chapter.

We now turn to the components of cash flow; then we explain the preparation of a cash flow statement. Finally, we explain how the cash flow statement can be used to assess the financial health of a company.

THE CASH FLOW STATEMENT

History

In 1985, the cash flow statement, then called the statement of changes in financial position, became a true cash flow statement. Prior to 1985, companies could prepare a cash flow statement or a statement of **working capital** flows. Working capital is current assets minus current liabilities. In 1985, companies no longer had a choice; they had to show the changes in cash flows. It was in 1985 that companies were first asked to show the changes in the cash flows through the three activities: operating, financing, and investing.

In 1998, some changes were introduced to the statement. First, the title "cash flow statement" replaced "statement of changes in financial position." As well, the articulation of what to include in operating, financing, and investing activities was more clearly defined. The cash flow statements from real companies and the discussions in this chapter follow the new guidelines.

Definition of Cash and Cash Equivalents

As we have seen above, proper management of cash is one of the critical tasks that management of all organizations must achieve. Having too little cash on hand results in not being able to pay liabilities and expenses. If this continues, bankruptcy will result. Having too much cash on hand is also a problem in that it is not efficient. Cash held in chequing accounts typically earns little or no interest. It is much better to invest excess cash in some kind of temporary investment that will earn interest. Thus, the proper management of cash involves the management of cash, short-term borrowings, and temporary investments.

Therefore, in considering cash flows that are to be summarized in the cash flow statement, rather than restricting our consideration to just cash, we must consider the broader concept of cash and cash equivalents, sometimes called the **cash position**. We use the term **cash equivalents** to include the short-term, highly liquid investments that are readily convertible into known amounts of cash. They also must be close enough to maturity that there is little risk of changes in their value due to changes in interest rates. The time frame suggested is three months or less. Items that commonly meet these criteria are Government of Canada Treasury Bills and demand loans of other companies. A demand loan is payable on demand, which means that it is very liquid. Cash equivalents also include short-term borrowings that companies use to cover their cash shortages for short periods of time, such as lines of credit. However, a normal short-term bank loan would not be called a cash equivalent. Rather, it would be a financing activity.

Components of Cash Flows

In discussing the components of cash flows, we are going back to Chapter 1 where we discussed the three components of the management of any business. First, you must find sufficient long-term financing from investments by shareholders or long-term borrowings to provide sufficient capitalization for the business. Next you must invest these funds in assets that you will use to produce revenues and profits. Finally, you must operate the business, carrying on the revenue generating activities for which the company was established.

The basic format of the cash flow statement summarizes all the cash flows into these three groups of activities. The cash flow statement for **Sears Canada** for the 52 weeks ended December 29, 2001, and December 30, 2000 is presented in Appendix A at the end of the book. We will use its cash flow statement as an example. Note that the cash flow statement is divided into the three activities: Operations with a net cash inflow of $241.7 million for 2001, Investment Activities with a net cash outflow of $113.8 million for 2001, and Financing Activities with a net cash inflow of $65.9 million for 2001. The net cash inflow for 2001 is $193.8 million. The final section of the cash flow statement shows how this net cash outflow, when added to the cash position at the beginning of the year of $135.5 million results in a cash position of $329.3 million at the end of the year. Sears Canada defines its cash equivalents as "cash and short-term investments." In summary, the cash flow statement summarizes all the cash flows for 2001 that resulted in the increase in cash position during the year.

Financing Activities

Financing activities are described as the activities involved in obtaining resources from shareholders and from lenders, and repaying those shareholders and lenders. Transactions classified as financing typically involve balance sheet accounts associated with equity capital and with short- and long-term borrowing. Typical cash inflows would be those from issuing shares, bonds, mortgages, notes, and other borrowings. Outflows include dividends paid to shareholders, repurchase of shares, and repayment of the principal of any debt obligation.

A special word is needed about interest and dividends. A company pays interest to lenders in exchange for the use of their money. Shareholders are repaid with dividends. Interest expense is associated with a debt which is a financing activity, but because interest is used in the determination of net income, interest payments are included in the operating section. Dividends, on the other hand, are not used in the determination of net income. They are therefore included in the financing section.

Some analysts (particularly bank lenders) would prefer, in their own analyses, to show the interest outflow in the financing section. They can accomplish this quite easily by simply moving the interest from the operating section to the financing section. This can readily be done because companies are required to disclose the amount of cash used for interest expense.

In the cash flow statement of Sears Canada found in Appendix A at the end of the book, the items included in the financing activities section are fairly typical:

> Issue of long-term obligations: inflows of $200 million; repayment of long-term obligations: outflow of $110.6 million; net proceeds from issue of capital stock: inflow of $2.1 million; and dividends paid: outflow of $25.6 million

Sears Canada used both debt and the issuance of shares as ways of raising additional cash in both 2001 and 2000. It has also been paying off substantial amounts of its long-term debt each year. In both 2001 and 2000, it paid dividends of $25.6 million. This is a sign of stability in a company. Investors who are interested in an annual dividend as a form of income would look for a company such as Sears Canada, which generates a positive cash flow and pays a regular dividend.

An International Perspective

Reports from Other Countries

The categorization of cash flows under Canadian GAAP is somewhat different from that in other countries. In the UK, for instance, cash flows are categorized under seven standard headings:

Operating activities
Returns on investments and servicing of finance
Taxation
Capital expenditures and financial investment
Acquisition and disposals
Equity dividends paid
Management of liquid resources
Financing

Cash is defined as "cash in hand and deposits repayable on demand at any qualifying institution less overdrafts from any qualifying institution repayable on demand."

Source: Financial Reporting Standards (FRS) 1: Cash Flow Statements, revised 1996.

Investing Activities

Transactions classified as **investing activities** typically involve balance sheet accounts classified as long-term assets. Typical transactions in this section would be investment in property, plant, and equipment and its subsequent sale or disposal, as well as investments in long-term marketable securities. The purchase or sale of any short-term investments which are not classified as cash equivalents would also be included in the investing section. In Sears Canada's cash flow statement, examples of these types of items are:

> Purchases of capital assets: outflows of $143.4 million; proceeds from sale of capital assets: inflows of $17.7 million; charge account receivables: inflows of $56.1 million; deferred charges: outflows of $13.4 million; acquisition of Eaton's: outflows of $23.5 million; investments and other assets: outflows of $7.3 million.

Note that Sears Canada had an outflow of cash for investment activities in 2001 and 2000. This is typical of companies. Usually, as companies are going through the normal process of replacing long-lived assets, they spend more for the new assets than they get for selling the old ones. This usually results in a net cash outflow for investing activities.

Before moving on to operating activities, we want to give you some more information about the acquisition of capital assets and investments. The amounts you see reported on the cash flow statement for the acquisition of capital assets and investments represent the amount of cash equivalents that was used by the company in the acquisition. For example, assume a company purchased a piece of land with a building for $500,000. The company paid 10% down ($50,000) and assumed a long-term mortgage for the balance ($450,000). The cash flow statement would only show the acquisition cash outflow of $50,000 under investing activities. Neither the remaining $450,000 of the acquisition nor the $450,000 representing the new mortgage would appear on the cash flow statement because cash did not flow in or out for the $450,000. Because the information about the new acquisition and the new debt do not appear on the cash flow statement, users need to be very vigilant about examining the assets and liabilities on the balance sheet and reading the notes to the financial statements in order to find information like this that is not specifically reported on one of the financial statements.

Operating Activities

Operating activities include all other transactions not covered by financing or investing activities. The operating section typically includes the cash flows that result directly from the sale of goods and services to customers. Transactions classified as operating activities typically involve balance sheet accounts classified as current assets and current liabilities. The major cash inflow is from the collection of revenues from customers. The major cash outflow is from payments to suppliers (for inventory, materials, labour, etc.). As mentioned earlier in the Financing Activities section, interest payments are also included in this section of the cash flow statement. One other cash flow worth noting in the operating section is related to taxes. Even though taxes are affected by all three types of activity, the net results of the taxes on the company are reported in the operating section of the cash flow statement.

A complete record of the gross amount of cash coming into the company from operating activities would show the total amount of cash received from revenues and collections from customers as inflows, and the total amount of cash paid out to suppliers for expenses and accounts payable as outflows. This approach, called the **direct approach**, is theoretically very informative, but is rarely used in the cash flow statement. When we prepared the cash flow statement for Demo Retail Company Ltd. in Chapter 2, we used the direct approach. The method normally used in published cash flow statements is the **indirect approach**. Note that these two approaches differ only in the format and content of the Operating Activities section. The Investing and Financing Activities sections are the same for both approaches.

The indirect approach does not report the full gross cash flows from operating activities; instead, it shows only the net cash flows. Using the indirect approach, the operating section starts with reported net income and then shows adjustments to net income to arrive at the net cash flows from operations. The adjustments are in two groups. The first group includes items from the income statement that do not involve cash flows. In the Sears Canada cash flow statement, note that the net income is adjusted by the items listed under the heading "Non-cash items included in earnings." The items in this group are depreciation, amortization gain on sale of receivables, and future income taxes. Depreciation and amortization do not involve a cash payment the way other expenses such as wages do. These expenses merely involve recognizing the use of a long-term asset. The cash outflow related to that asset occurred when the asset was purchased, which probably happened several years ago and was initially reported in the Investing Section of the cash flow statement as an outflow of cash. As a result of recognizing depreciation and amortization, the net income figure has been reduced by the amount of the expense that does not represent a current cash outflow. Note the journal entries in the following example:

A-Equipment	10,000	
A-Cash		10,000
SE-Amortization expense	1,000	
XA-Accumulated amortization		1,000

There was an outflow when the asset was purchased, but each time it is amortized there is no cash effect. The depreciation and amortization expenses are thus added back to net income to determine the actual net cash flows from operating activities for the year. The adding back of future income taxes is similar in nature. On the income statement, the income tax expense represents the amount of tax that will likely have to be paid on the revenues less expenses that are recognized in the current period. All of those income taxes may not be owed to the Canada Customs and Revenue Agency (CCRA) in the current year, because CCRA rules about recognition are not always the same as those in accounting. Income tax expense that is deducted to arrive at net income is the amount owed for this year (which is probably paid, and thus is a cash outflow) plus the amount that will be owed in future years (the future income taxes). To arrive at the net cash flow from operating activities, it is necessary to add the future income taxes to the net income amount because they do not represent a cash outflow yet. For now, we are going to leave aside the explanation of the gain on the sale of receivables.

Adjustments in the second group are needed because all revenues and expenses do not result in immediate cash flows. If accounts receivable increase, this means that not all of the revenues have been collected in cash; some will be collected later. Thus Sears Canada's cash flow statement shows an adjustment for net change in non-cash working capital of $28.8 million. Remember that working capital is current assets minus current liabilities. If we look at Note 12 referred to on the cash flow statement, the 2001 changes in the following current assets and liabilities are identified (in millions):

Accounts receivable	$ 70.2
Inventories	150.7
Prepaid expenses and other assets	(6.1)
Accounts payable	(204.7)
Accrued liabilities	0.1
Income and other taxes payable	18.6
	$ 28.8

On Sears Canada's balance sheet in Appendix A at the end of the book, the accounts receivable amount has decreased from $942 million in 2000 to $871.9 million in 2001, a decline of $70.1 million. (The discrepancy between the difference in the amounts on the balance sheet, $70.1 million, and the difference as reported in note 12, $70.2 million, is probably a result of rounding.) This means that $70.1 million more than the sales amount reported on the income statement was collected during the year. Fewer accounts receivable are owed at the end of the year than were owed at the beginning of the year. The cash flow is represented by the following formula:

Beginning A/R + Sales − Ending A/R = Cash Flow from Sales

When the amounts from Sears Canada's financial statements are slotted into this formula, the following emerges:

$942 million + $6,726.4 million − $871.9 million = $6,796.5 million

The cash flow from sales is $70.1 million more than the sales amount ($6,796.5 million − $6,726.4 million). To summarize, when there is a decrease in accounts receivable over the year, the sales figure that is included in the income statement does not represent the amount of cash flow from sales. It is too small. Thus a decrease in accounts receivable is added to the net income amount in order to determine the cash flow from operations.

Changes in other current assets and liabilities included in this second group follow similar reasoning. A decrease in current assets reflects an increase in the amount of cash inflow from operating activities. An increase in current assets reflects a decrease in the amount of cash inflow or a net cash outflow from operating activities. A decrease in current liabilities such as accounts payable means that cash was used to pay down the liabilities, which is a cash outflow adjustment. An increase in current liabilities indicates that cash was saved by not paying the liabilities this year. This cash saving is the same as an increase in cash from operations. The following chart should help you learn whether to add or subtract the change in the current assets and liabilities:

Current Account	Change in the Current Account	
	Increase	Decrease
Current Asset	Subtract	Add
Current Liability	Add	Subtract

Referring back to Note 12 from Sears Canada's financial statements, the prepaid expenses and other assets and accounts payable are negative. This means that the prepaid expenses and other assets increased, and the accounts payable decreased. The accounts receivable, inventories, accrued liabilities, and income and other payables are positive. This means that the accounts receivable and inventories decreased, and the accrued liabilities and income and other payables increased. You can verify this by calculating the changes in these accounts on the balance sheet in the Appendix at the end of the book.

AN INTERNATIONAL PERSPECTIVE

Reports from Other Countries

NAFTA Facts

United States—A cash flow statement is required and can be prepared using either the direct or indirect approach. As in Canada, the indirect approach is used most often. Cash flows are segregated into operating, investing, and financing activities. The disclosure requirements in the United States are very similar to those required in Canada under the 1998 changes.

Mexico—The statement of changes in financial position is typically presented as a cash flow statement. Mexican GAAP requires that the financial statements be adjusted for the effect of inflation. A portion of inflation adjustment is typically shown in the operating section, and another portion due to adjustments to the debt balances of the company is shown in the financing section.

PREPARATION OF THE CASH FLOW STATEMENT

Learning Objective

Prepare a cash flow statement from a company's balance sheet and income statement.

To illustrate the preparation of a cash flow statement, another example will be used. Exhibit 5-11 shows the balance sheet for Huskies Industries Ltd. (a fictitious company) for the year ended December 31, 20x1. Exhibit 5-12 shows the income statement for Huskies Industries for the same period.

HUSKIES INDUSTRIES LTD.

Balance Sheet

	Dec. 31, 20x1	Dec. 31, 20x0
Cash	$ 6,050	$ 19,500
Accounts receivable	10,000	20,000
Inventory	40,000	30,000
Prepaid rent	600	500
Total current assets	56,650	70,000
Property, plant, and equipment	159,000	100,000
Accumulated amortization	(69,200)	(50,000)
Net capital assets	89,800	50,000
Total assets	$146,450	$120,000
Accounts payable	$ 11,000	$ 6,000
Notes payable	200	100
Accrued salaries	400	300
Dividends payable	470	300
Total current liabilities	12,070	6,700
Bonds payable	46,000	40,000
Total liabilities	58,070	46,700
Common shares	29,000	25,000
Retained earnings	59,380	48,300
Total shareholders' equity	88,380	73,300
Total liabilities and shareholders' equity	$146,450	$120,000

HUSKIES INDUSTRIES LTD.

Income Statement
For the year ended December 31, 20x1

Sales revenue		$130,000
Cost of goods sold		80,000
Gross profit margin		50,000
Rent expense	$ 7,100	
Miscellaneous cash expenses	600	
Amortization	20,000	
Salaries expense	9,600	
Total expenses		37,300
Income from operations		12,700
Gain on sale of property, plant, and equipment		300
Income before income tax		13,000
Income tax		520
Net income		$ 12,480

In addition to the balance sheet and income statement, the following additional information applies to the transactions of Huskies Industries Ltd. for 20x1:

1. Huskies Industries is a retailer and, as such, all amounts added to its inventory reflect purchases at wholesale prices. All inventory is purchased on credit from suppliers.
2. Huskies Industries sells its products to customers on credit. There are no cash sales.
3. During the year, Huskies Industries sold (for $500 in cash) equipment that had an original cost of $1,000 and a book value of $200, thus recording a gain on sale of $300.
4. Huskies Industries borrowed an additional $8,000 by issuing bonds in 20x1.
5. Notes payable were used during 20x1 for short-term financing.

T-Account Approach

Our objective is to construct a cash flow statement from the information given above, which is typical of most companies, although simplified for illustrative purposes. We want to determine all of the cash flows that would have occurred to produce the balances shown above. Several methods can be used to determine the underlying cash flows, but all of them require, at a minimum, a balance sheet showing balances at the beginning and end of the year, plus an income statement for the current year. In addition, some additional information may be required.

Two of the common methods used to determine the underlying cash flows are to use a set of T-accounts or to use a work sheet. The T-account approach will be used here, but remember that a work sheet could also be used for the same task. Also, we will show the preparation of a cash flow statement using only the indirect approach, as virtually all published cash flow statements use this format. For completeness, we include the T-account preparation of the cash flow statement using the direct approach found on the *Accounting Perspectives CD*.

Cash Flow Statement: Direct Approach

Exhibit 5-13 shows the set-up of the T-account approach. Note that a large T-account has been included for cash because the objective of this exercise is to reconstruct all the transactions that affected cash in this account. All the accounts from the balance sheet are listed, including their beginning and ending balances. The objective is to reconstruct the transactions that occurred during 20x1 and to include as much detail as possible regarding the nature of the cash transactions. Within the cash account, the transactions are categorized into the three basic activities discussed above: operating, financing, and investing activities. Note that as we start to reconstruct the transactions, we are working outside the formal company records. The transactions that we are reconstructing already occurred during the year and were recorded as isolated transactions. We are trying to determine what the aggregate of those transactions is and how they are related to cash.

HUSKIES INDUSTRIES LTD.

Cash Flow T-Accounts

A-Cash	
✓ 19,500	
Operating:	
Financing:	
Investing:	
✓ 6,050	

A-Acc. Rec.		A-Inventory		A-Prepaid Rent	
✓ 20,000		✓ 30,000		✓ 500	
✓ 10,000		✓ 40,000		✓ 600	

A-PP&E		XA-Accum. Amort.		L-Acc. Pay.	
✓ 100,000			50,000 ✓		6,000 ✓
✓ 159,000			69,200 ✓		11,000 ✓

L-Notes Pay.		L-Accrued Salaries		L-Dividends Payable	
	100 ✓		300 ✓		300 ✓
	200 ✓		400 ✓		470 ✓

L-Bonds Payable		SE-Common Shares		SE-Retained Earnings	
	40,000 ✓		25,000 ✓		48,300 ✓
	46,000 ✓		29,000 ✓		59,380 ✓

In Exhibit 5-14, the analysis for the cash flow statement has been reconstructed for 20x1. The entries in the T-accounts have been given transaction numbers and each is discussed in its section.

HUSKIES INDUSTRIES LTD.

EXHIBIT 5-14

Cash Flow T-Accounts

A-Cash

✓	19,500					
Operating:			10,000	(3)	Increase in inventory	
Net income	(1)	12,480	100	(4)	Increase in ppd. rent	
Decrease in A/R	(2)	10,000	300	(8)	Gain on sale of equip.	
Increase in A/P	(5)	5,000				
Incr. in acc. sal.	(6)	100				
Amortization	(7)	20,000				
Financing:			2,000	(12)	Prepay. of bond	
Proceeds from note	(10)	100	1,230	(15)	Pay. of dividends	
Proceeds from bond	(11)	8,000				
Issue of shares	(13)	4,000				
Investing:			60,000	(9)	Purchase of PP&E	
Sale of equip.	(8)	500				
✓	6,050					

A-Acc. Rec.

✓	20,000		
		10,000	(2)
✓	10,000		

A-Inventory

✓	30,000	
(3)	10,000	
✓	40,000	

A-Prepaid Rent

✓	500	
(4)	100	
✓	600	

A-PP&E

✓	100,000			
(9)	60,000	1,000	(8)	
✓	159,000			

XA-Accum. Amort.

		50,000	✓	
(8)	800	20,000	(7)	
		69,200	✓	

L-Acc. Pay.

	6,000	✓
	5,000	(5)
	11,000	✓

L-Notes Pay.

	100	✓
	100	(10)
	200	✓

L-Accrued Salaries

	300	✓
	100	(6)
	400	✓

L-Dividends Payable

		300	✓
(15)	1,230	1,400	(14)
		470	✓

L-Bonds Payable

		40,000	✓
(12)	2,000	8,000	(11)
		46,000	✓

SE-Common Shares

	25,000	✓
	4,000	(13)
	29,000	✓

SE-Retained Earnings

		48,300	✓
(14)	1,400	12,480	(1)
		59,380	✓

In the indirect approach, the operating activities section is constructed by starting with net income and then reconciling it to its net cash flow equivalent. In this approach, net income is initially assumed to increase cash by the amount of the net income (or decrease cash by the amount of a net loss). This is not strictly true because many of the items in income do not represent cash flows. For example, as we discussed on page 277, amortization has no effect on cash. The remaining entries in the operating section, except for the gain on the sale of equipment, use the current asset and liability accounts to adjust all the items that compose the net income to the amount of the cash flows that actually occurred.

In using the T-account method, it is very convenient to reconstruct the summary journal entries that would have been recorded for each of the accounts to determine the resulting net cash flows. These reconstructed journal entries are not essential, but they are a convenient method of determining what happened. Remember that they are only intended for us to understand what occurred; they are not recorded in the accounting system. For example, the cash impact of net income on cash is as follows:

(1) The entry is:

A-Cash (Operating)	12,480	
SE-Retained Earnings		12,480

One of the adjustments that must be made when all the net income is assumed to increase cash results from the assumption that all the revenues included in net income are collected in cash. The change in the balance of accounts receivable shows the net effect of the difference between the sales revenue recorded during the period and the cash collected from customers.

In the case of Huskies Industries, the accounts receivable balance decreased during the year, which means that there were more collections (credit entries to the accounts receivable account) than sales (debit entries to the accounts receivable account). This, in turn, means that Huskies collected more cash than its sales figure shows. The adjustment to the cash account, therefore, shows an increase in cash over that represented by the revenues included in net income. In effect, this adjustment adds $10,000 to the revenues shown of $130,000 and is included in net income to produce a net figure of $140,000 in cash received from customers as follows:

Sales revenues	$130,000
Decrease in accounts receivable	10,000
Cash collections from sales	$140,000

The net or summary entry to represent this adjustment is as follows:

(2) The entry is:

A-Cash (Operating)	10,000	
A-Accounts receivable		10,000

A second assumption that requires an adjustment is that the cost of goods sold reduced cash during the period by the same amount. There are two reasons why this may be incorrect. The first is that the goods sold, represented by the amounts shown in cost of goods sold, may have come from the beginning inventory (i.e., purchases that were made last year) and may not have required an outflow of cash this year (assuming the accounts payable associated with the inventory purchased were paid last year). The change in the balance of inventory provides information about this potential adjustment.

A second reason would be the assumption that purchases of inventory during the period resulted in accounts payable, assuming all purchases are bought on credit. Therefore, if these accounts were not paid as at year end, the expenses reported would not yet have resulted in cash outflows. The effects of both these factors can be corrected by adjusting the net income number by the net change in the inventory balance and the net change in the accounts payable balance. The effect of these two entries is to adjust the cost of goods sold amount included in the net income ($80,000) to its cash equivalent of cash paid to suppliers ($85,000) as follows:

Cost of goods sold as reported (assumed cash outflow)	($80,000)
Increase in inventory (requiring extra cash outflow)	(10,000)
Increase in accounts payable (meaning less cash paid out)	5,000
Actual cash paid to suppliers	($85,000)

The entries to represent these adjustments are as follows:

(3) and (5) The entries are:

A-Inventory	10,000	
A-Cash (Operating)		10,000
A-Cash (Operating)	5,000	
L-Accounts payable		5,000

Two other expenses on the income statement have corresponding current assets or liabilities: rent expense (prepaid rent) and salaries expense (accrued salaries). Since there is prepaid rent on the balance sheet, Huskies evidently prepays its rent. The increase in the prepaid rent ($100) indicates that more cash was paid out than is reflected in the rent expense. The entry to represent this adjustment is as follows:

(4) The entry is:

A-Prepaid rent	100	
A-Cash (Operating)		100

The salaries expense account has a related liability account, accrued salaries. The increase in accrued salaries ($100) means that Huskies reduced the outflow of cash by owing more to employees at the end of the year than it owed at the beginning of the year. The salaries expense on the income statement is $100 larger than the actual cash outflow for salaries. The entry to represent this adjustment is as follows:

(6) The entry is:

A-Cash (Operating)	100	
L-Accrued salaries		100

A third type of adjustment results from the assumption that all other expenses represent cash outflows. Amortization expense is not a cash expense. Amortization is merely a recognition that part of the long-term assets are used up each year, but no cash flows are associated with amortization expense. The associated cash flow occurred years before when the assets were purchased. Therefore, because amortization expense is included in calculating net income and results in a decrease in net income, its effect must be removed by adding it back to net income to show the net income figure that would have resulted if we had not included amortization expense.

One caveat at this point: because this adjustment is on the debit side of the cash account, it looks as though amortization is a source of cash. This is not true. Cash collections from customers are the source of cash from operations. It is only because the indirect method is attempting to correct the misstatements made by assuming that all net income increases cash that this item appears as if it were a source of cash. Many analysts approximate the cash from operations of a company by adding amortization to the company's net income. This is a quick and reasonably close approximation to cash received from operations. However, this method ignores the adjustments due to the other accounts that are shown in Exhibit 5-14.

The entry to adjust for amortization is as follows:

(7) The entry is:

A-Cash (Operating)	20,000	
XA-Accumulated amortization		20,000

The last adjustment in the operating section adjusts the net income number for the gain from the sale of the equipment. The $300 gain shown in income assumes that $300 was received in cash. However, point 3 from the additional information provided at the outset of the example indicated that $500 cash was received on the disposal of the equipment. Thus the effect on cash is $500, not $300. Therefore, making the assumption that the $300 increase in the net income figure represents the cash inflow is not correct.

The original entry to record the sale was as follows:

A-Cash	500	
XA-Accumulated amortization	800	
A-PP&E		1,000
SE-Gain on sale of equipment		300

The second problem is that, even if this were the right amount, it would be reported in the wrong section of the cash flow statement. Companies invest in property, plant, and equipment, so cash flows resulting from disposals of property, plant, and equipment are also investing (or, more properly, disinvesting) activities. These are not operating cash flows. The entry to correct for these two misstatements makes two adjustments. It adjusts the amount of cash that actually was received, and it corrects the activity that was affected. The entry to represent these two items is as follows:

(8) The entry is:

A-Cash (Investing)	500	
XA-Accumulated amortization	800	
A-Cash (Operating)		300
A-PP&E		1,000

Remember when we were discussing **Sears Canada's** cash flow statement earlier? In the operating activities section, it had included "a gain on sale of receivables" as part of its adjustments for non-cash items included in net earnings. The gain means that more cash was received for the receivables that were sold than their carrying value (or book value). The actual cash received is shown in the investing section as "charge account receivables" of $56.1 million. If the receivables had been sold for a loss instead of a gain, the loss would have been added back to the operating section. Then the actual cash proceeds from the sale (including the gain or loss) would be included in the investing section.

The remaining items adjust for the cash flows that resulted from the financing and investing activities. To determine the cash flows for financing and investing activities, look for changes in long-term assets, financing liabilities (both short- and long-term), and shareholders' equity accounts. The amount of the purchases of new property, plant, and equipment can be determined by considering the beginning and ending balances in the property, plant, and equipment summary account and the credit entry made to this account in entry (8). Note that to reach the ending balance of $159,000 an additional debit of $60,000 is needed. We assume that additional assets were purchased for cash. This cash outflow is shown in the investing section. The entry is represented as follows:

(9) The entry is:

A-PP&E	60,000	
A-Cash (Investing)		60,000

The other accounts that still have changes that remain to be explained at this point are the notes payable, dividends payable, bonds payable, common shares, and retained earnings accounts. Using the extra information provided, an analysis is now made of each of these accounts.

The entry for notes payable is a net entry. It is net because not enough information is given to determine how many new notes were issued for cash or how many were retired (paid off by paying cash). All that is known is the net change in the notes payable account. The net change indicates that more notes were issued during this period than were retired because the balance in the account increased. This net effect is then shown as increasing the notes payable account. The net cash inflow appears in the financing section. The entry is represented as follows:

(10) The entry is:

A-Cash (Financing)	100	
L-Notes payable		100

Entry (11) for the bonds payable is similar to that in (10) except that, in this case, the additional information indicated that there was $8,000 in new long-term borrowings this year. Therefore, there would be a new credit of $8,000 to this account. However, the balance in this account only increased by $6,000. It can, therefore, be inferred that $2,000 worth of bonds were paid off during the year. The entries are represented as follows:

(11) The entry is:
A-Cash (Financing)   8,000
    L-Bonds payable   8,000

(12) The entry is:
L-Bonds payable   2,000
    A-Cash (Financing)   2,000

In the common shares account, credits represent a new issuance of shares, and debits represent a repurchase of shares. Again, because there is no explicit information that there were new issuances or repurchases, you can only infer the net effect. The net effect is that the account increased, indicating that more shares were issued than were repurchased. The entry is represented as follows:

(13) The entry is:
A-Cash (Financing)   4,000
    SE-Common shares   4,000

Because all of the income statement transactions have now been explained, attention can be turned to the retained earnings account to determine if the entire change in this account has been explained. The account needs an additional debit of $1,400 to explain the change in the balance. The logical assumption about this debit is that it represents the dividends declared during the period. The entry is represented as follows:

(14) The entry is:
SE-Retained earnings   1,400
    L-Dividends payable   1,400

When dividends are declared, they become legally payable, but there may be a lag between the time they are declared and the time they are paid. Therefore, the credit side of entry (14) is to a dividend payable account. The cash entry for dividends takes into consideration the change in the balance of the dividends payable account. The balance in the dividends payable account probably reflects the last quarter's dividend, which has yet to be paid. The entry is represented as follows:

(15) The entry is:
L-Dividends payable   1,230
    A-Cash (Financing)   1,230

Entry (15) completes the cash flow analysis. All the net changes in the balance sheet accounts have been explained. The cash account now contains all the information necessary to produce a cash flow statement. The net cash flows from the three types of activities, as taken from the Cash T-account, are as follows:

Huskies Industries Ltd.
Cash Flow Statement
For the Year Ended December 31, 20x1

Operating activities		
Net income	$ 12,480	
Add back items not representing cash flows:		
Amortization	20,000	
Gain on Disposal	(300)	
Adjustments for the effect of changes in working capital items:		
Decrease in Accounts Receivable	10,000	
Increase in Inventory	(10,000)	
Increase in Prepaid Rent	(100)	
Increase in Accounts Payable	5,000	
Increase in Salaries Payable	100	
Cash from operating activities		$ 37,180
Financing activities		
Issue of Notes Payable	$ 100	
Issue of Common Shares	4,000	
Issue of Bonds Payable	8,000	
Payment of Bonds Payable	(2,000)	
Payment of Dividends	(1,230)	
Cash from financing activities		8,870
Investing activities		
Purchase of Property, Plant, and Equipment	($60,000)	
Sale of Property, Plant, and Equipment	500	
Cash used for investing activities		(59,500)
Decrease in Cash		(13,450)
Cash – beginning of the year		19,500
Cash – end of the year		$ 6,050

The information from the Cash T-accounts was used to prepare a proper cash flow statement. The totals of the cash flows from the three types of activities, a net cash outflow of $13,450 ($37,180 + $8,870 − $59,500 = ($13,450)), must be the same as the net change in cash for the year, a $13,450 reduction ($19,500 − $6,050 = $13,450), which it is. Although the cash flow statement is technically finished with the Decrease in Cash amount, most companies will add the final two lines to the statement so that users can more easily verify the change in cash. In our example, we had cash but no cash equivalents. Many companies have cash equivalents added (or subtracted if they happen to be liabilities) to the cash to arrive at a change in cash and cash equivalents. Such companies must inform users as to which accounts are used for cash equivalents.

Remember that debits in the cash account represent sources or inflows of cash, and credits represent uses or outflows of cash. The formal cash flow statement shows the operating, investing, and financing activities separately.

INTERPRETATION OF CASH FLOW INFORMATION

Learning Objective

7

Provide a basic analysis of a company's financial health using a cash flow statement.

Once the cash flow statement has been prepared, users will want to interpret what the statement tells them about the company. While many users will be interested in what has happened to cash in the current period, they are likely to be more interested in predicting the future cash flows of the company. A bank loan officer, for example, wants to be sure that, if money is loaned to the company, the company will be able to pay it back. A stock analyst, on the other hand, will want to know what the cash flows will be over a long period of time to ensure an adequate return on the investment in shares. Users interested in the future of the company will try to decide which cash flows will continue in the future and which will not.

In addition to deciding which cash flows are likely to continue, users will want to make sure that cash from continuing operations is sufficient over the long run to pay for the continuing investing and financing activities. There is a limit to the cash inflows that can be achieved from investing and financing activities. Investing inflows are limited by the kinds of returns that can be earned from investments in long-term assets and the level of investment by the company. The financing inflows are limited by the willingness of lenders and investors to invest their money in the company. At some level of debt, the company becomes so risky that no lender will agree to lend more. Because the inflows from investing and financing are limited, the company, if it is to remain in business, must generate sufficient cash inflow from operating activities to pay the interest and dividends on the financing activities and to continue investing at appropriate levels in property, plant, and equipment and other long-term assets.

Huskies Industries, as an example, generated $37,180 from operations. Assuming that these are continuing operations (as opposed to discontinued operations) and that Huskies is in a fairly stable industry, you would expect this amount of cash flow to continue into the future. One way to evaluate this is to look at the trend in cash flow from operations over the last five years to see how stable this figure is. The next question to address is whether this flow is sufficient to cover the continuing cash needs of Huskies.

If you look at the uses of cash in the investing and financing sections, you will see that Huskies spent $60,000 to buy new equipment, $1,230 to pay dividends, and $2,000 to pay off debt. It is likely that purchasing new property, plant, and equipment will be a continuing need because buildings and equipment wear out over time. But does the company buy $60,000 in property, plant, and equipment every year, or is this year's purchase larger (or smaller) than usual? If Huskies buys $60,000 every year, you could quickly conclude that the cash from operations will not be sufficient in the long run to pay for this one need, not to mention other needs. If, however, Huskies has this large need only once every three years and if, in the other two years, the purchases are, say, $15,000, then the average amount of property, plant, and equipment purchased is $30,000 per year [($60,000 + 15,000 + 15,000)/3 = $30,000]. Cash flow from operations would be sufficient to pay for this need, with $10,000 left over to pay for other needs. Again, this can be learned by looking at the trend in property, plant, and equipment spending over the last five years to determine the average spending pattern.

Once started, the payment of dividends is generally a continuing need. Companies are reluctant to stop or reduce the payment of dividends because such action sends a negative signal to the market about the future profitability of the company. The amount of dividends paid, of course, is affected by the number of shares outstanding. If there was an additional issuance of shares in a given year, some growth in the total amount of dividend payments would be expected. Huskies is, in fact, in this position. New shares were issued in 20x1, and this could mean more dividends paid in future years.

The repayment of debt is another generally continuing item, but it is not dependent on cash from operations. Most companies maintain a certain amount of debt. The level of debt is sometimes measured by comparing the dollar amount of debt on the balance sheet to the total amount of debt plus shareholders' equity. This measure is called a **debt/equity ratio**.

$$\text{Debt/Equity ratio} = \frac{\text{Debt}}{\text{Debt} + \text{Shareholders' Equity}}$$

For Huskies, this ratio, at the end of the year, was $58,070/$146,450 = 39.7%. This measure indicates that 39.7% of Huskies' total financing is in the form of debt. As will be discussed in Chapter 12, there is a theoretical optimal level of debt that will maximize the return to shareholders. Most companies try to maintain this optimal level of debt. Therefore, if some debt must be paid off in a given year (which would lower the debt/equity ratio), it is generally replaced by a new borrowing (which would bring the debt/equity ratio back to its original value). This process of replacing old debt with new debt is sometimes called the rollover of debt. In the cash flow statement, this type of transaction would show up as both an inflow of cash and an outflow of cash in the financing section. If the financing activities involve short-term debt like the note payable used by Huskies, it is acceptable to show the net cash flow rather than the inflows and outflows separately.

With regard to debt, Huskies did pay off some long-term debt but at the same time borrowed additional long-term debt, increasing the long-term borrowings by $6,000. It may be that Huskies saw an opportunity to acquire long-term debt at acceptable interest rates. Huskies also took out some additional short-term borrowings to finance the company. Recognize that this short-term debt will probably require a cash payoff in a relatively short period of time, whereas the long-term borrowing will require cash payments over a longer period. If the company has some short-term cash inflow shortages, short-term debt can be a difficult problem. As the reader of the financial statements, you should have some understanding of how soon the debt of a company comes due because this will affect its need for cash. In the notes to the financial statements, companies usually describe their borrowings quite extensively, including information about interest rates and due dates.

In addition to the borrowing, Huskies generated cash from two other sources: the sale of equipment and the issuance of common shares. Neither of these is considered a continuing source of cash. In addition, the inflow of cash from the sale of the equipment is very small.

In summary, Huskies required $63,230 in cash to pay for the purchase of property, plant, and equipment, dividends, and the repayment of debt. It generated a total of $49,780 from operations, issuance of notes payable, issuance of common shares, and the sale of property, plant, and equipment. This produced a shortfall of $13,450 for the period, which was covered by the beginning cash balance. Cash declined during this period from $19,500 to $6,050. If all the items in the cash flow statement were continuing items, Huskies could continue to operate for only part of another year before it runs out of cash. Nothing definitive can be said about Huskies' cash flow health because not enough historical data are available. You can say that, if all items are continuing, Huskies will be in trouble next year. If, on the other hand, the purchase of property, plant, and equipment does not continue at its present level, then Huskies may be in reasonable shape.

Cash from operations can also be examined further to determine whether there are any problems in the company's operations. This analysis is easily done using the indirect format of the cash flow statement, where net income is reconciled to cash from operations. For Huskies Industries, the operating section shows that the two reasons for the increase in cash from operations during this period were that accounts receivable decreased and accounts payable increased. This gives some information about the management of the company's receivables and payables, which are critical in determining the lead/lag relationship in the cash-to-cash cycle. In general, these two accounts would be expected to move in unison. When business is growing, the company usually generates more receivables and more payables. When business contracts, both these accounts decrease. In the case of Huskies, they are moving in opposite directions with accounts receivable decreasing and accounts payable increasing. This should raise a red flag, leading the reader of the statement to question why these amounts are moving in opposite directions. It could mean that there is a problem in the management of receivables or payables, especially the accounts payable.

Another concern regarding cash from operating activities is that Huskies increased inventories during the period, causing cash from operations to decline. If a business was expanding, you would expect a larger inventory. But increased sales normally mean that a larger amount of accounts receivable should also be present, which was not the case. Again, this raises a red flag, which should prompt the user to ask why inventory has increased so much. It is possible that Huskies is stockpiling inventory in anticipation of a strike by employees, or it may be that its product is not selling and it has not adjusted inventory purchases sufficiently. This situation may lead to obsolete inventory that cannot be sold.

ANALYSIS OF THE CASH FLOW OF SEARS CANADA

Refer to Appendix A at the end of the book to find the cash flow statement for **Sears Canada**.

First of all, Sears Canada uses the indirect approach for the operating section. Note that the two adjustments to net income in 2001 are the non-cash items included in net earnings (depreciation, amortization, gain on sale of receivables, and future income taxes) and the changes in the non-cash working capital balances related to operations (the current assets and liabilities). Both of these items are produced as summary amounts and in order to get more information about the individual components, you will have to exam the notes to the financial statements. Also note that Sears Canada produces a substantial amount of cash from operations ($241.7 million in 2001) and that the amount has decreased from the prior year when it was $310.4 million. The two biggest uses of cash in 2001 are the purchases of capital assets ($143.4 million), and the repayment of long-term obligations ($110.6 million). The trend over the last two years in these items indicates that they are both continuing items, although in 2001 less cash was used than in 2000. With respect to purchases of capital assets, Sears Canada purchased Eaton's late in 2000, which would account for much of the purchase of capital assets in that year. It is unlikely that expenditures for capital assets in the future will be at the level they were at in 2000. To understand more fully the impact of these two items, the user would need to examine the balance sheet and the accompanying notes.

Let's look more closely at the cash flows associated with borrowings. To understand the net effects of borrowing, examine the information about debt included in Note 9:

(in millions)	2001	2002
Unsecured debentures:		
7.8% due March 1, 2001	$ -	$ 100.0
6.55% due November 5, 2007	125.0	125.0
Unsecured medium-term notes:		
7.45% due May 10, 2010	200.0	200.0
7.05% due September 20, 2010	100.0	100.0
6.75% due March 15, 2006	200.0	-
Proportionate share of long-term debt of joint ventures with a weighted average interest rate of 9.4% due 2002 to 2016	145.3	158.8
Capital lease obligations:		
Interest rates from 7% to 14%	42.5	14.8
	812.8	698.6
Less principal payments due within one year included in current liabilities	10.1	152.5
Total long-term liabilities	$ 802.7	$ 546.1

The information shows that Sears Canada has been rolling over its debt (using new debt issues to pay off debt that is due). It settled an unsecured debenture due in 2001 and replaced it with an unsecured medium-term note due in five years. Note as well that the principal repayment due in 2002 is only $10.1 million compared to $152.5 million the previous year. It is probable that Sears Canada will use the cash it generates from operations to make principal debt repayments in 2002. Operations have been a good source of cash over the last two years; this has enabled Sears to repay debt and, thereby, establish a credible credit rating. It will be able to borrow again in the future if the need arises.

Returning to the overall analysis, the cash flow from operations in 2001 ($241.7 million) was almost sufficient to cover the continuing needs for the repayment of debt and the purchases of capital assets. The inflow of cash from the disposition of capital assets ($17.7 million), the sale of charge account receivables ($56.1 million), and issues of new long-term debt ($200 million) was more than sufficient to cover the remaining needs for cash. Note that the cash received from the sale of capital assets is much less than the amount spent on new acquisitions. This is normal for most businesses. It could be concluded that Sears Canada performs quite well when it comes to cash generation. It also appears that, based on the past trend, this will continue into the future.

SUMMARY

This chapter opened with a discussion about the importance to organizations of effective cash management. We showed you how a company can be earning profits yet, at the same time, have serious cash flow problems. We outlined the information that users can obtain from the cash flows that are summarized in the cash flow statement. Remember that for a business to be successful, both cash flows and profits must be generated. We also went through the cash flow statement, describing the three essential components of the statement and the kinds of activity that are included in each section. We then described the procedure for preparing a cash flow statement. This statement is more complex than the balance sheet and the income statement in that you need to analyze the income statement and the balance sheet as well as seek out additional information before you can organize all the data that you need to prepare the statement. With the income statement and balance sheet, you mostly copy balances from accounts to the right place on the statement. Little analysis is required.

The last part of this chapter is more important than the actual preparation of the statement. It outlined for you how the cash flow statement could be used in assessing the future cash flow of a company. Remember that it is important to see a positive cash flow from operations. The operations are the lifeblood of the company; it is through them that the company will live or die.

The next chapters provide details of the items that appear in the balance sheet to give you a better understanding of the source of the amounts that appear in the financial statements.

Additional Demonstration Problems

SUMMARY PROBLEMS

1. The 2004 balance sheet and income statement of Hayes Industries, Inc. are provided in Exhibit 5-15. Hayes Industries manufactures and distributes a broad range of clothing and provides related services to retailers. Using these statements, construct the cash flow statement for Hayes for the year ended May 31, 2004. Use T-accounts and the indirect approach. The following additional information and assumptions are also provided (all numbers are in thousands unless otherwise indicated).

a. Dividends declared in fiscal 2004 totalled $6,594.

b. Amortization totalled $7,805 in 2004.

c. Purchases of new property, plant, and equipment totalled $14,790 in 2004.

d. Property, plant, and equipment sold in 2004 produced a gain of $1,169.

e. All changes in the shareholders' equity accounts other than earnings and dividends are due to the issuance of new common shares.

f. Treat the issuance and repayment of long-term debt on a net basis.

HAYES INDUSTRIES, INC.

EXHIBIT 5-15

Balance Sheet
($ in thousands)

	May 31, 2004	May 31, 2003
Assets		
Current Assets:		
Cash and equivalents	$ 2,225	$ 3,227
Accounts receivable	83,962	75,165
Inventories	169,978	114,465
Prepaid expenses	13,023	12,402
Other Assets	1,190	1,471
Total Current Assets	270,378	206,730
Property, plant, and equipment	110,343	102,870
Less: Accumulated amortization	(71,693)	(69,653)
Total Assets	$309,028	$239,947
Liabilities and Shareholders' Equity		
Current Liabilities:		
Notes payable	$ 43,500	$ 19,500
Accounts payable	54,331	45,023
Accrued salaries	8,235	11,687
Other accrued expenses	13,039	12,977
Income taxes	4,732	5,352
Dividends payable	1,739	1,555
Total Current Liabilities	125,576	96,094
Long-term debt	50,873	16,118
Total Liabilities	176,449	112,212
Shareholders' Equity		
Common shares	15,714	14,791
Retained earnings	116,865	112,944
Total Shareholders' Equity	132,579	127,735
Total Liabilities and Shareholders' Equity	$309,028	$239,947

HAYES INDUSTRIES, INC.

Income Statement
Consolidated Statements of Earnings
($ in thousands except per share amounts)

Year Ended	May 31, 2004	May 31, 2003
Net Sales	$656,987	$624,568
Costs and Expenses:		
Cost of goods sold	543,624	498,790
Selling, general, and administrative	91,601	91,209
Interest	4,136	2,297
	639,361	592,296
Earnings Before Income Taxes	17,626	32,272
Income Taxes	7,051	13,071
Net Earnings	$ 10,575	$ 19,201
Net Earnings Per Common Share	$ 1.22	$ 2.23

2. Based on the answer to Question 1 and the previous two years' cash flow statements for Hayes Industries shown in Exhibit 5-16, answer the following questions:

   a. Discuss the company's ability to meet its needs for cash over the last three years. Comment on the continuing nature of the major items that have appeared over the last three years.

   b. Explain why so much cash was generated from operations in 2004.

HAYES INDUSTRIES, INC.

Cash Flow Statements
($ in thousands)

Year Ended	May 31, 2003	May 31, 2002
Operating Activities:		
Net earnings	$ 19,201	$ 14,786
Adjustments to reconcile net earnings to net cash provided by operating activities:		
Amortization	7,041	6,457
(Gain) loss on sale of property, plant, and equipment	488	(211)
Changes in working capital:		
(Increase) decrease in:		
Receivables	(7,072)	(935)
Inventories	(11,872)	(19,687)
Prepaid expenses	(704)	(1,851)
(Decrease) increase in:		
Accounts payable	10,121	(3,734)
Accrued salaries and other current expenses	2,428	1,078
Income taxes payable	–	(402)
Other noncurrent assets	52	(513)
Net cash provided by operations	19,683	(5,012)

EXHIBIT 5-16
CONT.

Investing Activities:		
Purchase of property, plant, and equipment	(9,395)	(8,050)
Proceeds from sale of property, plant, and equipment	414	1,824
Net cash used in investing activities	(8,981)	(6,226)
Financing Activities:		
Short-term borrowings	1,000	18,500
Dividends on common shares	(5,956)	(5,486)
Payments on long-term debt	(4,913)	(14,733)
Addition to long-term debt	—	10,000
Purchase and retirement of common shares	(1,885)	(2,449)
Net cash used in financing activities	(11,754)	5,832
Net Change in Cash	(1,052)	(5,406)
Cash at Beginning of Period	4,279	9,685
Cash at End of Period	$ 3,227	$ 4,279

SUGGESTED SOLUTIONS TO SUMMARY PROBLEMS

1. T-Accounts:

A-Cash

✓		3,227			
Operations:					
Net income	(1)	10,575	8,797	(2)	Incr. in A/R
Increase in A/P	(5)	9,308	55,513	(3)	Incr. in inventories
Incr. other acc. exp.	(7)	62	621	(4)	Incr. in ppd. exp.
Decr. in other assets	(9)	281	3,452	(6)	Decr. in accrued sal.
Amortization	(10)	7,805	620	(8)	Decr. in inc. taxes
			1,169	(12)	Gain on sale of PP&E
Investing:					
Proceeds from sale of PP&E	(12)	2,721	14,790	(11)	Purchase of PP&E
Financing:					
Issuance of notes pay.	(13)	24,000	6,470	(15)	Dividends
Iss. of long-term debt	(16)	34,755			
Iss. of shares	(17)	923			
✓		2,225			

A-Accounts Receivable	
✓ 75,165	
(2) 8,797	
✓ 83,962	

A-Inventories	
✓ 114,465	
(3) 55,513	
✓ 169,978	

A-Prepaid Expenses	
✓ 12,402	
(4) 621	
✓ 13,023	

A-PP&E	
✓ 102,870	
(11) 14,790	7,317 (12)
✓ 110,343	

	XA-Accum. Amort.		
		69,653	✓
(12)	5,765	7,805	(10)
		71,693	✓

	A-Other Assets		
✓	1,471		
		281	(8)
✓	1,190		

	L-Notes Payable		
		19,500	✓
		24,000	(13)
		43,500	✓

	L-Accounts Payable		
		45,023	✓
		9,308	(5)
		54,331	✓

	L-Accrued Salaries		
		11,687	✓
(6)	3,452		
		8,235	✓

	L-Other Accrued Expenses		
		12,977	✓
		62	(7)
		13,039	✓

	L-Taxes Payable		
		5,352	✓
(8)	620		
		4,732	✓

	L-Dividends Payable		
		1,555	✓
(15)	6,470	6,654	(14)
		1,739	✓

	L-Long-term Debt		
		16,118	✓
		34,755	(16)
		50,873	✓

	SE-Common Shares		
		14,791	✓
		923	(17)
		15,714	✓

	SE-Retained Earnings		
		112,944	✓
(14)	6,654	10,575	(1)
		116,865	✓

Explanations of selected transactions.

Transaction 10. The debit entry to the cash account is the amortization of property, plant, and equipment, which is a non-cash expense and, therefore, it must be added back. The reconstruction entry is:

A-Cash (Operating)	7,805	
XA-Accumulated amortization		7,805

Transaction 12. The sale of property, plant, and equipment resulted in a gain of $1,169. The cost (in the PP&E account) and the accumulated amortization associated with this sale are determined by balancing these two accounts in the T-accounts. The reconstruction entry that results is as follows:

A-Cash (Investing)	2,721	
XA-Accumulated amortization	5,765	
A-Property, plant, and equipment		7,317
A-Cash (Operating)		1,169

Transactions 14 and 15. Determining the amount of dividends that were actually paid during 2004 involves first determining the amount of dividends declared. If you balance the retained earnings account, it is obvious that an additional debit of $6,654 is needed. This debit represents the dividends declared. The reconstruction entry to record this is as follows:

SE-Retained earnings	6,654	
L-Dividends payable		6,654

With the additional entry to the dividends payable account, it is now possible to determine the amount of dividends actually paid during the year by balancing the account. An additional debit of $6,470 is required to reach the end balance of $1,739. The reconstruction entry to record this is as follows:

L-Dividends payable	6,470	
A-Cash (Financing)		6,470

HAYES INDUSTRIES, INC.
Cash Flow Statement
For the Year Ended May 31, 2004

Operating activities		
Net income	$ 10,575	
Adjustments to reconcile net earnings to cash		
provided by operating activities:		
Amortization	7,805	
Gain on sale of equipment	(1,169)	
Effect from changes in working capital:		
Increase in accounts receivable	(8,797)	
Increase in inventory	(55,513)	
Increase in prepaid expenses	(621)	
Increase in accounts payable	9,308	
Decrease in accrued salaries	(3,452)	
Increase in other accrued expenses	62	
Decrease in income taxes	(620)	
Decrease in other assets	281	
Cash provided by operations		($42,141)
Investing		
Sale of property, plant, and equipment	2,721	
Purchase of property, plant, and equipment	(14,790)	
Cash provided by investing		(12,069)
Financing		
Issuance of notes payable	24,000	
Issuance of long-term debt	34,755	
Issuance of shares	923	
Payment of dividends	(6,470)	
Cash provided by financing		53,208
Decrease in cash		(1,002)
Beginning cash balance		3,227
Ending cash balance		$ 2,225

2. a. The two major continuing needs for cash over the last three years have been the purchase of property, plant, and equipment and the payment of dividends. The combination of these two items has averaged $16,715 over the last three years. Only in 2003 did Hayes produce enough cash from operations to cover these needs. In both 2002 and 2004, Hayes had to use cash in its operations (there was a negative amount), with a significant amount used in 2004.

In 2002, Hayes also used a significant amount of cash to retire long-term debt and buy back shares. Since operations did not provide cash in that year, short-term borrowings were used to meet Hayes' cash needs. Hayes also drew down its cash balance significantly in 2002 to pay for its cash needs. In 2003, Hayes continued to retire long-term debt and buy back shares. In that year, however, there was some extra cash left over from operations after paying for property, plant, and equipment and dividends. Additional cash was raised from short-term borrowings again, such that Hayes ended the year in about the same cash position as at the beginning of the year.

In 2004, cash from operations was significantly negative and the expenditures for property, plant, and equipment and dividends were the largest in the three-year period shown on the cash flow statements. Hayes primarily paid for these items by issuing more debt with more than half of the issuance being long-term and the rest short-term. A look at the balance sheet indicates that long-term debt increased approximately four-fold in 2004. Short-term debt more than doubled. This has significant implications for 2005, as this debt carries with it additional interest expense that will appear in the income statement next year.

b. In analyzing the operating section of Hayes' cash flow statements, it is clear that the biggest negative adjustment over the last three years has been the change in inventories. These changes represent increases in inventories. In 2004, inventories increase $55,513 or almost 49% over the levels in 2003 ($114,465). There is clearly a problem here as sales have not increased this dramatically, only increasing $32,419 or 5.2% in 2004. Receivables have also increased fairly dramatically, by $8,797 or 11.7% in 2004. As an offset to the increase in receivables, accounts payable have also increased by $9,308 or 20.7% in 2004. While this helps the cash flow of the company, it may also indicate that it is having trouble paying its bills and is slowing down payment on its accounts. The biggest concern is the increase in the level of inventory; you would want to investigate why inventories have grown this much.

GLOSSARY

Capitalization   The amount of resources contributed to the company by shareholders and debtholders. The term *capitalization* is used in several ways in accounting. Besides the definition given above, it can also mean the recording of an asset or the deferring of a cost.

Cash equivalents   Current assets and liabilities that are very liquid and readily convertible into cash or that may require the short-term use of cash. Examples are short-term investments and bank overdrafts or lines of credit.

Cash flow   The net change in cash that occurs from the beginning of an accounting period to the end of the period.

Cash position   The amount of cash and cash equivalents.

Debt/equity ratio   The ratio calculated by dividing total liabilities by the sum of total liabilities and shareholders' equity. It indicates whether the company relies more heavily on debt or equity for financing.

Direct approach   A method of calculating the cash from operations of a company in which the direct gross cash receipts and payments are shown.

Financing activities   The activities of a company that are directed to obtaining resources from investors or debtholders. The return of resources to shareholders and debtholders is also considered part of these activities.

Indirect approach   A method of calculating the cash from operations of a company in which the net income number is adjusted for all non-cash revenues or expenses to convert it from an accrual basis to its cash-basis equivalent.

Investing activities   The activities of a company that are directed to investing the resources of the company over extended periods of time in long-term assets.

Lead/lag relationship   The relationships between the recognition of revenues and expenses for income statement purposes and the recognition of their cash flow effects.

Line of credit   An arrangement with a financing institution that allows a company to overdraw its accounts. The overdrawn amounts become a loan that must be repaid.

Operating activities   The activities of a company that are directed to selling goods and services to customers.

Working capital   Current assets minus current liabilities.

ASSIGNMENT MATERIAL

Assessing Your Recall

5-1   Discuss why it is important for companies to prepare a cash flow statement in addition to an income statement.

Multiple Choice Quizzes

5-2   Discuss how a company's receivables, inventory, and payables policies affect cash flows relative to the income produced in a given period.

5-3   What is meant by a lead/lag relationship in terms of the cash flow statement?

5-4   For a company with a cash flow problem, list at least three potential reasons for the problem and suggest a possible solution for each.

5-5   Describe the three major categories of activities that are shown on the cash flow statement.

5-6   Discuss the major difference between the direct approach and the indirect approach for constructing the operating section of a cash flow statement.

5-7   "Amortization is a source of cash." Explain your reasons for agreeing or disagreeing with this statement.

5-8 In what section of the cash flow statement (operating, financing, or investing) would each of the following items appear:

    a. Purchase of new property, plant, and equipment

    b. Proceeds from a bank loan

    c. Collections from customers

    d. Dividends to shareholders

    e. Proceeds from the sale of marketable securities

    f. Retirement of debt

    g. Changes in accounts receivable

    h. Net income

    i. Gain or loss on the sale of property, plant, and equipment

5-9 Indicate whether each of the following items should be classified as an operating, investing, or financing activity on the cash flow statement. If an item does not belong on the statement indicate why.

    a. Payment of cash dividends on common shares

    b. Sale of a warehouse

    c. Interest payments on an outstanding long-term bank loan

    d. Purchase of a company's own common shares on the stock market

    e. Acquisition of land

    f. Obtaining cash through a long-term bank loan

    g. Purchase of an investment in another company by buying some of its shares

    h. Collection of an accounts receivable

    i. Declaration of dividends on common shares

    j. Purchase of operating equipment

5-10 When analyzing the cash flow statement, a user looks for a positive cash flow from operations. Explain why this is so important.

5-11 Explain why the total cash flows from investing are often negative.

Applying Your Knowledge

5-12 (Identification of sources and uses of cash)
In the chapter's opening story, Dorothy Hooper, controller of the **Manitoba Theatre Centre**, described the importance of cash to the viability of the company.

    Required:

    a. Identify three possible sources of cash and three possible uses of cash for the MTC.

    b. With respect to the acquisition of cash, describe how a not-for-profit organization is different from a profit-oriented organization.

5-13 (Cash flow and sales growth)
Explain why a high sales growth rate can create significant cash flow problems for a company.

5-14 (Cash flow and capital assets)
Explain how the timing of the cash flows relates to the purchase, use, and ultimate sale of property, plant, and equipment.

5-15 (Cash flow and interest)
Discuss the classification of interest cash flows in the cash flow statement and discuss whether you think this is appropriate.

5-16 (Effect of transactions on cash flows)
Classify each of the following transactions as increasing, decreasing, or having no effect on cash flows:

   a. Purchasing inventory on account

   b. Paying wages owed to employees

   c. Buying a new building by making a down payment and taking out a mortgage for the balance of the amount owed

   d. Receiving interest that is owed from a customer

   e. Prepaying rent that is owed for the month

   f. Purchasing office supplies and writing a cheque to cover the amount

   g. Selling inventory to a customer on account

   h. Making a monthly payment on a bank loan which included interest and principal repayment

   i. Declaring and paying a dividend to shareholders

   j. Issuing new shares

   k. Amortizing capital assets

5-17 (Effect of transactions on cash flows)
For each of the following items: (1) identify the accounts affected and give the amounts by which they would be increased or decreased; (2) state the amount of any cash flow and whether cash is increased or decreased; and (3) identify how each item would be reported in the cash flow statement.

   a. Two years ago a licence was purchased for $50,000. The licence is amortized over four years at a rate of $12,500 per year.

   b. A capital asset is sold for $90,000. The asset originally cost $165,000 and the accumulated amortization is $95,000.

   c. A capital asset is purchased for $250,000. A cash payment of $50,000 is made and the remainder is paid with a long-term note of $200,000.

   d. Annual interest of 7% is paid on bonds that were issued for $1,000,000.

   e. Income tax expense for the year is $95,000. The tax payment during the year was $80,000. The remainder will be paid next year.

5-18   (Effect of transactions on cash flows)
For each of the transactions listed below:

a. Indicate the effect on balance sheet categories by using the following format:

Trans. No.	Cash	Other Current Assets	Noncurrent Assets	Current Liabilities	Noncurrent Liabilities	Shareholders' Equity

b. For the transactions affecting cash shown below, state whether they relate to an operating, investing, or financing activity.

Transactions:

1. Borrowed $25,000 from the bank; amount is due in two years

2. Bought inventory on credit, $120,000

3. Sold inventory on credit, $175,000

4. Cash collected on accounts receivable, $172,000

5. Purchased a new machine for cash, $9,000

6. Cash paid on accounts payable, $110,000

7. Cost of goods sold, $105,000

8. Paid rent during the year, $24,000; the last payment of $2,000 was for the first month of the next year

9. Bought office supplies for cash, $8,000; at year end, $7,000 of the supplies had been used

10. Paid wages to employees, $12,000

11. At the end of the year, $1,000 was owed to the employees

12. Amortization expense on equipment, $1,500

13. Interest of $1,875 was paid on the amount borrowed

14. Issued new shares for $30,000 cash

15. Equipment having a book value (cost minus accumulated amortization) of $900 sold for $1,000 cash

16. Declared and paid dividends, $500

17. Paid for advertising, $575

18. Income taxes accrued and paid, $5,600

5-19   (Effect of transactions on cash flows)
For each of the transactions listed below:

a. Indicate the effect on balance sheet categories by using the following format:

Trans. No.	Cash	Other Current Assets	Noncurrent Assets	Current Liabilities	Noncurrent Liabilities	Shareholders' Equity

b. For the transactions affecting cash, state whether they relate to an operating, investing, or financing activity.

Transactions:

1. 5,000 common shares were issued at $30 per share.

2. Equipment worth $110,000 was purchased for $70,000 in cash and the balance in common shares.

3. Rent payment of $2,000 was received in advance.

4. Sales contracts for $150,000 were signed, and a $37,500 deposit was received in cash.

5. Merchandise inventory costing $210,000 was purchased on account.

6. Goods costing $10,000 were found defective and returned to suppliers. These goods had been purchased on account.

7. Sales were $450,000, of which $90,000 was on account.

8. Cash was paid to suppliers on account in the amount of $215,000.

9. Equipment recorded at $10,000 was destroyed by fire. The insurance company paid $9,000 for the loss.

10. The company purchased 100 shares of Allied Company at $9 per share for short-term investment purposes.

11. The company purchased 50,000 shares of Zider Company at $4 per share in an effort to buy a controlling interest in Zider (a supplier).

12. Interest expense for the year amounted to $2,500 and was paid in cash.

13. One of the sales contracts in transaction 4 was cancelled; $10,000 of the deposit was returned and the rest was forfeited.

14. A bank loan for $100,000 was taken out and is due in five years.

15. Equipment with a cost of $30,000 was sold for $35,000. The buyer agreed to pay $20,000 in the future and signed a note receivable which required interest payments.

16. During the year, warranty services costing $5,500 were provided to customers. A provision for warranty services was provided earlier in a separate transaction.

17. Amortization for the year totalled $20,000.

18. Dividends of $7,000 were declared, and $5,000 remained unpaid at year end.

19. Patents on a new manufacturing process were purchased for $15,000.

20. Research and development expenses amounted to $45,000 and were charged to expense as incurred.

5-20 (Cash flow from operations)

Calculate the cash flow from operations in each of the following cases:

	I	II	III
Sales revenues	$355,000	$575,000	$935,000
Cost of goods sold	210,000	320,000	620,000
Selling and admin. expenses	65,000	95,500	105,500
Amortization expense	6,500	18,000	28,000
Income tax expense	18,000	35,000	45,000
Dividends paid	7,000	5,000	25,000

Increase/(Decrease) in:

Accounts receivable	(2,500)	(5,000)	8,500
Inventories	4,000	8,000	(14,000)
Prepaid expenses	1,000	2,500	(2,400)
Accounts payable	(3,500)	6,500	(4,200)
Wages payable	2,500	(1,500)	3,500
Interest payable	1,500	1,200	(6,500)

5-21 (Cash flow from operations)
Calculate the cash flow from operations in each of the following cases:

	I	II	III
Sales revenues	$275,000	$375,000	$415,000
Cost of goods sold	150,000	205,000	260,000
Amortization expense	25,000	35,000	40,000
Interest expense	6,000	12,000	15,000
Gain/(loss) on sale of equipment	10,000	(8,000)	6,000
Dividends paid	——	10,000	5,000
Increase/(Decrease) in:			
Building and equipment	100,000	(60,000)	80,000
Common shares	20,000	40,000	50,000
Bonds payable	10,000	(30,000)	30,000
Interest payable	2,000	4,000	(1,000)
Accounts payable	6,000	(6,000)	(3,000)
Accounts receivable	(8,000)	8,000	(7,000)
Inventories	12,000	10,000	(12,000)

5-22 (Preparation of cash flow statement)
Financial statement data for First Moving Company for 2004 are as follows:

FIRST MOVING COMPANY
Comparative Balance Sheets

	Dec. 31, 2004	Dec. 31, 2003
Assets		
Cash	$ 88,600	$ 49,100
Accounts receivable	85,000	59,400
Prepaid insurance	70,000	60,000
Total current assets	243,600	168,500
Property, equipment, and vehicles	360,000	305,000
Accumulated amortization	(110,400)	(105,900)
Total noncurrent assets	249,600	199,100
Total assets	$493,200	$ 367,600
Liabilities and shareholders' equity		
Accounts payable	$ 21,500	$ 18,600
Wages payable	3,000	4,000
Total current liabilities	24,500	22,600
Bank loan	50,000	60,000
Total liabilities	74,500	82,600
Common shares	200,000	200,000
Retained earnings	218,700	85,000
Total liabilities and shareholders' equity	$493,200	$ 367,600

FIRST MOVING COMPANY
Income statement
For the year ended December 31, 2004

Moving revenue		$ 450,000
Expenses		
Vehicle maintenance	$ 102,400	
Wage expense	134,000	
Amortization expense	59,500	
Interest expense	5,400	
Gain on sale of vehicles	(5,000)	
Total expenses		296,300
Net income		$ 153,700

Additional information:

1. Vehicles originally costing $65,000 were sold for $15,000.

2. Dividends declared and paid during the year were $20,000.

Required:
Prepare a cash flow statement for First Moving Company for the year ended December 31, 2004, supported by a set of T-accounts.

5-23   (Preparation of financial statements)
Financial statement data for Matrix Incorporated are as follows:

MATRIX INCORPORATED
Balance sheet
December 31, 2003

Assets	
Cash	$ 15,500
Accounts receivable	10,000
Notes receivable	5,000
Inventories	20,500
Total current assets	51,000
Property, plant, and equipment	160,000
Accumulated amortization	(35,500)
Total noncurrent assets	124,500
Total assets	$175,500
Liabilities and shareholders' equity	
Accounts payable	$ 5,000
Salaries payable	18,000
Total current liabilities	23,000
Bonds payable	50,000
Total liabilities	73,000
Common shares	100,000
Retained earnings	2,500
Total liabilities and shareholders' equity	$175,500

MATRIX INCORPORATED
Trial Balance for the Year ended December 31, 2004

	Debits	Credits
Cash	$ 2,900	
Accounts receivable	12,500	
Prepaid rent	6,000	
Inventories	18,900	
Property, plant, and equipment	160,000	
Accumulated amortization		$ 45,500
Accounts payable		13,800
Interest payable		9,000
Salaries payable		6,000
Bonds payable		10,000
Common shares		100,000
Retained earnings		2,500
Sales		350,000
Cost of goods sold	275,500	
Amortization expense	10,000	
Rent expense	12,000	
Interest expense	15,000	
Salaries expense	24,000	
Totals	$536,800	$536,800

Required:

a. Prepare an income statement and a reconciliation of retained earnings for the year ended December 31, 2004.

b. Prepare a balance sheet as at December 31, 2004.

c. Prepare a cash flow statement for the year ended December 31, 2004.

5-24 (Preparation of cash flow statement)
Athabasca Company reported the following abbreviated balance sheet and income statement for 2004.

ATHABASCA COMPANY
Income Statement
For the year ended December 31, 2004

Sales		$450,000
Cost of goods sold		240,000
Gross profit		210,000
Other expenses:		
Supplies expense	$ 15,000	
Amortization expense	35,000	
Wages and salaries	110,000	
Interest expense	24,000	184,000
		26,000
Other income		21,000
Net income		$ 47,000

ATHABASCA COMPANY
Balance Sheets

	2004	2003
Cash	$ 80,000	$ 70,000
Accounts receivable	120,000	140,000
Inventory	320,000	280,000
Buildings and equipment (net)	440,000	420,000
Total Assets	$960,000	$910,000
Accounts payable	$ 90,000	$ 80,000
Wages and salaries payable	20,000	15,000
Bonds payable	350,000	400,000
Common shares	200,000	150,000
Retained earnings	300,000	265,000
Total Liabilities and Shareholders' Equity	$960,000	$910,000

Required:

a. Prepare a cash flow statement for Athabasca Company for the year ended December 31, 2004.

b. Did the working capital change by the same amount as cash generated by operations? Should these two be the same? Explain.

5-25 (Preparation of cash flow statement)
The balance sheets for Pentagon Company as at the beginning and end of 2004 are as follows:

PENTAGON COMPANY
Balance Sheets

	Dec. 31, 2004	Dec. 31, 2003
Assets		
Current assets		
Cash	$ 20,000	$ 28,000
Accounts receivable	66,000	80,000
Inventories	102,000	82,000
Prepaid expenses	20,000	30,000
Total current assets	208,000	220,000
Property, plant, and equipment	625,000	600,000
Accumulated amortization	(175,000)	(150,000)
Total noncurrent assets	450,000	450,000
Total assets	$ 658,000	$670,000
Liabilities and shareholders' equity		
Current liabilities		
Accounts payable	$ 68,000	$145,000
Wages payable	25,000	45,000
Total current liabilities	93,000	190,000
Bonds payable	125,000	100,000
Total liabilities	218,000	290,000

Shareholders' equity		
Common shares	225,000	200,000
Retained earnings	215,000	180,000
Total shareholders' equity	440,000	380,000
Total liabilities and shareholders' equity	$ 658,000	$670,000

Additional information:

1. No dividends were declared or paid.

2. No property, plant, or equipment was sold.

3. No long-term debt was repaid.

4. Net income was $35,000, including $25,000 of amortization expense.

Required:
Prepare a cash flow statement for the year ended December 31, 2004.

5-26   (Preparation of cash flow statement)
Comparative balance sheets of Janxen Jeans Company for 2004 and 2003 are as follows:

JANXEN JEANS COMPANY
Comparative Balance Sheets

	Dec. 31, 2004	Dec. 31, 2003
Assets		
Current assets		
Cash	$ 200,000	$ 188,000
Accounts receivable	120,000	133,000
Notes receivable	70,000	61,000
Inventories	439,000	326,000
Total current assets	829,000	708,000
Noncurrent assets		
Land	525,000	500,000
Machinery	483,000	238,000
Accumulated amortization	(143,000)	(97,500)
Total noncurrent assets	865,000	640,500
Total assets	$1,694,000	$1,348,500
Liabilities and shareholders' equity		
Current liabilities		
Accounts payable	$ 145,000	$ 158,000
Interest payable	17,500	10,000
Total current liabilities	162,500	168,000
Long-term debt	350,000	200,000
Total liabilities	512,500	368,000
Shareholders' equity		
Common shares	650,000	550,000
Retained earnings	531,500	430,500
Total shareholders' equity	1,181,500	980,500
Total liabilities and shareholders' equity	$ 1,694,000	$1,348,500

Additional information:

1. Net income is $145,000 and includes amortization expenses of $95,500.

2. Dividends declared and paid during the year were $44,000.

3. A machine costing $70,000 was sold at its book value (cost minus accumulated amortization) of $20,000.

4. No repayment of long-term debt occurred in 2004.

Required:
Prepare a cash flow statement for the year ended December 31, 2004.

5-27 (Preparation of income statement and cash flow statement)
The financial statement data for Pharmex Pharmaceutical Company for 2004 are as follows:

PHARMEX PHARMACEUTICAL COMPANY
Comparative Data

	Dec. 31, 2004	Dec. 31, 2003
Debits		
Cash	$ 80,000	$ 50,000
Accounts receivable	185,000	235,000
Inventories	296,000	325,000
Machinery	545,000	555,000
Totals	$1,106,000	$1,165,000
Credits		
Accumulated amortization	$ 122,500	$ 172,500
Accounts payable	97,500	82,500
Bonds payable	150,000	175,000
Common shares	350,000	400,000
Retained earnings	386,000	335,000
Total credits	$1,106,000	$ 1,165,000

Income Statement

Sales	$ 1,052,000
Gain on sale of machinery	15,000
Cost of goods sold	878,000
Amortization expense	75,000
Interest expense	60,000
Rent expense	85,000
Net Loss	$ (31,000)

Additional information:
Acquisition cost of new machinery is $135,000. Old machinery having an original cost of $125,000 was sold at a gain. Dividends were declared and paid.

Required:

a. Prepare a reconciliation of retained earnings for the year ended December 31, 2004.

b. Prepare a cash flow statement for Pharmex for the year ended December 31, 2004.

5-28 (Determine cash collected from customers and paid to suppliers)
Southbend Company had sales of $735,600 for the year. The company reported accounts receivable of $55,000 at the end of last year and $58,900 at the end of this year. Southbend's cost of goods sold this year was $440,000. In last year's balance sheet, Southbend reported

inventory of $62,000 and accounts payable of $32,400. In this year's balance sheet, Southbend reported inventory of $59,700 and accounts payable of $28,200.

Required:

a. How much cash did Southbend collect from customers during the year?

b. How much cash did Southbend pay to suppliers for inventory during the year?

5-29   (Preparation of cash flow statement)
Downsview Company had a $261,800 cash balance at the beginning of 2004. The company reported net income of $388,900 for 2004. Included in the company's income statement were amortization expense of $67,000, interest expense of $31,600, and income tax expense of $102,000. The following also occurred during 2004:

1. Accounts receivable increased by $13,000.

2. Inventory decreased by $7,000.

3. Accounts payable increased by $3,500.

4. Wages payable decreased by $1,300.

5. Income taxes payable increased by $3,100.

6. The patent account increased by $27,400. One patent was purchased during the year for $31,200.

7. The plant and equipment account increased by $465,000. One piece of equipment was sold during the year for $22,000. It had originally cost $51,000 and had a $17,000 book value at the time of the sale.

8. Downsview declared and paid cash dividends of $52,000 during 2004.

9. The company repurchased some of its common shares during the year for $44,000.

10. The company issued $100,000 of bonds during the year.

Required:
To help the management of Downsview Company better understand its sources and uses of cash, do the following:

a. Calculate the cash generated from operations.

b. Calculate the cash flow related to investing activities.

c. Calculate the cash flow related to financing activities.

d. Prepare a cash flow statement for Downsview for 2004 in good form.

5-30   (Interpretation of cash flow statement)
The following are the comparative cash flow statements for Yellow Spruce Incorporated:

YELLOW SPRUCE INCORPORATED
Comparative Cash Flow Statements
($ millions)

	2004	2003	2002
Operating activities			
Net income	57	86	98
Add back:			
Amortization	82	75	65

Loss (gain) on sale of investment	1	-0-	(11)
Effect from changes in working capital items:			
Receivables	(38)	20	(39)
Inventories	(21)	(17)	(21)
Prepaid expenses	4	23	(9)
Accounts payable	(7)	(12)	35
Cash from operations	78	175	118
Investing activities			
Acquisition of noncurrent assets	(54)	(61)	(52)
Acquisitions of investments	(123)	(151)	(172)
Proceeds from sale of noncurrent assets	16	11	27
Cash used for investing	(161)	(201)	(197)
Financing activities			
Issue in long-term debt	213	156	332
Repayment of long-term debt	(131)	(72)	(93)
Issuance of common shares	2	2	7
Repurchase of common shares	-0-	(38)	(84)
Dividends paid	(16)	(14)	(15)
Cash flow from financing	68	34	147
Net increase (decrease) in cash	(15)	8	68
Cash position at beginning of year	109	101	33
Cash position at end of year	94	109	101

Required:

a. Discuss the company's ability to meet its needs for cash over the last three years. Comment on the continuing nature of the major items that have appeared over the last three years.

b. Comment on Yellow Spruce's accounts receivable, accounts payable, and inventory policies.

c. How did Yellow Spruce finance its repayment of long-term debt and acquisition of noncurrent assets in 2004?

User Perspective Problems

5-31 (Cash flows from operations)
In this chapter, we have emphasized the importance of a careful analysis of the operating section of the cash flow statement. In fact, this section is the first one listed on the statement. From a user perspective, explain why this section is so important for an understanding of a company's financial health.

5-32 (Cash flow statement and lending decisions)
From the perspective of a bank loan officer, discuss why the cash flow statement may or may not be more important than the income statement in your analysis of a company that is applying for a loan.

5-33 (Cash flow statement and investing decisions)
From the perspective of a stock analyst, discuss why the cash flow statement may or may not be more important than the income statement in the analysis of a company for which you must make a recommendation.

5-34   (Cash flow and compensation plans)

If you were a CEO (Chief Executive Officer) of a company and wanted to use a management compensation plan to motivate your top management, would you want to base your performance targets on cash flows from operations or net income? Discuss the pros and cons of using these two measures of performance.

5-35   (Format of the cash flow statement from lending perspective)

As a lender, discuss whether you would be satisfied with the current method of classifying cash flows into only three categories. In particular, comment on the classification of interest cash flows and whether you think placing them under operating activities is appropriate.

5-36   (Cash flow analysis)

Jacques Rousseau is considering investing in Health Life Ltd., a pharmaceutical company. He read in the paper that this company is doing cancer research and is close to a breakthrough in developing a new drug that will be effective against bone cancer. The author of the article said that this was a good time to buy because, once the breakthrough happens, the share price is going to grow very rapidly. Jacques decided to look at the company's most recent financial statements. On the balance sheet, he saw that the company had a significant amount of cash and short-term investments. It had some assets listed as capital assets under capital leases, which he interpreted to mean that the company leased its buildings and equipment rather than buying them. When he looked at the income statement, he saw that there was no revenue. The largest expense was for research and development. The company had a loss last year and this year the total retained earnings on the balance sheet was in a deficit position. He thought that this made sense because the company had yet to make its first medical breakthrough. The company had very little debt, but its common shares totalled approximately $35 million. When he looked at the notes, he saw that there were about 7 million shares issued. In fact, one million of those shares were issued in the current year.

Required:

Help Jacques with his decision by answering the following questions:

a. Do you think that investing in this company would be risky? Explain your answer.

b. Does the fact that Health Life is holding a large amount of cash and short-term investments mean that management is doing a good job? Explain in detail.

c. Is it possible for Jacques to make a rough estimate as to how much longer the cash/short-term investments will last, assuming that the company does not get its breakthrough? What information would help him make this estimate?

d. Based on the number of shares that have been issued and the amount that is recorded in common shares, it is obvious that many investors have concluded that this is a good investment. Think carefully and then list three or four advantages and disadvantages to buying shares in Health Life right now.

5-37   (Cash flow analysis)

The 2004 financial statements of Green Company include the cash flow statement reproduced below.

GREEN COMPANY
Cash Flow Statement
For the year ended December 31, 2004

Operating:

Net income	$ 544,000	
Adjustments to convert to cash:		
Amortization	230,000	
Gain on sale of operating assets	(14,000)	
Change in current assets other than cash	(120,000)	
Change in current liabilities	80,000	
Cash provided by operations		720,000
Investing:		
Purchase of operating assets	($ 1,200,000)	
Sale of operating assets	400,000	
Cash used for investing		(800,000)
Financing:		
Issuance of common shares	1,000,000	
Retirement of bonds	(1,300,000)	
Dividends paid	(250,000)	
Cash used by financing		(550,000)
Decrease in cash		($630,000)

Required:

a. Did Green Company increase or decrease its current assets other than cash in 2004? Is this change consistent with an increase or a decrease in sales during the period? Explain.

b. Has Green Company become more or less risky during 2004 from an investor's point of view? Explain.

c. Does Green Company appear to be expanding or contracting its operations? How can you tell? What other financial statement information might you examine to determine whether Green is expanding?

d. Does Green appear to be able to maintain its productive capacity without additional financing? Explain.

5-38 (Operating section analysis)
The operating section of Johann Manufacturing Company's cash flow statement is shown below.

JOHANN MANUFACTURING COMPANY
Cash Flow Statement
For the year ended December 31, 2004

Cash flows from operations:		
Net income		$632,000
Adjustments to convert to cash:		
Amortization	110,000	
Loss on sale of investments	50,000	160,000

Change in current non-cash items:		
Accounts receivable	(80,000)	
Inventory	20,000	
Prepaid expenses	(15,000)	
Accounts payable	75,000	
Income tax payable	(4,000)	(4,000)
Cash provided by operations		788,000
Cash balance, January 1		566,000
Cash balance, December 31		$1,354,000

Required:

Using this information, answer the following questions. If a question cannot be answered from the information given, indicate why.

1. Have accounts receivable increased or decreased this year?

2. Does the company appear to be more or less inclined to prepay expenses than in the past? Does this help or hurt its cash position? Explain.

3. Has inventory increased or decreased this year? Explain how this affects cash.

4. Compared with last year, does the company seem to be relying more or less heavily on trade credit to finance its activities?

5. Has amortization expense increased from last year?

6. If you were a potential creditor of Johann, do you see any warning signs in the cash flow statement that you would want to investigate further before lending the company money? Explain.

7. Johann has $2,000,000 of bonds maturing on January 12, 2005. It does not have a bond sinking fund (cash fund used to repay the bond debt) established to pay off the bonds. Do you think Johann will be able to meet its obligation to pay off the bonds without additional long-term financing? Explain.

Reading and Interpreting Published Financial Statements

5-39   (Analysis of cash flow statement)
Exhibit 5-17 shows the consolidated statement of cash flow for **Purcell Energy Ltd.** at December 31, 2001 and 2000. There have been some dramatic changes in Purcell's cash position since the end of 2000. (Note that Purcell Energy has a total labelled "Cash flow from operations" of $20,717,339 in 2001. This is not the real cash flow from operations. The changes in non-cash working capital balances must be included. The cash flow from operating activities is $26,121,328 for 2001.)

Required:

a. Prepare a list of all of the sources of cash and the percentage of cash coming from each. Use "cash from operations" as one source.

b. Prepare a list of all of the uses of cash and the percentage going to each.

c. Describe the changes in each of the current non-cash assets and liabilities.

d. Comment on the change in cash position and sources and uses of cash during the year, including an explanation of the major changes that Purcell made during the year.

PURCELL ENERGY LTD. (2001)
CONSOLIDATED STATEMENTS OF CASHFLOWS
For the years ended December 31

EXHIBIT 5-17

	2001	2000
Cash flows from operating activities		
Net income for the year	$ 7,413,678	$ 8,225,838
Adjust for non-cash items:		
Gain of sale of marketable securities	(2,872)	–
Future income taxes	3,086,533	4,908,819
Depletion, amortization and site restoration	10,220,000	4,755,000
Cash flow from operations	20,717,339	17,889,657
Changes in non-cash working capital balances		
Accounts receivable	2,726,734	(4,698,110)
Prepaid expenses and deposits	4,733,661	(5,032,528)
Inventory	45,403	(69,765)
Accounts payable and accrued liabilities	(2,047,511)	384,147
Corporate taxes payable	(54,298)	(66,836)
	26,121,328	8,406,565
Cash flows from financing activities		
Payments from (to) Liard Resources Ltd.	6,862	(99,053)
Decrease in share purchase loans	73,250	–
Issue of common shares, net of related expenses	8,931,068	3,732,665
Repurchase of common shares	(7,815,836)	(7,151,416)
Issue of special warrants, net of related expenses	(65,050)	5,894,991
Repayment of capital leases	(79,287)	(215,756)
Increase in utilization of bank credit facilities	6,300,056	10,989,434
	7,351,063	13,150,865
Cash flows from investing activities		
Changes in non-cash working capital balances		
Accounts receivable	337,473	(402,521)
Accounts payable	3,181,290	1,032,532
Proceeds on disposition of marketable securities	118,699	–
Purchase of marketable securities	(22,233)	(93,594)
Purchases of property, plant and equipment	(39,764,985)	(22,651,319)
Proceeds on disposition of property, plant and equipment	2,671,680	547,500
	(33,478,076)	(21,567,402)
Decrease in cash	(5,685)	(9,972)
Cash, beginning of year	6,248	16,220
Cash, end of year	$ 563	$ 6,248
Cash flow from operations per share – basic	$ 0.821	$ 0.730
– diluted	$ 0.789	$ 0.697

5-40   (Analysis of cash flow statement)
Exhibit 5-18 shows the consolidated statements of cash flows for **CCL Industries Inc.**
at December 31, 2001 and 2000. CCL Industries uses "cash and short-term investments" for its definition of cash and cash equivalents.

Required:

a. Prepare a list of all of the sources of cash and the percentage of cash coming from each. Use "cash provided by operating activities" as one source.

b. Prepare a list of all of the uses of cash and the percentage going to each.

c. Comment on the change in cash position and sources and uses of cash during the year, including an explanation of the major changes that CCL Industries made during the year.

EXHIBIT 5-18

CCL INDUSTRIES INC. (2001)
CONSOLIDATED STATEMENTS OF CASH FLOWS

YEARS ENDED DECEMBER 31, 2001 AND 2000

(in thousands of dollars except per share data)	2001	2000
Cash provided by (used for)		
Operating activities		
Net earnings	$ 24,891	$ 26,654
Items not requiring cash:		
Depreciation and amortization	89,193	90,555
Future income taxes	7,047	5,240
Unusual items	780	18,776
	121,911	141,225
Net change in non-cash working capital	16,667	(8,263)
Cash provided by operating activities	138,578	132,962
Financing activities		
Proceeds of long-term debt	1,135	5,347
Retirement of long-term debt	(2,461)	(3,940)
Increase (decrease) in bank advances	3,070	(45,116)
Issue of shares	234	1,021
Repurchase of shares	(29,513)	(25,358)
Dividends	(11,350)	(12,077)
Cash used for financing activities	(38,885)	(80,123)
Investing activities		
Additions to capital assets	(55,595)	(61,086)
Proceeds on disposals	40,459	6,323
Other	(5,174)	2,373
Cash used for investing activities	(20,310)	(52,390)
Effect of exchange rate on cash	1,571	1,053
Increase in cash	80,954	1,502
Cash and cash equivalents at beginning of year	31,937	30,435
Cash and cash equivalents at end of year	$ 112,891	$ 31,937

5-41   (Analysis of cash flow statement)
Exhibit 5-19 shows the consolidated statements of cash flows for **Bema Gold Corporation** (a mining exploration company) at December 31, 2001, 2000, and 1999.

BEMA GOLD CORPORATION (2001)

EXHIBIT 5-19

CONSOLIDATED STATEMENTS OF CASH FLOWS

for the years ended December 31
(in thousands of United States dollars)

	2001	2000	1999
OPERATING ACTIVITIES			
Loss for the year	$(11,338)	$(51,139)	$(4,048)
Non-cash charges (credits)			
Depreciation and depletion	5,810	7,331	6,482
Amortization of deferred financing costs	2,231	1,512	1,509
Equity in losses of associated companies	100	928	809
Amortization of deferred revenue	(1,696)	(1,469)	(4,146)
Investment losses (gains)	(554)	9,331	–
Write-down of investments	–	11,773	–
Write-down of mineral properties	–	22,565	1,765
Write-down of inventory	2,248	–	–
Write-down of notes receivable	–	1,248	–
Other	673	676	569
Changes in non-cash working capital (*Note 15*)	2,388	(2,090)	326
	(138)	666	3,266
FINANCING ACTIVITIES			
Common shares issued, net of issue costs (*Note 9*)	4,609	–	540
Special warrants issued, net of issue costs (*Note 9*)	–	2,953	3,105
Convertible loan, net proceeds (*Note 8*)	–	7,593	4,842
Julietta project loans and overrun facility	21,200	17,800	–
Refugio loan repayments	(8,000)	(6,000)	(6,000)
Deferred financing costs	(1,840)	(4,758)	(604)
Capital lease repayments	(438)	(850)	(362)
Other	135	–	–
	15,666	16,738	1,521
INVESTING ACTIVITIES			
Refugio mine	(111)	(4,544)	(4,181)
Julietta development and construction	(20,064)	(18,706)	(3,189)
Acquisition, exploration and development	(1,082)	(1,136)	(3,002)
Promissory notes issued by associated companies, net	(283)	(2,120)	(3,447)
Proceeds on sale of investments	3,751	5,892	–
Proceeds from the sale of notes receivable	3,300	3,000	–
Restricted cash	–	484	(484)
Other	(132)	(453)	(647)
	(14,621)	(17,583)	(14,950)
Effect of exchange rate changes on cash and cash equivalents	1	4	59
Increase (decrease) in cash and cash equivalents	908	(175)	(10,104)
Cash and cash equivalents, beginning of year	3,225	3,400	13,504
Cash and cash equivalents, end of year	$ 4,133	$ 3,225	$ 3,400

See accompanying notes to consolidated financial statements.

Required:

a. Considering only the information presented in the cash flow statement, describe the apparent operations and cash management policies of Bema Gold over these three years.

b. Assume you are considering investing in shares of Bema Gold. What additional information would you require before you could make your decision?

5-42   (Analysis of cash flow statement)

Exhibit 5-20 shows the consolidated statements of cash flows for **Algoma Central Corporation** (a shipping and real estate company) at December 31, 2001 and 2000.

EXHIBIT 5-20

ALGOMA CENTRAL CORPORATION
Consolidated Statements of Cash Flows

Years ended December 31, 2001 and 2000
(In thousands of dollars)

	2001	2000
NET INFLOW (OUTFLOW) OF CASH RELATED TO THE FOLLOWING ACTIVITIES:		
OPERATING		
Net income	$ 31,619	$ 2,179
Items not affecting cash		
Amortization	28,555	27,991
Writedown of capital assets	-	23,587
Future income taxes	(9,697)	(12,367)
Other	(398)	(538)
	50,079	40,852
Net change in non-cash operating working capital *(Note 11)*	4,593	626
	54,672	41,478
INVESTING		
Additions to capital assets	(5,451)	(18,311)
Proceeds from sale of capital assets	1,343	429
Long-term receivables	(1,070)	189
Other assets	(594)	(388)
	(5,772)	(18,081)
FINANCING		
Repayment of long-term debt	(3,716)	(19,582)
Dividends paid	(3,794)	(3,801)
	(7,510)	(23,383)
GAIN ON CASH HELD IN FOREIGN CURRENCY	341	229
TOTAL CASH INCREASE FOR YEAR	41,731	243
CASH, BEGINNING OF YEAR	4,983	4,740
CASH, END OF YEAR	$ 46,714	$ 4,983

Required:

a. Discuss the company's ability to meet its need for cash over the last two years. Comment on the continuing nature of the major items that have appeared over these years.

b. Which items would require more investigation or further explanation, or both, to help you understand the company's financial health?

c. Explain why, although there is a $29-million difference in the amount of net income between the two years, the difference in cash from operations is only $13 million.

5-43 (Analysis of cash flow statement)
Exhibit 5-21 shows the consolidated statements of cash flows for **AT Plastics Inc.** for the years ended December 31, 2001, 2000, and 1999.

Required:

a. Discuss the company's ability to meet its needs for cash over the last three years. Comment on the continuing nature of the major items that have appeared over these years.

b. Which items would require more investigation or further explanation, or both, to help you understand the company's financial health?

c. Discuss why there was a significant increase in cash during 2001 although the company's net loss for 2001 was not that different from 2000.

d. In this chapter, we talked about the placement of interest expense within the operating section of the cash flow statement. Note at the bottom of the AT Plastics cash flow statement that both the interest and the income taxes paid during the year are disclosed. To whom do you think the company is aiming this information? Explain your answer.

5-44 (Analysis of cash flow statement)
Go to the *Accounting Perspectives CD* and find the cash flow statements for **Sun-Rype Products Ltd.** for the years 2001 and 2000.

**Sun-Rype
Products Ltd.
Annual Report**

Required:

a. Discuss the company's ability to meet its needs for cash over the last two years. Comment on the continuing nature of the major items that have appeared over these years.

b. Which items would require more investigation or further explanation, or both, to help you understand the company's financial health?

c. In this chapter, we talked about the placement of interest expense within the operating section of the cash flow statement. Note at the bottom of Sun-Rype's cash flow statement that both the interest and the income taxes paid during the year are disclosed. To whom do you think it is aiming this information? Explain your answer.

EXHIBIT 5-21

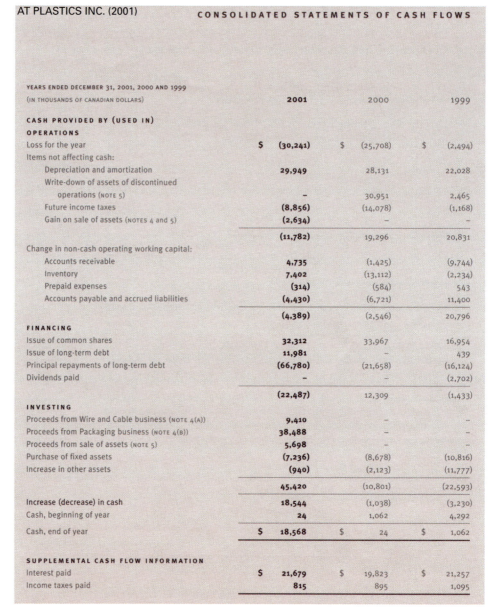

AT PLASTICS INC. (2001)   CONSOLIDATED STATEMENTS OF CASH FLOWS

YEARS ENDED DECEMBER 31, 2001, 2000 AND 1999

(IN THOUSANDS OF CANADIAN DOLLARS)	2001	2000	1999
CASH PROVIDED BY (USED IN)			
OPERATIONS			
Loss for the year	$ (30,241)	$ (25,708)	$ (2,494)
Items not affecting cash:			
Depreciation and amortization	29,949	28,131	22,028
Write-down of assets of discontinued operations (NOTE 5)	–	30,951	2,465
Future income taxes	(8,856)	(14,078)	(1,168)
Gain on sale of assets (NOTES 4 and 5)	(2,634)	–	–
	(11,782)	19,296	20,831
Change in non-cash operating working capital:			
Accounts receivable	4,735	(1,425)	(9,744)
Inventory	7,402	(13,112)	(2,234)
Prepaid expenses	(314)	(584)	543
Accounts payable and accrued liabilities	(4,430)	(6,721)	11,400
	(4,389)	(2,546)	20,796
FINANCING			
Issue of common shares	32,312	33,967	16,954
Issue of long-term debt	11,981	–	439
Principal repayments of long-term debt	(66,780)	(21,658)	(16,124)
Dividends paid	–	–	(2,702)
	(22,487)	12,309	(1,433)
INVESTING			
Proceeds from Wire and Cable business (NOTE 4(A))	9,410	–	–
Proceeds from Packaging business (NOTE 4(B))	38,488	–	–
Proceeds from sale of assets (NOTE 5)	5,698	–	–
Purchase of fixed assets	(7,236)	(8,678)	(10,816)
Increase in other assets	(940)	(2,123)	(11,777)
	45,420	(10,801)	(22,593)
Increase (decrease) in cash	18,544	(1,038)	(3,230)
Cash, beginning of year	24	1,062	4,292
Cash, end of year	$ 18,568	$ 24	$ 1,062
SUPPLEMENTAL CASH FLOW INFORMATION			
Interest paid	$ 21,679	$ 19,823	$ 21,257
Income taxes paid	815	895	1,095

Beyond the Book

5-45   (Analysis of cash flow statement)
For a company of your own choosing, answer the following questions related to its cash flow statement:

  a. Summarize the results for cash from operating, investing, and financing activities over the last two years.

  b. Explain any significant changes from last year to this year in the items listed in part a).

  c. What were the four most significant uses of cash (from the investing and financing sections)?

d. What were the four most significant sources of cash, including operations?

e. How is the company financing its investing activities, through operating or financing activities or both? Support your answer with numbers.

Cases

Additional Cases

5-46 Atlantic Service Company
Atlantic Service Company was established five years ago to provide services to the home construction industry. It has been very successful, with assets, sales, and profits increasing each year. However, Atlantic is experiencing serious cash shortages and is in danger of going into bankruptcy because it cannot pay its suppliers and already has a very substantial overdraft at its bank. The president has asked you to analyze the cash flow statement for the years ended December 31, 2004 and 2003, in Exhibit 5-22, to explain what appears to be causing the cash shortage, and to recommend a plan to save the company from bankruptcy.

ATLANTIC SERVICE COMPANY

EXHIBIT 5-22

Cash Flow Statement
For the years ended December 31, 2004 and 2003

	2004	2003
Operations:		
Net income	$150,000	$135,000
Adjustments to convert to cash:		
Amortization	25,000	20,000
Changes in non-cash working capital:		
Increase in accounts receivable	(35,000)	(30,000)
Increase in inventory	(30,000)	(25,000)
Increase in accounts payable	55,000	45,000
	165,000	145,000
Financing:		
Increase in one-year bank loan	50,000	30,000
Dividends paid	(15,000)	(10,000)
	35,000	20,000
Investing:		
Purchase of equipment	(300,000)	(250,000)
Net cash used in the year	(100,000)	(85,000)
Cash position, beginning of the year	(130,000)	(45,000)
Cash position, end of the year	($230,000)	($130,000)

5-47 Robertson Furniture Ltd.
Kayla Moss has just received a small inheritance from her grandparents' estate. She would like to invest the money and is currently reviewing several investment opportunities. A friend has brought her the financial statements of Robertson Furniture Ltd., a great company she found on the Internet. Kayla has reviewed the financial statements of Robertson Furniture and is ready to invest in this company.

Before she invests, Kayla comes to you for some financial advice because she knows you have just finished an accounting course and may be able to give her some insight into the financial statements. She is very certain that this company will be a profitable investment because the balance sheet indicates that the company has cash balances of over $300,000. She has copied Robertson's statement of cash flow so that you can see how much cash the company is able to generate each year.

EXHIBIT 5-23

ROBERTSON FURNITURE LTD.

Cash Flow Statement

For the year ended December 31, 2004

	2004	2003
Operations activities		
Net income (loss)	$ (5,000)	$ 1,000
Add back items not representing cash flows:		
Amortization	20,000	50,000
Loss on disposal	2,000	1,000
Adjustment for working capital items:		
Increase in accounts receivable	(40,000)	(36,000)
Increase in inventories	(56,000)	(42,000)
Decrease in prepaid insurance	8,000	2,000
Increase in accounts payable	45,000	28,000
Cash from operating activities	(26,000)	4,000
Financing activities		
Issue of bonds payable	100,000	-
Issue of common shares	50,000	50,000
Payment of dividends	(1,000)	(20,000)
Cash from financing activities	149,000	30,000
Investing activities		
Sale of property, plant, and equipment	70,500	22,400
Sale of investments	50,000	20,000
Cash from investing activities	120,500	42,400
Increase in cash	243,500	76,400
Cash—beginning of the year	84,950	8,550
Cash—end of the year	$ 328,450	$ 84,950

Required:

a. Comment on Robertson's Furniture's cash flow statement, keeping in mind Kayla's comments on the fact that the company must be a good investment given the amount of cash shown on the balance sheet.

b. Based on the results in the cash flow statement, outline several questions that Kayla should investigate before investing her inheritance in this company.

5-48   Vassar Inc.

The 2004 comparative income statement and balance sheet of Vassar Inc. have just been distributed at a meeting of the company's board of directors.

While discussing the business's year-end results, the board raises concerns over the year-end cash balance. They cannot understand why the cash balance is so low given the increase in profitability over the past year. As the chief financial officer, the board is looking to you for answers to their questions.

Required:

a. Using the indirect method, prepare a cash flow statement for the year ended December 31, 2004. In addition to the balance sheet and income statement presented below, you gather the following information (amounts in thousands):

- In 2003, the company sold capital assets for $2,500. These assets had originally cost $400 and had a net book value of $2,750. While no capital assets were sold in 2004, equipment costing $165 was purchased for use in the company's manufacturing facilities.

- Vassar paid dividends of $1,000 in 2004.

- The company sold no other long-term assets or investments.

- Vassar issued no common shares or long-term debt in 2004, but did issue bonds worth $10,000 in 2003.

b. Using all the information available to you, prepare an answer to the questions raised by the board explaining why the cash balance is low when the company is experiencing record profits.

VASSAR INC.

EXHIBIT 5-24

Balance Sheet
At August 31, 2004
(in thousands)

	2004	2003
Assets		
Cash	$ 89	$ 398
Accounts receivable	1,580	1,578
Inventory	9,852	8,750
Total current assets	11,521	10,726
Capital assets	10,917	10,752
Less: accumulated amortization	(862)	(745)
Total assets	$ 21,576	$ 20,733
Liabilities and Shareholders' Equity		
Accounts payable	$ 1,450	$ 1,276
Salaries payable	85	66
Interest payable	22	36
Total current liabilities	1,557	1,378
Bonds payable	10,000	10,000
Total liabilities	11,557	11,378
Common shares	8,000	8,000
Retained earnings	2,019	1,355
Total shareholders' equity	10,019	9,355
Total liabilities and shareholders' equity	$ 21,576	$ 20,733

EXHIBIT 5-24
CONT.

VASSAR INC.

Income Statement
For the year ended August 31, 2004
(in thousands)

	2004	2003
Sales revenue	$ 70,595	$ 56,238
Cost of goods sold	46,120	36,555
Gross profit	24,475	19,683
Salaries expense	10,586	9,265
Administrative expense	8,850	7,952
Rent and maintenance expense	1,620	1,541
Amortization	117	121
Insurance expense	52	66
Advertising expense	76	43
Income from operations	3,174	695
Other income (expenses)		
Gain on sale of capital assets	-	250
Interest expense	(1,000)	(375)
Income before income tax	2,174	570
Income tax	510	139
Net income	$ 1,664	$ 431

5-49   Ridlow Shipping

Jim Shea is an accountant at Powers, Barnes, and King, an accounting firm based in Halifax, Nova Scotia. The firm specializes in dealing with small business clients and, while most clients are very successful business people, many have limited accounting knowledge. Owen Ridlow is the sole owner of Ridlow Shipping and he recently called Jim with some questions about the financial statements prepared for the year ended December 31, 2004.

   Owen: "Jim, I am wondering why I have to pay you guys to prepare a cash flow statement. I understand the importance of the balance sheet and the income statement, but since I always know how much cash I have in the bank and I reconcile my accounts regularly, why do I need a cash flow statement? I feel that paying to have this statement prepared is an unnecessary expense."

Required:

Do you feel that Owen is justified in his comments? Outline several points that Jim should raise in his discussions with Owen to justify the need for a cash flow statement. The cash flow statement for Ridlow Shipping has been provided to assist you in preparing your answer.

RIDLOW SHIPPING LTD.

EXHIBIT 5-25

Cash Flow Statement
For the year ended December 31, 2004

	2004	2003
Operating activities		
Net income	$ 206,450	$ 254,560
Add back items not representing cash flows:		
Amortization	40,000	50,000
Loss on disposal	2,000	6,000
Adjustment for working capital items:		
Decrease (increase) in accounts receivable	(40,000)	16,000
Increase in inventories	(5,000)	(2,000)
Decrease in prepaid rent	500	200
Increase (decrease) in accounts payable	45,000	(28,000)
Cash from operating activities	248,950	296,760
Financing activities		
Payment of bonds	(100,000)	-
Issue of common shares	50,000	-
Payment of dividends	(75,000)	(75,000)
Cash from financing activities	(125,000)	(75,000)
Investing activities		
Sale of investments	50,000	20,000
Purchase of capital assets	(215,000)	(197,000)
Cash from investing activities	(165,000)	(177,000)
Increase in cash	(41,050)	44,760
Cash—beginning of the year	53,310	8,550
Cash—end of the year	$ 12,260	$ 53,310

5-50 Jones Printing

Ben Jones would like to expand his printing business to include a new computerized colour printing system. To finance the equipment, Ben has applied for a loan from a government venture capital agency. The agency requires a complete set of financial statements before it can approve any loan application and has employees assigned to each applicant to assist them in preparing the necessary financial statements.

You have been assigned to assist Ben and he has provided you with a basic income statement and balance sheet for his business. You explain to Ben that a complete set of financial statements includes a cash flow statement and that one will have to be prepared for his business before the loan application can be processed. Ben does not understand the purpose of the cash flow statement and what types of information he will have to gather in order to prepare it.

Required:

Prepare a brief memo to Ben Jones outlining the purpose and structure of the cash flow statement and any additional information beyond the income statement and balance sheet which he will have to provide to assist you in preparing a cash flow statement for his business.

Critical Thinking Question

5-51   (Universality of the definition of cash and cash equivalents)
As discussed in this chapter, the cash flow statement provides users of financial information with another "flow" measure of a company's performance. However, several issues have been raised in both academic and practitioner-oriented research relative to the meaning, usefulness, and calculation of cash flows. For example, Wallace and Collier ("The 'Cash' in Cash Flow Statements: A Multi-Country Comparison," *Accounting Horizons*, December 1991) describe how various countries, including Canada, have issued standards regarding the presentation of cash flows but have failed to define the term "cash" either consistently or adequately. The changes made in 1998 in Canada with respect to the cash flow statement define cash as "cash on hand and demand deposits" and cash equivalents as "short-term, highly liquid investments that are readily convertible to known amounts of cash and which are subject to an insignificant risk of changes in value" (*CICA Handbook*, Sec. 1540.06). It goes on to define "short-term" as three months or less, and to restrict investments to non-equity ones. It also includes bank overdrafts, which are payable on demand, in the cash equivalents.

Required:
Look up the Wallace and Collier article in your library, briefly summarize the authors' arguments, and discuss the potential problems associated with the lack of a uniform definition of cash both for companies that have only domestic operations and for those that have both domestic and foreign operations. Discuss whether the new Canadian requirements address their arguments or whether they are still deficient.

What If They Won't Pay?

Sales are brisk at Stiff Sentences, Inc.: the 12-person Ottawa company recorded receivables of about $1.2 million in 2001 and expected to reach $1.5 million in 2002. Its product? Words. Mostly strung together into sentences, as the company name suggests, to form annual reports, letters, speeches, advertising copy, and other communication tools—though Stiff Sentences also occasionally sells words in ones and twos, as it creates names for companies, products, and brands.

Most of the company's clients, which have included Bell Canada, Alcatel, Nokia, Canada Post, the CBC, the United Way, and numerous government departments and agencies, are satisfied customers who bring repeat business and keep the 10 seasoned writers busy. But because the company sells a creative process rather than a tangible item, judgements of the quality of its products are subjective.

So, despite strict quality control procedures—the company has been ISO-9000 [1] certified since 1999—"it can happen," says Deborah Johnson, co-owner and business manager, "that a client isn't happy with the final result. The biggest problems come when we don't find out about it until we're trying to find out why the bill hasn't been paid two months later." To avoid these situations, the company hired an outside receivables clerk who works from home and calls clients as soon as an invoice becomes overdue. As a result, late payments are usually collected before a problem arises.

Still, when it does, "we try to work something out," Ms. Johnson explains. Sometimes the work is redone; often, however, Stiff Sentences ends up writing off all or part of the fee as a bad debt. The writer(s) involved share in the responsibility in such cases. "They're not employees, but associates," Ms. Johnson says, explaining that the company's financial relationship with the writers is much like that of a real estate company with its agents. "They pay a fee to belong to the group, and they keep a percentage of the revenue from the work that they do."

Most of them make an excellent living (rare in the writing profession). But while they share in the profits at Stiff Sentences, they also share in the risk. Writers are paid twice a month for work completed to date; but if the fee for a job is written off and the writer has already been paid for working on it, he or she refunds the payment.

"It's important, therefore, that we keep focused on who's responsible for what in each job," stresses Ms. Johnson. Of course, it's also important to keep these uncollectible amounts to a minimum. "The best way to do that is to stay on top of our receivables," she explains. "The other thing that helps is to make sure you're serving people well. We've started doing customer satisfaction surveys and the feedback has been extremely valuable."

---

[1] ISO 9000 is an internationally recognized accreditation that signifies that the company has met a high standard of quality in its activities.

CASH, TEMPORARY INVESTMENTS, AND ACCOUNTS AND NOTES RECEIVABLE

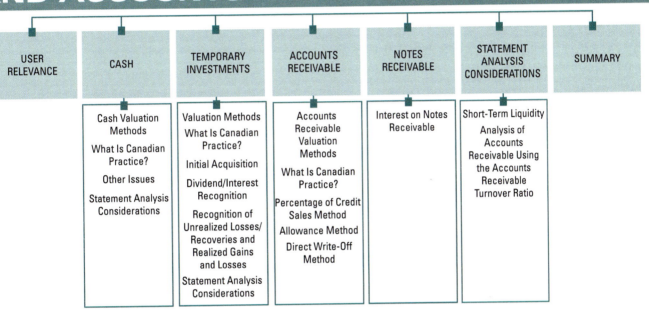

USER RELEVANCE	CASH	TEMPORARY INVESTMENTS	ACCOUNTS RECEIVABLE	NOTES RECEIVABLE	STATEMENT ANALYSIS CONSIDERATIONS	SUMMARY
	Cash Valuation Methods	Valuation Methods	Accounts Receivable Valuation Methods	Interest on Notes Receivable	Short-Term Liquidity Analysis of Accounts Receivable Using the Accounts Receivable Turnover Ratio	
	What Is Canadian Practice?	What Is Canadian Practice?	What Is Canadian Practice?			
	Other Issues	Initial Acquisition	Percentage of Credit Sales Method			
	Statement Analysis Considerations	Dividend/Interest Recognition	Allowance Method			
		Recognition of Unrealized Losses/ Recoveries and Realized Gains and Losses	Direct Write-Off Method			
		Statement Analysis Considerations				

Learning Objectives:

After studying this chapter, you should be able to:

1. *Discuss the control issues related to cash.*
2. *Recognize the importance of cash to the success of a business.*
3. *Prepare a simple bank reconciliation.*
4. *Identify the criteria for the classification of an investment as temporary.*
5. *Explain why temporary investments are recorded using the lower of cost and market.*
6. *Prepare the journal entries associated with the acquisition, holding, and selling of temporary investments.*
7. *Explain why estimating the potential uncollectibility of accounts receivable is required.*
8. *Identify two methods for recognizing uncollectibility and describe the circumstances under which each is appropriate.*
9. *Describe a note receivable and explain the circumstances under which it is used.*
10. *Calculate interest associated with notes receivable and prepare the necessary journal entries.*
11. *Using financial statement information, calculate the current ratio, the quick ratio, and the accounts receivable turnover ratio.*
12. *Explain how the current ratio, the quick ratio, and the accounts receivable turnover ratio help users to understand short-term liquidity issues.*

■ Our opening story talks about accounts receivable, one of the topics in this chapter. Stiff Sentences, Inc. describes its difficulty in collecting its accounts receivable. Remember that in Chapter 4 we discussed revenue recognition and the matching principle? If a company like Stiff Sentences wants to recognize revenue when it bills its customers, it will have to somehow measure the potential for uncollectibility to ensure that the revenues are not overstated. More will be said about this topic when we discuss accounts receivable later in the chapter. Stiff Sentences has contracted out the management of its accounts receivable to an outside person. This type of outsourcing of work that in the past used to be done by employees is becoming more and more common. Some companies contract out the total accounting system.

You should have noticed that this company is organized quite differently from most companies. The people who do the work are not employees. Stiff Sentences calls them associates. They pay a fee to Stiff Sentences to be part of the writing pool, and they earn a percentage of the revenue from each piece of writing they do. How much they earn is very much dependent on their understanding of what the customer wants and their skills as a writer. The writers are, in fact, independent contractors.

With the outsourcing of the accounts receivable collection and the pool of associates from which to obtain competent, experienced writers, the owners are able to devote their efforts to finding new clients and keeping in touch with old ones. Over the last three years the business has grown, which is an indication that the business model it uses is working.

USER RELEVANCE

The three topics discussed in this chapter—cash, temporary investments, and accounts and notes receivable—represent the most liquid of a company's assets. It is mainly from these items that the company is going to meet its immediate, short-term obligations. Users need to be aware of what these items are when they see them on financial statements. For example, cash seems to be very straightforward, but in reality it constitutes a series of things ranging from physical money to amounts in bank accounts to cheques and money orders. The temporary investments are an indication to the user that the company is managing its cash. It is taking cash that it does not need immediately and investing it, so that rather than lying idle, it is earning revenue. When the cash is needed, these investments are sold. Accounts receivable are usually collected within 30 days. However, as a user you need to be aware of potential uncollectibility and of agreements that allow the customer more than 30 days to pay.

The presence of these items on the financial statements enable users who are interested in the company's short-term ability to repay obligations to evaluate its capacity to do so. A deeper understanding of these items will improve your ability to assess the short-term vulnerability of a company. The assets discussed in this chapter have the unique property that all are either cash or will become cash very soon. In accounting terms, we often call them **monetary** assets because their value is fixed in current monetary terms. Obviously, they are very important to every business since, as we learned in Chapter 5, sufficient cash must be available at all times to pay for purchases and for obligations as they become due.

In this chapter, the accounting methods and principles that apply to cash, temporary investments, and accounts and notes receivable are considered. In each account category, recognition criteria, valuation methods, income statement implications, financial statement analysis considerations, and other issues that are important to understanding that account category are discussed. The complexities of financial statement analysis associated with this group of accounts are discussed in this chapter and each subsequent chapter in a section entitled "Statement Analysis Considerations."

CASH

In the first chapter of this book, we discussed the criteria that are used to decide whether, for accounting purposes, something is an asset. Assets are identified as items that: (1) have probable future value that can be measured, (2) the company owns or has the right to use, and (3) arose from a past event. In this chapter, we will use these criteria to decide whether and how we will categorize cash, temporary investments, and accounts and notes receivable as assets.

Cash meets the probable future value criterion. Cash does not have any intrinsic value other than the value of the paper or the metal from which it is made. It derives its value from its ability to be exchanged for goods and services in the future, which is also called its **purchasing power**. It serves as the medium of exchange in every economy. The ability of cash to serve as a medium of exchange depends on the faith in the economy of the individuals who use it. If there is a loss of confidence that the medium can be exchanged in the future, the currency loses its value. For example, Argentina has recently been experiencing difficulty making its international borrowing repayments. Up until early 2002, the country's currency, the peso, was tied one-to-one with the U.S. dollar. In an attempt to get greater control of its economy, Argentina delinked its currency from the U.S. dollar. People in Argentina immediately became concerned that the peso would lose value and attempted to withdraw their money from banks so that they could invest it in assets that would not lose value. A full run on the banks could have precipitated a complete collapse of the Argentine economy. To stop this happening, the country has on several occasions frozen bank accounts, preventing depositors from withdrawing their money. As of the end of April 2002, the Argentine peso has dropped to half its former value. One peso was worth US $0.50.

Learning Objective

Discuss the control issues related to cash.

Cash also meets the ownership/right-to-use criterion. Ownership of cash is generally evidenced by possession: currency, cheques, money orders, etc., in safes; money deposited in banks. One type of cash, currency (bills and coins), is difficult to differentiate except by using serial numbers on bills. It is therefore a very difficult asset to control. To deal with this problem, companies have learned to make extensive use of banks. As you are aware, more and more cash transactions are conducted electronically using credit or debit cards, thus eliminating the physical handling of cash. This makes the control of cash much easier and transactions much more efficient. All companies must establish effective internal control procedures to govern how they handle and control their cash. Auditors review the internal control systems established by a company and design special audit procedures to test whether these controls adequately safeguard the handling and recording of cash.

The third criterion, the occurrence of a past event that transferred the cash to the company, is also met. Cash flowing in or out of a company is a signal that a transaction has occurred. If cash is present, a past event has occurred.

Cash Valuation Methods

Knowing that cash meets the recognition criterion, the next problem is how to record the cash in the accounting system. For this account and for all other accounts discussed in this text, a number of possible valuation methods will be discussed. Some of these methods are not allowed under Canadian GAAP but are allowed in other countries. The purpose of discussing the range of possible methods is to lay out conceptually the possibilities that serve as the basis for current practice. A separate section is devoted to the requirements of Canadian GAAP. In some cases, the methods used under Canadian GAAP are a combination of the various possible valuation methods discussed here.

One possible method of valuing cash is to record it at its face value. This means that as long as cash is held, its value is assumed not to change. If we had $100 in cash, the cash would be valued at $100. If that same $100 was present several weeks later, it would still be valued at $100. Its face value does not change.

Even though the face value of the $100 does not change, its ability to be converted into goods and services may change. The ability to be exchanged for goods and service, or purchasing power, is affected by the level of inflation or deflation during the period. During periods of inflation, cash is said to have sustained a loss in purchasing power because of its relative loss in terms of exchangeability for goods and services. The $100 can buy fewer goods and services than it could before. In the example we are using here, the attribute of face value does not change, but the attribute of purchasing power does. If, however, the attribute of purchasing power is used to value cash, then income would have to be recognized for the change in purchasing power during the accounting period. Consequently, the choice of which attribute of cash to measure is critical to how it is represented on the balance sheet and how it affects the income statement.

accounting in the news

BURGERNOMICS 101—A LESSON IN PURCHASING POWER

Every year, *The Economist* magazine issues its much-anticipated Big Mac index, a survey of the purchasing power of currencies using the ubiquitous McDonald's burger for its standard. It's based on the idea of purchasing power parity, which predicts that the exchange rate between two countries eventually moves toward a rate equalizing prices for the same goods and services in each country.

The Big Mac is a useful standard because it's made from the same recipe around the world. The survey calculates the exchange rate that would make the cost of buying a Big Mac in the United States the same as buying one in another country. The rate can then be compared with actual exchange rates, giving one measure of how under- or overvalued a currency is.

In the April 2002 survey, an American Big Mac cost US $2.49. Compared to that, the least expensive Big Macs around the world were to be had in Argentina, China, Russia, South Africa, and Thailand; the most expensive, in Switzerland, Turkey, and Denmark. A Canadian Big Mac cost CDN $3.33, or US $2.12. Given an exchange rate of $1.57 at the time, a Big Mac in Canada was 15% cheaper than its southern brother—yet another (admittedly simplistic) measure of the extent to which the Canadian dollar has been undervalued.

Source: "Economics focus Big MacCurrencies," *The Economist*, April 27, 2002, p. 76.

What Is Canadian Practice?

In Canada, there is an underlying assumption, referred to as the **unit-of-measure assumption,** which specifies that the results of activities of the company should be measured in terms of a **monetary unit** (e.g., the Canadian dollar). This precludes the measurement of activities in terms of purchasing power, and cash is, therefore, measured at its face value rather than by any other method.

While the unit-of-measure assumption requires that Canadian currency be measured at face value, this is not the case for foreign currency. Suppose, for example, that a company does business with a Swiss customer and that the agreement with the customer is denominated in euros (the currency used by most European countries). This means that the customer is required to pay in euros rather than Canadian dollars. The company will receive euros and will probably hold a certain amount of euro currency at the beginning and the end of the accounting period. Because this asset is measured in a different monetary unit than the rest of the company's assets, a conversion will have to be made from euros to Canadian dollars.

Learning Objective

2

Recognize the importance of cash to the success of a business.

In Canada, the conversion of euros into dollars is done using the exchange rate that exists on the date of the balance sheet. For example, suppose the exchange rate is 1.0 euro = 1.5 Canadian dollars at the beginning of the year and 1.0 euro = 1.45 Canadian dollars at the end of the year. Further, suppose that the company holds 1,000 euros at the beginning and the end of the year. Exhibit 6-1 shows how the euro would be valued on the balance sheet. You can see that, while there is no gain or loss during the year in terms of euros (the face value does not change), there is a loss in terms of dollars. This loss will appear on the income statement and will be called a foreign currency transaction loss.

EXHIBIT 6-1	

■ FOREIGN CURRENCY VALUATION

Date	Amount of Foreign Currency	Amount of Exchange Rate	Cdn. Currency
Jan. 1, 20x1	1,000 euros	1.0 euro = $1.50	$1,500
Dec. 31, 20x1	1,000 euros	1.0 euro = $1.45	$1,450
Loss	0 euros		$50

Exchange rates are determined in the foreign currency markets. Reasons for changes in the exchange rates of currencies are difficult to pinpoint precisely but, in theory, one of the major causes is differential inflation rates in the two countries (the economic theory that describes this is called the *purchasing power parity theory*). Individuals who hold currencies in countries with high inflation rates lose more purchasing power than those in countries with low inflation rates. Exchange rates adjust to compensate for these differences in purchasing power. In effect, GAAP recognizes the changes in purchasing power of foreign currency by allowing the dollar value of the foreign currencies to rise and fall with the exchange rates.

One final note with regard to purchasing power. In the mid- to late 1970s and in the early 1980s, Canada experienced high rates of inflation (by Canadian standards). Accounting regulators became concerned with the problem that income, as measured by GAAP, did not take into consideration the changes in purchasing power of the assets and liabilities of the company. In 1982, the Canadian Institute of Chartered Accountants (CICA) adopted guidelines that requested that companies present supplementary information regarding the effects of changing price levels on the financial results. These requirements were dropped in 1992 when inflation was down to more normal levels. Therefore, in Canada, there is currently no systematic reporting of the effects of inflation or changing prices on companies' financial results.

Reports from Other Countries

NAFTA Facts

United States—Inflation levels are very low in the United States. Its accounting is based primarily on historical cost, similar to Canada. It currently does not require any inflation adjustments.

Mexico—In the past, Mexico has had relatively high inflation. In 1999, its inflation was approximately 13%. By 2001, it was down to 4.4%. Mexico's central bank is aiming to ensure that inflation does not rise above 4.5% in 2002. Even though inflation is much lower now, inflation adjustments are required for changes in the general price level. Inventory, fixed assets, and their related expenses may alternatively be adjusted to replacement costs.

Other Issues

Despite the issues discussed so far, accounting for cash is relatively straightforward—you simply report how much cash is owned by the company. By cash, we mean currency, cheques, money orders, and amounts in bank accounts that can be used with very short notice.

The main issues with cash are the control of cash to ensure that it is not lost or stolen, and the management of cash balances. Proper control of cash includes policies such as ensuring that all cash is deposited into bank accounts daily or even more frequently, using secure safes and tills to hold cash until it is deposited, writing cheques instead of using cash to pay expenses, and keeping as little cash on hand as possible.

Control of cash is one part of a company's **internal control system**. Management is responsible for safeguarding all of the assets of a company. To accomplish this, policies and procedures are established to help protect and manage assets like cash, inventory, supplies, equipment, and buildings. Besides the control features mentioned above, an effective control system should include the following:

1. Physical measures aimed at protecting the assets from theft or vandalism. Management needs to protect the assets by ensuring that premises are secure through the use of locks and/or alarms. In the case of cash, this means depositing cash in the bank regularly and keeping cash that is on the premises securely stored in tills and safes.

2. Separation of duties. Employees have the opportunity to defraud a company if they are in charge of purchasing assets, inspecting them on arrival to ensure that what has been ordered has been received, and entering the receipt of the assets in the accounting system. To reduce this opportunity for fraud, management

attempts to ensure that one person is not responsible for all of these activities. When one person is responsible for verifying the work of another, dishonest behaviour requires collusion, which is more difficult to plan and execute. With respect to cash, separation of duties means that one person receives cash, another is authorized to write cheques, and a third records the receipt or payment of cash in the accounting records. In a small company, separation of duties may be more difficult because of the limited number of employees. Then, management itself must periodically verify the work of employees.

3. An effective record keeping system. Management establishes an accounting system such that all transactions are recorded on a timely basis, only authorized personnel record transactions, and all personnel authorized to record transactions have the appropriate training to ensure that errors are minimized.

You may think that all of this concern about internal control is excessive. However, as the following summary indicates, Canadian companies lose profits annually due to fraud perpetrated by their employees.

accounting in the news

ONE COMPANY'S LOSS

CINAR Corp. demonstrated major weaknesses in internal control of its money when the company disclosed that US $122 million from its coffers had been invested without proper authorization. Further, the company did not know where most of the money had gone.

The company was able to account for some $36 million in Canadian government bonds. However, new CEO Barrie Usher admitted in a conference call with incredulous investment analysts that he did not know exactly where the rest had been invested—only that it was in investment-grade stocks or bonds meant to secure other investments.

CINAR, famous for popular children's television shows such as *Caillou* and *Arthur*, had been under fire over allegations of tax-credit fraud. The company was accused of crediting Canadians for scripts written by Americans and then collecting Canadian tax credits for the work. This precipitated the internal audit, which revealed that $122 million from a fund meant for acquisitions had been invested without approval by the Board of Directors.

Following the revelation, CINAR's chief financial officer was dismissed, while company founders Micheline Charest and Ron Weinberg resigned their posts as co-chief executive officers. Trading in the stock was also halted.

Source: "CINAR bosses resign; Financial officer fired; $86 million still missing," by Mary Lamey, *The Gazette* (Montreal), March 7, 2000, p. A1.

One control procedure used by virtually every company is the **bank reconciliation**, which ensures that the accounting records agree with the bank records. Every bank account has a corresponding general ledger account in the company's accounting system. The company's records and the bank ledgers reflect the same transactions such as cash deposits and cheques written, but the transactions may be recorded at different times. For example, a company may write, record, and mail a cheque on November 1, and the payee may receive it on November 7, and deposit it in its bank account on November 8. The payee's bank will forward the cheque to the company's bank, which will then withdraw the money from the company's account on November 9. The transaction takes a few days to be completed, so the cheque will be outstanding from the time the company records it on November 1 until the bank shows it as a withdrawal from the account on November 9. During the time in which the cheque is outstanding, the two accounts (the general ledger and the bank's records) will be different. The bank reconciliation is the process used to account for all such differences. To manage your cash most effectively as an individual, you should reconcile your personal bank balance every month.

The following information about Gelardi Company illustrates a bank reconciliation:

- The balance in Gelardi's cash account on March 31 was $9,763.42.
- The balance in Gelardi's bank account on March 31 was $9,043.92.
- The accountant reviewed the bank statement and the transactions in the cash account and discovered the following:
  - Cheque #8889 for $462.89, and #8891 for $65.78 were still outstanding (they had been mailed but they had not yet been presented to the bank for payment).
  - The last deposit of the month for $1,035.62 was made as a night deposit and the bank did not record it in Gelardi's bank account until April 2.
  - The bank had included a bank charge of $25.75 for March, but the accountant had not yet recorded it in the company's books.
  - The bank had returned a cheque from one of Gelardi's customers marked NSF (not sufficient funds). This was a cheque for $186.80 that a customer had given the company in exchange for some merchandise. Gelardi had accepted the cheque, recorded it as an increase to the cash account, and deposited it in its bank account. However, when Gelardi's bank presented the cheque to the customer's bank for payment, it was informed that the customer did not have enough money in his bank account to cover the cheque. Gelardi's bank returned the cheque to Gelardi and removed the amount from the bank account.

Using this information, the accountant would prepare the following bank reconciliation:

Learning Objective

Prepare a simple bank reconciliation.

Bank Reconciliation
For the month of March

Balance per bank statement		$ 9,043.92
Add: Outstanding deposit		1,035.62
		10,079.54
Deduct: Outstanding cheques		
#8889	$ 462.89	
#8891	65.78	528.67
Adjusted cash balance		$ 9,550.87
Balance per cash account		$ 9,763.42
Deduct: Bank charges	$ 25.75	
NSF cheque	186.80	212.55
Adjusted cash balance		$ 9,550.87

The accountant now knows that the appropriate cash balance is $9,550.87 and also that the company's records and the bank's records are in agreement with respect to cash. After the bank reconciliation is complete, the accountant needs to make a journal entry to adjust the cash account so that it reflects the information that was just received from the bank. The entry would be:

SE-Bank charge expense	25.75	
A-Accounts receivable	186.80	
A-Cash		212.55

After posting, the balance in the cash account would be $9,550.87.

Bank reconciliations are an important control procedure. They ensure that all transactions affecting the bank account have been properly recorded, so the company knows that no transactions have been missed. They are normally made every month for every bank account, as soon as the bank statement is received. The bank reconciliation procedure consists of reconciling the balance recorded by the company with the balance recorded by the bank. The main reconciling items are outstanding cheques, outstanding deposits, bank service charges that have been deducted from the bank account but not recorded by the company, errors in recording items, and any other item that affects cash and is recorded by either the company or the bank.

Another important control measure is to ensure that the person who reconciles the bank account is not the person who is responsible for the bank account or the accounting records. This will ensure that any error or discrepancy will be found and properly corrected. It also ensures that an individual is not given the opportunity to take cash and then change the books to cover the theft.

The other issue associated with cash is cash management. Proper cash management requires that sufficient cash be maintained in readily accessible bank accounts to pay expenses, while at the same time excess amounts of cash be kept neither on hand nor in bank accounts. Cash is a non-earning asset; that is, it is not earning a return. The company will want to keep as much of its cash invested in income-earning assets as possible. Income-earning assets include savings accounts and short-term investments. A company's cash management policies are critical to the effective management of its cash position and to the maximization of total earnings. Advanced cash management techniques are not discussed in this book but are very important to the shareholders and management of companies.

Statement Analysis Considerations

Concern might be expressed regarding restrictions placed on a company's use of cash. Sometimes a company's cash is restricted with regard to withdrawal from the bank because of a feature known as **compensating balances**. These are minimum balances that must be maintained in the bank account to avoid significant service charges or, in some cases, to satisfy restrictive loan covenants (which are clauses in loan agreements that are designed to reduce the risk to the lender). A company might also restrict cash for a specific use. In such cases, the restricted cash should be segregated from other amounts of cash. Other than these, and those discussed in conjunction with the understanding of the cash flow statement in Chapter 5, there are no special considerations with regard to cash for financial statement analysis.

ethics in accounting

Ethics in Accounting

■ Because of the easy portability of money and difficulty of identifying one owner's money from another's, the handling of cash in any business can be an ethical dilemma for managers and employees. Strict controls must be placed on who within the organization handles cash, and how they handle it. The set of controls put in place by a business to manage cash (or any other asset or liability) is referred to as the internal control system. Internal controls are not based on the assumption that people are dishonest. Rather, their purpose is to ensure that employees do not have the opportunity to become dishonest.

Suppose, for example, that you own a parking lot and have hired an employee to collect fees from individuals who park in the lot. What controls do you think would be necessary to ensure that you receive all the cash the employee collects? What characteristics would you look for in the person you hire to do this job?

There are certain basic guidelines on control issues that companies should consider. Control can provide assurance regarding a broad range of objectives in three general categories: the effectiveness and efficiency of operations, the reliability of financial and management reporting, and the compliance with applicable laws and regulations and with company policies.

Ethical questions arise with respect to management's attitude toward its employees. Should they assume all employees are dishonest and will steal if they think they can get away with it? Or should management establish controls to ensure that employees are not given any opportunity to steal?

TEMPORARY INVESTMENTS

Learning Objective

*Identify the criteria for
the classification of an
investment as temporary.*

As discussed in the last section, the management of cash is an important part of managing a company. One of its aspects is the company's need to minimize its cash balance, given that current or chequing accounts normally earn no returns. One way to convert cash into an earning asset is to invest it in temporary (short-term) marketable securities. **Marketable securities** are securities (i.e., assets that are publicly traded) that represent either a debt interest (Treasury Bills, bonds, or Guaranteed Investment Certificates) or an equity interest (shares) in another entity. The more active the trading in the security, the easier it is to convert back into cash when the cash is needed for other purposes. The ability to turn an investment back into cash quickly is known as *liquidity* and is an important aspect of managing the company's cash position. When a security has a maturity date of three months or less, it is often classified as a cash equivalent because it will quickly become cash.

Securities that are not marketable would likely not qualify as current assets of the company because they might not be easily converted into cash within a year. They would probably be classified as noncurrent investments. The discussion in this section is restricted to short-term marketable securities.

The probable future value associated with marketable securities comes from two sources. One source is the periodic payments that these securities produce while they are being held. If the security is a debt security, these payments are interest. If the debt security matures in three months or less, it would probably be classified as a cash equivalent by the company. Payments received from equity securities are dividends. Because equity securities do not have a maturity date, they are not classified as cash equivalents. The second source of value is the value of the securities when sold in the future. If the intention is to hold these securities for the short term (less than one year), then the resale price becomes very important. If the intention is to hold them for the long term (more than one year), the resale price is less important. Securities held for the long term are usually called long-term investments and do not appear under the heading of temporary investments in the balance sheet.

The uncertainty, or risk, associated with the future value of temporary investments relates to both the periodic payments and the ultimate sales value. For example, the issuers of debt may default on the interest payments. This not only causes uncertainty with regard to the periodic payments, but it also reduces the value of a security in terms of its final price. If a company cannot make interest payments, it is unlikely that it will be able to pay back the principal when the debt matures. With regard to equity securities, there is no guarantee that dividends will continue at present levels, nor is there any guarantee of the ultimate sales value. The company may grow, increasing its future selling price, or it may fail, rendering the equity shares worthless.

The uncertainty with regard to the future cash flows of a security is sometimes evidenced by the volatility of its price in the securities markets. If you read the business section of the newspaper, you are well aware of the volatility of the markets for equity securities (shares). The market prices of shares fluctuate for many reasons. For example, from May 1, 2001, to May 1, 2002, the shares of BCE Inc. (Bell Canada Enterprises) varied from a low of $23.00 to a high of $40.00. The variability in the price is partially a function of the highly competitive telecommunication market in which it operates. The terrorist acts of September 11, 2001, in the United

States sent most share prices tumbling as investor confidence was seriously shaken. Some companies' shares recovered quickly, while others are taking longer to reach pre–September 11 levels.

A similar volatility has been present in recent years in the markets for debt securities (bond markets). The degree of uncertainty depends on the type of security and on the financial health of the issuing entity. Debt securities, for example, may be viewed as quite safe if they are issued by the government. Canadian government bonds are an example. At the other extreme are corporate bonds issued by very highly leveraged companies (highly leveraged means total liabilities greatly exceed total shareholders' equity). These bonds are sometimes called junk bonds. Junk bonds pay very high interest rates to compensate for the high risk of their principal not being repaid. Equity securities offer a similar spectrum of risk.

The ownership criterion for these assets is relatively straightforward. For some securities, pieces of paper can be held by the owner that represent ownership (share certificates and bonds). In many cases, however, no certificates are issued and ownership is evidenced by entries in an account maintained by an outside party (such as a broker).

Valuation Methods

One method that could be used to value temporary investments is to record them at their original acquisition cost, or **historical cost**. With this method, changes in the market value of the investments have no effect on the balance sheet or income statement until the investment is actually sold. Income is recognized at the time the investment is sold and is termed a **realized gain** or **loss**. In addition, income is recognized with this method as periodic payments are received in the form of dividends or interest revenue.

A second method would be to value the temporary investments at their market value. In its pure form, this method means that changes in the market value of the investments would cause changes in the carrying value on the balance sheet and a corresponding recognition of a gain (or loss) on the income statement. The changes in market value are called **unrealized gains** or **losses**. If you have adjusted the value of the securities to market value and if the market value remains stable up to the point of sale, there will be no further recognition of income because the investment is already valued at its market value at the time of sale. In addition, the periodic receipts of interest and dividends are recognized as income.

What Is Canadian Practice?

The current method of accounting for temporary investments is a combination of the above methods. Temporary investments are held in place of cash, so the intention is to show them as the amount of cash that is expected to be received from them. However, this intention is modified to show a conservative figure. Therefore, temporary investments are shown at their cost—unless their market value has declined to below cost, in which case they are shown at the market value. We call this method the **lower of cost and market method (LCM)**. This is a hybrid of the

Learning Objective

5

Explain why temporary investments are recorded using the lower of cost and market.

two methods discussed earlier, historical cost (i.e., the amount paid for the securities when they were purchased) and market value. The lower of cost and market method uses cost, except in situations where the market value of the portfolio is less than the historical cost, in which case the market value is used. The gain resulting from a market value higher than cost is not recognized until the investment is sold. This one-sided rule with regard to market values was adopted based on the conservative principle in accounting which states, in essence, that losses should be recognized as soon as they can be estimated, but that gains should be deferred until they are realized.

AN INTERNATIONAL PERSPECTIVE

Reports from Other Countries

In the United States, all short-term marketable securities are carried at their market values. Accountants used the lower of cost and market method until 1994, but then they switched to market values. Canada has been discussing moving to market values for temporary investments, but so far has stayed with the lower of cost and market method. In Canada, however, companies are required to disclose the market value of the marketable securities if they are being carried at cost. In 2003, the AcSB in Canada plans to make some changes to financial instruments in which it intends to recommend that standards be harmonized with the United States. This means that marketable securities would be carried at market value, eliminating the need for the LCM.

The implementation of the lower of cost and market method presents several issues that must be resolved. The first is one of classification. When a company invests in a marketable security, it must first decide whether to classify the investment as a current or noncurrent asset. The classification is generally based on the intent of management and on the marketability of the asset. If management intends to hold the security for less than one year, and if it is readily marketable, it will be classified as a current asset. Otherwise, it will be classified as noncurrent, in which case the account will be called a long-term investment rather than a temporary or short-term investment.

A second issue that is important in accounting for investments arises with respect to equity securities. When a company buys shares in another company, the buyer will be able to have some voting power based on the number of shares it owns. The larger the proportion of shares owned by the buyer, the more control it can exercise over the other company. Most equity securities are shares that carry a vote entitling the owner to vote for the board of directors, which has direct authority over management. For short-term investments, there is usually no intention on the part of the buying company to exercise control. In fact, the number of shares usually purchased as a short-term investment (a relatively small number) does not allow a buying company to exercise much control. With long-term investments in shares, there may be some intention to control the company. In some cases, for example, the acquiring company will buy 100% of the outstanding shares of a company. In this case, the acquiring company exercises absolute control over the acquired company. The accounting for investments in which a company exercises significant control is different from that in which the company has little control (i.e., a passive investment). The accounting for investments in which there exists significant control is discussed in Appendix B at the end of the book. In this chapter, only passive investments in securities are considered.

The data in Exhibit 6-2 for Clifford Company illustrate the application of the lower of cost and market method to short-term investments. Assume that Clifford's year end is December 31, and that it prepares income statements on a quarterly basis. You will notice that Clifford buys three securities during the first quarter (the first three months in the year). The exhibit then tracks the performance of the portfolio during the year, valuing each security each quarter until it is sold. Dividend and interest payments received over the year are also included.

CLIFFORD COMPANY

Temporary Investment Data

Security	Type	Quarter Acquired	Acquisition Cost	Quarter Sold	Selling Price
HTMS Corp.	Bonds	1	$10,000	3	$12,000
ATS Inc.	Shares	1	$20,000	4	$18,000
LFS Ltd.	Shares	1	$30,000	-	NA

| | Values as at the End of | | | | | | | |
| | Quarter 1 | | Quarter 2 | | Quarter 3 | | Quarter 4 | |
Security	Cost	Market	Cost	Market	Cost	Market	Cost	Market
HTMS Corp.	$10,000	$11,000	$10,000	$13,000	NA	NA	NA	NA
ATS Inc.	20,000	17,000	20,000	21,000	$20,000	$17,000	NA	NA
LFS Ltd.	30,000	29,000	30,000	28,000	30,000	29,000	$30,000	$28,500
Portfolio	$60,000	$57,000	$60,000	$62,000	$50,000	$46,000	$30,000	$28,500

Dividends/Interest Received	
Quarter	Amount
1	$1,200
2	$1,200
3	$ 500
4	$ 500

Initial Acquisition

The initial acquisition entry is the same as the entry to acquire any other asset. The only distinction at this point is that each security must be classified as HTMS, ATS, or LFS. To illustrate, the following entry would record the acquisition of

Learning Objective
6

Prepare the journal entries associated with the acquisition, holding, and selling of temporary investments.

the temporary investments during the first quarter of the year:

A-Investment in HTMS	10,000
A-Investment in ATS	20,000
A-Investment in LFS	30,000
A-Cash	60,000

Notice that each investment is recorded in its own account. These accounts are **subsidiary accounts**. There is also a control account (probably called Short-term investments) which holds the sum of all of the subsidiary accounts (see below).

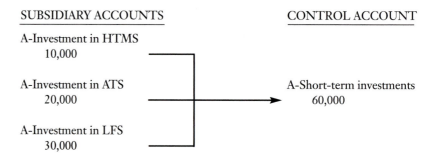

It is the control account that is reported in the financial statements. Transactions are recorded in the subsidiary accounts, which are then used to update the control account.

Dividend/Interest Recognition

Dividend and interest income is recognized each period as it is earned. In the case of Clifford Company, we will assume that all dividend and interest income is received in cash. However, recognize that the interest could be accrued and result in interest receivable rather than cash, and dividends could have only been declared and not paid, which would result in dividends receivable. In Exhibit 6-2, the dividends and interest from all three investments have been aggregated into one amount. The entry to record these dividends in Quarter 1 would be as follows:

A-Cash	1,200
SE-Dividend/interest income	1,200
(income statement account)	

Recognition of Unrealized Losses/Recoveries and Realized Gains and Losses

The lower of cost and market rule requires that, at any financial statement date, the company compares the aggregate market value of its portfolio to its original cost to determine the lower of the two. The company is then required to carry its portfolio at this lower value. Note that, for Quarter 1 at March 31 in Exhibit 6-2, the portfolio should be carried at $57,000 because this is the lower of cost and market value. The writedown from the cost of $60,000 would result in an unrealized loss of $3,000, which would appear in the income statement.

The lower of cost and market rule can be applied on one of two bases: either compare the totals for the entire portfolio of investments, or apply the rule to individual securities. For example, if we were to apply the lower of cost and market rule on an individual basis, the investments in ATS and LFS would be written down to their market values, but the investment in HTMS would remain at cost. This would result in an unrealized loss of $4,000, which is larger than the loss that results when the rule is applied on a portfolio basis. This occurs because the portfolio basis allows unrealized gains on some securities (such as HTMS) to offset unrealized losses on other securities (ATS and LFS). Most companies tend to use the portfolio basis because they manage their temporary investments on that basis. Therefore, this valuation method better reflects the value of the portfolio to the company.

The entry to record the reduction in the carrying value of the temporary investments and the unrealized loss would be:

SE-Unrealized loss on valuation of temporary investments	3,000	
XA-Valuation allowance for temporary investments		3,000

For the current portfolio, the preceding debit entry affects the income statement; that is, unrealized losses are shown on the income statement. The credit entry is to a contra-asset account (see Chapter 3 for contra-asset accounts). The account is reported contra to the temporary investments account and reduces the portfolio of securities to its aggregate market value. Notice that the original cost of the securities is unaffected by the above transaction. The **valuation allowance** account is sometimes called the *allowance for the excess of cost of marketable securities over market value* account. It is similar to an accumulated amortization account in that it preserves the historical cost amounts in the temporary investment accounts that are needed for disclosure and tax purposes. Unlike accumulated amortization, the allowance for the excess of cost of marketable securities over market value is rarely disclosed as a separate item on the balance sheet. Instead, companies will report the temporary investments as a *net* amount (the original cost less the allowance).

In Quarter 2, Clifford again recognizes dividend interest revenue. At the end of Quarter 2 at June 30, when the company applies the lower of cost and market rule again, you should note that the market value of the portfolio has recovered and, in fact, has gone up above the original cost of the securities purchased. Companies can recover unrealized losses but can never recognize unrealized gains above the original cost of the securities. This means that Clifford can recover the $3,000 unrealized loss it recorded in the first quarter to bring the portfolio back to its original cost of $60,000 but that it cannot recognize the unrealized gain of $2,000 above the original acquisition cost. The entry to record the recovery would be as follows:

XA-Valuation allowance for temporary
    investments   3,000
        SE-Recovery of unrealized loss on
            valuation of temporary investments   3,000

The *recovery of unrealized loss on valuation of temporary investments* is an income statement account and, like a gain, it increases net income, thereby offsetting the loss recorded in Quarter 1.

The effects on the balance sheet and income statement of the application of the lower of cost and market rule, as well as the other events that affect marketable securities, are summarized in Exhibit 6-3.

EXHIBIT 6-3

■ CLIFFORD COMPANY

Financial Statements (Partial)

Income Statement

For the Quarter	Quarter 1	Quarter 2	Quarter 3	Quarter 4
Unrealized holding loss on valuation of temporary investments	($3,000)	–	($4,000)	–
Recovery of unrealized holding loss on valuation of temporary investments	–	$ 3,000	–	$2,500
Realized gain (loss) on sale of temporary investments	–	–	2,000	(2,000)
Dividend/interest income	1,200	1,200	500	500
Effect on net income of temporary investments	($1,800)	$4,200	($1,500)	$1,000

Balance Sheet

As at the end of	Quarter 1	Quarter 2	Quarter 3	Quarter 4
Temporary investments (at cost)	$60,000	$60,000	$50,000	$30,000
Less valuation allowance	(3,000)	—	(4,000)	(1,500)
Temporary investments (at LCM)	$57,000	$60,000	$46,000	$28,500

As shown in Exhibit 6-3, the effect of the preceding entries would be to record a recovery (gain) on the income statement in Quarter 2, and the debit entry brings the balance in the valuation allowance account to zero.

In the third quarter, Clifford recognized dividend/interest revenue and sold investment HTMS for $12,000. Bonds have a face value (in this case $10,000) and the promise of the issuer is that the purchaser will be paid the face value when the bond matures. The fact that Clifford sold the bonds for $12,000 means that they had not reached maturity yet. If they had, Clifford would have only received $10,000. Between the date of issue and the date of maturity, it is possible that the value of the bond will change. The difference between the acquisition cost and the selling price ($2,000) represents a gain on the sale. It is appropriate to recognize a gain because a market transaction has occurred. To record this sale in the third quarter, the following entry would be made:

A-Cash	12,000	
A-Investment in HTMS		10,000
SE-Realized gain on sale of temporary investment		2,000

At the end of Quarter 3 at September 30, the company again applies the lower of cost and market rule. Recognize that the portfolio now has one less security, because HTMS was sold during the period. The analysis indicated that the portfolio should be carried at market because it is lower than cost. The adjustment to the allowance account is for the full difference between cost and market because the balance in the valuation allowance account from the previous quarter is zero. The entry at the end of Quarter 3 is:

SE-Unrealized loss on valuation of temporary investments	4,000	
XA-Valuation allowance for temporary investments		4,000

In the fourth quarter of the year, Clifford sells the investment in ATS for $18,000 and continues to hold the investment in LFS at the end of the quarter, which is also the year-end date of December 31. The sale of ATS results in a realized loss of $2,000 because its acquisition cost was $20,000. The amount of unrealized losses is not considered in calculating the realized loss. The determination of a realized gain or loss is always made by comparing the original acquisition cost with the selling price. The following entry is made for the sale of ATS:

A-Cash	18,000	
SE-Realized loss on sale of temporary investment	2,000	
A-Investment in ATS		20,000

The evaluation of the lower of cost and market rule at the end of Quarter 4 indicates that the market value of the portfolio (the portfolio now consists of only one security) is lower than the cost by $1,500. As the balance in the allowance account is $4,000, Clifford will have to recognize a recovery of $2,500 to bring the balance back to $1,500. The following entry will accomplish this:

XA-Valuation allowance for temporary investments	2,500	
SE-Recovery of unrealized loss on valuation of temporary investments		2,500

Again, Exhibit 6-3 summarizes the results of the transactions affecting the marketable securities in Quarter 4.

The disclosure of the effects of transactions involving temporary investments in a typical set of financial statements tends to be somewhat limited because of the insignificant nature of these transactions relative to the company's other transactions. Although Canada does not follow the United States' lead and maintain its temporary investments at market all of the time, it does require that companies disclose the market value of temporary investments. Many companies may simply list a line item for temporary investments on the balance sheet and have a note stating that the securities are carried at cost, which approximates market. No details may be provided concerning the amount of dividend or interest revenue or the amount of realized and unrealized gains and losses that are recognized. When the amounts are significant, however, a note to the financial statements generally provides the details.

Examples of disclosures of market values of temporary investments are shown in Exhibit 6-4.

EXHIBIT 6-4

EXAMPLES OF DISCLOSURE OF TEMPORARY INVESTMENTS

IEI Energy Inc. (2001)

	December 31 2001	December 31 2000
Marketable securities [Market value $3,834,249 (2000–$3,501,315)]	3,523,663	3,322,957

Note 1

Marketable Securities

Marketable securities are carried at the lower of cost and market value. Certain of the Company's marketable securities with a carring value of $2,035,884 (2000–$3,106,147) have been pledged as security for $4,951,415 (2000–$4,910,991) of amounts included in accounts payable and accrued liabilities.

IBEX Technologies Inc. (2001)

5. Marketable securities

(a) Marketable securities include the following:

	2001 $	2000 $
Bonds—at cost (which approximates market value)		
Canadian dollars	4,458,845	5,959,275
U.S. dollars ($1,009,050; 2000–$979,560)	1,566,626	1,436,535
	6,025,471	7,395,810

(b) The bonds mature at various dates through February 6, 2002. Annual interest rates on these bonds range between 4.8% and 8.0%.

The note disclosure used by IEI Energy is typical of many companies in Canada. The short-term nature of the investments means that there is often very little difference between original acquisition price and market value. This means that a note like the one used by IEI Energy is sufficient. The note issued by IBEX is a little more extensive. You will notice that IBEX has bonds denominated in Canadian and U.S. dollars. For the U.S.-dollar bonds, it has disclosed both the American amounts and the Canadian equivalents. The Canadian equivalents would have been translated at the exchange rate at the balance sheet date, July 31, 2001.

Long-Term Investments

Accounting rules for noncurrent investments are different from the rules for short-term investments and are discussed in Appendix B at the end of the book.

Statement Analysis Considerations

If temporary investments make up a significant portion of the current assets of the company, the potential effects that the unrecognized gains and losses have on the financial health of the company being analyzed should be recognized. If the portfolio is being held at the lower of cost and market, the user has some idea already of the loss potential of the securities as some portion of it has already been recognized. Remember, however, if the lower of cost and market rule is applied on a portfolio basis, gains on some securities can offset losses on others. Also, if the market value of the securities is above the cost, this unrealized gain will not have been recognized. Unrecorded gains or losses could make any ratio using net income misleading. The disclosure requirements for temporary investments are such that you can usually get information about both of these amounts from the notes to the financial statements, as Canadian GAAP requires that the market values be disclosed (see IEI Energy's disclosure in Exhibit 6-4). Because of this disclosure, it is possible for users to rely on the market value of the temporary investments in any financial statement analysis.

ACCOUNTS RECEIVABLE

Accounts receivable are amounts owed by customers that resulted from the normal business transactions of selling goods and services on credit. The ownership criterion for accounts receivable is evidenced either by a formal contractual agreement or by some other less formal arrangement, such as a sales invoice. The sale itself represents the past event that gave rise to the accounts receivable. The probable future value criterion would be met by the fact that a receivable is the right to receive payment at some future date. The cash that is received at that future date can then be exchanged for other goods and services. The value of the cash that is to be received in the future is affected by the same uncertainties that we described in the earlier section on cash. In addition to those uncertainties, there is also the uncertainty that the customer will pay the cash as agreed. A complete default by the customer would be called a **bad debt**. This makes the valuation of accounts receivable less certain than the valuation of cash.

Other uncertainties with accounts receivable are that the customer might return the goods for credit, the customer may request a price adjustment if the goods are damaged in shipment, or the customer may pay less than what is listed on the bill if allowed a discount for prompt payment. All of these factors can affect the uncertainty of collecting accounts receivable and complicate the determination of the appropriate recording amount.

Accounts Receivable Valuation Methods

An account receivable is an agreement to pay a certain amount at some point in the future. A simple way to value the receivable is to add up the gross payments called for in the agreement. This *gross payments method* ignores the effects of bad debts (customers that do not pay), returns, and so forth, as well as the effects of the *time value of money*.

A second method for valuing an account receivable is to take into consideration the time value of the gross payments to be received. The time value of money refers to the concept that a dollar paid tomorrow is worth less than a dollar paid today. The reasoning here is that an investor can invest the dollar received today and have more than a dollar by tomorrow. Therefore, if the company has a receivable for $100 to be received a month from now, it is worth less than $100 today. Using the terminology of the time value of money, we would want to calculate the *present value* of the future cash flows of the receivable. We would discount the future cash flows using an appropriate interest rate to arrive at this present value. See the *Accounting Perspectives CD* for a full discussion of the calculation of present values.

Time Value of Money

A third method is to take into consideration the possibility that the receivable may not be paid. This could result from a default by the customer or the return of the goods. Partial payment might also result if the customer pays early, taking advantage of a cash discount, or if the customer demands a price concession. Incorporating these events into the valuation would mean reducing the receivable. This alternative can be used in conjunction with either the first (gross payments) or the second (present value) method of valuing the receivable.

Finally, a valuation method based on the market value of the accounts receivable might also be considered. Accounts receivable can be sold to other parties, who then collect from the customer. The process of selling accounts receivable is referred to as **factoring**. If a ready market is available in which to sell a receivable, a market price can be used as a value for the receivable.

What Is Canadian Practice?

Most Canadian companies show receivables at the gross payments amount less appropriate allowances for bad debts, returns, and so forth. Ideally, the use of present value would be more appropriate, but there is a materiality consideration. If there is little difference between the present value and the gross payments, such as occurs with receivables expected to be paid in a relatively short period of time, the gross payments can be used. The use of present value adds some complications to the accounting for receivables and, unless the accounting for present value makes a significant difference, it is probably not worth the effort. For most companies, the time between sale and collection is relatively short (30 to 60 days). Unless interest rates are extremely high, the difference between the present value and the gross payments for these types of receivables is relatively small. This is why most companies account for their accounts receivable at the gross amount less the allowance for bad debts, returns, and so forth. The adjustment for these allowances is necessary because the company does not want to overstate its assets or its income from sales to customers. For example, consider a company that sells $10,000 worth of goods during the accounting period, all on account. The entry to record this transaction is:

A-Accounts receivable	10,000	
SE-Sales revenue		10,000

If the company anticipates that it will collect the entire $10,000, the preceding entry would appropriately state the effects of the transaction on assets and shareholders' wealth. However, if the company anticipates that some customers will not pay, this entry overstates the receivables as well as the shareholders' wealth.

The likelihood that a customer will default on payments depends on the customer's creditworthiness. A company can improve its chances of receiving payments by performing a credit check on its customers before it grants them credit. The company must balance its desire to sell its product to the customer against the likelihood that the customer will pay. Too strict a credit policy means that many customers will be denied credit and may, therefore, purchase their goods from other suppliers. Too loose a credit policy, and the company may lose more money from bad debts than it makes from good sales. The company should do a cost/benefit analysis to decide what its credit policy should be. The company must also stay aware of the changes in the industry in which it operates and the economy in general. Changes in interest rates, inflation, or the global economy can change the credit status of a customer within a short period of time. The following article summary illustrates how a changing economy can affect a company's ability to collect its accounts receivable.

accounting in the news

BAD DEBTS IN THE BANKING SECTOR

Banks always face exposure to bad debts because the major services they offer are loans to businesses and individuals. Each reporting period, banks review their outstanding loans and establish an appropriate loan-loss provision.

Early in the summer of 2001, Toronto-Dominion Bank, one of the major lenders to the telecom sector, increased its loan-loss provision by $140 million, bringing its total provision to $620 million. Each time the loan-loss provision is adjusted, it affects the profits earned in that period.

Sometimes, when banks determine that the probability of collecting on some of their loans is low, they sell their loans in the distress-loans market. This market for business loans is similar to collection agencies for individual loans. Whoever buys the loans understands that the chance of collection is low. To counter this risk, the purchaser buys the loans at amounts considerably below their carrying value. In this way, if they collect, they make money. If they don't, they do not lose a lot. From the banks perspective, they at least recover something where otherwise they might not recover anything.

Source: "Bad debts expected to erode banks' profits," by Paula Arab, Canadian Press, page B4, *globeandmail.com*, August 20, 2001.

In addition to a policy on bad debts, other policies can affect the amounts collected. One of these is the company's return policy. Can customers return goods, and under what circumstances? Again, the strictness or looseness of the policy will have an effect on whether customers will buy goods from the company. In 2002, a private publishing and distribution company owned by Jack Stoddart, General Publishing, filed for bankruptcy protection while it attempted to restructure its organization. One of the main causes of its financial difficulty arose from the demands placed on it by the mega bookstore company, Chapters Inc. Chapters extended its payment terms to 250 days (nine months) from its former 90 days (three months). Often, instead of making its payment in 250 days, Chapters returned unsold books to settle its debt. The long delay in receiving payment, coupled with the fact that General Publishing had to pay its own suppliers in 90 days, drained the company of cash, pushing it into financial difficulty. Here is a situation where customer returns affected not only the company's revenue picture but its cash flow as well.

A second policy that should be considered is that concerning cash discounts for early payment. If the company decides to offer a cash discount, the amount of cash that will be collected from the receivables will depend on the number of customers who pay early. The number of customers who pay early will depend on the attractiveness of the discount. Both of these policies require some adjustment to the amounts recorded in accounts receivable as well as in the sales revenue account.

The accounting methods for anticipated bad debts or doubtful (sometimes referred to as "uncollectible") accounts are illustrated in the next section. Recognize that similar methods could be used to account for the other adjustments to accounts receivable, such as cash discounts and sales returns. For a more complete description of the accounting for discounts and returns, refer to an intermediate accounting text.

Accounting for doubtful accounts requires adjustments to the accounts receivable account as well as the recognition of the related bad debt expense in the income statement. Some smaller businesses use the direct write-off method, but most medium and large companies use what is called the **allowance method** to recognize doubtful accounts.

Allowance Method

Let us review two key points already discussed earlier in the text. First, the matching concept requires that when a company recognizes revenue from a sale, it must also recognize all expenses relating to that sale. Second, bad debts are technically not expenses; they are reductions in revenues. These reductions in revenues should be recognized at the same time as the revenues are recognized. Because, at the point of sale, the company does not know which customers will end up as bad debts, it must make some estimates of what dollar amount of sales will ultimately be uncollectible. These estimates are usually based on the company's past experience with its customers. New businesses usually have little basis for initial estimates and so must use some other method of making an estimate.

Consider the example accompanying the preceding journal entry. Assume that the company estimates that, of the $10,000 in sales, $325 will ultimately prove to be uncollectible. One method used to arrive at this estimate is discussed later in the chapter. As the company is not able to identify the customers that will not pay, the $325 cannot directly reduce specific accounts receivable. Therefore, the following entry records this amount in an account that is contra to the accounts receivable account. This contra account, which is usually called the *allowance for doubtful accounts*, reduces the aggregate amount of accounts receivable by the anticipated effects of **uncollectible accounts**. The debit is to the bad debt expense account.

Learning Objective
7

Explain why estimating the potential uncollectibility of accounts receivable is required.

SE-Bad debt expense	325	
XA-Allowance for doubtful accounts		325

The allowance for doubtful accounts normally has a credit balance because its purpose is to show that the full debit balance amount in the accounts receivable will not be collected. In effect, it reduces the accounts receivable total to the net amount of cash that the company actually expects to receive. Remember that the allowance account is contra to accounts receivable and is grouped with that current asset on the balance sheet.

Note that this entry has the effect of reducing the net carrying value of the accounts receivable (the accounts receivable balance less the balance in the allowance account) from $10,000 to $9,675 ($10,000 − $325) and reducing net income by the same amount. Accounts receivable is now stated at the amount the company ultimately expects to collect in cash.

The actual **write-off** of an account receivable, under the allowance method, occurs when the cut-off date specified in the write-off policy is reached. The decision by the company that the account is uncollectible is usually based on a bad debt policy. For example, the policy may state that accounts will be declared uncollectible if they have been outstanding for more than 120 days. This policy is based on the company's experience with collecting from its customers and usually means that the probability of collecting the account after 120 days is so small that it is not worth pursuing. The company may still try to collect this account, but it will probably turn it over to a collection agency that will attempt to collect from the customer. Assume that we are using this policy for the company in our example; that is, accounts that have not been collected within 120 days are written off. Assume that nonpayments resulted in $300 in actual write-offs. With the allowance method, this means that we have now specifically identified customer accounts that are bad, which we were unable to identify at the time we recognized the bad debt expense. Because we recognized the expense when the estimate was made, no further expense should be recognized. We should simply remove the specific accounts from accounts receivable and remove an equivalent amount from the allowance account because some portion of the allowance account is no longer necessary. The entry is:

XA-Allowance for doubtful accounts	300	
A-Accounts receivable		300

What happens if one of the accounts we have written off is finally paid by the customer? This is called a **recovery**. Under the allowance method, recoveries are accounted for by reinstating the account receivable. This is accomplished by reversing the write-off entry and then showing the normal cash collection entry. The following two entries would be made if an account worth $50 was recovered after having been written off. Note that, whereas one net entry can be made to accomplish the recording of this transaction, if no entry is made to the accounts receivable account, the customer's account will always be shown in the records as having been a bad debt.

A-Accounts receivable	50	
XA-Allowance for doubtful accounts		50
A-Cash	50	
A-Accounts receivable		50

Assume that this was the first year of this company's operations and that the company had collected $8,500 from its customers by the end of the year. Exhibit 6-5 illustrates the entries and balances in the accounts receivable and the allowance for doubtful accounts.

The ending balance in the accounts receivable account ($1,200) represents those accounts that have not been collected as at the end of the accounting period. In our example, the maximum amount of time any of these accounts can have been outstanding is 120 days; any account beyond that time is written off. The ending balance in the allowance for doubtful accounts should be the remaining allowance that applies to the ending balance in accounts receivable. In other words, the company expects that, of the remaining $1,200 in accounts receivable, $75 will prove to be uncollectible.

ALLOWANCE METHOD FOR DOUBTFUL ACCOUNTS

EXHIBIT 6-5

A-Accounts Receivable

Beginning Balance	0		
Credit sales	10,000	8,500	Cash collections
Recoveries	50	300	Write-offs
		50	Collections from recoveries
Ending Balance	1,200		

XA-Allowance for Doubtful Accounts

		0	Beginning balance
Write-offs	300	325	Bad debt expense
		50	Recoveries
		75	Ending balance

In most financial statements, the allowance account is netted against the accounts receivable account to produce a single line item on the balance sheet. Few companies provide details of the amount of the allowance either by showing the balance in the allowance for doubtful accounts or by including information about it in the notes to the financial statements.

One final point to consider about the accounting for doubtful accounts is the method used to estimate the dollar amounts that are doubtful. A method that is commonly used is called the **percentage of credit sales method**. This method will be described below. Another method that is used is called the **ageing of accounts receivable method**. We will leave the discussion of this method to intermediate accounting texts.

Learning Objective

8

Identify two methods for recognizing uncollectibility and describe the circumstances under which each is appropriate.

Percentage of Credit Sales Method

The **percentage of credit sales method** is based on the assumption that the amount of bad debt expense is a function of the total sales made on credit. It estimates the bad debt expense for the period by multiplying the credit sales during the period by an appropriate percentage. The percentage is determined based on the past collection history of the company. In the example above, the $325 of bad debt expense that was used could have been the result of using 3.25% of credit sales as an estimate of the bad debts (3.25% of the $10,000 in credit sales would have resulted in the estimated bad debt expense of $325). In a new company, the percentage may be determined initially by considering the bad debt experience of other

OMIT

companies in the same industry. In an existing company, historical data is generally used to estimate this percentage as adjusted for present and anticipated future economic conditions. For example, during an economic downturn, bad debt percentages often rise.

The initial estimate of the percentage must be adjusted from time to time to reflect the company's recent credit experience. If the company is experiencing more write-offs than were estimated, the percentage should be increased. Companies typically do not go back to prior periods to adjust this percentage but adjust it on a prospective basis. Therefore, an overestimate or an underestimate in one period will be adjusted in the following period. The percentage can be affected by the types of customers that the company has, a change in credit policy, and general economic conditions, such as economic downturns and changes in unemployment.

Note that with the percentage of credit sales method, the ending balance in the allowance for doubtful accounts results from simply totalling the entries to the account. The percentage relationship between the ending balance in the allowance account and the accounts receivable account has nothing to do with the percentage used to estimate bad debt expense. In the example, the ratio of the ending balance in the allowance account to the accounts receivable account is 6.25% ($75/$1,200). This is considerably higher than the 3.25% bad debts the company estimated as its percentage of sales. This is not necessarily inconsistent, however, as a higher percentage of the accounts receivable that are left at the end of the period may not be paid. For example, many of them may be approaching the 120-day limit, which means that the probability of collecting them is becoming extremely small.

An International Perspective

Reports from Other Countries

The estimation of uncollectible accounts is accomplished in some countries, for example, France and Germany, by considering the circumstances of individual accounts rather than by estimating an overall percentage rate such as with the percentage of credit sales method. This method is similar to the ageing of accounts receivable used in Canada. The method is also used by some companies in Japan.

Direct Write-Off Method

The **direct write-off method** is often used by small companies. It recognizes the loss from the uncollectible account in the period in which the company decides the account is, in fact, uncollectible. Assume that we are using the same policy as with the allowance method, that is, that accounts are written off after 120 days. In our example, $300 worth of accounts receivable were identified as being more than 120 days overdue. These accounts should be written off. With the direct write-off method, the entry to record this is:

SE-Bad debt expense	300	
A-Accounts receivable (specific accounts)		300

Note that the debit to the bad debt expense account reduces net income in this period. Bad debt expense is somewhat different from other "expenses." It is not accompanied by a related cash outflow. It is more like a reduction in a revenue account in the sense that it represents revenues the company will never receive. In recognition of this, a few companies report this as a direct reduction in the sales revenue amount on the income statement. These companies report a line item which they call *net sales*, where *net* means that the bad debt expense has been netted out against the sales revenue amount. The majority of companies, however, show bad debts as an expense grouped with other expenses and not as a reduction of revenues.

The credit entries to the accounts receivable account refer to specific customer accounts; the company has identified exactly who it is that has not paid. For example, the $300 might be in two specific accounts, a $180 account from Joe Lee and a $120 account from Mary Smith. The accounts receivable balance is generally supported by what is called a subsidiary ledger, similar to the subsidiary ledger used with temporary investments, in which individual separate receivable accounts are maintained for each customer. This entry would cause reductions in the accounts of both Joe Lee and Mary Smith.

The direct write-off method is a simple way to account for bad debts. The company makes every reasonable effort to collect the account, and when it finally decides that an account is uncollectible, it records the preceding entry to remove it from the accounting system. The problem with this method is that it violates the matching concept discussed in Chapter 4. As you will recall, the matching concept states that all expenses related to the production of revenue should be matched with the revenue in the period in which the revenue is recognized. The direct write-off method could result in the revenue being recognized in one accounting period, and the associated bad debt expense recorded in the following period. If bad debts are not significant, then this mismatching can probably be ignored. If bad debts are significant, however, this mismatching can distort the measurement of performance enough that most accountants would find this method unacceptable. The more appropriate method when bad debts are significant is the allowance method that was discussed earlier.

NOTES RECEIVABLE

Notes receivable are very similar to accounts receivable in their fundamental characteristics. Therefore, we will not discuss the recognition criteria and valuation methods; they are the same as for accounts receivable. The difference between an account receivable and a note receivable is that the note receivable is evidenced by a more formal agreement referred to as a **promissory note**. A promissory note is

Learning Objective
9

Describe a note receivable and explain the circumstances under which it is used.

a written contract between two parties, the *maker* and the *payee*. The maker promises to pay specific amounts either upon demand by the payee or at a definite date in the future.

Interest may be shown explicitly as a part of the note, or it may be implicit in the contractual payments. When interest is explicit, it is typically calculated by multiplying the explicit interest rate times the face value of the note times the time factor. The presumption here is that the face value is the amount that has been borrowed via the note. A note in which the interest is implicit specifies the amount to be paid at maturity (the face value), which will be larger than the initial amount borrowed. The interest is the difference between the amount borrowed and the face value. These are sometimes called *discounted notes*.

The maturity of notes is generally longer than for accounts receivable, but is usually less than a year; hence, the notes are usually considered current assets. Long-term notes receivable are classified in the noncurrent assets section along with long-term investments.

Notes are most commonly arranged with banks or other financial institutions. These financial institutions may require that the maker of the note put up some type of **collateral** for the note. Collateral is some asset that the payee has the right to receive if the maker defaults on the note. As an example, think of an individual who purchases a car with a loan from a bank or finance company. The bank would use the new car as collateral for the loan. If the person defaults on the loan, the bank or finance company can reclaim the car and sell it to satisfy the outstanding debt.

A note secured by collateral is called a **secured note**. The collateral may be some type of real property, such as real estate, or personal property, such as equipment or inventory. Depending on the creditworthiness of the maker, a payee may agree to issue an unsecured note, which means no collateral is specified. Companies will sometimes agree to issue a note to a customer if the customer cannot pay an account receivable within the normal payment period. If the customer wants a longer period of time to pay, the company may agree to this arrangement provided the customer pays interest on the outstanding debt. Extending credit beyond the normal credit terms without demanding interest is not effective cash management.

Interest on Notes Receivable

Learning Objective
10

Calculate interest associated with notes receivable and prepare the necessary journal entries.

As stated earlier, interest on notes receivable can be either implied or explicit. A note with implied interest might state: "the maker of the note agrees to pay $1,050 at maturity in exchange for $1,000 today." The maker is borrowing $1,000 and, as the maturity payment is $1,050, the difference ($50) is interest. A note with explicit interest might state: "the maker agrees to pay the principal amount of $1,000 at maturity plus interest at a rate of 12% [always stated as an annual rate unless otherwise indicated] in exchange for $1,000 today." The dollar amount of interest in this case depends on how long the period is between now and maturity.

Short-term notes receivable generally require that interest payments be calculated using **simple interest** calculations. Long-term notes, on the other hand, generally use

compound interest calculations. Compound interest calculations are discussed in the Time Value of Money section on the *Accounting Perspectives CD*. Simple interest calculations are demonstrated in the following equation.

Time Value of Money

Interest charges are calculated based on the amount borrowed, the interest rate, and the amount of time that passes. The formula is:

> **Simple Interest Formula:**
> Interest = Principal × Interest Rate × Time

The principal is the amount borrowed, the interest rate is specified in the note and is stated as a yearly amount, and the time is the time that has elapsed, stated as a fraction of a year. The time that has elapsed is generally measured in days. While the actual number of days can be used, many lenders simplify the calculation by considering that each month is composed of 30 days and, therefore, 360 days is treated as being equivalent to one year. This convention is used in the calculations that follow.

To illustrate the calculation of interest and the accounting for notes, assume the following:

1. On November 30, 20x1, the Bierstaker Company agrees to accept a $1,000 note from the Wilkicki Company to satisfy an outstanding account receivable. (This could happen if Wilkicki is having trouble meeting its payments or temporarily has some more pressing needs for its cash.) The note has a maturity of two months (60 days) and an interest rate of 12%.

2. Bierstaker's fiscal year end is December 31, and Wilkicki does not pay the note until maturity.

On acceptance of the note from Wilkicki, Bierstaker makes the following entry:

A-Notes receivable	1,000	
A-Accounts receivable		1,000

Bierstaker's entry reflects receipt of the note from Wilkicki and the reduction in its accounts receivable.

On December 31, 20x1, one month after receiving the note, Bierstaker must close its books. This means that it must record the accrual of interest on the note from Wilkicki. The interest through December 31, 20x1, is calculated as follows:

> Interest = Principal × Interest Rate × Time
> = $1,000 × 12% × 30/360
> = $10

The entry to record this amount is:

A-Interest receivable	10	
SE-Interest revenue		10

At the end of January 20x2, Bierstaker will receive payment from Wilkicki of $1,020. Bierstaker will have to record the accrual of interest for the month of January and the receipt of cash. The calculation of interest is the same as the earlier one because another 30 days has passed. Two entries are shown on January 31, 20x2. The first records the accrual of the interest, and the second records the cash payment. Recognize that one combined entry could have been made. The entries are:

A-Interest receivable	10	
SE-Interest revenue		10
A-Cash	1,020	
A-Notes receivable		1,000
A-Interest receivable		20

Other entries are possible if the note has been paid off early or if it is extended for an additional period of time. Another possibility is that the note may be sold to another party. This is the same as factoring accounts receivable. The note may be sold with or without **recourse**, meaning that if the maker does not pay the note at maturity, the third party that bought the note will or will not have the right to collect the amount owed from the payee. Further information about the accounting for the factoring of notes receivable will be given in intermediate accounting courses.

Relatively few short-term notes receivable appear on balance sheets because they are not common and their amounts are relatively small. Normally notes receivable are grouped with accounts receivable.

STATEMENT ANALYSIS CONSIDERATIONS

Short-Term Liquidity

As discussed in Chapter 1, liquidity refers to the company's ability to convert assets into cash to pay liabilities. An important part of the analysis of short-term liquidity comes from considering the short-term monetary assets on the balance sheet. There are at least two ratios that provide quantitative measures of short-term liquidity: the current ratio and the quick ratio.

Current Ratio

The **current ratio** is measured by comparing the current assets directly with the current liabilities. It is calculated as:

$$\text{Current Ratio} = \frac{\text{Current Assets}}{\text{Current Liabilities}}$$

Remember that current assets are those that are going to be converted into cash in the next year or operating cycle of the company, and that current liabilities are going to require the use of cash in the next year or operating cycle. As such, this ratio should normally be greater than 1; otherwise, it is difficult to see how the company will remain solvent in the next year. The rule of thumb for this ratio is that to provide a margin of safety for most businesses, the ratio should be approximately 2 or greater. However, the size of this ratio depends on the type of business and the types of assets and liabilities that are considered current.

Refer to the balance sheet of **Sears Canada Inc.** in Appendix A at the end of the book. The current ratio for Sears Canada in 2001 is:

CURRENT RATIO—SEARS CANADA: 2001

$$\text{Current Ratio} = \frac{\$2,299.3}{\$1,343.7} = 1.7$$

Sears Canada's ratio is not quite 2.0. Last year, the current ratio was 1.4 ($2,416.8/$1,730.0). Although the ratio is below 2.0 in 2001, it has improved from 2000, which is a positive sign.

One caveat: the current ratio is sometimes subject to manipulation by a company at the end of the year. This ratio may not, therefore, be a very reliable measure of liquidity. For example: remember the two criteria for classifying a marketable security as a current asset? It must be possible to sell the security and management must intend to sell it within the next year. Management could declare that it intended to sell a long-term investment within the next year and reclassify it as short-term. This change in intent would have the effect of increasing the current ratio. Here is another example. Consider a company that has $100 in current assets and $50 in current liabilities just before the end of a given year. Its current ratio would be 2 ($100/$50). Suppose that $25 of the $100 is in cash and the rest is in inventory. Suppose further that the company uses up all its $25 in cash by paying off $25 worth of current liabilities at the end of the year. The current ratio becomes 3 ($75/$25); now the company looks more liquid. Notice, however, that the company is actually less liquid; in fact, it is virtually illiquid in the short term because it has no cash and must sell its inventory and wait until it collects on those sales before it will have any cash to pay its bills. In this case, the current ratio is deceptive. We have therefore developed a second short-term liquidity ratio, the quick ratio, to help provide more information on the company's liquidity.

Quick Ratio

As illustrated in the above example, one of the problems with the current ratio is that some assets in the current section may be much less liquid than others. For example, inventory is less liquid than accounts receivable, which is less liquid than cash. In some industries, inventory is very illiquid because of the long period of time that it may have to be held before sale. Consider, for example, the holding period in the manufacture of 12-year-old Scotch whisky. The current ratio in such cases will not adequately measure the short-term liquidity of the company. The quick ratio is used in this case to assess short-term liquidity. It differs from the current ratio in that inventories (and often prepaid expenses) are omitted from the numerator. It is calculated as:

Learning Objective

Explain how the current ratio, the quick ratio, and the accounts receivable turnover ratio help users to understand short-term liquidity issues.

$$\text{Quick Ratio} = \frac{\text{Current Assets} - \text{Inventory} - \text{Prepaid Expenses}}{\text{Current Liabilities}}$$

The rule of thumb for this ratio is that it should be approximately 1 or more. Again, the actual value depends somewhat on the type of industry. For Sears Canada, the calculation results in:

QUICK RATIO—SEARS CANADA: 2001

$$\text{Quick Ratio} = \frac{\$2,299.3 - \$864.5 - \$123.3 - \$110.3}{\$1,343.7} = .89$$

Note that a third amount was subtracted from the total current assets—the current portion of future income tax assets. This amount does not represent a future inflow of cash. Rather it represents a future reduction in taxes payable. As such, it should be deducted from total current assets in the calculation of the quick ratio. The current assets are listed in the order of liquidity. This means that all items listed after the inventory in this section should be subtracted along with the inventory when determining the quick ratio.

The quick ratio of Sears Canada is below 1.0. Last year, the quick ratio was .63 (($2,416.8 − $1,015.2 − $117.2 − $206.9)/$1,730.0). The quick ratio is below 1.0 in 2001 but, similar to the current ratio, it has improved from 2000, which is again a positive sign.

Analysis of Accounts Receivable Using the Accounts Receivable Turnover Ratio

A company's cash flows are critical to its profitability and even to its survival. Because most companies receive a significant amount of operating cash from the collection of their accounts receivable, the analysis of a company's short-term liquidity should consider its success in collecting its accounts receivable.

One of the common ratios used to assess the management of accounts receivable is the **accounts receivable turnover ratio**. This is calculated by dividing the credit sales for the period by the average accounts receivable, as follows:

$$\text{Accounts Receivable Turnover Ratio} = \frac{\text{Credit Sales}}{\text{Average Accounts Receivable}}$$

Calculating this ratio from financial statement data usually requires you to assume that all of the sales are credit sales. If the analyst has more detailed information about the composition of sales, then some adjustment can be made in the numerator to include only credit sales. In addition, information in the financial statements may indicate that not all receivables are from customers. Therefore, a more sophisticated calculation might include only customer receivables in the denominator, as only these relate to the credit sales figure in the numerator.

As an example, consider the information provided in Exhibit 6-6 from the 2001 and 2000 financial statements of **Sun-Rype Products Ltd.**

SUN-RYPE PRODUCTS LTD.

EXHIBIT 6-6

2001 and 2000 Financial Statements

BALANCE SHEET (Excerpts)

Current assets	2001	2000	1999
Accounts receivable	$10,068,000	$7,644,000	$8,018,000

INCOME STATEMENT (Excerpts)

Sales	$101,092,000	$94,670,000	$96,359,000

A quick review of this information shows that Sun-Rype's accounts receivable fell slightly in 2000 to $7,644,000 from $8,018,000 in 1999, but then grew significantly in 2001 to $10,068,000. This growth in accounts receivable should not be a surprise in that the sales grew as well, from $94,670,000 in 2000 to $101,092,000 in 2001. A detailed analysis in Exhibit 6-7 shows how this growth affected Sun-Rype's collection rate.

SUN-RYPE PRODUCTS LTD.

EXHIBIT 6-7

Accounts Receivable Turnover

$$2001 = \frac{101,092,000}{\frac{(10,068,000 + 7,644,000)}{2}} = \frac{101,092,000}{8,856,000} = 11.42$$

$$2000 = \frac{94,670,000}{\frac{(7,644,000 + 8,018,000)}{2}} = \frac{94,670,000}{7,831,000} = 12.09$$

In this context, "turnover" means how often the accounts receivable are "turned over": how often they are collected in full and replaced by new accounts. Thus, the turnover analysis shows that Sun-Rype's collection record was slightly better in 2000 than in 2001: the turnover decreased from 12.09 to 11.42.

Another way to analyze the performance of accounts receivable collection is to calculate the number of days to collect the average balance of the receivables. This analysis assumes that the sales are spread evenly over a 365-day year. The calculation divides the number of days in the year (365) by the accounts receivable turnover. Using this calculation, Sun-Rype's number of days to collect increased from 30.2 ($365/12.09) in 2000 to 32.0 (365/11.42) in 2001. Thus, Sun-Rype's days to collect increased by 1.8 days in 2001. Another comparison that should be made is with the company's normal credit terms. If normal credit terms are 30 days, then you would expect that the number of days to collect would be 30 days or fewer. Sun-Rype does not sell products directly to the end customer. Rather, it sells to retailers who then sell to the end customer. The credit terms for business to business sales may be longer than 30 days. Remember the earlier reference to General Publishing Co.? That company gave its business customers 90 days to pay.

Companies usually do not disclose their credit policy time frames. Sun-Rype's days to collect of 32 days in 2001 is very reasonable and is an indication of good collection management. One way to check the reasonableness of the ratio would be to compare it with a competitor.

In doing these analyses, several complicating factors should be considered. For example, some receivables such as "financing receivables" do not correspond directly to the revenues produced during the period. These financing receivables may reflect loans made by the company to its customers. These loans do not immediately generate an equivalent amount of revenue the way sales of goods or services do. Revenue from financing receivables is earned over time as the loans accrue interest. Therefore, an accounts receivable turnover based on these receivables would have little meaning.

Finally, trends over time should be considered. For example, in the analysis of a company, you may find that the amounts written off over the last several years have been increasing. Whether this is good or bad depends on how the accounts receivable balance has changed over the same period of time. To address this question, a ratio such as amounts written off to the balance in the receivables could be calculated. If this ratio is increasing over the last several years, it may represent some relative degradation in the quality of the receivables. If this were to continue, this would not be good news for the company.

Another way to address the same issue would be to compare the ratio of the ending balance in the allowance for doubtful accounts to the ending balance in the accounts receivable (before deducting the allowance). An increase in this ratio over time would indicate that a higher percentage of the ending accounts receivable was considered uncollectible. This, too, would be a negative indication.

SUMMARY

In this chapter, we have discussed four major types of current assets that are either cash, or about to become cash. We discussed how each could be valued and what the current Canadian practice is with respect to valuation. For cash, we spent some time outlining the importance of internal controls. For temporary investments, we outlined how the lower of cost and market is applied to their valuation. We discussed the measuring and recording of potential bad debts associated with accounts receivable. The discussion of notes receivable included a section on how to account for the interest that is earned on the notes.

The discussion of these four types of current assets was completed with the introduction of three ratios: the current ratio, the quick ratio, and the accounts receivable turnover ratio, which can be used to assess the short-term liquidity of a company.

The next chapter considers the last major component of current assets: inventory. Because of the complexities associated with inventory accounting, an entire chapter is devoted to this discussion. Other current assets that appear on balance sheets from time to time are considered in other chapters in this book. For the remaining current assets, reference to the notes to the company's financial statements, or to an intermediate accounting text, should help you understand their nature.

SUMMARY PROBLEMS

Additional Demonstration Problems

1. Exhibit 6-8 provides information about the transactions involving short-term investments for Labbé Ltée. Assuming that Labbé prepares financial statements on a quarterly basis, construct the journal entries that Labbé would make each quarter to record these transactions (do not bother making closing entries for income statement accounts). Assume that all dividends are received in cash during the quarter.

LABBÉ LTÉE

EXHIBIT 6-8

Temporary Investment Data

Security	Quarter Acquired	Acquisition Cost	Quarter Sold	Selling Price
Alpha Co.	1	$20,000	–	–
Beta Co.	1	$35,000	4	$29,000
Gamma Co.	1	$15,000	2	$19,000

	Values as at the End of							
	Quarter 1		Quarter 2		Quarter 3		Quarter 4	
Security	Cost	Market	Cost	Market	Cost	Market	Cost	Market
Alpha	$20,000	$21,000	$20,000	$22,000	$20,000	$17,000	$20,000	$15,000
Beta	35,000	32,000	35,000	36,000	35,000	37,000	–	–
Gamma	15,000	14,000	–	–	–	–	–	–
Portfolio	$70,000	$67,000	$55,000	$58,000	$55,000	$54,000	$20,000	$15,000

Dividends Received	
Quarter	Amount
1	$650
2	$525
3	$550
4	$150

2. The Gujarathi Company sells goods on credit to its customers. During 20x4, Gujarathi sold $150,000 worth of goods on credit and collected $125,000 from its customers. The company started the period with a balance of $15,000 in accounts receivable and a balance in the allowance for doubtful accounts of $450. During 20x4, Gujarathi wrote off $2,925 of accounts receivable. Gujarathi estimates that 2% of the sales amount will ultimately be uncollectible. Calculate the amount of bad debt expense that should be recorded. Also, show all journal entries that would be made during the period that would affect accounts receivable and the related allowance account.

3. Using the 2001 balance sheet and income statement of **Danier Leather Inc.** in Exhibit 6-9, calculate the current ratio, the quick ratio, and the accounts receivable turnover ratio for 2001. Write a brief interpretation of the ratios.

consolidated balance sheets

DANIER LEATHER INC. (2001)

(thousands of dollars)

	June 30, 2001	June 24, 2000
Assets		
Current Assets		
Cash	$ 1,663	$ 775
Accounts receivable	664	762
Inventories (Note 2)	39,227	35,124
Prepaid expenses	459	197
Current portion of future income tax asset (Note 8)	932	1,163
	42,945	38,021
Other Assets		
Capital assets (Note 3)	25,151	20,631
Goodwill (Note 4)	342	355
	$ 68,438	$ 59,007
Liabilities		
Current Liabilities		
Bank overdraft (Note 5)	$ 3,486	$ -
Accounts payable and accrued liabilities	11,945	13,208
Income taxes payable	1,184	3,251
Current portion of long-term debt	-	270
	16,615	16,729
Long-term debt	-	470
Future income tax liability (Note 8)	531	363
	17,146	17,562
Shareholders' Equity		
Share capital (Note 6)	23,412	24,236
Retained earnings	27,880	17,209
	51,292	41,445
	$ 68,438	$ 59,007

consolidated statements of earnings

(thousands of dollars, except per share amounts)

	For the Years Ended	
	June 30, 2001	June 24, 2000
	(53 weeks)	*(52 weeks)*
Revenue	$ 165,418	$ 143,011
Cost of sales (Note 7)	82,818	69,865
Gross profit	82,600	73,146
Selling, general and administrative expenses (Note 7)	60,902	54,051
Earnings before interest and income taxes	21,698	19,095
Interest expense – net	583	33
Earnings before income taxes	21,115	19,062
Provision for income taxes (Note 8)		
Current	9,090	8,166
Future	(53)	186
	9,037	8,352
Net earnings	$ 12,078	$ 10,710
Net earnings per share (Notes 1(i) & 9)		
Basic	**$1.75**	**$1.48**
Fully diluted	**$1.73**	**$1.48**

SUGGESTED SOLUTIONS TO SUMMARY PROBLEMS

1. The journal entries that Labbé Ltée. would make each quarter are as follows:

Quarter 1

Acquisition entry:		
A-Investment in Alpha	20,000	
A-Investment in Beta	35,000	
A-Investment in Gamma	15,000	
A-Cash		70,000
Dividend revenue:		
A-Cash	650	
SE-Dividend revenue		650
Unrealized loss/recovery:		
SE-Unrealized loss on valuation of temporary		
investment	3,000	
XA-Valuation allowance for temporary		
investment		3,000
Realized gain/loss on sale:		
No sales this quarter.		

Quarter 2

Acquisition entry:		
No acquisitions this quarter.		
Dividend revenue:		
A-Cash	525	
SE-Dividend revenue		525
Unrealized loss/recovery:		
XA-Valuation allowance for temporary		
investment	3,000*	
SE-Recovery of unrealized loss on		
valuation of temporary investment		3,000
Realized gain/loss on sale:		
A-Cash	19,000	
A-Investment in Gamma		15,000
SE-Realized gain on sale of temporary		
investment		4,000

*Because the portfolio has recovered from its loss position in Quarter 1, the portfolio should now be carried at cost, and the balance in the valuation allowance account ($3,000) should be reduced to zero.

Quarter 3

Acquisition entry:		
No acquisitions this quarter.		
Dividend revenue:		
A-Cash	550	
SE-Dividend revenue		550
Unrealized loss/recovery:		
SE-Unrealized loss on valuation of temporary investment	1,000	
XA-Valuation allowance for temporary investment		1,000
Realized gain/loss on sale:		
No sales this quarter.		

Quarter 4

Acquisition entry:		
No acquisitions this quarter.		
Dividend revenue:		
A-Cash	150	
SE-Dividend revenue		150
Unrealized loss/recovery:		
SE-Unrealized loss on valuation of temporary investment	4,000	
XA-Valuation allowance for temporary investment		4,000
Realized gain/loss on sale:		
A-Cash	29,000	
SE-Realized loss on sale of temporary investment	6,000	
A-Investment in Beta		35,000

2. The following journal entries would be made during the year by Gujarathi Company:

Credit sales:		
A-Accounts receivable	150,000	
SE-Sales revenue		150,000
Collections from customers:		
A-Cash	125,000	
A-Accounts receivable		125,000
Write-off of bad debts:		
XA-Allowance for doubtful accounts	2,925	
A-Accounts receivable		2,925
Recording of annual bad debt expense:		
SE-Bad debt expense	3,000	
XA-Allowance for doubtful accounts		3,000
($150,000 × .02 = $3,000)		

3. Current ratio
$$\frac{\$42,945}{\$16,615} = 2.58$$

Quick ratio
$$\frac{\$1,663 + \$664}{\$16,615} = .14$$

Accounts receivable turnover ratio
$$\frac{\$165,418}{(\$664 + 762)/2} = 232$$

$$365/232 = 1.57 \text{ days}$$

Interpretation:

The current ratio is well within the "rule of thumb" amount. It indicates that Danier Leather has more than twice as many current assets as liabilities. However, the quick ratio falls far below the "rule of thumb" ratio of 1.0. The reason that it is so low is that $32,227 of the current assets are held in inventory. The inventory level is consistent with the previous year and the company survived without running into financial difficulty. Danier Leather is a retailer, which means that the inventory will generate cash on a daily basis. The company probably relies on this cash inflow from sales to facilitate the payment of its current obligations.

The accounts receivable turnover ratio looks very favourable. It indicates that the accounts receivable are collected every 1.57 days. This is extremely fast, indicating that the ratio may be distorted. To calculate the ratio we used the revenue amount. We did not have the "credit" sales amount available. Danier Leather probably sells the majority of its merchandise for cash or by credit card. This means that the majority of its sales amount is probably cash sales. Because it is not possible to determine the credit sales amount, we cannot calculate a more accurate ratio and we should not put too much weight on the accounts receivable turnover ratio.

GLOSSARY

Accounts receivable   Assets of a seller that represent the promise by a buyer to pay the seller at some date in the future.

Accounts receivable turnover ratio   A ratio that divides the total credit sales (if known) by the average accounts receivable. It indicates how many times during the year the accounts receivable balance is collected in total.

Allowance method   A method used to value accounts receivable by estimating the amount of accounts receivable that will not be collected in the future.

Bank reconciliation   The procedure used to reconcile a company's record of its bank account balance to the record provided by the bank.

Collateral   An asset that is pledged against a debt. If the borrower defaults on the debt, the lender receives title to the asset, which can then be sold to cover the amount owed to the lender.

Compensating balances   Minimum balances that must be maintained in a bank account to avoid significant service charges or, in some cases, to satisfy restrictive loan covenants (which are clauses in loan agreements that are designed to reduce the risk to the lender).

Compound interest   Interest calculated by adding the interest earned in one period to the balance in the account and multiplying the total by the interest rate. The interest earned in one period then earns interest itself in the next period.

Current ratio   A ratio calculated by dividing the total current assets by the total current liabilities.

Direct write-off method   A method of recognizing bad debts. Bad debt expense is recognized under this method at the time the account receivable is written off.

Factoring   The process of selling the accounts receivable of a company to a third party.

Historical cost   A valuation attribute or method that values assets at the price paid to obtain those assets.

Lower of cost and market (LCM)   A valuation method that reports the value of an asset at the lower of its historical cost and its current market value.

Marketable securities   Shares or debt securities that actively trade in a market.

Monetary   An attribute of an asset or liability that indicates that the asset or liability represents a fixed number of monetary units.

Monetary unit   The nominal units used to measure assets and liabilities. The monetary unit used is usually the local currency unit (such as the Canadian dollar).

Note receivable   An asset that represents the right of the holder of the note to receive a fixed set of cash payments in the future.

Percentage of credit sales method   A method of estimating the bad debt expense of a company by estimating the expense as a percentage of the credit sales for the period.

Promissory note   A document in which the issuer of the note agrees to pay fixed amounts to the holder of the note at some point in the future.

Purchasing power   An attribute of an asset that measures its ability to be exchanged for goods and services.

Quick ratio   A ratio calculated by dividing the most liquid current assets (cash, temporary investments, accounts receivable) by the total current liabilities.

Realized gain/loss   A gain or loss from the sale or reacquisition of an asset or liability that is the result of a completed transaction (in general, it means that cash or an agreement to pay cash has been received in exchange for the asset or liability).

Recourse   A provision in agreements to sell receivables in which the buyer of the receivables has the right to return them to the seller if the buyer cannot collect the receivables.

Recovery (accounts receivable)   The reinstatement and collection of an account receivable that was previously written off.

Recovery (marketable securities)   An unrealized gain from revaluing the portfolio of marketable securities according to the lower of cost and market rule.

Secured note   A note receivable secured by collateral.

Security   A financial instrument, usually a share or a debt, that may be publicly traded.

Simple interest   Interest that is calculated by multiplying the interest rate in the agreement by the principal involved. Interest earned in one period does not earn interest in a subsequent period.

Uncollectible accounts   Accounts receivable that are deemed to be uncollectible. The point at which they are uncollectible is generally established by the company policy.

Unit-of-measure assumption   An assumption made under GAAP that all transactions should be measured using a common unit, the Canadian dollar.

Unrealized gain/loss   A gain or loss recognized in the financial statements that has not resulted in the receipt of cash or the right to receive cash, but represents a change in value of an asset.

Valuation allowance   An account used to hold the adjustments necessary to lower the carrying value of the temporary investments from historical cost to market value when the market value is lower.

Write-off   The process by which an account receivable is removed from the books of a company when it is deemed uncollectible.

ASSIGNMENT MATERIAL

Multiple Choice Quizzes

Assessing Your Recall

6-1   Briefly describe how cash, temporary investments, accounts receivable, and notes receivable meet the criteria of probable future value and ownership to qualify as assets.

6-2   Explain what the unit-of-measure assumption means in accounting.

6-3   Discuss why cash is subject to purchasing power risk and why inventory may or may not be subject to this risk.

6-4 Explain why internal control is so important, especially for cash. Describe three things that represent internal control measures that can be put in place by companies.

6-5 Describe the process that accountants use to establish the lower of cost and market value for temporary investments.

6-6 What are the guidelines accountants use to decide whether an investment should be classified as a temporary investment?

6-7 Describe and compare the allowance method and the direct write-off method for determining bad debt expense. Is either more consistent with GAAP than the other?

6-8 How is a note receivable different from an account receivable?

6-9 Describe two ratios that measure current liquidity and compare the information they provide.

6-10 Describe a ratio that measures the management of accounts receivable and explain what information it provides.

Applying Your Knowledge

6-11 (Preparation of a bank reconciliation)
William's Carpet Company received its monthly bank statement for its business bank account, with a balance of $54,622 for the month of March. The cash account in the company's accounting system at that date was $59,304. After a comparison of the cheques written by the company and those deducted from the bank account, William's accountant determined that five cheques, totalling $2,806, were outstanding on March 31. A review of the deposits showed that a deposit on March 1 for $12,610 was actually recorded in the company's accounting system on February 28 and a March 31 deposit of $10,200 was recorded in the company's system on that date but had not been recorded by the bank yet. The March bank statement showed a service fee of $18, a customer's cheque in the amount of $70 that had been returned NSF, a loan payment of $700 that was deducted automatically by the bank, and a note for $3,500 that was collected by the bank for William's Carpet.

Required:

a. Prepare a bank reconciliation at March 31.

b. How much cash does William's Carpet actually have in its cash account at March 31?

c. Prepare adjusting journal entries to record all necessary adjustments to bring the cash account to its adjusted balance.

6-12 (Placement of items on a bank reconciliation)
Henrietta Walters is attempting to prepare a bank reconciliation. Indicate whether each of the following items would be added to the bank balance, deducted from the bank balance, added to the cash account balance, or deducted from the cash account balance. If any items do not have to be included, explain why.

a. The bank indicates that two cheques received by Walters and deposited in her account had been returned as uncollectible (NSF).

b. A monthly service charge has been deducted from the account by the bank.

c. Two cheques written by Walters were paid by the bank; however, Walters had forgotten to record them in the cash account.

d. Cash received by Walters during the last day of the month and deposited that evening is not shown as deposits by the bank.

e. An automatic deduction for Walters' electricity bill was made by the bank. She had recorded the amount in the cash account earlier in the month.

f. A loan to Walters from the bank reached maturity during the month and was deducted by the bank from the bank account. Walters had forgotten about the loan coming due.

g. A customer deposited an amount owed to Walters directly into Walters' bank account. Walters had not recorded it yet.

h. An outstanding deposit from the previous month was shown as having been received by the bank at the beginning of the month.

i. Six cheques written by Walters during the month had not yet cleared the bank.

6-13   (Reconciliation of personal bank account)

Grace Ho notices that the balance recorded in her chequebook is $1,243, which is $320 less than the balance shown on her bank statement. Examining the cheques included on the bank statement, she sees that two cheques she wrote totalling $310 have not yet cleared the bank. Also, she notices that a cheque that did clear was written for $76 but was mistakenly recorded in her chequebook as $67. In addition, a $20 cheque given to her by a co-worker was returned for insufficient funds and the bank charged her $5 because of the NSF cheque. The bank had made an automatic deposit of $50 to her account that she had not yet recorded. The bank also deducted a monthly service charge, but the bank statement is smeared and she cannot determine the amount of the charge. Calculate the bank service charge.

6-14   (Temporary investments)

Duggan Company purchased 100 preferred shares of Green Company for $25 each on March 1, 2004. It also purchased 200 common shares of White Company for $40 per share on that date. At December 31, 2004, the preferred shares of Green were selling at $26 and the common shares of White were selling at $32. Duggan Company considers the shares to be a temporary investment.

Required:

a. At what amount will the investments be reported in the December 31, 2004, balance sheet?

b. Will any other balance sheet or income statement accounts be affected by the accounting treatment of these securities? If so, which accounts will be affected and what will the effect be?

6-15   (Dividends earned on temporary investments)

During 2004, Duggan received dividends from the two companies in Problem 6-14. Green Company paid preferred dividends of $2 per share, and White paid a common dividend of $3.50 per share.

Required:

a. If Duggan Company reports income of $45,000 from operations (before any financing income or expenses) during 2004, what amount of net income will it report for the year?

b. Duggan Company has a goal of attaining a 10% annual return on investments. Has Duggan accomplished its goal for 2004?

6-16 (Temporary investments)
The following transactions relate to the Abbe Investment Company for 20x1 and 20x2. Abbe closes its books on December 31 each year.

Transactions:
20x1

June 30	Abbe purchased 5,000 common shares of Signal Corp. at $12.50 per share. It also paid fees to its stockbroker of $0.15 per share.
September 1	Signal Corp. declared a dividend of $0.90 per share to be paid on September 24.
Septment 25	Abbe received the dividend cheque from Signal Corp.
December 31	The market value of Signal Corp.'s common shares was $13.95 per share.

20x2

January 16	Abbe sold 4,000 common shares of Signal Corp. at $14.25 per share. Brokerage fees were $0.15 per share.

Required:

a. Prepare journal entries to record all the preceding transactions in the books of Abbe Investment Company. Assume the shares purchased are considered to be temporary investments. Note that we have not discussed fees to stockbrokers or brokerage fees. In answering this question, use your knowledge of accounting to determine a logical method for recording them.

b. What amount of temporary investments would appear in Abbe's balance sheet at December 31, 20x1?

6-17 (Temporary investments and the lower of cost and market)
The Corona Company holds a portfolio of temporary investments. The aggregate cost and aggregate market value of the entire portfolio in four years is as follows:

Dates	Aggregate Cost	Aggregate Market Value
Dec. 31, 20x1	$450,000	$410,000
Dec. 31, 20x2	500,000	480,000
Dec. 31, 20x3	480,000	510,000
Dec. 31, 20x4	540,000	530,000

Required:

a. What amount of temporary investments would appear in Corona's balance sheets for each of these years?

b. Give the necessary journal entries for each year. The accounting period ends on December 31 each year.

6-18 (Temporary investments and the lower of cost and market)
Upper Company purchased 500 shares each of Jack, Queen, and King companies on June 30, 2004, at a cost of $55, $18, and $40 per share, respectively. On December 31, 2004, the market values of the shares were $58, $16, and $38, respectively. Upper Company considers the shares to be temporary investments.

Required:

a. At what amount will the investments be reported in the December 31, 2004, balance sheet of Upper Company?

b. Will any other balance sheet or income statement accounts be affected by the accounting treatment of these securities? If so, which accounts and what will the effect be?

6-19   (Dividends earned on temporary investments)
During 2004, Upper received dividends of $6, $2, and $5 per share, respectively, from the common shares of Jack, Queen, and King companies acquired in Problem 6-18.

Required:

a. If Upper Company reports income from operations of $640,000 for 2004, what amount will it report for net income for the year after the dividend revenue is added?

b. If Upper Company has a goal of earning a 12% annual return on its temporary investments, has it accomplished its goal for 2004?

6-20   (Temporary investments including lower of cost and market)
The following information relates to the temporary investments held by Anders Corp. as current assets.

Security	Acquisition Date	Acquisition Cost	Date Sold	Selling Price	Market Value Dec. 31		
					20x4	20x5	20x6
Alpha	Apr. 13/x4	$ 70,000	NA	NA	$ 68,000	$ 72,000	$ 69,000
Beta	Aug 24/x4	45,000	May 27/x5	52,000	48,000	NA	NA
Delta	Jan. 8/x5	35,000	NA	NA	32,000	38,000	41,000
Omega	Jan. 3/x6	95,000	June 30/x6	98,000	94,000	96,000	NA

The Anders Corp. closes its books on December 31 each year.

Required:

a. Prepare journal entries relating to these temporary investments for each year.

b. Show how the marketable securities would be presented on the income statement and balance sheet for each year.

6-21   (Temporary investments)
The following information relates to Faun & Faun Inc. for the year ended December 31, 20x4.

Balance sheet at December 31, 20x4
Current assets

Temporary investments—at cost	$313,000
Less: Valuation allowance for temporary investments	13,000
Net balance (lower of cost and market)	$300,000

The income statement includes the following:

	20x3	20x4
Unrealized loss on valuation of temporary investments		($3,850)
Recovery of unrealized loss on valuation of temporary investments	$ 2,000	
Realized loss on sale of temporary investments	(4,950)	(5,650)
Net income	96,325	103,825

During 20x4, the company sold temporary investments for $50,000 in cash. These investments had a market value of $53,000 on December 31, 20x3. The company also purchased new temporary investments at a cost of $85,000.

Required:

a. Calculate the cost of the temporary investments sold in 20x4, and create the necessary journal entry to show the sale of the investments.

b. Calculate the beginning balance (at cost) of the temporary investments for the year 20x4.

c. Calculate the beginning balance in the valuation allowance for temporary investments for the year 20x4.

6-22 (Accounts receivable and uncollectible accounts)
Dundee Company started business on January 1, 2004. The company made credit sales of $750,000 during 2004 and received payments of $680,000 to the end of the year. It also wrote off as uncollectible $12,000 of its receivables when it learned that the customer who owed the $12,000 had filed for bankruptcy. Other than the entry to write off the $12,000, Dundee Company has made no entries related to bad debt expense for the period. The industry average for bad debt expense for companies similar to Dundee is 3% of credit sales. If Dundee uses the allowance method of accounting for bad debts and adopts the industry percentage in estimating bad debt expense for 2004:

Required:

a. What should be the balance reported in the allowance for doubtful accounts at December 31, 2004?

b. What accounts receivable balance would be reported in the balance sheet at December 31, 2004?

c. Evaluate the reasonableness of the balance in the allowance for doubtful accounts at December 31, 2004.

6-23 (Accounts receivable and uncollectible accounts)
Supreme Equipment Sales Company had a balance in its accounts receivable account at December 31, 2003, of $120,000 and a $4,000 balance in its allowance for doubtful accounts. During 2004, the company sold equipment on credit in the amount of $820,000. Total cash collections during 2004 were $790,000. The company also determined that $5,000 of accounts would not be collectible, and it wrote them off. At the end of 2004, management determined that it should increase its allowance percentage to 1% of credit sales from the previous year's 0.5% because of a slowdown in the economy and the amount of accounts receivable that proved to be uncollectible during the year.

Required:

a. Prepare the necessary journal entries for recording all the 2004 transactions including the recording of the new allowance amount at the end of the year.

b. Show the accounts receivable section of the balance sheet at December 31, 2004.

6-24 (Accounts receivable and uncollectible accounts)
The Global Sales Company's accounts receivable show the following balances at October 31, 2004, before adjustment: accounts receivable: $1,638,000; allowance for doubtful accounts: $8,000 (credit balance). Total sales for the year then ended were $26,350,000. Global Sales has a policy that 1.5% of its sales on credit would be expected to be uncollectible. Of the total sales, 25% are cash sales and 75% are made on credit.

Required:

a. Prepare the necessary journal entry to record the bad debt expense for the year.

b. Show the accounts receivable section of Global Sales' balance sheet at October 31, 2004.

c. What amount of bad debt expense would appear in the income statement for the year ended October 31, 2004?

6-25   (Accounts receivable and uncollectible accounts)
Belkou Company began operations on January 1, 2004. Its first year's sales were $1,100,000, which were 60% on credit. On December 31, 2004, the accounts receivable had a debit balance of $55,000. The management estimated that 0.5% of all credit sales would probably be uncollectible. The company wrote off accounts worth $2,800 at the end of the first year.

At the end of 2005, the balances in selected accounts were: accounts receivable: $76,000; allowance for doubtful accounts: $4,200 (debit balance); sales: $1,540,000 (60% on credit). The bad debt expense for 2005 had not been determined or recorded.

After reviewing the write-off of accounts receivable during 2005, the company decided that the estimate of uncollectibility should be increased from 0.5% to 0.75%.

Required:

a. Give the journal entry to record the bad debt expense for 2005.

b. Prepare a T-account for the allowance for doubtful accounts and enter into the account all of the transactions that have affected it since the company started operations.

c. What is the net accounts receivable at the end of 2005?

6-26   (Note receivable with interest calculations)
On March 1, 2004, the Moon Company determined that it would not be able to pay the account receivable that was owed to Gamma Company. Moon was confident that it would have the necessary cash near the end of the year. It therefore signed a 10-month, 9% note for the $10,000 that was owed. This note was recorded at its face amount. On August 31, 2004, the Gamma Company closed its books for the year.

Required:

a. Prepare all of the necessary journal entries associated with this note up to the end of August 31, 2004, assuming that the interest that is owed on this note will be paid when the note matures (is due).

b. Prepare the journal entry to record the payment by Moon of the amount owed to Gamma on December 31, 2004.

6-27   (Note receivable with interest calculations)
On June 1, 2004, Active Networks sold a computer networking system to Finn Motors for $36,000. Finn Motors signed a note receivable with interest at 11%, agreeing to pay the $36,000 in eight months. Active Networks' year end is December 31.

Required:

a. Prepare all of the necessary journal entries associated with this note including the end of year entries and the receipt of payment from Finn Motors.

b. What items would be included on the balance sheet and income statement of Active Networks on December 31 with respect to this note?

6-28   (Note receivable with interest calculations)
Kristi Scudeler wanted to buy a laptop computer. She selected one priced at $2,770 including tax. She didn't have the money right then, but her friend, Carter Ng, agreed to loan her the money. On March 1, 2004, she signed a four-month note receivable with interest at 13%.

Required:

a. Calculate how much interest will have been earned by July 1, 2004, when the note is due.

b. Do you think that the 13% charged by Carter Ng is reasonable or unreasonable? Explain your answer. What things should Carter Ng consider when he determines how much interest to charge?

6-29   (Current and quick ratios)
The following amounts were reported by Liquid Company in its most recent balance sheet:

Cash	$ 45,000
Accounts receivable	130,000
Short-term investments	18,000
Inventory	390,000
Prepaid insurance	55,000
Accounts payable	85,000
Wages payable	37,000
Income tax payable	45,000
Sales tax payable	10,000
Short-term notes payable	115,000

Required:

a. Calculate the current ratio and the quick ratio for Liquid Company.

b. Based on a review of other companies in the industry, the management of Liquid Company thinks it should maintain a current ratio of 2 or more and a quick ratio of 1 or more. The ratios at the end of the prior year were 1.8 and 1.2, respectively. How successful has the company been in achieving the desired results in this period?

c. How could the company improve its current position? What risks, if any, are associated with the strategy you have suggested?

6-30   (Liquidity decisions)
The following balance sheet accounts and amounts were included in the balance sheet of Wanhill Processors Ltd.:

Equipment and vehicles	$205,000
Bank loan (long-term)	250,000
Prepaid expenses	2,000
Accumulated amortization	88,000
Taxes payable	14,000
Inventory	255,000
Wages payable	26,000
Accounts receivable	15,000
Unearned revenue	48,000
Retained earnings	60,000
Trademarks (capital assets)	45,000
Common shares	30,000
Cash	59,000
Accounts payable	65,000

Required:

a. Prepare a classified balance sheet in good form.

b. Calculate the amount of Wanhill's working capital (current assets minus current liabilities).

c. At the beginning of the period, Wanhill reported total current assets of $300,000 and current liabilities of $260,000. Calculate the current ratios for Wanhill at the beginning and end of the period. Has the current ratio improved or declined during the period?

d. At the beginning of the current period, working capital was $40,000. Have Wanhill's working capital position and its overall liquidity improved or declined during the period?

e. How might Wanhill evaluate whether or not its overall liquidity is adequate?

6-31   (Cash flow analysis)
The balance sheets and the income statement of the Smythe Company for the year 2004 are given here. In addition to these statements, the following information is available:

Transactions:

1. There were no sales of property, plant, and equipment during 2004.

2. No dividends were declared or paid during 2004.

3. Temporary investments costing $75 were sold for $100.

SMYTHE COMPANY
Balance Sheet
At December 31

	2004	2003
Assets		
Cash	$ 540	$ 500
Accounts receivable	900	850
Allowance for doubtful accounts	(15)	(10)
Temporary investments	600	500
Allowance for valuation of temporary investments	(100)	(50)
Inventory	1,800	1,350
Property, plant, and equipment	8,000	5,800
Accumulated amortization	(2,800)	(1,800)
Total assets	$ 8,925	$ 7,140
Liabilities and Shareholders' Equity		
Accounts payable	$ 1,700	$ 1,550
Common shares	3,000	3,000
Retained earnings	4,225	2,590
Total liabilities and shareholders' equity	$ 8,925	$ 7,140

SMYTHE COMPANY
Income Statement
For the year ended December 31, 2004

Revenues		$10,000
Cost of goods sold		6,500
Gross profit		3,500
Expenses:		
Bad debt expense	$ 150	
Amortization	1,000	1,150
Operating income		2,350
Unrealized loss on valuation of temporary investments		(50)
Realized gain on sale of temporary investments		25
Income before taxes		2,325
Income taxes		690
Net income		$ 1,635

Required:
Prepare a statement to show why cash increased from $500 to $540.

User Perspective Problems

6-32 (Internal control and the audit process)
You are the auditor of a medium-sized business (revenues of $10 million). Before you begin the audit, you review the company's internal control system. Why is this preliminary step necessary? What are you hoping to learn? If you had reviewed the internal control system last year before the audit, is it necessary to do it again this year? Explain your answer.

6-33 (Estimation of uncollectibility of accounts receivable)
Suppose that there is a stock option plan at the SeeSaw Company that rewards managers for achieving a certain level of reported net income. What incentives might management have to influence the estimation of uncollectibility of accounts receivable?

6-34 (Market value of temporary investments and decision-making)
As a loan officer at a bank, why would you be interested in the market value of a company's temporary investments? Would you want them *recorded* at their market value or would you be satisfied with just the disclosure of the market valuation? Explain your reasoning.

6-35 (Market value of temporary investments and decision-making)
As a shareholder, why would you be interested in the market value of a company's temporary investments?

6-36 (Impact of a negative cash balance)
You are one of the shareholders of a large retail company. When you received the annual report, you noticed that the company did not have any cash recorded on the balance sheet. Instead, there was an entry in the current liabilities called "Bank overdraft." What do you think happened to the cash? Should you be concerned? What ratio analysis could you do that might help you understand the seriousness of this situation?

6-37 (Bank reconciliation and decision-making)
As a manager of a company, explain why a bank reconciliation is important to your management of cash.

6-38 (Accounts receivable and uncollectibility)
Ontario Company is involved in the manufacture and sale of high-quality racing and mountain bicycles. At the end of 2003, Ontario's balance sheet reported total accounts receivable of $350,000 and an allowance for doubtful accounts of $28,000. During 2004, the following events occurred:

1. Credit sales in the amount of $1,350,000 were made.

2. Collections of $1,300,000 were received.

3. Ontario recorded bad debt expense for 2004 as 3% of credit sales.

4. Customers with total debts of $36,000 to Ontario were declared bankrupt and those accounts receivable were written off.

As the Director of Finance for Ontario, you have been asked by a member of the executive committee to:

a. Analyze the above activities by giving the journal entries to be recorded by Ontario for each of the transactions.

b. Illustrate Ontario's balance sheet disclosure of accounts receivable at December 31, 2004.

c. Evaluate the adequacy of Ontario's allowance for doubtful accounts at December 31, 2004.

6-39 (Accounts receivable and uncollectible accounts)
Lowrate Communications is involved in the telephone/cellular phone industry. The following selected information is taken from the financial statements of Lowrate (in thousands of dollars):

	2004	2003	2002
Accounts receivable (net)	$ 1,469.8	$ 1,230.6	$ 1,044.8
Allowance for doubtful accounts	128.9	21.9	118.0
Accounts written off	309.9	270.2	296.8
Bad debt expense	312.4	271.5	267.0
Sales	12,661.8	11,367.8	10,420.0

Required:
Based on the information from Lowrate's financial statements, answer the following questions:

a. What percentage of total accounts receivable is considered uncollectible in each of the three years presented?

b. What percentage of sales is bad debt expense in each of the three years presented?

c. Did Lowrate's collection of accounts receivable improve over the three-year period?

d. The cloning of cellular phones is currently a serious problem. Cloning involves copying access/billing codes from cellular phones belonging to others. Cellular phone companies typically absorb charges for unauthorized calls on cellular phones, amounts involving many thousands of dollars. If cloning continues to be a problem as the cellular business grows, how would this affect the financial statements of a company like Lowrate?

Reading and Interpreting Published Financial Statements

6-40 (Cash and temporary investments)

Information from the balance sheet of **Air Canada** at December 31, 2001, shows a cash and cash equivalents balance of $1,067 million in 2001 and $437 million in 2000. Note 1d to the financial statements states: "Cash and cash equivalents include short-term investments of $1,021 million (2000–$458 million). All short-term investments may be liquidated promptly and have maturities of less than 90 days. Reported cash and cash equivalents are netted against outstanding cheques."

Required:

a. Explain why the short-term investments are included with the cash and cash equivalents.

b. Describe what you think the cash management policies of Air Canada are.

6-41 (Cash and temporary investments)

In the 2001 balance sheet of **Mosaid Technologies Incorporated**, the first two current assets listed are "cash and cash equivalents" and "short-term marketable securities." Why are the short-term marketable securities not shown as a cash equivalent? Is it possible that there are short-term investments included in the cash equivalents? If so, what do you know about them?

6-42 (Accounts receivable turnover ratio)

Using data for **Mosaid Technologies Incorporated** (balance sheet and income statement in Exhibit 1-10), calculate the accounts receivable turnover ratios for 2001 and 2000, using balances of accounts receivable at each year end rather than average balances. Use revenues from operations rather than total revenues. Comment on the ratios and trend.

6-43 (Accounts receivable turnover ratio)

The following appeared in the 2001 balance sheet of **Domtar Inc.** (in millions of dollars):

	2001	2000
Receivables, net of allowance for doubtful accounts of $19 (2000—$18)	$300	$404
The following amounts were reported as Sales on the income statement (millions of dollars)	$4,377	$3,598

Required:

a. What percentage of accounts receivable is considered to be uncollectible in 2001 and 2000?

b. Calculate the accounts receivable turnover for 2001 and 2000 using the balance of the receivables for each year rather than the average receivables. Convert the turnover into the number of days that it takes to collect a receivable.

c. In December 2000, Domtar entered into an agreement to sell some of its Canadian accounts receivable on a limited recourse basis. Why would a company want to sell its accounts receivable? What does it mean to sell them on a limited recourse basis?

6-44   (Accounts receivable, uncollectible accounts, and the turnover ratio)
On the 2001 balance sheet of **Suncor Energy Inc.**, the accounts receivable balance is given as $306 million in 2001, $407 million in 2000, and $277 million in 1999. Note 4 to the financial statements states that the allowance for doubtful accounts for those years was $3 million, $3 million, and $3 million respectively. Sales on the income statement were reported as $3,990 million (2001), $3,385 million (2000), and $2,383 million (1999).

Required:

a. What percentage of accounts receivable is considered to be uncollectible in 2001, 2000, and 1999?

b. Although sales increased between 1999 and 2001, the allowance for doubtful accounts stayed the same. Suggest some reasons why this occurred.

c. Calculate the accounts receivable turnover for 2001 and 2000 using the average of the receivables. Convert the turnover into the number of days that it takes to collect a receivable. What do you observe?

d. For 2001, reconstruct the journal entries to record transactions relating to sales and collections of accounts receivable assuming that all sales were on account.

6-45   (Accounts receivable and the turnover ratio)
On the 2001 balance sheet of **Big Rock Brewery Ltd.**, the accounts receivable balance is given as $1,593,984 in 2001 and $1,872,064 in 2000. Net sales on the income statement were reported as $23,199,678 (2001) and $22,716,926 (2000).

Required:

a. Calculate the accounts receivable turnover for 2001 and 2000 using the single-year amounts of the receivables. Convert the turnover into the number of days that it takes to collect a receivable. What do you observe?

b. For 2001, reconstruct the journal entries to record transactions relating to sales and collections of accounts receivable, assuming that all sales were on account.

Beyond The Book

6-46   (Examination of a company's financial statements)
Acquire the financial statements of a large retail company such as the Hudson's Bay Company, a large resource industry company such as Weyerhaeuser Company Ltd., and a large bank such as the Royal Bank of Canada. Prepare a short report in which you include the following:

a. Do an in-depth analysis of the cash and other financial asset balances held by each company. Be sure to review the balance sheet accounts and all related notes.

b. Look at the cash flow statement to see if you can determine the major sources of cash inflows and outflows during the past year. Did the companies borrow money during the year? Did they issue shares?

c. Make a list comparing the operating characteristics of the companies that might affect the amount of financial assets they would have on hand. For example, which of the three businesses would be likely to have the most dependable and predictable cash inflows and outflows? Which of the companies would realize most of its profits from holding financial assets?

6-47 (Examination of a company's financial statements)

Choose a company as directed by your instructor and answer the following questions:

a. Prepare a quick analysis of the cash (and cash equivalents), marketable securities, accounts receivable (gross), and the allowance for doubtful accounts by listing the beginning and ending amounts in these accounts and calculating the net change in both dollar and percentage terms for the most recent year.

b. If any of the accounts in part a) has changed more than 10%, give an explanation for this change.

c. If the company has any temporary investments, list the cost and market value of the securities at the beginning and end of the current year and calculate any unrealized gain or loss (if possible) that was recognized during the year. If there was an unrealized gain or loss, describe where it was reported in the financial statements.

d. Calculate the following ratios for the most recent two years:

Bad debt expense divided by net sales

Allowance for doubtful accounts divided by gross accounts receivable

Accounts receivable turnover (in times and days)

Comment on both the reasonableness of these ratios and any significant changes in them.

Cases

Additional Cases

6-48 Saintjay Supplies Limited

Saintjay Supplies Limited is concerned about its ability to pay its debts. Analyze the information provided below and explain why Saintjay is experiencing problems with its cash balance. What can Saintjay do to reduce these problems?

SAINTJAY SUPPLIES LIMITED
Selected Financial Information (in thousands)

Years ended March 31	2004	2003	2002
Sales on credit	$12,700	$14,100	$17,100
Cash	310	50	10
Temporary investments	25	-----	-----
Accounts receivable	1,180	1,510	1,980
Inventories	940	1,250	1,470
Short-term bank loans	-----	240	760
Accounts payable	610	390	440
Other short-term liabilities	80	80	80

6-49 Versa Tools Inc.

Versa Tools Inc. is a small tool and die manufacturing shop located in southwestern Ontario. The company's main shareholder, Arthur Henderson, is becoming increasingly concerned over the safety and security of the company assets and, in particular, cash. In the past, Arthur or his wife, Jeannine, have handled all cash transactions. However, with increasing production and the possibility of expanding into a plastics division, Arthur realizes that he will be unable to continue with this hands-on approach.

Currently, there is only one person in the accounting department who is responsible for recording all cash receipts and disbursements and for depositing all cash. Because this person is so busy, cash is generally only deposited in the bank once a week. All cash collected is locked in a desk drawer in the main office.

The accounting clerk has no formal accounting education. In fact, she is a graduate of a local art school and is working at Versa to earn enough money to move to Toronto and begin a career as a graphic artist. She often writes cash receipts on slips of paper until she has time to enter them into the computer system several days later.

Finally, Arthur does not have time to prepare bank reconciliations. When asked about the bank reconciliation, Arthur replied, "I'm so busy running the business that I don't have time to check every item on the bank statement."

Required:

Prepare a memo to Arthur outlining basic cash controls that should be put into place at Versa Tools Inc. to ensure the protection and management of cash balances.

6-50   Beltway International

Beltway International is an import-export company. Due to the nature of the business, the company often has significant amounts of cash on hand. Some of this cash has been invested in other companies as a means of achieving vertical integration. These investments are intended to be held for many years. At other times, Beltway's management invests extra cash in temporary investments. Management believes that it is better to have excess cash earning some return rather than just sitting in a bank account.

At December 31, 2003, Beltway's year-end date, the company had the following investments:

Investment	Cost	Market Value at December 31, 2003
Equity investment in shares of Agway Ltd. Agway is an import company operating in Argentina. The shares were acquired to facilitate Beltway's entrance into the South American market.	Purchased 100,000 shares at $8 per share	$9 per share
Equity investment in the Royal Bank. These shares were purchased to be held for the short term.	Purchased 2,000 shares at $48 per share	$52
Equity investment in Fishery Products International. Purchased as a short-term investment.	Purchased 4,000 shares at $8.30 per share	$9.40

Beltway's CEO has recently approached you, the corporate controller, with some exciting news. The company plans to sell a significant bond issue in 2004 to provide funding for a large expansion into Eastern European markets. The CEO wants the income statement and balance sheet to be as strong as possible and tells you to write up all the investments to their market value at December 31, 2003.

He says, "we could easily sell the shares, so why shouldn't we record the earnings now rather than waiting until they are actually sold? I know that if the share price falls we would have to write down the investments, so it only seems fair to write them up to market when the share price increases."

Required:

Is the CEO correct in his comments? Prepare a response to the CEO's statement outlining proper accounting policies for temporary investments.

6-51 Heritage Mill Works

Heritage Mill Works sells finished lumber and mouldings to a variety of housing contractors. Given the nature of the business, most of its sales are on credit and management of credit and bad debts is a critical success factor for this business. The company owners place significant emphasis on the operations as they appear on the income statement. They believe that accurate net income is the best indicator of the success of a business. The owners are currently looking at revising their credit-granting policies in light of a number of large write-offs that were made in the past year.

Karen Starkly is the accounts receivable clerk for the business and has been asked by the controller to prepare an estimate of bad debt expense for the company. The estimate is to be used in preparing the 2004 annual financial statements. The company had sales of $1,495,000 in 2004, of which 90% were on credit. Historically, the percentage of bad debt has varied from 2% to 4% of credit sales. Bad debts are usually higher in times of economic downturns. Karen notes that business has been strong this year for the entire industry since interest rate reductions have led to a boom in new housing starts.

The balance in the accounts receivable at December 31, 2004, is $330,000. During 2004, the company wrote off $43,890 of accounts receivable as uncollectible.

Required:

a. Provide the controller with an estimate of bad debt expense. Be prepared to justify your recommendation to the controller.

b. Discuss the trade-off that must be considered when selecting a credit policy. Are there any steps that this company can take to reduce the risk of not collecting its accounts receivable in the future?

6-52 Braditch Global Manufacturing

Braditch Global Manufacturing produces a variety of products for the airline industry. It is the world's largest manufacturer of luggage carts and carriers and sells to both large and small airlines. Each airline will purchase anywhere from 15 to 200 carts at a given time, which leads to Braditch's carrying large balances in its accounts receivable.

With recent problems in the airline industry, Braditch's board of directors is becoming concerned over the collectibility of many of its larger receivables, some of which have been outstanding for several months. They are considering requesting that these customers convert their accounts receivable into 6-month, 10% notes receivable. As well, the board would like more of the company's larger sales to be negotiated using notes receivable in the future.

Required:

Discuss the difference between an account receivable and a note receivable. Discuss the benefits and risks associated with the proposed change in receivables policy so that the board can make a well-informed decision.

Critical Thinking Questions

6-53 (Temporary investments and accounts receivable)
The balance sheet and cash flow statement of **Sierra Wireless, Inc.** at December 31, 2001, are shown in Exhibit 6-10. Analyze the changes in the short-term investments.

Required:

a. Reconstruct the journal entries that would have been made by Sierra Wireless in 2001 relating to these temporary investments. Be careful. Sierra Wireless puts the most recent year's amounts in the outside column instead of the inside column.

b. The balance in Sierra Wireless's accounts receivable at the end of 2001 is less than half the balance at the end of 2000 ($10,504,000 as compared to $22,588,000). Has the allowance for doubtful accounts been reduced by half as well? What possible explanations can you suggest for the change in the allowance?

6-54 (Accounts receivable)
In its 2001 financial statements, **Cangene Corporation**, a pharmaceutical company, includes the following note about its accounts receivable:

2. ACCOUNTS RECEIVABLE
As of July 31, 2001, accounts receivable include approximately $3.8 million [2000–$4.1 million] due from a major customer and $2.4 million [2000–$1.5 million] due from Apotex Inc., a company under common control.

Its accounts receivable balances were as follows: 2001–$13,167,000 and 2000–$10,005,000.

Required:
Provide reasons why Cangene's disclosure about the components of accounts receivable is necessary.

SIERRA WIRELESS, INC.

Consolidated Balance Sheets

(Expressed in thousands of United States dollars)
(Prepared in accordance with United States GAAP)

December 31,		2000		2001
Assets				
Current assets:				
Cash and cash equivalents	$	6,891	$	12,085
Short-term investments		72,144		31,879
Accounts receivable, net of allowance for doubtful				
accounts of $5,169 (2000 — $1,320)		22,588		10,504
Inventories (note 4)		12,560		25,591
Deferred income taxes (note 10)		506		224
Prepaid expenses		1,239		1,180
		115,928		81,463
Fixed assets (note 5)		7,500		14,694
Deferred income taxes (note 10)		3,733		4,030
Intangible assets (note 6)		8,564		10,054
Other		340		483
	$	136,065	$	110,724
Liabilities and Shareholders' Equity				
Current liabilities:				
Accounts payable	$	11,301	$	4,356
Accrued liabilities		9,128		12,555
Deferred revenue and credits		750		1,050
Current portion of long-term liabilities		248		341
Current portion of obligations under capital lease (note 7)		323		947
		21,750		19,249
Long-term liabilities		419		671
Obligations under capital lease (note 7)		83		761
Shareholders' equity:				
Share capital (note 8)				
Authorized				
Unlimited number of common and preference shares with no par value				
Common shares, issued and outstanding		122,174		122,673
Deficit		(7,632)		(31,901)
Accumulated other comprehensive income				
Cumulative translation adjustments		(729)		(729)
		113,813		90,043
	$	136,065	$	110,724

Commitments and contingent liabilities (note 13)

See accompanying notes to consolidated financial statements.

DSutcliffe.

David B. Sutcliffe
Director

S. Jane Rowe

S. Jane Rowe
Director

EXHIBIT 6-10 CONT.

SIERRA WIRELESS, INC.

Consolidated Statements of Cash Flows

(Expressed in thousands of United States dollars)
(Prepared in accordance with United States GAAP)

Years ended December 31,	1999	2000	2001
Cash flows from operating activities:			
Net earnings (loss)	$ 3,212	$ (3,118)	$ (24,269)
Adjustments to reconcile net earnings (loss) to net cash provided by operating activities			
Loss on disposal	30	—	—
Amortization	892	3,068	6,661
Expense in-process research and development costs	—	1,000	—
Deferred income taxes	(1,100)	448	(15)
Accrued warrants	—	—	671
Changes in operating assets and liabilities			
Accounts receivable	(1,727)	(17,646)	12,084
Inventories	(537)	(5,644)	(13,031)
Prepaid expenses	(187)	(943)	59
Accounts payable	1,697	7,237	(6,945)
Accrued liabilities	226	7,069	3,420
Deferred revenue and credits	(6)	559	300
Net cash provided by (used in) operating activities	2,500	(7,970)	(21,065)
Cash flows from investing activities:			
Business acquisitions	(506)	(7,250)	—
Purchase of fixed assets	(1,261)	(6,692)	(10,523)
Increase in intangible assets	(624)	(3,118)	(3,328)
Increase in other assets	—	(340)	(143)
Purchase of short-term investments	(38,991)	(212,438)	(69,411)
Proceeds on maturity of short-term investments	42,615	140,294	109,676
Net cash provided by (used in) investing activities	1,233	(89,544)	26,271
Cash flows from financing activities:			
Issue of common shares	29,370	66,557	499
Increase in long-term liabilities	—	—	255
Repayment of long-term liabilities	(389)	(744)	(766)
Net cash provided by (used in) financing activities	28,981	65,813	(12)
Effect of foreign currency exchange rates on cash and cash equivalents	(37)	—	—
Net increase (decrease) in cash and cash equivalents	32,677	(31,701)	5,194
Cash and cash equivalents, beginning of year	5,915	38,592	6,891
Cash and cash equivalents, end of year	$ 38,592	$ 6,891	$ 12,085

Managing Inventory in York, P.E.I.

When Vesey's Seeds first began operations in 1939, orders were filled using a spoon and kitchen scale, and inventory was tracked on the backs of little cards. Sixty years later, the York, Prince Edward Island, mail order company processes more than 100,000 customer orders each year, shipping to gardeners across Canada and the United States. Today, using state-of-the-art inventory and bookkeeping software, it has a perpetual inventory system that is automatically updated with each and every transaction.

Over the years, Vesey's inventory has grown to include hundreds of different vegetable, flower, and herb seeds, as well as a wide range of bulbs, gardening accessories, and tools. Since seeds—which Vesey's purchases in bulk and packages on site—are sold in up to five different sizes of packets, the company has to keep track of thousands of individual items sold through its three printed catalogues, a retail outlet, and, since 1999, its website—which now brings in around 25% of total sales.

"Our entire inventory is stored in a database, so to create a purchase order, we simply type in a vendor name and item number and the current price and ordering information pops up," explains John Barrett, Sales and Marketing Director at Vesey's. "Meanwhile, it's not just a fancy way of typing up the order. When the product arrives, our receiver records the shipment against the original purchase order. As a result, at any given time our customer sales staff can tell whether an item is available or not, or if it's back-ordered."

Because Vesey's uses a just-in-time system—it buys seeds in large quantities but only packages them in increments—an item may occasionally show up as unavailable when in fact it is currently in packaging and will be on the shelf by the end of the day. "When that happens, our staff does an override and the sale goes through," says Mr. Barrett. But what happens with web-based orders coming in around the clock? For now, the system on its own can't make the call, and those transactions still have to be entered manually by staff each morning.

In addition to keeping track of inventory, the system also produces reports such as sales by week or by category. It can even show the number of items and dollar revenue per item on any page of Vesey's catalogues. "By comparing those figures with what we've bought so far, I can come up with a pretty good estimate of what we're going to need," Mr. Barrett says. "In the end, it will tell me whether I've bought too much or too little based on my projections. Due to the nature of our business, we can't have any surplus. Our product is alive, and it has to be sold and planted within a certain period of time or it's finished."

INVENTORY

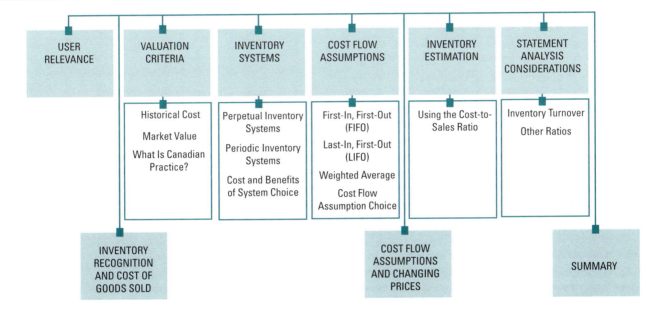

Learning Objectives:

After studying this chapter, you should be able to:

1. *Discuss the importance of inventory to the overall success of a company.*
2. *Describe the valuation criteria used for inventory in Canada.*
3. *Describe how the lower of cost and market rule is applied to inventory.*
4. *Explain the difference between the perpetual inventory system and the periodic inventory system.*
5. *Discuss some criteria used by companies when choosing an inventory system.*
6. *Describe the three cost flow assumptions and calculate cost of goods sold and ending inventory under each.*
7. *Explain the shortcomings of LIFO and why it is rarely used in Canada.*
8. *Describe the impact of inflation on each of the cost flow assumptions.*
9. *Estimate a value for ending inventory using the cost-to-sales ratio method.*
10. *Calculate the inventory turnover ratio and explain how it can be interpreted by users.*

Purchasing, stocking, and selling inventory is a complicated process. Vesey's Seeds is particularly vulnerable because its products have a short shelf life. Management must have enough seeds in stock to fill orders as they come in because customers want to get the seeds planted and growing. They are not willing to wait. At the same time, management must not overstock. Any seeds that are not sold will have to be discarded. Keeping the inventory at just the right level requires Vesey to generate up-to-date information about past sales, current demand, and current inventory levels. Vesey's uses a perpetual inventory system which gives management information about current inventory levels, enabling them to place orders with suppliers on a daily basis. Vesey's management of inventory is further complicated by its three modes of sales—store outlet, catalogue, and Internet. All customer personnel must have access to the same information and must update that information with each sale so that the next person has the most current information possible. Management of inventory is a complicated process, but is essential to the efficient sale of goods.

Inventory is any item purchased by a company for resale to customers or to be used in the manufacture of items to be sold to customers. Inventory is generally the most important asset to a retailer or manufacturer. The success or failure of the company depends upon buying or making inventory with a unit cost lower than its selling price. It also depends upon buying or making the inventory that people want to buy. Management must be very careful to buy or make the right items, at the right price, and in the right quantities so that sufficient profit can be made on their sales to cover all the other necessary business expenditures.

Visualize, for a moment, a music store that sells CDs, tapes, and movies. Imagine the complications that can arise with inventory: the store must select from its supplier the music and movies that people want to buy in quantities that will ensure it does not run out of stock of an item (called a **stockout**) and force buyers to go elsewhere—where they may buy more than just the item that was out of stock at the first store. It must make sure that it does not have too many items in inventory because there are storage and handling costs associated with inventory on hand, as well as the risk of obsolescence. It must also make sure that it sets prices that are competitive but at the same time high enough to provide sufficient profit for the company. The store must also provide safeguards so that people cannot steal the inventory. Complicating this activity even further are the variety and volume of items typically sold by any one company.

Learning Objective

1

Discuss the importance of inventory to the overall success of a company.

Managing inventory can sometimes run into unforeseen problems. Note what happened to the Sobeys grocery store chain:

accounting in the news

WHEN INVENTORY SOFTWARE FAILS

In the grocery business, failing to stock store shelves properly can be a costly mistake. In December 2000, Sobeys Inc. suffered a massive information-technology failure that left store shelves empty in the chain's Atlantic and Ontario stores. The crash disrupted merchandise traffic over five days leading into the crucial holiday season and it took several weeks for Canada's second-largest grocery store operator (after Loblaw) to recover.

The failure led to management's decision to scrap a database system that SAP AG in Germany had been developing for Sobeys. Though the company had already invested two years in the project, Sobeys president and CEO Bill McEwan said that SAP's software could not handle the high number of transactions that characterized Sobeys' retail operations.

As for the bottom line, McEwan said that costs related to the failure would be reflected in operating earnings well below expected results for that quarter. Sobeys took a writedown of $49.9 million to abandon the system. The company's stock also suffered, dropping 14% on the news of the breakdown.

Source: "Software snafu hurts Sobeys," Canadian Press, in *The Gazette* (Montreal), Jan. 26, 2001, p. C1.

USER RELEVANCE

When you think about inventory, you probably think about items you have purchased recently in stores. Inventory includes not only those items, but much more. To a property developer, inventory is land and buildings; to a forest products company, it is logs, lumber, and pulp; to a recycler, it is old newspapers and aluminum cans. Exhibit 7-1 includes two other examples of inventory.

EXAMPLES OF INVENTORY

Suncor Energy Inc. is an integrated oil and gas company operating in the tar sands in Northern Alberta. The first example shows note 7 from its 2001 annual report, which describes its inventory. **Comac Food Group Inc.** owns and holds franchise interests in a chain of retail bakery cafés, retail coffee shops, and restaurants in Canada. Note 4 from its 2001 annual report lists its inventory items. Note how the value of the stores held for resale has greatly declined from the previous year.

<table>
<tr><td>EXHIBIT 7-1
CONT.</td></tr>
</table>

Suncor Energy Inc.

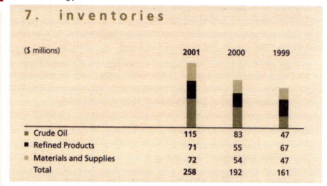

7.   inventories

($ millions)	2001	2000	1999
■ Crude Oil	115	83	47
■ Refined Products	71	55	67
▪ Materials and Supplies	72	54	47
Total	258	192	161

Comac Food Group Inc.

Excerpt from the Notes to the Statements

4. Inventories

Inventories are comprised of the following:

	2001	2000
Franchise stores under construction	$ 4,000	$166,000
Stores held for sale	65,000	535,000
Ingredients, uniforms and selling supplies	11,000	77,000
	$ 80,000	$778,000

==Investment in inventory can be substantial, so companies manage inventory levels carefully to maximize their return and minimize their costs.== For example, the following article about Wal-Mart Canada explains its strategy for inventory management:

accounting in the news

INVENTORY MANAGEMENT IN THE RETAIL BUSINESS

Only five years after stepping into the Canadian market, Wal-Mart Canada Inc. has changed the face of this country's retailing industry. With more than 150 outlets nationwide, Wal-Mart accounts for 30% of department store sales—and it continues to expand. The key to its success lies in great part in its distribution system, viewed as the world's most efficient: in Canada, Wal-Mart has the highest rate of stock turnover of all department stores.

The company invested billions of dollars to create Wal-Mart Retail Link, a computer system that tracks inventory from the point of shipping until the moment it leaves the store. The company has its own satellite to transmit the information. Suppliers are required to make deliveries to distribution centres within a 15- to 30-minute window; missing shipments can mean fines. Because Wal-Mart has 3,600 stores worldwide, it can negotiate cutthroat prices from suppliers that translate into retail prices for high-turnover items as low as some retailers pay wholesale.

Source: "The Retail Revolution," by John Schofield, *Maclean's*, March 1, 1999,

For companies whose major source of revenue is the sale of inventory, the management of the inventory inflows and outflows can mean the difference between success and failure. As a user, you should make yourself aware of the types of inventory that a company sells. You should also determine the margin (sales minus cost of goods sold) that the company earns in the current year and over the last several years. Has the company been earning enough margin to cover the rest of its costs? Has that margin been increasing, decreasing, or staying constant?

A variety of accounting methods for estimating the total cost of inventory have been developed and are acceptable under GAAP. This makes the accounting for inventory a fairly complicated process. As a user, you need to be aware of what those methods are and how each method affects the margin and the net income. Because companies are required to disclose their inventory costing method(s), once you know the method you can make some assumptions about how it is affecting income. The basics of inventory accounting are covered in this chapter so that you will have a reasonable understanding of how inventory is measured, recorded, and reported. You can then use this information to make informed evaluations of companies.

INVENTORY RECOGNITION AND COST OF GOODS SOLD

Does inventory meet the criteria for being an asset? The probable future value associated with inventory is measured by the company's ability to sell it in the future and to use the proceeds to buy other goods and services. Since inventory has not yet been sold, the collection of cash from its sale is even more uncertain than collecting accounts receivable. All the uncertainties associated with the collection of accounts receivable are present with inventory, as well as two others that are unique to this asset: finding buyers and obsolescence/spoilage. If a sufficient number of buyers cannot be found at the initial price set for the product or service, the price may have to change in order to attract buyers. A second uncertainty is obsolescence and spoilage. Computer hardware, for instance, is at considerable risk of technological obsolescence. Spoilage, on the other hand, is a major factor for food inventories.

Ownership of inventories is evidenced by possession and by legal title. Usually ownership of low-priced inventories is evidenced by possession because it is impractical to keep track of legal title to such items. It is very much like cash in terms of management. Adequate controls must be maintained so that the inventory is not lost or stolen. Ownership of high-priced inventories may also be evidenced by possession, but there are generally legal documents that also prove ownership. The ownership of automobiles, for instance, is evidenced by registration.

The fact that the company has possession of inventory indicates that a past transaction occurred. Inventory, therefore, meets the recognition criteria for an asset, and should be recorded as such in the company's accounts. The amount that is placed in the accounts then depends on the valuation or measurement criteria that are applied.

Cost of goods sold represents the expense side of the inventory asset. Once inventory is sold, it is no longer an asset. Its cost is reported on the income statement as cost of goods sold and is matched against the revenue that its sale generated. Determining what that cost is can be problematic. Much of the discussion in this chapter will centre around establishing an appropriate cost for the inventory and for the cost of goods sold.

VALUATION CRITERIA

Learning Objective

2

Describe the valuation criteria used for inventory in Canada.

The valuation method allowed under GAAP is a combination of several valuation approaches. GAAP generally specifies cost, but it recognizes that the cost figure used should not differ materially from more recent costs. If it does, the company can use one of a number of methods to recognize a decline in inventory value. Before GAAP is discussed in detail, however, we need to examine these different approaches to valuation.

Historical Cost

One possible valuation method is to carry inventory at its historical cost. According to this method, inventory is recorded at its cost on the date it was acquired. In the purest application of this method, no recognition is made of changes in the market value of the inventory while it is held. Income is recognized only when the inventory is sold. At that time, a profit or loss is recorded.

Market Value

A second possible valuation method is to carry inventory at its market value. To apply this method, the term **market** must be more clearly defined. Inventory really has two markets. The first is the market in which the company buys its products. In the case of a retailer, this is called the **wholesale market**. For a manufacturing company, there is no one market in which the company buys its inventory because numerous costs are incurred when constructing the product. If the market price can be found in the market where the inventory is bought (the wholesale market), the term **replacement cost** is used. Replacement cost refers to what it would cost the company to replace the product today. The market in which these products are acquired is called the **input market**, or the **entry market** since this is the market from which the products enter the company.

Another measure of market value might be obtained from the market in which the company sells its products. This is called the **retail market**. The company, of course, hopes prices in the retail market are higher than those in the wholesale market so that it can earn a profit. The markets in which companies sell their products are sometimes referred to as **output markets**, or **exit markets**. In accounting terminology, the exit price is sometimes referred to as the **net realizable value** (NRV), which is defined as the net amount that can be realized from the sale of the product in question. Net realizable value is not the same as selling price. The "net" part of NRV refers to the company's need to net some costs against the selling prices. For example, there are generally some selling costs that must be incurred to sell a product. Net realizable value is then the selling price less the costs necessary to sell the item. In a manufacturing company, some inventory is not ready for sale (work in process). Net realizable value, in this case, is the selling price less the selling costs as well as the costs necessary to complete the item.

There is one final issue with regard to the definition of market. The markets referred to in the preceding paragraphs are assumed to be the normal markets in which the company does normal business. There are also markets for goods that must be sold quickly (such as in a "fire sale") or in abnormally large or small quantities. The prices in these markets do not reflect the value of inventory in its normal use and should not be used in valuing inventory of a **going concern** (a company that will continue to operate in the foreseeable future). These markets may be important in valuing inventory, however, if the company is in bankruptcy or going out of business. Under these distress conditions, normal accounting procedures would not be appropriate because the conditions violate the going-concern assumption that underlies GAAP financial accounting.

Replacement Cost

If a company uses a pure replacement cost valuation system, inventory is carried at its replacement cost. At acquisition, replacement cost is the same as historical cost. As the company holds the inventory, however, unrealized increases and decreases in value are recognized as the replacement cost of the inventory changes. The balance sheet reflects the replacement cost of the inventory at the end of each period, and the income statement shows the unrealized profits and losses. At the time of sale, the only additional profit or loss that is recognized is the difference between the replacement cost at the date of sale and the selling price. This difference is called a realized profit or loss.

Net Realizable Value

A pure net realizable value system records inventory at its net realizable value. At the date of acquisition, this means that a profit or loss is recorded equal to the difference between the historical cost and the net realizable value. While the inventory is held, this system requires that changes in net realizable value be recognized as unrealized profits or losses. At the time of ultimate sale, no profit is recognized because the item has already been recorded at its net realizable value.

What Is Canadian Practice?

The application of cost is used extensively in Canada. When the use of cost results in a figure that is materially different from recent cost figures, companies should apply a lower of cost and market (LCM) rule at the end of the period. This treatment is very similar to that given to temporary investments. Market, as defined here, is most commonly either replacement cost or net realizable value. If market value is used, there is an impact on the inventory amount on the balance sheet and a loss is reflected on the income statement. In Canada, most companies describe their inventories as being valued at the lower of cost and market. In order to understand the implications for inventory, we will first discuss what should be included in the cost of inventory, and then consider how to apply the LCM rule.

Acquisition Costs

The value assigned to inventory should contain all **laid-down costs**. For a retailer, laid-down costs include the invoice price as well as any customs, tariff, and excise duties in addition to freight and cartage costs. As a practical matter, it is often difficult to assign the specific dollar amount of freight and cartage to a specific item of inventory. Imagine, for example, that a major grocery store received a new shipment of inventory that contained everything from cereal to heads of lettuce. It would be totally impractical to assign freight costs to a single head of lettuce. Therefore, many companies do not assign these costs to inventory, but treat them instead as period costs in the period in which they are incurred. The shipping costs, often called **transportation in** or **freight in**, may be assigned to inventory, but are more commonly treated as period costs in the cost of goods sold calculation. The calculation of cost of goods sold was first introduced in Chapter 2. With the inclusion of transportation costs, the calculation becomes:

	Beginning inventory
+	Purchases
+	Transportation in
=	Goods available for sale
−	Ending inventory
=	Cost of goods sold

For a manufacturing company the inventory costs are more complicated. Typically, a manufacturing company buys materials which it intends to use to make new products. These materials are called **raw materials** and their cost is kept in a raw materials inventory account. The cost assigned to this account includes the cost of the materials plus any transportation costs. The company takes the raw materials and begins to make its new products. The process of manufacturing involves additional costs such as the labour costs of the workers, the costs of the machines and buildings, the cost of utilities paid to run the facilities in which the manufacturing occurs, etc. The labour costs associated with manufacturing are referred to as **direct labour** and all of the other more indirect costs are referred to as **overhead**. A typical product includes raw materials, direct labour, and overhead.

A company uses three inventory accounts in the manufacturing process: the raw materials inventory account, a work-in-process account, and a finished goods account. The **work-in-process account** collects all of the costs (raw materials, direct labour, and overhead) that are incurred as the product is being made. Once the product is complete, the full cost of making the product is transferred from the work-in-process account to the **finished goods account**. Products that are sold are deducted from the finished goods account. Exhibit 7-2 diagrams how the costs flow through the three inventory accounts to cost of goods sold.

MANUFACTURING COST FLOWS

EXHIBIT 7-2

```
A-Raw materials            A-Work-in-process              A-Finished goods
     XX
                     XX  ──────▶  XX                      
                                  + Labour
                                  costs
                                  + Overhead
                                              YY  ──────▶  YY
                                          (finished
                                          product)                 YY  ┐
                                                                       │
                                            SE-Cost of goods sold  ◀───┘
                                          └──────▶  YY
```

Exhibit 7-3 includes the inventory disclosure of a manufacturing company, Cangene Corporation.

Cangene Corporation is a biopharmaceutical company that develops, manufactures, and markets specialty plasma products. It is also involved in developing genetic solutions to certain diseases. Its 2001 inventory disclosure is included below:

CANGENE CORPORATION

EXHIBIT 7-3

Excerpted from the Notes to the Statements

3. INVENTORIES in thousands of Cdn dollars	2001	2000
Raw materials	$ 3,742	$ 2,583
Work in process	8,272	2,736
Finished goods	246	419
	$ 12,260	$ 5,738

Lower of Cost and Market

Because inventory is crucial to the success of companies in the retail and manufacturing business, users are very interested in its value. When inventory is listed as a current asset on the balance sheet, users assume that it will be sold in the subsequent period for at least its stated value, but more optimistically, at a profit. During an accounting period, economic circumstances may arise that negatively affect the value of the inventory. At the end of every accounting period, most companies compare the cost of the inventory to its market value and apply the LCM rule. The rule is similar to that applied to temporary investments, discussed in Chapter 6. Companies can use either the **direct method** or the **allowance method**. Under the direct method, the ending inventory is reduced to the lower market value, which causes the cost of goods sold amount to rise in the income statement. In the subsequent year, the lower market value becomes part of the cost of goods sold when it becomes beginning inventory. Under the allowance method, the inventory

Learning Objective

3

Describe how the lower of cost and market rule is applied to inventory.

account remains at the original cost and an allowance account is used to hold the decline in value. The allowance account, which is shown contra to the inventory on the balance sheet, is usually adjusted each year to reflect the changing value of the inventory (similar to the treatment of the allowance used with temporary investments). LCM can be applied to individual items, to pools of similar items, or to the inventory as a whole. It is generally impractical to apply it on an individual item basis, so companies will use either pools of similar items or the total inventory.

An International Perspective

Reports from Other Countries

In Canada, the LCM rule is usually applied on a total inventory basis because companies are required to use the total inventory basis for tax purposes. It is more efficient to apply the same method for both purposes.

In the United States, the LCM rule is more commonly applied on an individual item basis because the U.S. tax department requires the application on an individual basis.

Under the direct method, the unrealized losses that result from the application of the LCM rule are often hidden in the cost of goods sold expense. Remember that the cost of goods sold calculation is:

	Beginning Inventory
+	Purchases
+	Transportation in
=	Goods available for sale
−	Ending inventory
=	Cost of goods sold

If the market value of the inventory is lower than the calculated cost amount, ending inventory is assigned the lower value. If the ending inventory value goes down, the cost of goods sold expense goes up, thereby incorporating the loss. Under this method, users will not know how large the loss was.

Under the allowance method, a separate loss account is created to hold the amount of the loss. It is usually called Loss Due to Market Decline of Inventory. This loss account could be listed separately on the income statement but is more frequently summarized with other expenses which are listed after Cost of Goods Sold. Similar to the direct method, the amount of the loss is frequently not disclosed as an individual item in the income statement. Companies would probably disclose the loss in inventory value as a separate item on the income statement if it was a material amount. They could also discuss it in a note to the financial statements.

To determine the appropriate market value to use in applying the LCM rule, we need to go back to the previous discussion about market value. In Canada, companies usually define market as net realizable value, net realizable value less a normal profit margin, or replacement cost. The most common is net realizable value. This makes sense, because if the selling price has dropped below the cost, the company may experience a loss next period when the inventory is sold. Because the decline in value occurred in the current period, we reduce the value of the inventory in the current period. Then when it is sold in the next period, it will sell at no profit if the selling price does not change. The option of net realizable value less a normal profit margin reduces the inventory value even more in the current period, so that when it is sold in the next period it will sell at a profit. This option is not used very often, but it is available to companies under GAAP. When replacement cost is used, it is often with inventory that is used to manufacture items rather than with inventory that is held for resale.

Exhibit 7-4 includes the inventory disclosure for **Finning International Inc.**, which distributes and services heavy equipment and related products. Note that it uses net realizable value as well as specific identification, first-in, first-out, and average cost in its inventory disclosure. More will be said about these other cost bases later in the chapter.

FINNING INTERNATIONAL INC. (2001)

EXHIBIT 7-4

Excerpted from the Notes to the Statements

Inventories

Inventories are stated at the lower of cost and net realizable value. Cost is determined on a specific item basis for on-hand equipment. For approximately two-thirds of parts and supplies, cost is determined on a first-in, first-out basis. An average cost basis is used for the remainder.

AN INTERNATIONAL PERSPECTIVE

Reports from Other Countries

Most countries require the application of a lower of cost and market rule. Some countries, such as the United States, refer to it as the lower of cost *or* market rule. The application of this rule, however, can vary across countries. The *market* value used in the rule is interpreted to mean replacement cost in a few countries (Italy and Japan, for example), whereas in many more countries it is interpreted as net realizable value (France, Germany, and the United Kingdom, for example). The **International Accounting Standards Board (IASB)** defines market value as net realizable value. Very few countries allow the flexibility that is available under Canadian GAAP. The United States uses all three values for market when it requires that, regardless of how high the replacement costs are, the company cannot carry the inventory at a value higher than net realizable value (called a ceiling value). In addition, the carrying value cannot be lower than net realizable value less a profit margin (called a floor value). Another difference is that the United States is somewhat alone in viewing the write-down of inventory as permanent. Most other countries, including Canada, either require or permit the recovery of value back to original cost if the market recovers.

INVENTORY SYSTEMS

Now that we have discussed the valuation of inventory in a general way, we need to look at various systems companies have developed to manage the volume and variety of inventory that they purchase and subsequently sell. Keeping track of inventory units and their associated costs is essential to the profitable management of the company. Information concerning the units sold and those in inventory is necessary for intelligent decisions about pricing, production, and reordering. An inventory system is needed to keep track of this information. As you saw in our opening story, computerized inventory systems are making the task of inventory management easier.

At least two types of information about inventory are needed. The first relates to the number of units sold during a period and the number that remain. This information is needed to establish a value for cost of goods sold, to trigger the reordering of inventory, or to set the level of production for the current period. It may also be necessary to fill sales orders. The second type of information is data about the cost of goods sold during the period and the cost of those that remain. This information is needed to prepare the financial statements, to evaluate performance, and to make pricing decisions.

Some inventory systems keep track of units of inventory but not their cost; others keep track of both units of inventory and cost. Systems that keep track of units but not costs are referred to as *physical inventory systems*. Major grocery chains, for example, have their cash registers connected to computers that record the sale of each item of inventory when the item is scanned for its bar code. The computerized inventory system is programmed to trigger new orders when the number of items remaining drops to a predetermined level. Unless the computer program is very sophisticated, it will not identify the purchase cost of the item sold.

Systems that keep track of the number of units and the costs associated with units of inventory are referred to as *cost inventory systems*. A cost inventory system can most easily be implemented when the inventory items are uniquely identifiable. For example, a car dealership records the unique characteristics of each vehicle that it buys for resale. When a vehicle is sold, it is relatively easy to record the sale of that specific vehicle and to record its original cost to the dealer. A grocery store, on the other hand, would not be able to determine the original cost of a can of peas because it would have no way of identifying the case from which the can was sold. The bar code on the can tells the computer simply that it is a can of a particular brand of peas. With the increasing sophistication of computer technology, more businesses will be able to convert to cost inventory systems and manage their inventories in a more detailed fashion.

In any inventory system, it is important for you to understand how inventory flows through it. To illustrate these flows, consider the inventory T-account in Exhibit 7-5. The company starts the period with a certain amount of beginning inventory which, in a physical inventory system, is the number of units and, in a cost inventory system, is the number of units multiplied by the cost of those units. These amounts are known from the end of the last period. The number of units purchased and the cost of those purchases are known from the invoices for the period (in the case of a manufacturer, the debits are for direct materials, labour, and overhead, all of which are known during the period). What is unknown is the cost of goods sold (the number of units sold in a physical system) and the cost (number) of units left in ending inventory. The sum of the cost of the beginning inventory and that of purchases is known as the cost of **goods available for sale**. The problem is deciding how to divide the total cost between the cost of goods sold and the cost of those that remain in ending inventory. Whatever inventory system is implemented, it must be able to allocate the goods available for sale between the cost of goods sold and ending inventory.

INVENTORY INFORMATION

A-Inventory			
Beginning balance	KNOWN		
Purchases	KNOWN	?????	Cost of goods sold
Ending balance	?????		

EXHIBIT 7-5

The type of inventory system used depends on the type and size of inventory involved and the cost of implementing the system. We will discuss two general types of inventory systems: perpetual and periodic systems.

Perpetual Inventory Systems

Perpetual inventory systems may be either physical inventory systems or cost inventory systems. They keep track of units or their associated costs, or both, on a continuous basis. Vesey's Seeds uses a perpetual system. This means that as soon as a unit is sold, it (or its cost) is immediately removed from the inventory account. In terms of the T-account in Exhibit 7-5, a credit is made to the account at the time of sale. The ending balance in the account can be calculated at any time to provide information about what is left in the account. In this type of system, the ending inventory balance and the cost of goods sold account are always up-to-date in terms of units and/or costs. Therefore, the information provided by this type of system is the most timely for decision purposes.

Learning Objective

4

Explain the difference between the perpetual inventory system and the periodic inventory system.

Up-to-date information, which is useful in any business, is crucial to some businesses, such as car dealerships. In the automobile business, the sales personnel must know what stock is still available for sale so that a car is not sold twice. Because selling prices are negotiated and the costs of different cars may vary dramatically, the cost of a specific car must be known at the time of sale so that an appropriate profit margin will be earned on the sale. The dealer's profitability depends on up-to-date information. Fortunately, the cost of keeping track of this information on a perpetual basis is not very high because the number of units of inventory is relatively small.

Contrast this with the decisions faced by the owner of a hardware store. Prices are not negotiated at the time of sale but rather each item is pre-priced and the stated price is what customers pay. Therefore, knowing the cost of each unit on a per-sale basis is not as important. The amount of inventory must be known in order to reorder stock, but reordering is probably not done on a daily basis. The cost of keeping track of each inventory item on a perpetual basis would be fairly substantial because the hardware store deals with numerous items in relatively large quantities. Consider, for example, using the perpetual system to keep track of all the types of nuts and bolts the store sells. The cost of implementing a perpetual system in this case would probably outweigh the benefits of having up-to-date information. Therefore, the hardware store would no doubt develop a periodic inventory system.

Periodic Inventory Systems

In a **periodic inventory system**, there is no entry to record the reduction in inventory at the time of sale. This may be because a perpetual inventory tracking system is too expensive to maintain, or because the cost of the item sold may not be known at the time of sale. In a retail store, for example, clerks know the retail price of an item because it is written on the sales tag, but they probably do not know the cost of the item to the store. To determine the amount sold and the amount left in inventory, the company must periodically stop business and physically count the units that are left, then assign costs to them. The cost of goods sold is then determined by subtracting the ending inventory value established by the count from the sum of the beginning inventory value and the purchases made during the period. This process assumes that all items included in the cost of goods sold were indeed sold, which may not always be the case. If items were stolen or misplaced, they would not be on the shelves or in the warehouse when the inventory was counted, and we would assume they had been sold. With a periodic inventory system, the company does not have up-to-date information during the period regarding the level of inventory or the cost of goods sold. It therefore needs to develop other methods to determine reorder points.

The counting and costing of ending inventory can be an expensive process, particularly for companies with large amounts of inventory. The company must close during the counting process and perhaps even turn away business. It must also pay individuals to do the counting. Because of the cost, it generally makes sense to count inventory only once a year. For internal control purposes, some companies count key items of inventory more frequently than once a year and often prepare financial statements more frequently than once a year. Accountants have therefore developed estimation methods that are used to establish inventory values for these interim reports.

A company may use a perpetual system to keep track of the physical units (remember the use of bar codes in the grocery store) but, because of the difficulty in determining unit costs, may use a periodic system to assign costs to units. This type of mixed system provides up-to-date information regarding the number of units available to aid in reordering or in production decisions. It does not provide up-to-date cost information. This may be perfectly acceptable to management if up-to-date unit information is more important than cost information.

Costs and Benefits of System Choice

One of the key factors in the choice of inventory systems is the cost of maintaining the system. The perpetual system provides better, more current information than the periodic system, but does so at a higher cost. However, as the cost of computer technology continues to decline, the implementation of perpetual systems has become a real possibility for companies that formerly would not have considered it. For example, the introduction of the bar code scanner in the grocery business has allowed businesses to keep track of units of inventory on a perpetual basis. Furthermore, with the introduction of **electronic data interchange** (EDI), some retailers use this information to automatically reorder inventory directly from the wholesaler or manufacturer.

With a perpetual system, management can make better business decisions. From the system, they know what items are selling and how many items they still have. They can more accurately determine what items to reorder and when that new order should be placed. In a periodic system, management must develop other techniques to determine the information that the perpetual system provides. For example, they might have a card placed near the bottom of a stack of merchandise. When the merchandise is sold and the card is visible, it is a signal that more must be ordered. This is a very crude system that depends on the card not being removed and on someone's noticing it when it becomes visible. Management also uses estimation methods in the periodic system to provide them with the information they need.

One advantage of the perpetual basis that we have not yet discussed is the identification of **inventory shrinkage**. *Shrinkage* is a general term that refers to losses of inventory due to theft, damage, and spoilage. Periodic systems are incapable of identifying shrinkage because shrinkage appears as a part of the cost of goods sold when the ending inventory value is subtracted from the beginning inventory plus purchases. A perpetual system can identify shrinkage because the system tells the company what the ending inventory should be. The company can then do a count to see what is actually left in its physical inventory. The difference is the shrinkage. Physically counting the inventory is necessary under both systems and the fact that shrinkage can be identified under the perpetual system is an added bonus. Companies with perpetual systems may, however, stagger the counting of inventories so that not all inventories are counted at the same time. The closest that a periodic system can come to the perpetual system in the identification of shrinkage is to use estimation methods. A company may be able to estimate how much inventory should be on hand. When it counts the inventory, it can then compare it with the estimated amount and get a crude measure of shrinkage.

Learning Objective

5

Discuss some criteria used by companies when choosing an inventory system.

accounting in the news

INVENTORY SHRINKAGE

Molson Inc. has decided it spills too much beer and wants to live up to the less messy standards of some of its competitors.

Reducing the shrinkage rate—the amount spilled and wasted during brewing and bottling operations—is one way the brewer expected to save money as part of an overall cost-cutting campaign. Company executives estimated that reducing shrinkage could save some $3 million per year. Molson's shrinkage rate was about 2%, compared to an industry average of 0.5% to 1.5%.

The company said it could save $100 million per year just by meeting the same operating standards as its top competitors. For example, the brewer expected to generate savings of $20 million by updating and improving processes in bottling and packaging, and another $20 million by replacing and taking care of equipment more diligently.

Source: "Spilled beer costs Molson millions a year," by Sean Silcoff, *National Post (Financial Post)*, March 2, 2002, p. FP4.

The cost of an inventory system must be balanced against the benefits of the information it provides. The main benefit of the perpetual system is its timely information. When inventory information is needed on a timely basis for pricing, reordering, or other important decisions, the benefits of the perpetual system must be carefully considered even though the system is likely to be more expensive.

COST FLOW ASSUMPTIONS

Learning Objective

6

Describe the three cost flow assumptions and calculate cost of goods sold and ending inventory under each.

In order to determine the cost of goods sold and the cost of ending inventory, the cost of specific units must somehow be linked to the actual physical units that either were sold (cost of goods sold) or remain in ending inventory. For some businesses, this is not difficult because the physical units are unique and records are kept that specifically identify the unit and its cost. Under these circumstances, the company can match the physical units with their costs using the **specific identification method**. Finning International Inc. (Exhibit 7-4) would be able to identify the cost of its on-hand equipment in its inventory. Each piece of equipment would have its own invoice price and registration number and, therefore, be unique.

In some businesses, the ability to specifically identify costs of individual physical units is not feasible. Consider a shoe retailer who buys multiple styles, sizes, and colours of shoes in a single order. If the retailer never ordered the same shoe again, it would be possible to determine the cost of a specific pair of shoes. However, once a second order is placed and arrives at the store, it is no longer possible to identify whether a specific pair of shoes came from the first order or from the second unless the retailer took the time to mark the second purchase to distinguish it from the first. It is unlikely that retailers would incur the additional cost of specifically identifying each new order. Therefore, in businesses in which specific identification is not feasible, a logical assumption is generally made about how costs flow through the company.

POSSIBLE COST-FLOW ASSUMPTIONS

1. The first item purchased is the first item sold (FIFO).

2. The last item purchased is the first item sold (LIFO).

3. The cost of the items is determined using an average of the cost of the items purchased.

As we get into the various cost flow possibilities, we are going to describe the **cost flow assumptions** related to a periodic inventory system only. The reason for restricting the choice to just the periodic system is that we want to concentrate on showing you the methods, and their financial statement implications, rather than working through six methods (three under each system). Under the perpetual system, LIFO and the average method will produce slightly different inventory cost amounts. FIFO will produce the same amounts under both the periodic and perpetual systems.

ethics in accounting

Ethics in Accounting

■ The determination of the ending balance in inventory is crucial not only for determining the balance sheet value for inventory, but also for establishing the cost of goods sold for the income statement. Any overstatement of ending inventory will result in an understatement of cost of goods sold and, therefore, an overstatement of income. There are many situations that put pressure on managers and employees to show higher net income, such as budget targets and bonus plans. There may also be incentives to overstate ending inventory if it is to serve as collateral for loans. Auditors are also interested in establishing ending inventory values and typically are required under audit guidelines to be present at the physical count of ending inventory to make sure inventory counts are accurate and values are appropriately determined.

Note as we go through the following assumptions that we are discussing *cost flows*, not *physical flows*. We will be suggesting logical assumptions for cost flows that may be entirely opposite to the way inventory physically flows through the company. To illustrate these assumptions, we will use the data in Exhibit 7-6 for Ted's Toasters, Inc.

Three cost flow assumptions—first-in, first-out (FIFO), last-in, first-out (LIFO), and weighted average—constitute three logical ways of assigning costs to units sold or remaining in inventory. FIFO assumes that the first unit purchased is also the first unit sold, hence first-in, first-out. LIFO assumes, however, that the last unit purchased is the first unit sold, hence last-in, first-out. Weighted average assigns an average cost to both cost of goods sold and ending inventory. Let's look at each of these approaches in more detail.

Ted's Toasters starts the period with six toasters in inventory. Note that the beginning inventory cost is $84 and that the unit cost is $14. Only in the very first period of operations are the beginning values in inventory the same under all three assumptions. Because different cost flow assumptions assign costs to units in different ways, in subsequent periods each assumption will result in different per-unit amounts being assigned to ending inventory, which in turn becomes beginning inventory for the next period. Each of these cost flow assumptions is discussed in the following subsections. Refer to Exhibit 7-6 as each method is discussed.

EXHIBIT 7-6	

■ TED'S TOASTERS, INC.

Inventory of Toasters

Date		Units	Unit cost	Total
January 1	Beginning inventory	6	$14.00	$ 84.00
January 10	Purchase #1	20	14.25	285.00
January 20	Purchase #2	10	14.50	145.00
Goods available for sale		36		$514.00

Sale record				
		Units	Unit price	Total
January 15	Sale #1	12	$32.00	$384.00
January 25	Sale #2	15	32.50	487.50
		27		$871.50

First-In, First-Out (FIFO)

The **first-in, first-out**, or **FIFO**, method is still the most commonly used method in Canada, although weighted average is a very close second. FIFO assigns the first costs to the first units sold. This means that ending inventory units will be matched to costs for the most recent purchases. One way to visualize this method is to consider the flow through a pipeline, as shown in Exhibit 7-7. Purchases enter one end of the pipeline. As new purchases are made, they enter the same end of the pipeline, pushing the first purchases further into the pipe. Goods that get sold come out the other end of the pipeline. Therefore, the ones that get sold first are also the ones that entered the pipeline first. The goods still left in the pipeline at the end of the period are the ending inventory. While the acronym FIFO is appropriate for this method, it refers to what happens to the cost of goods sold, not to the ending inventory. A more accurate acronym for ending inventory is LISH, for **last-in, still-here**.

FIFO VISUALIZATION

EXHIBIT 7-7

Using the Ted's Toasters data (Exhibit 7-6) and the FIFO assumption, we can assign a cost to the cost of goods sold and ending inventory as follows:

Cost of goods sold (27 units)

6	units @ $14.00 (beginning inventory)	$ 84.00
+ 20	units @ $14.25 (first purchase)	285.00
+ 1	unit @ $14.50 (second purchase)	14.50
27	units	$383.50

Ending inventory (9 units)

9	units @ $14.50 (second purchase)	$130.50

Note how the sum of units in cost of goods sold and ending inventory (27 + 9) equals the 36 units in goods available for sale. The sum of the dollar amounts ($383.50 + $130.50) equals the dollar amount of the goods available for sale, $514.00. If the dollar amount of ending inventory were to increase, the dollar amount of the cost of goods sold would have to decrease because the sum of the two must add up to the dollar amount of the goods available for sale. Any errors in counting ending inventory or assigning costs will have an immediate impact on the cost of goods sold and, therefore, net income.

FIFO describes fairly accurately the physical flow of goods in most businesses. For example, in grocery stores new items are put behind old items on the shelf so that old items are sold first. If the grocery store did not rotate inventory in this way, some items would sit on the shelf for months, risking spoilage.

Under GAAP, the matching of costs to physical units does not depend on the physical flow of goods. GAAP attempts to provide the best measure of periodic net income, which is not necessarily achieved by choosing a cost flow assumption that matches the physical flow of the goods. Under FIFO, the costs assigned to the cost of goods sold are the costs from beginning inventory and from earlier purchases.

Last-In, First-Out (LIFO)

The **last-in, first-out**, or **LIFO**, method is used very infrequently in Canada. It assigns the last costs in (i.e., the costs of the most recent purchases) to the first units sold. This means that ending inventory is assigned the costs associated with the first purchases (or beginning inventory). The LIFO method is visualized in Exhibit 7-8. Imagine inventory as something stored in a bin. New purchases are added to the bin from the top, adding new layers of inventory to what is already in the bin (beginning inventory). Goods sold are taken from the top layer of the bin. The costs associated with these units are, therefore, the costs associated with the most recent purchases. Ending inventory, on the other hand, is associated with the cost of the layers at the date each was purchased. The bottom layers could have been purchased in a much earlier period. The acronym used to refer to ending inventory is FISH, for **first-in, still-here**.

EXHIBIT 7-8

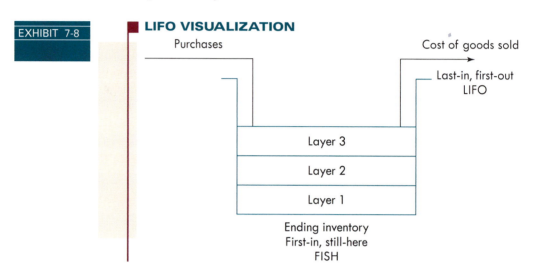

■ **LIFO VISUALIZATION**

Using Ted's Toasters (Exhibit 7-6) and the LIFO assumption, let us now assign a cost to cost of goods sold and ending inventory.

Cost of goods sold (27 units)

10	units @ $14.50 (second purchase)	$145.00
17	units @ $14.25 (first purchase)	242.25
27	units	$387.25

Ending inventory (9 units)

3	units @ $14.25 (first purchase)	$ 42.75
6	units @ $14.00 (beginning inventory)	84.00
9	units	$126.75

Note again how the sum of the units in cost of goods sold and ending inventory (27 + 9) equals the 36 units in goods available for sale. The sum of the dollar amounts ($387.25 + $126.75) equals the dollar amount of the goods available for sale, $514.00. Note also that the dollar amount of ending inventory is lower than it is under FIFO and that, therefore, the dollar amount of the cost of goods sold is higher. The unit cost of inventory has been rising through January, and because the cost of goods sold is assigned costs from the most recent purchases, it receives higher unit costs than under FIFO.

The main problem with LIFO is the cost assigned to ending inventory. In Ted's Toasters, the cost was the $14.00 from beginning inventory and the $14.25 from the first purchase. When purchases are made in February, LIFO will assign those new purchase costs to the cost of goods sold, and again assign the $14.00 and $14.25 to ending inventory. Several years from now, the unit costs assigned to ending inventory could still be the $14.00 and $14.25. These old costs will not show the inventory on the balance sheet at a very realistic value. In fact, if they were left unadjusted, the inventory costs could be substantially below market value. Recognizing this problem with LIFO, accountants have developed several techniques to adjust the inventory amount to a more realistic value while still assigning the most recent costs to the cost of goods sold. The discussion of these methods is, however, beyond the scope of an introductory textbook.

> **Learning Objective**
> **7**
> *Explain the shortcomings of LIFO and why it is rarely used in Canada.*

Remember that the diagram in Exhibit 7-8 is concerned with the flow of costs, not the physical flow of inventory. Not many inventories actually follow a LIFO physical flow, although there are a few examples: using steel plates from the top of a pile, taking coal from the top of a pile, or selling nails from a keg of nails. This, however, does not prevent companies from using the LIFO cost assumption to assign costs. LIFO represents a systematic, logical way of assigning costs. In fact, the cost of goods sold on the income statement includes the most recent costs and is, therefore, a good match to the revenue of the period.

LIFO and FIFO represent the two extremes of cost assumptions. LIFO will produce the highest cost of goods sold and, therefore, the lowest net income when unit costs are rising. This might be of interest to a manager who wants to discourage shareholders from requesting cash dividends. FIFO, on the other hand, will produce the lowest cost of goods sold and, therefore, the highest net income under the same conditions. This might be of interest to a manager who wants to attract new investors. Because these two assumptions produce dramatically different financial results during times of changing prices, it is important for users of financial statements to know which method is being used and to understand the managerial objectives that might underlie the selection of that method.

Of the three methods we have examined thus far (specific identification, FIFO, and LIFO), LIFO is used the least often in Canada for several reasons. First, it produces the lowest net income when costs are rising. Second, the value of inventory on the balance sheet quickly becomes unrealistic. Third, the Canada Customs and Revenue Agency does not accept it as a method for determining inventory costs for tax purposes, probably because it produces the lowest net income and would therefore produce the lowest taxable income. We now turn our attention to the fourth and final potential cost flow assumption: the weighted average method.

Weighted Average

The **weighted average** method, the second most commonly used method in Canada, calculates an average cost for all the units available for sale in a given period and assigns that average cost to both the units that are sold during the period, and those that remain in ending inventory. Exhibit 7-9 provides a visualization of this method. Imagine inventory as a liquid stored in a tank, such as gasoline at a service station. Purchases are dumped into the tank and mixed with beginning inventory and previous purchases. Inventory that is sold is therefore a mixture of beginning inventory and recent purchases.

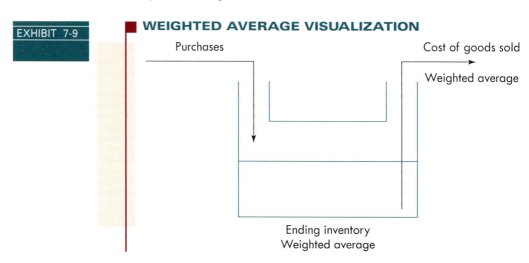

EXHIBIT 7-9

■ **WEIGHTED AVERAGE VISUALIZATION**

In Ted's Toasters, the average cost is calculated by taking the total cost of the goods available for sale ($514.00) and dividing it by the number of toasters available (36) to produce an average cost of $14.278 per unit. This unit cost is then assigned to all the units in ending inventory (9 × $14.278 = $128.50), and to the 27 units sold (27 × $14.278 = $385.51). Note that when the ending inventory of $128.50 is added to the cost of goods sold of $385.51, the total is $514.01—a one-cent difference in the total value of goods available for sale. This error occurred because we had to round the unit cost. When using the weighted average method, use the calculated unit cost to determine either the ending inventory or the cost of goods sold. Determine the other amount by subtracting your calculated amount from the value of goods available for sale.

Note that the weighted average method produces results on the income statement and balance sheet that lie somewhere between those of LIFO and FIFO. Because it produces a lower pre-tax income than FIFO, many companies in Canada choose it for tax purposes. They like the higher net income produced by FIFO for reporting purposes and so will maintain two sets of inventory records. This is acceptable practice. The recent increase in the use of the weighted average method for reporting purposes is an indication that companies are choosing to maintain only one set of inventory records.

Cost Flow Assumption Choice

All three of the cost flow assumptions we have discussed are in accordance with GAAP. Given free choice, which method should Ted's Toasters use to represent the operating results for the period? This depends on the fundamental objectives of management. Examine Exhibit 7-10 to see the different financial statement effects of each of the three assumptions.

FINANCIAL STATEMENT RESULTS

EXHIBIT 7-10

	FIFO	Cost flow assumption Weighted Average	LIFO
Sales revenue	$871.50	$871.50	$871.50
Cost of goods sold	383.50	385.50	387.25
Gross profit	$488.00	$486.00	$484.25
Balance sheet			
Inventory	$130.50	$128.50	$126.75

Ted's Toasters would probably like to use LIFO because it produces the smallest amount of profit and would therefore result in the smallest amount of tax liability. However, because the Canada Customs and Revenue Agency will not allow it, Ted's tax adviser would instead recommend weighted average.

Management in Ted's Toasters may, however, be more interested in getting a bonus to increase their own compensation. If Ted's managers calculate their bonuses based on reported net income, they would be more likely to choose FIFO, which produces the highest amount of net income. Management may also be tempted to use FIFO if the company has a loan agreement with a lender that requires it to maintain a specified current ratio (current assets/current liabilities) and the company is in danger of not meeting the required ratio test. When prices are rising, first-in, first-out produces the highest value of inventory that goes into the numerator of the current ratio.

Political sensitivity may also influence the cost flow decision. Suppose the company is in the oil and gas industry, and recent disruptions in world oil markets have caused the price of oil to rise significantly. Consumer advocates have been criticizing the oil and gas industry for profiting from this situation by raising prices beyond what is required by the change in world prices. They advocate an excess profits tax on the industry. In this situation, the company may want to avoid reporting income at any higher level than is necessary. Last-in, first-out may be the best choice to minimize the income effects of these changing prices.

Constraints on Selection

The choice of inventory methods is not entirely without constraints. First of all, GAAP requires the company to select the method that is the fairest matching of costs with revenues, regardless of the actual physical flow of inventory. To understand what is meant by fair matching, consider the situation at Ted's Toasters. It has been experiencing a rise in its costs, that is, a period of inflation. The selling price has risen, which means it has been able to adjust the prices it charges to customers to reflect this rise in costs.

Consider the income reported using the LIFO method. The $484.25 in the gross margin is a result of matching the cost of $387.25 (the most recent purchases) with the current revenue of $871.50. If prices were to stabilize at this point, Ted's could continue to produce a steady profit margin on future sales because it can continue to buy goods at $14.50. On the other hand, the gross margin of $488.00 produced by using FIFO matches a cost of $383.50 (old costs) against the current revenue. Considering that the current replacement cost of that unit is $14.50, the income produced under FIFO can be split up into a **current gross margin** and a **realized holding gain** as shown in Exhibit 7-11. The sum of the current gross margin and the realized holding gain is the amount of profit reported in Exhibit 7-10 under GAAP. The presentation in Exhibit 7-11 is shown for illustrative purposes and is not used under GAAP. It does illustrate that income produced using FIFO is a combination of a gross margin that can be expected to continue into the future and a realized holding gain that cannot be duplicated in the future. The holding gain is often referred to as a **paper profit**. Users should be aware that because lower, older costs form part of the cost of goods sold, some of the resulting gross margin is not a true profit because some of the profit must be used to replace the inventory sold with more expensive units.

EXHIBIT 7-11

■ FIFO INCOME AND HOLDING GAINS

Sales revenue	$871.50		
Replacement cost of goods sold	391.50	(27 @ $14.50)	
Current gross margin			$480.00
Replacement cost of goods sold	$391.50		
Historical cost of goods sold	383.50		
Realized holding gain			8.00
Reported gross margin			$488.00

As indicated in Exhibit 7-11, holding gains on inventory are, in fact, recognized at the time the item is sold. Holding gains on items in ending inventory are not recognized under GAAP. Holding losses on items in ending inventory are recognized to the extent that writedowns occur in the application of the lower of cost and market rule. Therefore, under GAAP, the only changes in the value of inventory that are not recognized are the unrealized holding gains on ending inventory. These holding gains are probably small for companies using FIFO because ending inventory is stated at the most recent prices. With LIFO, however, these unrealized holding gains can be large.

Given Ted's circumstances, it could be argued that LIFO produces a better measure of periodic net income because the realized holding gains that are contained in net income using FIFO will not persist into the future. It is generally true that during periods of inflation LIFO produces a better measure of net income. Note, however, that LIFO may also produce the least accurate measure of the value of ending inventory under such circumstances because the prices in inventory may be very old and very low compared to current prices.

Under another set of circumstances, LIFO might not be the best choice. For example, if prices had been stable throughout the period (say, all units had a cost of $14), then all the cost flow assumptions would produce the same income. The least expensive inventory method should be applied under these circumstances.

Reports from Other Countries

The predominant practice with regard to cost flow assumptions around the world is to assume either FIFO or weighted average. LIFO is not permitted in France and the United Kingdom and used only in limited situations in most countries other than the United States. The significant use of LIFO in the United States is partially driven by its allowance for tax purposes and the LIFO conformity rule (if you use LIFO for tax purposes, you must also use it for reporting purposes). In Germany, the reporting books are essentially the same as the tax books, and prior to 1990, LIFO was not permitted under the tax code. Starting in 1990, however, German law was changed to allow LIFO. Note the following inventory disclosure by DaimlerChrysler in its 2000 financial statements:

Inventories—Inventory is valued at the lower of acquisition or manufacturing cost or market, cost being generally determined on the basis of an average or first-in, first-out method (FIFO). Certain of the Group's U.S. businesses' inventories are valued using the last-in, first-out method (LIFO). Manufacturing costs comprise direct material and labour and applicable manufacturing overheads, including depreciation charges.

COST FLOW ASSUMPTIONS AND CHANGING PRICES

As the Ted's Toasters example illustrates, the use of LIFO during periods of rising prices generally produces the lowest net income, whereas the use of FIFO produces the highest net income. The reverse would be true during periods of deflation although the use of the lower of cost and market rule would tend to modify this. In Canada, there have been virtually no sustained periods of deflation in recent memory. However, that is not to say that some companies have not faced periods of decreasing unit prices in the goods they use or produce. Take, for example, the microchip industry, which has seen significant drops in the cost per unit of its products. For these types of business, FIFO would make sense for tax purposes: in cases of declining costs, FIFO would produce the highest cost of goods sold and the lowest net income.

In periods of stable prices, all three cost flow assumptions produce the same values for cost of goods sold and ending inventory. The differences among the assumptions are driven by changes in prices across time. The magnitude of the effect depends on the size of the change in prices and on the size and turnover characteristics of the inventory. Users of financial statements, therefore, need to know more than just the inventory method that is being used. They must also know the type of inventory being sold and how the economy may be affecting the cost of that inventory.

Learning Objective

Describe the impact of inflation on each of the cost flow assumptions.

Consider the use of FIFO and the effects of changing prices. The balance sheet reflects the most recent prices. The cost of goods sold reflects older prices. How old can these prices be? The oldest costs in the cost of goods sold figure are those that existed in beginning inventory. Those costs may have been incurred in the last month of the last year or even earlier, depending on how often the company turns over its inventory. Inventory turnover measures the number of times the total inventory is sold during the period.

If the inventory turnover ratio is 12, the inventory turns over on average once a month, and the ending inventory costs come from the purchases made in the last month of the year. If inventory turnover is four, the company turns over its inventory on average once a quarter, and the oldest costs in ending inventory could come from the beginning of the last quarter of the year. Therefore, while these costs are viewed as "old," in reality they are not very old. When prices are not rising very rapidly, the differences between current year prices and those from the end of the last year will be relatively small.

Now, consider LIFO. Cost of goods sold reflects the most recent prices. Inventory, on the other hand, reflects old prices. How old can these old prices be? The oldest prices in ending inventory are associated with the oldest layer of inventory, which could have been acquired in the first year the company was in business. For a 100-year-old company, these unit prices could be from a century ago. Even with small levels of annual inflation, the cumulative difference in prices for these layers and current prices can be very substantial. The effects of inflation can cause the LIFO inventory value of a company to be very different from the current replacement cost of the inventory. For this reason, LIFO companies often provide information in the footnotes to their annual reports to inform the reader of the current cost of their inventories.

The choice of cost flow assumption depends on the nature of the inventory, but the same assumption does not have to apply to all inventories held by the company. For example, note the multiple inventory methods used by **Suncor Energy Inc.** in Exhibit 7-12.

EXHIBIT 7-12

SUNCOR ENERGY INC. (2001)

Excerpted from the Notes to the Statements

Summary of significant accounting policies
(g) Inventories
Inventories of crude oil and refined products are valued at the lower of cost using the last-in, first-out (LIFO) method and net realizable value.
Materials and supplies are valued at the lower of average cost and net realizable value.

Reports from Other Countries

NAFTA Facts

United States—Inventory accounting is very similar to Canada except that LIFO is more commonly used because it is acceptable for tax purposes, and if it is used for tax purposes, it must also be used for reporting purposes.

Mexico—Inventory is initially recorded at its acquisition or production cost and then restated at the balance sheet date, using either price level adjusted or replacement cost amounts, subject to the constraint that this amount cannot exceed net realizable value. Cost flow methods are essentially the same as in Canada.

INVENTORY ESTIMATION

There are several circumstances in which a company needs the cost of goods sold or inventory value, but either chooses not to count inventory (too costly to close the business to count inventory) or simply cannot count it (it has been stolen or destroyed). In these cases, the company may attempt to estimate the cost of goods sold amount if it wants to prepare monthly income statements. It may need to estimate the amount and value of inventory for insurance purposes if the inventory is destroyed or stolen. As mentioned earlier, it is difficult to determine inventory shrinkage when using the periodic system. Companies will often estimate the inventory before they start the annual physical inventory count so that they can determine if shrinkage has occurred.

Using the Cost-to-Sales Ratio

One way to estimate the cost of goods sold is to multiply the sales revenue for the period (a figure that is readily determinable) by the normal **cost-to-sales ratio**. The normal cost-to-sales ratio reflects the normal markup that the company applies to its products. For example, a company that normally marks up its products by 50% prices an item that costs $60 at $90. The cost-to-sales ratio then is 67% ($60/$90). If the sales for a given month are $12,000, the estimated cost of goods sold is $8,000 (67% × $12,000).

This cost-to-sales ratio can be used to estimate ending inventory as well. The company would be able to determine the cost of the goods available for sale by referring to the accounting records and finding the beginning inventory and the

Learning Objective

9

Estimate a value for ending inventory using the cost-to-sales ratio method.

purchases for the period. For example, if the beginning inventory is $2,000 and the purchases for the period were $9,000, the goods available for sale would be $11,000. If we use the cost-to-sales ratio and the sales amount from the previous paragraph, we can determine that the cost of goods sold is $8,000 for the period. Because we know that goods available for sale must equal cost of goods sold plus ending inventory, all we need to do is subtract the calculated cost of goods sold ($8,000) from the goods available for sale ($11,000) to find the cost of ending inventory ($3,000). This method is often referred to as the **gross margin estimation method.**

STATEMENT ANALYSIS CONSIDERATIONS

Because of the diversity of cost flow assumptions that can be made by companies and the significant differences that these assumptions can cause in the financial statements, adjustments must be made when inventory ratios are compared across companies. Cross-industry analyses are most affected by cost flow assumptions. Analyses of the same company over time are not affected as much, as long as the inventory method has been consistently applied (the company used FIFO or weighted average all the time). Changes in the cost flow assumption across time make time series analyses difficult. When using the inventory or cost of goods sold amounts in ratio analysis, keep these points in mind as you evaluate your results.

Inventory Turnover

Learning Objective

10

Calculate the inventory turnover ratio and explain how it can be interpreted by users.

The one ratio that looks exclusively at inventory is the **inventory turnover ratio.** This ratio tells the user how fast inventory is sold or how long it is held before it is sold. It is calculated as:

$$\text{Inventory turnover} = \frac{\text{Cost of goods sold}}{\text{Average inventory}}$$

The numerator contains the cost of goods sold, which measures the costs assigned to all the items of inventory that were sold. The denominator contains the average inventory. Average inventory is used, where possible, rather than ending inventory because it represents a more appropriate measure of inventory levels if the inventory level has changed over the year. Average inventory is the beginning inventory plus the ending inventory in a year divided by two. Inventory turnover for **Sun-Rype Products Ltd.** for 2001 was:

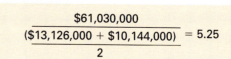

$$\frac{\$61,030,000}{\dfrac{(\$13,126,000 + \$10,144,000)}{2}} = 5.25$$

If the turnover is 5.25, it takes Sun-Rype Products about 70 days to sell an average-sized batch of inventory. In order to determine if a turnover of 5.25 is reasonable for Sun-Rype Products, you would need to calculate the ratio for previous years so that you could see if it was changing. You should also compare Sun-Rype's ratio with those of other companies in the same industry to see how it compares with its competitors. A look at the 2000 inventory turnover shows that turnover was the same in 2000:

$$\frac{\$58{,}464{,}000}{\dfrac{(\$10{,}144{,}000 + \$12{,}105{,}000)}{2}} = 5.25$$

The 70 days mentioned in the previous paragraph is calculated by dividing the number of days in a year (365) by the inventory turnover. This will tell you approximately how many days inventory is held before it is sold. For Sun-Rype Products, the number of days inventory was held in 2001 and 2000 was:

$$365/5.25 = 69.5 \text{ days}$$

One concern about this ratio exists when LIFO is used. The ratio attempts to provide information about how fast the physical inventory turns over. Ideally, the ratio would put the number of units sold in the numerator and the number of units in ending inventory in the denominator. Because information about the number of units sold or in ending inventory is not provided in the financial statements, we use the cost figures provided in the statements and divide cost of goods sold by the average cost of inventory. With FIFO and weighted average, we can use values in the numerator and denominator without risk of distortion since both values were determined in similar time frames. Because LIFO assigns the most recent costs to the cost of goods sold, the units in the numerator are stated at current prices. The units in the denominator, however, may be stated at very old unit prices because of the layers that exist with LIFO. Because of this, during periods of rising prices the ratio is likely to overstate the turnover since higher-priced units are in the numerator and lower-priced units are in the denominator. Because very few companies in Canada use LIFO, this will not pose a problem for most of the analyses that you do.

Other Ratios

Other ratios are affected by the use of LIFO versus FIFO if they contain inventory figures or the cost of goods sold. The most dramatic effects are in those ratios that use balance sheet information. The ratio that is probably most affected is the current ratio, which compares current assets to current liabilities (current assets/current liabilities). If costs are rising, the choice of LIFO can cause this ratio to be significantly lower than it would be with FIFO. Also, remember that the current ratio is used in many debt agreements. If a company using LIFO is in danger of violating the requirement for this ratio, a switch to FIFO might solve the problem.

On the income statement, the gross profit percentage (gross profit /sales) is also affected by the choice of FIFO versus LIFO. In Exhibit 7-10, the gross profit for Ted's Toasters varied from $488.00 under FIFO to $484.25 under LIFO. The difference is less than $4.00, but remember that we are dealing with the sale of only 27 units of a single type of inventory. The gross margin percentage is 56% under FIFO and 55% under LIFO. With a greater fluctuation in unit costs and more years of application of the individual methods, the difference between the two would be more dramatic.

SUMMARY

This chapter discussed inventory, a current asset that is vital to the health of a company, and its related expense, cost of goods sold. Because of the many kinds of inventory, managing all aspects of inventory is a very complex task. Managers need to order the right kind and amount of inventory, price it competitively (but high enough to ensure that the company makes a profit), and safeguard it so that it cannot be stolen. Over time, accountants have developed two major systems for accounting for inventory: the perpetual system, which keeps a continuous record of the inventory on hand, and the periodic system, which records the purchase of inventory but does not cost the amount that has been sold until the end of an accounting period. Within these two systems, four methods have developed for assigning costs to inventory: specific identification, FIFO, LIFO, and weighted average. Each of these methods results in a different cost for ending inventory and cost of goods sold. Users need to be aware of how these methods are used so that they can factor their effect into any ratio analysis that they perform. Because counting inventory to determine the amount on hand is a costly endeavour, accountants have developed methods for estimating inventory. Estimates are used for interim reports and for establishing a pre-count value against which management is able to compare the actual physical count of inventory. In this chapter, we described the cost-to-sales ratio method for estimating inventory. We finished the chapter by discussing the inventory turnover ratio, a ratio that helps users evaluate the management of inventory.

At this point, all the major current asset accounts have been covered, and attention turns next to the noncurrent assets, which have longer lives than current assets. The benefits of these assets are received over much longer periods of time than those of current assets. The next chapter considers the most common noncurrent asset accounts, with an emphasis on property, plant, and equipment.

**Additional
Demonstration
Problems**

SUMMARY PROBLEM

The income statement, balance sheet, and Note 4 from the 2001 annual report of **IPSCO Inc.** are shown in Exhibit 7-13. IPSCO is a Canadian company that manufactures steel products. Note 2 of the report states that "inventories are valued at the lowest of average cost, replacement cost, and net realizable value."

1. In 2001, IPSCO's net income declined from $46,848 thousand to $27,405 thousand. Based solely on the sale of inventory, can you suggest reasons why the net income declined in 2001?

2. Calculate the inventory turnover for IPSCO for 2001. Provide a brief discussion of what this ratio means.

3. Calculate the current ratio for IPSCO for 2001 and 2000. How important is the inventory value in this ratio?

IPSCO Consolidated Financial Statements 2001

EXHIBIT 7-13

IPSCO Inc. Consolidated Statements of Financial Position
As at 31 December
(thousands of United States dollars)

	Notes	2001	2000
CURRENT ASSETS			
Cash and cash equivalents		$ 37,492	$ 18,151
Accounts receivable			
Trade less allowances	3	106,770	135,412
Other		9,938	31,037
Inventories	4	239,394	225,958
Prepaid expenses		2,031	2,631
Income taxes allocated to future years	5	44,490	34,409
		440,115	447,598
CURRENT LIABILITIES			
Bank indebtedness	7	35,000	–
Accounts payable and accrued charges	6	129,366	133,799
Accrued payroll and related liabilities		15,315	16,838
Income and other taxes payable		2,111	–
Current portion of long-term debt	7	21,100	21,100
Other current liabilities		13,926	10,508
		216,818	182,245
WORKING CAPITAL		223,297	265,353
Capital assets	8	1,163,803	1,081,549
Deferred charges		2,026	2,695
Income taxes allocated to future years	5	126,123	88,066
		1,291,952	1,172,310
TOTAL INVESTMENT		1,515,249	1,437,663
Long-term debt	7	386,809	343,822
Deferred pension liability	9	234	4,365
Income taxes allocated to future years	5	142,668	104,842
		529,711	453,029
SHAREHOLDERS' EQUITY		$ 985,538	$ 984,634
Derived from			
Preferred shares	10	$ 98,545	$ 98,572
Common shares	11	256,163	255,772
Subordinated notes	12	104,250	104,250
Retained earnings	13	491,777	475,551
Cumulative translation adjustment		34,803	50,489
		$ 985,538	$ 984,634
Commitments and contingencies	17,19&22		

The accompanying notes are an integral part of the consolidated financial statements.

Approved by the Board

Burton Joyce, Director

David Sutherland, Director

EXHIBIT 7-13
CONT.

IPSCO Consolidated Financial Statements 2001

IPSCO Inc. Consolidated Statements of Income and Retained Earnings
Years Ended 31 December
(thousands of United States dollars except per share data)

	Notes	2001	2000	1999
Revenue				
Sales		$ 903,743	$ 949,263	$ 808,251
Expenses				
Cost of sales, exclusive of the following items		770,742	764,198	615,827
Selling, research and administration		57,527	62,076	46,122
Interest on long-term debt	7	6,634	6,934	19,067
Amortization of capital assets		37,107	35,257	29,670
Litigation settlement	22	(39,000)	–	–
Provision for loss on assets held for sale or redeployment	8	10,000	–	–
		843,010	868,465	710,686
Income before income taxes		60,733	80,798	97,565
Income taxes	5	21,865	23,125	23,283
NET INCOME		38,868	57,673	74,282
Dividends on preferred shares including part VI.I tax	10	5,692	5,935	5,895
Interest on subordinated notes net of income tax	12	5,771	4,890	133
NET INCOME AVAILABLE TO COMMON SHAREHOLDERS		$ 27,405	$ 46,848	$ 68,254
EARNINGS PER COMMON SHARE – Basic	14	$ 0.67	$ 1.15	$ 1.68
EARNINGS PER COMMON SHARE – Diluted	14	$ 0.66	$ 0.91	$ 1.58
RETAINED EARNINGS AT BEGINNING OF YEAR, as previously reported		$ 475,551	$ 451,548	$ 397,051
Cumulative effect of change in accounting policy	9	–	(8,977)	–
RETAINED EARNINGS AT BEGINNING OF YEAR, as adjusted		475,551	442,571	397,051
NET INCOME		38,868	57,673	74,282
		514,419	500,244	471,333
Dividends on preferred shares including part VI.I tax	10	5,692	5,935	5,895
Interest on subordinated notes net of income tax	12	5,771	4,890	133
Dividends on common shares	13	11,179	13,748	13,744
Issue costs net of income tax	10&12	–	120	13
RETAINED EARNINGS AT END OF YEAR		$ 491,777	$ 475,551	$ 451,548

The accompanying notes are an integral part of the consolidated financial statements.

27

SUGGESTED SOLUTION TO SUMMARY PROBLEM

All figures in the solution are in thousands.

1. In 1999, the gross margin on revenues of $808,251 was $192,424, or 23.8%. In 2000, the gross margin on $949,263 of revenues was $185,065, or 19.5%. Note that the revenue increased but the gross margin decreased. In 2001, the revenues decreased to $903,743. The gross margin also decreased to $133,001, or 14.7%. In other words, revenues decreased but the cost of sales increased, which caused the gross margin to decrease quite sharply. The decrease in the margin from 19.5% to 14.7% makes it more difficult for IPSCO to cover all of its other costs. IPSCO manufactures steel products and is, therefore, subject to international steel markets, which experienced declining prices in 2000 and 2001. When prices decline, it is important for companies to reduce their production costs so that they remain competitive.

2.
$$\frac{\$770,742}{\dfrac{(\$239,394 + \$225,958)}{2}} = 3.3$$

$$365 \,/\, 3.3 = 110.6 \text{ days}$$

IPSCO's inventory turnover is 3.3. It takes about 110 days for it to sell its inventory. IPSCO is an international supplier of steel products. It is probable that because of the nature of its product, it will hold inventory for several months without selling it. Without additional information about IPSCO's activities in previous years or about its competitors, it is not possible to comment further on this ratio.

3.
$$\text{Current ratio (2000)} = \frac{\$447,598}{\$182,245} = 2.46$$

$$\text{Current ratio (2001)} = \frac{\$440,115}{\$216,818} = 2.03$$

Inventory represents approximately 50% of the current assets in 2000 and approximately 54% in 2001. This means that it has a significant impact on this ratio. Without the inventory, the ratio in both years would be close to or below one. The company would have difficulty meeting its current liabilities without selling inventory.

ABBREVIATIONS USED

EDI   Electronic data interchange
FIFO   First-in, first-out
FISH   First-in, still-here
IASB   International Accounting Standards Board
LCM   Lower of cost and market
LIFO   Last-in, first-out
LISH   Last-in, still-here
NRV   Net realizable value

SYNONYMS

Entry market/Input market/Wholesale market
Exit Market/Output market/Retail market
Entry price/Input price/Replacement cost
Exit price/Output price/Net realizable value
Freight in/Transportation in

GLOSSARY

Cost flow assumption   An assumption made as to how the costs of inventory should be assigned to individual units when it is impossible or impractical to assign costs specifically to units.

Current gross margin   The difference between the current selling price of a unit of inventory and its current replacement cost.

Electronic data interchange   The linkage of two companies with computers such that inventory is ordered directly over the computer connection.

Entry market   The market from which goods or materials enter the company; sometimes also referred to as the *wholesale market.*

Exit market   The market in which goods exit the company; sometimes also referred to as the *retail market.*

FIFO   An acronym (first-in, first-out) for the cost flow assumption that assigns the cost of the first unit into the company to the first unit sold.

FISH   An acronym (first-in, still-here) that describes the ending inventory units with the LIFO cost flow assumption.

Freight in   The transportation cost paid when inventory is acquired.

Going-concern assumption   An assumption made in GAAP that the company for which the financial statements are being prepared will continue to exist into the foreseeable future.

Goods available for sale   The units of inventory available to be sold during the period. These units include those available from the beginning inventory plus those produced or purchased during the current period.

Input market   Another name for entry market.

Inventory shrinkage   The losses of inventory due to spoilage, damage, thefts, etc.

Laid-down cost   The costs including invoice cost plus customs, tariff, and excise duties, and transportation. Although transportation in should be included in the laid-down cost, it is often treated as a period cost because it is impractical to allocate it to inventory items. In a manufacturing company, the laid-down cost comprises direct materials, direct labour, and overhead.

LIFO   An acronym (last-in, first-out) for the cost flow assumption that assigns the cost of the last unit purchased by the company to the first unit sold.

LISH   An acronym (last-in, still-here) that describes the ending inventory units using the FIFO cost flow assumption.

Market   Net realizable value, net realizable value less a profit margin, or replacement cost.

Net realizable value (NRV)   A selling price of a unit of inventory less any costs necessary to complete and sell the unit.

Output market   Another name for exit market.

Periodic inventory system   An inventory system in which cost of goods sold is determined by counting ending inventory, assigning costs to these units and then subtracting the ending inventory value from the sum of the beginning inventory plus purchases for the period.

Perpetual inventory system   An inventory system in which the cost of goods sold is determined at the time of sale of the unit.

Realized holding gain   A gain that results from the sale of a unit of inventory that had been held during a period of time during which prices increased. The profits that result from the change in price are the portion referred to as a holding gain.

Replacement cost   The current price at which a unit of inventory can be replaced by the company.

Retail market   Another term for exit market.

Specific identification method   A method of assigning costs to units of inventory in which the cost of a unit can be specifically identified from the records of the company.

Stockout   A situation that arises when a company sells all of a specific item of inventory and has no more in stock.

Transportation in   A synonym for freight in.

Weighted average   A method of assigning costs to units of inventory in which each unit is assigned the average cost of the units available for sale during the period.

Wholesale market   Another term for entry market.

ASSIGNMENT MATERIAL

Assessing Your Recall

Multiple Choice Quizzes

7-1 Describe the inventory valuation methods allowed under GAAP.

7-2 Describe how the lower of cost and market rule is applied to inventory under GAAP, and how this application is similar to that used for temporary investments.

7-3 Define replacement cost and net realizable value, and explain the difference between them.

7-4 Describe the basic differences between the periodic and perpetual inventory systems.

7-5 Discuss the advantages and disadvantages of the periodic inventory system compared to the perpetual inventory system.

7-6 Describe the three major cost flow assumptions that are most commonly used for determining the value of ending inventory and cost of goods sold.

7-7 Discuss a company's incentives for choosing one cost flow assumption over another. Be sure to include a discussion of the choice from both a reporting and a tax perspective.

7-8 Explain the term "holding gain" and discuss how it might arise with various cost flow assumptions.

7-9 Under what circumstances would a company want or need to estimate the cost of goods sold or ending inventory?

7-10 Describe the effects the choice of LIFO or FIFO may have on the ratios related to inventory. Discuss specifically the inventory turnover ratio and the current ratio.

Applying Your Knowledge

7-11 (Calculation of ending inventory and cost of goods sold)
Burke Ltd. had 6,000 units, at a cost of $18.50 each, in its inventory at the beginning of August. The company's purchases during August were as follows:

August	7	8,000 units	@	$18.00
	14	4,000 units	@	$17.50
	23	12,000 units	@	$16.00
	28	6,000 units	@	$14.50
		30,000 units		

Burke uses a periodic inventory system. At the end of August, the company had 10,000 units of inventory on hand.

Required:

a. Calculate the cost of goods sold for August using the weighted average cost flow assumption.

b. Calculate the cost of goods sold for August using the first-in, first-out cost flow assumption.

c. Calculate the cost of goods sold for August using the last-in, first-out cost flow assumption.

d. Which inventory cost flow assumption results in the greatest net income for August? Which results in the smallest? (Note that prices *decreased* during the period.)

e. Which inventory cost flow assumption results in the largest inventory balance at August 31? Which results in the smallest?

f. Compare your answers in parts d) and e) above and comment on the relationship between these items.

7-12 (Calculation of ending inventory and cost of goods sold)
Exquisite Jewellers purchases chiming clocks from around the world for sale in Canada. According to its records, Exquisite Jewellers had the following purchases and sales of clocks in the current year:

Clock No.	Date Purchased	Amount Paid	Date Sold	Sale Price
423	Jan. 22	$1,750	Mar. 8	$3,200
424	Feb. 9	6,000		
425	April 6	2,800	June 16	4,900
426	June 6	3,000	Aug. 9	4,800
427	Sept. 27	2,000		
428	Dec. 8	1,200	Dec. 24	2,000

Exquisite Jewellers has used the average cost method in calculating its cost of goods sold and inventory balances, but is thinking of changing to specific identification.

Required:

a. Compare the dollar amounts that would be reported as cost of goods sold and ending inventory under the average cost and specific identification methods.

b. Is average cost an appropriate method to use in a situation such as this? Explain why or why not.

c. What conditions generally must exist for specific identification to be used? Explain why.

d. Which of the two methods best represents the operating results for Exquisite Jewellers? Explain your answer.

7-13 (Calculation of cost of goods sold and gross profit)
Yoder Company recorded the following inventory transactions during 2004:

	Unit Number of Units	Unit Purchase Price	Sale Price
Inventory balance, January 1, 2004	60	$4	
Purchase #1	200	$5	
Sale #1	100		$9
Purchase #2	40	$6	
Purchase #3	60	$7	
Sale #2	170		$10

Required:

a. Calculate the cost of goods sold and gross profit for Yoder Company for 2004 if Yoder uses a first-in, first-out cost flow assumption.

b. Calculate the cost of goods sold and gross profit for Yoder Company for 2004 if Yoder uses a last-in, first-out cost flow assumption.

c. Which of the two assumptions provides the most conservative estimate of the carrying value of inventory? Which provides the best estimate of the current cost of replacing the inventory? Explain your answers.

d. Which method provides the most conservative estimate of reported income? Under what circumstances would the opposite be true?

7-14 (Calculation of ending inventory and cost of goods sold)
The following information relates to the merchandise inventory of Aspen Company for the month of October:

				Cost
October	1	Beginning inventory	6,000 units	$60,000
October	3	Purchased	4,000 units	$44,000
October	7	Sold	5,500 units	
October	15	Sold	3,000 units	
October	23	Purchased	5,000 units	$60,000
October	29	Sold	3,500 units	
October	31	Purchased	4,500 units	$58,500

Required:
Calculate the cost of goods sold and ending inventory as at October 31 using the periodic inventory system and the following cost flow assumptions:

a. FIFO

b. LIFO

c. Weighted average

7-15 (Gross margin and the lower of cost and market)
The Corral Saddle Company's information about merchandise inventories is as follows:

			Ending Inventory	
Year	Purchases	Sales	Cost	Market Value
1	$140,000	$115,000	$75,000	$70,000
2	100,000	175,000	80,000	67,000
3	155,000	253,000	72,000	80,000
4	104,000	225,000	31,000	31,000

There was no beginning balance in inventories prior to Year 1.

Required:

a. Calculate the gross margin for each year using the acquisition cost basis for valuing inventory.

b. Calculate the same gross margin using the lower of cost and market basis for valuing inventory.

c. Compare the gross margin for each year using the two methods, and explain the reason(s) for any differences you observe.

d. Compare the total results (gross margins) for the four-year period, using the two methods of valuation.

7-16   (Lower of cost and market)

Canadian Lumber Company carries a number of different types of screwdrivers. At the end of 2003, the chief financial officer of Canadian Lumber noted that the international price of screwdrivers had been dropping appreciably. Screwdrivers currently on hand that had been purchased in July 2003 for $8 per unit could be replaced at the end of December for $6 per unit.

Required:

a. Why is the decline in the replacement cost of screwdrivers relevant in this type of situation?

b. If Canadian Lumber Company has 3,000 screwdrivers on hand at December 31, 2003, at what dollar amount should inventory be reported?

c. What other information would be relevant in determining the year-end reporting amount?

d. Which accounting concepts are relevant in deciding the dollar amount of inventory to be reported? Explain why these concepts are important.

7-17   (LIFO, FIFO, and the lower of cost and market)

The following presentation relates to the inventory valuations of Aurora Inc. using different inventory methods (the company started operations in 20x1):

Period	LIFO	FIFO	Lower of FIFO Cost and Market
December 31, 20x1	$ 65,000	$ 60,000	$ 55,000
December 31, 20x2	135,000	125,000	120,000
December 31, 20x3	150,000	143,000	130,000
December 31, 20x4	110,000	125,000	125,000

There was no beginning balance of inventory in 20x1.

Required:

a. For 20x1, state whether the prices for acquiring inventory went up or down.

b. For 20x4, state whether the prices went up or down.

c. State which method would show the highest income in each year.

d. Which method would show the lowest income for the four years combined?

7-18   (LIFO and the production of additional inventory)

In mid-September, Waterford Incorporated needed to decide how many units should be produced for the balance of the accounting year, which ends on December 31. The company began its operations in the current year with an inventory of 20,000 units at a unit cost of $15. Thus far during the year, it has produced 85,000 units at a unit cost of $18. The annual production capacity of the plant is 200,000 units. It is estimated that the unit cost of producing additional units (for the remaining part of the year) will be $20. The company, after doing time-series and cross-industry analyses, expects annual sales to be 125,000 units at a selling price of $30 per unit. The company uses a periodic LIFO inventory system.

Required:

a. Assume the company produces just enough units to cover the 125,000 units it sells (that is, it will end the year with no inventory). Determine the cost of goods sold and the gross profit at this level of production.

b. Assume the company produces the maximum that the plant can produce, but still sells only 125,000 units. Determine the cost of goods sold and the gross profit at this level of production.

c. If the company sold the same number of units under assumptions a) and b), why is there a difference in the value of cost of goods sold and gross profit?

d. What conclusion can you draw from this regarding the LIFO method?

7-19 (Inventory estimation)
On March 31, 20x2, Cedar Grove Ltd. had a major fire in its main lumberyard. All the inventory in that yard was destroyed. In order to complete the insurance claim, the accountant needed an estimate of the inventory that had been in the lumberyard at the time of the fire. A search through the accounting records (which, luckily, had been kept in another building that was not destroyed by the fire) produced the following information:

A cost-to-sales ratio of 64%

Purchases for the year up to March 31	$ 94,000
Sales for the year up to March 31	140,000
Inventory on hand on January 1, 20x2	28,000

Required:

a. Calculate how much inventory should be on hand.

b. Cedar Grove had two other small lumberyards. On April 1, it counted the inventory in the other yards and determined that there was $9,600 in inventory in the other yards. How much should the company claim from the insurance company?

c. What factors could make the estimate of ending inventory inaccurate?

7-20 (FIFO, LIFO, and holding gains)
At the beginning of the year, the Sintex Company had merchandise inventory consisting of 3,500 units at a cost of $350 per unit. During the year, the company produced 5,000 units at an average cost of $400. The company sold 4,000 units for $600 each. The replacement cost on December 31 was $500 per unit.

Required:

a. Calculate the cost of goods sold and gross margin using both the FIFO and LIFO cost flow assumptions.

b. Separate the gross margin on sales into operating gross margin and realized holding gains, using both FIFO and LIFO.

c. Calculate the unrealized holding gains and the total gains (operating margin + realized gain + unrealized gain), using both FIFO and LIFO.

d. Compare the total gains and explain why they are different.

7-21 (Inventory turnover and gross margin calculations)
Stream Ltd. reported total inventory at January 1 and December 31, 2004, of $120,000 and $100,000, respectively. Cost of goods sold for 2004 was $470,000. Stream's nearest competitor reported inventories of $280,000 and $250,000 at January 1 and December 31, 2004, respectively, and reported cost of goods sold of $900,000 for 2004. Total 2004 sales for Stream Ltd. and its competitor were $600,000 and $1,250,000, respectively.

Required:

a. Calculate the inventory turnover ratios for the two companies for 2004.

b. Calculate the gross margin percentage (gross margin divided by sales) for the two companies for 2004.

c. On the basis of inventory turnover, which company is superior?

d. On the basis of gross margin percentage, which company is superior?

e. Which company would you recommend as being better managed? Indicate why.

7-22 (Evaluation of the inventory turnover ratio)
The inventory turnover ratios for Canadian Manufacturing, Honest John's Car Dealership, and Sweet Green Grocery Ltd. are 4.5, 9.7, and 18.2, respectively.

Required:

a. How is the inventory turnover ratio calculated? What information is provided by this ratio?

b. Is the company with the highest turnover ratio being run the most efficiently? Explain your answer.

c. Evaluate the turnover ratios for the three companies. Are the differences in ratios consistent with what you would expect? Explain.

d. What other ratios would you examine in assessing the operating efficiency of the companies?

User Perspective Problems

7-23 (Measurement issues related to ending inventory)
As an auditor, what concerns might you have about the measurement of inventories at year end? What effects might misstatements in these amounts have on the financial statements of the company?

7-24 (Use of ratio analysis during audit procedures)
Auditors typically conduct a preliminary review of a company's financial statements using analytical procedures that include ratio analysis. As an auditor, why would you find ratio analysis useful in auditing financial statements?

7-25 (Ratio analysis and foreign currencies)
Suppose that you are analyzing two competitors, one a Canadian company and the other a company in Japan whose statements are expressed in yen. Discuss whether it is necessary to convert the statements of the Japanese company into Canadian dollars before calculating ratios.

7-26 (Inventory ratio analysis with international competitors)
Describe the concerns that you might have regarding the ratio analysis of inventories when comparing a Canadian company with a foreign competitor.

7-27 (Effects of changing inventory costing method)
Suppose that a company has used LIFO since it began operations, and that prices have generally risen from that point to the present. In one of the company's debt agreements, there is a restrictive covenant stating that the company must maintain a current ratio of 2, or it is in violation of the debt agreement and the debt immediately becomes due. If you represent the lender, what reaction would you have if the company wanted to change its inventory method from LIFO to FIFO? How would your answer change if you knew that the company was already financially distressed?

7-28 (Decision-making with respect to inventory valuation)
Your company manufactures a line of processed snack foods using a soybean base with a low fat content. The line was very popular until some negative publicity emphasized that the product is very high in salt and contains numerous chemical preservatives. Now you have inventory on hand that will be hard to sell. The inventory originally cost $3,500,000. Its wholesale selling price prior to the publicity had been $7,000,000. The sales division has presented the following alternative proposals to the executive committee, of which you are a member:

Proposal 1: Offer the product at deep discounts to regular customers. If the discounts are large enough, all of the inventory will probably sell. The selling price for the total inventory under these conditions is estimated to be $3,000,000.

Proposal 2: Market the product in third world countries as a nutritious soybean-based food. Marketing costs will probably be $1,000,000, but the entire inventory could be sold at the regular list price of $7,000,000. Nutrition disclosure requirements are virtually non-existent in most of these countries.

Required:

a. Do any accounting entries need to be made to reflect the inventory problem?

b. Which proposal would you favour? Would you suggest any other alternatives?

c. What type of financial disclosure would you expect your company to make, if financial statements were prepared prior to the selection of an alternative for disposing of the inventory?

7-29 (Decision-making with respect to inventory estimation)
Black Light Company reported sales of $700,000 in the first quarter of 2004. Because the company does not keep a running tally of the cost of the inventory sold, the controller does not know how much inventory is actually on hand at the end of the quarter. The company, for the first time, is going to prepare quarterly financial reports to issue to its shareholders, but counting the inventory at the end of each quarter is too costly. Therefore, the controller decides to estimate how much inventory is on hand. By looking at the last annual balance sheet, the controller is able to determine that inventory on hand on January 1, 2004, was $250,000, and he knows that an additional $650,000 of inventory was purchased during the first quarter. The company normally earns a 30% gross profit on sales. Based on this information, and using the cost-to-sales method, the controller arrives at what he thinks is a reasonable estimate of the cost of inventory on hand at the end of the first quarter of 2004.

Required:

a. What would you estimate as the cost of Black Light's inventory on hand at the end of the first quarter of 2004? Explain how you arrived at your estimate.

b. If the gross margin estimation method works reasonably well for interim estimates of inventory on hand, why not use it at year end as well and avoid altogether the cost of an annual inventory count?

c. Under what conditions might this method of estimating inventory provide reliable results?

d. Under what conditions might this method of estimating inventory provide unreliable results?

e. Based on your estimate of Black Light's inventory at the end of the first quarter, what is your assessment of the company's inventory position? What factors might have contributed to it?

7-30   (LIFO and ending inventory problems)
Suppose that your company has always used LIFO and that prices have been rising over the years. In order to increase efficiency you have recommended that the company change its manufacturing process and adopt a just-in-time process, in which the raw materials are purchased just in time for production and goods are produced just in time for sale. The new system will either eliminate or significantly reduce inventory levels. What are the financial statement implications of your decision, both during the change-over period and in subsequent periods? What might be the financial tradeoffs that you should consider in changing your manufacturing process to a just-in-time basis?

Reading and Interpreting Published Financial Statements

7-31   (Interpreting the inventory turnover ratio)
Big Rock Brewery Ltd.'s 2001 comparative balance sheet, income statement, and note 3 on inventory are presented in Exhibit 7-14.

EXHIBIT 7-14

BIG ROCK BREWERY LTD. (2001)

Consolidated Balance Sheets

As at March 31

	2001 $	2000 $
	(Denominated in Canadian Dollars)	
ASSETS *[notes 5 & 6]*		
Current		
Cash and cash equivalents	1,602,202	106,492
Accounts receivable	1,593,984	1,872,064
Inventories *[note 3]*	2,701,982	2,676,790
Prepaid expenses and other	400,985	237,656
Investments	156,035	19,060
	6,455,188	4,912,062
Capital assets *[note 4]*	24,844,994	24,954,398
Deferred charges and other	45,619	51,779
	31,345,801	29,918,239
LIABILITIES AND SHAREHOLDERS' EQUITY		
Current		
Bank indebtedness *[note 5]*	1,362,907	2,244,903
Accounts payable and accrued liabilities	1,393,068	1,264,073
Income tax payable	151,869	—
Current portion of long-term debt *[note 6]*	1,567,862	1,496,189
	4,475,706	5,005,165
Long-term debt *[note 6]*	3,469,976	4,378,224
Future income taxes *[note 8]*	4,362,400	3,905,400
Total liabilities	12,308,082	13,288,789
Commitments [note 9]		
Shareholders' equity		
Share capital *[note 7]*	11,553,637	10,077,900
Retained earnings	7,484,082	6,551,550
	19,037,719	16,629,450
	31,345,801	29,918,239

BIG ROCK BREWERY LTD. (2001)

EXHIBIT 7-14
CONT.

Consolidated Statements of Operations & Retained Earning

Years ended March 31

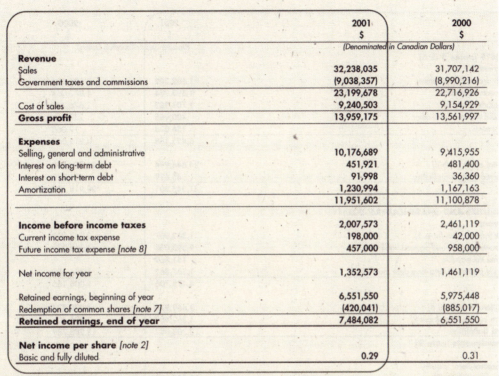

	2001 $	2000 $
	(Denominated in Canadian Dollars)	
Revenue		
Sales	32,238,035	31,707,142
Government taxes and commissions	(9,038,357)	(8,990,216)
	23,199,678	22,716,926
Cost of sales	9,240,503	9,154,929
Gross profit	13,959,175	13,561,997
Expenses		
Selling, general and administrative	10,176,689	9,415,955
Interest on long-term debt	451,921	481,400
Interest on short-term debt	91,998	36,360
Amortization	1,230,994	1,167,163
	11,951,602	11,100,878
Income before income taxes	2,007,573	2,461,119
Current income tax expense	198,000	42,000
Future income tax expense [note 8]	457,000	958,000
Net income for year	1,352,573	1,461,119
Retained earnings, beginning of year	6,551,550	5,975,448
Redemption of common shares [note 7]	(420,041)	(885,017)
Retained earnings, end of year	7,484,082	6,551,550
Net income per share [note 2]		
Basic and fully diluted	0.29	0.31

See accompanying notes

3. INVENTORIES

	2001 $	2000 $
Raw materials and returnable glass containers	1,162,917	1,195,338
Brews in progress	322,305	319,829
Finished product	804,479	635,726
Promotional goods and dispensing units	412,281	525,897
	2,701,982	2,676,790

Required:

Using the information in these statements, answer the following questions:

a. Calculate the inventory turnover ratios for Big Rock for 2001 and 2000. Knowing that Big Rock is a brewery company, how would you interpret the ratios?

b. Note 3 on inventory shows the components of the inventory amount. Three of those items are part of the manufacturing process; the other one is not. What impact did this other item have on the calculations and interpretation in part a)?

c. One of the items listed as a component of the inventory is returnable glass containers (bottles). Some of these bottles will be returned and re-used. Suggest some alternative ways that Big Rock could account for these bottles.

7-32 (Inventory turnover)

The balance sheet, statement of earnings, and excerpts from the notes accompanying the financial statements of **Danier Leather Inc.** are presented in Exhibit 7-15. Danier Leather is a vertically integrated designer, manufacturer, and retailer of specialty leather apparel.

Required:

Using the information in these statements, answer the following questions:

a. What costing method is Danier Leather using to value its inventory? Where did you find this information?

b. Calculate the inventory turnover ratio for 2001 and then convert it into days.

c. Knowing the type of merchandise that Danier Leather sells, does this ratio seem reasonable?

d. Question 7-31 includes the inventory turnover ratios for Big Rock Brewery. How do they compare with the ratios for Danier Leather? Is such a comparison useful? Explain why or why not.

EXHIBIT 7-15

consolidated balance sheets   DANIER LEATHER INC. (2001)

(thousands of dollars)

	June 30, 2001	June 24, 2000
Assets		
Current Assets		
Cash	$ 1,663	$ 775
Accounts receivable	664	762
Inventories (Note 2)	39,227	35,124
Prepaid expenses	459	197
Current portion of future income tax asset (Note 8)	932	1,163
	42,945	38,021
Other Assets		
Capital assets (Note 3)	25,151	20,631
Goodwill (Note 4)	342	355
	$ 68,438	$ 59,007
Liabilities		
Current Liabilities		
Bank overdraft (Note 5)	$ 3,486	$ -
Accounts payable and accrued liabilities	11,945	13,208
Income taxes payable	1,184	3,251
Current portion of long-term debt	-	270
	16,615	16,729
Long-term debt	-	470
Future income tax liability (Note 8)	531	363
	17,146	17,562
Shareholders' Equity		
Share capital (Note 6)	23,412	24,236
Retained earnings	27,880	17,209
	51,292	41,445
	$ 68,438	$ 59,007

Approved by the Board

Edwin F. Hawken, Director

Jeffrey Wortsman

Jeffrey Wortsman, Director

consolidated statements of earnings

(thousands of dollars, except per share amounts)

	For the Years Ended	
	June 30, 2001	June 24, 2000
	(53 weeks)	(52 weeks)
Revenue	$ 165,418	$ 143,011
Cost of sales (Note 7)	82,818	69,865
Gross profit	82,600	73,146
Selling, general and administrative expenses (Note 7)	60,902	54,051
Earnings before interest and income taxes	21,698	19,095
Interest expense – net	583	33
Earnings before income taxes	21,115	19,062
Provision for income taxes (Note 8)		
Current	9,090	8,166
Future	(53)	186
	9,037	8,352
Net earnings	$ 12,078	$ 10,710
Net earnings per share (Notes 1(i) & 9)		
Basic	**$1.75**	$1.48
Fully diluted	**$1.73**	$1.48

NOTE 1 SIGNIFICANT ACCOUNTING POLICIES

d) INVENTORIES

Inventories are valued at the lower of cost or market. Cost is determined on a first-in, first-out basis. For finished goods and work-in-process, market is defined as net realizable value; for raw materials, market is defined as replacement cost.

NOTE 2 INVENTORIES (THOUSANDS OF DOLLARS)

	June 30, 2001	June 24, 2000
Raw materials	$ 6,012	$ 5,129
Work-in-process	3,065	1,445
Finished goods	30,150	28,550
	$ 39,227	$ 35,124

7-33   (Inventory turnover)
Corel Corporation reported the following amounts for inventory and cost of sales in its 2001 financial statements:

Inventory:
2001 $799 thousand
2000 $3,117 thousand

Cost of sales:
2001 $25,927 thousand
2000 $47,025 thousand

Required:

a. Calculate the inventory turnover (by ratio and by days) for Corel for 2001 and 2000 using the inventory value at each year end instead of the average inventory amount. Comment on the results.

b. Corel is a Canadian company that offers software for home and small business users, creative professionals, and enterprise customers. Using this information about Corel's activities, evaluate the appropriateness of the inventory turnover that you calculated in part a).

7-34　(Components of inventory)

Comac Food Group Inc. owns the franchises of Domino's Pizza, Grabbajabba Fine Coffee, Pastel's Café, and Company's Coming Bakery Café. It builds the retail outlets and sells the franchise for operation to interested entrepreneurs. A franchisee buys the right to sell the merchandise sold by that outlet (pizza in the case of Domino's Pizza), but the franchisee must run the business under the direction of the franchisor (Comac), which establishes the ingredients, furnishings for the store, and even management style. In its 2001 financial statements, Comac has the following note on its inventory:

4. Inventories

Inventories are comprised of the following:

	2001	2000
Franchise stores under construction	$ 4,000	$166,000
Stores held for resale	65,000	535,000
Ingredients, uniforms, and selling supplies	11,000	77,000
	$80,000	$778,000

Required:

a. In most of the inventory examples that you have seen in this book, inventory has comprised retail items that we normally think of as inventory. Explain why it is appropriate for Comac to include the stores in its inventory.

b. Comac Food Group Inc. reports cost of sales at $4,617,000 and $3,875,000 for 2001 and 2000, respectively. Explain why calculating an inventory turnover for Comac would not be meaningful.

7-35　(Inventory turnover)

Moore Corporation is an international leader in the management and distribution of print-based and digital information. Because it is a manufacturing company, its inventory is composed of raw materials, work-in-process, and finished goods, as follows:

3. Inventories (in thousands of U.S. dollars)

	2001	2000
Raw materials	$ 39,452	$ 43,010
Work-in-process	10,048	14,612
Finished goods	75,149	93,441
Other	3,772	3,421
	$128,421	$154,484

The cost of sales was $1,552,561 thousand and $1,598,525 thousand for 2001 and 2000, respectively.

Required:

a. Calculate the inventory turnover for Moore Corporation in 2001 and 2000 using first cost of sales divided by total inventory and then cost of sales divided by finished goods. Use the inventory value for the given year rather than the average inventory.

b. The inventory turnover using total inventory is quite different from the inventory turnover using only finished goods. Which amount do you think is more useful? Why?

7-36 (Impact of inventory on current ratio; gross profit impact of changing sales levels) **Chai-Na-Ta Corp.** is the largest producer of ginseng in the world. It produces, markets, and distributes North American ginseng root and value-added products. Ginseng reaches maturity and can be harvested in three years, but Chai-Na-Ta sometimes allows the crops to mature longer to allow for higher yields and additional seed harvests. The balance sheet and statement of earnings for 2001 and 2000 are presented in Exhibit 7-16.

Required:

a. Calculate the current ratio (CA/CL) for both 2001 and 2000. Comment on the impact that inventory has on this ratio in each year.

b. Included with the current assets and long-term assets is an asset called Ginseng crops. This account collects all of the cost of growing the ginseng. The portion in the current asset section includes the accumulated costs associated with the ginseng that is expected to be sold in the following year. Is it appropriate to classify this as an inventory item? Explain why you think that it is or is not.

CHAI-NA-TA CORP (2001)

consolidated statements of operations

EXHIBIT 7-16

(Stated in Canadian Dollars)	Year ended December 31 2001	Thirteen-month period ended December 31 2000	Year ended November 30 1999
Revenue	$ 13,885,635	$ 12,221,235	$ 16,204,278
Cost of goods sold	11,680,559	11,463,521	16,153,852
	2,205,076	757,714	50,426
Selling, general and administrative expenses	2,883,611	4,157,615	4,628,349
Bad debts	-	-	131,903
Interest on short-term debt	151,854	207,925	105,577
Interest on long-term debt	-	-	3,049,883
Write-down of inventory and crop costs	1,573,466	1,207,501	9,902,734
	4,608,931	5,573,041	17,818,446
Operating loss	(2,403,855)	(4,815,327)	(17,768,020)
Write-down of investment in Dalian Pegasus Ginseng Pharmaceutical Co. Ltd. (Note 3(a))	-	-	(3,372,413)
Net gain on debt forgiveness (Note 1)	-	13,916,088	-
Other income (loss) (Note 14)	246,585	(788,232)	(138,392)
Earnings (loss) before income taxes	(2,157,270)	8,312,529	(21,278,825)
Provision for (recovery of) income taxes (Note 13)	-	1,462,000	(3,126,781)
NET EARNINGS (LOSS)	$ (2,157,270)	$ 6,850,529	$ (18,152,044)
Basic earnings (loss) per share (Note 2(n))	$ (0.15)	$ 0.65	$ (4.09)
Weighted average number of shares used to calculate basic earnings (loss) per share	14,264,508	10,611,211	4,440,303
Fully diluted earnings (loss) per share (Note 2(n))	$ (0.15)	$ 0.30	$ (4.09)
Weighted average number of shares used to calculate fully diluted earnings (loss) per share	14,264,508	22,943,190	4,440,303

EXHIBIT 7-16
CONT.

CHAI-NA-TA CORP (2001)

consolidated balance sheets

(Stated in Canadian Dollars)	As at December 31 **2001**		As at December 31 **2000**
ASSETS			
Current assets			
Cash and cash equivalents	$ 2,086,789	$	608,656
Accounts receivable	240,688		688,071
Inventory	10,746,183		11,507,038
Ginseng crops (Note 4)	8,098,718		9,290,369
Prepaid expenses and other assets	147,368		1,047,558
	21,319,746		23,141,692
Ginseng crops (Note 4)	11,712,809		11,625,652
Capital assets (Note 5)	8,095,118		9,535,140
Other assets (Note 6)	—		107,760
	$ 41,127,673	$	44,410,244
LIABILITIES			
Current liabilities			
Line of credit (Note 7)	$ 1,650,000	$	390,000
Short-term borrowings (Note 8)	6,423,845		5,910,020
Accounts payable and accrued liabilities	1,303,979		2,321,318
Customer deposits	1,356,302		—
Current portion of long-term debt (Note 9)	573,137		533,443
	11,307,263		9,154,781
Long-term debt (Note 9)	146,797		3,153,499
Other liabilities (Note 10(a))	—		433,836
Future income taxes (Note 13)	1,462,000		1,462,000
	12,916,060		14,204,116
SHAREHOLDERS' EQUITY			
Share capital (Notes 11 and 12)	38,200,398		38,200,398
Cumulative translation adjustments	(57,313)		(220,068)
Deficit	(9,931,472)		(7,774,202)
	28,211,613		30,206,128
	$ 41,127,673	$	44,410,244

APPROVED BY THE BOARD

c. Calculate the gross profit percentage for both 2001 and 2000. Sales declined in 2000 but then improved in 2001. What effect has this had on the gross profit? What conclusions can you draw from the results that you found?

Beyond the Book

7-37 (Examination of a company's financial statements)
Choose a Canadian company as directed by your instructor and answer the following questions:

a. What kind of inventory does your company carry?

b. Calculate the inventory turnover for each of the last two years, using the inventory of the year instead of the average inventory. Report any difficulties that you had in finding the appropriate numbers to make this calculation.

c. Describe any significant change that occurred in the inventory balance and try to determine what caused it.

d. Calculate a current ratio for each of the last two years. Describe the significance that inventory has on this ratio in each year.

Cases

7-38 Bema Gold Corporation
Bema Gold Corporation is a Canadian company headquartered in Vancouver, British Columbia. It explores and develops gold properties in South America. Rani, a Business Administration student, has recently inherited some money from a grandparent. She intends to create a diversified portfolio of share investments. Although they can be risky, she has heard that investing in gold properties can be quite profitable. Rani is contemplating investing in Bema Gold Corporation. She has the annual report, which includes the financial statements (see Exhibit 7-17). She is concerned because the company has not shown a profit for the last three years, yet issued 16,100,000 new shares for cash in 2001 and 10,000,000 new shares for cash in 2000. If other investors are willing to buy over 26,000,000 new shares over the last two years, they obviously have confidence in this company.

Required:

a. Knowing that Bema explores and develops gold properties, explain the significance of gold inventory on its balance sheet by calculating a current ratio for each year and explaining the impact that inventory has on this ratio.

b. Review the financial statements and draw up a list of questions you would like to ask an investment advisor about this company.

EXHIBIT 7-17

CONSOLIDATED BALANCE SHEETS

BEMA GOLD CORPORATION (2001)

as at December 31
(in thousands of United States dollars)

	2001	2000
ASSETS		
Current		
Cash and cash equivalents	$ **4,133**	$ 3,225
Accounts receivable	**2,529**	4,498
Marketable securities (at quoted market value)	**2,352**	3,265
Inventories *(Note 2)*	**6,405**	6,153
Assets held for sale *(Note 3)*	**-**	5,810
Other	**147**	216
	15,566	23,167
Investments *(Note 4)*	**2,525**	2,694
Property, plant and equipment *(Note 5)*	**149,160**	132,540
Other assets *(Note 6)*	**15,341**	17,549
	$182,592	$ 175,950
LIABILITIES		
Current		
Accounts payable	$ **5,426**	$ 6,543
Current portion of long-term debt *(Note 7)*	**9,584**	9,231
	15,010	15,774
Deferred revenue *(Notes 7 and 10)*	**103**	1,799
Long-term debt *(Note 7)*	**33,910**	24,145
Other liabilities	**3,937**	2,747
	52,960	44,465
SHAREHOLDERS' EQUITY		
Capital stock *(Note 9)*		
Authorized 300,000,000 common shares with no par value		
Issued 184,838,770 common shares (2000 – 159,056,898)	**265,080**	258,191
Equity portion of convertible debt *(Note 8)*	**13,697**	10,482
Deficit	**(149,145)**	(137,188)
	129,632	131,485
	$182,592	$ 175,950

Commitments *(Note 10)*
Subsequent events *(Notes 8 and 18)*

Approved by the Board

Director   Director

CONSOLIDATED STATEMENTS OF OPERATIONS — BEMA GOLD CORPORATION (2001)

EXHIBIT 7-17 CONT.

for the years ended December 31
(in thousands of United States dollars, except shares and per share amounts)

	2001	2000	1999
Gold revenue	$21,209	$30,630	$35,252
Expenses (Income)			
Operating costs	16,639	25,849	24,309
Depreciation and depletion	5,745	6,940	6,235
Insurance proceeds	(361)	(3,507)	(2,670)
Write-down of inventory	2,248	–	–
Other	845	(522)	1,995
	25,116	28,760	29,869
Operating earnings (loss)	(3,907)	1,870	5,383
Other expenses (Income)			
General and administrative	2,844	3,051	3,419
Interest on long-term debt	1,200	1,799	2,068
Amortization of deferred financing costs	2,231	1,512	1,509
General exploration	304	442	557
Other	1,277	509	(488)
	7,856	7,313	7,065
Loss before the undernoted items	11,763	5,443	1,682
Equity in losses of associated companies	129	779	601
Investment losses (gains) *(Note 4)*	(554)	9,331	–
Write-down of investments *(Notes 3 and 4)*	–	11,773	–
Write-down of mineral properties *(Note 5)*	–	22,565	1,765
Write-down of notes receivable *(Note 3)*	–	1,248	–
Net loss for the year	$11,338	$51,139	$ 4,048
Net loss per common share – basic and diluted	$ 0.07	$ 0.36	$ 0.03
Weighted average number of common shares outstanding (in thousands)	166,750	142,836	123,839

CONSOLIDATED STATEMENTS OF DEFICIT

for the years ended December 31
(in thousands of United States dollars)

	2001	2000	1999
Deficit, beginning of year	$137,188	$ 85,041	$80,929
Loss for the year	11,338	51,139	4,048
Charges related to convertible debt *(Note 8)*	619	1,008	64
Deficit, end of year	$149,145	$137,188	$85,041

See accompanying notes to consolidated financial statements.

EXHIBIT 7-17
CONT.

CONSOLIDATED STATEMENTS OF CASH FLOWS   BEMA GOLD CORPORATION (2001)

for the years ended December 31
(in thousands of United States dollars)

	2001	2000	1999
OPERATING ACTIVITIES			
Loss for the year	$(11,338)	$(51,139)	$(4,048)
Non-cash charges (credits)			
Depreciation and depletion	5,810	7,331	6,482
Amortization of deferred financing costs	2,231	1,512	1,509
Equity in losses of associated companies	100	928	809
Amortization of deferred revenue	(1,696)	(1,469)	(4,146)
Investment losses (gains)	(554)	9,331	–
Write-down of investments	–	11,773	–
Write-down of mineral properties	–	22,565	1,765
Write-down of inventory	2,248	–	–
Write-down of notes receivable	–	1,248	–
Other	673	676	569
Changes in non-cash working capital (*Note 15*)	2,388	(2,090)	326
	(138)	666	3,266
FINANCING ACTIVITIES			
Common shares issued, net of issue costs (*Note 9*)	4,609	–	540
Special warrants issued, net of issue costs (*Note 9*)	–	2,953	3,105
Convertible loan, net proceeds (*Note 8*)	–	7,593	4,842
Julietta project loans and overrun facility	21,200	17,800	–
Refugio loan repayments	(8,000)	(6,000)	(6,000)
Deferred financing costs	(1,840)	(4,758)	(604)
Capital lease repayments	(438)	(850)	(362)
Other	135	–	–
	15,666	16,738	1,521
INVESTING ACTIVITIES			
Refugio mine	(111)	(4,544)	(4,181)
Julietta development and construction	(20,064)	(18,706)	(3,189)
Acquisition, exploration and development	(1,082)	(1,136)	(3,002)
Promissory notes issued by associated companies, net	(283)	(2,120)	(3,447)
Proceeds on sale of investments	3,751	5,892	–
Proceeds from the sale of notes receivable	3,300	3,000	–
Restricted cash	–	484	(484)
Other	(132)	(453)	(647)
	(14,621)	(17,583)	(14,950)
Effect of exchange rate changes on cash and cash equivalents	1	4	59
Increase (decrease) in cash and cash equivalents	908	(175)	(10,104)
Cash and cash equivalents, beginning of year	3,225	3,400	13,504
Cash and cash equivalents, end of year	$ 4,133	$ 3,225	$ 3,400

See accompanying notes to consolidated financial statements.

7-39 Flick's Electronics

Jeff Stevenson was recently hired as a new manager for Flick's Electronics. His compensation is composed of a base salary and a bonus based on gross profit. The bonuses are to be paid monthly as determined by the gross profit for the preceding month.

Flick's Electronics currently uses a periodic inventory system but Jeff would like to see the company move to a perpetual system. The company's owners are willing to consider the change provided that Jeff prepares a written analysis outlining the two methods and detailing the benefits and costs of switching to the perpetual system.

Required:

Prepare a report that Jeff could present to the owner's of Flick's Electronics to support his request to change to a perpetual inventory system.

7-40 Park Avenue Tire Company

Park Avenue Tire Company has been operating in Winnipeg for over 30 years and has a very loyal customer base. The company sells and installs tires and the owners pride themselves on the excellent business relationships they have developed with both their customers and suppliers. The company often sells tires on credit, allowing customers to pay their balances within 30 days. Collection of accounts receivable has never been a problem, with most people paying their balances within 60 days.

Park Avenue purchases tires from most of the large national brands and, due to the nature of the business, generally maintains a fairly large inventory. It is essential that the company have the necessary tires on hand to meet customer needs due to increased competition from large retailers such as Canadian Tire and Wal-Mart.

The company has always had sufficient cash to pay its suppliers immediately and take advantage of cash discounts. However, this month, for the first time ever, Park Avenue does not have sufficient cash in the bank to meet its supplier payments. Chris Park, son of the original owner Ernest Park, is currently operating the business and is very concerned about the inability of the company to maintain what he feels are adequate levels of cash.

Your firm has been the accountants for Park Avenue Tire Company for the past 20 years. Chris has approached the firm expressing his concerns and asking for advice as to how the cash flow problems can be solved. As part of your analysis, you review the company's financial statements for the past three years. Excerpts from the financial statements are presented below.

	Dec. 31 2004	Dec. 31 2003	Dec. 31 2002
Current assets			
Cash	$ 10,000	$ 35,000	$ 31,500
Accounts receivable	15,000	12,000	9,000
Inventory	169,000	122,000	116,000
Prepaid expenses	6,000	8,000	6,500
Total current assets	$ 200,000	$177,000	$ 163,000
Current liabilities			
Accounts payable	$ 62,000	$ 47,000	$ 33,000
Salaries payable	4,200	5,850	3,775
Income tax payable	1,200	1,150	1,950
Total current liabilities	$ 67,400	$ 54,000	$ 38,725

During 2004, credit sales and cost of goods sold were $160,000 and $97,000, respectively. The 2003 and 2002 credit sales were $175,000 and $177,000 and cost of goods sold for the same periods were $93,000 and $95,000. The accounts receivable and inventory balances at the end of 2001 were $8,000 and $99,000, respectively.

Required:

Provide a report to Chris Park detailing options that he can take to alleviate the company's cash problems. Remember that you are to present options, not recommendations. As a basis for the report, you should calculate and comment on the following ratios:

1. Current ratio

2. Quick ratio

3. Receivables turnover ratio and Average collection period

4. Inventory turnover ratio and Days in inventory

7-41   North End Television Services

North End Television Services sells and services a variety of high-end home entertainment products. An inventory count is prepared at each year end for the purpose of verifying the information contained in the company's periodic inventory system. Once counted, the inventory is valued for purposes of preparing the financial statements. The following inventory items represent a cross-section of North End's inventory for the year ended June 30, 2004. Because computerized records are maintained and a specific identification method of inventory is applied, the historical cost of each inventory item can be easily determined.

In addition to the historical cost, the store management has also included information detailing net realizable value for each item.

Item	Quantity on hand June 30, 2004	Historical cost (per unit)	Net realizable value (per unit)
Sony DVD Player	4	$400	$325
RCA High Definition "52-Inch" Television	2	$2,100	$1,999
Sony High 8 Camcorder	3	$600	$200
JVC Surround Sound System	6	$700	$900
Nikon Digital Camera	4	$600	$750

Tim Cappelino, the manager of North End, is confused as to why there is a difference between historical cost and net realizable value. Tim is not an accountant and is unfamiliar with these terms. He is also wondering which number should be used to value the company's inventory at June 30, 2004.

Required:

For the purposes of this case, assume that the above items represent the total inventory of North End Television Services at June 30, 2004.

a. Define for Tim the meaning of historical cost and net realizable value in the context of inventory valuation.

b. Based on Canadian practice, determine for Tim the value of North End's ending inventory at June 30, 2004.

7-42

Jim Kennedy has been a public accountant for the past 20 years and is now a partner in a prominent accounting firm based in Truro, Nova Scotia. Recently, he was approached by the local chamber of commerce to be a guest speaker at its monthly meeting. Since many members of the chamber are small to mid-sized retailers, Jim decided to prepare a talk on determining inventory values and cost flow assumptions.

It is now Friday afternoon and Jim has just returned to his office following the presentation to the chamber. He is surprised to see messages from two clients who were at the meeting. The first message is from Bryan Cartel, who owns and operates the local Ford dealership. In addition to selling cars, the dealership also has a large service department and maintains an extensive inventory of parts and accessories. The second caller is Jenny Mead, who manages her family's grocery store. Jim returns the calls and discovers that both business people want further advice as to the best cost flow assumption they should be using in their respective inventory systems.

In particular, Jenny would like to know why her family is using the weighted average approach instead of LIFO. From Jim's chamber presentation, she learned that LIFO results in lower net income in times of rising prices, and since lower net income means less taxes, she is wondering why Jim has not previously recommended switching to LIFO.

Required:

a. Determine which inventory cost flow assumption would best suit the needs of each of these clients. Be prepared to support your recommendation.

b. Writing as Jim, draft a response to Jenny regarding her concerns about the use of LIFO in her business. Do you think that the business should change to this method? Why or why not?

7-43   Armstrong Hardware

Armstrong Hardware lost most of its inventory in an electrical fire that destroyed the company's warehouse and retail store. Fortunately, the accounting records were backed up on the owner's computer in her home office and could therefore be recovered. However, Armstrong uses a periodic inventory system, so without being able to perform a physical count, the company could not determine the amount of inventory lost in the fire. In order to process the insurance claim, the insurance company requires Armstrong to prepare a reasonable estimate of the lost inventory.

As Armstrong's accountant, you have been able to gather the following information:

1. Ending inventory, from the accounting records of last year was $85,800.

2. In the current year, purchases up to the time of the fire totalled $486,500.

3. According to last year's financial statements, sales and the cost of goods sold were $964,000 and $578,400, respectively.

4. According to this year's accounting records, sales in the current year were $678,000.

Required:

a. Prepare an estimate of the amount of inventory lost in the fire. To ensure the reasonableness of the amount claimed, write a brief memo to the insurance company outlining your approach for determining the amount of inventory destroyed. You should also specify any assumptions used in preparing your estimate.

b. How would this process have differed if Armstrong had used a perpetual instead of a periodic inventory system?

Critical Thinking Questions

7-44   (Inventory decision-making with respect to buying and selling)
You and two of your friends have decided to apply some of the knowledge that you are learning in your business classes. You plan to start a wholesale business, buying goods in the Czech Republic and selling them to small specialty stores. One of your friends has an uncle in the Czech Republic who has some contacts that will enable you to buy the merchandise you want. Another friend has an aunt who owns a trucking company that transports merchandise all over Europe. You hope to use the trucking company to transport your merchandise from the Czech Republic to Amsterdam for shipment to Canada.

You are going to have a meeting to discuss the necessary details surrounding the buying and selling of the inventory. In preparation for the meeting, write a short report outlining the items that you think should be discussed. To make this more realistic and to make your task easier, decide on what types of inventory you are going to buy. The type of inventory you import will affect some of the decisions you need to make.

7-45   (Impact of various definitions of "Market value" under LCM)
The management of Handy Hardware has collected the following information related to the lower of cost and market (LCM) valuation of a particular item of inventory at the end of 2003:

> 400 units on hand
> acquisition cost, $100 per unit
> replacement cost, $80 per unit
> expected selling price, $170 per unit
> expected selling expense, $37 per unit
> normal profit margin, 40% of the selling price

Required:

a. Determine the amount of the inventory write-down (if any) that would be recorded in 2003, using each of the following definitions of market value:

   1. Replacement cost

   2. Net realizable value

   3. Net realizable value less a normal profit margin

b. Assume that all these units are sold in the next accounting period, at the expected selling price and expected selling expense. Determine the amount of profit that would be recognized in 2004 (after taking into consideration the write-down in part a) under each of the three definitions of market value.

c. In your opinion, which of these definitions of market value resulted in the best financial reporting outcome, in terms of the profit or loss that was reported in 2003 and 2004? Explain your reasoning.

How Much Is That Whooping Crane Worth?

One of the most important concepts in accounting is that of value, which can have many different meanings, depending on the situation—especially when it comes to capital assets. At the Calgary Zoological Society, the question, "What is it worth?" has several answers, explains Annalise Van Ham, CGA, Manager Financial Services.

"Our office furnishings, vehicles, land, and buildings are all capital assets," she says. "We depreciate most equipment and furnishings over four years; for computers, it's two years, and software, 12 months," Which means that some assets are completely depreciated and have no net value on the books any longer.

The Zoo's facilities are treated slightly differently. "Prior to December 2000, our buildings and exhibits did not appear on our books at all because they're technically owned by the City of Calgary," explains Ms. Van Ham. "However, since we have free use of the city's assets and full responsibility to maintain, upkeep, and manage the facilities, it was deemed appropriate for us to show them on our balance sheet. We now include them, with a note explaining that it is beneficial ownership and not full legal title."

An example of such an item is Canadian Wilds, a large forest with various areas, each representing a different habitat and sheltering a number of species native to Canada: mountain goats, wolves, moose, buffalo, deer, and—rarest of all—whooping cranes. Completed in 1998, Canadian Wilds was built entirely with Zoological Society funds before being transferred to the city. "When we brought those assets back as an adjustment at the

end of 2000, the value on our balance sheet simply reflected the original cost less the accumulated depreciation to date and the net value going straight into our equity," says Ms. Van Ham.

The Zoo's newest addition, still under construction, is a vast multi-habitat display called Destination Africa. Scheduled to open in January 2003, the $31-million complex will include a large open area where the Zoo's giraffes, monkeys, and other African species can roam freely. "It's a new approach in the presentation of animals at a zoo," explains Ms. Van Ham. "They are free to intermingle in an open environment—it's the people who are in the enclosed area!" As construction proceeds, the value of the exhibit is being accumulated as work-in-process.

And what about the most important asset of all—the animals? "They don't appear on the balance sheet in any way, in part because they don't have an established market value," Ms. Van Ham points out. "It's a bit ironic, because that's what the Zoo is all about." In fact, if the Zoo buys an animal, it turns up as an expense, and similarly, a sale creates a revenue; they pretty much cancel each other out. In any case, zoos are more likely, these days, to lend or exchange animals than to buy and sell them.

CAPITAL ASSSETS—
TANGIBLE AND INTANGIBLE

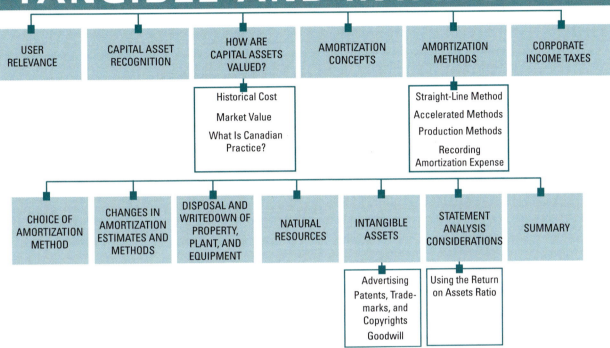

Learning Objectives:

After studying this chapter, you should be able to:

1. *Describe the valuation methods used for capital assets.*
2. *Identify the acquisition costs that are usually added to the capital asset account at acquisition.*
3. *Describe the purpose of amortization and identify and implement four methods of amortization, including capital cost allowance.*
4. *Identify the factors that influence the choice of amortization method.*
5. *Describe and implement changes in amortization estimates and methods.*
6. *Account for the disposal and writedown of capital assets.*
7. *Describe and implement the amortization method used most frequently for natural resources.*
8. *Explain the accounting difficulties associated with intangible assets.*
9. *Amortize intangible assets.*
10. *Calculate the return on assets ratio and discuss the potential implications of the results.*

Our opening story describes some difficulties associated with recording and reporting capital assets at the Calgary Zoological Society. The Zoo faces some unique problems because of the nature of the assets it has and its relationship with the City of Calgary. The Calgary Zoological Society is a not-for-profit entity similar to the Manitoba Theatre Centre described at the beginning of Chapter 5. Because it is a not-for-profit entity, it has some unique ways of accounting for things. Let's look at some of the unique capital asset issues it faces.

First, although the Calgary Zoological Society raises funds for capital expenditures like buildings and exhibits, the actual assets become the property of the City of Calgary as soon as they are complete. This type of arrangement is not uncommon for a public organization like a zoo. Because the assets are transferred to the city, you would expect to find them on the financial statements of the City of Calgary. Prior to December 2000, that is where they were. Now you will find them on the Zoo's balance sheet. Although the City of Calgary has legal title, the Zoo manages, maintains, and repairs them and has, therefore, decided to include them on its financial statements. The animals represent a whole different problem. Can we put a value on a life? Ms. Van Ham is right. The animals do not have an established market value. It is, therefore, very difficult to measure them. Can we value them? You know from your accounting studies so far that we do not record people as assets in the accounting system although they, like the animals, may be essential to the organization's operations. There may be some animals that the Zoo actually does buy, which would give you a starting point at valuation. For those animals, you could perhaps estimate their expected life and amortize the original cost over that lifetime. But there are probably more animals that the Zoo receives by trading with another zoo or that are born in the Zoo. How would we value those? This is a problem that accountants have not solved yet. Until they do, zoos like the Calgary Zoo will continue to expense the cost of animals when they are purchased instead of recording them in the accounting system as capital assets.

This chapter will discuss the measurement, recording, and reporting issues related to capital assets. In the previous two chapters, current assets whose value would be realized within one year (or operating cycle) of the company were studied. In this chapter, assets with lives longer than a year (or operating cycle) are discussed. We are going to focus on **capital assets**, those which management intends to use in the company's operations to generate revenue. Long-term investments that also have lives longer than a year are discussed briefly in Appendix B at the end of the text. You will be studying these assets if you take courses in intermediate financial accounting.

Of the capital assets that we are going to study, property, plant, and equipment are the most recognizable. These are a type of noncurrent asset called **tangible assets**, which are usually defined as those assets with some physical form (*tangible* comes from the Latin word meaning "to touch"). In other words, you can usually see them and touch them. **Intangible assets**, on the other hand, are noncurrent assets that are associated with certain rights or privileges of the company, such as patents, trademarks, leases, and goodwill.

In the sections that follow, the recognition and valuation issues for capital assets are discussed, much as they were for current assets. Because of the long-term nature of these assets, the issue of how to show the income statement effects (expensing of the cost) of the purchase of these assets over time must be addressed. The expense that is recorded is referred to as amortization or depreciation.

USER RELEVANCE

Capital assets provide the underlying infrastructure of many companies. They include the real estate, buildings, equipment, vehicles, computers, patents, etc., that companies need to carry out their day-to-day operations. They often require a substantial outlay of funds to acquire, which means that companies will often secure long-term mortgages to help spread the cost over several periods. Another common way to acquire long-lived assets is to lease them. You may find some assets on a balance sheet labelled as "assets under capital leases."

Because of their importance to the operations of the business, their high cost, and their long lives, it is essential that users understand the role capital assets play in a company's success. Users need to monitor the assets' lives so that they can anticipate the future outflow of cash to replace them. They need to know what methods a company is using to amortize its assets and what impact those methods have on the income statement. They need to understand that the value that is being carried for capital assets on the balance sheet represents a future benefit that the company expects to earn from using the assets. If the company did not expect to earn that much, it would be required to reduce the carrying value. In most instances, companies expect to earn amounts in excess of the carrying value of their capital assets.

This chapter will provide you, the user, with the background information about capital assets that will help you better understand the impact of these assets on financial statements.

CAPITAL ASSET RECOGNITION

Assets must have a future value for the company. The company must have the right to use them and must have earned that right through a past transaction. When a company buys a capital asset, it has the right to use it, and the transaction has occurred. Therefore, the only asset criterion that merits further discussion is the probable future value, which takes at least two forms. Capital assets are used, first and foremost, to generate revenue, usually by facilitating sales, producing products, or providing services. Therefore, the future value is represented by the cash that will be received from the sales of products and services in the future. Because of the long-term nature of capital assets, these cash flows will be received over several future periods. This type of value is sometimes referred to as **value in use**.

The second source of value for capital assets is their ultimate sales value. Many capital assets are used until the company decides to replace them with a new asset. For example, a business may use a truck for three or four years and then trade it in for a new one. This type of value is called **residual value** (or **resale value**) and can be very important, depending on the type of asset.

Value in use is normally the most appropriate concept for capital assets because companies usually invest in them to use them, not to sell them. Residual value cannot, however, be totally ignored because it affects the value of the asset at the end of the period for which the company uses it. You saw in Chapter 2 how we use residual value to determine amortization.

The difficulty with the value in use concept for capital assets is the inherent uncertainty with regard to future revenue generated by the sale of inventory or the provision of service. The company does not know whether the demand for its products or services will continue into the future. It also does not know what prices it will be able to command for its products or services. Other uncertainties relate to technology. Equipment can become obsolete as a result of technological change. New technology can give competitors a significant advantage in producing and pricing products. Technological change can also eliminate the need for the company's product. Consider the manufacturer of 8-track tapes when CDs came on the market, or the typewriter manufacturer with the advent of the personal computer.

The uncertainty of the ultimate residual value is similar to that of the value in use because the ultimate residual value depends on whether the asset has any value in use to the ultimate buyer. It is also a question of whether a buyer can even be found. Equipment that is made to the original buyer's specifications may not have much of a residual market because it may not meet the needs of other potential users.

Learning Objective

1

Describe the valuation methods used for capital assets.

HOW ARE CAPITAL ASSETS VALUED?

In the sections that follow, the discussion is limited to valuation issues regarding property, plant, and equipment, which are similar to those relating to other non-current capital assets. At the end of the chapter, specific concerns and issues with regard to natural resources and intangible assets are discussed.

In Canada, property, plant, and equipment are usually valued at the historical cost with no recognition of any other value unless the value of the asset becomes impaired (the value of the estimated future cash flows is less than its current carrying value). Some countries do allow for the recognition of changes in market values of property, plant, and equipment and there have been historical instances of companies disclosing information about the market values of these assets. Before Canadian practice is discussed in detail, several possible valuation methods will be considered.

Historical Cost

In a historical cost value system, the original cost of the asset is recorded at the time of acquisition. Changes in the market value of the asset are ignored in this system. During the period in which the asset is used, its cost is expensed (amortized) using an appropriate amortization method (these methods are discussed later). Market values are recognized only when the asset is sold. The company then recognizes a gain or loss on the sale, which is determined by the difference between the proceeds from the sale and the net book value (carrying value) of the asset at the time of sale. The **net book value** or **carrying value** is the original cost less any amortization that had been taken to the point of sale. This net book value is sometimes called the **amortized cost** of the asset.

Market Value

Another possible valuation method records capital assets at their market value. There are at least two types of market values: replacement cost and net realizable value.

Replacement Cost

In a replacement cost valuation system, the asset is carried at its replacement cost. By **replacement cost**, accountants mean the amount that would be needed to acquire an equivalent asset. At acquisition, the historical cost is recorded because this is the replacement cost at the time of purchase. As the asset is used, the carrying value of the asset is adjusted upward or downward to reflect changes in the replacement cost. Unrealized gains and losses are recognized for these changes. The periodic expensing of the asset in the form of amortization has to be adjusted to reflect the changes in the replacement cost. For example, if the replacement cost of the asset goes up, the amortization expense will also have to go up to reflect the higher replacement cost. A gain or loss is also recognized upon disposal of this asset. The amount of the gain or loss is determined by the difference between the proceeds from the sale and the amortized replacement cost at the time of sale. The Accounting Standards Board at one time recommended that companies report supplementary information on the replacement cost of their property, plant, and equipment. At that time, inflation in Canada exceeded 10% and users were expressing concern over the historical cost carrying values of capital assets. The level of inflation declined and users' interest in replacement cost declined along with it. The AcSB removed the recommendation from the *CICA Handbook*. In countries experiencing extreme rates of inflation, capital assets may be recorded at replacement value to provide a better measure of the results for the period. For example, in Mexico, replacement cost of property, plant, and equipment is required for companies whose shares trade on stock exchanges.

Net Realizable Value

With a **net realizable value** system, assets are recorded at the amount that could be received by converting them to cash in the normal course of business; in other words, selling them. During the periods in which assets are being used, gains and losses are recognized as the **net realizable value** changes over time. Amortization in this type of system is based on the net realizable value and is adjusted every year for the change in this value. At the time of sale, there is no further recognition of gain or loss, as the asset should be carried at net realizable value at that date. This system is not consistent with the notion of value in use, which assumes that the company has no intention of selling the asset. Therefore, this method is generally not used in Canada, even in times of higher inflation.

The word *market* must be used with some care. The preceding discussions assume that both the replacement market and the selling market are the markets in which the company normally trades. There are, however, special markets if a company must liquidate its assets quickly. The values in these markets can be significantly different from those in the normal market. As long as the company is a going concern, these specialty markets are not appropriate to establish values for the company's assets. On the other hand, if the company is bankrupt or going out of business, these specialty markets may be the most appropriate places to obtain estimates of the market values of the company's assets.

AN INTERNATIONAL PERSPECTIVE

Reports from Other Countries

While most countries value property, plant, and equipment at historical cost, a few (United Kingdom, France, Holland, and Switzerland) allow for revaluation of these assets based on current replacement cost. In France, these revaluations are seldom done because there is a conformity requirement between the reporting and tax books that would make such revaluations taxable. In the United Kingdom, such revaluations are quite common. The increase in the valuation of the assets that occurs under the replacement cost valuation does not typically pass through income but is recorded directly to the shareholders' equity section in an account called a *revaluation reserve*.

What Is Canadian Practice?

Capital assets are normally valued at their historical cost (their original acquisition cost). During the period of use, the cost of the asset is expensed using an amortization method that is rational, systematic, and appropriate to the asset. Changes in market values of assets are generally not recognized. If it is ever determined that the net recoverable amount of an asset is less than its net carrying value, the difference is recognized as a loss and the carrying value of the asset must be written down. The **net recoverable amount** is the total of all future cash flows without discounting them to present values. Unlike temporary investments and inventory, once a capital asset has been written down, it is not written back up if the net recoverable amount subsequently increases.

ethics in accounting

Ethics in
Accounting

■ The ability to control the timing of a writedown of property, plant, and equipment provides management with an opportunity to manage or manipulate earnings. The issue of earnings management has been studied by many researchers in an attempt to demonstrate its existence and to estimate its effects. In one study along these lines, Bruns and Merchant[1] surveyed 649 managers using a questionnaire that described 13 earnings-management situations and asked respondents to describe each as ethical, questionable, or unethical. To quote the authors directly:

> We found striking disagreements among managers in all groups. Furthermore, the liberal definitions revealed in many responses of what is moral or ethical should raise profound questions about the quality of financial information that is used for decision-making purposes by parties both inside and outside a company. It seems many managers are convinced that if a practice is not explicitly prohibited or is only a slight deviation from the rules, it is an ethical practice regardless of who might be affected either by the practice or the information that flows from it. This means that anyone who uses information on short-term earnings is vulnerable to misinterpretation, manipulation, or deliberate deception.

> The write-off of property, plant, and equipment is but one way that management may attempt to manipulate earnings. The reader of financial statements must be aware of this possibility to avoid being misled.

[1] Bruns, W.J., and Merchant, K.A., "The Dangerous Morality of Managing Earnings," *Management Accounting*, August 1990, pp. 22–25.

Capitalizable Costs

At the date of acquisition, the company must decide which costs associated with the purchase of the asset should be included or capitalized as a part of the asset's cost. The general guideline is that any cost that is necessary to acquire the asset and get it ready for use is a **capitalizable cost**. The following is a partial list of costs that would be considered capitalizable costs:

Learning Objective
2

Identify the acquisition costs that are usually added to the capital asset account at acquisition.

CAPITALIZABLE COSTS

Purchase price (less any discounts)
Installation costs
Transportation costs
Legal costs
Direct taxes
Interest cost (on self-constructed assets)

The determination of which costs appropriately belong in an asset account is not always easy. For example, the cost associated with the salaries of the employees who plan for and order the new asset are normally not included in the acquisition cost itself. This is true even though the time spent by the employees is necessary to acquire the asset. On the other hand, if employee time is required to install a new piece of equipment, the employees' wages usually are included. The costs associated with clearing land in preparation for constructing a new building are usually added to the land account. The cost of digging the hole to build the foundation of the building, on the other hand, is added to the building account. Land is a unique capital asset. Even though it is used by a company for several years, it is still there. Unlike other capital assets, it does not need to be replaced and, therefore, its original cost is not amortized. Assigning costs to land means that those costs will not appear in the future on the income statement.

Deciding which costs to capitalize is also influenced by the rules used for tax purposes. For tax purposes, the company would like to expense as many costs as possible to reduce taxable income and save on taxes. Capitalizing a cost means that the company will have to wait until the asset is amortized before the cost can be deducted for tax purposes. There is, therefore, an incentive to expense rather than to capitalize costs that are only indirectly related to the acquisition of the asset. A company may decide to expense a cost for reporting purposes to bolster its argument that the cost is an expense for tax purposes. The materiality criterion also plays a part in which costs are capitalized. Small expenditures related to the purchase of the asset may be expensed rather than capitalized because it is easier to expense them and the addition of the amount to the asset account would not change it significantly.

Basket Purchases

Sometimes a company acquires several assets in one transaction. This is called a **basket purchase**. For example, when a forest products company acquires timberland, it is buying both land and timber. The price paid for the timberland must then be divided between the land and the timber. In Canada, the price paid for these two assets must be divided between them on the basis of their relative fair values at the time of acquisitions for three reasons. First, full disclosure requires that each important type of asset should be shown separately. Second, assets that have different rates of amortization should be separated in the accounts. Third, some assets, like land, are not amortized at all.

Suppose that the purchase price of the timberland was $1 million and the relative fair values of the land and timber were assessed at $300,000 and $900,000 respectively. In this case, 25% [$300,000/($300,000 + $900,000)] of the cost, or $250,000, should be assigned to the land and the remaining 75%, or $750,000, should be assigned to the timber. In the case of timberland, splitting the cost has significant implications for the company because the cost of land is not amortized and the cost of timber can be expensed as the timber is harvested.

This example of a basket purchase used the purchase of timberland. Another example could be the purchase of a building. Part of the real estate cost must be allocated to the land on which the building is sitting and the remainder to the building. If the building includes various pieces of equipment or furniture, part of the purchase cost will have to be allocated to these items as well. Management's bias in favour of high profits would lead them to allocate less of the cost to the building. However, their conflicting interest in paying less tax would lead them to allocate more of the cost to the building.

Interest Capitalization

Interest capitalization deserves special consideration. Companies often borrow money to finance a capital asset. The interest paid on the borrowed money is capitalized when it is included in the capital asset account rather than expensing it. This is an issue for companies that construct some of their own capital assets. For example, some utility companies construct their own buildings. In addition to the costs incurred in the actual construction of the asset, such as raw materials, labour, and overhead, the company may also incur interest costs if it has to borrow money to pay for the materials, labour, and overhead. In Canada, companies can capitalize interest costs for capital assets that are constructed or acquired over time if the costs are directly attributable to the acquisition. The interest costs can only be capitalized until the capital asset is substantially complete and ready for use. For assets that are purchased rather than constructed, interest costs are usually not capitalized. The time period between acquisition and use is usually too short to make interest capitalization meaningful.

AN INTERNATIONAL PERSPECTIVE

Reports from Other Countries

NAFTA Facts

United States—The accounting for property, plant, and equipment is essentially the same as in Canada.

Mexico—Property, plant, and equipment are initially recorded at acquisition cost and then restated to current value at balance sheet dates, using either price indices or replacement cost.

AMORTIZATION CONCEPTS

Amortization or **depreciation** is a systematic and rational method of allocating the cost of capital assets to the periods in which the benefits from the assets are received. This matches, in a systematic way, the expense of the asset to the revenues earned from its use and therefore satisfies the matching principle described in Chapter 4. The allocation of any cost across multiple periods will always be somewhat arbitrary. In Canada, the amortization method used must be a rational and

Learning Objective

Describe the purpose of amortization and identify and implement four methods of amortization, including capital cost allowance.

systematic method appropriate to the nature of the capital asset with a limited life and to its use by the enterprise. In addition, the method of amortization and estimates of the useful life should be reviewed on a regular basis.

Amortization as used in accounting does not refer to valuation. While it is true that a company's capital assets generally decrease in value over time, amortization does not attempt to measure this change in value.

Matching some portion of a capital asset's cost to the company's revenues along with its other expenses results in a net profit or loss during the period. The company does not show the entire cost of the capital asset as an expense in the period of acquisition because the asset is expected to help generate revenues over multiple future periods. If these revenues do not materialize, the company will have overstated its profitability in earlier periods and will have to write off the remaining cost of the asset.

To allocate the expense systematically to the appropriate number of periods, the company must estimate the **useful life** of the asset; that is, the periods over which the company intends to use the asset to generate revenues. The company must also estimate the ultimate residual sales value of the asset at the end of its useful life.

Once the useful life and residual value of the asset have been estimated, the **amortizable cost** (cost minus the residual value) must then be allocated in a systematic and rational way to the years of useful life. Even though in Canada we do not specify which amortization methods may be used, most Canadian companies use one of three methods. These methods are discussed in the next section.

AMORTIZATION METHODS

As GAAP developed in the twentieth century, "rational and systematic" methods of amortizing capital assets were developed. The simplest and most commonly used method (used by more than 50% of Canadian companies) is the **straight-line method** (illustrated in Chapter 2), which allocates the amortizable cost of the asset evenly over its useful life. Many accountants have argued in favour of this method for two reasons. First, it is a very simple method to apply. Second, they argue that it properly matches expenses to revenues for costs associated with assets that generate revenues evenly throughout their lives. It might also be argued that, if an asset physically deteriorates evenly throughout its life, then straight-line amortization would capture this physical decline.

For certain assets, decline in revenue-generating capabilities (and physical deterioration) do not occur evenly over time. In fact, many assets are of most benefit to the company during the early years of their useful lives. In later years, when an asset is wearing out and requires more maintenance and perhaps produces inferior products, the value to the company declines significantly. This scenario argues for a more rapid amortization in the early years of the asset's life when a larger amortization expense is matched to the larger revenues produced. Methods that match this pattern are known as **accelerated** or **declining balance amortization** methods.

A third type of amortization recognizes that the usefulness or benefits derived from some capital assets can be measured fairly specifically. These methods are called **production** or **units-of-production** methods. Their use requires that the output or usefulness that will be derived from the asset be measured as a specific quantity. For example, a new truck might be expected to be used for a specific number of kilometres, perhaps 250,000. Then the amortization cost per kilometre can be calculated and used to determine amortization expense based on the number of kilometres driven in the accounting period.

A fourth, but rarely used, amortization method argues that, for some assets, the greatest change in usefulness and/or physical deterioration takes place in the last years of the asset's life rather than in the first few years. A method that captures this pattern is called **decelerated amortization**. Although this type of amortization method is not used much in practice, it is conceptually consistent with a **present-value method** of valuation of the asset. Present-value amortization methods, sometimes also called **compound interest methods**, are of this type.

Exhibit 8-1 illustrates the pattern of decline in the carrying value of an asset under three basic methods: straight-line, accelerated, and decelerated (these methods are discussed in detail later). Exhibit 8-2 illustrates the pattern of amortization expense recognition with the same methods. The graphs are based on a 40-year useful life, a zero residual value, and a $10,000 original cost. Note that Exhibits 8-1 and 8-2 do not show production methods because there is no consistent pattern with those methods. The amount of amortization expense depends on the actual usage each year.

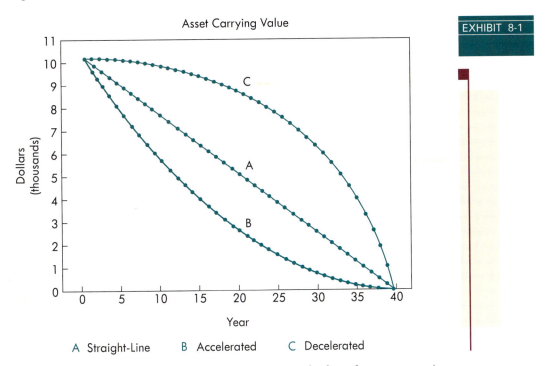

EXHIBIT 8-1

Asset Carrying Value

A Straight-Line   B Accelerated   C Decelerated

In Exhibit 8-1, note that using the straight-line method produces an even (or straight-line) decline in the carrying value of the asset. The accelerated method produces a more rapid decline in the carrying value, and the decelerated (present value) method shows a less rapid decline. Note that all methods start and end at the same value.

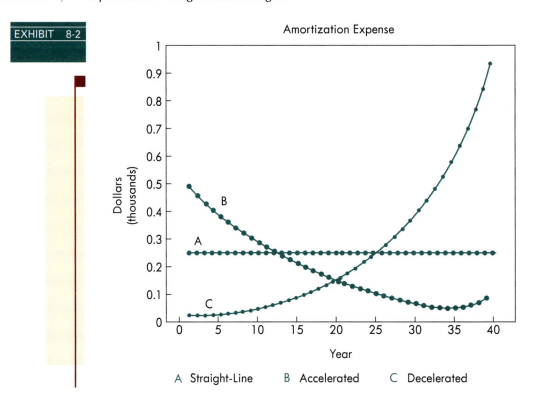

EXHIBIT 8-2

Amortization Expense

A Straight-Line   B Accelerated   C Decelerated

In Exhibit 8-2, you can see that the amortization expense for each period is the same with the straight-line method. With the accelerated method, the amortization expenses are higher in the earlier years of the asset's life, corresponding to the more rapid decline in carrying value as seen in Exhibit 8-1. The decelerated method, on the other hand, shows a slower decline in the carrying value of the asset and hence small amounts of amortization expense in the earlier years compared to the later years. Although the pattern of recognition is different, the total amount of the expense taken over the life of the asset will be the same for all methods.

Straight-Line Method

The most common method used for financial reporting is the straight-line method. It assumes that the cost of the asset should be allocated evenly over its life. Estimates must be made of the useful life and residual value. To illustrate the straight-line calculation and the calculation of amortization using other methods, a simple example is used. Assume that the company buys an asset for $10,000. The asset has an estimated useful life of five years and an estimated residual value of $1,000. Straight-line amortization would be calculated as shown in Exhibit 8-3.

STRAIGHT-LINE METHOD

EXHIBIT 8-3

Assumptions:

Original Cost	$10,000
Estimated Residual Value	$ 1,000
Estimated Useful Life	5 years

Calculation:

Straight-Line Amortization

$$\text{Amortization Expense} = \frac{\text{Original Cost} - \text{Estimated Residual Value}}{\text{Estimated Useful Life}}$$

$$= \frac{\$10,000 - \$1,000}{5 \text{ years}}$$

$$= \$1,800 \text{ per year}$$

Amortization Schedule:

Year	Book Value Beginning	Amortization Expense
1	$10,000	$1,800
2	8,200	1,800
3	6,400	1,800
4	4,600	1,800
5	2,800	1,800
		$9,000

The $1,800 of amortization expense is recorded each year for five years so that by the end of the useful life of the asset, the entire amortizable cost ($9,000 = $10,000 − 1,000) will have been expensed and the residual value of $1,000 will remain on the company's books.

Even though the straight-line method can be described by the estimated useful life and estimated residual value, it is sometimes characterized by a rate of amortization. The **rate of amortization** with the straight-line method is determined by taking the inverse of the number of years, 1/N, where N is the number of years of estimated useful life. In the case of the asset in the example, amortizing it over five years means a rate of 0.2 (1/5), or 20% per year. This will be referred to as the **straight-line rate**. Note that 20% of the amortizable cost, $9,000, is $1,800.

Accelerated Methods

The use of an accelerated method assumes that most of the benefits from the asset's use are realized in the early years. Most accelerated methods are calculated by multiplying the carrying value of the asset by a fixed percentage. Because the carrying value (cost less accumulated amortization) decreases each year (the accumulated amortization increases each year by the amount of the amortization recorded), the calculated amount of amortization to be recognized as an expense decreases each year.

The percentage used in these calculations is selected by management based on their judgement of the rapidity of the decline in usefulness of the asset. The faster the decline, the higher the percentage selected. Different types of capital assets have different percentages. A capital asset with a relatively long expected useful life (such as a building) would have a fairly small percentage (such as 5% or 10%). A capital asset with a relatively short expected useful life (such as equipment) would have a larger percentage (such as 20% or 30%).

One method of establishing the percentage rates to be used is called the **double declining balance method,** often referred to as the 200% declining balance method. With this method, the percentage selected is double the straight-line rate. Thus, using the example shown in Exhibit 8-3, the five-year expected useful life of an asset would be amortized over five years on a straight-line basis (that is, 1/5 per year, or 20%), but would be amortized at 40% using a double declining balance method (2 × 20%). However, even though this method appears to be based on fairly concrete numbers, it must be remembered that the 40% rate is still somewhat arbitrary (the 20% is an estimate).

Double declining balance amortization is calculated for our example asset in Exhibit 8-4. Note that the residual value of the asset does not enter into the calculation of the amortization expense. In some accelerated methods, the estimated residual value serves as a constraint; the net book value cannot drop below the residual value. In the example in Exhibit 8-4, this means that in Year 5 the company would not take the full amortization expense determined by the calculation because this would reduce the carrying value of the asset below the estimated residual value. In other cases, the residual value may not be reached prior to the end of the useful life so that additional amortization must be taken in the year of disposal of the asset. Alternatively, a loss on disposal could be recognized. In the example in Exhibit 8-4, suppose that the residual value was $500. The amortization schedule would be the same as in Exhibit 8-4 except that in Year 5 the company would have to recognize $796 in amortization expense so the carrying value of the asset would be $500, which is the amount of the residual value.

EXHIBIT 8-4

■ DOUBLE DECLINING BALANCE METHOD

Assumptions:

Original Cost	$10,000
Estimated Residual Value	$ 1,000
Estimated Useful Life	5 years
200% Declining Balance Method	

Calculation:

DB rate = DB% × SL rate

= 200% × 1/n

= 200% × 1/5 = 40%

Amortization Schedule:

At the beginning of the year

EXHIBIT 8-4

CONT.

Year	Balance in PP&E	Accumulated Amortization	Net Book Value	Calculation of Expense	Amortization Expense
1	$10,000	$ 0	$10,000	40% × 10,000 =	$4,000
2	10,000	4,000	6,000	40% × 6,000 =	2,400
3	10,000	6,400	3,600	40% × 3,600 =	1,440
4	10,000	7,840	2,160	40% × 2,160 =	864
5	10,000	8,704	1,296	40% × 1,296 =	296[a]
					$9,000

a The calculation of amortization expense in Year 5 results in a calculated amortization expense of $518, which would reduce the balance below the residual value. Therefore, only the amount of expense necessary to bring the balance to the residual value ($1,000) is recorded.

Production Methods

Another method used to calculate amortization is based on the assumption that benefits derived from a capital asset are related to the output or use of that asset. Note that the straight-line and accelerated methods of amortization assume that benefits derived from capital assets are related to time, disregarding how much the assets are actually used during the period. Production methods relate benefits to actual usage, which means that they best satisfy the matching principle.

The use of production methods requires that the useful life of the assets be known or can be estimated and expressed as units of output. For example, trucks can be amortized using a production method if their expected useful life can be expressed in kilometres driven or hours used. Machinery used in producing products may have an expected useful life based on the total number of units of output. Amortization expense is determined by calculating the amortization cost per unit, then multiplying this cost per unit by the actual number of units produced for the period. The formula for calculating amortization expense per unit for the production methods is as follows:

$$\text{Amortization expense per unit} = \frac{(\text{cost} - \text{residual value})}{\text{estimated total units of output}}$$

To calculate total amortization expense, simply multiply this per-unit cost by the total number of units produced. Exhibit 8-5 illustrates this method using our previous example.

■ PRODUCTION METHOD

Assumptions:

Original Cost	$10,000		
Estimated Residual Value	$ 1,000		
Estimated Usage	Year 1	5,000 units
	Year 2	4,500 units
	Year 3	5,500 units
	Year 4	3,000 units
	Year 5	2,000 units
		20,000 units

Calculation:

$$\text{Amortization Expense per Unit} = \frac{(\text{Cost} - \text{Residual Value})}{\text{Estimated Total Units of Output}}$$

$$= \frac{(\$10,000 - \$1,000)}{20,000 \text{ units}}$$

$$= \$0.45 \text{ per unit}$$

Amortization Schedule:

Year	Cost per Year	Units Used	Expense
1	$0.45 x	5,000	$2,250
2	$0.45 x	4,500	2,025
3	$0.45 x	5,500	2,475
4	$0.45 x	3,000	1,350
5	$0.45 x	2,000	900
			$9,000

Recording Amortization Expense

Regardless of the amortization method, the recording of the expense is the same. Amortization expense is debited and accumulated amortization is credited. The credit side of the entry is made to an accumulated amortization account and *not* to the asset account. The accumulated amortization account is a contra asset account that is used to accumulate the total amount of amortization expense that has been recorded for the capital asset over its lifetime. It might help you to think of the asset account being used to show the original historical cost of the asset, and the accumulated amortization account being used to show how much of the asset cost has already been expensed. The reason that we use the accumulated amortization account instead of reducing the asset directly is so that users have more information. If they can see what the original cost was, they will be able to estimate how much the company will probably have to pay to replace the assets. When the accumulated amortization is offset against the asset, users can determine how much of the asset has been amortized and can make a judgement about how soon the assets will need to be replaced.

In financial statements, companies normally show the total original costs of all tangible capital assets separately by category (such as land, buildings, and equipment) with accumulated amortization for each category. Some companies show only one total for accumulated amortization for all the various categories of assets. Some companies show capital assets grouped not by category but by operating division. Many companies show only the total net book value (cost less accumulated amortization) in the balance sheet with the details provided in a note to the financial statements.

Examples of disclosure of capital assets (sometimes called fixed assets) and related accumulated amortization (sometimes called depreciation) are shown in Exhibits 8-6 and 8-7. Note that **Cara Operations Limited** discloses that it is constructing some capital assets and that it is capitalizing the interest costs. The capitalization of interest was discussed earlier in this chapter. In 2000, **Algoma Central Corporation** disclosed that it wrote down the carrying value of some of its vessels. Companies must periodically review the carrying value of their assets to determine if there is any change in the future benefits they expect to derive from their use. If the future recoverable amount of the assets is less than their current carrying value, they must be written down to reflect the impairment in value.

CARA OPERATIONS LIMITED, 2001

EXHIBIT 8-6

Excerpted from the Notes to the Statements

Note ⑤ **Property, Plant and Equipment**

(in thousands of dollars)	2002 Cost	2002 Accumulated Amortization	2002 Net	2001 Cost	2001 Accumulated Amortization	2001 Net
Land	$ 19,710	$ —	$ 19,710	$ 20,239	$ —	$ 20,239
Buildings	105,163	33,740	71,423	103,753	30,958	72,795
Equipment	283,320	115,859	167,461	248,137	89,084	159,053
Leasehold improvements	159,539	54,228	105,311	134,547	44,093	90,454
Equipment under capital lease	20,312	12,487	7,825	20,355	10,660	9,695
Construction in progress	4,311	—	4,311	11,480	—	11,480
	$ 592,355	$ 216,314	$ 376,041	$ 538,511	$ 174,795	$ 363,716

Interest capitalized during the year was $0.5 million (2001 – $2.5 million).

ALGOMA CENTRAL CORPORATION, 2001

Excerpted from the Notes to the Statements

EXHIBIT 8-7

4. CAPITAL ASSETS

		Land		Amortizable Assets		Accumulated Amortization		Net
2001								
Marine	$	197	$	599,483	$	369,094	$	230,586
Real Estate		4,963		61,193		18,304		47,852
	$	5,160	$	660,676	$	387,398	$	278,438
2000								
Marine	$	197	$	592,179	$	345,908	$	246,468
Real Estate		4,963		61,146		16,711		49,398
	$	5,160	$	653,325	$	362,619	$	295,866

During 2000 the Corporation wrote down certain vessels in the domestic and ocean fleets to reflect a permanent impairment in their value. The amount of the write-down before income taxes was $23,587. The Corporation's share of the write-down attributable to two ocean-going vessels in the Marbulk Canada Inc. fleet was $12,205 and the balance of $11,382 relates to certain vessels in the domestic fleet.

CORPORATE INCOME TAXES

The issue of corporate income taxes arises quite naturally at this point and is therefore introduced here. The Canada Customs and Revenue Agency (CCRA) does not allow companies to deduct amortization expense when calculating **taxable income**. However, it does allow a similar type of deduction, called **capital cost allowance**. Capital cost allowance (CCA) is calculated in a manner similar to accelerated amortization, with several exceptions. The calculation of amortization expense for accounting income and CCA for taxable income means that the net carrying value of the capital asset under each calculation is different. This difference is known as a **temporary difference**. Although the amortization expense and the CCA will not necessarily be the same in a given year, over time, the net capital asset amount under both calculations will be the same. When there is a difference in the net capital asset amounts because accounting guidelines and tax rules are different, a **future income tax liability** or **asset** results which accounts for the difference.

While it is not the purpose of this text to teach you about income taxes, which are subject to very complex rules, you should understand the basics of how capital cost allowance works. Because CCA is required for tax purposes, many smaller companies use it for the accounting amortization calculation as well so that they only have to do one calculation. For tax purposes, capital assets are grouped into classes as defined by the CCRA. For example, most vehicles are grouped into Class 10 and

OMIT

most equipment into Class 8. Each class has a prescribed rate used to calculate the maximum amount that may be deducted. For example, Class 10 has a maximum rate of 30% and Class 8 has a 20% rate. Companies may deduct any amount of the **undepreciated capital cost** (UCC) in the class up to the stated maximum in a year, except for assets acquired in the current year. In the year of acquisition, the maximum CCA that may be deducted for new assets is restricted to 50% of the normal amount.

As an example, assume that Central Corp. purchases new equipment (Class 8) in Year 1 with a total cost of $20,000. For tax purposes, it may deduct a maximum of the following:

CCA Year 1	50% × $20,000 × 20% = $2,000
CCA Year 2	20% × ($20,000 − $2,000) = $3,600
CCA Year 3	20% × ($20,000 − $2,000 − $3,600) = $2,880

Note that the UCC declines each year by the amount of CCA claimed the previous year.

The cost of new capital assets is added to the class to increase the UCC. When capital assets are sold, the lesser of the original cost or the proceeds from the sale is deducted from the UCC.

The differences between tax and financial statement amounts can produce significant differences between the carrying value of the asset measured in accordance with accounting guidelines and the UCC used as the basis for the CCA reported to the CCRA. For example, assume that a company has only one asset. Assume further that there are no other differences in the revenues and expenses for accounting and tax purposes. For tax purposes, assume the maximum capital cost allowance rate is 30%. For financial statement purposes, assume the use of straight-line, and use the deductions shown in Exhibit 8-3. Exhibit 8-8 presents some additional data for this hypothetical company and the calculation of income before taxes for the first year of the asset's life.

FUTURE TAX CALCULATIONS

EXHIBIT 8-8

The calculation of CCA for the first year would be: $10,000 x .30 x .50 = $1,500

Income Statement

	Accounting	Tax
Revenues	$ 90,000	$90,000
Expenses (except amortization or CCA)	50,000	50,000
Income before amortization and taxes	40,000	40,000
Amortization/CCA	1,800	1,500
Income before taxes	$ 38,200	$38,500
Tax expense (30%)	$ 11,460	
Taxes payable (30%)		$11,550
Carrying value of the asset	$ 8,200	$ 8,500

Future tax asset = ($8,200 − $8,500) × 30% = $90

If the tax rate is 30%, the company will owe the CCRA $11,550 ($38,500 × 30%) in taxes based on the taxable income reported. What should the company report as tax expense to the shareholders? Some accountants would argue that the tax expense should be calculated based on the accounting income times the tax rate. In this case, the tax expense would be $11,460 ($38,200 × 30%). Others would argue that the company should report the actual taxes payable to the CCRA, $11,550, as the expense. In the second case, the tax expense for accounting purposes would not bear any relationship to the income before taxes; that is, $11,550/$38,200 = 30.2%, which would not reflect the actual tax rate of 30%.

In Canada, the tax expense reported in the income statement will be based on the difference between the income taxes payable and the future tax asset. The entry that would be recorded for our example company would therefore be:

SE-Tax expense	11,460	
A-Future tax asset	90	
L -Income taxes payable		11,550

As you can see in the preceding entry, the debit to tax expense would then be less than the credit to the taxes payable account, because the latter is based on what is actually owed to the CCRA. The difference between these two entries, the future tax asset, represents the difference between the carrying values of the asset under accounting and tax multiplied by the tax rate. If the future tax amount has a debit balance, it means that the carrying value of the asset for tax is larger than the carrying value for accounting and therefore, less tax will be paid in the future because there is still $8,500 of taxable asset remaining compared to $8,200 for the accounting asset. If the future tax amount has a credit balance (a future tax liability), it means that the carrying value of the asset for tax is smaller than the carrying value for accounting and therefore, more tax will be paid in the future because the smaller tax carrying amount represents a smaller future deduction. These taxes will have to be paid by the company later in the asset's life when the deduction for tax purposes is significantly less than the amortization for reporting purposes.

Future income tax, therefore, arises from differences in the carrying value of assets for tax purposes compared to the carrying value for financial statement purposes. The discussion of income taxes is continued in more detail in Chapter 9.

CHOICE OF AMORTIZATION METHOD

Learning Objective
4

Identify the factors that influence the choice of amortization method.

Companies are free to choose from the amortization methods that have been discussed. The majority of companies use the straight-line method, probably because of its simplicity and possibly because it usually produces the highest net income in the early years of an asset's life. Some small companies choose to calculate amortization expense using CCA to simplify bookkeeping and tax reporting.

CHANGES IN AMORTIZATION ESTIMATES AND METHODS

Because the amounts used for useful life and residual value are estimates, the assumptions used in their estimation may change over time. Companies must periodically revisit these estimates to ensure that they are still valid. For example, after an asset has been in service for several years, the company may change its estimate about the asset's remaining useful life. The asset may last longer or deteriorate faster than originally anticipated. Changes in the estimates used to calculate amortization expense are accounting estimate changes. Accounting estimate changes are handled prospectively (in current and future periods).

To illustrate a prospective change in amortization assumptions, the amortization example in Exhibit 8-3 will be used. Assume that during Year 4 the company decides that the asset has three more years of useful life left (i.e., it should have had an original life of six rather than five years), and that the residual value at the end of the sixth year will be $400. The company recalculates the amortization for Years 4, 5, and 6 based on these new assumptions. The new calculation is based on the remaining book value at the end of Year 3 of $4,600 [$10,000 − (3 × $1,800)]. The entire schedule of amortization, then, is as shown in Exhibit 8-9. Note that there is no restatement of prior periods with a change of estimate.

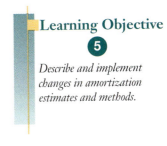

Learning Objective 5

Describe and implement changes in amortization estimates and methods.

STRAIGHT-LINE METHOD

EXHIBIT 8-9

Change in Estimate of Useful Life and Residual Value

Assumptions:

Original Cost	$10,000
Estimated Residual Value	$ 1,000
Estimated Useful Life	5 years

Change during Year 4:

Remaining Estimated Useful Life	3 years
Estimated Residual Value	$ 400

Calculation of Remaining Amortization (years 4–6):
Straight-Line Amortization

$$\text{Amortization Expense} = \frac{\text{Remaining Book Value} - \text{Estimated Residual Value}}{\text{Estimated Useful Life}}$$

$$= \frac{\$4,600 - \$400}{3 \text{ years}}$$

$$= \$1,400 \text{ per year}$$

Amortization Schedule:

Year	Book Value Beginning	Amortization Expense
1	$10,000	$1,800
2	8,200	1,800

EXHIBIT 8-9 CONT.			
	3	6,400	1,800
	4	4,600	1,400
	5	3,200	1,400
	6	1,800	1,400
			$9,600

The disclosure of changes in estimates in financial statements usually describes the nature of the change and the effects on the current year. Companies are not required to make this type of disclosure but voluntary disclosure improves the usefulness of the financial information.

Amortization amounts can also change as new costs are added to the asset account for major repairs and improvements. These generally will require new estimates of useful life and residual value and are handled as changes in accounting estimates.

A company may also decide that a different amortization method more appropriately aligns the amortization expense with the benefits received from the asset. If the decision to change comes from changed circumstances, experience, or new information, the change is treated in the same way as the changes in estimates were treated. The new amortization method is applied to the carrying value of the asset at the time that the change is made, and the company continues with the new method over the asset's remaining useful life. It is possible that changes in the useful life and residual value might also be applied with the new amortization method.

DISPOSAL AND WRITEDOWN OF PROPERTY, PLANT, AND EQUIPMENT

Learning Objective

6

Account for the disposal and writedown of capital assets.

At the end of an asset's useful life, the company usually sells it for another asset of similar productive capacity, especially if the line of business is growing and prospering. In lines of business that are on a decline or discontinued, old assets are not replaced and assets may be sold or written off before they reach the end of their useful lives.

Normally, at the end of an asset's life, it is sold. If the company has accurately projected the residual value, there is no gain or loss on the transaction. If the residual value was not estimated accurately, either a gain or a loss results from this transaction. For example, suppose that the asset in Exhibit 8-3 is sold at the end of its useful life for $1,200. Recall that its original cost was $10,000 and that its residual value was $1,000. The following entry would be made to record the transaction.

A-Cash	1,200	
XA-Accumulated amortization	9,000	
A-Property, plant, and equipment		10,000
SE-Gain on sale of property, plant, and equipment		200

In this entry, the accumulated amortization is removed from the account as well as the original cost in the equipment account. Note that the net of these two amounts is the carrying value of the asset at the point of sale, $1,000 ($10,000 − 9,000). This amount is also known as the **book value** or the **net book value** at the time of sale. Note also that you cannot credit the equipment account for the book value amount of $1,000, as that would leave $9,000 in the asset account and $9,000 in the accumulated amortization account, even though the asset is no longer owned by the company.

If the asset had been worthless at the end of its useful life, the disposal of the asset would be recorded as above, except that no cash is received. If we assume that no cash is received, then the write-off of the asset in our example results in the following entry:

XA-Accumulated amortization	9,000	
SE-Loss on disposal of property, plant, and equipment	1,000	
A-Property, plant, and equipment		10,000

Note that the remaining book value of $1,000 is recorded as a loss on disposal and not as an adjustment to the amortization that has been recorded.

Sometimes the future recoverable amount of a capital asset (reflecting its ability to generate revenue in the future) declines below its carrying value. Some of the reasons for this decline could be technological change, damage to the asset, or change in the market direction of the company. When the recoverable amount declines, the company must write down the carrying value of the asset to its new lower value. This is accomplished by recognizing a loss on the income statement and increasing the accumulated amortization account by the amount of the loss. Increasing the accumulated amortization decreases the net book value of the asset. For example, suppose that at the end of the third year, when the book value of the asset in Exhibit 8-3 is $4,600, the company determines that as a result of some damage the asset's future recoverable amount has declined to $3,600. The following entry would be made to record this change:

SE-Loss due to damage to equipment	1,000	
XA-Accumulated amortization		1,000

In all likelihood, subsequent to this decline in value, the company would review the estimated residual value and the useful life so that changes could be made to the amortization in future periods if they were necessary.

NATURAL RESOURCES

Companies that deal with natural resources face some unique problems not associated with investments in property, plant, and equipment. For example, consider the situation of an oil exploration company. The company incurs large costs to find oil. Some explorations are successful in finding oil and others are not. Should the costs of unsuccessful exploration be capitalized on the balance sheet as assets, or should they be written off? If these costs are capitalized as assets, that implies that they

Learning Objective

7

Describe and implement the amortization method used most frequently for natural resources.

have future value. But do they? On successful explorations, if the costs are capitalized, how should they be expensed? That is, what is the useful life of the asset created, and what is a reasonable pattern of expense allocation across the useful life?

In Canada, oil exploration companies have a choice of two methods to account for exploration costs: the **full costing method**, and the **successful efforts method**. The full costing method capitalizes the costs of all explorations, both successful and unsuccessful, as long as the expected revenues from all explorations are estimated to exceed the total costs. The successful efforts method, on the other hand, capitalizes only the cost of successful explorations and expenses unsuccessful exploration costs. Sufficient time is allowed to determine whether an effort is or is not successful. Generally, smaller oil companies use the full costing method because using the successful efforts method would make their income appear to be very uneven from year to year, depending on the results of the wells they drilled in the year. Larger oil companies drill more wells every year, so they tend to use the successful efforts method as it is simpler to apply and its use over a large base does not result in uneven results from year to year.

Exhibit 8-10 includes examples from two companies:

EXHIBIT 8-10

■ **EXAMPLES OF FULL COSTING AND SUCCESSFUL EFFORTS METHODS**

Excerpts from the Notes to the Statements

Purcell Energy Inc. (2001)

2. Summary of Significant accounting policies

(d) Property, plant and equipment

The Company follows the full cost method of accounting for oil and gas operations whereby all costs of exploring for and developing oil and gas reserves are initially capitalized. Such costs include land acquisition costs, geological and geophysical expenses, carrying charges on non-producing properties, costs of drilling, and overhead charges directly related to acquisition and exploration activities.

Costs capitalized, together with the cost of production equipment, are depleted on the unit-of-production method based on the estimated gross proven reserves. Petroleum products and reserves are converted to equivalent units of natural gas at approximately 6,000 cubic feet to 1 barrel of oil.

Suncor Energy Inc. (2001)

Summary of Significant Accounting Policies

(d) Property, Plant, and Equipment

The company follows the successful efforts method of accounting for its crude oil and natural gas operations. Under the successful efforts method, acquisition costs of proved and unproved properties are capitalized. Costs of unproved properties are transferred to proved properties when proved reserves are confirmed. Exploration costs, including geological and geophysical costs, are expensed as incurred. Exploration drilling costs are capitalized initially. If it is determined that the well does not contain proved reserves, the capitalized exploratory drilling costs are charged to expense, as dry hole costs, at that time. The related land costs are expensed through the amortization of unproved properties as covered under the Natural Gas section of the depreciation, depletion, and amortization policy below.

Note that Suncor Energy uses the successful efforts method for its acquisition costs and exploration drilling costs. Exploration costs, on the other hand, are expensed as they are incurred.

Under the full costing method, all capitalized costs are expensed over the life of the exploration site. Under the successful efforts method, only the capitalized costs associated with the successful site are amortized over the life of the exploration site. The amortization of natural resources is often referred to as **depletion.** The amortization method most commonly used is the units-of-production method. With this method, the total number of barrels of oil (in the case of an oil field) that exists in the field is estimated. The amortization expense is then calculated by dividing the number of barrels extracted during the period by the estimated total and multiplying this ratio by the capitalized costs. For example, assume a company estimates a field to have 2 million barrels of oil. In a given period, 500,000 barrels are extracted. If the capitalized costs are $6 million, then the amortization expense during the period would be $1.5 million ($500,000/2,000,000 x 6,000,000).

INTANGIBLE ASSETS

As discussed earlier in the chapter, some assets can have probable future value to the company but may not have any physical form. The knowledge gained from research and development, or the customer loyalty and awareness spawned by a well-run advertising campaign, are examples of intangible assets. The company certainly hopes that it benefits from having spent money on these things. The difficulty in trying to quantify the benefits and assess the costs of producing intangible assets, such as research and development or advertising, is what makes intangible assets a troublesome area for accountants. Although accountants would generally agree that these might constitute assets, the inability to provide reliable data concerning their costs and future value makes it hard to record these items objectively in the company's accounting system.

The capitalization guideline for intangible assets is that if an intangible asset is developed internally by the company, the costs associated with its production are generally expensed as incurred. If the intangible asset is purchased from an independent third party, however, the intangible asset can be capitalized at its acquisition cost.

An exception to this general guideline occurs with the **development costs** for a product or process. If certain guidelines are met, these development costs may be capitalized and amortized over the useful life of the product. However, the basic **research costs** that occurred prior to any decision to develop the product or process are still expensed. The guidelines are intended to ensure that development costs will be capitalized only if the product or process is actually marketable. The guidelines stipulate that the product or process be clearly definable, that technical feasibility be established, that management intend to market the product in a defined market, and that the company have the resources needed to complete the project. In the United States, both research and development costs are expensed. This can result in very large income differences between a Canadian company and an American company.

The amortization of the cost of an intangible asset is similar to the amortization of other capital assets. The company must estimate the useful life and residual value

Learning Objective

Explain the accounting difficulties associated with intangible assets.

Learning Objective

9

Amortize intangible assets.

(if any) of the asset. Because of the estimation problems associated with intangible assets, this is sometimes very difficult to do. Typically, the method used to amortize intangibles is the straight-line method, with an estimated residual value of zero. The useful life depends on the type of intangible. The one aspect of amortization that is different for intangibles is that the accumulated amortization account is rarely used. Most often the company reduces the intangible asset directly. Because of the uncertain valuation of intangibles and the fact that the asset normally cannot be replaced, it is not as important for users to know what the original cost was. For example, the journal entry to record the amortization of a patent would probably be:

SE-Amortization expense	xxx	
A-Patents		xxx

One additional point is worth noting. When estimating the useful life of an intangible asset, both economic life and legal life should be considered. Many intangible assets, such as patents, copyrights, and trademarks, have very well-defined legal lives, but may have less well-defined and much shorter economic lives. Intangible assets that have definite lives have to be amortized over the useful life or legal life of the asset, whichever is shorter. Intangible assets with indefinite lives are no longer amortized in a systematic, rational manner. Instead, they must be evaluated each year to determine whether there has been any impairment in the value of the asset. If there has, the asset should immediately be written down. If there has not, the asset remains at its current carrying amount until the following year when it is evaluated again. Note the following example:

accounting in the news

INTANGIBLES IN BIOTECH COMPANIES

Small biotech companies are often founded on the strength of intangible assets in the form of scientific patents that hold potential for drug discoveries. The costs associated with developing a drug, however, are high, and pharmaceutical companies can spend a lot of money with no guarantee of their drug's ever reaching the marketplace.

In 1997, Novopharm Biotech Inc., a drug development company in Toronto, acquired Genesys Pharma of Winnipeg, largely because of the potential of an anti-cancer drug being developed by the smaller company. Two years later, Novopharm stopped development following reports of side effects during Phase 1 clinical trials. Novopharm planned to account for the costs associated with GP1-2A's development by taking a $19.6-million writedown.

Source: "Novopharm Biotech suspends drug," by John Greenwood, *National Post* (*Financial Post*), Feb. 11, 1999, p. C9

Several types of intangible assets involve special problems. They are discussed in the following section.

Advertising

Companies spend enormous amounts of money advertising their products to increase current and future sales. Does the incurrence of advertising costs create an asset for the company? If the advertising is successful, then the answer is probably yes. But how will the company know if the advertising is successful, and what time periods will receive the benefits from advertisements that were purchased during the current period? If a customer buys a product, did he/she buy it because of the advertisement, because he/she happened to be in the store and saw it on the shelf, or because his/her neighbour has one? The answers to these questions are very difficult to address. The intent of advertising is clearly to create an asset, but measuring its value can be extremely difficult. These measurement uncertainties are so severe that accountants generally expense all advertising costs in the period in which the advertising occurs. If a company does capitalize this cost, it has to provide very strong evidence to support the creation of an asset.

Many companies spent advertising dollars for the 2002 Winter Olympics in Salt Lake City. The spending began in 2001 and continued into 2002. For many companies, the money was not just spent for advertisements during the games but rather to provide pre-game financial support to the athletes, who then wore clothing with the sponsor's logo on it.

accounting in the news

THE GAMES

Corporate sponsorship helps make going to the Olympics a reality for many amateur athletes. But what do corporations receive in return for their promotional dollars? For Visa Canada, sponsoring the Canadian bobsleigh teams at the Salt Lake City games was a chance to be connected with Olympians, who embody leadership and worldwide acceptance.

Promoting the sponsorship carried a $1.9-million price tag, but several factors helped justify the cost. First, the Olympics is a 17-day event followed around the world, drawing an audience of all ages and from all walks of life.

Then the company compared the volume of impressions of Visa that viewers would receive from television coverage of the bobsleigh teams to the volume of impressions from paid television advertising. Including the cost of a PR firm to promote the teams, the return in value was twice the cost, one Visa official said. Focus groups and telephone surveys also found that people who knew about the sponsorships reacted differently from those who didn't—another sign that the promotion was scoring.

> Finally, the sponsorship fit into a larger marketing strategy. A sweepstakes contest in malls, featuring cutouts of a bobsleigh in Visa's colours, offered a winning trip to the Winter Olympics. Visa also sponsored World Cup events in Calgary. And track-level footage to highlight the speed and risks that make the sport exciting was included in prime-time television commercials.
>
> Source: "The Final Push," by Michael Grange, *The Globe and Mail, Report on Business Magazine,* Jan. 25, 2002, p. 59.

Patents, Trademarks, and Copyrights

Patents, trademarks, and copyrights are legal agreements that give the owner rights to use protected information. If the protected information is valuable, then the agreements are considered assets. Of course, determining whether they have value or not is a difficult task, as is estimating the period over which the agreements will continue to have value. Each agreement may have a legal life associated with it. For example, a patent has a legal life of 20 years, but this does not mean that it will have an economic life of 20 years. The patent on a computer chip, for example, may have a useful economic life of only a year or two as a result of technological innovation. On the other hand, trademarks like Coca-Cola may have an indefinite life. Copyrights have a legal life of the life of the creator plus 50 years.

A company records these types of intangible assets only when it buys them from a third party. Development costs of most internally developed patents, trademarks, and copyrights are expensed. Some minor costs, such as registration and the legal costs of filing a patent, trademark, or copyright can be capitalized. The costs are then usually amortized on a straight-line basis over the estimated useful life of the asset. Legal life serves as a maximum in the determination of the asset's useful economic life.

It is sometimes difficult to establish and defend patents, trademarks, and copyrights. Note the following example:

accounting in the news

During the anthrax scare in Canada and the United States in 2001, Federal Health Minister Allan Rock ignored Bayer Inc.'s patent on the anti-anthrax antibiotic Cipro when he agreed to buy a cheaper generic version. He changed his mind following a high-profile protest over patent rights.

Patent protection can be a key factor in drug manufacturers' commitment to drug discovery. In Canada, drug companies are reaping the benefits of patent protection laws that give them exclusivity for 20 years before generic drug manufacturers can bring cheaper versions to market. This exclusivity can be traced back to 1987, the result of federal patent law changes geared to increase drug R&D in Canada.

In exchange for longer exclusivity, drug companies agreed that by 1996, their R&D budgets would almost double to 10% of sales. They kept the bargain. Federal figures show that total R&D spending grew 277% between 1988 and 1995, when spending for drug discovery represented 11.7% of sales.

Drug companies have reaped even better rewards—revenue growth from increased exclusivity has outpaced R&D spending. In 2000, while sales for the 79 patent holders reporting to the Federal Government rose 12%, R&D spending increased by only 5.6%, representing 10.1% of sales.

Source: "Swallow this: Drug R&D spending is waning," by Zena Olijnyk, *Canadian Business*, Dec. 10, 2001.

Goodwill

Goodwill is an asset that represents the above-average profits that a company can earn as a result of a number of factors. Above-average management expertise, for example, could give a company an advantage over another company in the same industry. An excellent location could provide a comparative advantage over other companies in the same business. Excellent employee or customer relations can also create an advantage in the marketplace.

Companies incur costs to create these types of goodwill. Advertising campaigns, public service programs, charitable gifts, and employee training programs all require outlays that to some extent develop goodwill. This type of goodwill is sometimes referred to as internally developed goodwill.

As with other intangible assets, the costs of developing internally developed goodwill are expensed as they are incurred. In practice, goodwill is recorded as an asset only when it is part of the purchase price paid to acquire another company. Goodwill is not an easily identifiable asset, but is represented by the dollar figure paid by the acquiring company for various valuable—but intangible—characteristics of the acquired company (such as good location, good management, etc.). These characteristics, in effect, give the acquired company more value than its identifiable assets (its buildings, inventory, etc.). Recorded goodwill arises only in situations in which one company buys ownership rights in another company. When the cost of the ownership right exceeds the fair value of the identifiable net assets acquired, then the company has purchased goodwill.

The recording of goodwill and its calculation are discussed in more detail in Appendix B at the end of the book. Once recorded, it is not amortized. Instead, management is required to periodically review the carrying value of the goodwill to determine whether the amount plus the fair value of the acquired net assets is still greater than the carrying value of the investment. If it is not, an impairment in goodwill has occurred and the goodwill should be written down and an impairment loss recognized.

During 2001 and 2002, many companies reviewed their acquisitions and recognized impairment losses.

accounting in the news

GOODWILL WRITEDOWNS IN GOOD COMPANY

In 2002, when AOL-Time Warner Inc. set a record by writing off up to US $60 billion in goodwill, analysts predicted other major companies would soon follow suit. Some estimated that goodwill writedowns could total more than $1 trillion by the end of the year.

Massive writedowns are a legacy of the late 1990s, as companies concede that acquisitions they paid dearly for during the high-tech go-go years will not deliver the returns they expected. Nortel Networks Corp., for instance, bought 20 companies in two years at the height of the market. It has since written off billions for its buying spree.

The incidence of writedowns is tied to changes in accounting rules. Goodwill is the amount a company pays that is higher than the value of the assets of a company it is acquiring. While companies used to be able to write off goodwill over several years, changes in American and Canadian standards now demand an assessment every year. If the company does not foresee recovering its investment (in other words, if it paid too much), it must acknowledge this by writing down "impaired assets."

Source: "Goodwill writedowns to hit $1 trillion," by Steve Maich, *National Post, Financial Post*, Jan. 10, 2002, p. FP2.

Examples of the disclosure of goodwill and other intangible assets are shown in Exhibit 8-11 for **METRO INC.**, and in Exhibit 8-12 for **AT Plastics Inc.** Note that AT Plastics includes accumulated amortization for its goodwill. Prior to July 2001, goodwill was systematically amortized.

STATEMENT ANALYSIS CONSIDERATIONS

The use of different amortization methods for capital assets can produce significantly different results in the financial statements of two otherwise similar companies. For the first few years, a company using the straight-line method will show higher carrying values for its capital assets than a similar company using the double declining balance method. This affects the balance sheet value as well as the amortization expense that is reported in the income statement. Unfortunately, there is no easy way for the user to convert from one method to another to make the statements more comparable.

7. CAPITAL ASSETS — METRO INC. (2001)

EXHIBIT 8-11

	2001			2000			1999
	Cost	Accu-mulated depre-ciation	Net book value	Cost	Accu-mulated depre-ciation	Net book value	Net book value
TANGIBLE ASSETS							
Land	$ 37.4	$ —	$ 37.4	$ 29.3	$ —	$ 29.3	$ 28.2
Buildings	134.7	47.4	87.3	122.4	43.6	78.8	79.5
Equipment	289.1	146.8	142.3	271.4	145.4	126.0	129.2
Leasehold improvements	113.2	54.5	58.7	104.3	53.6	50.7	49.5
	574.4	248.7	325.7	527.4	242.6	284.8	286.4
INTANGIBLE ASSETS							
Leasehold rights	54.8	16.9	37.9	53.6	15.2	38.4	40.1
Improvements and development of retail network loyalty, software and other	197.0	78.7	118.3	170.9	63.2	107.7	87.4
	251.8	95.6	156.2	224.5	78.4	146.1	127.5
	$826.2	**$344.3**	**$481.9**	$ 751.9	$ 321.0	$430.9	$ 413.9

The net acquisitions under capital leases and other acquisitions of assets excluded from the statement of cash flows totalled $6.0, $6.4 and $7.2 in 2001, 2000 and 1999 respectively.

8. OTHER ASSETS — AT PLASTICS INC. (2001)

EXHIBIT 8-12

2001	Cost	Accumulated amortization	Net book value
Development costs	$ 9,784	$ 7,238	$ 2,546
Deferred exchange	6,955	6,492	463
Deferred financing costs	5,270	3,347	1,923
Deferred pension costs	591	–	591
Goodwill	1,109	518	591
Investment tax credits recoverable	2,503	–	2,503
Pre-operating costs	7,215	4,288	2,927
	$ 33,427	$ 21,883	$ 11,544

2000	Cost	Accumulated amortization	Net book value
Development costs	$ 10,992	$ 5,235	$ 5,757
Deferred exchange	6,336	4,213	2,123
Deferred financing costs	4,216	1,425	2,791
Deferred pension costs	343	–	343
Goodwill	1,109	444	665
Investment tax credits recoverable	2,289	–	2,289
Pre-operating costs	7,215	2,937	4,278
	$ 32,500	$ 14,254	$ 18,246

Probably the biggest concerns in the analysis of capital assets are understanding which assets have been left out and what market values can be assigned to the assets listed. The historical cost figures for property, plant, and equipment may be very old. Even though the company is not holding these assets for resale, it will have to replace them at some point and, therefore, the replacement cost may be relevant. In Canada, companies are not required to disclose replacement cost information. If a company reports property, plant, and equipment as a single amount, the user is not able to determine how much is invested in each of the components. This information could be important to users as they attempt to anticipate future outflows of cash for the replacement of some of these assets. Even if a company assigns three separate amounts for property, plant, and equipment, the user is still missing some important pieces of information that could be useful in evaluating the company. For example, if a single amount for buildings is disclosed, the user still does not know: (1) how many buildings are included, (2) where the buildings are located, or (3) when the buildings were acquired. Without this information, the user does not have any way of determining replacement cost or market value.

Another problem is that many intangible assets that have been developed internally do not appear on the company's financial statements because their costs have been expensed as they were developed. It is possible for a company to have the rights to a patent that it has developed that will generate revenues for several years. This valuable asset is often not listed as an asset. The large dollar amounts that companies are willing to pay for goodwill when taking control of other companies testify to the substantial value of these unrecorded assets. A failure to consider these assets can lead different analysts to draw significantly different conclusions about the value of a company.

One final general concern with regard to financial statement analysis is whether the capital assets listed on the company's balance sheet are really worth the amounts recorded. For example, the conditions that gave rise to goodwill at the date of acquisition may have changed since acquisition. Suppose the goodwill was due to the technical expertise of a key employee of the business that was acquired. If the employee dies or otherwise leaves the company after acquisition, then the goodwill could be worth less. For this reason, analysts generally have a healthy scepticism about the value of goodwill and other intangibles.

Using the Return on Assets (ROA) Ratio

Despite the unknowns associated with the capital asset values, a ratio using assets has been developed. This ratio, called the return on assets ratio, or ROA, is used to calculate how well management managed the assets used in the company. This ratio simply expresses the total return earned as a percentage of total assets. The return on the investment in assets should be calculated prior to any payments or returns to the debtholders or shareholders. Net income has interest expense already deducted, but not dividends. Therefore, the net income, if it is to be used as a measure of return on assets, must be adjusted for the effects of interest expense so it is treated on a basis that is similar to the treatment of dividends.

A complicating factor exists because interest is a deductible expense in the calculation of income tax expense. Therefore, if interest expense is to be removed from the net income figure, we must also adjust the amount of income tax expense that would result. In other words, the tax savings (i.e., the reduction in income tax expense) associated with this interest deduction must also be removed. The ROA ratio is thus calculated as the ratio of the return (income before interest) divided by the investment in total assets as follows:

Learning Objective
10

Calculate the return on assets ratio and discuss the potential implications of the results.

$$ROA = \frac{\text{Income Before Interest}}{\text{Average Total Assets}}$$

$$= \frac{\text{Net Income} + \text{Interest Expense} - \text{Tax Savings of Interest Expense}}{\text{Average Total Assets}}$$

$$= \frac{\text{Net Income} + \text{Interest Expense} - (\text{Tax Rate} \times \text{Interest Expense})}{\text{Average Total Assets}}$$

$$ROA = \frac{\text{Net Income} + [\text{Interest Expense} \times (1 - \text{Tax Rate})]}{\text{Average Total Assets}}$$

For **Sears Canada Inc.**, the calculation of ROA for 2001 is as follows:

$$ROA = \frac{\text{Net Income} + [\text{Interest Expense} \times (1 - \text{Tax Rate})]}{\text{Average Total Assets}}$$

$$= \frac{\$94.1 + [\$64.2 \times (1 - .419)]}{(\$3,888 + \$3,955)/2}$$

$$= \frac{\$94.1 + \$37.3}{\$3,921.5}$$

$$ROA = .0335$$

Financial statement amounts are in millions of dollars.

Sears Canada's ROA of 3.35% seems low. Late in 2000, Sears Canada bought some of the Eaton's stores along with the right to use the Eaton's name. Sears anticipated that it would be able to continue the Eaton's tradition and capture some of the high-end department store market. Unfortunately, in 2001, it became apparent that the investment in Eaton's was not going to capture the returns that Sears Canada had anticipated. Sears Canada decided early in 2002 to convert its Eaton's stores to Sears stores. As a user of this information, you would be interested in following this ratio over the next few years to determine whether the company's decision with respect to the Eaton's investment results in an improvement in its ROA.

As with many ratios, the ROA alone is not as meaningful as a comparison over time or among companies. However, before using ROA to compare different companies, you should be sure their amortization policies are comparable, as different amortization policies will affect the total assets figure. As you saw with Sears Canada, you should also determine whether the companies you are comparing have recently invested in new assets. New assets will significantly increase the total asset amount and thus decrease the ROA.

SUMMARY

In this chapter, we described the initial acquisition of capital assets—both tangible and intangible—paying attention to the costs that are included in the asset account. Capital assets include land, buildings, vehicles, equipment, natural resources, intangibles, and many other assets that have a useful life of more than one year. We explored several systematic, rational methods of amortizing capital assets. Amortization of capital assets is an estimate of the expense that relates to the use of the assets each year. As an estimate, it is up to management to determine appropriate amortization rates incorporating useful lives and residual values. We took a brief look at what happens with respect to the CCRA and amortization. Because the CCRA has restricted the amortization method to CCA, there is often a difference between the income tax recorded on the accounting income statement and the income tax that is actually owed to the CCRA. This difference is referred to as a future tax asset or liability.

Because amortization methods are estimates, it is important to periodically review the useful life and residual value assumptions to determine if they are still appropriate. If new values are established, the book value of the asset is amortized over its remaining useful life using the new values. Also, if the company decides to change amortization methods, it will amortize the asset over its remaining useful life using the new method.

We completed the chapter with a discussion of the calculation of ROA and its limitations.

**Additional
Demonstration
Problems**

SUMMARY PROBLEM

Pete's Trucking Company has a fleet of 10 large trucks that cost a total of $1,410,000. The trucks have an estimated useful life of 10 years and an estimated residual value of 10%. For tax purposes, their Capital Cost Allowance (CCA) rate is 30%. The trucks are expected to be driven a total of 1,000,000 kilometres. At the end of the tenth year, the trucks were sold for $5,500 each.

Required:

1. Prepare a schedule showing the straight-line amortization that would be recorded over the life of these trucks.

2. Prepare a schedule showing the amortization that would result if Pete's had used the double declining balance method.

3. Prepare a schedule showing amortization on a production basis if the following usage was recorded:

Year 1:	125,000 km
Year 2:	120,000 km
Year 3:	115,000 km
Year 4:	110,000 km
Year 5:	105,000 km
Year 6:	100,000 km
Year 7:	90,000 km
Year 8:	80,000 km
Year 9:	70,000 km
Year 10:	60,000 km

4. Prepare journal entries to record the disposal of the trucks, assuming:

   a. Pete's used straight-line amortization

   b. Pete's used double declining balance amortization

   c. Pete's used a production method of amortization

5. Compare the difference in tax savings in the first two years if the CCRA accepted straight-line amortization rather than CCA. Assume a 34% tax rate.

SUGGESTED SOLUTION TO SUMMARY PROBLEM

All solutions in parts 1 and 2 are presented in thousands of dollars.

1. The residual value of the equipment would be $141 (10% of $1,410). The straight-line amortization would be:

$$\text{Amortization Expense} = \frac{\text{Original Cost} - \text{Estimated Residual Value}}{\text{Estimated Useful life}}$$

$$= (\$1,410 - \$141)/10 \text{ years}$$

$$= \$126.9 \text{ year}$$

2. Double declining balance method:
   Declining balance rate = 200% × straight-line rate
   $$= 200\% \times 1/10 = 20\%$$

   The amortization schedule for double declining balance is:

Year	Asset Balance		Calculation	Amortization Expense
1	1,410.0		20% × 1,410.0	$282.0
2	(1,410.0 − 282.0) =	1,128.0	20% × 1,128.0	225.6
3	(1,128.0 − 225.6) =	902.4	20% × 902.4	180.5
4	(902.4 − 180.5) =	721.9	20% × 721.9	144.4
5	(721.9 − 144.4) =	577.5	20% × 577.5	115.5
6	(577.5 − 115.5) =	462.0	20% × 462.0	92.4
7	(462.0 − 92.4) =	369.6	20% × 369.6	73.9
8	(369.6 − 73.9) =	295.7	20% × 295.7	59.1
9	(295.7 − 59.1) =	236.6	20% × 236.6	47.3
10	(236.6 − 47.3) =	189.3	See note	48.3

Note: The calculation in Year 10 would result in amortization of $37.8, which would be insufficient to reduce the carrying value of the asset to its residual value ($141). Therefore, additional amortization would be taken in Year 10 to bring the asset to its residual value of $141 at the end of Year 10.

3. Cost per km: ($1,410 − $141)/1,000 = $1.269
   Amortization in Year 1: $1.269 × 125,000 = $158,625
   Amortization in Year 2: $1.269 × 120,000 = $152,280
   Amortization in Year 3: $1.269 × 115,000 = $145,935
   Amortization in Year 4: $1.269 × 110,000 = $139,590
   Amortization in Year 5: $1.269 × 105,000 = $133,245
   Amortization in Year 6: $1.269 × 100,000 = $126,900
   Amortization in Year 7: $1.269 × 90,000 = $114,210
   Amortization in Year 8: $1.269 × 80,000 = $101,520
   Amortization in Year 9: $1.269 × 70,000 = $88,830
   Amortization in Year 10: $1.269 × 60,000 = $76,140

4. a.   Straight-line method:

A-Cash	55,000	
XA-Accumulated amortization	1,269,000	
SE-Loss on disposal	86,000	
A-Trucks		1,410,000

   b.   Double declining balance method:

A-Cash	55,000	
XA-Accumulated amortization	1,269,000	
SE-Loss on disposal	86,000	
A-Trucks		1,410,000

   c.   Production method:

A-Cash	55,000	
XA-Accumulated amortization	1,237,275	
SE-Loss on disposal	117,725	
A-Trucks		1,410,000

5. Year 1: Straight-line amortization: $126,900
   CCA: 50% × 30% × $1,410,000 =   211,500
                                              $ 84,600

   Difference in tax: 34% × $84,600 = $28,764 less tax paid under CCA.

   Year 2: Straight-line amortization: $126,900
   CCA: 30% × ($1,410,000 − $211,500) =   359,550
                                              $232,650

   Difference in tax: 34% × $232,650 = $79,101 less tax paid under CCA.

ABBREVIATIONS USED

AcSB	Accounting Standards Board
CCA	Capital cost allowance
CCRA	Canada Customs and Revenue Agency
DB	Declining balance
UCC	Undepreciated capital cost

SYNONYMS

Amortization/depreciation
Amortized cost/net book value/carrying value

GLOSSARY

Accelerated amortization   A method of amortization that allocates higher expenses to the earlier years of an asset's life than does the straight-line method.

Amortizable cost   The amount of an asset that can be amortized over its useful life. It is calculated as the original cost less residual value.

Amortization   The allocation of the cost of capital assets to expense over their useful lives.

Amortized cost   The amount of an asset's cost that remains after it has been amortized. It is another term for net book value or carrying value.

Basket purchase   A purchase of assets in which more than one asset is acquired for a single purchase price.

Book value   The value of an asset or liability carried on the books of a company. For capital assets, this value is the acquisition cost of the asset less the accumulated amortization.

Capital assets   Assets with expected useful lives of more than one year (or normal operating cycle, if longer) that are used in the business and are not intended for resale.

Capital cost allowance   The deduction permitted by the CCRA for tax purposes in place of amortization.

Capitalizable cost   A cost that can be recorded as an asset on the financial statements rather than being expensed immediately.

Carrying value   The acquisition cost of a capital asset minus its accumulated amortization. Synonym for book value.

Compound interest amortization   An amortization method that calculates the amortization expense for a period by the change in the present value of the asset.

Decelerated amortization   A method of amortization that allocates lower expenses to the earlier years of an asset's life than to the later years.

Declining balance amortization   Amortization methods that calculate the amortization each period by multiplying the rate of amortization by the carrying value of the asset.

Depletion   A term sometimes used to describe amortization of the cost of natural resources to expense over the useful life of the resource.

Depreciation   A term sometimes used for amortization, especially for tangible assets that are not natural resources.

Double declining balance method   A particular type of declining balance amortization method that is calculated by using a percentage rate that is double the rate that would be used for straight-line amortization.

Full costing method   A method of accounting for the drilling and exploration costs of an oil exploration company in which all costs of exploration are capitalized and amortized without regard to the success or failure of individual wells. Common in smaller oil and gas companies.

Future tax asset or liability   An asset or liability account that arises when there is a difference between the revenues or expenses used for tax purposes and book purposes. With respect to capital assets, it represents the tax effect of the temporary difference in the net carrying value of the capital assets under accounting versus the carrying value for tax purposes.

Goodwill   An intangible asset that represents the above-average earning capacity of a company as a result of reputation, advantageous location, superior sales staff, expertise of employees, etc. It is only recorded when a company acquires another company and pays more for it than the fair market value of its identifiable net assets.

Intangible asset   A nonphysical capital asset that usually involves a legal right.

Interest capitalization   The recording of interest as a part of the construction cost of a capital asset.

Net book value   The carrying value of an asset on the books of a company.

Net realizable value   The selling price of an asset less any costs to complete and sell the asset.

Net recoverable amount   The estimated future net cash flow from use of a capital asset together with its residual value.

Present-value amortization   An amortization method that calculates the amortization expense for a period by the change in the present value of the asset.

Production method   A method of amortization that allocates the amortizable cost of the asset to the years of its useful life as a function of the volume of production or usage for the period.

Rate of amortization   A ratio or percentage that describes the amount of amortization that may be taken during a given period. For straight-line amortization, the rate is the reciprocal of the number of years of useful life $(1/N)$.

Replacement cost   A market value of an asset determined from the market in which the asset can be purchased by the company. In a manufacturing company, replacement cost is the cost to reproduce the asset based on current prices of the inputs.

Resale value   The market value of an asset in the market in which it can be sold.

Residual value   The estimated net realizable value of a capital asset at the end of its useful life to the company.

Straight-line amortization   A method of amortization that allocates the amortizable cost of the asset evenly over its useful life.

Straight-line rate   The rate of amortization for the straight-line method. Calculated as the reciprocal of the number of years of useful life (1/N).

Successful efforts method   A method of accounting for the drilling and exploration costs of an oil exploration company in which the costs of exploration are capitalized and amortized only for successful wells.

Tangible asset   An asset that has a physical substance.

Undepreciated capital cost   The carrying value of an asset in a class that has not yet been deducted as capital cost allowance for tax purposes.

Useful life   An estimate of the period of time over which an asset will have economic value to the company.

Value in use   The value of an asset if the intent is to use the asset rather than sell it.

ASSIGNMENT MATERIAL

Multiple Choice Quizzes

Assessing Your Recall

8-1   Describe what is meant by "value in use" versus "resale value" as applied to capital assets.

8-2   Discuss the types of costs that should be capitalized for a piece of equipment.

8-3   Describe the procedure used in Canada to allocate the cost of a basket purchase of assets to the individual assets.

8-4   Explain why interest can be capitalized as part of the construction costs of an asset.

8-5   Discuss the purpose of amortization expense and the possible patterns of amortization for a company.

8-6   Discuss the motivations that a company might have for choosing one amortization method over another.

8-7   Describe how residual value and useful life are used in the calculation of amortization under the following methods: straight-line, production, and declining balance.

8-8   Explain what is done when a company changes its estimate of an asset's useful life and/or residual value partway through the asset's life.

8-9   Describe the differences between Capital Cost Allowance and accelerated amortization.

8-10   Discuss the nature of future income taxes in the context of differences between amortization and CCA.

8-11   Describe the conditions under which intangible assets can be recorded on the books of a company, and the guidelines under which their value can then be expensed over the life of the asset. Specifically, discuss goodwill, research and development, and patents.

8-12   Discuss the conditions under which a company is required to write down the value of its capital assets.

Applying Your Knowledge

8-13   (Acquisition cost and interest capitalization)
Cedar Homes Ltd. decided to upgrade some of its log preparation equipment and to expand its facilities. The following events occurred during the year:

Jan.	4	Equipment with an invoice price of $95,000 was received.
	9	Construction of a new addition to the main building was started. The estimated cost of the construction was $250,000.
	24	A bill in the amount of $2,400 was received for transporting the equipment (received Jan. 4) to Cedar Homes.
	27	Architect's fees of $7,500 were paid for the preliminary design of the addition to the building.
Feb.	3	Payment was made for the equipment and transportation.
May	9	Payment was made to the construction company in the amount of $250,000 following completion of the addition to the building.
	14	Work crews installed the equipment and were paid $2,000.
	15	A special ad was run in the local paper at a cost of $250 informing residents that the company would begin interviewing for new employees in two weeks.
	24	A party costing $850 was held to celebrate the completion of the new building.
June	7	Testing of the new equipment was completed and it was placed in service. Total testing costs were $1,000.

Required:

a. Determine the costs that should be capitalized as assets by Cedar Homes in the buildings and equipment accounts. (These must be accounted for separately, as they will be subject to different amortization rates.)

b. What should be done with any costs that are not capitalized?

c. If Cedar Homes had borrowed money to finance the expansion of the facilities, what two options would it have had with respect to the interest cost?

8-14   (Valuation of capital assets)
Lundon Company purchased a tract of land for $150,000 roughly 20 years ago and has now divided the land into two parcels. The company intends to sell one of the parcels and keep the other. Lundon estimates it can sell the one parcel for $240,000. It already has an offer of $180,000 from a local business, and it has a tentative offer from the brother of the president of Lundon Company for $300,000.

Required:

a. What accounting concepts and objectives might be used by the accountant in support of recognizing the value of the parcel at $240,000?

b. What accounting concepts and objectives might be used to argue against recognizing either of the proposed offers in the accounting records?

c. Would it be appropriate to revalue one of the parcels and not the other?

d. At what amount should the parcel in question be valued?

8-15 (Valuation of capital assets)

Four years ago, Litho Printers Ltd. purchased a large, four-colour printing press for $440,000 with the intent of using it for 10 years. Recently, the production manager learned that replacing the press with a comparable new one would cost $600,000. On the other hand, the production manager estimates that if the company were to sell the current machine it would receive $310,000. The manager also estimates that the company could make $950,000 from selling materials produced on the press over the next six years.

Required:

a. What should be the value assigned to the press in Litho Printers' financial statements?

b. Under what conditions should the press be valued at $950,000?

c. Under what conditions should the press be valued at $600,000?

d. Under what conditions should the press be valued at $310,000?

8-16 (Amortization calculations and journal entries)

Polar Company purchased a building with an expected useful life of 30 years for $650,000 on January 1, 2004. The building is expected to have a residual value of $50,000.

Required:

a. Give the journal entries that would be made by Polar to record the purchase of the building in 2004 and the amortization expense for 2004 and 2005, assuming straight-line amortization is used.

b. Give the journal entries that would be made by Polar to record the amortization expense for 2004 and 2005, assuming the double declining balance method is used.

8-17 (Calculation of amortization)

A machine is purchased on January 1, 20x1, for $95,000. It is expected to have a useful life of six years and a residual value of $5,000. The company closes its books on December 31.

Required:

a. Calculate the amount of amortization to be charged each year, using each of the following methods:

1. Straight-line method

2. Double declining balance method

b. Which method results in the highest amortization expense:

1. During the first three years

2. Over all six years

8-18 (Amortization [including CCA] and income calculation)

On January 1, 2001, Johnson Company invested $450,000 in equipment with an expected useful life of 20 years and an anticipated residual value of $50,000. For tax purposes, this is a Class 8 asset with a CCA rate of 20%. In 2004, Johnson reported sales of $1,100,000 and operating expenses other than amortization of $800,000. At December 31, 2004, Johnson held $750,000 of assets in addition to its equipment. Johnson's tax rate is 30%.

Required:

a. Assuming Johnson uses straight-line amortization, what amount of net income will it report for 2004? What will be the return on assets, using the total assets reported at December 31, 2004, and assuming there is no interest expense on the income statement?

b. What is the maximum amount of CCA (capital cost allowance) that Johnson would be able to claim for tax purposes in 2004? Assuming the company used straight-line amortization for accounting purposes, give the journal entry to record the company's income taxes for 2004.

c. Assuming Johnson uses double declining balance amortization, what amount of net income will it report for 2004? What will be the return on assets, using total assets reported at December 31, 2004?

d. For what type of asset would it be appropriate to use double declining balance amortization?

8-19 (Change in estimates)
On October 31, 2001, Steelman Company acquired a new machine for $125,000. The company estimated the useful life to be 10 years and expected a residual value of $5,000. During 2004, the company decided that the machine was to be used for another 10 years beyond that date (including all of 2004) and that the residual value would be $3,000. On June 30, 2006, the machine was sold for $82,000. The company uses the straight-line method of amortization and closes its books on December 31.

Required:
Give the necessary journal entries related to the acquisition, amortization, and disposal of this asset for the years 2001, 2004, and 2006.

8-20 (Straight-line amortization with disposal)
On June 1, 20x1, Sherman Bros. Corp. purchased a new machine for $30,000. A useful life of 10 years and a residual value of $1,200 were estimated. On November 30, 20x1, another machine was acquired for $75,000. Its useful life was estimated to be 12 years and its residual value $3,000. On April 30, 20x3, the first machine was sold for $20,000. Sherman Bros. closes its books on December 31 each year, uses the straight-line method of amortization, and calculates amortization on a monthly basis.

Required:
Give the necessary journal entries for the years 20x1 through 20x3 for both machines.

8-21 (Disposal of capital assets)
On March 31, 20x4, Hammer & Holding Inc. purchased new machinery. The company acquired the new machinery by trading in its old machine, paying $20,375 in cash and issuing a 12% note payable for $6,000. The old machinery was acquired on June 30, 20x1, for $22,000. At that time, its estimated useful life was 10 years, with a $1,000 residual value. The old asset's market value was approximately the same as its book value at the date of the trade-in. The new machinery's estimated life is six years, with a residual value of $3,000. The company uses the straight-line method of amortization and closes its books on December 31.

Required:

a. Give the necessary journal entry to record the amortization of the old asset up to the date of the trade-in in 20x4. Assume that the amortization was correctly recorded for 20x1, 20x2, and 20x3. Give the necessary journal entry to record the trade-in of the old asset and the acquisition of the new one. (*Hint:* The cost of the new asset includes the value of the old asset plus the cash and note given in payment for the new asset.)

b. Assume that on March 31, 20x9, the machinery acquired in 20x4 could not be sold and the company decided to write it off. Give the necessary journal entries for 20x9.

8-22 (Intangibles and amortization)

Pinetree Manufacturing Company reports both equipment and patents in its balance sheet.

Required:

a. Explain how the dollar amount for each type of asset is determined.

b. If both types of assets were purchased three years ago for $20,000 each and had estimated useful lives of 10 years, what amount would be reported in the balance sheet at the end of the current period? Explain.

c. Financial analysts sometimes ignore intangible assets in analyzing financial statements. Do you think this is appropriate? Explain.

8-23 (Intangibles and amortization)

Vinay Company purchases several intangible assets, as follows:

Asset	Cost
Patent	$ 60,000
Copyright	200,000
Licence	320,000

In addition to the purchase cost of each asset, legal fees associated with the acquisition of the licence are $24,000. While the patent has a legal life of 20 years, technological changes are expected to render it worthless after about five years. The copyright is good for another 30 years, but nearly all of the related sales are expected to occur during the next eight years. The licence is good in perpetuity, and sales under the licence are expected to continue at the same level for many decades.

Required:

a. Calculate the annual amortization, if any, for each of Vinay's intangible assets.

b. Show the balance sheet presentation of the Intangible Assets section of Vinay's balance sheet prepared at the end of the fourth year after acquisition of the intangible assets, assuming that there has been no evidence that their values have been impaired.

User Perspective Problems

8-24 (Valuation of assets in discontinued business)

Suppose that a company decides to discontinue a line of business and sell the related assets. Describe what you think would be the most appropriate valuation basis for the property, plant, and equipment for the discontinued operations. As an investor in the shares of the company, discuss what disclosure might be most useful to you in this circumstance.

8-25 (Capital assets as collateral for a loan)
As a lender, discuss how much comfort you might get from the existence of long-term assets, specifically plant and goodwill, in making a long-term loan to a company.

8-26 (Auditing and valuation of capital assets)
As an auditor, discuss how you might evaluate a company's property, plant, and equipment to decide whether it should write down the value of these assets.

8-27 (Goodwill's effect on financial statements)
In some countries (such as the United Kingdom), companies can write off goodwill at the date of acquisition by directly reducing shareholders' equity—that is, the write-off does not pass through net income. Suppose that a Canadian company and a UK company agreed to purchase the same company for the same amount of money. As a stock analyst, describe how the balance sheets and income statements would differ for the two companies after the acquisition. Discuss whether this provides any differential advantage for either of the two companies.

8-28 (Impact of writedowns on remuneration)
Suppose that you are the accounting manager of a division of a large company and your remuneration is partly based on meeting an income target. In the current year, it seems unlikely that your division will meet its target. You have some property, plant, and equipment that has been idle for a while but has not yet been written off. What incentives do you have to write off its value during the current year? If you do write it off, how will it affect your future ability to meet the income targets for your division?

8-29 (Basket purchase)
Companies that buy real estate often face a basket purchase situation. The purchase of real estate usually involves both the land that is purchased and the building that is on the land. If you are the accounting manager, how would you attempt to allocate the purchase price of the real estate between the land and the building? Why must you allocate the cost between the two assets? What incentives might you have to allocate a disproportionate amount to either the land or the building?

8-30 (Analysis of an R & D company)
As a stock analyst, discuss any difficulties or inadequacies that you might find with the financial statements of a company that is predominately a research and development company.

8-31 (Capital assets and company valuation)
Suppose that you have been asked to provide an analysis of a potential acquisition by your company. Which long-term assets on its financial statements are the most likely to be misstated by their book values, and why? Are there long-term assets of the potential acquire that might not be represented on the financial statements at all?

8-32 (Accounting for idle assets)
Conservative Company purchased a warehouse on January 1, 2000, for $750,000. At the time of purchase, Conservative anticipated that the warehouse would be used to facilitate its expanded product line. The warehouse is being amortized over 20 years and is expected to have a residual value of $100,000. On January 1, 2005, Conservative concluded that the warehouse would no longer be used and should be sold for its book value. At the end of 2005, the warehouse still had not been sold and its net realizable value was estimated to be only $450,000.

Required:

a. Calculate the book value of the warehouse on January 1, 2005.

b. Prepare all journal entries that Conservative would make during 2005 related to the warehouse.

c. If, during 2006, Conservative sells the warehouse for $400,000, what entry would be made for the sale?

d. During 2005, the financial vice-president expressed concern that if Conservative put the building up for sale, the company might have to report a loss, and he didn't want to reduce 2005 earnings; he wanted to continue treating the warehouse as an operating asset. How would the 2005 and 2006 financial statements be different if the warehouse were still treated as an operating asset during 2005? From a shareholder's perspective, do you think the treatment makes any difference? Explain.

8-33   (Analysis of a company with goodwill)

The 2004 annual report of Fedders Company contained the following financial statement information:

	2004	2003
Inventory	$19,270,000	$ 40,939,000
Net property, plant, and equipment	31,637,000	78,399,000
Other assets	8,125,000	35,236,000
Total assets	81,285,000	169,249,000
Net loss	1,775,000	24,931,000

The notes further indicate that the figures of $8,125,000 and $35,236,000 for other assets reported for 2004 and 2003, respectively, included goodwill of $5,823,000 and $17,670,000.

Fedders' sales are concentrated in room air conditioners. Sales are made directly to dealers and through private-label arrangements with major retailers and distributors.

Required:

a. What factor or factors are most likely to have led to the $46,762,000 reduction in net property, plant, and equipment?

b. According to the information in the annual report, a significant portion of the reduction in inventory was not directly related to the reduction in property, plant, and equipment. What factors might have led to such a large reduction in inventory?

c. As noted, more than half of other assets was goodwill. Given that the company reported a net loss in both 2003 and 2004, is it appropriate to continue to report goodwill in the balance sheet? Explain.

d. In light of the net loss for the year, ratios such as return on equity may not be meaningful. What ratios might be useful in evaluating Fedders' performance over the 2004 fiscal year?

e. What is your conclusion about Fedders' activities during 2004? What additional information would you like to have for analysis?

Reading and Interpreting Published Financial Statements

8-34   (Reconstruction of capital asset transactions)

Garneau Inc.'s primary business is the application of high-performance protective coatings and linings for oil and gas pipeline protection, plus the design and fabrication of oilfield equipment for both the Canadian and international markets. Its consolidated balance sheets, statements of earnings (loss), statements of cash flows, and note 3 regarding its capital assets are presented in Exhibit 8-13.

Required:

Prepare summary journal entries to reconstruct the transactions that affected Garneau's capital assets during the 2001 fiscal year (i.e., acquisitions, disposals, and amortization expense). Deal with the total capital assets, rather than with the individual components. (*Hint:* You may find the use of T-accounts helpful in reconstructing the events that affected the capital asset and accumulated amortization accounts during the year.)

GARNEAU INC. (2001)

CONSOLIDATED BALANCE SHEETS

EXHIBIT 8-13

(in thousands)	at December 31, 2001	at December 31, 2000
Assets		
Current assets:		
Cash	$ 121	$ —
Accounts receivable	6,821	3,916
Income taxes recoverable	—	145
Inventory	1930	2,206
Prepaid expenses and deposits	66	63
	8,938	6,330
Capital assets (note 3)	21,317	22,233
	$ 30,255	$ 28,563
Liabilities and shareholders' equity		
Current liabilities:		
Bank indebtedness (note 2)	$ —	$ 958
Accounts payable and accrued liabilities	3,841	2,937
Current portion of long-term debt	1,608	1,370
Current portion of capital lease obligations	223	146
	5,672	5,411
Long-term debt (note 4)	4,568	5,372
Capital lease obligations (note 4)	697	433
	10,937	11,216
Shareholders' equity:		
Share capital (note 5)	20,718	20,718
Deficit	(1,400)	(3,371)
	19,318	17,347
Commitments (note 6)		
	$ 30,255	$ 28,563

EXHIBIT 8-13 CONT.

GARNEAU INC. (2001)

CONSOLIDATED STATEMENTS OF EARNINGS (LOSS)

(in thousands except per share data)	Year Ended December 31, 2001	Year Ended December 31, 2000
Revenue	$ 29,320	$ 16,786
Operating costs	21,049	13,247
	8,271	3,539
Other expense (recoveries):		
Selling, general and administrative	3,288	3,543
Amortization	2,069	1,926
Research and development,		
net of investment tax credits	344	197
Bad debts (recovery)	48	(40)
Loss (gain) on disposal on capital assets	(15)	39
	5,734	5,665
Operating income (loss)	2,537	(2,126)
Financing:		
Interest on long-term debt	454	512
Interest on bank indebtedness	94	113
Interest income	(17)	(42)
Earnings (loss) before income taxes	2,006	(2,709)
Income taxes (note 7):		
Current	35	39
Future	—	(100)
	35	(61)
Net earnings (loss)	1,971	(2,648)
Deficit, beginning of year	(3,371)	(723)
Deficit, end of year	$ (1,400)	$ (3,371)
Earnings (loss) per share (note 5):		
Basic	$ 0.18	$ (0.24)
Diluted	$ 0.18	$ (0.24)

GARNEAU INC. (2001)

EXHIBIT 8-13
CONT.

CONSOLIDATED STATEMENTS OF CASH FLOWS

(in thousands)	Year Ended December 31, 2001	Five-Months Ended December 31, 2000
Cash provided by (used in):		
Operations (note 10):		
Net earnings (loss)	$ 1,971	$ (2,648)
Items not involving cash:		
Amortization	2,069	1,926
Loss (gain) on disposal of capital assets	(15)	39
Future income taxes	—	(100)
	4,025	(783)
Changes in non-cash operating working capital	(1,583)	(80)
	2,442	(863)
Financing:		
Repayment of long-term debt and capital leases	(1,618)	(1,195)
Increase (decrease) in bank indebtedness	(958)	(1,208)
Advances under term loan	897	3,761
Proceeds from sale and lease-back of assets	496	0
	(1,183)	1,358
Investments:		
Proceeds from disposal of capital assets	327	—
Additions to capital assets	(1,465)	(495)
	1,138	(495)
Increase in cash	121	—
Cash, beginning of year	—	—
Cash, end of year	121	—

EXHIBIT 8-13

CONT.

GARNEAU INC. (2001)

CAPITAL ASSETS

2001

(In thousands)	Cost	Accumulated amortization	Net book value
Land and land improvements	$ 3,398	$ 1,074	$ 2,324
Buildings and extrusion plant	9,413	2,304	7,109
Machinery and equipment	16,383	5,889	10,494
Leasehold improvements	264	243	21
Rental equipment	794	450	344
	$ 30,252	$ 9,960	$ 20,292
Equipment under capital lease	1,273	248	1,025
	$ 31,525	$ 10,208	$ 21,317

2000

(in thousands)	Cost	Accumulated amortization	Net book value
Land and land improvements	$ 3,398	$ 919	$ 2,479
Buildings and extrusion plant	9,296	1,959	7,337
Machinery and equipment	15,913	4,551	11,362
Leasehold improvements	251	237	14
Rental equipment	794	387	407
	$ 29,652	$ 8,053	$ 21,599
Equipment under capital lease	777	143	634
	$ 30,429	$ 8,196	$ 22,233

8-35   (Research and development costs)

The 2001 and 2000 consolidated statements of earnings for **MOSAID Technologies Incorporated** are shown in Exhibit 8-14. As one would expect for a company in the semiconductor business, it incurs substantial costs related to research and development. MOSAID has expensed all of these costs in the years in which they were incurred.

Required:

a. Calculate what MOSAID's earnings (loss) from operations would have been for 2001 and 2000 if it had capitalized its research and development costs and then amortized them on a straight-line basis over a five-year period. Note: In order to be able to do this with the data available, you will have to assume that 2000 was the company's first year of operations.

b. Compare your results in part a) to the earnings (loss) from operations shown in Exhibit 8-14. Are the differences significant?

c. Explain why MOSAID is not allowed, under GAAP, to capitalize these research and development costs.

MOSAID TECHNOLOGIES INCORPORATED

EXHIBIT 8-14

CONSOLIDATED STATEMENTS OF EARNINGS AND RETAINED EARNINGS

(in thousands, except per share amounts)

Year ended	April 27, 2001	April 28, 2000
REVENUES		
Operations	$ 81,640	$ 47,044
Interest	1,286	1,065
	82,926	48,109
EXPENSES		
Labour and materials	13,367	8,181
Research and development (NOTE 7)	31,428	18,450
Selling and marketing	18,250	11,839
General and administration	8,338	7,015
Bad debt	139	–
Unusual item (NOTE 8)	694	(206)
	72,216	45,279
Earnings from operations	10,710	2,830
Income tax expense (NOTE 9)	3,708	926
NET EARNINGS	7,002	1,904
RETAINED EARNINGS, beginning of year	17,550	15,646
RETAINED EARNINGS, end of year	$ 24,552	$ 17,550
EARNINGS PER SHARE (NOTE 10)		
Basic	$ 0.79	$ 0.26
Fully diluted	$ 0.76	$ 0.26
WEIGHTED AVERAGE NUMBER OF SHARES		
Basic	8,889,863	7,374,469
Fully diluted	10,445,596	8,880,413

See accompanying Notes to the Consolidated Financial Statements.

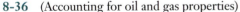

8-36 (Accounting for oil and gas properties)
Imperial Oil Limited is an integrated producer, refiner, and marketer of petroleum and petrochemical products. The portion of its summary of significant accounting policies that deals with property, plant, and equipment is shown in Exhibit 8-15.

Required:

a. What method does Imperial Oil use to account for its costs related to exploration and development activities? Explain in your own words how these costs are handled under this method.

b. Is the method that Imperial uses to account for exploration and development costs the method that you would expect a large oil and gas company to use? Explain why or why not.

c. Assume that a smaller company has been in operation for two years, during which it explored 10 sites each year at a cost of $2,000,000 per site. Only one of the sites each year proved to be economically viable; the remaining wells were dry. The reserves in each of the successful wells are estimated to be 600,000 barrels, extracted evenly over a six-year period commencing in the year of discovery.

Demonstrate your understanding of the full cost method of accounting for these expenditures by indicating what the company would report as:

1. The value of the asset on the balance sheet, at the end of each of the two years

2. The amount of expense on the income statement, for each of the two years

IMPERIAL OIL LTD. (2001)
Property, plant and equipment
Property, plant and equipment are recorded at cost.

The company follows the successful-efforts method of accounting for its exploration and development activities. Under this method, costs of exploration acreage are capitalized and amortized over the period of exploration or until a discovery is made. Costs of exploration wells are capitalized until their success can be determined. If the well is successful, the costs remain capitalized; otherwise they are expensed. Capitalized exploration costs are reevaluated annually. All other exploration costs are expensed as incurred. Development costs, including the cost of natural gas and natural gas liquids used as injectants in enhanced (tertiary) oil-recovery projects, are capitalized.

Imperial selected the successful-efforts method over the alternative full-cost method of accounting because it provides a more timely accounting of the success or failure of exploration and production activities.

Maintenance and repair costs are expensed as incurred. Improvements that increase or prolong the service life or capacity of an asset are capitalized.

Investment tax credits and other similar grants are treated as a reduction of the capitalized cost of the asset to which they apply.

Depreciation and depletion (the allocation of the cost of assets to expense over the period of their useful lives) are calculated using the unit-of-production method for producing properties. Depreciation of other plant and equipment is calculated using the straight-line method, based on the estimated service life of the asset. In general, refineries are depreciated over 25 years; other major assets, including chemical plants and service stations, are depreciated over 20 years.

Gains or losses on assets sold are included in "investment and other income" in the consolidated statement of earnings.

8-37   (Accounting for oil and gas properties)
Purcell Energy Ltd. is an Alberta-based oil and gas producer. Note 2 (d) from its financial statements describes its accounting policies for property, plant, and equipment and is shown in Exhibit 8-16.

Required:

a. What method does Purcell Energy use to account for its exploration and development costs? Explain in your own words how these costs are handled under this method.

b. Is the method that Purcell uses to account for exploration and development costs the method that you would expect smaller oil and gas companies to use? Explain why or why not.

c. Assume that a large company has been in operation for two years, during which it explored 20 sites each year at a cost of $4,000,000 per site. Only three of the sites each year proved to be economically viable; the remaining wells were dry. The reserves in each of the successful wells are estimated to be 800,000 barrels, extracted evenly over an eight-year period commencing in the year of discovery.

Demonstrate your understanding of the successful efforts method of accounting for these costs by indicating what the company would report as:

1. The value of the asset on the balance sheet at the end of each of the two years

2. The amount of expense on the income statement, for each of the two years

PURCELL ENERGY LTD. (2001)

EXHIBIT 8-16

(d)   Property, plant and equipment

The Company follows the full cost method of accounting for oil and gas operations whereby all costs of exploring for and developing oil and gas reserves are initially capitalized. Such costs include land acquisition costs, geological and geophysical expenses, carrying charges on non-producing properties, costs of drilling and overhead charges directly related to acquisition and exploration activities.

Costs capitalized, together with the costs of production equipment, are depleted on the unit-of-production method based on the estimated gross proved reserves. Petroleum products and reserves are converted to equivalent units of natural gas at approximately 6,000 cubic feet to 1 barrel of oil.

Costs of acquiring and evaluating unproved properties are initially excluded from depletion calculations. These unevaluated properties are assessed periodically to ascertain whether impairment has occurred. When proved reserves are assigned or the property is considered to be impaired, the cost of the property or the amount of the impairment is added to costs subject to depletion calculations.

Proceeds from a sale of petroleum and natural gas properties are applied against capitalized costs, with no gain or loss recognized, unless such a sale would significantly alter the rate of depletion. Alberta Royalty Tax Credits are included in oil and gas sales.

In applying the full cost method, the Company performs a ceiling test which restricts the capitalized costs less accumulated depletion and amortization from exceeding an amount equal to the estimated undiscounted value of future net revenues from proved oil and gas reserves, as determined by independent engineers, based on sales prices achievable under existing contracts and posted average reference prices in effect at the end of the year and current costs, and after deducting estimated future general and administrative expenses, production related expenses, financing costs, future site restoration costs and income taxes.

8-38   (Capitalization of labour costs)

In the notes accompanying its 2002 financial statements, **Big Rock Brewery Ltd.** includes the following statement:

During the year ended March 31, 2002, the Company capitalized labour of $60,854 (2001 − $41,002; 2000 − $34,296) relating to certain enhancements at its brewing facilities.

Required:

a. Is it acceptable accounting practice for a company to capitalize labour costs in certain circumstances? Explain why or why not.

b. How would the balance sheets and income statements have been different if Big Rock Brewery had not capitalized these labour costs?

8-39   (Accounting policies related to capital assets)

The notes dealing with significant accounting policies for capital assets and other assets and deferred charges accompanying the 2001 financial statements of **Fairmont Hotels and Resorts Inc.** are shown in Exhibit 8-17.

Required:

Examine the company's accounting policies with respect to capital assets and other assets and deferred charges and answer the following questions:

a. Hotel and resort operators such as Fairmont have significant amounts invested in property and equipment, which must be regularly maintained or repaired, and periodically renewed or replaced. How does Fairmont account for the costs of major renewals and replacements? What amount does it consider "major"? How does it account for the costs of maintenance, repairs, minor renewals, and replacements?

b. Does Fairmont capitalize interest costs or charge them directly to expense?

c. Hotel and resort operators also have significant amounts of what is referred to as "circulating operating equipment" such as tableware and bedding. How does Fairmont account for these costs?

d. How does Fairmont account for computer system development costs and for software to be used internally?

e. How does Fairmont account for the costs associated with its brand name and trademarks?

EXHIBIT 8-17

FAIRMONT HOTELS AND RESORTS LTD. (2001)

Capital assets

Property and equipment are recorded at cost. The Company's policy is to capitalize major renewals and replacements and interest incurred during the construction period on new facilities and during the renovation period of major renovations to existing facilities costing over $1.0. Interest is capitalized, based on the borrowing rate of debt related to the project or the Company's average cost of borrowing. Maintenance, repairs and minor renewals and replacements are charged against income when incurred.

Computer system development costs for internal use software are capitalized to the extent the project is expected to be of continuing benefit to the Company.

The cost of the initial complement of the circulating operating equipment, such as linens, china, glassware and silverware, is capitalized and then amortized by 33%. Replacements are expensed when placed in service.

Amortization is provided at rates designed to write off the assets over their estimated economic lives, except for buildings on leased land, which are amortized over the lesser of the term of the lease, including options, and the economic life of the building.

The unamortized portions of capital assets are reviewed regularly and compared with their net recoverable amounts. Based on management's projected undiscounted future cash flows from the related operations, any impairment in value is recorded as a charge to income. The annual rates of amortization are as follows:

Buildings	40 years straight-line
Building equipment	17-25 years straight-line
Furniture and equipment	5-17 years straight-line
Computer system software	2-7 years straight-line
Vehicles	3-5 years straight-line
Leasehold improvements	over the term of the leases

Other assets and deferred charges

The costs allocated to brand name and trademarks are amortized on a straight-line basis over 40 years. The recoverability of the unamortized costs of brand name and trademarks is evaluated on an annual basis to determine whether such costs will be recovered from cash flows of future operations.

Goodwill represents the excess of purchase price over fair value of identifiable assets acquired, and is amortized on a straight-line basis over the estimated periods of benefit of up to 40 years. FHR evaluates the carrying value of goodwill for possible impairment on an annual basis. Goodwill is written down to the net recoverable amount when declines in value are considered to be other than temporary, based upon expected cash flows of the respective operation.

Beyond the Book

8-40 (Financial statement disclosures)
Choose a company as directed by your instructor and answer the following:

a. Use the balance sheet and the notes to the financial statements to prepare an analysis of the capital assets, by listing the beginning and ending amounts in the various asset and accumulated amortization amounts and calculating the net change, in both dollar and percentage terms, for the most recent year.

b. If any of the amounts in part a) have changed more than 10%, provide an explanation for this change.

c. What percentage of the company's total assets is invested in property, plant, and equipment? Has this percentage changed significantly over the last year?

d. What amortization method(s) does the company use for its financial statements?

e. Use the following formulae to examine the property, plant, and equipment for the company:

Average Useful Life of PP&E = Total Gross PP&E / Annual Amort. Exp.

Average Age of PP&E = Total Accum. Amort. / Annual Amort. Expense

Note: Remember that amortization (depreciation) expense may not be disclosed in the income statement but will usually appear in the cash flow statement.

   Compare your results to any information disclosed in the notes. Do these results make sense?

f. Does the company have any significant intangible assets? If so, describe each of them.

Cases

8-41 Onta and KewBee Sales Companies
Summary balance sheet and income statement information for Onta Sales Company and KewBee Sales Company for the first year of operations for both are shown below. The operations of the two businesses are similar. Upon investigation, you find that Onta is financed mainly by shareholders' equity, KewBee mainly by long-term debt. Onta amortizes all equipment at 10% straight-line and buildings at 5% straight-line, while KewBee amortizes equipment at 20% declining balance and buildings at 10% declining balance. Both have effective corporate income tax rates of 25%.

Required:

a. Which company has the higher return on assets without adjusting for differences in amortization policy?

b. Using numbers from this example, explain why the ROA formula adjusts for interest after taxes in the numerator.

c. Which company has the higher return on assets after adjusting for differences in amortization policy? (Determine this using two different calculations: Onta's amortization method for KewBee, and KewBee's amortization method for Onta.)

d. Using numbers from this example, explain why you should adjust for differences in amortization policy when comparing different companies.

	Onta	KewBee
Balance Sheet Information		
Total current assets	$ 75,000	$ 80,000
Capital assets		
Land	140,000	125,000
Equipment	200,000	200,000
Accumulated amortization	(20,000)	(40,000)
Buildings	500,000	500,000
Accumulated amortization	(25,000)	(50,000)
Total assets	$ 870,000	$ 815,000
Total liabilities	$ 300,000	$ 700,000
Total shareholders' equity	570,000	115,000
Total liabilities and equity	$ 870,000	$ 815,000
Income Statement Information		
Revenues	$1,000,000	$1,000,000
Expenses		
Amortization	45,000	90,000
Interest	30,000	70,000
Other	770,000	770,000
Income taxes	38,750	17,500
Net income	$ 116,250	$ 52,500

8-42   Rolling Fields Nursing Home

Rolling Fields Nursing Home purchased land to use for a planned assisted-living community. As a condition of the sale, a title search had to be performed and a survey completed. Rolling Fields incurred both these costs. In order to prepare the land for new construction, a small barn that was on the land when it was purchased had to be torn down. Finally, a series of streets and roads through the planned community had to be constructed and paved.

The year after the land was purchased, construction of new homes began. The homes are to be owned by Rolling Fields and will be rented on a long-term basis to elderly residents who no longer feel they can live on their own but do not yet need nursing home care. Rolling Fields will be responsible for all maintenance and repair costs associated with the properties. By the end of the year, Phase 1 was complete and 28 homes had been constructed and were occupied. The average cost of each home was $50,000.

In the first year, repair and maintenance costs averaged $500 per property. The company also borrowed $450,000 to finance the construction of the homes. Interest on the loan for the year was $18,000.

Required:

a. Determine which of the above expenditures should be capitalized. For those expenditures that are capitalized, identify the appropriate account to which the costs should be charged.

b. How should each asset class be amortized?

8-43

Hugh White is a real estate developer with several properties located throughout St. John's, Newfoundland. Although Mr. White sells most properties upon completion, in some instances he arranges to purchase the property either by himself or in a consortium with other investors.

In 2004, Hugh White obtained two properties. The first property, a large residential rental complex that generates revenue of over $1,000,000 per year, was purchased solely by Mr. White. Because he pays personal income taxes on any profits earned by this property, Mr. White has a strong incentive to maximize expenses in order to minimize net income and consequently his tax liability.

The second property is owned by a group of professionals living in St. John's and is very similar in nature to the property owned by Mr. White. They have purchased the property as an investment opportunity and hired Mr. White to be the property manager. The group is very concerned with earning a reasonable return on the investment and Mr. White's compensation is based upon the profitability of the property.

During the year, both properties required a new parking lot to be constructed. The new parking lots replace existing dirt lots but are significantly improved in that they are now paved and lighted, with a security system installed.

Required:

a. In discussions with Mr. White, you discover that he would like to capitalize the costs of the parking lot for which he is the property manager and expense the parking lot for his own building. What is his rationale for wanting this accounting treatment?

b. What is the appropriate accounting treatment for the costs of both parking lots?

8-44   Rock Maple Development Co.

Rock Maple Development Co. recently purchased a property for use as a manufacturing facility. The company paid $850,000 for a building, warehouse, and 10 acres of land. When recording the purchase, the company accountant allocated $800,000 to the building and warehouse and $50,000 for the land. The warehouse is very old and after an independent appraisal, was deemed to have a value of only $35,000. The same appraisal valued the building at $650,000. The property is located near a major new highway and provides excellent access for shipping. Similar properties in the area have been selling for $30,000 per acre.

Rock Maple is a very successful company and has traditionally reported very high net income. Last year, the company paid over $200,000 in income taxes.

Required:

a. Determine the appropriate allocation between buildings and land for this basket purchase.

b. Why would the company accountant have wanted to allocate most of the costs to the building rather than the land?

8-45   Peterson Manufacturing

Peterson Manufacturing is a division of Wentworth Enterprises, a large multinational computer manufacturer. Peterson was acquired by Wentworth for its ability to manufacture high-quality, low-cost microchips. Wentworth has developed a compensation package whereby all division vice-presidents are compensated with a base salary and a bonus based on divisional performance as measured by the division's return on assets. If return on assets for the division exceeds the previous year's, the vice-president receives a $100,000 bonus. Wentworth allows it vice-presidents complete autonomy in running their divisions, with the guideline that the company considers any project with a projected ROA greater than 10% to be an excellent investment opportunity. Excerpts from the divisional financial statements for Peterson Manufacturing for the past three years are presented below.

The vice-president of Peterson Manufacturing, Haley Straub, is considering a new investment in equipment that will lead to higher quality chips that are able to process information much faster. The technology is very innovative and would revolutionize the industry. The cost of the related equipment will cause average total assets to increase by $8,500,000 and it is expected that net income before interest will increase by $975,000. The cost of financing the new project will cause interest expense to increase by $331,000.

Peterson Manufacturing
Selected Financial Information
For the year ended July 31

	2004	2003	2002
Net Income	$1,150,000	$ 985,000	$ 947,000
Interest Expense	$ 337,500	$ 326,800	$ 322,500
Total Assets	$8,675,000	$8,425,000	$8,524,000

The company has a tax rate of 30%. Total assets in 2001 were $8,346,000.

Required:

a. Calculate Peterson Manufacturing's return on assets for the past three years.

b. Calculate the return on assets of the new microchip project.

c. From a personal perspective, what do you think Haley Straub's decision will be regarding the new project? Is this decision good for the company as a whole?

8-46   Preakness Consulting and Bellevue Services

Preakness Consulting and Bellevue Services are two petroleum-engineering firms located in Calgary, Alberta. Both companies are very successful and are looking to attract additional investors to provide them with an infusion of capital for expansion purposes. In the past year, both companies had consulting revenue of $1.5 million. Expenses for both businesses are detailed below. Both companies have a tax rate of 25%.

On January 1, 2004, both companies purchased new computer systems. Currently, the only other asset owned by the companies is office equipment, which is fully amortized. The computer systems, related hardware, and installation cost each company $850,000 and the systems have an expected life of five years. The residual value at the end of the five-year period is expected to be $50,000 in each case.

Preakness has chosen to amortize the computer equipment using the straight-line method, while Bellevue has taken a more aggressive approach and is amortizing the system using the double declining balance method. Both companies have a December 31, 2004 year end.

Expense Information:

	Preakness	Bellevue
Salaries and wages	$650,250	$647,500
Rent	24,800	26,400
Office supplies	8,542	9,267
Other operating expenses	110,675	109,790

Required:

a. For each company, prepare an amortization schedule showing the amount of amortization to be charged each year for the computer system.

b. Prepare an income statement for the current year for both companies.

c. How might an unsophisticated investor interpret the financial results? Is one company really more profitable than the other?

Critical Thinking Question

8-47 (Classification of assets)
O&Y Properties Corporation is a leading Canadian office property owner, manager, and developer. Its balance sheet for December 31, 2001, is presented in Exhibit 8-18. Note that O&Y does not present its balance sheets in a classified format (that is, the company does not subdivide its assets and liabilities into current and long-term sections).

Required:
Should classified balance sheets be required for companies such as O&Y Properties? Why or why not?

0&Y PROPERTIES CORPORATION (2001)

BALANCE SHEET

(in thousands of dollars)

	NOTES	DEC. 31, 2001
ASSETS		
Rental properties	4	$ 508,941
Loans receivable	5	95,000
Deferred costs		2,127
Amounts receivable		3,428
Prepaid expenses and other assets		770
Cash and cash equivalents	6	7,321
		$ 617,587
LIABILITIES AND UNITHOLDERS' EQUITY		
Liabilities		
Secured debt	7	$ 198,847
Bank loan	8	28,600
Accounts payable and accrued liabilities		11,866
Convertible debentures – liability component	9	73,574
		312,887
Unitholders' Equity		304,700
		$ 617,587

See accompanying notes to financial statements.

On behalf of the Board of Trustees:

Joseph H. Wright, Chairman   Phineas Schwartz, Q.C., Trustee

Good Accounting Makes for Good Employee Relations

Mountain Equipment Co-op, which sells outdoor clothing and gear in stores across Canada as well as through its catalogue and website worldwide, has a reputation among its members for its helpful, knowledgeable staff. Founded in 1971, it now has more than 900 employees working at stores in Vancouver, Calgary, Edmonton, Toronto, Ottawa, and Halifax (the Co-op is planning to open a store in Winnipeg in 2002).

Treasury Manager Jennifer Henrey knows MEC's success depends on the dedication of its staff—which is why she considers payroll to be the most important aspect of its accounting for liabilities. "Payroll is a huge area," she explains. "In fact, it is our biggest expense. It's also an area where there is little margin for error—pay reflects how valued employees feel, and they are understandably sensitive about it. So we endeavour to have accurate payroll, and we do."

All payroll functions for MEC's stores across Canada are handled at the Vancouver head office by four staff members (three full-time and one part-time). Each store has salaried workers, hourly workers, full- and part-time employees. Sales staff, who are all active in outdoor activities themselves, do not receive commissions—because MEC is a co-operative, its primary goal is not to make a profit but to serve its members. All customers must be members; a lifetime membership costs $5.

While inventory, general accounting, and warehouse operations are managed by one program, MEC uses a separate system for payroll. The actual calculation of pay, deductions (for the Canada Pension Plan and Employment Insurance), and benefits (both statutory benefits and supplemental

disability and premium health-care plans), is pretty straightforward with today's computerized accounting systems, "but there are always exceptions—people leaving, provincial variations in rules for statutory holiday pay, hours to be keyed in—which require human intervention or additional calculations," says Ms. Henrey.

Previously, MEC had an outside firm take care of all its payroll functions. But it now does them in-house for greater flexibility. While external services have standardized reports, MEC wanted to focus on specific areas. For example, employees at each store report on how much of their time is spent on different functions: working the floor area, the cash area, the stock room, and so forth. The head office tracks and collates this information so store managers can keep informed about how their resources are allocated. "We're hoping in the next couple of years to move to a completely automated electronic time capture system that will make things even more efficient," says Ms. Henrey.

By taking care of payroll and other accounting functions at the central office, MEC can benefit from dealing with a single bank, and from economies of scale. More importantly, it can allow its store managers to focus on selling merchandise and serving members.

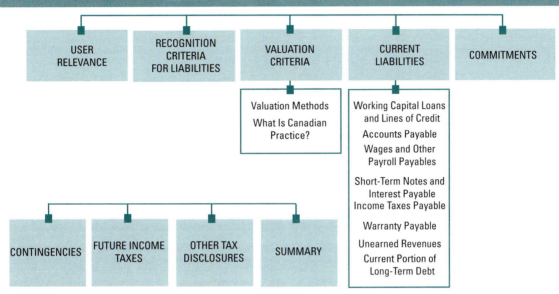

chapter 9

LIABILITIES

Learning Objectives:

After studying this chapter, you should be able to:

1. *Describe the valuation methods used for liabilities in Canada.*
2. *Explain why companies use working capital loans and lines of credit.*
3. *Explain why accounts payable are sometimes thought of as "free debt."*
4. *Prepare journal entries to record the payroll of a company.*
5. *Calculate the amount of interest that is owed on a short-term note payable.*
6. *Describe how warranties payable differ from current liabilities such as accounts payable.*
7. *Describe situations where unearned revenue must be recorded.*
8. *Explain why the portion of long-term debt that is due in the next year is recorded as a current liability.*
9. *Explain what a commitment is and how it is recognized by a company.*
10. *Explain the criteria necessary for a contingency and discuss when it is recorded.*
11. *Describe why future income taxes exist.*
12. *Calculate future income taxes in amortization and warranty situations.*

People like Jennifer Henrey of Mountain Equipment Co-op would agree that good employee relations are important to a successful business. One of the ways that MEC fosters good relations is through strict attention to detail with respect to payroll. Errors in payroll can affect morale. In the story about MEC, Ms. Henrey explained that it used to use an outside contractor to manage its payroll function. Smaller businesses and even some medium-sized and large companies may find it more cost-effective to use an outside group with expertise in an accounting area rather than to hire people as full-time employees. MEC has grown to the point where it wants more information from its payroll data and it has found it easier to customize its information flow by making the payroll function an internal one.

Successful businesses also pay attention to obligations owed to people outside the company. A good reputation for paying debts on time enables a company to use credit to operate effectively and to take on new initiatives. A poor credit rating, on the other hand, means a curtailment of options for outside financing.

In this and the next two chapters, our attention turns to the credit side of the balance sheet and the accounting for liabilities and shareholders' equity. Both liabilities and shareholders' equity can be viewed as sources of assets. Liability holders contribute assets in return for a promise of repayment at some future date, usually with interest. Shareholders contribute assets to the company in return for an ownership interest and the right to share in the future profits of the company.

The general nature of liabilities is discussed first, followed by a discussion of current liabilities, contingent liabilities, and future income taxes. Chapter 10 covers major noncurrent liabilities, such as bonds, leases, and pensions. In Chapter 11, shareholders' equity transactions are discussed.

USER RELEVANCE

Current liabilities represent obligations that the company must settle within the next year. Most of these obligations—accounts payable, income taxes payable, wages payable, notes payable—will require an outflow of cash. Users need to examine the current liabilities to determine how much cash will be required and to estimate when that cash will need to be paid—in one week, one month, three months, etc. An examination of the current assets, especially cash, accounts receivable, and temporary investments, will provide the user with information about the availability of cash. We have already talked about determining how quickly accounts receivable are collected and inventory is sold. These turnover ratios help the user estimate whether enough cash is going to be available when the various liabilities come due. If there does not appear to be enough cash available, the company will have to go to outside sources—short-term debt, long-term debt, issuing more shares—in order to raise additional cash. Understanding the short-term cash needs of a company is essential to determining its financial health and its long-term viability.

RECOGNITION CRITERIA FOR LIABILITIES

Liabilities represent obligations agreed to by the company through some past transaction. To be classified as a liability, an item must have three characteristics. First, it requires that the company settle the obligation through the transfer of assets, the performance of services, or the conferring of some other benefit specified in the transaction. There is usually a specific time when the settlement must occur. Second, companies usually have little or no discretion with respect to liabilities. If they do not satisfy the obligation, the creditor usually has the right to pursue legal action. Third, the transaction or event that gave rise to the obligation must have already occurred.

The transfer of assets or services criterion is similar to the probable future value criterion for the assets. The uncertainty associated with liabilities concerns the dollar value of the assets to be given up, and when that sacrifice will be made.

To avoid uncertainty about the amount and timing of the settlement, some liabilities have fixed payments and fixed due dates. Most loans and accounts payable are of this type. The interest and principal payments are specified in the loan agreement, as are the dates on which those payments will be made. Other liabilities, such as warranty liabilities, may have neither fixed payments nor fixed dates. The settlement of a warranty obligation will depend on when the customer detects a warranty problem and the cost incurred by the company to fix it. Liabilities, therefore, differ in the amount of uncertainty that is associated with them.

If the uncertainty associated with either the amount or the timing of the future transfer is sufficiently high, the liability will probably not be recognized in the financial statements. Suppose, for example, that the company is under investigation by the government for an alleged chemical spill into a river. Does the company have an obligation to transfer assets in the future? If the company is found negligent, there could be a significant liability if a fine is imposed or if the company is required to clean up the spill or both. The company may have a difficult time, however, predicting whether it will be found negligent and, if found negligent, how much it will cost to satisfy the obligation. In this case, it is likely that no liability will be recorded. However, because of the *possibility* of the future transfer of assets, the company could disclose information about the investigation in the notes to the financial statements. Such an item would be referred to as a **contingent liability** in that the future obligation is contingent on certain events occurring.

The ownership criterion that is used for assets does not strictly apply to liabilities, but a similar notion is present. Companies should record only those obligations that they will be required to satisfy. For example, if a customer falls on the company's sidewalk, sues the company for medical costs, and wins, the company may not be obligated to make the payment. If the company is insured against such claims, the insurance company will pay the claim. The company, therefore, does not record the obligation to pay this liability on its books because it is the insurance company's obligation. If the insurance does not cover all of the obligation, the company needs to record any excess as a liability.

The third characteristic of a liability, that is, proving that the transaction that gave rise to the obligation has already occurred, is sometimes difficult to evaluate. For example, in the case of the lawsuit mentioned in the preceding paragraph, what is the event that gave rise to the obligation? Is it the customer falling on the sidewalk, the filing of a lawsuit, or the decision of the court? In this case, the certainty of the obligation increases as each subsequent event occurs. However, the event that gives rise to the ultimate obligation depends on the sequence of events.

Another difficulty that can make evaluation difficult arises when the company signs a binding contract. Suppose, for example, the company signs a contract to purchase 1,000 units of inventory at $30 per unit, to be delivered 30 days from now. Is the signing of the contract the event that gives rise to the obligation to pay for the inventory, or is it the delivery of the inventory? The company's obligation is contingent upon the seller performing its part of the contract by delivering the goods on time. If the goods are not delivered, then the company is not obliged to pay. The signing of the contract creates what is known as a **mutually unexecuted contract** because, at the time of signing, neither the buyer nor the seller has performed its part of the contract. The seller has not delivered any inventory, and the buyer has not paid any cash. Such contracts are normally not recorded in the accounting system, although the company may include information about the contract in the notes to its financial statements.

A **partially executed contract** is one in which one party has performed all or part of its obligation. In the example just given, the contract would be viewed as partially executed if the buyer had made a $3,000 deposit. A partial transaction would then be recorded. In this case, the seller would show an inflow of cash of $3,000 and create a liability account to represent its obligation to deliver inventory valued at $3,000. The liability account would be called "unearned revenue." Once inventory valued at $3,000 was delivered to the customer, the obligation would be satisfied and the revenue would be earned. Note that only the amount of the deposit is recorded at this time, not the full amount of the contract ($30,000 = 1,000 units × $30 per unit). The buyer would show an outflow of cash of $3,000, and create an asset account for the right to receive the inventory valued at $3,000. The account would be called "deposits on purchase commitments."

VALUATION CRITERIA

Just as there are different methods for valuing assets, there are different methods for valuing liabilities. Theoretically, liabilities are valued at their net present value as at the date they are incurred. There are, however, several possible valuation methods to be considered before discussing Canadian practice in depth.

Valuation Methods

One way to value a liability is to record it at the *gross amount* of the obligation, that is, the total of the payments to be made. For example, if an obligation requires the company to pay $1,000 each month for the next three years, the gross obligation would be $36,000. While this amount accurately measures the total payments to be made, it may not accurately measure the company's obligation as at the date it is recorded on the balance sheet. For example, suppose the obligation is a rental agreement for a piece of machinery. If the company can cancel the rental agreement at any time, it is obligated to pay only $1,000 each month. The remaining payments are an obligation only if it decides to keep using the asset. If the contract was non-cancellable, the full $36,000 would make more sense.

Another reason why the gross obligation may not adequately measure the value of the liability is that it ignores the time value of money. Suppose that, in the example, the $1,000 a month is to repay a loan. The total payments of $36,000 include both the repayment of principal and the payment of interest. Interest is an obligation only as the company uses the money over time. If the company has the option to pay off the loan early, it merely has to pay off the principal balance and any accumulated interest. It does not have to pay the full amount. Suppose, for example, that the principal of the loan is $31,000. The difference ($5,000) between this amount and the gross amount is the interest that accrues over time. The company could settle the obligation today with a payment of $31,000. Therefore, recording the liability at $36,000 would overstate the company's obligation at the present time.

To recognize the time value of money, a company may record its obligations at their **net present value**. Both the future payments on the principal and the interest payments are discounted back to the current period using a discount rate. Chapter 10 will go into more detail about present value calculations. Under this valuation system, the company records the obligation at the net present value. As payments are made, the obligation is reduced and interest expense is recorded to represent the use of the money over time. It is important to remember that interest is only recorded as time passes.

Learning Objective

1

Describe the valuation methods used for liabilities in Canada.

What Is Canadian Practice?

In Canada, liabilities should be recorded at the present value of the future payments. The interest rate used depends on the type of liability, and the company's creditworthiness. It should be the appropriate interest rate for an arm's-length transaction of the type that gives rise to the obligation. However, accountants do not use present-value calculations for short-term liabilities such as accounts payable because the time to maturity is so short. Instead, current liabilities such as accounts payable and wages payable are recorded at the gross amount that is owed. Short-term notes payable that have an interest component are recorded at the total principal amount. The interest is recorded as it accrues.

Once a liability is recorded, the carrying value is not usually adjusted except when the liability is paid. One exception occurs when a company is in financial trouble and restructures its debt in negotiations with its creditors. Based on the concessions that the company may obtain from the lender, it may be able to reduce the amount owed on the obligation, or to reduce the interest rate used to calculate interest expense on the existing balance, or to extend the period over which the debt is to be paid. This is called **troubled debt restructuring**.

CURRENT LIABILITIES

Current liabilities are those obligations that require the transfer of assets or services within one year, or one operating cycle of the company. As just discussed, most of them are carried on the books at the gross amount. In order for a company to stay solvent (able to pay its debts as they fall due), it must have sufficient current assets and/or assets generated by operations to pay the current liabilities. Creditors, like bankers, will often use total current liabilities to assess the company's ability to remain viable. The most frequently encountered current liabilities are discussed in the following subsections.

Working Capital Loans and Lines of Credit

Learning Objective

2

Explain why companies use working capital loans and lines of credit.

As mentioned in the preceding paragraph, companies need to have sufficient current assets or inflows of cash from operations to pay debts as they fall due. However, some of those current assets may not be converted into cash fast enough to meet current debt obligation deadlines. To manage this shortfall, companies have a few options. For example, they can arrange a **working capital loan** with a bank. This short-term loan is often secured by customer balances in accounts receivable, by inventory, or both. As money is received from accounts receivable or as the inventory is sold, the amounts received are used to pay off the loan.

Another way that companies can deal with cash shortages is to arrange a **line of credit** with a bank. In this case, the bank assesses the company's ability to repay short-term debts and establishes a short-term debt balance that it feels is reasonable. This provides the company with more freedom to take advantage of opportunities and/or to settle debts. If cheques written by the company exceed the current cash balance in the bank, the bank covers the excess by immediately activating the line of credit and establishing a short-term loan. Subsequent cash deposits by the company are used by the bank to draw down the loan. A company that is using a working capital loan or has activated a line of credit might have a negative cash balance, which must be shown with the current liabilities. This negative cash balance would be obvious to users on the cash flow statement because the end cash balance would also be negative. For example, **Sun-Rype Products Ltd.** has a "$15 million operating line of credit with a Canadian bank." This line of credit bears interest at the bank's prime lending rate which at December 31, 2001, was 4.0%. (Sun-Rype Products' Annual Report, p. 18, included on the *Accounting Perspectives CD*.) Sun-Rype Products' line of credit has been steady at $15 million over the last several years. Its use of the line of credit, however, has been declining. In 1999, it owed

$1,607,000 on its line of credit. In 2000, that balance dropped to $800,000. In 2001, Sun-Rype Products did not owe anything on its line of credit. The bank has given Sun-Rype Products its line of credit at the prime rate. This is the rate that it offers to its very best customers.

Accounts Payable

Accounts payable occur when a company buys goods or services on credit. These are sometimes referred to as **trade accounts payable.** (For an example, see the excerpt from the liability section of **Domtar Inc.**, Exhibit 9-1). Payment is generally deferred for a relatively short period of time, such as 30 to 60 days. These accounts generally do not carry explicit interest charges and are sometimes thought of as "free" debt. Under some agreements, there can be either a penalty for late payment or a discount provision for early payment. The penalty and the difference between the discounted payment and the full payment can both be viewed as interest charges for delayed payments on these liabilities.

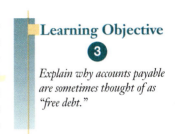

Learning Objective

3

Explain why accounts payable are sometimes thought of as "free debt."

DOMTAR INC. 2001

**Excerpted from the Consolidated Balance Sheets
As at December 31, 2001 and 2000**

(in millions of Canadian dollars, unless otherwise noted)

EXHIBIT 9-1

Liabilities and Shareholders' Equity

Current liabilities	2001 US$	2001	2000
Bank indebtedness	$ 28	$ 45	$ 47
Trade and other payables	452	719	532
Income and other taxes payable	12	19	20
Long-term debt due within one year	24	38	41
	$ 516	$ 821	$ 640
Long-term debt	$1,803	$2,872	$ 973

Wages and Other Payroll Payables

Wages owed to employees can be another significant current liability. The magnitude of the liability depends somewhat on how often the company pays its employees, because the balance in the account reflects the accrual of wages since the last pay period. In addition to the wages themselves, the company may also provide fringe benefits for employees that must also be quantified. These accruals for health care, pensions, vacation pay, and other benefits must also be recognized in the periods in which they occur. Because these may be paid in periods other than those in which they are earned, liabilities have to be recorded.

Learning Objective

4

Prepare journal entries to record the payroll of a company

Additionally, the company acts as a government agent (federal and provincial) in the collection of certain taxes. For example, income taxes must be withheld from employees' wages and remitted to the government. While this is not an expense to the company, the company must nevertheless keep track of the amounts deducted from employees' earnings and show the liability to pay these amounts to the government. The liability to pay the employee is reduced by the amount withheld. Other deductions, such as Canada Pension Plan (CPP) or Quebec Pension Plan (QPP) and Employment Insurance (EI), are also deducted from employees' total wages and remitted to the government. This further reduces the amount paid to employees. Beyond the amount deducted from employees' wages, companies must make additional payments to the government for CPP or QPP, EI, and Workers' Compensation. These amounts are shown as an expense to the employer and are recorded as liabilities until they are remitted to the government.

As an example, assume that Angelique's Autobody Shop has a two-week payroll of $7,500 for its seven employees. Income tax of $990 is deducted from the employees' cheques, as well as 4.7% for CPP and 2.2% for EI. The employer has to submit an additional 4.7% for CPP and 3.08% for EI on behalf of its employees. The journal entries to record the payroll would be:

DEDUCTIONS FROM EMPLOYEES' EARNED INCOME

SE-Wage expense	7,500.00	
L-Employee income tax payable		990.00
L-CPP contribution payable		352.50
L-EI taxes payable		165.00
A-Cash		5,992.50
Additional Deductions Paid by Employer:		
SE-Wage expense	583.50	
L-CPP contribution payable		352.50
L-EI taxes payable		231.00

The amounts in the three liability accounts are remitted periodically to the government according to its regulations. The following journal entry illustrates the remittance:

L-Employee income tax payable	990	
L-CPP contribution payable	705	
L-EI taxes payable	396	
A-Cash		2,091

Note that the total amount recorded by the employer as an expense ($8,083.50) exceeds the amount it has agreed to pay the employees ($7,500.00). Because of these extra amounts that the government requires companies to remit, businesses are concerned each time the government makes changes to the Canada Pension Plan or Employment Insurance (unless of course, the government reduces the rates as it has for EI in the last few years). These rates are set by the government each year, usually in November or December. The additional amounts must always be taken into account by an employer, whether it is considering hiring new employees or maintaining its current number of employees.

Short-Term Notes and Interest Payable

Short-term notes payable represent borrowings of the company that require repayment in the next year or operating cycle. They either carry explicit interest rates or are structured such that the difference between the original amount borrowed and the amount repaid represents implicit interest. Interest expense and interest payable should be recognized over the life of these loan agreements.

Assume that the Checkerboard Taxi Company borrowed $10,000 at 9% from the local bank. The loan was to be repaid in monthly instalments of $1,710.70 over six months. The monthly instalments included reductions of the principal ($10,000) as well as interest at 9% per annum. The interest is calculated on the decreasing amount of principal. The following amortization table illustrates the interest component and the reductions of the principal.

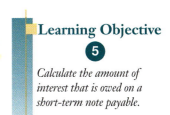

Learning Objective

5

Calculate the amount of interest that is owed on a short-term note payable.

Month	Payment	Interest	Principal Reduction	Principal Balance
				$10,000.00
1	$1,710.70	$75.00[a]	$1,635.70	$ 8,364.30
2	$1,710.70	$62.73	$1,647.97	$ 6,716.33
3	$1,710.70	$50.37	$1,660.33	$ 5,056.00
4	$1,710.70	$37.92	$1,672.78	$ 3,383.22
5	$1,710.70	$25.37	$1,685.33	$ 1,697.89
6	$1,710.70	$12.81[b]	$1,697.89	-0-

[a] $10,000 × .09 / 12 = $75.00
[b] rounding of $0.08

The journal entry at the end of the first month to record the first payment would be:

SE-Interest expense	75.00	
L-Short-term note payable	1,635.70	
A-Cash		1,710.70

Try to reconstruct the journal entries for the remaining months. The short-term note payable would initially have been recorded at the principal amount of $10,000, then gradually reduced as monthly payments were made.

Income Taxes Payable

Companies are subject to both federal corporate income taxes and provincial corporate taxes. As mentioned earlier in the book, the rules governing the calculation of income for tax purposes may differ from the accounting guidelines. The discussion in Chapter 8 concerning future income taxes highlighted this difference (future income taxes are discussed in greater detail later in this chapter). The taxes that become payable under the rules of the CCRA must be recorded as a liability of the company. Multinational companies may also be subject to taxation in the other countries in which they operate.

The payment of taxes does not always coincide with the incurrence of the tax. In Canada, companies are required to make monthly tax payments, usually based on taxes paid the previous year, so that the government has a steady flow of cash during the year on which to operate. The deadline for filing the yearly tax return is six months after the corporate year end, but the balance of taxes owed for a year must be paid within two months of the year end. Penalties are imposed if the company significantly underestimates the amount of tax payable.

Warranty Payable

Learning Objective

Describe how warranties payable differ from current liabilities such as accounts payable.

When a company sells a good or service, there are either explicit or implicit guarantees to the buyer. If the product or service fails to satisfy the customer, the seller may have to provide warranty service. Because the amount of warranty service is unknown at the time of sale, the company should estimate an amount in order to match the expense of the warranty to the revenue from the sale. Therefore, to satisfy the matching principle, at the time of sale a warranty expense and a warranty liability are recognized based on an estimate of future warranty costs for that sale. If the company has been in business for a reasonable length of time, this estimate can be made fairly easily, based on the past history of defects in the product. For new products and new companies, this may be much more difficult. As warranty service is provided (paid for by cash or other resources), the estimated liability amount is reduced.

As an example of a warranty situation, let us consider Hubble Appliance Company Ltd. It sells large appliances like stoves and refrigerators. During the month of January 20x2, it sold eight refrigerators, each of which carried a three-year warranty against mechanical defects. If the refrigerators sold for an average price of $1,150, Hubble would record revenues of $9,200 ($1,150 × 8). Although Hubble buys quality merchandise from its supplier, it is possible that within three years of sale, one or more of these refrigerators may break down. In reviewing its past record of mechanical breakdowns, Hubble estimates that, over the long term, it costs approximately 5% off every sticker price to fix all units that ultimately require repair work. Over the next three years, Hubble therefore expects to spend about $460 ($9,200 × .05) to fix one or more of the eight refrigerators just sold. Depending on the quality of the eight refrigerators, it may spend more than $460 or less than $460. Experience and knowledge of the merchandise make it possible for companies to make reasonably accurate estimates. To record the estimated warranty obligation in the year of the sale, Hubble makes the following journal entry:

SE-Warranty expense	460	
L -Estimated warranty obligation		460

If Hubble needed to spend $126 in 20x3 to replace a leaking seal on one of the refrigerators, it would record the repair work by reducing the liability account.

L -Estimated warranty obligation	126	
A-Cash		126

As you can see, an expense is not recorded when actual repair costs are incurred. By estimating its potential future obligation at the same time that it records revenue from the sale, Hubble is able to record the warranty expense in the same period that it records the revenue. This way, users get a clearer picture of the actual amount of revenue earned on the sale. If Hubble had delayed recognizing an expense until it actually incurred some warranty costs, that expense could easily appear in a period other than the one in which the revenue was recognized and the matching principle would have been violated. The profit reported for the sale would then have been overstated. For this reason, companies are asked to estimate the potential future warranty obligation and to record it at the time of sale if the amount of warranty costs is material.

In the airline industry, frequent flyer programs are treated in the same manner as warranties. As customers accrue travel miles, the company records an expense to represent the cost of providing a free flight and a liability to represent the company's future obligation to honour the credits earned by a customer. But some customers never collect enough points to earn a free flight. Others may not redeem their points even though they have enough for a free flight. Should the companies accrue a liability for all the potential free flights or would it be more appropriate to estimate future redemptions of points and accrue a liability to represent that estimate? The following article summary should provide some insight into this problem:

accounting in the news

FREQUENT FLYER POINTS

F requent flyer programs, which allow people to accumulate points they later trade in for air travel, are a good example of a future liability. Airlines need to account for them because people eventually redeem their points. By one estimate, two trillion points were outstanding in 1997—enough to fill 440,000 300-seat planes and send airlines into bankruptcy!

However, major airlines only rate the liability at 25 cents per $1,000 of outstanding cashable miles. Why? They don't expect to pay for every mile outstanding. Many people never claim their miles; some people forget and some never fly enough to reach minimum award levels.

Source: "Frequent travellers: How a frequent flyer can make a point," Advertising Special Report, *Globe and Mail*, April 25, 1997, p. C11.

Unearned Revenues

In many businesses, customers are required to make down payments prior to the receipt of goods or services. This creates partially executed contracts between buyers and sellers. Because the sellers have not fulfilled their part of the contract, it would be inappropriate for them to recognize revenue from the sale. Therefore, sellers must defer the recognition of revenue from down payments. These deferrals create liabilities that are known as **unearned revenues** or **deferred revenues**.

Businesses that require prepayments generally show unearned revenues as a part of the liability section. Magazine and newspaper publishers and airline companies are among these types of businesses. The current liability section of **Air Canada** in 2001 includes $481 million ($498 million in 2000) for Advance Ticket Sales. The note on air transportation revenue states that "Airline passenger and cargo sales are recognized as operating revenues when the transportation is provided. The value of unused transportation is included in current liabilities."

Current Portion of Long-Term Debt

When long-term debt (discussed in Chapter 10) comes within a year of being due, it must be reclassified as a current liability. This reclassification enables users to estimate more accurately the outflow of cash expected during the following year. Therefore, this account category, known as **current portion of long-term debt**, is used for all the debt that was originally long-term, but that is now within one year, or one operating cycle, of being paid off or retired. This account is also referred to as the *current maturity of long-term debt*. In the case of long-term mortgages or other debt obligations requiring monthly or annual payments, the current maturity part that is shown with the current liabilities represents the amount of principal that will be paid off in the next year. Remember that the interest paid on this debt is only recorded as it accrues or is paid. Note in Exhibit 9-1 that in 2001, about 1.3% of **Domtar's** long-term debt ($38/($38 + $2,872)) is due to be paid within the next year.

COMMITMENTS

In the course of business, many companies sign agreements committing them to certain transactions. A common type of **commitment** transaction is a **purchase commitment**, which is an agreement to purchase items in the future for a negotiated price. As discussed earlier, this is an example of a mutually unexecuted contract and, under Canadian accounting guidelines, is therefore not recorded on the books of the company. The company would, however, discuss it in a note to the financial statements if it thought that the commitment would have a material effect on future operations. An example of this type of disclosure can be seen in Exhibit 9-2, which is the Commitments and Contingencies footnote for **AT Plastics Inc.**

AT PLASTICS INC. 2001

EXHIBIT 9-2

Excerpted from the Notes to the Statements

Note 16. Commitments and contingencies

(a) Operating leases

Under the terms of operating leases, the Company is committed to rental payments until expiry of leases as follows:

2002	$3,915
2003	3,484
2004	3,039
2005	2,771
2006	2,529

(b) Purchases

The Company has entered into a new 15-year ethylene supply contract that commenced in 1999 for approximately 125,000 tonnes per year under a limited take-or-pay arrangement.

The Company has entered into a 10-year electrical energy supply contract that commenced in 2000 for a minimum of 1.57 billion kilowatts per year at a fixed rate per kilowatt.

(c) Other

Management believes that any costs resulting from environmental matters known to it will not have a material impact on the Company's financial position and results of operations.

AT Plastics disclosed the information about the leases because the Company is committed to the given outflows of cash as a result of the lease contracts. It disclosed the information about the ethylene supply contract probably because of the type of contract involved, and because it is committed for several years. A **take-or-pay contract** means that the company must pay for the 125,000 tonnes of ethylene whether it actually takes that much from the supplier or not. No monetary amounts are discussed, but the fact that the take-or-pay contract is *limited* may mean that the amount that must be paid each year has a top limit. The electrical supply contract states the minimum number of kilowatts that must be purchased each year. The disclosure of the information about the two supply commitments is useful to users in two ways. First, it lets them know of a possible future cost to the company whether an amount of the item is purchased or not. Second, and probably more importantly, it lets users know that the company is planning ahead and attempting to get long-term commitments at fixed prices for items that it knows it is going to need in its manufacturing process. Such commitments would be of concern to users if the price of these items started to fall in the marketplace, leaving the company committed to paying prices higher than would have been paid if no contract was in place.

accounting in the news

Technology equipment manufacturers, major casualties of the high-tech crash, have been left vulnerable by commitments they made to suppliers when the high-tech sector was at its peak.

One study estimates that manufacturers, especially those in the telecom industry, would have to write-off billions. The 2002 study by Booz Allen & Hamilton, a management consultancy firm, noted that seven companies in the technology equipment sector tallied up a US $5.4-billion inventory write-off for 2001.

Responding to a supply squeeze in 1999 to 2000, equipment manufacturers entered into contracts to buy a certain share of a supplier's production for a specified period. But demand collapsed, and these companies were locked into commitments that would result in mounting inventory—which can quickly become obsolete.

Renegotiating the terms of the commitments could mean cash charges for companies that agree to make payments to suppliers. A co-author of the study said these companies could put the lure of future contracts, as well as the possibility of withdrawing their business, on the renegotiating table with suppliers.

The analysis included Canadian companies Nortel Networks Inc., Celestica Inc., and JDS Uniphase Corp., though it did not identify which companies had the most exposure.

Source: "Huge writeoffs predicted to hit tech firms," by Patrick Brethour, *The Globe and Mail*, Jan. 29, 2002, p. B4.

When the financial statements of a company are analyzed, undisclosed purchase commitments are a significant risk to be considered. The problem this can pose for the reader of financial statements is illustrated by an international example from **Westinghouse Company** (which became CBS Company in 1997) in the United States in the mid-1970s. Westinghouse was in the business of building nuclear power plants for utility companies. To secure the construction business, Westinghouse offered utility companies fixed-price contracts to supply them with uranium after the plants were completed and running. The average prices stated in these contracts were approximately US $8 to $10 per pound of uranium. By the mid-1970s, Westinghouse was committed to providing a total of approximately 70 million pounds over a 20-year period. Since these were mutually unexecuted contracts, they were not recorded or disclosed in the financial statements.

When the market price of uranium was close to the fixed price in the contracts, these mutually unexecuted contracts were a break-even proposition for Westinghouse (i.e., no gain or loss would occur when the contracts were satisfied), and no disclosure was required. The problem began when a cartel formed in the uranium supply market and drove up the price of the fuel. When the price reached US $26 per pound in September 1975, Westinghouse informed the utility companies that it had to be excused from performing on its contracts because of a legal doctrine called "commercial impracticability." The utility companies then brought lawsuits against Westinghouse, alleging breach of contract. By 1978, the price of uranium had risen to US $45 per pound.

Because the price escalated so significantly above the contract price of US $8-$10 per pound, Westinghouse had to disclose the loss on these commitment contracts. In 1975, the estimated cost to Westinghouse of settling the contracts approached $2 billion, which was about 75% of its total equity at the time. Over the next 15 years, Westinghouse settled most of the lawsuits, the first of them in 1977 for $20.5 million. The audit opinion on Westinghouse was qualified by the auditors until 1979, when Westinghouse accrued a loss of $405 million (net of taxes) to cover the estimated costs of settling the remaining suits. Remember that auditors qualify their opinion about a company's financial statements if the company does not follow GAAP. Failing to accrue the potential liability for the lawsuits would have led to such a qualification. The effects of these suits lingered for 19 years as indicated by the note in Exhibit 9-3, excerpted from Westinghouse's 1994 annual report.

WESTINGHOUSE, 1994

EXHIBIT 9-3

Note 16: Contingent Liabilities and Commitments

Uranium Settlements

The Corporation had previously provided for the estimated future costs for the resolution of all uranium supply contract suits and related litigation. The remaining uranium reserve balance includes assets required for certain settlement obligations and reserves for estimated future costs. The reserve balance at December 31, 1994, is deemed adequate considering all facts and circumstances known to management. The future obligations require providing the remainder of the fuel deliveries running through 2013 and the supply of equipment and services through approximately 1995. Variances from estimates which may occur are considered in determining if an adjustment of the liability is necessary.

CONTINGENCIES

Contingent liabilities (also referred to as **contingent losses**) arise when the incurrence of the liability is contingent upon some future event. The settlement of a lawsuit, for example, is a situation in which the company may or may not incur a liability, depending upon the judgement in the case. The note in Exhibit 9-4 from the 2001 annual report of Canadian Pacific Railway Ltd. outlines one such contingency.

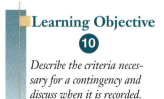

Learning Objective

10

Describe the criteria necessary for a contingency and discuss when it is recorded.

CANADIAN PACIFIC RAILWAY LTD. 2001

EXHIBIT 9-4

Excerpted from the Notes to the Statements

23. Major commitments and contingencies

In the normal course of its operations, the Company becomes involved in various legal actions, including claims relating to injuries and damage to property. The Company maintains provisions for such items, which it considers to be adequate. While the final outcome with respect to actions outstanding or pending as at December 31, 2001 cannot be predicted with certainty, it is the opinion of management that their resolution will not have a material adverse effect on the Company's financial position or results of operations.

In Canada, a contingent loss should be recognized as a loss on the income statement and a liability on the balance sheet if it meets the following criteria:

1. It is likely that some future event will result in the company's incurring an obligation which will require the use of assets or the performance of a service.

2. The amount of the loss can be reasonably estimated.

If either of these criteria are not met, but the potential for loss is significant, the company should provide users with information about the potential loss in a note disclosure similar to the two examples that follow.

Another kind of **contingency** is the guarantee of one company's loan by another company. This happens many times when a subsidiary company takes out a loan and the parent company (the company that owns most of the shares of the subsidiary) guarantees repayment of the loan. The liability to repay the loan is a contingent liability to the parent company because it is contingent upon the default of the subsidiary. Such a contingency is illustrated in the 2001 annual report for **Teck Cominco Limited**, shown in Exhibit 9-5.

EXHIBIT 9-5

■ TECK COMINCO LIMITED 2001

Excerpted from the Notes to the Statements

Note 5 Property, Plant and Equipment

Investment in Antamina
The company accounts for its 22.5% investment in Compania Minera Antamina S.A., the company holding the Antamina project, on an equity basis. In connection with the senior debt financing of the project the company has provided the lenders with a guarantee on its 22.5% share of the debt during the pre-completion period. The guarantee will be removed if the project meets certain completion tests which are expected to take place in the second half of 2002. At December 31, 2001 the senior project debt outstanding was US $1.22 billion in respect of which the company is responsible for and has guaranteed US $275 million.

As a third and final example, the selling of accounts receivable with recourse creates a contingent liability for the selling company because it may be required to buy back the receivables under the recourse provision if the customers default on their payments. A further discussion of the sale of receivables is located in Chapter 6. In its 2001 financial statements, IPSCO Inc. reports the existence of an agreement to sell its accounts receivable.

EXHIBIT 9-6

■ IPSCO INC. 2001

Excerpted from the Notes to the Statements

Note 3 Accounts Receivable

On 27 September 2001, the company amended an existing agreement to sell accounts receivable, on a revolving basis, up to a maximum value of CDN $75,000, with limited recourse. Through 31 December 2001, no accounts receivable have been sold pursuant to this agreement. The agreement may be terminated under certain conditions at any time by the company or the purchaser and in any event, on 31 January 2005.

FUTURE INCOME TAXES

Future income taxes arise because, although the company uses accounting revenues and expenses to determine income tax expense on the income statement, it also uses Canada Customs and Revenue Agency (CCRA) calculations of revenues and expenses to determine the income tax payable (that is, the amount that must actually be paid to the government). In Chapter 8, future income taxes were mentioned because companies must use capital cost allowance (CCA) for tax purposes. They can, however, use any one of several amortization methods to prepare financial statements. The use of the different methods for tax versus accounting results in an accounting asset balance that is different from a tax asset balance. The asset balances hold different future tax effects.

> **Learning Objective**
> **11**
>
> *Explain why future income taxes exist.*

Other areas that create differences between what is taxed by the government and what is reported in the accounting system include the warranty costs we mentioned earlier in this chapter. The warranty liability on the balance sheet is an estimate of future warranty costs based on revenue that was recognized in the current period. For tax purposes, there is no warranty liability. Rather, the actual amount that the company paid in the current period to repair items under warranty is used as a tax deduction. Amortization and warranties are examples of how an accounting asset/liability can have a future tax impact that is different from the future tax impact as measured by the CCRA.

The method used in Canada to measure future taxes is the **liability method**. This method focuses on the balance sheet. It attempts to measure the liability to pay taxes (or the future tax benefit to be derived from) the current imbalance in accounting and tax carrying amounts in the future, based on a set of assumptions about future revenues and expenses. Once the liability/benefit for these future taxes is calculated and the amounts currently payable to the CCRA are established, the tax expense to be reported on the income statement is determined based on the taxes owed to the CCRA plus/minus the future tax amount. There is no attempt to calculate tax expense using tax rates and income reported to shareholders with this method.

To illustrate the liability method, we will use the data and calculations in Exhibit 9-7. The data represent a company that sells fitness equipment. The motorized equipment, such as treadmills, carries a three-year warranty. The company estimates the probable future costs associated with the sale and records a liability (Obligations under warranties) and a warranty expense in the year of the sale. The CCRA allows a tax deduction for the actual costs incurred by the company to repair equipment under warranty. Assume that the warranty is the only difference between the accounting and tax methods of the company.

LIABILITY METHOD CALCULATIONS

EXHIBIT 9-7

Assumptions:

Income before tax and warranties	$10,000

Warranty expense (accounting purposes):
Year 1: $200

Actual warranty costs incurred:
Year 1: $50
Year 2: $70
Year 3: $80

Tax rate	40%

The liability method requires the company to do a *pro forma* (as if) calculation of the amounts of income tax that will be payable in the future based on the **temporary differences** that exist in the current period. The pro forma calculations require that the company prepare a schedule of the differences that exist and how they will reverse in future periods. In the case of warranties, the company accrues a warranty liability in the current period that will become a tax deduction in the current and future periods as actual costs are incurred. This creates a **future tax asset** because fewer taxes will be paid in the future as these deductions are included. Exhibit 9-8 will illustrate how this occurs.

EXHIBIT 9-8

■ **LIABILITY METHOD—FUTURE TAX ASSET CALCULATION**

	Year 1	Year 2	Year 3
Beginning warranty obligation	$200	$150	$ 80
Actual warranty costs incurred	50	70	80
Ending warranty obligation	$150	$ 80	$—
Tax rate	40%	40%	40%
Future tax asset	$ 60	$ 32	$—
Increase/(decrease) in future tax asset		($28)	($32)
Income tax payable calculation:			
Income before warranty costs and			
income tax	$10,000	$10,000	$10,000
Actual warranty costs	50	70	80
	9,950	9,930	9,920
Taxes payable	3,980	3,972	3,968
	$ 5,970	$ 5,958	$ 5,952
Taxes payable	$ 3,980	$ 3,972	$ 3,968
Less: Future tax asset			
increase/(decrease)	60	(28)	(32)
Accounting tax expense	$ 3,920	$ 4,000	$ 4,000

Note how the original difference of $150 (future tax obligation of $60) reverses in Years 2 and 3 as actual warranty costs are incurred. In years 2 and 3, the amount of actual taxes owed to the government is lower than the accounting tax expense because the actual warranty costs are deductible for tax purposes. This future reduction in actual taxes owed allows us to create the future tax asset of $60 in Year 1. Note as well that the accounting tax expense is less than taxes payable in Year 1 but higher than taxes payable in Years 2 and 3.

This example assumes that the original estimate in Year 1 was accurate (actual warranty costs over the three years were exactly $200). It also assumes that the tax rate of 40% does not change. Under the liability method, the company must review its estimates to ensure that the future tax asset still exists and that the amount estimated is still valid. In calculating the future tax asset, the company must also use the tax rate that will be in effect in Years 2 and 3. If there is a planned change in rates for Years 2 and 3, the new rates must be used. The purpose of these two provisions is to ensure that the amount represented on the balance sheet for the future tax asset or liability is as accurate as possible.

To keep the example simple, we created a warranty obligation in Year 1 and then traced it through Years 2 and 3. In reality, there would be more sales of inventory with warranty provisions in Years 2 and 3. These new sales would create new warranty obligations and actual warranty costs incurred in Years 2 and 3 would probably be incurred on inventory sold in any or all of the three years. Once we start to deal with multiple years the calculations become more complex, but the concept is the same. Warranty obligations are recognized in Year 1 and over the next two years of the warranty, and costs will be incurred as the obligations are met. A future tax asset is created in Year 1 that will be reversed over Years 2 and 3.

In Chapter 8 there is an example of how the liability method is applied when the source of the tax difference is the use of amortization for accounting and CCA for tax. Refer back there to see the illustration.

Some users misunderstand future income taxes on the balance sheet, especially if they have a credit balance and are included with the long-term liabilities. They incorrectly assume that these future income taxes represent an amount owed by the company to the CCRA. This assumption is incorrect. The amount owed is shown as taxes payable. Future income taxes on the balance sheet represent an amount that will *likely become payable* in the future if conditions continue unchanged. If we take the example of future income taxes arising because of amortization (CCA for tax and straight-line for accounting, as illustrated in Chapter 8), in the early period of a capital asset's life, the tax carrying value of the asset will be smaller than the accounting carrying value. This means that the company is paying less tax today than is measured for accounting purposes. In the latter part of the asset's life, CCA will be less than the accounting amortization, which means that the company will pay more in tax. Over the life of any asset, the total tax expense will be the same as total taxes payable.

Sears Canada has a substantial investment in capital assets. In 2000, it increased its investment in capital assets by $270.9 million. In 2001, that balance increased by just over $145 million. Sears Canada generally uses straight-line amortization for reporting purposes, but like every other company in Canada, must use CCA for tax. The future income tax assets balance fell by $121 million in 2000 and the future income tax liabilities fell by $5.7 million. In 2001, the future income tax assets fell by a further $73.6 million and the future income tax liabilities by $23.6. Although the company has been increasing its investment in assets, the previously accumulated temporary differences have been reversing faster than the new temporary differences are causing future income taxes to rise.

Future income taxes can represent a significant amount on the balance sheet (6.8% of Sears Canada's total assets in 2001 and 2% of its total liabilities). It is therefore important that you understand what they are, and what they are not. They are the difference between the accounting carrying value of assets and liabilities and the related tax carrying value of the same items. They are not the amount owed to the government for the current period. In fact, whether or not the company ever pays the amount to the government depends on the future activities of the business, and on whether or not the government keeps the same tax rules.

Future income taxes can appear in various parts of the balance sheet as current assets or liabilities, or as long-term assets or liabilities. Where they appear is a function of the differences that caused them, and whether they have a debit or credit balance. Future income taxes that arise from warranty costs are often classified as current because the actual costs for warranties (those that are deductible for tax purposes) are usually incurred during the same year as the expense, or in the following year. This is true if the warranty is a one-year warranty. For three-year warranties, the future income taxes would take longer to reverse, and are therefore classified as noncurrent. Future income taxes that result from the CCA/amortization situation are classified as noncurrent because it takes several years for the future income taxes to reverse. Sears Canada has a current portion of future income tax assets, noncurrent future income tax assets, and noncurrent future income tax liabilities.

One more issue regarding income taxes should be considered. Some differences between the methods used for accounting and tax purposes are considered **permanent differences**. One example is the recognition of dividend revenue received from an investment in another Canadian company. This is a legitimate revenue for accounting purposes. For tax purposes, however, it is not taxable income because the company that paid the dividend already paid taxes on it. To tax the recipient of the dividend would, in effect, tax the same income twice. If future income tax were to be calculated on this permanent difference, it would never reverse and the balance in the future income tax account would never disappear. Refer back to the example in Exhibit 9-7. In the example, the company earned $10,000 before tax and warranties. Assume that in Year 1 the source of $500 of that income was dividends from an investment in another company. The calculation of taxes payable and accounting tax expense under the liability method would be as follows:

EXHIBIT 9-9	

LIABILITY METHOD—FUTURE TAX ASSET CALCULATION INCLUDING A PERMANENT DIFFERENCE

	Year 1	Year 2	Year 3
Beginning warranty obligation	$200	$150	$ 80
Actual warranty costs incurred	50	70	80
Ending warranty obligation	$150	$80	$—
Tax rate	40%	40%	40%
Future tax asset	$ 60	$ 32	$—
Increase/(decrease) in future tax asset		($28)	($32)
Income tax payable calculation:			
Income before warranty costs and income tax	$10,000	$10,000	$10,000
Less: permanent difference	500		
	9,500		
Actual warranty costs	50	70	80
	9,450	9,930	9,920
Taxes payable	3,780	3,972	3,968
	$ 5,670	$5,958	$5,952
Taxes payable	$ 3,780	$ 3,972	$ 3,968
Less: Future tax asset increase/(decrease)			
	60	(28)	(32)
Accounting tax expense	$ 3,720	$ 4,000	$ 4,000

Note that the income before taxes is adjusted for the permanent difference before the taxes payable amount is determined.

An International Perspective

Reports from Other Countries

In some countries, such as Italy and Norway, accounting practices follow the tax requirements of the country. Therefore, no future income tax account is necessary since there are no differences between accounting and tax. In most other countries, such as Denmark, France, and Japan, the provision for income taxes is based on the taxable income and not on the accounting income reported to shareholders. Therefore, in these countries, no future income taxes will be shown either. Another group of countries (including the United States, Chile, and South Africa) follow the Canadian practice of calculating future income taxes on all temporary differences (excluding permanent differences). The United Kingdom follows the Canadian practice except that differences that will not reverse in the foreseeable future are not recorded as future income taxes but instead are treated as permanent differences. Virtually no country allows future income tax amounts to be present-valued. The International Accounting Standards Board (IASB) requires the use of the liability method for determining income tax expense. Unlike Canada, the IASB refers to the income tax difference as deferred income tax rather than future income tax.

NAFTA Facts

United States—The liability method is used.
Mexico—The liability method is also used.

OTHER TAX DISCLOSURES

Included in the usual tax disclosure of a company are three basic types of information. The first is often a breakdown of the tax expense (sometimes referred to as the tax provision) into the amounts currently payable and the amounts deferred. If the company has significant foreign operations, foreign taxes are sometimes broken down in this disclosure. **Canada Bread Company, Limited's** 2001 financial statements disclose this in Note 12, where the breakdown of the tax expense occurs in the second table (Exhibit 9-10).

The second major disclosure in the footnotes is a reconciliation of the difference between the tax expense reported and the amount that would have been reported based on statutory rates. This disclosure takes into consideration the tax credits and other items that cause the average (effective) rate to be different from the statutory CCRA rate.

The first table in Exhibit 9-10 shows that the differences are due mainly to a manufacturing and process credit (permanent difference), non-taxable gains (permanent difference), non-deductible goodwill amortization (permanent difference), the equity in earnings of an associated company, the large corporations tax, and other provisions.

The third tax disclosure is a discussion of the temporary differences creating the future income tax amounts. The major sources of temporary differences are depreciable capital assets, accrued assets, other assets, and taxes payable regarding accrued liabilities.

EXHIBIT 9-10

CANADA BREAD COMPANY, LIMITED (2001)

12. Income Taxes

Income tax expense varies from the amount that would be computed by applying the combined federal and provincial statutory income tax rate as a result of the following:

	2001	2000
Expected income tax expense based on statutory income tax rate of 41.9% (2000 – 44.5%)	$ 15,245	$ 10,761
Increase (reduction) in income taxes resulting from:		
Adjustment to net future tax liabilities for changes in tax laws and rates	—	(2,804)
Manufacturing and processing credit	(2,246)	(1,943)
Non-taxable gains	(12)	(87)
Non-deductible goodwill amortization	1,075	1,129
Equity in earnings of associated company	(541)	(748)
Large corporations tax	200	147
Other	1,540	510
	$ 15,261	$ 6,965

Income tax expense attributable to net income consists of:

	Current	Future	Total
2001	$ 15,399	$ (138)	$ 15,261
2000	7,275	(310)	6,965

The tax effects of temporary differences that give rise to significant portions of the future tax assets and future tax liabilities at December 31 are presented below:

	2001	2000
Future tax assets:		
Accrued assets	$ 3,120	$ 2,310
Other	2,000	779
	$ 5,120	$ 3,089
Future tax liabilities:		
Plant and equipment	$ 35,453	$ 24,275
Investments in associated company	—	7,966
Taxes payable regarding accrued liabilities	1,760	—
Other	2,995	2,332
	$ 40,208	$ 34,573
Classified in the consolidated financial statements as:		
Future tax asset current	$ 3,094	$ 2,655
Future tax liability non-current	38,182	34,139
Net future tax liability	$ 35,088	$ 31,484

SUMMARY

This chapter opened with a description of commonly reported current liabilities. It traced the financial statement impact of lines of credit, accounts payable, wages payable, short-term notes, income tax, warranties, and unearned revenue. It also described some of the anomalies that can affect the decisions made by users, but that may or may not be actually reflected on the balance sheet or income statement. These items are commitments (often described in notes to the financial statements) and loss contingencies (reported on the financial statements if they are likely to occur and are measurable, but in the notes to the financial statements if they are likely but not measurable). The chapter concluded with a discussion of future income taxes, an item that can be confusing to users because it can be either current or noncurrent depending on its source. Unlike previous chapters, this one did not include a discussion of financial statement analysis with respect to liabilities. This topic is deferred until the discussion of the remaining liabilities in Chapter 10 is complete. In Chapter 10, attention turns to the noncurrent liabilities, of which the primary accounts are bonds payable, pension liabilities, and lease liabilities.

SUMMARY PROBLEM

Additional Demonstration Problems

The Lundkvist Company purchased a piece of equipment on January 1, 20x2, for $21,000. The company will amortize the asset straight-line for book purposes over its useful life, which is estimated to be seven years. The residual value is estimated to be zero. The asset qualifies as a class 10 asset for tax purposes, with a 30% CCA rate. During 20x2, Lundkvist generated $4,500 in income before amortization and taxes. The tax rate in 20x2 is 25%. The amortization of the asset purchased in 20x2 is the only difference between the book methods and the tax methods used by Lundkvist.

1. Construct the entry for taxes that Lundkvist will make in 20x2 using the liability method of calculating future income taxes.

2. Prepare a footnote to accompany the 20x2 financial statements.

SUGGESTED SOLUTION TO SUMMARY PROBLEM

1. The future income tax liability and taxes payable for 20x2 are calculated as shown in Exhibit 9-11 under the liability method.

SE-Tax expense	375.00	
L-Tax payable		337.50
L-Future tax liability		37.50

LIABILITY METHOD CALCULATIONS

EXHIBIT 9-11

Amortization:

$21,000 / 7 = $3,000

Book value of asset at the end of 20x2 = $18,000

    ($21,000 − $3,000)

CCA:

$21,000 × 30% × 50% = $3,150

UCC at the end of 20x2 = $17,850

    ($21,000 − $3,150)

Calculation of future tax liability:

$18,000 − $17,850 = $150 Difference in ending asset carrying values

Tax rate = 25%

Future tax liability = $150 × 25% = $37.50

	Accounting	Tax
Income before amortization/CCA	$4,500	$4,500
Amortization/CCA	3,000	3,150
Income before taxes	1,500	1,350
Taxes	375	338
Net income	$1,125	$1,012

2. The following footnote could be included with Lundkvist Company's financial statements:

Income Taxes
Income taxes for 20x2 consist of:

Current	$338
Future	37
	$375

Future income taxes arise as a result of temporary differences from claiming capital cost allowance for income tax purposes in excess of amortization on capital assets.

Statutory rate	25.0%
Effect on taxes of capital cost allowance	(2.5)
Effective tax rate	22.5%

ABBREVIATIONS USED

CCA	Capital Cost Allowance
CCRA	Canada Customs and Revenue Agency
CPP	Canada Pension Plan
EI	Employment Insurance
IASB	International Accounting Standards Board
QPP	Quebec Pension Plan
UCC	Undepreciated Capital Cost

SYNONYMS

Contingent liability/Contingent loss
Current maturities of long-term debt/Current portion of long-term debt

GLOSSARY

Commitments   Obligations to which a company has agreed, but that do not yet meet the recognition criteria for liabilities.

Contingencies   Events or transactions whose effects on the financial statements depend on the outcome of some future event.

Contingent liability   A liability of a company that is contingent on some future event, such as the resolution of a lawsuit.

Contingent loss   Synonym for contingent liability.

Current portion of long-term debt   That portion of long-term debt that is within one year of being due.

Future tax asset/liability   Accounts used to record the future tax effect of the differences between the carrying values of assets/liabilities with respect to accounting records and tax records.

Liability   An obligation that will require a probable future sacrifice of resources of the company.

Liability method   A method of calculating deferred taxes in which the balance in the future tax asset/liability account is calculated based on the tax calculation of future years at future tax rates. The tax expense reported to shareholders is then determined based on the calculated future tax amount and the taxes owed to the CCRA.

Line of credit   A credit limit established by a bank that allows the company to write cheques for amounts greater than the amount of cash in its bank account.

Mutually unexecuted contract   A contract between two entities in which neither entity has performed its part of the agreement.

Net present value   The value today of an amount or series of amounts to be received or paid in the future.

Originating differences   The initial differences between book and tax reporting that arise in the accounting for the transactions of the company. When these differences reverse themselves, the reversals are referred to as reversing differences.

Partially executed contract   A contract between two entities in which one or both of the parties has performed a portion of its part of the agreement.

Permanent differences   Differences between book and tax reporting that never reverse themselves; that is, they are "permanent." For example, a manufacturing deduction that reduces taxable income but is not an accounting expense.

Purchase commitment   A contract between two entities in which one entity agrees to buy goods or services from another entity, but neither party has executed the contract.

Reversing differences   Temporary differences that are reversals of previously recognized originating differences.

Take-or-pay contract   A contract in which the buyer must pay for a minimum level of merchandise whether delivery of those goods is taken or not.

Temporary differences   Differences that arise because of the different carrying values of assets/liabilities as they are recorded in the accounting records versus as they are recorded in the tax records.

Troubled debt restructuring   The renegotiation of the terms of a debt agreement when the debtor is financially distressed.

Unearned revenues   Cash receipts from customers that have not yet met the criteria for revenue recognition. Also known as deferred revenues.

Working capital loan   A short-term loan, often a demand loan, that is arranged with a bank to cover short-term cash shortages experienced by a company.

ASSIGNMENT MATERIAL

Assessing Your Recall

Multiple Choice Quizzes

9-1   List three essential characteristics of a liability.

9-2   Describe the term *mutually unexecuted contract* and explain how it is accounted for in Canada.

9-3   Describe the appropriate valuation method for liabilities. Include a discussion of both current and noncurrent liabilities in your response.

9-4   Explain why warranty expense and the actual costs incurred with respect to warranties often do not occur in the same period.

9-5   Describe the nature of an account called *unearned revenues* and provide an example.

9-6   Explain why employers often object when the government changes CPP/QPP and/or EI rates.

9-7   What is the "current portion of long-term debt"? Why is it recorded with the current liabilities?

9-8   Describe the circumstances under which a commitment would be recognized in the financial statements.

9-9   Describe the circumstances under which a loss contingency would be recognized in the financial statements.

9-10   Explain how future income taxes are calculated.

9-11   Describe or discuss the meaning of the following terms: temporary differences, permanent differences, originating differences, and reversing differences.

Applying Your Knowledge

9-12   (Future tax liabilities)

Some accountants do not believe that future tax liabilities meet the criteria for recognition as liabilities. Discuss future tax liabilities in terms of the three criteria for a liability, and provide your own arguments in support of whether or not they meet the criteria.

9-13   (Recording and reporting current liabilities)

Shamous Ltd. operates on a calendar-year basis. At the beginning of December 2003, Shamous had the following current liabilities listed on its books:

Accounts payable	$82,700
Rent payable	24,000
Unearned revenue	4,500
Obligations under warranties	13,000

During December 2003, the following events occurred:

1. Shamous purchased a new computer system at a cost of $28,000 on account, payable on January 15, 2004. The company paid an installer $3,500 to set up the new system and train the employees.

2. Shamous purchased inventory for $94,000 on account and made payments of $86,000 to the suppliers.

3. Shamous borrowed $35,000 from the Sussex Bank on December 15 at 6% annual interest. Principal and interest are due three months from the date of the loan.

4. The rent that was owed at the beginning of December represented the rent payments that should have been made in October and November. In December, Shamous paid the past rent owed as well as the rent owed for December.

5. The company earned two thirds of the income for services that had been prepaid by a customer on November 30.

6. Shamous's products are sold with a two-year warranty. The company estimates its warranty expense for the year (not previously recorded) as $15,000. During December, the company paid $1,100 in warranty claims.

7. Employees of the company are paid a total of $1,900 per day. Three work days elapsed between the last payday and the end of the fiscal year. (Ignore deductions for income tax, CPP, and EI.)

8. Since January 2, 2003, Shamous has had a five-year bank loan of $20,000 outstanding. The loan requires that annual interest payments at 7.5% be paid each December 31. The loan further requires that $4,000 of the principal be repaid on January 1 of each year.

Required:

a. Prepare the journal entries to record the December transactions and adjustments. Ignore the income tax, CPP, and EI on the wages.

b. Prepare the current liability section of Shamous's balance sheet at December 31, 2003.

c. Explain your treatment of the five-year bank loan.

9-14 (Recording and reporting current liabilities)
Joan's Golf Shoppe had the following transactions involving current liabilities:

1. The company ordered golfing supplies from a supplier for $546,400. The parts were ordered on credit. During the year, $523,500 was paid to suppliers.

2. Joan offered her customers a one-year warranty on golf clubs. She estimated that warranty costs would total 2% of sales. Sales for the year were $2,108,200. During the year, she actually spent $39,240 to replace faulty golf clubs under warranty.

3. Joan has four employees involved in sales and one involved in accounting and marketing. During the year, they earned gross wages of $145,000. From this amount, Joan deducted 27% for income tax, 4.7% for Canada Pension deductions, and 2.2% for Employment Insurance contributions before giving the cheques to her staff. As an employer, she was also required to make additional contributions of 4.7% for Canada Pension and 3.08% for Employment Insurance on behalf of her employees.

Required:

a. Journalize the above transactions.

b. Prepare the current liability section of the balance sheet as it would appear at the end of the year, after these transactions had been made.

9-15 (Recording and reporting current liabilities)
The University Survival Magazine was a small operation run by two enterprising university students. They published a magazine once a month from September through April. The magazine reported on various university activities, providing tidbits of knowledge on how to get the best tickets, where the best beer was sold for the best price, where the good study spots were located, and how to get library personnel to help with research. They sold their magazine by single copy in the bookstore for $2.75 an issue or by subscription for $16.00 per year for eight issues. In August, they canvassed various local businesses and managed to raise $20,000 in advertising for the magazine. The advertisements were to be included in all eight issues of the magazine. In early September of 2003, they sold 3,000 subscriptions. Up to the end of December, they sold 5,000 single copies in each of the four months. The cost of printing the first four issues of the magazine was $66,000.

Required:

a. Journalize all of the transactions for August through to the end of December.

b. Prepare any necessary adjusting entries on December 31.

c. Prepare an income statement for the magazine for the period up to the end of December.

d. Write a brief memo to the students explaining why the net income amount on the balance sheet will not equal the cash balance in the bank account.

9-16   (Recording and reporting warranties)

Computers Galore Ltd. sold computers, computer accessories, and software. On its computers, the company offered a one-month warranty, which was covered in the cost of the computer, but offered extended warranties of one or two years for an additional charge. The company charged $79 for a one-year warranty and $129 for a two-year warranty. Most customers took advantage of this additional coverage and paid Computers Galore the extra amount. Claims against the warranty varied from replacing parts in computers to providing the customer with a new computer if repairs could not be made. During 2004, Computers Galore sold 1,300 one-year warranties and 850 two-year warranties. Also during 2004, costs associated with the warranties amounted to $61,200 and $59,100, respectively, for the one- and two-year warranties. The estimated cost related to the one-month warranties was $42,000, of which $39,000 had been incurred prior to year end.

Required:

a. Should Computers Galore classify the warranty obligation as current or noncurrent? Explain.

b. Should Computers Galore record a warranty expense associated with its computers? Explain.

c. Prepare journal entries to record the warranty transactions for 2004.

d. If the actual warranty costs incurred by the company are less than the amount collected from customers for the extended warranty coverage, how should the company account for the difference? How should the company account for the difference if the actual warranty costs are greater?

9-17   (Warranty obligations)

The Athletic Accountant Company produces exercise equipment for accountants. Its main product, the *pencil-pusher push-up platform*, is sold with a three-year warranty against defects. The company expects that 1% of the units sold will prove to be defective in the first year after they were sold, 2% will be prove defective in the second year, and 3% of the units sold will prove to be defective in the third year. The average cost to repair or replace a defective unit under the warranty is expected to be $50.

The company's sales and warranty costs incurred were as follows:

	Units sold	Actual costs of repairs and replacements under the warranty plan
2004	10,000 units	$ 6,000
2005	15,000 units	$20,000
2006	20,000 units	$49,000

Required:

a. Calculate the amount that should appear in the Warranty Obligation (Liability) account at the end of 2004.

b. Calculate the amount of warranty expense that should be recognized in 2005.

c. At the end of 2006, do the company's estimates regarding the warranty costs seem to have been too high, too low, or just about right? Explain your reasoning.

9-18   (Contingent liability)

On April 10, 2003, while shopping for new furniture for her home, Mia Thorne, a world-renowned pianist, cut her finger because some of the nails on the table she was looking at were not hammered in properly. On June 10, 2003, Ms. Thorne sued the furniture store for $5 million. The case came to trial on September 13, 2003, and the jury reached a decision on December 13, 2003, finding the store liable and awarding Ms. Thorne the sum of $1 million. On February 3, 2004, the furniture store, dissatisfied with the judgement, appealed to a higher court. The higher court reheard the case beginning on July 18, 2004. On November 25, 2004, a jury again found the store liable and awarded $4 million to Ms. Thorne. On January 15, 2005, the furniture store negotiated a reduced payment to Ms. Thorne and paid her the agreed amount of $3 million.

Required:

Using the stated events in the case, identify the various times at which a loss could be recognized. Using the criteria for a contingent liability, recommend and justify which of those times would be the most appropriate for reporting a note to the financial statements and for making an actual journal entry on the books, and indicate the appropriate amounts in each case. Assume the company's year end is December 31.

9-19   (Income taxes and capital assets)

On January 1, 20x1, the Precision Machining Company purchased a new machine costing $38,000. The company uses straight-line amortization for book purposes and CCA for tax purposes. The machine has an estimated useful life of eight years and a $2,000 residual value. For tax purposes, the machine is in the 20% asset class, and the company is in the 30% marginal tax bracket and closes its books on December 31.

Required:

a. Calculate the income tax asset/liability for 20x1 and 20x2, and give the necessary journal entries for recording the tax expense for each year. Assume that income before amortization and taxes is constant at $80,000 each year.

b. What amount would appear on the balance sheet for future tax assets/liabilities for 20x1 and 20x2? Where on the balance sheet would these amounts be reported?

c. If you were a banker reviewing this company's financial statements in anticipation of granting it a loan, what importance would you place on the future tax asset/liability balance? Explain.

9-20   (Income taxes and capital assets)

On January 1, 20x1, the Canadian Works Company purchased a new capital asset costing $18,000. The company estimated the useful life of the asset to be five years with a $3,000 residual value. The company uses straight-line amortization for book purposes and the asset qualifies for a 30% CCA rate for tax purposes. The company closes its books on December 31. The income before amortization and taxes in 20x1 is $75,000.

Required:

a. Calculate the future tax asset/liability amount, income tax expense, and taxes payable for 20x1. Assume a tax rate for 20x1 and all future years of 40%. Give the necessary journal entry.

b. Calculate the future tax asset/liability amount to the end of years 20x2 and 20x3.

c. Explain why the future tax account has changed over the three years.

9-21   (Future income taxes with changing tax rate)

At the beginning of 2003, Maritime Manufacturing Company acquired a capital asset costing $500,000 which was expected to have a residual value of approximately $50,000 at the end of its productive life. The company decided to amortize it using the production method, which resulted in amortization expense of $60,000 in 2003 and $70,000 in 2004.

For tax purposes, a capital cost allowance rate of 20% was applicable to this asset. The income tax rate was 45% for 2003; however, legislation had been passed reducing the rate to 40% for 2004 and subsequent years.

In 2003, the company had income before amortization and tax of $400,000.

Required:

a. Calculate the amount of income tax payable by the company for 2003.

b. What would be the balance in the Future Income Taxes account at the end of 2003? Be sure that you specify whether it would be an asset or a liability.

c. Explain briefly what this balance (in the Future Income Taxes account) represents.

d. Calculate the amount of income tax expense for the company in 2003.

e. What amount of capital cost allowance could be deducted in 2004?

f. By what amount would the Future Income Taxes account change during 2004?

g. What would be the balance in the Future Income Taxes account at the end of 2004? Again, be sure to specify whether it would be an asset or a liability.

h. Explain briefly how the balance in the Future Income Taxes account is related to the carrying values of the asset (i.e., the net book value for accounting purposes and the undepreciated capital cost for tax purposes).

9-22   (Income taxes and warranties)
The Hudson Motor Company manufactures engines for small airplanes and helicopters. The company offers its customers a warranty of five years or 7,500 flying hours. To maintain the warranty, customers must have their engines serviced every 1,000 flying hours. In 20x2, the company sold engines valued at $2,600,000. It estimates that the future warranty costs on these engines will be 4% of sales. During 20x2, it incurred costs of $25,000 associated with warranty work on engines, and $15,000 in 20x3.

Required:

a. Calculate the future tax asset/liability amount associated with the warranties in 20x2. The tax rate in effect in 20x2 and future years is 32%.

b. Where on the balance sheet would the future taxes balance be reported? Why?

c. If the tax rate changed to 40% in 20x3 and is expected to remain at 40% for the foreseeable future, explain what impact this would have on the calculation of the future tax asset/liability.

d. Calculate the future tax asset/liability balance that would appear on the balance sheet at the end of 20x3.

User Perspective Problems

9-23   (Future income taxes and investment decisions)
As a stock analyst, discuss how you might view the nature of future tax liabilities and whether you would treat them in the same way that you might a long-term bank loan.

9-24   (Contingent liabilities and investment decisions)
Suppose that you have been asked by your company to evaluate the potential purchase of another company. The company has been in the chemical business for more than 60 years and has several plants throughout Alberta, Ontario, Texas, and Mexico. Because of the nature of the chemical industry, every company must recognize the possibility of

environmental problems associated with the manufacture and transportation of its products. Describe what you might find in terms of disclosure in the company's financial statements relative to environmental liabilities, and what additional information you would like to have in assessing its liabilities.

9-25   (Commitments)
Suppose that you are the sales manager for a construction company and you are responsible for securing contracts. As a part of your negotiations with customers, you offer a "sweetener" to your contracts, which is an agreement to supply raw materials to the customer at a fixed price over an extended period of time. The price fixed in the contract is currently right at the fair market price for the raw materials.

Required:

a. What does the accounting department need to know about these "sweeteners" to appropriately account for these agreements?

b. How should the accounting department record these transactions?

c. Under what circumstances might your answer to part b) change?

d. What should shareholders know about these agreements?

9-26   (Effect of changes in the CPP and EI rates)
You are the manager of a company with approximately 20 employees. The government has just announced its new rates for CPP and EI. With respect to employee contributions, the CPP is going up from 4.7% to 5.6% and the EI is dropping from 2.2% to 1.8%. The company's contribution for CPP is rising from 4.7% to 6.0% and the EI is dropping, from 3.08% to 2.52%.

Required:

a. Assume a gross wages amount of $80,000 per month. Calculate the financial impact that this change in rates has on the company.

b. Write a memo to the President of the company explaining the financial impact of this change in rates.

c. Suggest some actions that the company could take to reduce the impact of this rate change.

Reading and Interpreting Published Financial Statements

9-27   (Future costs of reclamation)
IEI Energy Inc., a Canadian mining company with operations in Canada and the United States, included the following in its notes to the financial statements of its 2001 annual report:

FUTURE SITE RECLAMATION COSTS

The estimated costs for reclamation of producing resource properties are accrued and charged to operations over commercial production based upon total estimated reclamation costs and recoverable reserves. The estimated costs for reclamation of non-producing resource properties are accrued as liabilities when the costs of site clean-up and reclamation can be reasonably estimated. Actual site reclamation costs will be deducted from the accrual.

Required:

a. Explain how and why IEI Energy treats future reclamation costs for producing properties differently from reclamation costs for non-producing properties.

b. Using accounting concepts, explain why it is not appropriate for IEI Energy to wait until it actually incurs reclamation costs before it recognizes an expense on its income statement for reclamation.

9-28   (Lines of credit)

Note 10B of **CAE Inc.'s** 2002 financial statements describes details of its short-term debt. An excerpt appears below:

B. SHORT-TERM DEBT

The Company has unused unsecured bank lines of credit available in various currencies totalling $57.8 million (2001–$85 million). The effective interest rate on short-term borrowings was 5.6% (2001–8.4%).

Required:

a. What is a line of credit?

b. Why would CAE want to have lines of credit in various currencies?

c. The lines of credit are unsecured. What do you think this means? Would CAE be able to get a lower rate of interest if the debt was secured? Explain.

9-29   (Presentation of liabilities for an investment company)

The balance sheets for December 31, 2001, for **Investors Group Inc.** are presented in Exhibit 9-12. Investors Group is one of Canada's premier mutual fund, managed asset, and wealth creation companies. The company's two operating units, Investors Group and Mackenzie Financial Corporation, offer their products and services through thousands of consultants and independent financial advisors.

Required:

a. Investors has an item called "deposits and certificates" among its liabilities. Explain how a liability could arise related to deposits.

b. Like many companies in the financial services industry, Investors does not distinguish between current and noncurrent liabilities on its balance sheet. Why do you think this is so?

c. Investors has an item called "loans" among its assets. Usually, accounts called loans are liabilities. Explain the nature of this item and why it is listed with the assets.

INVESTORS GROUP INC. (2001)
CONSOLIDATED BALANCE SHEETS

EXHIBIT 9-12

As at December 31 (in thousands of dollars)	2001	2000
Assets		
Cash and short term investments	$ 854,275	$ 716,202
Securities (Note 2)	248,205	416,142
Loans (Note 3)	655,094	215,782
Investment in affiliate (Note 5)	297,810	293,481
Deferred selling commissions	657,221	70,771
Future income taxes	–	48,568
Other assets (Note 6)	388,941	201,268
Goodwill	3,020,922	22,998
	$ 6,122,468	$ 1,985,212
Liabilities		
Deposits and certificates (Note 7)	$ 671,248	$ 218,980
Bankers' acceptances (Note 8)	497,000	–
Other liabilities (Note 9)	779,853	501,512
Future income taxes (Note 11)	120,234	–
Long term debt (Note 12)	1,362,268	168,435
Non-controlling interest	13,621	–
	3,444,224	888,927
Shareholders' Equity		
Share capital (Note 13)		
Preferred	360,000	–
Common	1,431,163	272,756
Retained earnings	884,531	823,529
Foreign currency translation adjustment	2,550	–
	2,678,244	1,096,285
	$ 6,122,468	$ 1,985,212

9-30 (Interest rates and security)
Note 5 accompanying the 2002 financial statements of **Danier Leather Inc.** is presented below:

NOTE 5. BANK OVERDRAFT

As at June 29, 2002, the Company had credit facilities available to a maximum amount of $53.0 million. The credit facilities consist of an operating facility for working capital and for general corporate purposes to a maximum amount of $50 million, bearing interest at prime plus 0.25% and a $3.0 million revolving capital expenditure loan facility bearing interest at prime plus 0.75% which declines by $0.5 million per year beginning on June 30, 2003. The operating facility is committed until October 31, 2003, and the revolving capital expenditure loan facility expires on October 31, 2005. The Company is required to comply with covenants regarding financial performance.

Security provided includes a security interest over all personal property of the business and a mortgage over the land and building, comprising the Company's head office/distribution facility.

Required:

a. The information regarding the interest rates on Danier's short-term credit facilities refers to "prime." What does this term mean?

b. Danier's loan facilities bear interest at prime plus 0.25% and prime plus 0.75%. What can you infer from this about the bank's assessment of the company's creditworthiness?

c. Are these borrowings secured or unsecured? Explain what this means and why a company might prefer to have its debt secured.

9-31 (Income tax disclosure)

In Exhibit 9-13, Note 12 to **Dofasco Inc.'s** 2001 financial statements describes how the income tax on the income statement is determined.

EXHIBIT 9-13

DOFASCO INC. (2001)

12. Income Taxes

The income tax expense is comprised of:

(in millions)	2001	2000
Current	$ 61.5	$ 107.4
Future	(32.2)	(29.2)
	$ 29.3	$ 78.2

The income tax expense differs from the amount calculated by applying Canadian income tax rates (Federal and Provincial) to income before income taxes, as follows:

(in millions)	2001	2000
Income before income taxes	$ 56.3	$ 260.6
Income tax expense computed using statutory income tax rates	$ 24.2	$ 114.4
Add (deduct):		
Manufacturing and processing credit	(10.8)	(21.5)
Effect of different rates in foreign jurisdictions	4.2	(1.7)
Benefit of previously unrecognized losses of U.S. subsidiaries	—	(6.8)
Minimum taxes	4.5	2.8
Unrecorded income tax benefit arising from losses of foreign subsidiaries	11.7	—
Net future income tax benefit resulting from reduction in tax rates	(8.5)	(3.5)
Other	4.0	(5.5)
	5.1	(36.2)
Income tax expense	$ 29.3	$ 78.2

Components of future income taxes by jurisdiction are summarized as follows:

(in millions)	2001	2000
Canada		
Current Assets –		
Accounting provisions not currently deductible for tax purposes	$ 10.7	$ 12.9
Inventory of production rolls	(7.4)	(8.7)
Future income tax assets	$ 3.3	$ 4.2
Liabilities –		
Tax depreciation in excess of book depreciation	$ 250.4	$ 290.3
Accounting provisions not currently deductible for tax purposes	(118.1)	(116.5)
Other	5.5	(3.5)
Future income tax liabilities	$ 137.8	$ 170.3
Foreign		
Assets –		
Net operating loss carryforward	$ 109.1	$ 100.1
Tax depreciation in excess of book depreciation	(62.4)	(53.7)
Other	(1.0)	(3.4)
Future income tax assets	$ 45.7	$ 43.0

At December 31, 2001, U.S. subsidiaries have accumulated losses for tax purposes of approximately U.S. $53.4 million (2000 – U.S. $40.2 million) for which no future tax benefit has been recognized in the accounts. These losses expire between 2018 and 2021.

Additionally, a Mexican subsidiary has a tax loss of approximately 35 million pesos for which no future tax benefit has been recognized. This loss expires in 2011.

Required:

a. What were Dofasco's statutory rates for income tax in 2001 and 2000?

b. Dofasco's tax at statutory rates is adjusted by various items to arrive at an actual income tax expense of $29.3 million in 2001 and $78.2 million in 2000. Determine the actual tax rates for each year.

c. How much income tax did Dofasco actually have to pay for the years 2001 and 2000? Explain how you determined these amounts.

d. In the second table, several items are listed that explain how the income tax for 2000 of $114.4 million (calculated using statutory income tax rates) became $78.2 million. These items represent permanent differences. What are permanent differences? Select two of these items and explain why you think they are permanent differences.

9-32 (Contingent liabilities)
Note 20 accompanying the 2001 financial statements of **Canadian National Railway Company** provides details of its major commitments and contingencies. Sections C and D of this note are presented in Exhibit 9-14.

EXHIBIT 9-14

CANADIAN NATIONAL RAILWAY (2001)

C. Contingencies

In the normal course of its operations, the Company becomes involved in various legal actions, including claims relating to contractual obligations, personal injuries including occupational related claims, damage to property and environmental matters. The Company maintains provisions for such items which it considers to be adequate. The final outcome with respect to actions outstanding or pending as at December 31, 2001 cannot be predicted with certainty, and therefore, there can be no assurance that their resolution and any future claims will not have a material adverse effect on the Company's financial position or results of operations in a particular quarter or fiscal year.

D. Environmental matters

The Company's operations are subject to federal, provincial, state, municipal and local regulations under environmental laws and regulations concerning, among other things, emissions into the air; discharges into waters; the generation, handling, storage, transportation, treatment and disposal of waste, hazardous substances, and other materials; decommissioning of underground and aboveground storage tanks; and soil and groundwater contamination. A risk of environmental liability is inherent in the railroad and related transportation operations; real estate ownership, operation or control; and other commercial activities of the Company with respect to both current and past operations. As a result, the Company incurs significant compliance and capital costs, on an ongoing basis, associated with environmental regulatory compliance and clean-up requirements in its railroad operations and relating to its past and present ownership, operation or control of real property.

While the Company believes that it has identified the costs likely to be incurred in the next several years, based on known information, for environmental matters, the Company's ongoing efforts to identify potential environmental concerns that may be associated with its properties may lead to future environmental investigations, which may result in the identification of additional environmental costs and liabilities. The magnitude of such additional liabilities and the costs of complying with environmental laws and containing or remediating contamination cannot be reasonably estimated due to:

(i) the lack of specific technical information available with respect to many sites;

(ii) the absence of any government authority, third-party orders, or claims with respect to particular sites;

(iii) the potential for new or changed laws and regulations and for development of new remediation technologies and uncertainty regarding the timing of the work with respect to particular sites;

(iv) the ability to recover costs from any third parties with respect to particular sites; and

therefore, the likelihood of any such costs being incurred or whether such costs would be material to the Company cannot be determined at this time. There can thus be no assurance that material liabilities or costs related to environmental matters will not be incurred in the future, or will not have a material adverse effect on the Company's financial position or results of operations in a particular quarter or fiscal year, or that the Company's liquidity will not be adversely impacted by such environmental liabilities or costs. Although the effect on operating results and liquidity cannot be reasonably estimated, management believes, based on current information, that environmental matters will not have a material adverse effect on the Company's financial condition or competitive position. Costs related to any future remediation will be accrued in the year in which they become known.

As at December 31, 2001, the Company had aggregate accruals for environmental costs of $112 million ($85 million as at December 31, 2000). During 2001, payments of $14 million were applied to the provision for environmental costs compared to $11 million in 2000 and $16 million in 1999. In addition, related environmental capital expenditures were $19 million in 2001, $20 million in 2000 and $11 million in 1999. The Company also expects to incur capital expenditures relating to environmental matters of approximately $21 million in 2002 and $30 million in each of 2003 and 2004. The Company has not included any reduction in costs for anticipated recovery from insurance.

Required:

a. In your own words, summarize the key information contained in CNR's notes regarding contingencies and environmental matters. Specify whether the company has (1) fully recorded liabilities related to these in its accounts, (2) merely disclosed information about them in its notes, or (3) both recognized liabilities in the financial statements and provided additional footnote disclosure.

b. Under GAAP, contingent liabilities must be recorded in the accounts if they are considered likely to occur and can be reasonably estimated. Discuss the extent to which CNR focuses on each of these criteria (i.e., "considered likely to occur" and "can be reasonably estimated") in its discussion of environmental matters.

c. If you were a CNR shareholder or investment analyst, how would the information presented in these notes affect your assessment of the company's contingencies and environmental matters?

9-33 (Guarantees and commitments)
In the 2001 annual report of **Alcan Inc.**, the following note was included under Commitments and Contingencies (in millions of U.S. dollars):

> The Company has guaranteed the repayment of approximately $17 of indebtedness by third parties. Alcan believes that none of these guarantees is likely to be invoked. Commitments with third parties and certain related companies for supplies of goods and services are estimated at $175 in 2002, $94 in 2003, $103 in 2004, $86 in 2005, $86 in 2006, and $884 thereafter. Total payments to these entities, excluding $218 in relation to the smelter at Alma, were $36 in 2001, $106 in 2000 and $18 in 1999.
>
> In 1997, as part of the claim settlement arrangements related to the British Columbia Government's cancellation of the Kemano Completion Project, Alcan received the right to transfer a portion of a power supply contract with BC Hydro to a third party. Alcan sold the right to supply this portion to Enron Power Marketing Inc. (EPMI), a subsidiary of Enron Corporation (Enron) for cash consideration. In order to obtain the consent of BC Hydro to this sale, Alcan was required to retain residual liability for EPMI's obligations arising from the supply contract, including in the event that EPMI became unable to perform. This contingent liability is subject to a maximum aggregate amount of $100, with mitigation and subrogation rights. On December 2, 2001, EPMI and Enron filed for protection under Chapter 11 of the U.S. Bankruptcy Code. The Company is unable to estimate reasonably the amount of the contingent loss, if any, after mitigation, which might arise in respect of this matter.

Required:

a. What is meant by "guaranteeing the indebtedness of third parties"?

b. With respect to the guarantees, why was it important for Alcan to include a note about them with the financial statements?

c. With respect to the commitments for the supplies of goods and services, has Alcan recorded these transactions in its accounting records? If not, why not?

d. The second paragraph of the note relates to a transaction with a subsidiary of Enron Corporation. It notes that Alcan's residual liability could be as high as US $100 million, but concludes with the statement that Alcan is not able to reasonably estimate the amount of the contingent loss (if any) that will ultimately arise from it.

   Check the SEDAR website for any additional information regarding this contingency that may have become available subsequent to the release of Alcan's 2001 financial statements. Has the matter been resolved? What additional action, if any, has Alcan taken on this issue?

Beyond the Book

9-34 (Comparative treatment of contingent liabilities and losses)
During the year 2000, Bridgestone Corporation and Ford Motor Company were con-
fronted with a large public liability issue regarding Firestone AT, ATX, and ATX II
radial tires that were used on Ford Explorers. Many sudden failures of these tires had
occurred with Explorer vehicles, some of which resulted in serious accidents. Millions
of tires and thousands of vehicles were involved in the ensuing controversy and litigation alleging defective product design and/or manufacture.

> *Required:*
> Determine how Bridgestone Corporation and Ford Motor Company handled this
> liability question. Outline how each company dealt with this issue in its 2000 and
> subsequent annual reports. Be sure to specify, for each company, whether it recog-
> nized a loss and recorded a liability in the financial statements and/or disclosed a
> contingent loss and liability in the notes accompanying its statements.

9-35 (Financial statement disclosures)
Choose a company as directed by your instructor and do the following exercises:

a. Prepare a quick analysis of the current liability accounts by listing the beginning
   and ending amounts in these accounts and calculating the net change, in both
   dollar and percentage terms, for the most recent year. If the company you have
   selected does not prepare a classified balance sheet, you will need to determine
   which liabilities are current.

b. If any of the accounts changed by more than 10%, try to give an explanation for
   this change.

c. What percentage of the company's total assets are funded by current liabilities?
   Has this percentage changed significantly in the last year?

d. Does the company have any significant (greater than 3% of total liabilities)
   accrued liabilities, such as warranties? If so, read any notes discussing these items
   and summarize in a short paragraph the nature of these liabilities.

e. Does the company have unearned revenues? If so, explain the nature of these
   liabilities.

f. Read the note on income taxes and answer the following questions:

   1. What is the company's effective tax rate? What are the major items that cause
      it to be different from the statutory rate?

   2. What are the major items that result in future (or deferred) tax assets and lia-
      bilities for the company?

   3. Try to reconcile the total net future tax assets (liabilities) presented in the
      note with what is reported in the financial statements. Note: To do this, you
      will need to consolidate all of the future tax accounts from the balance sheet.

g. Does the company have any significant commitments or contingencies? Read
   any related notes and then write a short paragraph summarizing each significant

item. For the contingencies, are you aware of anything that has happened since the financial statements were issued related to these contingencies? If so, please describe.

Cases

9-36   Greenway Medical Equipment Corporation
At a recent meeting of the Board of Directors of Greenway Medical Equipment Corporation, Chief Financial Officer Robert Ables presented to the board a draft set of financial statements for the year ended December 31, 2004. It is Greenway's corporate policy that all directors be given an opportunity to review the financial statements before they are finalized.

Yesterday, Robert received a memo from Dr. Clarise Locklier posing some questions with regard to the draft financial statements. Dr. Locklier is a relatively new member to the board and is not familiar with some of the accounting terms and concepts used in the statements. She has several questions she would like Robert to answer before approving the financial statements at the next board meeting.

Memorandum

To: Robert Ables, CFO, Greenway Medical Equipment Corporation

From: Dr. Clarise Locklier, Board of Directors, Greenway Medical Equipment Corporation

Re: Draft financial statements

Dear Mr. Ables:

I have reviewed in depth the financial statements you presented to the board last week. As a physician, I do not have a lot of experience reading accounting information and I am confused about several items presented in the financial statements.

1. I have always been under the impression that revenues are reported on the income statement, which is why I was confused to see unearned revenues presented as a liability on the balance sheet. As well, if the revenues are unearned, shouldn't they be presented in the period when earned and not in the current year?

2. I notice that under current liabilities you have reported a current portion of long-term debt. How can debt be current and long-term at the same time? Are we overstating our liabilities if we report this?

3. In note 4 to the financial statements, you state that the liability for warranty costs is based on an estimate, not actual warranty repair costs. If we know what our actual costs are for the year, why do we need this estimated liability?

I would appreciate a response to these questions prior to our next board meeting so that I can feel more comfortable approving the financial statements.

Thank you for your time in addressing these matters.

Required:
As Robert Ables, review Dr. Locklier's letter and prepare a memo to the doctor addressing her concerns.

9-37 Altabet Company

Altabet Company is completing its financial statements for the year ended April 30, 2004. Janet Kramer, Altabet's controller, is reviewing the company's legal correspondence and trying to decide which, if any, of the potential contingencies facing the company need to be accrued in the financial statements. As part of her review, Kramer has identified three contingencies:

1. In May 2003, the company was sued for breach of contract concerning a sale of equipment to a local manufacturer. The manufacturer claims that because Altabet was unable to deliver the equipment in the time period specified in the contract, the manufacturer lost profits of $130,000. Correspondence with Altabet's attorney indicated that there was no breach of contract because the manufacturer failed to make all the required payments and therefore Altabet was under no obligation to deliver the equipment. The attorney feels this is a nuisance suit and believes there is little possibility of the manufacturer's being successful. Kramer does not consider the potential loss to be significant.

2. In January 2004, Terry Chambers fell on some ice in Altabet's parking lot. As a result of the fall, Chambers suffered a concussion and a broken arm that required a two-day hospital stay. She is suing Altabet for all medical bills, loss of wages, and personal suffering. Altabet's attorney feels that Altabet will probably lose the suit and has strongly advised them to settle out of court. On April 25, 2004, Altabet instructed its attorney to offer Chambers a settlement of $850,000. The attorney believes this is reasonable and that Chambers will probably accept the offer.

3. Jeff Altabet, son of the owner of the company, needed to borrow $800,000. The loan is a five-year, 10% term loan requiring monthly payments of principal and interest. Because Jeff has just graduated from college and has no credit history, the company guaranteed the note, stating that if Jeff failed to make three consecutive payments Altabet Company would repay the note in full. Jeff has invested the money in a business venture that is turning out to be very profitable. He has made every required payment on the loan and expects to be able to repay the full balance within the next six months. At April 30, 2004, Kramer still considers the balance of the loan to be significant.

Required:

How should each of the above contingencies be accounted for in the April 30, 2004, financial statements of Altabet Company?

9-38 Slip-n-Slide Water Park

It is now July 31 and Slip-n-Slide Water Park has just completed its first year of operations. The company's owners, Kelly and Derek Neil, are very pleased with the results of operations and are trying to prepare the company's first set of financial statements. You have been controller for a local manufacturing firm for several years and are good friends with Kelly and Derek. The couple approaches you one afternoon with some questions concerning how certain items should be recorded in their financial statements.

Derek: "I can figure out how to record revenues and expenses, but I don't know how to treat the revenues associated with season passes we sold back in June. The season passes sell for $30 each and are good for June, July, and August. Holders of season passes have unlimited access to the park for these three months. I believe we sold 350 season passes this year."

Kelly: "The other problem we have is that we have a $60,000 bank loan. The loan agreement requires us to repay the loan at $500 per month plus interest over the next 10 years. The interest rate on the loan is 7% annually. Since some of the loan has to be repaid in the next year, I want to record the $60,000 as a current liability, but Derek thinks that the entire amount should be recorded as a long-term liability since it does not have to be fully paid for ten years."

Required:

Provide the Neils with some advice on how the above transactions should be recorded in July 31, 20x1, financial statements. Be sure to explain to them why they should record the transactions in the manner you recommend.

9-39 Hanson's Consulting

Jenny Shea is in the process of renegotiating her annual employment contract with her employer, Hanson's Consulting. Jenny knows that it is important that she negotiate a good contract because the amount of her raise will become a benchmark for the raises to be received by the rest of Hanson's 15 consultants. Currently, Jenny and the other consultants are receiving a payroll transfer into their personal bank accounts of $2,500 per month.

Under her existing contract, Jenny is allowed to review Hanson's annual financial statements. She is aware that each of the 15 consultants receives the same monthly payments, which total $450,000 per year, and is therefore confused to see that Hanson is reporting over $600,000 in consulting wages on its annual income statement. Jenny approaches you, the company controller, to see why the consulting wages on the income statement are higher than the amounts paid to the employees. She is concerned that the company may be posting other expenses to the consulting salaries account in order to improve its bargaining position in contract negotiations.

Required:

Explain to Jenny why payroll costs as per the company's accounting records are higher than the net amounts being received by employees.

Critical Thinking Question

9-40   (Revenue recognition/expense accrual and income measurement)

Software Solutions produces inventory-tracking and supply-chain management software, which it sells to large commercial clients. Its main software packages sell for approximately $100,000 each and require the company to customize the programs to the buyers' operations and organizations. There is no additional charge for this customization service—it is included in the initial selling price. This work is done by a special team of employees, usually takes several months to complete, and involves significant costs (averaging approximately $20,000 per sale) for Software Solutions.

Required:

a. Discuss appropriate accounting treatments for handling the income measurement issues that arise in this type of situation. You should be able to describe at least two alternative approaches that could be taken within GAAP.

b. Which approach would be preferable if Software Solutions wants to treat the customization work as:

   1. a "cost centre" (i.e., the software customization team is not expected to generate a profit)?

   2. a "profit centre" (i.e., the customization work is treated as an income-generating line of business)?

9-41   (Recognition and disclosure of contingent liabilities)

An issue discussed in Chapter 9 is financial statement recognition and disclosure of contingent liabilities, such as the potential claims associated with litigation. Loss and liability recognition is a function of whether it is likely that an asset has been impaired or a liability has been incurred and the degree to which a loss can reasonably be estimated. Evaluating whether these conditions exist is often a matter of judgement by management and auditors, perhaps more so than with any other issue of recognition or disclosure. Research has shown that reliance on judgement leads to differences among companies regarding whether and how contingencies associated with lawsuits are disclosed.

Required:

a. As discussed in this chapter, some long-term liabilities are measured using present values. Discuss the appropriateness of using present values for long-term liabilities and whether liabilities that are recorded for lawsuits are, or should be, subject to present value measurement.

b. In today's environmentally conscious world, regulatory bodies are making more demands on resource companies to be environmentally responsible. For example, companies involved in mineral exploration are often required to plan for the cleanup and restoration of resource sites. A review of the annual reports of several resource companies reveals that some companies create liabilities each year in anticipation of this future event, some companies mention a contingent liability in the notes to the financial statements, and some companies do or say nothing about it. In a brief essay, discuss the criteria that a company should use when deciding on the kind of disclosure necessary to account for future cleanup and restoration costs.

Turning Short-Term into Long-Term Debt

When Bell Canada wanted to term out some short-term debt in early 2002, the Montreal-based telecommunications company did what it frequently does—it raised the funds by selling debt, specifically medium-term notes (MTNs). The issue, directed at retail investors, was carried out in January of the same year and consisted of $500 million in 10-year MTNs. At a time of record-low interest rates, it sold out within hours.

Part of the proceeds was used by Bell Canada to pay off some of its short-term notes as well as previously issued debt that had reached maturity. The rest of the funds were to be used to cover capital expenditures such as new high-speed digital telephone lines and switching equipment. On average, Bell spends about $4 billion a year on capital outlays. At the time of the issue, it had a total of $12.8 billion in outstanding debt.

"The first thing we always try to do when we have extra cash is pay down our commercial paper," says Len Ruggins, Vice-President of Financing and Treasury for BCE, Bell's parent company. "Exchanging short-term debt for long-term debt means we don't have to refinance it as frequently. It also allows us to lock in a fixed interest rate for a longer period of time."

Issued through a consortium of nine dealers led by CIBC World Markets, Bell's offering was one of the largest retail-directed issues of its kind ever carried out in Canada. The bonds, sold at a unit price of $99.40, had a coupon rate of 6.25%; with interest compounding semi-annually,

the effective yield will be slightly higher. Standard and Poor assigned the issue its A+ senior unsecured debt rating based on a number of factors, including the company's competitive position, increasing geographic diversity, and conservative financial policies.

But why raise funds through debt rather than issuing shares? As Mr. Ruggins explains, there are obvious benefits. "Common shares create dilution, and you often have to pay a dividend on them. In fact, they're a very expensive form of capital. With this latest issue of debentures, although there's a coupon rate of more than 6%, after tax it works out to around 3.8%, so that's very cheap money." Still, he points out, corporations cannot simply issue debt ad infinitum, since rating agencies and debt investors look closely at a company's financial ratios.

While most of Bell's debt usually goes to institutional investors—big mutual funds, life insurance companies, and the like—from time to time it borrows from the general public. "What's nice in this case is by issuing to retail investors, we're keeping the demand with the institutional investors unsatisfied, so next time we come out with an issue they will typically be more responsive to buying," says Mr. Ruggins. "We like to give retail investors the opportunity to buy our paper at least once a year, otherwise it's very hard for them to get a hold of it at a decent price. This helps us and it helps them."

chapter 10

LONG-TERM
LIABILITIES

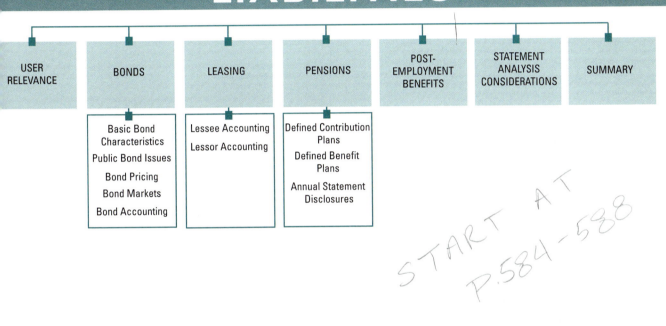

| USER RELEVANCE | BONDS | LEASING | PENSIONS | POST-EMPLOYMENT BENEFITS | STATEMENT ANALYSIS CONSIDERATIONS | SUMMARY |

Basic Bond Characteristics

Public Bond Issues

Bond Pricing

Bond Markets

Bond Accounting

Lessee Accounting

Lessor Accounting

Defined Contribution Plans

Defined Benefit Plans

Annual Statement Disclosures

START AT P.584-588

Learning Objectives:

After studying this chapter, you should be able to:

1. *Describe the basic characteristics of a bond.*
2. *Explain how bonds are issued and how the pricing of bonds is affected by risk.*
3. *Calculate the issue price of a bond and prepare journal entries for the issuance of the bond and interest payments subsequent to the issuance for bonds issued at par, below par, and above par.*
4. *Discuss the advantages and disadvantages of leasing.*
5. *Distinguish between an operating lease and a capital lease and prepare journal entries for a lessee under both conditions.*
6. *Explain the distinguishing features of a defined contribution pension plan and a defined benefit plan.*
7. *Describe other employment benefits and explain how they are treated in Canada.*
8. *Calculate the debt/equity ratio and the times-interest-earned ratio and write a statement describing the financial health of a company using the information from these ratios.*

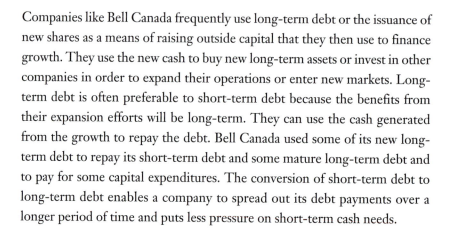

Companies like Bell Canada frequently use long-term debt or the issuance of new shares as a means of raising outside capital that they then use to finance growth. They use the new cash to buy new long-term assets or invest in other companies in order to expand their operations or enter new markets. Long-term debt is often preferable to short-term debt because the benefits from their expansion efforts will be long-term. They can use the cash generated from the growth to repay the debt. Bell Canada used some of its new long-term debt to repay its short-term debt and some mature long-term debt and to pay for some capital expenditures. The conversion of short-term debt to long-term debt enables a company to spread out its debt payments over a longer period of time and puts less pressure on short-term cash needs.

USER RELEVANCE

Users of financial statement information need to pay particular attention to the type and extent of debt within a company. All debt must be paid back at some time. There is often interest in addition to the principal amount. As Bell Canada has done, many companies will sell new debt to settle either short- or long-term debt as it reaches maturity. In the Bell Canada vignette, Mr. Ruggins stated that issuing debt is cheaper than issuing shares and it does not dilute the current shareholders' interests. However, a company cannot rely too extensively on debt for financing because investors and lenders become concerned if the proportion of debt to equity gets too high.

As a user, you should pay attention to the following items with respect to debt. First, what are the maturity dates and interest rates on the debt? Knowing these two things will enable you to determine the amount and timing of the future cash flows that will be necessary to meet the conditions of the debt. Second, are there any special conditions attached to the debt? For example, is the company required to maintain a certain debt/equity ratio or level of retained earnings? Failure to meet debt conditions (called covenants) could make the debt come due immediately, which could have a detrimental effect on the business operations. Third, what is the proportion of debt to equity? The higher the amount of debt to equity, the greater the risk that the company may have difficulty meeting the debt requirements as they fall due. Financial lenders will be watching this ratio as well. A high proportion of debt to equity may result in higher interest rates being charged to the company. It could also make lenders reluctant to extend further debt to the company, which could affect its future financial viability.

As you will see later in this chapter, it is possible for a company to borrow at a rate lower than the return it can earn by employing the money in revenue generating activities. We call this leverage. This return increases shareholder wealth. Bell Canada plans to gain leverage by borrowing at the after-tax rate of 3.8%. If it can earn a return greater than 3.8%, the return to shareholders grows. As a user, you will want to examine the company's financial statements to see if leverage is being used effectively.

In this chapter, we are going to illustrate for you some of the more common liabilities that will be repaid over a period of time longer than a year. The three major long-term debts discussed are bonds payable, lease liabilities, and pension and other employment benefit liabilities. The general nature of liabilities was discussed in Chapter 9, along with the recognition and valuation criteria for liabilities. You might want to refresh your memory before moving on.

BONDS

When a public company wants to raise long-term funds to support its operations, it has two basic alternatives: the equity (stock) market or the debt market. Issuing shares in the equity market is discussed in Chapter 11. Issuing debt in the debt market is the subject of this section. Within the debt market, there are various sources of funds. The company may borrow money from a commercial bank, much as individuals borrow money from the bank to buy a new home or car. These borrowings are often listed on a company's financial statements as notes payable. The term of the note can be short or long, and it may carry a fixed or floating interest rate. Another source of funds is what is known as the **commercial paper** market. Commercial paper is an unsecured promissory note that is generally sold to other businesses by a company that has a fairly high credit rating. In effect, one company borrows from another. Bell Canada uses commercial paper. In the vignette, it said that the company likes to use its extra cash to pay down its commercial paper.

Another market in which the company may borrow money is the **bond market**. Generally, **bonds** are sold initially to institutional and individual investors through an investment banker (who gets a commission for handling the transaction). The **investment banker**, or a group of investment bankers (sometimes known as a **syndicate**), works with the company to decide which bond terms will be most attractive to investors. In our opening vignette, you learned that Bell Canada used nine dealers led by CIBC World Markets when it issued its bonds. Once all the bonds have been sold by the investment bankers, they can be freely traded between investors in a bond market much as shares are traded on the stock market. The most widely known bond market is the New York Bond Market, which is a **public bond market**. Some bonds are sold to investors through what is referred to as a **private placement**. These types of bonds do not trade in public markets. Private placements are usually made to institutional investors such as trustees in charge of pension funds.

A full understanding of how the various debt markets differ is beyond the scope of this book. Various markets are mentioned so that you can gain some appreciation of the disclosures you will typically find as you read annual reports. Publicly traded bonds in Canada are used to illustrate the accounting issues surrounding long-term debt. There are some complex issues related to **foreign-denominated debt** that we will mention briefly, but in-depth coverage falls outside the parameters of this book.

Basic Bond Characteristics

Learning Objective

1

Describe the basic characteristics of a bond.

A bond is a formal agreement between a borrower (the company) and a lender (the investor) that specifies how the borrower is to pay back the lender and any conditions that the borrower must meet during the period of the loan. The conditions of the loan are stated in a document called the **indenture agreement**. The indenture agreement may specify certain restrictions on the company that are known as **bond covenants**. These covenants may limit the company's ability to borrow additional amounts, to sell or acquire assets, or to pay dividends. The restrictions placed in the bond covenants are intended to protect the investor against a default on the loan by the company.

Bonds that are traded in public markets are fairly standardized. The indenture agreement will state a **face value** for the bonds which, in almost all cases, is $1,000 per bond. The Bell Canada bonds were $100 per bond. Unless stated otherwise, you should assume that the face value of a bond is $1,000. The face value specifies the cash payment the borrower will make to the lender at the bond's **maturity date** (which is also specified in the indenture agreement). In addition to the cash payment at maturity, most bonds make semi-annual interest payments to the lender. The amount of these payments is determined by multiplying the bond interest rate times the face value and dividing by two (because they are semi-annual). The bond interest rate is stated as an annual percentage and is *not* an effective or true interest rate, but simply a rate that determines the periodic amount of the interest payments. The Bell Canada bonds will pay $3.125 per bond every six months ($100 × .0625 × 1/2).

One other important item described in the indenture agreement is the collateral the company pledges to the lenders. If collateral is pledged, it means that if the company defaults on the interest or maturity payment, the bondholders can demand that the pledged assets be sold in order to settle the debt. Some bonds specify particular assets as collateral. A bond known as a **mortgage bond** has some type of real property as collateral. A **collateral trust bond** provides shares and bonds of other companies as collateral. A bond that carries no specific collateral but is backed by the general creditworthiness of the company is known as a **debenture** bond. Bell Canada refers to its bonds as debentures. General debenture bonds can be either **senior debenture** bonds or **subordinated debenture** bonds. The distinction between senior and subordinated is the order in which creditors are paid in the event of bankruptcy: senior creditors are paid first.

Some indenture agreements specify special provisions that are designed to make the bonds more attractive to investors. **Convertible bonds**, for example, are convertible to a specified number of common shares in the company issuing the bond. In the 1970s and 1980s, investors became concerned about the effects of inflation on the fixed payments, particularly the large final payment that characterizes bond agreements. Remember from earlier chapters that in a period of inflation, fixed payments decline in terms of their purchasing power. Therefore, the payment the investor receives at the maturity date may be worth considerably less (in terms of purchasing power) than the dollars lent to the company initially. To protect investors from the effects of inflation, some companies have issued bonds that index the final payment to a commodity. **Sunshine Mining Corporation** issued one of the first of these bonds in 1980. It indexed the maturity payment to be the greater of $1,000 (the normal maturity payment of a bond) or the market value of 50 ounces of silver. If inflation was significant, the market value of silver would rise, and the investor would get that value at maturity. Since that time, other bonds have indexed maturity values to oil and other commodities.

accounting in the news

CONVERTIBLE BONDS TODAY

2001 was a record year for convertible bond sales, as stock sales plummeted and companies looked for cheaper ways to raise money.

Like other bonds, convertibles offer investors a return in interest payments, but they can also be exchanged for shares. Typically, convertible bonds pay lower interest than other forms of debt.

Sales were up 60% from 2000, according to Thomson Financial, a financial data provider, with investment banks underwriting US $145 billion of convertible bonds. In comparison, stock sales dropped by more than half to US $239 billion.

Many companies—such as Xerox Corp., Nortel Networks Corp. and Cendant Corp.—took advantage of the lowest interest rates in 41 years to raise capital. Convertible bond sales are also cheaper to arrange than a public offering of shares. Investment bankers say they charge an average fee of 2% for a convertible bond sale, compared to fees as high as 7% in the United States for initial public offerings of shares.

For some companies, convertible bonds provided access to capital they had difficulty finding elsewhere. Troubled Lucent Technologies Inc., for example, offered yields as high as 8%, with the potential for a handsome payoff if shares rebounded.

Source: "Issuers find convertibles easiest way to raise cash: Record underwritings," by Emma Moody, *National Post, Financial Post*, Dec. 11, 2001, p. FP13.

Public Bond Issues

When a company decides to issue bonds in the public bond market, it contacts an investment banker who will assist the company in issuing the securities. The investment banker will consult the company about its objectives, and will help design an issue that will both meet the company's objectives and attract investors. All the basic features of the bond that have been discussed will be considered when structuring the offering.

Learning Objective
2

Explain how bonds are issued and how the pricing of bonds is affected by risk.

The investment banker will not only help design the bond issue, but will also be responsible for the initial sale of the issue to its investor clients. Because most issues involve larger amounts than one investment banker can easily sell, the investment banker usually forms a syndicate with other investment bankers, who will be jointly responsible for selling the issue. The members of the syndicate are sometimes known as the **underwriters** of the issue.

The syndicate will agree on a price for the bond issue and will attempt to sell all the bonds to its clients. The price of the bonds is fixed at this point and will not change until the syndicate has sold all of its bonds. If events occur that make the price unattractive to the clients of the investment bankers, then it is likely that the syndicate will not sell the entire issue. In some cases, the syndicate agrees to sell the issue on what is known as a **best efforts basis**. If the syndicate cannot sell all the securities, it simply returns them to the company, which means that the company will not be able to raise the amount of money it had hoped to raise. For financially strong companies, however, the syndicate guarantees to sell the entire issue, thereby accepting the risk that it will not be able to sell all the issue to its clients.

Once all the bonds have been sold to the clients of the syndicate, they are "thrown on the open market." This means that holders of the bonds are free to trade them with any other investors. Prices of the bonds can then fluctuate with changes in economic conditions.

Bond Pricing

Learning Objective

3

Calculate the issue price of a bond and prepare journal entries for the issuance of the bond and interest payments subsequent to the issuance for bonds issued at par, below par, and above par.

The prices of bonds are established in the marketplace by negotiations between buyers and sellers. At the initial issuance of the bonds, the buyers are institutional and individual investors, and the seller is the company issuing the bonds. The buyers calculate the present value of the cash flows they will receive from the bond, then decide the amount they are willing to pay for it. The process of calculating the present value of the bond involves discounting (at the desired earning rate) the future cash flows (repayment of principal and periodic interest) from the bond. The seller does a similar calculation to decide what it is willing to accept for the bond. The buyer weighs the yield (desired) rate against the rate that could be earned from the next best alternative investment, and also against the risk involved with the particular bond issue. The higher the risk, the higher the yield rate should be. In other words, if buyers are going to accept a higher risk of default, they want to be compensated for that risk with a higher return. In addition to the calculation of the present value, the buyer also has to factor in any special features of the bond such as convertibility into shares or any indexing of the maturity value to a commodity. To keep things as simple as possible in the rest of this section, these special features are ignored as we discuss bond pricing.

The starting point in determining the value of a bond is to calculate the cash flows that will be received by the buyer (and paid by the seller). To illustrate the calculation of interest payments, assume a company issues bonds on January 1, 20x1, with a total face value of $100,000 and a **bond interest rate** of 10%. The company issues 100 bonds, each with a face value of $1,000 and a maturity date of December 31, 20x7. The company must make a $100,000 payment to the lenders on December 31, 20x7, and must make **interest payments** every six months of $5,000 each. The $5,000 amount is calculated as follows:

Interest Payment = Face Value × Bond Interest Rate × 1/2
= $100,000 x 10% x 1/2 = $5,000

There will be a total of 14 interest payments because there are seven years to maturity and two interest payments per year. The interest payments on a bond are typically structured to come at the end of each six-month period. In other words, the stream of interest payments is an annuity in arrears, meaning the payments are made at the end of the period.

To illustrate the pricing of a bond, we will use a very simple example. Suppose that Baum Company Ltd. wishes to issue a $1,000 bond (a single bond will be used to make it simple) with two years to maturity. The bond is to have an interest rate of 10% and pay interest semi-annually. Suppose that Baum expects the investor to demand a return of 8% compounded semi-annually from an investment in its bonds. What price can Baum expect to get from this offering? The cash flows that Baum will pay must be discounted using the yield rate of 8%. The yield rate is sometimes referred to as the **discount rate** or the **market rate**. Exhibit 10-1 shows the timeline and the cash flows that would result from this bond.

BAUM COMPANY LTD.

EXHIBIT 10-1

Assumptions:

Face value	$1,000
Bond interest rate	10%
Time to maturity	2 years
Yield rate	8%

Calculation:

Number of periods	= Time to maturity × 2
	= 2 years × 2 = 4
Yield rate per period	= Yield rate / 2
	= 8% / 2 = 4%
Interest payments	= Face amount × bond interest rate × 1/2
	= $1,000 × 10% × 1/2 = $50

					$1,000
Cash flows		$50	$50	$50	$50
End of period (semi-annual periods)	0	1	2	3	4

Note that the interest payments (the four payments of $50 each) are an annuity in arrears and that the maturity payment ($1,000) is a lump sum cash flow at the end of the fourth period. There are four periods because interest payments are made at the end of each six-month period. The total net present value of the bond, based on a 4% desired or yield rate, is calculated as follows. To calculate the net present value, we will use the Time Value of Money tables[1] found in the Appendix at the end of this chapter.

We need to calculate the present value of each of the future cash flows.

				$1,000
	$50	$50	$50	$50
1	4%			
2		4%		
3			4%	
4				4%

For illustrative purposes we will use Table 2, Present value of $1, found on pages 618 and 619.
($50 × 0.96154) + ($50 × 0.92456) + ($50 × 0.88900) + ($50 × 0.85480) + ($1,000 × 0.85480)
48.08 + 46.23 + 44.45 + 42.74 + 854.80 = $1,036.30

The result of this calculation means that Baum should expect buyers to pay up to $1,036.30 for this bond. If buyers pay exactly this amount, they will earn an 8% return (compounded semi-annually). If they pay more for this bond, they will earn less than 8% and, if they pay less than this amount, they will earn more than 8%. Note that because the payments to be made by Baum are fixed by the terms of the bonds, the only way buyers of the bonds can change the return is by changing the amount they invest initially (i.e., the price they pay). If Baum thinks that 8% is too high an interest rate to pay, it should not offer these bonds at the price calculated here. It should offer them at a higher price (which will lower the interest rate). Recognize, however, that buyers may not be willing to buy the bonds at that higher price.

An easier way to arrive at the above amount of $1,036.30 is to treat the interest payments of $50 as an annuity (calculate the present value by using Table 4 from the Appendix, Present Value of an Annuity in Arrears) and add to this calculation the present value of the payment at maturity ($1,000). The calculation would be as follows:

$50 × 3.62990 (present value for 4 periods at 4%) + ($1,000 × 0.85480)
$181.50 + $854.80 = $1,036.30

Technology Tools for Time Value of Money

This is the method we will use for subsequent calculations of the present value of a bond issue. These calculations can also be made using a financial calculator that has present value and future value functions.

How does a different desired or yield rate affect the value of the bond? Suppose that, instead of 8%, buyers demand a 12% return from this type of investment. The only thing that would change in the calculation would be the factors that enter the present-value calculation. The calculation would then be:

---

[1] There are four Time Value of Money Tables in the Appendix. We will be using Table 2, Present value of $1, and Table 4, Present value of an annuity in arrears. These tables contain pre-calculated factors for given interest rates and time periods. When the factors are multiplied times the cash flow amount, the present value of that cash flow is determined.

Present value of the Baum Company Ltd. bond at 12%:

PV of bond = PV of interest payments + PV of maturity payment

= PV of the annuity of $50 for 4 periods at 6% (Table 4) + PV of the $1,000 for 4 periods at 6% (Table 2)

= ($50 × 3.46511) + ($1,000 × 0.79209)

= $965.35

Consistent with the preceding explanation, if buyers pay less for the bond (in this case, $965.35), they earn a higher return (12%). Baum Company Ltd., in this case, receives a lower initial amount from this borrowing and effectively pays a higher interest rate (12%).

According to the terminology used to describe bond pricing, when the bond is issued (or sells) at a price higher than its face value (i.e., greater than $1,000), it is issued (sells) at a **premium.** When the bond is issued for less than its face value, it is issued at a **discount**. If it is issued for exactly its face value, it is said to be issued at **par**. You should avoid placing any connotations on the words premium and discount. They do not mean either that buyers paid too much or that they got a good deal. The price they pay, whether it is par, premium, or discount, is the appropriate value for the bond, given the desired or yield rate used. Bell Canada issued its bonds at $99.40 which is below the par value of $100. This means that the bonds were issued at a discount of $.60.

A question that might be asked is: what rate would have to be used to present-value or discount the cash flows in the example for the bonds to be issued at par? The answer is 10%. Whenever the yield rate of a bond is exactly equal to the bond interest rate, the bond will sell at par. Consequently, if the yield rate is higher than the bond interest rate, the bond sells at a discount and, when the yield rate is lower than the bond interest rate, it sells at a premium. This relationship is represented in Exhibit 10-2, which shows the price of the bond in the example for various combinations of bond interest rates and yield rates.

RELATIONSHIP OF BOND PRICE TO BOND INTEREST AND YIELD RATES

EXHIBIT 10-2

		Yield Rates			
		6%	8%	10%	12%
Bond Interest Rates	6%	$1,000.00	$963.70	$929.08	$896.05
	8%	$1,037.17	$1,000.00	$964.54	$930.70
	10%	$1,074.34	$1,036.30	$1,000.00	$965.35
	12%	$1,111.51	$1,072.60	$1,035.46	$1,000.00

Note that, in Exhibit 10-2, all the prices on the diagonal, which represent situations in which the bond interest rate equals the yield rate, are at par. Prices below the diagonal represent premium price situations, where the yield rate is below the bond interest rate, and the area above the diagonal represents discount prices.

Another question might be: why would a company agree to issue (sell) a bond at other than its par value? Remember the earlier discussion about how the company gets advice from investment bankers when it is initially deciding on the terms of a new bond issue? The investment bankers will provide information to the company about how the market is assessing its risk. The company takes this information into consideration, but it also assesses its ability to pay the interest and the length of time over which it needs the money. The interest rate set for the bond may or may not be close to the market's interest rate demands. The company takes this into consideration when it is trying to determine how much capital it will be able to raise by issuing the bonds. The other aspect of the issue price that must be considered is the time factor. When a company decides to issue bonds as a way of raising capital, it must get financial advice as to what interest rate it can afford and legal advice as to aspects of the indenture agreement. Once all of those decisions are made, it takes time to have the bond certificates printed and ready for issue. By the time the bonds are actually issued to investors, the market's risk assessment of the company may have changed, which will cause the issue price to change.

Bond Markets

All financial newspapers and several local newspapers provide information about bond prices to interested investors. Bond prices are quoted in the *Globe and Mail* in a section entitled "Canadian Bonds." An excerpt from this section on July 11, 2002, is shown in Exhibit 10-3. You will notice that it lists Government of Canada, Provincial, and Corporate bonds. Look for a moment at the Corporate section. The first column of the listing shows who is issuing each bond. An abbreviation of the company name is given, followed by a set of numbers, a date, and then numbers in the next three columns. These columns identify the bond interest rate of the issue (coupon rate), the maturity date, then in the last three columns, the current selling price, the yield rate at that selling price, and the change in the price since the last sale. For instance, locate the line "Air Canada 6.750 Feb 02/04 89.00 14.96 0.00." This is a bond from Air Canada that carries a 6.75% interest rate and that matures on February 2, 2004. Prices in the market are quoted as a percent of the face value. The bond is currently selling at 89.00, which means that investors are paying $890.00 for a $1,000 bond. In other words, the bond is selling at 89% of its face value: it is selling at a discount. When investors buy this bond at a discount, they will earn a return of 14.96%. The yield is higher than the actual interest on the bond because the bond sold for less than the face or principal value. This higher yield is likely demanded by investors because they can invest their money elsewhere at the same risk and earn a higher return. The last set of numbers indicates that the price has not changed from the last time Air Canada bonds were traded.

EXHIBIT   10-3   **CANADIAN BONDS**

Provided by RBC Capital Markets. Selected quotations, with changes since the previous day, on actively traded bond issues yesterday. Yields are calculated to full maturity. Price is the final bid-side price as of 5 pm yesterday.

issuer	coupon	maturity	price	yield	price $ chg	issuer	coupon	maturity	price	yield	price $ chg
GOVERNMENT OF CANADA						Canada	6.500	Jun 01/04	104.91	3.78	0.21
Canada	5.250	Sep 01/03	102.08	3.36	0.10	Canada	5.000	Sep 01/04	102.21	3.91	0.24
Canada	7.500	Dec 01/03	105.39	3.48	0.14	Canada	4.250	Dec 01/04	100.53	4.01	0.26
Canada	5.000	Dec 01/03	102.03	3.49	0.14	Canada	9.000	Dec 01/04	111.28	4.00	0.26
Canada	10.250	Feb 01/04	109.97	3.60	0.17	Canada	12.000	Mar 01/05	119.42	4.15	0.28
Canada	3.500	Jun 01/04	99.48	3.79	0.21	Canada	12.250	Sep 01/05	122.95	4.33	0.31

EXHIBIT 10-3 CONT.

issuer	coupon	maturity	price	yield	price $ chg	issuer	coupon	maturity	price	yield	price $ chg
Canada	6.000	Sep 01/05	104.78	4.35	0.31	New Brunswick	6.000	Dec 27/17	100.27	5.97	0.59
Canada	8.750	Dec 01/05	113.54	4.39	0.34	Newfoundland	6.150	Apr 17/28	97.29	6.36	0.47
Canada	5.750	Sep 01/06	104.17	4.63	0.39	Nova Scotia	5.250	Jun 02/03	101.64	3.34	0.02
Canada	14.000	Oct 01/06	135.39	4.65	0.42	Nova Scotia	6.600	Jun 01/27	103.06	6.35	0.53
Canada	7.000	Dec 01/06	109.09	4.68	0.41	Ontario	7.750	Dec 08-03	105.64	3.58	0.12
Canada	7.250	Jun 01/07	110.69	4.77	0.45	Ontario	4.875	Jun 02/04	101.80	3.87	0.21
Canada	4.500	Sep 01/07	98.57	4.82	0.44	Ontario	9.000	Sep 15/04	110.27	4.00	0.23
Canada	12.750	Mar 01/08	138.05	4.93	0.55	Ontario	6.250	Mar 08/05	105.00	4.23	0.29
Canada	10.000	Jun 01/08	125.58	4.93	0.55	Ontario	7.500	Jan 19/06	109.47	4.55	0.37
Canada	6.000	Jun 01/08	105.24	4.96	0.51	Ontario	5.900	Mar 08/06	104.30	4.61	0.39
Canada	5.500	Jun 01/09	102.06	5.14	0.49	Ontario	5.200	Mar 08/07	101.31	4.86	0.46
Canada	9.750	Mar 01/10	127.90	5.26	0.57	Ontario	6.125	Sep 12/07	105.13	4.98	0.47
Canada	9.500	Jun 01/10	127.23	5.24	0.59	Ontario	5.700	Dec 01/08	102.57	5.22	0.54
Canada	5.500	Jun 01/10	101.51	5.26	0.53	Ontario	6.200	Nov 19/09	104.77	5.40	0.51
Canada	9.000	Mar 01/11	124.94	5.35	0.59	Ontario	6.100	Nov 19/10	103.76	5.53	0.55
Canada	6.000	Jun 01/11	104.60	5.34	0.55	Ontario	6.100	Dec 02/11	103.44	5.62	0.58
Canada	5.250	Jun 01/12	98.99	5.38	0.57	Ontario	8.100	Sep 08/23	123.38	6.11	0.52
Canada	10.250	Mar 15/14	141.39	5.42	0.81	Ontario	7.600	Jun 02/27	118.01	6.17	0.60
Canada	11.250	Jun 01/15	153.33	5.44	0.92	Ontario	6.500	Mar 08/29	104.49	6.15	0.51
Canada	9.750	Jun 01/21	146.19	5.72	0.53	Ontario	6.200	Jun 02/31	100.88	6.13	0.52
Canada	9.250	Jun 01/22	141.25	5.74	0.54	Ontario Hyd	5.375	Jun 02/03	101.78	3.30	0.02
Canada	8.000	Jun 01/23	126.65	5.78	0.48	Ontario Hyd	7.750	Nov 03/05	109.91	4.48	0.36
Canada	9.000	Jun 01/25	139.95	5.82	0.51	Ontario Hyd	5.600	Jun 02/08	102.28	5.15	0.51
Canada	8.000	Jun 01/27	128.50	5.82	0.46	Ontario Hyd	8.250	Jun 22/26	125.48	6.19	0.56
Canada	5.750	Jun 01/29	99.80	5.76	0.45	Quebec	7.500	Dec 01/03	105.23	3.58	0.12
Canada	5.750	Jun 01/33	100.39	5.72	0.49	Quebec	6.500	Dec 01/05	106.06	4.54	0.34
CMBT	5.527	Jun 15/06	103.11	4.65	0.40	Quebec	6.500	Oct 01/07	106.76	5.01	0.44
CMBT	4.750	Mar 15/07	99.68	4.83	0.44	Quebec	11.000	Apr 01/09	131.47	5.35	0.52
CMHC	5.750	Dec 01/04	103.78	4.07	0.28	Quebec	5.500	Jun 01/09	100.42	5.42	0.48
CMHC	6.250	Dec 01/05	105.50	4.48	0.34	Quebec	6.250	Dec 01/10	104.08	5.63	0.55
CMHC	5.250	Dec 01/06	101.88	4.77	0.41	Quebec	6.000	Oct 01/12	101.73	5.77	0.59
CMHC	5.300	Dec 03/07	101.57	4.96	0.47	Quebec	8.500	Apr 01/26	126.82	6.30	0.56
CMHC	5.500	Jun 01/12	99.63	5.55	0.63	Quebec	6.000	Oct 01/29	96.05	6.30	0.48
Exp Dev	5.500	Jun 18/04	102.99	3.87	0.21	Quebec	6.250	Jun 01/32	99.48	6.29	0.48
Exp Dev	5.000	May 04/06	101.21	4.65	0.36	Saskatchewan	5.500	Jun 02/08	101.70	5.16	0.50
Exp Dev	5.000	Feb 09/09	98.76	5.22	0.49	Saskatchewan	8.750	May 30/25	130.51	6.23	0.56
						Toronto-Met	6.100	Aug 15/07	104.53	5.08	0.46
PROVINCIAL						Toronto-Met	6.100	Dec 12/17	100.69	6.03	0.59
Alberta	6.375	Jun 01/04	104.53	3.85	0.20						
B C	7.750	Jun 16/03	103.97	3.33	0.00	**CORPORATE**					
B C	5.250	Dec 01/06	101.72	4.81	0.41	AGT Limited	8.800	Sep 22/25	76.43	11.78	0.22
B C	6.000	Jun 09/08	104.22	5.16	0.48	Air Canada	6.750	Feb 02/04	89.00	14.96	0.00
B C	5.700	Jun 01/09	101.99	5.35	0.56	Avco Fin	5.750	Jun 02/03	102.00	3.43	0.03
B C	6.375	Aug 23/10	105.42	5.54	0.54	Bank of Mont	7.000	Jan 28/10	107.30	5.79	0.52
B C	5.750	Jan 09/12	100.71	5.65	0.57	Bank of Mont	6.903	Jun 30/10	103.15	6.39	0.51
B C	8.500	Aug 23/13	122.92	5.69	0.72	Bank of Mont	6.647	Dec 31/10	101.32	6.44	0.53
B C	6.150	Nov 19/27	98.94	6.23	0.53	Bank of Mont	6.685	Dec 31/11	101.00	6.54	0.40
B C	5.700	Jun 18/29	93.50	6.20	0.47	Bank of N S	6.250	Jul 16/07	103.47	5.45	0.44
B C Mun Fin	7.750	Dec 01/05	109.64	4.63	0.37	Bank of N S	7.310	Dec 31/10	105.46	6.46	0.54
B C Mun Fin	5.500	Mar 24/08	101.67	5.16	0.50	Bell Canada	6.250	Dec 01/03	102.40	4.43	-0.02
B C Mun Fin	5.900	Jun 01/11	101.60	5.67	0.56	Bell Canada	6.500	May 09/05	103.36	5.20	0.03
Hydro Quebec	5.500	May 15/03	101.83	3.25	0.02	Bell Canada	6.250	Apr 12/12	94.47	7.06	0.52
Hydro Quebec	7.000	Jun 01/04	105.62	3.87	0.19	Bell Canada	6.550	May 01/29	82.04	8.22	0.27
Hydro Quebec	6.500	Feb 15/11	105.76	5.64	0.57	Can Crd Tst	5.625	Mar 24/05	103.08	4.40	0.28
Hydro Quebec	10.250	Jul 16/12	134.21	5.71	0.67	Coca-Cola	5.650	Mar 17/04	102.47	4.10	0.16
Hydro Quebec	11.000	Aug 15/20	151.69	6.20	0.49	DlmrCCFin	6.600	Jun 21/04	103.14	4.88	0.20
Hydro Quebec	9.625	Jul 15/22	138.46	6.23	0.49	DlmrCCFin	5.940	Apr 22/05	101.63	5.30	0.29
Hydro Quebec	6.000	Aug 15/31	96.17	6.29	0.47	Domtar Inc	10.000	Apr 15/11	115.38	7.56	0.56
Manitoba	7.875	Apr 07/03	103.35	3.18	-0.01	Ford Credit	5.730	Dec 01/03	101.25	4.78	0.13
Manitoba	5.750	Jun 02/08	102.95	5.16	0.51	Ford Credit	6.000	Mar 08/04	101.74	4.88	0.16
Manitoba	7.750	Dec 22/25	118.47	6.24	0.53	Ford Credit	6.650	Jun 20/05	102.13	5.85	0.03
New Brunswick	8.000	Mar 17/03	103.19	3.17	-0.01	Genesis Trus	6.869	Feb 15/05	106.17	4.32	0.24
New Brunswick	5.700	Jun 02/08	102.47	5.21	0.51	GoldCred	5.700	Aug 15/06	103.21	4.82	0.40

EXHIBIT 10-3 CONT.	issuer	coupon	maturity	price	yield	price $ chg	issuer	coupon	maturity	price	yield	price $ chg
	Grtr TTO Air	5.400	Dec 03/02	100.85	3.15	-0.01	Oxford	6.860	Jul 21/04	105.44	4.03	0.21
	Grtr TTO Air	5.950	Dec 03/07	102.78	5.35	0.47	Renaissance	6.850	Feb 06/07	103.84	5.88	-0.39
	Grtr TTO Air	6.700	Jul 19/10	104.78	5.94	0.53	Rogers Cable	8.750	Jul 15/07	88.00	12.01	0.00
	Grtr TTO Air	6.250	Jan 30/12	101.06	6.10	0.55	Rogert Cant	10.500	Jun 01/05	80.00	17.85	0.00
	Grtr TTO Air	6.450	Dec 03/27	94.44	6.92	0.33	Royal Bank	6.400	Aug 15/05	104.51	4.81	0.31
	Grtr TTO Air	6.450	Jul 30/29	96.24	6.75	0.41	Royal Bank	6.750	Jun 04/07	105.87	5.37	0.44
	Grtr TTO Air	7.050	Jun 12/30	101.62	6.92	0.36	Royal Bank	6.100	Jan 22/08	102.98	5.47	0.48
	Grtr TTO Air	7.100	Jun 04/31	102.26	6.92	0.37	Royal Bank	7.400	Jan 25/10	107.27	5.89	0.52
	Gtc Trans	6.200	Jun 01/07	99.30	6.37	0.01	Royal Bank	7.288	Jun 30/10	105.71	6.36	0.52
	Gulf Can Res	6.450	Oct 01/07	106.75	4.96	0.00	Royal Bank	7.183	Jun 30/11	104.43	6.52	0.53
	HolRecTst	5.672	Apr 26/06	103.04	4.78	0.38	Sask Wheat	6.600	Jul 18/07	52.00	23.35	0.00
	HSBC	7.780	Dec 31/10	107.47	6.60	0.54	SNC Lavalin	7.700	Sep 20/10	102.96	7.21	0.51
	HydroOne	6.940	Jun 03/05	106.67	4.45	0.30	Sun Life	6.865	Dec 31/11	102.60	6.49	0.54
	HydroOne	7.150	Jun 03/10	107.71	5.91	0.53	Sun Life	6.150	Jun 30/12	98.30	6.38	0.55
	HydroOne	7.350	Jun 03/30	106.86	6.80	0.38	Suncor Inc	6.700	Aug 22/11	102.44	6.34	0.53
	IADB	5.625	Jun 29/09	102.02	5.27	0.49	T D Bank	6.600	Apr 14/05	104.97	4.65	0.27
	Interprv Pip	8.200	Feb 15/24	114.67	6.88	0.42	T D Bank	6.000	Jul 26/06	103.27	5.09	0.40
	Legacy	5.930	Nov 15/02	100.47	4.45	0.17	T D Bank	6.550	Jul 31/07	105.16	5.37	0.45
	Loblaws Co	6.650	Nov 08/27	96.58	6.94	0.11	T D Bank	7.600	Dec 31/09	107.40	6.34	0.51
	Milit-Air	5.750	Jun 30/19	98.81	5.86	0.81	TELUS	7.500	Jun 01/06	87.06	11.74	0.05
	MLI	5.700	Feb 16/06	102.79	4.84	0.36	Trizec Hahn	7.950	Jun 01/07	111.15	5.36	0.00
	MLI	6.240	Feb 16/11	100.84	6.11	0.51	Union Gas	8.650	Nov 10/25	120.57	6.87	0.39
	MLI	6.700	Jun 30/12	101.21	6.53	0.48	Weston Geo	7.450	Feb 09/04	105.42	3.85	0.17
	Morguard Ret	6.700	Oct 09/07	97.12	7.27	0.43	Wstcoast Ene	6.750	Dec 15/27	98.00	6.92	-0.24
	Mstr Cr Trus	6.150	Dec 21/04	104.33	4.26	0.21						
	Nav Canada	7.560	Mar 01/27	114.18	6.41	1.04	Real Return	4.250	Dec 01/21	111.46	3.43	0.11
	Nexen	6.300	Jun 02/08	99.46	6.41	0.00	Real Return	4.250	Dec 01/26	113.47	3.43	0.13
	Ontrea	5.700	Oct 31/11	100.26	5.66	0.55	Real Return	4.000	Dec 01/31	110.40	3.43	0.15

Bond Accounting

The accounting for bonds will be illustrated using the simple example developed earlier for a bond issued at par, at a discount, and at a premium. For each of the bonds, the entries made at issuance, to recognize the interest accrual and payments, and to record the final payment of the face amount at maturity will be illustrated.

Bonds Issued at Par

Consider the issuance of the Baum Company Ltd. bond (see data in Exhibit 10-1) when bond interest rates were 10%. To record the bond issued at par, the cash proceeds must be recorded in the cash account and the present value of the bond in the liability account. When bonds are issued at par, they are said to be issued at 100. Because the cash proceeds equal the present value at issuance, the following entry is made (any commissions that are paid to the underwriters are ignored to keep the entries simple):

BAUM COMPANY LTD. BOND ISSUED AT PAR—ISSUANCE ENTRY		
A-Cash	1,000	
L-Bond Payable		1,000

No interest is recognized on the date of issuance because interest accrues as time passes. The recognition of interest requires two entries. The first is to accrue the interest expense for the period and the amount payable to the bondholders. The second is to record the cash payment made. The recognition of expense should be based on a time value of money calculation using the yield rate (10% for the Baum Company Ltd. bond sold at par) and the carrying value of the bond ($1,000 when sold at par). The amount payable to the bondholders is dictated by the bond interest rate. The following calculations and entries would be made at the end of the first interest payment period (six months):

BAUM COMPANY LTD. BOND ISSUED AT PAR—INTEREST ENTRIES
(at end of first interest period)

SE-Interest Expense[a]	50	
L-Interest Payable[b]		50
L-Interest Payable	50	
A-Cash		50

[a]Interest expense = Carrying Value × Yield Rate × Time
           = $1,000 × 10% × 6/12 = $50
[b]Interest payable = Face Amount × Bond Interest Rate × Time
           = $1,000 × 10% × 6/12 = $50

The calculation of the interest expense (the interest incurred during the period) and interest payable (the cash amount owed based on the bond contract) results in the same number for a bond sold at par. This is not the case for bonds issued at a premium or a discount.

The calculation of the interest payable amount will be the same in all four interest periods over the life of the bond. The calculation of interest expense in each period will depend on the carrying value of the bond at the beginning of each period. The carrying value will equal the face value of the bond less the discount, or the face value of the bond plus the premium. The carrying value (book value) at the end of each period can be calculated using the following formula:

Carrying Value (ending) = Carrying Value (beginning) + Interest Expense − Interest Payments

In the first period:

Carrying Value (ending) = $1,000 + 50 − 50 = $1,000

Because the expense and the cash payment are the same in every period, a bond sold at par will have a carrying value of $1,000 at the end of every period. The entries for interest recognition, therefore, would be exactly the same at the end of each of the four interest periods.

At the end of the fourth period, the company will make the additional payment of the face value. The entry will be:

BAUM COMPANY LTD. BOND ISSUED AT PAR—MATURITY PAYMENT ENTRY (at maturity date)		
L-Bond Payable	1,000	
A-Cash		1,000

The carrying value of the bond over time can be shown graphically as in Exhibit 10-4. Note that the carrying value of the bond remains constant over the four six-month periods. The balance in the liability account at the end of the four interest periods is $1,000. This is the balance prior to the maturity payment and, therefore, should be exactly $1,000.

EXHIBIT   10-4

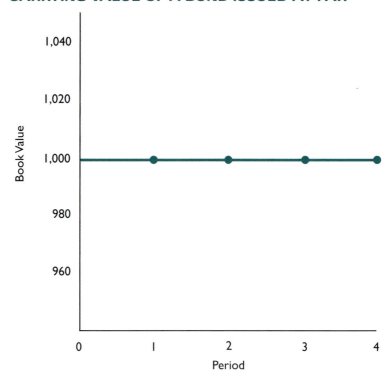

CARRYING VALUE OF A BOND ISSUED AT PAR

Sometimes, the change in the value of a bond over its life is also summarized in what is known as an amortization table. Exhibit 10-5 shows a typical amortization table for the bond issued at par.

AMORTIZATION TABLE—BOND ISSUED AT PAR

EXHIBIT 10-5

Period	Beginning Carrying Value	Interest	Payment	Ending Carrying Value
1	$1,000.00	$50.00	$50.00	$1,000.00
2	$1,000.00	$50.00	$50.00	$1,000.00
3	$1,000.00	$50.00	$50.00	$1,000.00
4	$1,000.00	$50.00	$1,050.00	$0.00

Bonds Issued at a Discount

Now assume that investors demanded a 12% return for the bond issued by Baum. As calculated earlier in the chapter, the bond would be issued at a price of $965.35 under these conditions. Another way of expressing the issue price would be to say that the bond sold at 96.535. The following entry would then be made by Baum Company Ltd. at issuance:

BAUM COMPANY LTD. BOND ISSUED AT A DISCOUNT—ISSUANCE ENTRY		
A-Cash	965.35	
XL-Discount on Bond Payable	34.65	
L-Bond Payable		1,000

In this case, the present value of the liability is $965.35, and this is the amount that should be recorded on Baum's books. This amount could be credited directly to the bond payable account. However, in Canada, we normally credit the bond payable account with the face value of the bond and then reduce the amount by creating a contra liability account called *discount on bond payable*. The contra account (note that the XL notation in the journal entry represents a contra liability account) is most commonly reported directly with the bond payable account.[2] The net of these two amounts is the present value, that is, $1,000 − $34.65 = $965.35. Note that this presentation allows for the disclosure of both the face amount of the bonds and the net present value at the date of issuance. Over the life of the bond, we will gradually reduce the discount on bond payable account such that at maturity the discount will be zero.

The interest entries for the bond issued at a discount are shown in the following box. Notice that the interest expense is now different from the amount payable. The reason for this is that the yield rate and the carrying value are now different from the bond interest rate and the face amount. The difference between the expense and the interest payable is credited to the discount account, which decreases the balance in the account. This is known as the **amortization of the discount**. This method of calculating interest expense is known as the **effective interest method**. The yield rate times the carrying value of the debt determines the interest expense for the period.

---

[2] The bond discount can also be reported under Other Assets in the long-term asset section of the balance sheet.

BAUM COMPANY LTD. BOND ISSUED AT A DISCOUNT—INTEREST ENTRIES
(at end of first interest period)

SE-Interest Expense[a]	57.92	
XL-Discount on Bond Payable		7.92
L-Interest Payable[b]		50.00
L-Interest Payable	50.00	
A-Cash		50.00

[a]Interest expense = Carrying Value × Yield Rate × Time
         = \$965.35 × 12% × 6/12 = \$57.92
[b]Interest payable = Face Amount × Bond Interest Rate × Time
         = \$1,000 × 10% × 6/12 = \$50

Because the discount is being amortized each period, the net carrying value changes from period to period. The discount can be amortized in a straight-line fashion, that is, the same amount each period, as long as the effect on the financial statements is not materially different from applying the effective interest method, which is illustrated in this section. The carrying value at the end of the period would be calculated as before:

Carrying Value (ending) = Carrying Value (beginning) + Interest Expense − Payments

In the first period:

Carrying Value (ending) = \$965.35 + 57.92 − 50.00 = \$973.27

Notice that the carrying value increases a little by the end of the first period. This new carrying value balance is used to calculate the interest expense in the second period. Therefore, the interest expense will increase slightly each period to reflect the increase in the carrying value. The ending carrying value could also be calculated by subtracting the balance in the discount account from the face amount in the bond payable account. The discount account will have a balance of \$26.73 (\$34.65 − \$7.92) at the end of the first period. The face amount minus this discount will give a carrying value of \$973.27, the same amount as calculated in the preceding equation.

Exhibit 10-6 shows graphically how the carrying value of the bond changes over time. Notice that because this bond is issued at a discount, the beginning carrying value is below \$1,000. As time passes, the discount is amortized (decreases) and the carrying value increases, eventually reaching \$1,000 by the maturity date, when the final payment of \$1,000 is made.

CARRYING VALUE OF A BOND ISSUED AT A DISCOUNT

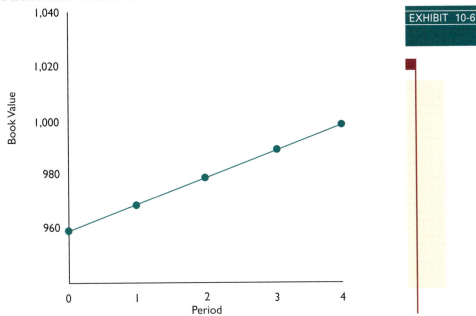

At the maturity date, the final maturity payment is made with the same entry as that made in the par case because the final carrying value is the same ($1,000). Recognize that what is happening is that the payments made at the interest dates are not sufficient to pay for the interest that has accrued during the period. Because the investors initially paid less than the face value for the bond but are being paid interest based on the face value and will receive the face value at maturity, the company is, in effect, paying a higher rate of interest than is reflected in the bond interest rate. This higher rate of interest needs to be reflected on the income statement. The excess of the interest expense over the payment decreases the discount, creating the rising carrying value shown in the graph. Exhibit 10-7 shows the amortization table for the bond issued at a discount.

AMORTIZATION TABLE—BOND ISSUED AT A DISCOUNT

Period	Beginning Carrying Value	Interest	Payment	Ending Carrying Value	Beginning Discount
1	$965.35	$57.92	$50.00	$973.27	($34.65)
2	$973.27	$58.40	$50.00	$981.67	($26.73)
3	$981.67	$58.90	$50.00	$990.57	($18.33)
4	$990.57	$59.43	$1,050.00	$0.00	($9.43)

Bonds Issued at a Premium

If the interest rate demanded by investors is 8%, then the Baum Company Ltd. bond would be issued at a premium. The issue price in this scenario was calculated earlier in the chapter as $1,036.30. Another way of expressing the issue price would be to say that the bond sold at 103.63. The following entry would be made at issuance by Baum Company Ltd.:

BAUM COMPANY LTD. BOND ISSUED AT A PREMIUM—ISSUANCE ENTRY

A-Cash	1,036.30	
L-Premium on Bond Payable		36.30
L-Bond Payable		1,000.00

A N I N T E R N A T I O N A L P E R S P E C T I V E

Reports from Other Countries

In Canada and the United States, the amortization of the discount (or premium) on a bond is calculated using effective interest methods, as described earlier. In some countries (Australia and Denmark, for example), the discount is typically amortized in a straight-line fashion, in much the same way as straight-line amortization of a capital asset. Straight-line amortization of the discount (or premium) is acceptable in Canada and the United States as long as the results of doing so are not materially different from the use of the effective interest method.

In some countries, the amount of the discount is written off in the year of issuance rather than being amortized to income over the life of the bond.

As in the case of the bond issued at a discount, the $1,000 face value is credited to the bond payable account. The excess of the proceeds over the face amount is credited to an account called *premium on bond payable*. This account is a liability account, but is also known as an **adjunct account**. The balance in this account is reported directly with the bond liability account; that is, the accounts are linked together. Adjunct accounts are used to contain balances that add to a related account in the same way that contra accounts subtract from related accounts. The sum of the two accounts creates a liability that is measured at its net present value.

The interest entries for the bond issued at a premium would be:

BAUM COMPANY LTD. BOND ISSUED AT A PREMIUM—INTEREST ENTRIES
(at end of first interest period)

SE-Interest Expense[a]	41.45	
L-Premium on Bond Payable	8.55	
L-Interest Payable[b]		50.00
L-Interest Payable	50.00	
A-Cash		50.00

---

[a]Interest expense = Carrying Value × Yield Rate × Time
= $1,036.30 × 8% × 6/12 = $41.45

[b]Interest payable = Face Amount × Bond Interest Rate × Time
= $1,000 × 10% × 6/12 = $50

The premium on the bond payable is amortized in much the same way as is a discount. As the premium is amortized, the premium account is reduced and, consequently, the carrying value of the bond is reduced from period to period. This should make sense because the cash payments made each period are more than enough to pay for the interest expense. The excess of the payments over the expense (i.e., the **amortization of the premium**) reduces the carrying value of the debt. The carrying value at the end of the period would be calculated as before:

Carrying Value (ending) = Carrying Value (beginning) + Interest Expense − Payments

In the first period:

Carrying Value (ending) = $1,036.30 + 41.45 − 50.00 = $1,027.75

Exhibit 10-8 shows graphically how the carrying value of the liability changes over time. Notice that, because this bond is issued at a premium, the beginning carrying value is above $1,000. As time passes, the premium is amortized (decreases), and the carrying value decreases, eventually reaching $1,000 by the maturity date. The payments made at the interest dates are higher than the interest expense that has accrued during the period. Because the investors initially paid more than the face value for the bond but are being paid interest based on the face value and will receive the face value at maturity, the company is, in effect, paying a lower rate of interest than is reflected by the bond interest rate. This lower rate of interest needs to be reflected on the income statement. The excess of the interest payment over the interest decreases the premium, creating the falling carrying value shown in the graph.

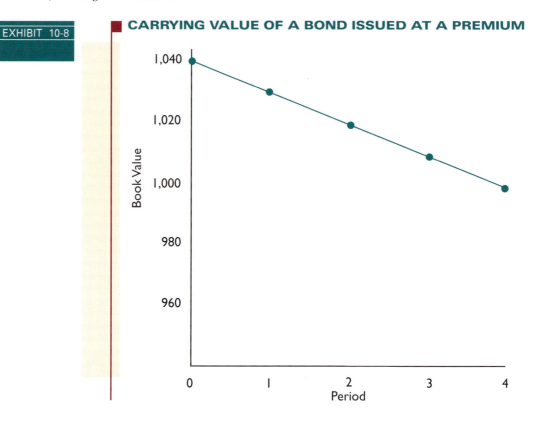

EXHIBIT 10-8

■ **CARRYING VALUE OF A BOND ISSUED AT A PREMIUM**

At the maturity date, the final maturity payment is made with the same entry as that made in the par case in that the final carrying value is the same ($1,000). Exhibit 10-9 shows the amortization table for the bond issued at a premium.

EXHIBIT 10-9

■ **AMORTIZATION TABLE—BOND ISSUED AT A PREMIUM**

Period	Beginning Carrying Value	Interest	Payment	Ending Carrying Value	Beginning Premium
1	$1,036.30	$41.45	$50.00	$1,027.75	$36.30
2	$1,027.75	$41.11	$50.00	$1,018.86	$27.75
3	$1,018.86	$40.75	$50.00	$1,009.62	$18.86
4	$1,009.62	$40.38	$1,050.00	$0.00	$9.62

Early Retirement of Debt

Although a company does not have to pay off its debts until maturity, there are times when it makes sense for it to pay the debt earlier. This transaction is known as **early retirement**, or **early extinguishment**, of debt. Bonds can be retired by buying them in the bond market or by **calling the bonds**. The bonds may have a *call* feature that allows the company to buy them back from the investors at a predetermined price. If the intention is to buy them in the bond market, it is likely that interest rates in the economy have changed between the issuance date and the date at which the company wants to buy back the debt. Because the interest rate used to account for the bond is fixed at the issuance date, it is likely that the carrying value of the bond will be different from the market value. A gain or loss will, consequently, result from this transaction. The gains and losses from the early retirement of debt are shown on the income statement.

To demonstrate the accounting for an early retirement, suppose the Baum Company Ltd. bond we discussed in the last section was issued when interest rates were 8%. Further, suppose that after one year Baum wishes to retire the bond. Interest rates in the economy have increased to 12% by this time. The carrying value at the end of Year 1 would be $1,018.86, as shown in Exhibit 10-9. The market value of the bond based on the 12% interest would be determined by discounting the remaining two coupon (interest) payments and the maturity value at 12%. This value would be the same as the value from the amortization table shown in Exhibit 10-7 for the bond, as if it were originally issued at 12%. Therefore, the market value would be $981.67 or, for clarification, the market value calculation would be as follows: $50 × 1.83339 (PV for 2 periods at 6%) + $1,000 × 0.8900 (PV for 2 periods at 6%) = $91.67 + $890.00 = $981.67. If Baum buys back the bond at this price, it will be satisfying an obligation on its books at $1,018.86 with a cash payment of $981.67. A gain will, therefore, result from this transaction. The entry to record this transaction would be:

EARLY RETIREMENT ENTRY

L-Bond Payable	1,000.00	
L-Premium on Bond Payable	18.86	
A-Cash		981.67
SE-Gain on Early Retirement of Bond		37.19

The example with Baum Company Ltd. illustrates one of the reasons that a company may decide to retire its debt early: the market value of the bond is lower than the maturity value. The company can pay off its debt with less money than would be required at maturity. The downside of this, however, is that if the company needs to raise more capital through the use of debt, it is probable that it will have to pay a higher rate of interest. The short-term gain on the retirement of the debt is replaced by higher interest costs over the long term. Under these circumstances, is the company better off (as reflected by the gain) for having retired its old debt?

LEASING

When a company needs to use an asset such as a piece of machinery, it can obtain the use of the asset in two ways. One is to purchase the asset outright. A second is to enter into a **lease agreement** in which another company (the **lessor**) buys the asset and the company that wants to use the asset (the **lessee**) makes periodic payments to the lessor in exchange for the use of the asset over the length of the lease agreement (**lease term**).

There are benefits and costs to both alternatives. One benefit of ownership is that the company can amortize the asset for tax purposes and, in some cases, obtain

Learning Objective
4

Discuss the advantages and disadvantages of leasing.

an investment tax credit for the purchase. Investment tax credits are incentives provided by the CCRA to encourage investment in certain types of assets. These credits usually take the form of a direct reduction in the company's tax bill based on a fixed percentage of the asset's acquisition cost.

Profit from appreciation in the value of the asset is another benefit of ownership. Loss from the amortization of the asset, which could be dramatic if the asset becomes technologically obsolete or loses its market popularity, is the downside. If the company has to borrow to buy the asset, the company's debt/equity and interest coverage ratios will change, which could affect its future borrowing capabilities (these ratios are discussed later in this chapter as well as in Chapter 12). This also ties up capital that might be used for other projects.

To the lessee, the benefits of leasing are several. The lessee does not have to put up its own capital to buy the asset. It also does not have to borrow to buy the asset, which means that its debt/equity and interest coverage ratios will not be affected. If the company is in a tax situation in which little taxable income is generated, the tax advantages of amortizing the asset or claiming an investment tax credit would be of limited value to the lessee. If the lessor can take advantage of the capital cost allowance deduction, then the lease payments that the lessee makes will be reduced as a result of the decrease in the lessor's costs. Because the lessee does not own the asset, the risk of loss from obsolescence falls on the lessor. Another advantage, along these same lines, is that the lessee may not want to use the asset for its full useful life. If the company wants to use the asset for only a short time, there is significant risk associated with the resale value if the company decides to buy the asset rather than to lease it.

Lessee Accounting

Learning Objective

Distinguish between an operating lease and a capital lease and prepare journal entries for a lessee under both conditions.

The accounting issues for a lessee can be illustrated using two extreme examples. At one extreme, suppose that the lease contract is signed for a relatively short period of time, say two years, whereas the useful life of the asset leased is eight years. In this case, it is clear that the lessee is not buying the asset, but is instead renting it for only a short period. The lease contract may be viewed as a mutually unexecuted contract, and the cash payments required by the lease are recorded by the lessee as rent expense and an outflow of cash. This type of lease is known as an **operating lease**.

Suppose at the other extreme that the lease contract was signed for the entire useful life of the asset and that the title to the asset passes to the lessee at the end of the lease term (not an uncommon event). In this case, the substance of the transaction is that the lessee has bought an asset and has agreed to pay for it in instalments. There is essentially no difference between this arrangement and one in which the lessee borrows the money and buys the asset for cash. The lender, in this case, is the lessor. It seems appropriate for the lessee to account for this as a borrowing and as a purchase of an asset. The asset is therefore recorded at its cost (in this case, the present value of the lease payments), and is amortized over time. The asset account name often includes the lease aspect (i.e., equipment under capital leases). The obligation to the lessor is recorded as a liability, and interest expense is recognized over time. This type of lease is known as a **capital lease**.

Although the appropriate accounting procedures for these extreme situations seem fairly clear, the question arises: what does the company do when the lease is somewhere in between these extremes? Suppose, for example, that the lease term is for 70% of the useful life of the asset and the company has an option to buy the asset at the end of the lease term. Should this qualify as a capital lease? In terms of the financial statement effects, a company would generally prefer to treat the lease as an operating lease. This would keep the lease obligation off the books, and there would be no effect on the debt/equity and interest coverage ratios. To address this issue, criteria have been developed to distinguish capital leases from operating leases. From the lessee's point of view, the lease qualifies as a capital lease if one of the following criteria is met:[3]

CAPITAL LEASE CRITERIA

1. The title to the asset passes to the lessee at the end of the lease term.

2. The lease term is equal to or greater than 75% of the useful life of the asset.

3. The present value of the minimum lease payments is greater than 90% of the fair value of the leased asset.

If the transaction does not meet any of the three criteria, the lease is an operating lease.

Criterion 1 indicates that the company will own the asset by the end of the lease term and, hence, is buying an asset. Many leases provide an option for the lessee to buy the asset at the end of the lease term. If the price to buy the asset is considered a bargain (i.e., the price is considered to be below the expected value at the end of the lease term, and therefore, it is likely that the company will exercise its option and buy the asset), then Criterion 1 would be met. Criterion 2 means that the company will have the use of the asset during most of its useful life, even though it may not retain title to it at the end of the lease term. Criterion 3 means that if the price the lessee pays to lease the asset is close to the price it would pay to buy the asset, it should account for the transaction as a purchase.

To illustrate the differences in accounting under a capital lease and an operating lease, let's consider the following simple situation. Suppose that an asset is leased for five years and requires quarterly lease payments of $2,000 each, payable in advance. The title does not pass at the end of the lease term, and there is no purchase option. The interest rate that is appropriate for this lease is 12%.

If the lease qualifies as an operating lease, the only entry to be made would be to record the payments as rent expense each quarter. The following entry would be made each quarter:

OPERATING LEASE ENTRY

SE-Rent expense (Lease expense)	2,000	
A-Cash		2,000

---

[3] *CICA Handbook*, Section 3065.06.

If the lease qualifies as a capital lease, the transaction must be recorded as the purchase of an asset and a related obligation. Both the asset and the obligation would be recorded at the present value of the lease payments. This transaction is structured as an annuity in advance (the first payment is made immediately and then there are 19 more payments). Because there are quarterly payments and the lease term is five years, there would be a total of 20 payments. The interest rate per period for use in discounting would be 3% (the quarterly rate based on the 12% annual rate). Using Table 4 from the Appendix at the end of the chapter for the present value of an annuity, the following would be the calculation of the present value:

$$
\begin{aligned}
\text{PV of lease payments} &= \text{First payment} + \text{PV of 19 payments at 3\%} \\
&= \$2,000 + (\$2,000 \times 14.32380) \\
&= \$2,000 + \$28,647.60 \\
&= \$30,647.60
\end{aligned}
$$

The entry to record the purchase of the asset and the related obligation at the time of contract signing would be:

CAPITAL LEASE ENTRY
(at date of signing)

A-Asset under capital lease	30,647.60	
L-Obligation under capital lease		30,647.60

The lease obligation would result in the recognition of interest expense similar to that generated by a bond. In the first quarter, two things happen. The first is that a payment is made at the beginning of the quarter (the first payment). This entire payment reduces the principal of the obligation because no time has passed and no interest has accrued. The principal at the beginning of the quarter is, therefore, $28,647.60 ($30,647.60 − $2,000). Interest is then calculated on this principal in the amount of $859.43 ($28,647.60 × 12% × 3/12). The entries to record these transactions in the first quarter are:

CAPITAL LEASE PAYMENT ENTRY
(on the first day of each quarter)

L-Obligation under capital lease	2,000	
A-Cash		2,000

CAPITAL LEASE EXPENSE ENTRY
(on the last day of the quarter)

SE-Interest expense	859.43	
L-Obligation under capital lease		859.43

An amortization table of the lease obligation, similar to those constructed earlier for bonds, could be prepared. By the end of the lease term, the lease obligation would be zero. Note that in the case of a lease, the interest is added directly to the lease obligation account and the cash payments directly reduce the balance.

In addition, subsequent to acquisition, the asset would be amortized over its useful life (in this case, the lease term, since the title does not pass at the end of the lease term). Assuming the company uses straight-line amortization, the amortization for the first quarter would be $1,532.38 ($30,647.60/20 quarters). Note that the residual value is zero in this calculation because the lessee does not retain title to the asset at the end of the lease term and, therefore, it is necessary to amortize the whole amount of the leased asset. The entry to record amortization would be:

CAPITAL LEASE EXPENSE ENTRY
(on the last day of the quarter)

SE-Amortization expense	1,532.38	
XA-Accumulated amortization		1,532.38
(on leased assets)		

These transactions have certain effects on the financial statements. If the asset qualifies as a capital lease, the company's assets and liabilities would be $30,647.60 higher than under an operating lease. On the income statement, the company would report both amortization expense and interest expense with the capital lease, whereas, with the operating lease, the company would report only rent expense. In the first quarter, the amortization plus interest would be $2,391.81 ($1,532.38 + $859.43). The expense under the operating lease would be $2,000. Therefore, in the first quarter, the capital lease results in higher expenses (they would be even higher if the company used an accelerated method of amortization). The total expenses reported over the life of the lease would be the same, however, regardless of which method is used to record the transaction. With the operating lease, the total expenses would be $40,000: $2,000 × 20 payments. The total capital lease expenses would also be $40,000: $30,647.60 in amortization and $9,352.40 in interest (total payments minus principal = $40,000 − $30,647.60). The difference, then, is in the pattern of expense recognition over the life of the lease, with operating leases showing a level amount of expense and capital leases showing larger expenses in the early years (when amortization and interest are high) and smaller expenses in later years. Exhibit 10-10 graphs the pattern of expense recognition over the life of the lease, treating the lease as an operating lease versus a capital lease.

PATTERNS OF EXPENSE RECOGNITION FOR LEASES

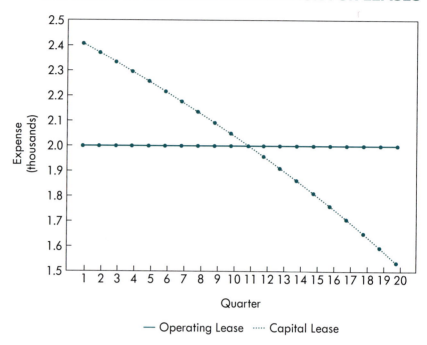

— Operating Lease   ····· Capital Lease

accounting in the news

NEW WAYS OF USING LEASES

Should a company buy or lease property? Some companies try to reap the accounting benefit of both by using "synthetic leases." A synthetic lease is an off-balance-sheet transaction that gives a company control over real estate without owning it outright.

Because the property is not an asset, the company avoids having to write-off an asset's depreciation against earnings. The synthetic lease is reported as an operating lease, with monthly payments treated as current expenses. But when it is time to pay the tax bill, the company can deduct interest and depreciation as if it owned the property.

Synthetic leases are relatively common, though Enron's failure—due in large part to such off-balance-sheet transactions—has generated criticism over their use to inflate earnings and the difficulty of finding them in financial reports. Companies ranging from telecommunications giant Cisco Systems to Krispy Kreme Doughnuts have been criticized for being less than transparent about their synthetic leases.

These transactions have their weaknesses. Typically, the loans are for relatively short terms—three to seven years—and the company agrees to a residual value. When the loan is due, the company can refinance or sell. If interest rates are high, refinancing is expensive; if real estate prices are falling, the company may not find a buyer who will pay the residual value it has guaranteed to its "landlord."

Source: "Debt? Who, Me?" by Seth Lubove and Elizabeth MacDonald, *Forbes*, Feb. 18, 2002, p. 56.

FYI: Krispy Kreme Doughnuts subsequently put its loan back on the balance sheet to satisfy the concerns of investors.

Because no asset or liability is recorded under operating leases in Canada, companies that have significant operating leases have to disclose their commitments to pay for these leases. Companies are required to disclose the future lease payments to be made in total and for each of the next five years. Capital leases also require similar disclosure. The obligations associated with leases would typically be shown in a footnote that relates either to long-term debt or to commitments or contingencies. In the financial statements for **CHC Helicopter Corporation**, these disclosures can be found in Note 22 (Exhibit 10-11).

CHC HELICOPTER CORPORATION, 2001

(tabular amounts in thousands)

EXHIBIT 10-11

22. Commitments

The Company has commitments with respect to operating leases for aircraft, buildings, and equipment. The minimum lease payments required under such leases were $188.4 million as at April 30, 2001 and are payable as follows:

2002	$42,883
2003	36,511
2004	34,129
2005	28,635
2006	22,809
and thereafter	23,388

Assets under capital leases are sometimes also segregated in the property, plant, and equipment section of the balance sheet. Note the example in Exhibit 10-12 from **WestJet Airlines Ltd.** WestJet leases some of its aircraft and computer hardware using capital leases.

EXHIBIT 10-12

WESTJET AIRLINES LTD., 2001

2. Capital assets:

	Cost	Accumulated depreciation	Net book value
Aircraft	$188,000	$49,912	$138,088
Spare engines and parts	42,628	5,551	37,077
Buildings	23,051	446	22,605
Flight simulators	19,455	670	18,785
Aircraft under capital lease	18,617	2,980	15,637
Computer hardware and software	12,388	3,732	8,656
Equipment	6,990	2,614	4,376
Leasehold improvements	3,539	1,421	2,118
Computer hardware under capital lease	643	494	149
	315,311	67,820	247,491
Deposits on aircraft	53,194	–	53,194
	$368,505	$67,820	$300,685

An International Perspective

Reports from Other Countries

Most developed countries have criteria for the capitalization of leased assets that are similar to Canada's. International accounting standards recommend capitalization for situations where substantially all of the risks and benefits of ownership are transferred to the lessee. Some countries (such as Spain and Sweden) require that the lease contain a bargain purchase option before capitalization is used.

Lessor Accounting

Lessor accounting is designed to be a mirror image of the accounting by the lessee. If the lessee qualifies for capital lease treatment, then the lessor should be viewed as having provided an asset to the lessee (the lessor will replace the capital asset with a receivable asset). If the lessee must treat the lease as an operating lease, then the lessor should retain the asset on its books as the owner and record lease revenue from the lease payments. In both of these situations, the lessor does not have a long-term liability (the subject of this chapter) on its books. An intermediate financial accounting courses will discuss lease accounting in more detail.

PENSIONS

Pensions are agreements between employers and employees that provide the latter with specified benefits (income) upon retirement. To the extent that the company is obligated to make payments under these agreements, some recognition should be given to their cost in the years when the company receives the benefits from the work of its employees. Because the payments to retired employees occur many years in the future, pensions represent an estimated future obligation. Two kinds of pension plans are commonly used by employers: **defined contribution plans** and **defined benefit plans**.

Defined Contribution Plans

In a **defined contribution plan**, the employer agrees to make a set (defined) contribution to a retirement fund for the employee (e.g., 10% of gross salary). The amount is usually set as a percentage of the employee's salary. Employees sometimes make their own contributions to the same fund to add to the amounts invested. The benefits to the employee at retirement depend on how well the investments in the retirement fund perform. The employer satisfies its obligation to the employee by payment into the fund. The fund is usually managed by a trustee (someone outside the employ and control of the company), and the assets are legally separated from the assets of the company, which means they are not reported with the other assets on the company's balance sheet.

The accounting for defined contribution funds is relatively straightforward. The company accrues the amount of its obligation to the pension fund, and then records a payment. Because the liability is settled, no other recognition is necessary in the financial statements. The entry to recognize pension expense and the related payment is:

SE-Pension expense	XXX	
L-Pension obligation		XXX
L-Pension obligation	XXX	
A-Cash		XXX

Companies generally make cash payments that coincide with the accruals because they cannot deduct the cost for tax purposes if no cash payment is made. Therefore, no net obligation usually remains with a defined contribution plan.

Defined Benefit Plans

A **defined benefit plan** guarantees to pay an employee a certain amount of money during each year of retirement. The formula used to calculate how much is paid usually takes into consideration the amount of time an employee has worked for the

Learning Objective

6

Explain the distinguishing features of a defined contribution pension plan and a defined benefit plan.

company as well as the highest salary (or an average of the highest salaries) that the employee earned while working for the company. For example, a plan might guarantee that the employee will receive 2% of the average of the highest three years of salaries multiplied by the number of years that the employee works for the company. If the employee worked for the company for 30 years and had an average salary of $40,000 for the highest three years, the pension benefit would be $24,000 per year [($40,000 × 2%) × 30 years].

Each year, as employees provide service to the company, they earn pension benefits which obligate the company to make cash payments at some point in the future. In estimating the cost of the obligation today (the present value of the liability), several projections must be included. These include: the length of time the employee will work for the company, the age at which the employee will retire, the employee's average salary during the highest salary years, the number of years the employee will live after retiring, and whether the employee will work for the company until retirement. All these factors will affect the amount and timing of the cash flows. In addition, the company must choose an appropriate rate of interest at which to calculate the net present value.

A given employee may leave the company at some point prior to retirement. If the pension benefits belong to employees only as long as they remain in the employment of the company, then there may be no obligation on the part of the company to pay out pension benefits. In most plans, however, there is a provision for **vesting** the benefits. Benefits that are vested belong to employees, even if they leave the company. In addition, while one employee may leave, many others will stay. Thus, even without vesting, it is likely that some fraction of the employees will continue to work for the company until retirement. The total obligation of the pension plan may, therefore, have to be estimated based on the characteristics of the average employee rather than on particular employees.

Calculating the present value of the future pension obligation generally requires the services of an **actuary**. The actuary is trained in the use of statistical procedures to make the types of estimates required for the pension calculation.

The accounting entries for defined benefit pension plans are essentially the same as the preceding entry for defined contribution plans. The company must make an accrual of the expense and the related obligation to provide pension benefits. The amounts are much more difficult to estimate in the case of defined benefit plans, but the concept is the same as for defined contribution plans. The entry made to recognize the pension expense is called the **accrual entry**. Setting aside cash to pay for these future benefits is done by making a cash entry. This is sometimes called the **funding entry**. Many employee pension plan agreements have clauses that require the company to fund the pension obligation. Because of the uncertainties associated with the amounts of the liabilities, some companies have been somewhat reluctant to fully fund their pension obligations. There is no accounting requirement that the amount expensed be the same as the amount funded. Therefore, a net pension obligation may result if more is expensed than funded, or a net pension asset may exist if funding is larger than the amount expensed. The actual calculation of the pension expense incorporates many factors and is beyond the scope of this book.

Pension funds are described as **overfunded** if the assets in the fund exceed the present value of future pension obligations. In **underfunded** pension plans, the present value of future obligations exceeds fund assets. Funds in which the assets actually equal the present value of the future obligations are called **fully funded** plans. The pension fund itself is usually handled by a trustee, and contributions to the fund cannot be returned to the employer except under extraordinary circumstances. To provide sufficient funds to pay benefits, the trustee invests the assets contributed to the fund. Benefits are then paid out of these fund assets.

accounting in the news

AN OVERFUNDED PENSION PLAN

Making decisions about pension funds can be difficult, but some tasks are less onerous than others. A few years ago, the province of Nova Scotia realized its pension fund for government employees was overfunded—that is, the fund had more money in assets than it needed to pay for employee retirements. Pension funds are not allowed to build up large surpluses. According to provincial figures, the fund had about 8% more than it needed.

The solution: pay out some of the surplus to government employees and put an equal amount back into government coffers. The government planned to give employees a total of $28 million. Each employee was to receive 6% of gross salary: a person who earned $30,000 would receive $1,800. Hence, a pension cheque before retirement!

Source: "Employees get windfall on pensions," by Brian Flinn, *Halifax Daily News*, March 21, 1998, p. 9.

Annual Statement Disclosures

In Canada, for a defined contribution plan, contribution amounts for the period are disclosed. For a defined benefit plan, the required disclosure is very extensive. Rather than list all of the requirements, look at the disclosure provided by **Petro-Canada** in Exhibit 10-13. Petro-Canada has both defined benefit and defined contribution pension plans, as well as some health care and life insurance benefits that it offers to its retired employees.

EXHIBIT 10-13

PETRO-CANADA (2001)
Note 18 EMPLOYEE FUTURE BENEFITS

The Company maintains pension plans with defined benefit and defined contribution provisions, and provides certain health care and life insurance benefits to its qualifying retirees. The actuarially determined cost of these benefits is accrued over the estimated service life of employees. The defined benefit provisions are generally based upon years of service and average salary during the final years of employment. Certain defined benefit options require employee contributions and the balance of the funding for the registered plans is provided by the Company, based upon the advice of an independent actuary. The defined contribution option provides for an annual contribution of 5% of each participating employee's pensionable earnings. Substantially all of the pension assets are invested in equity, fixed income and other marketable securities.

Benefit Plan Expense

	Pension Plans			Other Post-Retirement Plans		
	2001	2000	1999	**2001**	2000	1999
(a) Defined benefit plans						
Employer current service cost	$ **22**	$ 20	$ 18	$ **2**	$ 3	$ 2
Interest cost	**70**	69	67	**11**	10	8
Expected return on plan assets	**(88)**	(83)	(90)	—	—	—
Amortization of transitional (asset) obligation	**(5)**	(5)	—	**2**	1	—
Amortization of past service costs (gains)	—	—	4	—	—	(1)
Amortization of net actuarial gains	—	—	(1)	—	—	(1)
	(1)	1	(2)	**15**	14	8
(b) Defined contribution plans	**7**	6	6			
Total expense	$ **6**	$ 7	$ 4	$ **15**	$ 14	$ 8
Benefit Plan Funding	$ **9**	$ 6	$ 6	$ **7**	$ 6	$ 5

Financial Status of Defined Benefit Plans

	Pension Plans		Other Post-Retirement Plans	
	2001	2000	**2001**	2000
Fair value of plan assets	**$ 1 039**	$ 1 113	$ **—**	$ —
Accrued benefit obligation	**1 119**	1 047	**172**	160
Funded status — plan (deficit) surplus	**(80)**	66	**(172)**	(160)
Unamortized transitional (asset) obligation	**(44)**	(49)	**23**	25
Unamortized net actuarial losses	**173**	29	**16**	9
Accrued benefit asset (liability)	$ **49**	$ 46	$ **(133)**	$ (126)
Reconciliation of Plan Assets				
Fair value of plan assets at beginning of year	**$ 1 113**	$ 1 052	$ **—**	$ —
Contributions	**9**	7	—	—
Benefits paid	**(60)**	(55)	—	—
Actual (loss) return on plan assets	**(17)**	115	—	—
Other	**(6)**	(6)	—	—
Fair value of plan assets at end of year	**$ 1 039**	$ 1 113	$ **—**	$ —
Reconciliation of Accrued Benefit Obligation				
Accrued benefit obligation at beginning of year	**$ 1 047**	$ 951	$ **160**	$ 145
Current service cost	**22**	21	**2**	3
Interest cost	**70**	69	**11**	10
Benefits paid	**(60)**	(55)	**(7)**	(7)
Actuarial losses	**40**	61	**6**	9
Accrued benefit obligation at end of year	**$ 1 119**	$ 1 047	$ **172**	$ 160

Note 18 EMPLOYEE FUTURE BENEFITS (continued) | PETRO-CANADA (2001) |

EXHIBIT 10-13
CONT.

Funded Status

The funded status includes the following amounts in respect of plans that are not fully funded:

	Pension Plans		Other Post-Retirement Plans	
	2001	2000	**2001**	2000
Accrued benefit obligation	**$ (161)**	$ (67)	**$ (172)**	$ (160)
Fair value of plan assets	**67**	—	**—**	—
Plan deficit	**$ (94)**	$ (67)	**$ (172)**	$ (160)

Defined Benefit Plan Assumptions

	2001	2000	1999
Year-end obligation discount rate	**6.50%**	6.75%	8.00%
Pension expense discount rate	**6.75%**	7.25%	8.00%
Long-term rate of return on plan assets	**8.00%**	8.00%	8.00%
Rate of compensation increase, excluding merit increases	**3.00%**	2.50% [1]	2.00% [1]
Annual increase in the per capita cost of other post-retirement benefits	**6.20%** [2]	6.20%	4.80%

[1] 3.0% in 2001 and thereafter.
[2] 4.2% in 2005 and thereafter.

POST-EMPLOYMENT BENEFITS

As you just saw with Petro-Canada, employers sometimes offer other types of **post-employment benefits** in addition to pensions. Health-care benefits and life insurance are two of the most commonly offered benefits. In the past, the obligation to provide these benefits has, for the most part, been ignored in the financial statements of companies in Canada. The benefits used to be recorded on a pay-as-you-go basis; that is, the costs were expensed as the cash was paid out to insurance companies that cover the costs of the benefits. To date, corporate exposure in Canada has been limited because of publicly funded health care. This may not be true in the future. In Canada, as of January 1, 2000, companies are required to account for these items in much the same way as pensions.

Learning Objective
7

Describe other employment benefits and explain how they are treated in Canada.

An International Perspective

Reports from Other Countries

While a significant number of countries require accrual of pension costs, many other countries require only that the costs of pension plans be recognized as benefits are paid, the pay-as-you-go method. Countries with this type of accounting include Belgium, India, Norway, and Spain.

NAFTA Facts

The accounting for pension benefits in the United States and Mexico is essentially the same as in Canada. However, both Canada and the United States have additional requirements with respect to accruing of post-employment benefits.

Learning Objective

8

Calculate the debt/equity ratio and the times-interest-earned ratio and write a statement describing the financial health of a company using the information from these ratios.

STATEMENT ANALYSIS CONSIDERATIONS

Two ratios that are commonly used to evaluate a company's ability to repay its obligations are the debt/equity ratio and the times-interest-earned ratio. Using the balance sheet and income statement (Exhibit 10-14) of **METRO INC.**, a Montreal-based company that is a leader in the food distribution industry in Quebec, we will demonstrate how these two ratios can provide insights into the riskiness of a company.

METRO INC. (2001)

EXHIBIT 10-14

CONSOLIDATED BALANCE SHEETS

As at September 29, 2001
(Millions of dollars)

	2001	2000	1999
ASSETS			
CURRENT			
Accounts receivable	$ 236.1	$ 186.3	$ 177.7
Income taxes recoverable	10.3	–	–
Inventories	242.0	221.8	195.7
Prepaid expenses	3.0	4.3	1.2
Future income taxes *(note 5)*	13.1	9.4	–
	504.5	421.8	374.6
Investments and other assets *(note 6)*	28.3	23.1	26.9
Future income taxes *(note 5)*	–	7.8	–
Capital assets *(note 7)*	481.9	430.9	413.9
Goodwill	171.3	176.1	180.8
	$ 1,186.0	$ 1,059.7	$ 996.2
LIABILITIES AND SHAREHOLDERS' EQUITY			
CURRENT			
Bank loans *(note 8)*	$ 31.7	$ 1.7	$ 12.6
Accounts payable	455.4	427.6	387.8
Income taxes payable	–	12.0	19.7
Current portion of long-term debt *(note 8)*	5.0	6.3	4.9
	492.1	447.6	425.0
Long-term debt *(note 8)*	55.3	88.6	144.2
Future income taxes *(note 5)*	80.6	61.8	–
Deferred income taxes	–	–	34.7
	628.0	598.0	603.9
SHAREHOLDERS' EQUITY			
Capital stock *(note 9)*	162.3	160.1	159.3
Retained earnings	395.7	301.6	233.0
	558.0	461.7	392.3
	$ 1,186.0	$ 1,059.7	$ 996.2

See accompanying notes

CONSOLIDATED STATEMENTS OF EARNINGS

Year ended September 29, 2001
(Millions, except for earnings per share)

	2001 52 weeks	2000 53 weeks	1999 52 weeks
SALES	$ 4,868.9	$ 4,657.5	$ 3,995.5
Cost of sales and operating expenses	4,618.3	4,438.0	3,808.2
Depreciation and amortization *(note 3)*	61.4	52.5	44.3
	4,679.7	4,490.5	3,852.5
OPERATING INCOME	189.2	167.0	143.0
Financing costs			
Short-term	0.6	0.7	0.2
Long-term	4.6	8.5	5.7
	5.2	9.2	5.9
EARNINGS BEFORE INCOME TAXES AND UNUSUAL ITEMS	184.0	157.8	137.1
Unusual items *(note 4)*	–	–	15.0
EARNINGS BEFORE INCOME TAXES	184.0	157.8	122.1
Income taxes *(note 5)*	61.2	60.5	45.7
NET EARNINGS	$ 122.8	$ 97.3	$ 76.4
EARNINGS PER SHARE *(note 4)*			
Basic	$ 2.45	$ 1.94	$ 1.51
Fully diluted	$ 2.36	$ 1.86	$ 1.45
WEIGHTED AVERAGE NUMBER OF SHARES OUTSTANDING	50.1	50.2	50.5

See accompanying notes

The formula for the debt/equity ratio is:

$$\frac{\text{Total liabilities}}{\text{Total liabilities} + \text{Shareholders' equity}}$$

The 2001, 2000, and 1999 debt/equity ratios of METRO INC. are:

$$\frac{\$628.0}{\$628.0 + \$558.0} \qquad \frac{\$598.0}{\$598.0 + \$461.7} \qquad \frac{\$603.9}{\$603.9 + \$392.3}$$
$$= 53.0\% \qquad\qquad = 56.4\% \qquad\qquad = 60.6\%$$

These calculations demonstrate that in 1999, 60.6% of METRO INC.'s assets were financed through debt. The ratio dropped a little in 2000 to 56.4%, and then again in 2001 to 53.0%. From the balance sheet, we can see that, over the three years, METRO INC. increased its short-term liabilities by approximately $67 million, decreased its long-term liabilities by approximately $43 million, and increased its shareholders' equity by approximately $166 million, practically all of which was from earnings. The increase in the short-term liabilities puts increased demands on the company's cash flows in the short run. It would be important to continue to follow this ratio before drawing too many conclusions about any major shifts in financing strategy by the company.

The times-interest-earned ratio provides a measure of the company's ability to make interest payments out of earnings. It is calculated by the following formula:

$$\frac{\text{Income before interest and taxes}}{\text{Interest}} = \frac{\text{Net income} + \text{Taxes} + \text{Interest}}{\text{Interest}}$$

The calculation of the times-interest-earned ratio for METRO INC. for 2001, 2000, and 1999 would be:

$$2001 \quad \frac{\$122.8 + \$61.2 + \$5.2}{\$5.2} \quad = 36.4 \text{ times}$$

$$2000 \quad \frac{\$97.3 + \$60.5 + \$9.2}{\$9.2} \quad = 18.2 \text{ times}$$

and

$$1999 \quad \frac{\$76.4 + \$45.7 + \$5.9}{\$5.9} \quad = 21.7 \text{ times}$$

In 1999, METRO INC. could pay its interest obligation almost 22 times out of earnings. This is a very comfortable position. The risk of nonpayment of interest is very low. By the end of 2001, interest costs had declined such that METRO could now pay its interest obligations 36 times out of earnings. Any creditor would likely be very confident about lending funds to METRO. The increase in the times-interest-earned ratio, coupled with the decrease in the debt/equity ratio, demonstrates to creditors that the risk of nonpayment of interest or principal of the debt has declined over the three years.

The biggest concern for analysts regarding liabilities is the possibility of unrecorded liabilities. As we saw in the last chapter, commitments and contingent liabilities can have significant effects on the health of a company. In this chapter, a company's obligations under operating leases are an example of liabilities that are not reported on the financial statements. Unrecorded liabilities will cause the debt/equity ratio to be understated and the times-interest-earned ratio to be overstated. Certain disclosures give the analyst some help in understanding the effects of these unrecorded liabilities. For example, the disclosure of the next five years of lease payments for operating leases allows an analyst to approximate the present value of these lease payments for inclusion in ratio analysis. The effects of other commitments and other off-balance-sheet liabilities may be more difficult to estimate, but the analyst should have a good understanding of the company and the type of contracts it enters into with suppliers, customers, and employees so that these liabilities do not come as surprises.

Another concern is whether the book values of liabilities reflect their current market values. Because liabilities are recorded at the interest rates that were in effect when the debt was issued, changes in market rates can cause changes in the value of these liabilities that are not reflected on the company's books. This does not mean that the company will be paying more or less interest as a result of the market changes, but it does mean that the company may be paying more or less than it would have if it had taken out new debt today. Knowledge of this change in interest rates is particularly important when one company is trying to buy another. Book value can be adjusted either by looking at the market value of the debt (for publicly traded debt) or by recalculating the present value of the debt based on current market interest rates. This, of course, requires some detailed information about the terms of the outstanding debt. Another reason why it is important for users to know about changes in interest rates is that companies are often refinancing their debt. Users need to know what the potential costs are to the company the next time it uses debt financing to increase its cash flow.

Another risk that the analyst should consider is that posed by debt that is denominated in a foreign currency. As you can imagine, if the company is required to repay a debt in a foreign currency, fluctuations in the exchange rate for that currency can cause increases or decreases in the liability as expressed in dollars. When financial statements are prepared, any debt that is denominated in a foreign currency will be restated in Canadian dollars using the current exchange rate. This provides the user with some knowledge about future costs. Another risk is that the company may enter into debt agreements in which the interest rate is not fixed but floats with interest rates in the economy (sometimes called variable-rate debt). If interest rates go up, the company can find itself making significantly higher interest payments. Both these risks can be managed through the use of sophisticated hedging techniques involving financial instruments such as interest rate and foreign currency options, and swaps. To help readers of financial statements understand these complex transactions and the risks posed to the company, companies in Canada are required to disclose these types of transactions and to provide some details concerning the risks the company faces because of them. Many of these risks are associated with amounts that are off-balance-sheet. As an example, consider the disclosure made by **Intrawest Corporation** in its 2001 annual report (Exhibit 10-15).

INTRAWEST CORPORATION (2001)
9. BANK AND OTHER INDEBTEDNESS:

EXHIBIT 10-15

The Company has obtained financing for its ski and resort operations and properties from various financial institutions by pledging individual assets as security for such financing. Security for general corporate debt is provided by general security which includes a floating charge on the Company's assets and undertakings, fixed charges on real estate properties, and assignment of mortgages and notes receivable. The following table summarizes the primary security provided by the Company, where appropriate, and indicates the applicable type of financing, maturity dates and the weighted average interest rate at June 30, 2001:

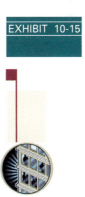

EXHIBIT 10-15

CONT.

INTRAWEST CORPORATION (2001)

	Maturity dates	Weighted average interest rate	2001	2000
Ski and resort operations:				
Mortgages and bank loans	Demand-2017	5.74%	$ 200,121	$ 211,561
Obligations under capital leases	2002-2005	7.75%	5,694	3,771
			205,815	215,332
Properties:				
Interim financing on properties under development and held for resale	2002-2017	7.36%	175,944	110,515
Resort club notes receivable credit facilities	2006	7.05%	21,399	1,094
Mortgages on revenue-producing properties	2002-2015	7.99%	10,952	12,425
			208,295	124,034
General corporate debt	2002	5.93%	31,803	59,210
Unsecured debentures	2002-2010	9.61%	564,081	434,585
			1,009,994	833,161
Current portion			201,640	158,228
			$ 808,354	$ 674,933

Principal repayments and the components related to either floating or fixed interest rates are as follows:

	Interest rates		Total
	Floating	Fixed	Repayments
Year ending June 30, 2002	$ 180,654	$ 20,986	$ 201,640
2003	146,104	111,362	257,466
2004	1,823	27,723	29,546
2005	245	14,420	14,665
2006	1,933	8,902	10,835
Subsequent to 2006	12,131	483,711	495,842
	$ 342,890	$ 667,104	$ 1,009,994

The Company has entered into a swap agreement to fix the interest rate on a portion of its floating rate debt. The Company had $14,000,000 (2000 – $26,262,000) of bank loans swapped against debt with a fixed interest rate ranging from 5.34% to 7.40% (2000 – 5.34% to 7.40%) per annum.

Bank and other indebtedness includes indebtedness in the amount of $342,206,000 (2000 – $349,277,000) which is repayable in Canadian dollars of $518,100,000 (2000 – $517,140,000).

The Company is subject to certain covenants in respect of some of the bank and other indebtedness which require the Company to maintain certain financial ratios. The Company is in compliance with these covenants at June 30, 2001.

SUMMARY

This chapter completes the discussion of liabilities. The risks associated with long-term liabilities are more extensive than those associated with the short-term liabilities discussed in the previous chapter because of the longer time frame, the larger amounts being borrowed, and the uncertainty of the future. Large companies use bonds as a way of raising additional funds for financing growth in the company. The issuance of bonds is a complex procedure involving the use of financial experts and investment bankers. Depending on the market's perception of the riskiness of the company, the bonds will be issued at par, above par, or below par. The chapter described the accounting for the bonds once they are issued.

The other two items described in the chapter are leases and pensions. Leasing is used extensively across Canada. When a company needs to buy or replace a capital asset, it will determine whether it is more advantageous to buy the asset or to lease it. The details of the leasing contract will determine whether the company must account for the lease as an operating lease or a capital lease.

Many large companies have pension plans for their employees. The two basic types of plans are defined contribution plans and defined benefit plans. We did not go into extensive detail about the accounting for either leases or pensions, but rather tried to give you an understanding of what these items are and how they are reported on the financial statements. Because these two items can have significant effects on the financial statements, knowledge of them is essential to any evaluation of the future profitability of an organization.

The two ratios that are important in this chapter are the debt/equity ratio and the times-interest-earned ratio. These ratios will provide users with an analysis of some of the risks associated with debt financing.

The discussion of balance sheet accounts concludes in the next chapter with a discussion of shareholders' equity. Following that, we provide a complete review of the ratio analysis used in this book.

SUMMARY PROBLEMS

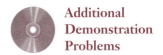

Additional Demonstration Problems

1. The Higgins Company Ltd. issued $100,000 face value bonds with a bond interest rate of 8% on January 1, 20x1. The bonds mature on December 31, 2x10 (i.e., there are 10 years to maturity) and pay interest semi-annually on June 30 and December 31. The issue price set for these bonds reflected an assumption that investors would need a 10% return (yield rate) in order to be convinced to buy the bonds.

   a. What issue price was set for these bonds under the assumptions set forth above? (Ignore commissions to the underwriters in your answer.)

   b. If the bonds were issued at the price calculated in part a), what entries would the Higgins Company make during 20x1 to account for these bonds?

   c. If, prior to the issuance of the bonds, interest rates increase in the economy such that investors demand a 12% return from investments such as Higgins' bonds, what price would they be willing to pay on January 1, 20x1, for these bonds?

2. The Acme Company Ltd. enters into a lease for the use of a computer system. The lessor paid $35,000 for the computer system and will lease the computer system to Acme for five years. At the end of the lease term, the computer will be returned to the lessor, who estimates that the computer will have a zero residual value. The lease contract will call for monthly payments of $778.56 to be made at the end of each month. These payments provide the lessor with a 12% return on the contract.

   a. Based on the above facts, how should Acme account for this lease?

   b. Construct the entries that Acme should make during the first two months of the lease, assuming that the lease is signed on January 1, 20x1, and that payments are made on the last day of each month.

   c. Give some reasons why Acme would choose to lease the computer system rather than buy it.

3. Exhibit 10-16 shows the pension footnote for **Teck Cominco Ltd.** (an integrated natural resource corporation involved in mineral exploration, mining, smelting, and refining).

   a. What kind of pension plan does Teck Cominco Ltd. have?

   b. How is Teck Cominco accounting for its non-pension retirement benefits?

   c. On its income statement, Teck Cominco does not disclose the total pension expense for 2001. On the balance sheet, it lists "Other liabilities" of $365 million. In the note with this amount it states that the accrued employee future benefits (a liability) are $121 million. This is up from the 2000 balance of $85 million. By listing this as an accrued future liability, what information is Teck Cominco giving users about its employee future benefits?

■ TECK COMINCO LTD.

Excerpted from the Notes to the 2001 Statements

1. Significant Accounting Policies

Employee Future Benefits

Pension expenses are based on actuarial determinations of current service costs. Certain actuarial assumptions used in the determination of future benefits and plan liabilities are based upon management's best estimates, including expected plan performance, salary escalation, and retirement dates of employees. The discount rate used to determine the accrued benefit obligation is determined by reference to market interest rates at the measurement date of high quality debt instruments. Differences between the actuarial liabilities and the amounts recorded in financial statements will arise from changes in plan assumptions, changes in benefits, or through experience as results differ from actuarial assumptions. These differences are taken into the determination of income over the average remaining service life of the related employees. Non-pension retirement benefits are accrued and are funded by the company as they become due.

SUGGESTED SOLUTIONS TO SUMMARY PROBLEMS

1. a. Present Value of the Higgins Company Bond at 10%:

PV of Bond = PV of Interest Payments + PV of Maturity Payment
= ($4,000 × 12.46221 (Table 4)) + ($100,000 × 0.37689 (Table 2))
= $87,537.84

b.

HIGGINS COMPANY BOND—ISSUANCE ENTRY
(at date of issuance)

A-Cash	87,537.84	
XL -Discount on Bond Payable	12,462.16	
L -Bond Payable		100,000.00

HIGGINS COMPANY BOND—INTEREST ENTRIES
(at the end of the first interest period)

SE-Interest Expense[a]	4,376.89	
XL -Discount on Bond Payable		376.89
L -Interest Payable[b]		4,000.00
L -Interest Payable	4,000.00	
A-Cash		4,000.00

[a]Interest Expense = Carrying Value × Yield Rate × Time
= $87,537.84 × 10% × 6/12 = $4,376.89

[b]Interest Payable = Face Amount × Bond Interest Rate × Time
= $100,000 × 8% × 6/12 = $4,000.00

Ending Carrying Value = Beginning Carrying Value + Interest − Payment
= $87,537.84 + 4,376.89 − 4,000 = $87,914.73

HIGGINS COMPANY BOND—INTEREST ENTRIES

SE-Interest Expense[a]	4,395.74	
XL -Discount on Bond Payable		395.74
L -Interest Payable[b]		4,000.00
L -Interest Payable	4,000.00	
A-Cash		4,000.00

---

[a]Interest Expense = Carrying Value × Yield Rate × Time
= $87,914.73 × 10% × 6/12 = $4,395.74

[b]Interest Payable = Face Amount × Bond Interest Rate × Time
= $1000,00 + 8% × 6/12 = $4,000.00

Ending Carrying Value = Beginning Carrying Value + Interest − Payment
= $87,914.73 + 4,395.74 − 4,000 = $88,310.47

c. Present Value of the Higgins Company Bond at 12%:

PV Bond = PV Interest of Payments + PV of Maturity Payment
= ($4,000.00 × 11.46994 (Table 4)) + ($100,000 × 0.31180 (Table 2))
= $77,059.68

2. a. Because the lease covers more than 75% of the useful life of the asset, Acme should account for it as a capital asset. You can assume that the useful life of the computer system is the full term of the lease because the residual value at the end of that time is zero.

b. The following entries should be made in the first two months:

The present value of the lease payments at 12% per year over 60 months is equal to $778.56 × 44.95504 (Table 4 (60 periods at 1%)) = $35,000

CAPITAL LEASE ENTRY
(at January 1, 20x1)

A-Asset under Lease	35,000	
L -Lease Obligation		35,000

The amortization of the obligation and the paying of the first lease payment must be recorded in the first month. Because this is an annuity in arrears, the first payment reduces the principal of the obligation at the end of the month. The following entries would be made:

CAPITAL LEASE EXPENSE ENTRY
(on January 31, 20x1)

L -Lease Obligation	778.56	
A-Cash		778.56
SE-Interest Expense[a]	350.00	
L -Lease Obligation		350.00

[a]Interest Expense = Carrying Value × Interest Rate × Time
= $35,000 × 12% × 1/12
= $350.00

Assuming that the corporation amortizes its leased assets straight-line over the lease term, the following entry would be made at the end of the first month:

CAPITAL LEASE EXPENSE ENTRY
(on January 31, 20x1)

SE-Amortization Expense[a]	583.33	
XA-Accumulated Amortization		583.33
(on leased assets)		

[a]Straight-Line Amortization = $35,000/60 months = $583.33 per month

In the second month, similar entries would be made as follows:

CAPITAL LEASE EXPENSE ENTRY
(on February 28, 20x1)

L -Lease Obligation	778.56	
A-Cash		778.56
SE-Interest Expense[a]	345.71	
L -Lease Obligation		345.71

[a]Interest Expense = Carrying Value × Interest Rate × Time
= ($35,000 − $778.56 + $350.00) × 12% × 1/12
= $34,571.44 × 12% × 1/12
= $345.71

CAPITAL LEASE EXPENSE ENTRY
(on February 28, 20x1)

SE-Amortization Expense[a]	583.33	
XA-Accumulated Amortization		583.33
(on leased assets)		

[a]Straight-Line Amortization = $35,000/60 months = $583.33 per month

c. There are several reasons why Acme might choose to lease the computer system:

1. Acme may not have $35,000 available to buy the system. Rather than borrow the $35,000 from the bank, it may choose to lease the asset and make monthly payments. The interest rate charged on the lease may be less than what the bank would charge.

2. Because Acme does not own the computer system, if something goes wrong with the system, the lessor is responsible for fixing it. It is likely that in the lease agreement there are clauses that outline the types of problems that the lessor agrees to fix and the types that are Acme's responsibility.

3. At the end of the five years, Acme is required to return the system to the lessor. This means that it will have to replace it. The end of the lease term forces Acme to stay technologically current (if you assume that five years is not too long to keep a computer system without replacing it). There may be clauses in the lease agreement about annual upgrades to the system and who is responsible for these upgrades. If the lessor is responsible, it is to Acme's advantage to lease the system.

3. a. Teck Cominco Ltd. appears to have a defined benefit pension plan. It mentions actuarial assumptions and the basis of those assumptions. If it had a defined contribution pension plan, it would need to disclose how much of the employee salaries are being contributed to the pension plan. There would be no need for information about actuarial assumptions.

b. Teck Cominco Ltd. is accounting for its post-employment benefits by accruing them as the employees are working but paying for them as they are incurred.

c. Teck Cominco Ltd. is telling users that its pension plan is not fully funded. The amount Teck Cominco has expensed for pension funds is greater than the amount that it has deposited in a pension fund to pay for those future benefits.

SYNONYMS

Bond interest rate/coupon rate/stated rate
Early retirement of debt/early extinguishment of debt
Market rate of interest/yield rate/effective rate/discount rate

 # GLOSSARY

Accrual entry   In the context of pension accounting, this is the entry to accrue pension cost and create the pension obligation.

Actuary   A professional trained in statistical methods who can make reasonable estimates of pension costs.

Adjunct account   An account that adds to a related account; it has the same type of balance as the related account. In this chapter, an example of this type of account is the premium on bond payable account.

Amortization of the discount   The systematic reduction of the discount account balance over the life of a bond. The reduction of the discount account each period adds to the interest expense recorded during the period.

Amortization of the premium   The systematic reduction of the premium account balance over the life of a bond. The reduction of the premium account each period reduces the interest expense recorded during this period.

Best efforts basis   The basis on which underwriters sometimes sell bonds for companies. The underwriters make their "best effort" to sell the bonds but, if they cannot sell them, the bonds are returned to the company.

Bond A long-term borrowing of a corporation that is evidenced by a bond certificate. The borrowing is characterized by a face value, interest rate, and maturity date.

Bond covenants Restrictions placed on a company that issues bonds. The restrictions usually apply to the company's ability to pay dividends or require that the company maintain certain minimum ratios.

Bond interest rate An interest rate specified in a bond used to determine the interest payments that are made on the bond.

Bond market A market in which bonds of companies are actively traded.

Capital lease A lease that the lessee must record as an asset and a related borrowing as if the transaction represented the purchase of the asset.

Collateral trust bond A bond that provides marketable securities as collateral in the event of default by the company.

Commercial paper A short-term borrowing in which the lender is another company rather than a financial institution.

Convertible bond A bond that is convertible, under certain conditions, into common shares.

Debenture A bond that is issued with no specific collateral.

Defined benefit plan A pension plan that specifies the benefits that retirees will receive upon retirement. The benefits are usually determined based on the number of years of service and the highest salary earned by the employee.

Defined contribution plan A pension plan that specifies how much the company will contribute to its employees' pension fund. No guarantee is made of the amount that will be available upon retirement.

Discount A term used to indicate that a bond is sold or issued at a value below its face value.

Early extinguishment of debt The settlement of debt (by paying the obligation) prior to its scheduled maturity date.

Early retirement of debt Synonym for early extinguishment of debt.

Effective interest method A method of calculating interest expense in which the interest is determined by multiplying the carrying value of the debt times the yield rate.

Face value A value specified in a bond that determines the cash payment that will be made on the bond's maturity date. The face value is also used to determine the periodic interest payments made on the bond.

Foreign-denominated debt Borrowings of a company that must be repaid in a foreign currency.

Fully funded Refers to a pension plan in which the pension plan assets equal the projected benefit obligation.

Funding entry In the context of pensions, this is the entry made to show the cash payment made to the pension plan to fund the obligation.

Indenture agreement An agreement that accompanies the issuance of a bond specifying all the terms and restrictions of the borrowing.

Interest payment The periodic interest payments made on a bond. The payments are typically made semi-annually. The amount is calculated by multiplying the face value of the bond by the bond interest rate.

Investment banker The intermediary who arranges the issuance of a bond in the public debt market on behalf of a company. The investment banker sells the bonds to its clients before the bond is traded in the open market.

Lease agreement An agreement between a lessee and a lessor for the rental or purchase of an asset, or both.

Lease term The period or term over which a lessee makes payments to a lessor in a lease.

Lessee The party or entity that is renting or purchasing the asset in a lease.

Lessor The party or entity that is selling or lending the asset in a lease.

Maturity date A date specified in a bond that determines the final payment date of the bond.

Mortgage bond A bond that provides some type of real asset as collateral in the event of a default by the company.

Note A long- or short-term borrowing.

Operating lease A lease in which the lessee does not record an asset and related obligation but treats the lease as a mutually unexecuted contract. Lease expense is then recognized as payments are made per the lease contract.

Overfunded Refers to a pension plan in which the plan assets exceed the projected benefit obligation.

Par A term used to indicate that a bond is sold or issued at its face value.

Pension A plan that provides benefits to employees upon retirement.

Post-employment benefits Benefits provided to retirees other than pensions. These benefits are typically health-care or life insurance benefits.

Premium A term used to indicate that a bond is sold or issued at a value above its face value.

Private placement A borrowing arranged privately between two companies or entities.

Projected benefit obligation The present value of the pension obligations under a defined benefit plan. The calculation includes all necessary actuarial assumptions and an assumption with regard to the escalation of salaries.

Public bond market A market in which bonds are publicly traded.

Senior debenture A general borrowing of the company that has priority over other types of long-term borrowings in the event of bankruptcy.

Subordinated debenture A general borrowing of the company that has a lower priority than senior debentures in the event of bankruptcy.

Syndicate A group of underwriters that collectively help a company sell its bonds.

Underfunded A pension plan in which the plan assets are less than the projected benefit obligation.

Underwriter An investment bank that arranges and agrees to sell the initial issuance of a company's bonds.

Vesting An event by which employees are granted pension benefits even if they leave the employ of the company.

ASSIGNMENT MATERIAL

Assessing Your Recall

Multiple Choice Quizzes

10-1 Describe the following terms relating to a bond: indenture agreement, bond covenants, face value, maturity date, bond interest rate, interest payments, and collateral.

10-2 Explain what is meant by the "yield" rate of interest with respect to bond issues.

10-3 Distinguish between the stated or nominal rate of interest on a bond and the effective or real rate.

10-4 Discuss the role of the investment banker in the issuance of bonds by a company.

10-5 Describe what the term "best efforts basis" means in the issuance of bonds and why it is important to a company.

10-6 Discuss how bonds are priced and how the price is affected by changes in market interest rates.

10-7 Describe the following terms as they relate to the issuance and sale of bonds: par, premium, and discount.

10-8 Discuss the meaning of the term "bond discount" and what is meant by the amortization of a bond discount.

10-9 Describe the procedure for the retirement of debt before maturity. Why would a company retire debt early?

10-10 Discuss the benefits of leasing, from the point of view of both the lessee and the lessor.

10-11 List and discuss the criteria used to distinguish capital leases from operating leases for lessees.

10-12 Differentiate between defined contribution pension plans and defined benefit plans.

10-13 Define the following terms: overfunded, underfunded, and fully funded.

10-14 What are post-employment benefits? Why are we now required to treat them similarly to pension obligations?

10-15 Explain what the following ratios tell you about a company's financial health: debt/equity ratio and times-interest-earned ratio.

Applying Your Knowledge

10-16 (Entries for bond transactions)
The Standard Mills Corporation issues 100 bonds, each with a face value of $1,000, that mature in 20 years. The bonds carry a 10% interest rate and are sold to yield 8%. They pay interest semi-annually.

Required:

a. Calculate the issuing price of the bonds, and show the journal entry to record the issuance of the bonds.

b. Calculate interest expense for the first year, and show the journal entries to record this expense and the corresponding interest payments.

10-17 (Entries for bond transactions)
Spring Water Company Ltd. needed to raise $1,000,000 of additional capital to finance the expansion of its bottled water company. After consulting an investment banker and the VP Finance of the company, it decided to issue bonds. The bonds had a maturity value of $1,000,000 and an annual interest rate of 9%, paid interest semi-annually, on June 30 and December 31, and matured on December 31, 2013. The bonds were issued on January 1, 2004, for $937,689, which represented a yield of 10%.

Required:

a. Show the journal entry to record the issuance of the bonds.

b. Calculate the interest expense for the first year and show the journal entries to record the interest expense and the corresponding interest payments.

c. Spring Water Company wanted to raise $1,000,000 but succeeded in raising only $937,689. Explain why the investors were not willing to pay $1,000,000 for the bonds.

10-18 (Issuance of bonds)
The Alphabet Toy Company has plans for a plant expansion and needs to raise additional capital to pay for the construction. The company is considering issuing six-year, 8% first mortgage bonds with a par value of $400,000. The bonds will pay interest semi-annually.

Required:

a. Calculate the amount of cash the company will receive if the bonds are sold at a yield rate of:

1. 6%

2. 10%

b. Prepare the journal entry Alphabet Toy would record at the time of the issuance under each of the alternative yields. Also prepare the journal entries to record the interest expense for the first two periods under each alternative.

c. What is a mortgage bond? Explain how the fact that this is a mortgage bond would affect the interest rate dictated by the market (the yield rate).

10-19 (Interest calculation on a bond)
Birch Company Ltd. issued bonds twice in recent years. The first issue has a $400,000 par value, a 10% bond interest rate, and a seven-year maturity; it sold on January 1, 2003, to yield 8%. The second issue has a $300,000 par value, a 6% bond interest rate, and a five-year maturity; it sold on January 1, 2004, to yield 8%. Both issues pay interest on July 1 and January 1.

Required:

a. What amount of interest payments will Birch Company make related to the year 2004?

b. What amount of interest expense will Birch report for the year 2004?

c. Prepare journal entries to record Birch's interest expense and payments in 2004.

d. Explain why it is reasonable that both bonds sold to yield 8%.

10-20   (Interest accrual with bond discount)
On January 1, 2004, Rupert Company Ltd. issued $300,000 of 10-year, 8% debentures. The effective yield on the bonds at the time of issue was 10%. Interest is paid semi-annually.

Required:

a. What amount of interest will Rupert pay every six months?

b. Calculate the issue price of the bonds and prepare the journal entry for the issuance.

c. Prepare the journal entries for June 30, 2004, and December 31, 2004, to record the accrual of interest expense and the payment of the interest owed.

d. Give the balance sheet presentation of the bond liability at December 31, 2004.

10-21   (Calculation of bond issuance and redemption amounts)
Fraser Equipment Company Inc. issues 500 $1,000, 10% bonds maturing in eight years. The bonds pay interest semi-annually and are issued to yield 8%.

Required:

a. Calculate the issue price of the bonds and the interest expense for the first year and give the journal entry to record the issuance.

b. Calculate the book value of the bonds two years after issuance—that is, at the beginning of the third year.

c. Calculate the market value of the bonds two years after issuance, if the market yield has increased to 12%.

d. Compare the book value (calculated in part b) and the market value (calculated in part c) at the end of five years. Explain why a difference exists.

e. Assume the company redeems the bonds at the beginning of the third year by purchasing them in the open market; give the journal entry to record this.

10-22   (Lease)
Dash Corporation leases automobiles from Speedy Leasing for use by its sales personnel. The leased vehicles are used for two years and then returned to Speedy Leasing. All maintenance and repair is done by Speedy. Dash makes a deposit of $4,000 at the beginning of the lease on each car and makes monthly payments of $500 per car. The deposit is refunded when the car is returned in reasonable condition. Dash currently has 20 cars under lease from Speedy.

Required:

a. Is the lease an operating lease or a capital lease? Explain.

b. What amount of expense related to the lease will Dash record for the current year?

c. How should the $4,000 deposit per car be reported by Dash?

10-23   (Capital lease)

On July 1, 2003, the Turlotec Manufacturing Corporation leased one of its machines to Start Mechanical Corporation. The machine had cost Turlotec $650,000 to manufacture, and would normally have sold for $800,000. The 10-year lease was classified as a capital lease for accounting purposes. The lease agreement required equal semi-annual payments of $70,795 payable on December 31 and June 30 each year, which reflected an interest rate of 14%. Start Mechanical closes its books annually on December 31.

Required:

Show the necessary journal entries relating to the lease in the books of Start Mechanical Corporation during 2003 and 2004. Assume that the machine has a useful life of 10 years and zero residual value, and that the company uses straight-line amortization.

10-24   (Lease)

Transprovincial Buslines experienced a major increase in people using the buses in the last three months of 2003. On January 1, 2004, Transprovincial entered into an agreement to lease four new buses from NewBus Leasing Ltd. The 10-year lease agreement on each bus requires Transprovincial to pay $1,000 per month at the end of each month starting January 31, 2004. At the end of the lease term, title to the buses transfers to Transprovincial. The lease is structured with a 12% interest rate. The buses have a useful life of 15 years and are amortized on a straight-line basis with no anticipated residual value.

Required:

a. Is the agreement a capital or an operating lease? Explain.

b. Assuming Transprovincial records the leases on the four buses as capital leases, calculate the present value of the lease payments.

c. Should Transprovincial amortize these buses over 10 years or over 15 years? Explain.

d. Present the amounts related to the lease that would appear on the income statements and balance sheets of Transprovincial Buslines at the end of January 2004 and February 2004.

10-25   (Operating or capital lease)

The *Provincial Star* newspaper has decided to lease a truck to deliver its newspapers. The company signs an agreement on January 1, 2004, to lease a truck for $650 per month for the next three years. The title to the truck reverts to the lessor at the end of the lease term. The lease calls for payments on the last day of the month starting on January 31, 2004. The *Provincial Star* closes its books monthly and believes that 9% is an appropriate yield rate for the lease.

Required:

a. Assuming that the fair market value of the truck is $35,000 and its expected useful life is 10 years, how should the *Provincial Star* account for this lease?

b. Assuming that the market value of the truck is $22,000 and that the lessor believes its useful life is five years, how should the *Provincial Star* account for this lease?

c. Show the appropriate accounting entries for the first two months of 2004 for the lease under both the operating lease method and the capital lease method. Assume that the *Provincial Star* amortizes its assets using the straight-line method.

User Perspective Problems

10-26 (Bond covenants)
As a bond investor, explain the importance of bond covenants in assessing the risk of a particular bond investment.

10-27 (Bond covenants)
Discuss the types of covenants bond investors might like to include in a bond indenture agreement to protect their investment. Explain why these covenants would be effective.

10-28 (Seniority of bond investments)
In assessing the riskiness of a particular bond, discuss the importance of the seniority of various liabilities of the company and how it affects your assessment.

10-29 (Collateral for long-term debt)
As a lender, discuss how much comfort you might get from knowing about the existence of long-term assets, specifically (1) property, plant, and equipment and (2) goodwill, in making a long-term loan to a company.

10-30 (Operating leases)
Suppose that you are a stock analyst and you are evaluating a company that has a significant number of operating leases.

> *Required:*
>
> a. Discuss the potential misstatement of the financial statements that may occur because of this treatment. Specifically, address the impact of this type of accounting on the debt/equity ratio and return on assets ratio.
>
> b. Using the disclosures provided in the financial statements, explain how you would adjust the statements to address the issues discussed in part a).

10-31 (Impact of lease treatment on net income)
Suppose that you are a manager whose remuneration is partially tied to meeting a particular income target for your company. How would the choice of an operating lease over a capital lease affect your ability to meet the target? Given a choice, which accounting treatment would you select? Does your answer depend on whether you are in the early years of the lease versus the later years?

10-32 (Lease or buy)
Starburst Brewery Ltd. must replace some of its old equipment with new stainless steel equipment to avoid losing its licence. The controller is unsure whether to purchase the equipment with borrowed money or to lease the equipment. If purchased, the equipment will cost $500,000 and have an estimated useful life of 20 years and no residual value. The Sussex Bank is willing to provide the $500,000 to Starburst. The terms of the loan are that the 10-year note would bear interest at 12%. Starburst would be required to pay the interest annually at the end of each year. The principal amount would be due at the end of the 10 years. A local rental company is willing to lease the equipment to Starburst for 15 years at an interest rate of 10%. At the end of each year, Starburst would be required to pay the leasing company $60,000. At the end of the lease period, title to the equipment would remain with the lessor.

> *Required:*
>
> a. Calculate the present value of the future cash flows under both arrangements.
>
> b. State what amounts would appear in Starburst's income statement and balance sheet for the first year, under both alternatives.

c. Which of the two financing alternatives would you recommend to the controller? Why? What factors, other than cash payments directly related to financing, might be important to the decision?

10-33   (Pension plans)
Describe the two main types of pension plans. As a manager, which plan would you recommend to the senior executives of the company? Explain your answer. As an employee, which plan would you prefer? Explain your answer.

10-34   (Post-employment benefits)
In Canada, accountants now have to record the future obligation for post-employment benefits. In the past, the cost of these benefits was recorded as it was incurred (pay-as-you-go). As a manager, explain why you would prefer to continue to use the pay-as-you-go method. What accounting concepts support the change in accounting method from pay-as-you-go to recording the future obligation before the employees retire?

10-35   (Liabilities not recorded)
In assessing the riskiness of a company, stock analysts are often concerned more with the liabilities that do not appear on the company's financial statements than with those that do appear. Discuss the major types of liabilities that might not appear on the company's financial statements. Describe the information that may be included in the notes to the financial statements concerning these liabilities.

10-36   (Interest capitalization and liquidity analysis)
Suppose that you are evaluating the liquidity of a company. What effect does the capitalization of interest have on your analysis—that is, how does it affect the ratios that you might calculate to evaluate liquidity?

Reading and Interpreting Published Financial Statements

10-37   (Long-term notes and debentures)
Notes 10 and 12 to the 2001 financial statements of **CHC Helicopter Corp.** (Exhibit 10-17) describe the senior subordinated notes and subordinated debentures currently held by the company.

Required:

a. What are senior subordinated notes and subordinated debentures?

b. The senior subordinated notes pay interest each January 15 and July 15. CHC Helicopter Corp.'s year end is April 30. Assume interest was paid on January 15, 2002, as required. Prepare the journal entry to accrue the interest to April 30, 2002, and then prepare the journal entry on July 15, 2002, to pay the second instalment of interest.

c. Note 12 states that the company "may redeem [buy back from the investors] the debentures at a redemption price ranging from 102.4% to 100% of the principal amount of the debentures being redeemed." Under what circumstances would the company want to exercise this option?

d. Are the debentures secured or unsecured? Explain.

CHC HELICOPTER CORP. (2001)
10. Senior subordinated notes

EXHIBIT 10-17

The €145.0 million ($197.6 million) senior subordinated notes bear interest at 11¾% per annum, payable semi-annually on January 15 and July 15, and are due July 2007.

The senior subordinated notes and the subsidiary guarantees are senior subordinated indebtedness and rank behind all of the Company's existing and future senior indebtedness including borrowings under the senior credit facilities (Note 9). The senior subordinated notes rank equally with other senior subordinated indebtedness and rank senior to subordinated indebtedness. The guarantees of the senior subordinated notes rank behind all existing and future guarantor senior indebtedness of the guarantor subsidiaries, including guarantees of borrowings under the senior credit facilities.

The Company may redeem the senior subordinated notes in whole or in part at any time on or after July 15, 2004 at a redemption price ranging from 105.875% to 100% of the principal amount of the senior subordinated notes being redeemed. In addition, at any time prior to July 15, 2003, the Company may redeem up to 35% of the original principal amount of the senior subordinated notes, within 90 days of one or more public equity offerings, with the net proceeds of such offerings at a redemption price equal to 111.75% of the principal amount provided that immediately after giving effect to such redemption at least 65% of the original principal amount of the senior subordinated notes remains outstanding.

12. Subordinated debentures

The subordinated debentures bear interest at 8% per annum, payable semi-annually on April 30 and October 31, and are due August 2007. The debentures are subordinated to all senior indebtedness including the senior credit facilities (Note 9) and the senior subordinated notes (Note 10). The Company may redeem the debentures at a redemption price ranging from 102.4% to 100% of the principal amount of the debentures being redeemed. The trust indenture requires mandatory sinking fund payments and equivalent subsequent redemptions of subordinated debentures of $743,000 on August 31 of each of the next six years. The sinking fund payment required on August 31, 2001 is included in current portion of long-term obligations. The Company has pledged its shares of CHC Helicopter Holdings Limited, a wholly-owned subsidiary, as collateral for the debentures.

10-38 (Short- and long-term debt)
Accompanying its 2001 financial statements, **Comac Food Group Inc.** presented Note 8 describing its long-term debt. This is reproduced in Exhibit 10-18.

Required:

a. The note reveals that $26,000 of the company's total debt as at March 31, 2001, was classified as short-term. Read the details provided in the note regarding the payments on the debt and present calculations to show how the $26,000 was determined.

b. The note makes frequent use of the term "collateralized." Explain in your own words what this means.

c. Identify the collateral attached to each category of Comac's debt.

d. What effect would the type of collateral have on a company's ability to borrow money?

EXHIBIT 10-18

COMAC FOOD GROUP INC. (2001)
8. LONG TERM DEBT
Long term debt is comprised of the following:

in dollars	2001	2000
a) Bank loan	**66,000**	78,000
b) Demand bank loans	**35,000**	49,000
c) Notes payable	–	44,000
	101,000	171,000
Less current portion	**26,000**	70,000
	75,000	101,000

a) The loan was issued under the Small Business Loan program to finance the construction of a corporate store. The loan is collateralized by a chattel mortgage on the store, bears interest at the bank's prime rate plus 3% and has principal repayments of $1,000 per month to August 2006.

b) The loan is collateralized by a security agreement covering the assets at a specific store location, bears interest at the bank's prime rate plus 1.5% and has principal repayments of $1,200 per month to September 2003. Providing the Company continues to satisfy the conditions of the loan agreement, the lender has indicated that they do not intend to demand repayment and accordingly the loan is classified as long term.

c) The notes payable are collateralized by a general security agreement covering all the assets of the Company, bear no interest and have monthly principal repayments of $4,200 to February 2001. The notes are also convertible at the holder's option into Class B common shares of the Company at a rate of $1.00 per share to March 3, 2001. The notes payable have been repaid in full and none were converted to shares.

The Company has calculated the debt component as the present value of the required interest and principal repayments discounted at a rate of 6% which approximates the interest rate that would have been applicable to non-convertible debt at the time of its issuance. The difference at acquisition date of $83,000 between the face amount of the loan and the calculated debt component has been presented as contributed surplus.

As at March 25, 2001 principal repayments are as follows:

in dollars	
2002	26,000
2003	26,000
2004	19,000
2005	12,000
2006	12,000
Thereafter	6,000
	101,000

Cash interest payments made during 2001 amounted to $6,000 (2000 - $31,000).

Operating Credit Facility
In addition to the long term credit facilities, the Company has a demand operating credit facility of $500,000 of which $200,000 is available for general operating purposes and $300,000 available to fund acquisition and development of franchise locations. The line of credit is due on demand and bears interest at the bank's prime rate plus 2%. A general security agreement and floating charge debenture covering all assets of the Company are pledged as collateral. At March 25, 2001, $nil (2000 - $nil) was drawn on the credit facility.

Lenders' Interest Rate
Lenders' prime rate at March 25, 2001 was 6.75% (2000 - 7.5%).

10-39 (Long-term debt)
In Exhibit 10-19, Note 9 to the 2002 financial statements of **Cara Operations Limited** describes the long-term debt currently held by the company.

Required:

a. Provide some reasons why the interest rate on the capital leases is higher than the interest rate on the medium-term notes.

b. In Note 9, Cara Operations discloses the principal repayments that will be made in each of the next five years as well as the aggregate amount due after the end of the five years. This is a required disclosure under GAAP. Explain why users need this information.

c. Of Cara's total debt of $163,904 thousand on March 31, 2001, $3,880 thousand is due within one year and therefore classified as a current liability. Normally, all debt not due within a year is simply classified as long-term. Accordingly, Cara reports long-term debt of $160,024 thousand. However, if we were to identify an intermediate range and define debt due within two to five years as "medium-term" rather than long-term, how much of Cara's debt could be considered medium-term? Similarly, if we were to redefine "long-term" liabilities as debt not due for more than five years, how much of Cara's debt would be considered long-term?

d. Do you think a classification system such as the one described in part c) would be useful to readers of financial statements? Explain why or why not.

Note ⑨ **Long-Term Debt**   CARA OPERATIONS LIMITED (2001) EXHIBIT 10-19

(in thousands of dollars)	2002	2001
Medium term notes	$ 149,550	$ 149,479
Obligations under capital lease	7,042	9,608
Other loans	7,312	8,030
	163,904	167,117
Less: Current portion	3,880	4,420
	$ 160,024	$ 162,697

Medium Term Notes

Unsecured medium term notes with a face value of $150 million bear interest at 5.95% per annum paid semi-annually in arrears on December 12 and June 12 and, unless prepaid, fall due in June 2008. The notes have been issued under a trust indenture and are net of a discount on issuance of $0.6 million which is being amortized over the term of the debt. The fair market value of these notes at year-end is estimated to be approximately $136.9 million (2001 – $140.5 million) at a rate of 7.75% (2001 – 7.1%) which is management's view of the rate that would be available for medium term notes with similar terms and maturity.

During the year, the Corporation entered into interest rate swap contracts to convert the current 5.95% fixed rate of interest paid by the Corporation on its medium term notes to a floating variable short-term rate based on 3 month bankers' acceptances for the term of the medium term notes. This is part of the Corporation's strategy to reduce interest cost in the context of current economic conditions. For the year ended March 31, 2002, a net interest differential of $2.3 million was recognized on the fixed-to-floating interest rate swap contract and reduced the net interest expense of the Corporation. The average effective rate of interest was 3.7%.

Obligations Under Capital Lease

Obligations under capital lease bear interest at an average rate of 7.3% (2001 – 7.3%) per annum; equipment under capital lease with a net book value of $7.8 million (2001 – $9.7 million) was pledged as security.

Other Loans

Other loans bear interest at rates ranging from 7.0% to 9.5% and mature between fiscal 2005 and fiscal 2012. The underlying property, plant and equipment acquired with the proceeds from these loans have been pledged as security.

The 5 year schedule of repayment of long-term debt is as follows (in millions of dollars): 2003 – $3.9; 2004 – $3.2; 2005 – $3.2; 2006 – $1.0; 2007 – $0.3 and thereafter – $152.3.

10-40   (Long-term debt)

Placer Dome Inc. includes information about its long-term debt in Note 11 of its 2001 financial statements. A portion of this note is included in Exhibit 10-20. Amounts are stated in millions of U.S. dollars.

Required:

a. Placer Dome Inc. has three bond issues outstanding at the end of 2001. Were these bonds issued at par, below par, or above par? How do you know?

b. Calculate the amount of bond interest that would be paid out by Placer Dome Inc. in 2002, assuming that no new bonds were issued and that none of the bonds were retired early.

c. Although the bonds have maturity dates several years apart, the bond interest being paid on each issue is very similar. Provide some reasons why the interest rates would be similar.

EXHIBIT 10-19

PLACER DOME INC. (2001)

Consolidated long-term debt and capital leases comprise the following:

December 31	2001	2000
Placer Dome Inc.		
Bonds, unsecured (note 14(d))		
May 15, 2003 at 7.125% per annum	$ 200	$ 200
June 15, 2007 at 7.125% per annum	100	100
June 15, 2015 at 7.75% per annum	100	100
Preferred Securities, unsecured (note 14(a, d))		
Series A, December 31, 2045 at 8.625%		
per annum	185	185
Series B, December 31, 2045 at 8.5%		
per annum	77	77
Medium–term notes, unsecured (note 14(b, d))	170	200
Capital leases (note 14(c))	10	16
	842	878
Current portion	(35)	(35)
	$ 807	$ 843

(b) The interest rates range from 6.1% to 8.0% and the notes mature between 2002 and 2026.

(c) The Group is obligated under capital leases for mobile mining equipment for remaining terms ranging from one to four years. All capital lease agreements provide that the Group can purchase the leased equipment at fair value at the end of the lease term. At December 31, 2001 and 2000, $4 million and $14 million respectively, of leased property was included in plant and equipment, net of $7 million and $17 million, respectively, of accumulated depreciation and depletion.

10-41   (Pension plans)

Aliant Inc. is a major telecommunications and information technology company in Atlantic Canada. Note 10 accompanying its 2001 financial statements dealing with its pension plan and other employee benefit obligations is presented in Exhibit 10-21.

Required:

a. What types of pension plans and other post-employment benefit plans does Aliant have?

b. At the end of 2001, was Aliant's pension plan underfunded or overfunded? By how much?

c. At the end of 2001, did Aliant's balance sheet show an asset or a liability related to its pension plans? In what amount?

d. Try to explain how a company could have underfunded pension plans and show an asset related to them on its balance sheet, or have overfunded pension plans and show a liability related to them on its balance sheet. Use the information in Aliant's note 10 and your answers to parts b) and c) above to illustrate this.

ALIANT INC. (2001)
NOTE 10
Accrued benefit obligation

The Company maintains both contributory defined contribution and non-contributory defined benefit final average pension plans for the benefit of employees of certain subsidiaries. The Company also offers other non-pension post employment benefits to employees of certain subsidiaries, including life insurance and health care plans.

The total expense for the Company's defined contribution plans providing pension benefits was $7,361,000 (2000 – $7,850,000).

Information about the Company's defined benefit plans in aggregate are as follows:

	Pension benefit plans		Other benefit plans	
(thousands of dollars)	**2001**	2000	**2001**	2000
Accrued benefit obligation				
Balance at beginning of year	**$1,157,699**	$ 932,087	**$ 132,641**	$ —
Adjustment to opening balance for change in accounting policy	**—**	182,515	**—**	121,290
Current service cost	**25,529**	19,358	**3,060**	2,738
Interest cost	**83,324**	80,630	**9,002**	8,613
Benefits paid	**(58,629)**	(56,891)	**(2,570)**	—
Actuarial (gains) losses	**60,619**	—	**(3,248)**	—
Balance at end of year	**$1,268,542**	$1,157,699	**$ 138,885**	132,641
Plan assets				
Fair value at beginning of year	**$1,294,629**	$1,276,611	**$ —**	$ —
Actual return on plan assets	**(26,746)**	78,980	**—**	—
Employer contributions	**4,428**	—	**2,570**	—
Benefits paid	**(58,629)**	(56,891)	**(2,570)**	—
Fund expenses	**(5,142)**	(4,071)	**—**	—
Fair value at end of year	**$1,208,540**	$1,294,629	**$ —**	$ —
Funded status – plan surplus (deficit)	**$ (60,002)**	$ 136,930	**$ (138,885)**	$ (132,641)
Unamortized net actuarial (gains) losses	**155,129**	(46,352)	**—**	—
Accrued benefit asset (liability)	**$ 95,127**	$ 90,578	**$ (138,885)**	$ (132,641)

The plan does not directly own common shares of the Company. The plan does own units of index funds which may hold shares of the Company by virtue of the fact that the shares of the Company are listed on the relevant index.

The significant actuarial assumptions adopted in measuring the Company's accrued benefit obligations are as follows (weighted-average assumptions as of December 31):

	Pension benefit plans		Other benefit plans	
	2001	2000	**2001**	2000
Discount rate	**7.00%**	7.25%	**7.00%**	7.25%
Expected long-term rate of return on plan assets	**9.00%**	9.00%	**—**	—
Rate of compensation increase	**3.00%**	3.00%	**3.00%**	3.00%

For measurement purposes, a 6.5 per cent annual rate of increase in the per capita cost of covered health care benefits was assumed for five years. The rate was assumed to decrease gradually to 4.5 per cent for

five years and then to 2.5 per cent and remain at that level thereafter.

The Company's net benefit plan expense is as follows:

	Pension benefit plans		Other benefit plans	
(thousands of dollars)	**2001**	2000	**2001**	2000
Current service cost	**$ 25,529**	$ 19,358	**$ 3,060**	$ 2,738
Interest cost	**83,324**	80,630	**9,002**	8,613
Expected return on plan assets	**(115,107)**	(111,754)	**—**	—
Net benefit plan (recovery) expense	**$ (6,254)**	$ (11,766)	**$ 12,062**	$ 11,351

10-42 (Pension plans and other post-retirement benefits)
Note 10 from the 2001 financial statements of **Investors Group Inc.** dealing with its employee pension plan, supplementary employee retirement plan, and other post-retirement benefit plans, is presented in Exhibit 10-22. Dollar amounts are in thousands.

Hint: In the Post-retirement benefit plans section of Note 10, the unlabelled subtotal (with the amounts $22,780 and $20,713 for 2001 and 2000, respectively) represents the plan deficit.

Required:

a. For each of Investors Group's three categories of future benefit plans:

  1. Identify whether the plan is underfunded or overfunded and by what amount.

  2. State whether an asset or a liability would be reflected on the balance sheet and in what amount.

b. Is there a significant difference between your answers for a1) and 2) for any of the individual plans? If so, comment on it.

c. For all of Investors Group's three categories of future benefit plans combined:

  1. Identify whether they are, in total, underfunded or overfunded and by what amount.

  2. State whether, overall, a net asset or a net liability would be reflected on the balance sheet, and in what amount.

d. Is there an anomaly between your answers for c1) and 2) for the three plans combined? If so, comment on it.

e. Many assumptions are required in accounting for pension plans and other post-retirement benefits. Review the information disclosed in Note 10 regarding key assumptions made by Investors Group, and answer the following questions:

  1. What is the average rate that the company estimates will be earned on the pension plan assets?

  2. By what average rate does the company estimate its salaries will rise?

  3. Why would the company use a different discount rate (for calculating the present value of the future obligations) from one year to another and from one plan to another?

INVESTORS GROUP INC. (2001)
NOTES TO CONSOLIDATED FINANCIAL STATEMENTS

EXHIBIT 10-22

December 31, 2001 (In thousands of dollars, except share amounts)

10. Pension plans and other post-retirement benefits

Employee pension plan

The Company maintains a defined benefit pension plan which covers substantially all of its eligible employees. Changes in the fair value of plan assets and the accrued pension obligation are as follows:

	2001	2000
Fair value of plan assets		
Balance, beginning of year	$ 145,797	$ 128,652
Employee contributions	2,909	2,186
Benefits paid	(7,358)	(5,913)
Return on plan assets	1,233	20,872
Balance, end of year	142,581	145,797
Accrued benefit obligation		
Balance, beginning of year	77,660	76,951
Benefits paid	(7,358)	(5,913)
Current service cost	2,519	1,569
Employee contributions	2,909	2,186
Interest cost	5,717	5,831
Actuarial losses (gains)	2,803	(2,964)
Balance, end of year	84,250	77,660
Funded status – plan surplus	58,331	68,137
Unamortized net actuarial gains	(21,499)	(36,435)
Accrued pension asset	$ 36,832	$ 31,702

Pension expense (income) was determined as follows:

	2001	2000
Current service cost	$ 2,519	$ 1,569
Interest cost	5,717	5,831
Expected return on plan assets	(10,032)	(8,875)
Amortization of net actuarial gains	(3,334)	(2,009)
	$ (5,130)	$ (3,484)

Significant weighted-average actuarial assumptions:

	2001	2000
Discount rate	6.95%	7.20%
Expected long-term rate of return on plan assets	7.00%	7.00%
Rate of compensation increase	6.10%	6.10%

Supplementary employee retirement plan

The Company maintains an unfunded supplementary pension plan for certain executive officers.

	2001	2000
Accrued benefit liability, end of year	$ 12,446	$ 10,321
Pension expense	$ 2,847	$ 1,352
Significant weighted-average actuarial assumptions		
Discount rate	6.88%	7.00%
Rate of compensation increase	6.10%	6.10%

EXHIBIT 10-22 CONT.

INVESTORS GROUP INC. (2001)
NOTES TO CONSOLIDATED FINANCIAL STATEMENTS

December 31, 2001 (In thousands of dollars, except share amounts)

10. Pension plans and other post-retirement benefits (cont'd)

Post-retirement benefit plans

The Company also provides certain unfunded post-retirement health care and life insurance benefits to eligible retirees.

	2001	2000
Accrued benefit liability		
Balance, beginning of year	$ **20,713**	$ 20,435
Benefits paid	**(835)**	(691)
Current service cost	**1,306**	1,639
Interest cost	**1,596**	1,630
Actuarial gains	**–**	(2,300)
	22,780	20,713
Unamortized actuarial gains	**2,158**	2,300
Balance, end of year	$ **24,938**	$ 23,013
Benefit expense was determined as follows:		
Current service cost	$ **1,306**	$ 1,639
Interest cost	**1,596**	1,630
Amortization of net actuarial gains	**(142)**	–
	$ **2,760**	$ 3,269

A discount rate of 7.25% was used to determine the non-pension post-retirement benefit obligation and a 10% trend rate was used to measure the per capita cost of covered health care benefits, declining to 4.5% annually after five years.

10-43   (Debt/equity ratio ratios)

The balance sheet from the 2001 annual report of **Xerox Inc.** is included in Exhibit 10-23.

Required:

a. Calculate the debt/equity ratios for 2000 and 2001.

b. Write a short report evaluating the ratios that you calculated in part a).

XEROX INC. (2001)
Consolidated Balance Sheets

EXHIBIT 10-23

(in millions)	December 31 2001	December 31 2000
		Restated Note 2
Assets		
Cash and cash equivalents	$ 3,990	$ 1,750
Accounts receivable, net	1,896	2,269
Finance receivables, net	3,922	4,392
Inventories	1,364	1,983
Deferred taxes and other current assets	1,428	1,078
Total Current Assets	12,600	11,472
Finance receivables due after one year, net	5,756	6,406
Equipment on operating leases, net	804	1,266
Land, buildings and equipment, net	1,999	2,527
Investments in affiliates, at equity	632	1,270
Intangible and other assets, net	4,453	3,763
Goodwill, net	1,445	1,549
Total Assets	**$27,689**	**$28,253**
Liabilities and Equity		
Short-term debt and current portion of long-term debt	$ 6,637	$ 3,080
Accounts payable	704	1,050
Accrued compensation and benefits costs	724	645
Unearned income	244	233
Other current liabilities	1,951	1,536
Total Current Liabilities	10,260	6,544
Long-term debt	10,128	15,557
Postretirement medical benefits	1,233	1,197
Deferred taxes and other liabilities	2,018	1,925
Total Liabilities	23,639	25,223
Deferred ESOP benefits	(135)	(221)
Minorities' interests in equity of subsidiaries	73	87
Obligation for equity put options	—	32
Company-obligated, mandatorily redeemable preferred securities of subsidiary trusts holding solely subordinated debentures of the Company	1,687	684
Preferred stock	605	647
Common stock, including additional paid in capital	2,622	2,231
Retained earnings	1,031	1,150
Accumulated other comprehensive loss	(1,833)	(1,580)
Total Liabilities and Equity	**$27,689**	**$28,253**

Shares of common stock issued and outstanding were (in thousands) 722,314 and 668,576 at December 31, 2001 and December 31, 2000, respectively.

The accompanying notes are an integral part of the consolidated financial statements.

10-44   (Debt/equity and times interest earned ratios)
The balance sheet and income statement from the 2001 annual report of **Talisman Energy Inc.** are included in Exhibit 10-24.

Required:

a. Calculate the debt/equity ratios and the times interest earned ratios for 2000 and 2001.

b. Write a short report evaluating the ratios you calculated in part a).

c. Talisman's amount of debt and shareholders' equity both increased between 2000 and 2001. Analyze the main components that caused these increases and comment on how these items might affect your evaluation of the health of this company.

    TALISMAN ENERGY INC. (2001)
EXHIBIT 10-24   **CONSOLIDATED BALANCE SHEETS**
(December 31)

(millions of Canadian dollars)	**2001**	2000
Assets		
Current		
Cash (note 14)	**17**	76
Accounts receivable	**654**	843
Inventories (note 3)	**99**	103
Prepaid expenses	**29**	20
	799	1,042
Accrued employee pension benefit asset (note 4)	**51**	52
Other assets	**128**	81
Goodwill (notes 1(o) and 2)	**467**	–
Property, plant and equipment (note 5)	**9,461**	7,501
	10,107	7,634
Total assets	**10,906**	8,676
Liabilities		
Current		
Accounts payable and accrued liabilities	**869**	1,031
Income and other taxes payable	**146**	250
Current portion of long-term debt (note 6)	**189**	30
	1,204	1,311
Deferred credits	**71**	44
Provision for future site restoration (note 10)	**619**	498
Long-term debt (note 6)	**2,794**	1,703
Future income taxes (note 13)	**1,989**	1,455
	5,473	3,700
Contingencies and commitments (notes 9 and 10)		
Shareholders' equity		
Preferred securities (note 7)	**431**	431
Common shares (note 8)	**2,831**	2,849
Contributed surplus	**77**	77
Retained earnings	**890**	308
	4,229	3,665
Total liabilities and shareholders' equity	**10,906**	8,676

TALISMAN ENERGY INC. (2001)

CONSOLIDATED STATEMENTS OF INCOME

(Years ended December 31)

EXHIBIT 10-24
CONT.

(millions of Canadian dollars except per share amounts)	2001	2000	1999
Revenue			
Gross sales	5,047	4,836	2,318
Less royalties	989	946	389
Net sales	4,058	3,890	1,929
Other (note 11)	82	99	46
Total revenue	4,140	3,989	1,975
Expenses			
Operating	946	827	603
General and administrative	108	95	70
Depreciation, depletion and amortization	1,313	1,153	747
Dry hole	113	77	51
Exploration	147	100	79
Interest on long-term debt (note 5)	139	136	120
Other (note 12)	25	15	(61)
Total expenses	2,791	2,403	1,609
Income before taxes	1,349	1,586	366
Taxes (note 13)			
Current income tax	342	334	49
Future income tax	72	196	109
Petroleum revenue tax	149	150	31
	563	680	189
Net income	786	906	177
Preferred security charges, net of tax	24	22	13
Net income available to common shareholders	762	884	164
Per common share (Canadian dollars)			
Net income	5.65	6.41	1.31
Diluted net income	5.55	6.32	1.30
Average number of common shares outstanding (millions)	135	138	125
Diluted number of common shares outstanding (millions)	137	140	126

Beyond the Book

10-45 (Analysis of a company's liabilities)
Choose a company as directed by your instructor and do the following exercises:

a. Prepare a quick analysis of the noncurrent liability accounts by listing the beginning and ending amounts in these accounts and calculating the net change, in both dollar and percentage terms, for the most recent year.

b. If any of the accounts changed by more than 10%, try to give an explanation for this change.

c. What percentage of the company's total liabilities comes from long-term bank loans? Long-term bonds? Has this percentage changed significantly over the last year?

d. Does the company have any other long-term liabilities? Is so, describe each of them.

e. What interest rates is the company paying on its long-term debt? (You will likely need to look in the notes to the financial statements to find the answer to this question.)

f. Calculate the debt/equity ratio and the times interest earned ratio for the company. Comment on the company's financial health.

Cases

10-46   Wasselec's Moving and Storage Corporation

Wasselec's Moving and Storage Corporation is a small company based in the Halifax area. It operates in both the residential and commercial markets. To serve its various clients, Wasselec's owns two large moving trucks (tractor and trailer units), six medium-sized cartage trucks, two large vans, and two cars. Because its business relies on its vehicles, it has always been the policy of the corporation to purchase new vehicles on a regular rotation basis. Its accountant and vehicle service manager have established guidelines that trigger when a new vehicle should be purchased. For example, the large vans are replaced every 200,000 kilometres, the tractors every nine years, and the trailers every 15 years. The President of the corporation recently read an article about the increasing trend towards leasing. She wonders if Wasselec should start leasing its vehicles instead of buying them, and has asked the accountant for some guidance in this matter. The accountant has asked you, a recent addition to the accounting department, for a summary of the advantages and disadvantages of ownership versus leasing.

Required:
Draft a memo to the accountant summarizing the advantages and disadvantages of ownership versus leasing with reference to the types of assets currently owned by Wasselec. Remember as well that the accountant is very busy. Therefore, your memo should be concise.

10-47   Grant's Homemade Ice Cream Shop

Jack and Gillian Grant, owners of Grant's Homemade Ice Cream Shop, have recently expanded their business by moving into a second location in a nearby town. To open the second location, the company had to obtain three large ice-cream machines. To buy the machines would have cost over $15,000, so Jack and Gillian instead decided to lease them.

The lease term is for five years and the machines are expected to have a useful life of 8 to 10 years. According to the lease contract, the present value of the lease payments over the lease term is $8,000 and the Grants can purchase the leased machines for $500 at the end of the five-year lease term. The market value of the leased assets is expected to be approximately $4,000 at the end the lease.

Jack Grant is thrilled with the arrangement: "not only do we get the machines we need, but we don't have to record any liabilities on the balance sheet since I can just report the annual lease payments as rental expense on the income statement."

Required:
Is Jack correct in assuming that the lease payments will be recorded as an expense and that no debt will have to be reported on Grant's balance sheet as a result of this transaction? Fully explain your answer using the three criteria for capital lease recognition presented in the text.

10-48   Regal Cars

Regal Cars has been manufacturing exotic automobiles for over 50 years. It has always prided itself on quality products and high customer satisfaction. All Regal Cars are hand-built to owner specifications. In the past year, the popularity of Regal Cars has increased dramatically following an advertising campaign whereby Regal provided complimentary cars to star members of the local NHL team. To meet this increasing demand, Mark Quaid, owner of Regal Cars, is considering partially automating the production line.

To finance the conversion of the manual line to a robotic system, Quaid will have to raise over $800,000 in capital. The company has been in the Quaid family for over 50 years and Mark is unwilling to sell shares and risk diluting his family's equity in the business. He has identified three potential sources of debt financing and has asked you, the company's accountant, to explain how each option would affect the company's financial statements.

Option 1   Bank Loan

A national bank has offered to lend Regal the necessary funds in the form of a 10-year, 12% bank loan. Annual payments of $80,000 plus interest will be required. Because of the size of the loan, the bank requires that Mark Quaid personally guarantee the loan with a mortgage on the family estate.

Option 2   Bond Issue

Regal can issue a 10-year, 10% bond for the amount required. Currently, similar bonds in the market are providing a return of 8%.

Option 3   Lease

Regal can lease the equipment. The terms of the lease state that annual lease payments of $137,000 must be made over a 10-year lease period. The present value of these payments, assuming an annual interest rate of 16%, would be $662,000. The equipment has a useful life of 12 years and is expected to be worth $100,000 at the end of the 10 years.

> **Required:**
> Prepare a memo to Mark Quaid discussing how each of these options would be reported in Regal Cars' financial statements. You should also include in your memo any other pertinent observations that could influence the financing decision.

10-49   Peterson Corporation

As part of recent contract negotiations, Peterson Corporation has presented two pension plan options to its employees. The employees are to vote on which plan they would like the company to implement. Peterson Corporation owns and operates a chain of grocery stores throughout western Canada and employs over 3,000 people. Most of the employees have little education and limited accounting knowledge.

Your cousin, Karen Cooper, is a cashier at a Peterson store located in Kamloops, B.C., and she has approached you asking for help in determining which pension option to select. She is confused over the terminology used in the proposal and would like you to explain both options in layman's terms so that she can make an informed decision.

Option 1

The company will establish a defined contribution pension plan. The company will contribute 10% of the employee's gross wages to the pension plan each pay period. Vesting will occur immediately and the funds will be placed with an independent trustee to be invested. Employees will have the option of contributing additional funds to the plan.

Option 2

The company will establish a defined benefit plan. The plan guarantees that the employees will receive 2% of the average of the highest five years of salary multiplied by the number of years the employee works for the company. The plan is fully employer funded and vests after five years of continuous service.

> **Required:**
> Briefly explain to Karen the difference between the two plan options. You should remember that Karen is unfamiliar with pension terminology and you may have to explain some terms used in the plan descriptions.

10-50

Jonah Fitzpatrick would like to start investing and is considering purchasing some of the bonds being issued by Jennings Financial. Details of the bond issue were outlined in a recent article in *Financial Times Magazine*. The following is an excerpt from the article:

> Jennings Financial is planning to issue a series of bonds to help finance the acquisition of a large manufacturing facility. In consultation with its investment bankers, the company has decided to issue $25,000,000 of 8%, five-year bonds. Each bond will be denominated at $1,000. The bonds will be classified as senior debenture bonds and will be sold to yield a return of 10%. Because this is such a large issue, the investment banker is required to underwrite the issue. However, given the historical performance and financial strength of the company, a syndicate is willing to guarantee the entire issue.

Jonah is unfamiliar with bond issues and approaches Mike Jacobs, his stockbroker, with some basic questions.

Jonah: "I have always invested in equity securities, but would like to consider investing in the bonds of Jennings Financial this time; however, since I know very little about bond trading, I have a few questions that need answering."

Mike: "Sure, Jonah, why don't you e-mail me a list of the questions and I'll get back to you later in the day."

Required:

Jonah has just sent Mike the following e-mail. Draft an appropriate response.

Mike, here is a list of my questions. I look forward to hearing from you.

1. The advertisement for the bonds issue states that the bonds will be 8% bonds but will yield 10%. Why are there two interest rates presented? Which interest rate should I use when determining my expected return on the bonds?

2. What is a debenture bond? Will I have any security if the company defaults on the bond?

3. What is the purpose of the investment banker? What does it mean to use a syndicate?

4. What if I need my money back before the five-year period? Does the five-year term mean I am locked into this investment for five years?

10-51   Fiche Limited

It is now January 1, 2004, and Fiche Limited is considering a $10-million share issue. The company would like to improve its debt/equity ratio before proceeding with the issue. Fiche's Chief Financial Officer has suggested to the Board of Directors that the company could retire its $5,000,000 of 9%, 10-year bonds. Currently, interest rates have risen, and therefore the bonds could be retired at 99. The board is willing to consider the proposal but would like to see the effect of the transaction on the company's debt/equity ratio.

The bonds were originally sold for 102 and pay interest semi-annually on June 30 and December 31. They will mature on June 30, 2005. The company has always maintained a bond sinking fund (a cash fund set aside specifically to repay the bonds at maturity) so it already has most of the cash needed to retire the bonds. Fiche Limited's accounting policy is to amortize any bond premium or discount using the straight-line method.

Debt and equity information for the company for the past three years is as follows:

FICHE LIMITED
Partial Balance Sheet
December 31

	2003	2002	2001
Current Liabilities	$ 2,650,555	$ 2,695,400	$ 2,873,650
Long-Term Debt			
Bank Loans	8,555,000	7,950,000	7,667,200
Bond Issue	5,015,000	5,025,000	5,035,000
Total Liabilities	$16,220,555	$15,670,400	$15,575,850
Total Equity	$13,520,000	$13,125,000	$12,998,000

Required:

a. Prepare the journal entry to record the retirement of the bond issue.

b. Calculate the effect of retiring the bonds on Fiche's debt/equity ratio.

Critical Thinking Question

10-52 (Pension plans)
For defined benefit pension plans, a formula has been devised for use in calculating the pension expense for each accounting period. When the calculated pension expense is compared to the amount of cash transferred to a trustee to invest in managing the future obligations of the pension plan, there could be a difference between the two amounts. If the amount of cash transferred is less than the pension expense, a liability for the difference results. If the amount of cash transferred is greater, an asset results. The difference between the two amounts is a reflection of either an overfunded or underfunded pension plan. However, these amounts are insignificant compared to the total liability of the corporation with respect to the pension plan.

Required:
Describe the current disclosure requirements for pensions in Canada. Should a company be required to include a liability on the balance sheet which reflects its future obligation with respect to its pension plan? What impact would such a requirement have on the debt/equity ratio? Are users being given enough information about pension plans to allow them to make informed decisions?

APPENDIX : Time Value of Money Tables

TABLE 1
Future Value of $1.00

Periods	0.50%	0.75%	1.00%	1.50%	2.00%	3.00%	4.00%	5.00%	6.00%	7.00%	8.00%
1	1.00500	1.00750	1.01000	1.01500	1.02000	1.03000	1.04000	1.05000	1.06000	1.07000	1.08000
2	1.01003	1.01506	1.02010	1.03023	1.04040	1.06090	1.08160	1.10250	1.12360	1.14490	1.16640
3	1.01508	1.02267	1.03030	1.04568	1.06121	1.09273	1.12486	1.15763	1.19102	1.22504	1.25971
4	1.02015	1.03034	1.04060	1.06136	1.08243	1.12551	1.16986	1.21551	1.26248	1.31080	1.36049
5	1.02525	1.03807	1.05101	1.07728	1.10408	1.15927	1.21665	1.27628	1.33823	1.40255	1.46933
6	1.03038	1.04585	1.06152	1.09344	1.12616	1.19405	1.26532	1.34010	1.41852	1.50073	1.58687
7	1.03553	1.05370	1.07214	1.10984	1.14869	1.22987	1.31593	1.40710	1.50363	1.60578	1.71382
8	1.04071	1.06160	1.08286	1.12649	1.17166	1.26677	1.36857	1.47746	1.59385	1.71819	1.85093
9	1.04591	1.06956	1.09369	1.14339	1.19509	1.30477	1.42331	1.55133	1.68948	1.83846	1.99900
10	1.05114	1.07758	1.10462	1.16054	1.21899	1.34392	1.48024	1.62889	1.79085	1.96715	2.15892
11	1.05640	1.08566	1.11567	1.17795	1.24337	1.38423	1.53945	1.71034	1.89830	2.10485	2.33164
12	1.06168	1.09381	1.12683	1.19562	1.26824	1.42576	1.60103	1.79586	2.01220	2.25219	2.51817
13	1.06699	1.10201	1.13809	1.21355	1.29361	1.46853	1.66507	1.88565	2.13293	2.40985	2.71962
14	1.07232	1.11028	1.14947	1.23176	1.31948	1.51259	1.73168	1.97993	2.26090	2.57853	2.93719
15	1.07768	1.11860	1.16097	1.25023	1.34587	1.55797	1.80094	2.07893	2.39656	2.75903	3.17217
16	1.08307	1.12699	1.17258	1.26899	1.37279	1.60471	1.87298	2.18287	2.54035	2.95216	3.42594
17	1.08849	1.13544	1.18430	1.28802	1.40024	1.65285	1.94790	2.29202	2.69277	3.15882	3.70002
18	1.09393	1.14396	1.19615	1.30734	1.42825	1.70243	2.02582	2.40662	2.85434	3.37993	3.99602
19	1.09940	1.15254	1.20811	1.32695	1.45681	1.75351	2.10685	2.52695	3.02560	3.61653	4.31570
20	1.10490	1.16118	1.22019	1.34686	1.48595	1.80611	2.19112	2.65330	3.20714	3.86968	4.66096
24	1.12716	1.19641	1.26973	1.42950	1.60844	2.03279	2.56330	3.22510	4.04893	5.07237	6.34118
36	1.19668	1.30865	1.43077	1.70914	2.03989	2.89828	4.10393	5.79182	8.14725	11.42394	15.96817
48	1.27049	1.43141	1.61223	2.04348	2.58707	4.13225	6.57053	10.40127	16.39387	25.72891	40.21057
60	1.34885	1.56568	1.81670	2.44322	3.28103	5.89160	10.51963	18.67919	32.98769	57.94643	101.2571
120	1.81940	2.45136	3.30039	5.96932	10.76516	34.71099	110.6626	348.9120	1088.188	3357.788	10252.99
240	3.31020	6.00915	10.89255	35.63282	115.8887	1204.853	12246.20	1.22E+05	1.18E+06	1.13E+07	1.05E+08
360	6.02258	14.73058	35.94964	212.7038	1247.561	41821.62	1.36E+06	4.25E+07	1.29E+09	3.79E+10	1.08E+12

(continued)

TABLE 1(continued)
Future Value of $1.00

Periods	9.00%	10.00%	11.00%	12.00%	13.00%	14.00%	15.00%	16.00%	18.00%	20.00%	25.00%
1	1.09000	1.10000	1.11000	1.12000	1.13000	1.14000	1.15000	1.16000	1.18000	1.20000	1.25000
2	1.18810	1.21000	1.23210	1.25440	1.27690	1.29960	1.32250	1.34560	1.39240	1.44000	1.56250
3	1.29503	1.33100	1.36763	1.40493	1.44290	1.48154	1.52088	1.56090	1.64303	1.72800	1.95313
4	1.41158	1.46410	1.51807	1.57352	1.63047	1.68896	1.74901	1.81064	1.93878	2.07360	2.44141
5	1.53862	1.61051	1.68506	1.76234	1.84244	1.92541	2.01136	2.10034	2.28776	2.48832	3.05176
6	1.67710	1.77156	1.87041	1.97382	2.08195	2.19497	2.31306	2.43640	2.69955	2.98598	3.81470
7	1.82804	1.94872	2.07616	2.21068	2.35261	2.50227	2.66002	2.82622	3.18547	3.58318	4.76837
8	1.99256	2.14359	2.30454	2.47596	2.65844	2.85259	3.05902	3.27841	3.75886	4.29982	5.96046
9	2.17189	2.35795	2.55804	2.77308	3.00404	3.25195	3.51788	3.80296	4.43545	5.15978	7.45058
10	2.36736	2.59374	2.83942	3.10585	3.39457	3.70722	4.04556	4.41144	5.23384	6.19174	9.31323
11	2.58043	2.85312	3.15176	3.47855	3.83586	4.22623	4.65239	5.11726	6.17593	7.43008	11.64153
12	2.81266	3.13843	3.49845	3.89598	4.33452	4.81790	5.35025	5.93603	7.28759	8.91610	14.55192
13	3.06580	3.45227	3.88328	4.36349	4.89801	5.49241	6.15279	6.88579	8.59136	10.69932	18.18989
14	3.34173	3.79750	4.31044	4.88711	5.53475	6.26135	7.07571	7.98752	10.14724	12.83918	22.73737
15	3.64248	4.17725	4.78459	5.47357	6.25427	7.13794	8.13706	9.26552	11.97375	15.40702	28.42171
16	3.97031	4.59497	5.31089	6.13039	7.06733	8.13725	9.35762	10.74800	14.12902	18.48843	35.52714
17	4.32763	5.05447	5.89509	6.86604	7.98608	9.27646	10.76126	12.46768	16.67225	22.18611	44.40892
18	4.71712	5.55992	6.54355	7.68997	9.02427	10.57517	12.37545	14.46251	19.67325	26.62333	55.51115
19	5.14166	6.11591	7.26334	8.61276	10.19742	12.05569	14.23177	16.77652	23.21444	31.94800	69.38894
20	5.60441	6.72750	8.06231	9.64629	11.52309	13.74349	16.36654	19.46076	27.39303	38.33760	86.73617
24	7.91108	9.84973	12.23916	15.17863	18.78809	23.21221	28.62518	35.23642	53.10901	79.49685	211.7582
36	22.25123	30.91268	42.81808	59.13557	81.43741	111.8342	153.1519	209.1643	387.0368	708.8019	3081.488
48	62.58524	97.10723	149.7970	230.3908	352.9923	538.8065	819.4007	1241.605	2820.567	6319.749	44841.55
60	176.0313	304.4816	524.0572	897.5969	1530.053	2595.919	4383.999	7370.201	20555.14	56347.51	652530.4
120	30987.02	92709.07	274636.0	805680.3	2.34E+06	6.74E+06	1.92E+07	5.43E+07	4.23E+08	3.18E+09	4.26E+11
240	9.60E+08	8.59E+09	7.54E+10	6.49E+11	5.48E+12	4.54E+13	3.69E+14	2.95E+15	1.79E+17	1.01E+19	1.81E+23
360	2.98E+13	7.97E+14	2.07E+16	5.23E+17	1.28E+19	3.06E+20	7.10E+21	1.60E+23	7.54E+25	3.20E+28	7.72E+34

TABLE 2
Present Value of $1.00

Periods	0.50%	0.75%	1.00%	1.50%	2.00%	3.00%	4.00%	5.00%	6.00%	7.00%	8.00%
1	0.99502	0.99256	0.99010	0.98522	0.98039	0.97087	0.96154	0.95238	0.94340	0.93458	0.92593
2	0.99007	0.98517	0.98030	0.97066	0.96117	0.94260	0.92456	0.90703	0.89000	0.87344	0.85734
3	0.98515	0.97783	0.97059	0.95632	0.94232	0.91514	0.88900	0.86384	0.83962	0.81630	0.79383
4	0.98025	0.97055	0.96098	0.94218	0.92385	0.88849	0.85480	0.82270	0.79209	0.76290	0.73503
5	0.97537	0.96333	0.95147	0.92826	0.90573	0.86261	0.82193	0.78353	0.74726	0.71299	0.68058
6	0.97052	0.95616	0.94205	0.91454	0.88797	0.83748	0.79031	0.74622	0.70496	0.66634	0.63107
7	0.96569	0.94904	0.93272	0.90103	0.87056	0.81309	0.75992	0.71068	0.66506	0.62275	0.58349
8	0.96089	0.94198	0.92348	0.88771	0.85349	0.78941	0.73069	0.67684	0.62741	0.58201	0.54027
9	0.95610	0.93496	0.91434	0.87459	0.83676	0.76642	0.70259	0.64461	0.59190	0.54393	0.50025
10	0.95135	0.92800	0.90529	0.86167	0.82035	0.74409	0.67556	0.61391	0.55839	0.50835	0.46319
11	0.94661	0.92109	0.89632	0.84893	0.80426	0.72242	0.64958	0.58468	0.52679	0.47509	0.42888
12	0.94191	0.91424	0.88745	0.83639	0.78849	0.70138	0.62460	0.55684	0.49697	0.44401	0.39711
13	0.93722	0.90743	0.87866	0.82403	0.77303	0.68095	0.60057	0.53032	0.46884	0.41496	0.36770
14	0.93256	0.90068	0.86996	0.81185	0.75788	0.66112	0.57748	0.50507	0.44230	0.38782	0.34046
15	0.92792	0.89397	0.86135	0.79985	0.74301	0.64186	0.55526	0.48102	0.41727	0.36245	0.31524
16	0.92330	0.88732	0.85282	0.78803	0.72845	0.62317	0.53391	0.45811	0.39365	0.33873	0.29189
17	0.91871	0.88071	0.84438	0.77639	0.71416	0.60502	0.51337	0.43630	0.37136	0.31657	0.27027
18	0.91414	0.87416	0.83602	0.76491	0.70016	0.58739	0.49363	0.41552	0.35034	0.29586	0.25025
19	0.90959	0.86765	0.82774	0.75361	0.68643	0.57029	0.47464	0.39573	0.33051	0.27651	0.23171
20	0.90506	0.86119	0.81954	0.74247	0.67297	0.55368	0.45639	0.37689	0.31180	0.25842	0.21455
24	0.88719	0.83583	0.78757	0.69954	0.62172	0.49193	0.39012	0.31007	0.24698	0.19715	0.15770
36	0.83564	0.76415	0.69892	0.58509	0.49022	0.34503	0.24367	0.17266	0.12274	0.08754	0.06262
48	0.78710	0.69861	0.62026	0.48936	0.38654	0.24200	0.15219	0.09614	0.06100	0.03887	0.02487
60	0.74137	0.63870	0.55045	0.40930	0.30478	0.16973	0.09506	0.05354	0.03031	0.01726	0.00988
120	0.54963	0.40794	0.30299	0.16752	0.09289	0.02881	0.00904	0.00287	0.00092	0.00030	0.00010
240	0.30210	0.16641	0.09181	0.02806	0.00863	0.00083	0.00008	0.00001	8.4E-07	8.9E-08	9.5E-09
360	0.16604	0.06789	0.02782	0.00470	0.00080	0.00002	7.4E-07	2.4E-08	7.8E-10	2.6E-11	9.3E-13

(continued)

TABLE 2 (continued)
Present Value of $1.00

Periods	9.00%	10.00%	11.00%	12.00%	13.00%	14.00%	15.00%	16.00%	18.00%	20.00%	25.00%
1	0.91743	0.90909	0.90090	0.89286	0.88496	0.87719	0.86957	0.86207	0.84746	0.83333	0.80000
2	0.84168	0.82645	0.81162	0.79719	0.78315	0.76947	0.75614	0.74316	0.71818	0.69444	0.64000
3	0.77218	0.75131	0.73119	0.71178	0.69305	0.67497	0.65752	0.64066	0.60863	0.57870	0.51200
4	0.70843	0.68301	0.65873	0.63552	0.61332	0.59208	0.57175	0.55229	0.51579	0.48225	0.40960
5	0.64993	0.62092	0.59345	0.56743	0.54276	0.51937	0.49718	0.47611	0.43711	0.40188	0.32768
6	0.59627	0.56447	0.53464	0.50663	0.48032	0.45559	0.43233	0.41044	0.37043	0.33490	0.26214
7	0.54703	0.51316	0.48166	0.45235	0.42506	0.39964	0.37594	0.35383	0.31393	0.27908	0.20972
8	0.50187	0.46651	0.43393	0.40388	0.37616	0.35056	0.32690	0.30503	0.26604	0.23257	0.16777
9	0.46043	0.42410	0.39092	0.36061	0.33288	0.30751	0.28426	0.26295	0.22546	0.19381	0.13422
10	0.42241	0.38554	0.35218	0.32197	0.29459	0.26974	0.24718	0.22668	0.19106	0.16151	0.10737
11	0.38753	0.35049	0.31728	0.28748	0.26070	0.23662	0.21494	0.19542	0.16192	0.13459	0.08590
12	0.35553	0.31863	0.28584	0.25668	0.23071	0.20756	0.18691	0.16846	0.13722	0.11216	0.06872
13	0.32618	0.28966	0.25751	0.22917	0.20416	0.18207	0.16253	0.14523	0.11629	0.09346	0.05498
14	0.29925	0.26333	0.23199	0.20462	0.18068	0.15971	0.14133	0.12520	0.09855	0.07789	0.04398
15	0.27454	0.23939	0.20900	0.18270	0.15989	0.14010	0.12289	0.10793	0.08352	0.06491	0.03518
16	0.25187	0.21763	0.18829	0.16312	0.14150	0.12289	0.10686	0.09304	0.07078	0.05409	0.02815
17	0.23107	0.19784	0.16963	0.14564	0.12522	0.10780	0.09293	0.08021	0.05998	0.04507	0.02252
18	0.21199	0.17986	0.15282	0.13004	0.11081	0.09456	0.08081	0.06914	0.05083	0.03756	0.01801
19	0.19449	0.16351	0.13768	0.11611	0.09806	0.08295	0.07027	0.05961	0.04308	0.03130	0.01441
20	0.17843	0.14864	0.12403	0.10367	0.08678	0.07276	0.06110	0.05139	0.03651	0.02608	0.01153
24	0.12640	0.10153	0.08170	0.06588	0.05323	0.04308	0.03493	0.02838	0.01883	0.01258	0.00472
36	0.04494	0.03235	0.02335	0.01691	0.01228	0.00894	0.00653	0.00478	0.00258	0.00141	0.00032
48	0.01598	0.01031	0.00668	0.00434	0.00283	0.00186	0.00122	0.00081	0.00035	0.00016	0.00002
60	0.00568	0.00328	0.00191	0.00111	0.00065	0.00039	0.00023	0.00014	0.00005	0.00002	1.5E-06
120	0.00003	0.00001	3.6E-06	1.2E-06	4.3E-07	1.5E-07	5.2E-08	1.8E-08	2.4E-09	3.1E-10	2.3E-12
240	1.0E-09	1.2E-10	1.3E-11	1.5E-12	1.8E-13	2.2E-14	2.7E-15	3.4E-16	5.6E-18	9.9E-20	5.5E-24
360	3.4E-14	1.3E-15	4.8E-17	1.9E-18	7.8E-13	3.3E-21	1.4E-22	6.2E-24	1.3E-26	3.1E-29	1.3E-35

TABLE 3
Future Value of an Annuity in Arrears

Periods	0.50%	0.75%	1.00%	1.50%	2.00%	3.00%	4.00%	5.00%	6.00%	7.00%	8.00%
1	1.00000	1.00000	1.00000	1.00000	1.00000	1.00000	1.00000	1.00000	1.00000	1.00000	1.00000
2	2.00500	2.00750	2.01000	2.01500	2.02000	2.03000	2.04000	2.05000	2.06000	2.07000	2.08000
3	3.01502	3.02256	3.03010	3.04522	3.06040	3.09090	3.12160	3.15250	3.18360	3.21490	3.24640
4	4.03010	4.04523	4.06040	4.09090	4.12161	4.18363	4.24646	4.31013	4.37462	4.43994	4.50611
5	5.05025	5.07556	5.10101	5.15227	5.20404	5.30914	5.41632	5.52563	5.63709	5.75074	5.86660
6	6.07550	6.11363	6.15202	6.22955	6.30812	6.46841	6.63298	6.80191	6.97532	7.15329	7.33593
7	7.10588	7.15948	7.21354	7.32299	7.43428	7.66246	7.89829	8.14201	8.39384	8.65402	8.92280
8	8.14141	8.21318	8.28567	8.43284	8.58297	8.89234	9.21423	9.54911	9.89747	10.25980	10.63663
9	9.18212	9.27478	9.36853	9.55933	9.75463	10.15911	10.58280	11.02656	11.49132	11.97799	12.48756
10	10.22803	10.34434	10.46221	10.70272	10.94972	11.46388	12.00611	12.57789	13.18079	13.81645	14.48656
11	11.27917	11.42192	11.56683	11.86326	12.16872	12.80780	13.48635	14.20679	14.97164	15.78360	16.64549
12	12.33556	12.50759	12.68250	13.04121	13.41209	14.19203	15.02581	15.91713	16.86994	17.88845	18.97713
13	13.39724	13.60139	13.80933	14.23683	14.68033	15.61779	16.62684	17.71298	18.88214	20.14064	21.49530
14	14.46423	14.70340	14.94742	15.45038	15.97394	17.08632	18.29191	19.59863	21.01507	22.55049	24.21492
15	15.53655	15.81368	16.09690	16.68214	17.29342	18.59891	20.02359	21.57856	23.27597	25.12902	27.15211
16	16.61423	16.93228	17.25786	17.93237	18.63929	20.15688	21.82453	23.65749	25.67253	27.88805	30.32428
17	17.69730	18.05927	18.43044	19.20136	20.01207	21.76159	23.69751	25.84037	28.21888	30.84022	33.75023
18	18.78579	19.19472	19.61475	20.48938	21.41231	23.41444	25.64541	28.13238	30.90565	33.99903	37.45024
19	19.87972	20.33868	20.81090	21.79672	22.84056	25.11687	27.67123	30.53900	33.75999	37.37896	41.44626
20	20.97912	21.49122	22.01900	23.12367	24.29737	26.87037	29.77808	33.06595	36.78559	40.99549	45.76196
24	25.43196	26.18847	26.97346	28.63352	30.42186	34.42647	39.08260	44.50200	50.81558	58.17667	66.76476
36	39.33610	41.15272	43.07688	47.27597	51.99437	63.27594	77.59831	95.83632	119.1209	148.9135	187.1021
48	54.09783	57.52071	61.22261	69.56522	79.35352	104.4084	139.2632	188.0254	256.5645	353.2701	490.1322
60	69.77003	75.42414	81.66967	96.21465	114.0515	163.0534	237.9907	353.5837	533.1282	813.5204	1253.213
120	163.8793	193.5143	230.0387	331.2882	488.2582	1123.700	2741.564	6958.240	18119.80	47954.12	128149.9
240	462.0409	667.8869	989.2554	2308.854	5744.437	40128.42	306130.1	2.43E+06	1.97E+07	1.61E+08	1.31E+09
360	1004.515	1830.743	3494.964	14113.59	62328.06	1.39E+06	3.39E+07	8.50E+08	2.15E+10	5.41E+11	1.35E+13

(continued)

TABLE 3 (continued)

Future Value of an Annuity in Arrears

Periods	9.00%	10.00%	11.00%	12.00%	13.00%	14.00%	15.00%	16.00%	18.00%	20.00%	25.00%
1	1.00000	1.00000	1.00000	1.00000	1.00000	1.00000	1.00000	1.00000	1.00000	1.00000	1.00000
2	2.09000	2.10000	2.11000	2.12000	2.13000	2.14000	2.15000	2.16000	2.18000	2.20000	2.25000
3	3.27810	3.31000	3.34210	3.37440	3.40690	3.43960	3.47250	3.50560	3.57240	3.64000	3.81250
4	4.57313	4.64100	4.70973	4.77933	4.84980	4.92114	4.99338	5.06650	5.21543	5.36800	5.76563
5	5.98471	6.10510	6.22780	6.35285	6.48027	6.61010	6.74238	6.87714	7.15421	7.44160	8.20703
6	7.52333	7.71561	7.91286	8.11519	8.32271	8.53552	8.75374	8.97748	9.44197	9.92992	11.25879
7	9.20043	9.48717	9.78327	10.08901	10.40466	10.73049	11.06680	11.41387	12.14152	12.91590	15.07349
8	11.02847	11.43589	11.85943	12.29969	12.75726	13.23276	13.72682	14.24009	15.32700	16.49908	19.84186
9	13.02104	13.57948	14.16397	14.77566	15.41571	16.08535	16.78584	17.51851	19.08585	20.79890	25.80232
10	15.19293	15.93742	16.72201	17.54874	18.41975	19.33730	20.30372	21.32147	23.52131	25.95868	33.25290
11	17.56029	18.53117	19.56143	20.65458	21.81432	23.04452	24.34928	25.73290	28.75514	32.15042	42.56613
12	20.14072	21.38428	22.71319	24.13313	25.65018	27.27075	29.00167	30.85017	34.93107	39.58050	54.20766
13	22.95338	24.52271	26.21164	28.02911	29.98470	32.08865	34.35192	36.78620	42.21866	48.49660	68.75958
14	26.01919	27.97498	30.09492	32.39260	34.88271	37.58107	40.50471	43.67199	50.81802	59.19592	86.94947
15	29.36092	31.77248	34.40536	37.27971	40.41746	43.84241	47.58041	51.65951	60.96527	72.03511	109.6868
16	33.00340	35.94973	39.18995	42.75328	46.67173	50.98035	55.71747	60.92503	72.93901	87.44213	138.1085
17	36.97370	40.54470	44.50084	48.88367	53.73906	59.11760	65.07509	71.67303	87.06804	105.9306	173.6357
18	41.30134	45.59917	50.39594	55.74971	61.72514	68.39407	75.83636	84.14072	103.7403	128.1167	218.0446
19	46.01846	51.15909	56.93949	63.43968	70.74941	78.96923	88.21181	98.60323	123.4135	154.7400	273.5558
20	51.16012	57.27500	64.20283	72.05244	80.94683	91.02493	102.4436	115.3797	146.6280	186.6880	342.9447
24	76.78981	88.49733	102.1742	118.1552	136.8315	158.6586	184.1678	213.9776	289.4945	392.4842	843.0329
36	236.1247	299.1268	380.1644	484.4631	618.7493	791.6729	1014.346	1301.027	2144.649	3539.009	12321.95
48	684.2804	960.1723	1352.700	1911.590	2707.633	3841.475	5456.005	7753.782	15664.26	31593.74	179362.2
60	1944.792	3034.816	4755.066	7471.641	11761.95	18535.13	29219.99	46057.51	114189.7	281732.6	2.61E+06
120	344289.1	927080.7	2.50E+06	6.71E+06	1.80E+07	4.81E+07	1.28E+08	3.39E+08	2.35E+09	1.59E+10	1.70E+12
240	1.07E+10	8.59E+10	6.86E+11	5.41E+12	4.22E+13	3.24E+14	2.46E+15	1.84E+16	9.92E+17	5.04E+19	7.25E+23
360	3.31E+14	7.97E+15	1.88E+17	4.36E+18	9.87E+19	2.19E+21	4.73E+22	1.00E+24	4.19E+26	1.60E+29	3.09E+35

TABLE 4
Present Value of an Annuity in Arrears

Periods	0.50%	0.75%	1.00%	1.50%	2.00%	3.00%	4.00%	5.00%	6.00%	7.00%	8.00%
1	0.99502	0.99256	0.99010	0.98522	0.98039	0.97087	0.96154	0.95238	0.94340	0.93458	0.92593
2	1.98510	1.97772	1.97040	1.95588	1.94156	1.91347	1.88609	1.85941	1.83339	1.80802	1.78326
3	2.97025	2.95556	2.94099	2.91220	2.88388	2.82861	2.77509	2.72325	2.67301	2.62432	2.57710
4	3.95050	3.92611	3.90197	3.85438	3.80773	3.71710	3.62990	3.54595	3.46511	3.38721	3.31213
5	4.92587	4.88944	4.85343	4.78264	4.71346	4.57971	4.45182	4.32948	4.21236	4.10020	3.99271
6	5.89638	5.84560	5.79548	5.69719	5.60143	5.41719	5.24214	5.07569	4.91732	4.76654	4.62288
7	6.86207	6.79464	6.72819	6.59821	6.47199	6.23028	6.00205	5.78637	5.58238	5.38929	5.20637
8	7.82296	7.73661	7.65168	7.48593	7.32548	7.01969	6.73274	6.46321	6.20979	5.97130	5.74664
9	8.77906	8.67158	8.56602	8.36052	8.16224	7.78611	7.43533	7.10782	6.80169	6.51523	6.24689
10	9.73041	9.59958	9.47130	9.22218	8.98259	8.53020	8.11090	7.72173	7.36009	7.02358	6.71008
11	10.67703	10.52067	10.36763	10.07112	9.78685	9.25262	8.76048	8.30641	7.88687	7.49867	7.13896
12	11.61893	11.43491	11.25508	10.90751	10.57534	9.95400	9.38507	8.86325	8.38384	7.94269	7.53608
13	12.55615	12.34235	12.13374	11.73153	11.34837	10.63496	9.98565	9.39357	8.85268	8.35765	7.90378
14	13.48871	13.24302	13.00370	12.54338	12.10625	11.29607	10.56312	9.89864	9.29498	8.74547	8.24424
15	14.41662	14.13699	13.86505	13.34323	12.84926	11.93794	11.11839	10.37966	9.71225	9.10791	8.55948
16	15.33993	15.02431	14.71787	14.13126	13.57771	12.56110	11.65230	10.83777	10.10590	9.44665	8.85137
17	16.25863	15.90502	15.56225	14.90765	14.29187	13.16612	12.16567	11.27407	10.47726	9.76322	9.12164
18	17.17277	16.77918	16.39827	15.67256	14.99203	13.75351	12.65930	11.68959	10.82760	10.05909	9.37189
19	18.08236	17.64683	17.22601	16.42617	15.67846	14.32380	13.13394	12.08532	11.15812	10.33560	9.60360
20	18.98742	18.50802	18.04555	17.16864	16.35143	14.87747	13.59033	12.46221	11.46992	10.59401	9.81815
24	22.56287	21.88915	21.24339	20.03041	18.91393	16.93554	15.24696	13.79864	12.55036	11.46933	10.52876
36	32.87102	31.44681	30.10751	27.66068	25.48884	21.83225	18.90828	16.54685	14.62099	13.03521	11.71719
48	42.58032	40.18478	37.97396	34.04255	30.67312	25.26671	21.19513	18.07716	15.65003	13.73047	12.18914
60	51.72556	48.17337	44.95504	39.38027	34.76089	27.67556	22.62349	18.92929	16.16143	14.03918	12.37655
120	90.07345	78.94169	69.70052	55.49845	45.35539	32.37302	24.77409	19.94268	16.65135	14.28146	12.49878
240	139.58077	111.14495	90.81942	64.79573	49.56855	33.30567	24.99796	19.99984	16.66665	14.28571	12.50000
360	166.79161	124.28187	97.21833	66.35324	49.95992	33.33254	24.99998	20.00000	16.66667	14.28571	12.50000

(continued)

TABLE 4 (continued)
Present Value of an Annuity in Arrears

Periods	9.00%	10.00%	11.00%	12.00%	13.00%	14.00%	15.00%	16.00%	18.00%	20.00%	25.00%
1	0.91743	0.90909	0.90090	0.89286	0.88496	0.87719	0.86957	0.86207	0.84746	0.83333	0.80000
2	1.75911	1.73554	1.71252	1.69005	1.66810	1.64666	1.62571	1.60523	1.56564	1.52778	1.44000
3	2.53129	2.48685	2.44371	2.40183	2.36115	2.32163	2.28323	2.24589	2.17427	2.10648	1.95200
4	3.23972	3.16987	3.10245	3.03735	2.97447	2.91371	2.85498	2.79818	2.69006	2.58873	2.36160
5	3.88965	3.79079	3.69590	3.60478	3.51723	3.43308	3.35216	3.27429	3.12717	2.99061	2.68928
6	4.48592	4.35526	4.23054	4.11141	3.99755	3.88867	3.78448	3.68474	3.49760	3.32551	2.95142
7	5.03295	4.86842	4.71220	4.56376	4.42261	4.28830	4.16042	4.03857	3.81153	3.60459	3.16114
8	5.53482	5.33493	5.14612	4.96764	4.79877	4.63886	4.48732	4.34359	4.07757	3.83716	3.32891
9	5.99525	5.75902	5.53705	5.32825	5.13166	4.94637	4.77158	4.60654	4.30302	4.03097	3.46313
10	6.41766	6.14457	5.88923	5.65022	5.42624	5.21612	5.01877	4.83323	4.49409	4.19247	3.57050
11	6.80519	6.49506	6.20652	5.93770	5.68694	5.45273	5.23371	5.02864	4.65601	4.32706	3.65640
12	7.16073	6.81369	6.49236	6.19437	5.91765	5.66029	5.42062	5.19711	4.79322	4.43922	3.72512
13	7.48690	7.10336	6.74987	6.42355	6.12181	5.84236	5.58315	5.34233	4.90951	4.53268	3.78010
14	7.78615	7.36669	6.98187	6.62817	6.30249	6.00207	5.72448	5.46753	5.00806	4.61057	3.82408
15	8.06069	7.60608	7.19087	6.81086	6.46238	6.14217	5.84737	5.57546	5.09158	4.67547	3.85926
16	8.31256	7.82371	7.37916	6.97399	6.60388	6.26506	5.95423	5.66850	5.16235	4.72956	3.88741
17	8.54363	8.02155	7.54879	7.11963	6.72909	6.37286	6.04716	5.74870	5.22233	4.77463	3.90993
18	8.75563	8.20141	7.70162	7.24967	6.83991	6.46742	6.12797	5.81785	5.27316	4.81219	3.92794
19	8.95011	8.36492	7.83929	7.36578	6.93797	6.55037	6.19823	5.87746	5.31624	4.84350	3.94235
20	9.12855	8.51356	7.96333	7.46944	7.02475	6.62313	6.25933	5.92884	5.35275	4.86958	3.95388
24	9.70661	8.98474	8.34814	7.78432	7.28288	6.83514	6.43377	6.07263	5.45095	4.93710	3.98111
36	10.61176	9.67651	8.87859	8.19241	7.59785	7.07899	6.62314	6.22012	5.54120	4.99295	3.99870
48	10.93358	9.89693	9.03022	8.29716	7.67052	7.12960	6.65853	6.24497	5.55359	4.99921	3.99991
60	11.04799	9.96716	9.07356	8.32405	7.68728	7.14011	6.66515	6.24915	5.55529	4.99991	3.99999
120	11.11075	9.99989	9.09088	8.33332	7.69230	7.14286	6.66667	6.25000	5.55556	5.00000	4.00000
240	11.11111	10.00000	9.09091	8.33333	7.69231	7.14286	6.66667	6.25000	5.55556	5.00000	4.00000
360	11.11111	10.00000	909091	8.33333	7.69231	7.14286	6.66667	6.25000	5.55556	5.00000	4.00000

* To calculate the present value factor for an annuity in advance, use the arrears factor for one less period and add one.

Taking Care
of Business

Since its founding in 1962, Shoppers Drug Mart (Pharmaprix in Quebec) has grown from a small family-run pharmacy on Toronto's Danforth Avenue to a nationwide network of more than 800 retail outlets with 30,000 employees. The success of the company, Canada's largest drugstore chain, is built on a franchising concept that combines an individual pharmacist-owner with the benefits of a corporate infrastructure.

In November 2001, Shoppers went public, issuing 30 million common shares at a price of $18 per share. Underwritten by a consortium of dealers led by CIBC World Markets, the initial public offering (IPO) raised $540 million, making it Canada's largest IPO in 2001. Proceeds were used to help pay back $591 million of the company's long-term debt, much of which was incurred in a leveraged buyout by a group of institutional investors the year before. As a result of the move, Shoppers improved its debt/equity ratio to 0.78:1 from 1.88:1. At the end of 2001, its balance of long-term debt was $1.1 billion.

The shares made their debut on the Toronto Stock Exchange on November 21, under the symbol SC. Criticized by some analysts as being too pricey, they initially fell in the first few weeks of trading but recovered by year end. Since then, they have been climbing steadily. In September 2002, SC was trading at over $23.

"Going public has given us more than just an opportunity to raise capital through a different market," says Arthur Konviser, Senior Vice President, Corporate Affairs.

"It also gives us greater exposure through wider shareholding. Obviously the more Canadians who own Shoppers Drug Mart shares, the better it is—in as much as they're consumers as well as shareholders, it gives them an affinity towards the company."

In its first set of financial results since it went public, Shoppers showed earnings of $22.91 million, or 12 cents a share, for the year ending December 29, 2001, compared with $16.09 million in 2000—a jump of 42%. Revenue increased to $3.63 billion from $3.18 billion a year earlier. The company's fourth quarter net earnings were $9 million or 5 cents per share compared with $5 million or 3 cents per share for the same period in 2000.

In the months leading up to the IPO, the company made significant changes in its senior management, downsized its corporate office, and redefined its objectives in a bid to pave the way for further expansion and increased profitability. Canada's $23-billion-a-year retail drugstore market is expected to grow in the coming decades as the population gets older and seeks more prescriptions. Shoppers plans to open 41 new stores in 2002 in addition to acquisitions of independent pharmacies. It also plans to spend $130 million on store renovations and expansions.

SHAREHOLDERS'
EQUITY

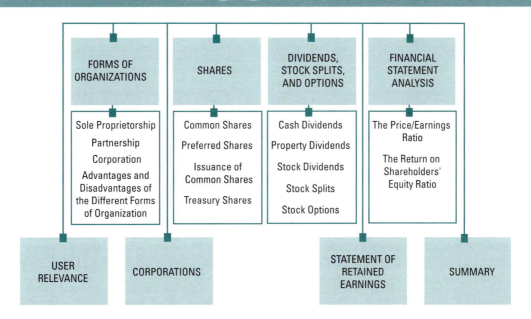

Learning Objectives:

After studying this chapter, you should be able to:

1. *Distinguish among different types of organizations and explain the advantages and disadvantages of each form.*

2. *Describe the different types of shares and explain why corporations choose to issue a variety of share types.*

3. *Prepare journal entries for share transactions, including the issuance and payment of dividends.*

4. *Describe the different types of dividends and explain why companies might opt to issue one type of dividend rather than another.*

5. *Explain the purpose of the statement of retained earnings.*

6. *Calculate and interpret the price/earnings ratio and the return on shareholders' equity ratio, which are often used for decision-making.*

The opening story describes how an established company, Shoppers Drug Mart, moved from being a private corporation to a public corporation. A private corporation has shareholders, but those shareholders are a controlled, usually relatively small group (compared to a publicly traded company). Because of the limited number of shareholders, it is more difficult to buy and/or sell an ownership interest. Once it went public, Shoppers Drug Mart increased its access to funds, increased its number of shareholders, and lost some control over who its shareholders are. Shoppers' financial statements are public information now and it must produce quarterly and annual reports for the stock exchange and its shareholders. When it was a private corporation, it produced financial information for its shareholders but not for the stock exchange or the general public. Shoppers saw the issuance of the IPO not just as an opportunity to expand its capital base, but also as an opportunity to expand its ownership base. It views new shareholders as probable new customers.

A company can also go from being a public company to becoming a private one. Note the following article:

accounting in the news

GOING PRIVATE

For many companies, going public is a desirable step, giving them access to a lot of money through the stock market. Less common are public companies that choose to go private. Among these is Sepp's Gourmet Foods Ltd., of Surrey, British Columbia, a company specializing in savoury foods. In July 2001, a group headed by chairman Peter Geib made a bid to take Sepp's private.

Since its creation in 1990, Sepp's had experienced handsome growth, with sales increasing from $2.4 million to $88 million in a decade. This was helped largely by the company's public offering in 1995, which raised money to help buy nine companies and expand product lines and distribution ability.

Despite being profitable, Sepp's stock performance had been lacklustre, dragged down by problems with a 1998 acquisition, Scottish food processor McIntosh of Dyce. By the summer of 2001, Sepp's was trading at 50 cents per share, down from $4 just three years before. Investors just were not interested; Sepp's was not reaping the big benefit of public ownership.

Further, the costs of being a public company were substantial. Investor relations and associated administrative costs accounted for an estimated 20% of company profits—not to mention the time that management was required to spend dealing with institutional and retail investors.

Finally, one expert pointed out a less tangible benefit of private ownership: without the pressure to meet quarterly earnings targets, a private company has more freedom to pursue longer-term goals.

Source: "A private decision," by Richard Wright, *Profit: The Magazine for Canadian Entrepreneurs*, Dec. 2001/Jan. 2002, p. 61.

In this chapter, we are going to delve more deeply into the components of shareholders' equity. Remember that shareholders' equity represents the residual amount (assets minus liabilities) and it measures the investment made by owners in the company. Before getting into a detailed discussion of the components of shareholders' equity in a corporation, we want to take a short detour in which we will briefly discuss why knowing more about shareholders' equity is important to users and also to look at alternative forms of business organization. Although many companies in Canada are established as corporations, they could have been established as proprietorships or partnerships.

USER RELEVANCE

The chances are relatively high that in the future you will invest in one or more companies, either directly by buying shares, or indirectly by buying mutual funds. As a future shareholder, you need to understand how your ownership interest is measured and disclosed in the financial statements. There is more than one type of share (ownership interest). With the help of financial experts, companies design and create financial instruments that have a variety of features that provide investors with specific rights and privileges. You should know what some of those features are so that you can assess the value of your ownership interest.

Sometimes investors buy shares to receive a periodic dividend payment. More frequently, however, shares are purchased in anticipation of the share value increasing so that the shares can be sold in the future for a profit. Buying and selling shares today is much easier than it was in the past, but investors need to do their homework. The information that you have gained by studying accounting should provide you with a reasonable level of knowledge so that you can assess a company's current and future financial health.

Let's take a brief look at some of the different forms of organizations.

FORMS OF ORGANIZATIONS

Learning Objective

Distinguish among different types of organizations and explain the advantages and disadvantages of each form.

Sole Proprietorship

As discussed briefly in Chapter 1, the simplest form of business is the **sole proprietorship**. The sole proprietorship is a single-owner business. All profits and losses belong to the owner, and all decisions are made either by the owner or under the owner's direction. It is probably this aspect of control that keeps the proprietorship form of business alive. Most owners like to be the ones making decisions and like to be active in the day-to-day operations. Proprietorships can be small, single-unit operations, or they can be larger operations with units in several places.

Proprietors must assume all the risk if the business runs into trouble. They have **unlimited liability.** Unlimited liability means that the sole proprietor is 100% liable for all debts of the business. Should a claim be made by a stakeholder against the company, both the business assets and the owner's personal property (if necessary) may be used to fulfill the obligation and satisfy the claim. It is this aspect of unlimited liability that makes many single owners consider establishing the business as a corporation rather than a proprietorship.

Because the sole proprietor does not have to report to shareholders, there is less concern about preparing reports according to Canadian standards. The sole proprietor might want to follow Canadian standards if the business is trying to obtain a loan from a bank, since loan officers could insist on financial statements prepared according to GAAP. GAAP statements might also be required if the sole proprietorship is regulated. The owner might want to deviate from Canadian standards if using a different method produced information that was more useful in making the decisions that need to be made to run the business.

The CCRA also wants information about the financial results of a sole proprietorship. Sole proprietors are required to combine the profits or losses from their businesses with their personal income for tax purposes. There is no separate taxation for sole proprietorships as there is for corporations. The rules for reporting income to the CCRA are, therefore, a motivator for producing financial statements. The accounting methods used by the sole proprietor are more likely to follow those used for tax purposes than those set forth under GAAP.

With regard to owner's equity accounts, there is little reason for the owner to distinguish the initial investment from the income retained in the business. For this reason, the owner's equity section of a sole proprietorship typically has only one account, which is sometimes called **owner's capital**. This account is used when the owner puts new capital into the business, when the business earns income (revenues and expenses are closed to this account), and when the owner withdraws cash from the business. Cash withdrawn from the business for personal use is usually referred to as a withdrawal by the owner. These withdrawals are the equivalent of dividends in a corporation. Because the owner is taxed on the combined basis of personal income and business income, these withdrawals are not taxed in the same manner as corporate dividends.

Partnership

A second form of business that is very similar to a sole proprietorship is a **partnership**. In a partnership, two or more individuals agree to conduct business under one name. The partner's involvement in the partnership can vary greatly. The rights and responsibilities of the partners are generally specified in a document called a **partnership agreement**. This document is very important because it specifies how the partners will make decisions about the business, including how they will share in the profits and losses of the partnership, as well as how the assets of the partnership will be distributed if the partnership dissolves. In the absence of a partnership agreement, the distribution of assets and profits is assumed to be equal for all partners. If the partners intend to share profits in some other proportion, this must be stated in a partnership agreement. For tax purposes, partnerships are not taxable entities; the income earned by the partners is passed through to them and must be reported on their personal tax returns, similar to the treatment of sole proprietorship income.

Partners can assume different responsibilities and risk in a partnership. **General partners** normally make day-to-day decisions about the business, share in profits and losses, and have unlimited liability. If the partnership defaults on its debts, creditors can sue one, more than one, or all of the general partners, taking both business assets and personal ones. **Limited partners**, on the other hand, have limited involvement in the partnership. Normally, they invest in the partnership but do not make day-to-day decisions about its operations. They share in profits and losses but creditors cannot normally sue them if the partnership runs into financial difficulty.

One of the major accounting problems in a partnership is distinguishing the roles that partners play as owners, creditors, and employees. For example, should the compensation paid to a partner who works as an employee of the partnership be treated as an expense of the partnership? That is, should all partners share in this expense, or should it be treated as a part of the partner's share of the profits from the business? As another example, suppose a partner lends money to the partnership. Should this be viewed as a liability of the partnership, or as part of the equity contributed by this partner? If the partnership liquidates, should this partner get paid back first as a creditor and then share in whatever is left, or should the loan be considered a part of the partner's equity? There is no single "right" answer to these questions, which is why these issues should all be addressed in the partnership agreement.

The accounting for the owners' equity section of a partnership requires that the partnership keep a separate account for each partner, usually called the partner's **capital account**. Each period, the profits or losses of the partnership must be distributed among the partners' capital accounts. This is usually a relatively complex process that takes into consideration the issues discussed in the preceding paragraph.

Sometimes there is also an account for each partner called a **drawing account**. This is an account that keeps track of the amounts withdrawn by the partner during the period. It is similar to a dividends declared account in a corporation, in that it collects payments made to owners. In the case of the drawings account, at the end of each accounting period it is closed into the capital account of the specific partner. As with sole proprietorships, such withdrawals are not taxable.

Detailed accounting rules for partnerships are sometimes covered in advanced accounting texts and will not be discussed here. The accounting for the transactions of a partnership other than owners' equity is essentially the same as that discussed in this book for corporations.

Corporation

The third major form of business organization is the **corporation**, which has been the focus of most of this book. It differs from sole proprietorships and partnerships in at least two significant ways. The first is that the corporation is legally separate from the shareholders. While the owners of sole proprietorships and partnerships can be held liable for the debts of their businesses, corporate shareholders have **limited liability** for the debts of the companies they own. Corporate shareholders cannot be made to pay for the company's debts out of their personal assets. Sole proprietors and partners do not enjoy this limited liability.

The second significant way in which corporations differ from proprietorships is the manner in which they are taxed. Because the corporation is viewed as a separate legal entity, the CCRA and provincial governments impose a corporate tax on the income it earns. This corporate tax is in addition to the personal income tax that shareholders pay on their personal income when they receive dividends or when they sell their shares and experience a gain or loss.

The basics of accounting for shareholders' equity in a company have been covered in preceding chapters of this book. Later in this chapter, details will be provided concerning more complex transactions that involve shareholders' equity.

accounting in the news

CORPORATIONS AND POLITICS

Typically, corporations run without the government interfering in management decisions. But the unusual history behind Fishery Products International (FPI) led to a much-publicized battle between the Newfoundland government and a seafood tycoon from Halifax over the future of Newfoundland's largest fish processor.

It started when John Risley, head of Clearwater Fine Foods Inc., won control of FPI's board of directors in a proxy battle and subsequently arranged a merger of the two companies. He later announced plans to upgrade three fish plants that would have cost almost half of the seasonal jobs there—reneging on an earlier promise not to lay off workers.

The plan provoked public anger and threats from the provincial government to block Risley's actions through legislation. Although a public company, FPI had originally been created from several failed fishing companies through an act of government as part of a bailout of the fishing industry. Premier Roger Grimes said that changing the rules governing the company was justified because FPI was a key element of an industry that sustains much of Newfoundland.

Risley said he was not prepared for the risks of running a company subject to political whim. He withdrew not only the plan but also the merger, saying it would be difficult to find investors if the province changed the legislation governing FPI.

Source: "Halifax's John Risley abandons merger," by Stephen Bornais, *The Daily News*, Halifax, Feb. 6, 2002.

Advantages and Disadvantages of the Different Forms of Organization

While there are many differences among sole proprietorships, partnerships, and corporations, the two primary differences just mentioned, legal liability and taxes, are sufficiently important to warrant detailed discussion here. With regard to legal liability, the owners of a sole proprietorship or partnership are fully liable for the debts of the business. If the business does not have sufficient assets to pay its debts, creditors have the right to try to collect from the personal assets of the owners. This feature is sometimes referred to as unlimited liability. The shareholders of corporations, on the other hand, enjoy limited liability unless required to give personal guarantees. The most a shareholder can lose is the amount of the investment in the shares. Creditors cannot seek satisfaction of their claims from the personal assets of corporate shareholders.

Limited liability is obviously an advantage of the corporate form of organization. There are some forms of partnerships, called **limited partnerships**, that share some of this advantage. In limited partnerships, there are general partners and limited partners. General partners have unlimited liability, whereas limited partners have limited liability. The downside for the limited partners is that they also have a limited say in making decisions within the partnership.

Where taxes are concerned, the income of partnerships and sole proprietorships is not taxed at the business level because it flows through to the individuals. Personal tax is then assessed according to the individual owner's tax bracket. Corporations, on the other hand, are subject to corporate taxation. An incorporated small business can obtain a tax advantage through tax deferral when profits are retained in the business. This occurs because the corporate tax rate is approximately 22% for a small business. The tax to be paid by the individual shareholders on dividends or capital gains (if they sell their shares), is deferred until dividends are received or the shares are sold. It is then taxed at the individual level. Corporate income is, therefore, subject to double taxation, once when the corporation pays taxes on corporate income and again when the shareholder pays taxes on a dividend distributed by the corporation. The income tax rules include methods intended to reduce the impact of this double taxation. This does not necessarily mean that the corporate form results in more tax being paid. The sum of the corporate tax and individual tax for a small business is approximately equal to the individual tax on business income. For larger corporations that cannot take advantage of the small business tax rate, the tax effect could be a disadvantage of the corporate form.

There are other advantages and disadvantages to each form of business. For example, incorporation requires a significant amount of paperwork and regulation, which makes a sole proprietorship or partnership easier to form. Although partnerships can be formed without any written agreement, a written partnership agreement prepared with legal assistance is advisable in order to avoid possible disagreements among the partners. Once established, corporations can raise additional capital much more easily than partnerships: they simply issue more shares or bonds. Partnerships and sole proprietorships are limited by the assets contributed by the owners and those earned by the business and not withdrawn. It is much easier to change your ownership interest if you are a shareholder than if you are a partner or a sole proprietor. You simply sell your shares on the stock market. If you no longer want to own a proprietorship, you must sell the whole business. If you are a partner and want to withdraw from the partnership, you must convince the other partners to buy you out or find another partner to buy your ownership interest. When establishing a new business, it is important to weigh all of the issues before deciding on the organizational form that will work best.

In Canada, corporations own the vast majority of business assets and almost all large businesses are organized as corporations. That is why we focus on accounting for corporations in this text.

CORPORATIONS

Let's look at corporations in more detail. Shareholders of corporations require certain types of legal protection, especially because the owners of most corporations are absentee shareholders; that is, they are not intimately involved in the day-to-day business of the company. This protection is provided by the laws of the jurisdiction under which the company is incorporated. In Canada, companies may be incorporated under the federal *Canada Business Corporations Act*, or under similar provincial acts that have been established in all 10 provinces. When investors decide to establish a business in the form of a corporation, they must first decide under which act they want to be incorporated. Normally, most companies in Canada are incorporated under the laws of the province in which the business, or at least the head office of the company, is to be located. Companies that intend to carry on business interprovincially or internationally may decide that being incorporated under federal legislation will provide them with more options. After deciding on where to be incorporated, the founding investors prepare a document called the **articles of incorporation**. The articles of incorporation include information about what type of business the company will conduct, how the board of directors will be organized, who the management will be, what kinds of shares will be issued, and other information. The exact content of the articles will depend on the decisions of the incorporating shareholders. Once the company has been incorporated, the articles of incorporation can generally be amended only by a vote of the shareholders.

SHARES

For accounting purposes, the most important section of the articles of incorporation is the description of the shares that will be issued. The maximum number of shares that the company can issue is specified in the articles. These are referred to as the **authorized shares**. In the past, companies would establish a fixed number of shares that they assumed would carry them for many years. When a company is first starting up, it is difficult to anticipate that you will ever issue the number of shares that you set as your authorized limit. (Remember our opening story? Shoppers Drug Mart issued 30 million shares in its first public offering.) However, companies found that issuing all of the authorized shares was not very hard to do. To increase the number of authorized shares, however, requires a change in the articles of incorporation, which requires a vote by the shareholders. To give you some perspective on numbers of shares, Sun-Rype Products, a medium-sized company, had 10,642,200 shares issued by the end of December 2001. Domtar Inc., one of the largest companies in Canada, had 226,202,379 common shares issued at the end of December 2001. In the United States, Microsoft had issued 5,383,000,000 shares by the end of June 2001. The magnitude of these numbers is difficult to conceive when you are starting a company. To overcome the problem of reaching the authorized limit set in the articles of incorporation, many companies today establish an *unlimited* number of authorized shares. This allows them the greatest freedom to use the issuance of shares as a means for raising capital.

Learning Objective

2

Describe the different types of shares and explain why corporations choose to issue a variety of share types.

In the past, the articles could also specify a dollar amount that was attached to each share. This dollar amount was known as the **par value**. Under most jurisdictions in Canada, par value shares are no longer permitted. Instead, most companies issue **no par value** shares. The original purpose of the par value was to protect the company's creditors by setting a limit on the dividends the company could pay. In most jurisdictions, a company was able to declare dividends only up to the value of the retained earnings. It could not pay dividends out of par value (i.e., the balance in the common shares account). If a company were allowed to declare a dividend equal to the total of retained earnings and the balance in the other equity accounts, the shareholders might then pay themselves a dividend of this amount (sometimes called a **liquidating dividend** because it liquidated the shareholders' investment). This might have left creditors with insufficient assets to satisfy their claims. Companies were able to avoid this constraint by setting very low par values and selling the shares at prices above the par value. Only the total of the par values was credited to the share account; the excess was credited to an account called paid-in capital, or premium on shares. Dividends paid out of this second account were permitted in some jurisdictions and were in fact liquidating dividends since they reduced the paid-in equity of the company.

While this is still theoretically true about par values today, the practical value of a par value is almost nonexistent. The par value of most shares is so small compared to the level of other shareholders' equity accounts and the level of liabilities that it provides very little protection to creditors. For this reason, when the *Canada Business Corporations Act* was changed in 1976, par value shares were no longer allowed. Instead, shares had to be no par value. When no par value shares are issued, the total amount received for the shares is put into one account, the share account. This larger amount is referred to as the **legal capital** and must be kept intact.

Except under specific circumstances, it cannot be paid out as dividends. This provides more protection for creditors. Once the *Canada Business Corporations Act* changed, most of the provincial acts were changed as well.

The articles of incorporation also specify the classes or types of shares that can be issued by the company if more than one class of shares is to be issued. **Sears Canada** has common shares and Class 1 preferred shares (which can be issued in more than one series). In 2000, Class 1, Preferred Shares, Series B were issued and immediately redeemed (bought back by the company as part of a restructuring process)[1]. In many companies, more than one class is authorized so that the company has more flexibility in attracting different kinds of investors. For example, some investors want the assurance of regular dividends to provide a steady income; others prefer no regular dividends but hope for increasing share values so that they can earn capital gains when they eventually sell their shares.

The different classes of shares differ in the rights that accrue to their holders. Two major classes of shares, **common shares** and **preferred shares**, are discussed in the following subsections. Different classes of shares can be authorized within each of these two major types. For example, some companies have multiple classes of common shares and multiple classes (sometimes these are called issues) of preferred shares. **BCE Inc.**, for example, had one class of common shares plus a Class B share class by the end of 2001 (none of the Class B shares were issued). It then had 10 series of preferred shares (Series Q, R, S, T, U, V, W, X, Y, and Z). BCE's board of directors has the power to set specific terms and conditions for each series. This allows for a great deal of flexibility in attracting investment in BCE.

Common Shares

Every corporation must have one class of shares that represents the basic voting ownership rights of the company. These shares are normally referred to as common shares. Corporations generally issue common shares through a firm of investment bankers, known as underwriters, in much the same way that bonds are issued (see Chapter 10 for a discussion of this process). When common or preferred shares are issued, the details and features of the shares being issued are discussed in a legal document called a **prospectus**, which is distributed to potential investors when shares (or a bond) are initially issued (sold).

Common shares carry a basic set of rights that allow the owner to share proportionately (based on the number of shares held) in:

1. Profits and losses
2. The selection of management of the corporation
3. Assets upon liquidation
4. Subsequent issues of shares (although not all jurisdictions in Canada provide for this basic right)

---

[1] Sears Canada is involved in joint venture real estate activities in which it jointly owns shopping malls that usually contain a Sears store. The issuance and immediate redemption of preferred shares enabled Sears Canada to facilitate a restructuring in one of these real estate joint ventures.

Rather than establishing complex income-sharing rules similar to a partnership, a corporation retains control over the distribution of its profits. It is sometimes useful to think of a corporation's profits or losses as being allocated to its shares, even if these earnings or losses are not actually paid out. The resulting per-share figure is useful in determining whether the corporation's profits are increasing or decreasing on an individual share basis. This earnings per share figure that corporations calculate provides a measure of performance that all shareholders can use. Recall from Chapter 3 that this is a calculation that consists of dividing the net income of the corporation by the average number of common shares outstanding during the year. A weighted average is used if the number of common shares outstanding changed during the year. Different classes of shares are entitled to different portions of the earnings. Normally, preferred shares are restricted to the amounts of their dividends and no more. Common shares normally have no restrictions on their rights to share in earnings once the claims of the creditors and the preferred shares have been satisfied.

If a corporation opts to pay dividends (it is not obligated to do so), shareholders of the same share class share proportionately in the distribution of earnings in the form of dividends. Corporations, in addition to reporting earnings per share, often report dividends per share. As will be seen shortly, the right to share in dividend distribution may be amended for different classes of shares, especially for preferred shares.

Common shareholders also have the right to vote on the selection of management for the corporation. The standard rule for voting is one share equals one vote. The more shares an individual owns, the greater the influence that individual has in the company. One of the shareholders' most important tasks is to elect members of the board of directors. The board of directors then represents the shareholders, and most decisions are made by a vote of the board of directors rather than by a vote of all shareholders. The board of directors hires (and fires) top-level management of the company and also declares the dividends that are paid to shareholders. Note the following example of how this right was exercised in **Spar Aerospace Ltd.**:

accounting in the news

SHAREHOLDER POWER

Shareholders wield great power. In 1999, Spar Aerospace Ltd. yielded to dissident shareholders who were demanding a new board of directors and a payout of the bulk of Spar's cash assets. The demands fuelled speculation that Spar's days were numbered.

The rebel shareholders, who represented 58% of outstanding shares, replaced seven of the nine-member board with five of their own choosing at Spar's annual meeting. The new board chairman, Eric Rosenfeld, was a principal in Spar's largest shareholder, Crescendo Partners LP, which held 19.9% of the company. Shareholders then voted for the board to initiate a shareholder payout of as much as $123 million of Spar's stated capital of $128 million, a move that would leave the maker of the famous Canadarm with virtually no growth potential.

> Analysts speculated that the board would sell Spar's aviation services company, its sole business asset following a major period of restructuring, and then shut the company down.
>
> Source: "Dissidents control Spar," by Peter Fitzpatrick, *National Post (Financial Post)*, May 14, 1999, p. C1, C6.
>
> Further to the story:
> On January 23, 2002, L-3 Communications Corporation, a New York company, purchased 71.9% of the outstanding shares of Spar Aerospace Ltd. Spar ceased trading on the Toronto Stock Exchange and became a subsidiary of L-3 Communications. Spar continues to operate as an aviation services company specializing in maintenance, repair and overhaul, and the upgrading of military and civilian aircraft.
>
> Source: News release, Investor Information, Frequently Asked Questions, www.spar.ca.

The third right of common shareholders is to share in assets upon liquidation. If a company goes bankrupt or otherwise liquidates, there is an established order in which creditors and shareholders are paid. Common shareholders come last on that list; whatever is left after creditors are paid is then divided proportionately among them based on their relative number of shares. This means that common shareholders bear the highest risk, since there may be nothing left over for them.

The fourth right of common shares is to share proportionately in any new issuance of shares. This is called the **preemptive right**. Preemptive rights are not automatic. They must be explicitly stated in the articles of incorporation. This right allows current holders of shares to retain their proportionate interest in the company when new shares are issued. For example, a shareholder owning 20% of a company's shares has the preemptive right to purchase 20% of any new shares of that class that may be issued. Without this right, an investor that had a **controlling interest** in a company (i.e., more than 50% of the outstanding shares) could lose that controlling interest if the new shares were issued to another investor. Of course, this scenario is unlikely as controlling interest includes the right to vote for the directors of the company so that directors who support the majority owner can be elected. The greatest protection is for shareholders who own a **minority** or **noncontrolling interest** in a company. Preemptive rights prevent their ownership interests from being diluted.

When more than one class of common shares is issued, each class is distinguished by some amendment to the fundamental rights just described. For example, a second class of non-voting common shares might be issued that may be entitled to conversion to voting common shares under certain conditions. This obviously affects the control that holders of the voting common shares have over the operations of the company. There might also be differences in the rights to share in the liquidation values of the assets. **Comac Food Group Inc.** provides an example of a company with two classes of common shares, Class A performance shares, which are non-voting, and Class B voting common shares, as shown in

Exhibit 11-1. The Class A performance shares are convertible on a one-for-one basis to Class B voting common shares when the company reaches certain performance levels, hence their name.

COMAC FOOD GROUP INC. (2001)

10. SHAREHOLDERS' EQUITY
Share capital authorized

CLASS A PERFORMANCE SHARES

900,000 Class A non voting performance shares, which convert on a one to one basis in increments of 150,000 shares to Class B common shares upon the Company reaching certain performance levels measured by funds from operations. Each performance level increases in increments of $100,000 with the first performance level starting at $300,000 per annum.

During the fiscal year ended March 26, 2000, all 900,000 Class A performance shares were converted to 900,000 Class B common shares.

CLASS B COMMON SHARES

Unlimited number of Class B voting common shares.

Dividends paid to different classes of common shares may also be paid on a different basis, although each outstanding share of any class of shares will be paid the same amount.

Preferred Shares

Preferred shares are shares that have preference over common shares with regard to dividends. This does not mean that preferred shareholders are guaranteed a dividend, but if dividends are declared, they will receive them before common shareholders. Many times, in addition to the preference for dividends, there is also some preference with regard to assets in the event of liquidation.

The amount of the preferred dividend is usually stated as a dollar amount per share, such as a "$2 preferred share issue." Such an issue would pay a dividend of $2 per share per year. For example, **BCE Inc.** has $1.5435 Series R, $1.385 Series U, $1.3625 series W, and $1.15 Series Y preferred shares.

Besides the difference in priority for dividends, another difference between common and preferred shares is that preferred shares are usually non-voting. One of the troubling issues in accounting is how to deal with securities such as preferred shares that have characteristics that make them look more like debt than common shares. Non-voting preferred shares with a fixed dividend amount are not much different from debt (which is also non-voting) that has a fixed interest payment. The only real difference is that the company is not obligated to pay the preferred dividend, whereas the interest on the debt is a true obligation and a legal liability.

Also, most preferred shares do not have a maturity date. Preferred shareholders often only receive the initial investment back when the company liquidates.

There are other features of preferred shares with which you should be familiar. Preferred dividends may be **cumulative**. Cumulative means that if a dividend is not declared on the preferred shares in one year, it carries over into the next year. In the second year, both the prior year's preferred dividend and the current year's preferred dividend must be declared before any common dividends can be declared. Dividends from prior years that have not been declared are called **dividends in arrears**. Note that for BCE, all of the series of preferred shares are cumulative. In fact, most preferred shares are cumulative.

Convertible preferred shares are convertible, at the option of the shareholder, into common shares (or other preferred shares) based on a ratio stated in the articles of incorporation. **CCL Industries Ltd.** has an interesting share capital arrangement. It has Class A shares that are voting and are convertible into Class B shares on a one-for-one basis. The Class B shares are non-voting but in all other respects rank equal to the Class A shares. Currently, the dividend on Class A shares has been set at 5 cents less than that for the Class B shares. As a result, some Class A shareholders have converted to Class B shares. All of BCE's preferred share series are convertible into another series of preferred shares at the holder's option.

Redeemable preferred shares can be bought back by the company (retired) at a price and time specified in the articles of incorporation, at the option of the issuing company. **Bombardier Inc.** has two preferred share issues, both of which are redeemable. The Series 2 shares are redeemable at $25.00 per share on August 1, 2002, or at $25.50 thereafter. The Series 3 shares are redeemable at $25.00 per share on August 1, 2007, and on August 1 of every fifth year thereafter. **Retractable preferred shares** can be sold back to the company (retired) at the option of the shareholder. The price that must be paid for them and the periods of time when they can be sold are specified in the articles of incorporation.

The last feature we are going to discuss is participation. **Participating preferred shares** are preferred shares that not only have a preference with regard to dividends but, if dividends are declared to common shareholders beyond the level declared to the preferred shareholders, the preferred shareholders share in the excess dividends. At one time, BCE had preferred shares that were participating. However, none of its current series of preferred shares has this feature. Most preferred shares are non-participating.

While the features of various classes of shares differ, the accounting issues relating to all of them are basically the same. Therefore, in the sections that follow, we limit the discussion to common shares.

Learning Objective
3

Prepare journal entries for share transactions, including the issuance and payment of dividends.

Issuance of Common Shares

When common shares are issued for cash, the company accounts for the proceeds from the issuance by debiting the cash account. The credit entry is then to a common shares account. This common shares account is sometimes referred to as **paid-in capital** or **legal capital**. Remember that, to provide protection for creditors, the amount credited to the common shares account cannot be paid out as dividends.

To illustrate the issuance entry, suppose that Rosman Company issues 1,000 common shares for $20 a share. The following entry would be made:

SHARE ISSUANCE ENTRY		
A-Cash	20,000	
SE-Common shares		20,000

Historically, companies were permitted to issue shares that had a stated or par value. With stated or par value shares, only the total of the stated or par value was credited to the common shares account, and any remaining amount was credited to another equity account. Although few jurisdictions now allow par value shares, you may still encounter them.

To illustrate the issuance entry for par value shares, suppose that Green Company issued 1,000 common shares for $15 a share that had a par value of $10 per share. The following entry would have been made:

SHARE ISSUANCE ENTRY		
A-Cash	15,000	
SE-Common shares		10,000
SE-Contributed capital		5,000

Note that the additional $5 per share (the amount in excess of par) is recorded in an account called Contributed capital. This account is sometimes called *contributed surplus in excess of par* or *additional paid-in capital*.

Treasury Shares

Subsequent to issuance, the company may decide to buy back some of its own shares. It might do this because it wants to reduce the number of shares outstanding, or because it wants to use those shares to satisfy its stock option plans rather than issue new shares. Shares that have been repurchased by the issuing company are called **treasury shares**. In most jurisdictions in Canada, treasury shares are cancelled immediately upon purchase. In a few jurisdictions, they are not cancelled immediately and are considered to be issued but not outstanding.

Three terms are used to refer to the number of shares of a company: **authorized shares**, **issued shares**, and **outstanding shares**. The maximum number of shares that can be issued by the company according to the articles of incorporation are the **authorized** shares. As mentioned earlier, many companies avoid the possible limitations that might result from an authorized limit by stating that they have the right to issue an unlimited number of shares. Those that have been sold (issued) by the company are considered **issued** shares. As long as the shares remain in the possession of shareholders outside the company, they are considered to be **outstanding**. If, however, the company purchases some of its own shares from the market, the shares remain issued but are no longer outstanding. If the company subsequently cancels the shares, they will cease to be issued and will revert to the status of only being authorized. If the company does not have to cancel the shares but instead holds them as treasury shares, the issued shares less those held as treasury shares are the outstanding shares. Examples of the use of these terms can be found in Note 9 of the financial statements of **METRO Inc.** shown in Exhibit 11-2. METRO has an unlimited number of First Preferred Shares, Class A Subordinate Shares, and Class B Shares. No preferred shares have been issued. The Class A shares have one voting right per share, are participating, and are convertible into Class B shares in case of a takeover bid. The Class B shares have 16 votes per share, are participating, and are convertible into Class A shares.

When a company repurchases its own shares and cancels them, a credit is made to cash for the cost of the shares. The debit entry then has to reduce shareholders' equity since the shares are no longer issued or outstanding. A problem arises if the cost of the shares repurchased is different from the amount received when the shares were originally issued. Shares that were issued in the past were issued perhaps at different times and for different amounts. If this is the case, then the average issue price must be determined by dividing the total amount in the shares account by the total number of shares outstanding before the repurchase.

As an example, suppose that Lee Industries Ltd. had 150,000 common shares outstanding and a balance of $1,500,000 in its Common Shares account. The average issue price is $10 ($1,500,000/150,000). If Lee repurchases 1,000 shares for $9 each, then it is paying $1 less than the average issue price. This $1 per share is not considered to be a profit or gain, and therefore does not appear on the income statement. The reason for this is that the $1 does not result from an activity that is part of the normal operations of the company. The company was not incorporated to earn money by trading in its own shares. As a general rule, companies never earn revenues or incur losses from transactions involving their own equities. Rather, the $1 is still part of shareholders' equity and is credited to a separate account called "Contributed Surplus." The entry to record this repurchase would be as follows:

SE-Common shares	10,000	
A-Cash		9,000
SE-Contributed surplus		1,000

EXHIBIT 11-2

METRO INC. (2001)

9.   CAPITAL STOCK

AUTHORIZED

Unlimited number of First Preferred Shares, non-voting, without par value, issuable in series.

Unlimited number of Class A Subordinate Shares, bearing one voting right per share, participating, convertible into Class B Shares in case of a takeover bid on Class B Shares, without par value.

Unlimited number of Class B Shares, bearing 16 voting rights per share, participating, convertible in case of disqualification into an equal number of Class A Subordinate Shares on the basis of one Class A Subordinate Share for each Class B Share held, without par value.

METRO INC. (2001)

EXHIBIT 11-2
CONT.

9. CAPITAL STOCK (cont'd)

ISSUED

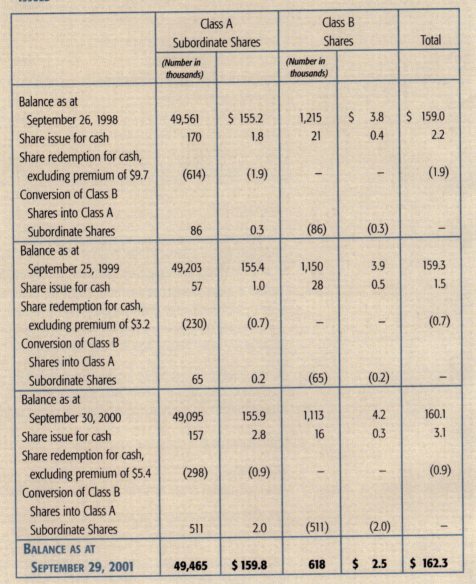

	Class A Subordinate Shares		Class B Shares		Total
	(Number in thousands)		*(Number in thousands)*		
Balance as at September 26, 1998	49,561	$ 155.2	1,215	$ 3.8	$ 159.0
Share issue for cash	170	1.8	21	0.4	2.2
Share redemption for cash, excluding premium of $9.7	(614)	(1.9)	–	–	(1.9)
Conversion of Class B Shares into Class A Subordinate Shares	86	0.3	(86)	(0.3)	–
Balance as at September 25, 1999	49,203	155.4	1,150	3.9	159.3
Share issue for cash	57	1.0	28	0.5	1.5
Share redemption for cash, excluding premium of $3.2	(230)	(0.7)	–	–	(0.7)
Conversion of Class B Shares into Class A Subordinate Shares	65	0.2	(65)	(0.2)	–
Balance as at September 30, 2000	49,095	155.9	1,113	4.2	160.1
Share issue for cash	157	2.8	16	0.3	3.1
Share redemption for cash, excluding premium of $5.4	(298)	(0.9)	–	–	(0.9)
Conversion of Class B Shares into Class A Subordinate Shares	511	2.0	(511)	(2.0)	–
BALANCE AS AT SEPTEMBER 29, 2001	**49,465**	**$ 159.8**	**618**	**$ 2.5**	**$ 162.3**

If Lee had paid $12 per share, it would have paid $2 more than the average issue price per share of $10. In this case, the $2 extra per share would reduce shareholders' equity. Normally, the $2 is debited to Retained Earnings as follows:

SE-Common shares	10,000	
SE-Retained earnings	2,000	
A-Cash		12,000

If there had been a previous repurchase and cancellation of treasury shares that created a contributed surplus account (similar to the first part of this example), the contributed surplus account could have been debited instead of retained earnings. Further details on the accounting for treasury share transactions can be found in more advanced accounting texts.

DIVIDENDS, STOCK SPLITS, AND OPTIONS

Learning Objective

4

Describe the different types of dividends and explain why companies might opt to issue one type of dividend rather than another.

Cash Dividends

Dividends are payments to shareholders from the total net income retained in a company in the Retained Earnings account. Dividends are a payment in return for the use of the shareholders' money by the company. They are paid to shareholders only if the board of directors has voted to declare a dividend. The declaration of a cash dividend makes the dividend a legal liability of the company. Dividends are not paid on treasury shares because these are held internally by the company, and companies cannot pay dividends to themselves. They are paid only on outstanding shares.

Here is an example of a dividend notice. On July 16, 2002, **Sears Canada** announced that it was paying a quarterly dividend on its common shares of $0.06. The dividend was payable on September 16, 2002, to shareholders of record on August 15, 2002. This announcement was made in several financial newspapers in Canada so that investors would know that a dividend was forthcoming.

Three dates are important in the **dividend declaration** process. The first is the **date of declaration**. This is the date on which the board of directors votes to declare a dividend. For Sears Canada, that date is July 16, 2002. On the date of declaration, the company records its obligation to pay the dividend by creating a dividends payable account and a dividends declared account. Suppose that Sears Canada had 106,750,000 common shares outstanding on July 16, 2002. The entry to record the declaration would be:

DIVIDEND DECLARATION ENTRY		
SE-Dividends declared	6,405,000	
L-Dividends payable		6,405,000

The debit is usually to a Dividends declared account, which is a temporary account that is closed to Retained Earnings at the end of the accounting period. Dividends declared does not appear on the income statement. It is not an expense of doing business; it is a return to shareholders on their investment. Companies typically declare dividends quarterly. Therefore, the Dividends declared account accumulates all four quarterly dividends by the end of the fiscal year. Not all companies use a Dividends declared account. Some debit dividends directly to Retained Earnings.

In the declaration of the dividend, the board of directors specifies that the dividend is payable to shareholders of record on the **date of record**. This second important date is the date on which a shareholder must own the shares in order to receive the dividend. For Sears Canada, that date is the close of business on August 15, 2002. The date of record is typically two weeks after the declaration date. Sears Canada's date is about a month later. This delay is needed because most public companies' shares are traded every day, so the company has no up-to-date record of the owners of its shares. The delay also allows new owners time to inform the company that they are owners of the shares. If a shareholder sells shares before the date of record, the new owner of the shares will then be entitled to receive the dividend.

In the shares market, traders talk about the **ex-dividend day**. The ex-dividend day is the day on which shares are sold without the right to receive the dividend. Purchasing the shares on the ex-dividend day means that the buyer will not receive the dividend; it belongs to the seller. As you might expect, the price of the shares decreases on the ex-dividend day to reflect the loss of this dividend.

A few weeks after the date of record, the company pays the dividend. This third important date is called the **date of payment**. Sears Canada's date of payment is September 16, 2002. Again, a delay is needed so the company can update its list of shareholders and calculate the total amount of dividends owed to each. This total amount is calculated as dividends per share times the number of shares owned.

At the date of record, no entry is made. The company is simply trying to find out who owns the shares on this date to determine who is entitled to receive a dividend cheque. On the payment date, the company sends out the cheques to the shareholders and must make an entry to record the reduction in cash and the payment of the liability. Sears Canada would make the following entry for the payment of the dividend declared:

DIVIDEND PAYMENT ENTRY		
L-Dividends payable	6,405,000	
A-Cash		6,405,000

Property Dividends

It is also possible for a company to declare a dividend that will be settled with some resource other than cash. Dividends of this type are called **property dividends** or **dividends in kind**. These dividends are rare, because the assets other than cash that can be paid out are necessarily limited to assets that can be divided into small, equal parts. A story is told of a liquor company that was short on cash but long on excess inventory and declared a dividend of one bottle per share. Whether this actually happened or not is not as important as the concept it illustrates. If a company issues a property dividend, it must be able to give the same amount per share to each shareholder. In May 2000, BCE owned approximately 37% of Nortel Networks. It decided to distribute 35% of its 37% investment to its shareholders in the form of a dividend. BCE shareholders received 1.57 Nortel shares for every BCE common share held.

The major accounting question for property dividends is how to value the dividend. Should the property be valued at its fair market value, or at its cost? In

Canada, property dividends are valued at their fair market value because this represents the value the company is giving up to pay the dividend. This means that if the property is currently being carried at cost, a gain or loss must be recognized to bring the property to its fair market value. Suppose that a company declares a property dividend that it will make by transferring inventory with a fair market value of $12,000 to its shareholders. The inventory is recorded at $9,000, which is the original cost to the company. The following entries would be made:

PROPERTY DIVIDEND ENTRIES		
Declaration of dividend (at fair market value)		
SE-Property dividend declared	12,000	
L-Dividend payable		12,000

Recognition of fair market value on declaration date and payment of dividend on payment date:

L-Dividend payable	12,000	
A-Inventory		9,000
SE-Gain on inventory		3,000

Stock Dividends

Stock dividends are dividends that are satisfied by issuing additional shares of the company to shareholders instead of cash or property. Stock dividends can be used to issue dividends when the company does not want to, or is not in a position to, use any of its assets for dividends. Shareholders who receive stock dividends have the option of keeping the new shares received or selling them for cash.

Whereas the issuance of a cash or property dividend reduces the overall value of the company (because cash or other assets have been removed), the issuance of a stock dividend does not. For example, assume that a company has 100 shares outstanding. These shares are held by 10 different people, each with 10 shares. In other words, each owns 10% of the company. If the company issues a 10% stock dividend, it will issue 10 additional shares (100 shares × 10%), one for every ten shares held. Each shareholder will now have 11 shares and the company will have 110 shares outstanding. Where before the company's value was divided among 100 shares, now the same value is divided among 110 shares. The overall value of the company has not changed, nor has the percentage ownership of each of the shareholders—they still own 10% each—but the value attached to each share is a little less.

If shareholders are no better off after a stock dividend than they were before, why would a company issue such a dividend? There are a couple of good reasons. First, it is possible that the shareholders *are* better off. Going back to our example, if the market value of the shares prior to the stock dividend was $10 a share, the market would have valued the company at $1,000 ($10 × 100 shares). After the stock dividend, there are 110 shares so the market value of the shares should drop to $9.09 ($1,000/110 shares). If the market price drops to $9.09, each shareholder is no better off. However, often the market price does not fully compensate for the increase in the number of shares. If the market price only drops to $9.15, the shareholders are better off. The market value of a 10% interest would now be $100.65 ($9.15 × 11 shares) where before it was $100 ($10 × 10).

The second reason is that issuing a stock dividend provides an opportunity for the company to *capitalize* its retained earnings. When cash or property dividends were declared and subsequently issued, a temporary account called dividends declared was used. At the end of the accounting period, this account is closed into retained earnings, causing it to decrease. When stock dividends are issued, the same procedure will be followed, and retained earnings will decrease. However, at the same time that retained earnings decreases, the share capital account will increase because more shares were issued. Because the amount in the share capital account represents stated or legal capital (meaning that it cannot be reduced to issue dividends), the company has taken an amount from an account from which dividends can be issued and put it in an account from which they cannot, thus *capitalizing* it. Companies that have a substantial accumulation of retained earnings but do not have cash available for a dividend will sometimes issue a stock dividend to reduce the retained earnings amount.

As with property dividends, the question that underlies stock dividends is: what value should be attached to the shares that are issued? Should the fair market value of the shares be used, or should some other value be selected?

To answer this question, consider the following extreme situations. When a stock dividend is declared, it is stated as a percent of the outstanding shares. Suppose a company declares a 100% stock dividend. This means that each shareholder will receive one additional share for each one that is currently held. No cash changes hands in this transaction. What would you expect to happen to the market value of the shares? It is likely that the value of a share would be cut in half. There is no change in the value of the company's assets or liabilities, only a doubling of the number of shares that represent ownership. If there is no change in the value of the company, then the price per share should adjust for the number of new shares that have been issued. This suggests that the value of the new shares issued is zero.

At the other extreme, suppose the company issues one additional share as a stock dividend. The recipient of the share can probably sell the share for the fair market value of the existing shares on that date. Assuming that there are large numbers of shares already on the market, it is unlikely that the price per share would adjust for the issuance of this one additional share. In this case, then, the fair market value of the share issued would seem to measure adequately the value of the dividend. In theory, the market price should adjust for the issuance of new shares in a stock dividend regardless of the number of shares issued. As a practical matter, however, it is unlikely that the market will fully adjust for very small stock dividends, which makes the fair market value of the shares a reasonable measure of the value given up by the company.

How, then, does the company value the shares that are issued in a stock dividend? Since most stock dividends are for relatively small percentages of the shares issued (similar to the second extreme example), most companies account for them by using the fair market value of the shares as at the date of declaration.

The market price that is used to record the issuance of a small stock dividend should be the market price on the date the dividend is declared. Unlike a cash or property dividend, the board of directors has the power to revoke the stock dividend at any time prior to its actual issuance. This means that the dividend does not represent a legal liability to the company on the date of declaration. For this reason, some companies do not record an entry on the date of declaration. If an entry is recorded, the credit part of the entry is made to a shareholders' equity account called Stock Dividends Issuable and not to a Dividends Payable account. Upon issuance, the credit is made to the shares account and the Stock Dividends Issuable account is removed.

To illustrate, let's suppose that a company decides to issue a 15% stock dividend when 100,000 shares are outstanding and the market price of a share is $30. The following entries would be made for the declaration and issuance:

SMALL STOCK DIVIDEND ENTRIES

Declaration		
SE-Dividends declared	450,000	
SE-Stock dividend issuable		450,000
Issuance		
SE-Stock dividend issuable	450,000	
SE-Common shares		450,000

Stock Splits

Another transaction that is very similar to a stock dividend is a **stock split**. A stock split is usually stated as a ratio. A two-for-one stock split is one in which each share currently held by shareholders is exchanged for two new shares. When this is done, the numbers of shares authorized and outstanding are adjusted to compensate for the increase in the number of shares. In a two-for-one split, the number of shares outstanding is doubled. Splits typically involve large numbers of shares, and the arguments discussed earlier with regard to large stock dividends apply here as well. The additional shares mean no increase or decrease in the value of the company, so the shares' market price simply adjusts to compensate for the split. Note the following example from **Bombardier Inc.**

EXHIBIT 11-3

BOMBARDIER INC., 2001

12. Share Capital

Share Split

On June 20, 2000, the shareholders of the Corporation approved a Class A (multiple voting) and Class B (subordinate voting) common share split on a two-for-one basis, effective as of the close of business on July 7, 2000. The number of shares and per share amounts included in these consolidated financial statements have been adjusted to give retroactive effect to the share split.

In accounting for a stock split, there is no change in the dollar amounts of any of the shareholders' equity accounts. No journal entry is made in the accounting system. The only change is that the number of shares issued and outstanding changes. This change can be accomplished with an informal or **memorandum entry** in the accounting system.

Why would a company want to double or triple the number of shares outstanding? The main reason is that a stock split improves the marketability of a company's shares. As a company grows, the market value of its shares generally rises. The share price can get quite high. As the price rises, fewer investors have the necessary funds to buy the shares. To lower the price so that it is within reach of more investors, the company may split its shares, which will cut the market price per share. IBM, for example, has split its shares numerous times since its incorporation as its price per share escalated.

Stock Options

A **stock option** on common shares is an agreement between two parties to either buy or sell shares at a fixed price at some future date. One type of option is granted by a company to an employee, which allows the employee to purchase the company's shares at a fixed price. This type of option is generally used as a form of compensation and as an incentive to employees. If employees are also shareholders, they may work harder for the company because they are owners as well. If the company grows because of their efforts, they can share in that growth by having shares that are increasing in value. For example, it was reported in many newspapers in 1996 that an executive with the **Potash Company of Saskatchewan** earned almost $3 million by cashing in stock options, buying 12,900 shares from the company at $17.50 and selling them the same day at $102.50 and then buying 22,500 shares at $25.50 and selling them at $104.125. You might wonder why the price the executive paid was so low. The stock option plans were probably created several years before the executive exercised the options. At the time the plans were created, those prices of $17.50 and $22.50 may not have been so different from the market price at the time. It is not uncommon for large corporations to compensate their senior executives with stock option plans. It is also not uncommon for the **exercise price** on those plans to be significantly below the market value. If, through effective management, the executive can increase the value of the company, which will translate into an increase in the market value of the company's shares, both the executive and the company benefit.

Stock option plans offered to employees who are not top executives often have exercise prices closer to the market price at the time the plan was created. The idea behind these plans is similar to the rationale behind the executive plans. The plan provides an incentive for the employees to work hard to improve the performance of the company so that the market price of the shares exceeds the exercise price. When the time comes for employees to exercise their options, they pay the exercise price, obtain the shares, and can either sell them for the current market price and realize a profit, or continue to hold the shares in hopes that the price will go up even further. Obviously, if the share price never exceeds the exercise price, the employees will not exercise their options.

Companies normally disclose details regarding their stock option plans. Exhibit 11-4 shows the stock option plan outstanding for **WestJet Airlines Ltd.** on December 31, 2001.

WESTJET AIRLINES LTD. (2001)
NOTES TO CONSOLIDATED FINANCIAL STATEMENTS

Years ended December 31, 2001 and 2000
(Tabular Amounts are Stated in Thousands of Dollars)

6. Share capital (continued):

(d) Stock Option Plan:

The Corporation has a Stock Option Plan, whereby up to a maximum of 4,565,693 common shares may be issued to directors, officers and employees of the Corporation subject to the following limitations:

(i)   the number of common shares reserved for issuance to any one optionee will not exceed 5% of the issued and outstanding common shares at any time;

(ii)   the number of common shares reserved for issuance to insiders shall not exceed 10% of the issued and outstanding common shares; and

(iii)   the number of common shares issuable under the Plan which may be issued within a one year period shall not exceed 10% of the issued and outstanding common shares at any time.

Stock options are granted at a price that equals the market value and have a term of four years.

Changes in the number of options, with their weighted average exercise prices, are summarized below:

	2001		2000	
	Number of options	Weighted average exercise price	Number of options	Weighted average exercise price
Stock options outstanding, beginning of year	3,358,121	$ 9.64	3,222,338	$ 2.84
Granted	1,787,734	21.96	1,272,850	20.48
Exercised	(1,346,015)	2.88	(1,120,944)	2.38
Cancelled	(80,162)	20.60	(16,123)	10.54
Stock options outstanding, end of year	3,719,678	$ 17.77	3,358,121	$ 9.64
Exercisable, end of year	552,886	$ 3.62	973,249	$ 3.02

Note that the plan is reserved for directors, officers, and employees of the company. The exercise price varies from a low of $2.38 to a high of $21.96 (each original issue price equalled the market price at the time of granting) and that the stock options are not exercisable for four years after the date of grant. The market price on December 31, 2001, was just under $16.00. At this time, there were stock options that were exercisable at an average price of $3.62 per share. The probability of these options being exercised is high. During 2001, 1,787,734 new options were granted, 1,346,015 were exercised, and 80,162 were cancelled or expired.

With respect to stock option plans, one of the major questions for accounting purposes is whether to record compensation expense for this type of incentive-based plan. When options are granted, most of them are not immediately worth anything since the exercise price may be close to, or even above, the current share price (WestJet's price equalled the market price). In addition, some stock option plans allow employees to exercise them only after a certain period of time, and only if they are still employed by the company (for WestJet, that is four years). So, even if the option appears to be worth something, an employee may not be able to benefit immediately from the granting of the option.

If an option is priced at or above the current market price, does that mean it is worthless? The answer is a qualified no. Employees may not be able to, nor do they have to, exercise the options immediately. There is generally an extended period of time over which the employees can exercise the option. There may, however, be an **expiration date** specified, after which the option can no longer be exercised. The option will be of some value (in present-value terms) if there is some probability that the share price will exceed the exercise price before the expiration date. The more likely this is, the higher the value of the option.

Regardless of whether the stock option plans appear to have value or not, they generally cannot be traded because they are restricted to the employees to whom they are issued. Therefore, the value of employee stock options is difficult to establish. Because they do not trade, the value of employee stock options can only be estimated. Financing methods have been developed that enable accountants to determine a value for the option. The difference between the calculated value and the exercise price is recorded as compensation expense by the company over the period of time between the date of the grant and the date when the options are exercisable.

On the date of exercise, the company normally recognizes the receipt of the proceeds from the employee and the issuance of common shares. The shares are valued at the amount of cash received by the company plus an amount equal to the amount that was recorded as compensation expense. Thus, the shares are recorded at or close to their fair value.

STATEMENT OF RETAINED EARNINGS

In the preceding discussions of shares and dividends, we made several references to the use of the retained earnings account. Many companies summarize the changes in their retained earnings in a separate statement, the Statement of Retained Earnings. The format of this statement is very simple. It starts with the opening balance of the retained earnings at the beginning of the year. Then it shows the net income or loss for the year, which comes directly from the income statement. This is followed by the dividends declared in the year. Next appear any other items that affect retained earnings. Finally, the balance of the retained earnings at the end of the year appears. The end balance is the one that appears on the current balance sheet.

An example is shown in Exhibit 11-5 for **Intrawest Corporation**. Note that the balance of the retained earnings at the beginning of the 2001 fiscal year was

Learning Objective
5

Explain the purpose of the statement of retained earnings.

$131,953 thousand, net income (net earnings) for the year was $60,587 thousand, and dividends of $4,618 thousand were declared. The end balance of $187,922 thousand is the amount that appears for retained earnings on the December 31, 2001, balance sheet.

EXHIBIT 11-5   INTRAWEST CORPORATION (2001)

CONSOLIDATED STATEMENTS OF RETAINED EARNINGS

For the years ended June 30, 2001 and 2000
(in thousands of United States dollars)

	2001	2000
Retained earnings, beginning of year	$ 131,953	$ 77,088
Net income	60,587	51,992
Reduction in redemption price of non-resort preferred shares (note 12(a))	–	7,588
Dividends	(4,618)	(4,715)
Retained earnings, end of year	$ 187,922	$ 131,953

AN INTERNATIONAL PERSPECTIVE

Reports from Other Countries

The accounting for the issuance and retirement of common shares is fairly standard across different countries. The biggest difference between Canada and some other countries is the establishment of reserves. Reserves in other countries can be used to set aside retained earnings in separate accounts so that they are unavailable to pay dividends. The part set aside is termed as "appropriated retained earnings" and the amount remaining is called "unappropriated retained earnings." Another way reserves can be used is to record changes in the value of assets or liabilities that do not pass through the income statement. In Canada, these reserves do not affect earnings for the period and are only allowed under very specific circumstances. In the United Kingdom, property, plant, and equipment can be revalued based on market values. The increase (or decrease) in value does not pass through the income statement, but is instead recorded in a separate account in shareholders' equity.

In Japan, several types of reserves are permitted in the shareholders' equity section. A portion of the balance sheet and a footnote for **Nippon Steel Corporation** are shown in Exhibit 11-6. These disclosures illustrate the use of shareholders' equity reserves. The "reserve for revaluation of land" arose when the company revalued its land according to the *Law concerning the Revaluation of Land*. The company determined that the market value of the land was higher than the current carrying value and, therefore, increased it on the balance sheet and recorded the reserve.

In Canada, the use of the word "reserve" is generally discouraged because users of financial statements may believe it refers to cash that has been set aside, which is erroneous. In Canada, its use is limited to references to appropriations of retained earnings.

NIPPON STEEL CORPORATION (2001)

EXHIBIT 11-6

SHAREHOLDERS' EQUITY

Common stock:			
Authorized — 9,917,077,000 shares			
Issued and outstanding, par value			
¥50 per share:			
6,806,980,977 shares as of March 31, 2002 and 2001	419,524	419,524	3,148,405
Additional paid-in capital	105,518	105,518	791,883
Unrealized gains on revaluation of land (Note 6)	7,488	5,675	56,200
Retained earnings (Note 9)	338,565	378,282	2,540,826
Unrealized gains on available-for-sale securities (Note 13)	54,898	94,187	411,992
Foreign currency translation adjustments	(18,822)	(23,491)	(141,260)
Less: Treasury stock, at cost	(21)	(1)	(163)
Total shareholders' equity	907,150	979,695	6,807,883
Total liabilities and shareholders' equity	¥4,030,596	¥4,232,011	$30,248,376

6. Revaluation of Land for Business

(Year ended March 31, 2002)
Revaluation of land used for business purpose was carried out in accordance with the 'Law concerning Revaluation of Land' and relating amendments for some Nippon Steel Corporation's consolidated subsidiaries and affiliates to which the equity method is applied.

Evaluation differences computed by consolidated subsidiaries, net of tax and minority interest, which were charged to "Deferred tax assets or liabilities" and "Minority interest in consolidated subsidiaries," respectively, were recorded as a separate component of shareholders' equity with a name of "Unrealized gains on revaluation of land."

Additionally, evaluation differences accounted for by affiliates were recorded as a separate component of shareholders' equity with a name of "Unrealized gains on revaluation of land" in proportion to equity rate.

• Method of revaluation
Calculations were made in accordance with the Law concerning Revaluation of Land.

(Revaluation made on March 31, 2000)
• Difference between the fair value and carrying amounts of the revalued land at the end of March 31, 2001: ¥10,936 million ($82,078 thousand)

(Revaluation made on March 31, 2002)
• Book-value of the land for business before the revaluation thereof: ¥2,199 million ($16,507 thousand)
• Book-value of the land for business after the revaluation thereof: ¥5,675 million ($42,596 thousand)

(Year ended March 31, 2001)
Revaluation of land used for business purpose was carried out in accordance with the 'Law concerning Revaluation of Land' and relating amendments for some Nippon Steel Corporation's consolidated subsidiaries and affiliates to which the equity method is applied.

Evaluation differences, net of tax and minority interest, which were charged to "Deferred tax assets or liabilities" and "Minority interest in consolidated subsidiaries," respectively, were recorded as a separate component of shareholders' equity with a name of "Unrealized gains on revaluation of land."

• Method of revaluation
Calculations were made in accordance with the Law concerning Revaluation of Land.
• Date of revaluation
March 31, 2000
• Difference between the fair value and carrying amounts of the revalued land at the end of March 31, 2001: ¥6,159 million

FINANCIAL STATEMENT ANALYSIS

Learning Objective

Calculate and interpret the price/earnings ratio and the return on shareholders' equity ratio, which are often used in decision-making.

The Price/Earnings Ratio

A key ratio that involves shareholders' equity is **earnings per share**. We introduced this ratio in Chapter 3, and are returning to it in this chapter. Earnings per share provides a measure of the earnings relative to the number of common shares outstanding. It is useful for tracking the return per share earned by the company over time. This ratio can also be related to the current market price per share by calculating the multiple or **price/earnings ratio**. This is calculated as:

$$\frac{\text{Market price per share}}{\text{Earnings per share}}$$

The ratio relates the accounting earnings to the market price at which the shares trade. If two companies in the same industry had the same earnings per share of $5, and Company A's shares were selling for $25 and Company B's shares were selling for $50, the price/earnings ratios would be different. Company A's price/earnings ratio would be 5 ($25/$5) and Company B's would be 10 ($50/$5). The market is placing a higher value on Company B's shares. There are probably many reasons for the higher valuation, such as an assessment of higher earning potential in the future, a lower risk with respect to debt repayment, or an assessment of future market share. When evaluating the price/earnings ratio of a company, it is important to compare the ratio with those of other companies in the same industry. This comparison gives the user information about how the market is valuing the company in relation to others.

The Return on Shareholders' Equity Ratio

Another useful indicator of return is **return on shareholders' equity**. This is a more general measure than earnings per share because it relates the net income available to common shares to the total of the common shareholders' equity. It is calculated as follows:

$$\text{ROE} = \frac{\text{Net income} - \text{Preferred dividends}}{\text{Average common shareholders' equity}}$$

Preferred dividends need to be subtracted from the net income because preferred shareholders have a prior claim on the income. Preferred dividends must be declared before dividends on common shares. We want this ratio to determine a measure of return to the common shares only. Common shareholders' equity is the shareholders' equity less any amounts that represent owners other than common shareholders. This means that the amount in the preferred shares account would need to be subtracted from the total shareholders' equity to arrive at common shareholders' equity.

This ratio tells you the return the common shareholder is earning on each dollar of income. For **Sears Canada** in 2001 and 2000, that return is $0.059 ($94.1/($1,619.9 + $1,549.3)/2) and $0.156 ($225.8/($1,549.3 + $1,346.3)/2), respectively. Sears Canada has no preferred shares issued so all of the net income accrues to the common shareholders. The return to common shareholders has declined in 2001 because of the decline in earnings in that year.

A more detailed discussion of other analyses that involve shareholders' equity can be found in Chapter 12.

SUMMARY

This chapter discussed the most common forms of business organizations—sole proprietorships, partnerships, and corporations. Advantages and disadvantages for each form were discussed. Because the predominant business structure is the corporation, this form was discussed in more detail. Particular attention was paid to shares. Corporations authorize different types or classes of shares with the intention of attracting capital investment. These shares come with different rights and privileges. The chapter outlined what some of those rights and privileges are.

Shareholders can be given a return from the company in the form of dividends. Dividends can come in various forms—cash, property, or stock. This section of the chapter concluded with a brief discussion about stock splits and employee stock option plans.

Because the chapter was discussing shareholders' equity, we discussed the fourth financial statement, the statement of retained earnings. An example from Intrawest Corporation was included as an illustration.

The chapter concluded with two ratios, the price/earnings ratio and the return on shareholders' equity ratio (ROE). These two ratios help investors evaluate the current return to common shareholders.

This concludes the discussion of the primary accounts on the balance sheet. In the final chapter of the book, financial statement analysis is summarized. You have already been introduced to most of the ratios discussed in Chapter 12. There is a further discussion of complex companies in Appendix B for those of you who are interested in understanding some of the issues behind consolidated financial statements. The discussion of complex organizations has been included in an appendix because it involves more complicated issues that require an understanding of the more basic issues that we have already discussed, and most introductory courses will not choose to include this topic.

SUMMARY PROBLEM

Additional Demonstration Problems

The Balukas Company had the following shareholders' equity section balances at December 31, 20x1:

Common shares	$4,700,000
(Unlimited number of common shares authorized, 240,000 shares issued)	
Retained earnings	4,000,000
Total shareholders' equity	$8,700,000

During 20x2, the following transactions occurred:

a. On January 2, 20x2, Balukas repurchased 5,000 of its own common shares at $35 per share and immediately cancelled them.

b. On March 15, 20x2, Balukas issued 10,000 new shares and received proceeds of $40 per share.

c. On June 29, 20x2, Balukas declared and paid a 10% stock dividend. The market price of Balukas's shares on June 29, 20x2, was $45 per share.

d. On June 30, 20x2, Balukas declared a cash dividend of $3.00 per share to shareholders of record on July 15, 20x2, payable on July 31, 20x2.

e. On September 1, 20x2, Balukas issued 100,000 new shares at a price of $50 per share.

f. On December 31, 20x2, Balukas declared a four-for-one stock split.

Required:

1. Construct journal entries for each of the transactions as they occurred during 20x2.

2. Explain why no journal entry was recorded for transaction f).

SUGGESTED SOLUTION TO SUMMARY PROBLEM

1. a. Repurchase of Common Shares and Cancellation Entry:

SE-Common shares	97,917[a]	
SE-Retained earnings	77,083	
A-Cash		175,000

[a]($4,700,000/240,000 × 5,000) = $97,917

b. Common Shares Issuance Entry:

A-Cash	400,000	
SE-Common shares		400,000

c. Small Stock Dividend Entries:

Declaration		
SE-Dividends declared	1,102,500 [b]	
SE-Stock dividend issuable		1,102,500

Issuance		
SE-Stock dividend issuable	1,102,500	
SE-Common shares		1,102,500

[b]Number of shares = 240,000 − 5,000 + 10,000 = 245,000 shares
245,000 shares × 10% × $45 per share = $1,102,500

d. On June 30, 20x2:

SE-Dividends declared	808,500 [c]	
L-Dividends payable		808,500

On July 31, 20x2:

L-Dividends payable	808,500	
A-Cash		808,500

[c](245,000 shares + 24,500 shares) = 269,500 shares
269,500 shares × $3.00 per share = $808,500

e. Issue of New Shares:

A-Cash	5,000,000	
SE-Common Shares		5,000,000

f. No entry is needed. However, a memorandum entry could be made to indicate that the number of shares outstanding has changed from 369,500 to 1,478,000.

2. During a stock split or a large stock dividend, the number of shares increases but the value of the company does not change. The purpose of the stock split is to lower the current market price of the company's shares. In the four-for-one split that was used in the sample problem, the market price would immediately drop to one quarter of the price before the split. The lower price would make the shares accessible to more investors.

SYNONYMS

Exercise price/Strike price/Option price
Property dividends/Dividends in kind

GLOSSARY

Articles of incorporation   A document filed with federal or provincial regulatory authorities when a business incorporates under that jurisdiction. The articles include, among other items, the authorized number of shares and dividend preferences for each class of shares that is to be issued.

Authorized shares   The maximum number of shares that a company is authorized to issue under its articles of incorporation.

Capital account   An account used in a partnership or proprietorship to record the investment and accumulated earnings of each owner.

Common shares   Certificates that represent portions of ownership in a corporation. These shares usually carry a right to vote.

Convertible preferred shares   Preferred shares that are exchangeable or convertible into a specified number of common shares.

Corporation   A form of business in which the shareholders have limited liability and the business entity is taxed directly. Shareholders receive distributions from the entity in the form of dividends.

Cumulative preferred shares   Preferred shares that accumulate dividends that are not declared from one period to the next. These accumulated dividends, called dividends in arrears, must be paid before a dividend can be declared for common shareholders.

Date of declaration   The date the board of directors votes to declare a dividend. On this date, the dividend becomes legally payable to shareholders.

Date of payment   The date on which a dividend is paid to shareholders.

Date of record   The date on which a shareholder must own the shares in order to receive the dividend from a share.

Dividend declaration   An action by the board of directors of a corporation that makes payment of a dividend a legal obligation of the corporation.

Dividends   Payments to shareholders from the total net income retained by a company in the Retained Earnings account.

Dividends in arrears   Dividends on cumulative preferred shares that have not yet been declared from a prior year.

Dividends in kind   Synonym for property dividend.

Drawing account   An account used in a partnership or proprietorship to record the cash withdrawals by owners.

Ex-dividend day   A date specified in the shares market on which the shares are sold without the most recently declared dividend.

Exercise price   The price per share that is required to be paid by the holder of a stock option upon exercise.

Expiration date   In the context of stock options, the date on which the option holder must either exercise the option or lose it.

General partners   The partners that have unlimited liability in a limited partnership.

Issued shares   The shares of a corporation that have been issued.

Limited liability   A feature of share ownership that restricts the liability of shareholders to the amount they have invested in the corporation.

Limited partners   The partners in a limited partnership that have limited liability.

Limited partnership   A partnership that allows some partners to have limited liability (limited partners) and others to have unlimited liability (general partners).

Memorandum entry   An entry made to record a stock split. No amounts are affected; only the record of the number of shares issued is affected.

No par value shares   Shares that have no par value associated with them.

Outstanding shares   The number of shares of a corporation that are held by individuals or entities outside the corporation (which does not include treasury shares).

Par value   A value per share of common shares set in the articles of incorporation.

Participating preferred shares   Preferred shares that can also participate in dividends declared beyond the level specified by the preferred shares, that is, beyond the fixed dividend payout specified in the preferred shares contract.

Partnership   A form of business in which the owners have unlimited legal liability and the business entity is not taxed directly; the income from the entity passes through to the partners' individual tax returns.

Partnership agreement   An agreement between the partners in a partnership that specifies how the individual partners will share in the risks and rewards of ownership of the partnership entity.

Preemptive right   The right of shareholders to share proportionately in new issuances of shares.

Preferred shares   An ownership right in which the shareholder has some preference as to dividends; that is, if dividends are declared, the preferred shareholders receive them first. Other rights that are normally held by common shareholders may also be changed in preferred shares; for example, many issues of preferred shares are non-voting.

Property dividend   A dividend that is satisfied with the transfer of some type of property other than cash.

Prospectus   A document filed with a securities commission by a corporation when it wants to issue public debt or shares.

Redeemable preferred shares   Preferred shares that can be bought back (redeemed) by the corporation under certain conditions and at a price stated in the articles of incorporation.

Retractable preferred shares   Shares that can be sold back to the company (retired) at the option of the shareholder. The price that must be paid for them and the periods of time within which they can be sold are specified in the articles of incorporation.

Sole proprietorship   A form of business in which there is a single owner (sole proprietor). This form is characterized by unlimited liability to the owner and exemption from corporate taxation.

Stock dividend   A distribution of additional common shares to shareholders. Existing shareholders receive shares in proportion to the number of shares they already own.

Stock option   An option granted to an employee to buy shares at a fixed price, usually as part of an incentive compensation plan.

Stock split   A distribution of new shares to shareholders. The new shares take the place of existing shares, and existing shareholders receive new shares in proportion to the number of old shares they already own.

Treasury shares   Shares that are repurchased by a corporation and held internally. Repurchased shares are normally cancelled immediately upon purchase.

Unlimited liability   A characteristic of sole proprietorships and partnerships that means the owners are personally responsible for the liabilities incurred by the business entity.

ASSIGNMENT MATERIAL

Multiple Choice Quizzes

Assessing Your Recall

11-1   Characterize the following forms of business in terms of the legal liability of the owners and their tax status: corporations, sole proprietorships, partnerships, and limited partnerships.

11-2   Discuss the purpose and importance of a partnership agreement.

11-3   Describe what is contained in a company's articles of incorporation and what significance they have for the accounting system.

11-4 List and briefly describe the four rights that common shareholders typically have in a corporation.

11-5 Discuss how preferred shares differ from common shares.

11-6 Briefly describe what each of the following features means in a preferred share issue:

a. Participating

b. Cumulative

c. Convertible

d. Redeemable

11-7 Briefly describe each of the following terms: authorized shares, issued shares, and outstanding shares.

11-8 Describe the process of declaring and paying a cash dividend, including information about the declaration date, date of record, and payment date.

11-9 Explain what property dividends are and why they are not used very often by companies.

11-10 Discuss the nature of a stock dividend and why a distinction is made between small and large stock dividends.

11-11 Compare and contrast a 100% stock dividend with a two-for-one stock split.

11-12 Explain why companies might declare a stock dividend rather than a cash dividend.

11-13 Discuss why companies issue employee stock options and what immediate and potential effects these options have on a company's financial results.

11-14 Explain why the shareholders of a company might want an expense to be recognized related to the company's employee stock option plans.

11-15 Describe what the price/earnings ratio is intended to tell users about a company.

11-16 Explain why the return on shareholders' equity provides information on the rate of return to common shareholders only.

Applying Your Knowledge

11-17 (Selecting a business entity)
Indicate whether each of the following business entities is more likely to be established as a sole proprietorship (SP), a partnership (P), or a corporation (C). Provide reasons for your choice.

a. A dental practice having five dentists

b. A clothing store that has six different locations in Ontario

c. A paint and body shop owned by Fred Weeks

d. A lumber company operating in British Columbia

e. A family of three brothers who decided to jointly operate a farm in Saskatchewan

f. A lobster fisher from Nova Scotia who owns two boats

11-18 (Selecting a business entity)

Indicate whether each of the following business entities is more likely to be established as a sole proprietorship (SP), a partnership (P), or a corporation (C). Provide reasons for your choice.

a. Mary's hairstyling salon

b. A local investment firm consisting of four financial advisors

c. A potash mining company

d. A real estate development company that specializes in shopping malls

e. One of the big four accounting firms

f. A car dealership owned by a mother and son

11-19 (Business formation)

Albert Wong just graduated from university and is planning to start his own software development company. He is trying to decide on the best form of business organization and is debating between setting up practice as a sole proprietor or establishing a corporate entity and serving as its president.

Required:

a. What advantages would there be to operating as a sole proprietorship?

b. What advantages would there be to operating as a corporation?

c. Which form of business organization would his customers likely prefer? Why?

d. Which form of business organization would his creditors likely prefer? Why?

e. Which form of business would be most advantageous to Albert Wong if he anticipated that the business would grow rapidly? Why?

11-20 (Business formation)

Janice Allen just inherited a large amount of money from her grandfather. She intends to start her own architectural company and plans within a few years to expand the operation by bringing in other architects.

Required:

a. What advantages would there be to operating as a sole proprietorship?

b. What advantages would there be to operating as a corporation?

c. What advantages would there be to begin operations as a sole proprietorship and then to switch to a partnership when she expands?

d. Which form of business organization would her customers likely prefer? Why?

e. Which form of business would be most advantageous to Janice Allen if she wanted to maintain control as the business expanded? Why?

11-21 (Equity transactions)

Southern Exposure Ltd. begins operations on January 2, 20x1. During the year, the following transactions occur that affected shareholders' equity:

1. Southern Exposure authorizes the issuance of 300,000 common shares and 80,000 preferred shares which pay a dividend of $2.50 per share.

2. 90,000 common shares are issued for $12 a share.

3. 25,000 preferred shares are issued for $18 per share.

4. The full annual dividend on the preferred shares is declared and paid.

5. A dividend of $0.25 per share is declared on the common shares but is not yet paid.

6. The company earns income of $220,000 for the year.

7. The dividends on the common shares are paid.

8. A 5% stock dividend is declared on the common shares and distributed. On the date of declaration, the market price of the shares was $15.

Required:

a. Prepare journal entries to record the above transactions.

b. Prepare the shareholders' equity section of the balance sheet as at December 31, 20x1.

11-22 (Equity transactions)
Marshall Investigations was owned by four retired police officers. They set up their business as a corporation and during the first year the following transactions occurred:

1. 10,000 common shares were issued to the four owners (2,500 shares each) at $35 per share. The company was authorized to issue up to 50,000 common shares.

2. 10,000 preferred shares were issued to people other than the owners at $50 per share. The company was authorized to issue 25,000 preferred shares.

3. A dividend of $4 per share was declared for the preferred shareholders.

4. The dividend declared in part c) was paid.

5. The company purchased 500 of its own common shares from one of its owners, at an agreed price of $40 per share, and immediately cancelled them.

6. During the first year of operations the company earned income of $110,000.

Required:

a. Prepare journal entries to record the above transactions.

b. Prepare the shareholders' equity section of the balance sheet at the end of the first year.

11-23 (Equity transactions)
Green Grocers Ltd. had been operating for several years. At the end of 2003, it had an unlimited number of common shares authorized and 750,000 shares issued at $10 per share. As well, there were 200,000 preferred shares authorized, 50,000 issued at $20 per share, and the balance in retained earnings was $5,350,000. The preferred shares paid a dividend of $2.00 per share. During 2004, the following transactions affecting shareholders' equity occurred:

1. 50,000 common shares were issued at $15 per share.

2. The preferred dividend for the year was declared and paid.

3. A 10% common stock dividend was declared when the market price of the shares was $17. The shares were distributed one month after the declaration.

4. At the very end of the year, a dividend of $1.00 per share was declared on the common shares. It would be paid in the following year.

5. The company earned income of $2,050,000.

Required:

a. Prepare journal entries to record the above transactions.

b. Prepare the shareholders' equity section of the balance sheet as at the end of 2004.

11-24   (Share issuance, repurchase, and cancellation)

On December 31, 2003, the shareholders' equity section of Ortegren Ltd.'s balance sheet appears as follows:

Preferred shares, no par, $8, redeemable, 50,000 shares	
authorized, 30,000 shares issued	$ 3,000,000
Common shares, no par, unlimited number	
authorized, 500,000 shares issued	5,820,000
Retained earnings	5,438,000
Total shareholders' equity	$14,258,000

During 2004, the following events occurred:

1. Ortegren issued 120,000 additional common shares for $25 per share.

2. The company declared and paid the dividend on the preferred shares for the first half of the year.

3. Immediately after paying the preferred dividend for the first half of the year, the company repurchased the shares on the market for $103 per share.

4. The company earned income of $966,000 for 2004.

Required:

a. Prepare journal entries to record the above transactions.

b. Prepare the shareholders' equity section of the balance sheet as at December 31, 2004.

c. Give possible reasons why Ortegren might change its equity financing by eliminating the preferred shares and issuing more common shares.

11-25   (Stock dividends)

Timmerman Company has 45,000 common shares outstanding. Because it wants to use its cash flow for other purposes, the company has decided to issue stock dividends to its shareholders. The market price of each of Timmerman Company's shares is $30. Give the journal entries recording the issuance of the stock dividend if:

a. The company decides to issue a 10% stock dividend.

b. The company decides to issue a 100% stock dividend.

11-26   (Change in shareholders' equity)

The shareholders' equity of Bamber Ltd. at the end of 2004 and 2003 appears as follows:

	2004	2003
Preferred shares, no par, 2,050,000 shares authorized, 10,000 shares issued	$ 100,000	$ 100,000
Common shares, no par, 1,000,000 shares authorized, 200,000 shares issued (2003 − 180,000 shares)	440,000	305,000
Retained earnings	510,000	430,000
Total shareholders' equity	$ 1,050,000	$ 835,000

During 2004, Bamber paid a total of $35,000 in cash dividends.

Required:

a. Assuming the preferred shares were not in arrears, how was the $35,000 in cash dividends distributed between the two classes of shares?

b. Both the common shares and the retained earnings changed during the year. Suggest explanations that would account for the changes and calculate the amount of each of the items that caused these changes.

11-27 (Equity transactions)
The following information relates to the shareholders' equity section of Johnson Ltd. (in thousands):

	December 31, 2004	December 31, 2003
Preferred shares (10,000 shares issued and outstanding)	$5,000	$ 5,000
Common shares (375,000 shares issued and outstanding at end of 2003)	?	7,500
Retained earnings	6,400	3,750
Total shareholders' equity	?	$16,250

During 2004, 10,000 common shares were issued at a price of $32 per share. Cash dividends of $250,000 and $500,000 were paid to common shareholders and preferred shareholders, respectively. The company acquired 15,000 treasury shares during the year at $30 per share and held them. The company issued 5,000 common shares under employee stock option plans at $25 per share.

Required:

a. Calculate the ending balance in common shares at the end of 2004.

b. Determine the number of common shares issued and the number outstanding at the end of 2004.

c. Calculate the amount of net income reported in 2004.

11-28 (Equity transactions)
Give the journal entries for the following shareholders' equity transactions of the Green Sleeves Apparel Company:

a. On January 10, 20x1, the articles of incorporation are filed with the provincial secretary. The company is authorized to issue 1,000,000 common shares and 100,000 cumulative preferred shares which carry a dividend of $10.00 per share.

b. On January 12, 20x1, the company issues 75,000 common shares at $25 each.

c. On January 20, 20x1, 25,000 of the preferred shares are issued at $100 per share.

d. On January 25, 20x1, the assets of Tritex Knits Ltd. are acquired in exchange for 20,000 common shares and 10,000 preferred shares. The market value of the common shares was $25 and that of the preferred shares $100 on this date. The assets acquired and their relative fair market values are: land, $400,000; equipment, $250,000; inventory, $200,000; building, $600,000; and accounts receivable, $50,000.

e. No dividends are declared in 20x1.

f. On December 2, 20x2, cash dividends are declared on the preferred shares. Once the dividends are paid on the date of payment, January 15, 20x3, no preferred dividends will be in arrears.

g. On December 2, 20x2, a 10% stock dividend is declared for the common shares. The market price of the common shares on this date is $52 per share. The shares are issued on December 15, 20x2, when the market price per share is $55.

11-29   (Income statement and statement of retained earnings)
The following are selected account balances from Darby Ltd.'s trial balance on December 31, 2003:

Amortization expense	$ 145,000
Common dividends declared	242,600
Common shares	11,407,000
Contributed surplus	57,000
Cost of goods sold	925,700
Interest expense	42,000
Miscellaneous expense	120,900
Preferred dividends declared	167,000
Preferred shares	2,087,500
Retained earnings, Jan. 1, 2003	4,239,500
Revenues	2,040,000
Wage expense	340,800

Required:

a. Prepare the 2003 income statement and retained earnings statement, in good form, for Darby Ltd.

b. Based on this information, how likely does the continuation of Darby's common dividend appear to be? Explain.

User Perspective Problems

11-30   (New share issuance)
You are a loan officer at a bank. You helped Cedar Ltd. arrange a $1.5-million, 20-year mortgage with your bank just six months ago. Cedar Ltd. has just announced an issuance of new shares from which it intends to raise $5 million. How do you think this new issuance will affect the bank's outstanding loan? Identify some positive outcomes and some negative ones.

11-31   (Price/earnings ratio)
As a stock analyst, explain the importance and limitations of the price/earnings ratio.

11-32 (Investment banker)
As an investment banker, describe some of the services that you would perform for a company.

11-33 (Cash dividends)
You have been considering buying some common shares of Basker Ltd. Basker has 1,000,000 common shares outstanding. The company has been through difficult times but is now doing better. Your main concern is whether you will receive cash dividends. In addition to the common shares, the company has 20,000 shares of $10, no par, Class A preferred outstanding which are noncumulative and nonparticipating. The company also has 60,000 shares of $6, no par, Class B preferred outstanding. These shares are nonparticipating but are cumulative. The normal dividend was paid on both classes of preferred shares until last year, when no dividends were paid. This year, however, Basker is doing well and is expecting net income of $2,000,000. The company has not yet declared its annual dividends but has indicated that it plans to pay total dividends equal to 40% of net income. If you immediately buy 100 shares of Basker Ltd. on the stock market:

a. What amount of common dividend would you expect to receive?

b. What amount of common dividend would you expect to receive if the Class B preferred shares were noncumulative?

11-34 (Stock dividends and splits)
The shareholders' equity section of Bonanza Ltd.'s balance sheet appears as follows on December 31, 2003:

Common shares, 1,000,000 authorized,	
100,000 issued and outstanding	$2,500,000
Retained earnings	2,345,000
Total shareholders' equity	$4,845,000

Near the beginning of 2004, Bonanza declared and distributed a 5% stock dividend. At the date of declaration, the common shares were selling for $89 per share. By the end of October, the price of the shares had risen to $124 per share. Bonanza's Board of Directors decided to split the shares four-for-one. Late in December, the Board declared a cash dividend on the common shares of $1 per share, payable in early January 2005. (In past years, the dividend had generally been about $3 per share.) During 2004, Bonanza Ltd. earned net income of $2,355,000.

Required:

a. What effect did each dividend (i.e., the stock dividend and the cash dividend) have on the individual shareholders' equity accounts of Bonanza and on Bonanza's total shareholders' equity?

b. Prepare the shareholders' equity section of Bonanza's balance sheet at December 31, 2004.

c. What reasons might the company have for declaring a stock dividend? What is your assessment of these reasons?

d. What reasons might the company have for splitting its shares? What is your assessment of these reasons?

e. If you were one of Bonanza's common shareholders, would you be happy or unhappy with the stock dividend and split? Why? What do you think about the reduction in the cash dividend from $3 to $1? Explain.

11-35   (Retained earnings and dividends)

You have recently been considering investing in some of Cascade Ltd.'s common shares. The company has been relatively profitable over the years and prospects for the future look good. However, it has recently had to make heavy expenditures for new capital assets. The company's summarized balance sheet at the end of 2003 is as follows:

Cash	$ 50,000
Other current assets	963,000
Capital assets (net)	8,259,000
Total	$9,272,000
Current liabilities	$ 586,000
Long-term debt	2,500,000
Common shares	4,000,000
Retained earnings	2,186,000
Total	$9,272,000

The company has 200,000 common shares outstanding and its earnings per share has increased by at least 10% in each of the last 10 years. In several recent years, earnings per share increased by more than 15%. Given the company's earnings and the amount of its retained earnings, you judge that it could easily pay cash dividends of $2 or $3 per share, resulting in hardly a dent in retained earnings.

Required:

a. Evaluate the prospects of your receiving a cash dividend from Cascade during the next year if you were to purchase its shares.

b. Evaluate the prospects of your receiving a cash dividend from Cascade during the next five years if you were to purchase its shares.

c. Suppose Cascade borrowed $2 million cash on a five-year bank loan to provide working capital and additional operating flexibility. While no collateral would be required, the loan would stipulate that no dividends be paid in any year in which the ratio of long-term debt to equity was greater than 2 to 3. Evaluate your prospects for receiving cash dividends from Cascade, in the short term and during the next five years, if Cascade were to enter into the loan agreement.

11-36   (Return on investment)

Stanley Corporation Ltd.'s balance sheet appears as follows:

Cash	$ 160,000
Other current assets	1,842,000
Capital assets (net)	7,841,000
Total	$9,843,000
Current liabilities	$ 912,000
Long-term debt	2,100,000
Preferred shares	1,200,000
Common shares	2,500,000
Retained earnings	3,131,000
Total	$9,843,000

For the year just ended, Stanley reported net income of $925,000. During the year, the company declared preferred dividends of $84,000 and common dividends of $300,000.

Required:

a. Calculate the following ratios for Stanley:

   1. Return on assets

   2. Return on long-term capital (long-term debt + shareholders' equity)

   3. Return on common shareholders' equity

b. If the company's interest expense related to its long-term debt was $105,000 for the year, after taxes, and the long-term debt could have been replaced by $2,100,000 worth of common shares, what would the return on common shareholders' equity have been for the year without debt financing? What does this imply about the desirability of this company's using long-term debt? Will this always be true? Explain.

c. Suppose the company had issued the long-term debt shown on the balance sheet, but had issued an additional $1,200,000 worth of common shares rather than the preferred shares. What would the return on common shareholders' equity have been? What does this imply about the desirability of this company's using preferred shares?

Reading and Interpreting Published Financial Statements

11-37 (Share transactions)
The consolidated balance sheet and statement of retained earnings for **Alcan Inc.**, together with note 16 and a portion of note 17 from its 2001 annual report, are shown in Exhibit 11-7.

Required:

a. Reconstruct all the journal entries that affected Alcan's common shares during the years ended December 31, 2001 and 2000. (*Hint:* For the entry involving shares "issued in exchange for tendered algroup shares," debit an account called "Investment in algroup.")

b. Reconstruct all the journal entries that affected Alcan's retained earnings during the years ended December 31, 2001 and 2000.

c. Calculate the return on Alcan's shareholders' equity for the years ended December 31, 2001 and 2000, and comment on the results.

d. Notice that the amount of preferred dividends was lower in 2001 than in 2000, even though the number of preferred shares was the same in both years. Explain how or why this occurred.

ALCAN INC. (2001)

EXHIBIT 11-7

CONSOLIDATED FINANCIAL STATEMENTS (cont'd)

CONSOLIDATED BALANCE SHEET *(in millions of US$)*

December 31	2001	2000	1999
ASSETS			
Current assets			
Cash and time deposits	$ 119	$ 261	$ 315
Trade receivables (net of allowances of $52 in 2001,			
$55 in 2000 and $31 in 1999) *(notes 2 and 10)*	1,216	1,721	1,019
Other receivables	532	559	280
Inventories			
– Aluminum operating segments			
– Aluminum	875	1,034	709
– Raw materials	413	414	294
– Other supplies	269	268	188
	1,557	1,716	1,191
– Packaging operating segment	393	399	85
	1,950	2,115	1,276
	3,817	4,656	2,890
Deferred charges and other assets *(note 11)*	737	719	525
Property, plant and equipment *(note 12)*			
Cost (excluding Construction work in progress)	16,225	14,807	11,771
Construction work in progress	613	1,979	1,220
Accumulated depreciation	(7,136)	(6,753)	(6,557)
	9,702	10,033	6,434
Intangible assets, net of accumulated amortization			
of $27 in 2001 and $5 in 2000	298	330	—
Goodwill, net of accumulated amortization			
of $92 in 2001 and $17 in 2000 *(note 5)*	2,925	2,669	—
Total assets	$17,479	$18,407	$ 9,849
LIABILITIES AND SHAREHOLDERS' EQUITY			
Current liabilities			
Payables	$ 2,328	$ 2,427	$ 1,268
Short-term borrowings	555	1,080	167
Debt maturing within one year *(note 15)*	652	333	311
	3,535	3,840	1,746
Debt not maturing within one year *(notes 15 and 21)*	2,884	3,195	1,011
Deferred credits and other liabilities *(note 14)*	1,131	874	563
Deferred income taxes *(note 8)*	1,006	1,227	781
Minority interests	132	244	207
Shareholders' equity			
Redeemable non-retractable preference shares *(note 16)*	160	160	160
Common shareholders' equity			
Common shares *(note 17)*	4,687	4,597	1,230
Retained earnings *(note 18)*	4,095	4,290	4,227
Deferred translation adjustments *(note 20)*	(151)	(20)	(76)
	8,631	8,867	5,381
	8,791	9,027	5,541
Commitments and contingencies *(note 19)*			
Total liabilities and shareholders' equity	$17,479	$18,407	$ 9,849

The accompanying notes are an integral part of the financial statements.

Approved by the Board:

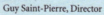

Travis Engen, Director   Guy Saint-Pierre, Director

EXHIBIT 11-7
CONT.

NOTES TO CONSOLIDATED FINANCIAL STATEMENTS (cont'd)

ALCAN INC. (2001)

(in millions of US$, except where indicated)

17. COMMON SHARES

The authorized common share capital is an unlimited number of common shares without nominal or par value. Changes in outstanding common shares are summarized below:

	Number (in thousands)			Stated Value		
	2001	2000	1999	**2001**	2000	1999
Outstanding – beginning of year	**317,921**	218,315	226,003	**$ 4,597**	$ 1,230	$ 1,251
Issued for cash:						
Executive share option plan	**2,158**	521	886	**55**	13	19
Dividend reinvestment and share purchase plans	**135**	237	271	**5**	8	8
Issued in exchange for tendered algroup shares	**688***	115,446**	—	**30**	3,476	—
Purchased for cancellation	**—**	(16,598)	(8,845)	**—**	(130)	(48)
Outstanding – end of year	**320,902**	317,921	218,315	**$ 4,687**	$ 4,597	$ 1,230

* The 688 common shares were issued to acquire the remaining algroup shares in accordance with the provisions of Swiss law.

** 115,386 common shares were issued in accordance with the Company's share exchange offer; 60 common shares were issued after the Company's share exchange offer.

Under the executive share option plan, certain employees may purchase common shares at market value on the effective date of the grant of each option. The vesting period for options granted beginning in 1998 is linked to Alcan's share price performance, but does not exceed nine years. Options granted before 1998 vest generally over a fixed period of four years from the grant date and expire at various dates during the next 10 years. Changes in the number of shares under option as well as average exercise price are summarized below:

	Average exercise price (CAN$)			Number (in thousands)		
	2001	2000	1999	**2001**	2000	1999
Outstanding – beginning of year	**$43.20**	$40.91	$38.16	**7,326**	5,472	5,156
Granted	**$50.96**	$46.52	$45.41	**1,945**	2,422	1,315
Exercised	**$39.85**	$35.75	$32.76	**(2,158)**	(521)	(886)
Cancelled	**$39.08**	$31.37	$31.80	**(5)**	(47)	(113)
Outstanding – end of year	**$46.34**	$43.20	$40.91	**7,108**	7,326	5,472

Range of Exercise Prices for Options Outstanding at December 31, 2001

Range of Exercise Prices (CAN$)	Number of Options (in thousands)
$21.94 – $34.00	93
$34.01 – $40.00	541
$40.01 – $46.00	1,378
$46.01 – $52.00	4,370
$52.01 – $59.35	726
	7,108

At December 31, 2001, approximately 4,665,000 (2000: 4,913,000; 1999: 3,099,000) of outstanding options with an average exercise price of CAN$44.91 (2000: CAN$41.56; 1999: CAN$38.12) were vested.

Upon consummation of the combination with Alusuisse Group Ltd, described in note 5, all options granted under the Company's executive share option plan prior to the consummation were vested.

At December 31, 2001, the Company had reserved for issue under the executive share option plan 15,700,844 shares.

The Company does not recognize compensation expense for options granted under the executive share option plan. If the Company had elected to recognize compensation expense for these options in accordance with the methodology prescribed by Statement No. 123 of the U.S. Financial Accounting Standards Board (FASB), net income would have been lower by $5, or $0.02 per share ($29, or $0.12 per share, in 2000 and $13, or $0.06 per share, in 1999).

The FASB provides the choice of either recognizing the compensation expense in the financial statements or disclosing it in the notes to the financial statements. To compute the notional compensation expense, the Black-Scholes valuation model was used to determine the fair value of the options granted. Using the model, the fair value of options averages approximately 31% to 37% of the exercise price.

In addition, a small number of employees are entitled to receive stock price appreciation units whereby they are entitled to receive cash in an amount equal to the excess of the market value of a share on the date of exercise over the market value of a share as of the date of grant of such units. In 2001, 311,060 such units were granted of which none were vested. The vesting period is linked to Alcan's share price performance, but does not exceed nine years.

In June 2000, the Company obtained authorization, which terminated on June 18, 2001, to repurchase up to 21,800,000 common shares under a normal course issuer bid. In 2001, no common shares were purchased under this authorization and in 2000, 16,598,100 common shares were purchased and cancelled at a cost of $530. In 1999, 8,845,000 common shares for an amount of $219 were purchased and cancelled under a previous authorization.

EXHIBIT 11-7
CONT.

CONSOLIDATED STATEMENT OF RETAINED EARNINGS *(in millions of US$)*		ALCAN INC.		
Year ended December 31	**2001**	2000	1999
Retained earnings – beginning of year	**$ 4,290**	$ 4,227	$ 4,078
Net income	**5**	618	460
	4,295	4,845	4,538
Amount related to common shares purchased for cancellation	**—**	400	171
Dividends – Common	**192**	145	131
– Preference	**8**	10	9
Retained earnings – end of year *(note 18)*	**$ 4,095**	$ 4,290	$ 4,227

16. PREFERENCE SHARES

AUTHORIZED

An unlimited number of preference shares issuable in series. All shares are without nominal or par value.

AUTHORIZED AND OUTSTANDING

In each of the years 2001, 2000 and 1999, there were authorized and outstanding 5,700,000 series C and 3,000,000 series E redeemable non-retractable preference shares with stated values of $106 and $54, respectively.

Preference shares, series C and E are eligible for quarterly dividends based on an amount related to the average of the Canadian prime interest rates quoted by two major Canadian banks for stated periods. The dividends on series C and E preference shares are cumulative.

Preference shares, series C and E may be called for redemption at the option of the Company on 30 days' notice at CAN$25.00 per share.

Any partial redemption of preference shares must be made on a pro rata basis or by lot.

11-38   (Stock options and warrants)

The consolidated balance sheets and statements of operations and accumulated deficit for **Ballard Power Systems Inc.**, together with excerpts from note 12 in its 2001 annual report, are presented in Exhibit 11-8.

Required:

a. Calculate Ballard's return on shareholders' equity for 2001.

b. Note that Ballard Power Systems has share options and warrants outstanding.

    1. Explain what stock options and warrants are.

    2. Who holds Ballard's options and warrants?

    3. Why would Ballard have issued these options and warrants?

c. Assume that all of the options and warrants that were outstanding on December 31, 2000, were exercised on January 1, 2001, at the applicable prices specified in Ballard's notes. (That is, assume that 5,042,649 options and 990,000 warrants were exercised during 2001, rather than 731,513 options and 540,000 warrants.)

    1. How much additional cash would Ballard have had available for use during 2001 as a result of this?

    2. Assume that Ballard could have earned a rate of return of 10% on the additional funds calculated in part 1 above. How much would Ballard's 2001 net income (loss) have been after taking these additional earnings into consideration?

    3. What would Ballard's revised rate of return on shareholders' equity for 2001 have been after taking these additional earnings into consideration? (*Hint:* Remember that the number of shares will also be increased in comparison to the number that was used in your calculation in part a) above.)

BALLARD POWER SYSTEMS INC. (2001)
CONSOLIDATED BALANCE SHEETS

EXHIBIT 11-8

	Change in currency – note 2	
December 31 *(Expressed in thousands of U.S. dollars)*	**2001**	2000
ASSETS		
Current assets:		
Cash and cash equivalents	$ **140,774**	$ 181,294
Short-term investments	**280,475**	301,987
Accounts receivable *(notes 4 and 15)*	**17,312**	14,476
Inventories *(note 5)*	**28,046**	11,078
Prepaid expenses	**873**	419
	467,480	509,254
Property, plant and equipment (note 6)	**109,006**	54,480
Intangible assets (note 7)	**170,453**	26,849
Goodwill (note 3)	**184,930**	—
Investments (note 8)	**26,241**	73,697
Other long-term assets	**1,209**	1,067
	$ **959,319**	$ 665,347
LIABILITIES AND SHAREHOLDERS' EQUITY		
Current liabilities:		
Accounts payable and accrued liabilities *(notes 9 and 15)*	$ **59,307**	$ 18,336
Deferred revenue	**1,944**	492
Accrued warranty liabilities	**16,622**	16,387
	77,873	35,215
Long-term liabilities (note 10)	**7,723**	3,881
Minority interest	**36,517**	10,294
	122,113	49,390
SHAREHOLDERS' EQUITY:		
Share capital (note 12)	**1,051,811**	734,165
Accumulated deficit	**(214,369)**	(118,208)
Cumulative translation adjustment	**(236)**	—
	837,206	615,957
	$ **959,319**	$ 665,347

Commitments and contingencies *(notes 12 and 13)*

See accompanying notes to consolidated financial statements.

Approved on behalf of the Board   *Director*   *Director*

EXHIBIT 11-8
CONT.

BALLARD POWER SYSTEMS INC. (2001)
CONSOLIDATED STATEMENTS OF OPERATIONS AND ACCUMULATED DEFICIT

		Change in currency – note 2	
Years ended December 31 *(Expressed in thousands of U.S. dollars, except per share amounts)*	**2001**	2000	1999
Product revenues	**$ 32,050**	$ 25,797	$ 20,815
Engineering service revenue	**4,154**	—	—
Investment and other income	**24,529**	27,902	9,893
	60,733	53,699	30,708
Cost of revenues and expenses:			
Cost of product revenues	**33,415**	34,578	18,695
Research and product development	**82,686**	54,315	38,945
General and administrative	**15,046**	8,952	7,281
Marketing	**3,450**	1,973	1,862
Amortization of intangible assets	**4,550**	2,302	2,301
Capital taxes	**444**	677	298
	139,591	102,797	69,382
Loss before undernoted	**(78,858)**	(49,098)	(38,674)
Equity in loss of associated companies	**(23,541)**	(21,947)	(12,814)
Minority interest	**8,002**	10,526	4,277
Business integration and restructuring costs (note 3)	**(3,700)**	—	—
Gain on issuance of shares by subsidiary (note 15)	**997**	15,561	2,721
License and royalty income (fees) (note 8)	**1,797**	(7,687)	(1,614)
Loss before income taxes	**(95,303)**	(52,645)	(46,104)
Income taxes (note 14)	**858**	1,187	480
Net loss	**(96,161)**	(53,832)	(46,584)
Accumulated deficit, beginning of year	**(118,208)**	(64,376)	(17,792)
Accumulated deficit, end of year	**$ (214,369)**	$ (118,208)	$ (64,376)
Loss per share (note 18)	**$ (1.05)**	$ (0.61)	$ (0.56)

See accompanying notes to consolidated financial statements.

12 SHARE CAPITAL

(a) Authorized: Unlimited number of common shares, voting, without par value
Unlimited number of preferred shares, issuable in series
1 Class A and 1 Class B share, convertible, redeemable and non-voting

(b) Issued:

	2001		2000		1999	
	Number of shares	**Amount**	Number of shares	Amount	Number of shares	Amount
Common shares						
Balance, beginning of year	89,064,938	$ 734,165	83,994,153	$ 415,559	83,331,883	$ 411,922
Issued for cash *(net of issue costs)*	2,023,173	34,535	3,293,750	299,987	—	—
Issued for long-term investment	12,205,525	270,315	—	—	—	—
Issued for intellectual property	—	—	4,779	437	—	—
Options exercised	731,513	9,900	1,265,794	16,455	525,010	3,637
Warrants exercised	540,000	2,896	300,000	1,727	—	—
Share distribution plan *(note 12(d))*	212,695	—	125,363	—	137,260	—
Share exchange plan *(note 12(e))*	36,230	—	81,099	—	—	—
Balance, end of year	104,814,074	$ 1,051,811	89,064,938	$ 734,165	83,994,153	$ 415,559

BALLARD POWER SYSTEMS INC. (2001)

EXHIBIT 11-8

CONT.

(c) Share option plans: The Company has four share option plans. All directors, officers, employees and consultants of the Company and its subsidiaries are eligible to participate in the share option plan. Option exercise prices are denominated in Canadian dollars but have been converted to U.S. dollars for presentation purposes.

(i) 2000 Share Option Plan: At December 31, 2001, 3,591,775 options to purchase common shares were outstanding. These options, when vested under the terms of the plan, are exercisable at prices ranging between $21.47 and $120.56 per common share. An additional 2,183,050 options may be granted in future years under this plan. All options have a term of ten years from the date of grant unless otherwise determined by the board of directors. 993,700 options vest and may be exercised in the 3rd year after granting. 252,500 options vest and may be exercised in the 4th year after granting. Of the remaining options, one-third vest and may be exercised in each of the 2nd, 3rd and 4th years after granting.

(ii) 1997 Share Option Plan: At December 31, 2001, 2,763,764 options to purchase common shares were outstanding. These options, when vested under the terms of the plan, are exercisable at prices ranging between $21.98 and $120.56 per common share. All options permitted to be granted under this plan have been granted. However, if options are surrendered, terminated or expire without being exercised new options may be granted covering common shares not purchased under such options. All options have a term of ten years from the date of grant unless otherwise determined by the board of directors. One third of the options vest and may be exercised in each of the 2nd, 3rd and 4th years after granting.

(iii) 1995 Share Option Plan: At December 31, 2001, options to purchase 609,060 common shares were outstanding and exercisable at prices ranging between $4.66 and $15.54 per common share. No additional options may be granted under this plan. All options have a term of ten years from the date of grant. One third of the options vest and may be exercised in each of the 1st, 2nd and 3rd years after granting.

(iv) 1993 Share Option Plan: At December 31, 2001, options to purchase 292,830 common shares were outstanding and exercisable at prices ranging between $1.48 and $2.88 per common share. No additional options may be granted under this plan. All options have a term of eight years from the date of grant. One third of the options vest and may be exercised in each of the 1st, 2nd and 3rd years after granting.

Share options	Options for Common shares	Weighted average exercise price
Balance, December 31, 1998	4,195,304	$ 11.25
Options granted	1,189,450	25.88
Options exercised	(525,010)	6.93
Options cancelled	(61,002)	21.20
Balance, December 31, 1999	4,798,742	15.22
Options granted	1,773,200	117.77
Options exercised	(1,265,794)	11.61
Options cancelled	(263,499)	22.57
Balance, December 31, 2000	5,042,649	51.80
Options granted	3,079,650	37.70
Options exercised	(731,513)	12.53
Options cancelled	(133,357)	93.67
Balance, December 31, 2001	7,257,429	$ 49.01

(h) Warrants: The following table summarizes information regarding the Company's warrants outstanding:

	2001	2000	1999
	Number of warrants	Number of warrants	Number of warrants
Balance, beginning of year	990,000	1,290,000	1,290,000
Exercised	(540,000)	(300,000)	—
Balance, end of year	450,000	990,000	1,290,000

In prior years the Company issued 1,890,000 warrants to joint development partners, of which 540,000 warrants were exercised in 2001, 300,000 warrants were exercised in 2000 and 600,000 warrants were exercised in 1998 leaving 450,000 warrants outstanding at December 31, 2001. Each warrant entitles the holder to purchase one common share of the Company upon completion of certain purchase commitments from the Company and upon payment of exercise prices of $16.34 per share before October 29, 2002.

11-39   (Effect of share issuances)

Excerpts from note 8 accompanying the financial statements of **Talisman Energy Inc.** for 2001 are presented in Exhibit 11-9.

There has been a movement towards requiring companies to recognize compensation expense arising from their stock option plans. In response to this, you should note that Talisman (in the portion of note 8 dealing with its stock option plans) provides pro forma figures showing what its net income would have been if it had recorded compensation expense related to the granting of stock options to employees.

Required:

a. Calculate the percentage by which the company's reported net income would have been reduced in each of the three years if Talisman had recognized compensation expense arising from its granting of employee stock options.

b. Do you think these differences in Talisman's income figures are significant?

TALISMAN ENERGY INC. (2001)

8.   Share Capital

Stock Option Plans

Talisman has stock option plans that allow employees and directors to receive options to purchase common shares of the Company. Options granted under the plans are generally exercisable after three years and expire 10 years after the grant date. Option exercise prices approximate the market price for the common shares on the date the options are issued.

No amount of compensation expense has been recognized in the financial statements for stock options granted to employees and directors. The following table provides pro forma measures of net income and net income per common share had stock options been recognized as compensation expense based on the estimated fair value of the options on the grant date.

	2001		2000		1999	
	As Reported	**Pro Forma**	As Reported	Pro Forma	As Reported	Pro Forma
Net income	**786**	**762**	906	890	177	150
Net income per common share	**5.65**	**5.47**	6.41	6.29	1.31	1.10

11-40   (Effect of share issuances)

An excerpt from note 9 accompanying the financial statements of **Corel Corporation** for 2001 is presented in Exhibit 11-10.

Required:

a. In its summary of the activity in its stock option plans, the terms "granted," "exercised," "forfeited," and "expired" are used.

1. Briefly explain what each of these terms mean in the context of stock option plans.

2. Why do you think some of the stock options would have been forfeited?

3. Why do you think some of the stock options would have been cancelled?

b. Calculate the percentage net change in the number of stock options outstanding during each of the three years for which data are given.

c. If all of the stock options outstanding on November 30, 2001, are exercised, how many shares would Corel issue and how much cash would it receive?

d. Explain how a company's earnings per share and its return on shareholders' equity are affected when stock options are exercised.

COREL CORPORATION (2001)

9. Share Capital
Stock option plans

EXHIBIT 11-10

The Company's stock option plans are administered by the Compensation Committee, which is a subcommittee of the Board of Directors. The Compensation Committee designates eligible participants to be included under the plans and designates the number of options and share price of the options, subject to applicable securities laws and stock exchange regulations. At November 30, 2001, there were approximately 13.9 million and 7.0 million common shares reserved for issuance under the Corel Corporation Stock Option Plan and the Corel Corporation Stock Option Plan 2000, respectively. Information with respect to stock option activity for 1999, 2000 and 2001 is as follows:

	Number of shares (000s)	Range	Weighted average
		Price per share (CDN$)	
Outstanding at November 30, 1998	8,281	$ 2.10 – $22.38	$ 8.65
Granted	3,022	3.37 – 11.70	3.41
Exercised	(5,054)	2.10 – 13.50	4.03
Forfeited	(1,883)	2.10 – 13.50	7.06
Expired	(1,313)	2.10 – 22.38	10.25
Outstanding at November 30, 1999	3,053	2.10 – 13.50	5.03
Granted	3,869	5.35 – 29.90	14.49
Exercised	(798)	2.06 – 13.50	4.08
Forfeited	(1,115)	2.10 – 15.25	14.44
Expired	(591)	7.70 – 13.50	7.88
Outstanding at November 30, 2000	4,418	3.00 – 29.90	10.65
Granted	2,840	3.30 – 4.80	4.22
Exercised	(174)	3.00 – 4.80	3.26
Forfeited	(2,198)	3.00 – 29.90	7.81
Expired	(364)	4.00 – 7.70	7.58
Outstanding at November 30, 2001	4,522	$ 3.00 – $15.25	$ 4.97

For various price ranges (in CDN$), weighted average characteristics of outstanding stock options at November 30, 2001 were as follows:

Range of grant price	Shares (000s)	Remaining life (years)	Weighted average
		Outstanding options	
$ 3.00 – $ 5.00	2,894	3.4	$4.09
5.01 – 8.00	1,228	2.3	5.68
8.01 – 15.25	400	2.8	9.10
Outstanding at November 30, 2001	4,522	3.06	$4.97

The outstanding options expire between April 15, 2002 and November 7, 2005.

11-41   (Effects of share issuances)

Note 6 accompanying the financial statements of **Danier Leather Inc.** for the year ended June 30, 2001, is presented in Exhibit 11-11.

Required:

a. Based upon the information presented in Exhibit 11-11, explain in your own words what is meant by the terms "multiple voting shares" and "subordinate voting shares."

b. What percentage of the total votes is held by the owners of Danier's multiple voting shares? By contrast, what percentage of the company's total share capital has been provided by these shareholders?

c. Reconstruct the journal entries affecting the subordinate voting shares during the year ended June 30, 2001. (For the stock options entry, round the amount to the nearest thousand dollars, in order to be consistent with the other amounts given.)

d. Danier Leather's note discloses that some of its outstanding options were "repriced" during the year. Explain what repricing means and why this is sometimes done.

EXHIBIT 11-11

DANIER LEATHER INC. (2001)
NOTE 6 CAPITAL STOCK (THOUSANDS OF DOLLARS, EXCEPT PER SHARE AMOUNTS)

	June 30, 2001	June 24, 2000
Authorized		
1,224,329 Multiple Voting Shares		
Unlimited Subordinate Voting Shares		
Unlimited Class A Preference Shares		
Issued and outstanding		
1,224,329 Multiple Voting Shares (June 24, 2000 – 1,224,329)	*	*
5,611,000 Subordinate Voting Shares (June 24, 2000 – 5,808,000)	23,412	24,236
	$23,412	$24,236

* Nominal

a) The Multiple Voting Shares and Subordinate Voting Shares have identical attributes except that the Multiple Voting Shares entitle the holder to ten votes per share and the Subordinate Voting Shares entitle the holder to one vote per share. Each Multiple Voting Share is convertible at any time, at the holder's option, into one fully paid and non-assessable Subordinate Voting Share. The Multiple Voting Shares are subject to provisions whereby, if a triggering event occurs then each Multiple Voting Share is converted into one fully paid and non-assessable Subordinate Voting Share. A triggering event may occur if Mr. Jeffrey Wortsman: (i) dies; (ii) ceases to be a senior officer of the Company; (iii) ceases to own less than 5% of the aggregate number of Multiple Voting Shares and Subordinate Voting Shares outstanding; or (iv) owns less than 918,247 Multiple Voting Shares and Subordinate Voting Shares combined.

b) The Company purchased for cancellation 197,500 (June 24, 2000 – 232,000) Subordinate Voting Shares at prevailing market prices for cash consideration of $2,231 (June 24, 2000 – $2,006). The excess of $1,407 (June 24, 2000 – $1,038) over the average paid-in value of the shares was charged to retained earnings.

c) The Company has reserved 700,000 Subordinate Voting Shares for issuance under its Stock Option Plan. The granting of options and the related vesting periods are at the discretion of the Board of Directors and have a maximum term of 10 years.

DANIER LEATHER INC. (2001)
NOTE 6 CAPITAL STOCK (CONTINUED)

EXHIBIT 11-11
CONT.

A summary of the status of the Company's Stock Option Plan as of June 30, 2001 and June 24, 2000 and changes during the years ending on those dates is presented below:

	June 30, 2001		June 24, 2000	
Stock Options	**Shares**	**Weighted-average exercise price**	**Shares**	**Weighted-average exercise price**
Outstanding at beginning of year	511,500	$ 9.10	507,500	$ 11.25
Granted	51,000	10.43	34,000	6.14
Exercised	(500)	6.85	-	-
Forfeited	(1,000)	10.40	(30,000)	11.25
Outstanding at end of year	561,000	9.22	511,500	10.91
Options exercisable at end of year	390,125	$ 9.12	250,750	$ 11.25

On January 19, 2000 the Board of Directors approved a resolution that was ratified by shareholders on October 19, 2000, to reduce the exercise price of 210,500 options to purchase Subordinate Voting Shares of the 511,500 options then outstanding. Options were **not** repriced for the President and Chief Executive Officer, the Vice-President and Chief Financial Officer and Secretary, or the Directors. The 210,500 options were originally issued in May 1998 and the exercise price was reduced from $11.25 to $6.85, being the average closing market price of the Corporation's Subordinate Voting Shares on the Toronto Stock Exchange for the 30 days from and including January 19, 2000, the date the resolution was approved by the Board and the date the Corporation announced to the public a 53% net earnings increase for the 26 weeks ended December 25, 1999. The effect of the repricing on the weighted average exercise price on options outstanding as at June 24, 2000 was a reduction of $1.81 per share.

Beyond the Book

11-42 (Examination of shareholders' equity for a real company)
Choose a company as directed by your instructor and answer the following questions:

a. Prepare a quick analysis of the shareholders' equity accounts by listing the beginning and ending amounts in these accounts and calculating the net change, in both dollar and percentage terms, for the most recent year.

b. If any of the accounts changed by more than 10%, give an explanation for this change.

c. For each type of share authorized by the company, list the nature of the issue, the number of shares (authorized, issued, and outstanding), par value or no-par value, market price at the end of the year, and any special features of the issue.

d. What was the market value of the company at the end of the most recent year? (Multiply the number of shares outstanding by the market price.) Compare this with the book value of the company and discuss the reasons why these amounts are different. Be as specific as possible.

e. Did the company pay dividends in the most recent year? If so, what was the dividend per share and has this amount changed over the past three years?

f. Did the company declare any stock dividends or have a stock split during the most recent year? If so, describe the nature of the event and the effects on the shareholders' equity section.

Cases

11-43   Manonta Sales Company

Manonta Sales Company's summary balance sheet and income statement as at December 31, 2003, are shown below:

Balance Sheet (in thousands)

Current assets	$178,000
Investments	1,000
Net property, plant, and equipment	56,000
Total assets	$235,000
Current liabilities	$105,000
Long-term debt	93,000
Shareholders' equity	37,000
Total liabilities and shareholders' equity	$235,000

Income Statement (in thousands)

Sales	$560,000
Cost of goods sold, operating and other expenses	525,000
Earnings before income taxes	35,000
Income taxes	15,000
Net income	$ 20,000
Earnings per share	$1.25

The long-term debt has an interest rate of 8% and is convertible into 9,300,000 common shares. After carefully analyzing all available information about Manonta, you decide the following events are likely to happen. First, Manonta will increase its earnings before income taxes by 10% next year because of increased sales. Second, the effective tax rate will stay the same. Third, the holders of long-term debt will convert it into shares on January 1, 2004. Fourth, the current multiple of earnings per share to market price of 20 will increase to 24 if the debt is converted, because of the reduced risk.

You own 100 common shares of Manonta and are trying to decide whether you should keep or sell them. You decide you will sell the shares if you think their market price is not likely to increase by at least 10% next year. Based on the information available should you keep the shares or sell them? Support your answer with a detailed analysis.

11-44   Tribec Wireless Inc.

Tribec Wireless Inc. had the following shareholders' equity section as at December 31, 2004:

Common Shares, authorized: an unlimited number of no par value common shares; issued and outstanding:	
2,000,000 shares	$ 4,000,000
Retained earnings	1,958,476
Total shareholders' equity	$ 5,958,476

In 2001 and 2002, Tribec paid a cash dividend of $0.75 per share. In 2003, the company expanded operations significantly and the board of directors decided to retain earnings in the business rather than pay them out as a cash dividend. In lieu of the cash dividend, the board voted to distribute a 10% stock dividend. In December 2004, the company returned to its previous dividend policy and again paid a $0.75 cash dividend.

In 2001 you inherited 5,000 shares of Tribec Wireless. At that time, the shares were trading at $5.00 per share. Given the tremendous growth in the wireless market by 2003 when the stock dividend was distributed, the company's shares were trading at $80 per share. After the stock dividend, the price of the shares dropped slightly but has since risen again, and as at December 31, 2004, they were trading at $82 per share.

Required:

a. From Tribec's perspective, how would the accounting for the stock dividend distributed in 2003 differ from that used for the cash dividends paid in the other years?

b. Immediately after the stock dividend, the price of the Tribec shares dropped slightly. Does this mean the value of the company (and your investment) decreased due to the payment of the stock dividend?

c. Prepare a schedule illustrating the total amount of cash dividends you have received since inheriting the Tribec shares. What is the value of your investment at December 31, 2004?

11-45 Blooming Valley Custom Landscaping

Blooming Valley Custom Landscaping provides landscaping services to a variety of clients in southern Ontario. The company's services include planting lawns and shrubs and the installation of outdoor lighting and irrigation systems as well as the construction of decks and gazebos. The company also remains very busy in the winter months by using its trucks for snow clearing. Blooming Valley would like to extend its operations into the northern United States, but Jack Langer, the owner, feels that the company would require at least $2 million in new capital before such a venture could be successful. Langer is excited about the prospects of expanding because his projections indicate that the company could earn an additional $750,000 in income before interest and taxes.

Currently, Blooming Valley has no long-term debt and the company is owned entirely by the Langer family. There are 300,000 common shares outstanding and the company currently has net income before tax of $900,000. The company's tax rate is 25% and is not expected to change as a result of the planned expansion. The family does not have sufficient financial resources to undertake the expansion, and therefore, it is essential to obtain outside financing. Mr. Langer is considering three financing options.

Option 1
The first option is to borrow, using a conventional bank loan. Interest on the loan would be 9% annually with monthly payments of principal and interest required.

Option 2
The second possibility is to issue 100,000 common shares to a local venture capitalist. As part of the plan, the venture capitalist would be given a seat on the board of directors and would also have a say in the day-to-day running of the company.

Option 3
The final option is to sell 100,000 of non-voting cumulative preferred shares. The preferred shares would have an annual dividend of $2.85. A number of investors have expressed interest in purchasing these shares.

Required:

a. Calculate the effect of each financing option on the company's earnings per share. Which option will result in the highest earnings per share?

b. Recommend an option to Mr. Langer. Be sure to consider both quantitative and qualitative factors as part of your analysis.

11-46

Sam Able, Abby Moss, and Kendra McDonald have just graduated from the Toronto Culinary Institute and are excited about opening their own restaurant. The three want to open a trendy Thai restaurant in Toronto and have been busy looking for the perfect location. Sam, who completed several business management courses as part of his degree, has estimated that the three will require $400,000 at a minimum to start the business. This would provide cash for rent, equipment, supplies, and advertising as well as small salaries for the three graduates until such time as the restaurant is up and running.

Having recently graduated, none of the three has significant assets to invest in the venture. Sam's parents are willing to loan them $50,000, but they want to see a solid business plan before committing to the loan. Sam and Abby are willing to work full-time in the business, but Kendra has a small child and feels that initially she may not be able to work full-time. Instead, she would be willing to work nights and weekends when her husband is home to take care of the baby.

The three friends recently had a meeting to discuss matters and to try to decide on how to form the business. Sam has proposed that they incorporate, but the others are concerned about the additional cost of incorporation and wonder if it would not be better to operate as a partnership. They feel that they need additional information before making this decision and decide to ask you, an independent business consultant, for advice.

Required:

a. Prepare a report for the three friends outlining how operating as a partnership differs from incorporating. Be sure to include the advantages and disadvantages of each form of organization.

b. Based on the information given above, make a preliminary recommendation as to which form of organization would best suit the needs of your clients.

11-47   Teed's Manufacturing Corporation

Teed's Manufacturing Corporation has the following shareholders' equity at December 1, 2004:

Shareholders' Equity

Share capital	
$4 preferred shares, no par value, cumulative,	
10,000 shares authorized, 8,000 shares issued	$ 360,000
Common shares, no par value, unlimited	
number of shares authorized, 60,000 shares issued	600,000
Total share capital	960,000
Retained earnings	687,500
Total shareholders' equity	$1,647,500

The company was formed in January 2002 and there has been no change in share capital since that time. It is now December 1, 2004, and after a very strong year the company has just declared a $150,000 cash dividend to shareholders of record as at February 10, 2005. The payment date of the dividend is February 28, 2005. Teed's has always used the earnings of the business for further expansion and has never paid a dividend before.

Jan Kielly owns 500 shares of Teed's Manufacturing common stock and is curious as to how much of a dividend she will receive. She is confused as to the difference between preferred and common stock and wonders why the preferred shareholders would purchase shares in a company without having the right to vote. Finally, she is confused as to the difference between the declaration date, date of record, and payment date. She wants to know when she will actually receive her dividend.

Required:

a. Determine how much of the dividend will be paid to the preferred shareholders and how much the common shareholders will receive.

b. Prepare a memo addressing Jan's questions.

Critical Thinking Question

11-48   (Stock Options)
Corporate executives are normally remunerated with a package that consists of a combination of one or more of the following:

a. Salary

b. "Perks" (a commonly used abbreviation for "perquisites") such as company cars, expense accounts, nice offices, and club memberships

c. Bonuses based on net income

d. Bonuses based on gross sales

e. Stock option plans

Required:
Discuss the impact of each of the above items on the actions of executives. What would each item encourage the executive to achieve? Which of these actions might be beneficial to the company? Which might be harmful? If you were designing a remuneration package for executives running a company you owned, what would you include? Explain why you included the items that you did.

Doing Your "Homework" on Investment Opportunities

Early every morning, at a time when most people can face little more than pop-music radio stations or the Weather Channel, Michael Decter sits down for half an hour with a cup of coffee, the business section of the morning paper, and a stack of quarterly and annual corporate reports. The habit has made him a millionaire.

When he first started out, Mr. Decter had no professional training or experience in investing or even accounting—his field is consultancy in the health-care sector. By simply researching businesses and analyzing financial statements, however, he has invested his way to an RRSP fund with a value of well over $1 million, ensuring that a comfortable retirement lies ahead. Today, he is also one of the founding partners of Lawrence Decter Investment Counsel, a Toronto-based firm that currently manages more than $70 million in assets.

Mr. Decter literally stumbled across his first big investment. Every day on his way to work, he would walk through Winnipeg's old Grain Exchange Building because it is connected to the city's underground tunnel system. "One day," he writes, "I noticed an annual report for a company called the Traders Building Association. I picked it up and discovered that this company owned the Grain Exchange Building as well as a portfolio of stocks and bonds."

Apparently, the Traders Building Association was set up as a corporation so that the tenants of the Grain Exchange Building, who were largely from the grain transport and related industries, could each own a piece of the action. Its shares were publicly traded on the tiny Winnipeg Stock

Exchange. Over the years, income from the building had been used to assemble a portfolio of stocks and bonds.

"As I began to analyze the report, I realized that the stocks and bonds had a combined value greater than the price of the shares. . . . After working over my logic a number of times, it seemed clear to me that if I could obtain shares in the Traders Building Association, eventually I would benefit from the unlocking of the company's hidden value."

Mr. Decter bought 300 shares of TBA. His stockbroker thought he was crazy, and assigned them a value on his monthly statement of US $1 each. After about a year and a half of almost no movement in the stock price, Mr. Decter unloaded 50 shares. Six months later, he regretted it; sure enough, a local entrepreneur made a takeover bid for TBA, and Mr. Decter sold his remaining shares for over twice their original price.

"My experience with TBA helped me formulate what I now think of as the two founding principles in my investment strategy," he says. "The first principle is to look under your nose. . . . I knew the territory. The second principle is to do your homework." The value of TBA's assets and of its shares was clearly outlined in the corporation's financial statements for anyone to see. The key is to look—and to have the confidence and initiative to follow through on your analysis.

FINANCIAL STATEMENT
ANALYSIS

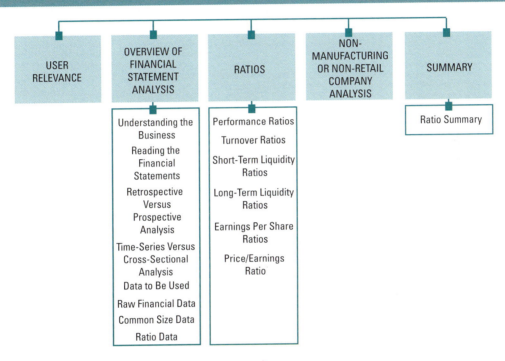

Learning Objectives:

After studying this chapter, you should be able to:

1. *Explain why knowledge of the business is important when attempting to draw conclusions about the future health of a company.*
2. *Describe the various ways of analyzing a company's financial statements.*
3. *Describe the types of ratios that are best suited to providing insight into specific decisions.*
4. *Calculate specific ratios and explain how the ratios can be interpreted.*
5. *Assess the financial health of a company through the use of ratios.*

Michael Decter picked up an annual report that someone had discarded, learned something about the company described in it, reviewed and analyzed its financial statements, and discovered that the shares were trading at a value lower than the value of its assets. Logic told him that if he invested at the current share price he would be able to sell them later at a higher price. And he did. He employed strategies that you have been learning throughout this book. You have an advantage over Mr. Decter. After studying this text, you know something about accounting, you can read financial statements, you are aware of the various methods that can be used to measure and report transactions, and you have some understanding of some of the limitations affecting the numbers on the statements.

In the first 11 chapters of this book, we described the basic components of the financial reporting system and how accounting numbers are accumulated and recorded. In most of these chapters we identified ratios that use the material that was being discussed. In this chapter, we pull all those ratios together and summarize how financial information can be analyzed. Here you will see how the various components of the reporting system work together.

USER RELEVANCE

As a user, you need to analyze financial information effectively. This involves more than a basic understanding of what each individual statement means. You need to understand the relationships among the three major financial statements and the methods that produce the numbers. You also need to compare and contrast these relationships over time and among different companies. This discussion was left until near the end of the book because proper analysis requires a good understanding of all components of all the financial statements.

As we worked through the material in the book, we introduced the ratios that pertained to the topics under discussion. This has given you some tools, but they are not organized cohesively. Now you need to think about analysis as a structured activity. You need to know what information would help you make informed decisions and then identify the tools (ratios) that will give you that information. The ratios in this chapter have been organized according to decision-making needs so that you can now pull together the tools you have aquired.

This chapter provides an overview of financial statement analysis and a discussion of the basic ratios used. However, because financial statement analysis is very complex, it can serve only as an introduction. Remember two basic facts as you work through this chapter. First, there is no definitive set of rules or procedures that dictate how to analyze financial statements. Second, every analysis should be tailored to suit the underlying reason for making the analysis. These two features make comprehensive analysis quite complex. A more detailed discussion of financial statement analysis is left to more advanced texts.

OVERVIEW OF FINANCIAL STATEMENT ANALYSIS

Financial statements are typically analyzed for a specific purpose. An investment analyst or a stockbroker, for example, may undertake an analysis in order to recommend that a client buy or sell shares. A bank's commercial loans officer may perform an analysis of a client's financial statements to decide whether the client will be capable of paying back a loan if the bank decides to lend the money. A student looking for a job may analyze a company to decide whether it is a suitable company for which to work.

Each analyst will tailor the analysis to the demands of the decision to be made. For example, a banker trying to decide whether to make a short-term loan may restrict the analysis to the company's short-term cash-producing capabilities. The investment analyst, on the other hand, may focus on its long-term financial health.

In this chapter, we take a very general approach to financial statement analysis. No particular decision is considered as the various ratios are discussed. However, we do attempt to discuss decision contexts in which one particular ratio may be more helpful than others in assessing the health of a company. Whatever the decision, one of the first things you have to do is come to some understanding of the business.

Understanding the Business

Understanding the business means more than understanding a company's financial statements. It means that you must have a grasp of the operating activities of the business, the underlying economics, the risks involved, and the economic factors that are crucial to the company's long- and short-term health. It means that you must understand the various types of businesses in which the company is engaged. For example, a large company such as **BCE Inc. (Bell Canada)** is involved in more than just telephones. It has businesses in many communications areas such as research (Bell-Northern Research), satellite mobile communications (TMI Communications), satellite television signals (Expressvu Inc.), cable television (Jones Intercable), and many other areas. An analyst who thinks that BCE is only in the telephone business has a very inaccurate view of the risks involved in lending BCE money, or in buying its shares.

A basic understanding of the range of businesses in which a company is engaged can be obtained by reading the first section of its annual report. In most annual reports, the first sections are devoted to describing the various businesses in which the company is involved, with their associated achievements and expectations. Usually, the financial statements are found in the second half of an annual report. Although this descriptive section of most annual reports does not explain everything you need to know about the company, it does provide some insight into what the company does and the types of risks it faces. You should also listen to the financial news and read financial newspapers and magazines to find additional information about the company and the industry in which it operates.

Once you have an overall view of the types of businesses operated by the com-

Learning Objective

1

Explain why knowledge of the business is important when attempting to draw conclusions about the future health of a company.

pany, you should next read the financial statements, including the auditor's report and the notes to the financial statements.

Reading the Financial Statements

The first thing that should be read in the financial statements is the auditor's report attached to them. The auditor's report states whether or not appropriate accounting policies were followed and whether or not the statements "present fairly" the financial position of the company. This report is important because the auditor is an independent third party who is stating a professional opinion on the fairness of the numbers and disclosures reported in the financial statements. Remember that the auditor's report is not a guarantee of the accuracy of the information contained in the financial statements. Financial statements are prepared by management, and management has primary responsibility for them. Auditors express their opinion on whether the financial statements present the information fairly according to generally accepted accounting principles. The auditor's report does not indicate if the information contained in the financial statements is good or bad. It is the reader's responsibility to interpret the information provided.

An example of a typical unqualified auditor's opinion provided by **PricewaterhouseCoopers**, Chartered Accountants for the 2002 financial statements of **Cara Operations Limited**, is shown in Exhibit 12-1.

EXHIBIT 12-1

Auditors' Report

To the Shareholders of Cara Operations Limited

We have audited the consolidated balance sheets of Cara Operations Limited as at March 31, 2002 and April 1, 2001, and the consolidated statements of earnings and retained earnings and cash flows for the years then ended. These financial statements are the responsibility of the Corporation's management. Our responsibility is to express an opinion on these financial statements based on our audits.

We conducted our audits in accordance with Canadian generally accepted auditing standards. Those standards require that we plan and perform an audit to obtain reasonable assurance whether the financial statements are free of material misstatement. An audit includes examining, on a test basis, evidence supporting the amounts and disclosures in the financial statements. An audit also includes assessing the accounting principles used and significant estimates made by management, as well as evaluating the overall financial statement presentation.

In our opinion, these consolidated financial statements present fairly, in all material respects, the financial position of the Corporation as at March 31, 2002 and April 1, 2001, and the results of its operations and its cash flows for the years then ended in accordance with Canadian generally accepted accounting principles.

Chartered Accountants
Toronto, Canada
May 22, 2002

The second step is to read each of the major financial statements to make sure that the results make sense for the types of activities in which the company is engaged. Use your knowledge from this course to look for unusual account titles and unusually large dollar items. For example, if there is a large loss item on the income statement, the nature of the loss is important. Is it an item that should be expected to continue into the future, or is it a noncontinuing item? Unusual account titles may indicate that the company is involved in a line of business that is new, which could have serious implications for future operations. For example, if a manufacturer suddenly shows lease receivables on its balance sheet, this probably indicates that it has started to lease assets as well as sell them. The leasing business is very different from the manufacturing business and exposes the company to different types of risk. You must take this new information into consideration in your evaluation of the company.

A reading of the financial statements is not complete unless the notes to the financial statements are read carefully. Because the major financial statements provide summary information only, there is not much room on the statements to provide all the details necessary for a full understanding of the company's transactions. Therefore, the notes provide a place for more details and discussion about many items on the financial statements. Also pay attention in the notes to the summary of the significant accounting policies used by the company. Remember that GAAP allows considerable flexibility in choosing accounting methods, so you should be aware of the choices that were made by management. These will generally be listed in the first note to the financial statements.

Once you have an overall understanding of the business and the financial statements, you can begin a detailed analysis of the financial results.

Retrospective Versus Prospective Analysis

As discussed earlier, most analysis is done with a particular objective in mind. Most objectives involve making decisions that have future consequences. Therefore, almost every analysis of a set of financial statements is, in one way or another, concerned with the future. Because of this, you should make a **prospective** (forward-looking) analysis of the company to try to determine what the future will bring. For example, commerical loans officers in banks try to forecast future cash flows of companies to ensure that loans will be repaid.

The problem with prospective analysis is that the world is an uncertain place; no one can predict the future with complete accuracy. Analysts, however, are expected to make recommendations based on their predictions of what the future outcomes will be for specified companies. In trying to predict the future, one of the most reliable sources of data you have is the results of a company's past operations as summarized in the financial statements. To the extent that the future follows the trends of the past, you can use these **retrospective** data to assist in predicting the future. You must also understand the economics of a company well enough to know when something fundamental has changed in the economic environment to make it unlikely that the company's past results will predict the future. In such a situation, you cannot rely on the retrospective data.

Learning Objective

2

Describe the various ways of analyzing a company's financial statements.

If you believe that retrospective data may be useful in predicting the future, a complete analysis of those data is in order. Two major types of analysis of retrospective data are **times-series** and **cross-sectional analyses**.

Time-Series Versus Cross-Sectional Analysis

In a time-series analysis, the analyst examines information from different time periods for the same company to look for any pattern in the data over time. For example, you may look at the sales data over a five-year period to determine whether sales are increasing, decreasing, or remaining stable. This would have important implications for future sales of the company. The assumption underlying a time-series analysis is that there is some predictability in the time series; that is, past data can be used to predict the future. Without this assumption, there is no reason to do a time-series analysis.

Many companies recognize the importance of time-series information and provide five- or ten-year summaries to assist in making this analysis. An example is shown in Exhibit 12-2 from the **Cara Operations Limited** 2002 annual report. The financial highlights report selected pieces of financial data across five years. In Cara's information, it is interesting to note that it sold its investment in Days Inn in 1998, incurred tax restructuring costs in 1999, experienced losses from its investment in Second Cup in both 2001 and 2000, and sold its investment in Beaver Foods at a gain in 2001. It considered all of these items unusual, which means that they result from normal operations but are abnormal in size and/or infrequent in occurrence. In the summary, it includes an earnings per share amount before unusual items so that users understand what its earnings are from operations before these items. Restructuring means that the company restructured its weighting of debt and equity. After the restructuring, the number of shares outstanding is down and the amount of long-term debt is up. From 1998 through to 2002, the number of shares outstanding has been declining.

A cross-sectional analysis compares the data from one company with the data from another company for the same time period. Usually, the comparison is with another company in the same industry (a competitor perhaps), or with an average of the other companies in the industry. For example, you might look at the growth in sales for General Motors Canada compared to the growth in sales for Ford Canada or DaimlerChrysler Canada. Other cross-sectional analyses might compare companies across different industries (General Motors Canada compared to BCE), countries (General Motors Canada compared to Nissan), and so forth. However, any such cross-sectional comparisons must consider that different industries may have slightly different accounting principles (for example, accounting principles for banks and insurance companies are slightly different from those for most other industries). Comparing across countries is much more difficult because of different accounting methods and sets of standards used in different countries. However, using as wide a range of investments as possible, investment analysts want to recommend the best investment strategy to their clients. To make the best recommendation, they must consider the return versus risk trade-off across many companies. They must, therefore, directly compare companies in different industries and different countries.

CARA OPERATIONS LIMITED (2002)

EXHIBIT 12-2

Five Year Financial Highlights

(in thousands of dollars, except for share data and ratios)	2002	2001	2000	1999	1998
System Sales	$ 1,548,745	$ 1,609,021	$ 1,526,220	$ 1,246,050	$ 1,188,490
Gross Revenue	1,036,749	1,127,460	1,088,813	864,890	801,193
EBITDA	109,108	115,844	105,229	81,462	84,743
EBIT	66,048	75,253	66,355	53,530	60,287
Earnings before Unusual Items[1]	35,654	39,139	32,858	28,229	35,380
Net Earnings	35,654	102,678	26,471	18,991	35,027
Capital Expenditures[2]	58,053	114,789	77,416	46,666	33,025
Capital Employed[3]	496,441	414,203	449,600	395,090	385,190
FINANCIAL POSITION					
Total Assets	746,638	688,727	603,337	561,111	496,048
Property, Plant and Equipment, net	376,041	363,716	323,127	249,808	228,655
Net Debt[4]	124,691	61,263	185,318	139,311	105,248
Shareholders' Equity	353,558	338,502	254,781	248,279	267,660
PER SHARE DATA					
Earnings per Share before Unusual Items[1] (¢)	38.7	42.2	35.1	29.5	36.0
Earnings per Share (¢)	38.7	110.6	28.3	19.9	35.7
Cash Flow per Share[5] (¢)	85.9	97.6	76.8	57.1	60.2
Dividends per Share (¢)	16.0	14.0	14.0	12.0	11.0
Book Value per Share	3.83	3.65	2.74	2.62	2.71
Share Price at Year-End					
Common	7.60	5.75	4.60	6.00	7.20
Class A	6.16	5.90	3.24	4.65	7.20
Weighted Average Shares Outstanding (000's)	92,249	92,846	93,585	95,563	98,197
Shares Outstanding at Year-End (000's)	91,895	92,836	92,864	94,638	98,859
OTHER RATIOS AND DATA					
Net Debt to Equity	35.3%	18.1%	72.7%	56.1%	39.3%
EBIT Interest Coverage (times)	11.09	7.76	5.78	6.01	9.79
EBITDA Interest Coverage (times)	18.32	11.95	9.16	9.15	13.75
Dividend Pay-out[1]	41.3%	33.2%	40.0%	40.5%	30.6%
Return on Capital Employed[6]	8.6%	10.1%	9.3%	8.5%	10.4%
Return on Shareholders' Equity[1]	10.3%	14.8%	13.1%	10.9%	14.0%
Number of Employees at Year End	38,000	28,500	33,400	27,400	26,000

[1] *Earnings before unusual items exclude: 2001 – after tax gain on sale of Beaver Foods of $65.5 million and Cara's share of The Second Cup's investment write-down of $2.0 million; 2000 – Cara's share of The Second Cup's divestment loss of $6.4 million; 1999 – after tax restructuring costs of $9.2 million and 1998 – loss on disposal of Days Inn of $0.3 million.*
[2] *Capital expenditures also include property, plant and equipment acquired by means of capital leases.*
[3] *Capital employed includes shareholders' equity, net debt, future income taxes and non-controlling shareholders' interest.*
[4] *Net debt includes long-term debt and bankers' acceptances less cash and marketable investment.*
[5] *Cash flow per share before unusual items excludes non-cash operating working capital. (Fiscal 2001 excludes the impact of the gain on sale of business.)*
[6] *Return on capital employed is based on after tax earnings before unusual items before interest.*

The choice of which type of analysis to conduct is driven, in part, by the type of decision that motivated the analysis. In a lending situation, for example, the commercial loans officer will use a time-series analysis of the company in conjunction with a cross-company comparison. The time-series analysis is important because it will help the lender determine the company's ability to repay any money loaned. As part of the decision-making process, the lender must also be aware of industry trends in the analysis of a particular company so as to get an overall assessment of how well this company performs relative to its competitors. This information will help ascertain its future viability.

Data to Be Used

The type of data used in a time-series or cross-sectional analysis will vary depending on the purpose of the analysis. Three general types of data that are frequently used are **raw financial data**, **common size data**, and **ratio data**.

Raw Financial Data

Raw financial data are the data that appear directly in the financial statements. An example of a time-series analysis of this type of data might be the time-series data from income statements, as shown for Cara Operations Limited in Exhibit 12-2, or the time-series of total net debt for the past five years. Cross-sectional analysis can also be used with this type of data. For example, you might compare total revenues across companies in the same industry for the past three years.

Time-series data are almost always available directly from financial statements, since they usually show data for a two-year period. In addition to the main financial statements, many annual reports contain additional time-series data in the form of a five- or ten-year summary such as that shown in Exhibit 12-2. Note that this summary does not include all items that appear on the income statement. Annual reports may also contain data other than strictly financial data, such as numbers of employees or sales volumes expressed in physical units rather than dollars.

In the remainder of the chapter, data from a set of financial statements will be used to illustrate various types of analyses. For purposes of illustration, we are going to continue to use the financial statement data of **Cara Operations Limited** for the year ended March 31, 2002. Cara Operations, with headquarters in Mississauga, Ontario, is the leading Canadian-owned and second largest food service company in Canada. The raw financial statement data for Cara Operations appear in Exhibit 12-3, which includes the balance sheets, statements of earnings and retained earnings, and statements of cash flows.

CARA OPERATIONS LIMITED (2002)

Consolidated Balance Sheets

As at March 31, 2002 and April 1, 2001

EXHIBIT 12-3
PART A

(in thousands of dollars)	2002	2001
ASSETS		
Current Assets		
Cash	$ 15,003	$ 106,429
Marketable investment *(note 3)*	75,710	–
Accounts receivable	68,793	64,138
Inventories	25,575	28,768
Prepaid expenses and other assets	6,972	5,866
Future income taxes *(note 11)*	9,500	6,414
Current portion of long-term receivables *(note 4)*	2,571	2,548
	204,124	214,163
Long-Term Receivables *(note 4)*	12,704	15,149
Property, Plant and Equipment *(note 5)*	376,041	363,716
Goodwill *(note 6)*	49,166	49,166
Brands and Other Intangible Assets *(note 6)*	90,309	8,549
Equity Investments *(note 7)*	14,294	37,984
	$ 746,638	$ 688,727
LIABILITIES		
Current Liabilities		
Bankers' acceptances *(note 8)*	$ 51,500	$ –
Accounts payable and accrued liabilities	123,740	117,553
Income taxes payable *(note 11)*	3,890	25,253
Current portion of long-term debt *(note 9)*	3,880	4,420
	183,010	147,226
Long-Term Debt *(note 9)*	160,024	162,697
Other Long-Term Liabilities *(note 10)*	22,354	19,450
Future Income Taxes *(note 11)*	18,382	15,052
	383,770	344,425
Non-Controlling Shareholders' Interest	9,310	5,800
SHAREHOLDERS' EQUITY		
Capital Stock *(note 12)*	30,708	30,438
Retained Earnings	322,850	308,064
	353,558	338,502
	$ 746,638	$ 688,727

Approved on behalf of the Board

M. BERNARD SYRON
Chairman of the Board

GABRIEL TSAMPALIEROS
President and Chief Executive Officer

EXHIBIT 12-3
PART B

CARA OPERATIONS LIMITED (2002)

Consolidated Statements of Cash Flows

For the years ended March 31, 2002 and April 1, 2001

(in thousands of dollars)	2002	2001
CASH FLOWS PROVIDED BY (USED IN) OPERATING ACTIVITIES		
Net earnings for the year	$ 35,654	$ 102,678
Adjustments for:		
Amortization of property, plant and equipment	41,830	36,008
Amortization of goodwill, brands and other intangible assets *(note 6)*	1,230	4,583
(Gain) loss on disposal of property, plant and equipment	(188)	3,219
(Gain) on sale of business *(note 2)*	–	(89,548)
Future income taxes	1,021	6,371
Equity (earnings) loss	(887)	927
Non-controlling shareholders' interest	2,360	1,866
Other non-cash items	(1,747)	430
Change in non-cash operating working capital *(note 14)*	(21,601)	14,811
	57,672	81,345
INVESTING ACTIVITIES		
Acquisition of marketable investment *(note 3)*	(74,602)	–
Purchase of property, plant and equipment	(58,053)	(114,789)
Proceeds on sale of business *(note 2)*	–	149,058
Business acquisition *(note 2)*	(50,254)	–
Cash distributions from equity investment *(note 7)*	–	7,326
Proceeds on disposal of property, plant and equipment	5,548	13,570
Purchase of intangible assets	(248)	(763)
Collection (issuance) of mortgages and notes	1,190	(2,518)
Collection of employee share purchase loans	1,232	3,426
	(175,187)	55,310
FINANCING ACTIVITIES		
Bankers' acceptances issued *(note 8)*	236,472	–
Repayment of bankers' acceptances *(note 8)*	(184,972)	–
Share repurchase under Normal Course Issuer Bid	(5,758)	(641)
Repayment of long-term debt	(5,963)	(20,086)
Dividends paid	(14,840)	(12,999)
Issuance of capital stock by subsidiary	1,150	–
Issuance of capital stock	–	283
	26,089	(33,443)
NET CHANGE IN CASH	(91,426)	103,212
CASH – BEGINNING OF YEAR	106,429	3,217
CASH – END OF YEAR	$ 15,003	$ 106,429

EXHIBIT 12-3
PART C

CARA OPERATIONS LIMITED (2002)

Consolidated Statements of Earnings and Retained Earnings

For the years ended March 31, 2002 and April 1, 2001

(in thousands of dollars, except earnings per share data)	2002	2001
SYSTEM SALES	$ 1,548,745	$ 1,609,021
GROSS REVENUE	$ 1,036,749	$ 1,127,460
Earnings before the following:	$ 109,108	$ 115,844
Amortization of property, plant and equipment	41,830	36,008
Amortization of goodwill, brands and other intangible assets *(note 6)*	1,230	4,583
	66,048	75,253
Interest expense net of investment income *(note 15)*	(5,487)	(7,173)
Gain on sale of business *(note 2)*	–	89,548
Equity earnings (loss) *(note 7)*	887	(927)
Earnings before income taxes and non-controlling shareholders' interest	61,448	156,701
Provision for income taxes *(note 11)*	23,434	52,157
Non-controlling shareholders' interest	2,360	1,866
Net earnings for the year	35,654	102,678
Retained Earnings – Beginning of Year	308,064	219,108
Share repurchase under Normal Course Issuer Bid	(5,228)	(578)
Issuance of capital stock on exercise of options *(note 12)*	(800)	(145)
Dividends	(14,840)	(12,999)
Retained Earnings – End of Year	$ 322,850	$ 308,064
Earnings per share *(note 13)*		
Basic	38.7¢	110.6¢
Diluted	38.3¢	110.3¢

Common Size Data

Although the raw data of a company can reveal much about its performance, certain relationships are more easily understood when some elements of the raw data are compared with other elements. For example, in the statement of earnings for Cara Operations in Exhibit 12-3, you can see that the gross revenue decreased from $1,127,460 thousand in 2001 to $1,036,749 thousand in 2002. Cost of goods sold and other operating expenses have also decreased over this same period from $1,011,616 thousand to $927,641 thousand. (The cost of goods sold and other operating expenses are not disclosed on the statement of earnings as a separate amount. Rather, Cara Operations discloses the "gross revenue" and then the "earnings before the following." The difference between these two amounts represents the cost of goods sold and other operating expenses.) The question is: what happened to profit margins on a relative basis? This is a question of the relationship of the costs to the revenues. One way to address this question is to compare the cost of goods sold and other income statement items expressed as a proportion of the sales revenue. Often, this is done by preparing a set of financial statements called common size statements.

In a common size statement of earnings, all line items are expressed as percentages of net revenues. In the case of Cara Operations, a common size income statement is shown in Exhibit 12-4 with every item calculated as a percentage of gross revenue.

CARA OPERATIONS LIMITED

Common Size Statements of Earnings

	2002	2001
Gross revenue	100.0%	100.0%
[Cost of goods sold and other operating expenses (not included)]	89.5%	89.7%]
Earnings before the following:	10.5%	10.3%
Amortization of property, plant, and equipment		
intangible assets	4.0%	3.2%
Amortization of goodwill, brands, and other intangible assets	0.1%	0.4%
	6.4%	6.7%
Interest expense, net of investment income	(0.5%)	(0.6%)
Gain on sale of business	–	7.9%
Equity earnings (loss)	0.1%	(0.1%)
Earnings before income taxes and non-controlling		
shareholders' interest	6.0%	13.9%
Provision for income taxes	2.3%	4.6%
Non-controlling shareholders' interest	0.2%	0.2%
Net earnings for the year	3.5%	9.1%

This common size statement of earnings shows that Cara's operations have been very stable. Sales have fallen, but the cost of those sales (cost of goods sold and other operating expenses) has fallen proportionately slightly more than the sales. This is a good sign because it means that Cara is controlling its major costs. An analyst will examine a company's financial statements carefully when sales are rising or falling. If they are rising and the cost of those sales rises proportionately more than the sales themselves, the new sales are costing the company more and management should be looking for ways to control the costs. Most of the items on the statement of earnings are proportionately very consistent with the previous year, although the amortization of property, plant, and equipment is slightly higher. A review of the balance sheet shows that the property, plant, and equipment increased by almost $10 million. Much of the increase in earnings in 2001 was a result of the gain on the sale of a business (Beaver Foods Limited). The notes to the financial statements state that in 2002, the company purchased all of the remaining shares of Second Cup Ltd. Prior to this acquisition, the company held a 39% interest in Second Cup. Because the acquisition was in February 2002 and the company's year end is March 2002, the financial statements reflect only two months of earnings from Second Cup. It will be interesting to read the financial statements in 2003 to see what impact this investment has on the company's earnings.

Common size statements could also be prepared for the balance sheet and the cash flow statement. The common size data can then be used in a time-series analysis, as they were earlier, or they could be used in a cross-sectional analysis of different companies. In fact, in cross-sectional analysis, common size statements allow one to compare of companies of different sizes.

Ratio Data

Common size data are useful for making comparisons of data items within a given financial statement. They are not useful for making comparisons across the various financial statements. Ratios compare a data element from one statement with an element from another statement, or with an element within the same statement. These ratios can then be used in a time-series or cross-sectional analysis. Ratio data are potentially the most useful because they reveal information about relationships between the financial statements. To further illustrate this, the remainder of the chapter is devoted to discussing various ratios, their calculation, and interpretation. Most of them have already been introduced throughout the book in previous chapters, but a discussion of the ratios as they relate to one another should help you understand the usefulness of ratio analysis.

Before you begin that analysis, it is important to remember that financial statements are based on GAAP. This means that they contain assumptions and estimates. As well, many of the assets and liabilities are reported at historical cost values rather than market values. Consequently, the limitations inherent in the financial statements are carried over into the ratios that are used to evaluate them.

RATIOS

Ratios explain relationships among data in the financial statements. The relationships differ across companies, if for no other reason than that the companies' underlying transactions are different. For example, a manufacturing company is very concerned about the management of inventory and focuses on various ratios related to inventory. A bank, on the other hand, has no inventory and would not be able to calculate a ratio involving inventory. It might, however, be very concerned about the loans that it makes, whereas the manufacturer might not have any items comparable to loans receivable.

Because of the differences across companies, it is impossible for us to address all the ratio issues related to all types of industries. The main focus of our discussion will, therefore, be restricted to Cara Operations. Most of our discussions are also applicable to companies in other industries, such as retailing. At the end of the chapter, we include a brief discussion of ratio analysis for non-retailing/manufacturing companies in areas where there may be differences in interpretation.

The ratios that will be discussed are divided into three general categories, but you will see that they are all related. The categories are performance, short-term liquidity, and long-term liquidity. Most of these ratios apply to any company regardless of the nature of its business, but some (such as inventory ratios) apply only to certain types of businesses.

Learning Objective

3

Describe the types of ratios that are best suited to providing insight into specific decisions.

Before the calculations of the various ratios are presented, one general caveat should be made. There are often several ways to calculate a given ratio. Therefore, it makes sense to understand the basis of a calculation before you attempt to interpret it. The use of ratios in this book will be consistent with the definitions given. However, if you use similar ratios from other sources, you should check the definition used in that source to make sure that it is consistent with your understanding of the ratio.

accounting in the news

COMPARISONS AMONG COMPANIES

Comparing a company with its competitors is a useful tool. For example, companies must report the depreciation periods of their different asset categories. Since the period chosen for depreciating an asset is a judgement call, comparing depreciation periods of different companies within an industry gives you a feel for the industry norm.

A big difference between a company and its competitors should raise questions. A company that depreciates an asset over a particularly long period reports lower yearly expense for that asset. This increases earnings.

Changing the depreciation period is another warning. During a difficult time in the late 1980s, General Motors Corp. increased the depreciation of its plants from 35 years to 45 years and gained $500 million more a year in income.

Source: "Don't Get Burned," by Shawn Tully, *Fortune*, Feb. 18, 2002, p. 88.

Performance Ratios

Learning Objective

4

Calculate specific ratios and explain how the ratios can be interpreted.

Net income and cash flow as measures of performance have already been discussed in Chapters 4 and 5. Although much can be learned from studying the income and cash flow statements, both in their raw data and common size forms, the ratios discussed in this section complement that understanding and also draw out some of the relationships between these statements and the balance sheet.

For example, in Chapter 4, a performance ratio called the **return on investment (ROI)** was briefly discussed. In that chapter, ROI was discussed in generic terms as a measure of the performance of an investment. The generic form of the ROI calculation can be used to formulate several different ratios depending on the perspective taken in measuring performance. For example, one perspective is that of the shareholders, who make an investment in the company and want to measure the performance of their investment. A form of the ROI measure that captures the return to shareholders is referred to as the **return on equity (ROE)**.

A second perspective is that of the debtholders, who make an investment in the company by lending money to it. The return they receive is the interest paid by the company. The interest rate paid to them is a measure of their ROI. This type of ROI calculation is not explicitly discussed in this chapter.

The third perspective is that of management. Management obtains resources from both shareholders and debtholders. Those resources are then invested in assets. The return generated by the investment in assets is then used to repay the debtholders and the shareholders. The performance of the investment in assets is, therefore, very important. This type of ROI is captured in a ratio referred to as the **return on assets (ROA)**.

In this chapter, both ROE and ROA are considered. In addition to these two overall measures of performance, three additional ratios, referred to as turnover ratios, are discussed. These turnover ratios provide additional insight into three major policy decisions management makes regarding accounts receivable, inventory, and accounts payable policies.

Return on Assets (ROA)

Management of a company must make two fundamental decisions regarding the company. The first is the type of assets in which the company should invest (sometimes referred to as the investment decision), and the second is whether to seek more financing to increase the amount the company can invest in assets (referred to as the financing decision). The ROA ratio, in this book, separates the investment decision from the financing decision. Regardless of the mix of debt and shareholder financing, this ratio asks: what type of return is earned on the investment in assets? From this perspective, the return on the investment in assets should be calculated prior to any payments or returns to the debtholders or shareholders. Net income is a measure of return on assets that is calculated prior to any returns to shareholders, but after the deduction of interest to the debtholders. Therefore, the net income, if it is to be used as a measure of return on assets, must be adjusted for the effects of interest expense so it is treated on a basis that is similar to the treatment of dividends.

A complicating factor exists because interest is deductible in the calculation of income tax expense. Therefore, if interest expense is to be removed from the net income figure, we must also adjust the amount of income tax expense that would result. In other words, the tax savings (i.e., the reduction in income tax expense) associated with this interest deduction must also be removed. The ROA ratio is then calculated as the ratio of the return (income before interest) divided by the investment in total assets, as follows:

$$ROA = \frac{\text{Income before interest}}{\text{Average total assets}}$$

$$= \frac{\text{Net income} + \text{Interest expense} - \text{Tax saving of interest expense}}{\text{Average total assets}}$$

$$= \frac{\text{Net income} + \text{Interest expense} - (\text{Tax rate} \times \text{Interest expense})}{\text{Average total assets}}$$

$$ROA = \frac{\text{Net income} + [\text{Interest expense} \times (1 - \text{Tax rate})]}{\text{Average total assets}}$$

Based on the data for Cara Operations in 2002, the calculation of the ROA has the following results. The income tax rate of 38.1% is found in a note to the financial statements.

ROA—CARA OPERATIONS LIMITED, 2002

$$\text{ROA} = \frac{\text{Net income} + [\text{Interest expense} \times (1 - \text{Tax rate})]}{\text{Average total assets}}$$

$$= \frac{\$35,654 + [\$5,487 \times (1 - 38.1\%)]}{\dfrac{\$746,638 + \$688,727}{2}}$$

$$= 5.44\%$$

This 5.44% ROA indicates that Cara Operations earned 5.44% on the average total assets before making any payments to the suppliers of capital. This 5.44% should be compared to the ROA earned by other similar companies and to Cara Operations' ROA in previous years to determine the trend.

The calculation of the appropriate tax rate to use in the ROA formula is somewhat problematic. The rate that should be used is the company's marginal tax rate. The marginal rate is the rate of tax the company would pay on an additional dollar of income before taxes. This marginal rate would be a combination of the federal and provincial corporate income tax rates. Many analysts use the effective tax rate, which is calculated by dividing the tax expense by the income before taxes. Many companies, including Cara Operations, show the effective tax rate in a note to the financial statements.

The ROA is useful as an overall measure of the performance of the investment in the assets of the company. However, cross-sectional comparisons of ROAs across industries must be made with care. The level of ROA reflects, to some extent, the risk inherent in the type of assets in which the company invests. Investors trade off the risk of an investment for the return on the investment. The more risk the investor takes, the higher the return demanded by the investor. If the company invested its assets in a bank account (a very low-risk investment), it would expect a lower return than if it invested in oil exploration equipment (a high-risk business). Although this factor cannot explain all the variations in ROA between companies, it must be kept in mind. It may be more appropriate either to do a time-series analysis of this ratio, or to compare it cross-sectionally with a direct competitor in the same business. Data obtained from a source of industry ratios such as Dun and Bradstreet can provide you with median measures of ROA that can be used for comparison purposes to determine if the calculated ROA is reasonable or not.

In addition, there is another useful breakdown of the ROA ratio that can provide insight into the cause of a change in this ratio. The most common breakdown of this ratio is as follows:

$$ROA = \frac{\text{Net income} + [\text{Interest expense} \times (1 - \text{Tax rate})]}{\text{Average total assets}}$$

$$= \frac{\text{Net income} + [\text{Interest expense} \times (1 - \text{Tax rate})]}{\text{Sales revenue}}$$

$$\times \frac{\text{Sales revenue}}{\text{Average total assets}}$$

$$= \text{Profit margin ratio} \times \text{Total asset turnover}$$

This breakdown of the ratio into a **profit margin ratio** and a **total asset turnover** allows the analyst to assess some of the reasons why the ROA of a company has gone up or down. The profit margin ratio is, of course, affected by the level of the company's costs relative to its revenues. Changes in this ratio would indicate a change in the profitability of the product and may indicate changes in the cost structure or pricing policy. The total asset turnover ratio is the ratio of sales to total assets, or the dollars of sales generated per dollar of investment in assets. Changes in this ratio could reflect an increase or decrease in sales volume or major changes in the level of investment in assets of the company.

The breakdown for Cara Operations in 2002 would be as follows:

ROA (BREAKDOWN)—CARA OPERATIONS LIMITED, 2002

$$ROA = \frac{\text{Net income} + [\text{Interest expense} \times (1 - \text{Tax rate})]}{\text{Sales revenue}}$$

$$\times \frac{\text{Sales revenue}}{\text{Average total assets}}$$

$$ROA = \frac{\$35,654 + [\$5,487 \times (1 - 38.1\%)]}{\$1,036,749} \times \frac{\$1,036,749}{\dfrac{\$746,638 + \$688,727}{2}}$$

$$= 3.77\% \times 1.44 = 5.44\%$$

These calculations indicate that Cara Operations earned the 5.44% ROA by achieving a profit margin ratio of 3.77% and a total asset turnover of 1.44. Note that the 5.44% could be increased by increasing either the profit margin ratio or the total asset turnover, or both.

Note that the same ROA could be achieved by companies in the same industry with different strategies. For example, a discount retailer operates on smaller profit margins and hopes to make that up by a larger volume of sales relative to investment in assets. Discounters generally have less invested in their retail stores. Other full-price retailers have a much larger investment in assets relative to their sales volume and, therefore, must charge higher prices to achieve a comparable ROA. Both businesses face the same general sets of risks and should earn comparable ROAs.

Return on Equity (ROE)

Return on equity (ROE), discussed earlier in this section, is the return the shareholders are earning on their investment in the company. There is one additional quirk that must be understood in calculating this ratio. If there is more than one class of shares (generally the second class would be preferred shares), the ROE calculation should be done from the point of view of the common shareholders. This means that any payments to the other classes of shares (preferred dividends, for example) should be deducted from net income in the numerator of this ratio because these amounts are not available to common shareholders. The denominator in such cases should include only the shareholders' equity accounts that belong to common shareholders. This usually means that the preferred shares equity account is subtracted from the total shareholders' equity to arrive at the common shareholders' equity.

The calculation of the ROE for a company is as follows:

$$ROE = \frac{\text{Net income} - \text{Preferred dividends}}{\text{Average common shareholders' equity}}$$

Cara Operations Limited has Class A non-voting shares as well as common shares. However, in the information accompanying the financial statements, management indicates that it paid dividends of $14,840 thousand. It does not distinguish between the dividends paid on the common shares and those on the non-voting shares. In its calculation of earnings per share (which is calculated on common shares), the company combined the two classes of shares when it calculated the weighted average number of shares outstanding. We can only conclude that the non-voting shares do not have a preferential right to dividends. Because we are unable to determine the exact status of the non-voting shares or the amount of dividends paid to this class of share, we are going to calculate the ROE without deducting the non-voting share dividends and we will use all of shareholders' equity, not just the common shareholders' equity. For Cara Operations, the calculation is as follows:

ROE—CARA OPERATIONS LIMITED, 2002

$$ROE = \frac{\text{Net income} - \text{Preferred dividends}}{\text{Average common shareholders' equity}}$$

$$= \frac{\$35,654 - 0}{\dfrac{\$353,558 + \$338,502}{2}}$$

$$= \frac{35,654}{346,030} = 10.3\%$$

This calculation shows that Cara Operations earned 10.3% ROE, indicating that it earned an average of 10.3% on the average shareholders' equity balances. This is down from the previous year's ROE of 34.6% (the net earnings were almost three times higher in 2001). Just as with the ROA, this 10.3% could be compared with other similar companies, or with the results of Cara Operations itself over time. Cross-sectional comparisons of ROE (among different companies) are also difficult for the same reason that ROA is difficult. Differences in the risks involved should result in differences in returns. Differences in the risks cannot, however, always explain large differences in return as there are many factors that affect ROE.

accounting in the news

WHY COMPANIES BUY BACK THEIR SHARES

Occasionally a company will buy back and cancel its own shares to boost its stock. In October 2001, Sears Canada Inc. announced that it would repurchase about 5.4 million shares, or up to 5% of its common shares outstanding.

The company said it wanted to make up for the dilution resulting from shares issued to compensate directors and employees.

A share buyback reduces a company's equity base, effectively increasing its earnings per share and return on equity. Investors use these measures to help them evaluate the financial health of a company.

The department store retailer also left the door open for another share buyback in the future, dependent on whether such action would enhance shareholder value.

Source: "Sears Canada to buyback five per cent of common shares," from *Canadian Press Newswire*, Oct. 31, 2001.

Leverage

Comparing the ROE calculated for Cara Operations with the associated ROA shows that the company, while earning only a 5.44% return on assets, showed a return of 10.3% on the shareholders' equity. This higher return on equity results from the company successfully applying financial **leverage**. Financial leverage simply means that some of the funds obtained to invest in assets came from debtholders rather than from shareholders. A company that has a larger proportion of debt to shareholders' equity is said to be highly leveraged.

In the case of a totally shareholder-financed company, that is, a company with no debt, the ROE (assuming only one class of shares) would equal the ROA. There would be no interest expense and, therefore, the numerators of both ratios would be the same. The denominators would be the same because the accounting equation (Assets = Liabilities − Shareholders' Equity) is adjusted for the assumed absence of any liabilities (Assets = Shareholders' Equity).

To understand the effects of leverage, consider first the data in Exhibit 12-5 for a 100% equity-financed company, Baker Company (a fictitious company). To keep the illustration simple, all liabilities are considered to be interest-bearing for Baker Company. Note that in this example, Baker generates a 16.67% return on its assets before taxes (income before interest and taxes/assets = $166.67/$1,000). After the 40% corporate income taxes, this translates into a 10% after-tax return (ROA). Note also that the ROE is the same as the after-tax ROA because there is no debt.

■ BAKER COMPANY (100% EQUITY-FINANCED)

Balance Sheet

Assets	Liabilities
$1,000	$ 0
	Shareholders' equity
	$1,000

Income Statement

Income before interest and taxes	$ 166.67
Interest	0.00
Income before taxes	166.67
Income taxes (40%)	66.67
Net income	$ 100.00

ROA = $100/$1,000 = 10%
ROE = $100/$1,000 = 10%

Now consider the data in Exhibit 12-6 for Baker Company, which now assumes that the company is only 90% shareholder-financed.

■ BAKER COMPANY (90% EQUITY-FINANCED) (16.67% INTEREST RATE)

Balance Sheet

Assets	Liabilities
$1,000	$ 100
	Shareholders' equity
	$ 900

Income Statement (assuming an interest rate of 16.67%)

Income before interest and taxes	$ 166.67
Interest	16.67
Income before taxes	150.00
Income taxes (40%)	60.00
Net income	$ 90.00

ROA = [$90 + {16.67 × (1 − .4)}]/$1,000 = $100/$1,000 = 10%
ROE = $90/$900 = 10%

In Exhibit 12-6, several things should be noted. The first is that the ROA is the same as in Exhibit 12-5, because the mix of assets has not changed; only the amount of debt in the balance sheet has changed. The assets should be earning exactly what they would have earned in a 100% shareholder-financed company. Second, note that the ROE is again the same as the ROA. This will be the case *only* if the after-tax borrowing rate is the same as the after-tax ROA. Note that the before-tax borrowing rate is 16.67%. To adjust the rate to an after-tax rate, multiply it by 1 minus the tax rate, or 16.67% × (1 − 40%) = 10%. This means that the company borrowed $100 at a net cost of 10% (the after-tax borrowing rate) and invested the $100 in assets that return 10% after taxes (ROA). Therefore, the company breaks even on the money it borrowed. The shareholders' return of 10% is the income after taxes ($90) divided by their investment ($900).

Next, consider Exhibit 12-7, in which a lower interest rate is assumed (12%). In Exhibit 12-7, note that the ROE is greater than the ROA. This occurs because the company was able to borrow at a rate that was less than the rate it could earn by investing in assets. The after-tax cost of borrowing is 7.2% [12% × (1 − 40%)], whereas the after-tax return on the assets is 10% (ROA). Therefore, when the company borrowed $100, it cost the company $7.20 in interest, but it was able to generate $10 in income. The difference is $2.80, which goes to the shareholders as an incremental return. Therefore, the shareholders earn a 10% (or $90) return on their investment of $900, plus they get the excess return of $2.80 that is earned on the money that was borrowed, for a total ROE of 10.3%. This improves their percentage return (ROE) over what they could have earned as a 100% equity-financed company without any further investment on their part.

BAKER COMPANY (90% EQUITY-FINANCED) (12% INTEREST RATE)

EXHIBIT 12-7

Balance Sheet

Assets	Liabilities
$1,000	$ 100
	Shareholders' equity
	$ 900

Income Statement (assuming an interest rate of 12%)

Income before interest and taxes	$ 166.67
Interest	12.00
Income before taxes	154.67
Income taxes (40%)	61.87
Net income	$ 92.80

ROA = [$92.80 + {12.00 × (1 − .4)}]/$1,000 = $100/$1,000 = 10%
ROE = $92.80/$900 = 10.3%

This, then, is the advantage of leverage. The shareholders can improve their return (ROE) if the company can borrow funds at an after-tax borrowing rate that is less than the after-tax ROA. This is a big "if." The company that leverages itself is committed to making fixed interest payments to debtholders prior to earning a return on its assets. It is betting that the return on assets will be higher than the after-tax cost of its borrowing. If it is wrong, the return to the shareholders (ROE) could fall below what they could have earned with no debt at all. Consider, for example, the results of Baker Company in Exhibit 12-8, where the company commits to paying lenders 20% (before taxes). Return on equity in this case falls below the ROA to 9.8%. This is the risk of leveraging a company.

BAKER COMPANY (90% EQUITY-FINANCED)
(20% INTEREST RATE)

Balance Sheet

Assets		Liabilities
$1,000		$ 100
		Shareholders' equity
		$ 900

Income Statement (assuming an interest rate of 20%)

Income before interest and taxes	$ 166.67
Interest	20.00
Income before taxes	146.67
Income taxes (40%)	58.67
Net income	$ 88.00

ROA = [$88 + {20 × (1 − .4)}]/$1,000 = $100/$1,000 = 10%
ROE = $88/$900 = 9.8%

If leveraging the company a little is potentially a good thing, as Exhibit 12-7 illustrated, why not leverage it a lot? In other words, why not borrow funds to buy most of the company's assets? In Exhibit 12-7, why not have 90% debt and 10% equity in the company? Exhibit 12-9 illustrates the kind of return the company could expect given 90% debt and the same interest rate as in Exhibit 12-7. A return of 35.2% is certainly very attractive compared to the ROE of 10% that could be achieved with a 100% equity-financed company. The problem with this financing strategy is that lenders will find the riskiness of their investment much higher in Exhibit 12-9 than they would in Exhibit 12-6. As the company adds more and more debt to its capital structure, it is committing itself to higher and higher fixed-interest payments. Therefore, lenders will start demanding higher and higher returns from their investments as the risk increases. The interest rates will rise, and Baker Company will no longer be able to borrow at the 12% that was assumed in Exhibit 12-7. When its average borrowing costs start to equal or exceed the ROA of the company, it will become unattractive to borrow any further funds.

EXHIBIT 12-9

BAKER COMPANY (10% EQUITY FINANCED)
(12% INTEREST RATE)

Balance Sheet

Assets		Liabilities
$1,000		$ 900
		Shareholders' equity
		$ 100

Income Statement (assuming an interest rate of 12%)

Income before interest and taxes	$ 166.67
Interest	108.00
Income before taxes	58.67
Income taxes (40%)	23.47
Net income	$ 35.20

ROA = [$35.20 + {108.00 × (1 − .4)}]/$1,000 = $100/$1,000 = 10%
ROE = $35.20/$100 = 35.2%

In theory, the increase in the borrowing rate would be an increasing function of the amount of leverage employed by the company. Return on equity would improve over that of a 100% equity-financed company up to some point. Exhibit 12-10 graphs the change (at least in theory) in ROE for various levels of leverage. Based on this graph, you can see that there is a point (at the top of the curve) at which ROE would be maximized. The amount of leverage that corresponds to this point has sometimes been called the **optimal capital structure** of the company. For the hypothetical company illustrated in the graph, the optimal capital structure would be approximately 40% debt and the rest equity. This point exists in theory, but is more difficult to determine in the real world. It is true, however, that as you look across industries, different industries have different average levels of leverage. This would indicate that, based on the risk characteristics of those industries, the companies in those industries borrow to the point they think is profitable, and no further.

LEVERAGE AND OPTIMAL CAPITAL STRUCTURE

EXHIBIT 12-10

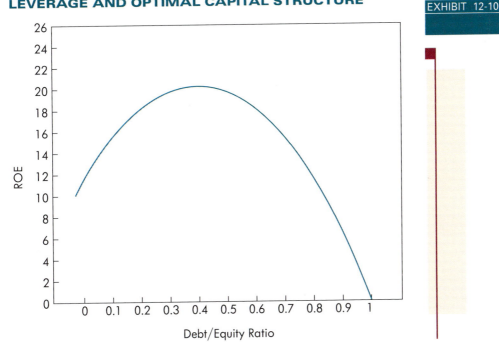

Debt/Equity Ratio

Cara Operations' interest rate on its debt varied from 3.7% to 9.5% before taxes. Its tax rate was approximately 40%, which means the after-tax interest rate ranged from 2.2% to 5.7%. If its ROA was 5.44%, it was earning a slightly higher return on its assets than it paid to borrow money except for the highest 9.5% debt. Its ROE of 10.33% illustrates how that slight increase in ROA translated into an increase in its return to shareholders.

The use of leverage by a company can be judged, to some extent, by the difference in the ROE of the company versus the ROA, as illustrated in the hypothetical example and by Cara Operations. In addition, several other ratios are used to measure the amount of leverage the company employs, as well as how well it uses that leverage. These ratios include the debt/equity ratio and the times interest earned ratio, which are discussed in a later section on liquidity.

accounting in the news

USE OF LEVERAGE

A company that has leveraged itself into massive debt faces tough decisions. It needs to reduce its level of leverage and debt without compromising its ability to function as a viable business. For Canadian-based Loewen Group, one of North America's largest providers of funeral-related services, reorganizing its debts under bankruptcy protection was the solution.

The company had incurred a staggering debt burden during an acquisition spree of funeral homes and cemeteries in the United States. By the time Loewen filed for bankruptcy protection in 1999, the over-leveraged company had an unwieldy empire of 400 cemeteries and 1,100 funeral homes—as well as a debt load of US $2.4 billion.

As part of its reorganization, the company shed close to 200 unprofitable funeral homes and 125 cemeteries. The company also reached agreements with creditors to reduce its debt to US $835 million. Creditors were to receive 40 million shares in the new company, now called Alderwoods Group, which had an estimated US $700 million in shareholders' equity. A leaner, more efficient, and economically viable company emerged from more than two years under bankruptcy protection.

Source: "U.S. court approves Loewen Group reincarnation as Alderwoods Group," by Gary Norris, *Canadian Press Newswire*, Dec. 4, 2001.

Turnover Ratios

In addition to the overall measures of performance, ROA and ROE, there are other measures that are helpful in understanding more specific items that make up the overall performance of the company. Three turnover measures are discussed in this book. They relate to the three policy decisions that were discussed in Chapter 5 with regard to the company's cash flow performance. They are the **accounts receivable**, **inventory**, and **accounts payable turnovers**. These ratios provide some quantitative measures of the lead/lag relationships that exist between the revenue and expense recognition and the cash flows related to these three items.

Accounts Receivable Turnover

The accounts receivable turnover ratio attempts to provide information about the accounts receivable policy of the company. This ratio measures how many times during a year the accounts receivable balance "turns over," that is, how many times old receivables are collected and replaced by new receivables. It is calculated as follows:

$$\text{Accounts receivable turnover} = \frac{\text{Sales on account}}{\text{Average accounts receivable}}$$

When data from financial statements are used, the assumption is usually made that all sales were on account because there is usually no information in the financial statements about the percentage of sales on account versus cash sales. If the turnover ratio was being prepared for internal use by management, this type of information would be available and would be used in the calculation of this ratio.

When the data from Cara Operations are used, the ratio for 2002 is:

ACCOUNTS RECEIVABLE TURNOVER—CARA OPERATIONS LIMITED, 2002

$$\text{Accounts receivable turnover} = \frac{\text{Sales on account}}{\text{Average accounts receivable}}$$

$$= \frac{\$1,036,749}{\dfrac{\$68,793 + \$64,138}{2}}$$

$$= 15.6 \text{ times}$$

The level of turnover of accounts receivable depends on several factors, especially the normal credit terms granted by the company. If the company normally allows 30 days for the customers to pay, and if customers pay in 30 days, the resulting accounts receivable turnover would be 12 because there would be 30 days' of sales always outstanding in accounts receivable. If the normal credit term is 60 days, the resulting accounts receivable turnover would be 6. With an accounts receivable turnover of 15.6, it appears that many of Cara Operations' receivables have 30-day credit terms. It is also probable that much of Cara Operations' sales are cash sales in that a large part of its sales are restaurant sales, which are cash or credit card. This means that the turnover ratio of 15.6 is probably higher than it would have been if we had used solely credit sales.

The turnover number can also be converted into a measure of the days necessary to collect the average receivable by dividing the numbers of days in one year by the turnover ratio. Users may find that the average days to collect is easier to interpret than accounts receivable turnover numbers, although they measure the same thing. To simplify calculations, the number of days in a year is sometimes assumed to be 360 rather than 365. The average days to collect for Cara Operations are:

DAYS TO COLLECT ACCOUNTS RECEIVABLE—CARA OPERATIONS LIMITED, 2002

$$\text{Days to collect} = \frac{365}{\text{Accounts receivable turnover}}$$

$$= \frac{365}{15.6}$$

$$= 23.4 \text{ days}$$

You cannot simply look at the 23.4 days and decide whether it is bad or good. You need to know what the normal credit terms are, if the average monthly sales are fairly equal, since large sales in the last month of the fiscal year would result in an apparently lower turnover and higher number of days' sales in the year-end balance, and what proportion of total sales are made on credit. To analyze this period, we should also consider a time-series analysis (the trend compared to previous years) and a cross-sectional analysis (a comparison with the competitors of Cara Operations).

Inventory Turnover

The inventory turnover ratio gives the analyst some idea of how fast inventory is sold or, alternatively, how long the inventory is held prior to sale. The calculation of the turnover is similar to that of the accounts receivable turnover, with a measure of the flow of inventory in the numerator (top number), and a measure of the balance in inventory in the denominator (bottom number). It is calculated as follows:

$$\text{Inventory turnover} = \frac{\text{Cost of goods sold}}{\text{Average inventory}}$$

Note that the numerator contains the cost of goods sold, not the sales value of the goods sold (revenues). Total sales revenue, while it does measure the flow of goods sold to customers, would be inappropriate in the numerator, because it is based on the selling price of the inventory while the denominator is measured at cost. Cost of goods sold is measured at cost and is therefore more appropriate.

The number of days for which inventory is held can be calculated from the turnover ratio in the same way as was the accounts receivable turnover ratio.

INVENTORY TURNOVER—CARA OPERATIONS LIMITED, 2002

$$\text{Inventory turnover} = \frac{\$927,641}{\dfrac{\$25,575 \ 1 \ \$28,768}{2}}$$

$$= 34.1 \text{ times}$$

$$\text{Days inventory held} = \frac{365}{\text{Inventory turnover}}$$

$$= \frac{365}{34.1}$$

$$= 10.7 \text{ days}$$

The average number of days that inventory is held depends on the type of inventory produced, used, or sold. In the ratio just calculated, the inventories of Cara Operations were used. Remember that Cara's major operations involve the sale of food products in restaurants, hospitals, schools, and airports. The 10.7 days, therefore, refers to the average length of time that costs remain in inventory from original purchase to use in food preparation. For Cara, this short period of time reflects the fact that its inventory is food.

There is one limitation that must be considered when interpreting the inventory turnover ratio for Cara Operations. Cara did not disclose its cost of goods sold amount on the statement of earnings. We determined the cost of goods sold and other operating expenses by subtracting "earnings before the following" from "gross revenue." Therefore, the amount we used in the denominator was larger than the actual cost of goods sold, which would make the inventory turnover higher than it would have been had we used just cost of goods sold. It is important, therefore, that we treat this ratio with some scepticism.

For a manufacturing company such as **Big Rock Brewery**, you would need to decide if you wanted to use all of the inventories (raw materials, work in process, and finished goods) or if you wanted to use only the finished goods in the denominator of the turnover ratio to assess how long it takes from completion of production to sale. From a note to its financial statements, the value of the finished goods inventories in 2002, 2001, and 2000 is $826,982, $804,479, and $635,726, respectively. From this information, we can calculate the finished goods inventory turnover as follows:

FINISHED GOODS INVENTORY TURNOVER—BIG ROCK BREWERY LTD., 2002 AND 2001

2002

$$\text{Inventory turnover} = \frac{\$10,167,456}{\dfrac{\$826,982 + \$804,479}{2}}$$

$$= 12.5 \text{ times}$$

$$\text{Days inventory held} = \frac{365}{\text{Inventory turnover}}$$

$$= \frac{365}{12.5}$$

$$= 29.2 \text{ days}$$

2001

$$\text{Inventory turnover} = \frac{\$9,240,503}{\dfrac{\$804,479 + \$635,726}{2}}$$

$$= 12.8 \text{ times}$$

$$\text{Days inventory held} = \frac{365}{\text{Inventory turnover}}$$

$$= \frac{365}{12.8}$$

$$= 28.5 \text{ days}$$

Based on these numbers, it seems obvious that the finished goods are not held for very long before they are sold (approximately 29 days). Knowing that Big Rock manufactures and sells beer, does the holding of the finished product for approximately 29 days seem reasonable? As with the accounts receivable turnover figures, deciding whether this is good or bad would require either a time-series or a cross-sectional analysis, as well as some detailed knowledge of the industry.

Accounts Payable Turnover

The accounts payable turnover ratio is similar to the accounts receivable ratio, but provides information about the company's accounts payable policy. In its ideal form, it would be calculated as follows:

$$\text{Accounts payable turnover} = \frac{\text{Credit purchases}}{\text{Average accounts payable}}$$

The problem with the preceding calculation is that the credit purchases of a company do not appear directly in the financial statements. It may be possible to approximate the credit purchases by finding the cash payments made to suppliers in the cash flow statement, assuming that the balance in accounts payable did not change drastically during the period. However, this requires that the company prepare its cash flow statement using the direct approach. As mentioned in Chapter 5, almost all companies use the indirect approach to the cash flow statement, and cash payments to suppliers do not appear directly in that statement.

Another alternative is to use the cost of goods sold figure in place of purchases on credit because cost of goods sold appears in the income statement. To the extent that the purchase of goods is the main item that affects cost of goods sold, this would be appropriate. In a retailing company, this would probably be a good approximation, again assuming that the level of inventories did not change dramatically during the period. For a manufacturing company, however, many items other than credit purchases affect the cost of goods sold. For example, a manufacturing company such as Big Rock Brewery will probably include the amortization of its production equipment in the cost assigned to the inventory it produces.

When this ratio is calculated, most analysts would use the cost of goods sold in the numerator. It would therefore be calculated as:

$$\text{Accounts payable turnover} = \frac{\text{Cost of goods sold}}{\text{Average accounts payable}}$$

For Cara Operations in 2002, this ratio is:

ACCOUNTS PAYABLE TURNOVER—CARA OPERATIONS LIMITED, 2002

$$\text{Accounts payable turnover} = \frac{\$927,641}{\frac{\$123,740 + \$117,553}{2}}$$

$$= 7.7 \text{ times}$$

$$\text{Days to pay} = \frac{365}{\text{Accounts payable turnover}}$$

$$= \frac{365}{7.7}$$

$$= 47 \text{ days}$$

For Cara Operations, the calculation of this ratio and the average days to pay appears to be high if the normal credit terms received by Cara Operations are 30 days. In this case, it may not be appropriate to use the cost of goods sold as an approximation of purchases on credit in that the amount we used was actually cost of goods sold plus other operating expenses. Also, you will notice that we used the "accounts payable and accrued liabilities" amount from the balance sheet because accounts payable were not listed separately. It is probable that the accrued charges include amounts such as interest payable, which are not included in the cost of goods sold and other operating expenses. However, we cannot really understand these numbers without knowing more details of the operations and the amounts that are included in the cost of goods sold and accrued liabilities. Again, cross-sectional and time-series analyses should be undertaken.

Short-Term Liquidity Ratios

As discussed in Chapter 1, liquidity refers to the ability of the company to convert assets into cash to pay liabilities. A basic understanding of the company's short-term liquidity position should result from a consideration of the financial statements, particularly the cash flow statement, as well as the turnover ratios discussed in the performance section. Understanding the liquidity position requires knowledge of the leads and lags in the company's cash-to-cash cycle. Additionally, there are at least two ratios that provide quantitative measures of short-term liquidity: the **current** and **quick ratios**.

Current Ratio

The current ratio is calculated by comparing the total current assets to the total current liabilities. It is calculated as follows:

$$\text{Current ratio} = \frac{\text{Current assets}}{\text{Current liabilities}}$$

Remember that current assets are those that are going to be converted into cash in the next year (or operating cycle of the company if it is longer than one year), and that current liabilities are going to require the use of cash in the next year. As such, this ratio should be greater than 1; otherwise, it is difficult to see how the company will remain solvent in the next year. The rule of thumb for this ratio for most industries is that it should be 1 or more, but, to be conservative, approximately 2 or more. However, the size of this ratio depends on the type of business and the types of assets and liabilities that are considered current.

One caveat: the current ratio is subject to manipulation by a company at the end of the year. This ratio may not, therefore, be a very reliable measure of liquidity. For example, consider a company that has $100 in current assets and $50 in current liabilities at the end of a given year. Its current ratio would be 2 ($100/$50). Suppose that $25 of the $100 is in cash and the rest is in inventory. Suppose further that the company uses up all of its $25 in cash to pay $25 of current liabilities at the end of the year. The current ratio becomes 3 ($75/$25); now the company looks more liquid. Notice, however, that it is actually less liquid; in fact, it is virtually illiquid in the short term because it has no cash and must sell its inventory and wait until it collects on the sale of that inventory before it will have any cash to pay its bills. In this case, the current ratio is deceptive.

The current ratios for Cara Operations in 2002 and 2001 are:

CURRENT RATIO—CARA OPERATIONS LIMITED, 2002 AND 2001

2002

$$\text{Current ratio} = \frac{\$204,124}{\$183,010} = 1.11$$

2001

$$\text{Current ratio} = \frac{\$214,163}{\$147,226} = 1.46$$

This current ratio of 1.11 in 2002 is not an improvement over the 1.46 of the previous year. Although this ratio appears to be low, it may be quite acceptable in this industry. Also, remember from the inventory turnover ratio that the inventory sells quite quickly, which means the company's ability to convert the inventory to cash is accelerated.

Quick Ratio

One of the problems with the current ratio is that some assets in the current section are less liquid than others. For example, inventory is usually less liquid than accounts receivable, which are less liquid than cash. In some industries, inventory is very illiquid because of the long period of time that it may have to be held before sale. Consider, for example, the holding period in the manufacture of 12-year-old Scotch whisky. The current ratio in such cases will not adequately measure the short-term liquidity of the company because the inventory will not be converted into cash for a long time. In this case, the quick ratio is a better measure of short-term liquidity. It differs from the current ratio in that only the most liquid current assets (cash, accounts receivable, and marketable securities) are included in the numerator. Prepaid expenses do not convert into cash. Instead they used cash in the past and the company will be saving cash because amounts have been paid in advance. The ratio is calculated as:

$$\text{Quick ratio} = \frac{\text{Cash} + \text{Accounts receivable} + \text{Marketable securities}}{\text{Current liabilities}}$$

The rule of thumb for this ratio is that it should be approximately 1 or more. A quick ratio of 1 means that the very short-term current assets are equal to the total current liabilities. Again, the actual value depends on the type of industry. For Cara Operations, the calculation results in:

QUICK RATIO—CARA OPERATIONS LIMITED, 2002 AND 2001

2002

$$\text{Quick ratio} = \frac{\$15,003 + \$68,793 + \$75,710}{\$183,010} = .87$$

2001

$$\text{Quick ratio} = \frac{\$106,429 + \$64,138 + \$0}{\$147,226} = 1.16$$

Just as with the current ratio, the quick ratio of 0.87 in 2002 is lower than the quick ratio of 1.16 in 2001. The quick ratio in 2002 is very close to the 1.0 rule of thumb amount. Taken together, the current ratio and quick ratio indicate that Cara Operations' liquidity position has declined in the last year. Just reviewing these two years illustrates the importance of time-series analyses in understanding a ratio. Going back further than the two years would enable you to see whether the quick ratio of .87 is normal or if the 1.16 is more common. Cross-sectional analyses should also be undertaken.

Long-Term Liquidity Ratios

Long-term liquidity refers to the ability of the company to pay its obligations in the long term (meaning more than one year in the future). This means its ability to pay its long-term debt. A time-series analysis of the cash flow statement and the patterns of cash flow over time should provide a lot of the insight you need to assess a company's abilities in this regard. There are at least two ratios that are generally used in the assessment of long-term liquidity: the **debt/equity ratio**, and the **times interest earned ratio**.

Debt/Equity Ratio

The debt/equity ratio is really a set of ratios that are used to assess the extent to which the company is leveraged. From our earlier discussion about leverage, you know that the more leverage a company has, the riskier its situation and the more fixed are its commitments to pay interest. Comparing the amount of debt to the amount of equity in a company is important in assessing its ability to pay off these debts in the long term.

Of the many different definitions of the debt/equity ratios that could be used here, we will show you three. They will be referred to as D/E(I), D/E(II), and D/E(III). D/E(I) expresses the total debt of the company as a percentage of total liabilities plus shareholders' equity (the same as total assets). The total liabilities are assumed to include all liabilities of the company, and the shareholders' equity to include all shareholders' equity accounts. This ratio is calculated as:

$$D/E(I) = \frac{\text{Total liabilities}}{\text{Total liabilities} + \text{Shareholders' equity}}$$

$$\text{Or} \quad \frac{\text{Total liabilities}}{\text{Total assets}}$$

For Cara Operations in 2002 and 2001, this ratio is:

D/E(I)—CARA OPERATIONS LIMITED, 2002 AND 2001

2002

$$D/E(I) = \frac{\$393,080}{\$746,638}$$

$$= 0.53$$

2001

$$D/E(I) = \frac{\$350,225}{\$688,727}$$

$$= 0.51$$

This first debt/equity ratio tells you that Cara's debt makes up just over half of total liabilities and shareholders' equity. In other words, Cara Operations uses equity and debt almost equally to finance its investment in assets. Note that for total liabilities we included total liabilities plus noncontrolling interest. The noncontrolling interest arises when Cara Operations buys over 50%, but not 100%, of other companies. The portion of the assets and liabilities that is not owned by Cara Operations is shown as noncontrolling interest. It is appropriate that the noncontrolling interest be included with the liabilities because the assets and liabilities of those other companies were included in Cara Operations' balance sheet at 100%.

The second debt-to-equity ratio provides the same information, but in a slightly different form. It is calculated as the ratio of the total liabilities to the total shareholders' equity, as follows:

$$D/E(II) = \frac{\text{Total liabilities}}{\text{Total shareholders' equity}}$$

For Cara Operations in 2002 and 2001, this ratio is:

D/E(II)—CARA OPERATIONS LIMITED, 2002 AND 2001

2002

$$D/E(II) = \frac{\$393,080}{\$353,558}$$

$$= 1.11$$

2001

$$D/E(II) = \frac{\$350,225}{\$338,502}$$

$$= 1.03$$

This ratio tells you, in a different way, that the debt and equity are almost equal. When the debt is compared to the equity, it represents just over 100% of the equity amount. In other words, Cara Operations uses debt slightly more often to finance its assets.

The third debt-to-equity ratio focuses on the long-term debt of the company relative to its equity. It is calculated as the ratio of the total long-term liabilities to the sum of the total long-term liabilities plus the shareholders' equity of the company, as follows:

$$D/E(III) = \frac{\text{Total long-term liabilities}}{\text{Total long-term liabilities} + \text{Shareholders' equity}}$$

For Cara Operations in 2002 and 2001, this ratio is:

D/E(III)—CARA OPERATIONS LIMITED, 2002 AND 2001

2002

$$D/E(III) = \frac{\$210,070}{\$210,070 + \$353,558}$$

$$= 0.37$$

2001

$$D/E(III) = \frac{\$202,999}{\$202,999 + \$338,502}$$

$$= 0.37$$

This ratio tells you that 37% of the long-term financing of the assets is achieved using long-term debt.

Is the level of debt represented in these ratios appropriate for Cara Operations? Again, a cross-sectional analysis could reveal whether or not Cara Operations has excessive debt compared to other companies. A time-series analysis could reveal the trend over time. As a general guide, however, the average of corporate debt on the books of nonfinancial companies is somewhere between 45% and 50%. Cara

Operations, with a ratio of 53%, appears to be very close to that average. An inspection of Cara Operations' long-term debt shows that 4.6% of the total liabilities ($18,382/$393,080) are future income taxes which, if you recall, are not contractual obligations with a fixed payment date. Therefore, the long-term liquidity position of Cara Operations without the future income taxes is even closer to 50%.

Times Interest Earned

The final ratio in the long-term liquidity section is the **times interest earned (TIE) ratio**. It compares the amount of earnings available to pay interest to the level of interest expense. Because interest is tax-deductible, the earnings available to pay interest would be the earnings prior to the payment of interest or taxes. One complication in the calculation of this ratio is that some companies capitalize interest when they construct long-term assets. This means that instead of expensing interest, a company can record the interest in an asset account. This generally happens only when a company is constructing an asset and incurs interest on money borrowed to finance the construction. The adjustment to the ratio is that the amount of interest capitalized should be added to the denominator. (Note: when we first introduced this ratio in Chapter 10, we did not bring capitalized interest into the calculation.) The numerator does not require adjustment if the amount of interest expensed is added back to net income. The ratio is therefore calculated as:

$$\text{Times interest earned} = \frac{\text{Income before interest and taxes}}{\text{Interest (including capitalized interest)}}$$

Cara Operations indicates in a note to the financial statements that its policy is to capitalize interest on "assets constructed over time." The notes to the financial statement indicate that in 2002, Cara Operations capitalized $500 thousand of interest, and in 2001, it was $2,500 thousand. Thus, to calculate this ratio for 2002 and 2001, we have included this amount in addition to the interest expense reported on the income statement. The ratio is therefore calculated as:

TIMES INTEREST EARNED—CARA OPERATIONS LIMITED, 2002 AND 2001

2002

$$\text{TIE} = \frac{\$35,654 + \$9,306 + \$23,434}{\$9,306 + \$500}$$

$$= 7.0$$

2001

$$\text{TIE} = \frac{\$102,678 + \$10,168 + \$52,157}{\$10,168 + \$2,500}$$

$$= 13.0$$

In Cara Operations' income statement, an amount is not given for income before income taxes. Therefore, we took the net income and added back the interest expense and the income taxes. As well, Cara Operations nets the interest expense and interest income together and reports the net amount, $5,487 and $7,173 in 2002 and 2001 respectively. In Note 15, it explained the components of the interest expense amount. For this ratio, we took the interest expense amounts from Note 15, which is why the amount included in this ratio is different from the income statement amount.

The resulting ratio of 7.0 in 2002 indicates that Cara Operations earned 7.0 times the amount it needed to pay its interest expense in 2002. This is a comfortable cushion. Income would have to drop to one-seventh of its current level before Cara Operations would have trouble paying the interest. In 2001, the cushion was even bigger when the times interest earned ratio was 13.0. When a company indicates that it has capitalized interest but does not disclose the amount of that capitalization, you need to remember that the times interest earned ratio will be overstated. Your problem as a user attempting to evaluate the company's ability to pay the interest owed is that you cannot determine by how much it is overstated. When any company shows a times interest earned ratio of close to 1, this indicates that the payment of the interest may be at risk. As a lender, a low times interest earned ratio should concern you.

Earnings Per Share Ratio

The **earnings per share ratio** is one that is quoted quite often in the financial press and one in which shareholders are very interested. In its simplest form, it is the earnings of the company divided by the weighted average number of common shares outstanding. Although this ratio may be of some help in analyzing a company's results, its usefulness is limited. The major problem with using it as a measure of performance is that it ignores the level of investment. Companies with the same earnings per share might have very different profitabilities, depending on their investment in net assets. The other limitation is that the shares of different companies are not equivalent, and companies with the same overall profitability may have different earnings per share figures because they have a different number of shares outstanding that represent ownership. The best use of the earnings per share figure is in a time-series analysis rather than in a cross-sectional analysis.

The earnings per share calculation represents the earnings per common share. Therefore, if the company also issues preferred shares, the effects of the preferred shares must be removed in calculating the ratio. With preferred shares outstanding, this means that any dividends that are paid to preferred shareholders should be deducted from net income because that amount of income is not available to common shareholders. The number of preferred shares outstanding should also be left out of the denominator. The calculation of basic earnings per share then becomes:

$$\text{Basic earnings per share} = \frac{\text{Net income} - \text{Preferred dividends}}{\text{Weighted average number of common shares outstanding}}$$

The preferred dividends that should be deducted are the cumulative preferred dividends, whether they are declared in the year or not, and any noncumulative preferred dividends that have been declared in the year. Recall from Chapter 11 that cumulative means that if a dividend is not declared on the preferred shares in one year, the dividends then carry over into the next year. In the second year, both the prior year's preferred dividends and the current year's preferred dividends must be declared before any common dividends can be declared.

In addition to preferred shares, another complicating factor in the calculation of earnings per share arises when the company issues any securities that are convertible into common shares. Examples of these types of securities are convertible debt, convertible preferred shares, and stock option plans. The key feature of these securities is that they are all convertible into common shares under certain conditions. If additional common shares are issued upon their conversion, the earnings per share number could decrease because of the larger number of shares that would be outstanding. This is called the potential dilution of earnings per share.

At the end of a given accounting period, the presence of convertible securities creates some uncertainty about how to report the earnings per share number. Should the company report earnings per share without considering the potentially dilutive effects of the convertible securities, or should it disclose some information that would allow readers of the financial statements to understand these effects? To provide the best information for users of financial statements, we should disclose information about the dilutive effects of convertible securities. Thus, financial statements may include several earnings per share figures, the main ones being the basic earnings per share and the fully diluted earnings per share.

Basic Earnings Per Share

Basic earnings per share is usually a very simple number that considers only the net income, preferred dividends, and weighted average number of common shares outstanding. Every published financial statement shows this figure. Note in Exhibit 12-3 on the statement of earnings for Cara Operations that there is a basic earnings per share of 38.7 cents. If Cara Operations had any extraordinary items or had discontinued some of its operations during the year, there would have been earnings per share amounts on the income statement balances both before the extraordinary items or discontinued operations and after. The reason for multiple amounts is that the company would have backed these amounts out of the normal continuing operations and showed them separately. When users review the financial statements, it is usually with two objectives in mind: first, to see how the company did during the last year, and second, to assess how it might do in the future. Because of this future focus, it is important for companies to isolate extraordinary items and discontinued operations that will not affect the future from continuing operations that may be a good measure of future operations. To help users in their evaluation, whenever there are non-future items like discontinued items or extraordinary items, multiple basic earnings per share figures are disclosed—one for continuing operations and one for net income. The basic earnings per share from continuing operations is probably more useful.

Fully Diluted Earnings Per Share

Fully diluted earnings per share is calculated under the worst-case scenario set of assumptions. The company identifies all of the dilutive securities that will have a negative effect on the earnings per share amount if they are converted. For example, if convertible preferred shares are converted to common shares, the number of common shares outstanding will increase. At the same time, the numerator will also increase because, if the preferred shares are now common shares, there will no longer be any preferred dividends and all of the net income will be available to the common shareholders. Because both the numerator and the denominator increase, the effect of a conversion on earnings per share is not always negative. Under the worst-case scenario for determining fully diluted earnings per share, the calculation includes only those conversions that will have a negative effect on earnings per share. The calculation of fully diluted earnings per share is a "heads-up" calculation for users. It attempts to tell them how much the earnings per share could decline in the future if all of the dilutive convertible securities were converted to common shares.

Cara Operations has stock option plans. As a result of the stock options, in 2002 it reported a fully diluted earnings per share amount of 38.3 cents (compared to the basic earnings per share of 38.7 cents). If the company had extraordinary items or discontinued operations, it would have disclosed a fully diluted earnings per share from continuing operations and from net earnings. Like the disclosure for basic earnings per share, it is important to distinguish between the amounts that reflect possible future earnings and those that represent net earnings. For Cara Operations the fully diluted earnings per share amounts are not much lower than the basic earnings per share amounts. In other words, although there will be a negative effect on earnings per share if the stock options are exercised, current shareholders can be assured that any such effect will not be very large.

Price/Earnings Ratio

The **price/earnings ratio**, or **multiple**, is a comparison of the price per share on the stock market with the earnings per share of the company. Many analysts think of this ratio as the price investors are willing to pay for a dollar's worth of earnings. The interpretation of this ratio is somewhat difficult because stock market price levels are not well understood. It might help to think of the multiple in terms of its inverse. If a company is earning $1.00 per common share and the shares are selling for $20 on the stock market, this indicates that the current multiple is 20. The inverse of this multiple is 1/20, or 5%. This indicates that the shares are returning 5% in the form of earnings per share when compared to the market price.

Many factors affect the level of stock market prices, including the interest rates prevailing in the economy and the future prospects of the company. It is sometimes useful to think that the market price reflects the present value of all future expected earnings of the company. Companies with a high growth potential tend to have a high price/earnings ratio. Companies with a low growth potential have a lower price/earnings ratio. The earnings per share figure serves as an important link between the accounting numbers produced in the financial statements and the stock market price of the company's shares.

NON-MANUFACTURING OR NON-RETAIL COMPANY ANALYSIS

Although the above discussion is applicable to most companies in most industries, some differences for non-manufacturing or non-retail companies should be noted. As an example of a non-manufacturing or non-retail company, consider the analysis of a financial services company such as a bank, an insurance company, or a finance company. These types of companies invest in very different kinds of assets than manufacturers or retailers, and they obtain their financing from different sources.

The assets of financial services companies consist of almost no inventories and relatively little property, plant, and equipment. The majority of their assets consist of loans that they made to their customers or other investments. The assets of most nonfinancial companies consist mainly of property, plant, and equipment, inventories, and receivables.

The liability sections of financial services companies' balance sheets are also very different from those of manufacturers or retailers. The first major difference is the debt/equity ratio. Financial services companies tend to have considerably higher debt/equity ratios than manufacturers or retailers because of the large amounts of cash received from depositors. In the insurance industry, the high ratio results from amounts owed to policyholders. Second, liabilities of financial services companies such as banks tend to be predominantly short-term in nature because of the deposits received from customers, which are normally payable upon demand. Many customers, however, leave amounts with these companies for long periods of time. This means that, although they are technically short-term because the customer can withdraw the funds at any time, in reality they are often long-term in nature.

The higher leverage employed by financial services companies reflects, in part, the lower risk of the types of assets in which these companies invest. In addition to employing financial leverage, manufacturers also employ something called **operating leverage**. Operating leverage involves investing in large amounts of property, plant, and equipment (capital assets with fixed amortization costs). The property, plant, and equipment allow manufacturers to make their own inventory rather than buying it from an outside supplier (variable costs). The risk is that the manufacturers must operate at a sufficient volume to allow their profit from the sale of goods to cover their fixed costs. At large volumes, this makes manufacturing companies very profitable, but at low volumes, they generate large losses because the fixed costs must be paid from the lower sales volumes. Partially because of the amount of operating leverage, lenders generally do not lend to manufacturers as much as they lend to financial services companies.

A complete analysis of financial services companies is beyond the scope of this book. It is hoped that this brief discussion of some of the differences between these companies and manufacturers and retailers will provide some insights into how an analysis of these companies may differ.

SUMMARY

At this point in the book, we have discussed all the major financial statements and specific accounting methods and principles that apply to each category within the asset, liability, and shareholders' equity sections of the balance sheet. We have devoted this final chapter to methods you can use to gain some insight into how to interpret the information that you find reported on the financial statements. By comparing amounts on one financial statement with related amounts on another financial statement, we are able to assess the impact of various items on the health and future prospects of a company. We restricted the discussion to fairly simple companies to make it easier for you to learn the basics.

In Appendix B at the back of the book, you will find additional information about complex organizations. These are companies (usually called parent companies) that buy an interest in other companies (called subsidiaries) to obtain control of the resources of the subsidiary. The majority of the real companies reported in this book are parent companies that have one or more subsidiaries. You can tell if a company is a parent company if it prepares "consolidated" financial statements. If you flip back through the examples of financial statements that we showed you in the book, you will see that most of them are consolidated. Complex issues face the accountant, such as how to represent the resources controlled by the shareholders of the parent company.

Ratio Summary

Exhibit 12-11 summarizes the ratios that were developed in the chapter.

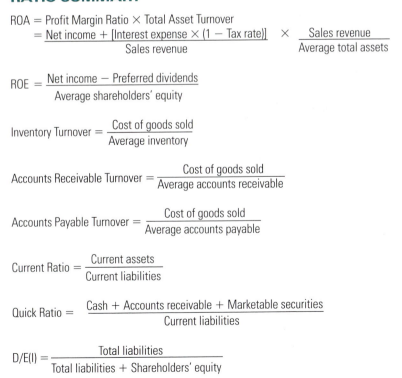

RATIO SUMMARY

$$\text{ROA} = \text{Profit Margin Ratio} \times \text{Total Asset Turnover}$$
$$= \frac{\text{Net income} + [\text{Interest expense} \times (1 - \text{Tax rate})]}{\text{Sales revenue}} \times \frac{\text{Sales revenue}}{\text{Average total assets}}$$

$$\text{ROE} = \frac{\text{Net income} - \text{Preferred dividends}}{\text{Average shareholders' equity}}$$

$$\text{Inventory Turnover} = \frac{\text{Cost of goods sold}}{\text{Average inventory}}$$

$$\text{Accounts Receivable Turnover} = \frac{\text{Cost of goods sold}}{\text{Average accounts receivable}}$$

$$\text{Accounts Payable Turnover} = \frac{\text{Cost of goods sold}}{\text{Average accounts payable}}$$

$$\text{Current Ratio} = \frac{\text{Current assets}}{\text{Current liabilities}}$$

$$\text{Quick Ratio} = \frac{\text{Cash} + \text{Accounts receivable} + \text{Marketable securities}}{\text{Current liabilities}}$$

$$\text{D/E(I)} = \frac{\text{Total liabilities}}{\text{Total liabilities} + \text{Shareholders' equity}}$$

EXHIBIT 12-11
CONT.

$$D/E(II) = \frac{\text{Total liabilities}}{\text{Shareholders' equity}}$$

$$D/E(III) = \frac{\text{Total long-term liabilities}}{\text{Total long-term liabilities} + \text{Shareholders' equity}}$$

$$\text{Times Interest Earned (TIE)} = \frac{\text{Net income} + \text{Taxes} + \text{Interest}}{\text{Interest}}$$

$$\text{Price/Earnings Ratio} = \frac{\text{Stock market price}}{\text{Earnings per share}}$$

Additional Demonstration Problems

SUMMARY PROBLEM

The income statement, balance sheet, and cash flow statement of **Canadian Tire Corporation, Limited** are shown in Exhibit 12-12. Calculate the following ratios for 2001 based on the data in the financial statements. Comment on what the ratios tell us about the financial position of Canadian Tire and what further analyses you should undertake.

Performance Ratios: Profitability

1. ROA (Break down into profit margin ratio and total asset turnover)
2. ROE
3. Accounts receivable turnover
4. Inventory turnover
5. Accounts payable turnover

Short-Term Liquidity Ratios:

6. Current ratio
7. Quick ratio

Long-Term Liquidity Ratios: Solvency
8. Debt/equity ratios
9. Times interest earned

CANADIAN TIRE CORPORATION, LIMITED (2001)

Consolidated Statements of Earnings and Retained Earnings

EXHIBIT 12-12

PART A

(Dollars in thousands except per share amounts) For the years ended		December 29, 2001		December 30, 2000
Gross operating revenue	$	**5,374,759**	$	5,207,574
Operating expenses				
Cost of merchandise sold and all other operating expenses except for the undernoted items		**4,854,801**		4,729,112
Interest				
Long-term debt		**81,389**		74,851
Short-term debt		**6,647**		19,836
Depreciation and amortization		**136,301**		127,021
Employee profit sharing plans (Note 8)		**18,645**		16,067
Total operating expenses		**5,097,783**		4,966,887
Earnings before income taxes		**276,976**		240,687
Income taxes (Note 9)				
Current		**102,445**		97,370
Future		**(2,733)**		(4,705)
Total income taxes		**99,712**		92,665
Net earnings before minority interest		**177,264**		148,022
Minority interest (Note 15)		**611**		—
Net earnings	$	**176,653**	$	148,022
Net earnings per share	$	**2.25**	$	1.89
Diluted earnings per share (Note 7)	$	**2.23**	$	1.89
Weighted average number of Common and Class A Non-Voting Shares outstanding		**78,652,610**		78,349,097
Retained earnings, beginning of year	$	**860,129**	$	763,651
Net earnings		**176,653**		148,022
Dividends		**(31,482)**		(31,328)
Repurchase of Class A Non-Voting Shares (Note 7)		**(32,250)**		(20,216)
Retained earnings, end of year	$	**973,050**	$	860,129

EXHIBIT 12-12
PART B

CANADIAN TIRE CORPORATION, LIMITED (2001)

Consolidated Statements of Cash Flows

(Dollars in thousands) For the years ended		**December 29, 2001**		December 30, 2000
Cash generated from (used for):				
Operating activities				
Net earnings	$	**176,653**	$	148,022
Items not affecting cash				
Depreciation and amortization of property and equipment		**125,592**		119,726
Net provision for credit charge receivables		**82,469**		73,665
Amortization of other assets		**10,709**		7,295
Post retirement benefits (Note 6)		**1,701**		1,432
Gain on sale of credit charge receivables (Note 2)		**(15,437)**		—
Gain on disposals of property and equipment		**(9,184)**		354
Gain on sale of subsidiary (Note 14)		**(8,128)**		—
Future tax liability		**(2,733)**		1,820
Cash generated from operations		**361,642**		352,314
Changes in other working capital components (Note 10)		**(174,699)**		150,024
Cash generated from operating activities		**186,943**		502,338
Investing activities				
Additions to property and equipment		**(358,229)**		(382,172)
Investment in credit charge receivables (Note 2)		**(317,597)**		(253,043)
Long-term receivables and other assets		**(22,256)**		(24,800)
Proceeds on sale of subsidiary (Note 14)		**135,590**		—
Proceeds on disposition of property and equipment		**93,659**		29,085
Cash used for investing activities		**(468,833)**		(630,930)
Financing activities				
Proceeds on sale of limited partnership interest (Note 15)		**300,000**		—
Issuance of long-term debt		**225,000**		65,000
Sale of Associate Dealer receivables (Note 10)		**188,594**		—
Securitization of credit charge receivables		**53,115**		115,217
Commercial paper		**—**		(234,025)
Dividends		**(31,482)**		(31,328)
Class A Non-Voting Share transactions (Note 7)		**(5,262)**		5,999
Repayment of long-term debt		**(315)**		(200,292)
Cash generated from (used for) financing activities		**729,650**		(279,429)
Cash generated (used) in the year		**447,760**		(408,021)
Cash and cash equivalents, beginning of year		**130,999**		539,020
Cash and cash equivalents, end of year (Note 10)	$	**578,759**	$	130,999

CANADIAN TIRE CORPORATION, LIMITED (2001)

Consolidated Balance Sheets

EXHIBIT 12-12
PART C

(Dollars in thousands) As at		December 29, 2001		December 30, 2000
ASSETS				
Current assets				
Cash and cash equivalents (Note 10)	$	578,759	$	130,999
Accounts receivable (Note 10)		433,825		515,130
Credit charge receivables (Note 2)		525,317		453,412
Merchandise inventories		440,935		412,381
Prepaid expenses and deposits		14,297		15,777
Total current assets		1,993,133		1,527,699
Long-term receivables and other assets (Note 3)		134,414		122,867
Property and equipment (Note 4)		2,243,609		2,097,095
Total assets	$	4,371,156	$	3,747,661
LIABILITIES				
Current liabilities				
Accounts payable and other	$	1,009,598	$	1,038,471
Income taxes payable		70,425		85,965
Current portion of long-term debt (Note 5)		30,027		315
Total current liabilities		1,110,050		1,124,751
Long-term debt (Note 5)		1,310,000		1,115,027
Long-term liability for post retirement benefits (Note 6)		28,280		26,579
Future tax liability (Note 9)		19,132		21,865
Total liabilities		2,467,462		2,288,222
Minority interest (Note 15)		300,000		—
SHAREHOLDERS' EQUITY				
Share capital (Note 7)		622,104		595,116
Accumulated foreign currency translation adjustment		8,540		4,194
Retained earnings		973,050		860,129
Total shareholders' equity		1,603,694		1,459,439
Total liabilities and shareholders' equity	$	4,371,156	$	3,747,661

Gilbert S. Bennett   **Director**

Maureen J. Sabia   **Director**

SUGGESTED SOLUTION TO SUMMARY PROBLEM

ROA:

ROA (BREAKDOWN)—CANADIAN TIRE CORPORATION, LIMITED, 2001

ROA = Profit Margin Ratio × Total Asset Turnover

$$= \frac{\text{Net income} + [\text{Interest expense} \times (1 - \text{Tax rate})]}{\text{Sales revenue}} \times \frac{\text{Sales revenue}}{\text{Average total assets}}$$

$$= \frac{\$176,653 + [\$88,036^* \times (1 - .36)]}{\$5,374,759} \times \frac{\$5,374,759}{\dfrac{\$4,371,156 + \$3,747,661}{2}}$$

$$= 4.34\% \times 1.32 = 5.73\%$$

*The interest expense is the sum of the short-term and long-term interest.

ROE:

ROE—CANADIAN TIRE CORPORATION, LIMITED, 2001

$$\text{ROE} = \frac{\text{Net income} - \text{Preferred dividends}}{\text{Average shareholders' equity}}$$

$$= \frac{\$176,653 - 0^*}{\dfrac{\$1,603,694 + \$1,459,439}{2}}$$

$$= 11.5\%$$

*Although the company had Class A Non-voting shares, it has always treated them as equivalent to common shares because they are fully participating. The earnings per share is calculated using both the Class A Non-voting shares and the Common shares.

Accounts Receivable Turnover:

A/R TURNOVER—CANADIAN TIRE CORPORATION, LIMITED, 2001

$$\text{Accounts Receivable Turnover} = \frac{\text{Credit sales}}{\text{Average accounts receivable}}$$

$$= \frac{\$5,374,759^*}{\dfrac{\$959,142 + \$968,542}{2}}$$

$$= 5.58 \text{ times}$$

$$\text{Days to collect} = \frac{365 \text{ days}}{\text{Receivable turnover}}$$

$$= \frac{365 \text{ days}}{5.58}$$

$$= 65.4 \text{ days}$$

*Total sales was used because no amount for credit sales was given. Because the total amount does include some cash sales, the accounts receivable turnover will be inflated. It will actually take longer to collect the accounts receivable than is indicated by this ratio. Average accounts receivable includes both accounts receivable and credit charge receivables. Because Canadian Tire has its own credit card, customers will be able to pay over a period of longer than 30 days.

Inventory Turnover:

INVENTORY TURNOVER—CANADIAN TIRE CORPORATION, LIMITED, 2001

$$\text{Inventory Turnover} = \frac{\text{Cost of goods sold}}{\text{Average inventory}}$$

$$= \frac{\$4,854,801^*}{\dfrac{\$440,935 + \$412,381}{2}}$$

$$= 11.37 \text{ times}$$

$$\text{Days Inventory Held} = \frac{365 \text{ days}}{\text{Inventory turnover}}$$

$$= \frac{365 \text{ days}}{11.37}$$

$$= 32.1 \text{ days}$$

*Cost of merchandise sold and all other operating expenses was used because the company did not disclose cost of goods sold separately. Because other operating expenses were included in the numerator, the inventory turnover will be inflated. It will actually take longer to sell the inventory than is indicated by this ratio.

Accounts Payable Turnover:

A/P TURNOVER—CANADIAN TIRE CORPORATION, LIMITED, 2001

$$\text{Accounts Payable Turnover} = \frac{\text{Cost of goods sold}}{\text{Average accounts payable}}$$

$$= \frac{\$4,854,801^*}{\dfrac{\$1,009,598 + \$1,038,471}{2}}$$

$$= 4.74$$

$$\text{Days to Pay} = \frac{365 \text{ days}}{\text{Payable turnover}}$$

$$= \frac{365 \text{ days}}{4.74}$$

$$= 77 \text{ days}$$

*The company does not disclose accounts payable as a separate item. It provides instead the sum of accounts payable and other (current) liabilities. This means that the average accounts payable amount used in the ratio is larger than accounts payable, and the number of days to pay is therefore much higher than would be the reality for the company. Because the cost of goods sold amount also includes additional expenses, it becomes even more difficult to interpret this ratio.

Current Ratio:

CURRENT RATIO—CANADIAN TIRE CORPORATION, LIMITED, 2001

$$\text{Current Ratio} = \frac{\text{Current assets}}{\text{Current liabilities}}$$

$$= \frac{\$1,993,133}{\$1,110,050}$$

$$= 1.8$$

Quick Ratio:

QUICK RATIO—CANADIAN TIRE CORPORATION, LIMITED, 2001

$$\text{Quick ratio} = \frac{\text{Cash and cash equivalents} + \text{Accounts receivable} + \text{Credit charge receivables}}{\text{Current liabilities}}$$

$$= \frac{\$578,759 + \$433,825 + \$525,317}{\$1,110,050}$$

$$= 1.39$$

D/E(I):

D/E(I)—CANADIAN TIRE CORPORATION, LIMITED, 2001

$$\text{D/E(I)} = \frac{\text{Total liabilities}}{\text{Total liabilities} + \text{Shareholders' equity}}$$

$$= \frac{\$2,767,462^*}{\$2,767,462 + \$1,603,694}$$

$$= 63.3\%$$

*Includes Minority Interest (the same as noncontrolling interest)

D/E(II):

D/E(II)—CANADIAN TIRE CORPORATION, LIMITED, 2001

$$\text{D/E(II)} = \frac{\text{Total liabilities}}{\text{Shareholders' equity}}$$

$$= \frac{\$2,767,462}{\$1,603,694}$$

$$= 1.73$$

D/E(III):

D/E(III)—CANADIAN TIRE CORPORATION, LIMITED, 2001

$$D/E(III) = \frac{\text{Total long-term liabilities}}{\text{Total long-term liabilities} + \text{Shareholders' equity}}$$

$$= \frac{\$1,657,412}{\$1,657,412 + \$1,603,694}$$

$$= 0.51$$

Times Interest Earned:

TIE—CANADIAN TIRE CORPORATION, LIMITED, 2001

$$TIE = \frac{\text{Net income} + \text{Taxes} + \text{Interest}}{\text{Interest}}$$

$$= \frac{\$176,653 + \$99,712 + \$81,389 + \$6,647}{\$81,389 + \$6,647}$$

$$= 4.14 \text{ times}$$

Performance Ratios

In analyzing the performance of any company, first consider the net income and its trend. For Canadian Tire, the net income is positive. It is up about 19% from 2000. This indicates that Canadian Tire is growing. It sells automotive and household goods, which do not fluctuate as much as clothing does. In 2002, Canadian Tire acquired **Mark's Work Wearhouse Limited**. This may cause some fluctuation in its earnings in the future. The earnings per share has been growing, reflecting the growth in earnings. Next, consider the ROA and ROE ratios. ROA is 5.73% and the ROE is 11.5%. The ROA of 5.73% indicates that Canadian Tire is earning a modest return on assets, although it is somewhat larger than could be earned if the assets were invested in bank deposits. From the breakdown in the ROA calculation, the performance by Canadian Tire can be seen to be in its profit margin (4.34) and not its asset turnover (1.32%). Canadian Tire has a reasonable markup on its automotive and household merchandise but it is much lower than many clothing or furniture stores. The ROE of 11.5% is significantly larger than the ROA and indicates the company is making use of leverage.

The turnover figures are interesting and some may be distorted. The calculation of the accounts receivable turnover of 5.58 times indicates there are 65.4 days' sales in accounts receivable. This is not within the normal credit term of 30 days. Because Canadian Tire has its own credit card, customers can probably take longer than 30 days to pay off the amount owed. However, in calculating the ratio we were not able to use "credit" sales because that amount was not disclosed. Canadian Tire accepts credit cards but also makes a large number of cash sales. Using the total sales amount to calculate this ratio has obviously inflated the turnover rate; by how much, we cannot determine.

The inventory turnover of 11.37 times indicates that there are 32.1 days' sales of inventory on hand. This indicates that the company is carrying just over a month of inventory. Considering that much of Canadian Tire's merchandise is not time-sensitive, this seems to be a very quick turnover.

The accounts payable turnover of 4.74 times indicates that the company pays its suppliers an average of 77 days after incurring the obligation. This ratio is obviously distorted by the inclusion of accrued liabilities in the denominator and the cost of merchandise sold and all other operating expenses in the numerator. There are more items included besides the amounts owed to suppliers of inventory, which makes this ratio impossible to interpret.

Further analyses would include common size financial statements to determine the trends in the cost of goods sold and other expenses (shown in Exhibit 12-13), and trend analyses of the ROA and ROE.

EXHIBIT 12-13

■ CANADIAN TIRE CORPORATION, LIMITED

Common Size Income Statement

	2001	2000	
Gross operating revenue	100.0%	100.0%	
Operating expenses			
Cost of merchandise sold and all other operating expenses except for the undernoted items	90.3%	90.8%	
Interest			
Long-term debt	1.5%	1.4%	
Short-term debt	.1%	.4%	
Depreciation and amortization	2.5%	2.4%	
Employee profit sharing plans	.4%	.3%	
Total operating expenses	94.8%	95.3%	
Earnings before income taxes	5.2%	4.7%	
Income taxes			
Current	1.9%	1.9%	
Future	(.1%)	(.1%)	
Total income taxes	1.8%	1.8%	
Net earnings before minority interest	3.4%	2.9%	
Minority interest	0%	—	
Net earnings	3.4%	2.9%	

These common size statements show that net earnings improved slightly in 2001. Sales have increased and supporting expenses, including cost of goods sold, have declined slightly, which enables the company to improve its net earnings. There are a few fluctuations in the other expenses, but where one has risen, another has fallen so that overall the total expense is relatively constant.

Short-Term Liquidity Ratios

The current ratio is reasonable at 1.8. The quick ratio at 1.39 shows that the company has a number of liquid assets which will enable it to pay its liabilities as they come due. Because of the large cash sales of this company, the cash inflow from inventory will probably improve the payment of liabilities even more. The cash flow from operations on the cash flow statement is positive and larger than the net income amount. This provides evidence that the company does not have a cash flow problem. The cash flow from operations is, however, much lower than it was last year. This drop can be explained by the gain amounts that were deducted from the net earnings in 2001 but then included in the sale amounts under investing, and by the net change in the components of the non-cash current assets and liabilities (working capital). In 2000, the net change increased cash from operations; in 2001, the net change decreased cash from operations.

Long-Term Liquidity

Canadian Tire Corporation is financed 63.3% by debt and 36.7% by equity. Approximately 60% of the total liabilities are in long-term debt. The moderately high debt/equity ratios result in an increment for leverage. The ROE of 11.5% is quite a bit higher than the ROA at 5.73%. This means that the company is able to make good use of leverage. High debt/equity ratios require a stable market for the products sold. The automotive and household products market is relatively stable. Canadian Tire must monitor its use of debt because it requires repayment.

Interesting information can be found in the cash flow statement. In 2001, the cash inflow from operating activities was positive, as it should be. The income was higher than the previous year but the cash flow from operations was just over $300,000 thousand lower. Last year, the working capital components (noncash current assets and liabilities) resulted in a positive amount of $150,024 thousand. In 2001, the working capital components generated a negative $174,699 thousand, which has caused a very different operating cash flow. Accounts receivable and inventory are up and accounts payable and income tax payable are down. All of these generate a negative working capital adjustment. The increase in sales has necessitated more inventory and it has also generated more accounts receivable. The fact that the current liabilities are down is an indication that the company is managing its debt repayment well.

Cash is being used for investing activities to invest in property and equipment, credit charge receivables, and long-term receivables, which is also a good sign. This new investment is being financed with long-term debt and a limited partnership interest. Because the company's times interest earned ratio indicates that it can cover the interest payment at least four times from earnings, the company should be able to handle this new debt quite readily. Some debt was paid off and dividends were paid. As an investor, if you were looking for an investment that would pay you periodically in the form of dividends, this may be what you are looking for.

ABBREVIATIONS USED

P/E Ratio	Price/earnings ratio
ROA	Return on assets
ROE	Return on equity
TIE	Times interest earned

 # GLOSSARY

Accounts payable turnover   The number of times that accounts payable are replaced during the accounting period. It is usually calculated as the cost of goods sold divided by the average accounts payable.

Accounts receivable turnover   The number of times that accounts receivable are replaced during the accounting period. It is calculated as the credit sales divided by the average accounts receivable.

Common size data   Data that are prepared from the financial statements (usually the income statement and balance sheet) in which each element of the financial statement is expressed as a percentage of some denominator value. On the income statement, the denominator value is usually the net sales revenues for the period and, on the balance sheet, the denominator is the total assets as at the year end.

Cross-sectional analysis   A type of financial statement analysis in which one company is compared with other companies, either within the same industry or across industries, for the same time period.

Current ratio   A measure of the short-term liquidity of the company. It is measured as the ratio of the current assets of the company divided by the current liabilities.

Debt/equity ratios   Measure the leverage of the company. There are numerous definitions of these ratios, but all of them attempt to provide a comparison of the amount of debt in the company compared to the amount of equity.

Earnings per share ratio   A measure of the performance of the company, calculated by dividing the earnings for the period available to common shares by the weighted average number of common shares that were outstanding during the period.

Fully diluted earnings per share   A type of earnings per share calculation that provides the lowest possible earnings per share figure under the assumption that all convertible securities and options of the company are converted into common shares. It measures the maximum potential dilution in earnings per share that would occur under these assumed conversions.

Inventory turnover   The number of times that inventory is replaced during the accounting period. It is calculated as the cost of goods sold divided by the average inventory.

Leverage   The use of debt in a company to improve the return to the shareholders.

Multiple   Synonym of Price/earnings ratio.

Operating leverage   The replacement of variable costs with fixed costs in the operation of the company. If a sufficient volume of sales is achieved, the investment in fixed costs can be very profitable.

Optimal capital structure   A theoretical point at which the leverage of the company maximizes the return to the shareholders (ROE).

Price/earnings ratio (P/E ratio)   A performance ratio that compares the market price per share with the earnings per share.

Profit margin ratio   A performance measure that compares the after-tax but before-interest income of a company with the revenues of the company.

Prospective analysis   A financial statement analysis of a company that attempts to look forward in time to predict future results.

Quick ratio   A measure of the short-term liquidity of a company calculated by dividing the current assets less inventories and, in most cases, prepaid items by the current liabilities.

Raw financial data   The data that appear directly in the financial statements.

Retrospective analysis   A financial statement analysis of a company that looks only at historical data.

Return on assets (ROA)   A measure of performance that measures the return on the investment in assets of the company. It is calculated by dividing the income after tax but before interest by the average total assets of the company during the accounting period. The ratio can be split into the profit margin ratio and the total asset turnover ratio.

Return on equity (ROE)   A measure of performance that measures the return on the investment made by common shareholders. It is calculated by dividing the net income less dividends for preferred shares by the average common shareholders' equity during the accounting period.

Time-series analysis   A financial statement analysis in which data are analyzed over time.

Times interest earned (TIE) ratio   A measure of the long-term liquidity of a company. It measures the ability of the company to make its interest payments. It is calculated by dividing the income before interest and taxes by the interest expense.

Total asset turnover   A measure of performance of a company that shows the number of dollars of sales that is generated per dollar of investment in total assets. It is calculated by dividing the sales revenue by the average total assets for the accounting period.

ASSIGNMENT MATERIAL

Assessing Your Recall

Multiple Choice Quizzes

12-1   Explain the difference between a retrospective analysis and a prospective analysis of a company.

12-2   Compare and contrast time-series analysis and cross-sectional analysis.

12-3   Describe the three major types of data that could be used in a time-series or cross-sectional analysis.

12-4   For each of the following ratios, reproduce the formula for their calculation:

a. ROA (Break down into profit margin percentage and total asset turnover rate)

b. ROE

c. Accounts receivable turnover

d. Inventory turnover

e. Accounts payable turnover

f. Current ratio

g. Quick ratio

h. D/E(I)

i. D/E(II)

j. D/E(III)

k. Times interest earned

12-5   Explain how the turnover ratios relate to the cash produced from the operations of a company.

12-6   Describe leverage, and explain how it is evidenced in the ROA and ROE ratios.

12-7   Explain, using the profit margin and total asset turnover ratios, how two companies in the same business (use retail clothing stores as an example) can earn the same ROA, yet have very different operating strategies.

12-8   What is the advantage of preparing common size statements in financial statement analysis?

12-9   Explain why the current ratio is subject to manipulation as a measure of liquidity.

12-10   Discuss the problems associated with calculating an accounts payable turnover ratio that make it difficult to interpret.

12-11   Describe how earnings per share is calculated, and discuss the purpose of producing basic and fully diluted earnings per share for a company.

12-12   Explain how the credit risk of a company can be assessed using the times interest earned ratio.

Applying Your Knowledge

12-13   (Common size analysis and differences in profitability)
Comparative financial statement data for First Company and Foremost Company, two competitors, appear below.

	First Company		Foremost Company	
	2004	2003	2004	2003
Net sales	$ 300,000		$1,440,000	
Cost of goods sold	192,000		864,000	
Operating expenses	61,200		302,400	
Interest expense	3,600		12,000	
Income tax expense	13,200		78,000	
Current assets	156,000	$132,000	840,000	$780,000
Capital assets (net)	366,000	324,000	960,000	900,000
Current liabilities	72,000	62,400	300,000	330,000
Long-term liabilities	60,000	81,600	240,000	180,000
Common stock	312,000	252,000	900,000	840,000
Retained earnings	78,000	60,000	360,000	330,000

Required:

a. Prepare a common size analysis of the 2004 income statement data for First Company and Foremost Company.

b. Calculate the return on assets and the return on shareholders' equity for both companies.

c. Comment on the relative profitability of these companies.

d. Identify two main reasons for the difference in profitability.

12-14   (Liquidity ratios)
The financial data for Spectrum Associates are as follows (amounts in thousands):

	Year 1	Year 2	Year 3	Year 4
Current assets				
Cash	$ 200	$ 100	$ 200	$ 150
Accounts receivable	700	800	700	650
Inventories	500	1,000	1,450	2,100
Other current assets	100	100	150	100
	$1,500	$2,000	$2,500	$3,000
Current liabilities				
Accounts payable	$ 600	$ 700	$ 825	$ 800
Accrued salaries	300	400	500	400
Other current liabilities	100	150	160	300
	$1,000	$1,250	$1,485	$1,500

Required:

a. Calculate the current and quick ratios for Years 1 through 4.

b. Comment on the short-term liquidity position of Spectrum Associates.

12-15 (Accounts receivable turnover)

The financial data for Campton Electric Company Inc. and Johnson Electrical Ltd. for the current year are as follows (amounts in thousands):

	Annual sales	Accounts receivable, Jan. 1	Accounts receivable, Dec. 31
Campton Electric	$3,893	$542	$628
Johnson Electrical	1,382	168	143

Required:

a. Calculate the accounts receivable turnover for each company.

b. Calculate the average number of days required by each company to collect the receivables.

c. Which company appears to be more efficient in terms of handling its accounts receivable?

d. What additional information would be helpful in evaluating management's handling of the collection of accounts receivable?

12-16 (Accounts receivable turnover)

The Super Gym Company Limited sells fitness equipment to retail outlets and fitness centres. The majority of these sales are on credit. The financial data related to accounts receivable over the last three years are as follows:

	2001	2002	2003
Accounts receivable	$ 350,600	$ 362,400	$ 358,500
Sales	3,218,400	3,585,300	3,988,400

Required:

a. Calculate the accounts receivable turnover for each year. In the year 2001, use the accounts receivable in 2001. For the other two years, use the average accounts receivable.

b. Calculate the average number of days required to collect the receivables in each year.

c. As a user of this information, describe what trends you see. What additional information would you like to know to help you understand the trends?

12-17 (Inventory turnover)

Information regarding the activities of Polymer Plastics Company is as follows:

	Year 1	Year 2	Year 3	Year 4	Year 5
Cost of goods sold	$463,827	$511,125	$593,350	$679,686	$708,670
Average inventory	65,537	81,560	110,338	166,072	225,295

Required:

a. Do a time-series analysis of the inventory turnover for each year. Also, calculate the average number of days that inventories are held for the respective years.

b. Is Polymer Plastics Company managing its inventories efficiently? Do you have enough information to answer this questions? If not, what else do you need to know?

12-18   (Inventory turnover)

The financial data for Green Grocers Limited and Fast Lane Foods Inc. for the current year are as follows:

	Annual cost of goods sold	Inventory Jan. 1	Inventory Dec. 31
Green Grocers Limited	$8,554,921	$580,633	$547,925
Fast Lane Foods Inc.	2,769,335	174,725	196,446

Required:

a. Calculate the inventory turnover for each company.

b. Calculate the average number of days the inventory is held by each company.

c. Knowing the type of inventory these companies sell, comment on the reasonableness of the inventory turnover. Which company manages its inventory more efficiently?

d. Are there any potential problems associated with fast inventory turnovers?

12-19   (Analysis using selected ratios)

The following ratios and other information are based on a company's comparative financial statements for a two-year period:

	Year 1	Year 2
Current ratio	1.84	2.20
Quick ratio	1.07	.89
D/E(I) ratio	.43	.58
D/E(II) ratio	.75	1.38
Earnings per share	.24	.15
Gross profit percentage	42.3%	45.6%
Total assets	$2,143,702	$3,574,825
Current assets	$ 965,118	$1,462,763

Required:

a. What is the amount of current liabilities at the end of Year 2?

b. What is the amount of total debt at the end of Year 2?

c. What is the total shareholders' equity at the end of Year 2?

d. Do you think this company is a retail company, a financial institution, or a service organization? Explain.

e. If the company has 1,650,200 common shares outstanding for most of Year 2 and has issued no other shares, what is its net income for Year 2?

f. Based on the information available, what is your assessment of the company's liquidity? Explain.

g. Given the limited information, what is your assessment of the company's overall financial position? Explain.

h. What changes do you see between Year 1 and Year 2 that appear particularly significant? What explanations might there be for these changes?

12-20 (ROE and ROA)

The following financial information relates to Stanton Publishing Inc. (amounts in thousands):

	Year 1	Year 2	Year 3	Year 4
Sales	$15,472	$19,558	$21,729	$28,793
Average total assets	19,645	25,227	33,146	67,185
Average shareholders' equity	6,278	9,614	13,619	24,729
Net income	200	503	1,105	2,913
Interest expense	50	55	96	89
Tax rate	40%	40%	40%	30%

Required:

For each year, calculate:

a. Return on shareholders' equity (ROE)

b. ROA

    1. Profit margin percentage

    2. Total asset turnover rate

c. Comment on the profitability of Stanton Publishing Inc.

12-21 (ROE and ROA)

The following financial information relates to Cool Cool Brewery Ltd. (amounts in thousands):

	Year 1	Year 2	Year 3
Sales	$42,798	$54,060	$76,023
Average total assets	48,774	65,258	98,654
Average shareholders' equity	24,664	32,415	51,515
Net income	1,583	3,830	6,755
Interest expense	896	1,441	2,112
Tax rate	25%	30%	30%

Required:

For each year, calculate:

a. Return on shareholders' equity (ROE)

b. ROA

    1. Profit margin percentage

    2. Total asset turnover rate

c. Comment on the profitability of Cool Cool Brewery Ltd.

12-22 (ROE and ROA)

Canadian Import Company's summarized balance sheet is as follows:

Total assets	$600,000	Liabilities	$300,000
		Shareholders' equity	300,000
	$600,000		$600,000

The interest rate on the liabilities is 8% and the income tax rate is 40%.

Required:

a. If the ROE is equal to the ROA, calculate the net income.

b. Calculate the ROE, using the net income determined in part a). Check this by calculating the ROA and confirming that it is equal to the ROE.

c. Explain what causes the ROE to be equal to the ROA.

d. Calculate the income before interest and taxes for the net income derived in part a).

e. Assume that the interest rate is now 6% and that the income tax rate remains at 40%. What is the net income if the ROA is the same as that calculated in part b)? What is the ROE?

f. Compare the ROE in both situations, and explain why there is a difference.

12-23 (D/E(I), D/E(II), D/E(III), and times interest earned)
Artscan Enterprises' financial data are as follows:

	Year 1	Year 2	Year 3
Income before interest and taxes	$ 500	$ 800	$1,000
Interest	60	100	135
Current liabilities	425	525	750
Noncurrent liabilities	600	1,000	1,400
Shareholders' equity	1,300	1,800	2,200

Required:

a. Calculate the debt/equity ratios (I, II, and III) and times interest earned ratio.

b. Comment on the long-term liquidity position of Artscan Enterprises.

12-24 (D/E(I), D/E(II), D/E(III), and times interest earned)
Waverly Company's financial data are as follows:

	Year 1	Year 2	Year 3
Income before interest and taxes	$1,000	$1,300	$1,600
Interest	120	150	165
Current liabilities	390	430	520
Noncurrent liabilities	700	1,170	1,200
Shareholders' equity	1,500	1,700	1,800

Required:

a. Calculate the debt/equity ratios (I, II, and III) and times interest earned ratio.

b. Comment on the long-term liquidity position of Waverly Company.

12-25 (Transaction effects on ratios)
State the immediate effect (increase, decrease, no effect) of the following transactions on the:

a. Current ratio

b. Quick ratio

c. Accounts receivable turnover

d. Inventory turnover

e. Debt/equity ratio (D/E(I))

f. ROA

g. ROE

Transactions:

1. Goods costing $350,000 are sold to customers on credit for $450,000.

2. Accounts receivable of $300,000 are collected.

3. Inventory costing $450,000 is purchased from suppliers.

4. A long-term bank loan for $760,000 is arranged with the bank, and the cash is received by the company.

5. The bank loan carries an interest rate of 10% and the interest payment is made at the end of the year.

6. The company uses $100,000 to buy temporary investments.

7. New common shares are issued for $550,000.

12-26 (Earnings per share)
Transland Equipment Ltd. has 400,000 common shares and 100,000 preferred shares outstanding. The preferred shares pay a dividend of $2.00 per share and are convertible into 300,000 common shares. During the year, Transland earned net income of $620,000.

Required:

a. Calculate the basic earnings per share that should be reported in the financial statements.

b. What relevance does the convertibility of the preferred shares have for reporting earnings per share?

12-27 (Earnings per share)
In 2003, Signal Communications Ltd. reported an earnings per share of $0.76. Signal had 28,500 common shares outstanding during 2003 and 2004, and no preferred shares. In 2004, Signal reported net income of $24,510.

Required:

a. What was the net income for 2003?

b. Calculate the earnings per share for 2004.

c. Where in the financial statements do you usually find the earnings per share amount?

d. Assume that in December 2004 Signal decided to split its common shares 2 for 1. What effect will this have on the earnings per share amount calculated in b)? Will the year 2003 earnings per share amount be affected as well? Explain.

12-28 (Analysis of assets)
You have inherited money from your grandparents and a friend suggests that you consider buying shares in Galena Ski Products. Because you may need to sell the shares within the next two years to finance your university education, you start your analysis of the company data by calculating (1) working capital, (2) the current ratio, and (3) the quick ratio. Galena's balance sheet is as follows:

Current assets	
Cash	$248,000
Inventory	320,000
Other current assets	32,000
Noncurrent assets	
Land	50,000
Building and equipment	266,000
Other	25,000
Total	$941,000
Current liabilities	$165,000
Long-term debt	400,000
Common shares	180,000
Retained earnings	196,000
Total	$941,000

Required:

a. What amount of working capital is currently maintained? Comment on the adequacy of the working capital.

b. Your preference is to have a quick ratio of at least 0.80 and a current ratio of at least 2.00. How do the existing ratios compare with your criteria? Using these two ratios, how would you evaluate the company's current asset position?

c. The company sells only on a cash basis currently and has sales of $900,000 this past year. How would you expect a change from cash to credit sales to affect the balance sheet ratios?

d. Galena's balance sheet is presented just before the start of shipments for its fall and winter season. How would your evaluation change if these balances existed in late February, following completion of its primary business for the skiing season?

12-29   (Ratio analysis of two companies)
You have obtained the financial statements of A-Tec and Bi-Sci, new companies in the high-tech industry. Both companies have just completed their second year of operations. You have acquired the following information for an analysis of the companies. All dollar amounts are stated in thousands.

	A-Tec		Bi-Sci	
	2004	2003	2004	2003
Cash	$ 3	$ 2	$ 1	$ 1
Accounts receivable	30	15	20	20
Inventory	40	20	30	30
Other current assets	5	1	3	1
Capital assets (net)	260	170	115	104
Current liabilities	67	40	24	24
Long-term debt	210	130	0	0
Common shares	28	18	72	72
Retained earnings	33	20	73	60
Sales (all credit sales)	950	675	610	600
Cost of goods sold	625	450	455	450
Net income	95	80	60	55

Required:

a. Calculate the following ratios for the two companies for the two years:

    1. Current ratio

2. Working capital (dollar amount)

3. Accounts receivable turnover

4. Inventory turnover

5. Asset turnover

6. D/E(I)

7. Shareholders' equity to total assets

8. Gross margin ratio

9. Return on sales

10. ROA

11. ROE

b. Write a brief analysis of the two companies based on the information given and the ratios calculated. Be sure to discuss issues of liquidity, leverage, and profitability. Which company appears to be the better investment for the shareholder? Explain. Which company appears to be the better credit risk for the lender? Explain.

12-30 (Comparative ratios and comments on results)
Selected financial data for two intense competitors in a recent year are presented below, in millions of dollars:

	X Corporation	Y Company
Income Statement data:		
Net sales	$ 5,030	$ 4,500
Cost of goods sold	4,550	3,970
Selling and administrative expenses	140	250
Interest expense	220	130
Other income (net)	10	0
Income taxes	50	60
Net income	$ 80	$ 90
Cash Flows Statement data:		
Net cash inflow from operating activities	$ 190	$ 170
Net increase in cash during the year	20	30
End-of-Year Balance Sheet data:		
Current assets	$ 1,570	$ 1,080
Property, plant, and equipment (net)	2,760	1,810
Other assets	1,050	660
Total assets	$ 5,380	$ 3,550
Current liabilities	900	570
Long-term debt	3,320	2,060
Total shareholders' equity	1,160	920
Total liabilities and shareholders' equity	$ 5,380	$ 3,550
Beginning-of-Year Balances:		
Total assets	$ 4,880	$ 3,440
Total shareholders' equity	700	620
Other Data:		
Average net receivables	$ 510	$ 520
Average inventory	770	400

Required:

a. For each company, calculate the following ratios:

    1. Average collection period (in days) for receivables

    2. Average holding period (in days) for inventory

    3. Current ratio

    4. Total debt to total assets

    5. Times interest earned

    6. Return on assets

    7. Return on equity

b. Compare the financial position and performance of the two companies, and comment on their relative strengths and weaknesses.

12-31 (Using ratios to calculate missing financial statement amounts)
Presented below are the incomplete income statement and comparative balance sheet of Labrador Corporation:

LABRADOR CORPORATION
Income Statement
For the Year Ended December 31, 2004

Sales	$23,650,000
Cost of goods sold	?
Gross profit	?
Operating expenses	3,579,750
Income from operations	?
Other expenses and losses	?
Interest expense	?
Income before income taxes	?
Income tax expense	1,204,000
Net income	$?

LABRADOR CORPORATION
Balance Sheet
December 31

	2004	2003
Assets		
Current assets		
Cash	$ 967,500	$ 806,250
Accounts receivable (net)	?	2,042,500
Inventory	?	3,698,000
Total current assets	?	6,546,750
Capital assets (net)	8,933,000	8,503,250
Total assets	$?	$15,050,000
Liabilities and Shareholders' Equity		
Current liabilities	$?	$ 1,773,750
Long-term notes payable	?	6,020,000
Total liabilities	?	7,793,750
Common stock	6,450,000	6,450,000
Retained earnings	860,000	806,250
Total shareholders' equity	7,310,000	7,256,250
Total liabilities and shareholders' equity	$?	$15,050,000

Additional data:

1. The current ratio on December 31, 2004, is 2.5:1.

2. All sales are on account.

3. The receivables turnover for 2004 is 11 times.

4. The inventory turnover for 2004 is 5.1 times.

5. Return on assets for 2004 is 20%.

6. The net profit margin on sales is 12.5%.

Required:
Calculate the missing amounts in Labrador's financial statements, using the ratios and additional data above. (*Hint:* You will not be able to calculate the missing amounts in the same sequence as they are presented above. Start with one of the ratios and derive as much information as possible from it before trying another ratio.)

User Perspective Problems

12-32   (Use of ratios in debt restrictions)
Contracts with lenders typically place restrictions on a company's activities in an attempt to ensure that the company will be able to repay both the interest and the principal on the debt covered by the restrictions. These restrictions are frequently stated in terms of ratios. For instance, a restriction could be that the debt/equity ratio (D/E(II)) cannot exceed 2.0. If it does exceed 2.0, the debt covered by the restrictions falls due immediately. Two commonly used ratios are the current ratio and the debt/equity ratio. Explain why these might appear as restrictions. How do they protect the lender?

12-33   (Use of ROA in performance measurement)
Management compensation plans typically specify performance criteria in terms of financial statement ratios. For instance, a plan might specify that management must achieve a certain level of return on investment, for example, ROA. If management were trying to maximize their compensation, how could they manipulate the ROA ratio to achieve this goal?

12-34   (Use of ratios for investing decisions)
You are considering investing in the stock market. As a potential investor, choose four ratios that you think would be most helpful to you in making your investment decision. Explain your choices.

12-35   (Ratio analysis and auditors)
Auditors review the financial statements to determine whether the information reported has been collected, summarized, and reported according to generally accepted accounting principles. Although auditors are not expected to identify fraud, they do perform tests to see if there are any apparent abnormalities. What ratios or forms of ratio analysis do you think would be helpful to auditors in identifying abnormalities?

12-36   (Using ratios to evaluate creditworthiness)
You are the sales manager in a company that sells automotive supplies to service stations and car dealerships. You have been contacted by a large car dealership that wants you to supply its service department with automotive parts. The dealership would like to purchase on credit, with 30 days to pay from the date of invoice. You have access to the dealership's financial statements for last year. Which ratios could be useful to you in making the decision about whether to sell on credit? Explain your choices.

12-37   (Use of ratios in decision-making)

Managers, investors, and creditors usually have a specific focus when making decisions about a business.

Required:

For each of the following cases, identify the ratio or ratios that would help the user in making a decision or in identifying areas for further analysis:

a. A company's net income has declined. Is the decrease in net income from:

   1. a decrease in sales or an increase in cost of goods sold?

   2. an increase in total operating expenses?

   3. an increase in a specific expense, such as tax expense?

b. Does a company generate sufficient cash to pay the debts that come due without having to borrow additional money?

c. Does a company rely more heavily on long-term debt financing than other companies in the same industry?

d. In a comparison of two companies, how would you decide which company utilizes its assets most effectively?

e. In a comparison of two companies, how would you decide which company has been more profitable in relation to invested capital?

f. Has the decline in the economy affected a company's ability to collect its accounts receivable?

g. Has a company been successful in reducing its investment in inventories as a result of installing a new ordering system?

h. From a group of companies, which company provides the best earnings per share? (Remember that a share in one company likely does not represent the same proportion of ownership interest as a share in another company.)

Reading and Interpreting Published Financial Statements

12-38   (Ratio analysis for Sleeman Breweries Ltd. and Big Rock Brewery Ltd.)

The 2001 financial statements of **Sleeman Breweries Ltd.** and **Big Rock Brewery Ltd.** are shown in Exhibits 12-14 and 12-15, respectively.

Required:

Based on these financial statements, answer each of the following questions:

a. Calculate the following ratios for 2001 for Sleeman Breweries:

   1. ROA (split into profit margin percentage and total asset turnover rate)

   2. ROE (there are no preferred shares outstanding)

   3. Inventory turnover

   4. Accounts receivable turnover

b. Calculate the following ratios for both 2001 and 2000 for Sleeman:

   1. Current ratio

   2. D/E(I)

3. Times interest earned

c. Comment on the use of leverage by Sleeman Breweries.

d. Assume you are thinking of investing in Sleeman Breweries. Comment on its financial health, highlighting any areas that might be of concern. Use not only the ratios, but also the information from all three financial statements in your analysis.

e. Big Rock Brewery, like Sleeman Breweries, brews beer. Calculate the same ratios in a) and b) for Big Rock Brewery that you did for Sleeman Breweries. Compare the two companies. Which do you think is the better investment? Why?

EXHIBIT 12-14
PART A

SLEEMAN BREWERIES LTD.
Consolidated Balance Sheets
(in thousands of dollars)

	December 29, 2001	December 30, 2000
ASSETS		
CURRENT		
Accounts receivable	$ $24,030	$ $22,010
Income taxes recoverable	-	226
Inventories (Note 4)	19,296	13,641
Prepaid expenses	1,185	2,122
	44,511	37,999
PROPERTY, PLANT AND EQUIPMENT (Note 5)	67,569	58,407
LONG-TERM INVESTMENTS (Note 6)	8,090	8,090
INTANGIBLE ASSETS (Note 7)	77,472	77,683
	$ 197,642	$ 182,179
LIABILITIES		
CURRENT		
Bank indebtedness (Note 8)	$ 16,063	$ 9,885
Accounts payable and accrued liabilities	19,144	14,547
Income taxes payable	2,748	-
Current portion of long-term debt (Note 9)	8,360	15,342
	46,315	39,774
LONG-TERM DEBT (Note 9)	71,933	74,645
FUTURE INCOME TAXES (Note 10)	6,306	5,206
	124,554	119,625
CONTINGENCY (Note 17)		
SHAREHOLDERS' EQUITY		
SHARE CAPITAL (Note 11)	38,965	38,196
RETAINED EARNINGS	34,123	24,358
	73,088	62,554
	$ 197,642	$ 182,179

EXHIBIT 12-14
PART B

SLEEMAN BREWERIES LTD.
Consolidated Statements of Earnings and Retained Earnings
(in thousands of dollars except per share amounts)

	Fiscal Year Ended	
	December 29, 2001	December 30, 2000
NET REVENUE	$ **143,637**	$ 134,439
COST OF GOODS SOLD	**75,937**	70,082
GROSS MARGIN	**67,700**	64,357
SELLING, GENERAL AND ADMINISTRATION	**39,248**	37,894
EARNINGS BEFORE THE UNDERNOTED	**28,452**	26,463
DEPRECIATION AND AMORTIZATION	**7,087**	6,371
INTEREST EXPENSE	**6,545**	6,773
EARNINGS BEFORE INCOME TAXES	**14,820·**	13,319
INCOME TAXES (NOTES 2 g) and 10)	**5,055** ·	4,350
NET EARNINGS	**9,765**	8,969
RETAINED EARNINGS, BEGINNING OF YEAR	**24,358**	18,602
ADJUSTMENT RELATED TO SHARES REPURCHASED (NOTE 11)	**-**	(3,213)
RETAINED EARNINGS, END OF YEAR	$ **34,123**	$ 24,358
EARNINGS PER SHARE		
BASIC (NOTES 2 h) and 13)	$ **0.64**	$ 0.58
DILUTED (NOTES 2 h) and 13)	$ **0.63**	$ 0.58

SLEEMAN BREWERIES LTD.
Consolidated Statements of Cash Flows
(in thousands of dollars)

EXHIBIT 12-14

PART C

	Fiscal Year Ended	
	December 29, 2001	December 30, 2000
NET INFLOW (OUTFLOW) OF CASH RELATED TO THE FOLLOWING ACTIVITIES:		
OPERATING		
Net earnings	**$ 9,765**	$ 8,969
Items not affecting cash		
Depreciation and amortization	**7,087**	6,371
Future income taxes	**1,100**	3,100
Gain on disposal of equipment	**-**	(586)
	17,952	17,854
Changes in non-cash operating working capital items (Note 14)	**1,032**	(5,432)
	18,984	12,422
INVESTING		
Business acquisitions (Note 3)	**(2,179)**	(1,054)
Additions to property, plant and equipment	**(12,677)**	(11,433)
Additions to intangible assets	**(1,402)**	(846)
Additions to long term investments (Note 6)	**-**	(4,780)
Proceeds from disposal of equipment	**22**	807
	(16,236)	(17,306)
FINANCING		
Net proceeds from bank operating loans	**6,179**	1,438
Stock options exercised	**769**	-
Common shares repurchased (Note 11)	**-**	(5,168)
Long-term debt - proceeds	**9,343**	15,280
Long-term debt - principal repayments	**(19,039)**	(6,666)
	(2,748)	4,884
NET CASH FLOW AND CASH BALANCE, END OF YEAR	**-**	-
Supplemental disclosures of cash flows:		
Interest paid	**$ 6,620**	$6,663
Income taxes paid, net of cash refunds of $898 (2000 -$225)	**$ 1,016**	$858

EXHIBIT 12-15

PART A

BIG ROCK BREWERY LTD. (2001)

Consolidated Balance Sheets

As at March 31

	2001 $	2000 $
	(Denominated in Canadian Dollars)	
ASSETS *[notes 5 & 6]*		
Current		
Cash and cash equivalents	1,602,202	106,492
Accounts receivable	1,593,984	1,872,064
Inventories *[note 3]*	2,701,982	2,676,790
Prepaid expenses and other	400,985	237,656
Investments	156,035	19,060
	6,455,188	4,912,062
Capital assets *[note 4]*	24,844,994	24,954,398
Deferred charges and other	45,619	51,779
	31,345,801	29,918,239
LIABILITIES AND SHAREHOLDERS' EQUITY		
Current		
Bank indebtedness *[note 5]*	1,362,907	2,244,903
Accounts payable and accrued liabilities	1,393,068	1,264,073
Income tax payable	151,869	—
Current portion of long-term debt *[note 6]*	1,567,862	1,496,189
	4,475,706	5,005,165
Long-term debt *[note 6]*	3,469,976	4,378,224
Future income taxes *[note 8]*	4,362,400	3,905,400
Total liabilities	12,308,082	13,288,789
Commitments *[note 9]*		
Shareholders' equity		
Share capital *[note 7]*	11,553,637	10,077,900
Retained earnings	7,484,082	6,551,550
	19,037,719	16,629,450
	31,345,801	29,918,239

BIG ROCK BREWERY LTD. (2001)

EXHIBIT 12-15

PART B

Consolidated Statements of Cash Flows

Years ended March 31

	2001 $	2000 $
	(Denominated in Canadian Dollars)	
OPERATING ACTIVITIES		
Net income for year	1,352,573	1,461,119
Items not affecting cash		
Amortization	1,230,994	1,167,163
Future income taxes	457,000	958,000
	3,040,567	3,586,282
Net change in non-cash working capital [note 12]	370,423	(1,150,883)
Cash provided by operating activities	3,410,990	2,435,399
FINANCING ACTIVITIES		
Increase (decrease) in bank indebtedness	(881,996)	1,619,994
Repayment of long term debt	(836,575)	(1,601,587)
Share repurchase [note 7]	(744,304)	(1,358,205)
Shares issued by private placement [note 7]	1,800,000	—
Shares issued on exercise of options [note 7]	—	78,879
Cash used in financing activities	(662,875)	(1,260,919)
INVESTING ACTIVITIES		
Aquisition of investments	(136,975)	—
Additions to capital assets	(1,121,590)	(1,143,222)
Deferred charges and other assets	6,160	—
Cash used in investing activities	(1,252,405)	(1,143,222)
Net increase in cash	1,495,710	31,258
Cash and cash equivalents, beginning of year	106,492	75,234
Cash and cash equivalents, end of year	1,602,202	106,492

EXHIBIT 12-15

PART C

BIG ROCK BREWERY LTD. (2001)

Consolidated Statements of Operations & Retained Earning

Years ended March 31

	2001 $	2000 $
	(Denominated in Canadian Dollars)	
Revenue		
Sales	32,238,035	31,707,142
Government taxes and commissions	(9,038,357)	(8,990,216)
	23,199,678	22,716,926
Cost of sales	9,240,503	9,154,929
Gross profit	13,959,175	13,561,997
Expenses		
Selling, general and administrative	10,176,689	9,415,955
Interest on long-term debt	451,921	481,400
Interest on short-term debt	91,998	36,360
Amortization	1,230,994	1,167,163
	11,951,602	11,100,878
Income before income taxes	2,007,573	2,461,119
Current income tax expense	198,000	42,000
Future income tax expense *[note 8]*	457,000	958,000
Net income for year	1,352,573	1,461,119
Retained earnings, beginning of year	6,551,550	5,975,448
Redemption of common shares *[note 7]*	(420,041)	(885,017)
Retained earnings, end of year	7,484,082	6,551,550
Net income per share *[note 2]*		
Basic and fully diluted	0.29	0.31

See accompanying notes

12-39 (Ratio analysis for Corel Corporation)
The 2001 financial statements of **Corel Corporation** are shown in Exhibit 12-16.

Required:
Based on these financial statements, answer each of the following questions:

a. Calculate the following ratios for 2001:

1. Inventory turnover

2. Accounts receivable turnover

b. Calculate the following ratios for both 2001 and 2000:

1. Current ratio

2. Quick ratio

3. D/E(I)

4. D/E(III)

c. Prepare a common size or vertical analysis of Corel's consolidated balance sheets and income statements (statements of operations) for 2001 and 2000, and comment on any significant differences that you observe.

d. Examine Corel's consolidated statements of cash flows and comment on any significant differences in the company's cash-related activities during the three-year period.

e. Assume you are thinking of investing in Corel. Comment on its financial health, highlighting any areas that might be of concern. Use not only the ratios, but also the information from all three financial statements in your analysis.

f. Notice that in the years in which Corel reported a *net loss* before tax, it also reported income *tax expense*. Conversely, in the year in which it reported *net income* before tax, it also reported an income *tax recovery*. Explain how this could happen.

Consolidated Balance Sheets
(in thousands of US$)

COREL CORPORATION (2001)

EXHIBIT 12-16

PART A

	As at November 30	
	2001	2000
Assets		
Current assets:		
Cash and cash equivalents	$ 24,924	$ 127,430
Restricted cash	19,367	1,136
Short-term investments	78,076	
Accounts receivable		
Trade	18,689	28,620
Other	1,272	773
Inventory	799	3,117
Future tax asset		479
Prepaid expenses	1,779	1,050
Total current assets	144,906	162,605
Investments	9,886	11,996
Future income tax asset		965
Deferred financing charges	250	550
Capital assets	43,123	42,471
Goodwill	37,534	
Total assets	$ 235,699	$ 218,587
Liabilities and shareholders' equity		
Current liabilities:		
Accounts payable and accrued liabilities	$ 27,862	$ 28,441
Participation rights obligation	16,338	
Novell obligations		10,000
Income taxes payable	4,749	6,595
Deferred revenue	10,160	10,907
Total current liabilities	59,109	55,943
Future income tax liability	4,967	
Total liabilities	64,076	55,943
Commitments and contingencies		
Shareholders' equity		
Share capital		
Issued and outstanding (000s): 80,709 common shares (73,641 in 2000); 24,000 Series A preferred shares (24,000 in 2000)	$ 388,193	$ 371,890
Contributed surplus	4,990	4,990
Deficit	(221,560)	(214,236)
Total shareholders' equity	171,623	162,644
Total liabilities and shareholders' equity	$ 235,699	$ 218,587

EXHIBIT 12-16

PART B

COREL CORPORATION (2001)
Consolidated Statements of Operations
(in thousands of US$, except share and per share data)

	Year ended November 30		
	2001	**2000**	**1999**
Sales	$134,320	$157,487	$243,051
Cost of sales	25,927	47,025	59,516
Gross profit	108,393	110,462	183,535
Expenses:			
Advertising	22,091	33,258	47,964
Selling, general and administrative	61,828	85,662	82,229
Research and development	25,251	43,867	40,049
Depreciation and amortization	5,577	7,354	6,443
Settlement proceeds	(409)		(6,342)
Loss (gain) on foreign exchange	(71)	1,371	(246)
	114,267	171,512	170,097
Income (loss) from operations	(5,874)	(61,050)	13,438
Gain (loss) on investments	(2,359)	14,585	
Interest income (expense)	5,420	(1,305)	(190)
Income (loss) before the undernoted	(2,813)	(47,770)	13,248
Income tax expense (recovery)	4,039	4,705	(3,946)
Share of loss of equity investments	472	2,873	478
Net income (loss)	$ (7,324)	$(55,348)	$ 16,716
Income (loss) per share:			
Basic	$ (0.10)	$ (0.80)	$ 0.27
Diluted	$ (0.10)	$ (0.80)	$ 0.27
Weighted average number of common shares outstanding (000s):			
Basic	74,325	69,498	62,194
Diluted	74,325	69,498	63,042

COREL CORPORATION (2001)
Consolidated Statements of Cash Flows
(in thousands of US$)

EXHIBIT 12-16

PART C

	Year ended November 30		
	2001	**2000**	**199**
Operating activities:			
Net income (loss)	$ (7,324)	$ (55,348)	$ 16,71
Items which do not involve cash or cash equivalents:			
Depreciation and amortization	16,347	17,904	15,53
Bad debt expense	3,197	2,357	3
Write down of assets		984	
Future income taxes	1,444	198	85
Loss (gain) on investments	2,359	(14,585)	
Gain on disposal of assets	(306)		(80
Share of loss of equity investments	472	2,873	47
Changes in operating assets and liabilities:			
Restricted cash	(1,893)	(1,136)	
Accounts receivable	10,277	26,974	(12,15
Inventory	2,836	10,450	3,15
Income taxes recoverable		5,135	(5,13
Prepaid expenses	430	992	2,57
Accounts payable and accrued liabilities	(9,897)	(25,843)	(7,92
Income taxes payable	(2,051)	6,595	(7,54
Deferred revenue	(747)	(7,565)	53
Net cash provided by (used in) operating activities	15,144	(30,015)	6,30
Financing activities:			
Issuance of common shares	265	19,056	12,76
Issuance of preferred shares		130,679	
Issuance of warrants		3,291	
Reduction of Novell obligations	(10,000)	(6,594)	(5,72
Net cash provided by (used in) financing activities	(9,735)	146,432	7,03
Investing activities:			
Proceeds on sale of investments		14,585	2,92
Purchase of investments	(909)	(2,356)	(1,56
Purchase of short-term investments	(78,076)		
Purchase of capital assets	(7,817)	(19,511)	(19,19
Cash restricted for participation rights obligation	(16,338)		
Proceeds on disposal of assets	818	274	11
Acquisition of Micrografx, Inc.	(5,593)		
Net cash used in investing activities	(107,915)	(7,008)	(17,71
Increase (decrease) in cash and cash equivalents	(102,506)	109,409	(4,37
Cash and cash equivalents at beginning of year	127,430	18,021	22,39
Cash and cash equivalents at end of year	$ 24,924	$ 127,430	$ 18,02
Supplemental non-cash information:			
Purchase of Micrografx, Inc.	$ 32,376		
Investment in Hemera Technologies, Inc.		$ 9,727	
Purchase of MetaCreations assets		$ 4,000	

12-40   (Ratio analysis for Enerflex Systems Ltd.)

The 2001 financial statements of **Enerflex Systems Ltd.** (headquartered in Calgary, Alberta), which produces compressor equipment used in the natural gas industry, are shown in Exhibit 12-17.

Required:

Based on these financial statements, answer each of the following questions:

a. Calculate the following ratios for 2001:

   1. ROA (split into profit margin percentage and total asset turnover rate)

   2. ROE (there are no preferred shares outstanding)

b. Calculate the following ratios for both 2001 and 2000:

   1. Current ratio

   2. D/E(II)

   3. Times interest earned

c. Comment on the use of leverage by Enerflex Systems.

d. Prepare a common size or vertical analysis of Enerflex's consolidated balance sheets and statements of income for 2001 and 2000, and comment on any significant differences that you observe.

e. Examine Enerflex's consolidated statements of cash flows and note any differences that you observe, in terms of how the data are presented, compared to the usual format. Can you determine the company's cash position? Reformat the lower portion of Enerflex's statements of cash flows (from Financing Activities to Cash, end of year), treating the increase or decrease in the bank loan as the change in cash during the period.

f. Enerflex purchased some of its common shares and cancelled them during 2001. Reconstruct the journal entry that would have been made to record this transaction. Would you expect this reduction in the number of shares to have a positive or a negative effect on the company's earnings per share? Explain.

g. Assume you are thinking of investing in Enerflex. Comment on its financial health, highlighting any areas that might be of concern. Use not only the ratios, but also the information from all three financial statements in your analysis.

ENERFLEX SYSTEMS LTD. (2001)

EXHIBIT 12-17
PART A

CONSOLIDATED BALANCE SHEETS

(Thousands)		December 31 2001	December 31 2000
Assets			
Current assets			
Accounts receivable		$ 67,987	$ 58,842
Inventory	(Note 3)	59,343	51,136
Future income taxes	(Note 9)	2,521	1,812
Total current assets		129,851	111,790
Rental equipment	(Note 4)	39,042	31,740
Property, plant and equipment	(Note 5)	45,149	47,273
Future income taxes	(Note 9)	1,138	639
Intangible assets		2,815	—
Goodwill, net of accumulated amortization		4,151	1,299
		$ 222,146	$ 192,741
Liabilities and Shareholders' Equity			
Current liabilities			
Bank loans	(Note 6)	$ 23,886	$ 24,638
Accounts payable and accrued liabilities		43,880	29,075
Current portion of long-term debt	(Note 6)	—	200
Total current liabilities		67,766	53,913
Long-term debt	(Note 6)	30,000	30,000
Future income taxes	(Note 9)	5,879	4,717
		103,645	88,630
Commitments and contingencies	(Note 8)		
Shareholders' equity			
Share capital	(Note 7)	35,412	35,617
Retained earnings		83,089	68,494
		118,501	104,111
		$ 222,146	$ 192,741

See accompanying notes to the Consolidated Financial Statements.

CONSOLIDATED STATEMENTS OF INCOME

(Thousands, except share amounts)		Years Ended December 31 2001	Years Ended December 31 2000
Revenue		$ 375,040	$ 286,283
Cost of goods sold		301,816	232,369
Gross margin		73,224	53,914
Selling, general and administrative expenses		35,151	33,227
Gain on sale of assets		(1,088)	(599)
Income before interest and taxes		39,161	21,286
Interest, net		2,680	3,583
Income before income taxes		36,481	17,703
Income taxes	(Note 9)	14,027	6,391
Net income		$ 22,454	$ 11,312
Net income per common share — basic		$ 1.51	$ 0.76
— diluted		$ 1.49	$ 0.75
Weighted average number of common shares		14,916,964	14,968,887

EXHIBIT 12-17
PART B

ENERFLEX SYSTEMS LTD. (2001)

CONSOLIDATED STATEMENTS OF RETAINED EARNINGS

		Years Ended December 31	
(Thousands)		**2001**	2000
Retained earnings, beginning of year		$ **68,494**	$ 67,763
Net income		**22,454**	11,312
Common shares purchased for cancellation	(Note 7)	**(1,807)**	(3,125)
Stock options purchased	(Note 7)	**(87)**	(1,467)
Dividends		**(5,965)**	(5,989)
Retained earnings, end of year		$ **83,089**	$ 68,494

CONSOLIDATED STATEMENTS OF CASH FLOWS

		Years Ended December 31	
(Thousands)		**2001**	2000
Operating Activities			
Net income		$ **22,454**	$ 11,312
Depreciation and amortization		**8,636**	7,570
Future income taxes		**(46)**	200
Gain on sale of assets		**(1,088)**	(599)
		29,956	18,483
Changes in non-cash working capital		**(889)**	(2,324)
		29,067	16,159
Investing Activities			
Acquisition of Landré Ruhaak bv	(Note 2)	**(9,154)**	—
Purchase of:			
Rental equipment		**(16,293)**	(12,443)
Property, plant and equipment		**(3,150)**	(4,503)
Proceeds on disposal of:			
Rental equipment		**6,310**	4,558
Property, plant and equipment		**678**	185
		(21,609)	(12,203)
Changes in non-cash working capital		**126**	(922)
		(21,483)	(13,125)
Financing Activities			
(Decrease) increase in bank loan		**(752)**	9,398
Repayment of long-term debt		**(200)**	(2,000)
Common shares purchased for cancellation		**(2,012)**	(3,369)
Stock options purchased		**(141)**	(2,482)
Stock options exercised		**—**	657
Dividends		**(5,965)**	(5,989)
		(9,070)	(3,785)
Changes in non-cash working capital		**1,486**	751
		(7,584)	(3,034)
Increase in cash		**—**	—
Cash, beginning of year		**—**	—
Cash, end of year		$ **—**	$ —

12-41 (Ratio analysis for MOSAID Technologies Incorporated)
The 2002 financial statements of **MOSAID Technologies Incorporated** are shown in
Exhibit 12-18.

Required:

Based on these financial statements, answer each of the following questions:

a. Calculate the following ratios for 2002:

1. ROE (there are no preferred shares outstanding)

2. Accounts receivable turnover

b. Calculate the following ratios for both 2002 and 2001:

1. Current ratio

2. Quick ratio

3. D/E(I)

4. D/E(II)

c. Prepare a common size or vertical analysis of MOSAID's consolidated balance
sheets and income statements (statements of earnings) for 2002 and 2001, and
comment on any significant differences that you observe.

d. Examine MOSAID's consolidated statements of cash flows and comment on any
significant differences that you observe in 2002 versus 2001.

e. Compare the ratios calculated for MOSAID with the ratios calculated in Problem
12-40 for Enerflex Systems Ltd. and compare the use of leverage by the two
companies. Explain why a comparison of the leverage of these two companies
may not be appropriate.

f. Notice that MOSAID issued approximately $40,000,000 of additional common
shares during the year ended April 26, 2002. What effect would you expect this
to have on the company's earnings per share?

12-42 (Ratio analysis for Aliant Inc.)
The 2001 financial statements of **Aliant Inc.** are shown in Exhibit 12-19, as is a portion
of note 12 related to capital stock.

Required:

Based on these financial statements, answer each of the following questions:

a. Calculate the following ratios for 2001:

1. ROA (split into profit margin percentage and total asset turnover rate)

2. ROE

b. Calculate the following ratios for both 2001 and 2000:

1. Current ratio

2. Quick ratio

3. D/E(I)

4. Times interest earned

c. Comment on the use of leverage by Aliant Inc.

d. Prepare a common size or vertical analysis of Aliant's consolidated balance sheets and statements of income for 2001 and 2000, and comment on any significant differences that you observe.

e. Examine Aliant's consolidated statements of cash flows and comment on any significant differences that you observe in 2001 versus 2000.

f. Assume you are thinking of investing in Aliant. Comment on its financial health, highlighting any areas that might be of concern. Use not only the ratios, but also the information from all three financial statements in your analysis.

EXHIBIT 12-18
PART A

MOSAID TECHNOLOGIES INCORPORATED
(incorporated under the Ontario Business Corporations Act)

CONSOLIDATED BALANCE SHEETS
(in thousands)

As at	April 27, 2001	April 28, 2000
CURRENT ASSETS		
Cash and cash equivalents	$ 5,769	$ 6,046
Short-term marketable securities	13,470	25,101
Accounts receivable	23,112	9,486
Income taxes receivable	–	1,721
Revenues recognized in excess of amounts billed	78	1,860
Inventories (NOTE 2)	6,144	4,690
Prepaid expenses	2,075	1,163
	50,648	50,067
CAPITAL ASSETS (NOTE 3)	22,996	18,107
LONG-TERM INVESTMENTS (NOTE 4)	6,897	1,482
FUTURE INCOME TAXES RECOVERABLE (NOTE 9)	8,462	4,627
	$ 89,003	$ 74,283
CURRENT LIABILITIES		
Accounts payable and accrued liabilities	$ 13,897	$ 10,836
Mortgage payable (NOTE 5)	163	150
Deferred revenue	1,030	1,618
	15,090	12,604
MORTGAGE PAYABLE (NOTE 5)	5,390	5,553
	20,480	18,157
SHAREHOLDERS' EQUITY		
Share capital (NOTE 6)	43,971	38,576
Retained earnings	24,552	17,550
	68,523	56,126
	$ 89,003	$ 74,283

See accompanying Notes to the Consolidated Financial Statements.

Thomas I. Csathy
Director

Robert F. Harland
Director

MOSAID TECHNOLOGIES INCORPORATED

EXHIBIT 12-18

PART B

CONSOLIDATED STATEMENTS OF EARNINGS AND RETAINED EARNINGS

(in thousands, except per share amounts)

Year ended	April 27, 2001	April 28, 2000
REVENUES		
Operations	$ 81,640	$ 47,044
Interest	1,286	1,065
	82,926	48,109
EXPENSES		
Labour and materials	13,367	8,181
Research and development (NOTE 7)	31,428	18,450
Selling and marketing	18,250	11,839
General and administration	8,338	7,015
Bad debt	139	–
Unusual item (NOTE 8)	694	(206)
	72,216	45,279
Earnings from operations	10,710	2,830
Income tax expense (NOTE 9)	3,708	926
NET EARNINGS	7,002	1,904
RETAINED EARNINGS, beginning of year	17,550	15,646
RETAINED EARNINGS, end of year	$ 24,552	$ 17,550
EARNINGS PER SHARE (NOTE 10)		
Basic	$ 0.79	$ 0.26
Fully diluted	$ 0.76	$ 0.26
WEIGHTED AVERAGE NUMBER OF SHARES		
Basic	8,889,863	7,374,469
Fully diluted	10,445,596	8,880,413

See accompanying Notes to the Consolidated Financial Statements.

MOSAID TECHNOLOGIES INCORPORATED

CONSOLIDATED STATEMENTS OF CASH FLOWS
(in thousands)

Year ended	April 27, 2001	April 28, 2000
OPERATING		
Net earnings	$ 7,002	$ 1,904
Items not affecting cash		
Amortization	7,146	5,361
Loss on disposal of capital assets	22	23
Future income taxes recoverable	(3,835)	(2,179)
	10,335	5,109
Change in non-cash working capital items (NOTE 11)	(10,016)	1,875
	319	6,984
INVESTING		
Acquisition of capital assets – net	(12,057)	(7,966)
Acquisition of short-term marketable securities	(19,674)	(26,651)
Proceeds on maturity/disposal of short-term marketable securities	31,305	14,677
Long-term investments	(5,415)	(1,566)
	(5,841)	(21,506)
FINANCING		
Repayment of mortgage	(150)	(139)
Repurchase of shares	–	(271)
Issue of common shares and warrants	5,395	17,402
	5,245	16,992
NET CASH (OUTFLOW) INFLOW	(277)	2,470
CASH AND CASH EQUIVALENTS, beginning of year	6,046	3,576
CASH AND CASH EQUIVALENTS, end of year	$ 5,769	$ 6,046

See accompanying Notes to the Consolidated Financial Statements.

ALIANT INC. (2001)

EXHIBIT 12-19
PART A

Consolidated balance sheets

As at December 31 (thousands of dollars)	2001	2000
ASSETS		
Current assets		
Cash and short term investments	$ 131,558	$ 80,492
Accounts receivable	482,454	628,377
Inventory	36,046	45,528
Prepayments	34,947	30,247
Future income tax asset (note 4)	17,500	—
	702,505	784,644
Capital assets – net (note 5)	2,346,599	2,355,145
Other assets		
Long-term investments (note 6)	65,501	80,058
Deferred charges	147,997	47,733
Future income tax asset (note 4)	10,897	9,439
Goodwill (note 7)	418,286	452,616
	642,681	589,846
Total assets	$ 3,691,785	$ 3,729,635
LIABILITIES AND SHAREHOLDERS' EQUITY		
Current liabilities		
Bank indebtedness	$ 11,722	$ 46,826
Notes payable (note 8)	4,907	235,317
Payables and accruals	398,446	396,871
Long-term debt due within one year (note 9)	84,788	58,880
	499,863	737,894
Long-term debt (note 9)	1,460,741	1,509,391
Future income tax liability (note 4)	—	5,631
Accrued benefit obligation (note 10)	43,758	42,063
Deferred credits	15,878	8,767
Non-controlling interest (note 11)	71,738	82,486
Shareholders' equity		
Capital stock (note 12)	1,186,680	922,601
Contributed surplus	69,320	69,320
Retained earnings	343,807	351,482
	1,599,807	1,343,403
Total liabilities and shareholders' equity	$ 3,691,785	$ 3,729,635

See accompanying notes to the consolidated financial statements

Signed on behalf of the board of directors:

Charles White
Chairman

Edward Reevey
Director

EXHIBIT 12-19
PART B

ALIANT INC. (2001)

Consolidated statements of income

For the years ended December 31 (thousands of dollars)	2001	2000
Operating revenues (note 18)	$ 2,601,566	$ 2,274,180
Expenses		
Cost of operating revenues	710,639	565,901
Operating expenses	913,890	849,457
Depreciation and amortization	439,368	357,855
Restructuring charge (note 2)	111,237	—
	2,175,134	1,773,213
Operating income	426,432	500,967
Other income (expenses)	(16,821)	16,872
Interest charges		
Interest on long-term debt	148,732	106,729
Other interest	8,757	17,658
	157,489	124,387
Income before underlisted items	252,122	393,452
Income taxes (note 4)	145,023	183,890
Income before non-controlling interest	107,099	209,562
Non-controlling interest share of losses	(13,829)	(7,559)
Net income	$ 120,928	$ 217,121
Earnings per common share (note 19)		
Basic	$ 0.84	$ 1.65
Diluted	$ 0.83	$ 1.64

See accompanying notes to the consolidated financial statements

Consolidated statements of retained earnings

For the years ended December 31 (thousands of dollars)	2001	2000
Balance, beginning of year	$ 351,482	$ 253,636
Net income	120,928	217,121
Preferred share dividends	(6,619)	—
Common share dividends	(121,984)	(119,275)
Balance, end of year	$ 343,807	$ 351,482

ALIANT INC. (2001)

Consolidated statements of cash flows

EXHIBIT 12-19
PART C

For the years ended December 31 (thousands of dollars)	2001	2000
Cash and cash equivalents from (used in) operations		
Net income	$ 120,928	$ 217,121
Add (deduct) non-cash items		
Depreciation and amortization	441,987	359,049
Other non cash items	(57,305)	(23,424)
Share in losses of equity accounted investments	6,217	1,141
Non-controlling interest share of losses	(13,829)	(7,559)
	497,998	546,328
Change in non-cash working capital balances related to operations	10,111	(76,628)
	508,109	469,700
Cash and cash equivalents from (used in) financing		
Proceeds from issue of preferred shares	172,264	—
Proceeds from issue of common shares	91,815	231,188
Proceeds from long-term debt	155,323	552,639
Repayment of long-term debt	(208,225)	(171,941)
Sale (repurchase) of accounts receivable	150,000	(50,000)
Preferred dividends	(6,619)	—
Common dividends	(121,984)	(119,275)
Increase in non-controlling interest	3,081	60,327
Increase (decrease) in notes payable	(216,372)	66,611
	19,283	569,549
Cash and cash equivalents from (used in) investing		
Capital expenditures	(465,642)	(437,665)
Decrease in other deferred charges	(51,455)	(22,103)
Proceeds on sale of investments	68,918	93,865
Purchase of subsidiaries' net assets and goodwill (note 3)	(2,539)	(582,482)
Non-controlling interest acquired	—	(22,821)
Investments	9,496	(15,667)
	(441,222)	(986,873)
Change in cash and cash equivalents	86,170	52,376
Cash and cash equivalents, beginning of period	33,666	(18,710)
Cash and cash equivalents, end of period	$ 119,836	$ 33,666
Cash and cash equivalents consist of:		
Cash and short term investments	$ 131,558	$ 80,492
Bank indebtedness	(11,722)	(46,826)
	$ 119,836	$ 33,666
Supplementary disclosure		
Interest paid	$ 165,693	$ 126,246
Income taxes paid	$ 202,787	$ 185,641

ALIANT INC. (2001)

NOTE 12
Capital stock
Authorized
Unlimited number of preference shares, issuable in series.
Unlimited number of common shares.

Issued

(thousands of dollars)		2001			2000
	Number of shares	Value	Number of shares		Value
Preference shares, series 2	7,000,000	$ 172,264	—	$	—
Common shares without par value	137,526,147	1,014,416	134,336,983		922,601
		$1,186,680		$	922,601

Beyond the Book

12-43 (Ratio analysis of a company)
Choose a company as directed by your instructor and answer the following questions:

a. Using the ratios given in the text, prepare an analysis of the company for the past two years with respect to performance, short-term liquidity, long-term liquidity, and earnings per share ratios.

b. Even though the ratios do not span a long period of time, discuss the financial health of the company. Would you invest in it? Why or why not?

Cases

12-44 Wineland Appliance Sales and Service Limited
Wineland Appliance Sales and Service Limited owns several retail and service centres in northern British Columbia. Financial ratios for the company for the years ended December 31, 2004 and 2003, are provided below. For comparative purposes, industry averages have also been provided.

Ratio	2004	2003	Industry average
Current ratio	1.6:1	1.7:1	2:1
Quick ratio	0.75:1	0.80:1	1:1
Accounts receivable turnover	8 times	7.75 times	12 times
Inventory turnover	4 times	3.8 times	7 times

The company is in the process of opening two new retail outlets and will need to obtain a line of credit to finance receivables and inventory. To receive a competitive interest rate on its line of credit, it needs to ensure that its liquidity ratios are close to the average for the industry. In particular, the company would like to see the current ratio at 2:1. The company has hired you, an independent consultant, to suggest how it might improve its liquidity ratios.

In preparing your report, you have gathered the following additional information:

1. The company's credit terms to its customers are net 45 days—no discounts are provided for early payment.

2. The company policy is to pay accounts payable every 45 days regardless of the credit terms. Many supplier invoices offer discounts for payments within 30 days.

3. Wineland's policy is to keep high amounts of inventory on hand to ensure that customers will have maximum selection.

Required:
Propose several steps that Wineland Appliance Sales and Services Ltd. might take to improve its liquidity. All suggestions must be ethical

12-45 Wildings Furniture and Guild Custom Furniture

Kelly Connors is considering investing in one of two furniture-manufacturing companies. The first company, Wildings Furniture, is a national manufacturer that has been in business for 25 years. It manufactures reasonably priced, comfortable furniture with a price range that is attractive to the general public. Retailers sell its furniture nationwide, including large department stores such as Sears Canada. After a slow start, Wildings has enjoyed considerable success over the past five years. The company is publicly traded and its shares are currently selling for $12.

The second company, Guild Custom Furniture, also manufactures furniture, but has traditionally catered to the more discriminating buyer who is willing to pay a high price for custom designs. Recently, however, the company has started to manufacture a variety of retail lines, but it is still very selective as to the retailers with whom it will deal. Retailers must meet high quality standards before they are able to carry the Guild brand. Guild has been in business for over 100 years. The company went public five years ago, which coincided with the decision to carry the retail lines of furniture. The movement to retail sales has been very successful for Guild Custom Furniture and the company's share price is now $32.

In order to make an informed investment decision, Kelly has obtained the most recent annual reports for both companies. She has summarized the following financial information for use in her analysis:

	Wildings Furniture (in thousands)	Guild Custom Furniture (in thousands)
Sales	$45,600	$6,798
Net Income	$3,200	$876
Average Inventory	$12,500	$1,542
Average Accounts Receivable	$4,700	$575
Average Current Assets	$29,450	$3,967
Average Total Assets	$36,475	$5,285
Average Current Liabilities	$13,658	$726
Average Total Liabilities	$16,266	$836
Average Common Shareholders' Equity	$20,209	$4,449

In addition to the above financial information, Karen learns that both companies make all of their sales on account and that the cost of sales is about 30% for Wildings and 40% for Guild. Both companies have a corporate tax rate of 30%. The most recent annual reports available to the public show that Wildings has 4,000,000 common shares outstanding while Guild has 500,000 common shares outstanding.

Through her research, Kelly has also obtained the following industry averages for furniture manufacturers:

Ratio	Industry Average
Current Ratio	4:1
Accounts Receivable Turnover	30 days
Inventory Turnover	180 days
Debt/Equity Ratio	25%
Return on Equity	22%
Earnings Per Share	$1.25
Price/Earnings Ratio	16 times

Required:

a. Based on raw data such as net income and sales, which company appears to be the better investment?

b. Prepare a ratio analysis of the two companies. Does your answer from part a) differ after studying the financial ratios?

c. Explain any difference between your answers in parts a) and b). Which approach offers the better analysis of these two companies? Why would the two analyses produce such different results?

12-46

Albert Long has just been awarded a large academic scholarship. Luckily, he had saved enough from his summer job to pay for his current year's expenses. Consequently, he has decided to invest the scholarship to maximize the funds he will have available for the next school year. Because he will need the money in about a year, Albert wants to invest in a fairly stable company and has decided that RBC Financial seems to be a very profitable investment.

Albert has obtained the company's annual report and has completed a very thorough ratio analysis. However, he has relied heavily on financial statements to perform the ratio analysis and only skimmed the other components of the annual report.

You are a good friend of Albert's and explain to him that, although ratio analysis will provide a good indication as to the financial strength of a company, there is much more information available that an informed investor should consider before making any investment decisions.

Required:

Albert has asked you to help him investigate the Royal Bank further. Other than ratio analysis, give him four examples of information that an investor might want to examine in order to fully understand a business. Where might such information be available?

12-47   Hencky Corporation

The management of Hencky Corporation is in the process of developing a loan proposal to present to a local investor. The company is looking for a $1-million loan to finance the research and development costs of producing a revolutionary new hand-held computer. Most of the loan proceeds will be spent on intangible costs, such as salaries, and this will therefore be a very risky investment. Because of the risk associated with the project, the investor is requiring some assurance that the company is currently solvent and operating as a going concern.

As the accountant for Hencky Corporation, you have used the most recent financial statements to calculate the following ratios:

	2004	2003
Current Ratio	1.8:1	1.7:1
Quick Ratio	1.10:1	1.08:1
Receivable Turnover	10 times	11 times
Inventory Turnover	6 times	5 times
Debt/Equity Ratio	25.2%	35.8%

Required:
Provide an explanation of how each of the above ratios should be interpreted and any indication they provide as to the company's solvency and ability to continue as a going concern.

Critical Thinking Questions

12-48   (Discussion of the value of comparability)
One of the qualitative characteristics underlying financial accounting is comparability. As you will recall, comparability refers to similarities of financial information between different companies, and consistency of the financial information produced by a company over time. Two of the many ways of achieving comparability are by limiting the number of different ways transactions may be recorded, and by specifying how assets, liabilities, equities, revenues, and expenses will be disclosed in the financial statements.

One of the arguments against comparability is that it limits the ability of companies to choose among accounting methods, and thus may result in disclosures that may not be agreeable to management or best suited to the particular circumstances.

Required:
Discuss the pros and cons of comparability, with reference to the analysis of financial statements.

12-49   (Use of subsidiaries to manage debt financing)
A major reason that companies such as General Motors form finance subsidiaries (separate companies that they control) is the potential to increase leverage as they seek ways to finance the manufacture and sale of their products. Such subsidiaries are referred to as "captive" finance subsidiaries.

Required:
Explain why a company that finances its operations through a subsidiary has greater debt capacity than a similar company that finances its operations internally.

PHOTO CREDITS

Care has been taken to trace ownership of copyright material contained in this textbook. The publisher will gladly take any information that will enable them to rectify any erroneous reference or credit in subsequent printings. Please note that products shown in photographs in this textbook do not reflect an endorsement by the publisher of those specific brand names.

All images copyright (c) 2002 Photo Disc, Inc., unless otherwise noted.

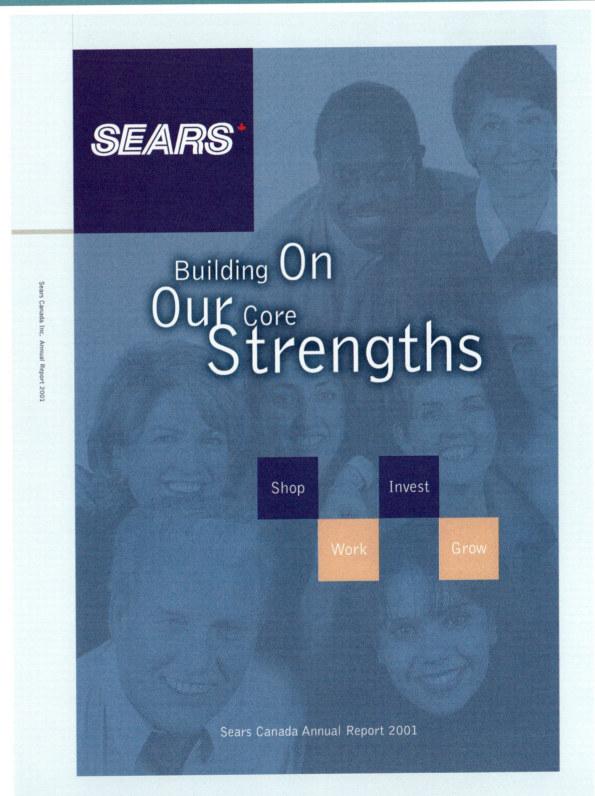

SEARS

Sears Canada Inc. Annual Report 2001

Building On Our Core Strengths

Shop

Invest

Work

Grow

Sears Canada Annual Report 2001

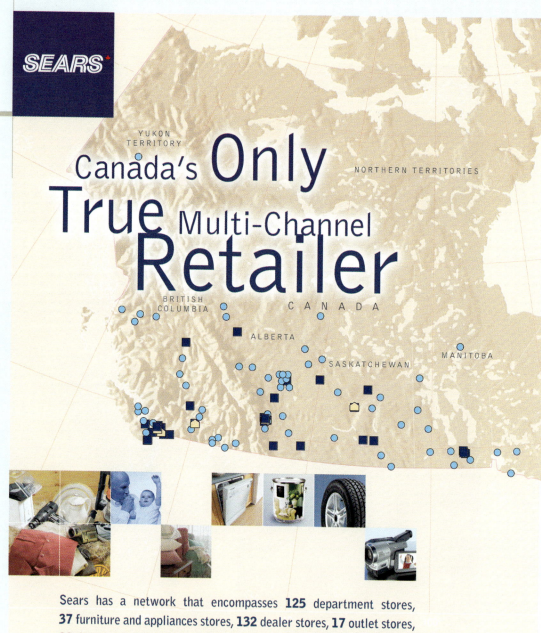

Sears has a network that encompasses **125** department stores, **37** furniture and appliances stores, **132** dealer stores, **17** outlet stores, **38** floor covering centers, **52** auto centers and **110** travel offices. Sears publishes Canada's largest general merchandise catalogue, offers online shopping at www.sears.ca and has over **2,157** catalogue/online order pick-up locations.

■ Department Stores	**125**	Locations
⌂ Furniture & Appliances Stores	**37**	Locations
○ Dealer Stores	**132**	Locations
▢ Catalogue	**2157**	Locations

Building On Our Core Strengths

In a very challenging year for the retail sector, our core values were our greatest asset. Throughout 2001, across the Company, across Canada, we continued to strive to be "A Great Place to Shop," "A Great Place to Work,"

"A Great Place to Invest" and a "Great Place to Grow". These goals are the driving force behind our business. They are the "Calls to Action" that shape all of our behaviours.

Building on Our Core Strengths

Canada's economy slowed throughout 2001. Further, the effects of a broad economic downturn were heightened by the tragic events of September 11th in the United States. All sectors of the economy were affected including the retail sector we occupy.

However, despite the weakness in consumer spending, Sears core strengths remained our most important focus.

We are Canada's only true multi-channel retailer. More than 93 per cent of Canadians live within a 10 minute drive of a Sears location. More fashion dollars are spent at Sears than at any other Canadian retailer, yet we also sell more furniture and appliances than any competitor. We publish the largest general merchandise catalogue in Canada and our web site, www.sears.ca, is Canada's preferred online retail destination.

Our core strengths and operating disciplines enabled the Company to respond quickly to decelerating market conditions. We moved aggressively to tighten merchandise assortments, bring inventory levels into line with consumer demand and reduced and reallocated expenses so as to be more efficient and strategically sound.

Despite a difficult year, Sears made considerable progress in positioning itself for the future. We continued to invest in our successful off mall formats, developed important new systems applications and continued to build on our unique capabilities with regard to e-commerce.

Contents Sears Canada Annual Report 2001

Financial Highlights

For the 52 week periods ended December 29, 2001 and December 30, 2000	2001	2000
Results for the year *(in millions)*		
Total revenues	$ 6,726	$ 6,356
Interest expense	64	66
Earnings before unusual items and income taxes	172	321
Unusual items gain	5	13
Income tax expense	83	108
Net earnings	94	226
Year end position *(in millions)*		
Working capital	$ 955	$ 687
Total assets	3,880	3,955
Shareholders' equity	1,620	1,549
Per share of capital stock *(in dollars)*		
Net earnings	$ 0.88	$ 2.12
Dividends declared	0.24	0.24
Shareholders' equity	15.18	14.55

Letter to Our Shareholders

"2001 was a challenging year for both the Company and the industry at large; a year characterized by a declining economy, considerable uncertainty and intense competition. While consumer confidence appears to be recovering from the impact of the tragic terrorist attacks of September 11th, it is still below the levels of the prior two years."

Mark A. Cohen, *Chairman and Chief Executive Officer*

Throughout the year, my first at the helm of the Company, we sought to re-assess our goals, tighten our merchandise assortments and more rigorously control our spending – efforts pointed at strengthening the fundamentals of our business. Growth remains imperative at Sears Canada, but growth that is profitable and sustainable over the longer-term.

I am pleased to report that, while we continue to face considerable challenges in this ever-changing, highly competitive retail environment, we have made substantial progress throughout 2001 in improving our underlying opportunity for success.

The Company recognized the adverse market conditions early in 2001 and began taking appropriate measures by focusing on inventory management as well as by reducing expenses and capital expenditures. For the year, we reduced expenses by almost $200 million from our original plan. Our inventory levels at the end of the year were $150 million less than the previous year. We also reduced capital expenditures by $57 million from plan and our total debt, net of cash, was down $88 million from last year.

We could not have made such important strides without the commitment of our 51,000 associates. They have been supportive of new leadership and have stood behind our vision of building for the future with a renewed commitment to profitable growth, service excellence and expense management.

In keeping with our focus on business fundamentals and after careful consideration of all strategic alternatives, in mid-February we announced our decision to convert our Eatons department stores to the Sears banner by the end of July 2002. The Yorkdale Shopping Centre in Toronto and the Polo Park Shopping Centre in Winnipeg have both an Eatons and a Sears department store. The Company will determine which one of the two stores will be retained as a Sears store at each of these locations. We will continue to provide many of the top brands that our customers have favoured, while adding an assortment of Sears merchandise categories including major appliances, hardware, electronics and sporting goods.

Our strongest asset is our people. Their dedication, combined with their product knowledge and customer service orientation is unparalleled. They also have big hearts as evidenced when associates, customers and suppliers from across the country joined with the Company to raise money for the Canadian Red Cross appeal in support of families whose loved ones senselessly perished on September 11th. Sears contribution of $200,000 was met with an outpouring of support of $800,000 totalling $1 million.

Sears has been an integral part of the fabric of the Canadian business community and Canadian society for almost 50 years.

We will continue to grow by building on our core strengths and remaining focused on sustainable, profitable growth to provide our shareholders with the return on their investment that they expect and deserve.

As we continue to leverage the unique strengths of Sears Canada, we intend on retaining our hard-won industry leadership position as a Great Place to Shop, Work, Invest and Grow.

In closing, I would like to express our gratitude to an important member of our Board of Directors, Alf Powis, who retired from the Board after 22 years of distinguished service and dedication to the Corporation. We will miss his wise counsel and tireless dedication to the Company.

On a sadder note, I would like to extend our condolences to the family of Mr. James W. Button, who passed away in December 2001. Mr. Button was former President of Sears Canada, an active member of the Board for 17 years, and an honorary director of Sears Canada for 22 years.

Both Alf and Jim will remain an important part of Sears history.

[signature]

Mark A. Cohen
Chairman & Chief Executive Officer

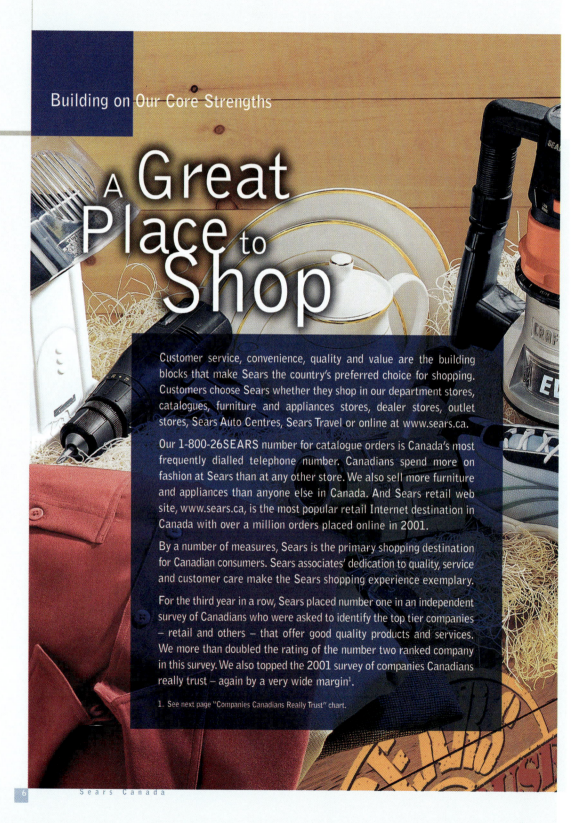

Building on Our Core Strengths

A Great Place to Shop

Customer service, convenience, quality and value are the building blocks that make Sears the country's preferred choice for shopping. Customers choose Sears whether they shop in our department stores, catalogues, furniture and appliances stores, dealer stores, outlet stores, Sears Auto Centres, Sears Travel or online at www.sears.ca.

Our 1-800-26SEARS number for catalogue orders is Canada's most frequently dialled telephone number. Canadians spend more on fashion at Sears than at any other store. We also sell more furniture and appliances than anyone else in Canada. And Sears retail web site, www.sears.ca, is the most popular retail Internet destination in Canada with over a million orders placed online in 2001.

By a number of measures, Sears is the primary shopping destination for Canadian consumers. Sears associates' dedication to quality, service and customer care make the Sears shopping experience exemplary.

For the third year in a row, Sears placed number one in an independent survey of Canadians who were asked to identify the top tier companies – retail and others – that offer good quality products and services. We more than doubled the rating of the number two ranked company in this survey. We also topped the 2001 survey of companies Canadians really trust – again by a very wide margin[1].

1. See next page "Companies Canadians Really Trust" chart.

Over 93 percent of Canadians are within a 10 minute drive of a Sears location. Sears exclusive brands – Kenmore, Craftsman, Nevada, Jessica and Diehard to name a few – enjoy national brand status among Canadians. Customer loyalty to these brands is an enduring competitive edge for Sears.

In 2001, Sears made several significant decisions to enhance the shopping experience for our customers. We introduced a Segmented Service program that addresses customers' needs for varying levels of service based on the products they want. Segmented Service adds more sales associates in customer areas that tend to require more knowledgeable and intensive customer service. At the same time, we relocated point-of-sale terminals to service multiple areas. This ensures faster and more efficient checkout for customers.

In 2001, we introduced better in-store information technology. This technology offers richer product information for customers and gives associates much better information to encourage better cross selling across product categories and business channels.

In our catalogue channel in 2001, Sears reduced the number of catalogues and redesigned them to make them easier to shop. Sears has 2,157 pick-up locations across the country and can deliver a catalogue order to almost all of them within 48 hours.

During the year, Sears announced new alliances with Pharmasave, Via Rail, Ticketking and Admission, a ticket agent in Quebec.

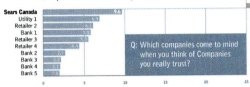

Companies Canadians Really Trust

Q: Which companies come to mind when you think of Companies you really trust?

NFO CF group multifacts study 7/01 - 1016 Canadians 18+, nationally representative

We also teamed up with Petro-Canada to offer customers the option of exchanging Petro-Points for Sears Club points and vice versa. Starting in March 2002, Sears Card holders can begin using their Sears Card as another payment option at more than 1,700 Petro-Canada stations nationwide.

These relationships enable Sears Card holders to earn Sears Club points on purchases of goods and services. Sears strategic partners also include Choice Hotels Canada, Roots Canada, Bell World, Bell Mobility, Bell Sympatico, AMJ Campbell Van Lines, Ticketmaster Canada, Medieval Times (Toronto, Ontario), and IBM Canada.

In this fiercely competitive retail environment, the quality and dedication of our associates gives Sears an important edge. As our customers' expectations grow, our associates must be increasingly professional and knowledgeable.

To give associates the tools they need to create a great shopping experience, we introduced a new associate development program in 2001 entitled Creating Customer Enthusiasm.

In 2001, more than 18,000 associates received training to build their leadership and customer service skills.

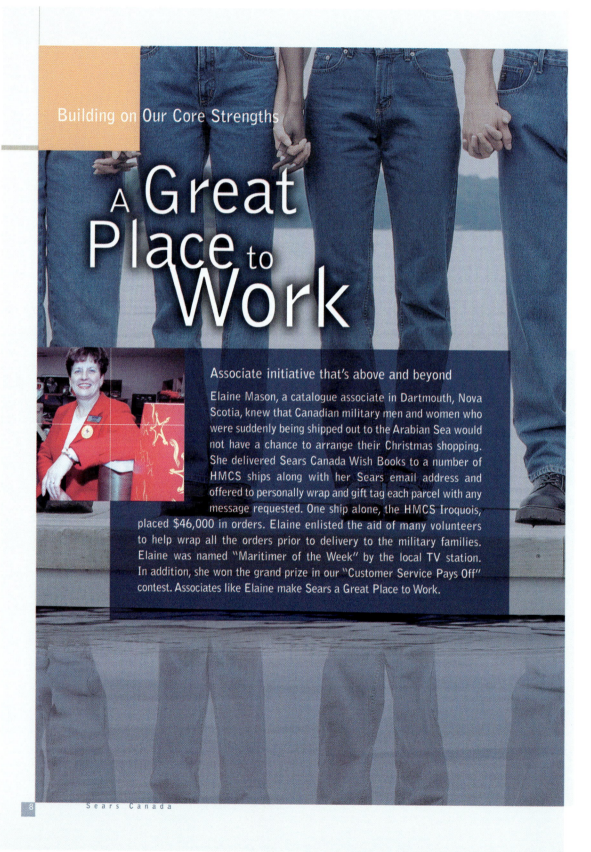

Building on Our Core Strengths

A Great Place to Work

Associate initiative that's above and beyond

Elaine Mason, a catalogue associate in Dartmouth, Nova Scotia, knew that Canadian military men and women who were suddenly being shipped out to the Arabian Sea would not have a chance to arrange their Christmas shopping. She delivered Sears Canada Wish Books to a number of HMCS ships along with her Sears email address and offered to personally wrap and gift tag each parcel with any message requested. One ship alone, the HMCS Iroquois, placed $46,000 in orders. Elaine enlisted the aid of many volunteers to help wrap all the orders prior to delivery to the military families. Elaine was named "Maritimer of the Week" by the local TV station. In addition, she won the grand prize in our "Customer Service Pays Off" contest. Associates like Elaine make Sears a Great Place to Work.

Companies Canadians Perceive as Offering Good Quality Products or Services

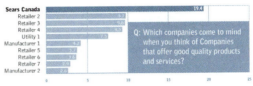

Q: Which companies come to mind when you think of Companies that offer good quality products and services?

NFO CF group multifacts study 7/01 - 1016 Canadians 18+, nationally representative

The value and connection of associate engagement to business success is well understood throughout Sears. Staying on top of what makes Sears a Great Place to Work is an ongoing priority. We know that just as customer expectations change, so do our associates' expectations of us. Our extensive survey process allows associates to assess their work environment and communicate with their manager and the Company so that we can respond quickly to their needs.

One example of the teamwork that helps make Sears a Great Place to Work was the way our associates rallied behind the organization during the 2001 holiday season. Our part-time associates enthusiastically agreed to increase their hours, which meant we were able to dramatically reduce the number of seasonal associates Sears normally hires. As a result of this dedication, we had our most experienced associates on the sales floor during peak demand periods, which translated into higher levels of service for our customers.

Companies Canadians Perceive as Having Good Customer Service

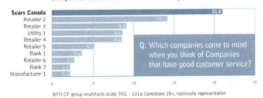

Q: Which companies come to mind when you think of Companies that have good customer service?

NFO CF group multifacts study 7/01 - 1016 Canadians 18+, nationally representative

The Company also has a number of programs that award service excellence, including the Gold Badge program. This is a prestigious award based on customer ratings on dimensions of customer attention, knowledge of associates, handling of out of stocks and the checkout process. Ratings are accumulated at the store level and recognize excellent levels of customer service throughout the entire store.

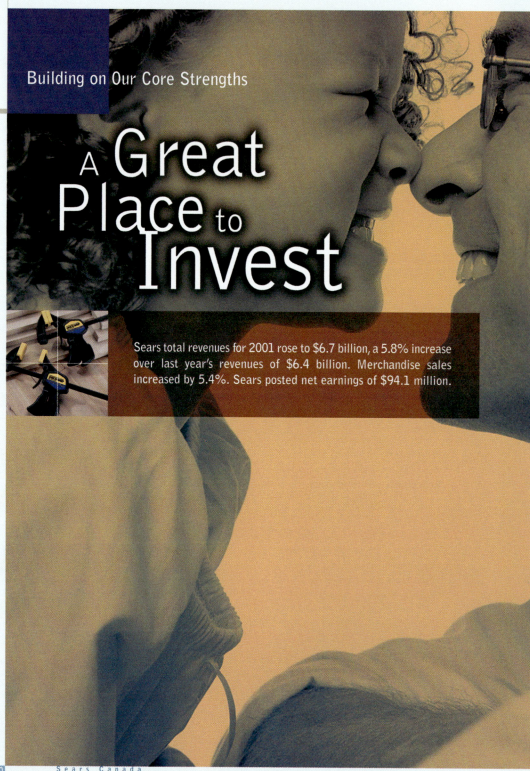

Building on Our Core Strengths

A Great Place to Invest

Sears total revenues for 2001 rose to $6.7 billion, a 5.8% increase over last year's revenues of $6.4 billion. Merchandise sales increased by 5.4%. Sears posted net earnings of $94.1 million.

The Company has invested resources to become more productive and efficient by finding ways to take costs out of our system, while constantly increasing our customer satisfaction levels. We took aim at inventory, one of our largest manageable assets, and by year-end had brought overall inventories down by $150 million. New technology now enables us to report on the profitability of every sales transaction. We believe this will provide significant added performance improvement.

We developed an ambitious department store remodeling program that will be launched in 2002. It will create a regular cycle of sales floor refreshment, with opportunities for enhanced revenues. This program, once underway, will enable us to refresh or remodel every one of our stores at reasonable cost every seven years. As well, we continued fine-tuning our two state-of-the-art distribution facilities in Vaughan, Ontario and in Calgary, Alberta.

We continued to leverage our existing assets, encouraging greater cross-channel shopping activity by increasing our associates' awareness of our multi-channel capabilities. This has proven to be a highly effective strategy, with the number of customers who purchase across all channels increasing from 99,000 in 1999 to 270,000 in 2001.

Technological improvements are helping us achieve incremental sales, support cost reduction in various areas of our business and improve customer service. For example, in 2001, we successfully transformed our call centre operations from an order-taking approach to a selling mode. This gives our call centre associates greater up sell and cross sell ability. Sears expects this initiative to result in $30 million of incremental sales annually.

Sears Canada has over 70% of Canadian homes in its databases, a considerable competitive advantage. More than 38% of all Canadian households receive Sears catalogues and the Sears Card is Canada's number one, single-issue proprietary credit card. More than 60% of our sales are charged to the Sears Card.

Because of these capabilities, Sears Canada is well positioned to respond as the economy and consumer confidence rebound.

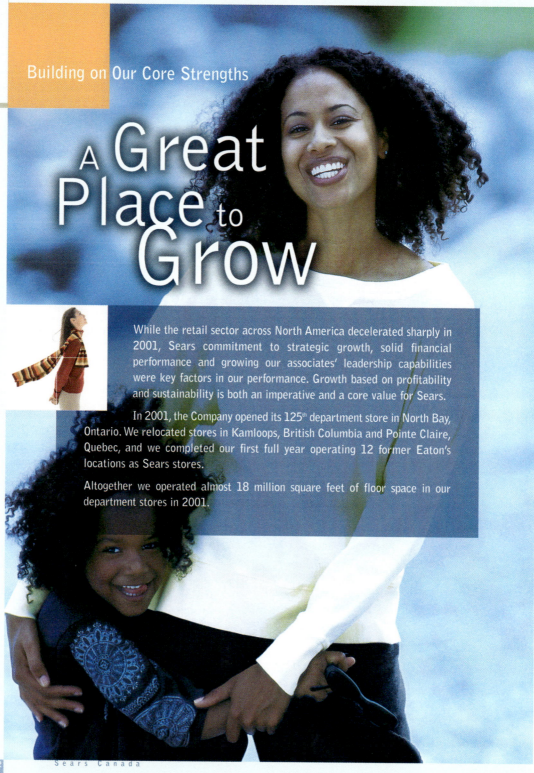

Building on Our Core Strengths

A Great Place to Grow

While the retail sector across North America decelerated sharply in 2001, Sears commitment to strategic growth, solid financial performance and growing our associates' leadership capabilities were key factors in our performance. Growth based on profitability and sustainability is both an imperative and a core value for Sears.

In 2001, the Company opened its 125th department store in North Bay, Ontario. We relocated stores in Kamloops, British Columbia and Pointe Claire, Quebec, and we completed our first full year operating 12 former Eaton's locations as Sears stores.

Altogether we operated almost 18 million square feet of floor space in our department stores in 2001.

We finalized expansion plans for our large distribution centres in Vaughan, Ontario and Calgary, Alberta. Operations at these centres, designed to enhance our ability to serve customers more quickly, were optimized in 2001. At the same time, we began construction of a terminal facility in Port Coquitlam, British Columbia to consolidate a number of secondary facilities in that province.

Sears off mall channel was a strong performer in 2001, including furniture and appliances stores, dealer stores and outlet stores. The Company opened four new Sears Furniture and Appliances Stores, in Saskatoon, Windsor, Moncton and Victoria. We expanded six furniture stores to include our Sears Brand Central selection of major appliances. We will convert our last furniture-only store in Whitby, Ontario to add major appliances when it is moved to a larger location in 2002. The Company plans to open six new furniture and appliances stores in 2002.

We opened eight new dealer stores in 2001. We also opened four new outlet stores to strengthen our ability to offer more customers a broad assortment of value-priced retail and catalogue surplus goods.

We closed 14 poorly performing auto centres in 2001 in order to focus efforts on improving profitability for the 52 remaining auto centres across the country.

We opened a new Sears HomeCentral showroom in 2001 and added service and repair programs for major appliances sold by other retailers.

Our travel business was considerably affected by the decline in the travel industry following September 11th. By the end of the year, however, bookings began to recover.

We also acquired a state-of-the-art web site, Tripeze.com. Our customers can now book travel via the Internet, by phone, or by visiting one of our Sears stores.

Sears online channel, www.sears.ca, was a bright spot, receiving over a million online orders in 2001.

We also grew our leadership capabilities internally. Over 70% of our managers completed leadership programs, while our associates grew their capabilities by participating in continuous learning programs offered by the Company.

Building on Our Core Strengths

Showing
We
Care

Whether it be a crippling ice storm, a raging flood or the tragic terrorist attacks of September 11th, Sears and its associates have been there to help in a meaningful way. We also have ongoing programs that contribute significantly to Canadian communities.

Sears Young Futures Program is a multifaceted program focused on promoting the positive development of children and youth. Sears worked with local charity partners to contribute over $3 million in cash and in kind to support the efforts of this program in 2001. Included in the total sum donated to children's charities was the more than $500,000 raised from Sears fourth annual plush toy program.

In addition to the above, Sears associates have the opportunity to give to charities of their choice through the Sears Employees Charitable Fund (SECF). The SECF raised over $1 million in 2001 through lump sum donations or payroll deductions.

2001 Financial Information

MD&A and Financial Highlights

2001 was a challenging year for Sears Canada, but the Company responded proactively to a slowing economy by reducing inventory and expense levels. Investments were made in new systems that will lead to greater inventory productivity, and enable the Company to respond quickly to an economic recovery.

The decision made in February 2002 to convert the Eatons department stores to the Sears banner reflects the Company's response to changing customer demand and the weaker than anticipated financial performance of these seven stores. This conversion is expected to improve future earnings and enable the Company to focus on long-term profitable growth through leveraging the strength and marketing reach of the Sears brand.

The Company's renovation and upgrade plan for its department stores, the continued growth of Sears off-mall channels, the Company's national network of catalogue selling locations and distribution capabilities, and the value, trust, and quality associated with Sears products and services positions the Company to continue to capture additional market share, and increase shareholder value in the future.

John T. Butcher
Executive Vice-President and Chief Financial Officer

Eleven Year Summary[1]

Fiscal Year	2001	2000	1999	1998	1997	1996	1995	1994	1993	1992	1991
Results for the Year *(in millions)*											
Total revenues[2]	$6,726	$6,356	$5,777	$5,132	$4,752	$4,120	$4,027	$4,168	$4,138	$4,147	$4,259
Depreciation and amortization	169	130	113	96	78	78	74	67	69	70	56
Earnings (loss) before unusual											
items and income taxes	172	321	345	269	215	70	43	88	15	(101)	(31)
Unusual items gain (loss)	5	13	–	–	–	(45)	(21)	(5)	(5)	(46)	(8)
Earnings (loss) before											
income taxes	177	334	345	269	215	25	22	83	10	(147)	(39)
Income taxes (recovery)	83	108	145	123	99	16	10	38	6	(56)	(10)
Net earnings (loss)	94	226	200	146	116	9	12	45	4	(91)	(29)
Dividends declared	26	26	26	25	25	23	23	23	23	21	20
Capital expenditures	143	447	231	142	160	63	76	60	37	55	235
Year End Position *(in millions)*[3]											
Accounts receivable	$ 872	$ 942	$1,070	$1,100	$1,225	$1,033	$ 926	$1,324	$1,101	$ 909	$1,090
Inventories	865	1,015	814	716	624	476	492	541	545	611	676
Capital assets	1,189	1,199	984	868	825	744	763	800	813	941	997
Total assets	3,880	3,955	3,767	3,198	3,007	2,734	2,554	2,949	2,746	2,796	3,069
Working capital	955	687	516	898	971	741	661	1,016	888	885	1,112
Debt	813	699	686	844	848	817	789	1,253	947	1,063	1,245
Shareholders' equity	1,620	1,549	1,346	1,164	1,042	949	856	867	845	863	900
Per Share of Capital Stock *(in dollars)*											
Net earnings	$ 0.88	$ 2.12	$ 1.88	$ 1.38	$ 1.10	$ 0.09	$ 0.13	$ 0.47	$ 0.05	$ (1.04)	$ (0.34)
Dividends declared	0.24	0.24	0.24	0.24	0.24	0.24	0.24	0.24	0.24	0.24	0.24
Shareholders' equity	15.18	14.55	12.67	10.98	9.84	8.98	9.02	9.13	8.90	9.10	10.67
Financial Ratios[2,3]											
Return on average											
shareholders' equity (%)	5.9	15.6	15.9	13.3	11.7	1.0	1.4	5.3	0.5	(10.3)	(3.1)
Current ratio	1.7	1.4	1.3	1.7	1.9	1.7	1.7	2.0	2.0	2.1	2.4
Return on total revenues (%)	1.4	3.6	3.5	2.8	2.4	0.2	0.3	1.1	0.1	(2.2)	(0.7)
Debt/Equity ratio	33/67	31/69	34/66	42/58	45/55	46/54	48/52	59/41	53/47	55/45	58/42
Pre-tax margin (%)	2.6	5.3	6.0	5.2	4.5	0.6	0.5	2.0	0.2	(3.5)	(0.9)
Number of Selling Units											
Department stores	125	125	110	109	110	110	110	110	110	109	106
Furniture stores	37	33	25	20	8	4	1	0	0	0	0
Outlet stores	17	15	12	12	8	9	10	11	12	13	15
Dealer stores	132	128	110	93	79	60	19	4	0	0	0
Catalogue selling locations	2,157	2,103	2,005	1,898	1,752	1,746	1,623	1,542	1,483	1,579	1,701

1   Certain amounts have been restated to reflect accounting changes related to the consolidation of the Company's proportionate share of the assets, liabilities, revenues and expenses of real estate joint ventures as recommended by the Canadian Institute of Chartered Accountants. The change in policy, effective in 1995, has been applied retroactively.

2   Total revenues and cost of merchandise sold have been restated to reflect new guidance on recording of revenues. Revenues relating to the travel business and licensed department businesses are now recorded in revenues net of cost of sales. The restatement had no impact on net earnings. The change in policy, effective in 2000, has been applied retroactively.

3   The 1999 balance sheet has been restated to reflect the finalization of the accounting for the acquisition of Eaton's.

Management's Discussion & Analysis

Sears offers Canadian consumers a diverse array of shopping options, with department and specialty stores, Canada's largest general merchandise catalogue, a comprehensive website, and a broad range of home-related services. The Company emphasizes quality, value, and service in appealing to a broad cross-section of Canadian consumers.

The Company's vision is to be Canada's most successful retailer by providing customers with total shopping satisfaction, associates with opportunities for career advancement and personal growth, and shareholders with superior returns on their investment.

Overview of Consolidated Results

For purposes of this discussion, "Sears" or the "Company" refers to Sears Canada Inc. and its subsidiaries, together with the Company's proportionate share of the assets, liabilities, revenues and expenses of joint venture interests in shopping centres.

The 2001 fiscal year refers to the 52 week period ended December 29, 2001 and, comparatively, the 2000 fiscal year refers to the 52 week period ended December 30, 2000.

The following table summarizes the Company's operating results for 2001 and 2000.

(in millions, except per share amounts)	2001	2000
Total revenues	$ 6,726.4	$ 6,355.8
Earnings before interest, unusual items and income taxes	236.2	388.0
Interest expense	64.2	66.4
Unusual items (gain)	(5.5)	(12.5)
Earnings before income taxes	177.5	334.1
Income taxes	83.4	108.3
Net earnings	$ 94.1	$ 225.8
Earnings per share	$ 0.88	$ 2.12

The Company reported earnings before interest, income taxes and unusual items of $236.2 million, a decrease of 39.1% from 2000. Included in this year's results is a pre-tax gain of $54.0 million from the sale of charge account receivables under the Company's securitization program.

Effective July 1, 2001, the Company adopted prospectively the new recommendations of the Canadian Institute of Chartered Accountants for recording the sale of securitized receivables. These recommendations require that gains or losses on the transfer of receivables be recognized at the time of sale. Additional information is found in Note 3 to the Financial Statements.

The 17 new department store locations opened in 2000 completed their first year of operations in 2001, and the Company's results reflect the additional fixed costs associated with the increased square footage. Merchandise sales were weaker than expected, and gross margins were under pressure throughout the year as a result of intense competition in the Canadian retail environment.

Over the course of 2001, a number of economic factors affected the Canadian retail environment. The economic slowdown that started late in 2000 continued into 2001, with the economy exhibiting recessionary characteristics. In 2001, growth in GDP and consumer spending was at a five-year low, unemployment rose, and demand for Canadian exports weakened. However, the year ended on a positive note, with interest rates at record low levels, continuing strength in housing starts and re-sales, and healthy gains in personal disposable income. Consumer confidence, although below 1999 and 2000 levels, appeared to recover from the impact of September 11.

The Company recognized the adverse market conditions early, and focused on productivity by reducing inventory, operating expenses, and capital expenditures throughout 2001. Ending inventory levels were $150.7 million lower than in 2000, operating expenses were more than $180.0 million below originally anticipated levels, and capital expenditures were $57.0 million below the 2001 plan. The Company believes that its early recognition of, and response to, the adverse market conditions will better enable it to benefit from any improvement in the economy.

Management's Discussion & Analysis

Unusual Items

The Company realized a gain of $8.3 million on the sale of its Underhill distribution facility in Vancouver, British Columbia, and incurred a charge of $2.8 million related to the closing of 14 of its 66 auto centres in the fourth quarter.

(in millions)	2001	2000
Gain on sale of distribution facility	$ 8.3	$ –
Cost of closing 14 auto centres	(2.8)	–
Gain on sale of shopping centre investments	–	25.3
Cost of exiting gas bar operations	–	(7.6)
Costs related to the restructuring of distribution operations	–	(3.4)
Other restructuring initiatives	–	(1.8)
Unusual gain	$ 5.5	$ 12.5

Number of Associates

	2001	2000
Full-time associates	13,363	13,906
Part-time associates	37,189	42,433
Total associates	50,552	56,339

In light of the uncertain economic environment, the Company offered more hours of work to its associates rather than hiring a large seasonal component as is customary. The reduction in full-time associates was largely due to attrition. These changes are reflected in a 10.3% reduction in the size of the workforce from last year.

Segmented Business Analysis

The Company's operations are classified into three major businesses: merchandising, credit, and real estate joint venture operations.

Merchandising Operations

(in millions)	2001	2000
Revenues	$ 6,290.5	$ 5,971.4
Earnings before interest, unusual items, and income taxes	$ 87.9	$ 280.9
Average capital employed	$ 1,333.4	$ 1,038.3

The merchandising segment includes the Company's department stores, catalogue operations, furniture and appliances stores, dealer stores, and outlet stores, as well as the products and services offered under the Sears HomeCentral banner and on the website, www.sears.ca.

Merchandising revenues were $6.3 billion in 2001, an increase of 5.3% over 2000. Most of the growth was related to the increase in new merchandise selling space added late in the year 2000. Same store sales decreased by 0.4%. During the year, several merchandise categories exhibited strong performance, including jewellery, cosmetics, major appliances, and women's wear. Weak sales were experienced in children's wear, and bed and bath.

Merchandising earnings before interest, unusual items, and income taxes were $87.9 million, compared to $280.9 million in 2000. Higher costs associated with additional selling space, surplus inventory at the beginning of the year, and weaker than expected sales and gross margins contributed to the decline in merchandising earnings.

The Canadian retailing environment remains highly competitive. The trend of lower gross margins started to abate late in the third quarter, but remained below expectations. The Company also reduced the level of inventory over the course of the year, and expects to improve inventory productivity further in 2002.

On February 18, 2002, the Company announced that it had made a decision to convert its Eatons department stores to the Sears banner by the end of July 2002. The seven Eatons department stores are located in Toronto and Ottawa, Ontario; Vancouver and Victoria, British Columbia; Winnipeg, Manitoba; and Calgary, Alberta. The Yorkdale Shopping Centre in Toronto, Ontario, and the Polo Park Shopping Centre in Winnipeg, Manitoba have both an Eatons and a Sears department store. The Company will determine which store will be retained as a Sears store at each of these locations.

The decision to convert the stores was made after careful consideration of strategic alternatives and was based on current conditions in the Canadian retail environment and changes in consumer spending, as well as a customer base and financial performance that were below expectations.

The conversion is expected to have a positive impact on future earnings through the reduction of corporate overhead, advertising costs, and improved margins. A one-time, pre-tax charge will be recorded in the first quarter of 2002 for an estimated amount of $180 million, consisting of $30 million in cash for severance payments, third party commitments, and closing costs, and a $150 million non-cash write-down of fixtures and leasehold improvements. Also refer to "Note 18 – Subsequent Event" on page 48.

Operating these seven locations under the Sears banner will better leverage the Company's buying and advertising efforts, and will take advantage of the equity of the Sears brand. By focusing on the Sears brand, the Company believes it will be better able to meet its long-term business goal of sustained and profitable growth.

Merchandising Revenues by Region

(in millions)	2001	% of Total	% of Total Households[1]	2000	% of Total	% of Total Households[1]
Atlantic	$ 551.3	9%	7.5%	$ 576.0	10%	7.6%
Quebec	1,177.1	19%	25.4%	1,153.9	19%	25.6%
Ontario	2,648.9	42%	36.7%	2,540.7	43%	36.6%
Prairies	1,151.9	18%	16.6%	1,034.8	17%	16.6%
BC/Territories[2]	761.3	12%	13.8%	666.0	11%	13.6%
Total	**$ 6,290.5**	100%	100%	$ 5,971.4	100%	100%

1   MapInfo Compusearch Estimates, based on Statistics Canada data.

2   Territories include the Yukon, Northwest and Nunavut.

The regional distribution of merchandising revenues for 2001 was similar to that in 2000. Growth was greatest in western Canada, while there was some reduction in eastern Canada. The addition of new merchandise selling space late in 2000 and the regional differences in the strength of the Canadian economy influenced the different rates of growth.

Number of Selling Units

As at December 29, 2001

	Atlantic	Quebec	Ontario	Prairies	BC and Territories	2001 Total	2000 Total
Department Stores	11	27	52	18	17	**125**	125
Furniture & Appliances	2	9	19	3	4	**37**	33
Dealer	18	17	32	49	16	**132**	128
Outlet	1	1	12	2	1	**17**	15
Catalogue	327	542	594	495	199	**2,157**	2,103

Department Stores – 125 department stores ranging in size from 25,757 to 702,629 square feet. In 2001, the Company opened one new Sears department store in North Bay, Ontario and closed a Sears department store in Edmonton, Alberta. Two Sears department stores were relocated in 2001: one in Pointe Claire, Quebec, and the other in Kamloops, British Columbia. In 2002, the Company plans to open a new Sears department store in Cambridge, Ontario, and in Montreal (Rosemere), Quebec. The Company also plans to relocate its Sears department store in Sarnia, Ontario, in 2002.

Management's Discussion & Analysis

Furniture and Appliances Stores – 37 stores ranging in size from 34,244 to 61,253 square feet and featuring an expanded selection of furniture, decorator rugs, and major appliances. Four new stores were opened 2001: Saskatoon, Saskatchewan; Windsor, Ontario; Moncton, New Brunswick; and Victoria, British Columbia. Appliances were added to six furniture stores that previously did not carry them. Appliances will be added to the Whitby, Ontario location when it moves to larger premises in 2002. Appliances will be featured in all furniture stores after this move. The Company plans to open six new furniture and appliances stores in 2002.

Dealer Stores – 132 independent, locally operated stores serving smaller population centres, selling home appliances and electronics, as well as lawn and garden furniture, garden and snow removal equipment, and in 18 locations, furniture. Eight new dealer stores were opened in 2001: High River, Drumheller, Olds, Canmore, and Athabasca, Alberta; Winkler, Manitoba; Digby, Nova Scotia; and Perth, Ontario. Three dealer stores were closed in Ontario in 2001: North Bay, Fort Frances, and Bowmanville, and one dealer store was closed in Fort McMurray, Alberta. The Company plans to open eight new dealer stores in 2002.

Outlet Stores – 17 stores ranging in size from 31,934 to 195,000 square feet, selling returned and surplus merchandise.

Catalogue Selling Locations – consist of 1,839 independent catalogue agent locations, plus catalogue selling locations within 118 Sears department stores, and selected outlet stores, dealer stores, and furniture and appliances stores.

Early in 2002, the Company announced that it will not be renewing the leases on its Sears department stores located in Welland and St. Thomas, Ontario, and Rouyn-Noranda, Quebec. The Welland and St. Thomas stores will be closed by the end of 2002, while the Rouyn-Noranda store will be closed early in 2003. It is the Company's intention to maintain a presence in these markets by opening a dealer store in each of these communities. The Company also announced that it plans to convert its Sears department store in Surrey, British Columbia to an outlet store in May 2002.

Merchandising Gross Floor Area

(square feet - in millions)	**2001**	2000
Sears Department Stores	**15.4**	15.4
Eatons Department Stores	**2.4**	2.4
Furniture	**1.7**	1.5
Outlet	**1.6**	1.4
Total	**21.1**	20.7
Merchandise service centres:		
Active	**7.8**	8.3
Subleased or dormant	**0.8**	1.4
Total merchandise service centres	**8.6**	9.7

Recent Merchandising Initiatives

- In 2001, the Company implemented new merchandise productivity software that provides detailed information about merchandise sales and gross profit performance at the item level. Traditionally, retail applications tend to aggregate information into general product categories. The new system provides greater detail in a timely fashion, will indicate which products are in high demand and the locations in which they are needed, and will lead to a more profitable merchandising mix. The Company believes that this is leading-edge technology for the retail sector.

- The Company implemented its Segmented Service program, which involved a re-definition of roles and responsibilities of its retail sales associates, as well as the relocation of the point of sale terminals within the department stores. This program is based on the customer's need for different levels of service across departments, and is designed to increase customer satisfaction with service levels.

- Working with Ryerson University in Toronto, Ontario, the Company enhanced its comprehensive training program for furniture and appliances store managers and associates. This program was used as the foundation to create a similar program to provide training across the dealer store network.

- The Company focused on delivering a more streamlined catalogue to its customers. The catalogue offerings in 2002 will have fewer pages, an improved layout and presentation, and a more focused selection of goods.

- New software was installed in the Company's call centres to facilitate the customer order process and to provide sales associates the opportunity to offer the customer additional products that complement the customer's order.

- The Company developed a renovation and upgrade plan for its department stores, with each store planned to be renovated over the course of a seven year cycle. Each store falls into one of four different upgrade categories, with improvements ranging from simple re-touching to a complete re-design. Ten stores are expected to be renovated in 2002 under this new plan.

- In July 2001, Sears opened a new Sears HomeCentral showroom in Windsor, Ontario. At the end of 2001, there were six Sears HomeCentral showroom locations, and the Company plans to open four more in 2002. These showrooms feature home products and services including windows, window coverings, doors and floor coverings, gas fireplaces, and kitchen and bath vignettes, and complement the wide assortment of Sears HomeCentral services such as appliance repairs, parts, heating and cooling services, and carpet cleaning.

- The Company opened five new Sears Floor Covering Centres in 2001, bringing the total number of locations to 38. In 2002, the Company plans to open 15 locations. The concept of combining the expertise of the independent, local floor covering merchant with the trust and convenience associated with shopping at Sears has been well received by customers.

- In September 2001, after evaluating the profitability of its auto centres, the Company decided to close 14 auto centres and focus on the remaining 52 auto centres to improve the performance of the automotive channel.

- In 2002, the Company plans to implement a program which will provide detailed information on the effectiveness of marketing expenditures.

Credit Operations

(in millions)	2001	2000
Service charge revenue before gain on sale of receivables	$ 325.8	$ 308.3
Gain on sale of receivables	54.0	–
Revenues	$ 379.8	$ 308.3
Earnings before interest, unusual items, and income taxes	$ 118.9	$ 70.0
Average capital employed	$ 850.1	$ 893.0

Sears credit operations finance and manage customer charge account receivables generated from the sale of goods and services charged on the Sears Card and on the Eatons Card.

Through its securitization program, the Company securitizes customer charge account receivables in order to obtain a more favourable overall cost of funding. The cost of the funding related to the securitization program is deducted from the total service charge revenues earned on the portfolio. (Refer to the section entitled "Securitization of Charge Account Receivables" on page 24).

Net service charge revenues earned on customer charge account receivables increased by $71.5 million or 23.2% in 2001, and includes a gain of $54.0 million on the sale of customer charge account receivables as a result of adopting prospectively the new recommendations of the Canadian Institute of Chartered Accountants for the sale of securitized receivables.

Credit operations contributed $118.9 million to the Company's 2001 consolidated earnings before interest, unusual items, and income taxes, compared to $70.0 million in 2000. The increase in earnings is primarily attributed to the above-mentioned gain on the sale of charge account receivables.

Net write-offs as a percentage of the average amounts outstanding were 4.1% in 2001 compared to 4.0% in 2000 and 3.2% in 1999. This write-off rate continues to be at the low end of industry norms. The Company maintains a low write-off rate through continued innovation of its portfolio management strategies.

Management's Discussion & Analysis

Charge Account Receivables Analysis

(in millions - except average outstanding account balance per customer)	2001	2000
Active customer accounts	4.3	4.3
Average outstanding balance per customer account at year end	$ 445	$ 459
Charge account receivables written-off during the year (net of recoveries)	$ 74.2	$ 70.2

Sears continues to have the largest single-issuer proprietary card in Canada. Sears accepts third party credit cards in addition to the Sears Card and Eatons Card. Debit cards are accepted in all of the Company's department stores, furniture and appliances stores, dealer stores, and outlet stores. The chart below reflects the trend in method of payment.

	2001	2000
Sears Card & Eatons Card	60.5%	61.5%
Third Party Credit Cards	15.6%	14.3%
Debit Cards	8.5%	7.9%
Cash	15.4%	16.3%
Total	100.0%	100.0%

Recent Credit Initiatives

The following initiatives have been directed at increasing usage of the Sears Card:

- Sears continues to form strategic alliances with other companies to enhance the benefits offered by the Sears Card and Sears Club to cardholders. In 2001, Sears announced new alliances with Via Rail, Pharmasave, TicketKing, and Admission, a ticketing agent in Quebec. These relationships enable Sears Card holders to earn Sears Club points on purchases of goods and services. Sears strategic partners also include Choice Hotels Canada, Bell World, Bell Mobility, Bell Sympatico, AMJ Campbell Van Lines, Ticketmaster Canada, Medieval Times (Toronto, Ontario), Roots Canada, and IBM Canada.

- In August 2001, the Company announced an initiative that offers Sears Club and Petro-Points members the value-added option to exchange their points between the two loyalty programs. In March 2002, the Company plans to add Petro Canada to its list of strategic partners so that in addition to points exchange, customers will be able to use their Sears Card to pay for purchases at Petro Canada, and earn valuable Sears Club points.

- In 2001, SearsConnect launched paging and cellular services in response to customer demand for wireless offerings. SearsConnect was created in 1998 through the combination of Sears PhonePlan and Sears EasyTalk, which provide flat rate long distance calling services. All services provided by SearsConnect earn Sears Club points.

- Sears continues to invest in technology in order to increase customer convenience. In 2001, Sears completed the preliminary phases of a new customer data warehouse. In addition, Sears will be developing a new credit platform in 2002 for implementation in early 2003. These initiatives will enable the Company to better tailor its products and services to meet the needs of its customers.

- In January 2002, the Company announced that it is formulating a strategic plan to enable the issuance of a general purpose credit card in addition to the Sears Card.

- The Eatons Card will be accepted at Sears and Eatons locations both during and after the conversion of the Eatons department stores to the Sears banner. Refer to the section "Merchandising Operations" on pages 18 and 19 for information relating to the Company's decision to convert the Eatons department stores.

Real Estate Joint Venture Operations

(in millions)	2001	2000
Revenues[3]	$ **56.1**	$ 76.1
Earnings before interest, unusual items, and income taxes	$ **29.4**	$ 37.1
Average capital employed	$ **156.9**	$ 208.6

3 Excluded from revenues is the Company's proportionate share of rental revenues earned from department stores of Sears Canada Inc. of $3.0 million (2000 - $3.8 million).

As at December 29, 2001, the Company held joint venture interests in 16 shopping centres, 14 of which contain a Sears store. The Company has 15% to 50% interests in these joint ventures. Accordingly, the Company carries its proportionate share of the assets, liabilities, revenues and expenses of these joint ventures on its books.

The Company sold its interests in three properties in 2000. The sale of its interests in Shops on Steeles, Markham, Ontario; Northumberland Mall, Cobourg, Ontario; and St. Laurent Shopping Centre in Ottawa, Ontario, was completed on March 31, 2000, December 1, 2000, and December 11, 2000, respectively. The Sears department stores at these shopping centres continue to operate as leased locations. No significant transactions took place in 2001.

The market value of Sears interest in its real estate joint venture properties is estimated to be approximately $324 million (2000 - $320 million). It is the Company's policy to have one-third of the properties independently appraised each year, while the appraisals of the remaining two-thirds are reviewed and updated by management. Sears portion of the debt of these properties is $145.3 million (2000 - $158.8 million).

Overview of the Consolidated Statements of Financial Position

Assets

(in millions)	2001	2000
Cash	$ **329.3**	$ 135.5
Accounts receivable	**871.9**	942.0
Inventories	**864.5**	1,015.2
Capital assets	**1,188.7**	1,199.2
Other assets	**625.6**	663.1
Total assets	$ **3,880.0**	$ 3,955.0

Accounts Receivable

(in millions)	2001	2000
Charge account receivables - current	$ **1,885.9**	$ 1,949.3
Charge account receivables - deferred	**755.7**	737.9
Managed accounts	**2,641.6**	2,687.2
Less: co-ownership interest held by third parties	**(1,804.2)**	(1,813.7)
Co-ownership retained by the Company	**837.4**	873.5
Interest-only strip receivable	**36.1**	–
Miscellaneous receivables	**(1.6)**	68.5
Total	$ **871.9**	$ 942.0

Total assets decreased by $75.0 million or 1.9% in 2001.

Cash increased by $193.8 million primarily due to proceeds of $276.6 million received from the securitization of charge account receivables on November 1, 2001.

Current receivables decreased by $63.4 million, or 3.3% while deferred receivables increased by $17.8 million or 2.4%. Deferred receivables represent credit sales not yet billed to customer accounts. Deferred credit sales are billed to customer accounts at the end of an interest-free deferral period.

Year-end inventories decreased by $150.7 million, or 14.8% as a result of the Company's efforts to improve inventory productivity.

Liabilities

(in millions)	2001	2000
Accounts payable	$ **769.9**	$ 974.6
Accrued liabilities	**422.1**	440.3
Long-term obligations due within one year	**10.1**	152.5
Long-term obligations	**802.7**	546.1
Other liabilities	**255.3**	292.2
Total liabilities	$ **2,260.1**	$ 2,405.7

Total liabilities decreased by $145.6 million or 6.1% in 2001.

Management's Discussion & Analysis

Accounts payable decreased by $204.7 million in 2001 as a result of the reduction in merchandise purchased by the Company in the latter part of the year.

Including amounts due within one year, long-term obligations increased by $114.2 million due to the issuance of $200.0 million in medium-term notes on March 15, 2001, upon maturity of $100.0 million of unsecured debentures.

The decrease in other liabilities is related to the recognition of a portion of the deferred credit arising from the acquisition of The T. Eaton Company Limited (Eaton's). Please refer to the section "Acquisition of Tax Loss – Eaton's" on page 27 for a detailed explanation.

Liquidity

As at December 29, 2001, the ratio of current assets to current liabilities was 1.7:1 compared to 1.4:1 at the end of 2000. Working capital was $955.6 million as at December 29, 2001, compared to $686.8 million as at December 30, 2000.

Financing Activities

The Company has the flexibility to raise funds through bank borrowings, by issuing equity and corporate debt securities, and through the securitization of charge account receivables.

In 2001, the Company carried out the following significant financing activities:

- On March 1, 2001, the outstanding 7.8% unsecured debentures of Sears Canada Inc. in the amount of $100 million matured and were repaid.

- On March 15, 2001, Sears Canada Inc. issued $200 million of 6.75% medium term notes due March 15, 2006 under the shelf prospectus filed on February 9, 2001 that qualified the issuance of up to $500 million in medium term notes (debt with a term to maturity in excess of one year) over the subsequent two years.

- On April 1, 2001, a 4.95% interest rate swap in the principal amount of $150 million matured.

- On August 16, 2001, a new securitization vehicle, SCORE Trust, was established. (See SCORE Trust in the section titled "Securitization of Charge Account Receivables".)

- On September 5, 2001, SCORE Trust completed its initial financing by issuing $504.5 million in commercial paper and $44.7 million in subordinated notes.

- On November 1, 2001, SCORE Trust issued $260 million in senior notes and $16.6 million in subordinated notes.

- During 2001, $53.7 million of joint venture debt matured, of which $40.1 million was refinanced.

Securitization of Charge Account Receivables

Securitization is an important financing vehicle which enables the Company to obtain favourable interest rates because of its structure and the high quality of the portfolio of charge account receivables backing its debt. Securitization provides the Company with a diversified source of funds for the operation of its business.

Under the Company's securitization programs, undivided co-ownership interests in the charge account receivables (excluding deferred receivables) are sold to Sears Canada Receivables Trust (Trust 1) and Sears Canada Receivables Trust - 1992 (Trust 2), and undivided co-ownership interests in its portfolio of charge account receivables (including deferred receivables) are sold to Sears Canada Receivables Trust - 1996 (Trust 3), (collectively referred to as SCRT) and to SCORE Trust.

The assets and liabilities of these trusts are not reflected in the Company's consolidated financial statements. The cost to the Company of the securitization program is reflected as a reduction in the Company's share of Sears Card and Eatons Card service charge revenues. Since July 1, 2001, as a result of prospectively adopting new recommendations of the Canadian Institute of Chartered Accountants, a gain or loss is recognized on the transfer of receivables at the date of transfer. For balances transferred prior to July 1, 2001, and subsequent transfers committed to before that date, the Company will continue to follow the previous accounting guidance, and will not recognize any gains or losses at the date of transfer. As at December 29, 2001, $852.0 million of the securitized receivables were subject to these new rules.

Trust 1 – Trust 1, which was established in 1991, issued short-term commercial paper and subordinated debentures to finance the purchase of undivided co-ownership interests in charge account receivables (excluding deferred receivables). As a result of the creation of SCORE Trust, Trust 1 was terminated on December 31, 2001.

Trust 2 – Trust 2, which was established in 1993, issued long-term senior and subordinated debentures to finance the purchase of undivided co-ownership interests in charge account receivables (excluding deferred receivables). As a result of the creation of SCORE Trust, it is expected that new debt will no longer be issued by Trust 2.

Trust 3 – Trust 3, which was established in 1996, finances the purchase of undivided co-ownership interests in charge account receivables (including deferred receivables) through drawdowns under revolving senior and subordinated note facilities. There may be further drawdowns under these facilities.

SCORE Trust – On August 16, 2001, SCORE Trust, a new securitization vehicle, was established. This new vehicle will expand the Company's ability to finance both current and deferred charge account receivables. SCORE Trust will issue both short and long-term senior and subordinated debt backed by undivided co-ownership interests in a designated pool of charge account receivables (including deferred receivables). On September 5, 2001, SCORE Trust launched its initial financing through the issuance of $504.5 million in commercial paper and $44.7 million in subordinated notes, the proceeds of which were used to purchase an undivided co-ownership interest in receivables. On November 1, 2001, SCORE Trust issued $260.0 million in senior notes and $16.6 million in subordinated notes.

Summary of Securitized Obligations

(in millions)	2001	2000
Commercial paper	$ 393.1	$ 385.3
Senior debt:		
Floating rate, due April 1, 2001	–	150.0
5.34%, due December 16, 2003	150.0	150.0
8.95%, due June 1, 2004	175.0	175.0
5.42%, due December 15, 2004	200.0	200.0
6.681%, due June 15, 2005	250.0	250.0
Floating rate, due June 30, 2006	243.0	390.1
5.035%, due November 15, 2006	260.0	–
	1,278.0	1,315.1
Subordinated debt:		
9.18%, due June 1, 2004	3.9	3.9
Floating rate, due 2001 to 2005	74.7	50.5
Floating rate, due June 30, 2006	2.5	4.0
6.235%, due November 15, 2006	16.6	–
	97.7	58.4
Accrued liabilities	0.6	5.1
Trust units (floating rate, due 2003 to 2006)	34.8	49.8
Total obligations	$ 1,804.2	$ 1,813.7

Debt Ratings

On February 20, 2001, Standard and Poor's (S&P) announced its A- harmonized corporate credit and senior unsecured debt rating for the Company. On November 16, 2001, S&P downgraded this debt rating to BBB+.

Dominion Bond Rating Service Limited (DBRS) has assigned a BBB (High) rating for the Company's senior unsecured debt.

Management's Discussion & Analysis

Analysis of Funding Costs

The following table summarizes the Company's total funding costs, including the cost of the securitization program:

(in millions)	2001	2000
Interest costs		
Total debt at end of year	$ 812.8	$ 698.6
Average debt for year	771.0	786.0
Interest expense	64.2	66.4
Average rate of debt	8.3%	8.4%
Securitization costs		
Amount securitized at end of year	$ 1,804.2	$ 1,813.7
Average amount securitized for year	1,805.8	1,576.3
Cost of funding[4]	101.9	99.7
Average rate of securitized funding	5.6%	6.3%
Total funding		
Total funding at the end of year	$ 2,617.0	$ 2,512.3
Total average funding for year	2,576.8	2,362.3
Total funding costs for year	166.1	166.1
Average rate of total funding	6.4%	7.0%

4   *Reported as a reduction of credit revenues.*

Average total funding increased by $214.5 million in 2001, but total funding costs remained at 2000 levels as a result of lower short-term interest rates.

Capital Structure

(in millions)	2001	% of Total	2000	% of Total
Long-term debt due within one year	$ 10.1	0.4	$ 152.5	6.8
Long-term debt	802.7	33.0	546.1	24.3
Total debt	812.8	33.4	698.6	31.1
Shareholders' equity	1,619.9	66.6	1,549.3	68.9
Total capital	$ 2,432.7	100.0	$ 2,247.9	100.0

The Company's debt to equity ratio increased in 2001, but remained within the Company's target levels.

Normal Course Issuer Bid

On October 31, 2001, the Company announced its intention to purchase for cancellation up to 5% of its issued and outstanding common shares, representing up to 5,336,681 of the issued and outstanding common shares. The purchases were eligible to commence on November 2, 2001 and must terminate by November 1, 2002 pursuant to the Notice of Intention filed with The Toronto Stock Exchange. The price which the Company will pay for any such shares will be the market price at the time of acquisition.

By purchasing common shares under this Normal Course Issuer Bid, the Company intends to offset the dilutive effect of common shares issued as equity-based compensation of employees and directors and may purchase additional common shares if, in the opinion of management, the additional purchases can be made on terms that enhance the value of the remaining common shares.

As at February 27, 2002, the Company has not purchased any shares under the Normal Course Issuer Bid. Shareholders may obtain a copy of the Notice of Intention, without charge, by contacting the Secretary.

Capital Expenditures

The Company expects to commit approximately $200.0 million for capital expenditures in 2002, compared to actual capital expenditures of $143.4 million in 2001 and $447.3 million in 2000. Throughout 2001, the Company focused on containing capital expenditures. Capital expenditures in 2000 were higher than customary levels due to the significant expansion of merchandise space resulting from the launching of the Eatons banner and the opening of new store locations.

Analysis of Total Taxes

Total taxes decreased by $8.8 million in 2001. Income taxes decreased by $24.9 million primarily as a result of lower operating income and corporate tax rates.

(in millions)	2001	2000
Provincial capital tax	$ 8.5	$ 8.6
Property tax	65.0	53.5
Payroll taxes[5]	95.1	90.4
Total taxes expensed in cost of merchandise sold, operating administrative and selling expenses	168.6	152.5
Corporate income taxes	83.4	108.3
Total taxes	$ 252.0	$ 260.8

5 *Represents contributions to the Canada and Quebec Pension Plans, Employment Insurance, health care levies and workplace insurance premiums.*

Acquisition of Tax Loss - Eaton's

On December 30, 1999, the Company acquired all of the outstanding common shares of Eaton's. The acquisition included 19 Eaton's store locations and selected other assets, including intellectual property and future income tax assets.

The future income tax assets acquired were valued at $310.0 million, which exceeded the total acquisition cost by $130.0 million. This amount was recorded as a deferred credit and is recognized proportionally as a reduction to income taxes as the future income tax asset is drawn down. Income taxes for the year 2001 included a charge of $20.9 million related to a reduction in the valuation of future income tax assets due to lower income in the current period and lower statutory rates of tax for future years. This is net of recognition of $15.1 million of the deferred credit relating to the acquisition of Eaton's. In addition, income taxes were reduced by the recognition of $16.8 million of the deferred credit.

Included in the acquisition cost is $20.0 million, which is payable to former Eaton's shareholders, contingent upon realization of the Eaton's tax losses. This amount was deposited into an escrow account in July 2001.

Risks and Uncertainties

Eaton's Tax Losses

Management believes the Company will be entitled to realize the Eaton's tax losses. In the event that the utilization of Eaton's tax losses is disallowed, tax reductions claimed in prior periods, plus applicable interest, would become payable. These amounts, and any related amounts remaining in the future income tax asset, would be recorded as tax expense in the then current year.

Interest Rates

Through the Company's securitization vehicles (SCRT, SCORE Trust) purchases of undivided co-ownership interests in the portfolio of charge account receivables are financed with the issuance of short-term commercial paper, long-term debt, and trust units, some of which are subject to floating interest rates. To reduce the risk associated with fluctuating interest rates, floating-to-fixed interest rate swap transactions in the notional amount of $100 million (2000 - $250 million) have been utilized. This brings the Company's fixed-to-floating funding ratio, including securitized funding, to 71/29, which is within the Company's target ratios.

Foreign Exchange

The Company's foreign exchange risk is limited to currency fluctuations between the Canadian and U.S. dollar. The Company's forecast for its total requirement of foreign funds in 2002 is approximately U.S. $500 million. From time to time the Company uses forward contracts to fix the exchange rate on a portion of its expected requirement for U.S. dollars. As at December 29, 2001, there were no foreign exchange contracts outstanding.

Management's Discussion & Analysis

Concentration of Credit Risk

The Company's exposure to credit risk relates mainly to customer charge account receivables. Sears Card customers are a large and diverse group. The average balance per customer account at year-end was $445.

Leases

The Company owns 19 Sears department store locations, one Eatons store location, and one furniture and appliances store location. The Company expects that store rental expense will remain stable since most of its remaining locations are held under long-term leases.

Merchandise Sources

A major aim of the merchandise procurement process is to ensure that Sears, together with its merchandise sources, fulfills its promises and obligations to its customers. Sears will continue to work with its merchandise sources to ensure that they share this commitment.

Sears is confident in its ability to continue providing consumers with high quality merchandise at competitive prices. While the Company purchases most of its consumer goods through Canadian companies, Sears shops the world to provide its customers with the best value for their dollar.

Competitive and Economic Environment

Retail sales are influenced by changes in economic variables and consumer confidence. There are a number of external factors which affect economic variables and consumer confidence over which the Company exerts no influence, including interest rates, personal debt levels, unemployment rates, and levels of personal disposable income.

The past year has been a challenging one, not only for the Company, but also for the economy in general. Consumer confidence appears to have recovered from the impact of September 11, but still remains below the level of the prior two years. Consumers are expected to continue to be cautious in their spending. The Company believes that the economy will continue to be difficult during 2002, with some recovery anticipated in the latter half of the year.

The Canadian retail market remains highly competitive. The Company's competitors include traditional Canadian department stores, discount department stores, "big box" retailers, and specialty stores that offer alternative retail formats to traditional department stores.

Outlook

Sears continues to position itself to capture a larger share of consumer spending through its program of store renovations and expansions, by offering an enhanced merchandise assortment and presentation, and through its adoption of emerging trends in retailing.

Sears strengths include an extensive customer reach and one of the strongest brands in Canada. Through the conversion of its Eatons store locations to the Sears banner, the Company expects to broaden its customer appeal in these seven urban locations through leveraging the Sears brand and the Company's strengths as a multi-channel retailer.

By meeting the needs of customers in terms of merchandise selection, pricing, store environment, and service, Sears anticipates growth in revenues and profits into the future.

Forward Looking Statements

A number of matters discussed in this Management's Discussion and Analysis and elsewhere in this Annual Report that are not historical or current facts deal with potential future circumstances and developments. Discussion of such matters is qualified by the inherent risks and uncertainties surrounding future expectations generally, which discussion also may materially differ from the Company's actual future experience involving any one or more of such matters.

Quarterly Results (Unaudited)

(in millions except per share amounts)	First Quarter		Second Quarter		Third Quarter		Fourth Quarter	
	2001	2000	**2001**	2000	**2001**	2000	**2001**	2000
Total revenues	**$ 1,427.3**	$ 1,329.0	**$ 1,584.6**	$ 1,462.0	**$ 1,581.7**	$ 1,456.0	**$ 2,132.8**	$ 2,108.8
Earnings (loss) before income taxes	**$ (17.2)**	$ 41.3	**$ 17.5**	$ 65.8	**$ 33.1**	$ 61.5	**$ 144.1**	$ 165.5
Net earnings (loss)	**$ (11.2)**	$ 23.5	**$ 8.8**	$ 45.9	**$ 17.9**	$ 36.2	**$ 78.6**	$ 120.2
Earnings (loss) per share	**$ (0.10)**	$ 0.22	**$ 0.08**	$ 0.43	**$ 0.17**	$ 0.34	**$ 0.73**	$ 1.13

Common Share Market Information*

	First Quarter		Second Quarter		Third Quarter		Fourth Quarter	
	2001	2000	**2001**	2000	**2001**	2000	**2001**	2000
High	**$ 26.95**	$ 42.50	**$ 25.00**	$ 37.50	**$ 24.09**	$ 36.00	**$ 19.15**	$ 34.00
Low	**$ 19.92**	$ 33.00	**$ 18.55**	$ 32.80	**$ 12.50**	$ 32.00	**$ 13.03**	$ 19.60
Close	**$ 20.00**	$ 34.05	**$ 21.80**	$ 34.25	**$ 13.85**	$ 34.00	**$ 18.75**	$ 21.55
Avg. daily trading volume	**227,635**	136,898	**86,177**	155,500	**162,651**	90,833	**265,786**	201,959

* The Toronto Stock Exchange

Statement of Management Responsibility

The accompanying consolidated financial statements of Sears Canada Inc. and all information in this Annual Report are the responsibility of management. The consolidated financial statements and the information contained in this Management's Discussion and Analysis have been approved by the Board of Directors. The consolidated financial statements have been prepared in accordance with Canadian generally accepted accounting principles and include certain amounts that are based on estimates and judgments. Financial information used elsewhere in the Annual Report is consistent with that contained in the consolidated financial statements.

Management is responsible for the accuracy, integrity, and objectivity of the financial statements and has developed, maintains, and supports an extensive program of internal controls and audits that provide reasonable assurance that financial records are reliable and that assets are safeguarded.

The Board of Directors carries out its responsibility for the financial statements in this Annual Report principally through the activities of its Audit Committee, all of whom are outside Directors. In monitoring the fulfillment by management of its

responsibilities for financial reporting and internal control, the Audit Committee meets periodically with senior officers, finance management, and internal and external auditors to discuss audit activities, internal accounting controls, and financial reporting matters. The Audit Committee has reviewed these consolidated financial statements and has recommended their approval by the Board of Directors.

The Company's external auditors, Deloitte & Touche LLP, have conducted audits of the financial records of the Company in accordance with Canadian generally accepted auditing standards.
Their report is as follows.

*Executive Vice-President and
Chief Financial Officer*

*Chairman of the Board and
Chief Executive Officer*

Auditors' Report to the Shareholders of Sears Canada Inc.

We have audited the consolidated statements of financial position of Sears Canada Inc. as at December 29, 2001 and December 30, 2000 and the consolidated statements of earnings, retained earnings and cash flows for the 52 week periods then ended. These financial statements are the responsibility of the Company's management. Our responsibility is to express an opinion on these financial statements based on our audits.

We conducted our audits in accordance with Canadian generally accepted auditing standards. Those standards require that we plan and perform an audit to obtain reasonable assurance whether the financial statements are free of material misstatement. An audit includes examining, on a test basis, evidence supporting the amounts and disclosures in the financial statements. An audit also includes assessing the accounting principles used and significant estimates made by

management, as well as evaluating the overall financial statement presentation.

In our opinion, these consolidated financial statements present fairly, in all material respects, the financial position of the Company as at December 29, 2001 and December 30, 2000 and the results of its operations and its cash flows for the 52 week periods then ended in accordance with Canadian generally accepted accounting principles.

Deloitte & Touche LLP
Chartered Accountants

*Toronto, Ontario
February 4, 2002,
except as to Note 18
which is as of
February 27, 2002*

Consolidated Statements of Financial Position

As at December 29, 2001 and December 30, 2000 (in millions)	2001	2000
Assets		
Current Assets		
Cash and short-term investments	$ 329.3	$ 135.5
Accounts receivable (Note 2)	871.9	942.0
Inventories	864.5	1,015.2
Prepaid expenses and other assets	123.3	117.2
Current portion of future income tax assets (Note 4)	110.3	206.9
	2,299.3	2,416.8
Investments and Other Assets *(Note 5)*	81.5	71.3
Capital Assets *(Note 6)*	1,188.7	1,199.2
Deferred Charges *(Note 7)*	157.8	138.0
Future Income Tax Assets *(Note 4)*	152.7	129.7
	$ 3,880.0	$ 3,955.0
Liabilities		
Current Liabilities		
Accounts payable	$ 769.9	$ 974.6
Accrued liabilities	422.1	440.3
Income and other taxes payable	127.9	109.3
Principal payments on long-term obligations due within one year (Note 9)	10.1	152.5
Current portion of deferred credit (Note 4)	13.7	53.3
	1,343.7	1,730.0
Long-term Obligations *(Note 9)*	802.7	546.1
Deferred Credit *(Note 4)*	61.7	54.0
Future Income Tax Liabilities *(Note 4)*	52.0	75.6
	2,260.1	2,405.7
Shareholders' Equity		
Capital Stock *(Note 10)*	457.7	455.6
Retained Earnings	1,162.2	1,093.7
	1,619.9	1,549.3
	$ 3,880.0	$ 3,955.0

Approved by the Board:

M.A. Cohen
Director

J.H. Bennett
Director

Consolidated Statements of Earnings

For the 52 week periods ended December 29, 2001 and December 30, 2000
(in millions, except per share amounts)

	2001	2000
Total revenues	$ 6,726.4	$ 6,355.8
Cost of merchandise sold, operating, administrative and selling expenses	6,320.9	5,838.0
Depreciation and amortization	169.3	129.8
Interest	64.2	66.4
Unusual items (gain) (Note 11)	(5.5)	(12.5)
	6,548.9	6,021.7
Earnings before income taxes	177.5	334.1
Income taxes (Note 4)		
Current	62.0	15.9
Future	21.4	92.4
	83.4	108.3
Net earnings	$ 94.1	$ 225.8
Earnings per share (Note 17)	$ 0.88	$ 2.12
Diluted earnings per share (Note 17)	$ 0.88	$ 2.11

Consolidated Statements of Retained Earnings

For the 52 week periods ended December 29, 2001 and December 30, 2000
(in millions)

	2001	2000
Opening balance	$ 1,093.7	$ 893.5
Net earnings	94.1	225.8
	1,187.8	1,119.3
Dividends declared and paid	(25.6)	(25.6)
Closing balance	$ 1,162.2	$ 1,093.7

Consolidated Statements of Cash Flows

For the 52 week periods ended December 29, 2001 and December 30, 2000
(in millions)

	2001	2000
Cash Flows Generated From (Used for) Operations		
Net earnings	$ 94.1	$ 225.8
Non-cash items included in net earnings, principally depreciation, amortization,		
gain on sale of receivables and future income taxes	118.8	166.6
Changes in non-cash working capital balances related to operations (Note 12)	28.8	(82.0)
	241.7	310.4
Cash Flow Generated From (Used for) Investment Activities		
Purchases of capital assets	(143.4)	(447.3)
Proceeds from sale of capital assets	17.7	84.5
Charge account receivables	56.1	132.3
Deferred charges	(13.4)	(2.2)
Acquisition of Eaton's	(23.5)	(141.0)
Investments and other assets	(7.3)	(10.3)
	(113.8)	(384.0)
Cash Flow Generated From (Used for) Financing Activities		
Issue of long-term obligations	200.0	320.5
Repayment of long-term obligations	(110.6)	(236.7)
Net proceeds from issue of capital stock	2.1	2.8
Dividends paid	(25.6)	(25.6)
	65.9	61.0
Increase (decrease) in cash and short-term investments	193.8	(12.6)
Cash and short-term investments at beginning of year	135.5	148.1
Cash and short-term investments at end of year	$ 329.3	$ 135.5

Notes to the Financial Statements

1. Summary of Accounting Policies

Principles of Consolidation

The consolidated financial statements include the accounts of Sears Canada Inc. and its subsidiaries together with its proportionate share of the assets, liabilities, revenues and expenses of real estate joint ventures (the "Company").

Fiscal Year

The fiscal year of the Company consists of a 52 or 53 week period ending on the Saturday closest to December 31. The fiscal years for the consolidated statements presented for 2001 and 2000 are the 52 week periods ended December 29, 2001 and December 30, 2000, respectively.

Cash & Short Term Investments

Cash and short term investments include all highly liquid investments with maturities of three months or less at the date of purchase.

Inventories

Inventories are valued at the lower of cost and net realizable value. Effective December 31, 2000, the Company changed its method of determining cost for retail store inventories from the retail inventory method to the average cost method, based on individual items. This change, applied retroactively, resulted in no material changes to the consolidated statements of financial position, results of operations, or cash flows in the current or preceding periods. Catalogue order and miscellaneous inventories are valued by the average cost method, based on individual items.

Prepaid Advertising Expense

Catalogue production costs are deferred and amortized over the life of each catalogue on the basis of the estimated sales from that catalogue.

Transfer of Receivables

Effective July 1, 2001, the Company adopted, on a prospective basis, the new accounting guideline, Accounting Guideline - 12 Transfers of Receivables, issued by The Canadian Institute of Chartered Accountants. For balances transferred prior to July 1, 2001, and subsequent transfers committed to before that date, the Company will continue to follow the previous accounting guidance, and will not recognize any gains or losses at the date of transfer. Under the new policy, the Company recognizes gains or losses on transfers of receivables that qualify as sales and recognizes certain financial components that are created as a result of such sales, which consist primarily of the retained interest in the form of a cash reserve account and the retained rights to future excess yield from the transferred receivables (interest-only strip). A gain or loss on sale of the receivables depends in part on the previous carrying amount of the receivables involved in the transfer, allocated between the assets sold and the retained interests based on their relative fair value at the date of transfer. Retained interests are initially recorded at fair value, which is estimated based upon the present value of the expected future cash flows and discount rates. Any subsequent decline in the value of the retained interest, other than a temporary decline, will be recorded as a reduction to income. The impact of the change in 2001 was an increase in net earnings of $32.4 million.

Deferred Receivables

Deferred receivables represent credit sales not yet billed to customer accounts. Service charges are not accrued on these accounts over the deferral period which generally ranges from 6 to 24 months.

Capital Assets

Capital assets are stated at cost. Depreciation and amortization provisions are generally computed by the straight-line method based on estimated useful lives of 2 to 10 years for equipment and fixtures, and of 10 to 40 years for buildings and improvements.

The Company's proportionate share of buildings held in joint ventures is generally depreciated by the sinking fund method over 20 to 40 years.

The Company capitalizes interest charges for major construction projects and depreciates these charges over the life of the related assets.

Associate Future Benefits

The Company maintains a defined benefit, final average pension plan which covers substantially all of its regular full-time associates as well as some of its part-time associates. The plan provides pensions based on length of service and final average earnings. The Company provides life insurance, medical and dental benefits to eligible retired associates. The Company has adopted the following accounting policies:

- The cost of pensions and other retirement benefits earned by associates is actuarially determined using the projected benefit method pro-rated on service and management's best estimate of expected plan investment performance, salary escalation, retirement ages of associates and expected health care costs.

- For the purpose of calculating the expected return on plan assets, those assets are valued at market value.

- Past service costs from plan amendments are amortized on a straight-line basis over the average remaining service period of associates active at the date of amendment.

- The excess of the net actuarial gain (loss) over 10% of the greater of the accrued benefit obligation and the fair value of plan assets is amortized over the average remaining service period of active associates. The average remaining service period of the active associates covered by the pension plan is eight years. The average remaining service period of the active associates covered by the other retirement benefits plan is 13 years.

Deferred Charges

The cumulative excess of contributions to the Company's pension plan over the amounts expensed is included in deferred charges.

Debt issuance costs are deferred and amortized by the straight-line method to the due dates of the respective debt issues. Securitization set up costs are amortized on a straight-line basis over a maximum of five years.

Other costs are deferred and amortized by the straight-line method over the remaining life of the related asset.

Foreign Currency Translation

Obligations payable in U.S. dollars are translated at the exchange rate in effect at the balance sheet date or at the rates fixed by forward exchange contracts.

Transactions in foreign currencies are translated into Canadian dollars at the rate in effect on the date of the transaction.

Estimates

The preparation of the Company's financial statements, in accordance with Canadian generally accepted accounting principles, requires management to make estimates and assumptions that affect the reported amounts of assets and liabilities and disclosure of contingent assets and liabilities at the date of the financial statements and the reported amounts of revenue and expenses during the reporting period. Actual results could differ from those estimates.

Earnings per Share

Effective December 31, 2000, the Company elected early adoption, on a retroactive basis, of the new recommendations issued by The Canadian Institute of Chartered Accountants relating to the calculation of earnings per share. Earnings per share is calculated using the weighted average number of shares outstanding during the period. Under the new standard, the diluted earnings per share calculation increases the number of shares used in the calculation, determined using the treasury stock method. The impact of the adoption of the new accounting standard, resulted in no change to the calculation of diluted earnings per share for the 52 week period ended December 30, 2000.

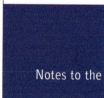

Notes to the Financial Statements

Revenue Recognition

Revenues from merchandise sales and services are net of estimated returns and allowances, exclude sales taxes and are recorded upon delivery to the customer. Revenues relating to the travel business and licensed department businesses are recorded in revenues net of cost of sales.

Finance charge revenues are recorded on an accrual basis, including unbilled finance charges based on actual finance charges on the most recent billing cycles.

Joint venture revenues are recorded based on monthly rentals.

The Company sells extended service contracts with terms of coverage generally between 12 and 36 months. Revenues from the sale of these contracts are deferred and amortized in proportion to the anticipated expenses.

Comparative Figures

Certain of last year's figures have been reclassified to conform with the current year's presentation.

2.   Accounts Receivable

(in millions)	2001	2000
Charge account receivables - current	$ **1,885.9**	$ 1,949.3
Charge account receivables - deferred	**755.7**	737.9
Managed accounts	**2,641.6**	2,687.2
Less: co-ownership interest held by third parties (Note 3)	**(1,804.2)**	(1,813.7)
Co-ownership retained by the Company	**837.4**	873.5
Interest-only strip receivable (Note 3)	**36.1**	–
Miscellaneous receivables	**(1.6)**	68.5
Total	$ **871.9**	$ 942.0

The total credit losses for the year on managed accounts, net of recoveries, were $74.2 million (2000 - $70.2 million). Of the current charge account receivables 72.9% (2000 - 70.7%) have a payment status that is current.

3.   Transfer of Receivables

The Company sells an undivided co-ownership interest in a pool of current and deferred charge account receivables on a fully serviced basis in securitization transactions and receives no fee for ongoing servicing responsibilities. The Company receives proceeds equal to fair value for the assets sold and retained rights to future cash flows arising after the investors in the securitization trusts have received the return for which they contracted. The co-owners have no recourse to the Company's retained interest in the receivables sold other than in respect of amounts in the cash reserve account (Note 5) and the interest-only strip receivable. The co-owners have no recourse to the Company's other assets.

During the year ended December 29, 2001, the Company recognized a pre-tax gain of $54.0 million on the securitization of charge account receivables. As at December 29, 2001, the interest-only strip was recorded at $36.1 million. The following table shows the key economic assumptions used in measuring the interest-only strip and securitization gains. The table also displays the sensitivity of the current fair value of residual cash flows to immediate 10% and 20% adverse changes in yield, payment rate, net charge-off rate and discount rate assumptions.

Effects of Adverse Changes
(in millions)

	Assumptions	10%	20%
Yield (annual rate)	24.14%	$ 5.7	$ 11.3
Principal payment rate (monthly)	24.07%	4.8	8.9
Net change-off rate (annual rate)	4.06%	0.9	1.8
Discount rate (annual rate)	12.00%	–	–

The table below summarizes certain cash flows related to the transfer of receivables during 2001, which have been accounted for under the provisions of Accounting Guideline – 12:

(in millions)

Proceeds from new transfers	$ 1,022.0
Proceeds from collections	259.4
Other cash flows relating to retained interests	30.6

4. Future Income Taxes

The tax effects of the significant components of temporary differences giving rise to the Company's net income tax assets and liabilities are as follows:

	2001		2000	
(in millions)	**Current**	**Long-Term**	*Current*	*Long-Term*
Future income tax assets:				
Items not deducted for				
tax purposes	**$ 94.5**	**$ –**	*$ 71.2*	*$ –*
Amounts related to				
tax losses carried forward	**32.7**	**152.7**	*127.0*	*129.7*
Deductible acquisition costs	**4.7**	**–**	*8.7*	*–*
(Gain) on securitization	**(21.6)**	**–**	*–*	*–*
Total	**$110.3**	**$152.7**	*$ 206.9*	*$ 129.7*
Future income tax liabilities:				
Depreciable capital assets	**$ –**	**$ 10.5**	*$ –*	*$ 27.6*
Deductible deferred charges	**–**	**40.1**	*–*	*46.3*
Other	**–**	**1.4**	*–*	*1.7*
Total	**$ –**	**$ 52.0**	*$ –*	*$ 75.6*

The average combined federal and provincial statutory income tax rate, excluding Large Corporations Tax, applicable to the Company was 41.9% for 2001 (2000 - 43.4%).

A reconciliation of income taxes at the average statutory tax rate to the actual income taxes is as follows:

(in millions)	**2001**		*2000*	
Earnings before income taxes	**$**	**177.5**	*$*	*334.1*
Income taxes at average				
statutory tax rate	**$**	**74.4**	*$*	*144.9*
Increase (decrease) in income				
taxes resulting from:				
Prior year recovery		**–**		*(5.6)*
Non-taxable portion				
of capital gains		**(0.8)**		*(13.6)*
Non-deductible items		**1.1**		*1.3*
Reduction in value of future				
income tax assets		**20.9**		*–*
Deferred credit drawdown		**(16.8)**		*(22.9)*
Large Corporations Tax		**4.6**		*4.2*
Income taxes	**$**	**83.4**	*$*	*108.3*
Effective tax rate		**47.0%**		*32.4%*

Income taxes for the year included a charge of $20.9 million relating to a reduction in the valuation of future income tax assets due to lower income in the current period and lower statutory rates of tax for future years. This is net of recognition of $15.1 million of the deferred credit relating to the acquisition of Eaton's. The future income tax assets acquired were valued at $310.0 million, which exceeded the total acquisition cost by $130.0 million. This amount was recorded as a deferred credit and is recognized proportionally as a reduction to income taxes as the future income tax asset is drawn down. In addition, income taxes were reduced by the recognition of deferred credit in the amount of $16.8 million (2000 - $22.9 million) for the year.

The Company's total cash payments for income taxes in 2001 were $34.1 million (2000 - $101.4 million).

Notes to the Financial Statements

5.   Investments and Other Assets

(in millions)	2001	2000
Unsecured debentures	$ 34.6	$ 49.7
Subordinated loans	13.4	21.6
Retained interest in transferred receivables		
- cash reserve account	33.5	–
Total	$ 81.5	$ 71.3

Unsecured debentures, which represent investments made by the Company in the independent trusts referred to in Note 16, in the amounts of $14.2 million, $5.9 million, $3.0 million, and $11.5 million, are due in 2010, 2011, 2013 and 2014 respectively. Subordinated loans, which represent loans to one of the independent trusts, are due in 2006. All bear interest at floating rates.

6.   Capital Assets

(in millions)	2001	2000
Land	$ 68.6	$ 62.4
Buildings and improvements	877.1	861.1
- held by joint ventures	175.4	181.3
Equipment and fixtures	1,237.4	1,108.4
Gross capital assets	2,358.5	2,213.2
Accumulated depreciation		
Buildings and improvements	370.3	322.1
- held by joint ventures	38.3	34.6
Equipment and fixtures	761.2	657.3
Total accumulated depreciation	1,169.8	1,014.0
Capital assets	$ 1,188.7	$ 1,199.2

The carrying values of land and buildings are evaluated by management on an on-going basis as to their net recoverable amounts. This is a function of their average remaining useful lives, market valuations, cash flows, and capitalization rate models. Situations giving rise to a shortfall in the net recoverable amounts are assessed as either temporary or permanent declines in the carrying values; permanent declines are adjusted.

7.   Deferred Charges

(in millions)	2001	2000
Excess of contributions to associate future benefits over amounts expensed	$ 109.6	$ 107.1
Tenant allowances for proportionate interests in joint ventures	6.5	6.6
Debt issuance and securitization set up costs	14.0	5.9
Other deferred charges	27.7	18.4
Total deferred charges	$ 157.8	$ 138.0

8. Associate Future Benefits

Information about the Company's defined benefit plans in aggregate, is as follows:

(in millions)	2001 Pension Plans		2001 Other Benefit Plans		2000 Pension Plans		2000 Other Benefit Plans	
Plan Assets								
Market value at beginning of year	$	1,387.6	$	91.7	$	1,318.6	$	93.7
Actual return on plan assets		(28.7)		(2.0)		100.2		7.1
Employer contributions		1.5		1.2		1.5		0.6
Associate contributions		19.3		–		16.5		–
Benefits paid[1]		(58.2)		(10.9)		(49.2)		(9.7)
Market value at end of year[2]		1,321.5		80.0		1,387.6		91.7
Plan Obligation								
Accrued benefit obligation at beginning of year[3]	$	969.4	$	201.5	$	885.0	$	173.2
Total current service cost		45.2		3.7		37.9		2.9
Interest cost		65.0		14.0		63.3		13.1
Benefits paid[1]		(58.2)		(11.3)		(49.2)		(10.3)
Actuarial losses		30.0		9.7		32.4		22.6
Accrued benefit obligation at end of year		1,051.4		217.6		969.4		201.5
Accrued Benefit Asset (Liability)								
End of year market value less accrued benefit obligation	$	270.1	$	(137.6)	$	418.2	$	(109.8)
Unamortized net actuarial (gain) loss		(26.6)		3.7		(188.1)		(13.1)
Unamortized past service costs		–		–		–		–
Accrued benefit asset (liability)		243.5		(133.9)		230.1		(122.9)
Valuation allowance[4]		–		–		–		–
Accrued benefit asset (liability), net of valuation allowance[5]	$	243.5	$	(133.9)	$	230.1	$	(122.9)

1 Benefits paid include amounts paid from funded assets. Other benefits are paid directly by the Company.

2 There are no plan assets invested in parties related to the plan.

3 Accrued benefit obligation represents the actuarial present value of benefits attributed to associate service rendered to a particular date.

4 The valuation allowance represents the amount of surplus not recognized on the Company's balance sheet.

5 The accrued benefit asset (liability), net of valuation allowance, represents the amount of the asset (liability) recognized on the Company's balance sheet.

Notes to the Financial Statements

Benefit Plan Expense

(in millions)	2001 Pension Plans	2001 Other Benefit Plans	2000 Pension Plans	2000 Other Benefit Plans
Company current service cost	$ 25.9	$ 3.7	$ 21.4	$ 2.9
Interest cost	65.0	14.0	63.2	13.1
Expected return on plan assets	(95.9)	(6.2)	(91.2)	(6.2)
Amortization of net actuarial (gain) loss	(6.6)	–	(10.8)	(0.6)
Net benefit plan expense	$ (11.6)	$ 11.5	$ (17.4)	$ 9.2

The significant actuarial assumptions adopted in measuring the Company's accrued benefit obligations are as follows (weighted-average assumptions as at year end):

	2001 Pension Plans	2001 Other Benefit Plans	2000 Pension Plans	2000 Other Benefit Plans
Discount rate	6.50%	6.75%	6.75%	6.75%
Expected long-term rate of return on plan assets	7.00%	N/A	7.00%	N/A
Rate of compensation increase	3.5%+ merit	3.5%+ merit	3.5%+ merit	3.5%+ merit

For measurement purposes a 6.6% annual rate of increase in the per capita cost of covered health care benefits was assumed for 2002. The rate of increase was assumed to decrease gradually to 4.0% for 2010 and remain at that level thereafter.

9. Long-Term Obligations

(in millions)	2001	2000
Unsecured debentures:		
7.80% due March 1, 2001	$ –	$ 100.0
6.55% due November 5, 2007	125.0	125.0
Unsecured medium term notes:		
7.45% due May 10, 2010	200.0	200.0
7.05% due September 20, 2010	100.0	100.0
6.75% due March 15, 2006	200.0	–
Proportionate share of long-term debt of joint ventures with a weighted average interest rate of 9.4% due 2002 to 2016	145.3	158.8
Capital lease obligations:		
Interest rates from 7% to 14%	42.5	14.8
	812.8	698.6
Less principal payments due within one year included in current liabilities	10.1	152.5
Total long-term obligations	$ 802.7	$ 546.1

The Company's proportionate share of the long-term debt of joint ventures is secured by the shopping malls owned by the joint ventures. The Company's total principal payments due within one year include $6.0 million (2000 - $51.5 million) of the proportionate share of the current debt obligations of joint ventures.

Interest on long-term debt amounted to $63.2 million (2000 - $67.7 million).

The Company's total cash payments for interest in 2001 were $56.6 million (2000 - $67.2 million)

Principal Payments

For fiscal years subsequent to the fiscal year ended December 29, 2001, principal payments required on the Company's total long-term obligations are as follows:

(in millions)	
2002	$ *10.1*
2003	*8.9*
2004	*10.8*
2005	*25.2*
2006	*210.8*
Subsequent years	*547.0*
Total debt outstanding	$ *812.8*

Significant Financing Transactions

During 2000, long-term financing for new capital projects of real estate joint ventures was obtained in the amount of $20.5 million. Due to the sale of two joint ventures, $70.7 million was released from the Company's obligations. In addition, $6.0 million of joint venture debt matured and was repaid.

The Company completed two issues of notes totaling $300 million in 2000, under the shelf prospectus filed on December 23,1998 that qualified the issuance of up to $500 million in medium term notes (debt with a term to maturity in excess of one year) over the subsequent two years.

• On May 10, 2000, $200 million of 7.45% medium term notes due May 10, 2010 were issued.

• On September 18, 2000, $100 million of 7.05% medium term notes due September 20, 2010 were issued.

On July 10, 2000, the outstanding 11.7% unsecured debentures of Sears Canada Inc. in the amount of $100 million matured and were repaid.

On December 11, 2000, the outstanding 8.25% unsecured debentures of Sears Canada Inc. in the amount of $125 million matured and were repaid.

On February 9, 2001, the Company filed a new shelf prospectus with securities commissions in Canada that qualifies the issuance of up to $500 million in medium term notes (debt with a term to maturity in excess of one year) over the next two years.

• On March 15, 2001, $200 million of 6.75% medium term notes due March 15, 2006 were issued.

On March 1, 2001, the outstanding unsecured 7.80% debentures of Sears Canada Inc. in the amount of $100 million matured and were repaid.

During 2001, $53.7 million of joint venture debt matured, of which $40.1 million was refinanced.

10. Capital Stock

The Company is authorized to issue an unlimited number of common shares and an unlimited number of non-voting, redeemable and retractable Class 1 Preferred Shares in one or more series. On December 22, 2000, a total of 25,633,934 Class 1 Preferred Shares, Series B were issued and immediately redeemed as part of a real estate joint-venture restructuring. As at December 29, 2001, the only shares outstanding were the common shares of the Company. Changes in the number of outstanding common shares and their stated values since January 1, 2000 are as follows:

	2001		2000	
	Number of Shares	**Stated Value (millions)**	*Number of Shares*	*Stated Value (millions)*
Beginning balance	**106,469,652**	**$ 455.6**	*106,258,828*	*$ 452.8*
Issued pursuant to Special Incentive Awards	**75,000**	**–**	*–*	*–*
Issued pursuant to stock options	**188,966**	**2.1**	*210,824*	*2.8*
Ending balance	**106,733,618**	**$ 457.7**	*106,469,652*	*$ 455.6*

Notes to the Financial Statements

During 2001, the Company announced its intention to purchase for cancellation up to 5% of its issued and outstanding common shares, representing up to 5,336,681 of the issued and outstanding common shares. The purchases were eligible to commence on November 2, 2001 and must terminate by November 1, 2002 pursuant to the Notice of Intention filed with The Toronto Stock Exchange. The price which the Company will pay for any such shares will be the market price at the time of acquisition. No shares had been purchased as at December 29, 2001.

Details of stock option transactions under the Company's Employees Stock Plan, including Special Incentive Awards, as at December 29, 2001, are set out below.

Special Incentive Awards of options and shares are awarded to Officers of the Company on a conditional basis, subject to achievement of specified performance criteria and specified vesting periods in the case of options. In 2001, 120,000 shares were awarded as Special Incentive Awards. In addition, 75,000 Special Incentive Award shares were issued during 2001.

Options granted and accepted	Option price	Expiry date	Options exercised	Options outstanding
232,301	$ 5.58	Feb. 2001	228,151	–
276,440	$ 5.58	Feb. 2006	165,985	110,455
60,000	$ 9.72	Nov. 2006	60,000	–
286,870	$ 10.65	Jan. 2007	151,456	135,414
30,000	$ 10.82	Feb. 2007	30,000	–
306,870	$ 19.63	Jan. 2008	66,702	240,168
26,000	$ 24.73	Apr. 2008	17,000	9,000
316,830	$ 21.19	Jan. 2009	36,911	279,919
324,740	$ 40.68	Jan. 2010	–	324,740
540,150	$ 21.72	Jan. 2011	–	540,150
3,000	$ 21.51	Mar. 2011	–	3,000

Special Incentive Award Options

170,000	$ 22.75	Feb. 2008	–	170,000
825,000	$ 28.75	Jul. 2008	–	825,000

As at December 29, 2001, 2,637,846 options were outstanding of which 777,592 are exercisable under the Employees Stock Plan, and 190,000 Special Incentive Awards shares were granted but unearned under the Employees Stock Plan.

Options to purchase 516,520 common shares have been authorized to be granted under the Employees Stock Plan in 2002.

Under the Directors' Stock Option Plan, stock options are granted to Directors who are not employees of the Company or Sears, Roebuck and Co.

Directors' Stock Option Plan:

Granted and accepted	Option price	Expiry date	Options exercised	Options cancelled	Options outstanding
9,000	$ 25.98	Apr. 2008	2,000	4,000	3,000
10,500	$ 29.96	Apr. 2009	500	4,000	6,000
9,000	$ 36.23	Apr. 2010	–	3,000	6,000
9,750	$ 21.32	Jul. 2011	–	–	9,750

As at December 29, 2001, 24,750 options were outstanding of which 9,000 are exercisable under the plan.

11. Unusual Items

The Company recorded a pre-tax gain of $5.5 million in 2001 (2000 - $12.5 million) comprised of the following unusual items:

(in millions)	2001	2000
Gain on sale of distribution facility	$ 8.3	$ –
Cost of closing 14 auto centres	(2.8)	–
Gain on sale of shopping centre investments	–	25.3
Cost of exiting gas bar operations	–	(7.6)
Costs related to the restructuring of distribution operations	–	(3.4)
Other restructuring initiatives	–	(1.8)
Unusual gain	$ 5.5	$ 12.5

During 2001, the Company recorded the following:

- A gain of $8.3 million on the sale of the Underhill distribution terminal.

- An expense of $2.8 million in relation to the closure of 14 auto centres, which includes severance and site restoration.

During 2000, the Company recorded the following:

- A gain of $25.3 million on the disposition of interests in three shopping centres.

- An expense of $7.6 million for the cost of exiting gas bar operations which includes site restoration.

- A loss of $3.4 million for the restructuring of distribution operations.

- An expense of $1.8 million, including severance, for the restructuring of business processes.

12. Changes in Non-Cash Working Capital

The cash generated from (used for) non-cash working capital is made up of changes related to operations in the following accounts:

(in millions)	2001	2000
Accounts receivable	$ 70.2	$ (4.4)
Inventories	150.7	(200.9)
Prepaid expenses and other assets	(6.1)	(18.4)
Accounts payable	(204.7)	164.7
Accrued liabilities	0.1	38.3
Income and other taxes payable	18.6	(61.3)
Cash generated from (used for) working capital	$ 28.8	$ (82.0)

13. Commitments and Contingencies

Minimum capital and operating lease payments, exclusive of property taxes, insurance and other expenses payable directly by the Company, having an initial term of more than one year as at December 29, 2001 are as follows:

(in millions)	Capital Leases	Operating Leases
2002	$ 7.5	$ 99.5
2003	7.5	91.7
2004	7.5	87.5
2005	7.5	82.2
2006	7.5	76.7
Subsequent years	23.5	658.1
Minimum lease payments	61.0	$ 1,095.7
Less imputed weighted average interest of 8.4%	18.5	
Total capital lease obligations	$ 42.5	

Total rentals charged to earnings under all operating leases for the year ended December 29, 2001 amounted to $125.2 million (2000 - $108.7 million).

The Company is party to a number of legal proceedings. The Company believes that each such proceeding constitutes routine litigation incidental to the business conducted by the Company and that the ultimate disposition of these matters will not have a material adverse effect on its consolidated earnings, cash flows or financial position.

Notes to the Financial Statements

14. Segmented Information

The Company has three reportable operating segments: merchandising, credit, and real estate joint venture operations.

- The merchandising segment includes the Company's department stores, catalogue operations, furniture and appliances stores, dealer stores, and outlet stores, as well as the products and services offered under the Sears HomeCentral banner and on its website, www.sears.ca.

- The credit segment finances and manages customer charge account receivables generated from the sale of goods and services charged on the Sears Card and Eatons Card.

- The real estate joint venture segment consists of the Company's joint venture interests in shopping centres, most of which contain a Sears store.

The reportable segments have been determined on the basis on which management measures performance and makes decisions on allocations of resources. The accounting policies of the segments are the same as those described in the Summary of Accounting Policies. During the preparation of the consolidated financial statements the revenues and expenses between segments are eliminated. The Company evaluates the performance of each segment based on earnings before interest expense and income taxes, as well as capital employed. The Company does not allocate interest expense or income taxes to segments.

Segmented Statements of Earnings for the 52 week periods ended December 29, 2001 and December 30, 2000

			2001					2000
			Real Estate				**Real Estate**	
			Joint				**Joint**	
(in millions)	**Mdse.**	**Credit**	**Ventures**[7]	**Total**	Mdse.	Credit	Ventures[7]	Total
Total Revenues[6]	$ 6,290.5	$ 379.8	$ 56.1	$ 6,726.4	$ 5,971.4	$ 308.3	$ 76.1	$ 6,355.8
Segment operating profit	87.9	118.9	29.4	236.2	280.9	70.0	37.1	388.0
Interest expense				64.2				66.4
Unusual items (gains)				(5.5)				(12.5)
Income taxes				83.4				108.3
Net earnings				$ 94.1				$ 225.8

6 The real estate joint venture revenues are net of $3.0 million (2000 - $3.8 million) representing the elimination of rental revenues earned from Sears department stores. Rental expense of the real estate joint venture segment has been decreased by the same amount having no effect on overall segment operating profit.

7 The real estate joint ventures had cash generated from operations of $15.3 million (2000 - $2.1 million), cash used for investments activities of $0.3 million (2000 - cash generated from investment activities of $84.6 million), and cash used for financing activities of $15.3 million (2000 - $85.8 million).

Segmented Statements of Financial Position as at December 29, 2001 and December 30, 2000

(in millions)	Mdse.	Credit	Real Estate Joint Ventures	Total	Mdse.	Credit	Real Estate Joint Ventures	Total
				2001				**2000**
Assets								
Cash and short-term investments	$ 325.4	$ –	$ 3.9	$ 329.3	$ 131.3	$ –	$ 4.2	$ 135.5
Accounts receivable	8.1	859.3	4.5	871.9	116.9	821.2	3.9	942.0
Inventories	864.5	–	–	864.5	1,015.2	–	–	1,015.2
Capital assets	1,022.4	–	166.3	1,188.7	1,022.6	–	176.6	1,199.2
Other	570.6	50.9	4.1	625.6	643.4	15.3	4.4	663.1
Total assets	$ 2,791.0	$ 910.2	$ 178.8	$ 3,880.0	$ 2,929.4	$ 836.5	$ 189.1	$ 3,955.0
Liabilities								
Accounts payable	$ 765.6	$ 0.4	$ 3.9	$ 769.9	$ 968.6	$ 1.0	$ 5.0	$ 974.6
Accrued liabilities	386.4	28.1	7.6	422.1	411.3	22.3	6.7	440.3
Other	232.8	7.6	14.9	255.3	289.0	(12.9)	16.1	292.2
Total liabilities excluding debt	$ 1,384.8	$ 36.1	$ 26.4	$ 1,447.3	$ 1,668.9	$ 10.4	$ 27.8	$ 1,707.1
Capital employed	$ 1,406.2	$ 874.1	$ 152.4	$ 2,432.7	$ 1,260.5	$ 826.1	$ 161.3	$ 2,247.9
Average capital employed	$ 1,333.4	$ 850.1	$ 156.9	$ 2,340.4	$ 1,038.3	$ 893.0	$ 208.6	$ 2,139.9
Capital expenditures	$ 141.7	$ –	$ 1.7	$ 143.4	$ 437.5	$ –	$ 9.8	$ 447.3
Depreciation and amortization	$ 165.6	$ –	$ 3.7	$ 169.3	$ 124.3	$ –	$ 5.5	$ 129.8

Notes to the Financial Statements

15. Related Party Transactions

Sears, Roebuck and Co. is the beneficial holder of the majority of the outstanding common shares of Sears Canada Inc., holding approximately 54% of the common shares of the Company.

During 2001, Sears, Roebuck and Co. charged the Company $14.8 million (2000 - $13.0 million) in the ordinary course of business for shared merchandise purchasing services. These amounts are included in the cost of merchandise sold, operating, administrative, and selling expenses.

Sears, Roebuck and Co. charged the Company $11.1 million (2000 - $19.4 million) and the Company charged Sears, Roebuck and Co. $4.6 million (2000 - $5.0 million) for other reimbursements. These reimbursements were primarily in respect of customer cross-border purchases made on the Sears Card, and the Sears, Roebuck and Co. charge card, as well as software and support services.

During 2001, the Company purchased an aircraft from Sears, Roebuck and Co. for $12.5 million. This transaction was recorded at fair market value.

There were no significant commitments, receivables or payables between the companies at the end of 2001 or 2000.

16. Financial Instruments

In the ordinary course of business, the Company enters into financial agreements with banks and other financial institutions to reduce underlying risks associated with interest rates and foreign currency. The Company does not hold or issue derivative financial instruments for trading or speculative purposes and controls are in place to prevent and detect these activities. The financial instruments do not require the payment of premiums or cash margins prior to settlement. These financial instruments can be summarized as follows:

Foreign Exchange Risk

From time to time the Company enters into foreign exchange contracts to reduce the foreign exchange risk with respect to U.S. dollar denominated goods purchased for resale. There were no such contracts outstanding at the end of 2001 or 2000.

Securitization of Charge Account Receivables

Securitization is an important financial vehicle which provides the Company with access to funds at a low cost. The Company sells undivided co-ownership interests in its portfolio of current and deferred charge account receivables to independent trusts and retains the income generated by the undivided co-ownership interests sold to the trusts in excess of the trusts' stipulated share of service charge revenues (refer to Notes 2 and 3).

Interest Rate Risk

To manage the Company's exposure to interest rate risks, the Company has entered into interest rate swap contracts with Schedule "A" Banks. Neither the notional principal amounts nor the current replacement value of these financial instruments are carried on the consolidated statements of financial position.

As at December 29, 2001, the Company had one interest rate swap contract in place to reduce the risk associated with variable interest rates associated with the floating rate debt issued by the trusts. For the year ended December 29, 2001, a net interest differential of $4.8 million (2000 - $3.0 million) was paid on the floating-to-fixed interest rate swap contracts and was recorded as an increase in interest expense of the Company.

Credit Risk

The Company's exposure to concentration of credit risk is limited. Accounts receivable are primarily from Sears Card and Eatons Card customers, a large and diverse group.

Interest Rate Sensitivity Position

Interest rate risk reflects the sensitivity of the Company's financial condition to movements in interest rates.

The table below identifies the Company's financial assets and liabilities which are sensitive to interest rate movements and those which are non-interest rate sensitive. Financial assets and liabilities which do not bear interest or which bear interest at fixed rates are classified as non-interest rate sensitive.

(in millions)	2001		2000	
	Interest Sensitive	Non-Interest Sensitive	Interest Sensitive	Non-Interest Sensitive
Cash and short-term investments	$ 329.3	$ –	$ 135.5	$ –
Investments and other assets	81.5	–	71.3	–
Accounts receivable[8]	36.1	835.8	–	942.0
Long-term obligations (including current portion)[9]	(1.9)	(810.9)	(148.8)	(549.8)
Net balance sheet interest rate sensitivity position	$ 445.0	$ 24.9	$ 58.0	$ 392.2

8   Interest sensitive portion relates to the interest-only- strip receivable described in Note 3 – Transfer of receivables

9   Interest sensitive portion includes long-term prime-rate based debt and current portion of long-term debt due to be renegotiated.

In addition to the net balance sheet interest rate sensitivity position, the Company is also affected by interest rate sensitive debt outstanding in the independent securitization trusts, where transfers are not subject to Accounting Guideline-12 (see Note 1, Summary of Accounting Policies). Any change in short-term interest rates will impact floating rate debt and debt with maturities of less than one year held by the trusts, which totaled $748.7 million at

December 29, 2001 (2000 - $1,034.8 million). An increase in the cost of this off-balance sheet debt will result in a decrease in the Company's share of service charge revenues. This interest rate exposure is offset, in part, by interest rate swap contracts held by the Company in the notional amount of $100 million (2000 - $250 million).

Fair Value of Financial Instruments

The estimated fair values of financial instruments as at December 29, 2001 and December 30, 2000 are based on relevant market prices and information available at that time. As a significant number of the Company's assets and liabilities, including inventory and capital assets, do not meet the definition of financial instruments, the fair value estimates below do not reflect the fair value of the Company as a whole.

Carrying value approximates fair value for financial instruments which are short-term in nature. These include cash and short-term investments, accounts receivable, prepaid expenses and other assets, accounts payable, accrued liabilities, income and other taxes payable, and principal payments on long-term obligations due within one year. For financial instruments which are long-term in nature, fair value estimates are as follows:

(in millions)	2001		2000	
	Carrying or Notional Amount	Fair Value	Carrying or Notional Amount	Fair Value
Financial Assets and Liabilities				
Investments and other assets	$ 81.5	$ 81.5	$ 71.3	$ 71.3
Long-term obligations	$ 802.7	$ 803.3	$ 546.1	$ 557.6

Notes to the Financial Statements

(in millions)	2001		2000	
	Carrying or Notional Amount	Fair Value Premium/ (Discount)	Carrying or Notional Amount	Fair Value Premium/ (Discount)
Off-Balance Sheet Interest Rate Swaps				
4.95%, expiring April 2001	$ –	$ –	$ 150.0	$ 0.6
9.54%, expiring April 2002	100.0	(3.4)	100.0	(5.9)
	$ 100.0	$ (3.4)	$ 250.0	$ (5.3)

The fair value of investments and other assets and long-term obligations was estimated based on quoted market prices, when available, or discounted cash flows using discount rates based on market interest rates and the Company's credit rating. As long-term debt coupon rates are higher than current market interest rates, the fair value of the Company's long-term debt exceeds its carrying value.

The fair value of the interest rate swap contracts was estimated by referring to the appropriate yield curves with matching terms of maturity. A fair value discount reflects the estimated amount that the Company would pay to terminate the contracts at the reporting date.

17. Earnings Per Share

A reconciliation of the number of shares used in the earnings per share calculation is as follows:

	2001	2000
	Number of shares	
Average number of shares per basic earnings per share calculation	106,690,685	106,397,789
Effect of dilutive options outstanding	185,298	759,842
Average number of shares per diluted earnings per share calculation	106,875,983	107,157,631

18. Subsequent Event

On February 18, 2002, after careful consideration of strategic alternatives, the Company announced that it had made a decision to convert its seven Eatons department stores to the Sears banner by the end of July 2002.

A one-time, pre-tax charge will be recorded in the first quarter of 2002 for an estimated amount of $180 million, consisting of $30 million in cash for severance payments, third party commitments, and closing costs, and a $150 million non-cash write-down of fixtures and leasehold improvements.

Interest Coverage Exhibit to the Financial Statements

The Company's earnings before interest and income taxes for the 52 week period ended December 29, 2001 were $240.7 million, which is 3.8 times the Company's long-term interest requirements of $63.2 million for this period.

Interest coverage on long-term debt is equal to net income before interest expense on long-term debt and income taxes, divided by annual interest requirements on long-term debt.

Corporate Governance

The Corporation, the Board of Directors and management are committed to maintaining high standards of corporate governance. The Board believes that strong corporate governance practices are essential to the success of the Corporation, to effective corporate performance and to the best interests of shareholders.

The Board of Directors is responsible for overseeing the business and affairs of the Corporation, acting with a view to the best interests of the Corporation, providing guidance and direction to the management of the Corporation in order to attain corporate objectives and maximize shareholder value. The Board carries out its stewardship functions directly and through its Committees.

The Board of Directors has five regularly scheduled meetings each year with additional meetings held as required. The Board has the opportunity to meet in camera (without management present) at each meeting. In 2001, there were six meetings of the Board, five meetings of the Audit Committee, four meetings of the Compensation Committee, four meetings of the Investment Committee and six meetings of the Nominating and Corporate Governance Committee. Attendance of the Directors at these meetings averaged approximately 90%. The Board has assigned the responsibility for corporate governance to the Nominating and Corporate Governance Committee (the "Nominating Committee").

The Board of Directors and the Audit, Compensation and Nominating Committees of the Board are each responsible for certain corporate governance functions in accordance with their respective mandates. The Nominating Committee is responsible for monitoring and guiding the corporate governance approach and practices of the Corporation. This Committee is satisfied that the Corporation is in conformance with the recommended practices of The Toronto Stock Exchange.

The Directors are elected annually by the shareholders. The Board is currently composed of eleven Directors. The Corporation's significant shareholder, Sears, Roebuck and Co., beneficially holds approximately 54% of the common shares of the Corporation. Three Directors are executive

officers of Sears, Roebuck and Co., and seven Directors (or 64% of the total number of Directors) are independent of the Corporation and its affiliates ("Independent Directors"). The Board's composition fairly reflects the investment in the Corporation by minority shareholders and the independence of the Board from management.

The Corporation has designed the Directors' compensation to align the Directors' interest with corporate performance and the return to shareholders. Independent Directors receive an annual equity grant of common shares and stock options under plans established by the Corporation. In addition to equity compensation, Independent Directors receive cash compensation and an administration and expense allowance, as more particularly set out in the Management Proxy Circular of the Corporation dated March 4, 2002, a copy of which may be obtained from the Secretary.

The Corporation has adopted a Corporate Disclosure, Confidentiality and Insider Trading Policy ("Policy") which reflects its commitment to providing timely and accurate corporate information to the capital markets, including its shareholders, and to the general public. The Policy provides direction and guidance to its directors, officers and employees regarding confidentiality and disclosure of company information and insider trading obligations. The Policy requires prompt general disclosure of any material information. It also sets out the procedures to be followed in communicating with investors, analysts and the media, including press conferences and media debriefings via webcast.

The Board of Directors believes that the Policy reflects the Corporation's commitment to timely disclosure, to maintaining a best practices approach to corporate governance and to compliance with continuous disclosure requirements.

A more detailed Statement of Corporate Governance Practices is contained in the Management Proxy Circular of the Corporation dated March 4, 2002. The Directors of the Corporation, their principal occupations and Committee appointments are listed on page 51 of this Report.

Corporate Information

Head Office
Sears Canada Inc.
222 Jarvis Street
Toronto, Ontario
Canada M5B 2B8

Transfer Agent and Registrar
CIBC Mellon Trust Company
Toronto, Ontario
Montreal, Quebec

Answerline: (416) 643-5500 or 1-800-387-0825

Website: www.cibcmellon.com
E-mail: inquiries@cibcmellon.com

Stock Exchange Listing
The Toronto Stock Exchange

Trading Symbol
SCC

Annual and Special Meeting
The Annual and Special Meeting of Shareholders
of Sears Canada Inc. will be held on
Monday, April 15, 2002 at 10:00 a.m. in the
Burton-Wood Auditorium
Main Floor
222 Jarvis Street
Toronto, Ontario, Canada

Édition française du Rapport annuel
On peut se procurer l'édition française de ce rapport
en écrivant au:
S/728, Relations Publiques
Sears Canada Inc.
222 Jarvis Street
Toronto, Ontario
Canada M5B 2B8

Pour de plus amples renseignements au sujet de la
Société, veuillez écrire au Service des relations
publiques, ou composer le (416) 941-4425

For More Information
Additional copies of the Annual Report can be
obtained through the Public Affairs Department at
the Head Office of Sears Canada Inc.

For more information about the Company, write to
Public Affairs, or call (416) 941-4425

Website: www.sears.ca
E-mail: home@sears.ca

Produced by Sears Canada Inc.
Public Affairs

Design by Compendium Design International Inc.

Printed in Canada by Kempenfelt Graphics Group

Certain brands mentioned in this report are the
trademarks of Sears Canada Inc., Sears, Roebuck
and Co., or used under license. Others are the
property of their owner.

Directors and Officers *(as at February 4, 2002)*

Board of Directors

Jalynn H. Bennett ◆ ■ ▲
President, Jalynn H. Bennett and Associates Ltd.

Micheline Bouchard ◆
*Corporate Vice President and General Manager,
Enterprise Services Organization, Motorola Inc.*

Mark A. Cohen ■ ●
*Chairman of the Board and Chief Executive Officer
of the Corporation*

Alan J. Lacy ■
*Chairman of the Board, President and
Chief Executive Officer, Sears, Roebuck and Co.*

Greg A. Lee
*Senior Vice President, Human Resources,
Sears, Roebuck and Co.*

Paul J. Liska ◆
*Executive Vice President and Chief Financial Officer,
Sears, Roebuck and Co.*

Brian F. MacNeill ■
Chairman of the Board, Petro-Canada

Mary Mogford ◆ ■ ▲ ●
Corporate Director

James W. Moir, Jr. ◆ ▲ ●
Corporate Director

C. Wesley M. Scott ● ▲
Corporate Director

Carol M. Stephenson ●
*President and Chief Executive Officer,
Lucent Technologies Canada Corp.*

Honorary Director

C. Richard Sharpe
*Former Chairman of the Board and
Chief Executive Officer,
Sears Canada Inc.*

Officers

Mark A. Cohen
Chairman of the Board and Chief Executive Officer

Richard A. Brown
Senior Vice-President, Strategic Initiatives

John T. Butcher
Executive Vice-President and Chief Financial Officer

G. Bruce Clark
Senior Vice-President, Credit

Barbara L. Duffy
Senior Vice-President, Human Resources

Brent V. Hollister
President, Sales, Service and Store Planning

John D. Smith
Senior Vice-President and Chief Information Officer

William R. Turner
President, Merchandising, Marketing and Logistics

Rudolph R. Vezér
Senior Vice-President, Secretary and General Counsel

Committees

■ Compensation ◆ Audit ▲ Investment
● Nominating and Corporate Governance

Mark A. Cohen is an ex officio member of the
Nominating and Corporate Governance Committee.

Sears Canada Inc. Annual Report 2001

APPENDIX B
COMPLEX ORGANIZATIONS

Throughout this text we have shown you excerpts from financial statements from various Canadian and international companies. Without exception, all of those financial statements were *consolidated* financial statements. Consolidated financial statements become necessary when one company buys a controlling ownership interest in another company, thus creating a complex organization. Before we end this text, we want to provide you with a broad understanding of how financial statements become consolidated, and the implications of using consolidated statements for decision-making. Because an investment in the common shares of a company carries with it a right to vote, one company can influence and, under the right circumstances, control the activities of another company. In this section, we also consider accounting issues related to organizations that are considered complex due to intercompany investments. We start with a brief discussion of the purpose of such intercompany investments, and then turn to their accounting and analysis aspects.

PURPOSE OF INTERCOMPANY INVESTMENTS

A company may have many reasons for acquiring an ownership interest in another company. Buying the shares of another company may be viewed as a good short-term or long-term investment. The equity securities that a company carries in its current asset account, called temporary investments, are an example of this type of investment. If the shares are bought for this reason, the number of shares purchased is usually small compared to the number of outstanding shares in the purchased company. Consequently, the acquiring company has little influence or control over the affairs of the company in which it has invested. Such investments are sometimes called **passive investments** or

portfolio investments because the acquiring company cannot exercise any control over the decisions of the acquired company. Some passive investments can also be long term if the intention of management is to hold the security for long-term returns.

A second major reason for obtaining ownership of the shares of another company is to influence or control the decisions made by that other company. Common targets for this kind of purchase are competitors, suppliers, and customers. Acquiring a block of shares in a supplier or customer allows the acquiring company to exercise some influence over the production, buying, and selling decisions of the acquired company, which may benefit the acquiring company. If the block of shares purchased is large enough, the acquiring company could have a controlling interest in a competitor, which would allow it to increase its market share by increasing its productive capacity, its geographic market, or both. Buying a controlling interest in a supplier or customer allows the company to ensure a market in which to buy its raw materials (in the case of a supplier), or to sell and distribute its product (in the case of a customer). Buying a supplier or customer is sometimes referred to as **vertical integration**. **Weyerhaeuser Company Limited** is an example of a company that is vertically integrated. Together with the various companies that it controls, it is involved in growing and harvesting trees, producing and selling forest products, collecting and recycling paper products, and building homes and developing land. Combining with a competitor is sometimes referred to as **horizontal integration**. Horizontal integration may also offer other benefits that come from economies of scale. The company may be able to reduce its workforce or use a single distribution system to avoid duplication of effort.

Another reason for buying and controlling another company is **diversification**. If a company is in a cyclical business, it can protect itself from cyclical declines in one business by investing in another business that is counter-cyclical. **Cyclical businesses** are those that have significant peaks and valleys of activity. A greeting card company is an example of a cyclical business. Some cards, like birthday cards, are purchased relatively evenly throughout the year. Other cards, like Christmas cards and Valentine cards, cause peaks in revenue generation. Such a company may wish to diversify by buying into an automobile dealership business. The peak times for the dealership are likely to be the late summer when the new cars are introduced and early spring when people are anticipating travelling over the summer. The greeting card business and the automobile dealership would have peak activities at different times, which would help to even out the revenue flows for the whole business.

Algoma Central Company is an example of a diversified Canadian business. Its main focus of operation is marine transportation. It operates several ships, and organizes the transportation of goods, provides for the repair and maintenance of ships, and provides marine-engineering services. This business is dependent not only upon the type of goods shipped, but also upon the economic environment of the countries to and from which goods are transported. Algoma has countered some of the cyclical nature of the shipping business by investing in commercial real estate. It owns and manages various commercial properties in Ontario. This business is also subject to the economic environment, but is much more localized and would be unlikely to experience the same peaks and valleys as marine transportation.

METHODS OF OBTAINING INFLUENCE AND CONTROL

Perhaps the simplest way to obtain control of the assets of another company is to purchase the assets directly from that company. This is called an **asset purchase**. The accounting for asset purchases is discussed in Chapter 8. If several assets are acquired at one time, such as in the acquisition of an entire division or plant, a single price may be negotiated. As discussed in Chapter 8, this type of purchase is called a *basket purchase*. The total cost of the assets purchased must be allocated to the individual assets acquired on the basis of their relative fair market values. Even if one company buys all of the assets of another company, it is not able to either influence or control the second company. Because it has purchased the assets, it controls only the assets it has purchased. The company from which it has purchased the assets can continue to operate, but now it has different assets that it must use to generate revenue. An asset purchase does not require consolidated financial statements. Once the new assets are recorded in the accounting system of the buying company, there are no further accounting complications.

The only way to obtain influence or control over another company is to buy common shares in a **share acquisition**. For the sake of this discussion, we will refer to the acquiring company as the **investor**, and to the company whose shares are acquired as the **investee**.

One way the shares can be obtained is through payment of cash by the investor to the shareholders of the investee (i.e., the shares are bought on the stock market). Another way is an exchange of the investor's shares for shares of the investee. This form of investment is called a **stock swap**. A variation of this is an exchange of the investor's debt (bonds) for shares of the investee in a transaction that may be called a **debt for equity swap**. In fact, some investments involve the exchange of all three (cash, shares, and debt) for the shares of the investee.

In a share acquisition, the investor can obtain a large degree of influence or control over the investee by buying (or swapping) more shares. That influence or control is obtained by exercising the voting rights that the investor obtains when buying the shares. Ultimate control over the assets and liabilities of the investee will occur when the percentage ownership of the voting rights is greater than 50%. This is called a **controlling interest**. An investor can sometimes effectively control an investee even though it owns less than 50% of the shares. This can occur in situations where the remainder of the shares are owned by a large number of investors, none of whom has a very large percentage ownership in the investee (the shares are said to be **widely held** in such situations). Therefore, if an investor owns 30% to 50% of an investee and the rest of the shares are widely held, the investor may be able to effectively control the assets and liabilities of the investee. Because it is possible to control with less than 50%, GAAP defines control as occurring when one company can make "strategic operating, investing and financing policies without the co-operation of others."[1] If a company owns 40% of the shares of another company, it may be able to elect a majority of people to the board of directors. It has, however, elected them with the co-operation of the other shareholders. If those shareholders became dissatisfied with

---

[1]*CICA Handbook*, para. 1590.03(b).

the way the board manages the company, they could get together and outvote the 40% shareholder. For this reason, a company with a 40% interest in another company would probably not prepare consolidated financial statements, but a company that owned 51% probably would.

In a share acquisition, the investee remains a legal entity separate from the investor. The investor company is like any other owner in that it has limited liability with regard to the debts of the investee. The investor's liability is limited to the amount invested in the shares. The separation of the legal status of the two companies is one reason this form of acquisition is appealing. The tax status of each company is also separate. Each company must file its own return. For accounting purposes, the separate legal status also means that the investor and the investee each keeps its own set of accounting records, even if the investor has acquired 100% of the investee's shares. This presents an accounting problem if the investor controls the investee because they are, in substance, one accounting entity.

VALUATION ISSUES AT DATE OF ACQUISITION

In any type of acquisition, whether the purchase of a single asset or of an entire company, the fundamental accounting valuation method is historical cost. The new asset or the investment in the investee is recorded at its cost. If the asset is acquired with a payment of cash, the amount of cash serves as the proper measure of the cost. If debt is exchanged for the asset or company, the value of the debt should be used as the measure of cost. Under GAAP, debt is usually measured at its net present value. The net present value of the debt at the date of issuance is used to measure the cost of an acquisition in which debt is exchanged.

When shares are issued in the acquisition, their fair market value should be used as the measure of cost at the date of acquisition. A problem exists in valuing shares when the issue is large because the number of shares outstanding increases significantly and the value of the investment acquired is not exact. How the market will adjust the existing share price to reflect this acquisition is not known at the date of the transaction. In these situations, instead of using the value of the shares to measure the acquisition, accountants sometimes turn to the fair market value of the assets acquired to measure the value of the shares given up. If the shares are used to swap for the shares of another company, the value of the shares of the other company may not be estimated easily. Stock swaps involving 100% of the shares of another company present the most difficulty in measuring the value of the transaction.

Share Acquisition

In a share acquisition, the investor records the cost of the acquisition in an investment account. There is no breakdown of this cost into individual assets and liabilities because the assets and liabilities do not technically belong to the investor; they remain the legal property or legal obligation of the investee. An investor that owns a large enough percentage of the investee's shares may control the assets economically through its voting rights, but it does not hold the title to the assets, nor is it legally obligated to settle the liabilities. Under GAAP, we currently use the **purchase method** to account for an acquisition of a controlling interest.

Purchase Method

The purchase method assumes that after the shares are purchased or exchanged, one company can be identified as an **acquirer**. This method is used when the investor pays cash or issues debt in exchange for the shares of the investee. When shares are swapped for the shares of the investee, this method is used when the original shareholders of the investor company control more shares than the new shareholders from the investee company. For example, assume that Company A has 500,000 common shares currently issued. It is interested in purchasing all of the shares of Company B, which has 100,000 common shares currently issued.

COMPANY A	COMPANY B
500,000 shares issued	100,000 shares issued
Company A issues 100,000 new shares and exchanges them with the shareholders of Company B on a 1-for-1 basis	
After the exchange	
600,000 shares issued	100,000 shares issued, now owned
(500,000 shares held by the original	by Company A
shareholders of Company A;	
100,000 held by the old	
shareholders of Company B)	

Result: The original shareholders of Company A still hold most of the shares of Company A and therefore still control Company A, which now controls Company B.

The purpose of most share exchanges in Canada is to gain control of another company. When this is achieved, the acquiring company is called the **parent** and the acquired company is called the **subsidiary**. The subsidiary is an integral part of the total operations of the parent company and, therefore, users need to know how it is performing. Both parent and subsidiary are separate legal entities that keep separate books, prepare separate financial statements, and pay separate taxes. To provide users with information about the whole entity (parent and subsidiaries), accountants prepare consolidated financial statements, which add the components of the various financial statements of the parent and the subsidiaries together. Users see the total cash controlled by the entity, the total inventory owned by the entity, the total revenues earned by the entity, and so forth. Complications in this addition arise if there have been transactions between the parent and the subsidiaries. Because such transactions occur within the total accounting entity (parent and subsidiaries), they are deemed not to have occurred—they must be eliminated. More will be said about this later.

As well as providing information about the total entity, consolidated financial statements hide information about the individual companies in the group. Because users are often not given information about these individual companies, they have difficulty determining the risks and rewards contributed by each. If a company, through its activities, is involved in various industries or geographic locations, it is required to disclose segmented information in the notes to its financial statements. The segmented information provides some breakdown of accounts in the different segments so that users can evaluate the potential future impact of the segments on the total entity.

As mentioned earlier, when the parent purchases a controlling number of shares in a subsidiary company, it has an investment on its books that it has recorded at the cost of the purchase. Because another company is being controlled and consolidated financial statements are going to be prepared, the transaction is viewed like a basket purchase. The cost to acquire the subsidiary needs to be allocated to the individual assets and liabilities of the subsidiary based on their relative fair market values at the date of acquisition, just as with any other basket purchase. This allocation is not recorded on the actual books of either the parent or the subsidiary, but instead is determined during the worksheet preparation of the financial statements. When the assets and liabilities of the subsidiary are added to the assets and liabilities of the parent so that consolidated financial statements can be prepared, it is the fair values of the subsidiary's assets and liabilities that are added to the historical cost assets and liabilities of the parent.

In the allocation of the purchase price, all the assets and liabilities in the subsidiary are first measured at their fair market values. Some assets that did not exist on the books of the subsidiary may be found and included in this measurement process. For example, if the subsidiary developed a patent or a trademark internally, the costs of such an item would have been expensed (see Chapter 8 for a discussion of whether to capitalize or expense the costs of these types of assets). The parent would need to identify all assets that the subsidiary owned or had the right to use, and establish values for those items using current items similar to them in the market, estimations of future benefits, or appraisals as a guide. By buying the shares, the parent is now also controlling these assets, and part of the acquisition cost should be allocated to them if they have a measurable market value. All of these assets and liabilities, those on the books and those that have value but are not on the books, are known as the **identifiable net assets** of the subsidiary. In the year that a parent buys a subsidiary, the components of the assets and liabilities that were purchased will be disclosed in the notes to the consolidated financial statements. Exhibit B-1 includes an example of this disclosure from the financial statements of **Domtar Inc.**

DOMTAR INC., 2001

EXHIBIT B-1

4. Business Acquisitions

2001

Four U.S. mills and related costs from Georgia-Pacific

On August 7, 2001, Domtar acquired from Georgia-Pacific Corporation four integrated pulp and paper mills and related assets, located in Ashdown, Arkansas, Nekoosa and Port Edwards, Wisconsin, and Woodland, Maine, for a consideration of cash of $2,531 million (US $1,650 million) and $38 million of transaction related costs. The acquisition has been accounted for using the purchase method and, accordingly, the purchase price was allocated to the assets acquired and the liabilities assumed based on their estimated fair value as of the acquisition date. The results of operations of these acquired mills were included in the consolidated financial statements from the date of acquisition. Details of the acquisition at the effective date are as follows:

	$
Net assets acquired at assigned values:	
Current assets	388
Current liabilities	(124)
Operating working capital	264
Property, plant, and equipment	2,461
Other assets	2
Other liabilities	(158)
	2,569
Consideration:	
Cash, including transaction related costs	2,569

The allocation of the purchase price has not been completed as of year end, and the assigned values may be modified once the ongoing study on the integration and restructuring of assets acquired is completed and a formal plan is approved.

You should note from Domtar's description that values have been assigned to three asset groups and two liability groups. By far the most valuable asset acquired was property, plant, and equipment. The fair value of the identifiable net assets was $2,531 million. Domtar's acquisition did not result in goodwill since the purchase price was negotiated at the fair value of the net assets of the four mills.

However, if the purchase price is more than the fair market value of the identifiable net assets, another asset called **goodwill** must be reported (refer to Chapter 8). It represents all the intangible reasons that motivated the investor to pay more for the investee than the sum of the fair market values of its individual assets and liabilities. Perhaps the acquirer expects to earn extra future cash flows, or perhaps the business is located in a high traffic area and so has a greater chance at higher revenues than businesses located elsewhere. Perhaps the sales personnel in the business have created a loyal customer following which leads to consistent revenues, or previous advertising campaigns may have made this a well-known business. If, on the other hand, the purchase price is less than the fair value of the identifiable net assets, negative goodwill is created. This negative goodwill must be allocated proportionately to the fair values of the noncurrent, nonmonetary assets. This is a topic for an advanced accounting course.

INCOME RECOGNITION ISSUES SUBSEQUENT TO ACQUISITION

Income recognition issues subsequent to acquisition are a consequence of the valuation decisions made at the date of acquisition. In the following subsections, these issues are discussed for asset acquisitions and share acquisitions.

Asset Purchases

Subsequent to purchase, asset acquisitions are accounted for in the same way as any other acquisition of assets. If the asset acquired is property, plant, or equipment, it is amortized like any other such asset. If the asset purchased is inventory, it ultimately affects cost of goods sold when it is sold.

Share Acquisitions

The accounting treatment of income subsequent to a share acquisition depends on the level of control the investor exerts over the investee. As examples of the conceptual differences, consider two extreme cases. The first case is one in which the investor owns only a few shares in the investee, and the second is one in which the investor buys 100% of the shares of the investee.

Case 1

If the investor buys only a few shares of the investee, it has virtually no control or influence over the investee. The investor may not dictate the dividend policy or any other strategic policy to the investee. As indicated earlier, this is a passive investment. The shareholders of the investor company in such a situation are unlikely to be interested in the full details of the investee's operating performance. They are probably more interested in the cash flows that have come in from their investment (dividends) and in its current market value. Therefore, income recognition should probably show dividend revenue.

Case 2

In this case, where the investor owns 100% of the shares of the investee, the investor's shareholders will likely want to know the operating details of the investee's performance, because they economically control all of its the assets and liabilities. For example, if the investee purchased was a competitor, the results of sales of the company's product are the combined results of the investor and the investee. To show only the details for the investor would be misleading in terms of the resources controlled by the shareholders. The investor's shareholders would probably find information about the combined assets and liabilities of the two companies more useful than simply a listing of the investor's assets and liabilities. A set of statements that conveys this information is a set of **consolidated financial statements**. Consolidated financial statements are prepared as if the investor and investee were one legal company. Under GAAP, the two companies represent one economic accounting entity. In this situation, the investor is typically referred to as the **parent company** and the investee as the **subsidiary**.

What Is Canadian Practice?

This section of the chapter will describe the guidelines that have been established under Canadian GAAP for the acquisition of various blocks of shares. It is important to understand these guidelines because companies will describe their various acquisitions and tell you how they are accounting for them. You will need to know the various methods used so that you can understand each one's effects on the financial statements.

Under Canadian GAAP, control is determined by the investor's ability to determine the strategic operating, investing, and financing activities of the investee without seeking the permission of any others. This usually means that the investor owns more than 50% of the voting shares of the investee.

Because control is evidenced by the ability to determine certain activities in another company, GAAP provides guidelines for recommended cutoffs for the percentage ownership (in voting shares) that require different accounting treatment. Exhibit B-2 outlines these cutoffs. For small investments (less than 20%), GAAP specifies the **cost method**. Small investments are also subdivided into those that are current, which we usually label temporary investments, and those that are noncurrent, which are generally labelled investments. Larger investments (greater than 50%) require **consolidation**; that is, consolidated financial statements must be prepared. For investments that fall between these two extremes, the acquirer is considered to have **significant influence** over activities in the investee. Significant influence is evidenced by being able to elect a person to the board of directors, having significant transactions between the two companies, or having an exchange of technology or managerial personnel. When significant influence exists, another method, called the **equity method**, is required. Each of these methods is discussed in detail in the following pages.

ACCOUNTING METHODS FOR INVESTMENTS

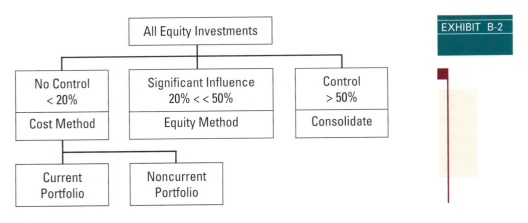

EXHIBIT B-2

The percentage cutoffs identified in Exhibit B-2 are only a guide. If a company can demonstrate that it possesses either more or less control than the percentage ownership indicates, it can apply a different method. For example, if a wholly owned subsidiary (100% ownership) goes into receivership, control often passes from the parent company to a trustee. The investment in the subsidiary should then be carried using the cost method. Also, an investor that owns less than 50% of an investee's voting shares, but also owns convertible rights on other securities which, if converted, would increase its ownership beyond 50%, would be required to prepare consolidated financial statements. Each method carries its own set of implications for the company, as discussed in the following subsections.

COST METHOD   The cost method was discussed in Chapter 6. To refresh your memory, the investment is carried in the investment account at its cost. During the period in which the investment is held, dividend revenue is recognized. If the investment is in marketable securities (short-term), at the end of each period the portfolio of securities is valued at the lower of its cost and market value. The unrealized losses (or recoveries) are shown in the income statement. If the investment is long-term, the portfolio is compared to market, but written down only if the decline is a permanent one. Once a long-term investment is written down, it is not written back up. To review the details of these accounting procedures, see Chapter 6. Note that no recognition is made of the net income results of the investee during the period except to the extent that these results are captured by its willingness to pay dividends.

CONSOLIDATION METHOD   Consolidation is required when an investor (parent company) controls the activities of an investee (subsidiary). For instructional purposes here, we will assume that the investor owns more than 50% of the outstanding shares of an investee. Because the subsidiary is still a legally separate company, the parent company records its investment in the subsidiary company in an investment account in its accounting system. However, because the parent company economically controls the assets and liabilities of the subsidiary, it is probably more useful to the parent company's shareholders to report the full details of the assets, liabilities, and income statement items rather than a single amount in the investment account and a single amount of income from the subsidiary on the income statement. The purpose of consolidating, therefore, is to replace the investment account with the individual assets and liabilities of the subsidiary. On the consolidated financial statements, it then looks as though the two companies are legally one, that is, as if they had merged. You must recognize, however, that this is simply an "as if" representation of the combined company. The accounting systems are not merged. In fact, the consolidated statements are prepared "on working papers"; no actual entries are made to either company's accounting system.

Because a consolidation tries to make it look as though the two companies were merged, the consolidated statements are prepared using the fair market value of the assets and liabilities acquired as well as any goodwill. These amounts are combined with the book values of the parent's assets and liabilities.

EQUITY METHOD   Between the two extremes of no control and complete control lies the situation in which the investor can significantly influence the investee but not completely control its decisions. The accounting method used, the equity method, tries to strike some middle ground between showing the results of all the assets, liabilities, and income items in the financial statements (consolidation) and showing only the dividend revenue from the investment (cost method). The equity method requires that the investor show the effects of its share of the investee's financial results, that is, as if it consolidated its share of the assets, liabilities, and income statement items. The difference is that its share of the net assets (assets minus liabilities) is reported as a single line item, "Investment in shares," on the investor's balance sheet. Its share of the net income is also reported as a single revenue item, "Equity in earnings of investment" or simply "Income from investment," on the income statement. Because of the netting of assets and liabilities as well as revenues and expenses, this method is sometimes referred to as a **one-line consolidation**.

To illustrate the entries made in a simple case using the cost method and the equity method, let us assume the following facts. Assume that the investor bought 30% of the outstanding shares of an investee for $10,000. During the first year of the investment, the investee's earnings were $3,000 and dividends of $1,500 were declared. We will assume that in Case A, the 30% does not give the investor significant influence (cost method required), and in Case B significant influence is present (equity method required). The entries the investor makes to account for the investment in the first year are as follows:

CASE A (COST METHOD)		CASE B (EQUITY METHOD)	
Investor's entry for acquisition:			
A-Investment in Shares 10,000		A-Investment in Shares 10,000	
A-Cash	10,000	A-Cash	10,000
Investor's entry to record earnings from investee:			
No entry		A-Investment in Shares 900	
		SE-Equity in Earnings of	
		Investment	900[a]
Investor's entry to record dividends from investee:			
A-Cash	450[b]	A-Cash	450
SE-Dividend Revenue	450	A-Investment in Shares	450

[a]Investor's percentage ownership × Earnings of investee = 30% × $3,000
[b]Investor's percentage ownership × Dividends of investee = 30% × $1,500

Under the equity method, the entry to record the earnings shows that the investment account increases by the investor's share of the earnings of the investee. The investment account represents the investor's investment in the investee and, as the investee earns income and increases its shareholders' equity, the investor's investment also increases in value. The credit part of this entry is to the income statement in a revenue line item called **Equity in earnings of investment**. We will subsequently abbreviate this as **EEI**.

The entry to record the dividends of the investee causes a decrease in the investor's investment account. This should make sense because, on the investee's books, the declaration of dividends causes a decrease in the shareholders' equity of the company. Because the investor's investment account measures its share of that equity, the investment account should decrease with the declaration of dividends. Another way to think about this is to imagine that the investment represents a deposit in a savings account. The interest on the savings account would be equivalent to the earnings of the subsidiary. Withdrawals from the savings account would be the equivalent of the dividends declared. Withdrawals decrease the balance in the savings account in the same way that dividends reduce the investment account.

CONSOLIDATION PROCEDURES AND ISSUES

Numerous procedures and issues are important to understanding consolidated statements, but they are complex enough that an advanced accounting course is usually necessary to thoroughly understand them. To give you a general idea of the procedures necessary for consolidation, we will show you the consolidation of a 100%-owned subsidiary. This will be followed by a discussion of the issues surrounding the handling of intercompany transactions.

Consolidation Procedures—100% Acquisition

To illustrate the concepts behind the preparation of a consolidated set of financial statements, let's consider a share acquisition in which the parent acquires a 100% interest in the subsidiary. To make the example as concrete as possible, let's assume that the balance sheet of the parent (referred to as Parent Company) and the subsidiary (referred to as Sub Company) just prior to the acquisition are as shown in Exhibit B-3.

EXHIBIT B-3

■ PARENT AND SUBSIDIARY BALANCE SHEETS

Prior to Acquisition

Balance Sheets

	Parent Company	Sub Company
Assets other than PP&E	$2,200	$2,500
Property, plant, and equipment	$1,800	$1,500
Total assets	$4,000	$4,000
Total liabilities	$2,000	$3,000
Shareholders' equity	$2,000	$1,000
Total liabilities and shareholders' equity	$4,000	$4,000

Assume that, at acquisition, Parent Company pays $1,400 in cash for all the outstanding shares of Sub Company. Because the book value of Sub Company's equity (net assets) is $1,000 at the date of acquisition, Parent Company has paid $400 more than the book value for Sub Company's assets and liabilities. Assume further that $250 of this $400 relates to the additional fair market value of Sub's property, plant, and equipment. It will be assumed that the fair market value of the other assets and liabilities of Sub are equal to their book values. This means that the remainder of the $400, or $150, is due to goodwill. Exhibit B-4 represents these assumptions.

REPRESENTATION OF THE PURCHASE PRICE COMPOSITION

Parent Company's 100% Acquisition of Sub Company

Note: Boxes are not scaled proportionately to dollar amounts.

Parent Company records its investment in an account called Investment in Sub Company. Because Parent Company owns more than 50% of the shares of Sub Company, it controls Sub Company and will have to prepare consolidated financial statements. Because Sub Company remains a separate legal entity, it will continue to record its transactions in its own accounting system. Parent Company will also continue to keep track of its own transactions on what are known as the **parent-only books**. At the end of each accounting period, the separate financial statements of the two entities will be combined on a worksheet to produce the consolidated financial statements, as if the two companies were one legal entity. One question that arises is how Parent Company should account for its Investment in Sub Company on its parent-only books. Because the Investment in Sub Company account will be replaced in the consolidation process by the individual assets and liabilities of Sub Company, it does not really matter, from a consolidated point of view, how Parent accounts for its investment on the parent-only statements. However, it will make a difference in the parent-only financial statements. GAAP is somewhat silent on this issue, and there is some diversity in practice. Some companies use the equity method to account for the investment, and some use the cost method. It will be assumed that Parent Company uses the equity method. The investment entry would be:

INVESTMENT ENTRY		
A-Investment in Sub Company	1,400	
A-Cash		1,400

The above entry would be the same if the company was intending to use the cost method. After recording the investment, the balance sheets of Parent Company and Sub Company will appear as in Exhibit B-5.

EXHIBIT B-5

■ PARENT AND SUBSIDIARY BALANCE SHEETS AT DATE OF ACQUISITION

Balance Sheets

	Parent Company	Sub Company
Assets other than PP&E	$ 800	$2,500
Property, plant, and equipment	1,800	1,500
Investment in Sub Company	1,400	–
	$4,000	$4,000
Total liabilities	$2,000	$3,000
Shareholders' equity	2,000	1,000
Total liabilities and shareholders' equity	$4,000	$4,000

To prepare a consolidated balance sheet for Parent Company at the date of acquisition, the Investment in Sub Company account must be replaced by the individual assets and liabilities of Sub Company. This would normally be done on a set of **consolidating working papers**, and no entries would be made directly in either the parent company's or the subsidiary company's accounting system. The consolidating entries that are discussed next are made on the consolidating working papers. The accountant starts the working papers by placing the financial statements as prepared by the parent company and the subsidiary side by side as shown in Exhibit B-6. The working papers will then have columns for the consolidating entries and for the consolidated totals. Note that the exhibit shows debit and credit columns for all four items.

EXHIBIT B-6

■ CONSOLIDATING WORKING PAPERS

Account	Parent Company Debit	Parent Company Credit	Sub Company Debit	Sub Company Credit	Consolidating Entries Debit	Consolidating Entries Credit	Consolidated Totals Debit	Consolidated Totals Credit
Assets other than PP&E	800		2,500					
Property, plant, and equipment	1,800		1,500					
Investment in Sub Company	1,400							
Liabilities		2,000		3,000				
Shareholders' equity		2,000		1,000				
Totals	4,000	4,000	4,000	4,000				

On the consolidating working papers, each row will be added across to obtain the consolidated totals. If no adjustments are made to the balances as stated in Exhibit B-6, several items will be double-counted. In the first place, the net assets of the subsidiary will be counted twice, once in the individual accounts of Sub and again as the net amount in Parent's investment account. One or the other of these two must be eliminated. Because the idea of consolidated statements is to show the individual assets and liabilities of the subsidiary in the consolidated totals, the best option is to eliminate the parent's investment account. The second item that will be counted twice is the shareholders' equity section. The only outside shareholders of the consolidated company are the parent company's shareholders. The shareholders' equity represented by the subsidiary's balances is held by the parent company. The shareholders' equity section of the subsidiary must, therefore, be eliminated. Both of these are eliminated in a working paper entry called the **elimination entry**. The elimination entry in the example would be:

WORKING PAPER ELIMINATION ENTRY

SE-Shareholders' Equity (Sub Company)	1,000	
???	400	
A-Investment in Sub Company		1,400

In the preceding entry you can see that, in order to balance the entry, a debit of $400 has been made. What does this represent? It represents the excess amount that Parent Company paid for its interest in Sub Company over the book value of the net assets. Remember the assumption that this excess is broken down into $250 for **excess fair market value** of property, plant, and equipment over its book value and $150 for goodwill. Therefore, the complete entry would be:

WORKING PAPER ELIMINATION ENTRY (ENTRY 1)

SE-Shareholders' Equity (Sub Company)	1,000	
A-Property, plant, and equipment	250	
A-Goodwill	150	
A-Investment in Sub Company		1,400

As a result of the elimination entry, the consolidating working papers would appear as in Exhibit B-7. The working paper entries are numbered so that you can follow them from the journal entry form to the working paper form.

CONSOLIDATING WORKING PAPERS (BALANCE SHEET ONLY)

EXHIBIT B-7

Account	Parent Company Debit	Parent Company Credit	Sub Company Debit	Sub Company Credit	Consolidating Entries Debit	Consolidating Entries Credit	Consolidated Totals Debit	Consolidated Totals Credit
Assets other than PP&E	800		2,500				3,300	
Property, plant, and equipment	1,800		1,500		(1) 250		3,550	
Goodwill	–		–		(1) 150		150	
Investment in Sub Company	1,400					1,400 (1)	–	
Liabilities		2,000		3,000				5,000
Shareholders' equity		2,000		1,000	(1) 1,000			2,000
Totals	4,000	4,000	4,000	4,000	1,400	1,400	7,000	7,000

Note that shareholders' equity on a consolidated basis is the same as on the parent company's books. This is true because all that consolidation has really done is replace the net assets represented in the investment account with the individual assets and liabilities that make up the net assets of the subsidiary. In this sense, the statements of the parent company (which are referred to as the *parent-only statements*) portray the same net results to the shareholders as a consolidation. However, the consolidated statements present somewhat different information to the shareholders in that ratios, such as the debt/equity ratio, can be quite different from those found in parent-only statements. For example, from Exhibit B-7 you can calculate the debt/equity ratio for the parent-only statements as 1.0 ($2,000/$2,000) whereas, in the consolidated statements, it is 2.5 ($5,000/$2,000). This occurs because Parent Company has acquired a subsidiary that is more highly leveraged than it is [note that the debt/equity ratio for Sub Company is 3.0 ($3,000/$1,000)]. The consolidation of the two companies produces a leverage ratio that is a weighted average of the two ratios. Although the debt/equity ratio appears to be less favourable on the consolidated statements, users must remember that Sub Company is a separate legal entity and is responsible for its own debts. Parent Company has limited liability. For this reason, creditors such as banks prefer to see parent-only financial statements when they assess a company's ability to repay debt.

Now consider what the financial statements of Parent Company and Sub Company might look like one year after acquisition. The accounts of the two companies are shown in Exhibit B-8 (remember that EEI stands for equity in earnings of the investment).

EXHIBIT B-8

PARENT AND SUBSIDIARY BALANCE SHEETS & INCOME STATEMENTS

One Year Subsequent to Acquisition

Balance Sheet

	Parent Company	Sub Company
Assets other than PP&E	$ 1,440	$ 3,000
Property, plant, and equipment	1,850	1,600
Investment in Sub Company	1,500	–
Total assets	$ 4,790	$ 4,600
Total liabilities	$ 2,420	$ 3,450
Shareholders' equity	2,370	1,150
Total liabilities and shareholders' equity	$ 4,790	$ 4,600

Income Statement

	Parent Company	Sub Company
Revenues	$ 1,500	$ 2,000
Expenses	(1,010)	(1,475)
Amortization	(250)	(225)
EEI	250	–
Net income	$ 490	$ 301
Dividends declared	$ 120	$ 150

Using the equity method, Parent Company would make the following entries during the year to account for its investment:

ENTRIES USING THE EQUITY METHOD (ON PARENT COMPANY'S BOOKS)

Parent's share of Sub's income:

A-Investment in Sub Company	300	
SE-EEI		300

Parent's share of Sub's dividends:

A-Cash	150	
A-Investment in Sub Company		150

After these entries, the ending balance in the investment account would be $1,550 ($1,400 + $300 − $150). You will note in the statements in Exhibit B-8 that the investment account has a balance of $1,500. The difference in these amounts is due to the fact that Parent Company paid more than the book value for the net assets of Sub Company. As we assumed earlier, Parent Company paid $400 more than the book value ($1,000). The $400 is due to the extra fair market value of property, plant, and equipment ($250) and goodwill ($150). Subsequent to acquisition, the property, plant, and equipment must be amortized and the amortization is shown as part of the EEI. Companies will establish amortization periods based on the expected useful life of the assets acquired. Assume that the property, plant, and equipment have a remaining useful life of five years, have a residual value of zero, and are amortized straight-line. Therefore, Parent Company must take an additional $50 ($250/5 years) in amortization expense over that shown on the books of Sub Company. The $150 of goodwill is not amortized. Instead, it is checked each year to determine if its value is impaired. To keep our example simple, we are going to assume that the goodwill is still worth $150. The amortization of the property, plant, and equipment means that Parent Company has to report an additional $50 in expenses during the year subsequent to acquisition. Using the equity method, Parent Company shows these additional expenses as a part of the EEI. The following entry is made (in addition to those shown earlier):

AMORTIZATION ENTRY UNDER EQUITY METHOD (ON PARENT COMPANY'S BOOKS)

SE-EEI	50	
A-Investment in Sub Company		50

With this additional entry, the balance in the Investment in Sub Company account is $1,500, exactly the balance shown in Exhibit B-8.

The consolidated working papers at the end of the first year are presented in Exhibit B-9. You should note that they are shown in the **trial balance phase**. In the trial balance phase, the temporary income statement and dividends declared accounts still have balances that have not been closed to retained earnings (refer to Chapter 3 if you need to refresh your memory concerning the meaning of the trial balance phase). Note that shareholders' equity has the same balance as at the beginning of the year. This is how the accounts must be listed in order to correctly prepare the consolidated financial statements.

| EXHIBIT B-9 | **CONSOLIDATING WORKING PAPERS (YEAR SUBSEQUENT TO ACQUISITION)** |

	Parent Company		Sub Company		Consolidating Entries		Consolidated Totals	
Account	Debit	Credit	Debit	Credit	Debit	Credit	Debit	Credit
Assets other than PP&E	1,440		3,000					
Property, plant, and equipment	1,850		1,600					
Goodwill								
Investment in Sub Company	1,500							
Liabilities		2,420		3,450				
Shareholders' equity		2,000[a]		1,000[a]				
Revenues		1,500		2,000				
Expenses	1,010		1,475					
Amortization expense	250		225					
Amortization expense—goodwill								
EEI		250						
Dividends declared	120		150					
Totals	6,170	6,170	6,450	6,450				

[a]Beginning of period balances (trial balance phase).

In the year subsequent to acquisition, three basic consolidating working paper entries are made if the parent company is using the equity method to account for the investment on the parent-only financial statements. In addition to eliminating the investment account and the shareholders' equity accounts discussed earlier, the EEI must be eliminated, as must the dividends declared account of the subsidiary. Otherwise, the income of the subsidiary would be counted twice, once as EEI and a second time as the individual revenue and expense items. Dividends declared by the subsidiary are intercompany transfers of cash from a consolidated point of view. They are not dividends to outside shareholders and, as such, they should be eliminated in the consolidation process. The entry to eliminate EEI and dividends will be called the *reversal of current year entries* because the entry is, in effect, removing income and dividends recognized during the period. Once these two entries have been made, the third set of entries recognizes the extra amortization expense discussed earlier. The consolidating working paper entries are as follows:

CONSOLIDATING WORKING PAPER ENTRIES

Reversal of current year entries (Entry 1):

SE-EEI	250	
SE-Dividends Declared		150
A-Investment in Sub Company		100

Investment elimination entry (Entry 2):

SE-Shareholders' Equity	1000	
A-Property, Plant, and Equipment	250	
A-Goodwill	150	
A-Investment in Sub Company		1,400

Amortization of PP&E (Entry 3):

SE-Amortization Expense	50	
A-Property, Plant, and Equipment		50
(or XA-Accumulated Amortization)		

The preceding entries are added to the consolidating working papers as shown in Exhibit B-10. Note that a separate accumulated amortization account has not been provided and that the amount of extra amortization for the period has simply been credited to the property, plant, and equipment account. You can think of property, plant, and equipment as a net account, that is, net of accumulated amortization.

Income, on a consolidated basis, is as follows:

PARENT COMPANY—CONSOLIDATED NET INCOME

Revenues	$3,500
Expenses	(2,485)
Amortization expense	(525)
Net Income	$ 490

Note that this is exactly the same as the net income that was reported by Parent Company using the equity method as shown in Exhibit B-8. This will always be the case. As mentioned earlier, the equity method is sometimes referred to as a *one-line consolidation*. It is a one-line consolidation because the balance sheet effects of consolidation are captured in the one-line item called the investment account. The income statement effects of consolidation are captured in the one-line item called EEI. The only difference, then, between the equity method and a full consolidation is that the one-line items are replaced with the full detail of the subsidiary's assets and liabilities on the balance sheet and the full detail of the subsidiary's revenues and expenses on the income statement.

EXHIBIT B-10	**CONSOLIDATING WORKING PAPERS (YEAR SUBSEQUENT TO ACQUISITION)**							
	Parent Company		Sub Company		Consolidating Entries		Consolidated Totals	
Account	Debit	Credit	Debit	Credit	Debit	Credit	Debit	Credit
Assets other than PP&E	1,440		3,000				4,440	
Property, plant, and equipment	1,850		1,600		(2) 250	50 (3)	3,650	
Goodwill					(2) 150		150	
Investment in Sub Company	1,500					100 (1)	—	
						1,400 (2)		
Liabilities		2,420		3,450				5,870
Shareholders' equity		2,000a		1,000a	(2) 1,000			2,000
Revenues		1,500		2,000				3,500
Expenses	1,010		1,475				2,485	
Amortization expense	250		225		(3) 50		525	
EEI		250			(1) 250			—
Dividends declared	120		150			150 (1)	120	
Totals	6,170	6,170	6,450	6,450	1,700	1,700	11,370	11,370

aBeginning of period balances (trial balance phase).

Consolidation Procedures—Less Than 100% Acquisition

One complication that arises in many acquisitions is that the parent company does not always acquire 100% of the shares of the subsidiary. Suppose, for example, that Parent Company buys 80% of the shares of Sub Company for $1,120. The balance sheets of Parent Company and Sub Company immediately after acquisition are shown in Exhibit B-11. A column that represents 80% of the balance sheet of Sub Company is also presented for future reference.

Assume that the same fair market values of the assets and liabilities apply to Sub Company as before. The only asset that had extra fair market value is property, plant, and equipment, with an excess value of $250. Since Parent Company purchased only 80% of the subsidiary, it acquired only 80% of this extra fair market value, or $200. The calculation of goodwill would be made as follows:

PARENT COMPANY—CONSOLIDATED NET INCOME	
Purchase price	$1,120
Less 80% of book value acquired (80% of $1,000)	(800)
Less 80% of extra fair market value (80% of $250)	(200)
Goodwill	$ 120

PARENT AND SUBSIDIARY BALANCE SHEETS AT DATE OF ACQUISITION (80% ACQUISITION)

Balance Sheet

	Parent Company	Sub Company	80% of Sub Company
Assets other than PP&E	$1,080	$2,500	$2,000
Property, plant, and equipment	1,800	1,500	1,200
Investment in Sub Company	1,120	–	–
Total assets	$4,000	$4,000	$3,200
Total liabilities	$2,000	$3,000	$2,400
Shareholders' equity	2,000	1,000	800
Total liabilities and shareholders' equity	$4,000	$4,000	$3,200

If Parent Company owns 80% of Sub Company, who owns the other 20%? The answer is other shareholders. Because Parent Company controls Sub Company, it must prepare consolidated financial statements. When consolidated financial statements are prepared, Parent Company adds 100% of Sub Company's assets, liabilities, revenues, and expenses to its own accounts. But Parent Company does not own 100% of Sub Company. It must, therefore, show 20% as being owned by the other shareholders. It does this by creating an account called **non-controlling interest** (NCI) or sometimes **minority interest**. The NCI account on the balance sheet is located at the end of the long-term liabilities. It contains 20% of the book value of Sub Company, $200 (20% of $1,000). There is another NCI account on the income statement that holds 20% of Sub Company's net income. It appears as an expense and reduces the income by 20% so that consolidated net income represents only the 80% that belongs to Parent Company. These two NCI accounts allow the parent to consolidate 100% of its subsidiaries and then to back out the part that does not belong to it.

To illustrate NCI (minority interest) disclosure, we have included the 2001 balance sheet and income statement of **Teck Cominco Limited** in Exhibit B-12. The non-controlling interest on the income statement in fiscal 2001 is a loss of $50 million. This amount of the combined incomes and losses from Teck Cominco's subsidiaries represents the amount that Teck Cominco does not own. The non-controlling interest on the balance sheet is $31 million. Teck Cominco has several subsidiaries but only one in which it does not own 100%.

EXHIBIT B-12

TECK COMINICO LIMITED (2001)

Consolidated Balance Sheets

As at December 31

($ in millions)	2001	2000
ASSETS		
Current Assets		
Cash	$ 101	$ 266
Accounts and settlements receivable	242	292
Production inventories	540	466
Supplies and prepaid expenses	161	172
	1,044	1,196
Investments (Note 4)	606	454
Property, Plant and Equipment (Note 5)	3,298	3,283
Other Assets (Note 6)	205	169
	$5,153	$5,102
LIABILITIES AND SHAREHOLDERS' EQUITY		
Current Liabilities		
Short-term bank loans	$ 80	$ 5
Accounts payable and accrued liabilities	310	391
Current portion of long-term debt (Note 7)	45	40
	435	436
Long-Term Debt (Notes 5 and 7)	1,005	875
Other Liabilities (Note 8)	365	347
Future Income and Resource Taxes (Note 14)	509	494
Debentures Exchangeable for Inco Shares (Note 9)	248	248
Minority Interests (Note 10)	31	1,007
Shareholders' Equity (Note 11)	2,560	1,695
	$5,153	$5,102

Commitments and contingencies (Notes 5 and 18)

Approved by the Directors

ROBERT J. WRIGHT   NORMAN B. KEEVIL

TECK COMINICO LIMITED (2001)
Consolidated Statements of Earnings

Years ended December 31

($ in millions, except per share data)	2001	2000
Revenues	$ 2,379	$1,206
Cost of operations	(1,751)	(820)
Depreciation and amortization	(226)	(139)
Operating profit	402	247
Other Expenses		
General, administration and marketing	(58)	(36)
Interest on long-term debt	(77)	(57)
Exploration	(59)	(32)
Research and development	(15)	(8)
Other income and expense	62	18
	255	132
Asset valuation writedowns (Note 12)	(169)	–
Income and resource taxes (Note 14)		
On earnings from operations	(103)	(41)
On asset valuation writedowns (Note 12)	47	–
Minority interests	(50)	(43)
Equity earnings (loss)	(1)	37
Net Earnings (Loss) (Note 13)	$ (21)	$ 85
Basic Earnings (Loss) Per Share	$ (0.17)	$ 0.77
Diluted Earnings (Loss) Per Share (Note 1)	$ (0.17)	$ 0.71

When a parent owns less than 100% of a subsidiary, the accounting can become quite complex. The discussion of these aspects will be left to more advanced texts. It is enough that you understand what the NCI account represents.

Consolidations—Intercompany Transactions

One final complication that deserves mentioning is the impact that intercompany transactions have on the consolidated financial statements. When a parent company buys a controlling interest in a supplier or a customer, it is likely that there are many transactions between the two companies. Prior to the acquisition, these transactions are viewed as taking place between two independent parties but, after the acquisition, they are viewed as intercompany transactions. Sales of goods and services between a parent and a subsidiary cannot be viewed as completed transactions unless there has been a sale of the goods or services outside the consolidated entity. Therefore, any profits (revenues and expenses) from those transactions that are not completed by a sale outside the consolidated entity must be eliminated. If there are remaining balances in accounts receivable and accounts payable that relate to intercompany transactions, these, too, must be removed.

To show you briefly this elimination process, let us consider the following example. Company A owns 100% of Company B. During 20x1, Company A sells a parcel of land to Company B for $60,000. This land had originally cost Company A $45,000. Company A records the transaction on its books in the following manner:

A-Cash	60,000	
A-Land		45,000
SE-Gain on sale of land		15,000

Company B records the acquisition of the land as follows:

A-Land	60,000	
A-Cash		60,000

Note that Cash went out of one entity and into the other entity. The consolidated entity still has the same amount of cash. Land went from $45,000 on one entity's books to $60,000 on the other entity's books. To the consolidated entity, this is the same parcel of land that was on last year's consolidated balance sheet at its historical cost of $45,000. If it is not reduced back to $45,000 on the consolidated balance sheet, it will be overstated. If we allowed the sale price of items sold intercompany to appear at the sale price on the consolidated financial statements, the two entities could sell items back and forth merely to increase asset value and to record revenue when, in reality, no external transactions with independent third parties took place. The last item, the Gain on the sale of land, must also be removed from the consolidated income statement. No gain can be recognized by the consolidated entity because the land has not been sold to an outside party. The journal entry to eliminate this unrealized gain on the consolidating working papers would be:

SE-Gain on sale of land	15,000	
A-Land		15,000

An entry similar to this would have to be repeated each year on the consolidating working papers when the consolidated financial statements are prepared. The entry in subsequent years would have a debit to Retained earnings rather than Gain on sale of land because in future years the income statement does not have the gain reported. The gain caused the retained earnings of Company A to increase in the year that the land was sold to Company B. Entries similar to these are prepared for all the intercompany transactions that occur between the two entities.

STATEMENT ANALYSIS CONSIDERATIONS

The consolidation of a subsidiary considerably changes the appearance of both the income statement and the balance sheet from the parent-only financial statements under equity. The income statement is different only in its detail; the net income for the period is the same regardless of whether or not the subsidiary is consolidated. Also, because the balances in the shareholders' equity accounts are the same with either method, ratios such as return on equity are unaffected by the consolidation policy.

Other ratios that involve other balance sheet figures can be dramatically affected. Earlier in the chapter, the effect that consolidation has on the debt/equity ratio was described using the information provided in Exhibit B-7. The debt/equity for Parent Company was 1.0, whereas the debt/equity for the consolidated entity was 2.5. Users who need information about an entity's ability to repay debt should not rely on consolidated financial statements. These statements contain the liabilities of all the companies in the consolidated entity, but each of those companies is responsible for only its own debt. A parent and its subsidiaries may guarantee each other's debt. This would reduce the risk of nonpayment and could result in lending institutions charging lower interest rates or loaning larger amounts. When the debt is guaranteed, the debt/equity ratio of the consolidated entity is useful. All of the assets are available to service the debt.

Other ratios will also be affected. The ROA ratio, for example, divides the net income before interest by the average total assets. The numerator changes to the extent that the interest expense of the subsidiary is included on the consolidated income statement and is, therefore, added back to the net income. The denominator (average total assets) also changes because the investment account is replaced by the individual assets and liabilities of the subsidiary. In the example in Exhibit B-8, the total assets of the parent prior to consolidation were \$4,790. After consolidation, the total assets were \$8,240 (Exhibit B-10). This dramatic increase would certainly affect the ROA. The ROA prior to consolidation would have been 10.2% (\$490 / \$4,790). After consolidation, the ROA was 6.0% (\$490 / \$8,240).

The current ratio will also be affected. The current assets and liabilities that are embedded in the investment account are shown in full detail when they are consolidated. The current assets and liabilities of the subsidiary would be added to the parent's when they are consolidated. Because our example in Exhibit B-7 does not distinguish current liabilities from long-term liabilities, it is not possible to demonstrate the change that would occur. Obviously, the quick ratio will also be affected by consolidation for the same reason as the current ratio.

Shareholders, potential investors, and most other outside users may not be able to determine the impact that various subsidiaries have on the consolidated financial statements. If a parent owns 100% of a subsidiary, the subsidiary will often not publish financial statements for external users other than the CCRA. A lender would be able to request individual financial statements for any company that wanted to borrow funds, but most other external users would not have this luxury. This means that users should have some understanding of which ratios are affected by the consolidation process. If the parent owns less than 100% of the shares, the subsidiary must publish publicly available financial statements if it is traded on the stock market. Users then have the opportunity to get more information about the components of the consolidated entity. A 100%-owned subsidiary does not trade on the stock exchange and does not need to make its financial statements public. Parent companies often have many subsidiaries. Evaluating each subsidiary individually is usually not necessary. Rather, users determine the ratios but keep in mind that each company is responsible for its own debt and taxes.

SUMMARY

In this Appendix, we provided more background to improve your understanding of consolidated financial statements. You learned about the different levels of investments in other companies, from portfolio investments to significant influence investments to controlled subsidiaries. Through simple examples, we demonstrated the acquisition of a 100%-owned subsidiary. We expanded your knowledge through a discussion of non-wholly-owned subsidiaries and of intercompany transactions. We concluded the Appendix with a brief discussion of the impact of the consolidation process on ratio analysis.

The environment of corporate financial reporting is one of constant change and growing complexity. This book has introduced you to most of the fundamental concepts and principles that guide standard-setting bodies, such as the Accounting Standards Board, as they consider new business situations and issues. You should think of the completion of this Appendix as the end of the beginning of your understanding of corporate financial reporting. As accounting standard-setting bodies and regulators adjust and change the methods and guidelines used to prepare financial statements, you must constantly educate yourself so that you understand the impacts of these changes on the financial statements of your company or of other companies you need to understand.

AN INTERNATIONAL PERSPECTIVE

Reports from Other Countries

In 1991, the FASB in the United States issued a discussion memorandum entitled "International Accounting Research Project: Consolidations/Equity Accounting" that concerned consolidation issues. Conducted by Price Waterhouse, the study surveyed practices in Australia, Canada, France, Germany, Italy, Japan, the Netherlands, the United Kingdom, and the United States as of November 1990.

In its findings, Price Waterhouse concluded that, in virtually all of the countries surveyed, consolidated financial statements were required for companies that were publicly traded on securities exchanges. In some countries, however, the consolidated statements are not considered the primary financial statements. In Japan, for instance, consolidated statements are provided as supplementary information. In many of the countries surveyed, non-publicly traded companies did not prepare consolidated financial statements.

The survey also found widespread use of a criterion of control rather than ownership in deciding whether to consolidate an entity. France, for instance, explicitly allows subsidiaries in which the parent owns more than 40% to be consolidated if no other group of shareholders has a greater share. Finance subsidiaries were generally not consolidated in countries other than the United States, but within seven months after the survey had been completed, Canada, New Zealand, and the United Kingdom had revised their standards to require consolidation of these subsidiaries. The revised international standard, IAS 22, on business combinations requires the use of the purchase method with the criterion of control and the consolidation of all subsidiaries.

In 2001, standard-setters in Canada and the United States introduced new consolidation standards that resulted in greater similarities between the two countries in the guidelines for consolidation. As a result of the changes, both countries now require the exclusive use of purchase accounting for acquisitions. Prior to the change, both countries allowed a second method called pooling, but that method is no longer used. The second change was the treatment of goodwill. Prior to the change, goodwill was amortized within a maximum period of 40 years. With the 2001 changes, goodwill is no longer amortized. Instead, it is checked periodically for impairment.

SUMMARY PROBLEM

Peck Company (parent) bought 100% of the shares of Spruce Company (subsidiary) on January 1, 20x1, for $600,000. On January 1, 20x1, the shareholders' equity section of Spruce Company was as follows:

Common shares	$125,000
Retained earnings	75,000
Total shareholders' equity	$200,000

The amount paid by Peck for Spruce was larger than the book value of the assets acquired. This excess amount was attributed partially to land ($50,000) and equipment ($250,000). The equipment had a remaining useful life of 10 years and an assumed residual value of zero. Peck amortizes its assets straight-line.

The following represents the trial balance of Peck and Spruce as at December 31, 20x1 (the end of the fiscal year).

Trial Balance, December 31, 20x1

	Peck Company		Spruce Company	
Account	Debit	Credit	Debit	Credit
Cash	$ 780,000		$ 240,000	
Accounts receivable	400,000		200,000	
Inventory	525,000		350,000	
Investment in Spruce	695,000		–	
PP&E	800,000		600,000	
Accumulated amortization		$ 300,000		$ 200,000
Accounts payable		425,000		290,000
Long-term debt		900,000		580,000
Common shares		700,000		125,000
Retained earnings (1/1)		400,000		75,000
Revenues		5,000,000		2,000,000
Expenses (other than amort'n)	4,200,000		1,700,000	
Amortization	100,000		100,000	
Equity in Spruce earnings		175,000		–
Dividends declared	400,000		80,000	
Totals	$7,900,000	$7,900,000	$3,270,000	$3,270,000

Required:

a. Reconstruct the entries that Peck made during 20x1 to account for its investment in Spruce using the equity method.

b. Prepare a set of consolidating working papers for Peck and Spruce for 20x1. Separately, show the consolidating entries in journal entry form.

c. Calculate the following ratios for Peck Company using its parent-only financial statement information and the consolidated entity information:

    1. Debt/equity

    2. Return on equity

    3. Return on assets

    4. Current ratio

SUGGESTED SOLUTION TO SUMMARY PROBLEM

a. Using the equity method, the following entries would be made:

At acquisition:

A-Investment in Spruce	600,000	
A-Cash		600,000

At year end:

To recognize income: The net income of Spruce is calculated as follows:

Revenues	$2,000,000
Expenses	1,700,000
Amortization	100,000
Net income	$ 200,000

Since Peck's share of Spruce's income is 100%, the following entry would be made:

A-Investment in Spruce	200,000	
SE-Equity in Spruce Earnings		200,000

To recognize dividends: Spruce declared $80,000 in dividends and Peck's share is 100%; therefore, the following entry would be made:

A-Cash	80,000	
A-Investment in Spruce		80,000

To recognize amortization of the fair value increment on the equipment: At the date of acquisition, Peck paid $400,000 more for the shares of Spruce than the book value ($200,000) of the net assets. This excess amount would be attributable to the following balance sheet items:

Land	$ 50,000
Equipment	250,000
Goodwill	100,000
Total	$400,000

The land is not amortized, but the excess amount due to the equipment must be amortized. Since Peck uses straight-line amortization, the extra amortization expense would be $25,000 per year ($250,000/10 years). The goodwill is not amortized. Using the equity method, the extra expenses would be recognized with the following entry:

SE-Equity in Spruce Earnings	25,000	
A-Investment in Spruce		25,000

Based on these entries, the investment account balance would be $695,000 and the equity in Spruce earnings would be $175,000, as shown in the trial balance.

b. The consolidating working papers are shown in Exhibit B-13.

CONSOLIDATING WORKING PAPERS, PECK COMPANY AND SPRUCE COMPANY, 20X1—100% ACQUISITION

EXHIBIT B-13

Account	Peck Company Debit	Peck Company Credit	Spruce Company Debit	Spruce Company Credit	Consolidating Entries Debit	Consolidating Entries Credit	Consolidated Totals Debit	Consolidated Totals Credit
Cash	780,000		240,000				1,020,000	
Accounts receivable	400,000		200,000				600,000	
Inventory	525,000		350,000				875,000	
Property, plant, & equipment	800,000		600,000		(2) 300,000		1,700,000	
Accumulated amortization		300,000		200,000		25,000 (3)		525,000
Goodwill					(2) 100,000		100,000	
Investment in Spruce	695,000					95,000 (1) 600,000 (2)	–	
Accounts payable		425,000		290,000				715,000
Long-term debt		900,000		580,000				1,480,000
Common shares		700,000		125,000	(2) 125,000			700,000
Retained earnings		400,000[a]		75,000[a]	(2) 75,000			400,000
Revenues		5,000,000		2,000,000				7,000,000
Expenses	4,200,000		1,700,000				5,900,000	
Amortization expense	100,000		100,000		(3) 25,000		225,000	
EEI		175,000			(1) 175,000			–
Dividends declared	400,000		80,000			80,000 (1)	400,000	
Totals	7,900,000	7,900,000	3,270,000	3,270,000	800,000	800,000	10,820,000	10,820,000

[a]Beginning of period balances (trial balance phase).

The consolidating working paper entries are as follows:
1. To reverse current income and dividends:

SE-Equity in Spruce Earnings	175,000	
SE-Dividends Declared		80,000
A-Investment in Spruce		95,000

2. To eliminate the investment account and shareholders' equity and to create extra fair market value and goodwill:

SE-Common Shares	125,000	
SE-Retained Earnings	75,000	
A-Land (PP&E)	50,000	
A-Equipment (PP&E)	250,000	
A-Goodwill	100,000	
A-Investment in Spruce		600,000

3. To amortize the extra fair market value of the equipment:

SE-Amortization Expense	25,000	
XA-Accumulated Amortization		25,000

   c. Parent-only   Consolidated entity

1. Debt/equity

$1,325,000/1,575,000^a = 0.84$ $2,195,000/1,575,000^b = 1.39$

[a] $700,000 + 400,000 + 5,000,000 − 4,200,000 − 100,000 + 175,000 − 400,000 = \$1,575,000$
[b] $700,000 + 400,000 + 7,000,000 − 5,900,000 − 225,000 − 400,000 = \$1,575,000$

2. Return on equity

$875,000^a/1,575,000 = 0.56$ $875,000^b/1,575,000 = 0.56$

[a] $\$5,000,000 − 4,200,000 − 100,000 + 175,000 = \$875,000$
[b] $\$7,000,000 − 5,900,000 − 225,000 = \$875,000$

3. Return on assets

$875,000/2,900,000^a = 0.30$ $875,000/3,770,000^b = 0.23$

[a] $\$780,000 + 400,000 + 525,000 + 800,000 − 300,000 + 695,000 = \$2,900,000$
[b] $\$1,020,000 + 600,000 + 875,000 + 1,700,000 − 525,000 + 100,000 = \$3,770,000$

4. Current ratio

$1,705,000^a/425,000 = 4.0$ $2,495,000^b/715,000 = 3.5$

[a] $\$780,000 + 400,000 + 525,000 = \$1,705,000$
[b] $\$1,020,000 + 600,000 + 875,000 = \$2,495,000$

ABBREVIATIONS USED

CCRA	Canada Customs and Revenue Agency
EEI	Equity in earnings of investment
NCI	Noncontrolling interest
PP&E	Property, plant, and equipment

GLOSSARY

Asset purchase   An acquisition of assets from another company in which the acquiring company purchases the assets directly rather than buying a controlling interest in the shares of the other company. Title to the assets passes to the acquiring company.

Consolidated financial statements   Financial statements that represent the total financial results of a parent company and its various subsidiaries as if they were one company, even though they are separate legal entities.

Consolidating working papers   A worksheet that adjusts the financial statements of a parent and its subsidiaries so that the statements can be combined to show the consolidated financial statements.

Consolidation   An accounting method that companies are required to use to represent their ownership in other companies when they have control over the activities in other companies. The method requires the preparation of consolidated financial statements.

Controlling interest   The amount of ownership of a subsidiary that a parent company must have in order to control the subsidiary's strategic operating, financing, and investing activities. An ownership interest of greater than 50% usually meets this criterion.

Cyclical business   A business that is subject to significant swings in the level of its activity, such as the greeting card business.

Debt for equity swap   A transaction in which debt securities are exchanged for equity securities.

Diversification   A reason for acquiring ownership in another company. Diversification typically implies that the new company acquired is in a business very different from the company's current business. The idea is to find a business that is countercyclical to the company's current business.

Elimination entry   A working paper consolidating entry that eliminates the balance in the investment in subsidiary account against the shareholders' equity accounts of the subsidiary. At the same time, if the price paid by the parent company exceeds the book value of the subsidiary's shareholders' equity section, the excess fair market value of the net assets acquired and goodwill are recognized as part of the entry.

Equity in earnings of investment (EEI)   An account used in a parent company's books to record its share of the subsidiary's net income for the period using the equity method.

Equity method   An accounting method that companies use to represent their ownership in companies in which

they have significant influence. This is usually true when the percentage of ownership is between 20% and 50%. In addition, this method is often used in parent-only statements to account for the investment in a subsidiary. In the latter case, the account will be eliminated on the consolidating working papers at the end of the year when consolidated financial statements are prepared.

Excess fair market value   The difference between the fair market value and book value of the assets of a subsidiary company whose shares are acquired by a parent company. The difference is measured at the date of acquisition.

Goodwill   An intangible asset that arises when a parent company acquires ownership in a subsidiary company and pays more for the shares than the fair market value of the underlying net identifiable assets at the date of acquisition. The difference between the price paid and the fair market value of the identifiable net assets at the date of acquisition is the value of the goodwill. It can represent expected excess earnings that result from the reputation of the subsidiary, its exceptional sales staff, or an advantageous location.

Horizontal integration   A type of acquisition in which a parent company buys a competitor company in order to gain a larger market share or to expand its markets geographically.

Identifiable net assets   The assets and liabilities that can be specifically identified at the date of a merger or acquisition. Some of the identifiable assets may not have been recorded on the subsidiary's books, such as patents and trademarks.

Investee   A company whose shares are being acquired by another company.

Investor   A company that acquires shares of another company as an investment.

Minority interest   A synonym for noncontrolling interest.

Non-controlling interest (NCI)   The portion of a less-than-100%-owned subsidiary that is owned by other shareholders.

One-line consolidation   The equity method is referred to as a one-line consolidation method because it produces the same net results as the full consolidation method except that the subsidiary's results are shown in a single line on the balance sheet (the investment account) and a single line on the income statement (the equity in earnings of investment).

Parent company   A company that acquires control (usually can elect a majority of the board of directors) of another company. The acquired company is referred to as a subsidiary.

Parent-only books   The accounting records of a parent company that have not been combined with its subsidiary's records in consolidated financial statements.

Passive investment   An investment by one company in another company in which the acquiring company has no capability of controlling or influencing the decisions of the acquired company.

Portfolio investment   Synonym for passive investment.

Purchase method   An accounting method used to record the acquisition of another company. The acquisition is treated as a purchase, and the assets and liabilities acquired are measured at their fair market value. Because this is typically a basket purchase, the cost is allocated to the individual assets and liabilities on the basis of their relative fair market values.

Share acquisition   An acquisition of another company that is accomplished through the acquisition of shares of the acquired company. The acquired company continues as a separate legal entity.

Stock swap   An acquisition in which an acquiring company exchanges its shares for the shares of the acquired company.

Subsidiary   A company controlled by another company (the parent), which usually owns more than 50% of its outstanding shares and controls its strategic operating, financing, and investing decisions.

Trial balance phase   A phase in the preparation of financial statements in which the temporary accounts still contain income statement and dividend information from the period and have not been closed out to retained earnings.

Vertical integration   A type of merger or acquisition in which a parent company buys a supplier or customer company in order to ensure a supply of raw materials or a market for its end product.

Widely held shares   Shares of a company that are held by a large number of individuals or institutions such that no one shareholder has significant influence on the decisions of the company.

ASSIGNMENT MATERIAL

Assessing Your Recall

B-1   Identify and briefly explain the major reasons why a company might want to buy shares in another company.

B-2   Compare and contrast a share acquisition and an asset acquisition in terms of their effects on the financial statements.

B-3   Explain the financial statement implications of accounting for an acquisition using the purchase method:

    a. At the date of acquisition

    b. Subsequent to the date of acquisition

B-4   Briefly describe the GAAP guidelines for accounting for long-term acquisitions in the shares of other companies. In your description, identify the criteria used to distinguish the various accounting methods.

B-5   Explain the nature of goodwill and how it arises in the context of an acquisition.

B-6   The equity method is sometimes referred to as a one-line consolidation. Explain.

B-7   Discuss what a consolidation is trying to accomplish.

B-8   The consolidating working paper entries are needed to eliminate double accounting for certain items on the parent's and subsidiary's books. Explain which items would
be accounted for twice if the subsidiary company's books were added directly to the parent's books.

B-9   The consolidated balances in the asset and liability accounts do not exist in either
the parent company's or the subsidiary company's accounting systems. Explain why you
agree or disagree with this statement.

Applying Your Knowledge

B-10   (Acquisition of 100%-owned subsidiaries)
Down Company purchased 100% ownership of Topp Company for $80,000 and 100%
of Steady Company for $240,000 on January 1, 2004. Immediately after the purchases
the companies reported the following amounts:

Company	Total Assets	Total Liabilities	Total Shareholders' Equity
Down Company	$950,000	$250,000	$700,000
Topp Company	120,000	40,000	80,000
Steady Company	370,000	130,000	40,000

Required:
If a consolidated balance sheet is prepared immediately after the purchase of the two
companies:
   a. What amount of total assets will be reported?

   b. What amount of total liabilities will be reported?

   c. What amount of total shareholders' equity will be reported?

   d. Why is it necessary to eliminate the balance in Down's investment account for
       each of the two subsidiaries when a consolidated balance sheet is prepared?

B-11   (Investments ranging from 10% to 100%)
On April 1, the Red Tin Company acquired some common shares of the Timber Steel
Company. The book value of the Timber Steel Company's net assets on April 1 was
$10 million, and the market value of the net assets was $12.5 million. During the year,
the Timber Steel Company had net earnings of $1 million and declared dividends of
$600,000.

Required:
For each of the following assumptions, give the amount of income recognized by the
Red Tin Company from its investment in Timber Steel Company and show the
beginning and ending balances for the investment account on Red Tin's books. Both
companies close their books annually on December 31. Assume that any excess fair
market value is to be amortized straight-line over five years. Goodwill, if any, is not
amortized. Assume in each case that the market value of the shares on December
31 is the same as the acquisition price.

   a. The acquisition price is $1,250,000 for 10% of the common shares of Timber
       Steel.

   b. The acquisition price is $1,500,000 for 15% of the common shares of Timber
       Steel.

c. The acquisition price is $3,125,000 for 25% of the common shares of Timber Steel.

d. The acquisition price is $6,000,000 for 45% of the common shares of Timber Steel.

e. The acquisition price is $13,000,000 for 100% of the common shares of Timber Steel.

B-12   (Acquisition alternatives for a 100% purchase)

Popular Limited decided to acquire 100% of the Wallflower Company for $250,000. To pay for the acquisition, Popular's management concluded it could (1) sell temporary investments it holds and pay cash, (2) issue new bonds and use the cash receipts, or (3) issue common shares with a market value of $250,000 in exchange for the shares of Wallflower.

Required:

Answer each of the following questions and explain why your answer is appropriate.

a. Under which of the alternatives will total liabilities in the consolidated balance sheet be greater than the amount reported by Popular prior to the purchase of Wallflower's shares?

b. Under which of the alternatives will total assets in the consolidated balance sheet be greater than the amount reported by Popular prior to the purchase of Wallflower's shares?

c. Under which of the alternatives will total shareholders' equity in the consolidated balance sheet be greater than the amount reported by Popular prior to the purchase of Wallflower's shares?

d. Which of the alternatives would appear to increase the risk of investing in Popular Company?

e. Which of the alternatives would appear to reduce the risk of investing in Popular Company?

B-13   (Portfolio investment and significant influence investment)

On January 1, Nix Company acquired portions of the common shares of two companies, Cal Company and Lake Company. The data relating to the acquisition and the first year of operations are as follows:

Company	Common Shares Acquired	Book Value of Net Assets as of 1/1	Market Value of Net Assets as of 1/1	Acquisition Price	Net Income for the Year	Dividends Declared for the Year
Cal Company	18%	$3,500,000	$5,000,000	$ 900,000	$1,250,000	$ 800,000
Lake Company	40%	$8,000,000	$9,500,000	$4,800,000	$3,000,000	$2,000,000

All the companies close their books annually on December 31. Goodwill, if any, is not amortized. Property, plant, and equipment acquired have a remaining useful life of six years, have a residual value of zero, and are amortized using the straight-line method. Any excess fair market value in the transaction relates to property, plant, and equipment. The market values of the Cal Company and the Lake Company shares held on December 31 were $850,000 and $4,500,000, respectively.

Required:

Show the journal entries (including the acquisition) to account for these two investments during the year.

B-14 (Consolidation of a 100%-owned subsidiary)

Large Company owns all of the common shares of Small Company. Income statements for the companies for 2004 contained the following amounts:

	Large Co.	Small Co.
Sales revenue	$600,000	$300,000
Cost of goods sold	400,000	160,000
Gross profit	200,000	140,000
Dividend income from subsidiary	90,000	
Operating expenses	(130,000)	(50,000)
Net income	$160,000	$ 90,000

During 2004 Small Company purchased inventory for $10,000 and immediately sold it to Large at cost. Large has not sold this inventory yet.

Required:

In the consolidated income statement for 2004:

a. What amount will be reported as sales revenue?

b. What amount will be reported as cost of goods sold?

c. What amount will be reported as dividend income from subsidiary?

d. What amount will be reported as operating expenses?

e. Why are some amounts reported in the consolidated income statement not equal to the sum of the amounts from the statements of the parent and subsidiary?

B-15 (Consolidation of a 100%-owned subsidiary)

On January 1, Lid Company acquired 100% of the common shares of Ant Company at a price of $1,500,000. The book value of the net assets of Ant Company on January 1 was $1,250,000. The book value of the net assets approximates the fair value at the date of acquisition. During the year, Ant earned $340,000 and declared dividends of $290,000. At the end of the year, the dividends receivable of Lid Company included an amount of $290,000 that was due from Ant Company. (*Hint*: Lid's balance sheet would have a dividend receivable and Ant's would have a dividend payable. The consolidated entity cannot owe money to itself. Therefore, both of these accounts must be removed on the working papers before consolidated financial statements are prepared.) Goodwill, if any, will not be amortized.

Required:

a. Show the journal entries for the acquisition of the common shares and other entries during the year, assuming that Lid uses the equity method on its own books.

b. Prepare the consolidating working paper entries.

B-16 (Consolidation of a 100%-owned subsidiary)

Jennie's Plumbing and Heating recently purchased 100% of the shares of Ron's Repair Service. The balance sheets for the two companies immediately after the purchase of Ron's shares were:

	Jennie's Plumbing	Ron's Repair
Cash	$ 20,000	$ 8,000
Accounts receivable	50,000	30,000
Inventory	80,000	72,000
Investment in Ron's Repair	150,000	
Buildings and equipment	300,000	240,000
Less: accumulated amortization	(110,000)	(80,000)
Total assets	$490,000	$270,000
Accounts payable	$ 60,000	$ 75,000
Taxes payable	70,000	45,000
Common shares	200,000	100,000
Retained earnings	160,000	50,000
Total liabilities and equity	$490,000	$270,000

At the balance sheet date, Ron's Repair owes Jennie's Plumbing $15,000 on accounts payable.

Required:

a. Prepare a consolidated balance sheet for Jennie's Plumbing and its subsidiary.

b. Why are the shareholders' equity balances of Ron's Repair not included in the consolidated balance sheet?

c. Monona Wholesale Supply has extended credit of $10,000 to Jennie's Plumbing, and Winona Supply Company has extended credit of $10,000 to Ron's Repair. Which supplier has the stronger claim on the consolidated cash balance? Explain.

d. Jennie's Plumbing has applied to the Sussex Bank for a $75,000 short-term loan to open a showroom for bathroom and kitchen fixtures. Accounts receivable will be used as collateral and Jennie's Plumbing has provided the bank with its consolidated balance sheet prepared immediately after the acquisition of Ron's Repair. From the bank's perspective, how would you rate the sufficiency of the collateral? Explain.

e. If Jennie's Plumbing had purchased only 80% of the shares of Ron's Repair, an item labelled "Noncontrolling Interest" would have been reported on the balance sheet. What does the amount assigned to the noncontrolling interest represent?

B-17   (Consolidation of a 100%-owned subsidiary)
The following are the balance sheets and income statements for Jungle Company and Forest Company as at December 31, 20x1:

Balance Sheet as at December 31, 20x1

	Jungle Company	Forest Company
Assets		
Cash	$ 29,000	$ 15,000
Accounts Receivable	35,000	45,500
Investment in Forest Company	130,000	–
Other Assets	61,000	74,500
Total Assets	$255,000	$135,000

Liabilities and Shareholders' Equity

Accounts Payable	$ 39,500	$ 20,000
Other Current Liabilities	10,500	10,000
Common Shares	150,000	80,000
Retained Earnings	55,000	25,000
Total Liabilities and Shareholders' Equity	$255,000	$135,000

Income Statement for the Year Ended December 31, 20x1

	Jungle Company	Forest Company
Sales Revenue	$100,000	$ 60,000
Cost of Goods Sold	(55,000)	(35,000)
Amortization	(25,000)	(5,000)
EEI	20,000	–
Net Income	$ 40,000	$ 20,000
Dividends Declared	$ 25,000	$ 15,000

On January 1, 20x1, Jungle had acquired 100% of the common shares of Forest Company. The acquisition price was $125,000. The shareholders' equity section of Forest Company on January 1 was as follows:

Forest Company

Common Shares	$ 80,000
Retained Earnings	20,000
Total	$100,000

The fair market value of Forest's net assets equalled their book values at the date of acquisition. Goodwill, if any, will not be amortized.

Required:

a. Prepare the consolidating working papers supported by the necessary working paper journal entries.

b. Prepare the consolidated balance sheet and income statement.

B-18 (Accounting for a subsidiary)

Varwood Company Ltd. is a subsidiary of Tabor Company Ltd. The balance sheets for Varwood Company and for the consolidated entity at December 31, 2004, contained the following balances:

	Varwood Company	Consolidated Amounts for Tabor Co. and Subsidiary
Cash and receivables	$ 80,000	$120,000
Inventory	150,000	260,000
Land	70,000	200,000
Building and equipment	150,000	450,000
Less: accumulated amortization	(70,000)	(210,000)
Total assets	$380,000	$820,000
Accounts payable	$ 40,000	$ 70,000
Notes payable	90,000	290,000
Noncontrolling interest		100,000
Common shares	80,000	180,000
Retained earnings	170,000	180,000
Total liabilities and equity	$380,000	$820,000

Required:

a. Does Tabor own 100% or less than 100% of Varwood's common shares? How do you know?

b. What percentage of Varwood's assets and liabilities is included in the consolidated balance sheet? Explain.

c. What is the amount of cash and accounts receivable reported by Tabor at December 31, 2004, if (1) there are no intercompany receivables and payables, and (2) Tabor's accounts receivable include a $20,000 receivable from Varwood?

d. Must Tabor share a portion of Varwood's net income with others? Explain. What portion of the income from Tabor's separate operations must be shared with the other shareholders of Varwood?

e. Which of questions a) through d) could be answered only if the consolidated financial statements were available?

B-19   (Consolidation of a 100%-owned subsidiary)
On January 1, 20x1, Neptune Company Ltd. acquired 100% of the outstanding shares of Baker Company Ltd. The acquisition price was $250,000, which included $20,000 related to the excess fair market value of the capital assets acquired. The shareholders' equity as at January 1, 20x1, was as follows:

	Neptune Co.	Baker Co.
Common shares	$500,000	$150,000
Retained earnings	10,000	50,000
Total	$510,000	$200,000

During the year, Neptune Company lent $50,000 to Baker Company, which was to be repaid by December 31, 20x1; however, $20,000 was still due from Baker at the end of the year. The trial balances of Neptune and Baker on December 31, 20x1, were as follows:

Trial Balance, December 31, 20x1

	Neptune Co.		Baker Co.	
Account	Debit	Credit	Debit	Credit
Current assets	$ 150,000		$ 90,000	
Capital assets	350,000		200,000	
Investment in Baker	251,000		–	
Cost of goods sold	200,000		75,000	
Other expenses	25,000		10,000	
Dividends declared	50,000		30,000	
Current liabilities		$ 85,000		$ 35,000
Noncurrent liabilities		100,000		50,000
Common shares		500,000		150,000
Retained earnings		10,000		50,000
Sales revenue		300,000		120,000
EEI		31,000		
Totals	$1,026,000	$1,026,000	$405,000	$405,000

The entire fair market value of the capital assets is to be amortized using the straight-line method. The remaining useful life is five years, and the residual value is zero. Goodwill, if any, will not be amortized.

Required:

a. Prepare the consolidating working papers supported by the necessary working paper journal entries.

b. Prepare the consolidated balance sheet.

B-20 (Equity method and consolidation of a 100%-owned subsidiary)
On January 1, 20x1, Casey Incorporated acquired 100% of the outstanding common shares of Smith Company Ltd. and List Company Ltd. The details of the acquisitions and the earnings of both companies are as follows:

	Smith Co.	List Co.
Book value of net assets as of 1/1/x1	$140,000	$175,000
Acquisition price	150,000	200,000
Earnings (loss) for 20x1	(20,000)	15,000
Dividends declared for 20x1	–	10,000

Goodwill, if any, will not be amortized. Assume that the fair market value of the net assets on 1/1/x1 is adequately measured by the book values.

Required:

a. Construct the journal entries that Casey will make in 20x1 to account for these investments on its own books assuming it uses the equity method.

b. Prepare the consolidating working paper entries for the consolidation of these investments as of 12/31/x1 assuming the entries in part a) have been recorded.

B-21 (Acquisition of a subsidiary)
The following are the balance sheets for Trident Inc. and Gum Company Ltd. as at December 31, 20x1 (prior to any acquisition):

Balance Sheet as at December 31, 20x1

	Trident Inc.	Gum Co.
Assets		
Current Assets	$175,000	$ 65,000
Noncurrent Assets	500,000	130,000
Total Assets	$675,000	$195,000
Liabilities and Shareholders' Equity		
Current Liabilities	$ 85,000	$ 28,000
Noncurrent Liabilities	190,000	57,000
Common Shares	350,000	100,000
Retained Earnings	50,000	10,000
Total Liabilities and Shareholders' Equity	$675,000	$195,000

On December 31, 20x1, Trident Inc. issued 5,000 shares having a market value of $300,000 in exchange for all 7,500 shares of Gum. The value of the shares exchanged over the book value of Gum includes $100,000 of excess fair market value of the non-current assets. All other assets and liabilities of Gum were properly valued on its books.

Required:

a. Construct the entry that Trident would make on its books to account for its investment in Gum.

b. Prepare a consolidated balance sheet as at December 31, 20x1.

B-22   (Calculation of consolidated net income)
Refer to the data in Problem B-21. For 20x1, the details of the net income and dividends reported by the two companies were as follows:

	Trident Inc.	Gum Co.
Net Income for 20x1	$250,000	$75,000
Dividends Declared for 20x1	$225,000	$65,000

Required:
What is the net income of Trident Inc. on a consolidated basis?

B-23   (Preparation of a consolidated income statement)
Refer to the data in Problem B-21 and assume that the net income and dividends declared for 20x2 are as follows:

	Trident Inc.	Gum Co.
Revenues	$700,000	$280,000
Cost of Goods Sold	400,000	160,000
Other Expenses	95,000	30,000
Net Income	$205,000	$ 90,000
Dividends Declared	$150,000	$ 75,000

Trident's net income excludes the income from its investment in Gum. Goodwill is not amortized, and any excess fair market value of noncurrent assets is to be amortized using the straight-line method over a 10-year useful life with a zero residual value.

Required:
Prepare a consolidated income statement for 20x2.

Reading and Interpreting Published Financial Statements

B-24   (Business acquisitions)
In its 2001 annual report, **Canadian Tire Corporation Ltd.** described its acquisition of **Mark's Work Wearhouse Ltd.** The details are described in Exhibit B-14.

EXHIBIT B-14

CANADIAN TIRE CORPORATION LTD. (2001)

17. SUBSEQUENT EVENT

On December 19, 2001, the Corporation announced an all cash offer to acquire all of the outstanding common shares of Mark's Work Wearhouse Ltd. ("Mark's"). The offer was conditional on 66 2/3rds of the outstanding common shares on a fully diluted basis being deposited in acceptance of the offer. On December 27, 2001, the Corporation mailed to shareholders of Mark's its offer to acquire all of the outstanding common shares of Mark's on the basis of $4.10 cash per common share. The offer was open for acceptance until February 1, 2002 and on February 4, 2002, the Corporation announced the successful completion of the offer. The Corporation initially took up all Mark's shares deposited to the offer (26,050,615 common shares or 98.3 percent of the outstanding shares) at $4.10 per share for a cost of $106.8 million. The Corporation also exercised its compulsory acquisition rights and took up all Mark's shares that were not deposited to the offer, which brought the total cost to $108.7 million. Mark's results will be included as a separate segment within the consolidated results of the corporation as of February 1, 2002.

Required:

a. What accounting method is Canadian Tire most likely to use to account for its investment in Mark's Work Wearhouse Ltd.? What items in the note led you to that conclusion?

b. Why is this item described in a note called "Subsequent Event" rather than in a separate note about a new acquisition?

c. Canadian Tire sells automotive parts and household goods and services vehicles. Mark's Work Wearhouse sells clothing for working people. Knowing these facts about the two companies, explain whether this is horizontal integration, vertical integration, or diversification.

B-25 (Business acquisitions)
Cara Operations acquired all of the remaining shares of **The Second Cup Ltd.** as of February 2002. This acquisition is described in Note 2 of its 2002 annual report. Note 2 is reproduced in Exhibit B-15.

CARA OPERATIONS (2001)

Note ② **Business Acquisition and Disposal**

Acquisition – Second Cup

Effective February 9, 2002, the Corporation acquired all the remaining issued and outstanding common shares of The Second Cup Ltd. ("Second Cup") pursuant to an offer of $8.00 cash per share made by the Corporation. Previously, the Corporation had an equity investment of approximately 39% in Second Cup. The purchase price consisted of $50.3 million cash consideration paid for common shares and related acquisition costs. In addition, $7.0 million was accrued on acquisition to provide for restructuring costs and certain liabilities assumed. The fair value assigned to the brand has an indefinite life and accordingly is not subject to amortization and has been presented net of a future income tax liability of approximately $14 million. The acquisition has been accounted for by the purchase method and the Corporation has included the results of operations in its consolidated financial statements, from the effective date of acquisition.

The net assets consolidated at the date of acquisition were as follows:

(in thousands of dollars)

Current assets	$ 4,785
Property, plant and equipment	1,462
Other non-current assets	575
Brands	82,745
	89,567
Liabilities	14,036
Total acquisition cost	$ 75,531
Represented by:	
Cash consideration	$ 50,254
Previously acquired equity investment	25,277
	$ 75,531

Sale of Business – Beaver Foods

In December 2000, the Corporation sold substantially all of the contract food catering business operated by the Corporation's wholly owned subsidiary, Beaver Foods Limited. The net proceeds included $4.6 million in deferred consideration, discounted at 7% and payable annually over 5 years. The sale resulted in an after tax gain of $65.5 million (70.6 cents per share).

Required:

a. Back in 1999, Cara Operations first acquired an equity interest in The Second Cup Ltd. What accounting method would Cara Operations have been using to account for this original investment? Explain.

b. With the completion of its total acquisition of The Second Cup Ltd. in 2002, what accounting method will Cara Operations now have to employ?

c. Cara Operations describes itself as being in the food services business. Does this investment represent horizontal integration, vertical integration, or diversification?

d. In 1993, Cara Operations described itself as having two core businesses: food services and office products. It subsequently sold its investments in office products. Why do you think Cara Operations exited the office products business?

B-26   (Acquisition of a subsidiary)

In August 1999, **CHC Helicopter Corporation** acquired 91.3% of the outstanding shares of **Helicopter Services Group (HSG)**. In September 1999, it acquired the remaining shares. CHC Helicopter Corporation provides helicopter transportation service to the oil and gas industry and for emergency services. Part of note 7 from the company's 2001 annual report describes the transaction (Exhibit B-16):

CHC HELICOPTER CORPORATION (2001)

Notes to the Consolidated Financial Statements

April 30, 2001 and 2000 (Tabular amounts in thousands, except per share amounts)

7. Long-term investments and acquisitions (*cont'd*)

As of August 11, 1999 the Company had acquired 91.3% of the outstanding shares of Helicopter Services Group ("HSG") and the remaining shares were acquired on September 30, 1999. The total cash consideration, including transaction costs, for the acquisition of the HSG shares was $229.5 million. The acquisition has been accounted for as a purchase, with the results of operations of HSG included in the consolidated financial statements from August 11, 1999. The purchase price was allocated based on the fair value of the net identifiable assets acquired as follows:

Cash (net of bank indebtedness)	$ 45,100
Other current assets	184,800
Capital assets	457,000
Other long-term assets	92,700
Current liabilities	(108,600)
Long-term debt	(325,300)
Other long-term obligations	(116,200)
Total consideration	$229,500

Required:

a. From the information given in Exhibit B-16, how would CHC Helicopter Corporation account for its investment in HSG?

b. Was there any goodwill that arose from this acquisition? How do you know?

c. Explain whether the purchase of HSG by CHC Helicopter is an example of horizontal integration, vertical integration, or diversification.

B-27 (Business acquisitions)

In its 2001 annual report, **Brampton Brick Limited** describes investments that it holds in two companies, **Richvale York Block Inc.** and **Futureway Communications Inc.** (Exhibit B-17). Brampton Brick's core business is the manufacture and sale of clay bricks. It has subsidiaries in the brick business but also one in medical waste management, **Sharpsmart Canada Ltd.**

BRAMPTON BRICK LIMITED (2001)

EXHIBIT B-17

3 Investment in Richvale York Block Inc.

The Company holds a 38.2% equity investment in Richvale York Block Inc., a concrete block manufacturer with two plants in the Greater Toronto area. The controlling 61.8% interest is held by Lafarge Canada Inc. The investment is accounted for on the equity basis, as follows:

	2001 $	2000 $
Investment at January 1	7,361	8,215
Share of income for the year	1,261	1,169
Dividends received	(1,145)	(2,023)
Investment at December 31	7,477	7,361

Additional information with respect to the operations and financial position of Richvale York Block Inc. is as follows:

	2001 $	2000 $
Net income for the year	3,302	3,063
Cash flow from operations	3,583	4,157
Working capital	5,494	4,703
Total assets	23,409	24,349
Shareholders' equity	19,409	19,066

4 Investment in Futureway Communications Inc.

The Company holds 517,660 shares of Futureway Communications Inc., a Canadian based competitive local exchange carrier that provides broadband voice, video and data communications services. This represents approximately a 1.2% interest. The investment is carried at cost.

Required:

a. What accounting methods is Brampton Brick using to account for its two investments described in Notes 3 and 4? Explain why these methods are appropriate.

b. Do the investments in these two companies represent horizontal integration, vertical integration, or diversification?

c. Brampton Brick holds investments in companies that are outside its core business. Explain why a company would make investments such as these.

B-28 (Business acquisition)

Cangene Corporation is a biopharmaceutical company that develops, manufactures, and sells specialty plasma products and recombinant therapeutic products. In January 2001, it acquired 100% of another biopharmaceutical company. The acquisition is described in Exhibit B-18.

Required:

a. Is this transaction an example of a share exchange or a cash purchase?

b. Explain why it is reasonable that there is goodwill in this acquisition.

c. The note explains that the new subsidiary has "non-capital loss carryforwards." In this text, we have not talked about loss carryforwards. What do you think they are and why do you think they could have value?

CANGENE CORPORATION (2001)

11. BUSINESS ACQUISITION

Effective January 31, 2001, the corporation, through its wholly-owned subsidiary Cangene U.S. Incorporated, acquired 100% of the outstanding shares of Chesapeake, which operates a biopharmaceutical contract manufacturing facility in Baltimore, Maryland. This transaction has been accounted for using the purchase method. Chesapeake's net assets acquired at assigned values and the consideration given are as follows:

in thousands of Cdn dollars

Net assets acquired, at fair values:	
Working capital	$ 134
Capital assets	14,870
Long-term debt	(13,967)
Goodwill	51,790
Consideration – cash	$ 52,827

Chesapeake has $8.1 million U.S. in pre-acquisition non-capital loss carry forwards that are available for federal carryforward purposes. They are partially restricted and to that extent, may not be entirely available for use in future years. The benefit of these losses has not been given recognition in the financial statements. Should they be recognized in the future, they will be offset by a corresponding decrease in the value of goodwill.

B-29   (Business acquisition)
Finning International Inc. had a 29.4% investment in **Hewden Stuart**. In January 2001, it purchased the remaining 70.6% interest. The acquisition is described in its 2001 annual report (see Exhibit B-19).

FINNING INTERNATIONAL INC. (2001)

5. ACQUISITION OF HEWDEN STUART

At December 31, 2000 Finning had an investment in Hewden of $218,050 representing 29.4% of the issued ordinary share capital. The Consolidated Financial Statements give effect to the acquisition of the remaining 70.6% of Hewden which was completed on January 26, 2001. Hewden is in the equipment rental and related services business, operating throughout Scotland, England, Wales and Northern Ireland. The results of Hewden's operations have been included in the Company's Consolidated Financial Statements from January 26, 2001. The purchase of Hewden is accounted for under the purchase method of accounting. The aggregate purchase price of $729,111 (including acquisition costs of $19,700) was paid in cash. Goodwill arising on the acquisition is amortized on a straight-line basis over its estimated useful life of 40 years.

The net assets acquired at their fair values comprised the following:

Net assets acquired	
Total assets	$ 704,995
Total liabilities	307,968
Net assets acquired	397,027
Goodwill	332,084
Total purchase price	$ 729,111

Required:

a. Finning's original investment in Hewden Stuart was 29.4%. What accounting method do you think Finning used prior to its acquisition of the remaining 70.6% interest? Explain your answer.

b. Finning International rents and services large construction equipment. Does this new acquisition represent horizontal integration, vertical integration, or diversification? Explain.

c. Hewden Stuart operates in Great Britain. Identify some difficulties that Finning might encounter when it prepares its consolidated financial statements.

B-30 (Business acquisition)

Enerflex Systems Ltd. acquired **Landré Ruhaak bv**, a Dutch company, in 2001. The acquisition is described in Exhibit B-20.

ENERFLEX SYSTEMS LTD. (2001)			EXHIBIT B-20
NOTE 2. ACQUISITION OF LANDRÉ RUHAAK bv			

On October 29, 2001, Enerflex Systems Ltd., through its wholly owned subsidiary, Enerflex European Holdings bv, acquired 100% of the issued and outstanding shares of Landré Ruhaak bv, a Netherlands company, for cash consideration of $8,566,000 including acquisition costs. The results of the operations of Landré Ruhaak bv have been included in the consolidated statement of income from the acquisition date. The acquisition was accounted for under the purchase method and is summarized as follows:

Non-cash working capital	$	3,216
Fixed assets		230
Intangible assets		2,815
Goodwill		2,893
Total assets acquired		9,154
Bank overdraft assumed		588
Net assets acquired	$	8,566

Required:

a. Enerflex Systems acquired Landré Ruhaak through its wholly owned European subsidiary, Enerflex European Holdings bv. Is Landré Ruhaak a subsidiary of Enerflex Systems Ltd.? Or is it only a subsidiary of Enerflex European Holdings bv?

b. What difficulties will Enerflex Systems encounter when it attempts to consolidate Landré Ruhaak at the year end?

c. Did any goodwill arise from this acquisition? If so, how much? If not, what reasons could you suggest for there not being any?

Critical Thinking Question

B-31 (Strategic planning of future growth)

As explained at the beginning of this chapter, companies buy all or parts of other companies for many reasons. You might assume that this type of activity is undertaken only by large corporations, but that is not the case. Many owners of small businesses will establish or buy subsidiaries as they start to expand. Often these small subsidiaries will represent a specific niche in the owner's business. This enables the owner to undertake various activities without exposing the whole organization to the risk of failure.

Assume that you are the owner of a small business. Your initial business is installing carpets. You have a crew of three people who do the installation for you. Your ultimate goal is to do finishing contract work on residential and commercial construction. You hope eventually to control a multimillion-dollar operation. Think about the path that could be taken so that you can expand your business from carpet installation to your eventual goal. Draft an expansion plan that would take you gradually from one to the other. Include in your plan the purchase or establishment of subsidiaries.

COMPANY
INDEX

SUBJECT INDEX